CRIME STATE RANKINGS
1995

Crime in the 50 United States

Editors:

Kathleen O'Leary Morgan, Scott Morgan and Neal Quitno

Morgan Quitno Press
© Copyright 1995, All Rights Reserved

512 East 9th Street, P.O. Box 1656, Lawrence, KS 66044
800-457-0742 or 913-841-3534

Crime State Rankings 1995 sells for $43.95 paper, $67.95 cloth. For those who prefer ranking information tailored to a particular state, we also offer *Crime State Perspectives*, state-specific reports for each of the 50 states. These individual guides provide information on a state's data and rank for each of the categories featured in the national *Crime State Rankings* volume. Perspectives sell for $18.00, $9.00 if ordered with *Crime State Rankings*. If you are interested in city and metropolitan crime data, we offer *City Crime Rankings* for $19.95. If you are interested in a general view of the states, please ask about our annual *State Rankings*. If health care statistics are your interest, please ask about our annual *Health Care State Rankings*. We also offer the data in our books on diskette (.dbf format).

Second Edition
Printed in the United States of America
March 1995

PREFACE

The level of concern Americans have when it comes to the issue of crime is nothing if not remarkable. When we introduced *Crime State Rankings* last year we did not realize how many readers would share our interest in having access to clear, straightforward and easy-to-understand crime statistics. We believe this, the second edition of *Crime State Rankings,* builds on the solid foundation of the inaugural volume and takes crime statistics to a new level of ease of use.

We have made some significant changes to this latest edition of *Crime State Rankings.* The most noteable change is its format. Data are now presented in both alphabetical and rank order. The two columns are presented side-by-side so you can quickly find information for a particular state and then just as quickly look up which states rank above and below that state.

While the format of *Crime State Rankings* has changed, we have continued many of the other features of last year's book that made it a hit with both reviewers and users. Among these are the prominent placement of national totals, rates and percentages at the top of each table to allow for easy comparison. In addition, all source and other explanatory footnotes are included on the same page as the data. Every other line is shaded in gray for easier reading. Tables show complete numbers with all of their "zeroes," making it easier to figure out if a number is thousands, hundreds, millions etc.

As in our previous edition, rankings of states are listed from highest to lowest for each category. Any ties among states are shown alphabetically for a given ranking. Numbers reported in parentheses "( )" are negative numbers. For tables with national totals (as opposed to rates, per capita's, etc.) we include a separate column showing what percent of the national total each individual state's total represents. This column is headed by "% of USA." This percentage figure is particularly interesting when compared with a state's share of the nation's population for a particular year. The appendix contains population tables and other helpful background information to aid in these comparisons.

For those interested in focusing on crime information for just one state, we once again are offering our *State Perspective* series of publications. These 21-page, comb-bound reports feature data and ranking information for an individual state, pulled from *Crime State Rankings 1995.* (For example, *New York Crime in Perspective* contains crime information about the state of New York only.) When purchased individually, *Crime State Perspectives* sell for $18. When purchased with a copy of *Crime State Rankings 1995,* these handy quick reference guides are just $9.

Crime State Rankings proved to be so popular its first year that we have since launched a companion volume of crime data, *City Crime Rankings.* Making its debut in February of 1995, this newest reference book was created in response to the large number of requests we received for crime data broken down by city and metropolitan area. *City Crime Rankings* ranks the 100 largest cities (down to a population of approximately 175,000) and 274 metropolitan areas (some as small as 65,000 population) in 40 categories of crime each. Numbers of crimes, crime rates, changes in crime rates over one and five years are presented for all major crime categories reported by the FBI. This book sells for $19.95.

Our company also continues to offer two other publications, *State Rankings* and *Health Care State Rankings.* In its sixth edition in 1995, *State Rankings* provides a general view of the states by featuring state statistics in categories ranging from agriculture to transportation, taxes to education and social welfare to health. This book has received great acclaim for its ease of use and simple presentation of state data. Also continued this year is *Health Care State Rankings,* a series now in its third edition. Following the same format as the book you are holding, *Health Care State Rankings* focuses on state health issues instead of crime. Included in this volume are data on health care facilities, providers, insurance and finance, incidence of disease, mortality, physical fitness, natality and reproductive health. Both *State Rankings* and *Health Care State Rankings* sell for $43.95 ($67.95 cloth) each including shipping. *State Perspectives* are also available for each of these books, selling for $18 individually and $9 if purchased with their corresponding national volume. We also offer the data in our books on diskette (.dbf format). If you would like a brochure or further information, please call us at 1-800-457-0742.

Finally, many thanks to all of the hard working librarians and government workers who so willingly helped us in developing, designing and producing this book. A continued special thanks to the very helpful librarians at the Kansas State Library for their feedback and encouragement. Most of all, thanks to you, our readers. We enjoy doing this and appreciate your comments -- so please give us a call or write us with your suggestions.

THE EDITORS

WHICH STATE IS THE MOST DANGEROUS?

For the second year in a row, the state of Louisiana has the troublesome distinction of being designated the "Most Dangerous State." The Bayou State earned the number one ranking based on statistics in *Crime State Rankings 1995*. At the other end, Maine is the safest state, edging out last year's winner, Vermont.

Using 14 basic criteria (listed below) the "Most Dangerous State" was determined by comparing state crime rates, juvenile crime statistics, corrections data, police protection and expenditures. These factors provide a statistical basis for comparing states' abilities to keep their streets safe for the average citizen.

Our methodology was fairly simple. Once the 14 factors were determined, we averaged each state's ranking for all 14 categories. Based on this composite number (the "AVG" in the table to the right), states were then ranked from "most dangerous" (lowest average ranking) to "safest" (highest average ranking). States with no data available for a given category were assigned a zero for that category and ranked on the remaining factors.

1995 MOST DANGEROUS STATE

RANK	STATE	AVG	RANK	STATE	AVG
1	Louisiana	10.21	26	Arkansas	25.71
2	Maryland	11.86	27	Washington	26.36
3	Nevada	13.07	28	Massachusetts	26.57
4	Florida	13.93	29	Ohio	26.64
5	Illinois	14.83	30	Hawaii	26.93
6	Texas	15.36	31	Indiana	27.57
7	Arizona	15.86	32	Virginia	28.93
8	California	16.79	33	Utah	29.14
9	New Mexico	16.86	34	Wisconsin	29.21
10	South Carolina	17.29	35	Idaho	30.50
11	New York	19.29	36	Connecticut	30.57
12	Delaware	19.79	37	South Dakota	30.86
13	Michigan	20.07	38	Montana	31.36
14	Alaska	20.50	38	Pennsylvania	31.36
15	Oklahoma	20.86	40	Wyoming	31.43
16	Tennessee	21.14	41	Rhode Island	31.50
17	Missouri	21.21	42	Minnesota	32.43
18	Colorado	22.00	43	Nebraska	33.50
19	North Carolina	22.21	44	Kentucky	34.36
20	Alabama	22.43	45	Iowa	35.79
21	Georgia	22.50	46	North Dakota	36.79
22	New Jersey	23.36	47	New Hampshire	38.50
23	Kansas	23.67	48	West Virginia	39.79
24	Oregon	25.14	49	Vermont	42.21
25	Mississippi	25.57	50	Maine	43.71

Morgan Quitno Press prides itself on presenting facts in a nonbiased, objective manner. A central theme of our books is our clear presentation of data, with the analysis left to our readers. However, with each new edition, we incorporate what we determine to be the most critical statistical measurements into our computer program and present an "award" based on the results. Annually since 1991 we have named the "Most Livable State" based on data from our *State Rankings* series. In 1993, we began the "Healthiest State" award based on data from our *Health Care State Rankings* series. With the debut of our third series of books in 1994, *Crime State Rankings*, we designated the "Most Dangerous State." This year we began two new awards, "Safest City" and "Safest Metropolitan Area" based on our latest book *City Crime Rankings*.

FACTORS CONSIDERED:
1. Crime Rate in 1993 (Table 279)
2. Violent Crime Rate in 1993 (Table 285)
3. Murder Rate in 1993 (Table 293)
4. Rape Rate in 1993 (Table 312)
5. Robbery Rate in 1993 (Table 318)
6. Aggravated Assault Rate in 1993 (Table 333)
7. Property Crime Rate in 1993 (Table 348)
8. Percent Change in Crime Rate: 1989 to 1993 (Table 434)
9. Percent Change in Violent Crime Rate: 1989 to 1993 (Table 438)
10. State Prisoner Incarceration Rate in 1994 (Table 84)
11. Reported Arrests of Youths 17 Years and Younger as a Percent of All Arrests in 1993 (Table 38)
12. Reported Arrests of Youths 17 Years and Younger for Violent Crime as a Percent of All Such Arrests in 1993 (Table 42)
13. State-Local Government Expenditures for Police Protection as a Percent of All Direct Expenditures in 1992 (Table 199)
14. Full-Time Sworn Officers in Law Enforcement Agencies per 10,000 Population in 1992 (Table 237)

We realize that our designation of the "Most Dangerous State" is not without controversy. There are some that take issue with our methodology and choice of factors. However, we have been successful in our primary goal: bringing to the attention of the average citizen an overall picture of crime in his or her home state. Our intent is not to anger, but rather to provoke and facilitate a productive discussion on a problem of great concern to us all.

THE EDITORS

TABLE OF CONTENTS

I. Arrests

Juvenile Arrests

TABLE OF CONTENTS (continued)

II. Corrections

TABLE OF CONTENTS (continued)

III. Drugs and Alcohol

TABLE OF CONTENTS (continued)

IV. Finance

TABLE OF CONTENTS (continued)

V. Law Enforcement

VI. Offenses

TABLE OF CONTENTS (continued)

TABLE OF CONTENTS (continued)

Urban/Rural Crime

TABLE OF CONTENTS (continued)

TABLE OF CONTENTS (continued)

VIII. Sources

IX. Index

I. ARRESTS

Juvenile Arrests

I. ARRESTS (continued)

Reported Arrests in 1993

National Total = 11,765,764 Reported Arrests*

ALPHA ORDER

RANK	STATE	ARRESTS	% of USA
19	Alabama	186,681	1.59%
40	Alaska	37,959	0.32%
15	Arizona	251,159	2.13%
23	Arkansas	177,421	1.51%
1	California	1,621,970	13.79%
16	Colorado	236,309	2.01%
20	Connecticut	182,472	1.55%
46	Delaware	10,026	0.09%
4	Florida	613,331	5.21%
8	Georgia	382,825	3.25%
34	Hawaii	63,805	0.54%
38	Idaho	46,760	0.40%
NA	Illinois**	NA	NA
25	Indiana	156,497	1.33%
33	Iowa	71,555	0.61%
NA	Kansas**	NA	NA
29	Kentucky	124,556	1.06%
21	Louisiana	181,388	1.54%
41	Maine	37,662	0.32%
13	Maryland	270,465	2.30%
27	Massachusetts	146,305	1.24%
9	Michigan	367,814	3.13%
18	Minnesota	195,717	1.66%
35	Mississippi	61,591	0.52%
14	Missouri	261,934	2.23%
47	Montana	9,677	0.08%
32	Nebraska	72,944	0.62%
31	Nevada	91,696	0.78%
43	New Hampshire	24,368	0.21%
10	New Jersey	363,846	3.09%
37	New Mexico	54,263	0.46%
3	New York	1,004,521	8.54%
5	North Carolina	484,583	4.12%
45	North Dakota	21,105	0.18%
11	Ohio	335,272	2.85%
28	Oklahoma	143,221	1.22%
26	Oregon	150,584	1.28%
12	Pennsylvania	327,567	2.78%
39	Rhode Island	39,900	0.34%
24	South Carolina	173,194	1.47%
42	South Dakota	32,380	0.28%
22	Tennessee	177,697	1.51%
2	Texas	1,032,728	8.78%
30	Utah	110,511	0.94%
48	Vermont	4,235	0.04%
7	Virginia	387,552	3.29%
17	Washington	231,989	1.97%
36	West Virginia	59,769	0.51%
6	Wisconsin	402,491	3.42%
44	Wyoming	23,648	0.20%

RANK ORDER

RANK	STATE	ARRESTS	% of USA
1	California	1,621,970	13.79%
2	Texas	1,032,728	8.78%
3	New York	1,004,521	8.54%
4	Florida	613,331	5.21%
5	North Carolina	484,583	4.12%
6	Wisconsin	402,491	3.42%
7	Virginia	387,552	3.29%
8	Georgia	382,825	3.25%
9	Michigan	367,814	3.13%
10	New Jersey	363,846	3.09%
11	Ohio	335,272	2.85%
12	Pennsylvania	327,567	2.78%
13	Maryland	270,465	2.30%
14	Missouri	261,934	2.23%
15	Arizona	251,159	2.13%
16	Colorado	236,309	2.01%
17	Washington	231,989	1.97%
18	Minnesota	195,717	1.66%
19	Alabama	186,681	1.59%
20	Connecticut	182,472	1.55%
21	Louisiana	181,388	1.54%
22	Tennessee	177,697	1.51%
23	Arkansas	177,421	1.51%
24	South Carolina	173,194	1.47%
25	Indiana	156,497	1.33%
26	Oregon	150,584	1.28%
27	Massachusetts	146,305	1.24%
28	Oklahoma	143,221	1.22%
29	Kentucky	124,556	1.06%
30	Utah	110,511	0.94%
31	Nevada	91,696	0.78%
32	Nebraska	72,944	0.62%
33	Iowa	71,555	0.61%
34	Hawaii	63,805	0.54%
35	Mississippi	61,591	0.52%
36	West Virginia	59,769	0.51%
37	New Mexico	54,263	0.46%
38	Idaho	46,760	0.40%
39	Rhode Island	39,900	0.34%
40	Alaska	37,959	0.32%
41	Maine	37,662	0.32%
42	South Dakota	32,380	0.28%
43	New Hampshire	24,368	0.21%
44	Wyoming	23,648	0.20%
45	North Dakota	21,105	0.18%
46	Delaware	10,026	0.09%
47	Montana	9,677	0.08%
48	Vermont	4,235	0.04%
NA	Illinois**	NA	NA
NA	Kansas**	NA	NA
	District of Columbia	51,805	0.44%

Source: U.S. Department of Justice, Federal Bureau of Investigation
   "Crime in the United States 1993" (Uniform Crime Reports, December 4, 1994)
*By law enforcement agencies submitting complete reports to the F.B.I. for 12 months in 1993. The F.B.I. estimates
14,036,300 reported and unreported arrests occurred in 1993.
**Not available.

Reported Arrest Rate in 1993

National Rate = 5,495.5 Reported Arrests per 100,000 Population*

ALPHA ORDER				RANK ORDER		
RANK	STATE	RATE		RANK	STATE	RATE
33	Alabama	4,718.9		1	Wisconsin	8,045.0
13	Alaska	6,694.7		2	Colorado	7,945.8
11	Arizona	6,733.5		3	Missouri	7,930.2
5	Arkansas	7,346.6		4	Nevada	7,622.3
26	California	5,218.7		5	Arkansas	7,346.6
2	Colorado	7,945.8		6	Mississippi	7,212.1
14	Connecticut	6,580.3		7	North Carolina	7,171.6
46	Delaware	2,687.9		8	Louisiana	7,033.3
31	Florida	4,787.2		9	Georgia	6,836.2
9	Georgia	6,836.2		10	Kentucky	6,832.5
24	Hawaii	5,444.1		11	Arizona	6,733.5
25	Idaho	5,393.3		12	New Mexico	6,732.4
NA	Illinois**	NA		13	Alaska	6,694.7
34	Indiana	4,533.5		14	Connecticut	6,580.3
41	Iowa	3,581.3		15	South Dakota	6,502.0
NA	Kansas**	NA		16	New York	6,467.4
10	Kentucky	6,832.5		17	Utah	6,436.3
8	Louisiana	7,033.3		18	Washington	6,046.1
42	Maine	3,580.0		19	Tennessee	6,003.3
23	Maryland	5,450.7		20	Virginia	5,973.4
45	Massachusetts	3,287.0		21	Texas	5,918.6
37	Michigan	4,385.5		22	Wyoming	5,824.6
36	Minnesota	4,408.0		23	Maryland	5,450.7
6	Mississippi	7,212.1		24	Hawaii	5,444.1
3	Missouri	7,930.2		25	Idaho	5,393.3
47	Montana	2,566.8		26	California	5,218.7
29	Nebraska	4,898.9		27	Oregon	5,139.4
4	Nevada	7,622.3		28	Ohio	5,038.7
43	New Hampshire	3,301.9		29	Nebraska	4,898.9
32	New Jersey	4,766.7		30	South Carolina	4,873.2
12	New Mexico	6,732.4		31	Florida	4,787.2
16	New York	6,467.4		32	New Jersey	4,766.7
7	North Carolina	7,171.6		33	Alabama	4,718.9
39	North Dakota	3,944.9		34	Indiana	4,533.5
28	Ohio	5,038.7		35	Oklahoma	4,518.0
35	Oklahoma	4,518.0		36	Minnesota	4,408.0
27	Oregon	5,139.4		37	Michigan	4,385.5
40	Pennsylvania	3,642.1		38	Rhode Island	4,109.2
38	Rhode Island	4,109.2		39	North Dakota	3,944.9
30	South Carolina	4,873.2		40	Pennsylvania	3,642.1
15	South Dakota	6,502.0		41	Iowa	3,581.3
19	Tennessee	6,003.3		42	Maine	3,580.0
21	Texas	5,918.6		43	New Hampshire	3,301.9
17	Utah	6,436.3		44	West Virginia	3,298.5
48	Vermont	1,557.0		45	Massachusetts	3,287.0
20	Virginia	5,973.4		46	Delaware	2,687.9
18	Washington	6,046.1		47	Montana	2,566.8
44	West Virginia	3,298.5		48	Vermont	1,557.0
1	Wisconsin	8,045.0		NA	Illinois**	NA
22	Wyoming	5,824.6		NA	Kansas**	NA

	District of Columbia	8,962.8

Source: Morgan Quitno Corporation using data from U.S. Department of Justice, Federal Bureau of Investigation
"Crime in the United States 1993" (Uniform Crime Reports, December 4, 1994)
*By law enforcement agencies submitting complete reports to the F.B.I. for 12 months in 1993. These rates based on
population estimates for areas under the jurisdiction of those agencies reporting. Arrest rate based on the F.B.I. estimate
of total arrests is 5,442.4 reported and unreported arrests per 100,000 population.
**Not available.

2

Reported Arrests for Crime Index Offenses in 1993

National Total = 2,422,839 Reported Arrests*

<u>ALPHA ORDER</u>

RANK	STATE	ARRESTS	% of USA
24	Alabama	34,942	1.44%
40	Alaska	8,300	0.34%
14	Arizona	55,035	2.27%
29	Arkansas	23,476	0.97%
1	California	422,796	17.45%
16	Colorado	45,300	1.87%
21	Connecticut	39,701	1.64%
46	Delaware	2,305	0.10%
3	Florida	171,877	7.09%
9	Georgia	70,176	2.90%
34	Hawaii	12,632	0.52%
38	Idaho	8,725	0.36%
NA	Illinois**	NA	NA
26	Indiana	32,204	1.33%
32	Iowa	13,453	0.56%
NA	Kansas**	NA	NA
30	Kentucky	22,486	0.93%
20	Louisiana	39,893	1.65%
39	Maine	8,357	0.34%
11	Maryland	64,492	2.66%
22	Massachusetts	38,596	1.59%
8	Michigan	71,946	2.97%
18	Minnesota	42,513	1.75%
35	Mississippi	12,571	0.52%
17	Missouri	45,267	1.87%
47	Montana	1,738	0.07%
33	Nebraska	13,097	0.54%
31	Nevada	16,761	0.69%
43	New Hampshire	4,331	0.18%
7	New Jersey	74,435	3.07%
36	New Mexico	10,518	0.43%
4	New York	170,313	7.03%
5	North Carolina	85,610	3.53%
44	North Dakota	3,973	0.16%
13	Ohio	57,480	2.37%
28	Oklahoma	26,915	1.11%
19	Oregon	40,040	1.65%
6	Pennsylvania	75,987	3.14%
41	Rhode Island	8,199	0.34%
23	South Carolina	35,135	1.45%
42	South Dakota	5,234	0.22%
25	Tennessee	33,724	1.39%
2	Texas	189,257	7.81%
27	Utah	28,354	1.17%
48	Vermont	1,141	0.05%
12	Virginia	63,543	2.62%
15	Washington	50,980	2.10%
37	West Virginia	9,293	0.38%
10	Wisconsin	68,042	2.81%
45	Wyoming	3,021	0.12%

<u>RANK ORDER</u>

RANK	STATE	ARRESTS	% of USA
1	California	422,796	17.45%
2	Texas	189,257	7.81%
3	Florida	171,877	7.09%
4	New York	170,313	7.03%
5	North Carolina	85,610	3.53%
6	Pennsylvania	75,987	3.14%
7	New Jersey	74,435	3.07%
8	Michigan	71,946	2.97%
9	Georgia	70,176	2.90%
10	Wisconsin	68,042	2.81%
11	Maryland	64,492	2.66%
12	Virginia	63,543	2.62%
13	Ohio	57,480	2.37%
14	Arizona	55,035	2.27%
15	Washington	50,980	2.10%
16	Colorado	45,300	1.87%
17	Missouri	45,267	1.87%
18	Minnesota	42,513	1.75%
19	Oregon	40,040	1.65%
20	Louisiana	39,893	1.65%
21	Connecticut	39,701	1.64%
22	Massachusetts	38,596	1.59%
23	South Carolina	35,135	1.45%
24	Alabama	34,942	1.44%
25	Tennessee	33,724	1.39%
26	Indiana	32,204	1.33%
27	Utah	28,354	1.17%
28	Oklahoma	26,915	1.11%
29	Arkansas	23,476	0.97%
30	Kentucky	22,486	0.93%
31	Nevada	16,761	0.69%
32	Iowa	13,453	0.56%
33	Nebraska	13,097	0.54%
34	Hawaii	12,632	0.52%
35	Mississippi	12,571	0.52%
36	New Mexico	10,518	0.43%
37	West Virginia	9,293	0.38%
38	Idaho	8,725	0.36%
39	Maine	8,357	0.34%
40	Alaska	8,300	0.34%
41	Rhode Island	8,199	0.34%
42	South Dakota	5,234	0.22%
43	New Hampshire	4,331	0.18%
44	North Dakota	3,973	0.16%
45	Wyoming	3,021	0.12%
46	Delaware	2,305	0.10%
47	Montana	1,738	0.07%
48	Vermont	1,141	0.05%
NA	Illinois**	NA	NA
NA	Kansas**	NA	NA
	District of Columbia	11,676	0.48%

Source: U.S. Department of Justice, Federal Bureau of Investigation
 "Crime in the United States 1993" (Uniform Crime Reports, December 4, 1994)
*By law enforcement agencies submitting complete reports to the F.B.I. for 12 months in 1993. The F.B.I. estimates 2,848,400 reported and unreported arrests for crime index offenses occurred in 1993. Crime index offenses consist of murder, forcible rape, robbery, aggravated assault, burglary, larceny-theft, motor vehicle theft and arson.
**Not available.

3

Reported Arrest Rate for Crime Index Offenses in 1993

National Rate = 1,131.6 Reported Arrests per 100,000 Population*

ALPHA ORDER			RANK ORDER		
RANK	STATE	RATE	RANK	STATE	RATE
32	Alabama	883.3	1	Utah	1,651.4
6	Alaska	1,463.8	2	Louisiana	1,546.8
4	Arizona	1,475.5	3	Colorado	1,523.2
29	Arkansas	972.1	4	Arizona	1,475.5
11	California	1,360.3	5	Mississippi	1,472.0
3	Colorado	1,523.2	6	Alaska	1,463.8
7	Connecticut	1,431.7	7	Connecticut	1,431.7
44	Delaware	618.0	8	Nevada	1,393.3
13	Florida	1,341.5	9	Missouri	1,370.5
18	Georgia	1,253.1	10	Oregon	1,366.6
23	Hawaii	1,077.8	11	California	1,360.3
25	Idaho	1,006.3	12	Wisconsin	1,360.0
NA	Illinois**	NA	13	Florida	1,341.5
31	Indiana	932.9	14	Washington	1,328.6
43	Iowa	673.3	15	New Mexico	1,305.0
NA	Kansas**	NA	16	Maryland	1,299.7
19	Kentucky	1,233.5	17	North Carolina	1,267.0
2	Louisiana	1,546.8	18	Georgia	1,253.1
40	Maine	794.4	19	Kentucky	1,233.5
16	Maryland	1,299.7	20	Tennessee	1,139.3
34	Massachusetts	867.1	21	New York	1,096.5
36	Michigan	857.8	22	Texas	1,084.6
30	Minnesota	957.5	23	Hawaii	1,077.8
5	Mississippi	1,472.0	24	South Dakota	1,051.0
9	Missouri	1,370.5	25	Idaho	1,006.3
47	Montana	461.0	26	South Carolina	988.6
33	Nebraska	879.6	27	Virginia	979.4
8	Nevada	1,393.3	28	New Jersey	975.2
45	New Hampshire	586.9	29	Arkansas	972.1
28	New Jersey	975.2	30	Minnesota	957.5
15	New Mexico	1,305.0	31	Indiana	932.9
21	New York	1,096.5	32	Alabama	883.3
17	North Carolina	1,267.0	33	Nebraska	879.6
42	North Dakota	742.6	34	Massachusetts	867.1
35	Ohio	863.8	35	Ohio	863.8
37	Oklahoma	849.1	36	Michigan	857.8
10	Oregon	1,366.6	37	Oklahoma	849.1
38	Pennsylvania	844.9	38	Pennsylvania	844.9
39	Rhode Island	844.4	39	Rhode Island	844.4
26	South Carolina	988.6	40	Maine	794.4
24	South Dakota	1,051.0	41	Wyoming	744.1
20	Tennessee	1,139.3	42	North Dakota	742.6
22	Texas	1,084.6	43	Iowa	673.3
1	Utah	1,651.4	44	Delaware	618.0
48	Vermont	419.5	45	New Hampshire	586.9
27	Virginia	979.4	46	West Virginia	512.9
14	Washington	1,328.6	47	Montana	461.0
46	West Virginia	512.9	48	Vermont	419.5
12	Wisconsin	1,360.0	NA	Illinois**	NA
41	Wyoming	744.1	NA	Kansas**	NA

District of Columbia	2,020.1

Source: Morgan Quitno Corporation using data from U.S. Department of Justice, Federal Bureau of Investigation "Crime in the United States 1993" (Uniform Crime Reports, December 4, 1994)

By law enforcement agencies submitting complete reports to the F.B.I. for 12 months in 1993. These rates based on population estimates for areas under the jurisdiction of those agencies reporting. Arrest rate based on the F.B.I. estimate of reported and unreported arrests for crime index offenses is 1,104.4 arrests per 100,000 population.

**Not available.*

4

Reported Arrests for Violent Crime in 1993

National Total = 648,416 Reported Arrests*

ALPHA ORDER

RANK	STATE	ARRESTS	% of USA
14	Alabama	11,347	1.75%
36	Alaska	1,606	0.25%
18	Arizona	9,657	1.49%
28	Arkansas	5,123	0.79%
1	California	146,320	22.57%
21	Colorado	8,760	1.35%
20	Connecticut	8,803	1.36%
42	Delaware	762	0.12%
3	Florida	52,229	8.05%
9	Georgia	20,208	3.12%
39	Hawaii	1,233	0.19%
40	Idaho	1,147	0.18%
NA	Illinois**	NA	NA
23	Indiana	8,501	1.31%
31	Iowa	2,638	0.41%
NA	Kansas**	NA	NA
25	Kentucky	7,716	1.19%
15	Louisiana	11,266	1.74%
41	Maine	826	0.13%
11	Maryland	14,433	2.23%
10	Massachusetts	16,450	2.54%
6	Michigan	22,759	3.51%
22	Minnesota	8,533	1.32%
34	Mississippi	2,153	0.33%
16	Missouri	10,251	1.58%
46	Montana	194	0.03%
38	Nebraska	1,499	0.23%
30	Nevada	3,003	0.46%
43	New Hampshire	583	0.09%
8	New Jersey	20,757	3.20%
35	New Mexico	1,851	0.29%
2	New York	67,467	10.40%
5	North Carolina	27,195	4.19%
48	North Dakota	173	0.03%
12	Ohio	13,981	2.16%
27	Oklahoma	5,868	0.90%
29	Oregon	4,533	0.70%
7	Pennsylvania	21,480	3.31%
33	Rhode Island	2,395	0.37%
17	South Carolina	10,092	1.56%
44	South Dakota	578	0.09%
19	Tennessee	8,876	1.37%
4	Texas	39,526	6.10%
32	Utah	2,592	0.40%
47	Vermont	185	0.03%
13	Virginia	12,771	1.97%
26	Washington	6,672	1.03%
37	West Virginia	1,506	0.23%
24	Wisconsin	7,947	1.23%
45	Wyoming	481	0.07%

RANK ORDER

RANK	STATE	ARRESTS	% of USA
1	California	146,320	22.57%
2	New York	67,467	10.40%
3	Florida	52,229	8.05%
4	Texas	39,526	6.10%
5	North Carolina	27,195	4.19%
6	Michigan	22,759	3.51%
7	Pennsylvania	21,480	3.31%
8	New Jersey	20,757	3.20%
9	Georgia	20,208	3.12%
10	Massachusetts	16,450	2.54%
11	Maryland	14,433	2.23%
12	Ohio	13,981	2.16%
13	Virginia	12,771	1.97%
14	Alabama	11,347	1.75%
15	Louisiana	11,266	1.74%
16	Missouri	10,251	1.58%
17	South Carolina	10,092	1.56%
18	Arizona	9,657	1.49%
19	Tennessee	8,876	1.37%
20	Connecticut	8,803	1.36%
21	Colorado	8,760	1.35%
22	Minnesota	8,533	1.32%
23	Indiana	8,501	1.31%
24	Wisconsin	7,947	1.23%
25	Kentucky	7,716	1.19%
26	Washington	6,672	1.03%
27	Oklahoma	5,868	0.90%
28	Arkansas	5,123	0.79%
29	Oregon	4,533	0.70%
30	Nevada	3,003	0.46%
31	Iowa	2,638	0.41%
32	Utah	2,592	0.40%
33	Rhode Island	2,395	0.37%
34	Mississippi	2,153	0.33%
35	New Mexico	1,851	0.29%
36	Alaska	1,606	0.25%
37	West Virginia	1,506	0.23%
38	Nebraska	1,499	0.23%
39	Hawaii	1,233	0.19%
40	Idaho	1,147	0.18%
41	Maine	826	0.13%
42	Delaware	762	0.12%
43	New Hampshire	583	0.09%
44	South Dakota	578	0.09%
45	Wyoming	481	0.07%
46	Montana	194	0.03%
47	Vermont	185	0.03%
48	North Dakota	173	0.03%
NA	Illinois**	NA	NA
NA	Kansas**	NA	NA
	District of Columbia	5,485	0.85%

Source: U.S. Department of Justice, Federal Bureau of Investigation
   "Crime in the United States 1993" (Uniform Crime Reports, December 4, 1994)
*By law enforcement agencies submitting complete reports to the F.B.I. for 12 months in 1993. The F.B.I. estimates
754,100 reported and unreported arrests for violent crimes occurred in 1993. Violent crimes are offenses of murder,
forcible rape, robbery and aggravated assault.
**Not available.

5

Reported Arrest Rate for Violent Crime in 1993

National Rate = 302.9 Reported Arrests per 100,000 Population*

ALPHA ORDER

RANK ORDER

RANK	STATE	RATE
14	Alabama	286.8
16	Alaska	283.2
19	Arizona	258.9
27	Arkansas	212.1
1	California	470.8
12	Colorado	294.6
9	Connecticut	317.5
29	Delaware	204.3
5	Florida	407.7
8	Georgia	360.9
41	Hawaii	105.2
37	Idaho	132.3
NA	Illinois**	NA
23	Indiana	246.3
38	Iowa	132.0
NA	Kansas**	NA
4	Kentucky	423.3
2	Louisiana	436.8
45	Maine	78.5
13	Maryland	290.9
7	Massachusetts	369.6
18	Michigan	271.4
31	Minnesota	192.2
20	Mississippi	252.1
10	Missouri	310.4
47	Montana	51.5
42	Nebraska	100.7
21	Nevada	249.6
44	New Hampshire	79.0
17	New Jersey	271.9
25	New Mexico	229.7
3	New York	434.4
6	North Carolina	402.5
48	North Dakota	32.3
28	Ohio	210.1
32	Oklahoma	185.1
35	Oregon	154.7
24	Pennsylvania	238.8
22	Rhode Island	246.7
15	South Carolina	284.0
40	South Dakota	116.1
11	Tennessee	299.9
26	Texas	226.5
36	Utah	151.0
46	Vermont	68.0
30	Virginia	196.8
33	Washington	173.9
43	West Virginia	83.1
34	Wisconsin	158.8
39	Wyoming	118.5

RANK	STATE	RATE
1	California	470.8
2	Louisiana	436.8
3	New York	434.4
4	Kentucky	423.3
5	Florida	407.7
6	North Carolina	402.5
7	Massachusetts	369.6
8	Georgia	360.9
9	Connecticut	317.5
10	Missouri	310.4
11	Tennessee	299.9
12	Colorado	294.6
13	Maryland	290.9
14	Alabama	286.8
15	South Carolina	284.0
16	Alaska	283.2
17	New Jersey	271.9
18	Michigan	271.4
19	Arizona	258.9
20	Mississippi	252.1
21	Nevada	249.6
22	Rhode Island	246.7
23	Indiana	246.3
24	Pennsylvania	238.8
25	New Mexico	229.7
26	Texas	226.5
27	Arkansas	212.1
28	Ohio	210.1
29	Delaware	204.3
30	Virginia	196.8
31	Minnesota	192.2
32	Oklahoma	185.1
33	Washington	173.9
34	Wisconsin	158.8
35	Oregon	154.7
36	Utah	151.0
37	Idaho	132.3
38	Iowa	132.0
39	Wyoming	118.5
40	South Dakota	116.1
41	Hawaii	105.2
42	Nebraska	100.7
43	West Virginia	83.1
44	New Hampshire	79.0
45	Maine	78.5
46	Vermont	68.0
47	Montana	51.5
48	North Dakota	32.3
NA	Illinois**	NA
NA	Kansas**	NA

District of Columbia   949.0

Source: Morgan Quitno Corporation using data from U.S. Department of Justice, Federal Bureau of Investigation "Crime in the United States 1993" (Uniform Crime Reports, December 4, 1994)
By law enforcement agencies submitting complete reports to the F.B.I. for 12 months in 1993. These rates based on population estimates for areas under the jurisdiction of those agencies reporting. Arrest rate based on the F.B.I. estimate of reported and unreported arrests for violent crimes is 292.4 arrests per 100,000 population.
**Not available.*

6

Reported Arrests for Murder in 1993

National Total = 20,285 Reported Arrests*

ALPHA ORDER

RANK	STATE	ARRESTS	% of USA
15	Alabama	450	2.22%
38	Alaska	22	0.11%
20	Arizona	245	1.21%
19	Arkansas	282	1.39%
1	California	3,297	16.25%
24	Colorado	208	1.03%
27	Connecticut	153	0.75%
47	Delaware	2	0.01%
5	Florida	1,177	5.80%
7	Georgia	718	3.54%
34	Hawaii	52	0.26%
40	Idaho	15	0.07%
NA	Illinois**	NA	NA
23	Indiana	221	1.09%
39	Iowa	21	0.10%
NA	Kansas**	NA	NA
26	Kentucky	156	0.77%
14	Louisiana	497	2.45%
47	Maine	2	0.01%
9	Maryland	632	3.12%
29	Massachusetts	146	0.72%
3	Michigan	1,704	8.40%
22	Minnesota	231	1.14%
25	Mississippi	189	0.93%
10	Missouri	547	2.70%
41	Montana	10	0.05%
36	Nebraska	49	0.24%
31	Nevada	133	0.66%
46	New Hampshire	4	0.02%
18	New Jersey	368	1.81%
33	New Mexico	58	0.29%
4	New York	1,612	7.95%
6	North Carolina	876	4.32%
44	North Dakota	7	0.03%
13	Ohio	516	2.54%
21	Oklahoma	243	1.20%
30	Oregon	136	0.67%
8	Pennsylvania	672	3.31%
37	Rhode Island	25	0.12%
16	South Carolina	411	2.03%
41	South Dakota	10	0.05%
17	Tennessee	379	1.87%
2	Texas	1,898	9.36%
35	Utah	50	0.25%
45	Vermont	6	0.03%
11	Virginia	534	2.63%
28	Washington	147	0.72%
32	West Virginia	120	0.59%
12	Wisconsin	521	2.57%
43	Wyoming	9	0.04%

RANK ORDER

RANK	STATE	ARRESTS	% of USA
1	California	3,297	16.25%
2	Texas	1,898	9.36%
3	Michigan	1,704	8.40%
4	New York	1,612	7.95%
5	Florida	1,177	5.80%
6	North Carolina	876	4.32%
7	Georgia	718	3.54%
8	Pennsylvania	672	3.31%
9	Maryland	632	3.12%
10	Missouri	547	2.70%
11	Virginia	534	2.63%
12	Wisconsin	521	2.57%
13	Ohio	516	2.54%
14	Louisiana	497	2.45%
15	Alabama	450	2.22%
16	South Carolina	411	2.03%
17	Tennessee	379	1.87%
18	New Jersey	368	1.81%
19	Arkansas	282	1.39%
20	Arizona	245	1.21%
21	Oklahoma	243	1.20%
22	Minnesota	231	1.14%
23	Indiana	221	1.09%
24	Colorado	208	1.03%
25	Mississippi	189	0.93%
26	Kentucky	156	0.77%
27	Connecticut	153	0.75%
28	Washington	147	0.72%
29	Massachusetts	146	0.72%
30	Oregon	136	0.67%
31	Nevada	133	0.66%
32	West Virginia	120	0.59%
33	New Mexico	58	0.29%
34	Hawaii	52	0.26%
35	Utah	50	0.25%
36	Nebraska	49	0.24%
37	Rhode Island	25	0.12%
38	Alaska	22	0.11%
39	Iowa	21	0.10%
40	Idaho	15	0.07%
41	Montana	10	0.05%
41	South Dakota	10	0.05%
43	Wyoming	9	0.04%
44	North Dakota	7	0.03%
45	Vermont	6	0.03%
46	New Hampshire	4	0.02%
47	Delaware	2	0.01%
47	Maine	2	0.01%
NA	Illinois**	NA	NA
NA	Kansas**	NA	NA
	District of Columbia	283	1.40%

Source: U.S. Department of Justice, Federal Bureau of Investigation
   "Crime in the United States 1993" (Uniform Crime Reports, December 4, 1994)
*By law enforcement agencies submitting complete reports to the F.B.I. for 12 months in 1993. The F.B.I. estimates 23,400 reported and unreported arrests for murder occurred in 1993. Murder includes nonnegligent manslaughter.
**Not available.

7

Reported Arrest Rate for Murder in 1993

National Rate = 9.5 Reported Arrests per 100,000 Population*

RANK	STATE	RATE
11	Alabama	11.4
33	Alaska	3.9
25	Arizona	6.6
9	Arkansas	11.7
14	California	10.6
24	Colorado	7.0
28	Connecticut	5.5
46	Delaware	0.5
17	Florida	9.2
6	Georgia	12.8
32	Hawaii	4.4
43	Idaho	1.7
NA	Illinois**	NA
27	Indiana	6.4
45	Iowa	1.1
NA	Kansas**	NA
18	Kentucky	8.6
3	Louisiana	19.3
48	Maine	0.2
8	Maryland	12.7
35	Massachusetts	3.3
2	Michigan	20.3
29	Minnesota	5.2
1	Mississippi	22.1
4	Missouri	16.6
38	Montana	2.7
35	Nebraska	3.3
12	Nevada	11.1
46	New Hampshire	0.5
30	New Jersey	4.8
23	New Mexico	7.2
15	New York	10.4
5	North Carolina	13.0
44	North Dakota	1.3
20	Ohio	7.8
21	Oklahoma	7.7
31	Oregon	4.6
22	Pennsylvania	7.5
39	Rhode Island	2.6
10	South Carolina	11.6
42	South Dakota	2.0
6	Tennessee	12.8
13	Texas	10.9
37	Utah	2.9
40	Vermont	2.2
19	Virginia	8.2
34	Washington	3.8
25	West Virginia	6.6
15	Wisconsin	10.4
40	Wyoming	2.2

RANK	STATE	RATE
1	Mississippi	22.1
2	Michigan	20.3
3	Louisiana	19.3
4	Missouri	16.6
5	North Carolina	13.0
6	Georgia	12.8
6	Tennessee	12.8
8	Maryland	12.7
9	Arkansas	11.7
10	South Carolina	11.6
11	Alabama	11.4
12	Nevada	11.1
13	Texas	10.9
14	California	10.6
15	New York	10.4
15	Wisconsin	10.4
17	Florida	9.2
18	Kentucky	8.6
19	Virginia	8.2
20	Ohio	7.8
21	Oklahoma	7.7
22	Pennsylvania	7.5
23	New Mexico	7.2
24	Colorado	7.0
25	Arizona	6.6
25	West Virginia	6.6
27	Indiana	6.4
28	Connecticut	5.5
29	Minnesota	5.2
30	New Jersey	4.8
31	Oregon	4.6
32	Hawaii	4.4
33	Alaska	3.9
34	Washington	3.8
35	Massachusetts	3.3
35	Nebraska	3.3
37	Utah	2.9
38	Montana	2.7
39	Rhode Island	2.6
40	Vermont	2.2
40	Wyoming	2.2
42	South Dakota	2.0
43	Idaho	1.7
44	North Dakota	1.3
45	Iowa	1.1
46	Delaware	0.5
46	New Hampshire	0.5
48	Maine	0.2
NA	Illinois**	NA
NA	Kansas**	NA

District of Columbia 49.0

Source: Morgan Quitno Corporation using data from U.S. Department of Justice, Federal Bureau of Investigation "Crime in the United States 1993" (Uniform Crime Reports, December 4, 1994)

*By law enforcement agencies submitting complete reports to the F.B.I. for 12 months in 1993. These rates based on population estimates for areas under the jurisdiction of those agencies reporting. Arrest rate based on the F.B.I. estimate of reported and unreported arrests for murder is 9.1 arrests per 100,000 population.

**Not available.

Reported Arrests for Rape in 1993

National Total = 32,523 Reported Arrests*

ALPHA ORDER

RANK	STATE	ARRESTS	% of USA
19	Alabama	644	1.98%
34	Alaska	163	0.50%
29	Arizona	297	0.91%
23	Arkansas	477	1.47%
1	California	3,570	10.98%
21	Colorado	530	1.63%
25	Connecticut	438	1.35%
39	Delaware	101	0.31%
3	Florida	2,253	6.93%
14	Georgia	841	2.59%
36	Hawaii	129	0.40%
42	Idaho	80	0.25%
NA	Illinois**	NA	NA
31	Indiana	243	0.75%
38	Iowa	110	0.34%
NA	Kansas**	NA	NA
27	Kentucky	344	1.06%
24	Louisiana	462	1.42%
40	Maine	95	0.29%
11	Maryland	958	2.95%
17	Massachusetts	730	2.24%
4	Michigan	1,982	6.09%
9	Minnesota	1,070	3.29%
33	Mississippi	203	0.62%
15	Missouri	786	2.42%
48	Montana	11	0.03%
32	Nebraska	221	0.68%
28	Nevada	300	0.92%
42	New Hampshire	80	0.25%
8	New Jersey	1,151	3.54%
45	New Mexico	73	0.22%
5	New York	1,978	6.08%
13	North Carolina	847	2.60%
47	North Dakota	40	0.12%
7	Ohio	1,198	3.68%
26	Oklahoma	429	1.32%
22	Oregon	497	1.53%
6	Pennsylvania	1,208	3.71%
37	Rhode Island	112	0.34%
16	South Carolina	735	2.26%
41	South Dakota	87	0.27%
20	Tennessee	532	1.64%
2	Texas	2,653	8.16%
30	Utah	251	0.77%
44	Vermont	75	0.23%
10	Virginia	1,001	3.08%
12	Washington	954	2.93%
35	West Virginia	133	0.41%
18	Wisconsin	689	2.12%
46	Wyoming	41	0.13%

RANK ORDER

RANK	STATE	ARRESTS	% of USA
1	California	3,570	10.98%
2	Texas	2,653	8.16%
3	Florida	2,253	6.93%
4	Michigan	1,982	6.09%
5	New York	1,978	6.08%
6	Pennsylvania	1,208	3.71%
7	Ohio	1,198	3.68%
8	New Jersey	1,151	3.54%
9	Minnesota	1,070	3.29%
10	Virginia	1,001	3.08%
11	Maryland	958	2.95%
12	Washington	954	2.93%
13	North Carolina	847	2.60%
14	Georgia	841	2.59%
15	Missouri	786	2.42%
16	South Carolina	735	2.26%
17	Massachusetts	730	2.24%
18	Wisconsin	689	2.12%
19	Alabama	644	1.98%
20	Tennessee	532	1.64%
21	Colorado	530	1.63%
22	Oregon	497	1.53%
23	Arkansas	477	1.47%
24	Louisiana	462	1.42%
25	Connecticut	438	1.35%
26	Oklahoma	429	1.32%
27	Kentucky	344	1.06%
28	Nevada	300	0.92%
29	Arizona	297	0.91%
30	Utah	251	0.77%
31	Indiana	243	0.75%
32	Nebraska	221	0.68%
33	Mississippi	203	0.62%
34	Alaska	163	0.50%
35	West Virginia	133	0.41%
36	Hawaii	129	0.40%
37	Rhode Island	112	0.34%
38	Iowa	110	0.34%
39	Delaware	101	0.31%
40	Maine	95	0.29%
41	South Dakota	87	0.27%
42	Idaho	80	0.25%
42	New Hampshire	80	0.25%
44	Vermont	75	0.23%
45	New Mexico	73	0.22%
46	Wyoming	41	0.13%
47	North Dakota	40	0.12%
48	Montana	11	0.03%
NA	Illinois**	NA	NA
NA	Kansas**	NA	NA
	District of Columbia	134	0.41%

Source: U.S. Department of Justice, Federal Bureau of Investigation
"Crime in the United States 1993" (Uniform Crime Reports, December 4, 1994)
*By law enforcement agencies submitting complete reports to the F.B.I. for 12 months in 1993. The F.B.I. estimates 38,420 reported and unreported arrests for rape occurred in 1993. Forcible rape is the carnal knowledge of a female forcibly and against her will. Assaults or attempts to commit rape by force or threat of force are included.
**Not available.

9

Reported Arrest Rate for Rape in 1993

National Rate = 15.2 Reported Arrests per 100,000 Population*

ALPHA ORDER

RANK	STATE	RATE
22	Alabama	16.3
1	Alaska	28.7
43	Arizona	8.0
11	Arkansas	19.8
35	California	11.5
17	Colorado	17.8
23	Connecticut	15.8
3	Delaware	27.1
18	Florida	17.6
27	Georgia	15.0
37	Hawaii	11.0
40	Idaho	9.2
NA	Illinois**	NA
46	Indiana	7.0
47	Iowa	5.5
NA	Kansas**	NA
13	Kentucky	18.9
16	Louisiana	17.9
42	Maine	9.0
12	Maryland	19.3
21	Massachusetts	16.4
9	Michigan	23.6
6	Minnesota	24.1
7	Mississippi	23.8
7	Missouri	23.8
48	Montana	2.9
28	Nebraska	14.8
4	Nevada	24.9
38	New Hampshire	10.8
26	New Jersey	15.1
41	New Mexico	9.1
33	New York	12.7
34	North Carolina	12.5
44	North Dakota	7.5
14	Ohio	18.0
31	Oklahoma	13.5
20	Oregon	17.0
32	Pennsylvania	13.4
35	Rhode Island	11.5
10	South Carolina	20.7
19	South Dakota	17.5
14	Tennessee	18.0
25	Texas	15.2
29	Utah	14.6
2	Vermont	27.6
24	Virginia	15.4
4	Washington	24.9
45	West Virginia	7.3
30	Wisconsin	13.8
39	Wyoming	10.1

RANK ORDER

RANK	STATE	RATE
1	Alaska	28.7
2	Vermont	27.6
3	Delaware	27.1
4	Nevada	24.9
4	Washington	24.9
6	Minnesota	24.1
7	Mississippi	23.8
7	Missouri	23.8
9	Michigan	23.6
10	South Carolina	20.7
11	Arkansas	19.8
12	Maryland	19.3
13	Kentucky	18.9
14	Ohio	18.0
14	Tennessee	18.0
16	Louisiana	17.9
17	Colorado	17.8
18	Florida	17.6
19	South Dakota	17.5
20	Oregon	17.0
21	Massachusetts	16.4
22	Alabama	16.3
23	Connecticut	15.8
24	Virginia	15.4
25	Texas	15.2
26	New Jersey	15.1
27	Georgia	15.0
28	Nebraska	14.8
29	Utah	14.6
30	Wisconsin	13.8
31	Oklahoma	13.5
32	Pennsylvania	13.4
33	New York	12.7
34	North Carolina	12.5
35	California	11.5
35	Rhode Island	11.5
37	Hawaii	11.0
38	New Hampshire	10.8
39	Wyoming	10.1
40	Idaho	9.2
41	New Mexico	9.1
42	Maine	9.0
43	Arizona	8.0
44	North Dakota	7.5
45	West Virginia	7.3
46	Indiana	7.0
47	Iowa	5.5
48	Montana	2.9
NA	Illinois**	NA
NA	Kansas**	NA

District of Columbia 23.2

Source: Morgan Quitno Corporation using data from U.S. Department of Justice, Federal Bureau of Investigation
"Crime in the United States 1993" (Uniform Crime Reports, December 4, 1994)
*By law enforcement agencies submitting complete reports to the F.B.I. for 12 months in 1993. These rates based on population estimates for areas under the jurisdiction of those agencies reporting. Arrest rate based on the F.B.I. estimate of reported and unreported arrests for rape is 14.9 arrests per 100,000 population.
**Not available.

Reported Arrests for Robbery in 1993

National Total = 153,533 Reported Arrests*

<u>ALPHA ORDER</u>

RANK	STATE	ARRESTS	% of USA
18	Alabama	1,948	1.27%
39	Alaska	174	0.11%
21	Arizona	1,563	1.02%
29	Arkansas	990	0.64%
2	California	29,568	19.26%
28	Colorado	1,002	0.65%
17	Connecticut	2,003	1.30%
40	Delaware	111	0.07%
3	Florida	10,682	6.96%
10	Georgia	4,174	2.72%
32	Hawaii	460	0.30%
43	Idaho	55	0.04%
NA	Illinois**	NA	NA
30	Indiana	963	0.63%
38	Iowa	241	0.16%
NA	Kansas**	NA	NA
25	Kentucky	1,191	0.78%
14	Louisiana	2,322	1.51%
41	Maine	90	0.06%
8	Maryland	4,693	3.06%
16	Massachusetts	2,237	1.46%
7	Michigan	4,819	3.14%
22	Minnesota	1,426	0.93%
31	Mississippi	524	0.34%
13	Missouri	2,582	1.68%
47	Montana	9	0.01%
34	Nebraska	360	0.23%
26	Nevada	1,081	0.70%
42	New Hampshire	59	0.04%
6	New Jersey	5,930	3.86%
37	New Mexico	242	0.16%
1	New York	31,284	20.38%
11	North Carolina	3,960	2.58%
45	North Dakota	21	0.01%
9	Ohio	4,548	2.96%
27	Oklahoma	1,032	0.67%
23	Oregon	1,315	0.86%
5	Pennsylvania	7,259	4.73%
35	Rhode Island	274	0.18%
20	South Carolina	1,692	1.10%
44	South Dakota	27	0.02%
19	Tennessee	1,866	1.22%
4	Texas	8,994	5.86%
33	Utah	389	0.25%
48	Vermont	4	0.00%
12	Virginia	2,797	1.82%
24	Washington	1,239	0.81%
36	West Virginia	260	0.17%
15	Wisconsin	2,300	1.50%
46	Wyoming	19	0.01%

<u>RANK ORDER</u>

RANK	STATE	ARRESTS	% of USA
1	New York	31,284	20.38%
2	California	29,568	19.26%
3	Florida	10,682	6.96%
4	Texas	8,994	5.86%
5	Pennsylvania	7,259	4.73%
6	New Jersey	5,930	3.86%
7	Michigan	4,819	3.14%
8	Maryland	4,693	3.06%
9	Ohio	4,548	2.96%
10	Georgia	4,174	2.72%
11	North Carolina	3,960	2.58%
12	Virginia	2,797	1.82%
13	Missouri	2,582	1.68%
14	Louisiana	2,322	1.51%
15	Wisconsin	2,300	1.50%
16	Massachusetts	2,237	1.46%
17	Connecticut	2,003	1.30%
18	Alabama	1,948	1.27%
19	Tennessee	1,866	1.22%
20	South Carolina	1,692	1.10%
21	Arizona	1,563	1.02%
22	Minnesota	1,426	0.93%
23	Oregon	1,315	0.86%
24	Washington	1,239	0.81%
25	Kentucky	1,191	0.78%
26	Nevada	1,081	0.70%
27	Oklahoma	1,032	0.67%
28	Colorado	1,002	0.65%
29	Arkansas	990	0.64%
30	Indiana	963	0.63%
31	Mississippi	524	0.34%
32	Hawaii	460	0.30%
33	Utah	389	0.25%
34	Nebraska	360	0.23%
35	Rhode Island	274	0.18%
36	West Virginia	260	0.17%
37	New Mexico	242	0.16%
38	Iowa	241	0.16%
39	Alaska	174	0.11%
40	Delaware	111	0.07%
41	Maine	90	0.06%
42	New Hampshire	59	0.04%
43	Idaho	55	0.04%
44	South Dakota	27	0.02%
45	North Dakota	21	0.01%
46	Wyoming	19	0.01%
47	Montana	9	0.01%
48	Vermont	4	0.00%
NA	Illinois**	NA	NA
NA	Kansas**	NA	NA
	District of Columbia	1,275	0.83%

Source: U.S. Department of Justice, Federal Bureau of Investigation
   "Crime in the United States 1993" (Uniform Crime Reports, December 4, 1994)
*By law enforcement agencies submitting complete reports to the F.B.I. for 12 months in 1993. The F.B.I. estimates 173,620 reported and unreported arrests for robbery occurred in 1993. Robbery is the taking or attempting to take anything of value by force or threat of force.

**Not available.

11

Reported Arrest Rate for Robbery in 1993

National Rate = 71.7 Reported Arrests per 100,000 Population*

ALPHA ORDER			RANK ORDER		
RANK	STATE	RATE	RANK	STATE	RATE
20	Alabama	49.2	1	New York	201.4
32	Alaska	30.7	2	California	95.1
25	Arizona	41.9	3	Maryland	94.6
26	Arkansas	41.0	4	Louisiana	90.0
2	California	95.1	5	Nevada	89.9
28	Colorado	33.7	6	Florida	83.4
11	Connecticut	72.2	7	Pennsylvania	80.7
34	Delaware	29.8	8	Missouri	78.2
6	Florida	83.4	9	New Jersey	77.7
10	Georgia	74.5	10	Georgia	74.5
27	Hawaii	39.2	11	Connecticut	72.2
43	Idaho	6.3	12	Ohio	68.3
NA	Illinois**	NA	13	Kentucky	65.3
36	Indiana	27.9	14	Tennessee	63.0
40	Iowa	12.1	15	Mississippi	61.4
NA	Kansas**	NA	16	North Carolina	58.6
13	Kentucky	65.3	17	Michigan	57.5
4	Louisiana	90.0	18	Texas	51.5
41	Maine	8.6	19	Massachusetts	50.3
3	Maryland	94.6	20	Alabama	49.2
19	Massachusetts	50.3	21	South Carolina	47.6
17	Michigan	57.5	22	Wisconsin	46.0
31	Minnesota	32.1	23	Oregon	44.9
15	Mississippi	61.4	24	Virginia	43.1
8	Missouri	78.2	25	Arizona	41.9
47	Montana	2.4	26	Arkansas	41.0
37	Nebraska	24.2	27	Hawaii	39.2
5	Nevada	89.9	28	Colorado	33.7
42	New Hampshire	8.0	29	Oklahoma	32.6
9	New Jersey	77.7	30	Washington	32.3
33	New Mexico	30.0	31	Minnesota	32.1
1	New York	201.4	32	Alaska	30.7
16	North Carolina	58.6	33	New Mexico	30.0
46	North Dakota	3.9	34	Delaware	29.8
12	Ohio	68.3	35	Rhode Island	28.2
29	Oklahoma	32.6	36	Indiana	27.9
23	Oregon	44.9	37	Nebraska	24.2
7	Pennsylvania	80.7	38	Utah	22.7
35	Rhode Island	28.2	39	West Virginia	14.3
21	South Carolina	47.6	40	Iowa	12.1
44	South Dakota	5.4	41	Maine	8.6
14	Tennessee	63.0	42	New Hampshire	8.0
18	Texas	51.5	43	Idaho	6.3
38	Utah	22.7	44	South Dakota	5.4
48	Vermont	1.5	45	Wyoming	4.7
24	Virginia	43.1	46	North Dakota	3.9
30	Washington	32.3	47	Montana	2.4
39	West Virginia	14.3	48	Vermont	1.5
22	Wisconsin	46.0	NA	Illinois**	NA
45	Wyoming	4.7	NA	Kansas**	NA

District of Columbia 220.6

Source: Morgan Quitno Corporation using data from U.S. Department of Justice, Federal Bureau of Investigation "Crime in the United States 1993" (Uniform Crime Reports, December 4, 1994)
By law enforcement agencies submitting complete reports to the F.B.I. for 12 months in 1993. These rates based on population estimates for areas under the jurisdiction of those agencies reporting. Arrest rate based on the F.B.I. estimate of reported and unreported arrests for robbery is 67.3 arrests per 100,000 population.
**Not available.*

12

Reported Arrests for Aggravated Assault in 1993

National Total = 442,075 Reported Arrests*

<u>ALPHA ORDER</u>

RANK	STATE	ARRESTS	% of USA
12	Alabama	8,305	1.88%
35	Alaska	1,247	0.28%
16	Arizona	7,552	1.71%
28	Arkansas	3,374	0.76%
1	California	109,885	24.86%
19	Colorado	7,020	1.59%
21	Connecticut	6,209	1.40%
42	Delaware	548	0.12%
2	Florida	38,117	8.62%
6	Georgia	14,475	3.27%
41	Hawaii	592	0.13%
37	Idaho	997	0.23%
NA	Illinois**	NA	NA
18	Indiana	7,074	1.60%
30	Iowa	2,266	0.51%
NA	Kansas**	NA	NA
23	Kentucky	6,025	1.36%
14	Louisiana	7,985	1.81%
40	Maine	639	0.14%
13	Maryland	8,150	1.84%
8	Massachusetts	13,337	3.02%
7	Michigan	14,254	3.22%
24	Minnesota	5,806	1.31%
36	Mississippi	1,237	0.28%
20	Missouri	6,336	1.43%
46	Montana	164	0.04%
39	Nebraska	869	0.20%
33	Nevada	1,489	0.34%
44	New Hampshire	440	0.10%
9	New Jersey	13,308	3.01%
34	New Mexico	1,478	0.33%
3	New York	32,593	7.37%
5	North Carolina	21,512	4.87%
47	North Dakota	105	0.02%
15	Ohio	7,719	1.75%
27	Oklahoma	4,164	0.94%
29	Oregon	2,585	0.58%
10	Pennsylvania	12,341	2.79%
31	Rhode Island	1,984	0.45%
17	South Carolina	7,254	1.64%
43	South Dakota	454	0.10%
22	Tennessee	6,099	1.38%
4	Texas	25,981	5.88%
32	Utah	1,902	0.43%
48	Vermont	100	0.02%
11	Virginia	8,439	1.91%
26	Washington	4,332	0.98%
38	West Virginia	993	0.22%
25	Wisconsin	4,437	1.00%
45	Wyoming	412	0.09%

<u>RANK ORDER</u>

RANK	STATE	ARRESTS	% of USA
1	California	109,885	24.86%
2	Florida	38,117	8.62%
3	New York	32,593	7.37%
4	Texas	25,981	5.88%
5	North Carolina	21,512	4.87%
6	Georgia	14,475	3.27%
7	Michigan	14,254	3.22%
8	Massachusetts	13,337	3.02%
9	New Jersey	13,308	3.01%
10	Pennsylvania	12,341	2.79%
11	Virginia	8,439	1.91%
12	Alabama	8,305	1.88%
13	Maryland	8,150	1.84%
14	Louisiana	7,985	1.81%
15	Ohio	7,719	1.75%
16	Arizona	7,552	1.71%
17	South Carolina	7,254	1.64%
18	Indiana	7,074	1.60%
19	Colorado	7,020	1.59%
20	Missouri	6,336	1.43%
21	Connecticut	6,209	1.40%
22	Tennessee	6,099	1.38%
23	Kentucky	6,025	1.36%
24	Minnesota	5,806	1.31%
25	Wisconsin	4,437	1.00%
26	Washington	4,332	0.98%
27	Oklahoma	4,164	0.94%
28	Arkansas	3,374	0.76%
29	Oregon	2,585	0.58%
30	Iowa	2,266	0.51%
31	Rhode Island	1,984	0.45%
32	Utah	1,902	0.43%
33	Nevada	1,489	0.34%
34	New Mexico	1,478	0.33%
35	Alaska	1,247	0.28%
36	Mississippi	1,237	0.28%
37	Idaho	997	0.23%
38	West Virginia	993	0.22%
39	Nebraska	869	0.20%
40	Maine	639	0.14%
41	Hawaii	592	0.13%
42	Delaware	548	0.12%
43	South Dakota	454	0.10%
44	New Hampshire	440	0.10%
45	Wyoming	412	0.09%
46	Montana	164	0.04%
47	North Dakota	105	0.02%
48	Vermont	100	0.02%
NA	Illinois**	NA	NA
NA	Kansas**	NA	NA
	District of Columbia	3,793	0.86%

Source: U.S. Department of Justice, Federal Bureau of Investigation
    "Crime in the United States 1993" (Uniform Crime Reports, December 4, 1994)
*By law enforcement agencies submitting complete reports to the F.B.I. for 12 months in 1993. The F.B.I. estimates
518,670 reported and unreported arrests for aggravated assault occurred in 1993. Aggravated assault is an attack for the
purpose of inflicting severe bodily injury.
**Not available.   13

Reported Arrest Rate for Aggravated Assault in 1993

National Rate = 206.5 Reported Arrests per 100,000 Population*

<u>ALPHA ORDER</u>

RANK	STATE	RATE
11	Alabama	209.9
10	Alaska	219.9
17	Arizona	202.5
26	Arkansas	139.7
1	California	353.6
8	Colorado	236.0
9	Connecticut	223.9
24	Delaware	146.9
6	Florida	297.5
7	Georgia	258.5
45	Hawaii	50.5
33	Idaho	115.0
NA	Illinois**	NA
14	Indiana	204.9
34	Iowa	113.4
NA	Kansas**	NA
2	Kentucky	330.5
4	Louisiana	309.6
41	Maine	60.7
22	Maryland	164.2
5	Massachusetts	299.6
21	Michigan	170.0
29	Minnesota	130.8
25	Mississippi	144.8
18	Missouri	191.8
46	Montana	43.5
43	Nebraska	58.4
31	Nevada	123.8
42	New Hampshire	59.6
20	New Jersey	174.3
19	New Mexico	183.4
12	New York	209.8
3	North Carolina	318.4
48	North Dakota	19.6
32	Ohio	116.0
28	Oklahoma	131.4
40	Oregon	88.2
27	Pennsylvania	137.2
15	Rhode Island	204.3
16	South Carolina	204.1
38	South Dakota	91.2
13	Tennessee	206.0
23	Texas	148.9
36	Utah	110.8
47	Vermont	36.8
30	Virginia	130.1
35	Washington	112.9
44	West Virginia	54.8
39	Wisconsin	88.7
37	Wyoming	101.5

<u>RANK ORDER</u>

RANK	STATE	RATE
1	California	353.6
2	Kentucky	330.5
3	North Carolina	318.4
4	Louisiana	309.6
5	Massachusetts	299.6
6	Florida	297.5
7	Georgia	258.5
8	Colorado	236.0
9	Connecticut	223.9
10	Alaska	219.9
11	Alabama	209.9
12	New York	209.8
13	Tennessee	206.0
14	Indiana	204.9
15	Rhode Island	204.3
16	South Carolina	204.1
17	Arizona	202.5
18	Missouri	191.8
19	New Mexico	183.4
20	New Jersey	174.3
21	Michigan	170.0
22	Maryland	164.2
23	Texas	148.9
24	Delaware	146.9
25	Mississippi	144.8
26	Arkansas	139.7
27	Pennsylvania	137.2
28	Oklahoma	131.4
29	Minnesota	130.8
30	Virginia	130.1
31	Nevada	123.8
32	Ohio	116.0
33	Idaho	115.0
34	Iowa	113.4
35	Washington	112.9
36	Utah	110.8
37	Wyoming	101.5
38	South Dakota	91.2
39	Wisconsin	88.7
40	Oregon	88.2
41	Maine	60.7
42	New Hampshire	59.6
43	Nebraska	58.4
44	West Virginia	54.8
45	Hawaii	50.5
46	Montana	43.5
47	Vermont	36.8
48	North Dakota	19.6
NA	Illinois**	NA
NA	Kansas**	NA

District of Columbia 656.2

Source: Morgan Quitno Corporation using data from U.S. Department of Justice, Federal Bureau of Investigation
"Crime in the United States 1993" (Uniform Crime Reports, December 4, 1994)
*By law enforcement agencies submitting complete reports to the F.B.I. for 12 months in 1993. These rates based on
population estimates for areas under the jurisdiction of those agencies reporting. Arrest rate based on the F.B.I. estimate
of reported and unreported arrests for aggravated assault is 201.1 arrests per 100,000 population.
**Not available.

Reported Arrests for Property Crime in 1993

National Total = 1,774,423 Reported Arrests*

ALPHA ORDER

RANK	STATE	ARRESTS	% of USA
26	Alabama	23,595	1.33%
40	Alaska	6,694	0.38%
13	Arizona	45,378	2.56%
29	Arkansas	18,353	1.03%
1	California	276,476	15.58%
16	Colorado	36,540	2.06%
20	Connecticut	30,898	1.74%
47	Delaware	1,543	0.09%
3	Florida	119,648	6.74%
11	Georgia	49,968	2.82%
33	Hawaii	11,399	0.64%
38	Idaho	7,578	0.43%
NA	Illinois**	NA	NA
25	Indiana	23,703	1.34%
34	Iowa	10,815	0.61%
NA	Kansas**	NA	NA
30	Kentucky	14,770	0.83%
21	Louisiana	28,627	1.61%
39	Maine	7,531	0.42%
10	Maryland	50,059	2.82%
27	Massachusetts	22,146	1.25%
12	Michigan	49,187	2.77%
19	Minnesota	33,980	1.91%
35	Mississippi	10,418	0.59%
18	Missouri	35,016	1.97%
46	Montana	1,544	0.09%
32	Nebraska	11,598	0.65%
31	Nevada	13,758	0.78%
44	New Hampshire	3,748	0.21%
8	New Jersey	53,678	3.03%
36	New Mexico	8,667	0.49%
4	New York	102,846	5.80%
6	North Carolina	58,415	3.29%
43	North Dakota	3,800	0.21%
15	Ohio	43,499	2.45%
28	Oklahoma	21,047	1.19%
17	Oregon	35,507	2.00%
7	Pennsylvania	54,507	3.07%
41	Rhode Island	5,804	0.33%
23	South Carolina	25,043	1.41%
42	South Dakota	4,656	0.26%
24	Tennessee	24,848	1.40%
2	Texas	149,731	8.44%
22	Utah	25,762	1.45%
48	Vermont	956	0.05%
9	Virginia	50,772	2.86%
14	Washington	44,308	2.50%
37	West Virginia	7,787	0.44%
5	Wisconsin	60,095	3.39%
45	Wyoming	2,540	0.14%

RANK ORDER

RANK	STATE	ARRESTS	% of USA
1	California	276,476	15.58%
2	Texas	149,731	8.44%
3	Florida	119,648	6.74%
4	New York	102,846	5.80%
5	Wisconsin	60,095	3.39%
6	North Carolina	58,415	3.29%
7	Pennsylvania	54,507	3.07%
8	New Jersey	53,678	3.03%
9	Virginia	50,772	2.86%
10	Maryland	50,059	2.82%
11	Georgia	49,968	2.82%
12	Michigan	49,187	2.77%
13	Arizona	45,378	2.56%
14	Washington	44,308	2.50%
15	Ohio	43,499	2.45%
16	Colorado	36,540	2.06%
17	Oregon	35,507	2.00%
18	Missouri	35,016	1.97%
19	Minnesota	33,980	1.91%
20	Connecticut	30,898	1.74%
21	Louisiana	28,627	1.61%
22	Utah	25,762	1.45%
23	South Carolina	25,043	1.41%
24	Tennessee	24,848	1.40%
25	Indiana	23,703	1.34%
26	Alabama	23,595	1.33%
27	Massachusetts	22,146	1.25%
28	Oklahoma	21,047	1.19%
29	Arkansas	18,353	1.03%
30	Kentucky	14,770	0.83%
31	Nevada	13,758	0.78%
32	Nebraska	11,598	0.65%
33	Hawaii	11,399	0.64%
34	Iowa	10,815	0.61%
35	Mississippi	10,418	0.59%
36	New Mexico	8,667	0.49%
37	West Virginia	7,787	0.44%
38	Idaho	7,578	0.43%
39	Maine	7,531	0.42%
40	Alaska	6,694	0.38%
41	Rhode Island	5,804	0.33%
42	South Dakota	4,656	0.26%
43	North Dakota	3,800	0.21%
44	New Hampshire	3,748	0.21%
45	Wyoming	2,540	0.14%
46	Montana	1,544	0.09%
47	Delaware	1,543	0.09%
48	Vermont	956	0.05%
NA	Illinois**	NA	NA
NA	Kansas**	NA	NA
	District of Columbia	6,191	0.35%

Source: U.S. Department of Justice, Federal Bureau of Investigation
"Crime in the United States 1993" (Uniform Crime Reports, December 4, 1994)
*By law enforcement agencies submitting complete reports to the F.B.I. for 12 months in 1993. The F.B.I. estimates 2,094,300 reported and unreported arrests for property crime occurred in 1993. Property crimes are offenses of burglary, larceny-theft, motor vehicle theft and arson.
**Not available.

15

Reported Arrest Rate for Property Crime in 1993

National Rate = 828.8 Reported Arrests per 100,000 Population*

ALPHA ORDER				RANK ORDER		
RANK	STATE	RATE		RANK	STATE	RATE
40	Alabama	596.4		1	Utah	1,500.4
7	Alaska	1,180.6		2	Colorado	1,228.6
4	Arizona	1,216.6		3	Mississippi	1,219.9
28	Arkansas	760.0		4	Arizona	1,216.6
19	California	889.6		5	Oregon	1,211.8
2	Colorado	1,228.6		6	Wisconsin	1,201.2
10	Connecticut	1,114.2		7	Alaska	1,180.6
46	Delaware	413.7		8	Washington	1,154.8
17	Florida	933.9		9	Nevada	1,143.6
18	Georgia	892.3		10	Connecticut	1,114.2
15	Hawaii	972.6		11	Louisiana	1,110.0
20	Idaho	874.0		12	New Mexico	1,075.3
NA	Illinois**	NA		13	Missouri	1,060.1
33	Indiana	686.6		14	Maryland	1,008.8
42	Iowa	541.3		15	Hawaii	972.6
NA	Kansas**	NA		16	South Dakota	934.9
24	Kentucky	810.2		17	Florida	933.9
11	Louisiana	1,110.0		18	Georgia	892.3
29	Maine	715.9		19	California	889.6
14	Maryland	1,008.8		20	Idaho	874.0
44	Massachusetts	497.6		21	North Carolina	864.5
41	Michigan	586.5		22	Texas	858.1
27	Minnesota	765.3		23	Tennessee	839.5
3	Mississippi	1,219.9		24	Kentucky	810.2
13	Missouri	1,060.1		25	Virginia	782.6
47	Montana	409.5		26	Nebraska	778.9
26	Nebraska	778.9		27	Minnesota	765.3
9	Nevada	1,143.6		28	Arkansas	760.0
43	New Hampshire	507.9		29	Maine	715.9
32	New Jersey	703.2		30	North Dakota	710.3
12	New Mexico	1,075.3		31	South Carolina	704.6
35	New York	662.2		32	New Jersey	703.2
21	North Carolina	864.5		33	Indiana	686.6
30	North Dakota	710.3		34	Oklahoma	663.9
36	Ohio	653.7		35	New York	662.2
34	Oklahoma	663.9		36	Ohio	653.7
5	Oregon	1,211.8		37	Wyoming	625.6
38	Pennsylvania	606.0		38	Pennsylvania	606.0
39	Rhode Island	597.7		39	Rhode Island	597.7
31	South Carolina	704.6		40	Alabama	596.4
16	South Dakota	934.9		41	Michigan	586.5
23	Tennessee	839.5		42	Iowa	541.3
22	Texas	858.1		43	New Hampshire	507.9
1	Utah	1,500.4		44	Massachusetts	497.6
48	Vermont	351.5		45	West Virginia	429.7
25	Virginia	782.6		46	Delaware	413.7
8	Washington	1,154.8		47	Montana	409.5
45	West Virginia	429.7		48	Vermont	351.5
6	Wisconsin	1,201.2		NA	Illinois**	NA
37	Wyoming	625.6		NA	Kansas**	NA
					District of Columbia	1,071.1

Source: Morgan Quitno Corporation using data from U.S. Department of Justice, Federal Bureau of Investigation
    "Crime in the United States 1993" (Uniform Crime Reports, December 4, 1994)
*By law enforcement agencies submitting complete reports to the F.B.I. for 12 months in 1993. These rates based on
population estimates for areas under the jurisdiction of those agencies reporting. Arrest rate based on the F.B.I. estimate
of reported and unreported arrests for property crime is 812.0 arrests per 100,000 population.
**Not available.

Reported Arrests for Burglary in 1993

National Total = 338,238 Reported Arrests*

<table>
<tr><td colspan="4">ALPHA ORDER</td><td colspan="4">RANK ORDER</td></tr>
<tr><td>RANK</td><td>STATE</td><td>ARRESTS</td><td>% of USA</td><td>RANK</td><td>STATE</td><td>ARRESTS</td><td>% of USA</td></tr>
<tr><td>25</td><td>Alabama</td><td>3,941</td><td>1.17%</td><td>1</td><td>California</td><td>74,564</td><td>22.04%</td></tr>
<tr><td>38</td><td>Alaska</td><td>1,123</td><td>0.33%</td><td>2</td><td>Florida</td><td>27,391</td><td>8.10%</td></tr>
<tr><td>13</td><td>Arizona</td><td>7,061</td><td>2.09%</td><td>3</td><td>Texas</td><td>25,956</td><td>7.67%</td></tr>
<tr><td>27</td><td>Arkansas</td><td>3,387</td><td>1.00%</td><td>4</td><td>New York</td><td>18,209</td><td>5.38%</td></tr>
<tr><td>1</td><td>California</td><td>74,564</td><td>22.04%</td><td>5</td><td>North Carolina</td><td>15,847</td><td>4.69%</td></tr>
<tr><td>26</td><td>Colorado</td><td>3,774</td><td>1.12%</td><td>6</td><td>Maryland</td><td>10,907</td><td>3.22%</td></tr>
<tr><td>18</td><td>Connecticut</td><td>5,548</td><td>1.64%</td><td>7</td><td>New Jersey</td><td>10,389</td><td>3.07%</td></tr>
<tr><td>44</td><td>Delaware</td><td>433</td><td>0.13%</td><td>8</td><td>Pennsylvania</td><td>10,239</td><td>3.03%</td></tr>
<tr><td>2</td><td>Florida</td><td>27,391</td><td>8.10%</td><td>9</td><td>Georgia</td><td>9,380</td><td>2.77%</td></tr>
<tr><td>9</td><td>Georgia</td><td>9,380</td><td>2.77%</td><td>10</td><td>Michigan</td><td>9,377</td><td>2.77%</td></tr>
<tr><td>35</td><td>Hawaii</td><td>1,549</td><td>0.46%</td><td>11</td><td>Ohio</td><td>8,058</td><td>2.38%</td></tr>
<tr><td>41</td><td>Idaho</td><td>875</td><td>0.26%</td><td>12</td><td>Virginia</td><td>7,351</td><td>2.17%</td></tr>
<tr><td>NA</td><td>Illinois**</td><td>NA</td><td>NA</td><td>13</td><td>Arizona</td><td>7,061</td><td>2.09%</td></tr>
<tr><td>28</td><td>Indiana</td><td>3,133</td><td>0.93%</td><td>14</td><td>Wisconsin</td><td>6,922</td><td>2.05%</td></tr>
<tr><td>33</td><td>Iowa</td><td>1,740</td><td>0.51%</td><td>15</td><td>Washington</td><td>5,963</td><td>1.76%</td></tr>
<tr><td>NA</td><td>Kansas**</td><td>NA</td><td>NA</td><td>16</td><td>South Carolina</td><td>5,906</td><td>1.75%</td></tr>
<tr><td>29</td><td>Kentucky</td><td>3,095</td><td>0.92%</td><td>17</td><td>Massachusetts</td><td>5,714</td><td>1.69%</td></tr>
<tr><td>19</td><td>Louisiana</td><td>5,539</td><td>1.64%</td><td>18</td><td>Connecticut</td><td>5,548</td><td>1.64%</td></tr>
<tr><td>34</td><td>Maine</td><td>1,658</td><td>0.49%</td><td>19</td><td>Louisiana</td><td>5,539</td><td>1.64%</td></tr>
<tr><td>6</td><td>Maryland</td><td>10,907</td><td>3.22%</td><td>20</td><td>Missouri</td><td>5,294</td><td>1.57%</td></tr>
<tr><td>17</td><td>Massachusetts</td><td>5,714</td><td>1.69%</td><td>21</td><td>Minnesota</td><td>4,762</td><td>1.41%</td></tr>
<tr><td>10</td><td>Michigan</td><td>9,377</td><td>2.77%</td><td>22</td><td>Oregon</td><td>4,579</td><td>1.35%</td></tr>
<tr><td>21</td><td>Minnesota</td><td>4,762</td><td>1.41%</td><td>23</td><td>Tennessee</td><td>4,303</td><td>1.27%</td></tr>
<tr><td>32</td><td>Mississippi</td><td>1,892</td><td>0.56%</td><td>24</td><td>Oklahoma</td><td>4,069</td><td>1.20%</td></tr>
<tr><td>20</td><td>Missouri</td><td>5,294</td><td>1.57%</td><td>25</td><td>Alabama</td><td>3,941</td><td>1.17%</td></tr>
<tr><td>47</td><td>Montana</td><td>238</td><td>0.07%</td><td>26</td><td>Colorado</td><td>3,774</td><td>1.12%</td></tr>
<tr><td>37</td><td>Nebraska</td><td>1,306</td><td>0.39%</td><td>27</td><td>Arkansas</td><td>3,387</td><td>1.00%</td></tr>
<tr><td>30</td><td>Nevada</td><td>2,892</td><td>0.86%</td><td>28</td><td>Indiana</td><td>3,133</td><td>0.93%</td></tr>
<tr><td>43</td><td>New Hampshire</td><td>461</td><td>0.14%</td><td>29</td><td>Kentucky</td><td>3,095</td><td>0.92%</td></tr>
<tr><td>7</td><td>New Jersey</td><td>10,389</td><td>3.07%</td><td>30</td><td>Nevada</td><td>2,892</td><td>0.86%</td></tr>
<tr><td>40</td><td>New Mexico</td><td>1,013</td><td>0.30%</td><td>31</td><td>Utah</td><td>2,707</td><td>0.80%</td></tr>
<tr><td>4</td><td>New York</td><td>18,209</td><td>5.38%</td><td>32</td><td>Mississippi</td><td>1,892</td><td>0.56%</td></tr>
<tr><td>5</td><td>North Carolina</td><td>15,847</td><td>4.69%</td><td>33</td><td>Iowa</td><td>1,740</td><td>0.51%</td></tr>
<tr><td>45</td><td>North Dakota</td><td>421</td><td>0.12%</td><td>34</td><td>Maine</td><td>1,658</td><td>0.49%</td></tr>
<tr><td>11</td><td>Ohio</td><td>8,058</td><td>2.38%</td><td>35</td><td>Hawaii</td><td>1,549</td><td>0.46%</td></tr>
<tr><td>24</td><td>Oklahoma</td><td>4,069</td><td>1.20%</td><td>36</td><td>West Virginia</td><td>1,408</td><td>0.42%</td></tr>
<tr><td>22</td><td>Oregon</td><td>4,579</td><td>1.35%</td><td>37</td><td>Nebraska</td><td>1,306</td><td>0.39%</td></tr>
<tr><td>8</td><td>Pennsylvania</td><td>10,239</td><td>3.03%</td><td>38</td><td>Alaska</td><td>1,123</td><td>0.33%</td></tr>
<tr><td>39</td><td>Rhode Island</td><td>1,103</td><td>0.33%</td><td>39</td><td>Rhode Island</td><td>1,103</td><td>0.33%</td></tr>
<tr><td>16</td><td>South Carolina</td><td>5,906</td><td>1.75%</td><td>40</td><td>New Mexico</td><td>1,013</td><td>0.30%</td></tr>
<tr><td>42</td><td>South Dakota</td><td>671</td><td>0.20%</td><td>41</td><td>Idaho</td><td>875</td><td>0.26%</td></tr>
<tr><td>23</td><td>Tennessee</td><td>4,303</td><td>1.27%</td><td>42</td><td>South Dakota</td><td>671</td><td>0.20%</td></tr>
<tr><td>3</td><td>Texas</td><td>25,956</td><td>7.67%</td><td>43</td><td>New Hampshire</td><td>461</td><td>0.14%</td></tr>
<tr><td>31</td><td>Utah</td><td>2,707</td><td>0.80%</td><td>44</td><td>Delaware</td><td>433</td><td>0.13%</td></tr>
<tr><td>48</td><td>Vermont</td><td>228</td><td>0.07%</td><td>45</td><td>North Dakota</td><td>421</td><td>0.12%</td></tr>
<tr><td>12</td><td>Virginia</td><td>7,351</td><td>2.17%</td><td>46</td><td>Wyoming</td><td>290</td><td>0.09%</td></tr>
<tr><td>15</td><td>Washington</td><td>5,963</td><td>1.76%</td><td>47</td><td>Montana</td><td>238</td><td>0.07%</td></tr>
<tr><td>36</td><td>West Virginia</td><td>1,408</td><td>0.42%</td><td>48</td><td>Vermont</td><td>228</td><td>0.07%</td></tr>
<tr><td>14</td><td>Wisconsin</td><td>6,922</td><td>2.05%</td><td>NA</td><td>Illinois**</td><td>NA</td><td>NA</td></tr>
<tr><td>46</td><td>Wyoming</td><td>290</td><td>0.09%</td><td>NA</td><td>Kansas**</td><td>NA</td><td>NA</td></tr>
<tr><td></td><td></td><td></td><td></td><td></td><td>District of Columbia</td><td>1,038</td><td>0.31%</td></tr>
</table>

Source: U.S. Department of Justice, Federal Bureau of Investigation
"Crime in the United States 1993" (Uniform Crime Reports, December 4, 1994)
*By law enforcement agencies submitting complete reports to the F.B.I. for 12 months in 1993. The F.B.I. estimates 402,700 reported and unreported arrests for burglary occurred in 1993. Burglary is the unlawful entry of a structure to commit a felony or theft. Attempts are included.
**Not available.

Reported Arrest Rate for Burglary in 1993

National Rate = 158.0 Reported Arrests per 100,000 Population*

ALPHA ORDER

RANK	STATE	RATE
39	Alabama	99.6
9	Alaska	198.1
10	Arizona	189.3
21	Arkansas	140.2
2	California	239.9
28	Colorado	126.9
8	Connecticut	200.1
32	Delaware	116.1
7	Florida	213.8
12	Georgia	167.5
25	Hawaii	132.2
38	Idaho	100.9
NA	Illinois**	NA
40	Indiana	90.8
42	Iowa	87.1
NA	Kansas**	NA
11	Kentucky	169.8
6	Louisiana	214.8
16	Maine	157.6
5	Maryland	219.8
26	Massachusetts	128.4
36	Michigan	111.8
37	Minnesota	107.3
4	Mississippi	221.5
14	Missouri	160.3
47	Montana	63.1
41	Nebraska	87.7
1	Nevada	240.4
48	New Hampshire	62.5
23	New Jersey	136.1
29	New Mexico	125.7
31	New York	117.2
3	North Carolina	234.5
44	North Dakota	78.7
30	Ohio	121.1
26	Oklahoma	128.4
17	Oregon	156.3
33	Pennsylvania	113.8
34	Rhode Island	113.6
13	South Carolina	166.2
24	South Dakota	134.7
20	Tennessee	145.4
19	Texas	148.8
15	Utah	157.7
43	Vermont	83.8
35	Virginia	113.3
18	Washington	155.4
45	West Virginia	77.7
22	Wisconsin	138.4
46	Wyoming	71.4

RANK ORDER

RANK	STATE	RATE
1	Nevada	240.4
2	California	239.9
3	North Carolina	234.5
4	Mississippi	221.5
5	Maryland	219.8
6	Louisiana	214.8
7	Florida	213.8
8	Connecticut	200.1
9	Alaska	198.1
10	Arizona	189.3
11	Kentucky	169.8
12	Georgia	167.5
13	South Carolina	166.2
14	Missouri	160.3
15	Utah	157.7
16	Maine	157.6
17	Oregon	156.3
18	Washington	155.4
19	Texas	148.8
20	Tennessee	145.4
21	Arkansas	140.2
22	Wisconsin	138.4
23	New Jersey	136.1
24	South Dakota	134.7
25	Hawaii	132.2
26	Massachusetts	128.4
26	Oklahoma	128.4
28	Colorado	126.9
29	New Mexico	125.7
30	Ohio	121.1
31	New York	117.2
32	Delaware	116.1
33	Pennsylvania	113.8
34	Rhode Island	113.6
35	Virginia	113.3
36	Michigan	111.8
37	Minnesota	107.3
38	Idaho	100.9
39	Alabama	99.6
40	Indiana	90.8
41	Nebraska	87.7
42	Iowa	87.1
43	Vermont	83.8
44	North Dakota	78.7
45	West Virginia	77.7
46	Wyoming	71.4
47	Montana	63.1
48	New Hampshire	62.5
NA	Illinois**	NA
NA	Kansas**	NA

District of Columbia   179.6

Source: Morgan Quitno Corporation using data from U.S. Department of Justice, Federal Bureau of Investigation "Crime in the United States 1993" (Uniform Crime Reports, December 4, 1994)

*By law enforcement agencies submitting complete reports to the F.B.I. for 12 months in 1993. These rates based on population estimates for areas under the jurisdiction of those agencies reporting. Arrest rate based on the F.B.I. estimate of reported and unreported arrests for burglary is 156.1 arrests per 100,000 population.

**Not available.

Reported Arrests for Larceny and Theft in 1993

National Total = 1,251,277 Reported Arrests*

ALPHA ORDER

RANK	STATE	ARRESTS	% of USA
25	Alabama	17,870	1.43%
40	Alaska	5,056	0.40%
13	Arizona	34,762	2.78%
28	Arkansas	14,110	1.13%
1	California	155,343	12.41%
16	Colorado	29,977	2.40%
20	Connecticut	22,588	1.81%
47	Delaware	997	0.08%
3	Florida	79,087	6.32%
9	Georgia	36,218	2.89%
34	Hawaii	8,137	0.65%
37	Idaho	6,138	0.49%
NA	Illinois**	NA	NA
24	Indiana	18,385	1.47%
33	Iowa	8,377	0.67%
NA	Kansas**	NA	NA
30	Kentucky	10,297	0.82%
21	Louisiana	21,623	1.73%
39	Maine	5,360	0.43%
14	Maryland	32,060	2.56%
29	Massachusetts	14,094	1.13%
11	Michigan	35,932	2.87%
19	Minnesota	25,322	2.02%
35	Mississippi	7,745	0.62%
18	Missouri	25,740	2.06%
46	Montana	1,147	0.09%
32	Nebraska	9,700	0.78%
31	Nevada	10,141	0.81%
44	New Hampshire	3,090	0.25%
6	New Jersey	40,083	3.20%
36	New Mexico	7,321	0.59%
4	New York	72,000	5.75%
7	North Carolina	39,779	3.18%
43	North Dakota	3,099	0.25%
15	Ohio	30,918	2.47%
27	Oklahoma	14,131	1.13%
17	Oregon	26,958	2.15%
10	Pennsylvania	36,031	2.88%
41	Rhode Island	3,928	0.31%
26	South Carolina	17,757	1.42%
42	South Dakota	3,729	0.30%
23	Tennessee	18,960	1.52%
2	Texas	108,529	8.67%
22	Utah	21,315	1.70%
48	Vermont	654	0.05%
8	Virginia	39,341	3.14%
12	Washington	35,762	2.86%
38	West Virginia	5,750	0.46%
5	Wisconsin	47,674	3.81%
45	Wyoming	2,077	0.17%

RANK ORDER

RANK	STATE	ARRESTS	% of USA
1	California	155,343	12.41%
2	Texas	108,529	8.67%
3	Florida	79,087	6.32%
4	New York	72,000	5.75%
5	Wisconsin	47,674	3.81%
6	New Jersey	40,083	3.20%
7	North Carolina	39,779	3.18%
8	Virginia	39,341	3.14%
9	Georgia	36,218	2.89%
10	Pennsylvania	36,031	2.88%
11	Michigan	35,932	2.87%
12	Washington	35,762	2.86%
13	Arizona	34,762	2.78%
14	Maryland	32,060	2.56%
15	Ohio	30,918	2.47%
16	Colorado	29,977	2.40%
17	Oregon	26,958	2.15%
18	Missouri	25,740	2.06%
19	Minnesota	25,322	2.02%
20	Connecticut	22,588	1.81%
21	Louisiana	21,623	1.73%
22	Utah	21,315	1.70%
23	Tennessee	18,960	1.52%
24	Indiana	18,385	1.47%
25	Alabama	17,870	1.43%
26	South Carolina	17,757	1.42%
27	Oklahoma	14,131	1.13%
28	Arkansas	14,110	1.13%
29	Massachusetts	14,094	1.13%
30	Kentucky	10,297	0.82%
31	Nevada	10,141	0.81%
32	Nebraska	9,700	0.78%
33	Iowa	8,377	0.67%
34	Hawaii	8,137	0.65%
35	Mississippi	7,745	0.62%
36	New Mexico	7,321	0.59%
37	Idaho	6,138	0.49%
38	West Virginia	5,750	0.46%
39	Maine	5,360	0.43%
40	Alaska	5,056	0.40%
41	Rhode Island	3,928	0.31%
42	South Dakota	3,729	0.30%
43	North Dakota	3,099	0.25%
44	New Hampshire	3,090	0.25%
45	Wyoming	2,077	0.17%
46	Montana	1,147	0.09%
47	Delaware	997	0.08%
48	Vermont	654	0.05%
NA	Illinois**	NA	NA
NA	Kansas**	NA	NA
	District of Columbia	3,152	0.25%

Source: U.S. Department of Justice, Federal Bureau of Investigation
    "Crime in the United States 1993" (Uniform Crime Reports, December 4, 1994)
*By law enforcement agencies submitting complete reports to the F.B.I. for 12 months in 1993. The F.B.I. estimates
1,476,300 reported and unreported arrests for larceny and theft occurred in 1993. Larceny and theft is the unlawful taking
of property without use of force, violence or fraud. Attempts are included. Motor vehicle thefts are excluded.
**Not available.

Reported Arrest Rate for Larceny and Theft in 1993

National Rate = 584.4 Reported Arrests per 100,000 Population*

ALPHA ORDER

RANK ORDER

RANK	STATE	RATE		RANK	STATE	RATE
37	Alabama	451.7		1	Utah	1,241.4
9	Alaska	891.7		2	Colorado	1,008.0
4	Arizona	932.0		3	Wisconsin	952.9
25	Arkansas	584.3		4	Arizona	932.0
33	California	499.8		4	Washington	932.0
2	Colorado	1,008.0		6	Oregon	920.1
12	Connecticut	814.6		7	New Mexico	908.3
47	Delaware	267.3		8	Mississippi	906.9
22	Florida	617.3		9	Alaska	891.7
18	Georgia	646.8		10	Nevada	843.0
16	Hawaii	694.3		11	Louisiana	838.4
15	Idaho	708.0		12	Connecticut	814.6
NA	Illinois**	NA		13	Missouri	779.3
29	Indiana	532.6		14	South Dakota	748.8
40	Iowa	419.3		15	Idaho	708.0
NA	Kansas**	NA		16	Hawaii	694.3
28	Kentucky	564.8		17	Nebraska	651.4
11	Louisiana	838.4		18	Georgia	646.8
32	Maine	509.5		19	Maryland	646.1
19	Maryland	646.1		20	Tennessee	640.5
45	Massachusetts	316.6		21	Texas	622.0
39	Michigan	428.4		22	Florida	617.3
27	Minnesota	570.3		23	Virginia	606.4
8	Mississippi	906.9		24	North Carolina	588.7
13	Missouri	779.3		25	Arkansas	584.3
46	Montana	304.2		26	North Dakota	579.3
17	Nebraska	651.4		27	Minnesota	570.3
10	Nevada	843.0		28	Kentucky	564.8
41	New Hampshire	418.7		29	Indiana	532.6
30	New Jersey	525.1		30	New Jersey	525.1
7	New Mexico	908.3		31	Wyoming	511.6
36	New York	463.6		32	Maine	509.5
24	North Carolina	588.7		33	California	499.8
26	North Dakota	579.3		34	South Carolina	499.6
35	Ohio	464.7		35	Ohio	464.7
38	Oklahoma	445.8		36	New York	463.6
6	Oregon	920.1		37	Alabama	451.7
43	Pennsylvania	400.6		38	Oklahoma	445.8
42	Rhode Island	404.5		39	Michigan	428.4
34	South Carolina	499.6		40	Iowa	419.3
14	South Dakota	748.8		41	New Hampshire	418.7
20	Tennessee	640.5		42	Rhode Island	404.5
21	Texas	622.0		43	Pennsylvania	400.6
1	Utah	1,241.4		44	West Virginia	317.3
48	Vermont	240.4		45	Massachusetts	316.6
23	Virginia	606.4		46	Montana	304.2
4	Washington	932.0		47	Delaware	267.3
44	West Virginia	317.3		48	Vermont	240.4
3	Wisconsin	952.9		NA	Illinois**	NA
31	Wyoming	511.6		NA	Kansas**	NA

District of Columbia   545.3

Source: Morgan Quitno Corporation using data from U.S. Department of Justice, Federal Bureau of Investigation
"Crime in the United States 1993" (Uniform Crime Reports, December 4, 1994)
*By law enforcement agencies submitting complete reports to the F.B.I. for 12 months in 1993. These rates based on
population estimates for areas under the jurisdiction of those agencies reporting. Arrest rate based on the F.B.I. estimate
of reported and unreported arrests for larceny and theft is 572.4 arrests per 100,000 population.
**Not available.

Reported Arrests for Motor Vehicle Theft in 1993

National Total = 168,795 Reported Arrests*

RANK	STATE	ARRESTS	% of USA
25	Alabama	1,637	0.97%
38	Alaska	476	0.28%
15	Arizona	3,198	1.89%
31	Arkansas	719	0.43%
1	California	44,172	26.17%
18	Colorado	2,459	1.46%
17	Connecticut	2,475	1.47%
47	Delaware	100	0.06%
3	Florida	12,563	7.44%
8	Georgia	3,971	2.35%
24	Hawaii	1,653	0.98%
36	Idaho	503	0.30%
NA	Illinois**	NA	NA
23	Indiana	2,041	1.21%
35	Iowa	579	0.34%
NA	Kansas**	NA	NA
30	Kentucky	1,170	0.69%
28	Louisiana	1,256	0.74%
40	Maine	406	0.24%
6	Maryland	6,611	3.92%
22	Massachusetts	2,169	1.28%
14	Michigan	3,210	1.90%
12	Minnesota	3,555	2.11%
32	Mississippi	706	0.42%
10	Missouri	3,601	2.13%
45	Montana	135	0.08%
39	Nebraska	474	0.28%
33	Nevada	659	0.39%
45	New Hampshire	135	0.08%
16	New Jersey	2,690	1.59%
41	New Mexico	294	0.17%
4	New York	11,822	7.00%
20	North Carolina	2,266	1.34%
42	North Dakota	265	0.16%
9	Ohio	3,889	2.30%
19	Oklahoma	2,389	1.42%
13	Oregon	3,509	2.08%
5	Pennsylvania	7,469	4.42%
34	Rhode Island	654	0.39%
29	South Carolina	1,205	0.71%
43	South Dakota	199	0.12%
27	Tennessee	1,387	0.82%
2	Texas	14,019	8.31%
26	Utah	1,549	0.92%
48	Vermont	45	0.03%
11	Virginia	3,583	2.12%
21	Washington	2,236	1.32%
37	West Virginia	497	0.29%
7	Wisconsin	4,953	2.93%
44	Wyoming	155	0.09%

RANK	STATE	ARRESTS	% of USA
1	California	44,172	26.17%
2	Texas	14,019	8.31%
3	Florida	12,563	7.44%
4	New York	11,822	7.00%
5	Pennsylvania	7,469	4.42%
6	Maryland	6,611	3.92%
7	Wisconsin	4,953	2.93%
8	Georgia	3,971	2.35%
9	Ohio	3,889	2.30%
10	Missouri	3,601	2.13%
11	Virginia	3,583	2.12%
12	Minnesota	3,555	2.11%
13	Oregon	3,509	2.08%
14	Michigan	3,210	1.90%
15	Arizona	3,198	1.89%
16	New Jersey	2,690	1.59%
17	Connecticut	2,475	1.47%
18	Colorado	2,459	1.46%
19	Oklahoma	2,389	1.42%
20	North Carolina	2,266	1.34%
21	Washington	2,236	1.32%
22	Massachusetts	2,169	1.28%
23	Indiana	2,041	1.21%
24	Hawaii	1,653	0.98%
25	Alabama	1,637	0.97%
26	Utah	1,549	0.92%
27	Tennessee	1,387	0.82%
28	Louisiana	1,256	0.74%
29	South Carolina	1,205	0.71%
30	Kentucky	1,170	0.69%
31	Arkansas	719	0.43%
32	Mississippi	706	0.42%
33	Nevada	659	0.39%
34	Rhode Island	654	0.39%
35	Iowa	579	0.34%
36	Idaho	503	0.30%
37	West Virginia	497	0.29%
38	Alaska	476	0.28%
39	Nebraska	474	0.28%
40	Maine	406	0.24%
41	New Mexico	294	0.17%
42	North Dakota	265	0.16%
43	South Dakota	199	0.12%
44	Wyoming	155	0.09%
45	Montana	135	0.08%
45	New Hampshire	135	0.08%
47	Delaware	100	0.06%
48	Vermont	45	0.03%
NA	Illinois**	NA	NA
NA	Kansas**	NA	NA
	District of Columbia	1,969	1.17%

Source: U.S. Department of Justice, Federal Bureau of Investigation
    "Crime in the United States 1993" (Uniform Crime Reports, December 4, 1994)
*By law enforcement agencies submitting complete reports to the F.B.I. for 12 months in 1993. The F.B.I. estimates
195,900 reported and unreported arrests for murder occurred in 1993. Motor vehicle theft includes the theft or attempted
theft of a self-propelled vehicle. Excludes motorboats, construction equipment, airplanes and farming equipment.
**Not available.

21

Reported Arrest Rate for Motor Vehicle Theft in 1993

National Rate = 78.8 Reported Arrests per 100,000 Population*

ALPHA ORDER				RANK ORDER		
RANK	STATE	RATE		RANK	STATE	RATE
32	Alabama	41.4		1	California	142.1
11	Alaska	84.0		2	Hawaii	141.0
10	Arizona	85.7		3	Maryland	133.2
43	Arkansas	29.8		4	Oregon	119.8
1	California	142.1		5	Missouri	109.0
13	Colorado	82.7		6	Wisconsin	99.0
9	Connecticut	89.3		7	Florida	98.1
46	Delaware	26.8		8	Utah	90.2
7	Florida	98.1		9	Connecticut	89.3
19	Georgia	70.9		10	Arizona	85.7
2	Hawaii	141.0		11	Alaska	84.0
25	Idaho	58.0		12	Pennsylvania	83.0
NA	Illinois**	NA		13	Colorado	82.7
22	Indiana	59.1		13	Mississippi	82.7
44	Iowa	29.0		15	Texas	80.3
NA	Kansas**	NA		16	Minnesota	80.1
21	Kentucky	64.2		17	New York	76.1
29	Louisiana	48.7		18	Oklahoma	75.4
34	Maine	38.6		19	Georgia	70.9
3	Maryland	133.2		20	Rhode Island	67.4
29	Massachusetts	48.7		21	Kentucky	64.2
35	Michigan	38.3		22	Indiana	59.1
16	Minnesota	80.1		23	Ohio	58.4
13	Mississippi	82.7		24	Washington	58.3
5	Missouri	109.0		25	Idaho	58.0
38	Montana	35.8		26	Virginia	55.2
42	Nebraska	31.8		27	Nevada	54.8
27	Nevada	54.8		28	North Dakota	49.5
47	New Hampshire	18.3		29	Louisiana	48.7
39	New Jersey	35.2		29	Massachusetts	48.7
37	New Mexico	36.5		31	Tennessee	46.9
17	New York	76.1		32	Alabama	41.4
41	North Carolina	33.5		33	South Dakota	40.0
28	North Dakota	49.5		34	Maine	38.6
23	Ohio	58.4		35	Michigan	38.3
18	Oklahoma	75.4		36	Wyoming	38.2
4	Oregon	119.8		37	New Mexico	36.5
12	Pennsylvania	83.0		38	Montana	35.8
20	Rhode Island	67.4		39	New Jersey	35.2
40	South Carolina	33.9		40	South Carolina	33.9
33	South Dakota	40.0		41	North Carolina	33.5
31	Tennessee	46.9		42	Nebraska	31.8
15	Texas	80.3		43	Arkansas	29.8
8	Utah	90.2		44	Iowa	29.0
48	Vermont	16.5		45	West Virginia	27.4
26	Virginia	55.2		46	Delaware	26.8
24	Washington	58.3		47	New Hampshire	18.3
45	West Virginia	27.4		48	Vermont	16.5
6	Wisconsin	99.0		NA	Illinois**	NA
36	Wyoming	38.2		NA	Kansas**	NA

District of Columbia   340.7

*Source: Morgan Quitno Corporation using data from U.S. Department of Justice, Federal Bureau of Investigation
"Crime in the United States 1993" (Uniform Crime Reports, December 4, 1994)*
*By law enforcement agencies submitting complete reports to the F.B.I. for 12 months in 1993. These rates based on
population estimates for areas under the jurisdiction of those agencies reporting. Arrest rate based on the F.B.I. estimate
of reported and unreported arrests for motor vehicle theft is 76.0 arrests per 100,000 population.
**Not available.

Reported Arrests for Arson in 1993

National Total = 16,113 Reported Arrests*

ALPHA ORDER

RANK	STATE	ARRESTS	% of USA
28	Alabama	147	0.91%
42	Alaska	39	0.24%
17	Arizona	357	2.22%
30	Arkansas	137	0.85%
1	California	2,397	14.88%
20	Colorado	330	2.05%
21	Connecticut	287	1.78%
48	Delaware	13	0.08%
7	Florida	607	3.77%
15	Georgia	399	2.48%
40	Hawaii	60	0.37%
38	Idaho	62	0.38%
NA	Illinois**	NA	NA
29	Indiana	144	0.89%
32	Iowa	119	0.74%
NA	Kansas**	NA	NA
23	Kentucky	208	1.29%
22	Louisiana	209	1.30%
35	Maine	107	0.66%
12	Maryland	481	2.99%
27	Massachusetts	169	1.05%
5	Michigan	668	4.15%
19	Minnesota	341	2.12%
36	Mississippi	75	0.47%
16	Missouri	381	2.36%
45	Montana	24	0.15%
34	Nebraska	118	0.73%
37	Nevada	66	0.41%
38	New Hampshire	62	0.38%
10	New Jersey	516	3.20%
42	New Mexico	39	0.24%
3	New York	815	5.06%
9	North Carolina	523	3.25%
47	North Dakota	15	0.09%
6	Ohio	634	3.93%
14	Oklahoma	458	2.84%
13	Oregon	461	2.86%
4	Pennsylvania	768	4.77%
32	Rhode Island	119	0.74%
26	South Carolina	175	1.09%
41	South Dakota	57	0.35%
24	Tennessee	198	1.23%
2	Texas	1,227	7.61%
25	Utah	191	1.19%
44	Vermont	29	0.18%
11	Virginia	497	3.08%
18	Washington	347	2.15%
31	West Virginia	132	0.82%
8	Wisconsin	546	3.39%
46	Wyoming	18	0.11%

RANK ORDER

RANK	STATE	ARRESTS	% of USA
1	California	2,397	14.88%
2	Texas	1,227	7.61%
3	New York	815	5.06%
4	Pennsylvania	768	4.77%
5	Michigan	668	4.15%
6	Ohio	634	3.93%
7	Florida	607	3.77%
8	Wisconsin	546	3.39%
9	North Carolina	523	3.25%
10	New Jersey	516	3.20%
11	Virginia	497	3.08%
12	Maryland	481	2.99%
13	Oregon	461	2.86%
14	Oklahoma	458	2.84%
15	Georgia	399	2.48%
16	Missouri	381	2.36%
17	Arizona	357	2.22%
18	Washington	347	2.15%
19	Minnesota	341	2.12%
20	Colorado	330	2.05%
21	Connecticut	287	1.78%
22	Louisiana	209	1.30%
23	Kentucky	208	1.29%
24	Tennessee	198	1.23%
25	Utah	191	1.19%
26	South Carolina	175	1.09%
27	Massachusetts	169	1.05%
28	Alabama	147	0.91%
29	Indiana	144	0.89%
30	Arkansas	137	0.85%
31	West Virginia	132	0.82%
32	Iowa	119	0.74%
32	Rhode Island	119	0.74%
34	Nebraska	118	0.73%
35	Maine	107	0.66%
36	Mississippi	75	0.47%
37	Nevada	66	0.41%
38	Idaho	62	0.38%
38	New Hampshire	62	0.38%
40	Hawaii	60	0.37%
41	South Dakota	57	0.35%
42	Alaska	39	0.24%
42	New Mexico	39	0.24%
44	Vermont	29	0.18%
45	Montana	24	0.15%
46	Wyoming	18	0.11%
47	North Dakota	15	0.09%
48	Delaware	13	0.08%
NA	Illinois**	NA	NA
NA	Kansas**	NA	NA
	District of Columbia	32	0.20%

Source: U.S. Department of Justice, Federal Bureau of Investigation
    "Crime in the United States 1993" (Uniform Crime Reports, December 4, 1994)
*By law enforcement agencies submitting complete reports to the F.B.I. for 12 months in 1993. The F.B.I. estimates 19,400 reported and unreported arrests for arson occurred in 1993. Arson is the willful burning or attempt to burn of a building, vehicle or another's personal property.
**Not available.

23

Reported Arrest Rate for Arson in 1993

National Rate = 7.5 Reported Arrests per 100,000 Population*

<u>ALPHA ORDER</u>

RANK	STATE	RATE
46	Alabama	3.7
31	Alaska	6.9
14	Arizona	9.6
36	Arkansas	5.7
23	California	7.7
7	Colorado	11.1
11	Connecticut	10.3
47	Delaware	3.5
42	Florida	4.7
29	Georgia	7.1
39	Hawaii	5.1
28	Idaho	7.2
NA	Illinois**	NA
44	Indiana	4.2
35	Iowa	6.0
NA	Kansas**	NA
5	Kentucky	11.4
20	Louisiana	8.1
12	Maine	10.2
13	Maryland	9.7
45	Massachusetts	3.8
21	Michigan	8.0
23	Minnesota	7.7
17	Mississippi	8.8
4	Missouri	11.5
34	Montana	6.4
22	Nebraska	7.9
37	Nevada	5.5
19	New Hampshire	8.4
32	New Jersey	6.8
41	New Mexico	4.8
38	New York	5.2
23	North Carolina	7.7
48	North Dakota	2.8
15	Ohio	9.5
2	Oklahoma	14.4
1	Oregon	15.7
18	Pennsylvania	8.5
3	Rhode Island	12.3
40	South Carolina	4.9
5	South Dakota	11.4
33	Tennessee	6.7
30	Texas	7.0
7	Utah	11.1
10	Vermont	10.7
23	Virginia	7.7
16	Washington	9.0
27	West Virginia	7.3
9	Wisconsin	10.9
43	Wyoming	4.4

<u>RANK ORDER</u>

RANK	STATE	RATE
1	Oregon	15.7
2	Oklahoma	14.4
3	Rhode Island	12.3
4	Missouri	11.5
5	Kentucky	11.4
5	South Dakota	11.4
7	Colorado	11.1
7	Utah	11.1
9	Wisconsin	10.9
10	Vermont	10.7
11	Connecticut	10.3
12	Maine	10.2
13	Maryland	9.7
14	Arizona	9.6
15	Ohio	9.5
16	Washington	9.0
17	Mississippi	8.8
18	Pennsylvania	8.5
19	New Hampshire	8.4
20	Louisiana	8.1
21	Michigan	8.0
22	Nebraska	7.9
23	California	7.7
23	Minnesota	7.7
23	North Carolina	7.7
23	Virginia	7.7
27	West Virginia	7.3
28	Idaho	7.2
29	Georgia	7.1
30	Texas	7.0
31	Alaska	6.9
32	New Jersey	6.8
33	Tennessee	6.7
34	Montana	6.4
35	Iowa	6.0
36	Arkansas	5.7
37	Nevada	5.5
38	New York	5.2
39	Hawaii	5.1
40	South Carolina	4.9
41	New Mexico	4.8
42	Florida	4.7
43	Wyoming	4.4
44	Indiana	4.2
45	Massachusetts	3.8
46	Alabama	3.7
47	Delaware	3.5
48	North Dakota	2.8
NA	Illinois**	NA
NA	Kansas**	NA

District of Columbia 5.5

Source: Morgan Quitno Corporation using data from U.S. Department of Justice, Federal Bureau of Investigation
"Crime in the United States 1993" (Uniform Crime Reports, December 4, 1994)
*By law enforcement agencies submitting complete reports to the F.B.I. for 12 months in 1993. These rates based on population estimates for areas under the jurisdiction of those agencies reporting. Arrest rate based on the F.B.I. estimate of reported and unreported arrests for arson is 7.5 arrests per 100,000 population.
**Not available.

Reported Arrests for Weapons Violations in 1993

National Total = 224,395 Reported Arrests*

ALPHA ORDER

RANK	STATE	ARRESTS	% of USA
25	Alabama	2,660	1.19%
36	Alaska	607	0.27%
15	Arizona	4,243	1.89%
20	Arkansas	3,054	1.36%
1	California	41,803	18.63%
16	Colorado	4,158	1.85%
19	Connecticut	3,208	1.43%
46	Delaware	112	0.05%
6	Florida	8,649	3.85%
7	Georgia	8,365	3.73%
35	Hawaii	703	0.31%
40	Idaho	450	0.20%
NA	Illinois**	NA	NA
27	Indiana	2,032	0.91%
37	Iowa	597	0.27%
NA	Kansas**	NA	NA
28	Kentucky	1,929	0.86%
18	Louisiana	3,654	1.63%
41	Maine	237	0.11%
13	Maryland	5,161	2.30%
30	Massachusetts	1,543	0.69%
4	Michigan	8,950	3.99%
24	Minnesota	2,718	1.21%
34	Mississippi	1,151	0.51%
11	Missouri	6,573	2.93%
47	Montana	44	0.02%
33	Nebraska	1,156	0.52%
29	Nevada	1,696	0.76%
45	New Hampshire	116	0.05%
10	New Jersey	7,197	3.21%
39	New Mexico	572	0.25%
3	New York	15,838	7.06%
5	North Carolina	8,948	3.99%
43	North Dakota	136	0.06%
12	Ohio	6,468	2.88%
21	Oklahoma	2,884	1.29%
26	Oregon	2,367	1.05%
14	Pennsylvania	4,392	1.96%
38	Rhode Island	587	0.26%
23	South Carolina	2,737	1.22%
42	South Dakota	204	0.09%
17	Tennessee	3,888	1.73%
2	Texas	24,204	10.79%
31	Utah	1,463	0.65%
48	Vermont	3	0.00%
8	Virginia	8,353	3.72%
22	Washington	2,880	1.28%
32	West Virginia	1,402	0.62%
9	Wisconsin	8,265	3.68%
44	Wyoming	125	0.06%

RANK ORDER

RANK	STATE	ARRESTS	% of USA
1	California	41,803	18.63%
2	Texas	24,204	10.79%
3	New York	15,838	7.06%
4	Michigan	8,950	3.99%
5	North Carolina	8,948	3.99%
6	Florida	8,649	3.85%
7	Georgia	8,365	3.73%
8	Virginia	8,353	3.72%
9	Wisconsin	8,265	3.68%
10	New Jersey	7,197	3.21%
11	Missouri	6,573	2.93%
12	Ohio	6,468	2.88%
13	Maryland	5,161	2.30%
14	Pennsylvania	4,392	1.96%
15	Arizona	4,243	1.89%
16	Colorado	4,158	1.85%
17	Tennessee	3,888	1.73%
18	Louisiana	3,654	1.63%
19	Connecticut	3,208	1.43%
20	Arkansas	3,054	1.36%
21	Oklahoma	2,884	1.29%
22	Washington	2,880	1.28%
23	South Carolina	2,737	1.22%
24	Minnesota	2,718	1.21%
25	Alabama	2,660	1.19%
26	Oregon	2,367	1.05%
27	Indiana	2,032	0.91%
28	Kentucky	1,929	0.86%
29	Nevada	1,696	0.76%
30	Massachusetts	1,543	0.69%
31	Utah	1,463	0.65%
32	West Virginia	1,402	0.62%
33	Nebraska	1,156	0.52%
34	Mississippi	1,151	0.51%
35	Hawaii	703	0.31%
36	Alaska	607	0.27%
37	Iowa	597	0.27%
38	Rhode Island	587	0.26%
39	New Mexico	572	0.25%
40	Idaho	450	0.20%
41	Maine	237	0.11%
42	South Dakota	204	0.09%
43	North Dakota	136	0.06%
44	Wyoming	125	0.06%
45	New Hampshire	116	0.05%
46	Delaware	112	0.05%
47	Montana	44	0.02%
48	Vermont	3	0.00%
NA	Illinois**	NA	NA
NA	Kansas**	NA	NA
	District of Columbia	1,737	0.77%

Source: U.S. Department of Justice, Federal Bureau of Investigation
   "Crime in the United States 1993" (Uniform Crime Reports, December 4, 1994)
*By law enforcement agencies submitting complete reports to the F.B.I. for 12 months in 1993. The F.B.I. estimates 262,300 reported and unreported arrests for weapons violations occurred in 1993. Weapons violations include illegal carrying and possession.
**Not available.

Reported Arrest Rate for Weapons Violations in 1993

National Rate = 104.8 Reported Arrests per 100,000 Population*

ALPHA ORDER

RANK	STATE	RATE
32	Alabama	67.2
16	Alaska	107.1
15	Arizona	113.8
13	Arkansas	126.5
9	California	134.5
6	Colorado	139.8
14	Connecticut	115.7
42	Delaware	30.0
31	Florida	67.5
3	Georgia	149.4
35	Hawaii	60.0
37	Idaho	51.9
NA	Illinois**	NA
36	Indiana	58.9
43	Iowa	29.9
NA	Kansas**	NA
18	Kentucky	105.8
4	Louisiana	141.7
45	Maine	22.5
19	Maryland	104.0
40	Massachusetts	34.7
17	Michigan	106.7
33	Minnesota	61.2
8	Mississippi	134.8
1	Missouri	199.0
47	Montana	11.7
26	Nebraska	77.6
5	Nevada	141.0
46	New Hampshire	15.7
22	New Jersey	94.3
30	New Mexico	71.0
20	New York	102.0
10	North Carolina	132.4
44	North Dakota	25.4
21	Ohio	97.2
23	Oklahoma	91.0
25	Oregon	80.8
38	Pennsylvania	48.8
34	Rhode Island	60.5
28	South Carolina	77.0
39	South Dakota	41.0
11	Tennessee	131.4
7	Texas	138.7
24	Utah	85.2
48	Vermont	1.1
12	Virginia	128.7
29	Washington	75.1
27	West Virginia	77.4
2	Wisconsin	165.2
41	Wyoming	30.8

RANK ORDER

RANK	STATE	RATE
1	Missouri	199.0
2	Wisconsin	165.2
3	Georgia	149.4
4	Louisiana	141.7
5	Nevada	141.0
6	Colorado	139.8
7	Texas	138.7
8	Mississippi	134.8
9	California	134.5
10	North Carolina	132.4
11	Tennessee	131.4
12	Virginia	128.7
13	Arkansas	126.5
14	Connecticut	115.7
15	Arizona	113.8
16	Alaska	107.1
17	Michigan	106.7
18	Kentucky	105.8
19	Maryland	104.0
20	New York	102.0
21	Ohio	97.2
22	New Jersey	94.3
23	Oklahoma	91.0
24	Utah	85.2
25	Oregon	80.8
26	Nebraska	77.6
27	West Virginia	77.4
28	South Carolina	77.0
29	Washington	75.1
30	New Mexico	71.0
31	Florida	67.5
32	Alabama	67.2
33	Minnesota	61.2
34	Rhode Island	60.5
35	Hawaii	60.0
36	Indiana	58.9
37	Idaho	51.9
38	Pennsylvania	48.8
39	South Dakota	41.0
40	Massachusetts	34.7
41	Wyoming	30.8
42	Delaware	30.0
43	Iowa	29.9
44	North Dakota	25.4
45	Maine	22.5
46	New Hampshire	15.7
47	Montana	11.7
48	Vermont	1.1
NA	Illinois**	NA
NA	Kansas**	NA

District of Columbia	300.5

Source: Morgan Quitno Corporation using data from U.S. Department of Justice, Federal Bureau of Investigation
"Crime in the United States 1993" (Uniform Crime Reports, December 4, 1994)
*By law enforcement agencies submitting complete reports to the F.B.I. for 12 months in 1993. These rates based on population estimates for areas under the jurisdiction those agencies reporting. Arrest rate based on the F.B.I. estimate of reported and unreported arrests for weapons violations is 101.7 arrests per 100,000 population.
**Not available.

Reported Arrests for Driving Under the Influence in 1993

National Total = 1,229,971 Reported Arrests*

ALPHA ORDER

RANK ORDER

RANK	STATE	ARRESTS	% of USA
22	Alabama	19,708	1.60%
39	Alaska	5,366	0.44%
15	Arizona	25,980	2.11%
23	Arkansas	19,567	1.59%
1	California	230,329	18.73%
12	Colorado	28,769	2.34%
31	Connecticut	10,503	0.85%
48	Delaware	0	0.00%
7	Florida	36,969	3.01%
4	Georgia	52,048	4.23%
41	Hawaii	5,177	0.42%
34	Idaho	8,982	0.73%
NA	Illinois**	NA	NA
25	Indiana	18,106	1.47%
27	Iowa	12,577	1.02%
NA	Kansas**	NA	NA
26	Kentucky	16,516	1.34%
30	Louisiana	10,984	0.89%
36	Maine	6,581	0.54%
18	Maryland	23,198	1.89%
28	Massachusetts	12,471	1.01%
5	Michigan	46,380	3.77%
11	Minnesota	32,261	2.62%
37	Mississippi	6,278	0.51%
19	Missouri	23,118	1.88%
46	Montana	2,043	0.17%
29	Nebraska	11,858	0.96%
38	Nevada	6,236	0.51%
43	New Hampshire	4,220	0.34%
16	New Jersey	24,640	2.00%
32	New Mexico	9,612	0.78%
8	New York	36,716	2.99%
3	North Carolina	70,863	5.76%
44	North Dakota	2,398	0.19%
14	Ohio	26,738	2.17%
17	Oklahoma	24,635	2.00%
21	Oregon	21,067	1.71%
13	Pennsylvania	27,521	2.24%
45	Rhode Island	2,309	0.19%
24	South Carolina	18,428	1.50%
40	South Dakota	5,293	0.43%
20	Tennessee	21,802	1.77%
2	Texas	101,978	8.29%
35	Utah	8,004	0.65%
47	Vermont	955	0.08%
9	Virginia	35,304	2.87%
6	Washington	38,785	3.15%
33	West Virginia	9,087	0.74%
10	Wisconsin	35,073	2.85%
42	Wyoming	4,499	0.37%

RANK	STATE	ARRESTS	% of USA
1	California	230,329	18.73%
2	Texas	101,978	8.29%
3	North Carolina	70,863	5.76%
4	Georgia	52,048	4.23%
5	Michigan	46,380	3.77%
6	Washington	38,785	3.15%
7	Florida	36,969	3.01%
8	New York	36,716	2.99%
9	Virginia	35,304	2.87%
10	Wisconsin	35,073	2.85%
11	Minnesota	32,261	2.62%
12	Colorado	28,769	2.34%
13	Pennsylvania	27,521	2.24%
14	Ohio	26,738	2.17%
15	Arizona	25,980	2.11%
16	New Jersey	24,640	2.00%
17	Oklahoma	24,635	2.00%
18	Maryland	23,198	1.89%
19	Missouri	23,118	1.88%
20	Tennessee	21,802	1.77%
21	Oregon	21,067	1.71%
22	Alabama	19,708	1.60%
23	Arkansas	19,567	1.59%
24	South Carolina	18,428	1.50%
25	Indiana	18,106	1.47%
26	Kentucky	16,516	1.34%
27	Iowa	12,577	1.02%
28	Massachusetts	12,471	1.01%
29	Nebraska	11,858	0.96%
30	Louisiana	10,984	0.89%
31	Connecticut	10,503	0.85%
32	New Mexico	9,612	0.78%
33	West Virginia	9,087	0.74%
34	Idaho	8,982	0.73%
35	Utah	8,004	0.65%
36	Maine	6,581	0.54%
37	Mississippi	6,278	0.51%
38	Nevada	6,236	0.51%
39	Alaska	5,366	0.44%
40	South Dakota	5,293	0.43%
41	Hawaii	5,177	0.42%
42	Wyoming	4,499	0.37%
43	New Hampshire	4,220	0.34%
44	North Dakota	2,398	0.19%
45	Rhode Island	2,309	0.19%
46	Montana	2,043	0.17%
47	Vermont	955	0.08%
48	Delaware	0	0.00%
NA	Illinois**	NA	NA
NA	Kansas**	NA	NA
	District of Columbia	3,560	0.29%

Source: U.S. Department of Justice, Federal Bureau of Investigation
"Crime in the United States 1993" (Uniform Crime Reports, December 4, 1994)
*By law enforcement agencies submitting complete reports to the F.B.I. for 12 months in 1993. The F.B.I. estimates
1,524,800 reported and unreported arrests for driving under the influence occurred in 1993. Includes driving any vehicle
while drunk or under the influence of liquor or narcotics.
**Not available.

Reported Arrest Rate for Driving Under the Influence in 1993

National Rate = 574.5 Reported Arrests per 100,000 Population*

ALPHA ORDER				RANK ORDER		
RANK	STATE	RATE		RANK	STATE	RATE
33	Alabama	498.2		1	New Mexico	1,192.6
8	Alaska	946.4		2	Wyoming	1,108.1
21	Arizona	696.5		3	South Dakota	1,062.9
11	Arkansas	810.2		4	North Carolina	1,048.7
14	California	741.1		5	Idaho	1,036.0
7	Colorado	967.4		6	Washington	1,010.8
40	Connecticut	378.8		7	Colorado	967.4
48	Delaware	0.0		8	Alaska	946.4
44	Florida	288.5		9	Georgia	929.4
9	Georgia	929.4		10	Kentucky	906.0
37	Hawaii	441.7		11	Arkansas	810.2
5	Idaho	1,036.0		12	Nebraska	796.4
NA	Illinois**	NA		13	Oklahoma	777.1
29	Indiana	524.5		14	California	741.1
22	Iowa	629.5		15	Tennessee	736.6
NA	Kansas**	NA		16	Mississippi	735.1
10	Kentucky	906.0		17	Minnesota	726.6
38	Louisiana	425.9		18	Oregon	719.0
23	Maine	625.6		19	Wisconsin	701.0
34	Maryland	467.5		20	Missouri	699.9
45	Massachusetts	280.2		21	Arizona	696.5
26	Michigan	553.0		22	Iowa	629.5
17	Minnesota	726.6		23	Maine	625.6
16	Mississippi	735.1		24	Texas	584.4
20	Missouri	699.9		25	New Hampshire	571.8
28	Montana	541.9		26	Michigan	553.0
12	Nebraska	796.4		27	Virginia	544.1
31	Nevada	518.4		28	Montana	541.9
25	New Hampshire	571.8		29	Indiana	524.5
42	New Jersey	322.8		30	South Carolina	518.5
1	New Mexico	1,192.6		31	Nevada	518.4
47	New York	236.4		32	West Virginia	501.5
4	North Carolina	1,048.7		33	Alabama	498.2
36	North Dakota	448.2		34	Maryland	467.5
39	Ohio	401.8		35	Utah	466.2
13	Oklahoma	777.1		36	North Dakota	448.2
18	Oregon	719.0		37	Hawaii	441.7
43	Pennsylvania	306.0		38	Louisiana	425.9
46	Rhode Island	237.8		39	Ohio	401.8
30	South Carolina	518.5		40	Connecticut	378.8
3	South Dakota	1,062.9		41	Vermont	351.1
15	Tennessee	736.6		42	New Jersey	322.8
24	Texas	584.4		43	Pennsylvania	306.0
35	Utah	466.2		44	Florida	288.5
41	Vermont	351.1		45	Massachusetts	280.2
27	Virginia	544.1		46	Rhode Island	237.8
6	Washington	1,010.8		47	New York	236.4
32	West Virginia	501.5		48	Delaware	0.0
19	Wisconsin	701.0		NA	Illinois**	NA
2	Wyoming	1,108.1		NA	Kansas**	NA

District of Columbia   615.9

Source: Morgan Quitno Corporation using data from U.S. Department of Justice, Federal Bureau of Investigation "Crime in the United States 1993" (Uniform Crime Reports, December 4, 1994)

*By law enforcement agencies submitting complete reports to the F.B.I. for 12 months in 1993. These rates based on population estimates for areas under the jurisdiction of those agencies reporting. Arrest rate based on the F.B.I. estimate of reported and unreported arrests for driving under the influence is 591.2 arrests per 100,000 population.

**Not available.

Reported Arrests for Drug Abuse Violations in 1993

National Total = 968,606 Reported Arrests*

<u>ALPHA ORDER</u>

RANK	STATE	ARRESTS	% of USA
24	Alabama	9,774	1.01%
41	Alaska	1,120	0.12%
14	Arizona	18,232	1.88%
27	Arkansas	7,931	0.82%
1	California	234,475	24.21%
22	Colorado	10,223	1.06%
15	Connecticut	18,092	1.87%
45	Delaware	556	0.06%
4	Florida	63,721	6.58%
7	Georgia	29,298	3.02%
33	Hawaii	3,372	0.35%
44	Idaho	749	0.08%
NA	Illinois**	NA	NA
29	Indiana	6,336	0.65%
40	Iowa	1,243	0.13%
NA	Kansas**	NA	NA
25	Kentucky	9,744	1.01%
17	Louisiana	14,105	1.46%
39	Maine	1,622	0.17%
6	Maryland	35,647	3.68%
13	Massachusetts	18,558	1.92%
8	Michigan	27,499	2.84%
26	Minnesota	9,234	0.95%
31	Mississippi	4,560	0.47%
16	Missouri	14,130	1.46%
48	Montana	278	0.03%
32	Nebraska	4,346	0.45%
28	Nevada	7,129	0.74%
38	New Hampshire	1,701	0.18%
5	New Jersey	42,105	4.35%
36	New Mexico	2,344	0.24%
2	New York	111,096	11.47%
9	North Carolina	26,931	2.78%
46	North Dakota	429	0.04%
11	Ohio	25,091	2.59%
23	Oklahoma	10,140	1.05%
21	Oregon	11,390	1.18%
10	Pennsylvania	26,032	2.69%
34	Rhode Island	3,251	0.34%
35	South Carolina	2,415	0.25%
42	South Dakota	842	0.09%
19	Tennessee	12,178	1.26%
3	Texas	72,103	7.44%
30	Utah	5,421	0.56%
47	Vermont	347	0.04%
12	Virginia	20,227	2.09%
20	Washington	11,804	1.22%
37	West Virginia	2,165	0.22%
18	Wisconsin	12,600	1.30%
43	Wyoming	771	0.08%

<u>RANK ORDER</u>

RANK	STATE	ARRESTS	% of USA
1	California	234,475	24.21%
2	New York	111,096	11.47%
3	Texas	72,103	7.44%
4	Florida	63,721	6.58%
5	New Jersey	42,105	4.35%
6	Maryland	35,647	3.68%
7	Georgia	29,298	3.02%
8	Michigan	27,499	2.84%
9	North Carolina	26,931	2.78%
10	Pennsylvania	26,032	2.69%
11	Ohio	25,091	2.59%
12	Virginia	20,227	2.09%
13	Massachusetts	18,558	1.92%
14	Arizona	18,232	1.88%
15	Connecticut	18,092	1.87%
16	Missouri	14,130	1.46%
17	Louisiana	14,105	1.46%
18	Wisconsin	12,600	1.30%
19	Tennessee	12,178	1.26%
20	Washington	11,804	1.22%
21	Oregon	11,390	1.18%
22	Colorado	10,223	1.06%
23	Oklahoma	10,140	1.05%
24	Alabama	9,774	1.01%
25	Kentucky	9,744	1.01%
26	Minnesota	9,234	0.95%
27	Arkansas	7,931	0.82%
28	Nevada	7,129	0.74%
29	Indiana	6,336	0.65%
30	Utah	5,421	0.56%
31	Mississippi	4,560	0.47%
32	Nebraska	4,346	0.45%
33	Hawaii	3,372	0.35%
34	Rhode Island	3,251	0.34%
35	South Carolina	2,415	0.25%
36	New Mexico	2,344	0.24%
37	West Virginia	2,165	0.22%
38	New Hampshire	1,701	0.18%
39	Maine	1,622	0.17%
40	Iowa	1,243	0.13%
41	Alaska	1,120	0.12%
42	South Dakota	842	0.09%
43	Wyoming	771	0.08%
44	Idaho	749	0.08%
45	Delaware	556	0.06%
46	North Dakota	429	0.04%
47	Vermont	347	0.04%
48	Montana	278	0.03%
NA	Illinois**	NA	NA
NA	Kansas**	NA	NA
	District of Columbia	8,234	0.85%

Source: U.S. Department of Justice, Federal Bureau of Investigation
  "Crime in the United States 1993" (Uniform Crime Reports, December 4, 1994)
*By law enforcement agencies submitting complete reports to the F.B.I. for 12 months in 1993. The F.B.I. estimates 1,126,300 reported and unreported arrests for drug abuse violations occurred in 1993. Includes offenses relating to possession, sale, use, growing and manufacturing of narcotic drugs.
**Not available.

29

Reported Arrest Rate for Drug Abuse Violations in 1993

National Rate = 452.4 Reported Arrests per 100,000 Population*

ALPHA ORDER			RANK ORDER		
RANK	STATE	RATE	RANK	STATE	RATE
33	Alabama	247.1	1	California	754.4
36	Alaska	197.5	2	Maryland	718.4
12	Arizona	488.8	3	New York	715.3
22	Arkansas	328.4	4	Connecticut	652.4
1	California	754.4	5	Nevada	592.6
20	Colorado	343.7	6	New Jersey	551.6
4	Connecticut	652.4	7	Louisiana	546.9
41	Delaware	149.1	8	Kentucky	534.5
11	Florida	497.4	9	Mississippi	534.0
10	Georgia	523.2	10	Georgia	523.2
31	Hawaii	287.7	11	Florida	497.4
44	Idaho	86.4	12	Arizona	488.8
NA	Illinois**	NA	13	Missouri	427.8
38	Indiana	183.5	14	Massachusetts	416.9
48	Iowa	62.2	15	Texas	413.2
NA	Kansas**	NA	16	Tennessee	411.4
8	Kentucky	534.5	17	North Carolina	398.6
7	Louisiana	546.9	18	Oregon	388.7
40	Maine	154.2	19	Ohio	377.1
2	Maryland	718.4	20	Colorado	343.7
14	Massachusetts	416.9	21	Rhode Island	334.8
23	Michigan	327.9	22	Arkansas	328.4
35	Minnesota	208.0	23	Michigan	327.9
9	Mississippi	534.0	24	Oklahoma	319.9
13	Missouri	427.8	25	Utah	315.7
46	Montana	73.7	26	Virginia	311.8
28	Nebraska	291.9	27	Washington	307.6
5	Nevada	592.6	28	Nebraska	291.9
34	New Hampshire	230.5	29	New Mexico	290.8
6	New Jersey	551.6	30	Pennsylvania	289.4
29	New Mexico	290.8	31	Hawaii	287.7
3	New York	715.3	32	Wisconsin	251.8
17	North Carolina	398.6	33	Alabama	247.1
45	North Dakota	80.2	34	New Hampshire	230.5
19	Ohio	377.1	35	Minnesota	208.0
24	Oklahoma	319.9	36	Alaska	197.5
18	Oregon	388.7	37	Wyoming	189.9
30	Pennsylvania	289.4	38	Indiana	183.5
21	Rhode Island	334.8	39	South Dakota	169.1
47	South Carolina	68.0	40	Maine	154.2
39	South Dakota	169.1	41	Delaware	149.1
16	Tennessee	411.4	42	Vermont	127.6
15	Texas	413.2	43	West Virginia	119.5
25	Utah	315.7	44	Idaho	86.4
42	Vermont	127.6	45	North Dakota	80.2
26	Virginia	311.8	46	Montana	73.7
27	Washington	307.6	47	South Carolina	68.0
43	West Virginia	119.5	48	Iowa	62.2
32	Wisconsin	251.8	NA	Illinois**	NA
37	Wyoming	189.9	NA	Kansas**	NA

District of Columbia   1,424.6

Source: Morgan Quitno Corporation using data from U.S. Department of Justice, Federal Bureau of Investigation
"Crime in the United States 1993" (Uniform Crime Reports, December 4, 1994)
*By law enforcement agencies submitting complete reports to the F.B.I. for 12 months in 1993. These rates based on population estimates for areas under the jurisdiction of those agencies reporting. Arrest rate based on the F.B.I. estimate of reported and unreported arrests for drug abuse violations is 436.7 arrests per 100,000 population.
**Not available.

Reported Arrests for Sex Offenses in 1993

National Total = 87,712 Reported Arrests*

ALPHA ORDER

RANK	STATE	ARRESTS	% of USA
32	Alabama	520	0.59%
36	Alaska	364	0.41%
14	Arizona	2,188	2.49%
34	Arkansas	409	0.47%
1	California	16,323	18.61%
17	Colorado	1,892	2.16%
24	Connecticut	967	1.10%
47	Delaware	91	0.10%
5	Florida	4,480	5.11%
6	Georgia	3,808	4.34%
31	Hawaii	576	0.66%
39	Idaho	244	0.28%
NA	Illinois**	NA	NA
19	Indiana	1,442	1.64%
38	Iowa	268	0.31%
NA	Kansas**	NA	NA
21	Kentucky	1,080	1.23%
25	Louisiana	958	1.09%
35	Maine	369	0.42%
16	Maryland	1,959	2.23%
26	Massachusetts	878	1.00%
8	Michigan	2,696	3.07%
22	Minnesota	1,069	1.22%
41	Mississippi	206	0.23%
13	Missouri	2,237	2.55%
45	Montana	122	0.14%
28	Nebraska	749	0.85%
29	Nevada	717	0.82%
40	New Hampshire	224	0.26%
15	New Jersey	2,141	2.44%
43	New Mexico	153	0.17%
3	New York	6,182	7.05%
9	North Carolina	2,662	3.03%
48	North Dakota	80	0.09%
12	Ohio	2,263	2.58%
23	Oklahoma	1,006	1.15%
18	Oregon	1,750	2.00%
10	Pennsylvania	2,562	2.92%
33	Rhode Island	417	0.48%
27	South Carolina	765	0.87%
42	South Dakota	188	0.21%
30	Tennessee	635	0.72%
2	Texas	6,740	7.68%
20	Utah	1,378	1.57%
46	Vermont	102	0.12%
7	Virginia	3,426	3.91%
11	Washington	2,431	2.77%
37	West Virginia	296	0.34%
4	Wisconsin	4,630	5.28%
44	Wyoming	128	0.15%

RANK ORDER

RANK	STATE	ARRESTS	% of USA
1	California	16,323	18.61%
2	Texas	6,740	7.68%
3	New York	6,182	7.05%
4	Wisconsin	4,630	5.28%
5	Florida	4,480	5.11%
6	Georgia	3,808	4.34%
7	Virginia	3,426	3.91%
8	Michigan	2,696	3.07%
9	North Carolina	2,662	3.03%
10	Pennsylvania	2,562	2.92%
11	Washington	2,431	2.77%
12	Ohio	2,263	2.58%
13	Missouri	2,237	2.55%
14	Arizona	2,188	2.49%
15	New Jersey	2,141	2.44%
16	Maryland	1,959	2.23%
17	Colorado	1,892	2.16%
18	Oregon	1,750	2.00%
19	Indiana	1,442	1.64%
20	Utah	1,378	1.57%
21	Kentucky	1,080	1.23%
22	Minnesota	1,069	1.22%
23	Oklahoma	1,006	1.15%
24	Connecticut	967	1.10%
25	Louisiana	958	1.09%
26	Massachusetts	878	1.00%
27	South Carolina	765	0.87%
28	Nebraska	749	0.85%
29	Nevada	717	0.82%
30	Tennessee	635	0.72%
31	Hawaii	576	0.66%
32	Alabama	520	0.59%
33	Rhode Island	417	0.48%
34	Arkansas	409	0.47%
35	Maine	369	0.42%
36	Alaska	364	0.41%
37	West Virginia	296	0.34%
38	Iowa	268	0.31%
39	Idaho	244	0.28%
40	New Hampshire	224	0.26%
41	Mississippi	206	0.23%
42	South Dakota	188	0.21%
43	New Mexico	153	0.17%
44	Wyoming	128	0.15%
45	Montana	122	0.14%
46	Vermont	102	0.12%
47	Delaware	91	0.10%
48	North Dakota	80	0.09%
NA	Illinois**	NA	NA
NA	Kansas**	NA	NA
	District of Columbia	134	0.15%

Source: U.S. Department of Justice, Federal Bureau of Investigation
"Crime in the United States 1993" (Uniform Crime Reports, December 4, 1994)
*By law enforcement agencies submitting complete reports to the F.B.I. for 12 months in 1993. The F.B.I. estimates 104,100 reported and unreported arrests for sex offenses occurred in 1993. Excludes forcible rape, prostitution and commercialized vice. Includes statutory rape and offenses against chastity, common decency, morals and the like.
**Not available.

Reported Arrest Rate for Sex Offenses in 1993

National Rate = 41.0 Reported Arrests per 100,000 Population*

ALPHA ORDER

RANK	STATE	RATE
48	Alabama	13.1
5	Alaska	64.2
11	Arizona	58.7
44	Arkansas	16.9
13	California	52.5
6	Colorado	63.6
27	Connecticut	34.9
37	Delaware	24.4
26	Florida	35.0
3	Georgia	68.0
15	Hawaii	49.1
35	Idaho	28.1
NA	Illinois**	NA
17	Indiana	41.8
47	Iowa	13.4
NA	Kansas**	NA
10	Kentucky	59.2
24	Louisiana	37.1
25	Maine	35.1
19	Maryland	39.5
42	Massachusetts	19.7
30	Michigan	32.1
38	Minnesota	24.1
38	Mississippi	24.1
4	Missouri	67.7
29	Montana	32.4
14	Nebraska	50.3
9	Nevada	59.6
33	New Hampshire	30.4
36	New Jersey	28.0
43	New Mexico	19.0
18	New York	39.8
20	North Carolina	39.4
46	North Dakota	15.0
28	Ohio	34.0
31	Oklahoma	31.7
8	Oregon	59.7
34	Pennsylvania	28.5
16	Rhode Island	42.9
40	South Carolina	21.5
22	South Dakota	37.8
40	Tennessee	21.5
21	Texas	38.6
2	Utah	80.3
23	Vermont	37.5
12	Virginia	52.8
7	Washington	63.4
45	West Virginia	16.3
1	Wisconsin	92.5
32	Wyoming	31.5

RANK ORDER

RANK	STATE	RATE
1	Wisconsin	92.5
2	Utah	80.3
3	Georgia	68.0
4	Missouri	67.7
5	Alaska	64.2
6	Colorado	63.6
7	Washington	63.4
8	Oregon	59.7
9	Nevada	59.6
10	Kentucky	59.2
11	Arizona	58.7
12	Virginia	52.8
13	California	52.5
14	Nebraska	50.3
15	Hawaii	49.1
16	Rhode Island	42.9
17	Indiana	41.8
18	New York	39.8
19	Maryland	39.5
20	North Carolina	39.4
21	Texas	38.6
22	South Dakota	37.8
23	Vermont	37.5
24	Louisiana	37.1
25	Maine	35.1
26	Florida	35.0
27	Connecticut	34.9
28	Ohio	34.0
29	Montana	32.4
30	Michigan	32.1
31	Oklahoma	31.7
32	Wyoming	31.5
33	New Hampshire	30.4
34	Pennsylvania	28.5
35	Idaho	28.1
36	New Jersey	28.0
37	Delaware	24.4
38	Minnesota	24.1
38	Mississippi	24.1
40	South Carolina	21.5
40	Tennessee	21.5
42	Massachusetts	19.7
43	New Mexico	19.0
44	Arkansas	16.9
45	West Virginia	16.3
46	North Dakota	15.0
47	Iowa	13.4
48	Alabama	13.1
NA	Illinois**	NA
NA	Kansas**	NA

District of Columbia   23.2

Source: Morgan Quitno Corporation using data from U.S. Department of Justice, Federal Bureau of Investigation
"Crime in the United States 1993" (Uniform Crime Reports, December 4, 1994)
*By law enforcement agencies submitting complete reports to the F.B.I. for 12 months in 1993. These rates based on
population estimates for areas under the jurisdiction of those agencies reporting. Arrest rate based on the F.B.I. estimate
of reported and unreported arrests for sex offenses is 40.4 arrests per 100,000 population.
**Not available.

Reported Arrests for Prostitution and Commercialized Vice in 1993

National Total = 88,850 Reported Arrests*

ALPHA ORDER

RANK	STATE	ARRESTS	% of USA
31	Alabama	405	0.46%
38	Alaska	99	0.11%
13	Arizona	1,792	2.02%
29	Arkansas	477	0.54%
1	California	17,657	19.87%
16	Colorado	1,485	1.67%
24	Connecticut	879	0.99%
40	Delaware	69	0.08%
4	Florida	6,119	6.89%
14	Georgia	1,684	1.90%
26	Hawaii	628	0.71%
44	Idaho	5	0.01%
NA	Illinois**	NA	NA
21	Indiana	998	1.12%
35	Iowa	256	0.29%
NA	Kansas**	NA	NA
28	Kentucky	490	0.55%
33	Louisiana	359	0.40%
42	Maine	12	0.01%
17	Maryland	1,383	1.56%
7	Massachusetts	2,993	3.37%
8	Michigan	2,737	3.08%
18	Minnesota	1,367	1.54%
38	Mississippi	99	0.11%
9	Missouri	2,714	3.05%
47	Montana	1	0.00%
34	Nebraska	316	0.36%
10	Nevada	2,691	3.03%
41	New Hampshire	14	0.02%
6	New Jersey	3,047	3.43%
27	New Mexico	602	0.68%
2	New York	12,310	13.85%
19	North Carolina	1,254	1.41%
47	North Dakota	1	0.00%
5	Ohio	4,301	4.84%
32	Oklahoma	362	0.41%
22	Oregon	968	1.09%
11	Pennsylvania	1,902	2.14%
36	Rhode Island	254	0.29%
30	South Carolina	455	0.51%
43	South Dakota	8	0.01%
20	Tennessee	1,136	1.28%
3	Texas	7,311	8.23%
25	Utah	732	0.82%
46	Vermont	2	0.00%
12	Virginia	1,834	2.06%
23	Washington	948	1.07%
37	West Virginia	129	0.15%
15	Wisconsin	1,556	1.75%
45	Wyoming	3	0.00%

RANK ORDER

RANK	STATE	ARRESTS	% of USA
1	California	17,657	19.87%
2	New York	12,310	13.85%
3	Texas	7,311	8.23%
4	Florida	6,119	6.89%
5	Ohio	4,301	4.84%
6	New Jersey	3,047	3.43%
7	Massachusetts	2,993	3.37%
8	Michigan	2,737	3.08%
9	Missouri	2,714	3.05%
10	Nevada	2,691	3.03%
11	Pennsylvania	1,902	2.14%
12	Virginia	1,834	2.06%
13	Arizona	1,792	2.02%
14	Georgia	1,684	1.90%
15	Wisconsin	1,556	1.75%
16	Colorado	1,485	1.67%
17	Maryland	1,383	1.56%
18	Minnesota	1,367	1.54%
19	North Carolina	1,254	1.41%
20	Tennessee	1,136	1.28%
21	Indiana	998	1.12%
22	Oregon	968	1.09%
23	Washington	948	1.07%
24	Connecticut	879	0.99%
25	Utah	732	0.82%
26	Hawaii	628	0.71%
27	New Mexico	602	0.68%
28	Kentucky	490	0.55%
29	Arkansas	477	0.54%
30	South Carolina	455	0.51%
31	Alabama	405	0.46%
32	Oklahoma	362	0.41%
33	Louisiana	359	0.40%
34	Nebraska	316	0.36%
35	Iowa	256	0.29%
36	Rhode Island	254	0.29%
37	West Virginia	129	0.15%
38	Alaska	99	0.11%
38	Mississippi	99	0.11%
40	Delaware	69	0.08%
41	New Hampshire	14	0.02%
42	Maine	12	0.01%
43	South Dakota	8	0.01%
44	Idaho	5	0.01%
45	Wyoming	3	0.00%
46	Vermont	2	0.00%
47	Montana	1	0.00%
47	North Dakota	1	0.00%
NA	Illinois**	NA	NA
NA	Kansas**	NA	NA
	District of Columbia	1,352	1.52%

Source: U.S. Department of Justice, Federal Bureau of Investigation
  "Crime in the United States 1993" (Uniform Crime Reports, December 4, 1994)
*By law enforcement agencies submitting complete reports to the F.B.I. for 12 months in 1993. The F.B.I. estimates 97,800 reported and unreported arrests for prostitution and commercialized vice occurred in 1993. Includes keeping a bawdy house, procuring or transporting women for immoral purposes. Attempts are included.
**Not available.

Reported Arrest Rate for Prostitution and Commercialized Vice in 1993

National Rate = 41.5 Reported Arrests per 100,000 Population*

<u>ALPHA ORDER</u>

RANK	STATE	RATE
39	Alabama	10.2
33	Alaska	17.5
10	Arizona	48.0
30	Arkansas	19.8
7	California	56.8
9	Colorado	49.9
18	Connecticut	31.7
32	Delaware	18.5
11	Florida	47.8
21	Georgia	30.1
8	Hawaii	53.6
46	Idaho	0.6
NA	Illinois**	NA
22	Indiana	28.9
35	Iowa	12.8
NA	Kansas**	NA
25	Kentucky	26.9
34	Louisiana	13.9
43	Maine	1.1
24	Maryland	27.9
5	Massachusetts	67.2
17	Michigan	32.6
20	Minnesota	30.8
37	Mississippi	11.6
2	Missouri	82.2
47	Montana	0.3
28	Nebraska	21.2
1	Nevada	223.7
41	New Hampshire	1.9
14	New Jersey	39.9
4	New Mexico	74.7
3	New York	79.3
31	North Carolina	18.6
48	North Dakota	0.2
6	Ohio	64.6
38	Oklahoma	11.4
16	Oregon	33.0
29	Pennsylvania	21.1
26	Rhode Island	26.2
35	South Carolina	12.8
42	South Dakota	1.6
15	Tennessee	38.4
13	Texas	41.9
12	Utah	42.6
44	Vermont	0.7
23	Virginia	28.3
27	Washington	24.7
40	West Virginia	7.1
19	Wisconsin	31.1
44	Wyoming	0.7

<u>RANK ORDER</u>

RANK	STATE	RATE
1	Nevada	223.7
2	Missouri	82.2
3	New York	79.3
4	New Mexico	74.7
5	Massachusetts	67.2
6	Ohio	64.6
7	California	56.8
8	Hawaii	53.6
9	Colorado	49.9
10	Arizona	48.0
11	Florida	47.8
12	Utah	42.6
13	Texas	41.9
14	New Jersey	39.9
15	Tennessee	38.4
16	Oregon	33.0
17	Michigan	32.6
18	Connecticut	31.7
19	Wisconsin	31.1
20	Minnesota	30.8
21	Georgia	30.1
22	Indiana	28.9
23	Virginia	28.3
24	Maryland	27.9
25	Kentucky	26.9
26	Rhode Island	26.2
27	Washington	24.7
28	Nebraska	21.2
29	Pennsylvania	21.1
30	Arkansas	19.8
31	North Carolina	18.6
32	Delaware	18.5
33	Alaska	17.5
34	Louisiana	13.9
35	Iowa	12.8
35	South Carolina	12.8
37	Mississippi	11.6
38	Oklahoma	11.4
39	Alabama	10.2
40	West Virginia	7.1
41	New Hampshire	1.9
42	South Dakota	1.6
43	Maine	1.1
44	Vermont	0.7
44	Wyoming	0.7
46	Idaho	0.6
47	Montana	0.3
48	North Dakota	0.2
NA	Illinois**	NA
NA	Kansas**	NA

District of Columbia   233.9

Source: Morgan Quitno Corporation using data from U.S. Department of Justice, Federal Bureau of Investigation
    "Crime in the United States 1993" (Uniform Crime Reports, December 4, 1994)
*By law enforcement agencies submitting complete reports to the F.B.I. for 12 months in 1993. These rates based on
population estimates for areas under the jurisdiction those agencies reporting. Arrest rate based on the F.B.I. estimate
of reported and unreported arrests for prostitution and commercialized vice is 37.9 arrests per 100,000 population.
**Not available.

Reported Arrests for Offenses Against Families and Children in 1993

National Total = 89,157 Reported Arrests*

ALPHA ORDER					RANK ORDER			
RANK	STATE	ARRESTS	% of USA		RANK	STATE	ARRESTS	% of USA
21	Alabama	1,057	1.19%		1	New Jersey	15,524	17.41%
43	Alaska	129	0.14%		2	Ohio	9,663	10.84%
17	Arizona	1,497	1.68%		3	Texas	7,780	8.73%
27	Arkansas	784	0.88%		4	North Carolina	6,329	7.10%
31	California	586	0.66%		5	Wisconsin	4,564	5.12%
15	Colorado	1,736	1.95%		6	Georgia	3,615	4.05%
12	Connecticut	2,072	2.32%		7	Massachusetts	3,590	4.03%
48	Delaware	40	0.04%		8	New York	2,994	3.36%
18	Florida	1,289	1.45%		9	Michigan	2,419	2.71%
6	Georgia	3,615	4.05%		10	Missouri	2,257	2.53%
11	Hawaii	2,096	2.35%		11	Hawaii	2,096	2.35%
44	Idaho	123	0.14%		12	Connecticut	2,072	2.32%
NA	Illinois**	NA	NA		13	Maryland	1,927	2.16%
28	Indiana	765	0.86%		14	Kentucky	1,873	2.10%
42	Iowa	157	0.18%		15	Colorado	1,736	1.95%
NA	Kansas**	NA	NA		16	Virginia	1,652	1.85%
14	Kentucky	1,873	2.10%		17	Arizona	1,497	1.68%
20	Louisiana	1,187	1.33%		18	Florida	1,289	1.45%
41	Maine	187	0.21%		19	Nebraska	1,212	1.36%
13	Maryland	1,927	2.16%		20	Louisiana	1,187	1.33%
7	Massachusetts	3,590	4.03%		21	Alabama	1,057	1.19%
9	Michigan	2,419	2.71%		21	Tennessee	1,057	1.19%
33	Minnesota	524	0.59%		23	New Mexico	1,052	1.18%
34	Mississippi	476	0.53%		24	Pennsylvania	996	1.12%
10	Missouri	2,257	2.53%		25	South Carolina	916	1.03%
46	Montana	83	0.09%		26	Nevada	846	0.95%
19	Nebraska	1,212	1.36%		27	Arkansas	784	0.88%
26	Nevada	846	0.95%		28	Indiana	765	0.86%
47	New Hampshire	46	0.05%		29	Oklahoma	719	0.81%
1	New Jersey	15,524	17.41%		30	Washington	650	0.73%
23	New Mexico	1,052	1.18%		31	California	586	0.66%
8	New York	2,994	3.36%		32	Utah	546	0.61%
4	North Carolina	6,329	7.10%		33	Minnesota	524	0.59%
38	North Dakota	215	0.24%		34	Mississippi	476	0.53%
2	Ohio	9,663	10.84%		35	Rhode Island	424	0.48%
29	Oklahoma	719	0.81%		36	Wyoming	337	0.38%
37	Oregon	311	0.35%		37	Oregon	311	0.35%
24	Pennsylvania	996	1.12%		38	North Dakota	215	0.24%
35	Rhode Island	424	0.48%		39	Vermont	192	0.22%
25	South Carolina	916	1.03%		40	West Virginia	189	0.21%
45	South Dakota	109	0.12%		41	Maine	187	0.21%
21	Tennessee	1,057	1.19%		42	Iowa	157	0.18%
3	Texas	7,780	8.73%		43	Alaska	129	0.14%
32	Utah	546	0.61%		44	Idaho	123	0.14%
39	Vermont	192	0.22%		45	South Dakota	109	0.12%
16	Virginia	1,652	1.85%		46	Montana	83	0.09%
30	Washington	650	0.73%		47	New Hampshire	46	0.05%
40	West Virginia	189	0.21%		48	Delaware	40	0.04%
5	Wisconsin	4,564	5.12%		NA	Illinois**	NA	NA
36	Wyoming	337	0.38%		NA	Kansas**	NA	NA
						District of Columbia	16	0.02%

Source: U.S. Department of Justice, Federal Bureau of Investigation
    "Crime in the United States 1993" (Uniform Crime Reports, December 4, 1994)
*By law enforcement agencies submitting complete reports to the F.B.I. for 12 months in 1993. The F.B.I. estimates
109,100 reported and unreported arrests for offenses against families and children occurred in 1993. Includes nonsupport,
neglect, desertion or abuse of family and children.
**Not available.

35

Reported Arrest Rate for Offenses Against Families and Children in 1993

National Rate = 41.6 Reported Arrests per 100,000 Population*

ALPHA ORDER

RANK ORDER

RANK	STATE	RATE		RANK	STATE	RATE
28	Alabama	26.7		1	New Jersey	203.4
31	Alaska	22.8		2	Hawaii	178.8
22	Arizona	40.1		3	Ohio	145.2
25	Arkansas	32.5		4	New Mexico	130.5
48	California	1.9		5	Kentucky	102.7
16	Colorado	58.4		6	North Carolina	93.7
11	Connecticut	74.7		7	Wisconsin	91.2
42	Delaware	10.7		8	Wyoming	83.0
45	Florida	10.1		9	Nebraska	81.4
15	Georgia	64.6		10	Massachusetts	80.7
2	Hawaii	178.8		11	Connecticut	74.7
39	Idaho	14.2		12	Vermont	70.6
NA	Illinois**	NA		13	Nevada	70.3
33	Indiana	22.2		14	Missouri	68.3
46	Iowa	7.9		15	Georgia	64.6
NA	Kansas**	NA		16	Colorado	58.4
5	Kentucky	102.7		17	Mississippi	55.7
18	Louisiana	46.0		18	Louisiana	46.0
37	Maine	17.8		19	Texas	44.6
23	Maryland	38.8		20	Rhode Island	43.7
10	Massachusetts	80.7		21	North Dakota	40.2
27	Michigan	28.8		22	Arizona	40.1
40	Minnesota	11.8		23	Maryland	38.8
17	Mississippi	55.7		24	Tennessee	35.7
14	Missouri	68.3		25	Arkansas	32.5
34	Montana	22.0		26	Utah	31.8
9	Nebraska	81.4		27	Michigan	28.8
13	Nevada	70.3		28	Alabama	26.7
47	New Hampshire	6.2		29	South Carolina	25.8
1	New Jersey	203.4		30	Virginia	25.5
4	New Mexico	130.5		31	Alaska	22.8
36	New York	19.3		32	Oklahoma	22.7
6	North Carolina	93.7		33	Indiana	22.2
21	North Dakota	40.2		34	Montana	22.0
3	Ohio	145.2		35	South Dakota	21.9
32	Oklahoma	22.7		36	New York	19.3
43	Oregon	10.6		37	Maine	17.8
41	Pennsylvania	11.1		38	Washington	16.9
20	Rhode Island	43.7		39	Idaho	14.2
29	South Carolina	25.8		40	Minnesota	11.8
35	South Dakota	21.9		41	Pennsylvania	11.1
24	Tennessee	35.7		42	Delaware	10.7
19	Texas	44.6		43	Oregon	10.6
26	Utah	31.8		44	West Virginia	10.4
12	Vermont	70.6		45	Florida	10.1
30	Virginia	25.5		46	Iowa	7.9
38	Washington	16.9		47	New Hampshire	6.2
44	West Virginia	10.4		48	California	1.9
7	Wisconsin	91.2		NA	Illinois**	NA
8	Wyoming	83.0		NA	Kansas**	NA

District of Columbia   2.8

Source: Morgan Quitno Corporation using data from U.S. Department of Justice, Federal Bureau of Investigation "Crime in the United States 1993" (Uniform Crime Reports, December 4, 1994)
By law enforcement agencies submitting complete reports to the F.B.I. for 12 months in 1993. These rates based on population estimates for areas under the jurisdiction of those agencies reporting. Arrest rate based on the F.B.I. estimate of reported and unreported arrests for offenses against families and children is 42.3 arrests per 100,000 population.
**Not available.

Reported Arrests of Youths 17 Years and Younger in 1993

National Total = 2,014,472 Reported Arrests*

ALPHA ORDER

RANK	STATE	ARRESTS	% of USA
33	Alabama	13,719	0.68%
43	Alaska	6,155	0.31%
9	Arizona	60,361	3.00%
29	Arkansas	17,365	0.86%
1	California	254,585	12.64%
11	Colorado	52,887	2.63%
22	Connecticut	29,043	1.44%
47	Delaware	1,810	0.09%
5	Florida	83,605	4.15%
17	Georgia	41,626	2.07%
28	Hawaii	19,246	0.96%
34	Idaho	13,523	0.67%
NA	Illinois**	NA	NA
20	Indiana	37,293	1.85%
32	Iowa	13,977	0.69%
NA	Kansas**	NA	NA
35	Kentucky	13,056	0.65%
24	Louisiana	24,547	1.22%
40	Maine	7,490	0.37%
16	Maryland	42,814	2.13%
27	Massachusetts	19,392	0.96%
10	Michigan	53,269	2.64%
12	Minnesota	51,849	2.57%
39	Mississippi	7,798	0.39%
21	Missouri	32,594	1.62%
46	Montana	2,387	0.12%
31	Nebraska	14,909	0.74%
30	Nevada	15,412	0.77%
44	New Hampshire	5,329	0.26%
6	New Jersey	82,454	4.09%
36	New Mexico	9,437	0.47%
3	New York	157,215	7.80%
15	North Carolina	44,251	2.20%
42	North Dakota	6,459	0.32%
8	Ohio	64,180	3.19%
23	Oklahoma	24,909	1.24%
19	Oregon	40,899	2.03%
7	Pennsylvania	76,406	3.79%
38	Rhode Island	8,746	0.43%
26	South Carolina	20,397	1.01%
37	South Dakota	8,922	0.44%
25	Tennessee	20,749	1.03%
2	Texas	185,336	9.20%
18	Utah	41,591	2.06%
48	Vermont	467	0.02%
13	Virginia	49,401	2.45%
14	Washington	45,612	2.26%
41	West Virginia	6,742	0.33%
4	Wisconsin	121,288	6.02%
45	Wyoming	5,164	0.26%

RANK ORDER

RANK	STATE	ARRESTS	% of USA
1	California	254,585	12.64%
2	Texas	185,336	9.20%
3	New York	157,215	7.80%
4	Wisconsin	121,288	6.02%
5	Florida	83,605	4.15%
6	New Jersey	82,454	4.09%
7	Pennsylvania	76,406	3.79%
8	Ohio	64,180	3.19%
9	Arizona	60,361	3.00%
10	Michigan	53,269	2.64%
11	Colorado	52,887	2.63%
12	Minnesota	51,849	2.57%
13	Virginia	49,401	2.45%
14	Washington	45,612	2.26%
15	North Carolina	44,251	2.20%
16	Maryland	42,814	2.13%
17	Georgia	41,626	2.07%
18	Utah	41,591	2.06%
19	Oregon	40,899	2.03%
20	Indiana	37,293	1.85%
21	Missouri	32,594	1.62%
22	Connecticut	29,043	1.44%
23	Oklahoma	24,909	1.24%
24	Louisiana	24,547	1.22%
25	Tennessee	20,749	1.03%
26	South Carolina	20,397	1.01%
27	Massachusetts	19,392	0.96%
28	Hawaii	19,246	0.96%
29	Arkansas	17,365	0.86%
30	Nevada	15,412	0.77%
31	Nebraska	14,909	0.74%
32	Iowa	13,977	0.69%
33	Alabama	13,719	0.68%
34	Idaho	13,523	0.67%
35	Kentucky	13,056	0.65%
36	New Mexico	9,437	0.47%
37	South Dakota	8,922	0.44%
38	Rhode Island	8,746	0.43%
39	Mississippi	7,798	0.39%
40	Maine	7,490	0.37%
41	West Virginia	6,742	0.33%
42	North Dakota	6,459	0.32%
43	Alaska	6,155	0.31%
44	New Hampshire	5,329	0.26%
45	Wyoming	5,164	0.26%
46	Montana	2,387	0.12%
47	Delaware	1,810	0.09%
48	Vermont	467	0.02%
NA	Illinois**	NA	NA
NA	Kansas**	NA	NA
	District of Columbia	4,391	0.22%

Source: U.S. Department of Justice, Federal Bureau of Investigation
"Crime in the United States 1993" (Uniform Crime Reports, December 4, 1994)
By law enforcement agencies submitting complete reports to the F.B.I. for 12 months in 1993.
**Not available.*

Reported Arrests of Youths 17 Years and Younger
As a Percent of All Arrests in 1993
National Percent = 17.12% of All Reported Arrests*

ALPHA ORDER

RANK	STATE	PERCENT
48	Alabama	7.35
28	Alaska	16.21
10	Arizona	24.03
46	Arkansas	9.79
31	California	15.70
14	Colorado	22.38
29	Connecticut	15.92
23	Delaware	18.05
34	Florida	13.63
44	Georgia	10.87
3	Hawaii	30.16
5	Idaho	28.92
NA	Illinois**	NA
11	Indiana	23.83
21	Iowa	19.53
NA	Kansas**	NA
45	Kentucky	10.48
35	Louisiana	13.53
19	Maine	19.89
30	Maryland	15.83
36	Massachusetts	13.25
33	Michigan	14.48
8	Minnesota	26.49
38	Mississippi	12.66
39	Missouri	12.44
9	Montana	24.67
18	Nebraska	20.44
27	Nevada	16.81
16	New Hampshire	21.87
13	New Jersey	22.66
25	New Mexico	17.39
32	New York	15.65
47	North Carolina	9.13
2	North Dakota	30.60
22	Ohio	19.14
25	Oklahoma	17.39
7	Oregon	27.16
12	Pennsylvania	23.33
15	Rhode Island	21.92
40	South Carolina	11.78
6	South Dakota	27.55
41	Tennessee	11.68
24	Texas	17.95
1	Utah	37.64
43	Vermont	11.03
37	Virginia	12.75
20	Washington	19.66
42	West Virginia	11.28
4	Wisconsin	30.13
17	Wyoming	21.84

RANK ORDER

RANK	STATE	PERCENT
1	Utah	37.64
2	North Dakota	30.60
3	Hawaii	30.16
4	Wisconsin	30.13
5	Idaho	28.92
6	South Dakota	27.55
7	Oregon	27.16
8	Minnesota	26.49
9	Montana	24.67
10	Arizona	24.03
11	Indiana	23.83
12	Pennsylvania	23.33
13	New Jersey	22.66
14	Colorado	22.38
15	Rhode Island	21.92
16	New Hampshire	21.87
17	Wyoming	21.84
18	Nebraska	20.44
19	Maine	19.89
20	Washington	19.66
21	Iowa	19.53
22	Ohio	19.14
23	Delaware	18.05
24	Texas	17.95
25	New Mexico	17.39
25	Oklahoma	17.39
27	Nevada	16.81
28	Alaska	16.21
29	Connecticut	15.92
30	Maryland	15.83
31	California	15.70
32	New York	15.65
33	Michigan	14.48
34	Florida	13.63
35	Louisiana	13.53
36	Massachusetts	13.25
37	Virginia	12.75
38	Mississippi	12.66
39	Missouri	12.44
40	South Carolina	11.78
41	Tennessee	11.68
42	West Virginia	11.28
43	Vermont	11.03
44	Georgia	10.87
45	Kentucky	10.48
46	Arkansas	9.79
47	North Carolina	9.13
48	Alabama	7.35
NA	Illinois**	NA
NA	Kansas**	NA

	District of Columbia	8.48

Source: Morgan Quitno Corporation using data from U.S. Department of Justice, Federal Bureau of Investigation
"Crime in the United States 1993" (Uniform Crime Reports, December 4, 1994)
*By law enforcement agencies submitting complete reports to the F.B.I. for 12 months in 1993.
**Not available.

Reported Arrests of Youths 17 Years and Younger for Crime Index Offenses in 1993

National Total = 710,916 Reported Arrests*

ALPHA ORDER

RANK	STATE	ARRESTS	% of USA
30	Alabama	5,791	0.81%
38	Alaska	3,373	0.47%
12	Arizona	18,803	2.64%
27	Arkansas	6,197	0.87%
1	California	107,736	15.15%
15	Colorado	16,053	2.26%
23	Connecticut	9,365	1.32%
47	Delaware	700	0.10%
3	Florida	48,733	6.85%
19	Georgia	14,323	2.01%
34	Hawaii	4,762	0.67%
33	Idaho	4,819	0.68%
NA	Illinois**	NA	NA
21	Indiana	11,451	1.61%
32	Iowa	4,980	0.70%
NA	Kansas**	NA	NA
29	Kentucky	5,893	0.83%
24	Louisiana	9,244	1.30%
37	Maine	3,643	0.51%
13	Maryland	17,701	2.49%
26	Massachusetts	7,312	1.03%
8	Michigan	21,937	3.09%
11	Minnesota	18,887	2.66%
39	Mississippi	3,165	0.45%
22	Missouri	10,750	1.51%
46	Montana	729	0.10%
31	Nebraska	5,685	0.80%
35	Nevada	4,588	0.65%
44	New Hampshire	1,632	0.23%
6	New Jersey	23,251	3.27%
36	New Mexico	3,673	0.52%
4	New York	42,293	5.95%
16	North Carolina	15,811	2.22%
43	North Dakota	2,152	0.30%
10	Ohio	18,915	2.66%
20	Oklahoma	11,724	1.65%
18	Oregon	15,258	2.15%
7	Pennsylvania	22,564	3.17%
40	Rhode Island	2,793	0.39%
25	South Carolina	9,106	1.28%
41	South Dakota	2,646	0.37%
28	Tennessee	5,981	0.84%
2	Texas	60,876	8.56%
14	Utah	16,222	2.28%
48	Vermont	248	0.03%
17	Virginia	15,570	2.19%
9	Washington	20,990	2.95%
42	West Virginia	2,449	0.34%
5	Wisconsin	31,534	4.44%
45	Wyoming	1,276	0.18%

RANK ORDER

RANK	STATE	ARRESTS	% of USA
1	California	107,736	15.15%
2	Texas	60,876	8.56%
3	Florida	48,733	6.85%
4	New York	42,293	5.95%
5	Wisconsin	31,534	4.44%
6	New Jersey	23,251	3.27%
7	Pennsylvania	22,564	3.17%
8	Michigan	21,937	3.09%
9	Washington	20,990	2.95%
10	Ohio	18,915	2.66%
11	Minnesota	18,887	2.66%
12	Arizona	18,803	2.64%
13	Maryland	17,701	2.49%
14	Utah	16,222	2.28%
15	Colorado	16,053	2.26%
16	North Carolina	15,811	2.22%
17	Virginia	15,570	2.19%
18	Oregon	15,258	2.15%
19	Georgia	14,323	2.01%
20	Oklahoma	11,724	1.65%
21	Indiana	11,451	1.61%
22	Missouri	10,750	1.51%
23	Connecticut	9,365	1.32%
24	Louisiana	9,244	1.30%
25	South Carolina	9,106	1.28%
26	Massachusetts	7,312	1.03%
27	Arkansas	6,197	0.87%
28	Tennessee	5,981	0.84%
29	Kentucky	5,893	0.83%
30	Alabama	5,791	0.81%
31	Nebraska	5,685	0.80%
32	Iowa	4,980	0.70%
33	Idaho	4,819	0.68%
34	Hawaii	4,762	0.67%
35	Nevada	4,588	0.65%
36	New Mexico	3,673	0.52%
37	Maine	3,643	0.51%
38	Alaska	3,373	0.47%
39	Mississippi	3,165	0.45%
40	Rhode Island	2,793	0.39%
41	South Dakota	2,646	0.37%
42	West Virginia	2,449	0.34%
43	North Dakota	2,152	0.30%
44	New Hampshire	1,632	0.23%
45	Wyoming	1,276	0.18%
46	Montana	729	0.10%
47	Delaware	700	0.10%
48	Vermont	248	0.03%
NA	Illinois**	NA	NA
NA	Kansas**	NA	NA
	District of Columbia	1,642	0.23%

Source: U.S. Department of Justice, Federal Bureau of Investigation
   "Crime in the United States 1993" (Uniform Crime Reports, December 4, 1994)
*By law enforcement agencies submitting complete reports to the F.B.I. for 12 months in 1993. Crime index offenses consist of murder, forcible rape, robbery, aggravated assault, burglary, larceny-theft, motor vehicle theft and arson.
**Not available.

Reported Arrests of Youths 17 Years and Younger for Crime Index Offenses
As a Percent of All Such Arrests in 1993
National Percent = 29.34% of Reported Arrests for Crime Index Offenses*

ALPHA ORDER

RANK	STATE	PERCENT
48	Alabama	16.57
13	Alaska	40.64
21	Arizona	34.17
32	Arkansas	26.40
36	California	25.48
19	Colorado	35.44
41	Connecticut	23.59
27	Delaware	30.37
29	Florida	28.35
44	Georgia	20.41
15	Hawaii	37.70
2	Idaho	55.23
NA	Illinois**	NA
18	Indiana	35.56
17	Iowa	37.02
NA	Kansas**	NA
34	Kentucky	26.21
42	Louisiana	23.17
7	Maine	43.59
30	Maryland	27.45
45	Massachusetts	18.94
26	Michigan	30.49
6	Minnesota	44.43
37	Mississippi	25.18
40	Missouri	23.75
11	Montana	41.94
9	Nebraska	43.41
31	Nevada	27.37
16	New Hampshire	37.68
25	New Jersey	31.24
20	New Mexico	34.92
38	New York	24.83
46	North Carolina	18.47
3	North Dakota	54.17
23	Ohio	32.91
8	Oklahoma	43.56
14	Oregon	38.11
28	Pennsylvania	29.69
22	Rhode Island	34.07
35	South Carolina	25.92
4	South Dakota	50.55
47	Tennessee	17.74
24	Texas	32.17
1	Utah	57.21
43	Vermont	21.74
39	Virginia	24.50
12	Washington	41.17
33	West Virginia	26.35
5	Wisconsin	46.34
10	Wyoming	42.24

RANK ORDER

RANK	STATE	PERCENT
1	Utah	57.21
2	Idaho	55.23
3	North Dakota	54.17
4	South Dakota	50.55
5	Wisconsin	46.34
6	Minnesota	44.43
7	Maine	43.59
8	Oklahoma	43.56
9	Nebraska	43.41
10	Wyoming	42.24
11	Montana	41.94
12	Washington	41.17
13	Alaska	40.64
14	Oregon	38.11
15	Hawaii	37.70
16	New Hampshire	37.68
17	Iowa	37.02
18	Indiana	35.56
19	Colorado	35.44
20	New Mexico	34.92
21	Arizona	34.17
22	Rhode Island	34.07
23	Ohio	32.91
24	Texas	32.17
25	New Jersey	31.24
26	Michigan	30.49
27	Delaware	30.37
28	Pennsylvania	29.69
29	Florida	28.35
30	Maryland	27.45
31	Nevada	27.37
32	Arkansas	26.40
33	West Virginia	26.35
34	Kentucky	26.21
35	South Carolina	25.92
36	California	25.48
37	Mississippi	25.18
38	New York	24.83
39	Virginia	24.50
40	Missouri	23.75
41	Connecticut	23.59
42	Louisiana	23.17
43	Vermont	21.74
44	Georgia	20.41
45	Massachusetts	18.94
46	North Carolina	18.47
47	Tennessee	17.74
48	Alabama	16.57
NA	Illinois**	NA
NA	Kansas**	NA

District of Columbia   14.06

Source: Morgan Quitno Corporation using data from U.S. Department of Justice, Federal Bureau of Investigation "Crime in the United States 1993" (Uniform Crime Reports, December 4, 1994)

*By law enforcement agencies submitting complete reports to the F.B.I. for 12 months in 1993. Crime index offenses consist of murder, forcible rape, robbery, aggravated assault, burglary, larceny-theft, motor vehicle theft and arson.

**Not available.

Reported Arrests of Youths 17 Years and Younger for Violent Crime in 1993

National Total = 119,678 Reported Arrests*

<table>
<tr><td colspan="4">ALPHA ORDER</td><td colspan="4">RANK ORDER</td></tr>
<tr><td>RANK</td><td>STATE</td><td>ARRESTS</td><td>% of USA</td><td>RANK</td><td>STATE</td><td>ARRESTS</td><td>% of USA</td></tr>
<tr><td>28</td><td>Alabama</td><td>920</td><td>0.77%</td><td>1</td><td>California</td><td>21,046</td><td>17.59%</td></tr>
<tr><td>39</td><td>Alaska</td><td>250</td><td>0.21%</td><td>2</td><td>New York</td><td>17,504</td><td>14.63%</td></tr>
<tr><td>14</td><td>Arizona</td><td>2,256</td><td>1.89%</td><td>3</td><td>Florida</td><td>8,947</td><td>7.48%</td></tr>
<tr><td>29</td><td>Arkansas</td><td>818</td><td>0.68%</td><td>4</td><td>Texas</td><td>8,796</td><td>7.35%</td></tr>
<tr><td>1</td><td>California</td><td>21,046</td><td>17.59%</td><td>5</td><td>New Jersey</td><td>5,438</td><td>4.54%</td></tr>
<tr><td>19</td><td>Colorado</td><td>1,752</td><td>1.46%</td><td>6</td><td>Pennsylvania</td><td>5,120</td><td>4.28%</td></tr>
<tr><td>23</td><td>Connecticut</td><td>1,458</td><td>1.22%</td><td>7</td><td>Michigan</td><td>3,849</td><td>3.22%</td></tr>
<tr><td>40</td><td>Delaware</td><td>164</td><td>0.14%</td><td>8</td><td>Maryland</td><td>3,495</td><td>2.92%</td></tr>
<tr><td>3</td><td>Florida</td><td>8,947</td><td>7.48%</td><td>9</td><td>North Carolina</td><td>3,110</td><td>2.60%</td></tr>
<tr><td>11</td><td>Georgia</td><td>2,853</td><td>2.38%</td><td>10</td><td>Ohio</td><td>2,854</td><td>2.38%</td></tr>
<tr><td>38</td><td>Hawaii</td><td>272</td><td>0.23%</td><td>11</td><td>Georgia</td><td>2,853</td><td>2.38%</td></tr>
<tr><td>35</td><td>Idaho</td><td>362</td><td>0.30%</td><td>12</td><td>Massachusetts</td><td>2,503</td><td>2.09%</td></tr>
<tr><td>NA</td><td>Illinois**</td><td>NA</td><td>NA</td><td>13</td><td>Wisconsin</td><td>2,305</td><td>1.93%</td></tr>
<tr><td>18</td><td>Indiana</td><td>1,820</td><td>1.52%</td><td>14</td><td>Arizona</td><td>2,256</td><td>1.89%</td></tr>
<tr><td>31</td><td>Iowa</td><td>584</td><td>0.49%</td><td>15</td><td>Minnesota</td><td>2,196</td><td>1.83%</td></tr>
<tr><td>NA</td><td>Kansas**</td><td>NA</td><td>NA</td><td>16</td><td>Louisiana</td><td>2,005</td><td>1.68%</td></tr>
<tr><td>27</td><td>Kentucky</td><td>971</td><td>0.81%</td><td>17</td><td>Missouri</td><td>1,841</td><td>1.54%</td></tr>
<tr><td>16</td><td>Louisiana</td><td>2,005</td><td>1.68%</td><td>18</td><td>Indiana</td><td>1,820</td><td>1.52%</td></tr>
<tr><td>43</td><td>Maine</td><td>114</td><td>0.10%</td><td>19</td><td>Colorado</td><td>1,752</td><td>1.46%</td></tr>
<tr><td>8</td><td>Maryland</td><td>3,495</td><td>2.92%</td><td>20</td><td>Washington</td><td>1,665</td><td>1.39%</td></tr>
<tr><td>12</td><td>Massachusetts</td><td>2,503</td><td>2.09%</td><td>21</td><td>Virginia</td><td>1,572</td><td>1.31%</td></tr>
<tr><td>7</td><td>Michigan</td><td>3,849</td><td>3.22%</td><td>22</td><td>South Carolina</td><td>1,505</td><td>1.26%</td></tr>
<tr><td>15</td><td>Minnesota</td><td>2,196</td><td>1.83%</td><td>23</td><td>Connecticut</td><td>1,458</td><td>1.22%</td></tr>
<tr><td>36</td><td>Mississippi</td><td>334</td><td>0.28%</td><td>24</td><td>Oklahoma</td><td>1,270</td><td>1.06%</td></tr>
<tr><td>17</td><td>Missouri</td><td>1,841</td><td>1.54%</td><td>25</td><td>Oregon</td><td>1,122</td><td>0.94%</td></tr>
<tr><td>47</td><td>Montana</td><td>33</td><td>0.03%</td><td>26</td><td>Utah</td><td>1,040</td><td>0.87%</td></tr>
<tr><td>37</td><td>Nebraska</td><td>300</td><td>0.25%</td><td>27</td><td>Kentucky</td><td>971</td><td>0.81%</td></tr>
<tr><td>33</td><td>Nevada</td><td>473</td><td>0.40%</td><td>28</td><td>Alabama</td><td>920</td><td>0.77%</td></tr>
<tr><td>44</td><td>New Hampshire</td><td>112</td><td>0.09%</td><td>29</td><td>Arkansas</td><td>818</td><td>0.68%</td></tr>
<tr><td>5</td><td>New Jersey</td><td>5,438</td><td>4.54%</td><td>30</td><td>Tennessee</td><td>589</td><td>0.49%</td></tr>
<tr><td>34</td><td>New Mexico</td><td>383</td><td>0.32%</td><td>31</td><td>Iowa</td><td>584</td><td>0.49%</td></tr>
<tr><td>2</td><td>New York</td><td>17,504</td><td>14.63%</td><td>32</td><td>Rhode Island</td><td>530</td><td>0.44%</td></tr>
<tr><td>9</td><td>North Carolina</td><td>3,110</td><td>2.60%</td><td>33</td><td>Nevada</td><td>473</td><td>0.40%</td></tr>
<tr><td>46</td><td>North Dakota</td><td>52</td><td>0.04%</td><td>34</td><td>New Mexico</td><td>383</td><td>0.32%</td></tr>
<tr><td>10</td><td>Ohio</td><td>2,854</td><td>2.38%</td><td>35</td><td>Idaho</td><td>362</td><td>0.30%</td></tr>
<tr><td>24</td><td>Oklahoma</td><td>1,270</td><td>1.06%</td><td>36</td><td>Mississippi</td><td>334</td><td>0.28%</td></tr>
<tr><td>25</td><td>Oregon</td><td>1,122</td><td>0.94%</td><td>37</td><td>Nebraska</td><td>300</td><td>0.25%</td></tr>
<tr><td>6</td><td>Pennsylvania</td><td>5,120</td><td>4.28%</td><td>38</td><td>Hawaii</td><td>272</td><td>0.23%</td></tr>
<tr><td>32</td><td>Rhode Island</td><td>530</td><td>0.44%</td><td>39</td><td>Alaska</td><td>250</td><td>0.21%</td></tr>
<tr><td>22</td><td>South Carolina</td><td>1,505</td><td>1.26%</td><td>40</td><td>Delaware</td><td>164</td><td>0.14%</td></tr>
<tr><td>42</td><td>South Dakota</td><td>129</td><td>0.11%</td><td>41</td><td>West Virginia</td><td>145</td><td>0.12%</td></tr>
<tr><td>30</td><td>Tennessee</td><td>589</td><td>0.49%</td><td>42</td><td>South Dakota</td><td>129</td><td>0.11%</td></tr>
<tr><td>4</td><td>Texas</td><td>8,796</td><td>7.35%</td><td>43</td><td>Maine</td><td>114</td><td>0.10%</td></tr>
<tr><td>26</td><td>Utah</td><td>1,040</td><td>0.87%</td><td>44</td><td>New Hampshire</td><td>112</td><td>0.09%</td></tr>
<tr><td>48</td><td>Vermont</td><td>19</td><td>0.02%</td><td>45</td><td>Wyoming</td><td>66</td><td>0.06%</td></tr>
<tr><td>21</td><td>Virginia</td><td>1,572</td><td>1.31%</td><td>46</td><td>North Dakota</td><td>52</td><td>0.04%</td></tr>
<tr><td>20</td><td>Washington</td><td>1,665</td><td>1.39%</td><td>47</td><td>Montana</td><td>33</td><td>0.03%</td></tr>
<tr><td>41</td><td>West Virginia</td><td>145</td><td>0.12%</td><td>48</td><td>Vermont</td><td>19</td><td>0.02%</td></tr>
<tr><td>13</td><td>Wisconsin</td><td>2,305</td><td>1.93%</td><td>NA</td><td>Illinois**</td><td>NA</td><td>NA</td></tr>
<tr><td>45</td><td>Wyoming</td><td>66</td><td>0.06%</td><td>NA</td><td>Kansas**</td><td>NA</td><td>NA</td></tr>
<tr><td></td><td></td><td></td><td></td><td></td><td>District of Columbia</td><td>746</td><td>0.62%</td></tr>
</table>

Source: U.S. Department of Justice, Federal Bureau of Investigation
 "Crime in the United States 1993" (Uniform Crime Reports, December 4, 1994)
*By law enforcement agencies submitting complete reports to the F.B.I. for 12 months in 1993. Violent crimes are offenses of murder, forcible rape, robbery and aggravated assault.
**Not available.

Reported Arrests of Youths 17 Years and Younger for Violent Crime
As a Percent of All Such Arrests in 1993
National Rate = 18.46% of Reported Arrests for Violent Crime*

ALPHA ORDER

RANK ORDER

RANK	STATE	PERCENT	RANK	STATE	PERCENT
47	Alabama	8.11	1	Utah	40.12
34	Alaska	15.57	2	Idaho	31.56
12	Arizona	23.36	3	North Dakota	30.06
32	Arkansas	15.97	4	Wisconsin	29.00
38	California	14.38	5	New Jersey	26.20
24	Colorado	20.00	6	New York	25.94
31	Connecticut	16.56	7	Minnesota	25.74
19	Delaware	21.52	8	Washington	24.96
28	Florida	17.13	9	Oregon	24.75
39	Georgia	14.12	10	Maryland	24.22
17	Hawaii	22.06	11	Pennsylvania	23.84
2	Idaho	31.56	12	Arizona	23.36
NA	Illinois**	NA	13	South Dakota	22.32
20	Indiana	21.41	14	Texas	22.25
15	Iowa	22.14	15	Iowa	22.14
NA	Kansas**	NA	16	Rhode Island	22.13
42	Kentucky	12.58	17	Hawaii	22.06
27	Louisiana	17.80	18	Oklahoma	21.64
40	Maine	13.80	19	Delaware	21.52
10	Maryland	24.22	20	Indiana	21.41
36	Massachusetts	15.22	21	New Mexico	20.69
30	Michigan	16.91	22	Ohio	20.41
7	Minnesota	25.74	23	Nebraska	20.01
35	Mississippi	15.51	24	Colorado	20.00
26	Missouri	17.96	25	New Hampshire	19.21
29	Montana	17.01	26	Missouri	17.96
23	Nebraska	20.01	27	Louisiana	17.80
33	Nevada	15.75	28	Florida	17.13
25	New Hampshire	19.21	29	Montana	17.01
5	New Jersey	26.20	30	Michigan	16.91
21	New Mexico	20.69	31	Connecticut	16.56
6	New York	25.94	32	Arkansas	15.97
44	North Carolina	11.44	33	Nevada	15.75
3	North Dakota	30.06	34	Alaska	15.57
22	Ohio	20.41	35	Mississippi	15.51
18	Oklahoma	21.64	36	Massachusetts	15.22
9	Oregon	24.75	37	South Carolina	14.91
11	Pennsylvania	23.84	38	California	14.38
16	Rhode Island	22.13	39	Georgia	14.12
37	South Carolina	14.91	40	Maine	13.80
13	South Dakota	22.32	41	Wyoming	13.72
48	Tennessee	6.64	42	Kentucky	12.58
14	Texas	22.25	43	Virginia	12.31
1	Utah	40.12	44	North Carolina	11.44
45	Vermont	10.27	45	Vermont	10.27
43	Virginia	12.31	46	West Virginia	9.63
8	Washington	24.96	47	Alabama	8.11
46	West Virginia	9.63	48	Tennessee	6.64
4	Wisconsin	29.00	NA	Illinois**	NA
41	Wyoming	13.72	NA	Kansas**	NA

District of Columbia   13.60

Source: Morgan Quitno Corporation using data from U.S. Department of Justice, Federal Bureau of Investigation
"Crime in the United States 1993" (Uniform Crime Reports, December 4, 1994)
*By law enforcement agencies submitting complete reports to the F.B.I. for 12 months in 1993. Violent crimes are offenses of murder, forcible rape, robbery and aggravated assault.
**Not available.

Reported Arrests of Youths 17 Years and Younger for Murder in 1993

National Total = 3,284 Reported Arrests*

<u>ALPHA ORDER</u>

RANK	STATE	ARRESTS	% of USA
18	Alabama	43	1.31%
37	Alaska	5	0.15%
17	Arizona	46	1.40%
16	Arkansas	48	1.46%
1	California	621	18.91%
21	Colorado	35	1.07%
24	Connecticut	26	0.79%
46	Delaware	0	0.00%
5	Florida	205	6.24%
11	Georgia	91	2.77%
40	Hawaii	1	0.03%
40	Idaho	1	0.03%
NA	Illinois**	NA	NA
28	Indiana	20	0.61%
35	Iowa	7	0.21%
NA	Kansas**	NA	NA
29	Kentucky	16	0.49%
9	Louisiana	103	3.14%
46	Maine	0	0.00%
7	Maryland	138	4.20%
24	Massachusetts	26	0.79%
4	Michigan	208	6.33%
22	Minnesota	34	1.04%
26	Mississippi	25	0.76%
6	Missouri	142	4.32%
40	Montana	1	0.03%
37	Nebraska	5	0.15%
31	Nevada	12	0.37%
46	New Hampshire	0	0.00%
15	New Jersey	63	1.92%
34	New Mexico	9	0.27%
3	New York	264	8.04%
10	North Carolina	96	2.92%
40	North Dakota	1	0.03%
14	Ohio	76	2.31%
18	Oklahoma	43	1.31%
30	Oregon	13	0.40%
12	Pennsylvania	82	2.50%
32	Rhode Island	11	0.33%
18	South Carolina	43	1.31%
40	South Dakota	1	0.03%
27	Tennessee	24	0.73%
2	Texas	367	11.18%
36	Utah	6	0.18%
40	Vermont	1	0.03%
13	Virginia	77	2.34%
23	Washington	28	0.85%
33	West Virginia	10	0.30%
8	Wisconsin	118	3.59%
39	Wyoming	3	0.09%

<u>RANK ORDER</u>

RANK	STATE	ARRESTS	% of USA
1	California	621	18.91%
2	Texas	367	11.18%
3	New York	264	8.04%
4	Michigan	208	6.33%
5	Florida	205	6.24%
6	Missouri	142	4.32%
7	Maryland	138	4.20%
8	Wisconsin	118	3.59%
9	Louisiana	103	3.14%
10	North Carolina	96	2.92%
11	Georgia	91	2.77%
12	Pennsylvania	82	2.50%
13	Virginia	77	2.34%
14	Ohio	76	2.31%
15	New Jersey	63	1.92%
16	Arkansas	48	1.46%
17	Arizona	46	1.40%
18	Alabama	43	1.31%
18	Oklahoma	43	1.31%
18	South Carolina	43	1.31%
21	Colorado	35	1.07%
22	Minnesota	34	1.04%
23	Washington	28	0.85%
24	Connecticut	26	0.79%
24	Massachusetts	26	0.79%
26	Mississippi	25	0.76%
27	Tennessee	24	0.73%
28	Indiana	20	0.61%
29	Kentucky	16	0.49%
30	Oregon	13	0.40%
31	Nevada	12	0.37%
32	Rhode Island	11	0.33%
33	West Virginia	10	0.30%
34	New Mexico	9	0.27%
35	Iowa	7	0.21%
36	Utah	6	0.18%
37	Alaska	5	0.15%
37	Nebraska	5	0.15%
39	Wyoming	3	0.09%
40	Hawaii	1	0.03%
40	Idaho	1	0.03%
40	Montana	1	0.03%
40	North Dakota	1	0.03%
40	South Dakota	1	0.03%
40	Vermont	1	0.03%
46	Delaware	0	0.00%
46	Maine	0	0.00%
46	New Hampshire	0	0.00%
NA	Illinois**	NA	NA
NA	Kansas**	NA	NA
	District of Columbia	34	1.04%

Source: U.S. Department of Justice, Federal Bureau of Investigation
"Crime in the United States 1993" (Uniform Crime Reports, December 4, 1994)
*By law enforcement agencies submitting complete reports to the F.B.I. for 12 months in 1993. Includes nonnegligent manslaughter.
**Not available.

Reported Arrests of Youths 17 Years and Younger for Murder
As a Percent of All Such Arrests in 1993
National Percent = 16.19% of Reported Arrests for Murder*

ALPHA ORDER

RANK ORDER

RANK	STATE	PERCENT		RANK	STATE	PERCENT
38	Alabama	9.56		1	Rhode Island	44.00
5	Alaska	22.73		2	Iowa	33.33
12	Arizona	18.78		2	Wyoming	33.33
17	Arkansas	17.02		4	Missouri	25.96
11	California	18.84		5	Alaska	22.73
19	Colorado	16.83		6	Wisconsin	22.65
18	Connecticut	16.99		7	Maryland	21.84
46	Delaware	0.00		8	Louisiana	20.72
15	Florida	17.42		9	Texas	19.34
28	Georgia	12.67		10	Washington	19.05
45	Hawaii	1.92		11	California	18.84
43	Idaho	6.67		12	Arizona	18.78
NA	Illinois**	NA		13	Massachusetts	17.81
40	Indiana	9.05		14	Oklahoma	17.70
2	Iowa	33.33		15	Florida	17.42
NA	Kansas**	NA		16	New Jersey	17.12
34	Kentucky	10.26		17	Arkansas	17.02
8	Louisiana	20.72		18	Connecticut	16.99
46	Maine	0.00		19	Colorado	16.83
7	Maryland	21.84		20	Vermont	16.67
13	Massachusetts	17.81		21	New York	16.38
29	Michigan	12.21		22	New Mexico	15.52
24	Minnesota	14.72		23	Ohio	14.73
27	Mississippi	13.23		24	Minnesota	14.72
4	Missouri	25.96		25	Virginia	14.42
36	Montana	10.00		26	North Dakota	14.29
35	Nebraska	10.20		27	Mississippi	13.23
41	Nevada	9.02		28	Georgia	12.67
46	New Hampshire	0.00		29	Michigan	12.21
16	New Jersey	17.12		30	Pennsylvania	12.20
22	New Mexico	15.52		31	Utah	12.00
21	New York	16.38		32	North Carolina	10.96
32	North Carolina	10.96		33	South Carolina	10.46
26	North Dakota	14.29		34	Kentucky	10.26
23	Ohio	14.73		35	Nebraska	10.20
14	Oklahoma	17.70		36	Montana	10.00
38	Oregon	9.56		36	South Dakota	10.00
30	Pennsylvania	12.20		38	Alabama	9.56
1	Rhode Island	44.00		38	Oregon	9.56
33	South Carolina	10.46		40	Indiana	9.05
36	South Dakota	10.00		41	Nevada	9.02
44	Tennessee	6.33		42	West Virginia	8.33
9	Texas	19.34		43	Idaho	6.67
31	Utah	12.00		44	Tennessee	6.33
20	Vermont	16.67		45	Hawaii	1.92
25	Virginia	14.42		46	Delaware	0.00
10	Washington	19.05		46	Maine	0.00
42	West Virginia	8.33		46	New Hampshire	0.00
6	Wisconsin	22.65		NA	Illinois**	NA
2	Wyoming	33.33		NA	Kansas**	NA

District of Columbia   12.01

Source: Morgan Quitno Corporation using data from U.S. Department of Justice, Federal Bureau of Investigation
   "Crime in the United States 1993" (Uniform Crime Reports, December 4, 1994)
*By law enforcement agencies submitting complete reports to the F.B.I. for 12 months in 1993. Includes nonnegligent manslaughter.
**Not available.

Reported Arrests of Youths 17 Years and Younger for Rape in 1993

National Total = 5,303 Reported Arrests*

ALPHA ORDER				RANK ORDER			
RANK	STATE	ARRESTS	% of USA	RANK	STATE	ARRESTS	% of USA
25	Alabama	59	1.11%	1	California	532	10.03%
37	Alaska	20	0.38%	2	Florida	403	7.60%
28	Arizona	39	0.74%	3	Texas	383	7.22%
22	Arkansas	78	1.47%	4	Michigan	321	6.05%
1	California	532	10.03%	5	New York	309	5.83%
20	Colorado	82	1.55%	6	Ohio	274	5.17%
23	Connecticut	77	1.45%	7	New Jersey	220	4.15%
31	Delaware	34	0.64%	7	Pennsylvania	220	4.15%
2	Florida	403	7.60%	9	Washington	214	4.04%
16	Georgia	111	2.09%	10	Minnesota	204	3.85%
44	Hawaii	11	0.21%	11	Maryland	181	3.41%
41	Idaho	14	0.26%	12	Wisconsin	135	2.55%
NA	Illinois**	NA	NA	13	Missouri	133	2.51%
27	Indiana	49	0.92%	14	South Carolina	127	2.39%
34	Iowa	28	0.53%	15	Virginia	118	2.23%
NA	Kansas**	NA	NA	16	Georgia	111	2.09%
32	Kentucky	32	0.60%	17	Massachusetts	95	1.79%
24	Louisiana	63	1.19%	17	North Carolina	95	1.79%
40	Maine	16	0.30%	19	Utah	91	1.72%
11	Maryland	181	3.41%	20	Colorado	82	1.55%
17	Massachusetts	95	1.79%	21	Oregon	81	1.53%
4	Michigan	321	6.05%	22	Arkansas	78	1.47%
10	Minnesota	204	3.85%	23	Connecticut	77	1.45%
34	Mississippi	28	0.53%	24	Louisiana	63	1.19%
13	Missouri	133	2.51%	25	Alabama	59	1.11%
48	Montana	2	0.04%	26	Oklahoma	56	1.06%
29	Nebraska	37	0.70%	27	Indiana	49	0.92%
30	Nevada	36	0.68%	28	Arizona	39	0.74%
41	New Hampshire	14	0.26%	29	Nebraska	37	0.70%
7	New Jersey	220	4.15%	30	Nevada	36	0.68%
39	New Mexico	17	0.32%	31	Delaware	34	0.64%
5	New York	309	5.83%	32	Kentucky	32	0.60%
17	North Carolina	95	1.79%	33	Tennessee	29	0.55%
46	North Dakota	8	0.15%	34	Iowa	28	0.53%
6	Ohio	274	5.17%	34	Mississippi	28	0.53%
26	Oklahoma	56	1.06%	36	Rhode Island	21	0.40%
21	Oregon	81	1.53%	37	Alaska	20	0.38%
7	Pennsylvania	220	4.15%	38	South Dakota	18	0.34%
36	Rhode Island	21	0.40%	39	New Mexico	17	0.32%
14	South Carolina	127	2.39%	40	Maine	16	0.30%
38	South Dakota	18	0.34%	41	Idaho	14	0.26%
33	Tennessee	29	0.55%	41	New Hampshire	14	0.26%
3	Texas	383	7.22%	41	West Virginia	14	0.26%
19	Utah	91	1.72%	44	Hawaii	11	0.21%
45	Vermont	9	0.17%	45	Vermont	9	0.17%
15	Virginia	118	2.23%	46	North Dakota	8	0.15%
9	Washington	214	4.04%	47	Wyoming	6	0.11%
41	West Virginia	14	0.26%	48	Montana	2	0.04%
12	Wisconsin	135	2.55%	NA	Illinois**	NA	NA
47	Wyoming	6	0.11%	NA	Kansas**	NA	NA
					District of Columbia	26	0.49%

Source: U.S. Department of Justice, Federal Bureau of Investigation
     "Crime in the United States 1993" (Uniform Crime Reports, December 4, 1994)
*By law enforcement agencies submitting complete reports to the F.B.I. for 12 months in 1993. Forcible rape is the carnal knowledge of a female forcibly and against her will. Assaults or attempts to commit rape by force or threat of force are included. However, statutory rape without force and other sex offenses are excluded.
**Not available.

Reported Arrests of Youths 17 Years and Younger for Rape
As a Percent of All Such Arrests in 1993
National Percent = 16.31% of Arrests for Rape*

ALPHA ORDER

RANK ORDER

RANK	STATE	PERCENT	RANK	STATE	PERCENT
46	Alabama	9.16	1	Utah	36.25
39	Alaska	12.27	2	Delaware	33.66
36	Arizona	13.13	3	Iowa	25.45
25	Arkansas	16.35	4	New Mexico	23.29
30	California	14.90	5	Ohio	22.87
29	Colorado	15.47	6	Washington	22.43
18	Connecticut	17.58	7	South Dakota	20.69
2	Delaware	33.66	8	Indiana	20.16
17	Florida	17.89	9	North Dakota	20.00
35	Georgia	13.20	10	Wisconsin	19.59
47	Hawaii	8.53	11	New Jersey	19.11
19	Idaho	17.50	12	Minnesota	19.07
NA	Illinois**	NA	13	Maryland	18.89
8	Indiana	20.16	14	Rhode Island	18.75
3	Iowa	25.45	15	Pennsylvania	18.21
NA	Kansas**	NA	16	Montana	18.18
45	Kentucky	9.30	17	Florida	17.89
34	Louisiana	13.64	18	Connecticut	17.58
23	Maine	16.84	19	Idaho	17.50
13	Maryland	18.89	19	New Hampshire	17.50
38	Massachusetts	13.01	21	South Carolina	17.28
27	Michigan	16.20	22	Missouri	16.92
12	Minnesota	19.07	23	Maine	16.84
33	Mississippi	13.79	24	Nebraska	16.74
22	Missouri	16.92	25	Arkansas	16.35
16	Montana	18.18	26	Oregon	16.30
24	Nebraska	16.74	27	Michigan	16.20
40	Nevada	12.00	28	New York	15.62
19	New Hampshire	17.50	29	Colorado	15.47
11	New Jersey	19.11	30	California	14.90
4	New Mexico	23.29	31	Wyoming	14.63
28	New York	15.62	32	Texas	14.44
43	North Carolina	11.22	33	Mississippi	13.79
9	North Dakota	20.00	34	Louisiana	13.64
5	Ohio	22.87	35	Georgia	13.20
37	Oklahoma	13.05	36	Arizona	13.13
26	Oregon	16.30	37	Oklahoma	13.05
15	Pennsylvania	18.21	38	Massachusetts	13.01
14	Rhode Island	18.75	39	Alaska	12.27
21	South Carolina	17.28	40	Nevada	12.00
7	South Dakota	20.69	40	Vermont	12.00
48	Tennessee	5.45	42	Virginia	11.79
32	Texas	14.44	43	North Carolina	11.22
1	Utah	36.25	44	West Virginia	10.53
40	Vermont	12.00	45	Kentucky	9.30
42	Virginia	11.79	46	Alabama	9.16
6	Washington	22.43	47	Hawaii	8.53
44	West Virginia	10.53	48	Tennessee	5.45
10	Wisconsin	19.59	NA	Illinois**	NA
31	Wyoming	14.63	NA	Kansas**	NA

District of Columbia   19.40

Source: Morgan Quitno Corporation using data from U.S. Department of Justice, Federal Bureau of Investigation
"Crime in the United States 1993" (Uniform Crime Reports, December 4, 1994)
*By law enforcement agencies submitting complete reports to the F.B.I. for 12 months in 1993. Forcible rape is the carnal knowledge of a female forcibly and against her will. Assaults or attempts to commit rape by force or threat of force are included. However, statutory rape without force and other sex offenses are excluded.
**Not available.

Reported Arrests of Youths 17 Years and Younger for Robbery in 1993

National Total = 43,340 Reported Arrests*

ALPHA ORDER

RANK	STATE	ARRESTS	% of USA
26	Alabama	268	0.62%
38	Alaska	55	0.13%
16	Arizona	495	1.14%
28	Arkansas	217	0.50%
2	California	8,254	19.04%
24	Colorado	299	0.69%
20	Connecticut	401	0.93%
40	Delaware	39	0.09%
4	Florida	2,930	6.76%
11	Georgia	774	1.79%
30	Hawaii	150	0.35%
41	Idaho	34	0.08%
NA	Illinois**	NA	NA
27	Indiana	230	0.53%
37	Iowa	62	0.14%
NA	Kansas**	NA	NA
25	Kentucky	274	0.63%
15	Louisiana	548	1.26%
43	Maine	11	0.03%
8	Maryland	1,069	2.47%
17	Massachusetts	468	1.08%
8	Michigan	1,069	2.47%
18	Minnesota	437	1.01%
34	Mississippi	91	0.21%
14	Missouri	558	1.29%
47	Montana	1	0.00%
32	Nebraska	132	0.30%
29	Nevada	182	0.42%
45	New Hampshire	9	0.02%
5	New Jersey	1,999	4.61%
35	New Mexico	75	0.17%
1	New York	11,389	26.28%
12	North Carolina	673	1.55%
42	North Dakota	14	0.03%
7	Ohio	1,218	2.81%
22	Oklahoma	353	0.81%
21	Oregon	379	0.87%
6	Pennsylvania	1,939	4.47%
36	Rhode Island	68	0.16%
23	South Carolina	311	0.72%
44	South Dakota	10	0.02%
33	Tennessee	126	0.29%
3	Texas	2,983	6.88%
31	Utah	138	0.32%
48	Vermont	0	0.00%
13	Virginia	579	1.34%
19	Washington	431	0.99%
38	West Virginia	55	0.13%
10	Wisconsin	876	2.02%
46	Wyoming	3	0.01%

RANK ORDER

RANK	STATE	ARRESTS	% of USA
1	New York	11,389	26.28%
2	California	8,254	19.04%
3	Texas	2,983	6.88%
4	Florida	2,930	6.76%
5	New Jersey	1,999	4.61%
6	Pennsylvania	1,939	4.47%
7	Ohio	1,218	2.81%
8	Maryland	1,069	2.47%
8	Michigan	1,069	2.47%
10	Wisconsin	876	2.02%
11	Georgia	774	1.79%
12	North Carolina	673	1.55%
13	Virginia	579	1.34%
14	Missouri	558	1.29%
15	Louisiana	548	1.26%
16	Arizona	495	1.14%
17	Massachusetts	468	1.08%
18	Minnesota	437	1.01%
19	Washington	431	0.99%
20	Connecticut	401	0.93%
21	Oregon	379	0.87%
22	Oklahoma	353	0.81%
23	South Carolina	311	0.72%
24	Colorado	299	0.69%
25	Kentucky	274	0.63%
26	Alabama	268	0.62%
27	Indiana	230	0.53%
28	Arkansas	217	0.50%
29	Nevada	182	0.42%
30	Hawaii	150	0.35%
31	Utah	138	0.32%
32	Nebraska	132	0.30%
33	Tennessee	126	0.29%
34	Mississippi	91	0.21%
35	New Mexico	75	0.17%
36	Rhode Island	68	0.16%
37	Iowa	62	0.14%
38	Alaska	55	0.13%
38	West Virginia	55	0.13%
40	Delaware	39	0.09%
41	Idaho	34	0.08%
42	North Dakota	14	0.03%
43	Maine	11	0.03%
44	South Dakota	10	0.02%
45	New Hampshire	9	0.02%
46	Wyoming	3	0.01%
47	Montana	1	0.00%
48	Vermont	0	0.00%
NA	Illinois**	NA	NA
NA	Kansas**	NA	NA
	District of Columbia	232	0.54%

Source: U.S. Department of Justice, Federal Bureau of Investigation
   "Crime in the United States 1993" (Uniform Crime Reports, December 4, 1994)
*By law enforcement agencies submitting complete reports to the F.B.I. for 12 months in 1993. Robbery is the taking or attempting to take anything of value by force or threat of force.
**Not available.

Reported Arrests of Youths 17 Years and Younger for Robbery
As a Percent of All Such Arrests in 1993
National Percent = 28.23% of Reported Arrests for Robbery*

ALPHA ORDER

RANK ORDER

RANK	STATE	PERCENT		RANK	STATE	PERCENT
44	Alabama	13.76		1	North Dakota	66.67
15	Alaska	31.61		2	Idaho	61.82
14	Arizona	31.67		3	Wisconsin	38.09
31	Arkansas	21.92		4	South Dakota	37.04
20	California	27.92		5	Nebraska	36.67
18	Colorado	29.84		6	New York	36.41
36	Connecticut	20.02		7	Utah	35.48
8	Delaware	35.14		8	Delaware	35.14
21	Florida	27.43		9	Washington	34.79
37	Georgia	18.54		10	Oklahoma	34.21
13	Hawaii	32.61		11	New Jersey	33.71
2	Idaho	61.82		12	Texas	33.17
NA	Illinois**	NA		13	Hawaii	32.61
26	Indiana	23.88		14	Arizona	31.67
24	Iowa	25.73		15	Alaska	31.61
NA	Kansas**	NA		16	New Mexico	30.99
28	Kentucky	23.01		17	Minnesota	30.65
27	Louisiana	23.60		18	Colorado	29.84
45	Maine	12.22		19	Oregon	28.82
29	Maryland	22.78		20	California	27.92
34	Massachusetts	20.92		21	Florida	27.43
30	Michigan	22.18		22	Ohio	26.78
17	Minnesota	30.65		23	Pennsylvania	26.71
39	Mississippi	17.37		24	Iowa	25.73
32	Missouri	21.61		25	Rhode Island	24.82
46	Montana	11.11		26	Indiana	23.88
5	Nebraska	36.67		27	Louisiana	23.60
41	Nevada	16.84		28	Kentucky	23.01
43	New Hampshire	15.25		29	Maryland	22.78
11	New Jersey	33.71		30	Michigan	22.18
16	New Mexico	30.99		31	Arkansas	21.92
6	New York	36.41		32	Missouri	21.61
40	North Carolina	16.99		33	West Virginia	21.15
1	North Dakota	66.67		34	Massachusetts	20.92
22	Ohio	26.78		35	Virginia	20.70
10	Oklahoma	34.21		36	Connecticut	20.02
19	Oregon	28.82		37	Georgia	18.54
23	Pennsylvania	26.71		38	South Carolina	18.38
25	Rhode Island	24.82		39	Mississippi	17.37
38	South Carolina	18.38		40	North Carolina	16.99
4	South Dakota	37.04		41	Nevada	16.84
47	Tennessee	6.75		42	Wyoming	15.79
12	Texas	33.17		43	New Hampshire	15.25
7	Utah	35.48		44	Alabama	13.76
48	Vermont	0.00		45	Maine	12.22
35	Virginia	20.70		46	Montana	11.11
9	Washington	34.79		47	Tennessee	6.75
33	West Virginia	21.15		48	Vermont	0.00
3	Wisconsin	38.09		NA	Illinois**	NA
42	Wyoming	15.79		NA	Kansas**	NA

District of Columbia   18.20

Source: Morgan Quitno Corporation using data from U.S. Department of Justice, Federal Bureau of Investigation
"Crime in the United States 1993" (Uniform Crime Reports, December 4, 1994)
*By law enforcement agencies submitting complete reports to the F.B.I. for 12 months in 1993. Robbery is the taking or attempting to take anything of value by force or threat of force.
**Not available.

Reported Arrests of Youths 17 Years and Younger for Aggravated Assault in 1993

National Total = 67,751 Reported Arrests*

ALPHA ORDER

RANK ORDER

RANK	STATE	ARRESTS	% of USA		RANK	STATE	ARRESTS	% of USA
28	Alabama	550	0.81%		1	California	11,639	17.18%
37	Alaska	170	0.25%		2	New York	5,542	8.18%
12	Arizona	1,676	2.47%		3	Florida	5,409	7.98%
30	Arkansas	475	0.70%		4	Texas	5,063	7.47%
1	California	11,639	17.18%		5	New Jersey	3,156	4.66%
15	Colorado	1,336	1.97%		6	Pennsylvania	2,879	4.25%
22	Connecticut	954	1.41%		7	Michigan	2,251	3.32%
41	Delaware	91	0.13%		8	North Carolina	2,246	3.32%
3	Florida	5,409	7.98%		9	Maryland	2,107	3.11%
11	Georgia	1,877	2.77%		10	Massachusetts	1,914	2.83%
39	Hawaii	110	0.16%		11	Georgia	1,877	2.77%
33	Idaho	313	0.46%		12	Arizona	1,676	2.47%
NA	Illinois**	NA	NA		13	Indiana	1,521	2.24%
13	Indiana	1,521	2.24%		13	Minnesota	1,521	2.24%
29	Iowa	487	0.72%		15	Colorado	1,336	1.97%
NA	Kansas**	NA	NA		16	Louisiana	1,291	1.91%
26	Kentucky	649	0.96%		17	Ohio	1,286	1.90%
16	Louisiana	1,291	1.91%		18	Wisconsin	1,176	1.74%
43	Maine	87	0.13%		19	South Carolina	1,024	1.51%
9	Maryland	2,107	3.11%		20	Missouri	1,008	1.49%
10	Massachusetts	1,914	2.83%		21	Washington	992	1.46%
7	Michigan	2,251	3.32%		22	Connecticut	954	1.41%
13	Minnesota	1,521	2.24%		23	Oklahoma	818	1.21%
36	Mississippi	190	0.28%		24	Utah	805	1.19%
20	Missouri	1,008	1.49%		25	Virginia	798	1.18%
46	Montana	29	0.04%		26	Kentucky	649	0.96%
38	Nebraska	126	0.19%		26	Oregon	649	0.96%
35	Nevada	243	0.36%		28	Alabama	550	0.81%
42	New Hampshire	89	0.13%		29	Iowa	487	0.72%
5	New Jersey	3,156	4.66%		30	Arkansas	475	0.70%
34	New Mexico	282	0.42%		31	Rhode Island	430	0.63%
2	New York	5,542	8.18%		32	Tennessee	410	0.61%
8	North Carolina	2,246	3.32%		33	Idaho	313	0.46%
46	North Dakota	29	0.04%		34	New Mexico	282	0.42%
17	Ohio	1,286	1.90%		35	Nevada	243	0.36%
23	Oklahoma	818	1.21%		36	Mississippi	190	0.28%
26	Oregon	649	0.96%		37	Alaska	170	0.25%
6	Pennsylvania	2,879	4.25%		38	Nebraska	126	0.19%
31	Rhode Island	430	0.63%		39	Hawaii	110	0.16%
19	South Carolina	1,024	1.51%		40	South Dakota	100	0.15%
40	South Dakota	100	0.15%		41	Delaware	91	0.13%
32	Tennessee	410	0.61%		42	New Hampshire	89	0.13%
4	Texas	5,063	7.47%		43	Maine	87	0.13%
24	Utah	805	1.19%		44	West Virginia	66	0.10%
48	Vermont	9	0.01%		45	Wyoming	54	0.08%
25	Virginia	798	1.18%		46	Montana	29	0.04%
21	Washington	992	1.46%		46	North Dakota	29	0.04%
44	West Virginia	66	0.10%		48	Vermont	9	0.01%
18	Wisconsin	1,176	1.74%		NA	Illinois**	NA	NA
45	Wyoming	54	0.08%		NA	Kansas**	NA	NA
					District of Columbia		454	0.67%

Source: U.S. Department of Justice, Federal Bureau of Investigation
   "Crime in the United States 1993" (Uniform Crime Reports, December 4, 1994)
*By law enforcement agencies submitting complete reports to the F.B.I. for 12 months in 1993. Aggravated assault is an attack for the purpose of inflicting severe bodily injury.
**Not available.

Reported Arrests of Youths 17 Years and Younger for Aggravated Assault
As a Percent of All Such Arrests in 1993
National Percent = 15.33% of Reported Arrests for Aggravated Assault*

ALPHA ORDER

RANK ORDER

RANK	STATE	PERCENT		RANK	STATE	PERCENT
48	Alabama	6.62		1	Utah	42.32
37	Alaska	13.63		2	Idaho	31.39
11	Arizona	22.19		3	North Dakota	27.62
36	Arkansas	14.08		4	Wisconsin	26.50
42	California	10.59		5	Minnesota	26.20
20	Colorado	19.03		6	Maryland	25.85
30	Connecticut	15.36		7	Oregon	25.11
25	Delaware	16.61		8	New Jersey	23.72
34	Florida	14.19		9	Pennsylvania	23.33
40	Georgia	12.97		10	Washington	22.90
21	Hawaii	18.58		11	Arizona	22.19
2	Idaho	31.39		12	South Dakota	22.03
NA	Illinois**	NA		13	Rhode Island	21.67
14	Indiana	21.50		14	Indiana	21.50
15	Iowa	21.49		15	Iowa	21.49
NA	Kansas**	NA		16	New Hampshire	20.23
41	Kentucky	10.77		17	Oklahoma	19.64
27	Louisiana	16.17		18	Texas	19.49
38	Maine	13.62		19	New Mexico	19.08
6	Maryland	25.85		20	Colorado	19.03
33	Massachusetts	14.35		21	Hawaii	18.58
29	Michigan	15.79		22	Montana	17.68
5	Minnesota	26.20		23	New York	17.00
30	Mississippi	15.36		24	Ohio	16.66
28	Missouri	15.91		25	Delaware	16.61
22	Montana	17.68		26	Nevada	16.32
32	Nebraska	14.50		27	Louisiana	16.17
26	Nevada	16.32		28	Missouri	15.91
16	New Hampshire	20.23		29	Michigan	15.79
8	New Jersey	23.72		30	Connecticut	15.36
19	New Mexico	19.08		30	Mississippi	15.36
23	New York	17.00		32	Nebraska	14.50
43	North Carolina	10.44		33	Massachusetts	14.35
3	North Dakota	27.62		34	Florida	14.19
24	Ohio	16.66		35	South Carolina	14.12
17	Oklahoma	19.64		36	Arkansas	14.08
7	Oregon	25.11		37	Alaska	13.63
9	Pennsylvania	23.33		38	Maine	13.62
13	Rhode Island	21.67		39	Wyoming	13.11
35	South Carolina	14.12		40	Georgia	12.97
12	South Dakota	22.03		41	Kentucky	10.77
46	Tennessee	6.72		42	California	10.59
18	Texas	19.49		43	North Carolina	10.44
1	Utah	42.32		44	Virginia	9.46
45	Vermont	9.00		45	Vermont	9.00
44	Virginia	9.46		46	Tennessee	6.72
10	Washington	22.90		47	West Virginia	6.65
47	West Virginia	6.65		48	Alabama	6.62
4	Wisconsin	26.50		NA	Illinois**	NA
39	Wyoming	13.11		NA	Kansas**	NA

District of Columbia   11.97

*Source: Morgan Quitno Corporation using data from U.S. Department of Justice, Federal Bureau of Investigation
"Crime in the United States 1993" (Uniform Crime Reports, December 4, 1994)*
*By law enforcement agencies submitting complete reports to the F.B.I. for 12 months in 1993. Aggravated assault is an attack for the purpose of inflicting severe bodily injury.
**Not available.

Reported Arrests of Youths 17 Years and Younger for Property Crime in 1993

National Total = 591,238 Reported Arrests*

ALPHA ORDER					RANK ORDER			
RANK	STATE	ARRESTS	% of USA		RANK	STATE	ARRESTS	% of USA
30	Alabama	4,871	0.82%		1	California	86,690	14.66%
38	Alaska	3,123	0.53%		2	Texas	52,080	8.81%
11	Arizona	16,547	2.80%		3	Florida	39,786	6.73%
28	Arkansas	5,379	0.91%		4	Wisconsin	29,229	4.94%
1	California	86,690	14.66%		5	New York	24,789	4.19%
14	Colorado	14,301	2.42%		6	Washington	19,325	3.27%
23	Connecticut	7,907	1.34%		7	Michigan	18,088	3.06%
47	Delaware	536	0.09%		8	New Jersey	17,813	3.01%
3	Florida	39,786	6.73%		9	Pennsylvania	17,444	2.95%
19	Georgia	11,470	1.94%		10	Minnesota	16,691	2.82%
32	Hawaii	4,490	0.76%		11	Arizona	16,547	2.80%
33	Idaho	4,457	0.75%		12	Ohio	16,061	2.72%
NA	Illinois**	NA	NA		13	Utah	15,182	2.57%
21	Indiana	9,631	1.63%		14	Colorado	14,301	2.42%
34	Iowa	4,396	0.74%		15	Maryland	14,206	2.40%
NA	Kansas**	NA	NA		16	Oregon	14,136	2.39%
29	Kentucky	4,922	0.83%		17	Virginia	13,998	2.37%
25	Louisiana	7,239	1.22%		18	North Carolina	12,701	2.15%
36	Maine	3,529	0.60%		19	Georgia	11,470	1.94%
15	Maryland	14,206	2.40%		20	Oklahoma	10,454	1.77%
31	Massachusetts	4,809	0.81%		21	Indiana	9,631	1.63%
7	Michigan	18,088	3.06%		22	Missouri	8,909	1.51%
10	Minnesota	16,691	2.82%		23	Connecticut	7,907	1.34%
39	Mississippi	2,831	0.48%		24	South Carolina	7,601	1.29%
22	Missouri	8,909	1.51%		25	Louisiana	7,239	1.22%
46	Montana	696	0.12%		26	Tennessee	5,392	0.91%
27	Nebraska	5,385	0.91%		27	Nebraska	5,385	0.91%
35	Nevada	4,115	0.70%		28	Arkansas	5,379	0.91%
44	New Hampshire	1,520	0.26%		29	Kentucky	4,922	0.83%
8	New Jersey	17,813	3.01%		30	Alabama	4,871	0.82%
37	New Mexico	3,290	0.56%		31	Massachusetts	4,809	0.81%
5	New York	24,789	4.19%		32	Hawaii	4,490	0.76%
18	North Carolina	12,701	2.15%		33	Idaho	4,457	0.75%
43	North Dakota	2,100	0.36%		34	Iowa	4,396	0.74%
12	Ohio	16,061	2.72%		35	Nevada	4,115	0.70%
20	Oklahoma	10,454	1.77%		36	Maine	3,529	0.60%
16	Oregon	14,136	2.39%		37	New Mexico	3,290	0.56%
9	Pennsylvania	17,444	2.95%		38	Alaska	3,123	0.53%
42	Rhode Island	2,263	0.38%		39	Mississippi	2,831	0.48%
24	South Carolina	7,601	1.29%		40	South Dakota	2,517	0.43%
40	South Dakota	2,517	0.43%		41	West Virginia	2,304	0.39%
26	Tennessee	5,392	0.91%		42	Rhode Island	2,263	0.38%
2	Texas	52,080	8.81%		43	North Dakota	2,100	0.36%
13	Utah	15,182	2.57%		44	New Hampshire	1,520	0.26%
48	Vermont	229	0.04%		45	Wyoming	1,210	0.20%
17	Virginia	13,998	2.37%		46	Montana	696	0.12%
6	Washington	19,325	3.27%		47	Delaware	536	0.09%
41	West Virginia	2,304	0.39%		48	Vermont	229	0.04%
4	Wisconsin	29,229	4.94%		NA	Illinois**	NA	NA
45	Wyoming	1,210	0.20%		NA	Kansas**	NA	NA
						District of Columbia	896	0.15%

Source: U.S. Department of Justice, Federal Bureau of Investigation
"Crime in the United States 1993" (Uniform Crime Reports, December 4, 1994)
*By law enforcement agencies submitting complete reports to the F.B.I. for 12 months in 1993. Property crimes are
offenses of burglary, larceny-theft, motor vehicle theft and arson.
**Not available.

Reported Arrests of Youths 17 Years and Younger for Property Crime
As a Percent of All Such Arrests in 1993
National Percent = 33.32% of Reported Arrests for Property Crime*

ALPHA ORDER

RANK	STATE	PERCENT
48	Alabama	20.64
10	Alaska	46.65
24	Arizona	36.46
35	Arkansas	29.31
31	California	31.36
19	Colorado	39.14
39	Connecticut	25.59
26	Delaware	34.74
28	Florida	33.25
44	Georgia	22.95
18	Hawaii	39.39
2	Idaho	58.81
NA	Illinois**	NA
15	Indiana	40.63
14	Iowa	40.65
NA	Kansas**	NA
27	Kentucky	33.32
41	Louisiana	25.29
9	Maine	46.86
36	Maryland	28.38
46	Massachusetts	21.71
23	Michigan	36.77
6	Minnesota	49.12
38	Mississippi	27.17
40	Missouri	25.44
12	Montana	45.08
11	Nebraska	46.43
33	Nevada	29.91
16	New Hampshire	40.55
29	New Jersey	33.18
21	New Mexico	37.96
42	New York	24.10
45	North Carolina	21.74
3	North Dakota	55.26
22	Ohio	36.92
5	Oklahoma	49.67
17	Oregon	39.81
30	Pennsylvania	32.00
20	Rhode Island	38.99
32	South Carolina	30.35
4	South Dakota	54.06
47	Tennessee	21.70
25	Texas	34.78
1	Utah	58.93
43	Vermont	23.95
37	Virginia	27.57
13	Washington	43.62
34	West Virginia	29.59
7	Wisconsin	48.64
8	Wyoming	47.64

RANK ORDER

RANK	STATE	PERCENT
1	Utah	58.93
2	Idaho	58.81
3	North Dakota	55.26
4	South Dakota	54.06
5	Oklahoma	49.67
6	Minnesota	49.12
7	Wisconsin	48.64
8	Wyoming	47.64
9	Maine	46.86
10	Alaska	46.65
11	Nebraska	46.43
12	Montana	45.08
13	Washington	43.62
14	Iowa	40.65
15	Indiana	40.63
16	New Hampshire	40.55
17	Oregon	39.81
18	Hawaii	39.39
19	Colorado	39.14
20	Rhode Island	38.99
21	New Mexico	37.96
22	Ohio	36.92
23	Michigan	36.77
24	Arizona	36.46
25	Texas	34.78
26	Delaware	34.74
27	Kentucky	33.32
28	Florida	33.25
29	New Jersey	33.18
30	Pennsylvania	32.00
31	California	31.36
32	South Carolina	30.35
33	Nevada	29.91
34	West Virginia	29.59
35	Arkansas	29.31
36	Maryland	28.38
37	Virginia	27.57
38	Mississippi	27.17
39	Connecticut	25.59
40	Missouri	25.44
41	Louisiana	25.29
42	New York	24.10
43	Vermont	23.95
44	Georgia	22.95
45	North Carolina	21.74
46	Massachusetts	21.71
47	Tennessee	21.70
48	Alabama	20.64
NA	Illinois**	NA
NA	Kansas**	NA

District of Columbia   14.47

Source: Morgan Quitno Corporation using data from U.S. Department of Justice, Federal Bureau of Investigation
"Crime in the United States 1993" (Uniform Crime Reports, December 4, 1994)
*By law enforcement agencies submitting complete reports to the F.B.I. for 12 months in 1993. Property crimes are offenses of burglary, larceny-theft, motor vehicle theft and arson.
**Not available.

Reported Arrests of Youths 17 Years and Younger for Burglary in 1993

National Total = 116,024 Reported Arrests*

ALPHA ORDER					RANK ORDER			
RANK	STATE	ARRESTS	% of USA		RANK	STATE	ARRESTS	% of USA
33	Alabama	776	0.67%		1	California	23,228	20.02%
36	Alaska	604	0.52%		2	Texas	10,622	9.16%
9	Arizona	3,263	2.81%		3	Florida	10,400	8.96%
27	Arkansas	1,147	0.99%		4	New York	4,794	4.13%
1	California	23,228	20.02%		5	New Jersey	3,824	3.30%
21	Colorado	1,735	1.50%		6	North Carolina	3,669	3.16%
22	Connecticut	1,605	1.38%		7	Wisconsin	3,644	3.14%
45	Delaware	167	0.14%		8	Michigan	3,342	2.88%
3	Florida	10,400	8.96%		9	Arizona	3,263	2.81%
14	Georgia	2,402	2.07%		10	Pennsylvania	3,190	2.75%
34	Hawaii	678	0.58%		11	Washington	3,150	2.71%
38	Idaho	530	0.46%		12	Ohio	3,013	2.60%
NA	Illinois**	NA	NA		13	Maryland	2,663	2.30%
26	Indiana	1,338	1.15%		14	Georgia	2,402	2.07%
32	Iowa	834	0.72%		15	Virginia	2,313	1.99%
NA	Kansas**	NA	NA		16	Minnesota	2,101	1.81%
28	Kentucky	1,089	0.94%		17	South Carolina	2,086	1.80%
23	Louisiana	1,472	1.27%		18	Oregon	2,000	1.72%
29	Maine	861	0.74%		19	Oklahoma	1,889	1.63%
13	Maryland	2,663	2.30%		20	Utah	1,766	1.52%
25	Massachusetts	1,340	1.15%		21	Colorado	1,735	1.50%
8	Michigan	3,342	2.88%		22	Connecticut	1,605	1.38%
16	Minnesota	2,101	1.81%		23	Louisiana	1,472	1.27%
35	Mississippi	617	0.53%		24	Missouri	1,346	1.16%
24	Missouri	1,346	1.16%		25	Massachusetts	1,340	1.15%
47	Montana	99	0.09%		26	Indiana	1,338	1.15%
37	Nebraska	559	0.48%		27	Arkansas	1,147	0.99%
30	Nevada	857	0.74%		28	Kentucky	1,089	0.94%
44	New Hampshire	173	0.15%		29	Maine	861	0.74%
5	New Jersey	3,824	3.30%		30	Nevada	857	0.74%
39	New Mexico	506	0.44%		31	Tennessee	840	0.72%
4	New York	4,794	4.13%		32	Iowa	834	0.72%
6	North Carolina	3,669	3.16%		33	Alabama	776	0.67%
43	North Dakota	195	0.17%		34	Hawaii	678	0.58%
12	Ohio	3,013	2.60%		35	Mississippi	617	0.53%
19	Oklahoma	1,889	1.63%		36	Alaska	604	0.52%
18	Oregon	2,000	1.72%		37	Nebraska	559	0.48%
10	Pennsylvania	3,190	2.75%		38	Idaho	530	0.46%
41	Rhode Island	412	0.36%		39	New Mexico	506	0.44%
17	South Carolina	2,086	1.80%		40	West Virginia	479	0.41%
42	South Dakota	361	0.31%		41	Rhode Island	412	0.36%
31	Tennessee	840	0.72%		42	South Dakota	361	0.31%
2	Texas	10,622	9.16%		43	North Dakota	195	0.17%
20	Utah	1,766	1.52%		44	New Hampshire	173	0.15%
48	Vermont	45	0.04%		45	Delaware	167	0.14%
15	Virginia	2,313	1.99%		46	Wyoming	109	0.09%
11	Washington	3,150	2.71%		47	Montana	99	0.09%
40	West Virginia	479	0.41%		48	Vermont	45	0.04%
7	Wisconsin	3,644	3.14%		NA	Illinois**	NA	NA
46	Wyoming	109	0.09%		NA	Kansas**	NA	NA
						District of Columbia	47	0.04%

Source: U.S. Department of Justice, Federal Bureau of Investigation
  "Crime in the United States 1993" (Uniform Crime Reports, December 4, 1994)
By law enforcement agencies submitting complete reports to the F.B.I. for 12 months in 1993. Burglary is the unlawful entry of a structure to commit a felony or theft. Attempts are included.
**Not available.*

Reported Arrests of Youths 17 Years and Younger for Burglary
As a Percent of All Such Arrests in 1993
National Percent = 34.30% of Reported Burglary Arrests*

ALPHA ORDER			RANK ORDER		
RANK	STATE	PERCENT	RANK	STATE	PERCENT
47	Alabama	19.69	1	Utah	65.24
4	Alaska	53.78	2	Idaho	60.57
12	Arizona	46.21	3	South Dakota	53.80
32	Arkansas	33.86	4	Alaska	53.78
36	California	31.15	5	Washington	52.83
13	Colorado	45.97	6	Wisconsin	52.64
38	Connecticut	28.93	7	Maine	51.93
21	Delaware	38.57	8	New Mexico	49.95
22	Florida	37.97	9	Iowa	47.93
41	Georgia	25.61	10	Oklahoma	46.42
15	Hawaii	43.77	11	North Dakota	46.32
2	Idaho	60.57	12	Arizona	46.21
NA	Illinois**	NA	13	Colorado	45.97
18	Indiana	42.71	14	Minnesota	44.12
9	Iowa	47.93	15	Hawaii	43.77
NA	Kansas**	NA	16	Oregon	43.68
30	Kentucky	35.19	17	Nebraska	42.80
39	Louisiana	26.58	18	Indiana	42.71
7	Maine	51.93	19	Montana	41.60
43	Maryland	24.42	20	Texas	40.92
44	Massachusetts	23.45	21	Delaware	38.57
28	Michigan	35.64	22	Florida	37.97
14	Minnesota	44.12	23	Wyoming	37.59
33	Mississippi	32.61	24	New Hampshire	37.53
42	Missouri	25.43	25	Ohio	37.39
19	Montana	41.60	26	Rhode Island	37.35
17	Nebraska	42.80	27	New Jersey	36.81
37	Nevada	29.63	28	Michigan	35.64
24	New Hampshire	37.53	29	South Carolina	35.32
27	New Jersey	36.81	30	Kentucky	35.19
8	New Mexico	49.95	31	West Virginia	34.02
40	New York	26.33	32	Arkansas	33.86
45	North Carolina	23.15	33	Mississippi	32.61
11	North Dakota	46.32	34	Virginia	31.47
25	Ohio	37.39	35	Pennsylvania	31.16
10	Oklahoma	46.42	36	California	31.15
16	Oregon	43.68	37	Nevada	29.63
35	Pennsylvania	31.16	38	Connecticut	28.93
26	Rhode Island	37.35	39	Louisiana	26.58
29	South Carolina	35.32	40	New York	26.33
3	South Dakota	53.80	41	Georgia	25.61
48	Tennessee	19.52	42	Missouri	25.43
20	Texas	40.92	43	Maryland	24.42
1	Utah	65.24	44	Massachusetts	23.45
46	Vermont	19.74	45	North Carolina	23.15
34	Virginia	31.47	46	Vermont	19.74
5	Washington	52.83	47	Alabama	19.69
31	West Virginia	34.02	48	Tennessee	19.52
6	Wisconsin	52.64	NA	Illinois**	NA
23	Wyoming	37.59	NA	Kansas**	NA
				District of Columbia	4.53

Source: Morgan Quitno Corporation using data from U.S. Department of Justice, Federal Bureau of Investigation
    "Crime in the United States 1993" (Uniform Crime Reports, December 4, 1994)
*By law enforcement agencies submitting complete reports to the F.B.I. for 12 months in 1993. Burglary is the unlawful
entry of a structure to commit a felony or theft. Attempts are included.
**Not available.

Reported Arrests of Youths 17 Years and Younger for Larceny and Theft in 1993

National Total = 391,950 Reported Arrests*

ALPHA ORDER

RANK	STATE	ARRESTS	% of USA
29	Alabama	3,594	0.92%
38	Alaska	2,229	0.57%
11	Arizona	11,286	2.88%
28	Arkansas	3,850	0.98%
1	California	45,237	11.54%
12	Colorado	11,081	2.83%
24	Connecticut	4,989	1.27%
47	Delaware	300	0.08%
3	Florida	23,125	5.90%
19	Georgia	7,343	1.87%
33	Hawaii	3,187	0.81%
30	Idaho	3,517	0.90%
NA	Illinois**	NA	NA
20	Indiana	7,161	1.83%
32	Iowa	3,195	0.82%
NA	Kansas**	NA	NA
31	Kentucky	3,279	0.84%
23	Louisiana	5,119	1.31%
37	Maine	2,422	0.62%
18	Maryland	7,877	2.01%
36	Massachusetts	2,511	0.64%
7	Michigan	12,839	3.28%
8	Minnesota	12,236	3.12%
40	Mississippi	1,855	0.47%
22	Missouri	5,985	1.53%
46	Montana	505	0.13%
26	Nebraska	4,499	1.15%
34	Nevada	2,975	0.76%
44	New Hampshire	1,224	0.31%
9	New Jersey	12,211	3.12%
35	New Mexico	2,595	0.66%
5	New York	16,476	4.20%
17	North Carolina	8,085	2.06%
41	North Dakota	1,729	0.44%
14	Ohio	10,477	2.67%
21	Oklahoma	6,824	1.74%
15	Oregon	10,350	2.64%
13	Pennsylvania	10,581	2.70%
43	Rhode Island	1,523	0.39%
25	South Carolina	4,897	1.25%
39	South Dakota	1,976	0.50%
27	Tennessee	3,998	1.02%
2	Texas	34,267	8.74%
10	Utah	12,112	3.09%
48	Vermont	166	0.04%
16	Virginia	9,822	2.51%
6	Washington	14,549	3.71%
42	West Virginia	1,559	0.40%
4	Wisconsin	21,963	5.60%
45	Wyoming	1,015	0.26%

RANK ORDER

RANK	STATE	ARRESTS	% of USA
1	California	45,237	11.54%
2	Texas	34,267	8.74%
3	Florida	23,125	5.90%
4	Wisconsin	21,963	5.60%
5	New York	16,476	4.20%
6	Washington	14,549	3.71%
7	Michigan	12,839	3.28%
8	Minnesota	12,236	3.12%
9	New Jersey	12,211	3.12%
10	Utah	12,112	3.09%
11	Arizona	11,286	2.88%
12	Colorado	11,081	2.83%
13	Pennsylvania	10,581	2.70%
14	Ohio	10,477	2.67%
15	Oregon	10,350	2.64%
16	Virginia	9,822	2.51%
17	North Carolina	8,085	2.06%
18	Maryland	7,877	2.01%
19	Georgia	7,343	1.87%
20	Indiana	7,161	1.83%
21	Oklahoma	6,824	1.74%
22	Missouri	5,985	1.53%
23	Louisiana	5,119	1.31%
24	Connecticut	4,989	1.27%
25	South Carolina	4,897	1.25%
26	Nebraska	4,499	1.15%
27	Tennessee	3,998	1.02%
28	Arkansas	3,850	0.98%
29	Alabama	3,594	0.92%
30	Idaho	3,517	0.90%
31	Kentucky	3,279	0.84%
32	Iowa	3,195	0.82%
33	Hawaii	3,187	0.81%
34	Nevada	2,975	0.76%
35	New Mexico	2,595	0.66%
36	Massachusetts	2,511	0.64%
37	Maine	2,422	0.62%
38	Alaska	2,229	0.57%
39	South Dakota	1,976	0.50%
40	Mississippi	1,855	0.47%
41	North Dakota	1,729	0.44%
42	West Virginia	1,559	0.40%
43	Rhode Island	1,523	0.39%
44	New Hampshire	1,224	0.31%
45	Wyoming	1,015	0.26%
46	Montana	505	0.13%
47	Delaware	300	0.08%
48	Vermont	166	0.04%
NA	Illinois**	NA	NA
NA	Kansas**	NA	NA
	District of Columbia	183	0.05%

Source: U.S. Department of Justice, Federal Bureau of Investigation
"Crime in the United States 1993" (Uniform Crime Reports, December 4, 1994)
*By law enforcement agencies submitting complete reports to the F.B.I. for 12 months in 1993. Larceny and theft is the unlawful taking of property without use of force, violence or fraud. Attempts are included. Motor vehicle thefts are excluded.
**Not available.

Reported Arrests of Youths 17 Years and Younger for Larceny and Theft
As a Percent of All Such Arrests in 1993
National Percent = 31.32% of Reported Larceny and Theft Arrests*

ALPHA ORDER			RANK ORDER		
RANK	STATE	PERCENT	RANK	STATE	PERCENT
47	Alabama	20.11	1	Idaho	57.30
11	Alaska	44.09	2	Utah	56.82
24	Arizona	32.47	3	North Dakota	55.79
34	Arkansas	27.29	4	South Dakota	52.99
32	California	29.12	5	Wyoming	48.87
20	Colorado	36.97	6	Minnesota	48.32
43	Connecticut	22.09	7	Oklahoma	48.29
28	Delaware	30.09	8	Nebraska	46.38
31	Florida	29.24	9	Wisconsin	46.07
46	Georgia	20.27	10	Maine	45.19
15	Hawaii	39.17	11	Alaska	44.09
1	Idaho	57.30	12	Montana	44.03
NA	Illinois**	NA	13	Washington	40.68
16	Indiana	38.95	14	New Hampshire	39.61
19	Iowa	38.14	15	Hawaii	39.17
NA	Kansas**	NA	16	Indiana	38.95
25	Kentucky	31.84	17	Rhode Island	38.77
40	Louisiana	23.67	18	Oregon	38.39
10	Maine	45.19	19	Iowa	38.14
38	Maryland	24.57	20	Colorado	36.97
48	Massachusetts	17.82	21	Michigan	35.73
21	Michigan	35.73	22	New Mexico	35.45
6	Minnesota	48.32	23	Ohio	33.89
39	Mississippi	23.95	24	Arizona	32.47
41	Missouri	23.25	25	Kentucky	31.84
12	Montana	44.03	26	Texas	31.57
8	Nebraska	46.38	27	New Jersey	30.46
30	Nevada	29.34	28	Delaware	30.09
14	New Hampshire	39.61	29	Pennsylvania	29.37
27	New Jersey	30.46	30	Nevada	29.34
22	New Mexico	35.45	31	Florida	29.24
42	New York	22.88	32	California	29.12
45	North Carolina	20.32	33	South Carolina	27.58
3	North Dakota	55.79	34	Arkansas	27.29
23	Ohio	33.89	35	West Virginia	27.11
7	Oklahoma	48.29	36	Vermont	25.38
18	Oregon	38.39	37	Virginia	24.97
29	Pennsylvania	29.37	38	Maryland	24.57
17	Rhode Island	38.77	39	Mississippi	23.95
33	South Carolina	27.58	40	Louisiana	23.67
4	South Dakota	52.99	41	Missouri	23.25
44	Tennessee	21.09	42	New York	22.88
26	Texas	31.57	43	Connecticut	22.09
2	Utah	56.82	44	Tennessee	21.09
36	Vermont	25.38	45	North Carolina	20.32
37	Virginia	24.97	46	Georgia	20.27
13	Washington	40.68	47	Alabama	20.11
35	West Virginia	27.11	48	Massachusetts	17.82
9	Wisconsin	46.07	NA	Illinois**	NA
5	Wyoming	48.87	NA	Kansas**	NA

District of Columbia   5.81

Source: Morgan Quitno Corporation using data from U.S. Department of Justice, Federal Bureau of Investigation
    "Crime in the United States 1993" (Uniform Crime Reports, December 4, 1994)
*By law enforcement agencies submitting complete reports to the F.B.I. for 12 months in 1993. Larceny and theft is the unlawful taking of property without use of force, violence or fraud. Attempts are included. Motor vehicle thefts are excluded.
**Not available.

Reported Arrests of Youths 17 Years and Younger for Motor Vehicle Theft in 1993

National Total = 75,315 Reported Arrests*

ALPHA ORDER

RANK	STATE	ARRESTS	% of USA
29	Alabama	477	0.63%
35	Alaska	267	0.35%
10	Arizona	1,771	2.35%
33	Arkansas	342	0.45%
1	California	16,827	22.34%
19	Colorado	1,275	1.69%
20	Connecticut	1,196	1.59%
47	Delaware	63	0.08%
3	Florida	6,027	8.00%
13	Georgia	1,623	2.15%
25	Hawaii	587	0.78%
31	Idaho	362	0.48%
NA	Illinois**	NA	NA
22	Indiana	1,064	1.41%
34	Iowa	300	0.40%
NA	Kansas**	NA	NA
30	Kentucky	468	0.62%
27	Louisiana	558	0.74%
40	Maine	172	0.23%
4	Maryland	3,403	4.52%
23	Massachusetts	891	1.18%
11	Michigan	1,649	2.19%
9	Minnesota	2,129	2.83%
32	Mississippi	345	0.46%
16	Missouri	1,457	1.93%
45	Montana	76	0.10%
36	Nebraska	262	0.35%
37	Nevada	258	0.34%
46	New Hampshire	75	0.10%
14	New Jersey	1,516	2.01%
41	New Mexico	164	0.22%
7	New York	3,162	4.20%
24	North Carolina	754	1.00%
42	North Dakota	163	0.22%
8	Ohio	2,242	2.98%
17	Oklahoma	1,430	1.90%
15	Oregon	1,468	1.95%
5	Pennsylvania	3,373	4.48%
38	Rhode Island	245	0.33%
26	South Carolina	563	0.75%
43	South Dakota	140	0.19%
28	Tennessee	497	0.66%
2	Texas	6,688	8.88%
21	Utah	1,179	1.57%
48	Vermont	16	0.02%
12	Virginia	1,645	2.18%
18	Washington	1,411	1.87%
39	West Virginia	220	0.29%
6	Wisconsin	3,257	4.32%
44	Wyoming	78	0.10%

RANK ORDER

RANK	STATE	ARRESTS	% of USA
1	California	16,827	22.34%
2	Texas	6,688	8.88%
3	Florida	6,027	8.00%
4	Maryland	3,403	4.52%
5	Pennsylvania	3,373	4.48%
6	Wisconsin	3,257	4.32%
7	New York	3,162	4.20%
8	Ohio	2,242	2.98%
9	Minnesota	2,129	2.83%
10	Arizona	1,771	2.35%
11	Michigan	1,649	2.19%
12	Virginia	1,645	2.18%
13	Georgia	1,623	2.15%
14	New Jersey	1,516	2.01%
15	Oregon	1,468	1.95%
16	Missouri	1,457	1.93%
17	Oklahoma	1,430	1.90%
18	Washington	1,411	1.87%
19	Colorado	1,275	1.69%
20	Connecticut	1,196	1.59%
21	Utah	1,179	1.57%
22	Indiana	1,064	1.41%
23	Massachusetts	891	1.18%
24	North Carolina	754	1.00%
25	Hawaii	587	0.78%
26	South Carolina	563	0.75%
27	Louisiana	558	0.74%
28	Tennessee	497	0.66%
29	Alabama	477	0.63%
30	Kentucky	468	0.62%
31	Idaho	362	0.48%
32	Mississippi	345	0.46%
33	Arkansas	342	0.45%
34	Iowa	300	0.40%
35	Alaska	267	0.35%
36	Nebraska	262	0.35%
37	Nevada	258	0.34%
38	Rhode Island	245	0.33%
39	West Virginia	220	0.29%
40	Maine	172	0.23%
41	New Mexico	164	0.22%
42	North Dakota	163	0.22%
43	South Dakota	140	0.19%
44	Wyoming	78	0.10%
45	Montana	76	0.10%
46	New Hampshire	75	0.10%
47	Delaware	63	0.08%
48	Vermont	16	0.02%
NA	Illinois**	NA	NA
NA	Kansas**	NA	NA
	District of Columbia	666	0.88%

Source: U.S. Department of Justice, Federal Bureau of Investigation
   "Crime in the United States 1993" (Uniform Crime Reports, December 4, 1994)
*By law enforcement agencies submitting complete reports to the F.B.I. for 12 months in 1993. Motor vehicle theft include the theft or attempted theft of a self-propelled vehicle. Excludes motorboats, construction equipment, airplanes and farming equipment.
**Not available.

57

Reported Arrests of Youths 17 Years and Younger for Motor Vehicle Theft As a Percent of All Such Arrests in 1993
National Percent = 44.62% of Reported Motor Vehicle Theft Arrests*

<u>ALPHA ORDER</u>

RANK	STATE	PERCENT
47	Alabama	29.14
13	Alaska	56.09
16	Arizona	55.38
28	Arkansas	47.57
41	California	38.09
19	Colorado	51.85
25	Connecticut	48.32
6	Delaware	63.00
26	Florida	47.97
37	Georgia	40.87
45	Hawaii	35.51
2	Idaho	71.97
NA	Illinois**	NA
18	Indiana	52.13
20	Iowa	51.81
NA	Kansas**	NA
39	Kentucky	40.00
32	Louisiana	44.43
34	Maine	42.36
21	Maryland	51.47
36	Massachusetts	41.08
22	Michigan	51.37
8	Minnesota	59.89
24	Mississippi	48.87
38	Missouri	40.46
12	Montana	56.30
17	Nebraska	55.27
40	Nevada	39.15
15	New Hampshire	55.56
11	New Jersey	56.36
14	New Mexico	55.78
48	New York	26.75
46	North Carolina	33.27
7	North Dakota	61.51
10	Ohio	57.65
9	Oklahoma	59.86
35	Oregon	41.84
31	Pennsylvania	45.16
42	Rhode Island	37.46
29	South Carolina	46.72
3	South Dakota	70.35
43	Tennessee	35.83
27	Texas	47.71
1	Utah	76.11
44	Vermont	35.56
30	Virginia	45.91
5	Washington	63.10
33	West Virginia	44.27
4	Wisconsin	65.76
23	Wyoming	50.32

<u>RANK ORDER</u>

RANK	STATE	PERCENT
1	Utah	76.11
2	Idaho	71.97
3	South Dakota	70.35
4	Wisconsin	65.76
5	Washington	63.10
6	Delaware	63.00
7	North Dakota	61.51
8	Minnesota	59.89
9	Oklahoma	59.86
10	Ohio	57.65
11	New Jersey	56.36
12	Montana	56.30
13	Alaska	56.09
14	New Mexico	55.78
15	New Hampshire	55.56
16	Arizona	55.38
17	Nebraska	55.27
18	Indiana	52.13
19	Colorado	51.85
20	Iowa	51.81
21	Maryland	51.47
22	Michigan	51.37
23	Wyoming	50.32
24	Mississippi	48.87
25	Connecticut	48.32
26	Florida	47.97
27	Texas	47.71
28	Arkansas	47.57
29	South Carolina	46.72
30	Virginia	45.91
31	Pennsylvania	45.16
32	Louisiana	44.43
33	West Virginia	44.27
34	Maine	42.36
35	Oregon	41.84
36	Massachusetts	41.08
37	Georgia	40.87
38	Missouri	40.46
39	Kentucky	40.00
40	Nevada	39.15
41	California	38.09
42	Rhode Island	37.46
43	Tennessee	35.83
44	Vermont	35.56
45	Hawaii	35.51
46	North Carolina	33.27
47	Alabama	29.14
48	New York	26.75
NA	Illinois**	NA
NA	Kansas**	NA
	District of Columbia	33.82

Source: Morgan Quitno Corporation using data from U.S. Department of Justice, Federal Bureau of Investigation
"Crime in the United States 1993" (Uniform Crime Reports, December 4, 1994)
*By law enforcement agencies submitting complete reports to the F.B.I. for 12 months in 1993. Motor vehicle theft include the theft or attempted theft of a self-propelled vehicle. Excludes motorboats, construction equipment, airplanes and farming equipment.
**Not available.

Reported Arrests of Youths 17 Years and Younger for Arson in 1993

National Total = 7,949 Reported Arrests*

ALPHA ORDER

RANK	STATE	ARRESTS	% of USA
41	Alabama	24	0.30%
42	Alaska	23	0.29%
13	Arizona	227	2.86%
36	Arkansas	40	0.50%
1	California	1,398	17.59%
17	Colorado	210	2.64%
21	Connecticut	117	1.47%
47	Delaware	6	0.08%
12	Florida	234	2.94%
22	Georgia	102	1.28%
38	Hawaii	38	0.48%
33	Idaho	48	0.60%
NA	Illinois**	NA	NA
27	Indiana	68	0.86%
28	Iowa	67	0.84%
NA	Kansas**	NA	NA
24	Kentucky	86	1.08%
23	Louisiana	90	1.13%
26	Maine	74	0.93%
9	Maryland	263	3.31%
28	Massachusetts	67	0.84%
11	Michigan	258	3.25%
14	Minnesota	225	2.83%
44	Mississippi	14	0.18%
20	Missouri	121	1.52%
43	Montana	16	0.20%
30	Nebraska	65	0.82%
39	Nevada	25	0.31%
33	New Hampshire	48	0.60%
10	New Jersey	262	3.30%
39	New Mexico	25	0.31%
4	New York	357	4.49%
18	North Carolina	193	2.43%
45	North Dakota	13	0.16%
5	Ohio	329	4.14%
7	Oklahoma	311	3.91%
6	Oregon	318	4.00%
8	Pennsylvania	300	3.77%
25	Rhode Island	83	1.04%
32	South Carolina	55	0.69%
36	South Dakota	40	0.50%
31	Tennessee	57	0.72%
2	Texas	503	6.33%
19	Utah	125	1.57%
48	Vermont	2	0.03%
15	Virginia	218	2.74%
16	Washington	215	2.70%
35	West Virginia	46	0.58%
3	Wisconsin	365	4.59%
46	Wyoming	8	0.10%

RANK ORDER

RANK	STATE	ARRESTS	% of USA
1	California	1,398	17.59%
2	Texas	503	6.33%
3	Wisconsin	365	4.59%
4	New York	357	4.49%
5	Ohio	329	4.14%
6	Oregon	318	4.00%
7	Oklahoma	311	3.91%
8	Pennsylvania	300	3.77%
9	Maryland	263	3.31%
10	New Jersey	262	3.30%
11	Michigan	258	3.25%
12	Florida	234	2.94%
13	Arizona	227	2.86%
14	Minnesota	225	2.83%
15	Virginia	218	2.74%
16	Washington	215	2.70%
17	Colorado	210	2.64%
18	North Carolina	193	2.43%
19	Utah	125	1.57%
20	Missouri	121	1.52%
21	Connecticut	117	1.47%
22	Georgia	102	1.28%
23	Louisiana	90	1.13%
24	Kentucky	86	1.08%
25	Rhode Island	83	1.04%
26	Maine	74	0.93%
27	Indiana	68	0.86%
28	Iowa	67	0.84%
28	Massachusetts	67	0.84%
30	Nebraska	65	0.82%
31	Tennessee	57	0.72%
32	South Carolina	55	0.69%
33	Idaho	48	0.60%
33	New Hampshire	48	0.60%
35	West Virginia	46	0.58%
36	Arkansas	40	0.50%
36	South Dakota	40	0.50%
38	Hawaii	38	0.48%
39	Nevada	25	0.31%
39	New Mexico	25	0.31%
41	Alabama	24	0.30%
42	Alaska	23	0.29%
43	Montana	16	0.20%
44	Mississippi	14	0.18%
45	North Dakota	13	0.16%
46	Wyoming	8	0.10%
47	Delaware	6	0.08%
48	Vermont	2	0.03%
NA	Illinois**	NA	NA
NA	Kansas**	NA	NA
	District of Columbia	0	0.00%

Source: U.S. Department of Justice, Federal Bureau of Investigation
"Crime in the United States 1993" (Uniform Crime Reports, December 4, 1994)
*By law enforcement agencies submitting complete reports to the F.B.I. for 12 months in 1993. Arson is the willful burning or attempt to burn of a building, vehicle or another's personal property.
**Not available.

Reported Arrests of Youths 17 Years and Younger for Arson
As a Percent of All Such Arrests in 1993
National Percent = 49.33% of Reported Arson Arrests*

ALPHA ORDER

RANK ORDER

RANK	STATE	PERCENT	RANK	STATE	PERCENT
47	Alabama	16.33	1	North Dakota	86.67
18	Alaska	58.97	2	Idaho	77.42
15	Arizona	63.59	2	New Hampshire	77.42
43	Arkansas	29.20	4	South Dakota	70.18
19	California	58.32	5	Rhode Island	69.75
14	Colorado	63.64	6	Maine	69.16
33	Connecticut	40.77	7	Oregon	68.98
26	Delaware	46.15	8	Oklahoma	67.90
37	Florida	38.55	9	Wisconsin	66.85
45	Georgia	25.56	10	Montana	66.67
16	Hawaii	63.33	11	Minnesota	65.98
2	Idaho	77.42	12	Utah	65.45
NA	Illinois**	NA	13	New Mexico	64.10
25	Indiana	47.22	14	Colorado	63.64
20	Iowa	56.30	15	Arizona	63.59
NA	Kansas**	NA	16	Hawaii	63.33
31	Kentucky	41.35	17	Washington	61.96
30	Louisiana	43.06	18	Alaska	58.97
6	Maine	69.16	19	California	58.32
22	Maryland	54.68	20	Iowa	56.30
34	Massachusetts	39.64	21	Nebraska	55.08
36	Michigan	38.62	22	Maryland	54.68
11	Minnesota	65.98	23	Ohio	51.89
46	Mississippi	18.67	24	New Jersey	50.78
41	Missouri	31.76	25	Indiana	47.22
10	Montana	66.67	26	Delaware	46.15
21	Nebraska	55.08	27	Wyoming	44.44
38	Nevada	37.88	28	Virginia	43.86
2	New Hampshire	77.42	29	New York	43.80
24	New Jersey	50.78	30	Louisiana	43.06
13	New Mexico	64.10	31	Kentucky	41.35
29	New York	43.80	32	Texas	40.99
39	North Carolina	36.90	33	Connecticut	40.77
1	North Dakota	86.67	34	Massachusetts	39.64
23	Ohio	51.89	35	Pennsylvania	39.06
8	Oklahoma	67.90	36	Michigan	38.62
7	Oregon	68.98	37	Florida	38.55
35	Pennsylvania	39.06	38	Nevada	37.88
5	Rhode Island	69.75	39	North Carolina	36.90
42	South Carolina	31.43	40	West Virginia	34.85
4	South Dakota	70.18	41	Missouri	31.76
44	Tennessee	28.79	42	South Carolina	31.43
32	Texas	40.99	43	Arkansas	29.20
12	Utah	65.45	44	Tennessee	28.79
48	Vermont	6.90	45	Georgia	25.56
28	Virginia	43.86	46	Mississippi	18.67
17	Washington	61.96	47	Alabama	16.33
40	West Virginia	34.85	48	Vermont	6.90
9	Wisconsin	66.85	NA	Illinois**	NA
27	Wyoming	44.44	NA	Kansas**	NA
				District of Columbia	0.00

Source: Morgan Quitno Corporation using data from U.S. Department of Justice, Federal Bureau of Investigation
"Crime in the United States 1993" (Uniform Crime Reports, December 4, 1994)
*By law enforcement agencies submitting complete reports to the F.B.I. for 12 months in 1993. Arson is the willful burning or attempt to burn of a building, vehicle or another's personal property.
**Not available.

Reported Arrests of Youths 17 Years and Younger for Weapons Violations in 1993

National Total = 52,352 Reported Arrests*

<table>
<tr><td colspan="4"><u>ALPHA ORDER</u></td><td colspan="4"><u>RANK ORDER</u></td></tr>
<tr><td>RANK</td><td>STATE</td><td>ARRESTS</td><td>% of USA</td><td>RANK</td><td>STATE</td><td>ARRESTS</td><td>% of USA</td></tr>
<tr><td>25</td><td>Alabama</td><td>565</td><td>1.08%</td><td>1</td><td>California</td><td>10,476</td><td>20.01%</td></tr>
<tr><td>39</td><td>Alaska</td><td>99</td><td>0.19%</td><td>2</td><td>Texas</td><td>5,011</td><td>9.57%</td></tr>
<tr><td>17</td><td>Arizona</td><td>974</td><td>1.86%</td><td>3</td><td>New York</td><td>3,386</td><td>6.47%</td></tr>
<tr><td>27</td><td>Arkansas</td><td>473</td><td>0.90%</td><td>4</td><td>New Jersey</td><td>2,888</td><td>5.52%</td></tr>
<tr><td>1</td><td>California</td><td>10,476</td><td>20.01%</td><td>5</td><td>Wisconsin</td><td>2,620</td><td>5.00%</td></tr>
<tr><td>15</td><td>Colorado</td><td>1,129</td><td>2.16%</td><td>6</td><td>Florida</td><td>1,902</td><td>3.63%</td></tr>
<tr><td>18</td><td>Connecticut</td><td>964</td><td>1.84%</td><td>7</td><td>Michigan</td><td>1,809</td><td>3.46%</td></tr>
<tr><td>46</td><td>Delaware</td><td>21</td><td>0.04%</td><td>8</td><td>Virginia</td><td>1,562</td><td>2.98%</td></tr>
<tr><td>6</td><td>Florida</td><td>1,902</td><td>3.63%</td><td>9</td><td>Georgia</td><td>1,559</td><td>2.98%</td></tr>
<tr><td>9</td><td>Georgia</td><td>1,559</td><td>2.98%</td><td>10</td><td>Pennsylvania</td><td>1,555</td><td>2.97%</td></tr>
<tr><td>41</td><td>Hawaii</td><td>85</td><td>0.16%</td><td>11</td><td>North Carolina</td><td>1,405</td><td>2.68%</td></tr>
<tr><td>36</td><td>Idaho</td><td>152</td><td>0.29%</td><td>12</td><td>Ohio</td><td>1,316</td><td>2.51%</td></tr>
<tr><td>NA</td><td>Illinois**</td><td>NA</td><td>NA</td><td>13</td><td>Maryland</td><td>1,216</td><td>2.32%</td></tr>
<tr><td>28</td><td>Indiana</td><td>444</td><td>0.85%</td><td>14</td><td>Minnesota</td><td>1,147</td><td>2.19%</td></tr>
<tr><td>38</td><td>Iowa</td><td>125</td><td>0.24%</td><td>15</td><td>Colorado</td><td>1,129</td><td>2.16%</td></tr>
<tr><td>NA</td><td>Kansas**</td><td>NA</td><td>NA</td><td>16</td><td>Missouri</td><td>1,084</td><td>2.07%</td></tr>
<tr><td>33</td><td>Kentucky</td><td>226</td><td>0.43%</td><td>17</td><td>Arizona</td><td>974</td><td>1.86%</td></tr>
<tr><td>21</td><td>Louisiana</td><td>752</td><td>1.44%</td><td>18</td><td>Connecticut</td><td>964</td><td>1.84%</td></tr>
<tr><td>43</td><td>Maine</td><td>43</td><td>0.08%</td><td>19</td><td>Washington</td><td>911</td><td>1.74%</td></tr>
<tr><td>13</td><td>Maryland</td><td>1,216</td><td>2.32%</td><td>20</td><td>Utah</td><td>818</td><td>1.56%</td></tr>
<tr><td>29</td><td>Massachusetts</td><td>383</td><td>0.73%</td><td>21</td><td>Louisiana</td><td>752</td><td>1.44%</td></tr>
<tr><td>7</td><td>Michigan</td><td>1,809</td><td>3.46%</td><td>22</td><td>South Carolina</td><td>672</td><td>1.28%</td></tr>
<tr><td>14</td><td>Minnesota</td><td>1,147</td><td>2.19%</td><td>23</td><td>Oklahoma</td><td>609</td><td>1.16%</td></tr>
<tr><td>34</td><td>Mississippi</td><td>201</td><td>0.38%</td><td>24</td><td>Tennessee</td><td>581</td><td>1.11%</td></tr>
<tr><td>16</td><td>Missouri</td><td>1,084</td><td>2.07%</td><td>25</td><td>Alabama</td><td>565</td><td>1.08%</td></tr>
<tr><td>47</td><td>Montana</td><td>19</td><td>0.04%</td><td>26</td><td>Oregon</td><td>491</td><td>0.94%</td></tr>
<tr><td>30</td><td>Nebraska</td><td>282</td><td>0.54%</td><td>27</td><td>Arkansas</td><td>473</td><td>0.90%</td></tr>
<tr><td>31</td><td>Nevada</td><td>280</td><td>0.53%</td><td>28</td><td>Indiana</td><td>444</td><td>0.85%</td></tr>
<tr><td>45</td><td>New Hampshire</td><td>33</td><td>0.06%</td><td>29</td><td>Massachusetts</td><td>383</td><td>0.73%</td></tr>
<tr><td>4</td><td>New Jersey</td><td>2,888</td><td>5.52%</td><td>30</td><td>Nebraska</td><td>282</td><td>0.54%</td></tr>
<tr><td>37</td><td>New Mexico</td><td>145</td><td>0.28%</td><td>31</td><td>Nevada</td><td>280</td><td>0.53%</td></tr>
<tr><td>3</td><td>New York</td><td>3,386</td><td>6.47%</td><td>32</td><td>Rhode Island</td><td>244</td><td>0.47%</td></tr>
<tr><td>11</td><td>North Carolina</td><td>1,405</td><td>2.68%</td><td>33</td><td>Kentucky</td><td>226</td><td>0.43%</td></tr>
<tr><td>42</td><td>North Dakota</td><td>62</td><td>0.12%</td><td>34</td><td>Mississippi</td><td>201</td><td>0.38%</td></tr>
<tr><td>12</td><td>Ohio</td><td>1,316</td><td>2.51%</td><td>35</td><td>West Virginia</td><td>161</td><td>0.31%</td></tr>
<tr><td>23</td><td>Oklahoma</td><td>609</td><td>1.16%</td><td>36</td><td>Idaho</td><td>152</td><td>0.29%</td></tr>
<tr><td>26</td><td>Oregon</td><td>491</td><td>0.94%</td><td>37</td><td>New Mexico</td><td>145</td><td>0.28%</td></tr>
<tr><td>10</td><td>Pennsylvania</td><td>1,555</td><td>2.97%</td><td>38</td><td>Iowa</td><td>125</td><td>0.24%</td></tr>
<tr><td>32</td><td>Rhode Island</td><td>244</td><td>0.47%</td><td>39</td><td>Alaska</td><td>99</td><td>0.19%</td></tr>
<tr><td>22</td><td>South Carolina</td><td>672</td><td>1.28%</td><td>40</td><td>South Dakota</td><td>87</td><td>0.17%</td></tr>
<tr><td>40</td><td>South Dakota</td><td>87</td><td>0.17%</td><td>41</td><td>Hawaii</td><td>85</td><td>0.16%</td></tr>
<tr><td>24</td><td>Tennessee</td><td>581</td><td>1.11%</td><td>42</td><td>North Dakota</td><td>62</td><td>0.12%</td></tr>
<tr><td>2</td><td>Texas</td><td>5,011</td><td>9.57%</td><td>43</td><td>Maine</td><td>43</td><td>0.08%</td></tr>
<tr><td>20</td><td>Utah</td><td>818</td><td>1.56%</td><td>44</td><td>Wyoming</td><td>38</td><td>0.07%</td></tr>
<tr><td>48</td><td>Vermont</td><td>0</td><td>0.00%</td><td>45</td><td>New Hampshire</td><td>33</td><td>0.06%</td></tr>
<tr><td>8</td><td>Virginia</td><td>1,562</td><td>2.98%</td><td>46</td><td>Delaware</td><td>21</td><td>0.04%</td></tr>
<tr><td>19</td><td>Washington</td><td>911</td><td>1.74%</td><td>47</td><td>Montana</td><td>19</td><td>0.04%</td></tr>
<tr><td>35</td><td>West Virginia</td><td>161</td><td>0.31%</td><td>48</td><td>Vermont</td><td>0</td><td>0.00%</td></tr>
<tr><td>5</td><td>Wisconsin</td><td>2,620</td><td>5.00%</td><td>NA</td><td>Illinois**</td><td>NA</td><td>NA</td></tr>
<tr><td>44</td><td>Wyoming</td><td>38</td><td>0.07%</td><td>NA</td><td>Kansas**</td><td>NA</td><td>NA</td></tr>
<tr><td></td><td></td><td></td><td></td><td colspan="2">District of Columbia</td><td>263</td><td>0.50%</td></tr>
</table>

Source: U.S. Department of Justice, Federal Bureau of Investigation
  "Crime in the United States 1993" (Uniform Crime Reports, December 4, 1994)
*By law enforcement agencies submitting complete reports to the F.B.I. for 12 months in 1993. Weapons violations include illegal carrying and possession.
**Not available.

Reported Arrests of Youths 17 Years and Younger for Weapons Violations
As a Percent of All Such Arrests in 1993
National Percent = 23.33% of Reported Weapons Violations*

ALPHA ORDER

RANK ORDER

RANK	STATE	PERCENT	RANK	STATE	PERCENT
26	Alabama	21.24	1	Utah	55.91
41	Alaska	16.31	2	North Dakota	45.59
22	Arizona	22.96	3	Montana	43.18
43	Arkansas	15.49	4	South Dakota	42.65
17	California	25.06	5	Minnesota	42.20
15	Colorado	27.15	6	Rhode Island	41.57
13	Connecticut	30.05	7	New Jersey	40.13
34	Delaware	18.75	8	Pennsylvania	35.41
23	Florida	21.99	9	Idaho	33.78
36	Georgia	18.64	10	Wisconsin	31.70
45	Hawaii	12.09	11	Washington	31.63
9	Idaho	33.78	12	Wyoming	30.40
NA	Illinois**	NA	13	Connecticut	30.05
24	Indiana	21.85	14	New Hampshire	28.45
28	Iowa	20.94	15	Colorado	27.15
NA	Kansas**	NA	16	New Mexico	25.35
46	Kentucky	11.72	17	California	25.06
31	Louisiana	20.58	18	Massachusetts	24.82
37	Maine	18.14	19	South Carolina	24.55
21	Maryland	23.56	20	Nebraska	24.39
18	Massachusetts	24.82	21	Maryland	23.56
33	Michigan	20.21	22	Arizona	22.96
5	Minnesota	42.20	23	Florida	21.99
38	Mississippi	17.46	24	Indiana	21.85
40	Missouri	16.49	25	New York	21.38
3	Montana	43.18	26	Alabama	21.24
20	Nebraska	24.39	27	Oklahoma	21.12
39	Nevada	16.51	28	Iowa	20.94
14	New Hampshire	28.45	29	Oregon	20.74
7	New Jersey	40.13	30	Texas	20.70
16	New Mexico	25.35	31	Louisiana	20.58
25	New York	21.38	32	Ohio	20.35
42	North Carolina	15.70	33	Michigan	20.21
2	North Dakota	45.59	34	Delaware	18.75
32	Ohio	20.35	35	Virginia	18.70
27	Oklahoma	21.12	36	Georgia	18.64
29	Oregon	20.74	37	Maine	18.14
8	Pennsylvania	35.41	38	Mississippi	17.46
6	Rhode Island	41.57	39	Nevada	16.51
19	South Carolina	24.55	40	Missouri	16.49
4	South Dakota	42.65	41	Alaska	16.31
44	Tennessee	14.94	42	North Carolina	15.70
30	Texas	20.70	43	Arkansas	15.49
1	Utah	55.91	44	Tennessee	14.94
48	Vermont	0.00	45	Hawaii	12.09
35	Virginia	18.70	46	Kentucky	11.72
11	Washington	31.63	47	West Virginia	11.48
47	West Virginia	11.48	48	Vermont	0.00
10	Wisconsin	31.70	NA	Illinois**	NA
12	Wyoming	30.40	NA	Kansas**	NA

District of Columbia   15.14

Source: Morgan Quitno Corporation using data from U.S. Department of Justice, Federal Bureau of Investigation
"Crime in the United States 1993" (Uniform Crime Reports, December 4, 1994)
*By law enforcement agencies submitting complete reports to the F.B.I. for 12 months in 1993. Weapons violations include illegal carrying and possession.
**Not available.

Reported Arrests of Youths 17 Years & Younger for Driving Under the Influence in 1993

National Total = 10,722 Reported Arrests*

ALPHA ORDER

RANK	STATE	ARRESTS	% of USA
27	Alabama	149	1.39%
39	Alaska	57	0.53%
12	Arizona	243	2.27%
13	Arkansas	202	1.88%
1	California	1,696	15.82%
7	Colorado	366	3.41%
35	Connecticut	74	0.69%
48	Delaware	0	0.00%
28	Florida	123	1.15%
4	Georgia	433	4.04%
44	Hawaii	36	0.34%
32	Idaho	87	0.81%
NA	Illinois**	NA	NA
31	Indiana	103	0.96%
25	Iowa	165	1.54%
NA	Kansas**	NA	NA
18	Kentucky	191	1.78%
33	Louisiana	83	0.77%
34	Maine	77	0.72%
22	Maryland	178	1.66%
29	Massachusetts	108	1.01%
5	Michigan	409	3.81%
8	Minnesota	350	3.26%
41	Mississippi	54	0.50%
16	Missouri	196	1.83%
42	Montana	50	0.47%
20	Nebraska	185	1.73%
45	Nevada	33	0.31%
42	New Hampshire	50	0.47%
21	New Jersey	179	1.67%
24	New Mexico	168	1.57%
17	New York	195	1.82%
2	North Carolina	955	8.91%
40	North Dakota	55	0.51%
9	Ohio	314	2.93%
10	Oklahoma	273	2.55%
13	Oregon	202	1.88%
23	Pennsylvania	170	1.59%
46	Rhode Island	19	0.18%
26	South Carolina	164	1.53%
37	South Dakota	70	0.65%
30	Tennessee	104	0.97%
3	Texas	816	7.61%
19	Utah	186	1.73%
47	Vermont	17	0.16%
15	Virginia	198	1.85%
11	Washington	261	2.43%
36	West Virginia	71	0.66%
6	Wisconsin	385	3.59%
38	Wyoming	58	0.54%

RANK ORDER

RANK	STATE	ARRESTS	% of USA
1	California	1,696	15.82%
2	North Carolina	955	8.91%
3	Texas	816	7.61%
4	Georgia	433	4.04%
5	Michigan	409	3.81%
6	Wisconsin	385	3.59%
7	Colorado	366	3.41%
8	Minnesota	350	3.26%
9	Ohio	314	2.93%
10	Oklahoma	273	2.55%
11	Washington	261	2.43%
12	Arizona	243	2.27%
13	Arkansas	202	1.88%
13	Oregon	202	1.88%
15	Virginia	198	1.85%
16	Missouri	196	1.83%
17	New York	195	1.82%
18	Kentucky	191	1.78%
19	Utah	186	1.73%
20	Nebraska	185	1.73%
21	New Jersey	179	1.67%
22	Maryland	178	1.66%
23	Pennsylvania	170	1.59%
24	New Mexico	168	1.57%
25	Iowa	165	1.54%
26	South Carolina	164	1.53%
27	Alabama	149	1.39%
28	Florida	123	1.15%
29	Massachusetts	108	1.01%
30	Tennessee	104	0.97%
31	Indiana	103	0.96%
32	Idaho	87	0.81%
33	Louisiana	83	0.77%
34	Maine	77	0.72%
35	Connecticut	74	0.69%
36	West Virginia	71	0.66%
37	South Dakota	70	0.65%
38	Wyoming	58	0.54%
39	Alaska	57	0.53%
40	North Dakota	55	0.51%
41	Mississippi	54	0.50%
42	Montana	50	0.47%
42	New Hampshire	50	0.47%
44	Hawaii	36	0.34%
45	Nevada	33	0.31%
46	Rhode Island	19	0.18%
47	Vermont	17	0.16%
48	Delaware	0	0.00%
NA	Illinois**	NA	NA
NA	Kansas**	NA	NA
	District of Columbia	0	0.00%

Source: U.S. Department of Justice, Federal Bureau of Investigation
  "Crime in the United States 1993" (Uniform Crime Reports, December 4, 1994)
*By law enforcement agencies submitting complete reports to the F.B.I. for 12 months in 1993. Includes driving any
vehicle while drunk or under the influence of liquor or narcotics.
**Not available.

Reported Arrests of Youths 17 Years and Younger for Driving Under the Influence
As a Percent of All Such Arrests in 1993
National Percent = 0.87% of Reported Arrests for Driving Under the Influence*

ALPHA ORDER

RANK ORDER

RANK	STATE	PERCENT		RANK	STATE	PERCENT
34	Alabama	0.76		1	Montana	2.45
19	Alaska	1.06		2	Utah	2.32
23	Arizona	0.94		3	North Dakota	2.29
20	Arkansas	1.03		4	Vermont	1.78
36	California	0.74		5	New Mexico	1.75
11	Colorado	1.27		6	Nebraska	1.56
38	Connecticut	0.70		7	North Carolina	1.35
48	Delaware	0.00		8	South Dakota	1.32
47	Florida	0.33		9	Iowa	1.31
29	Georgia	0.83		10	Wyoming	1.29
38	Hawaii	0.70		11	Colorado	1.27
21	Idaho	0.97		12	New Hampshire	1.18
NA	Illinois**	NA		13	Maine	1.17
42	Indiana	0.57		13	Ohio	1.17
9	Iowa	1.31		15	Kentucky	1.16
NA	Kansas**	NA		16	Oklahoma	1.11
15	Kentucky	1.16		17	Wisconsin	1.10
34	Louisiana	0.76		18	Minnesota	1.08
13	Maine	1.17		19	Alaska	1.06
33	Maryland	0.77		20	Arkansas	1.03
26	Massachusetts	0.87		21	Idaho	0.97
25	Michigan	0.88		22	Oregon	0.96
18	Minnesota	1.08		23	Arizona	0.94
27	Mississippi	0.86		24	South Carolina	0.89
28	Missouri	0.85		25	Michigan	0.88
1	Montana	2.45		26	Massachusetts	0.87
6	Nebraska	1.56		27	Mississippi	0.86
44	Nevada	0.53		28	Missouri	0.85
12	New Hampshire	1.18		29	Georgia	0.83
37	New Jersey	0.73		30	Rhode Island	0.82
5	New Mexico	1.75		31	Texas	0.80
44	New York	0.53		32	West Virginia	0.78
7	North Carolina	1.35		33	Maryland	0.77
3	North Dakota	2.29		34	Alabama	0.76
13	Ohio	1.17		34	Louisiana	0.76
16	Oklahoma	1.11		36	California	0.74
22	Oregon	0.96		37	New Jersey	0.73
41	Pennsylvania	0.62		38	Connecticut	0.70
30	Rhode Island	0.82		38	Hawaii	0.70
24	South Carolina	0.89		40	Washington	0.67
8	South Dakota	1.32		41	Pennsylvania	0.62
46	Tennessee	0.48		42	Indiana	0.57
31	Texas	0.80		43	Virginia	0.56
2	Utah	2.32		44	Nevada	0.53
4	Vermont	1.78		44	New York	0.53
43	Virginia	0.56		46	Tennessee	0.48
40	Washington	0.67		47	Florida	0.33
32	West Virginia	0.78		48	Delaware	0.00
17	Wisconsin	1.10		NA	Illinois**	NA
10	Wyoming	1.29		NA	Kansas**	NA

District of Columbia   0.00

Source: Morgan Quitno Corporation using data from U.S. Department of Justice, Federal Bureau of Investigation
     "Crime in the United States 1993" (Uniform Crime Reports, December 4, 1994)
*By law enforcement agencies submitting complete reports to the F.B.I. for 12 months in 1993. Includes driving any
vehicle while drunk or under the influence of liquor or narcotics.
**Not available.

Reported Arrests of Youths 17 Years and Younger for Drug Abuse Violations in 1993

National Total = 93,316 Reported Arrests*

ALPHA ORDER

RANK	STATE	ARRESTS	% of USA
27	Alabama	674	0.72%
40	Alaska	121	0.13%
8	Arizona	2,790	2.99%
28	Arkansas	659	0.71%
1	California	17,557	18.81%
17	Colorado	1,638	1.76%
12	Connecticut	2,232	2.39%
45	Delaware	72	0.08%
5	Florida	5,245	5.62%
13	Georgia	1,996	2.14%
30	Hawaii	479	0.51%
42	Idaho	98	0.11%
NA	Illinois**	NA	NA
26	Indiana	747	0.80%
43	Iowa	96	0.10%
NA	Kansas**	NA	NA
29	Kentucky	630	0.68%
20	Louisiana	1,242	1.33%
38	Maine	174	0.19%
6	Maryland	4,631	4.96%
15	Massachusetts	1,804	1.93%
9	Michigan	2,646	2.84%
19	Minnesota	1,360	1.46%
34	Mississippi	361	0.39%
18	Missouri	1,414	1.52%
47	Montana	39	0.04%
35	Nebraska	345	0.37%
31	Nevada	464	0.50%
37	New Hampshire	220	0.24%
4	New Jersey	5,538	5.93%
32	New Mexico	419	0.45%
2	New York	10,173	10.90%
11	North Carolina	2,248	2.41%
46	North Dakota	46	0.05%
10	Ohio	2,634	2.82%
25	Oklahoma	774	0.83%
23	Oregon	978	1.05%
7	Pennsylvania	3,064	3.28%
33	Rhode Island	403	0.43%
36	South Carolina	229	0.25%
41	South Dakota	105	0.11%
24	Tennessee	808	0.87%
3	Texas	8,004	8.58%
22	Utah	1,170	1.25%
48	Vermont	13	0.01%
16	Virginia	1,800	1.93%
21	Washington	1,183	1.27%
39	West Virginia	171	0.18%
14	Wisconsin	1,822	1.95%
44	Wyoming	90	0.10%

RANK ORDER

RANK	STATE	ARRESTS	% of USA
1	California	17,557	18.81%
2	New York	10,173	10.90%
3	Texas	8,004	8.58%
4	New Jersey	5,538	5.93%
5	Florida	5,245	5.62%
6	Maryland	4,631	4.96%
7	Pennsylvania	3,064	3.28%
8	Arizona	2,790	2.99%
9	Michigan	2,646	2.84%
10	Ohio	2,634	2.82%
11	North Carolina	2,248	2.41%
12	Connecticut	2,232	2.39%
13	Georgia	1,996	2.14%
14	Wisconsin	1,822	1.95%
15	Massachusetts	1,804	1.93%
16	Virginia	1,800	1.93%
17	Colorado	1,638	1.76%
18	Missouri	1,414	1.52%
19	Minnesota	1,360	1.46%
20	Louisiana	1,242	1.33%
21	Washington	1,183	1.27%
22	Utah	1,170	1.25%
23	Oregon	978	1.05%
24	Tennessee	808	0.87%
25	Oklahoma	774	0.83%
26	Indiana	747	0.80%
27	Alabama	674	0.72%
28	Arkansas	659	0.71%
29	Kentucky	630	0.68%
30	Hawaii	479	0.51%
31	Nevada	464	0.50%
32	New Mexico	419	0.45%
33	Rhode Island	403	0.43%
34	Mississippi	361	0.39%
35	Nebraska	345	0.37%
36	South Carolina	229	0.25%
37	New Hampshire	220	0.24%
38	Maine	174	0.19%
39	West Virginia	171	0.18%
40	Alaska	121	0.13%
41	South Dakota	105	0.11%
42	Idaho	98	0.11%
43	Iowa	96	0.10%
44	Wyoming	90	0.10%
45	Delaware	72	0.08%
46	North Dakota	46	0.05%
47	Montana	39	0.04%
48	Vermont	13	0.01%
NA	Illinois**	NA	NA
NA	Kansas**	NA	NA
	District of Columbia	732	0.78%

Source: U.S. Department of Justice, Federal Bureau of Investigation
   "Crime in the United States 1993" (Uniform Crime Reports, December 4, 1994)
*By law enforcement agencies submitting complete reports to the F.B.I. for 12 months in 1993. Includes offenses relating to possession, sale, use, growing and manufacturing of narcotic drugs.
**Not available.

Reported Arrests of Youths 17 Years and Younger for Drug Abuse Violations
As a Percent of All Such Arrests in 1993
National Percent = 9.63% of Reported Drug Abuse Violation Arrests*

ALPHA ORDER

RANK ORDER

RANK	STATE	PERCENT		RANK	STATE	PERCENT
43	Alabama	6.90		1	Utah	21.58
21	Alaska	10.80		2	New Mexico	17.88
4	Arizona	15.30		3	Colorado	16.02
35	Arkansas	8.31		4	Arizona	15.30
42	California	7.49		5	Minnesota	14.73
3	Colorado	16.02		6	Wisconsin	14.46
16	Connecticut	12.34		7	Hawaii	14.21
12	Delaware	12.95		8	Montana	14.03
36	Florida	8.23		9	New Jersey	13.15
44	Georgia	6.81		10	Idaho	13.08
7	Hawaii	14.21		11	Maryland	12.99
10	Idaho	13.08		12	Delaware	12.95
NA	Illinois**	NA		13	New Hampshire	12.93
17	Indiana	11.79		14	South Dakota	12.47
40	Iowa	7.72		15	Rhode Island	12.40
NA	Kansas**	NA		16	Connecticut	12.34
47	Kentucky	6.47		17	Indiana	11.79
32	Louisiana	8.81		18	Pennsylvania	11.77
22	Maine	10.73		19	Wyoming	11.67
11	Maryland	12.99		20	Texas	11.10
27	Massachusetts	9.72		21	Alaska	10.80
28	Michigan	9.62		22	Maine	10.73
5	Minnesota	14.73		23	North Dakota	10.72
38	Mississippi	7.92		24	Ohio	10.50
26	Missouri	10.01		25	Washington	10.02
8	Montana	14.03		26	Missouri	10.01
37	Nebraska	7.94		27	Massachusetts	9.72
46	Nevada	6.51		28	Michigan	9.62
13	New Hampshire	12.93		29	South Carolina	9.48
9	New Jersey	13.15		30	New York	9.16
2	New Mexico	17.88		31	Virginia	8.90
30	New York	9.16		32	Louisiana	8.81
34	North Carolina	8.35		33	Oregon	8.59
23	North Dakota	10.72		34	North Carolina	8.35
24	Ohio	10.50		35	Arkansas	8.31
41	Oklahoma	7.63		36	Florida	8.23
33	Oregon	8.59		37	Nebraska	7.94
18	Pennsylvania	11.77		38	Mississippi	7.92
15	Rhode Island	12.40		39	West Virginia	7.90
29	South Carolina	9.48		40	Iowa	7.72
14	South Dakota	12.47		41	Oklahoma	7.63
45	Tennessee	6.63		42	California	7.49
20	Texas	11.10		43	Alabama	6.90
1	Utah	21.58		44	Georgia	6.81
48	Vermont	3.75		45	Tennessee	6.63
31	Virginia	8.90		46	Nevada	6.51
25	Washington	10.02		47	Kentucky	6.47
39	West Virginia	7.90		48	Vermont	3.75
6	Wisconsin	14.46		NA	Illinois**	NA
19	Wyoming	11.67		NA	Kansas**	NA

District of Columbia   8.89

Source: Morgan Quitno Corporation using data from U.S. Department of Justice, Federal Bureau of Investigation
   "Crime in the United States 1993" (Uniform Crime Reports, December 4, 1994)
*By law enforcement agencies submitting complete reports to the F.B.I. for 12 months in 1993. Includes offenses relating to possession, sale, use, growing and manufacturing of narcotic drugs.
**Not available.

Reported Arrests of Youths 17 Years and Younger for Sex Offenses in 1993

National Total = 16,393 Reported Arrests*

<u>ALPHA ORDER</u>

RANK	STATE	ARRESTS	% of USA
44	Alabama	27	0.16%
34	Alaska	58	0.35%
16	Arizona	390	2.38%
39	Arkansas	44	0.27%
1	California	2,669	16.28%
15	Colorado	395	2.41%
22	Connecticut	228	1.39%
47	Delaware	13	0.08%
7	Florida	572	3.49%
14	Georgia	401	2.45%
26	Hawaii	118	0.72%
29	Idaho	80	0.49%
NA	Illinois**	NA	NA
20	Indiana	255	1.56%
35	Iowa	56	0.34%
NA	Kansas**	NA	NA
28	Kentucky	90	0.55%
24	Louisiana	131	0.80%
30	Maine	79	0.48%
5	Maryland	679	4.14%
31	Massachusetts	71	0.43%
8	Michigan	540	3.29%
19	Minnesota	345	2.10%
41	Mississippi	34	0.21%
18	Missouri	354	2.16%
37	Montana	51	0.31%
25	Nebraska	129	0.79%
35	Nevada	56	0.34%
40	New Hampshire	40	0.24%
12	New Jersey	443	2.70%
45	New Mexico	21	0.13%
3	New York	1,230	7.50%
21	North Carolina	253	1.54%
42	North Dakota	31	0.19%
16	Ohio	390	2.38%
27	Oklahoma	103	0.63%
13	Oregon	413	2.52%
6	Pennsylvania	597	3.64%
33	Rhode Island	59	0.36%
23	South Carolina	153	0.93%
38	South Dakota	46	0.28%
32	Tennessee	62	0.38%
4	Texas	1,097	6.69%
9	Utah	507	3.09%
48	Vermont	10	0.06%
11	Virginia	462	2.82%
10	Washington	477	2.91%
42	West Virginia	31	0.19%
2	Wisconsin	1,882	11.48%
46	Wyoming	19	0.12%

<u>RANK ORDER</u>

RANK	STATE	ARRESTS	% of USA
1	California	2,669	16.28%
2	Wisconsin	1,882	11.48%
3	New York	1,230	7.50%
4	Texas	1,097	6.69%
5	Maryland	679	4.14%
6	Pennsylvania	597	3.64%
7	Florida	572	3.49%
8	Michigan	540	3.29%
9	Utah	507	3.09%
10	Washington	477	2.91%
11	Virginia	462	2.82%
12	New Jersey	443	2.70%
13	Oregon	413	2.52%
14	Georgia	401	2.45%
15	Colorado	395	2.41%
16	Arizona	390	2.38%
16	Ohio	390	2.38%
18	Missouri	354	2.16%
19	Minnesota	345	2.10%
20	Indiana	255	1.56%
21	North Carolina	253	1.54%
22	Connecticut	228	1.39%
23	South Carolina	153	0.93%
24	Louisiana	131	0.80%
25	Nebraska	129	0.79%
26	Hawaii	118	0.72%
27	Oklahoma	103	0.63%
28	Kentucky	90	0.55%
29	Idaho	80	0.49%
30	Maine	79	0.48%
31	Massachusetts	71	0.43%
32	Tennessee	62	0.38%
33	Rhode Island	59	0.36%
34	Alaska	58	0.35%
35	Iowa	56	0.34%
35	Nevada	56	0.34%
37	Montana	51	0.31%
38	South Dakota	46	0.28%
39	Arkansas	44	0.27%
40	New Hampshire	40	0.24%
41	Mississippi	34	0.21%
42	North Dakota	31	0.19%
42	West Virginia	31	0.19%
44	Alabama	27	0.16%
45	New Mexico	21	0.13%
46	Wyoming	19	0.12%
47	Delaware	13	0.08%
48	Vermont	10	0.06%
NA	Illinois**	NA	NA
NA	Kansas**	NA	NA
	District of Columbia	14	0.09%

Source: U.S. Department of Justice, Federal Bureau of Investigation
"Crime in the United States 1993" (Uniform Crime Reports, December 4, 1994)

By law enforcement agencies submitting complete reports to the F.B.I. for 12 months in 1993. Excludes forcible rape, prostitution and commercialized vice. Includes statutory rape and offenses against chastity, common decency, morals and the like.

**Not available.*

67

Reported Arrests of Youths 17 Years and Younger for Sex Offenses
As a Percent of All Such Arrests in 1993
National Percent = 18.69% of Reported Sex Offense Arrests*

ALPHA ORDER				RANK ORDER		
RANK	STATE	PERCENT		RANK	STATE	PERCENT
48	Alabama	5.19		1	Montana	41.80
29	Alaska	15.93		2	Wisconsin	40.65
22	Arizona	17.82		3	North Dakota	38.75
38	Arkansas	10.76		4	Utah	36.79
27	California	16.35		5	Maryland	34.66
14	Colorado	20.88		6	Idaho	32.79
10	Connecticut	23.58		7	Minnesota	32.27
32	Delaware	14.29		8	South Dakota	24.47
37	Florida	12.77		9	Oregon	23.60
39	Georgia	10.53		10	Connecticut	23.58
16	Hawaii	20.49		11	Pennsylvania	23.30
6	Idaho	32.79		12	Maine	21.41
NA	Illinois**	NA		13	Iowa	20.90
23	Indiana	17.68		14	Colorado	20.88
13	Iowa	20.90		15	New Jersey	20.69
NA	Kansas**	NA		16	Hawaii	20.49
45	Kentucky	8.33		17	Michigan	20.03
35	Louisiana	13.67		18	South Carolina	20.00
12	Maine	21.41		19	New York	19.90
5	Maryland	34.66		20	Washington	19.62
46	Massachusetts	8.09		21	New Hampshire	17.86
17	Michigan	20.03		22	Arizona	17.82
7	Minnesota	32.27		23	Indiana	17.68
26	Mississippi	16.50		24	Ohio	17.23
30	Missouri	15.82		25	Nebraska	17.22
1	Montana	41.80		26	Mississippi	16.50
25	Nebraska	17.22		27	California	16.35
47	Nevada	7.81		28	Texas	16.28
21	New Hampshire	17.86		29	Alaska	15.93
15	New Jersey	20.69		30	Missouri	15.82
34	New Mexico	13.73		31	Wyoming	14.84
19	New York	19.90		32	Delaware	14.29
44	North Carolina	9.50		33	Rhode Island	14.15
3	North Dakota	38.75		34	New Mexico	13.73
24	Ohio	17.23		35	Louisiana	13.67
41	Oklahoma	10.24		36	Virginia	13.49
9	Oregon	23.60		37	Florida	12.77
11	Pennsylvania	23.30		38	Arkansas	10.76
33	Rhode Island	14.15		39	Georgia	10.53
18	South Carolina	20.00		40	West Virginia	10.47
8	South Dakota	24.47		41	Oklahoma	10.24
43	Tennessee	9.76		42	Vermont	9.80
28	Texas	16.28		43	Tennessee	9.76
4	Utah	36.79		44	North Carolina	9.50
42	Vermont	9.80		45	Kentucky	8.33
36	Virginia	13.49		46	Massachusetts	8.09
20	Washington	19.62		47	Nevada	7.81
40	West Virginia	10.47		48	Alabama	5.19
2	Wisconsin	40.65		NA	Illinois**	NA
31	Wyoming	14.84		NA	Kansas**	NA
					District of Columbia	10.45

Source: Morgan Quitno Corporation using data from U.S. Department of Justice, Federal Bureau of Investigation
"Crime in the United States 1993" (Uniform Crime Reports, December 4, 1994)
*By law enforcement agencies submitting complete reports to the F.B.I. for 12 months in 1993. Excludes forcible rape, prostitution and commercialized vice. Includes statutory rape and offenses against chastity, common decency, morals and the like.
**Not available.

Reported Arrests of Youths 17 & Younger for Prostitution & Commercialized Vice in 1993

National Total = 994 Reported Arrests*

ALPHA ORDER					RANK ORDER			
RANK	STATE		ARRESTS	% of USA	RANK	STATE	ARRESTS	% of USA
33	Alabama		3	0.30%	1	California	197	19.82%
37	Alaska		1	0.10%	2	Texas	99	9.96%
22	Arizona		14	1.41%	3	Florida	81	8.15%
19	Arkansas		16	1.61%	4	New York	65	6.54%
1	California		197	19.82%	5	Massachusetts	38	3.82%
29	Colorado		6	0.60%	6	Ohio	37	3.72%
25	Connecticut		9	0.91%	7	New Jersey	36	3.62%
42	Delaware		0	0.00%	8	Utah	28	2.82%
3	Florida		81	8.15%	9	Michigan	27	2.72%
15	Georgia		20	2.01%	9	Washington	27	2.72%
29	Hawaii		6	0.60%	9	Wisconsin	27	2.72%
37	Idaho		1	0.10%	12	Pennsylvania	25	2.52%
NA	Illinois**		NA	NA	13	Minnesota	24	2.41%
23	Indiana		12	1.21%	14	Oregon	23	2.31%
37	Iowa		1	0.10%	15	Georgia	20	2.01%
NA	Kansas**		NA	NA	15	North Carolina	20	2.01%
28	Kentucky		8	0.80%	17	Missouri	18	1.81%
25	Louisiana		9	0.91%	18	Nevada	17	1.71%
42	Maine		0	0.00%	19	Arkansas	16	1.61%
19	Maryland		16	1.61%	19	Maryland	16	1.61%
5	Massachusetts		38	3.82%	19	New Mexico	16	1.61%
9	Michigan		27	2.72%	22	Arizona	14	1.41%
13	Minnesota		24	2.41%	23	Indiana	12	1.21%
33	Mississippi		3	0.30%	24	South Carolina	10	1.01%
17	Missouri		18	1.81%	25	Connecticut	9	0.91%
42	Montana		0	0.00%	25	Louisiana	9	0.91%
37	Nebraska		1	0.10%	25	Oklahoma	9	0.91%
18	Nevada		17	1.71%	28	Kentucky	8	0.80%
36	New Hampshire		2	0.20%	29	Colorado	6	0.60%
7	New Jersey		36	3.62%	29	Hawaii	6	0.60%
19	New Mexico		16	1.61%	29	Virginia	6	0.60%
4	New York		65	6.54%	32	Tennessee	5	0.50%
15	North Carolina		20	2.01%	33	Alabama	3	0.30%
42	North Dakota		0	0.00%	33	Mississippi	3	0.30%
6	Ohio		37	3.72%	33	Rhode Island	3	0.30%
25	Oklahoma		9	0.91%	36	New Hampshire	2	0.20%
14	Oregon		23	2.31%	37	Alaska	1	0.10%
12	Pennsylvania		25	2.52%	37	Idaho	1	0.10%
33	Rhode Island		3	0.30%	37	Iowa	1	0.10%
24	South Carolina		10	1.01%	37	Nebraska	1	0.10%
42	South Dakota		0	0.00%	37	West Virginia	1	0.10%
32	Tennessee		5	0.50%	42	Delaware	0	0.00%
2	Texas		99	9.96%	42	Maine	0	0.00%
8	Utah		28	2.82%	42	Montana	0	0.00%
42	Vermont		0	0.00%	42	North Dakota	0	0.00%
29	Virginia		6	0.60%	42	South Dakota	0	0.00%
9	Washington		27	2.72%	42	Vermont	0	0.00%
37	West Virginia		1	0.10%	42	Wyoming	0	0.00%
9	Wisconsin		27	2.72%	NA	Illinois**	NA	NA
42	Wyoming		0	0.00%	NA	Kansas**	NA	NA
						District of Columbia	10	1.01%

Source: U.S. Department of Justice, Federal Bureau of Investigation
   "Crime in the United States 1993" (Uniform Crime Reports, December 4, 1994)
*By law enforcement agencies submitting complete reports to the F.B.I. for 12 months in 1993. Includes keeping a bawdy house, procuring or transporting women for immoral purposes. Attempts are included.
**Not available.

69

Reported Arrests of Youths 17 Years & Younger for Prostitution & Commercialized Vice
As a Percent of All Such Arrests in 1993
National Percent = 1.12% of Reported Prostitution & Commercialized Vice Arrests*

ALPHA ORDER

RANK ORDER

RANK	STATE	PERCENT		RANK	STATE	PERCENT
33	Alabama	0.74		1	Idaho	20.00
27	Alaska	1.01		2	New Hampshire	14.29
31	Arizona	0.78		3	Utah	3.83
4	Arkansas	3.35		4	Arkansas	3.35
25	California	1.12		5	Mississippi	3.03
38	Colorado	0.40		6	Washington	2.85
26	Connecticut	1.02		7	New Mexico	2.66
42	Delaware	0.00		8	Louisiana	2.51
17	Florida	1.32		9	Oklahoma	2.49
21	Georgia	1.19		10	Oregon	2.38
29	Hawaii	0.96		11	South Carolina	2.20
1	Idaho	20.00		12	Minnesota	1.76
NA	Illinois**	NA		13	Wisconsin	1.74
20	Indiana	1.20		14	Kentucky	1.63
39	Iowa	0.39		15	North Carolina	1.59
NA	Kansas**	NA		16	Texas	1.35
14	Kentucky	1.63		17	Florida	1.32
8	Louisiana	2.51		18	Pennsylvania	1.31
42	Maine	0.00		19	Massachusetts	1.27
24	Maryland	1.16		20	Indiana	1.20
19	Massachusetts	1.27		21	Georgia	1.19
28	Michigan	0.99		22	New Jersey	1.18
12	Minnesota	1.76		22	Rhode Island	1.18
5	Mississippi	3.03		24	Maryland	1.16
34	Missouri	0.66		25	California	1.12
42	Montana	0.00		26	Connecticut	1.02
41	Nebraska	0.32		27	Alaska	1.01
35	Nevada	0.63		28	Michigan	0.99
2	New Hampshire	14.29		29	Hawaii	0.96
22	New Jersey	1.18		30	Ohio	0.86
7	New Mexico	2.66		31	Arizona	0.78
36	New York	0.53		31	West Virginia	0.78
15	North Carolina	1.59		33	Alabama	0.74
42	North Dakota	0.00		34	Missouri	0.66
30	Ohio	0.86		35	Nevada	0.63
9	Oklahoma	2.49		36	New York	0.53
10	Oregon	2.38		37	Tennessee	0.44
18	Pennsylvania	1.31		38	Colorado	0.40
22	Rhode Island	1.18		39	Iowa	0.39
11	South Carolina	2.20		40	Virginia	0.33
42	South Dakota	0.00		41	Nebraska	0.32
37	Tennessee	0.44		42	Delaware	0.00
16	Texas	1.35		42	Maine	0.00
3	Utah	3.83		42	Montana	0.00
42	Vermont	0.00		42	North Dakota	0.00
40	Virginia	0.33		42	South Dakota	0.00
6	Washington	2.85		42	Vermont	0.00
31	West Virginia	0.78		42	Wyoming	0.00
13	Wisconsin	1.74		NA	Illinois**	NA
42	Wyoming	0.00		NA	Kansas**	NA

District of Columbia   0.74

Source: Morgan Quitno Corporation using data from U.S. Department of Justice, Federal Bureau of Investigation "Crime in the United States 1993" (Uniform Crime Reports, December 4, 1994)
*By law enforcement agencies submitting complete reports to the F.B.I. for 12 months in 1993. Includes keeping a bawdy house, procuring or transporting women for immoral purposes. Attempts are included.
**Not available.

Reported Arrests of Youths 17 Years and Younger for
Offenses Against Families and Children in 1993
National Total = 3,940 Reported Arrests*

<table>
<tr><td colspan="4">ALPHA ORDER</td><td colspan="4">RANK ORDER</td></tr>
<tr><td>RANK</td><td>STATE</td><td>ARRESTS</td><td>% of USA</td><td>RANK</td><td>STATE</td><td>ARRESTS</td><td>% of USA</td></tr>
<tr><td>35</td><td>Alabama</td><td>5</td><td>0.13%</td><td>1</td><td>Ohio</td><td>1,017</td><td>25.81%</td></tr>
<tr><td>39</td><td>Alaska</td><td>3</td><td>0.08%</td><td>2</td><td>Texas</td><td>570</td><td>14.47%</td></tr>
<tr><td>44</td><td>Arizona</td><td>0</td><td>0.00%</td><td>3</td><td>Wisconsin</td><td>361</td><td>9.16%</td></tr>
<tr><td>33</td><td>Arkansas</td><td>7</td><td>0.18%</td><td>4</td><td>New York</td><td>297</td><td>7.54%</td></tr>
<tr><td>26</td><td>California</td><td>16</td><td>0.41%</td><td>5</td><td>Georgia</td><td>206</td><td>5.23%</td></tr>
<tr><td>19</td><td>Colorado</td><td>41</td><td>1.04%</td><td>6</td><td>Massachusetts</td><td>163</td><td>4.14%</td></tr>
<tr><td>9</td><td>Connecticut</td><td>103</td><td>2.61%</td><td>7</td><td>Louisiana</td><td>149</td><td>3.78%</td></tr>
<tr><td>44</td><td>Delaware</td><td>0</td><td>0.00%</td><td>8</td><td>Hawaii</td><td>131</td><td>3.32%</td></tr>
<tr><td>26</td><td>Florida</td><td>16</td><td>0.41%</td><td>9</td><td>Connecticut</td><td>103</td><td>2.61%</td></tr>
<tr><td>5</td><td>Georgia</td><td>206</td><td>5.23%</td><td>10</td><td>North Carolina</td><td>85</td><td>2.16%</td></tr>
<tr><td>8</td><td>Hawaii</td><td>131</td><td>3.32%</td><td>10</td><td>North Dakota</td><td>85</td><td>2.16%</td></tr>
<tr><td>35</td><td>Idaho</td><td>5</td><td>0.13%</td><td>12</td><td>Missouri</td><td>83</td><td>2.11%</td></tr>
<tr><td>NA</td><td>Illinois**</td><td>NA</td><td>NA</td><td>13</td><td>New Mexico</td><td>73</td><td>1.85%</td></tr>
<tr><td>16</td><td>Indiana</td><td>58</td><td>1.47%</td><td>14</td><td>Pennsylvania</td><td>66</td><td>1.68%</td></tr>
<tr><td>42</td><td>Iowa</td><td>2</td><td>0.05%</td><td>15</td><td>South Carolina</td><td>62</td><td>1.57%</td></tr>
<tr><td>NA</td><td>Kansas**</td><td>NA</td><td>NA</td><td>16</td><td>Indiana</td><td>58</td><td>1.47%</td></tr>
<tr><td>31</td><td>Kentucky</td><td>10</td><td>0.25%</td><td>17</td><td>Rhode Island</td><td>50</td><td>1.27%</td></tr>
<tr><td>7</td><td>Louisiana</td><td>149</td><td>3.78%</td><td>18</td><td>Nevada</td><td>42</td><td>1.07%</td></tr>
<tr><td>37</td><td>Maine</td><td>4</td><td>0.10%</td><td>19</td><td>Colorado</td><td>41</td><td>1.04%</td></tr>
<tr><td>33</td><td>Maryland</td><td>7</td><td>0.18%</td><td>20</td><td>Oklahoma</td><td>33</td><td>0.84%</td></tr>
<tr><td>6</td><td>Massachusetts</td><td>163</td><td>4.14%</td><td>21</td><td>Utah</td><td>24</td><td>0.61%</td></tr>
<tr><td>44</td><td>Michigan</td><td>0</td><td>0.00%</td><td>22</td><td>Minnesota</td><td>22</td><td>0.56%</td></tr>
<tr><td>22</td><td>Minnesota</td><td>22</td><td>0.56%</td><td>22</td><td>Virginia</td><td>22</td><td>0.56%</td></tr>
<tr><td>29</td><td>Mississippi</td><td>13</td><td>0.33%</td><td>24</td><td>Washington</td><td>21</td><td>0.53%</td></tr>
<tr><td>12</td><td>Missouri</td><td>83</td><td>2.11%</td><td>25</td><td>New Jersey</td><td>17</td><td>0.43%</td></tr>
<tr><td>44</td><td>Montana</td><td>0</td><td>0.00%</td><td>26</td><td>California</td><td>16</td><td>0.41%</td></tr>
<tr><td>28</td><td>Nebraska</td><td>15</td><td>0.38%</td><td>26</td><td>Florida</td><td>16</td><td>0.41%</td></tr>
<tr><td>18</td><td>Nevada</td><td>42</td><td>1.07%</td><td>28</td><td>Nebraska</td><td>15</td><td>0.38%</td></tr>
<tr><td>43</td><td>New Hampshire</td><td>1</td><td>0.03%</td><td>29</td><td>Mississippi</td><td>13</td><td>0.33%</td></tr>
<tr><td>25</td><td>New Jersey</td><td>17</td><td>0.43%</td><td>29</td><td>Wyoming</td><td>13</td><td>0.33%</td></tr>
<tr><td>13</td><td>New Mexico</td><td>73</td><td>1.85%</td><td>31</td><td>Kentucky</td><td>10</td><td>0.25%</td></tr>
<tr><td>4</td><td>New York</td><td>297</td><td>7.54%</td><td>32</td><td>Oregon</td><td>8</td><td>0.20%</td></tr>
<tr><td>10</td><td>North Carolina</td><td>85</td><td>2.16%</td><td>33</td><td>Arkansas</td><td>7</td><td>0.18%</td></tr>
<tr><td>10</td><td>North Dakota</td><td>85</td><td>2.16%</td><td>33</td><td>Maryland</td><td>7</td><td>0.18%</td></tr>
<tr><td>1</td><td>Ohio</td><td>1,017</td><td>25.81%</td><td>35</td><td>Alabama</td><td>5</td><td>0.13%</td></tr>
<tr><td>20</td><td>Oklahoma</td><td>33</td><td>0.84%</td><td>35</td><td>Idaho</td><td>5</td><td>0.13%</td></tr>
<tr><td>32</td><td>Oregon</td><td>8</td><td>0.20%</td><td>37</td><td>Maine</td><td>4</td><td>0.10%</td></tr>
<tr><td>14</td><td>Pennsylvania</td><td>66</td><td>1.68%</td><td>37</td><td>Vermont</td><td>4</td><td>0.10%</td></tr>
<tr><td>17</td><td>Rhode Island</td><td>50</td><td>1.27%</td><td>39</td><td>Alaska</td><td>3</td><td>0.08%</td></tr>
<tr><td>15</td><td>South Carolina</td><td>62</td><td>1.57%</td><td>39</td><td>South Dakota</td><td>3</td><td>0.08%</td></tr>
<tr><td>39</td><td>South Dakota</td><td>3</td><td>0.08%</td><td>39</td><td>Tennessee</td><td>3</td><td>0.08%</td></tr>
<tr><td>39</td><td>Tennessee</td><td>3</td><td>0.08%</td><td>42</td><td>Iowa</td><td>2</td><td>0.05%</td></tr>
<tr><td>2</td><td>Texas</td><td>570</td><td>14.47%</td><td>43</td><td>New Hampshire</td><td>1</td><td>0.03%</td></tr>
<tr><td>21</td><td>Utah</td><td>24</td><td>0.61%</td><td>44</td><td>Arizona</td><td>0</td><td>0.00%</td></tr>
<tr><td>37</td><td>Vermont</td><td>4</td><td>0.10%</td><td>44</td><td>Delaware</td><td>0</td><td>0.00%</td></tr>
<tr><td>22</td><td>Virginia</td><td>22</td><td>0.56%</td><td>44</td><td>Michigan</td><td>0</td><td>0.00%</td></tr>
<tr><td>24</td><td>Washington</td><td>21</td><td>0.53%</td><td>44</td><td>Montana</td><td>0</td><td>0.00%</td></tr>
<tr><td>44</td><td>West Virginia</td><td>0</td><td>0.00%</td><td>44</td><td>West Virginia</td><td>0</td><td>0.00%</td></tr>
<tr><td>3</td><td>Wisconsin</td><td>361</td><td>9.16%</td><td>NA</td><td>Illinois**</td><td>NA</td><td>NA</td></tr>
<tr><td>29</td><td>Wyoming</td><td>13</td><td>0.33%</td><td>NA</td><td>Kansas**</td><td>NA</td><td>NA</td></tr>
<tr><td></td><td></td><td></td><td></td><td></td><td>District of Columbia</td><td>0</td><td>0.00%</td></tr>
</table>

Source: U.S. Department of Justice, Federal Bureau of Investigation
  "Crime in the United States 1993" (Uniform Crime Reports, December 4, 1994)
*By law enforcement agencies submitting complete reports to the F.B.I. for 12 months in 1993. Includes nonsupport, neglect, desertion or abuse of family and children.
**Not available.

Reported Arrests of Youths 17 Years and Younger for Offenses Against Families And Children as a Percent of All Such Arrests in 1993

National Percent = 4.42% of Reported Offenses Against Families & Children Arrests*

ALPHA ORDER

RANK ORDER

RANK	STATE	PERCENT		RANK	STATE	PERCENT
40	Alabama	0.47		1	North Dakota	39.53
29	Alaska	2.33		2	Louisiana	12.55
44	Arizona	0.00		3	Rhode Island	11.79
38	Arkansas	0.89		4	Ohio	10.52
25	California	2.73		5	New York	9.92
28	Colorado	2.36		6	Wisconsin	7.91
14	Connecticut	4.97		7	Indiana	7.58
44	Delaware	0.00		8	Texas	7.33
36	Florida	1.24		9	New Mexico	6.94
13	Georgia	5.70		10	South Carolina	6.77
12	Hawaii	6.25		11	Pennsylvania	6.63
20	Idaho	4.07		12	Hawaii	6.25
NA	Illinois**	NA		13	Georgia	5.70
7	Indiana	7.58		14	Connecticut	4.97
35	Iowa	1.27		15	Nevada	4.96
NA	Kansas**	NA		16	Oklahoma	4.59
39	Kentucky	0.53		17	Massachusetts	4.54
2	Louisiana	12.55		18	Utah	4.40
31	Maine	2.14		19	Minnesota	4.20
41	Maryland	0.36		20	Idaho	4.07
17	Massachusetts	4.54		21	Wyoming	3.86
44	Michigan	0.00		22	Missouri	3.68
19	Minnesota	4.20		23	Washington	3.23
25	Mississippi	2.73		24	South Dakota	2.75
22	Missouri	3.68		25	California	2.73
44	Montana	0.00		25	Mississippi	2.73
36	Nebraska	1.24		27	Oregon	2.57
15	Nevada	4.96		28	Colorado	2.36
30	New Hampshire	2.17		29	Alaska	2.33
43	New Jersey	0.11		30	New Hampshire	2.17
9	New Mexico	6.94		31	Maine	2.14
5	New York	9.92		32	Vermont	2.08
33	North Carolina	1.34		33	North Carolina	1.34
1	North Dakota	39.53		34	Virginia	1.33
4	Ohio	10.52		35	Iowa	1.27
16	Oklahoma	4.59		36	Florida	1.24
27	Oregon	2.57		36	Nebraska	1.24
11	Pennsylvania	6.63		38	Arkansas	0.89
3	Rhode Island	11.79		39	Kentucky	0.53
10	South Carolina	6.77		40	Alabama	0.47
24	South Dakota	2.75		41	Maryland	0.36
42	Tennessee	0.28		42	Tennessee	0.28
8	Texas	7.33		43	New Jersey	0.11
18	Utah	4.40		44	Arizona	0.00
32	Vermont	2.08		44	Delaware	0.00
34	Virginia	1.33		44	Michigan	0.00
23	Washington	3.23		44	Montana	0.00
44	West Virginia	0.00		44	West Virginia	0.00
6	Wisconsin	7.91		NA	Illinois**	NA
21	Wyoming	3.86		NA	Kansas**	NA
					District of Columbia	0.00

Source: Morgan Quitno Corporation using data from U.S. Department of Justice, Federal Bureau of Investigation
 "Crime in the United States 1993" (Uniform Crime Reports, December 4, 1994)
*By law enforcement agencies submitting complete reports to the F.B.I. for 12 months in 1993. Includes nonsupport, neglect, desertion or abuse of family and children.
**Not available.

Percent of Crimes Cleared in 1993

National Percent = 21.1% of Crimes*

ALPHA ORDER				RANK ORDER		
RANK	STATE	PERCENT		RANK	STATE	PERCENT
NA	Alabama**	NA		1	South Dakota	32.5
7	Alaska	27.3		2	Wyoming	30.5
37	Arizona	19.6		3	Maine	29.4
5	Arkansas	28.7		4	Utah	28.9
34	California	20.6		5	Arkansas	28.7
12	Colorado	25.4		6	Delaware	27.6
38	Connecticut	19.5		7	Alaska	27.3
6	Delaware	27.6		8	Idaho	26.9
33	Florida	20.9		9	Wisconsin	26.3
25	Georgia	22.1		10	Virginia	26.1
46	Hawaii	15.3		11	Kentucky	25.6
8	Idaho	26.9		12	Colorado	25.4
32	Illinois	21.2		13	Pennsylvania	24.7
42	Indiana	18.1		14	North Dakota	24.4
40	Iowa	18.3		15	Nebraska	23.9
48	Kansas	13.8		15	Oregon	23.9
11	Kentucky	25.6		17	New Mexico	23.8
23	Louisiana	22.2		18	Massachusetts	23.4
3	Maine	29.4		19	Montana	22.8
27	Maryland	21.8		19	Washington	22.8
18	Massachusetts	23.4		21	Tennessee	22.4
47	Michigan	13.9		22	Ohio	22.3
23	Minnesota	22.2		23	Louisiana	22.2
30	Mississippi	21.6		23	Minnesota	22.2
26	Missouri	22.0		25	Georgia	22.1
19	Montana	22.8		26	Missouri	22.0
15	Nebraska	23.9		27	Maryland	21.8
45	Nevada	16.5		28	North Carolina	21.7
40	New Hampshire	18.3		28	South Carolina	21.7
39	New Jersey	18.8		30	Mississippi	21.6
17	New Mexico	23.8		31	Texas	21.3
43	New York	17.8		32	Illinois	21.2
28	North Carolina	21.7		33	Florida	20.9
14	North Dakota	24.4		34	California	20.6
22	Ohio	22.3		35	Oklahoma	20.3
35	Oklahoma	20.3		36	West Virginia	20.0
15	Oregon	23.9		37	Arizona	19.6
13	Pennsylvania	24.7		38	Connecticut	19.5
44	Rhode Island	16.9		39	New Jersey	18.8
28	South Carolina	21.7		40	Iowa	18.3
1	South Dakota	32.5		40	New Hampshire	18.3
21	Tennessee	22.4		42	Indiana	18.1
31	Texas	21.3		43	New York	17.8
4	Utah	28.9		44	Rhode Island	16.9
49	Vermont	12.0		45	Nevada	16.5
10	Virginia	26.1		46	Hawaii	15.3
19	Washington	22.8		47	Michigan	13.9
36	West Virginia	20.0		48	Kansas	13.8
9	Wisconsin	26.3		49	Vermont	12.0
2	Wyoming	30.5		NA	Alabama**	NA
					District of Columbia	17.1

Source: U.S. Department of Justice, Federal Bureau of Investigation (unpublished data)
*Includes murder, rape, robbery, aggravated assault, burglary, larceny-theft and motor vehicle theft. A crime is considered cleared when at least one person is arrested, charged and turned over to the court for prosecution. Clearances recorded in 1993 may be for crimes which occurred in prior years. Several crimes may be cleared by the arrest of one person while the arrest of many persons may clear only one crime.
**Not available.

Percent of Violent Crimes Cleared in 1993

National Percent = 44.2% Cleared*

ALPHA ORDER			RANK ORDER		
RANK	**STATE**	**PERCENT**	**RANK**	**STATE**	**PERCENT**
NA	Alabama**	NA	1	South Dakota	70.8
18	Alaska	50.6	2	Nebraska	69.3
36	Arizona	44.1	2	Wyoming	69.3
10	Arkansas	56.1	4	Maine	67.5
33	California	45.3	5	Delaware	62.4
8	Colorado	57.3	6	Idaho	59.5
39	Connecticut	41.8	7	Virginia	58.5
5	Delaware	62.4	8	Colorado	57.3
27	Florida	47.0	9	Utah	56.4
30	Georgia	46.0	10	Arkansas	56.1
45	Hawaii	35.8	11	North Dakota	55.2
6	Idaho	59.5	12	Kentucky	55.0
44	Illinois	37.8	13	Massachusetts	54.9
43	Indiana	38.0	13	Vermont	54.9
28	Iowa	46.8	15	Wisconsin	53.3
48	Kansas	28.9	16	Oklahoma	51.9
12	Kentucky	55.0	17	Montana	51.4
38	Louisiana	42.1	18	Alaska	50.6
4	Maine	67.5	19	South Carolina	50.0
37	Maryland	42.7	20	New Mexico	49.4
13	Massachusetts	54.9	20	Pennsylvania	49.4
47	Michigan	29.1	22	Rhode Island	49.0
25	Minnesota	48.0	22	Texas	49.0
42	Mississippi	39.0	24	North Carolina	48.9
40	Missouri	41.7	25	Minnesota	48.0
17	Montana	51.4	26	Washington	47.1
2	Nebraska	69.3	27	Florida	47.0
49	Nevada	22.4	28	Iowa	46.8
35	New Hampshire	44.9	29	Tennessee	46.6
41	New Jersey	39.7	30	Georgia	46.0
20	New Mexico	49.4	31	Ohio	45.8
46	New York	34.0	32	Oregon	45.6
24	North Carolina	48.9	33	California	45.3
11	North Dakota	55.2	34	West Virginia	45.2
31	Ohio	45.8	35	New Hampshire	44.9
16	Oklahoma	51.9	36	Arizona	44.1
32	Oregon	45.6	37	Maryland	42.7
20	Pennsylvania	49.4	38	Louisiana	42.1
22	Rhode Island	49.0	39	Connecticut	41.8
19	South Carolina	50.0	40	Missouri	41.7
1	South Dakota	70.8	41	New Jersey	39.7
29	Tennessee	46.6	42	Mississippi	39.0
22	Texas	49.0	43	Indiana	38.0
9	Utah	56.4	44	Illinois	37.8
13	Vermont	54.9	45	Hawaii	35.8
7	Virginia	58.5	46	New York	34.0
26	Washington	47.1	47	Michigan	29.1
34	West Virginia	45.2	48	Kansas	28.9
15	Wisconsin	53.3	49	Nevada	22.4
2	Wyoming	69.3	NA	Alabama**	NA
				District of Columbia	38.3

Source: U.S. Department of Justice, Federal Bureau of Investigation (unpublished data)

*Includes murder, rape, robbery and aggravated assault. A crime is considered cleared when at least one person is arrested, charged and turned over to the court for prosecution. Clearances recorded in 1993 may be for crimes which occurred in prior years. Several crimes may be cleared by the arrest of one person while the arrest of many persons may clear only one crime.

**Not available.

Percent of Murders Cleared in 1993

National Percent = 65.6% Cleared*

ALPHA ORDER		
RANK	STATE	PERCENT
NA	Alabama**	NA
47	Alaska	48.0
20	Arizona	73.4
4	Arkansas	87.0
44	California	55.5
38	Colorado	60.3
39	Connecticut	59.2
12	Delaware	80.0
34	Florida	67.0
28	Georgia	71.3
21	Hawaii	73.3
26	Idaho	71.4
46	Illinois	48.2
45	Indiana	52.7
49	Iowa	43.2
35	Kansas	66.7
16	Kentucky	77.4
41	Louisiana	58.9
30	Maine	70.0
24	Maryland	72.3
33	Massachusetts	68.6
42	Michigan	58.8
8	Minnesota	84.5
13	Mississippi	78.3
29	Missouri	70.5
35	Montana	66.7
2	Nebraska	89.3
43	Nevada	56.9
40	New Hampshire	59.1
22	New Jersey	73.0
11	New Mexico	80.2
37	New York	62.4
17	North Carolina	75.5
1	North Dakota	100.0
23	Ohio	72.6
7	Oklahoma	84.6
25	Oregon	72.1
18	Pennsylvania	75.2
32	Rhode Island	69.2
9	South Carolina	82.5
15	South Dakota	77.8
26	Tennessee	71.4
31	Texas	69.3
19	Utah	74.6
48	Vermont	45.5
10	Virginia	80.7
14	Washington	77.9
6	West Virginia	86.5
5	Wisconsin	86.9
3	Wyoming	87.5

RANK ORDER		
RANK	STATE	PERCENT
1	North Dakota	100.0
2	Nebraska	89.3
3	Wyoming	87.5
4	Arkansas	87.0
5	Wisconsin	86.9
6	West Virginia	86.5
7	Oklahoma	84.6
8	Minnesota	84.5
9	South Carolina	82.5
10	Virginia	80.7
11	New Mexico	80.2
12	Delaware	80.0
13	Mississippi	78.3
14	Washington	77.9
15	South Dakota	77.8
16	Kentucky	77.4
17	North Carolina	75.5
18	Pennsylvania	75.2
19	Utah	74.6
20	Arizona	73.4
21	Hawaii	73.3
22	New Jersey	73.0
23	Ohio	72.6
24	Maryland	72.3
25	Oregon	72.1
26	Idaho	71.4
26	Tennessee	71.4
28	Georgia	71.3
29	Missouri	70.5
30	Maine	70.0
31	Texas	69.3
32	Rhode Island	69.2
33	Massachusetts	68.6
34	Florida	67.0
35	Kansas	66.7
35	Montana	66.7
37	New York	62.4
38	Colorado	60.3
39	Connecticut	59.2
40	New Hampshire	59.1
41	Louisiana	58.9
42	Michigan	58.8
43	Nevada	56.9
44	California	55.5
45	Indiana	52.7
46	Illinois	48.2
47	Alaska	48.0
48	Vermont	45.5
49	Iowa	43.2
NA	Alabama**	NA
	District of Columbia	52.2

Source: U.S. Department of Justice, Federal Bureau of Investigation
    unpublished data

*Includes nonnegligent manslaughter. A crime is considered cleared when at least one person is arrested, charged and turned over to the court for prosecution. Clearances recorded in 1993 may be for crimes which occurred in prior years. Several crimes may be cleared by the arrest of one person while the arrest of many persons may clear only one crime.

**Not available.

Percent of Rapes Cleared in 1993

National Percent = 52.8% Cleared*

ALPHA ORDER

RANK	STATE	PERCENT
NA	Alabama**	NA
39	Alaska	36.5
42	Arizona	32.9
5	Arkansas	61.0
25	California	52.6
14	Colorado	56.7
28	Connecticut	50.8
3	Delaware	65.1
19	Florida	54.6
8	Georgia	60.3
35	Hawaii	43.7
16	Idaho	55.7
43	Illinois	32.7
33	Indiana	46.1
40	Iowa	35.6
46	Kansas	28.8
17	Kentucky	55.4
31	Louisiana	46.8
4	Maine	64.8
10	Maryland	58.3
6	Massachusetts	60.7
NA	Michigan**	NA
NA	Minnesota**	NA
32	Mississippi	46.3
12	Missouri	56.9
44	Montana	31.7
26	Nebraska	51.9
47	Nevada	19.8
41	New Hampshire	33.9
13	New Jersey	56.8
37	New Mexico	37.3
30	New York	47.0
24	North Carolina	53.1
36	North Dakota	43.1
21	Ohio	53.8
9	Oklahoma	60.0
33	Oregon	46.1
7	Pennsylvania	60.6
38	Rhode Island	36.7
15	South Carolina	56.3
1	South Dakota	72.2
18	Tennessee	55.3
23	Texas	53.4
22	Utah	53.7
45	Vermont	31.5
2	Virginia	70.5
27	Washington	51.2
29	West Virginia	48.4
11	Wisconsin	57.1
20	Wyoming	54.3

RANK ORDER

RANK	STATE	PERCENT
1	South Dakota	72.2
2	Virginia	70.5
3	Delaware	65.1
4	Maine	64.8
5	Arkansas	61.0
6	Massachusetts	60.7
7	Pennsylvania	60.6
8	Georgia	60.3
9	Oklahoma	60.0
10	Maryland	58.3
11	Wisconsin	57.1
12	Missouri	56.9
13	New Jersey	56.8
14	Colorado	56.7
15	South Carolina	56.3
16	Idaho	55.7
17	Kentucky	55.4
18	Tennessee	55.3
19	Florida	54.6
20	Wyoming	54.3
21	Ohio	53.8
22	Utah	53.7
23	Texas	53.4
24	North Carolina	53.1
25	California	52.6
26	Nebraska	51.9
27	Washington	51.2
28	Connecticut	50.8
29	West Virginia	48.4
30	New York	47.0
31	Louisiana	46.8
32	Mississippi	46.3
33	Indiana	46.1
33	Oregon	46.1
35	Hawaii	43.7
36	North Dakota	43.1
37	New Mexico	37.3
38	Rhode Island	36.7
39	Alaska	36.5
40	Iowa	35.6
41	New Hampshire	33.9
42	Arizona	32.9
43	Illinois	32.7
44	Montana	31.7
45	Vermont	31.5
46	Kansas	28.8
47	Nevada	19.8
NA	Alabama**	NA
NA	Michigan**	NA
NA	Minnesota**	NA

District of Columbia	62.3

Source: U.S. Department of Justice, Federal Bureau of Investigation (unpublished data)
*Forcible rape including attempts. However, statutory rape without force and other sex offenses are excluded. A crime is considered cleared when at least one person is arrested, charged and turned over to the court for prosecution. Clearances recorded in 1993 may be for crimes which occurred in prior years. Several crimes may be cleared by the arrest of one person while the arrest of many persons may clear only one crime.
**Not available.

Percent of Robberies Cleared in 1993

National Percent = 23.5% Cleared*

<table>
<tr><td colspan="3">ALPHA ORDER</td><td colspan="3">RANK ORDER</td></tr>
<tr><th>RANK</th><th>STATE</th><th>PERCENT</th><th>RANK</th><th>STATE</th><th>PERCENT</th></tr>
<tr><td>NA</td><td>Alabama**</td><td>NA</td><td>1</td><td>South Dakota</td><td>48.0</td></tr>
<tr><td>44</td><td>Alaska</td><td>18.9</td><td>2</td><td>Nebraska</td><td>44.4</td></tr>
<tr><td>27</td><td>Arizona</td><td>26.2</td><td>3</td><td>Maine</td><td>41.8</td></tr>
<tr><td>11</td><td>Arkansas</td><td>31.5</td><td>4</td><td>Oklahoma</td><td>40.2</td></tr>
<tr><td>31</td><td>California</td><td>23.2</td><td>5</td><td>Kentucky</td><td>36.4</td></tr>
<tr><td>17</td><td>Colorado</td><td>29.9</td><td>6</td><td>Virginia</td><td>35.7</td></tr>
<tr><td>38</td><td>Connecticut</td><td>21.3</td><td>7</td><td>Idaho</td><td>33.3</td></tr>
<tr><td>14</td><td>Delaware</td><td>30.8</td><td>7</td><td>Vermont</td><td>33.3</td></tr>
<tr><td>30</td><td>Florida</td><td>23.9</td><td>9</td><td>Oregon</td><td>32.9</td></tr>
<tr><td>22</td><td>Georgia</td><td>28.2</td><td>10</td><td>North Carolina</td><td>31.7</td></tr>
<tr><td>32</td><td>Hawaii</td><td>23.1</td><td>11</td><td>Arkansas</td><td>31.5</td></tr>
<tr><td>7</td><td>Idaho</td><td>33.3</td><td>12</td><td>Wisconsin</td><td>31.4</td></tr>
<tr><td>47</td><td>Illinois</td><td>15.3</td><td>13</td><td>South Carolina</td><td>31.1</td></tr>
<tr><td>39</td><td>Indiana</td><td>20.7</td><td>14</td><td>Delaware</td><td>30.8</td></tr>
<tr><td>39</td><td>Iowa</td><td>20.7</td><td>14</td><td>North Dakota</td><td>30.8</td></tr>
<tr><td>46</td><td>Kansas</td><td>17.7</td><td>16</td><td>Utah</td><td>30.1</td></tr>
<tr><td>5</td><td>Kentucky</td><td>36.4</td><td>17</td><td>Colorado</td><td>29.9</td></tr>
<tr><td>29</td><td>Louisiana</td><td>24.1</td><td>18</td><td>Wyoming</td><td>29.6</td></tr>
<tr><td>3</td><td>Maine</td><td>41.8</td><td>19</td><td>Pennsylvania</td><td>29.5</td></tr>
<tr><td>43</td><td>Maryland</td><td>20.4</td><td>20</td><td>Texas</td><td>29.1</td></tr>
<tr><td>24</td><td>Massachusetts</td><td>26.9</td><td>21</td><td>Ohio</td><td>28.9</td></tr>
<tr><td>49</td><td>Michigan</td><td>11.3</td><td>22</td><td>Georgia</td><td>28.2</td></tr>
<tr><td>28</td><td>Minnesota</td><td>25.8</td><td>23</td><td>New Hampshire</td><td>27.4</td></tr>
<tr><td>34</td><td>Mississippi</td><td>22.4</td><td>24</td><td>Massachusetts</td><td>26.9</td></tr>
<tr><td>32</td><td>Missouri</td><td>23.1</td><td>24</td><td>West Virginia</td><td>26.9</td></tr>
<tr><td>41</td><td>Montana</td><td>20.6</td><td>26</td><td>Washington</td><td>26.4</td></tr>
<tr><td>2</td><td>Nebraska</td><td>44.4</td><td>27</td><td>Arizona</td><td>26.2</td></tr>
<tr><td>48</td><td>Nevada</td><td>12.2</td><td>28</td><td>Minnesota</td><td>25.8</td></tr>
<tr><td>23</td><td>New Hampshire</td><td>27.4</td><td>29</td><td>Louisiana</td><td>24.1</td></tr>
<tr><td>41</td><td>New Jersey</td><td>20.6</td><td>30</td><td>Florida</td><td>23.9</td></tr>
<tr><td>45</td><td>New Mexico</td><td>18.2</td><td>31</td><td>California</td><td>23.2</td></tr>
<tr><td>37</td><td>New York</td><td>21.5</td><td>32</td><td>Hawaii</td><td>23.1</td></tr>
<tr><td>10</td><td>North Carolina</td><td>31.7</td><td>32</td><td>Missouri</td><td>23.1</td></tr>
<tr><td>14</td><td>North Dakota</td><td>30.8</td><td>34</td><td>Mississippi</td><td>22.4</td></tr>
<tr><td>21</td><td>Ohio</td><td>28.9</td><td>35</td><td>Tennessee</td><td>22.3</td></tr>
<tr><td>4</td><td>Oklahoma</td><td>40.2</td><td>36</td><td>Rhode Island</td><td>21.7</td></tr>
<tr><td>9</td><td>Oregon</td><td>32.9</td><td>37</td><td>New York</td><td>21.5</td></tr>
<tr><td>19</td><td>Pennsylvania</td><td>29.5</td><td>38</td><td>Connecticut</td><td>21.3</td></tr>
<tr><td>36</td><td>Rhode Island</td><td>21.7</td><td>39</td><td>Indiana</td><td>20.7</td></tr>
<tr><td>13</td><td>South Carolina</td><td>31.1</td><td>39</td><td>Iowa</td><td>20.7</td></tr>
<tr><td>1</td><td>South Dakota</td><td>48.0</td><td>41</td><td>Montana</td><td>20.6</td></tr>
<tr><td>35</td><td>Tennessee</td><td>22.3</td><td>41</td><td>New Jersey</td><td>20.6</td></tr>
<tr><td>20</td><td>Texas</td><td>29.1</td><td>43</td><td>Maryland</td><td>20.4</td></tr>
<tr><td>16</td><td>Utah</td><td>30.1</td><td>44</td><td>Alaska</td><td>18.9</td></tr>
<tr><td>7</td><td>Vermont</td><td>33.3</td><td>45</td><td>New Mexico</td><td>18.2</td></tr>
<tr><td>6</td><td>Virginia</td><td>35.7</td><td>46</td><td>Kansas</td><td>17.7</td></tr>
<tr><td>26</td><td>Washington</td><td>26.4</td><td>47</td><td>Illinois</td><td>15.3</td></tr>
<tr><td>24</td><td>West Virginia</td><td>26.9</td><td>48</td><td>Nevada</td><td>12.2</td></tr>
<tr><td>12</td><td>Wisconsin</td><td>31.4</td><td>49</td><td>Michigan</td><td>11.3</td></tr>
<tr><td>18</td><td>Wyoming</td><td>29.6</td><td>NA</td><td>Alabama**</td><td>NA</td></tr>
<tr><td></td><td></td><td></td><td></td><td>District of Columbia</td><td>16.3</td></tr>
</table>

Source: U.S. Department of Justice, Federal Bureau of Investigation (unpublished data)
*Robbery is the taking of anything of value by force or threat of force. Attempts are included. A crime is considered cleared when at least one person is arrested, charged and turned over to the court for prosecution. Clearances recorded in 1993 may be for crimes which occurred in prior years. Several crimes may be cleared by the arrest of one person while the arrest of many persons may clear only one crime.
**Not available.

Percent of Aggravated Assaults Cleared in 1993

National Percent = 55.5% Cleared*

ALPHA ORDER				RANK ORDER		
RANK	STATE	PERCENT		RANK	STATE	PERCENT
NA	Alabama**	NA		1	Maine	75.5
18	Alaska	60.1		2	Nebraska	75.2
40	Arizona	50.3		3	Delaware	74.1
14	Arkansas	62.3		3	Wyoming	74.1
22	California	59.1		5	South Dakota	72.6
9	Colorado	65.5		5	Virginia	72.6
23	Connecticut	57.9		7	Wisconsin	71.8
3	Delaware	74.1		8	Vermont	70.4
29	Florida	56.6		9	Colorado	65.5
33	Georgia	54.7		10	Pennsylvania	65.1
46	Hawaii	43.3		11	Utah	64.8
16	Idaho	61.4		12	North Dakota	63.7
34	Illinois	54.4		13	Massachusetts	63.1
45	Indiana	44.1		14	Arkansas	62.3
37	Iowa	52.6		15	Minnesota	61.5
48	Kansas	32.7		16	Idaho	61.4
21	Kentucky	59.4		17	Rhode Island	60.4
41	Louisiana	49.7		18	Alaska	60.1
1	Maine	75.5		19	New Hampshire	60.0
20	Maryland	59.9		20	Maryland	59.9
13	Massachusetts	63.1		21	Kentucky	59.4
47	Michigan	37.5		22	California	59.1
15	Minnesota	61.5		23	Connecticut	57.9
43	Mississippi	47.9		23	Montana	57.9
38	Missouri	50.4		23	Ohio	57.9
23	Montana	57.9		26	Texas	57.5
2	Nebraska	75.2		27	Tennessee	57.2
49	Nevada	30.4		28	New Mexico	56.7
19	New Hampshire	60.0		29	Florida	56.6
30	New Jersey	56.4		30	New Jersey	56.4
28	New Mexico	56.7		31	North Carolina	55.4
44	New York	47.4		32	Washington	54.9
31	North Carolina	55.4		33	Georgia	54.7
12	North Dakota	63.7		34	Illinois	54.4
23	Ohio	57.9		35	South Carolina	53.7
36	Oklahoma	53.5		36	Oklahoma	53.5
38	Oregon	50.4		37	Iowa	52.6
10	Pennsylvania	65.1		38	Missouri	50.4
17	Rhode Island	60.4		38	Oregon	50.4
35	South Carolina	53.7		40	Arizona	50.3
5	South Dakota	72.6		41	Louisiana	49.7
27	Tennessee	57.2		42	West Virginia	48.4
26	Texas	57.5		43	Mississippi	47.9
11	Utah	64.8		44	New York	47.4
8	Vermont	70.4		45	Indiana	44.1
5	Virginia	72.6		46	Hawaii	43.3
32	Washington	54.9		47	Michigan	37.5
42	West Virginia	48.4		48	Kansas	32.7
7	Wisconsin	71.8		49	Nevada	30.4
3	Wyoming	74.1		NA	Alabama**	NA

	District of Columbia	54.1

Source: U.S. Department of Justice, Federal Bureau of Investigation (unpublished data)
*Aggravated assault is an attack for the purpose of inflicting severe bodily injury. A crime is considered cleared when at least one person is arrested, charged and turned over to the court for prosecution. Clearances recorded in 1993 may be for crimes which occurred in prior years. Several crimes may be cleared by the arrest of one person while the arrest of many persons may clear only one crime.
**Not available.

Percent of Property Crimes Cleared in 1993

National Percent = 17.4% Cleared*

ALPHA ORDER

RANK ORDER

RANK	STATE	PERCENT		RANK	STATE	PERCENT
NA	Alabama**	NA		1	Illinois	37.8
9	Alaska	23.6		2	South Dakota	29.6
35	Arizona	16.9		3	Maine	27.8
6	Arkansas	24.8		4	Wyoming	27.6
40	California	15.6		5	Utah	27.2
14	Colorado	21.7		6	Arkansas	24.8
32	Connecticut	17.1		7	Wisconsin	24.4
12	Delaware	22.0		8	Idaho	24.2
36	Florida	16.5		9	Alaska	23.6
24	Georgia	18.8		10	North Dakota	23.5
44	Hawaii	14.4		11	Virginia	22.9
8	Idaho	24.2		12	Delaware	22.0
1	Illinois	37.8		13	Oregon	21.9
40	Indiana	15.6		14	Colorado	21.7
40	Iowa	15.6		15	Montana	21.4
48	Kansas	11.1		15	Nebraska	21.4
18	Kentucky	20.7		17	Pennsylvania	21.0
26	Louisiana	18.5		18	Kentucky	20.7
3	Maine	27.8		19	Washington	20.5
29	Maryland	17.7		20	Minnesota	20.3
33	Massachusetts	17.0		21	Mississippi	19.7
47	Michigan	11.5		22	Ohio	19.1
20	Minnesota	20.3		23	New Mexico	19.0
21	Mississippi	19.7		24	Georgia	18.8
25	Missouri	18.6		25	Missouri	18.6
15	Montana	21.4		26	Louisiana	18.5
15	Nebraska	21.4		27	Tennessee	18.0
40	Nevada	15.6		28	North Carolina	17.9
33	New Hampshire	17.0		29	Maryland	17.7
38	New Jersey	15.7		29	West Virginia	17.7
23	New Mexico	19.0		31	Texas	17.6
45	New York	13.7		32	Connecticut	17.1
28	North Carolina	17.9		33	Massachusetts	17.0
10	North Dakota	23.5		33	New Hampshire	17.0
22	Ohio	19.1		35	Arizona	16.9
37	Oklahoma	16.0		36	Florida	16.5
13	Oregon	21.9		37	Oklahoma	16.0
17	Pennsylvania	21.0		38	New Jersey	15.7
45	Rhode Island	13.7		38	South Carolina	15.7
38	South Carolina	15.7		40	California	15.6
2	South Dakota	29.6		40	Indiana	15.6
27	Tennessee	18.0		40	Iowa	15.6
31	Texas	17.6		40	Nevada	15.6
5	Utah	27.2		44	Hawaii	14.4
49	Vermont	10.6		45	New York	13.7
11	Virginia	22.9		45	Rhode Island	13.7
19	Washington	20.5		47	Michigan	11.5
29	West Virginia	17.7		48	Kansas	11.1
7	Wisconsin	24.4		49	Vermont	10.6
4	Wyoming	27.6		NA	Alabama**	NA
					District of Columbia	10.2

Source: U.S. Department of Justice, Federal Bureau of Investigation (unpublished data)

*Property crimes are offenses of burglary, larceny-theft and motor vehicle theft. A crime is considered cleared when at least one person is arrested, charged and turned over to the court for prosecution. Clearances recorded in 1993 may be for crimes which occurred in prior years. Several crimes may be cleared by the arrest of one person while the arrest of many persons may clear only one crime.

**Not available.

Percent of Burglaries Cleared in 1993

National Percent = 13.1% Cleared*

ALPHA ORDER

RANK	STATE	PERCENT
NA	Alabama**	NA
6	Alaska	18.9
39	Arizona	9.8
10	Arkansas	16.9
31	California	12.4
22	Colorado	14.6
37	Connecticut	11.0
5	Delaware	19.0
19	Florida	14.9
25	Georgia	13.4
45	Hawaii	8.1
16	Idaho	15.4
41	Illinois	9.2
39	Indiana	9.8
41	Iowa	9.2
49	Kansas	5.3
7	Kentucky	17.6
27	Louisiana	13.1
3	Maine	21.3
17	Maryland	15.0
21	Massachusetts	14.7
47	Michigan	7.7
35	Minnesota	11.2
30	Mississippi	12.5
26	Missouri	13.3
7	Montana	17.6
13	Nebraska	16.4
46	Nevada	7.9
41	New Hampshire	9.2
33	New Jersey	12.2
44	New Mexico	8.4
37	New York	11.0
19	North Carolina	14.9
14	North Dakota	15.9
24	Ohio	13.5
32	Oklahoma	12.3
17	Oregon	15.0
10	Pennsylvania	16.9
36	Rhode Island	11.1
28	South Carolina	12.9
2	South Dakota	21.4
15	Tennessee	15.6
23	Texas	13.8
10	Utah	16.9
48	Vermont	7.1
1	Virginia	21.9
33	Washington	12.2
29	West Virginia	12.6
9	Wisconsin	17.0
4	Wyoming	19.9

RANK ORDER

RANK	STATE	PERCENT
1	Virginia	21.9
2	South Dakota	21.4
3	Maine	21.3
4	Wyoming	19.9
5	Delaware	19.0
6	Alaska	18.9
7	Kentucky	17.6
7	Montana	17.6
9	Wisconsin	17.0
10	Arkansas	16.9
10	Pennsylvania	16.9
10	Utah	16.9
13	Nebraska	16.4
14	North Dakota	15.9
15	Tennessee	15.6
16	Idaho	15.4
17	Maryland	15.0
17	Oregon	15.0
19	Florida	14.9
19	North Carolina	14.9
21	Massachusetts	14.7
22	Colorado	14.6
23	Texas	13.8
24	Ohio	13.5
25	Georgia	13.4
26	Missouri	13.3
27	Louisiana	13.1
28	South Carolina	12.9
29	West Virginia	12.6
30	Mississippi	12.5
31	California	12.4
32	Oklahoma	12.3
33	New Jersey	12.2
33	Washington	12.2
35	Minnesota	11.2
36	Rhode Island	11.1
37	Connecticut	11.0
37	New York	11.0
39	Arizona	9.8
39	Indiana	9.8
41	Illinois	9.2
41	Iowa	9.2
41	New Hampshire	9.2
44	New Mexico	8.4
45	Hawaii	8.1
46	Nevada	7.9
47	Michigan	7.7
48	Vermont	7.1
49	Kansas	5.3
NA	Alabama**	NA

District of Columbia   9.8

Source: U.S. Department of Justice, Federal Bureau of Investigation (unpublished data)
Burglary is the unlawful entry of a structure to commit a felony or theft. Attempts are included. A crime is considered cleared when at least one person is arrested, charged and turned over to the court for prosecution. Clearances recorded in 1993 may be for crimes which occurred in prior years. Several crimes may be cleared by the arrest of one person while the arrest of many persons may clear only one crime.
**Not available.

80

Percent of Larcenies and Thefts Cleared in 1993

National Percent = 19.8% Cleared*

ALPHA ORDER				RANK ORDER		
RANK	STATE	PERCENT		RANK	STATE	PERCENT
NA	Alabama**	NA		1	South Dakota	30.9
8	Alaska	25.1		2	Maine	29.1
27	Arizona	20.4		3	Utah	28.8
5	Arkansas	27.3		4	Wyoming	28.3
36	California	18.9		5	Arkansas	27.3
12	Colorado	23.8		6	Wisconsin	26.5
24	Connecticut	21.1		7	Idaho	26.1
13	Delaware	23.7		8	Alaska	25.1
39	Florida	17.6		9	Oregon	24.5
31	Georgia	19.8		10	New Mexico	24.2
45	Hawaii	16.0		11	North Dakota	24.1
7	Idaho	26.1		12	Colorado	23.8
23	Illinois	21.2		13	Delaware	23.7
39	Indiana	17.6		14	Pennsylvania	23.4
38	Iowa	17.7		15	Washington	23.1
47	Kansas	14.1		16	Mississippi	23.0
19	Kentucky	21.8		17	Minnesota	22.9
19	Louisiana	21.8		18	Virginia	22.5
2	Maine	29.1		19	Kentucky	21.8
35	Maryland	19.2		19	Louisiana	21.8
42	Massachusetts	17.5		21	Nebraska	21.7
48	Michigan	13.2		22	Missouri	21.3
17	Minnesota	22.9		23	Illinois	21.2
16	Mississippi	23.0		24	Connecticut	21.1
22	Missouri	21.3		25	Montana	21.0
25	Montana	21.0		26	Ohio	20.8
21	Nebraska	21.7		27	Arizona	20.4
30	Nevada	19.9		28	New Jersey	20.1
33	New Hampshire	19.4		28	Tennessee	20.1
28	New Jersey	20.1		30	Nevada	19.9
10	New Mexico	24.2		31	Georgia	19.8
44	New York	16.7		32	West Virginia	19.5
37	North Carolina	18.5		33	New Hampshire	19.4
11	North Dakota	24.1		34	Texas	19.3
26	Ohio	20.8		35	Maryland	19.2
39	Oklahoma	17.6		36	California	18.9
9	Oregon	24.5		37	North Carolina	18.5
14	Pennsylvania	23.4		38	Iowa	17.7
45	Rhode Island	16.0		39	Florida	17.6
43	South Carolina	16.9		39	Indiana	17.6
1	South Dakota	30.9		39	Oklahoma	17.6
28	Tennessee	20.1		42	Massachusetts	17.5
34	Texas	19.3		43	South Carolina	16.9
3	Utah	28.8		44	New York	16.7
49	Vermont	11.8		45	Hawaii	16.0
18	Virginia	22.5		45	Rhode Island	16.0
15	Washington	23.1		47	Kansas	14.1
32	West Virginia	19.5		48	Michigan	13.2
6	Wisconsin	26.5		49	Vermont	11.8
4	Wyoming	28.3		NA	Alabama**	NA
					District of Columbia	10.3

Source: U.S. Department of Justice, Federal Bureau of Investigation (unpublished data)
*Larceny and theft is the unlawful taking of property without use of force, violence or fraud. Attempts are included. Motor vehicle thefts are excluded. A crime is considered cleared when at least one person is arrested, charged and turned over to the court for prosecution. Clearances recorded in 1993 may be for crimes which occurred in prior years. Several crimes may be cleared by the arrest of one person while the arrest of many persons may clear only one crime.
**Not available.

Percent of Motor Vehicle Thefts Cleared in 1993

National Percent = 13.6% Cleared*

ALPHA ORDER				RANK ORDER		
RANK	STATE	PERCENT		RANK	STATE	PERCENT
NA	Alabama**	NA		1	Wyoming	46.3
20	Alaska	19.9		2	Maine	43.5
39	Arizona	11.6		3	South Dakota	42.9
9	Arkansas	30.4		4	Montana	36.4
43	California	10.0		5	Nebraska	35.3
14	Colorado	21.7		6	Utah	34.7
44	Connecticut	9.5		7	North Dakota	33.7
31	Delaware	14.8		8	Idaho	31.4
34	Florida	14.5		9	Arkansas	30.4
12	Georgia	24.7		10	Virginia	28.9
33	Hawaii	14.6		11	North Carolina	27.1
8	Idaho	31.4		12	Georgia	24.7
36	Illinois	13.1		13	Kentucky	22.7
35	Indiana	14.2		14	Colorado	21.7
21	Iowa	18.8		15	Wisconsin	21.6
41	Kansas	11.3		16	Vermont	21.0
13	Kentucky	22.7		17	Minnesota	20.7
40	Louisiana	11.4		18	Mississippi	20.6
2	Maine	43.5		19	Ohio	20.3
30	Maryland	14.9		20	Alaska	19.9
23	Massachusetts	18.5		21	Iowa	18.8
46	Michigan	9.4		21	West Virginia	18.8
17	Minnesota	20.7		23	Massachusetts	18.5
18	Mississippi	20.6		24	Oregon	17.7
32	Missouri	14.7		25	Washington	16.7
4	Montana	36.4		26	Pennsylvania	16.6
5	Nebraska	35.3		27	Oklahoma	16.4
47	Nevada	9.1		28	Texas	15.7
38	New Hampshire	12.2		29	South Carolina	15.4
49	New Jersey	5.1		30	Maryland	14.9
42	New Mexico	11.2		31	Delaware	14.8
48	New York	7.5		32	Missouri	14.7
11	North Carolina	27.1		33	Hawaii	14.6
7	North Dakota	33.7		34	Florida	14.5
19	Ohio	20.3		35	Indiana	14.2
27	Oklahoma	16.4		36	Illinois	13.1
24	Oregon	17.7		37	Tennessee	13.0
26	Pennsylvania	16.6		38	New Hampshire	12.2
44	Rhode Island	9.5		39	Arizona	11.6
29	South Carolina	15.4		40	Louisiana	11.4
3	South Dakota	42.9		41	Kansas	11.3
37	Tennessee	13.0		42	New Mexico	11.2
28	Texas	15.7		43	California	10.0
6	Utah	34.7		44	Connecticut	9.5
16	Vermont	21.0		44	Rhode Island	9.5
10	Virginia	28.9		46	Michigan	9.4
25	Washington	16.7		47	Nevada	9.1
21	West Virginia	18.8		48	New York	7.5
15	Wisconsin	21.6		49	New Jersey	5.1
1	Wyoming	46.3		NA	Alabama**	NA
					District of Columbia	9.8

Source: U.S. Department of Justice, Federal Bureau of Investigation (unpublished data)
*Motor vehicle theft includes the theft or attempted theft of a self-propelled vehicle. Excludes motorboats, construction equipment, airplanes and farming equipment. A crime is considered cleared when at least one person is arrested, charged and turned over to the court for prosecution. Clearances recorded in 1993 may be for crimes which occurred in prior years. Several crimes may be cleared by the arrest of one person while the arrest of many persons may clear only one crime.
**Not available.

II. CORRECTIONS

II. CORRECTIONS (continued)

Prisoners in State Correctional Institutions in 1994

National Total = 919,143 State Prisoners*

ALPHA ORDER

RANK	STATE	PRISONERS	% of USA
16	Alabama	19,098	2.08%
41	Alaska	2,738	0.30%
17	Arizona	18,809	2.05%
29	Arkansas	8,916	0.97%
1	California	124,813	13.58%
27	Colorado	9,954	1.08%
21	Connecticut	14,427	1.57%
35	Delaware	4,324	0.47%
4	Florida	56,052	6.10%
8	Georgia	30,292	3.30%
37	Hawaii	3,246	0.35%
40	Idaho	2,861	0.31%
7	Illinois	35,614	3.87%
20	Indiana	14,826	1.61%
33	Iowa	5,090	0.55%
32	Kansas	6,090	0.66%
23	Kentucky	10,724	1.17%
12	Louisiana	23,333	2.54%
47	Maine	1,468	0.16%
14	Maryland	20,887	2.27%
26	Massachusetts	10,072	1.10%
6	Michigan	40,220	4.38%
34	Minnesota	4,573	0.50%
25	Mississippi	10,631	1.16%
18	Missouri	16,957	1.84%
45	Montana	1,654	0.18%
42	Nebraska	2,449	0.27%
30	Nevada	6,745	0.73%
44	New Hampshire	1,895	0.21%
11	New Jersey	24,471	2.66%
36	New Mexico	3,704	0.40%
3	New York	65,962	7.18%
13	North Carolina	22,650	2.46%
50	North Dakota	522	0.06%
5	Ohio	41,156	4.48%
19	Oklahoma	16,306	1.77%
31	Oregon	6,723	0.73%
9	Pennsylvania	27,071	2.95%
38	Rhode Island	3,049	0.33%
15	South Carolina	19,646	2.14%
46	South Dakota	1,636	0.18%
22	Tennessee	14,397	1.57%
2	Texas	100,136	10.89%
39	Utah	2,948	0.32%
48	Vermont	1,182	0.13%
10	Virginia	24,822	2.70%
24	Washington	10,650	1.16%
43	West Virginia	1,941	0.21%
28	Wisconsin	9,206	1.00%
49	Wyoming	1,174	0.13%

RANK ORDER

RANK	STATE	PRISONERS	% of USA
1	California	124,813	13.58%
2	Texas	100,136	10.89%
3	New York	65,962	7.18%
4	Florida	56,052	6.10%
5	Ohio	41,156	4.48%
6	Michigan	40,220	4.38%
7	Illinois	35,614	3.87%
8	Georgia	30,292	3.30%
9	Pennsylvania	27,071	2.95%
10	Virginia	24,822	2.70%
11	New Jersey	24,471	2.66%
12	Louisiana	23,333	2.54%
13	North Carolina	22,650	2.46%
14	Maryland	20,887	2.27%
15	South Carolina	19,646	2.14%
16	Alabama	19,098	2.08%
17	Arizona	18,809	2.05%
18	Missouri	16,957	1.84%
19	Oklahoma	16,306	1.77%
20	Indiana	14,826	1.61%
21	Connecticut	14,427	1.57%
22	Tennessee	14,397	1.57%
23	Kentucky	10,724	1.17%
24	Washington	10,650	1.16%
25	Mississippi	10,631	1.16%
26	Massachusetts	10,072	1.10%
27	Colorado	9,954	1.08%
28	Wisconsin	9,206	1.00%
29	Arkansas	8,916	0.97%
30	Nevada	6,745	0.73%
31	Oregon	6,723	0.73%
32	Kansas	6,090	0.66%
33	Iowa	5,090	0.55%
34	Minnesota	4,573	0.50%
35	Delaware	4,324	0.47%
36	New Mexico	3,704	0.40%
37	Hawaii	3,246	0.35%
38	Rhode Island	3,049	0.33%
39	Utah	2,948	0.32%
40	Idaho	2,861	0.31%
41	Alaska	2,738	0.30%
42	Nebraska	2,449	0.27%
43	West Virginia	1,941	0.21%
44	New Hampshire	1,895	0.21%
45	Montana	1,654	0.18%
46	South Dakota	1,636	0.18%
47	Maine	1,468	0.16%
48	Vermont	1,182	0.13%
49	Wyoming	1,174	0.13%
50	North Dakota	522	0.06%
	District of Columbia	11,033	1.20%

Source: U.S. Department of Justice, Bureau of Justice Statistics
   Press Release (October 27, 1994)
*As of June 30, 1994. Totals include inmates sentenced to more than one year and those sentenced to a year or less or with no sentence. Does not include 93,708 prisoners under federal jurisdiction. State and federal prisoners combined total 1,012,851.

State Prisoner Incarceration Rate in 1994

National Rate = 343 State Prisoners per 100,000 Population*

ALPHA ORDER

RANK ORDER

RANK	STATE	RATE		RANK	STATE	RATE
7	Alabama	439		1	Texas	545
27	Alaska	256		2	Louisiana	514
6	Arizona	448		3	South Carolina	504
18	Arkansas	355		4	Oklahoma	501
14	California	382		5	Nevada	456
26	Colorado	272		6	Arizona	448
19	Connecticut	331		7	Alabama	439
12	Delaware	391		8	Michigan	423
10	Florida	404		9	Georgia	417
9	Georgia	417		10	Florida	404
40	Hawaii	170		11	Maryland	392
29	Idaho	253		12	Delaware	391
23	Illinois	302		13	Mississippi	385
27	Indiana	256		14	California	382
38	Iowa	180		15	Virginia	374
31	Kansas	239		16	Ohio	369
24	Kentucky	281		17	New York	361
2	Louisiana	514		18	Arkansas	355
47	Maine	113		19	Connecticut	331
11	Maryland	392		20	Missouri	321
43	Massachusetts	165		21	North Carolina	314
8	Michigan	423		22	New Jersey	307
49	Minnesota	100		23	Illinois	302
13	Mississippi	385		24	Kentucky	281
20	Missouri	321		25	Tennessee	278
36	Montana	192		26	Colorado	272
45	Nebraska	148		27	Alaska	256
5	Nevada	456		27	Indiana	256
42	New Hampshire	167		29	Idaho	253
22	New Jersey	307		30	Wyoming	247
34	New Mexico	216		31	Kansas	239
17	New York	361		32	South Dakota	227
21	North Carolina	314		33	Pennsylvania	224
50	North Dakota	75		34	New Mexico	216
16	Ohio	369		35	Washington	198
4	Oklahoma	501		36	Montana	192
41	Oregon	169		37	Rhode Island	185
33	Pennsylvania	224		38	Iowa	180
37	Rhode Island	185		39	Wisconsin	172
3	South Carolina	504		40	Hawaii	170
32	South Dakota	227		41	Oregon	169
25	Tennessee	278		42	New Hampshire	167
1	Texas	545		43	Massachusetts	165
44	Utah	154		44	Utah	154
46	Vermont	138		45	Nebraska	148
15	Virginia	374		46	Vermont	138
35	Washington	198		47	Maine	113
48	West Virginia	106		48	West Virginia	106
39	Wisconsin	172		49	Minnesota	100
30	Wyoming	247		50	North Dakota	75

District of Columbia   1,578

Source: U.S. Department of Justice, Bureau of Justice Statistics
    Press Release (October 27, 1994)

*As of June 30, 1994. Includes only inmates sentenced to more than one year. Does not include federal incarceration rate of 30 prisoners per 100,000 population. State and federal combined incarceration rate is 373 prisoners per 100,000 population.

Prisoners in State Correctional Institutions in 1993

National Total = 854,844 State Prisoners*

<table>
<tr><td colspan="4">ALPHA ORDER</td><td colspan="4">RANK ORDER</td></tr>
<tr><td>RANK</td><td>STATE</td><td>PRISONERS</td><td>% of USA</td><td>RANK</td><td>STATE</td><td>PRISONERS</td><td>% of USA</td></tr>
<tr><td>16</td><td>Alabama</td><td>18,349</td><td>2.15%</td><td>1</td><td>California</td><td>115,534</td><td>13.52%</td></tr>
<tr><td>38</td><td>Alaska</td><td>2,928</td><td>0.34%</td><td>2</td><td>Texas</td><td>84,551</td><td>9.89%</td></tr>
<tr><td>17</td><td>Arizona</td><td>16,998</td><td>1.99%</td><td>3</td><td>New York</td><td>63,875</td><td>7.47%</td></tr>
<tr><td>28</td><td>Arkansas</td><td>8,736</td><td>1.02%</td><td>4</td><td>Florida</td><td>50,603</td><td>5.92%</td></tr>
<tr><td>1</td><td>California</td><td>115,534</td><td>13.52%</td><td>5</td><td>Michigan</td><td>39,893</td><td>4.67%</td></tr>
<tr><td>27</td><td>Colorado</td><td>9,188</td><td>1.07%</td><td>6</td><td>Ohio</td><td>39,792</td><td>4.65%</td></tr>
<tr><td>22</td><td>Connecticut</td><td>12,067</td><td>1.41%</td><td>7</td><td>Illinois</td><td>33,072</td><td>3.87%</td></tr>
<tr><td>35</td><td>Delaware</td><td>4,284</td><td>0.50%</td><td>8</td><td>Georgia</td><td>27,004</td><td>3.16%</td></tr>
<tr><td>4</td><td>Florida</td><td>50,603</td><td>5.92%</td><td>9</td><td>Pennsylvania</td><td>25,588</td><td>2.99%</td></tr>
<tr><td>8</td><td>Georgia</td><td>27,004</td><td>3.16%</td><td>10</td><td>New Jersey</td><td>22,837</td><td>2.67%</td></tr>
<tr><td>37</td><td>Hawaii</td><td>3,079</td><td>0.36%</td><td>11</td><td>Louisiana</td><td>21,915</td><td>2.56%</td></tr>
<tr><td>41</td><td>Idaho</td><td>2,602</td><td>0.30%</td><td>12</td><td>Virginia</td><td>21,857</td><td>2.56%</td></tr>
<tr><td>7</td><td>Illinois</td><td>33,072</td><td>3.87%</td><td>13</td><td>North Carolina</td><td>21,086</td><td>2.47%</td></tr>
<tr><td>20</td><td>Indiana</td><td>14,221</td><td>1.66%</td><td>14</td><td>Maryland</td><td>20,173</td><td>2.36%</td></tr>
<tr><td>33</td><td>Iowa</td><td>4,695</td><td>0.55%</td><td>15</td><td>South Carolina</td><td>18,892</td><td>2.21%</td></tr>
<tr><td>32</td><td>Kansas</td><td>6,230</td><td>0.73%</td><td>16</td><td>Alabama</td><td>18,349</td><td>2.15%</td></tr>
<tr><td>23</td><td>Kentucky</td><td>10,526</td><td>1.23%</td><td>17</td><td>Arizona</td><td>16,998</td><td>1.99%</td></tr>
<tr><td>11</td><td>Louisiana</td><td>21,915</td><td>2.56%</td><td>18</td><td>Missouri</td><td>16,540</td><td>1.93%</td></tr>
<tr><td>46</td><td>Maine</td><td>1,470</td><td>0.17%</td><td>19</td><td>Oklahoma</td><td>15,676</td><td>1.83%</td></tr>
<tr><td>14</td><td>Maryland</td><td>20,173</td><td>2.36%</td><td>20</td><td>Indiana</td><td>14,221</td><td>1.66%</td></tr>
<tr><td>25</td><td>Massachusetts</td><td>9,950</td><td>1.16%</td><td>21</td><td>Tennessee</td><td>12,567</td><td>1.47%</td></tr>
<tr><td>5</td><td>Michigan</td><td>39,893</td><td>4.67%</td><td>22</td><td>Connecticut</td><td>12,067</td><td>1.41%</td></tr>
<tr><td>34</td><td>Minnesota</td><td>4,286</td><td>0.50%</td><td>23</td><td>Kentucky</td><td>10,526</td><td>1.23%</td></tr>
<tr><td>26</td><td>Mississippi</td><td>9,586</td><td>1.12%</td><td>24</td><td>Washington</td><td>10,349</td><td>1.21%</td></tr>
<tr><td>18</td><td>Missouri</td><td>16,540</td><td>1.93%</td><td>25</td><td>Massachusetts</td><td>9,950</td><td>1.16%</td></tr>
<tr><td>47</td><td>Montana</td><td>1,445</td><td>0.17%</td><td>26</td><td>Mississippi</td><td>9,586</td><td>1.12%</td></tr>
<tr><td>42</td><td>Nebraska</td><td>2,544</td><td>0.30%</td><td>27</td><td>Colorado</td><td>9,188</td><td>1.07%</td></tr>
<tr><td>31</td><td>Nevada</td><td>6,512</td><td>0.76%</td><td>28</td><td>Arkansas</td><td>8,736</td><td>1.02%</td></tr>
<tr><td>44</td><td>New Hampshire</td><td>1,765</td><td>0.21%</td><td>29</td><td>Wisconsin</td><td>8,397</td><td>0.98%</td></tr>
<tr><td>10</td><td>New Jersey</td><td>22,837</td><td>2.67%</td><td>30</td><td>Oregon</td><td>6,626</td><td>0.78%</td></tr>
<tr><td>36</td><td>New Mexico</td><td>3,440</td><td>0.40%</td><td>31</td><td>Nevada</td><td>6,512</td><td>0.76%</td></tr>
<tr><td>3</td><td>New York</td><td>63,875</td><td>7.47%</td><td>32</td><td>Kansas</td><td>6,230</td><td>0.73%</td></tr>
<tr><td>13</td><td>North Carolina</td><td>21,086</td><td>2.47%</td><td>33</td><td>Iowa</td><td>4,695</td><td>0.55%</td></tr>
<tr><td>50</td><td>North Dakota</td><td>491</td><td>0.06%</td><td>34</td><td>Minnesota</td><td>4,286</td><td>0.50%</td></tr>
<tr><td>6</td><td>Ohio</td><td>39,792</td><td>4.65%</td><td>35</td><td>Delaware</td><td>4,284</td><td>0.50%</td></tr>
<tr><td>19</td><td>Oklahoma</td><td>15,676</td><td>1.83%</td><td>36</td><td>New Mexico</td><td>3,440</td><td>0.40%</td></tr>
<tr><td>30</td><td>Oregon</td><td>6,626</td><td>0.78%</td><td>37</td><td>Hawaii</td><td>3,079</td><td>0.36%</td></tr>
<tr><td>9</td><td>Pennsylvania</td><td>25,588</td><td>2.99%</td><td>38</td><td>Alaska</td><td>2,928</td><td>0.34%</td></tr>
<tr><td>40</td><td>Rhode Island</td><td>2,824</td><td>0.33%</td><td>39</td><td>Utah</td><td>2,827</td><td>0.33%</td></tr>
<tr><td>15</td><td>South Carolina</td><td>18,892</td><td>2.21%</td><td>40</td><td>Rhode Island</td><td>2,824</td><td>0.33%</td></tr>
<tr><td>45</td><td>South Dakota</td><td>1,538</td><td>0.18%</td><td>41</td><td>Idaho</td><td>2,602</td><td>0.30%</td></tr>
<tr><td>21</td><td>Tennessee</td><td>12,567</td><td>1.47%</td><td>42</td><td>Nebraska</td><td>2,544</td><td>0.30%</td></tr>
<tr><td>2</td><td>Texas</td><td>84,551</td><td>9.89%</td><td>43</td><td>West Virginia</td><td>1,859</td><td>0.22%</td></tr>
<tr><td>39</td><td>Utah</td><td>2,827</td><td>0.33%</td><td>44</td><td>New Hampshire</td><td>1,765</td><td>0.21%</td></tr>
<tr><td>48</td><td>Vermont</td><td>1,222</td><td>0.14%</td><td>45</td><td>South Dakota</td><td>1,538</td><td>0.18%</td></tr>
<tr><td>12</td><td>Virginia</td><td>21,857</td><td>2.56%</td><td>46</td><td>Maine</td><td>1,470</td><td>0.17%</td></tr>
<tr><td>24</td><td>Washington</td><td>10,349</td><td>1.21%</td><td>47</td><td>Montana</td><td>1,445</td><td>0.17%</td></tr>
<tr><td>43</td><td>West Virginia</td><td>1,859</td><td>0.22%</td><td>48</td><td>Vermont</td><td>1,222</td><td>0.14%</td></tr>
<tr><td>29</td><td>Wisconsin</td><td>8,397</td><td>0.98%</td><td>49</td><td>Wyoming</td><td>1,060</td><td>0.12%</td></tr>
<tr><td>49</td><td>Wyoming</td><td>1,060</td><td>0.12%</td><td>50</td><td>North Dakota</td><td>491</td><td>0.06%</td></tr>
<tr><td></td><td></td><td></td><td></td><td></td><td>District of Columbia</td><td>11,295</td><td>1.32%</td></tr>
</table>

Source: U.S. Department of Justice, Bureau of Justice Statistics
  Press Release (October 27, 1994)
*As of June 30, 1993. Totals include inmates sentenced to more than one year and those sentenced to a year or less or with no sentence. Does not include 86,972 prisoners under federal jurisdiction. State and federal prisoners combined total 941,816.

Percent Change in Number of State Prisoners: 1993 to 1994

National Percent Change = 7.5% Increase*

ALPHA ORDER

RANK	STATE	PERCENT CHANGE
31	Alabama	4.1
50	Alaska	(6.5)
10	Arizona	10.7
40	Arkansas	2.1
15	California	8.0
14	Colorado	8.3
1	Connecticut	19.6
44	Delaware	0.9
8	Florida	10.8
6	Georgia	12.2
27	Hawaii	5.4
11	Idaho	10.0
17	Illinois	7.7
29	Indiana	4.3
13	Iowa	8.4
47	Kansas	(2.2)
41	Kentucky	1.9
23	Louisiana	6.5
46	Maine	(0.1)
35	Maryland	3.5
43	Massachusetts	1.2
45	Michigan	0.8
22	Minnesota	6.7
7	Mississippi	10.9
39	Missouri	2.5
4	Montana	14.5
49	Nebraska	(3.7)
34	Nevada	3.6
19	New Hampshire	7.4
21	New Jersey	7.2
17	New Mexico	7.7
37	New York	3.3
19	North Carolina	7.4
25	North Dakota	6.3
36	Ohio	3.4
32	Oklahoma	4.0
42	Oregon	1.5
26	Pennsylvania	5.8
15	Rhode Island	8.0
32	South Carolina	4.0
24	South Dakota	6.4
3	Tennessee	14.6
2	Texas	18.4
29	Utah	4.3
48	Vermont	(3.3)
5	Virginia	13.6
38	Washington	2.9
28	West Virginia	4.4
12	Wisconsin	9.6
8	Wyoming	10.8

RANK ORDER

RANK	STATE	PERCENT CHANGE
1	Connecticut	19.6
2	Texas	18.4
3	Tennessee	14.6
4	Montana	14.5
5	Virginia	13.6
6	Georgia	12.2
7	Mississippi	10.9
8	Florida	10.8
8	Wyoming	10.8
10	Arizona	10.7
11	Idaho	10.0
12	Wisconsin	9.6
13	Iowa	8.4
14	Colorado	8.3
15	California	8.0
15	Rhode Island	8.0
17	Illinois	7.7
17	New Mexico	7.7
19	New Hampshire	7.4
19	North Carolina	7.4
21	New Jersey	7.2
22	Minnesota	6.7
23	Louisiana	6.5
24	South Dakota	6.4
25	North Dakota	6.3
26	Pennsylvania	5.8
27	Hawaii	5.4
28	West Virginia	4.4
29	Indiana	4.3
29	Utah	4.3
31	Alabama	4.1
32	Oklahoma	4.0
32	South Carolina	4.0
34	Nevada	3.6
35	Maryland	3.5
36	Ohio	3.4
37	New York	3.3
38	Washington	2.9
39	Missouri	2.5
40	Arkansas	2.1
41	Kentucky	1.9
42	Oregon	1.5
43	Massachusetts	1.2
44	Delaware	0.9
45	Michigan	0.8
46	Maine	(0.1)
47	Kansas	(2.2)
48	Vermont	(3.3)
49	Nebraska	(3.7)
50	Alaska	(6.5)

District of Columbia (2.3)

*Source: U.S. Department of Justice, Bureau of Justice Statistics
   Press Release (October 27, 1994)*
From June 30, 1993 to June 30, 1994. Includes inmates sentenced to more than one year and those sentenced to a year or less or with no sentence. The percent change in number of prisoners under federal jurisdiction during the same period was a 7.7% increase. The combined state and federal increase was 7.5%.

State Prison Population as a Percent of Highest Capacity in 1993

National Percent = 118% of Highest Capacity*

ALPHA ORDER

RANK	STATE	PERCENT
11	Alabama	124
16	Alaska	118
21	Arizona	111
38	Arkansas	99
1	California	190
17	Colorado	117
30	Connecticut	103
33	Delaware	101
39	Florida	98
35	Georgia	100
13	Hawaii	120
13	Idaho	120
8	Illinois	131
45	Indiana	94
3	Iowa	150
48	Kansas	87
26	Kentucky	105
45	Louisiana	94
25	Maine	109
35	Maryland	100
4	Massachusetts	146
5	Michigan	143
21	Minnesota	111
24	Mississippi	110
31	Missouri	102
18	Montana	115
13	Nebraska	120
43	Nevada	96
19	New Hampshire	113
7	New Jersey	135
39	New Mexico	98
26	New York	105
31	North Carolina	102
50	North Dakota	84
2	Ohio	180
12	Oklahoma	123
33	Oregon	101
6	Pennsylvania	138
47	Rhode Island	91
19	South Carolina	113
26	South Dakota	105
42	Tennessee	97
39	Texas	98
49	Utah	86
43	Vermont	96
10	Virginia	125
29	Washington	104
35	West Virginia	100
9	Wisconsin	129
21	Wyoming	111

RANK ORDER

RANK	STATE	PERCENT
1	California	190
2	Ohio	180
3	Iowa	150
4	Massachusetts	146
5	Michigan	143
6	Pennsylvania	138
7	New Jersey	135
8	Illinois	131
9	Wisconsin	129
10	Virginia	125
11	Alabama	124
12	Oklahoma	123
13	Hawaii	120
13	Idaho	120
13	Nebraska	120
16	Alaska	118
17	Colorado	117
18	Montana	115
19	New Hampshire	113
19	South Carolina	113
21	Arizona	111
21	Minnesota	111
21	Wyoming	111
24	Mississippi	110
25	Maine	109
26	Kentucky	105
26	New York	105
26	South Dakota	105
29	Washington	104
30	Connecticut	103
31	Missouri	102
31	North Carolina	102
33	Delaware	101
33	Oregon	101
35	Georgia	100
35	Maryland	100
35	West Virginia	100
38	Arkansas	99
39	Florida	98
39	New Mexico	98
39	Texas	98
42	Tennessee	97
43	Nevada	96
43	Vermont	96
45	Indiana	94
45	Louisiana	94
47	Rhode Island	91
48	Kansas	87
49	Utah	86
50	North Dakota	84
	District of Columbia	105

Source: U.S. Department of Justice, Bureau of Justice Statistics
"Prisoners in 1993" (Bulletin, June 1994, NCJ-147036)
*As of December 31, 1993. Federal prison population is at 136% of highest rated capacity.

Prisoners in State Correctional Institutions: Year End 1993

National Total = 859,295 State Prisoners*

<table>
<tr><td colspan="4"><u>ALPHA ORDER</u></td><td colspan="4"><u>RANK ORDER</u></td></tr>
<tr><th>RANK</th><th>STATE</th><th>PRISONERS</th><th>% of USA</th><th>RANK</th><th>STATE</th><th>PRISONERS</th><th>% of USA</th></tr>
<tr><td>16</td><td>Alabama</td><td>18,624</td><td>2.17%</td><td>1</td><td>California</td><td>119,951</td><td>13.96%</td></tr>
<tr><td>38</td><td>Alaska</td><td>3,068</td><td>0.36%</td><td>2</td><td>Texas</td><td>71,103</td><td>8.27%</td></tr>
<tr><td>17</td><td>Arizona</td><td>17,811</td><td>2.07%</td><td>3</td><td>New York</td><td>64,569</td><td>7.51%</td></tr>
<tr><td>29</td><td>Arkansas</td><td>8,628</td><td>1.00%</td><td>4</td><td>Florida</td><td>53,048</td><td>6.17%</td></tr>
<tr><td>1</td><td>California</td><td>119,951</td><td>13.96%</td><td>5</td><td>Ohio</td><td>40,641</td><td>4.73%</td></tr>
<tr><td>27</td><td>Colorado</td><td>9,462</td><td>1.10%</td><td>6</td><td>Michigan</td><td>39,529</td><td>4.60%</td></tr>
<tr><td>21</td><td>Connecticut</td><td>13,691</td><td>1.59%</td><td>7</td><td>Illinois</td><td>34,495</td><td>4.01%</td></tr>
<tr><td>35</td><td>Delaware</td><td>4,237</td><td>0.49%</td><td>8</td><td>Georgia</td><td>27,783</td><td>3.23%</td></tr>
<tr><td>4</td><td>Florida</td><td>53,048</td><td>6.17%</td><td>9</td><td>Pennsylvania</td><td>26,050</td><td>3.03%</td></tr>
<tr><td>8</td><td>Georgia</td><td>27,783</td><td>3.23%</td><td>10</td><td>New Jersey</td><td>23,831</td><td>2.77%</td></tr>
<tr><td>37</td><td>Hawaii</td><td>3,155</td><td>0.37%</td><td>11</td><td>Virginia</td><td>22,850</td><td>2.66%</td></tr>
<tr><td>41</td><td>Idaho</td><td>2,606</td><td>0.30%</td><td>12</td><td>Louisiana</td><td>22,532</td><td>2.62%</td></tr>
<tr><td>7</td><td>Illinois</td><td>34,495</td><td>4.01%</td><td>13</td><td>North Carolina</td><td>21,889</td><td>2.55%</td></tr>
<tr><td>20</td><td>Indiana</td><td>14,470</td><td>1.68%</td><td>14</td><td>Maryland</td><td>20,264</td><td>2.36%</td></tr>
<tr><td>33</td><td>Iowa</td><td>4,898</td><td>0.57%</td><td>15</td><td>South Carolina</td><td>18,704</td><td>2.18%</td></tr>
<tr><td>32</td><td>Kansas</td><td>5,727</td><td>0.67%</td><td>16</td><td>Alabama</td><td>18,624</td><td>2.17%</td></tr>
<tr><td>23</td><td>Kentucky</td><td>10,440</td><td>1.21%</td><td>17</td><td>Arizona</td><td>17,811</td><td>2.07%</td></tr>
<tr><td>12</td><td>Louisiana</td><td>22,532</td><td>2.62%</td><td>18</td><td>Oklahoma</td><td>16,409</td><td>1.91%</td></tr>
<tr><td>46</td><td>Maine</td><td>1,469</td><td>0.17%</td><td>19</td><td>Missouri</td><td>16,178</td><td>1.88%</td></tr>
<tr><td>14</td><td>Maryland</td><td>20,264</td><td>2.36%</td><td>20</td><td>Indiana</td><td>14,470</td><td>1.68%</td></tr>
<tr><td>26</td><td>Massachusetts</td><td>10,055</td><td>1.17%</td><td>21</td><td>Connecticut</td><td>13,691</td><td>1.59%</td></tr>
<tr><td>6</td><td>Michigan</td><td>39,529</td><td>4.60%</td><td>22</td><td>Tennessee</td><td>12,827</td><td>1.49%</td></tr>
<tr><td>34</td><td>Minnesota</td><td>4,415</td><td>0.51%</td><td>23</td><td>Kentucky</td><td>10,440</td><td>1.21%</td></tr>
<tr><td>25</td><td>Mississippi</td><td>10,116</td><td>1.18%</td><td>24</td><td>Washington</td><td>10,419</td><td>1.21%</td></tr>
<tr><td>19</td><td>Missouri</td><td>16,178</td><td>1.88%</td><td>25</td><td>Mississippi</td><td>10,116</td><td>1.18%</td></tr>
<tr><td>47</td><td>Montana</td><td>1,454</td><td>0.17%</td><td>26</td><td>Massachusetts</td><td>10,055</td><td>1.17%</td></tr>
<tr><td>42</td><td>Nebraska</td><td>2,408</td><td>0.28%</td><td>27</td><td>Colorado</td><td>9,462</td><td>1.10%</td></tr>
<tr><td>31</td><td>Nevada</td><td>6,198</td><td>0.72%</td><td>28</td><td>Wisconsin</td><td>8,783</td><td>1.02%</td></tr>
<tr><td>44</td><td>New Hampshire</td><td>1,775</td><td>0.21%</td><td>29</td><td>Arkansas</td><td>8,628</td><td>1.00%</td></tr>
<tr><td>10</td><td>New Jersey</td><td>23,831</td><td>2.77%</td><td>30</td><td>Oregon</td><td>6,560</td><td>0.76%</td></tr>
<tr><td>36</td><td>New Mexico</td><td>3,498</td><td>0.41%</td><td>31</td><td>Nevada</td><td>6,198</td><td>0.72%</td></tr>
<tr><td>3</td><td>New York</td><td>64,569</td><td>7.51%</td><td>32</td><td>Kansas</td><td>5,727</td><td>0.67%</td></tr>
<tr><td>13</td><td>North Carolina</td><td>21,889</td><td>2.55%</td><td>33</td><td>Iowa</td><td>4,898</td><td>0.57%</td></tr>
<tr><td>50</td><td>North Dakota</td><td>498</td><td>0.06%</td><td>34</td><td>Minnesota</td><td>4,415</td><td>0.51%</td></tr>
<tr><td>5</td><td>Ohio</td><td>40,641</td><td>4.73%</td><td>35</td><td>Delaware</td><td>4,237</td><td>0.49%</td></tr>
<tr><td>18</td><td>Oklahoma</td><td>16,409</td><td>1.91%</td><td>36</td><td>New Mexico</td><td>3,498</td><td>0.41%</td></tr>
<tr><td>30</td><td>Oregon</td><td>6,560</td><td>0.76%</td><td>37</td><td>Hawaii</td><td>3,155</td><td>0.37%</td></tr>
<tr><td>9</td><td>Pennsylvania</td><td>26,050</td><td>3.03%</td><td>38</td><td>Alaska</td><td>3,068</td><td>0.36%</td></tr>
<tr><td>40</td><td>Rhode Island</td><td>2,782</td><td>0.32%</td><td>39</td><td>Utah</td><td>2,888</td><td>0.34%</td></tr>
<tr><td>15</td><td>South Carolina</td><td>18,704</td><td>2.18%</td><td>40</td><td>Rhode Island</td><td>2,782</td><td>0.32%</td></tr>
<tr><td>45</td><td>South Dakota</td><td>1,553</td><td>0.18%</td><td>41</td><td>Idaho</td><td>2,606</td><td>0.30%</td></tr>
<tr><td>22</td><td>Tennessee</td><td>12,827</td><td>1.49%</td><td>42</td><td>Nebraska</td><td>2,408</td><td>0.28%</td></tr>
<tr><td>2</td><td>Texas</td><td>71,103</td><td>8.27%</td><td>43</td><td>West Virginia</td><td>1,805</td><td>0.21%</td></tr>
<tr><td>39</td><td>Utah</td><td>2,888</td><td>0.34%</td><td>44</td><td>New Hampshire</td><td>1,775</td><td>0.21%</td></tr>
<tr><td>48</td><td>Vermont</td><td>1,223</td><td>0.14%</td><td>45</td><td>South Dakota</td><td>1,553</td><td>0.18%</td></tr>
<tr><td>11</td><td>Virginia</td><td>22,850</td><td>2.66%</td><td>46</td><td>Maine</td><td>1,469</td><td>0.17%</td></tr>
<tr><td>24</td><td>Washington</td><td>10,419</td><td>1.21%</td><td>47</td><td>Montana</td><td>1,454</td><td>0.17%</td></tr>
<tr><td>43</td><td>West Virginia</td><td>1,805</td><td>0.21%</td><td>48</td><td>Vermont</td><td>1,223</td><td>0.14%</td></tr>
<tr><td>28</td><td>Wisconsin</td><td>8,783</td><td>1.02%</td><td>49</td><td>Wyoming</td><td>1,081</td><td>0.13%</td></tr>
<tr><td>49</td><td>Wyoming</td><td>1,081</td><td>0.13%</td><td>50</td><td>North Dakota</td><td>498</td><td>0.06%</td></tr>
<tr><td></td><td></td><td></td><td></td><td></td><td>District of Columbia</td><td>10,845</td><td>1.26%</td></tr>
</table>

Source: U.S. Department of Justice, Bureau of Justice Statistics
    "Prisoners in 1993" (Bulletin, June 1994, NCJ-147036)

*Advance figures as of December 31, 1993. Totals reflect all prisoners, including those sentenced to a year or less and those unsentenced. National total does not include 89,586 prisoners under federal jurisdiction. State and federal prisoners combined total 948,881.

State Prisoners Sentenced to More than One Year in 1993

National Total = 836,064 State Prisoners*

ALPHA ORDER

RANK	STATE	PRISONERS	% of USA
15	Alabama	18,169	2.17%
41	Alaska	1,954	0.23%
17	Arizona	17,160	2.05%
29	Arkansas	8,567	1.02%
1	California	115,573	13.82%
26	Colorado	9,462	1.13%
22	Connecticut	10,508	1.26%
37	Delaware	2,796	0.33%
4	Florida	53,041	6.34%
8	Georgia	27,079	3.24%
40	Hawaii	2,026	0.24%
38	Idaho	2,606	0.31%
7	Illinois	34,495	4.13%
20	Indiana	14,364	1.72%
33	Iowa	4,898	0.59%
31	Kansas	5,727	0.68%
23	Kentucky	10,440	1.25%
12	Louisiana	21,499	2.57%
47	Maine	1,446	0.17%
14	Maryland	19,121	2.29%
27	Massachusetts	9,315	1.11%
6	Michigan	39,529	4.73%
34	Minnesota	4,415	0.53%
25	Mississippi	9,798	1.17%
19	Missouri	16,178	1.94%
46	Montana	1,454	0.17%
39	Nebraska	2,360	0.28%
30	Nevada	6,198	0.74%
43	New Hampshire	1,775	0.21%
10	New Jersey	23,689	2.83%
35	New Mexico	3,373	0.40%
3	New York	64,569	7.72%
13	North Carolina	21,358	2.55%
50	North Dakota	446	0.05%
5	Ohio	40,641	4.86%
18	Oklahoma	16,409	1.96%
32	Oregon	5,118	0.61%
9	Pennsylvania	26,045	3.12%
44	Rhode Island	1,716	0.21%
16	South Carolina	17,896	2.14%
45	South Dakota	1,553	0.19%
21	Tennessee	12,827	1.53%
2	Texas	71,103	8.50%
36	Utah	2,871	0.34%
49	Vermont	893	0.11%
11	Virginia	22,635	2.71%
24	Washington	10,419	1.25%
42	West Virginia	1,805	0.22%
28	Wisconsin	8,757	1.05%
48	Wyoming	1,080	0.13%

RANK ORDER

RANK	STATE	PRISONERS	% of USA
1	California	115,573	13.82%
2	Texas	71,103	8.50%
3	New York	64,569	7.72%
4	Florida	53,041	6.34%
5	Ohio	40,641	4.86%
6	Michigan	39,529	4.73%
7	Illinois	34,495	4.13%
8	Georgia	27,079	3.24%
9	Pennsylvania	26,045	3.12%
10	New Jersey	23,689	2.83%
11	Virginia	22,635	2.71%
12	Louisiana	21,499	2.57%
13	North Carolina	21,358	2.55%
14	Maryland	19,121	2.29%
15	Alabama	18,169	2.17%
16	South Carolina	17,896	2.14%
17	Arizona	17,160	2.05%
18	Oklahoma	16,409	1.96%
19	Missouri	16,178	1.94%
20	Indiana	14,364	1.72%
21	Tennessee	12,827	1.53%
22	Connecticut	10,508	1.26%
23	Kentucky	10,440	1.25%
24	Washington	10,419	1.25%
25	Mississippi	9,798	1.17%
26	Colorado	9,462	1.13%
27	Massachusetts	9,315	1.11%
28	Wisconsin	8,757	1.05%
29	Arkansas	8,567	1.02%
30	Nevada	6,198	0.74%
31	Kansas	5,727	0.68%
32	Oregon	5,118	0.61%
33	Iowa	4,898	0.59%
34	Minnesota	4,415	0.53%
35	New Mexico	3,373	0.40%
36	Utah	2,871	0.34%
37	Delaware	2,796	0.33%
38	Idaho	2,606	0.31%
39	Nebraska	2,360	0.28%
40	Hawaii	2,026	0.24%
41	Alaska	1,954	0.23%
42	West Virginia	1,805	0.22%
43	New Hampshire	1,775	0.21%
44	Rhode Island	1,716	0.21%
45	South Dakota	1,553	0.19%
46	Montana	1,454	0.17%
47	Maine	1,446	0.17%
48	Wyoming	1,080	0.13%
49	Vermont	893	0.11%
50	North Dakota	446	0.05%
	District of Columbia	8,908	1.07%

Source: U.S. Department of Justice, Bureau of Justice Statistics
"Prisoners in 1993" (Bulletin, June 1994, NCJ-147036)
*Advance figures as of December 31, 1993. Does not include 74,398 prisoners under federal jurisdiction sentenced to more than one year. State and federal prisoners sentenced to more than one year total 910,462.

Female Prisoners in State Correctional Institutions in 1993

National Total = 48,474 State Female Prisoners*

<u>ALPHA ORDER</u>

RANK	STATE	PRISONERS	% of USA
13	Alabama	1,131	2.33%
NA	Alaska***	NA	NA
17	Arizona	1,037	2.14%
NA	Arkansas***	NA	NA
1	California	7,580	15.64%
26	Colorado	542	1.12%
18	Connecticut	994	2.05%
NA	Delaware***	NA	NA
4	Florida	2,696	5.56%
7	Georgia	1,760	3.63%
NA	Hawaii***	NA	NA
NA	Idaho***	NA	NA
8	Illinois	1,688	3.48%
21	Indiana	778	1.60%
NA	Iowa***	NA	NA
NA	Kansas***	NA	NA
25	Kentucky	545	1.12%
14	Louisiana	1,119	2.31%
NA	Maine***	NA	NA
19	Maryland	976	2.01%
23	Massachusetts	622	1.28%
6	Michigan	1,801	3.72%
NA	Minnesota***	NA	NA
24	Mississippi	589	1.22%
20	Missouri	920	1.90%
NA	Montana***	NA	NA
NA	Nebraska***	NA	NA
NA	Nevada***	NA	NA
NA	New Hampshire***	NA	NA
12	New Jersey	1,134	2.34%
NA	New Mexico***	NA	NA
3	New York	3,528	7.28%
14	North Carolina	1,119	2.31%
NA	North Dakota***	NA	NA
5	Ohio	2,584	5.33%
9	Oklahoma	1,582	3.26%
NA	Oregon***	NA	NA
11	Pennsylvania	1,194	2.46%
NA	Rhode Island***	NA	NA
16	South Carolina	1,105	2.28%
NA	South Dakota***	NA	NA
27	Tennessee	521	1.07%
2	Texas**	4,015	8.28%
NA	Utah***	NA	NA
NA	Vermont***	NA	NA
10	Virginia	1,219	2.51%
22	Washington	666	1.37%
NA	West Virginia***	NA	NA
NA	Wisconsin***	NA	NA
NA	Wyoming***	NA	NA

<u>RANK ORDER</u>

RANK	STATE	PRISONERS	% of USA
1	California	7,580	15.64%
2	Texas**	4,015	8.28%
3	New York	3,528	7.28%
4	Florida	2,696	5.56%
5	Ohio	2,584	5.33%
6	Michigan	1,801	3.72%
7	Georgia	1,760	3.63%
8	Illinois	1,688	3.48%
9	Oklahoma	1,582	3.26%
10	Virginia	1,219	2.51%
11	Pennsylvania	1,194	2.46%
12	New Jersey	1,134	2.34%
13	Alabama	1,131	2.33%
14	Louisiana	1,119	2.31%
14	North Carolina	1,119	2.31%
16	South Carolina	1,105	2.28%
17	Arizona	1,037	2.14%
18	Connecticut	994	2.05%
19	Maryland	976	2.01%
20	Missouri	920	1.90%
21	Indiana	778	1.60%
22	Washington	666	1.37%
23	Massachusetts	622	1.28%
24	Mississippi	589	1.22%
25	Kentucky	545	1.12%
26	Colorado	542	1.12%
27	Tennessee	521	1.07%
NA	Alaska***	NA	NA
NA	Arkansas***	NA	NA
NA	Delaware***	NA	NA
NA	Hawaii***	NA	NA
NA	Idaho***	NA	NA
NA	Iowa***	NA	NA
NA	Kansas***	NA	NA
NA	Maine***	NA	NA
NA	Minnesota***	NA	NA
NA	Montana***	NA	NA
NA	Nebraska***	NA	NA
NA	Nevada***	NA	NA
NA	New Hampshire***	NA	NA
NA	New Mexico***	NA	NA
NA	North Dakota***	NA	NA
NA	Oregon***	NA	NA
NA	Rhode Island***	NA	NA
NA	South Dakota***	NA	NA
NA	Utah***	NA	NA
NA	Vermont***	NA	NA
NA	West Virginia***	NA	NA
NA	Wisconsin***	NA	NA
NA	Wyoming***	NA	NA
	District of Columbia	687	1.42%

Source: U.S. Department of Justice, Bureau of Justice Statistics
    "Prisoners in 1993" (Bulletin, June 1994, NCJ-147036)

*As of December 31, 1993. States shown have at least 500 female inmates. Total includes 4,342 female inmates in states not shown separately. Total does not include 6,891 federal female inmates. Combined state and federal total is 55,365 female inmates. **Texas' total does not include 3,363 female inmates in local jails awaiting transport.
***Not available, fewer than 500 female inmates.

Female Prisoners in State Correctional Institutions as a Percent of All Prisoners: 1993

National Percent = 5.6% of State Prisoners are Female*

ALPHA ORDER				RANK ORDER		
RANK	STATE	PERCENT		RANK	STATE	PERCENT
8	Alabama	6.1		1	Oklahoma	9.6
NA	Alaska**	NA		2	Connecticut	7.3
10	Arizona	5.8		3	Ohio	6.4
NA	Arkansas**	NA		3	Washington	6.4
5	California	6.3		5	California	6.3
12	Colorado	5.7		5	Georgia	6.3
2	Connecticut	7.3		7	Massachusetts	6.2
NA	Delaware**	NA		8	Alabama	6.1
19	Florida	5.1		9	South Carolina	5.9
5	Georgia	6.3		10	Arizona	5.8
NA	Hawaii**	NA		10	Mississippi	5.8
NA	Idaho**	NA		12	Colorado	5.7
22	Illinois	4.9		12	Missouri	5.7
16	Indiana	5.4		14	Texas	5.6
NA	Iowa**	NA		15	New York	5.5
NA	Kansas**	NA		16	Indiana	5.4
18	Kentucky	5.2		17	Virginia	5.3
21	Louisiana	5.0		18	Kentucky	5.2
NA	Maine**	NA		19	Florida	5.1
23	Maryland	4.8		19	North Carolina	5.1
7	Massachusetts	6.2		21	Louisiana	5.0
25	Michigan	4.6		22	Illinois	4.9
NA	Minnesota**	NA		23	Maryland	4.8
10	Mississippi	5.8		23	New Jersey	4.8
12	Missouri	5.7		25	Michigan	4.6
NA	Montana**	NA		25	Pennsylvania	4.6
NA	Nebraska**	NA		27	Tennessee	4.1
NA	Nevada**	NA		NA	Alaska**	NA
NA	New Hampshire**	NA		NA	Arkansas**	NA
23	New Jersey	4.8		NA	Delaware**	NA
NA	New Mexico**	NA		NA	Hawaii**	NA
15	New York	5.5		NA	Idaho**	NA
19	North Carolina	5.1		NA	Iowa**	NA
NA	North Dakota**	NA		NA	Kansas**	NA
3	Ohio	6.4		NA	Maine**	NA
1	Oklahoma	9.6		NA	Minnesota**	NA
NA	Oregon**	NA		NA	Montana**	NA
25	Pennsylvania	4.6		NA	Nebraska**	NA
NA	Rhode Island**	NA		NA	Nevada**	NA
9	South Carolina	5.9		NA	New Hampshire**	NA
NA	South Dakota**	NA		NA	New Mexico**	NA
27	Tennessee	4.1		NA	North Dakota**	NA
14	Texas	5.6		NA	Oregon**	NA
NA	Utah**	NA		NA	Rhode Island**	NA
NA	Vermont**	NA		NA	South Dakota**	NA
17	Virginia	5.3		NA	Utah**	NA
3	Washington	6.4		NA	Vermont**	NA
NA	West Virginia**	NA		NA	West Virginia**	NA
NA	Wisconsin**	NA		NA	Wisconsin**	NA
NA	Wyoming**	NA		NA	Wyoming**	NA
					District of Columbia	6.3

Source: U.S. Department of Justice, Bureau of Justice Statistics
  "Prisoners in 1993" (Bulletin, June 1994, NCJ-147036)
*As of December 31, 1993. States shown have at least 500 female inmates. National rate reflects 4,342 female inmates in states not shown separately. Rate does not include federal female inmates. Federal female inmates constitute 7.7% of federal inmates. The federal/state combined rate is 5.8%.
**Not available, fewer than 500 female inmates.

Percent Change in Female Prisoner Population: 1992 to 1993

National Percent Change = 9.9% Increase*

ALPHA ORDER				RANK ORDER		
RANK	STATE	PERCENT CHANGE		RANK	STATE	PERCENT CHANGE
20	Alabama	2.7		1	Texas	61.4
NA	Alaska**	NA		2	Connecticut	40.0
17	Arizona	3.6		3	Georgia	21.0
NA	Arkansas**	NA		4	North Carolina	17.8
8	California	12.3		5	Mississippi	16.6
19	Colorado	2.8		6	Illinois	15.9
2	Connecticut	40.0		7	Oklahoma	13.0
NA	Delaware**	NA		8	California	12.3
16	Florida	3.7		9	Massachusetts	10.3
3	Georgia	21.0		10	Louisiana	9.5
NA	Hawaii**	NA		11	Pennsylvania	8.0
NA	Idaho**	NA		12	Washington	7.8
6	Illinois	15.9		13	Ohio	6.8
14	Indiana	5.4		14	Indiana	5.4
NA	Iowa**	NA		15	Virginia	4.8
NA	Kansas**	NA		16	Florida	3.7
23	Kentucky	0.0		17	Arizona	3.6
10	Louisiana	9.5		17	New Jersey	3.6
NA	Maine**	NA		19	Colorado	2.8
21	Maryland	2.3		20	Alabama	2.7
9	Massachusetts	10.3		21	Maryland	2.3
26	Michigan	(2.2)		22	New York	0.8
NA	Minnesota**	NA		23	Kentucky	0.0
5	Mississippi	16.6		24	Tennessee	(1.3)
NA	Missouri**	NA		25	South Carolina	(2.0)
NA	Montana**	NA		26	Michigan	(2.2)
NA	Nebraska**	NA		NA	Alaska**	NA
NA	Nevada**	NA		NA	Arkansas**	NA
NA	New Hampshire**	NA		NA	Delaware**	NA
17	New Jersey	3.6		NA	Hawaii**	NA
NA	New Mexico**	NA		NA	Idaho**	NA
22	New York	0.8		NA	Iowa**	NA
4	North Carolina	17.8		NA	Kansas**	NA
NA	North Dakota**	NA		NA	Maine**	NA
13	Ohio	6.8		NA	Minnesota**	NA
7	Oklahoma	13.0		NA	Missouri**	NA
NA	Oregon**	NA		NA	Montana**	NA
11	Pennsylvania	8.0		NA	Nebraska**	NA
NA	Rhode Island**	NA		NA	Nevada**	NA
25	South Carolina	(2.0)		NA	New Hampshire**	NA
NA	South Dakota**	NA		NA	New Mexico**	NA
24	Tennessee	(1.3)		NA	North Dakota**	NA
1	Texas	61.4		NA	Oregon**	NA
NA	Utah**	NA		NA	Rhode Island**	NA
NA	Vermont**	NA		NA	South Dakota**	NA
15	Virginia	4.8		NA	Utah**	NA
12	Washington	7.8		NA	Vermont**	NA
NA	West Virginia**	NA		NA	West Virginia**	NA
NA	Wisconsin**	NA		NA	Wisconsin**	NA
NA	Wyoming**	NA		NA	Wyoming**	NA
					District of Columbia	(4.6)

Source: U.S. Department of Justice, Bureau of Justice Statistics
"Prisoners in 1993" (Bulletin, June 1994, NCJ-147036)

*As of December 31, 1993. States shown have at least 500 female inmates. National rate reflects 4,342 female inmates in states not shown separately. Rate does not include federal female inmates. Federal female inmate population increased by 7.7%. The combined federal/state female inmate population grew by 9.6%.

**Not available, fewer than 500 female inmates.

White Prisoners in State Correctional Institutions in 1992

National Total = 357,333 White State Prisoners*

<u>ALPHA ORDER</u>

RANK	STATE	PRISONERS	% of USA
20	Alabama	6,045	1.69%
42	Alaska	1,459	0.41%
7	Arizona	12,872	3.60%
29	Arkansas	3,525	0.99%
1	California	66,815	18.70%
19	Colorado	6,340	1.77%
32	Connecticut	3,218	0.90%
44	Delaware	1,284	0.36%
3	Florida	19,047	5.33%
13	Georgia	8,094	2.27%
49	Hawaii	605	0.17%
37	Idaho	2,094	0.59%
11	Illinois	8,284	2.32%
10	Indiana	8,330	2.33%
30	Iowa	3,329	0.93%
31	Kansas	3,267	0.91%
15	Kentucky	7,008	1.96%
24	Louisiana	4,806	1.34%
41	Maine	1,467	0.41%
27	Maryland	4,645	1.30%
23	Massachusetts	4,981	1.39%
6	Michigan	15,790	4.42%
36	Minnesota	2,112	0.59%
34	Mississippi	2,296	0.64%
9	Missouri	8,418	2.36%
46	Montana	1,208	0.34%
40	Nebraska	1,560	0.44%
28	Nevada	3,646	1.02%
39	New Hampshire	1,686	0.47%
18	New Jersey	6,628	1.85%
33	New Mexico	2,771	0.78%
2	New York	29,699	8.31%
16	North Carolina	6,998	1.96%
50	North Dakota	375	0.10%
4	Ohio	17,717	4.96%
12	Oklahoma	8,147	2.28%
25	Oregon	4,802	1.34%
8	Pennsylvania	8,602	2.41%
38	Rhode Island	1,861	0.52%
22	South Carolina	5,980	1.67%
47	South Dakota	1,079	0.30%
21	Tennessee	5,981	1.67%
5	Texas	17,373	4.86%
35	Utah	2,287	0.64%
45	Vermont	1,254	0.35%
14	Virginia	7,436	2.08%
17	Washington	6,941	1.94%
43	West Virginia	1,426	0.40%
26	Wisconsin	4,710	1.32%
48	Wyoming	847	0.24%

<u>RANK ORDER</u>

RANK	STATE	PRISONERS	% of USA
1	California	66,815	18.70%
2	New York	29,699	8.31%
3	Florida	19,047	5.33%
4	Ohio	17,717	4.96%
5	Texas	17,373	4.86%
6	Michigan	15,790	4.42%
7	Arizona	12,872	3.60%
8	Pennsylvania	8,602	2.41%
9	Missouri	8,418	2.36%
10	Indiana	8,330	2.33%
11	Illinois	8,284	2.32%
12	Oklahoma	8,147	2.28%
13	Georgia	8,094	2.27%
14	Virginia	7,436	2.08%
15	Kentucky	7,008	1.96%
16	North Carolina	6,998	1.96%
17	Washington	6,941	1.94%
18	New Jersey	6,628	1.85%
19	Colorado	6,340	1.77%
20	Alabama	6,045	1.69%
21	Tennessee	5,981	1.67%
22	South Carolina	5,980	1.67%
23	Massachusetts	4,981	1.39%
24	Louisiana	4,806	1.34%
25	Oregon	4,802	1.34%
26	Wisconsin	4,710	1.32%
27	Maryland	4,645	1.30%
28	Nevada	3,646	1.02%
29	Arkansas	3,525	0.99%
30	Iowa	3,329	0.93%
31	Kansas	3,267	0.91%
32	Connecticut	3,218	0.90%
33	New Mexico	2,771	0.78%
34	Mississippi	2,296	0.64%
35	Utah	2,287	0.64%
36	Minnesota	2,112	0.59%
37	Idaho	2,094	0.59%
38	Rhode Island	1,861	0.52%
39	New Hampshire	1,686	0.47%
40	Nebraska	1,560	0.44%
41	Maine	1,467	0.41%
42	Alaska	1,459	0.41%
43	West Virginia	1,426	0.40%
44	Delaware	1,284	0.36%
45	Vermont	1,254	0.35%
46	Montana	1,208	0.34%
47	South Dakota	1,079	0.30%
48	Wyoming	847	0.24%
49	Hawaii	605	0.17%
50	North Dakota	375	0.10%
	District of Columbia	188	0.05%

Source: U.S. Department of Justice, Bureau of Justice Statistics
"Correctional Populations in the United States, 1992" (February 1995, NCJ 146413)
As of December 31, 1992. National total does not include 51,932 white federal prisoners.

White Prisoners in State Correctional Institutions as a Percent of All Prisoners: 1992

National Percent = 44.48% White *

ALPHA ORDER				RANK ORDER		
RANK	STATE	PERCENT		RANK	STATE	PERCENT
37	Alabama	34.64		1	Vermont	100.00
28	Alaska	50.92		2	Maine	96.58
11	Arizona	78.12		3	New Hampshire	94.88
33	Arkansas	42.55		4	Idaho	92.82
20	California	61.02		5	West Virginia	85.19
15	Colorado	70.47		6	Utah	84.74
45	Connecticut	28.22		7	New Mexico	84.71
42	Delaware	31.70		8	Montana	80.64
35	Florida	39.43		9	Wyoming	79.68
41	Georgia	32.00		10	North Dakota	78.62
50	Hawaii	20.68		11	Arizona	78.12
4	Idaho	92.82		12	Iowa	73.68
46	Illinois	26.18		13	Oregon	72.95
22	Indiana	59.73		14	South Dakota	72.56
12	Iowa	73.68		15	Colorado	70.47
25	Kansas	54.20		16	Washington	69.70
17	Kentucky	67.62		17	Kentucky	67.62
49	Louisiana	23.00		18	Rhode Island	67.06
2	Maine	96.58		19	Nebraska	62.05
48	Maryland	23.25		20	California	61.02
30	Massachusetts	49.55		21	Nevada	60.27
34	Michigan	40.37		22	Indiana	59.73
23	Minnesota	55.26		23	Minnesota	55.26
47	Mississippi	26.15		24	Oklahoma	54.97
27	Missouri	52.00		25	Kansas	54.20
8	Montana	80.64		26	Wisconsin	52.85
19	Nebraska	62.05		27	Missouri	52.00
21	Nevada	60.27		28	Alaska	50.92
3	New Hampshire	94.88		29	Tennessee	50.48
43	New Jersey	29.26		30	Massachusetts	49.55
7	New Mexico	84.71		31	New York	48.11
31	New York	48.11		32	Ohio	46.16
39	North Carolina	34.21		33	Arkansas	42.55
10	North Dakota	78.62		34	Michigan	40.37
32	Ohio	46.16		35	Florida	39.43
24	Oklahoma	54.97		36	Virginia	35.08
13	Oregon	72.95		37	Alabama	34.64
38	Pennsylvania	34.44		38	Pennsylvania	34.44
18	Rhode Island	67.06		39	North Carolina	34.21
40	South Carolina	32.08		40	South Carolina	32.08
14	South Dakota	72.56		41	Georgia	32.00
29	Tennessee	50.48		42	Delaware	31.70
44	Texas	28.40		43	New Jersey	29.26
6	Utah	84.74		44	Texas	28.40
1	Vermont	100.00		45	Connecticut	28.22
36	Virginia	35.08		46	Illinois	26.18
16	Washington	69.70		47	Mississippi	26.15
5	West Virginia	85.19		48	Maryland	23.25
26	Wisconsin	52.85		49	Louisiana	23.00
9	Wyoming	79.68		50	Hawaii	20.68

District of Columbia   1.73

Source: Morgan Quitno Corporation using data from U.S. Department of Justice, Bureau of Justice Statistics
"Correctional Populations in the United States, 1992" (February 1995, NCJ 146413)
*As of December 31, 1992. National percent does not include white federal prisoners. Federal prison population is 64.71% white. Combined state and federal percentage is 46.31% white.

Black Prisoners in State Correctional Institutions in 1992

National Total = 398,923 Black State Prisoners*

ALPHA ORDER					RANK ORDER			
RANK	STATE	PRISONERS	% of USA		RANK	STATE	PRISONERS	% of USA
16	Alabama	11,371	2.85%		1	California	36,650	9.19%
40	Alaska	355	0.09%		2	New York	31,126	7.80%
27	Arizona	2,888	0.72%		3	Texas	28,885	7.24%
23	Arkansas	4,731	1.19%		4	Florida	28,424	7.13%
1	California	36,650	9.19%		5	Michigan	22,401	5.62%
31	Colorado	2,089	0.52%		6	Ohio	20,661	5.18%
22	Connecticut	5,202	1.30%		7	Illinois	20,394	5.11%
28	Delaware	2,665	0.67%		8	Georgia	17,064	4.28%
4	Florida	28,424	7.13%		9	Louisiana	16,090	4.03%
8	Georgia	17,064	4.28%		10	Maryland	15,260	3.83%
43	Hawaii	168	0.04%		11	New Jersey	14,747	3.70%
47	Idaho	27	0.01%		12	Pennsylvania	14,156	3.55%
7	Illinois	20,394	5.11%		13	Virginia	13,634	3.42%
20	Indiana	5,567	1.40%		14	North Carolina	12,744	3.19%
34	Iowa	1,076	0.27%		15	South Carolina	12,597	3.16%
29	Kansas	2,264	0.57%		16	Alabama	11,371	2.85%
25	Kentucky	3,352	0.84%		17	Missouri	7,726	1.94%
9	Louisiana	16,090	4.03%		18	Mississippi	6,422	1.61%
46	Maine	33	0.01%		19	Tennessee	5,816	1.46%
10	Maryland	15,260	3.83%		20	Indiana	5,567	1.40%
26	Massachusetts	3,175	0.80%		21	Oklahoma	5,295	1.33%
5	Michigan	22,401	5.62%		22	Connecticut	5,202	1.30%
33	Minnesota	1,190	0.30%		23	Arkansas	4,731	1.19%
18	Mississippi	6,422	1.61%		24	Wisconsin	3,961	0.99%
17	Missouri	7,726	1.94%		25	Kentucky	3,352	0.84%
48	Montana	25	0.01%		26	Massachusetts	3,175	0.80%
37	Nebraska	860	0.22%		27	Arizona	2,888	0.72%
32	Nevada	1,766	0.44%		28	Delaware	2,665	0.67%
44	New Hampshire	79	0.02%		29	Kansas	2,264	0.57%
11	New Jersey	14,747	3.70%		30	Washington	2,205	0.55%
39	New Mexico	365	0.09%		31	Colorado	2,089	0.52%
2	New York	31,126	7.80%		32	Nevada	1,766	0.44%
14	North Carolina	12,744	3.19%		33	Minnesota	1,190	0.30%
49	North Dakota	8	0.00%		34	Iowa	1,076	0.27%
6	Ohio	20,661	5.18%		35	Oregon	911	0.23%
21	Oklahoma	5,295	1.33%		36	Rhode Island	891	0.22%
35	Oregon	911	0.23%		37	Nebraska	860	0.22%
12	Pennsylvania	14,156	3.55%		38	South Dakota	369	0.09%
36	Rhode Island	891	0.22%		39	New Mexico	365	0.09%
15	South Carolina	12,597	3.16%		40	Alaska	355	0.09%
38	South Dakota	369	0.09%		41	Utah	252	0.06%
19	Tennessee	5,816	1.46%		42	West Virginia	247	0.06%
3	Texas	28,885	7.24%		43	Hawaii	168	0.04%
41	Utah	252	0.06%		44	New Hampshire	79	0.02%
50	Vermont	0	0.00%		45	Wyoming	52	0.01%
13	Virginia	13,634	3.42%		46	Maine	33	0.01%
30	Washington	2,205	0.55%		47	Idaho	27	0.01%
42	West Virginia	247	0.06%		48	Montana	25	0.01%
24	Wisconsin	3,961	0.99%		49	North Dakota	8	0.00%
45	Wyoming	52	0.01%		50	Vermont	0	0.00%
						District of Columbia	10,687	2.68%

Source: U.S. Department of Justice, Bureau of Justice Statistics
"Correctional Populations in the United States, 1992" (February 1995, NCJ 146413)
*As of December 31, 1992. National total does not include 25,763 black federal prisoners.

Black Prisoners in State Correctional Institutions as a Percent of All Prisoners: 1992

National Percent = 49.65% Black*

ALPHA ORDER				RANK ORDER		
RANK	STATE	PERCENT		RANK	STATE	PERCENT
7	Alabama	65.15		1	Louisiana	77.00
40	Alaska	12.39		2	Maryland	76.39
37	Arizona	17.53		3	Mississippi	73.14
14	Arkansas	57.10		4	South Carolina	67.57
27	California	33.47		5	Georgia	67.47
35	Colorado	23.22		6	Delaware	65.79
21	Connecticut	45.62		7	Alabama	65.15
6	Delaware	65.79		8	New Jersey	65.10
12	Florida	58.85		9	Illinois	64.46
5	Georgia	67.47		10	Virginia	64.31
43	Hawaii	5.74		11	North Carolina	62.31
49	Idaho	1.20		12	Florida	58.85
9	Illinois	64.46		13	Michigan	57.27
23	Indiana	39.92		14	Arkansas	57.10
34	Iowa	23.82		15	Pennsylvania	56.68
24	Kansas	37.56		16	Ohio	53.84
28	Kentucky	32.34		17	New York	50.42
1	Louisiana	77.00		18	Tennessee	49.08
46	Maine	2.17		19	Missouri	47.72
2	Maryland	76.39		20	Texas	47.21
30	Massachusetts	31.58		21	Connecticut	45.62
13	Michigan	57.27		22	Wisconsin	44.45
31	Minnesota	31.14		23	Indiana	39.92
3	Mississippi	73.14		24	Kansas	37.56
19	Missouri	47.72		25	Oklahoma	35.73
48	Montana	1.67		26	Nebraska	34.21
26	Nebraska	34.21		27	California	33.47
32	Nevada	29.19		28	Kentucky	32.34
45	New Hampshire	4.45		29	Rhode Island	32.11
8	New Jersey	65.10		30	Massachusetts	31.58
41	New Mexico	11.16		31	Minnesota	31.14
17	New York	50.42		32	Nevada	29.19
11	North Carolina	62.31		33	South Dakota	24.82
47	North Dakota	1.68		34	Iowa	23.82
16	Ohio	53.84		35	Colorado	23.22
25	Oklahoma	35.73		36	Washington	22.14
39	Oregon	13.84		37	Arizona	17.53
15	Pennsylvania	56.68		38	West Virginia	14.76
29	Rhode Island	32.11		39	Oregon	13.84
4	South Carolina	67.57		40	Alaska	12.39
33	South Dakota	24.82		41	New Mexico	11.16
18	Tennessee	49.08		42	Utah	9.34
20	Texas	47.21		43	Hawaii	5.74
42	Utah	9.34		44	Wyoming	4.89
50	Vermont	0.00		45	New Hampshire	4.45
10	Virginia	64.31		46	Maine	2.17
36	Washington	22.14		47	North Dakota	1.68
38	West Virginia	14.76		48	Montana	1.67
22	Wisconsin	44.45		49	Idaho	1.20
44	Wyoming	4.89		50	Vermont	0.00
					District of Columbia	98.27

Source: Morgan Quitno Corporation using data from U.S. Department of Justice, Bureau of Justice Statistics
   "Correctional Populations in the United States, 1992" (February 1995, NCJ 146413)
*As of December 31, 1992. National percent does not include black federal prisoners. Federal prison population is 32.10% black. Combined state and federal percentage is 48.06% black.

Average Annual Operating Expenditures per Inmate in 1990

National Average = $15,586 per Inmate*

ALPHA ORDER			RANK ORDER		
RANK	STATE	AVG EXPENDITURE	RANK	STATE	AVG EXPENDITURE
48	Alabama	$8,718	1	Alaska	$28,214
1	Alaska	28,214	2	Minnesota	26,661
41	Arizona	10,311	3	Maine	22,656
50	Arkansas	7,557	4	California	21,816
4	California	21,816	5	New Jersey	20,703
29	Colorado	14,180	6	Tennessee	20,048
15	Connecticut	17,002	7	Washington	19,742
37	Delaware	11,208	8	Hawaii	19,542
30	Florida	13,902	9	Wisconsin	18,965
33	Georgia	12,930	10	New York	18,670
8	Hawaii	19,542	11	North Carolina	18,486
45	Idaho	9,450	12	Iowa	18,304
20	Illinois	15,980	13	Maryland	17,214
25	Indiana	14,822	14	New Hampshire	17,208
12	Iowa	18,304	15	Connecticut	17,002
26	Kansas	14,670	16	New Mexico	16,711
38	Kentucky	11,118	17	Michigan	16,649
46	Louisiana	9,337	18	Rhode Island	16,497
3	Maine	22,656	19	Virginia	16,145
13	Maryland	17,214	20	Illinois	15,980
24	Massachusetts	15,152	21	Vermont	15,905
17	Michigan	16,649	22	Pennsylvania	15,438
2	Minnesota	26,661	23	Utah	15,251
47	Mississippi	9,133	24	Massachusetts	15,152
44	Missouri	9,766	25	Indiana	14,822
27	Montana	14,590	26	Kansas	14,670
31	Nebraska	13,012	27	Montana	14,590
49	Nevada	8,630	28	North Dakota	14,581
14	New Hampshire	17,208	29	Colorado	14,180
5	New Jersey	20,703	30	Florida	13,902
16	New Mexico	16,711	31	Nebraska	13,012
10	New York	18,670	32	Texas	12,988
11	North Carolina	18,486	33	Georgia	12,930
28	North Dakota	14,581	34	Wyoming	12,151
39	Ohio	11,028	35	West Virginia	11,699
43	Oklahoma	9,919	36	Oregon	11,516
36	Oregon	11,516	37	Delaware	11,208
22	Pennsylvania	15,438	38	Kentucky	11,118
18	Rhode Island	16,497	39	Ohio	11,028
42	South Carolina	10,268	40	South Dakota	10,859
40	South Dakota	10,859	41	Arizona	10,311
6	Tennessee	20,048	42	South Carolina	10,268
32	Texas	12,988	43	Oklahoma	9,919
23	Utah	15,251	44	Missouri	9,766
21	Vermont	15,905	45	Idaho	9,450
19	Virginia	16,145	46	Louisiana	9,337
7	Washington	19,742	47	Mississippi	9,133
35	West Virginia	11,699	48	Alabama	8,718
9	Wisconsin	18,965	49	Nevada	8,630
34	Wyoming	12,151	50	Arkansas	7,557
				District of Columbia	13,894

Source: U.S. Department of Justice, Bureau of Justice Statistics
    "Census of State and Federal Correctional Facilities, 1990" (1992, NCJ-137003)
*For fiscal year 1990. Determined by dividing the amount spent on salaries, wages, supplies, utilities, transportation,
contractual services and other current operating items by the average daily inmate population. Federal average is $14,456,
combined federal/state average is $15,496.

State Prison Inmates Serving Life Sentences in 1992

National Total = 66,585 Inmates*

ALPHA ORDER

RANK	STATE	INMATES	% of USA
8	Alabama	2,606	3.91%
NA	Alaska**	NA	NA
20	Arizona	763	1.15%
27	Arkansas	494	0.74%
1	California	11,767	17.67%
25	Colorado	512	0.77%
35	Connecticut	152	0.23%
29	Delaware	403	0.61%
3	Florida	4,912	7.38%
5	Georgia	3,381	5.08%
47	Hawaii	3	0.00%
32	Idaho	195	0.29%
23	Illinois	565	0.85%
NA	Indiana**	NA	NA
30	Iowa	391	0.59%
26	Kansas	507	0.76%
22	Kentucky	586	0.88%
11	Louisiana	2,230	3.35%
41	Maine	44	0.07%
NA	Maryland**	NA	NA
17	Massachusetts	949	1.43%
6	Michigan	3,193	4.80%
34	Minnesota	160	0.24%
40	Mississippi	49	0.07%
15	Missouri	1,218	1.83%
44	Montana	27	0.04%
38	Nebraska	84	0.13%
18	Nevada	934	1.40%
43	New Hampshire	28	0.04%
19	New Jersey	910	1.37%
33	New Mexico	165	0.25%
2	New York	9,477	14.23%
10	North Carolina	2,237	3.36%
46	North Dakota	13	0.02%
7	Ohio	3,078	4.62%
16	Oklahoma	991	1.49%
28	Oregon	462	0.69%
9	Pennsylvania	2,417	3.63%
39	Rhode Island	83	0.12%
12	South Carolina	1,357	2.04%
37	South Dakota	102	0.15%
13	Tennessee	1,290	1.94%
4	Texas	4,237	6.36%
42	Utah	41	0.06%
45	Vermont	14	0.02%
14	Virginia	1,273	1.91%
21	Washington	608	0.91%
31	West Virginia	260	0.39%
24	Wisconsin	523	0.79%
36	Wyoming	111	0.17%

RANK ORDER

RANK	STATE	INMATES	% of USA
1	California	11,767	17.67%
2	New York	9,477	14.23%
3	Florida	4,912	7.38%
4	Texas	4,237	6.36%
5	Georgia	3,381	5.08%
6	Michigan	3,193	4.80%
7	Ohio	3,078	4.62%
8	Alabama	2,606	3.91%
9	Pennsylvania	2,417	3.63%
10	North Carolina	2,237	3.36%
11	Louisiana	2,230	3.35%
12	South Carolina	1,357	2.04%
13	Tennessee	1,290	1.94%
14	Virginia	1,273	1.91%
15	Missouri	1,218	1.83%
16	Oklahoma	991	1.49%
17	Massachusetts	949	1.43%
18	Nevada	934	1.40%
19	New Jersey	910	1.37%
20	Arizona	763	1.15%
21	Washington	608	0.91%
22	Kentucky	586	0.88%
23	Illinois	565	0.85%
24	Wisconsin	523	0.79%
25	Colorado	512	0.77%
26	Kansas	507	0.76%
27	Arkansas	494	0.74%
28	Oregon	462	0.69%
29	Delaware	403	0.61%
30	Iowa	391	0.59%
31	West Virginia	260	0.39%
32	Idaho	195	0.29%
33	New Mexico	165	0.25%
34	Minnesota	160	0.24%
35	Connecticut	152	0.23%
36	Wyoming	111	0.17%
37	South Dakota	102	0.15%
38	Nebraska	84	0.13%
39	Rhode Island	83	0.12%
40	Mississippi	49	0.07%
41	Maine	44	0.07%
42	Utah	41	0.06%
43	New Hampshire	28	0.04%
44	Montana	27	0.04%
45	Vermont	14	0.02%
46	North Dakota	13	0.02%
47	Hawaii	3	0.00%
NA	Alaska**	NA	NA
NA	Indiana**	NA	NA
NA	Maryland**	NA	NA
	District of Columbia	784	1.18%

Source: "Corrections Compendium" (Lincoln, NE) (January 1993)

*As of September 30, 1992. Total does not include states without data.
**Not available.

Percent of State Prison Inmates Serving Life Sentences in 1992

National Percent = 8.29% of Inmates*

ALPHA ORDER				RANK ORDER		
RANK	**STATE**	**PERCENT**		**RANK**	**STATE**	**PERCENT**
3	Alabama	14.93		1	Nevada	15.44
NA	Alaska**	NA		2	New York	15.35
33	Arizona	4.63		3	Alabama	14.93
28	Arkansas	5.86		4	West Virginia	14.90
9	California	10.75		5	Georgia	13.37
30	Colorado	5.69		6	North Carolina	10.94
44	Connecticut	1.33		7	Tennessee	10.89
12	Delaware	10.13		8	Wyoming	10.86
11	Florida	10.17		9	California	10.75
5	Georgia	13.37		10	Louisiana	10.72
47	Hawaii	0.10		11	Florida	10.17
19	Idaho	7.88		12	Delaware	10.13
40	Illinois	1.79		13	Pennsylvania	9.68
NA	Indiana**	NA		14	Massachusetts	9.44
15	Iowa	8.65		15	Iowa	8.65
16	Kansas	8.41		16	Kansas	8.41
31	Kentucky	5.65		17	Michigan	8.18
10	Louisiana	10.72		18	Ohio	8.02
38	Maine	2.90		19	Idaho	7.88
NA	Maryland**	NA		20	Missouri	7.52
14	Massachusetts	9.44		21	South Carolina	7.28
17	Michigan	8.18		22	Oregon	7.00
34	Minnesota	4.19		23	Texas	6.93
46	Mississippi	0.54		24	South Dakota	6.86
20	Missouri	7.52		25	Oklahoma	6.69
41	Montana	1.74		26	Washington	6.11
36	Nebraska	3.27		27	Virginia	6.01
1	Nevada	15.44		28	Arkansas	5.86
42	New Hampshire	1.58		29	Wisconsin	5.78
35	New Jersey	4.02		30	Colorado	5.69
32	New Mexico	5.04		31	Kentucky	5.65
2	New York	15.35		32	New Mexico	5.04
6	North Carolina	10.94		33	Arizona	4.63
39	North Dakota	2.80		34	Minnesota	4.19
18	Ohio	8.02		35	New Jersey	4.02
25	Oklahoma	6.69		36	Nebraska	3.27
22	Oregon	7.00		37	Rhode Island	2.99
13	Pennsylvania	9.68		38	Maine	2.90
37	Rhode Island	2.99		39	North Dakota	2.80
21	South Carolina	7.28		40	Illinois	1.79
24	South Dakota	6.86		41	Montana	1.74
7	Tennessee	10.89		42	New Hampshire	1.58
23	Texas	6.93		43	Utah	1.52
43	Utah	1.52		44	Connecticut	1.33
45	Vermont	1.10		45	Vermont	1.10
27	Virginia	6.01		46	Mississippi	0.54
26	Washington	6.11		47	Hawaii	0.10
4	West Virginia	14.90		NA	Alaska**	NA
29	Wisconsin	5.78		NA	Indiana**	NA
8	Wyoming	10.86		NA	Maryland**	NA
				District of Columbia		7.21

Source: Morgan Quitno Corporation using data from U.S. Department of Justice, Bureau of Justice Statistics
"Prisoners in 1992" (Bulletin, May 1993, NCJ-141874) and
"Corrections Compendium" (Lincoln, NE) (January 1993)
*National percent does not include states without data.
**Not available.

Prisoners Under Sentence of Death in 1993

National Total = 2,710 State Prisoners*

ALPHA ORDER					RANK ORDER			
RANK	STATE	PRISONERS	% of USA		RANK	STATE	PRISONERS	% of USA
8	Alabama	120	4.43%		1	California	363	13.39%
NA	Alaska**	NA	NA		2	Texas	357	13.17%
9	Arizona	112	4.13%		3	Florida	324	11.96%
20	Arkansas	33	1.22%		4	Pennsylvania	169	6.24%
1	California	363	13.39%		5	Illinois	152	5.61%
32	Colorado	3	0.11%		6	Ohio	129	4.76%
31	Connecticut	5	0.18%		7	Oklahoma	122	4.50%
23	Delaware	15	0.55%		8	Alabama	120	4.43%
3	Florida	324	11.96%		9	Arizona	112	4.13%
12	Georgia	96	3.54%		10	North Carolina	99	3.65%
NA	Hawaii**	NA	NA		11	Tennessee	98	3.62%
22	Idaho	22	0.81%		12	Georgia	96	3.54%
5	Illinois	152	5.61%		13	Missouri	80	2.95%
17	Indiana	47	1.73%		14	Nevada	65	2.40%
NA	Iowa**	NA	NA		15	Mississippi	50	1.85%
NA	Kansas**	NA	NA		16	Virginia	49	1.81%
21	Kentucky	30	1.11%		17	Indiana	47	1.73%
19	Louisiana	45	1.66%		17	South Carolina	47	1.73%
NA	Maine**	NA	NA		19	Louisiana	45	1.66%
23	Maryland	15	0.55%		20	Arkansas	33	1.22%
NA	Massachusetts**	NA	NA		21	Kentucky	30	1.11%
NA	Michigan**	NA	NA		22	Idaho	22	0.81%
NA	Minnesota**	NA	NA		23	Delaware	15	0.55%
15	Mississippi	50	1.85%		23	Maryland	15	0.55%
13	Missouri	80	2.95%		25	Oregon	13	0.48%
29	Montana	8	0.30%		26	Nebraska	11	0.41%
26	Nebraska	11	0.41%		26	Utah	11	0.41%
14	Nevada	65	2.40%		28	Washington	10	0.37%
35	New Hampshire	0	0.00%		29	Montana	8	0.30%
30	New Jersey	7	0.26%		30	New Jersey	7	0.26%
34	New Mexico	1	0.04%		31	Connecticut	5	0.18%
NA	New York**	NA	NA		32	Colorado	3	0.11%
10	North Carolina	99	3.65%		33	South Dakota	2	0.07%
NA	North Dakota**	NA	NA		34	New Mexico	1	0.04%
6	Ohio	129	4.76%		35	New Hampshire	0	0.00%
7	Oklahoma	122	4.50%		35	Wyoming	0	0.00%
25	Oregon	13	0.48%		NA	Alaska**	NA	NA
4	Pennsylvania	169	6.24%		NA	Hawaii**	NA	NA
NA	Rhode Island**	NA	NA		NA	Iowa**	NA	NA
17	South Carolina	47	1.73%		NA	Kansas**	NA	NA
33	South Dakota	2	0.07%		NA	Maine**	NA	NA
11	Tennessee	98	3.62%		NA	Massachusetts**	NA	NA
2	Texas	357	13.17%		NA	Michigan**	NA	NA
26	Utah	11	0.41%		NA	Minnesota**	NA	NA
NA	Vermont**	NA	NA		NA	New York**	NA	NA
16	Virginia	49	1.81%		NA	North Dakota**	NA	NA
28	Washington	10	0.37%		NA	Rhode Island**	NA	NA
NA	West Virginia**	NA	NA		NA	Vermont**	NA	NA
NA	Wisconsin**	NA	NA		NA	West Virginia**	NA	NA
35	Wyoming	0	0.00%		NA	Wisconsin**	NA	NA
					District of Columbia**		NA	NA

Source: U.S. Department of Justice, Bureau of Justice Statistics
    "Capital Punishment 1993" (Bulletin, December 1994, NCJ-150042)
*As of December 31, 1993. Does not includes six federal prisoners under sentence of death. There were 38 executions in 1993.
**No death penalty.

Male Prisoners Under Sentence of Death in 1993

National Total = 2,675 Male State Prisoners*

ALPHA ORDER

RANK	STATE	PRISONERS	% of USA
8	Alabama	116	4.34%
NA	Alaska**	NA	NA
9	Arizona	111	4.15%
20	Arkansas	33	1.23%
1	California	359	13.42%
32	Colorado	3	0.11%
31	Connecticut	5	0.19%
23	Delaware	15	0.56%
3	Florida	320	11.96%
12	Georgia	96	3.59%
NA	Hawaii**	NA	NA
22	Idaho	21	0.79%
5	Illinois	148	5.53%
17	Indiana	47	1.76%
NA	Iowa**	NA	NA
NA	Kansas**	NA	NA
21	Kentucky	30	1.12%
19	Louisiana	45	1.68%
NA	Maine**	NA	NA
23	Maryland	15	0.56%
NA	Massachusetts**	NA	NA
NA	Michigan**	NA	NA
NA	Minnesota**	NA	NA
15	Mississippi	49	1.83%
13	Missouri	78	2.92%
29	Montana	8	0.30%
26	Nebraska	11	0.41%
14	Nevada	64	2.39%
35	New Hampshire	0	0.00%
30	New Jersey	7	0.26%
34	New Mexico	1	0.04%
NA	New York**	NA	NA
10	North Carolina	97	3.63%
NA	North Dakota**	NA	NA
6	Ohio	129	4.82%
7	Oklahoma	118	4.41%
25	Oregon	13	0.49%
4	Pennsylvania	166	6.21%
NA	Rhode Island**	NA	NA
17	South Carolina	47	1.76%
33	South Dakota	2	0.07%
10	Tennessee	97	3.63%
2	Texas	354	13.23%
26	Utah	11	0.41%
NA	Vermont**	NA	NA
15	Virginia	49	1.83%
28	Washington	10	0.37%
NA	West Virginia**	NA	NA
NA	Wisconsin**	NA	NA
35	Wyoming	0	0.00%

RANK ORDER

RANK	STATE	PRISONERS	% of USA
1	California	359	13.42%
2	Texas	354	13.23%
3	Florida	320	11.96%
4	Pennsylvania	166	6.21%
5	Illinois	148	5.53%
6	Ohio	129	4.82%
7	Oklahoma	118	4.41%
8	Alabama	116	4.34%
9	Arizona	111	4.15%
10	North Carolina	97	3.63%
10	Tennessee	97	3.63%
12	Georgia	96	3.59%
13	Missouri	78	2.92%
14	Nevada	64	2.39%
15	Mississippi	49	1.83%
15	Virginia	49	1.83%
17	Indiana	47	1.76%
17	South Carolina	47	1.76%
19	Louisiana	45	1.68%
20	Arkansas	33	1.23%
21	Kentucky	30	1.12%
22	Idaho	21	0.79%
23	Delaware	15	0.56%
23	Maryland	15	0.56%
25	Oregon	13	0.49%
26	Nebraska	11	0.41%
26	Utah	11	0.41%
28	Washington	10	0.37%
29	Montana	8	0.30%
30	New Jersey	7	0.26%
31	Connecticut	5	0.19%
32	Colorado	3	0.11%
33	South Dakota	2	0.07%
34	New Mexico	1	0.04%
35	New Hampshire	0	0.00%
35	Wyoming	0	0.00%
NA	Alaska**	NA	NA
NA	Hawaii**	NA	NA
NA	Iowa**	NA	NA
NA	Kansas**	NA	NA
NA	Maine**	NA	NA
NA	Massachusetts**	NA	NA
NA	Michigan**	NA	NA
NA	Minnesota**	NA	NA
NA	New York**	NA	NA
NA	North Dakota**	NA	NA
NA	Rhode Island**	NA	NA
NA	Vermont**	NA	NA
NA	West Virginia**	NA	NA
NA	Wisconsin**	NA	NA
	District of Columbia**	NA	NA

Source: Morgan Quitno Corporation using data from U.S. Department of Justice, Bureau of Justice Statistics
"Capital Punishment 1993" (Bulletin, December 1994, NCJ-150042)
*As of December 31, 1993. Does not includes six federal male prisoners under sentence of death. There were 38 executions in 1993. All were male.
**No death penalty.

Female Prisoners Under Sentence of Death in 1993

National Total = 35 Female State Prisoners*

ALPHA ORDER				RANK ORDER			
RANK	STATE	PRISONERS	% of USA	RANK	STATE	PRISONERS	% of USA
1	Alabama	4	11.43%	1	Alabama	4	11.43%
NA	Alaska**	NA	NA	1	California	4	11.43%
10	Arizona	1	2.86%	1	Florida	4	11.43%
15	Arkansas	0	0.00%	1	Illinois	4	11.43%
1	California	4	11.43%	1	Oklahoma	4	11.43%
15	Colorado	0	0.00%	6	Pennsylvania	3	8.57%
15	Connecticut	0	0.00%	6	Texas	3	8.57%
15	Delaware	0	0.00%	8	Missouri	2	5.71%
1	Florida	4	11.43%	8	North Carolina	2	5.71%
15	Georgia	0	0.00%	10	Arizona	1	2.86%
NA	Hawaii**	NA	NA	10	Idaho	1	2.86%
10	Idaho	1	2.86%	10	Mississippi	1	2.86%
1	Illinois	4	11.43%	10	Nevada	1	2.86%
15	Indiana	0	0.00%	10	Tennessee	1	2.86%
NA	Iowa**	NA	NA	15	Arkansas	0	0.00%
NA	Kansas**	NA	NA	15	Colorado	0	0.00%
15	Kentucky	0	0.00%	15	Connecticut	0	0.00%
15	Louisiana	0	0.00%	15	Delaware	0	0.00%
NA	Maine**	NA	NA	15	Georgia	0	0.00%
15	Maryland	0	0.00%	15	Indiana	0	0.00%
NA	Massachusetts**	NA	NA	15	Kentucky	0	0.00%
NA	Michigan**	NA	NA	15	Louisiana	0	0.00%
NA	Minnesota**	NA	NA	15	Maryland	0	0.00%
10	Mississippi	1	2.86%	15	Montana	0	0.00%
8	Missouri	2	5.71%	15	Nebraska	0	0.00%
15	Montana	0	0.00%	15	New Hampshire	0	0.00%
15	Nebraska	0	0.00%	15	New Jersey	0	0.00%
10	Nevada	1	2.86%	15	New Mexico	0	0.00%
15	New Hampshire	0	0.00%	15	Ohio	0	0.00%
15	New Jersey	0	0.00%	15	Oregon	0	0.00%
15	New Mexico	0	0.00%	15	South Carolina	0	0.00%
NA	New York**	NA	NA	15	South Dakota	0	0.00%
8	North Carolina	2	5.71%	15	Utah	0	0.00%
NA	North Dakota**	NA	NA	15	Virginia	0	0.00%
15	Ohio	0	0.00%	15	Washington	0	0.00%
1	Oklahoma	4	11.43%	15	Wyoming	0	0.00%
15	Oregon	0	0.00%	NA	Alaska**	NA	NA
6	Pennsylvania	3	8.57%	NA	Hawaii**	NA	NA
NA	Rhode Island**	NA	NA	NA	Iowa**	NA	NA
15	South Carolina	0	0.00%	NA	Kansas**	NA	NA
15	South Dakota	0	0.00%	NA	Maine**	NA	NA
10	Tennessee	1	2.86%	NA	Massachusetts**	NA	NA
6	Texas	3	8.57%	NA	Michigan**	NA	NA
15	Utah	0	0.00%	NA	Minnesota**	NA	NA
NA	Vermont**	NA	NA	NA	New York**	NA	NA
15	Virginia	0	0.00%	NA	North Dakota**	NA	NA
15	Washington	0	0.00%	NA	Rhode Island**	NA	NA
NA	West Virginia**	NA	NA	NA	Vermont**	NA	NA
NA	Wisconsin**	NA	NA	NA	West Virginia**	NA	NA
15	Wyoming	0	0.00%	NA	Wisconsin**	NA	NA
					District of Columbia**	NA	NA

Source: U.S. Department of Justice, Bureau of Justice Statistics
   "Capital Punishment 1993" (Bulletin, December 1994, NCJ-150042)
*As of December 31, 1993. There were 38 executions in 1993. All were male. Since 1977 one woman has been executed.
**No death penalty.

102

Percent of Prisoners Under Sentence of Death Who Are Female: 1993

National Percent = 1.29% of State Prisoners*

ALPHA ORDER

RANK	STATE	PERCENT
2	Alabama	3.33
NA	Alaska**	NA
13	Arizona	0.89
15	Arkansas	0.00
11	California	1.10
15	Colorado	0.00
15	Connecticut	0.00
15	Delaware	0.00
10	Florida	1.23
15	Georgia	0.00
NA	Hawaii**	NA
1	Idaho	4.55
4	Illinois	2.63
15	Indiana	0.00
NA	Iowa**	NA
NA	Kansas**	NA
15	Kentucky	0.00
15	Louisiana	0.00
NA	Maine**	NA
15	Maryland	0.00
NA	Massachusetts**	NA
NA	Michigan**	NA
NA	Minnesota**	NA
7	Mississippi	2.00
5	Missouri	2.50
15	Montana	0.00
15	Nebraska	0.00
9	Nevada	1.54
15	New Hampshire	0.00
15	New Jersey	0.00
15	New Mexico	0.00
NA	New York**	NA
6	North Carolina	2.02
NA	North Dakota**	NA
15	Ohio	0.00
3	Oklahoma	3.28
15	Oregon	0.00
8	Pennsylvania	1.78
NA	Rhode Island**	NA
15	South Carolina	0.00
15	South Dakota	0.00
12	Tennessee	1.02
14	Texas	0.84
15	Utah	0.00
NA	Vermont**	NA
15	Virginia	0.00
15	Washington	0.00
NA	West Virginia**	NA
NA	Wisconsin**	NA
15	Wyoming	0.00

RANK ORDER

RANK	STATE	PERCENT
1	Idaho	4.55
2	Alabama	3.33
3	Oklahoma	3.28
4	Illinois	2.63
5	Missouri	2.50
6	North Carolina	2.02
7	Mississippi	2.00
8	Pennsylvania	1.78
9	Nevada	1.54
10	Florida	1.23
11	California	1.10
12	Tennessee	1.02
13	Arizona	0.89
14	Texas	0.84
15	Arkansas	0.00
15	Colorado	0.00
15	Connecticut	0.00
15	Delaware	0.00
15	Georgia	0.00
15	Indiana	0.00
15	Kentucky	0.00
15	Louisiana	0.00
15	Maryland	0.00
15	Montana	0.00
15	Nebraska	0.00
15	New Hampshire	0.00
15	New Jersey	0.00
15	New Mexico	0.00
15	Ohio	0.00
15	Oregon	0.00
15	South Carolina	0.00
15	South Dakota	0.00
15	Utah	0.00
15	Virginia	0.00
15	Washington	0.00
15	Wyoming	0.00
NA	Alaska**	NA
NA	Hawaii**	NA
NA	Iowa**	NA
NA	Kansas**	NA
NA	Maine**	NA
NA	Massachusetts**	NA
NA	Michigan**	NA
NA	Minnesota**	NA
NA	New York**	NA
NA	North Dakota**	NA
NA	Rhode Island**	NA
NA	Vermont**	NA
NA	West Virginia**	NA
NA	Wisconsin**	NA
	District of Columbia**	NA

Source: Morgan Quitno Corporation using data from U.S. Department of Justice, Bureau of Justice Statistics "Capital Punishment 1993" (Bulletin, December 1994, NCJ-150042)

*As of December 31, 1993. There were 38 executions in 1993. All were male. Since 1977 one woman has been executed.

**No death penalty.

White Prisoners Under Sentence of Death in 1993

National Total = 1,563 White State Prisoners*

ALPHA ORDER

RANK	STATE	PRISONERS	% of USA
7	Alabama	64	4.09%
NA	Alaska**	NA	NA
4	Arizona	96	6.14%
20	Arkansas	20	1.28%
1	California	217	13.88%
30	Colorado	3	0.19%
30	Connecticut	3	0.19%
25	Delaware	7	0.45%
3	Florida	205	13.12%
12	Georgia	48	3.07%
NA	Hawaii**	NA	NA
19	Idaho	22	1.41%
10	Illinois	59	3.77%
15	Indiana	31	1.98%
NA	Iowa**	NA	NA
NA	Kansas**	NA	NA
17	Kentucky	23	1.47%
22	Louisiana	16	1.02%
NA	Maine**	NA	NA
30	Maryland	3	0.19%
NA	Massachusetts**	NA	NA
NA	Michigan**	NA	NA
NA	Minnesota**	NA	NA
20	Mississippi	20	1.28%
13	Missouri	47	3.01%
28	Montana	6	0.38%
25	Nebraska	7	0.45%
14	Nevada	42	2.69%
35	New Hampshire	0	0.00%
29	New Jersey	4	0.26%
34	New Mexico	1	0.06%
NA	New York**	NA	NA
11	North Carolina	55	3.52%
NA	North Dakota**	NA	NA
8	Ohio	63	4.03%
5	Oklahoma	80	5.12%
23	Oregon	12	0.77%
9	Pennsylvania	62	3.97%
NA	Rhode Island**	NA	NA
17	South Carolina	23	1.47%
33	South Dakota	2	0.13%
6	Tennessee	66	4.22%
2	Texas	215	13.76%
24	Utah	9	0.58%
NA	Vermont**	NA	NA
16	Virginia	25	1.60%
25	Washington	7	0.45%
NA	West Virginia**	NA	NA
NA	Wisconsin**	NA	NA
35	Wyoming	0	0.00%

RANK ORDER

RANK	STATE	PRISONERS	% of USA
1	California	217	13.88%
2	Texas	215	13.76%
3	Florida	205	13.12%
4	Arizona	96	6.14%
5	Oklahoma	80	5.12%
6	Tennessee	66	4.22%
7	Alabama	64	4.09%
8	Ohio	63	4.03%
9	Pennsylvania	62	3.97%
10	Illinois	59	3.77%
11	North Carolina	55	3.52%
12	Georgia	48	3.07%
13	Missouri	47	3.01%
14	Nevada	42	2.69%
15	Indiana	31	1.98%
16	Virginia	25	1.60%
17	Kentucky	23	1.47%
17	South Carolina	23	1.47%
19	Idaho	22	1.41%
20	Arkansas	20	1.28%
20	Mississippi	20	1.28%
22	Louisiana	16	1.02%
23	Oregon	12	0.77%
24	Utah	9	0.58%
25	Delaware	7	0.45%
25	Nebraska	7	0.45%
25	Washington	7	0.45%
28	Montana	6	0.38%
29	New Jersey	4	0.26%
30	Colorado	3	0.19%
30	Connecticut	3	0.19%
30	Maryland	3	0.19%
33	South Dakota	2	0.13%
34	New Mexico	1	0.06%
35	New Hampshire	0	0.00%
35	Wyoming	0	0.00%
NA	Alaska**	NA	NA
NA	Hawaii**	NA	NA
NA	Iowa**	NA	NA
NA	Kansas**	NA	NA
NA	Maine**	NA	NA
NA	Massachusetts**	NA	NA
NA	Michigan**	NA	NA
NA	Minnesota**	NA	NA
NA	New York**	NA	NA
NA	North Dakota**	NA	NA
NA	Rhode Island**	NA	NA
NA	Vermont**	NA	NA
NA	West Virginia**	NA	NA
NA	Wisconsin**	NA	NA
	District of Columbia**	NA	NA

Source: U.S. Department of Justice, Bureau of Justice Statistics
"Capital Punishment 1993" (Bulletin, December 1994, NCJ-150042)
*As of December 31, 1993. Does not includes three white federal prisoners under sentence of death. There were 38 executions in 1993, 23 of whom were white prisoners.
**No death penalty.

Percent of Prisoners Under Sentence of Death Who Are White: 1993

National Percent = 57.68% of State Prisoners*

ALPHA ORDER				RANK ORDER		
RANK	**STATE**	**PERCENT**		**RANK**	**STATE**	**PERCENT**
24	Alabama	53.33		1	Colorado	100.00
NA	Alaska**	NA		1	Idaho	100.00
6	Arizona	85.71		1	New Mexico	100.00
17	Arkansas	60.61		1	South Dakota	100.00
20	California	59.78		5	Oregon	92.31
1	Colorado	100.00		6	Arizona	85.71
19	Connecticut	60.00		7	Utah	81.82
29	Delaware	46.67		8	Kentucky	76.67
16	Florida	63.27		9	Montana	75.00
26	Georgia	50.00		10	Washington	70.00
NA	Hawaii**	NA		11	Tennessee	67.35
1	Idaho	100.00		12	Indiana	65.96
31	Illinois	38.82		13	Oklahoma	65.57
12	Indiana	65.96		14	Nevada	64.62
NA	Iowa**	NA		15	Nebraska	63.64
NA	Kansas**	NA		16	Florida	63.27
8	Kentucky	76.67		17	Arkansas	60.61
33	Louisiana	35.56		18	Texas	60.22
NA	Maine**	NA		19	Connecticut	60.00
34	Maryland	20.00		20	California	59.78
NA	Massachusetts**	NA		21	Missouri	58.75
NA	Michigan**	NA		22	New Jersey	57.14
NA	Minnesota**	NA		23	North Carolina	55.56
30	Mississippi	40.00		24	Alabama	53.33
21	Missouri	58.75		25	Virginia	51.02
9	Montana	75.00		26	Georgia	50.00
15	Nebraska	63.64		27	South Carolina	48.94
14	Nevada	64.62		28	Ohio	48.84
35	New Hampshire	0.00		29	Delaware	46.67
22	New Jersey	57.14		30	Mississippi	40.00
1	New Mexico	100.00		31	Illinois	38.82
NA	New York**	NA		32	Pennsylvania	36.69
23	North Carolina	55.56		33	Louisiana	35.56
NA	North Dakota**	NA		34	Maryland	20.00
28	Ohio	48.84		35	New Hampshire	0.00
13	Oklahoma	65.57		35	Wyoming	0.00
5	Oregon	92.31		NA	Alaska**	NA
32	Pennsylvania	36.69		NA	Hawaii**	NA
NA	Rhode Island**	NA		NA	Iowa**	NA
27	South Carolina	48.94		NA	Kansas**	NA
1	South Dakota	100.00		NA	Maine**	NA
11	Tennessee	67.35		NA	Massachusetts**	NA
18	Texas	60.22		NA	Michigan**	NA
7	Utah	81.82		NA	Minnesota**	NA
NA	Vermont**	NA		NA	New York**	NA
25	Virginia	51.02		NA	North Dakota**	NA
10	Washington	70.00		NA	Rhode Island**	NA
NA	West Virginia**	NA		NA	Vermont**	NA
NA	Wisconsin**	NA		NA	West Virginia**	NA
35	Wyoming	0.00		NA	Wisconsin**	NA
					District of Columbia**	NA

Source: Morgan Quitno Corporation using data from U.S. Department of Justice, Bureau of Justice Statistics
    "Capital Punishment 1993" (Bulletin, December 1994, NCJ-150042)
*As of December 31, 1993. Does not includes three white federal prisoners under sentence of death. There were 38 executions in 1993, 23 of whom were white prisoners.
**No death penalty.

Black Prisoners Under Sentence of Death in 1993

National Total = 1,106 Black State Prisoners*

ALPHA ORDER

RANK	STATE	PRISONERS	% of USA
7	Alabama	54	4.88%
NA	Alaska**	NA	NA
19	Arizona	13	1.18%
19	Arkansas	13	1.18%
1	California	138	12.48%
29	Colorado	0	0.00%
27	Connecticut	2	0.18%
22	Delaware	8	0.72%
3	Florida	119	10.76%
8	Georgia	48	4.34%
NA	Hawaii**	NA	NA
29	Idaho	0	0.00%
5	Illinois	93	8.41%
18	Indiana	16	1.45%
NA	Iowa**	NA	NA
NA	Kansas**	NA	NA
23	Kentucky	7	0.63%
14	Louisiana	29	2.62%
NA	Maine**	NA	NA
21	Maryland	12	1.08%
NA	Massachusetts**	NA	NA
NA	Michigan**	NA	NA
NA	Minnesota**	NA	NA
12	Mississippi	30	2.71%
10	Missouri	33	2.98%
29	Montana	0	0.00%
24	Nebraska	3	0.27%
17	Nevada	23	2.08%
29	New Hampshire	0	0.00%
24	New Jersey	3	0.27%
29	New Mexico	0	0.00%
NA	New York**	NA	NA
9	North Carolina	42	3.80%
NA	North Dakota**	NA	NA
6	Ohio	65	5.88%
10	Oklahoma	33	2.98%
29	Oregon	0	0.00%
4	Pennsylvania	102	9.22%
NA	Rhode Island**	NA	NA
15	South Carolina	24	2.17%
29	South Dakota	0	0.00%
12	Tennessee	30	2.71%
2	Texas	137	12.39%
27	Utah	2	0.18%
NA	Vermont**	NA	NA
15	Virginia	24	2.17%
24	Washington	3	0.27%
NA	West Virginia**	NA	NA
NA	Wisconsin**	NA	NA
29	Wyoming	0	0.00%

RANK ORDER

RANK	STATE	PRISONERS	% of USA
1	California	138	12.48%
2	Texas	137	12.39%
3	Florida	119	10.76%
4	Pennsylvania	102	9.22%
5	Illinois	93	8.41%
6	Ohio	65	5.88%
7	Alabama	54	4.88%
8	Georgia	48	4.34%
9	North Carolina	42	3.80%
10	Missouri	33	2.98%
10	Oklahoma	33	2.98%
12	Mississippi	30	2.71%
12	Tennessee	30	2.71%
14	Louisiana	29	2.62%
15	South Carolina	24	2.17%
15	Virginia	24	2.17%
17	Nevada	23	2.08%
18	Indiana	16	1.45%
19	Arizona	13	1.18%
19	Arkansas	13	1.18%
21	Maryland	12	1.08%
22	Delaware	8	0.72%
23	Kentucky	7	0.63%
24	Nebraska	3	0.27%
24	New Jersey	3	0.27%
24	Washington	3	0.27%
27	Connecticut	2	0.18%
27	Utah	2	0.18%
29	Colorado	0	0.00%
29	Idaho	0	0.00%
29	Montana	0	0.00%
29	New Hampshire	0	0.00%
29	New Mexico	0	0.00%
29	Oregon	0	0.00%
29	South Dakota	0	0.00%
29	Wyoming	0	0.00%
NA	Alaska**	NA	NA
NA	Hawaii**	NA	NA
NA	Iowa**	NA	NA
NA	Kansas**	NA	NA
NA	Maine**	NA	NA
NA	Massachusetts**	NA	NA
NA	Michigan**	NA	NA
NA	Minnesota**	NA	NA
NA	New York**	NA	NA
NA	North Dakota**	NA	NA
NA	Rhode Island**	NA	NA
NA	Vermont**	NA	NA
NA	West Virginia**	NA	NA
NA	Wisconsin**	NA	NA
	District of Columbia**	NA	NA

Source: U.S. Department of Justice, Bureau of Justice Statistics
"Capital Punishment 1993" (Bulletin, December 1994, NCJ-150042)
As of December 31, 1993. Does not includes three black federal prisoners under sentence of death. There were 38 executions in 1993, 14 of whom were black prisoners.
**No death penalty.*

Percent of Prisoners Under Sentence of Death Who Are Black: 1993

National Percent = 40.81% of State Prisoners*

ALPHA ORDER

RANK ORDER

RANK	STATE	PERCENT		RANK	STATE	PERCENT
11	Alabama	45.00		1	Maryland	80.00
NA	Alaska**	NA		2	Louisiana	64.44
28	Arizona	11.61		3	Illinois	61.18
16	Arkansas	39.39		4	Pennsylvania	60.36
18	California	38.02		5	Mississippi	60.00
29	Colorado	0.00		6	Delaware	53.33
15	Connecticut	40.00		7	South Carolina	51.06
6	Delaware	53.33		8	Ohio	50.39
19	Florida	36.73		9	Georgia	50.00
9	Georgia	50.00		10	Virginia	48.98
NA	Hawaii**	NA		11	Alabama	45.00
29	Idaho	0.00		12	New Jersey	42.86
3	Illinois	61.18		13	North Carolina	42.42
21	Indiana	34.04		14	Missouri	41.25
NA	Iowa**	NA		15	Connecticut	40.00
NA	Kansas**	NA		16	Arkansas	39.39
26	Kentucky	23.33		17	Texas	38.38
2	Louisiana	64.44		18	California	38.02
NA	Maine**	NA		19	Florida	36.73
1	Maryland	80.00		20	Nevada	35.38
NA	Massachusetts**	NA		21	Indiana	34.04
NA	Michigan**	NA		22	Tennessee	30.61
NA	Minnesota**	NA		23	Washington	30.00
5	Mississippi	60.00		24	Nebraska	27.27
14	Missouri	41.25		25	Oklahoma	27.05
29	Montana	0.00		26	Kentucky	23.33
24	Nebraska	27.27		27	Utah	18.18
20	Nevada	35.38		28	Arizona	11.61
29	New Hampshire	0.00		29	Colorado	0.00
12	New Jersey	42.86		29	Idaho	0.00
29	New Mexico	0.00		29	Montana	0.00
NA	New York**	NA		29	New Hampshire	0.00
13	North Carolina	42.42		29	New Mexico	0.00
NA	North Dakota**	NA		29	Oregon	0.00
8	Ohio	50.39		29	South Dakota	0.00
25	Oklahoma	27.05		29	Wyoming	0.00
29	Oregon	0.00		NA	Alaska**	NA
4	Pennsylvania	60.36		NA	Hawaii**	NA
NA	Rhode Island**	NA		NA	Iowa**	NA
7	South Carolina	51.06		NA	Kansas**	NA
29	South Dakota	0.00		NA	Maine**	NA
22	Tennessee	30.61		NA	Massachusetts**	NA
17	Texas	38.38		NA	Michigan**	NA
27	Utah	18.18		NA	Minnesota**	NA
NA	Vermont**	NA		NA	New York**	NA
10	Virginia	48.98		NA	North Dakota**	NA
23	Washington	30.00		NA	Rhode Island**	NA
NA	West Virginia**	NA		NA	Vermont**	NA
NA	Wisconsin**	NA		NA	West Virginia**	NA
29	Wyoming	0.00		NA	Wisconsin**	NA
					District of Columbia**	NA

Source: Morgan Quitno Corporation using data from U.S. Department of Justice, Bureau of Justice Statistics
"Capital Punishment 1993" (Bulletin, December 1994, NCJ-150042)
*As of December 31, 1993. Does not includes three black federal prisoners under sentence of death. There were 38
executions in 1993, 14 of whom were black prisoners.
**No death penalty.

Prisoners Executed: 1930 to 1993

National Total = 4,085 Prisoners*

<u>ALPHA ORDER</u>

RANK	STATE	EXECUTIONS	% of USA
12	Alabama	145	3.55%
43	Alaska	0	0.00%
25	Arizona	41	1.00%
13	Arkansas	122	2.99%
4	California	294	7.20%
23	Colorado	47	1.15%
29	Connecticut	21	0.51%
33	Delaware	15	0.37%
6	Florida	202	4.94%
1	Georgia	383	9.38%
43	Hawaii	0	0.00%
40	Idaho	3	0.07%
17	Illinois	91	2.23%
24	Indiana	43	1.05%
31	Iowa	18	0.44%
33	Kansas	15	0.37%
15	Kentucky	103	2.52%
10	Louisiana	154	3.77%
43	Maine	0	0.00%
20	Maryland	68	1.66%
28	Massachusetts	27	0.66%
43	Michigan	0	0.00%
43	Minnesota	0	0.00%
9	Mississippi	158	3.87%
19	Missouri	73	1.79%
37	Montana	6	0.15%
38	Nebraska	4	0.10%
27	Nevada	34	0.83%
41	New Hampshire	1	0.02%
18	New Jersey	74	1.81%
35	New Mexico	8	0.20%
3	New York	329	8.05%
5	North Carolina	268	6.56%
43	North Dakota	0	0.00%
7	Ohio	172	4.21%
21	Oklahoma	63	1.54%
30	Oregon	19	0.47%
11	Pennsylvania	152	3.72%
43	Rhode Island	0	0.00%
8	South Carolina	166	4.06%
41	South Dakota	1	0.02%
16	Tennessee	93	2.28%
2	Texas	368	9.01%
32	Utah	17	0.42%
38	Vermont	4	0.10%
14	Virginia	114	2.79%
22	Washington	48	1.18%
26	West Virginia	40	0.98%
43	Wisconsin	0	0.00%
35	Wyoming	8	0.20%

<u>RANK ORDER</u>

RANK	STATE	EXECUTIONS	% of USA
1	Georgia	383	9.38%
2	Texas	368	9.01%
3	New York	329	8.05%
4	California	294	7.20%
5	North Carolina	268	6.56%
6	Florida	202	4.94%
7	Ohio	172	4.21%
8	South Carolina	166	4.06%
9	Mississippi	158	3.87%
10	Louisiana	154	3.77%
11	Pennsylvania	152	3.72%
12	Alabama	145	3.55%
13	Arkansas	122	2.99%
14	Virginia	114	2.79%
15	Kentucky	103	2.52%
16	Tennessee	93	2.28%
17	Illinois	91	2.23%
18	New Jersey	74	1.81%
19	Missouri	73	1.79%
20	Maryland	68	1.66%
21	Oklahoma	63	1.54%
22	Washington	48	1.18%
23	Colorado	47	1.15%
24	Indiana	43	1.05%
25	Arizona	41	1.00%
26	West Virginia	40	0.98%
27	Nevada	34	0.83%
28	Massachusetts	27	0.66%
29	Connecticut	21	0.51%
30	Oregon	19	0.47%
31	Iowa	18	0.44%
32	Utah	17	0.42%
33	Delaware	15	0.37%
33	Kansas	15	0.37%
35	New Mexico	8	0.20%
35	Wyoming	8	0.20%
37	Montana	6	0.15%
38	Nebraska	4	0.10%
38	Vermont	4	0.10%
40	Idaho	3	0.07%
41	New Hampshire	1	0.02%
41	South Dakota	1	0.02%
43	Alaska	0	0.00%
43	Hawaii	0	0.00%
43	Maine	0	0.00%
43	Michigan	0	0.00%
43	Minnesota	0	0.00%
43	North Dakota	0	0.00%
43	Rhode Island	0	0.00%
43	Wisconsin	0	0.00%
	District of Columbia	40	0.98%

Source: U.S. Department of Justice, Bureau of Justice Statistics
   "Capital Punishment 1993" (Bulletin, December 1994, NCJ-150042)
*Includes 33 executions by the federal government. Does not include 160 executions carried out under military authority.
There were no executions from 1968 to 1976. Of the total, 3,560 were executed for murder, 455 for rape and 70 for other
offenses (armed robbery (25), kidnapping (20), burglary (11), sabotage (6), aggravated assault (6) and espionage (2)).

Prisoners Executed: 1977 to 1993

National Total = 226 Prisoners*

<u>ALPHA ORDER</u>

RANK	STATE	EXECUTIONS	% of USA
7	Alabama	10	4.42%
22	Alaska	0	0.00%
14	Arizona	3	1.33%
10	Arkansas	4	1.77%
17	California	2	0.88%
22	Colorado	0	0.00%
22	Connecticut	0	0.00%
14	Delaware	3	1.33%
2	Florida	32	14.16%
5	Georgia	17	7.52%
22	Hawaii	0	0.00%
22	Idaho	0	0.00%
19	Illinois	1	0.44%
17	Indiana	2	0.88%
22	Iowa	0	0.00%
22	Kansas	0	0.00%
22	Kentucky	0	0.00%
4	Louisiana	21	9.29%
22	Maine	0	0.00%
22	Maryland	0	0.00%
22	Massachusetts	0	0.00%
22	Michigan	0	0.00%
22	Minnesota	0	0.00%
10	Mississippi	4	1.77%
6	Missouri	11	4.87%
22	Montana	0	0.00%
22	Nebraska	0	0.00%
8	Nevada	5	2.21%
22	New Hampshire	0	0.00%
22	New Jersey	0	0.00%
22	New Mexico	0	0.00%
22	New York	0	0.00%
8	North Carolina	5	2.21%
22	North Dakota	0	0.00%
22	Ohio	0	0.00%
14	Oklahoma	3	1.33%
22	Oregon	0	0.00%
22	Pennsylvania	0	0.00%
22	Rhode Island	0	0.00%
10	South Carolina	4	1.77%
22	South Dakota	0	0.00%
22	Tennessee	0	0.00%
1	Texas	71	31.42%
10	Utah	4	1.77%
22	Vermont	0	0.00%
3	Virginia	22	9.73%
19	Washington	1	0.44%
22	West Virginia	0	0.00%
22	Wisconsin	0	0.00%
19	Wyoming	1	0.44%

<u>RANK ORDER</u>

RANK	STATE	EXECUTIONS	% of USA
1	Texas	71	31.42%
2	Florida	32	14.16%
3	Virginia	22	9.73%
4	Louisiana	21	9.29%
5	Georgia	17	7.52%
6	Missouri	11	4.87%
7	Alabama	10	4.42%
8	Nevada	5	2.21%
8	North Carolina	5	2.21%
10	Arkansas	4	1.77%
10	Mississippi	4	1.77%
10	South Carolina	4	1.77%
10	Utah	4	1.77%
14	Arizona	3	1.33%
14	Delaware	3	1.33%
14	Oklahoma	3	1.33%
17	California	2	0.88%
17	Indiana	2	0.88%
19	Illinois	1	0.44%
19	Washington	1	0.44%
19	Wyoming	1	0.44%
22	Alaska	0	0.00%
22	Colorado	0	0.00%
22	Connecticut	0	0.00%
22	Hawaii	0	0.00%
22	Idaho	0	0.00%
22	Iowa	0	0.00%
22	Kansas	0	0.00%
22	Kentucky	0	0.00%
22	Maine	0	0.00%
22	Maryland	0	0.00%
22	Massachusetts	0	0.00%
22	Michigan	0	0.00%
22	Minnesota	0	0.00%
22	Montana	0	0.00%
22	Nebraska	0	0.00%
22	New Hampshire	0	0.00%
22	New Jersey	0	0.00%
22	New Mexico	0	0.00%
22	New York	0	0.00%
22	North Dakota	0	0.00%
22	Ohio	0	0.00%
22	Oregon	0	0.00%
22	Pennsylvania	0	0.00%
22	Rhode Island	0	0.00%
22	South Dakota	0	0.00%
22	Tennessee	0	0.00%
22	Vermont	0	0.00%
22	West Virginia	0	0.00%
22	Wisconsin	0	0.00%
	District of Columbia	0	0.00%

Source: U.S. Department of Justice, Bureau of Justice Statistics
"Capital Punishment 1993" (Bulletin, December 1994, NCJ-150042)
*As of December 31, 1993. All executions since 1977 have been for murder.

Prisoners Sentenced to Death: 1973 to 1993

National Total = 4,977 Death Sentences*

<table>
<tr><td colspan="4">ALPHA ORDER</td><td colspan="4">RANK ORDER</td></tr>
<tr><td>RANK</td><td>STATE</td><td>SENTENCES</td><td>% of USA</td><td>RANK</td><td>STATE</td><td>SENTENCES</td><td>% of USA</td></tr>
<tr><td>10</td><td>Alabama</td><td>206</td><td>4.14%</td><td>1</td><td>Florida</td><td>664</td><td>13.34%</td></tr>
<tr><td>NA</td><td>Alaska**</td><td>NA</td><td>NA</td><td>2</td><td>Texas</td><td>576</td><td>11.57%</td></tr>
<tr><td>11</td><td>Arizona</td><td>176</td><td>3.54%</td><td>3</td><td>California</td><td>512</td><td>10.29%</td></tr>
<tr><td>20</td><td>Arkansas</td><td>67</td><td>1.35%</td><td>4</td><td>North Carolina</td><td>343</td><td>6.89%</td></tr>
<tr><td>3</td><td>California</td><td>512</td><td>10.29%</td><td>5</td><td>Ohio</td><td>267</td><td>5.36%</td></tr>
<tr><td>31</td><td>Colorado</td><td>14</td><td>0.28%</td><td>6</td><td>Georgia</td><td>240</td><td>4.82%</td></tr>
<tr><td>34</td><td>Connecticut</td><td>5</td><td>0.10%</td><td>7</td><td>Oklahoma</td><td>224</td><td>4.50%</td></tr>
<tr><td>25</td><td>Delaware</td><td>31</td><td>0.62%</td><td>8</td><td>Pennsylvania</td><td>223</td><td>4.48%</td></tr>
<tr><td>1</td><td>Florida</td><td>664</td><td>13.34%</td><td>9</td><td>Illinois</td><td>211</td><td>4.24%</td></tr>
<tr><td>6</td><td>Georgia</td><td>240</td><td>4.82%</td><td>10</td><td>Alabama</td><td>206</td><td>4.14%</td></tr>
<tr><td>NA</td><td>Hawaii**</td><td>NA</td><td>NA</td><td>11</td><td>Arizona</td><td>176</td><td>3.54%</td></tr>
<tr><td>24</td><td>Idaho</td><td>32</td><td>0.64%</td><td>12</td><td>Tennessee</td><td>159</td><td>3.19%</td></tr>
<tr><td>9</td><td>Illinois</td><td>211</td><td>4.24%</td><td>13</td><td>Louisiana</td><td>137</td><td>2.75%</td></tr>
<tr><td>19</td><td>Indiana</td><td>78</td><td>1.57%</td><td>14</td><td>Mississippi</td><td>127</td><td>2.55%</td></tr>
<tr><td>NA</td><td>Iowa**</td><td>NA</td><td>NA</td><td>15</td><td>South Carolina</td><td>122</td><td>2.45%</td></tr>
<tr><td>NA</td><td>Kansas**</td><td>NA</td><td>NA</td><td>16</td><td>Missouri</td><td>110</td><td>2.21%</td></tr>
<tr><td>21</td><td>Kentucky</td><td>54</td><td>1.08%</td><td>17</td><td>Nevada</td><td>87</td><td>1.75%</td></tr>
<tr><td>13</td><td>Louisiana</td><td>137</td><td>2.75%</td><td>18</td><td>Virginia</td><td>86</td><td>1.73%</td></tr>
<tr><td>NA</td><td>Maine**</td><td>NA</td><td>NA</td><td>19</td><td>Indiana</td><td>78</td><td>1.57%</td></tr>
<tr><td>22</td><td>Maryland</td><td>37</td><td>0.74%</td><td>20</td><td>Arkansas</td><td>67</td><td>1.35%</td></tr>
<tr><td>35</td><td>Massachusetts</td><td>4</td><td>0.08%</td><td>21</td><td>Kentucky</td><td>54</td><td>1.08%</td></tr>
<tr><td>NA</td><td>Michigan**</td><td>NA</td><td>NA</td><td>22</td><td>Maryland</td><td>37</td><td>0.74%</td></tr>
<tr><td>NA</td><td>Minnesota**</td><td>NA</td><td>NA</td><td>22</td><td>New Jersey</td><td>37</td><td>0.74%</td></tr>
<tr><td>14</td><td>Mississippi</td><td>127</td><td>2.55%</td><td>24</td><td>Idaho</td><td>32</td><td>0.64%</td></tr>
<tr><td>16</td><td>Missouri</td><td>110</td><td>2.21%</td><td>25</td><td>Delaware</td><td>31</td><td>0.62%</td></tr>
<tr><td>32</td><td>Montana</td><td>13</td><td>0.26%</td><td>25</td><td>Oregon</td><td>31</td><td>0.62%</td></tr>
<tr><td>30</td><td>Nebraska</td><td>20</td><td>0.40%</td><td>27</td><td>Utah</td><td>23</td><td>0.46%</td></tr>
<tr><td>17</td><td>Nevada</td><td>87</td><td>1.75%</td><td>27</td><td>Washington</td><td>23</td><td>0.46%</td></tr>
<tr><td>39</td><td>New Hampshire</td><td>0</td><td>0.00%</td><td>29</td><td>New Mexico</td><td>22</td><td>0.44%</td></tr>
<tr><td>22</td><td>New Jersey</td><td>37</td><td>0.74%</td><td>30</td><td>Nebraska</td><td>20</td><td>0.40%</td></tr>
<tr><td>29</td><td>New Mexico</td><td>22</td><td>0.44%</td><td>31</td><td>Colorado</td><td>14</td><td>0.28%</td></tr>
<tr><td>36</td><td>New York</td><td>3</td><td>0.06%</td><td>32</td><td>Montana</td><td>13</td><td>0.26%</td></tr>
<tr><td>4</td><td>North Carolina</td><td>343</td><td>6.89%</td><td>33</td><td>Wyoming</td><td>9</td><td>0.18%</td></tr>
<tr><td>NA</td><td>North Dakota**</td><td>NA</td><td>NA</td><td>34</td><td>Connecticut</td><td>5</td><td>0.10%</td></tr>
<tr><td>5</td><td>Ohio</td><td>267</td><td>5.36%</td><td>35</td><td>Massachusetts</td><td>4</td><td>0.08%</td></tr>
<tr><td>7</td><td>Oklahoma</td><td>224</td><td>4.50%</td><td>36</td><td>New York</td><td>3</td><td>0.06%</td></tr>
<tr><td>25</td><td>Oregon</td><td>31</td><td>0.62%</td><td>37</td><td>Rhode Island</td><td>2</td><td>0.04%</td></tr>
<tr><td>8</td><td>Pennsylvania</td><td>223</td><td>4.48%</td><td>37</td><td>South Dakota</td><td>2</td><td>0.04%</td></tr>
<tr><td>37</td><td>Rhode Island</td><td>2</td><td>0.04%</td><td>39</td><td>New Hampshire</td><td>0</td><td>0.00%</td></tr>
<tr><td>15</td><td>South Carolina</td><td>122</td><td>2.45%</td><td>NA</td><td>Alaska**</td><td>NA</td><td>NA</td></tr>
<tr><td>37</td><td>South Dakota</td><td>2</td><td>0.04%</td><td>NA</td><td>Hawaii**</td><td>NA</td><td>NA</td></tr>
<tr><td>12</td><td>Tennessee</td><td>159</td><td>3.19%</td><td>NA</td><td>Iowa**</td><td>NA</td><td>NA</td></tr>
<tr><td>2</td><td>Texas</td><td>576</td><td>11.57%</td><td>NA</td><td>Kansas**</td><td>NA</td><td>NA</td></tr>
<tr><td>27</td><td>Utah</td><td>23</td><td>0.46%</td><td>NA</td><td>Maine**</td><td>NA</td><td>NA</td></tr>
<tr><td>NA</td><td>Vermont**</td><td>NA</td><td>NA</td><td>NA</td><td>Michigan**</td><td>NA</td><td>NA</td></tr>
<tr><td>18</td><td>Virginia</td><td>86</td><td>1.73%</td><td>NA</td><td>Minnesota**</td><td>NA</td><td>NA</td></tr>
<tr><td>27</td><td>Washington</td><td>23</td><td>0.46%</td><td>NA</td><td>North Dakota**</td><td>NA</td><td>NA</td></tr>
<tr><td>NA</td><td>West Virginia**</td><td>NA</td><td>NA</td><td>NA</td><td>Vermont**</td><td>NA</td><td>NA</td></tr>
<tr><td>NA</td><td>Wisconsin**</td><td>NA</td><td>NA</td><td>NA</td><td>West Virginia**</td><td>NA</td><td>NA</td></tr>
<tr><td>33</td><td>Wyoming</td><td>9</td><td>0.18%</td><td>NA</td><td>Wisconsin**</td><td>NA</td><td>NA</td></tr>
<tr><td></td><td></td><td></td><td></td><td></td><td>District of Columbia**</td><td>NA</td><td>NA</td></tr>
</table>

Source: U.S. Department of Justice, Bureau of Justice Statistics
  "Capital Punishment 1993" (Bulletin, December 1994, NCJ-150042)
As of December 31, 1993. Does not include seven federal prisoners sentenced to death.
**No death penalty.*

Death Sentences Overturned or Commuted: 1973 to 1993

National Total = 1,906 Sentences*

<table>
<tr><td colspan="4">ALPHA ORDER</td><td colspan="4">RANK ORDER</td></tr>
<tr><td>RANK</td><td>STATE</td><td>SENTENCES</td><td>% of USA</td><td>RANK</td><td>STATE</td><td>SENTENCES</td><td>% of USA</td></tr>
<tr><td>8</td><td>Alabama</td><td>73</td><td>3.83%</td><td>1</td><td>Florida</td><td>292</td><td>15.32%</td></tr>
<tr><td>NA</td><td>Alaska**</td><td>NA</td><td>NA</td><td>2</td><td>North Carolina</td><td>235</td><td>12.33%</td></tr>
<tr><td>12</td><td>Arizona</td><td>57</td><td>2.99%</td><td>3</td><td>Texas</td><td>136</td><td>7.14%</td></tr>
<tr><td>16</td><td>Arkansas</td><td>29</td><td>1.52%</td><td>4</td><td>Ohio</td><td>133</td><td>6.98%</td></tr>
<tr><td>5</td><td>California</td><td>128</td><td>6.72%</td><td>5</td><td>California</td><td>128</td><td>6.72%</td></tr>
<tr><td>28</td><td>Colorado</td><td>10</td><td>0.52%</td><td>6</td><td>Georgia</td><td>120</td><td>6.30%</td></tr>
<tr><td>37</td><td>Connecticut</td><td>0</td><td>0.00%</td><td>7</td><td>Oklahoma</td><td>95</td><td>4.98%</td></tr>
<tr><td>25</td><td>Delaware</td><td>13</td><td>0.68%</td><td>8</td><td>Alabama</td><td>73</td><td>3.83%</td></tr>
<tr><td>1</td><td>Florida</td><td>292</td><td>15.32%</td><td>9</td><td>Mississippi</td><td>69</td><td>3.62%</td></tr>
<tr><td>6</td><td>Georgia</td><td>120</td><td>6.30%</td><td>10</td><td>South Carolina</td><td>68</td><td>3.57%</td></tr>
<tr><td>NA</td><td>Hawaii**</td><td>NA</td><td>NA</td><td>11</td><td>Louisiana</td><td>67</td><td>3.52%</td></tr>
<tr><td>29</td><td>Idaho</td><td>9</td><td>0.47%</td><td>12</td><td>Arizona</td><td>57</td><td>2.99%</td></tr>
<tr><td>15</td><td>Illinois</td><td>47</td><td>2.47%</td><td>13</td><td>Tennessee</td><td>55</td><td>2.89%</td></tr>
<tr><td>18</td><td>Indiana</td><td>26</td><td>1.36%</td><td>14</td><td>Pennsylvania</td><td>48</td><td>2.52%</td></tr>
<tr><td>NA</td><td>Iowa**</td><td>NA</td><td>NA</td><td>15</td><td>Illinois</td><td>47</td><td>2.47%</td></tr>
<tr><td>NA</td><td>Kansas**</td><td>NA</td><td>NA</td><td>16</td><td>Arkansas</td><td>29</td><td>1.52%</td></tr>
<tr><td>19</td><td>Kentucky</td><td>23</td><td>1.21%</td><td>17</td><td>New Jersey</td><td>28</td><td>1.47%</td></tr>
<tr><td>11</td><td>Louisiana</td><td>67</td><td>3.52%</td><td>18</td><td>Indiana</td><td>26</td><td>1.36%</td></tr>
<tr><td>NA</td><td>Maine**</td><td>NA</td><td>NA</td><td>19</td><td>Kentucky</td><td>23</td><td>1.21%</td></tr>
<tr><td>20</td><td>Maryland</td><td>21</td><td>1.10%</td><td>20</td><td>Maryland</td><td>21</td><td>1.10%</td></tr>
<tr><td>34</td><td>Massachusetts</td><td>4</td><td>0.21%</td><td>20</td><td>New Mexico</td><td>21</td><td>1.10%</td></tr>
<tr><td>NA</td><td>Michigan**</td><td>NA</td><td>NA</td><td>22</td><td>Oregon</td><td>18</td><td>0.94%</td></tr>
<tr><td>NA</td><td>Minnesota**</td><td>NA</td><td>NA</td><td>23</td><td>Missouri</td><td>15</td><td>0.79%</td></tr>
<tr><td>9</td><td>Mississippi</td><td>69</td><td>3.62%</td><td>24</td><td>Nevada</td><td>14</td><td>0.73%</td></tr>
<tr><td>23</td><td>Missouri</td><td>15</td><td>0.79%</td><td>25</td><td>Delaware</td><td>13</td><td>0.68%</td></tr>
<tr><td>32</td><td>Montana</td><td>5</td><td>0.26%</td><td>26</td><td>Virginia</td><td>11</td><td>0.58%</td></tr>
<tr><td>32</td><td>Nebraska</td><td>5</td><td>0.26%</td><td>26</td><td>Washington</td><td>11</td><td>0.58%</td></tr>
<tr><td>24</td><td>Nevada</td><td>14</td><td>0.73%</td><td>28</td><td>Colorado</td><td>10</td><td>0.52%</td></tr>
<tr><td>37</td><td>New Hampshire</td><td>0</td><td>0.00%</td><td>29</td><td>Idaho</td><td>9</td><td>0.47%</td></tr>
<tr><td>17</td><td>New Jersey</td><td>28</td><td>1.47%</td><td>30</td><td>Utah</td><td>8</td><td>0.42%</td></tr>
<tr><td>20</td><td>New Mexico</td><td>21</td><td>1.10%</td><td>31</td><td>Wyoming</td><td>7</td><td>0.37%</td></tr>
<tr><td>35</td><td>New York</td><td>3</td><td>0.16%</td><td>32</td><td>Montana</td><td>5</td><td>0.26%</td></tr>
<tr><td>2</td><td>North Carolina</td><td>235</td><td>12.33%</td><td>32</td><td>Nebraska</td><td>5</td><td>0.26%</td></tr>
<tr><td>NA</td><td>North Dakota**</td><td>NA</td><td>NA</td><td>34</td><td>Massachusetts</td><td>4</td><td>0.21%</td></tr>
<tr><td>4</td><td>Ohio</td><td>133</td><td>6.98%</td><td>35</td><td>New York</td><td>3</td><td>0.16%</td></tr>
<tr><td>7</td><td>Oklahoma</td><td>95</td><td>4.98%</td><td>36</td><td>Rhode Island</td><td>2</td><td>0.10%</td></tr>
<tr><td>22</td><td>Oregon</td><td>18</td><td>0.94%</td><td>37</td><td>Connecticut</td><td>0</td><td>0.00%</td></tr>
<tr><td>14</td><td>Pennsylvania</td><td>48</td><td>2.52%</td><td>37</td><td>New Hampshire</td><td>0</td><td>0.00%</td></tr>
<tr><td>36</td><td>Rhode Island</td><td>2</td><td>0.10%</td><td>37</td><td>South Dakota</td><td>0</td><td>0.00%</td></tr>
<tr><td>10</td><td>South Carolina</td><td>68</td><td>3.57%</td><td>NA</td><td>Alaska**</td><td>NA</td><td>NA</td></tr>
<tr><td>37</td><td>South Dakota</td><td>0</td><td>0.00%</td><td>NA</td><td>Hawaii**</td><td>NA</td><td>NA</td></tr>
<tr><td>13</td><td>Tennessee</td><td>55</td><td>2.89%</td><td>NA</td><td>Iowa**</td><td>NA</td><td>NA</td></tr>
<tr><td>3</td><td>Texas</td><td>136</td><td>7.14%</td><td>NA</td><td>Kansas**</td><td>NA</td><td>NA</td></tr>
<tr><td>30</td><td>Utah</td><td>8</td><td>0.42%</td><td>NA</td><td>Maine**</td><td>NA</td><td>NA</td></tr>
<tr><td>NA</td><td>Vermont**</td><td>NA</td><td>NA</td><td>NA</td><td>Michigan**</td><td>NA</td><td>NA</td></tr>
<tr><td>26</td><td>Virginia</td><td>11</td><td>0.58%</td><td>NA</td><td>Minnesota**</td><td>NA</td><td>NA</td></tr>
<tr><td>26</td><td>Washington</td><td>11</td><td>0.58%</td><td>NA</td><td>North Dakota**</td><td>NA</td><td>NA</td></tr>
<tr><td>NA</td><td>West Virginia**</td><td>NA</td><td>NA</td><td>NA</td><td>Vermont**</td><td>NA</td><td>NA</td></tr>
<tr><td>NA</td><td>Wisconsin**</td><td>NA</td><td>NA</td><td>NA</td><td>West Virginia**</td><td>NA</td><td>NA</td></tr>
<tr><td>31</td><td>Wyoming</td><td>7</td><td>0.37%</td><td>NA</td><td>Wisconsin**</td><td>NA</td><td>NA</td></tr>
<tr><td></td><td></td><td></td><td></td><td></td><td>District of Columbia**</td><td>NA</td><td>NA</td></tr>
</table>

Source: Morgan Quitno Corporation using data from U.S. Department of Justice, Bureau of Justice Statistics
  "Capital Punishment 1993" (Bulletin, December 1994, NCJ-150042)
*As of December 31, 1993. Does not include one federal prisoner whose sentence was overturned.
**No death penalty.

Percent of Death Penalty Sentences Overturned or Commuted: 1973 to 1993

National Percent = 38.30% of Sentences*

ALPHA ORDER				RANK ORDER		
RANK	STATE	PERCENT		RANK	STATE	PERCENT
23	Alabama	35.44		1	Massachusetts	100.00
NA	Alaska**	NA		1	New York	100.00
27	Arizona	32.39		1	Rhode Island	100.00
18	Arkansas	43.28		4	New Mexico	95.45
29	California	25.00		5	Wyoming	77.78
7	Colorado	71.43		6	New Jersey	75.68
37	Connecticut	0.00		7	Colorado	71.43
21	Delaware	41.94		8	North Carolina	68.51
17	Florida	43.98		9	Oregon	58.06
13	Georgia	50.00		10	Maryland	56.76
NA	Hawaii**	NA		11	South Carolina	55.74
28	Idaho	28.13		12	Mississippi	54.33
32	Illinois	22.27		13	Georgia	50.00
26	Indiana	33.33		14	Ohio	49.81
NA	Iowa**	NA		15	Louisiana	48.91
NA	Kansas**	NA		16	Washington	47.83
19	Kentucky	42.59		17	Florida	43.98
15	Louisiana	48.91		18	Arkansas	43.28
NA	Maine**	NA		19	Kentucky	42.59
10	Maryland	56.76		20	Oklahoma	42.41
1	Massachusetts	100.00		21	Delaware	41.94
NA	Michigan**	NA		22	Montana	38.46
NA	Minnesota**	NA		23	Alabama	35.44
12	Mississippi	54.33		24	Utah	34.78
35	Missouri	13.64		25	Tennessee	34.59
22	Montana	38.46		26	Indiana	33.33
29	Nebraska	25.00		27	Arizona	32.39
34	Nevada	16.09		28	Idaho	28.13
37	New Hampshire	0.00		29	California	25.00
6	New Jersey	75.68		29	Nebraska	25.00
4	New Mexico	95.45		31	Texas	23.61
1	New York	100.00		32	Illinois	22.27
8	North Carolina	68.51		33	Pennsylvania	21.52
NA	North Dakota**	NA		34	Nevada	16.09
14	Ohio	49.81		35	Missouri	13.64
20	Oklahoma	42.41		36	Virginia	12.79
9	Oregon	58.06		37	Connecticut	0.00
33	Pennsylvania	21.52		37	New Hampshire	0.00
1	Rhode Island	100.00		37	South Dakota	0.00
11	South Carolina	55.74		NA	Alaska**	NA
37	South Dakota	0.00		NA	Hawaii**	NA
25	Tennessee	34.59		NA	Iowa**	NA
31	Texas	23.61		NA	Kansas**	NA
24	Utah	34.78		NA	Maine**	NA
NA	Vermont**	NA		NA	Michigan**	NA
36	Virginia	12.79		NA	Minnesota**	NA
16	Washington	47.83		NA	North Dakota**	NA
NA	West Virginia**	NA		NA	Vermont**	NA
NA	Wisconsin**	NA		NA	West Virginia**	NA
5	Wyoming	77.78		NA	Wisconsin**	NA
					District of Columbia**	NA

Source: Morgan Quitno Corporation using data from U.S. Department of Justice, Bureau of Justice Statistics
   "Capital Punishment 1993" (Bulletin, December 1994, NCJ–150042)
*As of December 31, 1993. Does not include one federal prisoner whose sentence was overturned.
**No death penalty.

Sentenced Prisoners Admitted to State Correctional Institutions in 1992

National Total = 495,756 Prisoners Admitted*

ALPHA ORDER

RANK	STATE	ADMISSIONS	% of USA
17	Alabama	8,219	1.66%
38	Alaska	1,491	0.30%
19	Arizona	7,705	1.55%
27	Arkansas	4,600	0.93%
1	California	94,477	19.06%
30	Colorado	4,359	0.88%
14	Connecticut	9,778	1.97%
41	Delaware	1,323	0.27%
3	Florida	34,626	6.98%
8	Georgia	16,423	3.31%
37	Hawaii	1,537	0.31%
39	Idaho	1,456	0.29%
7	Illinois	19,929	4.02%
22	Indiana	6,522	1.32%
32	Iowa	3,340	0.67%
31	Kansas	3,705	0.75%
23	Kentucky	5,872	1.18%
12	Louisiana	10,407	2.10%
44	Maine	831	0.17%
16	Maryland	9,124	1.84%
25	Massachusetts	5,402	1.09%
9	Michigan	13,891	2.80%
34	Minnesota	2,918	0.59%
29	Mississippi	4,494	0.91%
15	Missouri	9,251	1.87%
46	Montana	698	0.14%
40	Nebraska	1,411	0.28%
33	Nevada	3,230	0.65%
42	New Hampshire	916	0.18%
11	New Jersey	12,495	2.52%
35	New Mexico	2,255	0.45%
4	New York	32,027	6.46%
5	North Carolina	24,850	5.01%
50	North Dakota	317	0.06%
6	Ohio	23,452	4.73%
20	Oklahoma	7,228	1.46%
28	Oregon	4,513	0.91%
13	Pennsylvania	10,063	2.03%
45	Rhode Island	829	0.17%
18	South Carolina	8,154	1.64%
43	South Dakota	854	0.17%
21	Tennessee	6,764	1.36%
2	Texas	39,886	8.05%
36	Utah	1,670	0.34%
48	Vermont	482	0.10%
10	Virginia	13,235	2.67%
24	Washington	5,476	1.10%
47	West Virginia	587	0.12%
26	Wisconsin	4,696	0.95%
49	Wyoming	406	0.08%

RANK ORDER

RANK	STATE	ADMISSIONS	% of USA
1	California	94,477	19.06%
2	Texas	39,886	8.05%
3	Florida	34,626	6.98%
4	New York	32,027	6.46%
5	North Carolina	24,850	5.01%
6	Ohio	23,452	4.73%
7	Illinois	19,929	4.02%
8	Georgia	16,423	3.31%
9	Michigan	13,891	2.80%
10	Virginia	13,235	2.67%
11	New Jersey	12,495	2.52%
12	Louisiana	10,407	2.10%
13	Pennsylvania	10,063	2.03%
14	Connecticut	9,778	1.97%
15	Missouri	9,251	1.87%
16	Maryland	9,124	1.84%
17	Alabama	8,219	1.66%
18	South Carolina	8,154	1.64%
19	Arizona	7,705	1.55%
20	Oklahoma	7,228	1.46%
21	Tennessee	6,764	1.36%
22	Indiana	6,522	1.32%
23	Kentucky	5,872	1.18%
24	Washington	5,476	1.10%
25	Massachusetts	5,402	1.09%
26	Wisconsin	4,696	0.95%
27	Arkansas	4,600	0.93%
28	Oregon	4,513	0.91%
29	Mississippi	4,494	0.91%
30	Colorado	4,359	0.88%
31	Kansas	3,705	0.75%
32	Iowa	3,340	0.67%
33	Nevada	3,230	0.65%
34	Minnesota	2,918	0.59%
35	New Mexico	2,255	0.45%
36	Utah	1,670	0.34%
37	Hawaii	1,537	0.31%
38	Alaska	1,491	0.30%
39	Idaho	1,456	0.29%
40	Nebraska	1,411	0.28%
41	Delaware	1,323	0.27%
42	New Hampshire	916	0.18%
43	South Dakota	854	0.17%
44	Maine	831	0.17%
45	Rhode Island	829	0.17%
46	Montana	698	0.14%
47	West Virginia	587	0.12%
48	Vermont	482	0.10%
49	Wyoming	406	0.08%
50	North Dakota	317	0.06%
	District of Columbia	7,582	1.53%

Source: U.S. Department of Justice, Bureau of Justice Statistics
   "Correctional Populations in the United States, 1992" (February 1995, NCJ 146413)
*Includes sentenced prisoners admitted because of new court commitments, parole violators returned, escapees returned and others.

New State Prisoners Admitted Through New Court Commitments in 1992

National Total = 334,301 New Prisoners

ALPHA ORDER

RANK	STATE	PRISONERS	% of USA
18	Alabama	5,970	1.79%
36	Alaska	1,220	0.36%
20	Arizona	5,823	1.74%
27	Arkansas	3,300	0.99%
1	California	40,158	12.01%
28	Colorado	3,262	0.98%
21	Connecticut	5,049	1.51%
39	Delaware	1,018	0.30%
2	Florida	29,976	8.97%
8	Georgia	12,121	3.63%
40	Hawaii	921	0.28%
38	Idaho	1,073	0.32%
7	Illinois	15,783	4.72%
19	Indiana	5,944	1.78%
32	Iowa	2,168	0.65%
31	Kansas	2,186	0.65%
23	Kentucky	4,363	1.31%
12	Louisiana	8,055	2.41%
44	Maine	601	0.18%
13	Maryland	7,472	2.24%
29	Massachusetts	2,575	0.77%
11	Michigan	8,935	2.67%
33	Minnesota	2,144	0.64%
25	Mississippi	4,035	1.21%
14	Missouri	6,671	2.00%
46	Montana	514	0.15%
37	Nebraska	1,075	0.32%
30	Nevada	2,497	0.75%
42	New Hampshire	728	0.22%
10	New Jersey	9,056	2.71%
35	New Mexico	1,435	0.43%
3	New York	25,153	7.52%
5	North Carolina	20,282	6.07%
49	North Dakota	243	0.07%
6	Ohio	19,335	5.78%
15	Oklahoma	6,538	1.96%
34	Oregon	2,049	0.61%
16	Pennsylvania	6,407	1.92%
45	Rhode Island	575	0.17%
17	South Carolina	6,328	1.89%
43	South Dakota	683	0.20%
24	Tennessee	4,314	1.29%
4	Texas	23,903	7.15%
41	Utah	745	0.22%
50	Vermont	232	0.07%
9	Virginia	11,031	3.30%
22	Washington	4,796	1.43%
47	West Virginia	489	0.15%
26	Wisconsin	3,792	1.13%
48	Wyoming	378	0.11%

RANK ORDER

RANK	STATE	PRISONERS	% of USA
1	California	40,158	12.01%
2	Florida	29,976	8.97%
3	New York	25,153	7.52%
4	Texas	23,903	7.15%
5	North Carolina	20,282	6.07%
6	Ohio	19,335	5.78%
7	Illinois	15,783	4.72%
8	Georgia	12,121	3.63%
9	Virginia	11,031	3.30%
10	New Jersey	9,056	2.71%
11	Michigan	8,935	2.67%
12	Louisiana	8,055	2.41%
13	Maryland	7,472	2.24%
14	Missouri	6,671	2.00%
15	Oklahoma	6,538	1.96%
16	Pennsylvania	6,407	1.92%
17	South Carolina	6,328	1.89%
18	Alabama	5,970	1.79%
19	Indiana	5,944	1.78%
20	Arizona	5,823	1.74%
21	Connecticut	5,049	1.51%
22	Washington	4,796	1.43%
23	Kentucky	4,363	1.31%
24	Tennessee	4,314	1.29%
25	Mississippi	4,035	1.21%
26	Wisconsin	3,792	1.13%
27	Arkansas	3,300	0.99%
28	Colorado	3,262	0.98%
29	Massachusetts	2,575	0.77%
30	Nevada	2,497	0.75%
31	Kansas	2,186	0.65%
32	Iowa	2,168	0.65%
33	Minnesota	2,144	0.64%
34	Oregon	2,049	0.61%
35	New Mexico	1,435	0.43%
36	Alaska	1,220	0.36%
37	Nebraska	1,075	0.32%
38	Idaho	1,073	0.32%
39	Delaware	1,018	0.30%
40	Hawaii	921	0.28%
41	Utah	745	0.22%
42	New Hampshire	728	0.22%
43	South Dakota	683	0.20%
44	Maine	601	0.18%
45	Rhode Island	575	0.17%
46	Montana	514	0.15%
47	West Virginia	489	0.15%
48	Wyoming	378	0.11%
49	North Dakota	243	0.07%
50	Vermont	232	0.07%
	District of Columbia	900	0.27%

Source: U.S. Department of Justice, Bureau of Justice Statistics
"Correctional Populations in the United States, 1992" (February 1995, NCJ 146413)

Parole Violators Returned to State Prison in 1992

National Total = 141,961 Prisoners*

<table>
<tr><td colspan="4"><u>ALPHA ORDER</u></td><td colspan="4"><u>RANK ORDER</u></td></tr>
<tr><th>RANK</th><th>STATE</th><th>PRISONERS</th><th>% of USA</th><th>RANK</th><th>STATE</th><th>PRISONERS</th><th>% of USA</th></tr>
<tr><td>18</td><td>Alabama</td><td>1,783</td><td>1.26%</td><td>1</td><td>California</td><td>53,225</td><td>37.49%</td></tr>
<tr><td>40</td><td>Alaska</td><td>256</td><td>0.18%</td><td>2</td><td>Texas</td><td>15,937</td><td>11.23%</td></tr>
<tr><td>21</td><td>Arizona</td><td>1,528</td><td>1.08%</td><td>3</td><td>New York</td><td>4,483</td><td>3.16%</td></tr>
<tr><td>25</td><td>Arkansas</td><td>1,169</td><td>0.82%</td><td>4</td><td>Florida</td><td>4,399</td><td>3.10%</td></tr>
<tr><td>1</td><td>California</td><td>53,225</td><td>37.49%</td><td>5</td><td>North Carolina</td><td>4,327</td><td>3.05%</td></tr>
<tr><td>28</td><td>Colorado</td><td>822</td><td>0.58%</td><td>6</td><td>Georgia</td><td>4,189</td><td>2.95%</td></tr>
<tr><td>7</td><td>Connecticut</td><td>4,049</td><td>2.85%</td><td>7</td><td>Connecticut</td><td>4,049</td><td>2.85%</td></tr>
<tr><td>47</td><td>Delaware</td><td>97</td><td>0.07%</td><td>8</td><td>Illinois</td><td>3,937</td><td>2.77%</td></tr>
<tr><td>4</td><td>Florida</td><td>4,399</td><td>3.10%</td><td>9</td><td>Ohio</td><td>3,894</td><td>2.74%</td></tr>
<tr><td>6</td><td>Georgia</td><td>4,189</td><td>2.95%</td><td>10</td><td>Michigan</td><td>3,590</td><td>2.53%</td></tr>
<tr><td>33</td><td>Hawaii</td><td>611</td><td>0.43%</td><td>11</td><td>New Jersey</td><td>3,142</td><td>2.21%</td></tr>
<tr><td>36</td><td>Idaho</td><td>353</td><td>0.25%</td><td>12</td><td>Tennessee</td><td>2,334</td><td>1.64%</td></tr>
<tr><td>8</td><td>Illinois</td><td>3,937</td><td>2.77%</td><td>13</td><td>Oregon</td><td>2,311</td><td>1.63%</td></tr>
<tr><td>34</td><td>Indiana</td><td>552</td><td>0.39%</td><td>14</td><td>Missouri</td><td>2,179</td><td>1.53%</td></tr>
<tr><td>29</td><td>Iowa</td><td>779</td><td>0.55%</td><td>15</td><td>Louisiana</td><td>2,057</td><td>1.45%</td></tr>
<tr><td>22</td><td>Kansas</td><td>1,468</td><td>1.03%</td><td>16</td><td>Pennsylvania</td><td>1,848</td><td>1.30%</td></tr>
<tr><td>23</td><td>Kentucky</td><td>1,347</td><td>0.95%</td><td>17</td><td>Virginia</td><td>1,808</td><td>1.27%</td></tr>
<tr><td>15</td><td>Louisiana</td><td>2,057</td><td>1.45%</td><td>18</td><td>Alabama</td><td>1,783</td><td>1.26%</td></tr>
<tr><td>41</td><td>Maine</td><td>208</td><td>0.15%</td><td>19</td><td>South Carolina</td><td>1,675</td><td>1.18%</td></tr>
<tr><td>20</td><td>Maryland</td><td>1,547</td><td>1.09%</td><td>20</td><td>Maryland</td><td>1,547</td><td>1.09%</td></tr>
<tr><td>24</td><td>Massachusetts</td><td>1,296</td><td>0.91%</td><td>21</td><td>Arizona</td><td>1,528</td><td>1.08%</td></tr>
<tr><td>10</td><td>Michigan</td><td>3,590</td><td>2.53%</td><td>22</td><td>Kansas</td><td>1,468</td><td>1.03%</td></tr>
<tr><td>30</td><td>Minnesota</td><td>765</td><td>0.54%</td><td>23</td><td>Kentucky</td><td>1,347</td><td>0.95%</td></tr>
<tr><td>39</td><td>Mississippi</td><td>283</td><td>0.20%</td><td>24</td><td>Massachusetts</td><td>1,296</td><td>0.91%</td></tr>
<tr><td>14</td><td>Missouri</td><td>2,179</td><td>1.53%</td><td>25</td><td>Arkansas</td><td>1,169</td><td>0.82%</td></tr>
<tr><td>46</td><td>Montana</td><td>138</td><td>0.10%</td><td>26</td><td>Utah</td><td>914</td><td>0.64%</td></tr>
<tr><td>37</td><td>Nebraska</td><td>323</td><td>0.23%</td><td>27</td><td>Wisconsin</td><td>900</td><td>0.63%</td></tr>
<tr><td>32</td><td>Nevada</td><td>677</td><td>0.48%</td><td>28</td><td>Colorado</td><td>822</td><td>0.58%</td></tr>
<tr><td>44</td><td>New Hampshire</td><td>176</td><td>0.12%</td><td>29</td><td>Iowa</td><td>779</td><td>0.55%</td></tr>
<tr><td>11</td><td>New Jersey</td><td>3,142</td><td>2.21%</td><td>30</td><td>Minnesota</td><td>765</td><td>0.54%</td></tr>
<tr><td>31</td><td>New Mexico</td><td>757</td><td>0.53%</td><td>31</td><td>New Mexico</td><td>757</td><td>0.53%</td></tr>
<tr><td>3</td><td>New York</td><td>4,483</td><td>3.16%</td><td>32</td><td>Nevada</td><td>677</td><td>0.48%</td></tr>
<tr><td>5</td><td>North Carolina</td><td>4,327</td><td>3.05%</td><td>33</td><td>Hawaii</td><td>611</td><td>0.43%</td></tr>
<tr><td>49</td><td>North Dakota</td><td>65</td><td>0.05%</td><td>34</td><td>Indiana</td><td>552</td><td>0.39%</td></tr>
<tr><td>9</td><td>Ohio</td><td>3,894</td><td>2.74%</td><td>35</td><td>Washington</td><td>476</td><td>0.34%</td></tr>
<tr><td>38</td><td>Oklahoma</td><td>303</td><td>0.21%</td><td>36</td><td>Idaho</td><td>353</td><td>0.25%</td></tr>
<tr><td>13</td><td>Oregon</td><td>2,311</td><td>1.63%</td><td>37</td><td>Nebraska</td><td>323</td><td>0.23%</td></tr>
<tr><td>16</td><td>Pennsylvania</td><td>1,848</td><td>1.30%</td><td>38</td><td>Oklahoma</td><td>303</td><td>0.21%</td></tr>
<tr><td>42</td><td>Rhode Island</td><td>197</td><td>0.14%</td><td>39</td><td>Mississippi</td><td>283</td><td>0.20%</td></tr>
<tr><td>19</td><td>South Carolina</td><td>1,675</td><td>1.18%</td><td>40</td><td>Alaska</td><td>256</td><td>0.18%</td></tr>
<tr><td>45</td><td>South Dakota</td><td>155</td><td>0.11%</td><td>41</td><td>Maine</td><td>208</td><td>0.15%</td></tr>
<tr><td>12</td><td>Tennessee</td><td>2,334</td><td>1.64%</td><td>42</td><td>Rhode Island</td><td>197</td><td>0.14%</td></tr>
<tr><td>2</td><td>Texas</td><td>15,937</td><td>11.23%</td><td>43</td><td>Vermont</td><td>180</td><td>0.13%</td></tr>
<tr><td>26</td><td>Utah</td><td>914</td><td>0.64%</td><td>44</td><td>New Hampshire</td><td>176</td><td>0.12%</td></tr>
<tr><td>43</td><td>Vermont</td><td>180</td><td>0.13%</td><td>45</td><td>South Dakota</td><td>155</td><td>0.11%</td></tr>
<tr><td>17</td><td>Virginia</td><td>1,808</td><td>1.27%</td><td>46</td><td>Montana</td><td>138</td><td>0.10%</td></tr>
<tr><td>35</td><td>Washington</td><td>476</td><td>0.34%</td><td>47</td><td>Delaware</td><td>97</td><td>0.07%</td></tr>
<tr><td>48</td><td>West Virginia</td><td>85</td><td>0.06%</td><td>48</td><td>West Virginia</td><td>85</td><td>0.06%</td></tr>
<tr><td>27</td><td>Wisconsin</td><td>900</td><td>0.63%</td><td>49</td><td>North Dakota</td><td>65</td><td>0.05%</td></tr>
<tr><td>50</td><td>Wyoming</td><td>22</td><td>0.02%</td><td>50</td><td>Wyoming</td><td>22</td><td>0.02%</td></tr>
<tr><td></td><td></td><td></td><td></td><td></td><td>District of Columbia</td><td>2,345</td><td>1.65%</td></tr>
</table>

Source: U.S. Department of Justice, Bureau of Justice Statistics
"Correctional Populations in the United States, 1992" (February 1995, NCJ 146413)
*Includes other conditional release violators.

Escapees Returned to State Prison in 1992

National Total = 10,031 Prisoners*

ALPHA ORDER					RANK ORDER			
RANK	STATE	PRISONERS	% of USA		RANK	STATE	PRISONERS	% of USA
11	Alabama	208	2.07%		1	New York	1,566	15.61%
45	Alaska	8	0.08%		2	Michigan	816	8.13%
7	Arizona	313	3.12%		3	Connecticut	673	6.71%
46	Arkansas	6	0.06%		4	California	654	6.52%
4	California	654	6.52%		5	Oklahoma	387	3.86%
8	Colorado	254	2.53%		6	Missouri	351	3.50%
3	Connecticut	673	6.71%		7	Arizona	313	3.12%
23	Delaware	86	0.86%		8	Colorado	254	2.53%
12	Florida	199	1.98%		9	North Carolina	220	2.19%
18	Georgia	113	1.13%		10	Iowa	217	2.16%
48	Hawaii	5	0.05%		11	Alabama	208	2.07%
46	Idaho	6	0.06%		12	Florida	199	1.98%
13	Illinois	183	1.82%		13	Illinois	183	1.82%
35	Indiana	16	0.16%		14	New Jersey	171	1.70%
10	Iowa	217	2.16%		15	Washington	155	1.55%
33	Kansas	36	0.36%		16	Kentucky	137	1.37%
16	Kentucky	137	1.37%		17	South Carolina	116	1.16%
21	Louisiana	100	1.00%		18	Georgia	113	1.13%
42	Maine	9	0.09%		18	Tennessee	113	1.13%
20	Maryland	103	1.03%		20	Maryland	103	1.03%
25	Massachusetts	66	0.66%		21	Louisiana	100	1.00%
2	Michigan	816	8.13%		22	Pennsylvania	89	0.89%
42	Minnesota	9	0.09%		23	Delaware	86	0.86%
26	Mississippi	60	0.60%		24	Oregon	70	0.70%
6	Missouri	351	3.50%		25	Massachusetts	66	0.66%
30	Montana	40	0.40%		26	Mississippi	60	0.60%
37	Nebraska	13	0.13%		27	Nevada	56	0.56%
27	Nevada	56	0.56%		28	Vermont	48	0.48%
39	New Hampshire	12	0.12%		29	Rhode Island	47	0.47%
14	New Jersey	171	1.70%		30	Montana	40	0.40%
30	New Mexico	40	0.40%		30	New Mexico	40	0.40%
1	New York	1,566	15.61%		32	Texas	38	0.38%
9	North Carolina	220	2.19%		33	Kansas	36	0.36%
42	North Dakota	9	0.09%		34	Virginia	22	0.22%
40	Ohio	11	0.11%		35	Indiana	16	0.16%
5	Oklahoma	387	3.86%		36	South Dakota	15	0.15%
24	Oregon	70	0.70%		37	Nebraska	13	0.13%
22	Pennsylvania	89	0.89%		37	West Virginia	13	0.13%
29	Rhode Island	47	0.47%		39	New Hampshire	12	0.12%
17	South Carolina	116	1.16%		40	Ohio	11	0.11%
36	South Dakota	15	0.15%		41	Utah	10	0.10%
18	Tennessee	113	1.13%		42	Maine	9	0.09%
32	Texas	38	0.38%		42	Minnesota	9	0.09%
41	Utah	10	0.10%		42	North Dakota	9	0.09%
28	Vermont	48	0.48%		45	Alaska	8	0.08%
34	Virginia	22	0.22%		46	Arkansas	6	0.06%
15	Washington	155	1.55%		46	Idaho	6	0.06%
37	West Virginia	13	0.13%		48	Hawaii	5	0.05%
NA	Wisconsin**	NA	NA		49	Wyoming	3	0.03%
49	Wyoming	3	0.03%		NA	Wisconsin**	NA	NA
					District of Columbia		2,139	21.32%

Source: U.S. Department of Justice, Bureau of Justice Statistics
   "Correctional Populations in the United States, 1992" (February 1995, NCJ 146413)
*Includes AWOLs returned.
**Not available.

Prisoners Released from State Correctional Institutions in 1992

National Total = 447,105 Prisoners*

ALPHA ORDER					RANK ORDER			
RANK	STATE	PRISONERS	% of USA		RANK	STATE	PRISONERS	% of USA
18	Alabama	7,681	1.72%		1	California	87,525	19.58%
37	Alaska	1,387	0.31%		2	Florida	32,872	7.35%
19	Arizona	6,698	1.50%		3	Texas	30,385	6.80%
28	Arkansas	4,127	0.92%		4	New York	28,153	6.30%
1	California	87,525	19.58%		5	North Carolina	23,157	5.18%
29	Colorado	3,754	0.84%		6	Ohio	20,818	4.66%
13	Connecticut	9,569	2.14%		7	Illinois	17,404	3.89%
41	Delaware	1,088	0.24%		8	Georgia	14,584	3.26%
2	Florida	32,872	7.35%		9	New Jersey	13,325	2.98%
8	Georgia	14,584	3.26%		10	Virginia	11,906	2.66%
39	Hawaii	1,381	0.31%		11	Michigan	11,201	2.51%
40	Idaho	1,343	0.30%		12	Louisiana	9,598	2.15%
7	Illinois	17,404	3.89%		13	Connecticut	9,569	2.14%
21	Indiana	6,307	1.41%		14	Missouri	8,967	2.01%
33	Iowa	2,967	0.66%		15	Pennsylvania	8,483	1.90%
31	Kansas	3,580	0.80%		16	Maryland	8,140	1.82%
23	Kentucky	5,307	1.19%		17	South Carolina	7,750	1.73%
12	Louisiana	9,598	2.15%		18	Alabama	7,681	1.72%
42	Maine	897	0.20%		19	Arizona	6,698	1.50%
16	Maryland	8,140	1.82%		20	Tennessee	6,389	1.43%
27	Massachusetts	4,558	1.02%		21	Indiana	6,307	1.41%
11	Michigan	11,201	2.51%		22	Oklahoma	5,747	1.29%
34	Minnesota	2,568	0.57%		23	Kentucky	5,307	1.19%
26	Mississippi	4,583	1.03%		24	Oregon	4,852	1.09%
14	Missouri	8,967	2.01%		25	Washington	4,673	1.05%
45	Montana	678	0.15%		26	Mississippi	4,583	1.03%
38	Nebraska	1,382	0.31%		27	Massachusetts	4,558	1.02%
32	Nevada	3,004	0.67%		28	Arkansas	4,127	0.92%
46	New Hampshire	672	0.15%		29	Colorado	3,754	0.84%
9	New Jersey	13,325	2.98%		30	Wisconsin	3,634	0.81%
35	New Mexico	2,117	0.47%		31	Kansas	3,580	0.80%
4	New York	28,153	6.30%		32	Nevada	3,004	0.67%
5	North Carolina	23,157	5.18%		33	Iowa	2,967	0.66%
50	North Dakota	330	0.07%		34	Minnesota	2,568	0.57%
6	Ohio	20,818	4.66%		35	New Mexico	2,117	0.47%
22	Oklahoma	5,747	1.29%		36	Utah	1,588	0.36%
24	Oregon	4,852	1.09%		37	Alaska	1,387	0.31%
15	Pennsylvania	8,483	1.90%		38	Nebraska	1,382	0.31%
43	Rhode Island	868	0.19%		39	Hawaii	1,381	0.31%
17	South Carolina	7,750	1.73%		40	Idaho	1,343	0.30%
44	South Dakota	741	0.17%		41	Delaware	1,088	0.24%
20	Tennessee	6,389	1.43%		42	Maine	897	0.20%
3	Texas	30,385	6.80%		43	Rhode Island	868	0.19%
36	Utah	1,588	0.36%		44	South Dakota	741	0.17%
49	Vermont	350	0.08%		45	Montana	678	0.15%
10	Virginia	11,906	2.66%		46	New Hampshire	672	0.15%
25	Washington	4,673	1.05%		47	Wyoming	442	0.10%
48	West Virginia	415	0.09%		48	West Virginia	415	0.09%
30	Wisconsin	3,634	0.81%		49	Vermont	350	0.08%
47	Wyoming	442	0.10%		50	North Dakota	330	0.07%
						District of Columbia	7,160	1.60%

Source: U.S. Department of Justice, Bureau of Justice Statistics
   "Correctional Populations in the United States, 1992" (February 1995, NCJ 146413)
*Includes conditional releases, unconditional releases, escapees, out on appeal, deaths and other releases.

State Prisoners Released with Conditions in 1992

National Total = 357,731 Prisoners*

ALPHA ORDER

RANK	STATE	PRISONERS	% of USA
21	Alabama	5,100	1.43%
41	Alaska	733	0.20%
17	Arizona	6,042	1.69%
26	Arkansas	3,027	0.85%
1	California	81,142	22.68%
30	Colorado	2,365	0.66%
15	Connecticut	6,796	1.90%
44	Delaware	514	0.14%
5	Florida	21,680	6.06%
7	Georgia	12,486	3.49%
37	Hawaii	1,225	0.34%
38	Idaho	1,147	0.32%
6	Illinois	16,562	4.63%
18	Indiana	5,788	1.62%
29	Iowa	2,600	0.73%
24	Kansas	3,412	0.95%
25	Kentucky	3,252	0.91%
12	Louisiana	8,811	2.46%
43	Maine	516	0.14%
14	Maryland	7,099	1.98%
36	Massachusetts	1,400	0.39%
11	Michigan	9,219	2.58%
31	Minnesota	2,316	0.65%
32	Mississippi	2,290	0.64%
13	Missouri	7,914	2.21%
42	Montana	539	0.15%
39	Nebraska	812	0.23%
33	Nevada	1,604	0.45%
46	New Hampshire	438	0.12%
8	New Jersey	10,847	3.03%
35	New Mexico	1,407	0.39%
3	New York	23,656	6.61%
4	North Carolina	22,554	6.30%
49	North Dakota	226	0.06%
10	Ohio	9,248	2.59%
27	Oklahoma	2,877	0.80%
22	Oregon	4,701	1.31%
16	Pennsylvania	6,498	1.82%
40	Rhode Island	779	0.22%
20	South Carolina	5,284	1.48%
45	South Dakota	490	0.14%
19	Tennessee	5,348	1.49%
2	Texas	25,645	7.17%
34	Utah	1,422	0.40%
50	Vermont	222	0.06%
9	Virginia	10,808	3.02%
28	Washington	2,833	0.79%
47	West Virginia	302	0.08%
23	Wisconsin	3,495	0.98%
48	Wyoming	254	0.07%

RANK ORDER

RANK	STATE	PRISONERS	% of USA
1	California	81,142	22.68%
2	Texas	25,645	7.17%
3	New York	23,656	6.61%
4	North Carolina	22,554	6.30%
5	Florida	21,680	6.06%
6	Illinois	16,562	4.63%
7	Georgia	12,486	3.49%
8	New Jersey	10,847	3.03%
9	Virginia	10,808	3.02%
10	Ohio	9,248	2.59%
11	Michigan	9,219	2.58%
12	Louisiana	8,811	2.46%
13	Missouri	7,914	2.21%
14	Maryland	7,099	1.98%
15	Connecticut	6,796	1.90%
16	Pennsylvania	6,498	1.82%
17	Arizona	6,042	1.69%
18	Indiana	5,788	1.62%
19	Tennessee	5,348	1.49%
20	South Carolina	5,284	1.48%
21	Alabama	5,100	1.43%
22	Oregon	4,701	1.31%
23	Wisconsin	3,495	0.98%
24	Kansas	3,412	0.95%
25	Kentucky	3,252	0.91%
26	Arkansas	3,027	0.85%
27	Oklahoma	2,877	0.80%
28	Washington	2,833	0.79%
29	Iowa	2,600	0.73%
30	Colorado	2,365	0.66%
31	Minnesota	2,316	0.65%
32	Mississippi	2,290	0.64%
33	Nevada	1,604	0.45%
34	Utah	1,422	0.40%
35	New Mexico	1,407	0.39%
36	Massachusetts	1,400	0.39%
37	Hawaii	1,225	0.34%
38	Idaho	1,147	0.32%
39	Nebraska	812	0.23%
40	Rhode Island	779	0.22%
41	Alaska	733	0.20%
42	Montana	539	0.15%
43	Maine	516	0.14%
44	Delaware	514	0.14%
45	South Dakota	490	0.14%
46	New Hampshire	438	0.12%
47	West Virginia	302	0.08%
48	Wyoming	254	0.07%
49	North Dakota	226	0.06%
50	Vermont	222	0.06%
	District of Columbia	2,006	0.56%

Source: U.S. Department of Justice, Bureau of Justice Statistics
"Correctional Populations in the United States, 1992" (February 1995, NCJ 146413)
Released on parole, probation, supervised mandatory release or other conditions.

State Prisoners Released Conditionally as a Percent of All Releases in 1992

National Percent = 80.01% of Prisoners Released*

<table>
<tr><th colspan="3">ALPHA ORDER</th><th colspan="3">RANK ORDER</th></tr>
<tr><th>RANK</th><th>STATE</th><th>PERCENT</th><th>RANK</th><th>STATE</th><th>PERCENT</th></tr>
<tr><td>33</td><td>Alabama</td><td>66.40</td><td>1</td><td>North Carolina</td><td>97.40</td></tr>
<tr><td>45</td><td>Alaska</td><td>52.85</td><td>2</td><td>Oregon</td><td>96.89</td></tr>
<tr><td>10</td><td>Arizona</td><td>90.21</td><td>3</td><td>Wisconsin</td><td>96.18</td></tr>
<tr><td>27</td><td>Arkansas</td><td>73.35</td><td>4</td><td>Kansas</td><td>95.31</td></tr>
<tr><td>6</td><td>California</td><td>92.71</td><td>5</td><td>Illinois</td><td>95.16</td></tr>
<tr><td>38</td><td>Colorado</td><td>63.00</td><td>6</td><td>California</td><td>92.71</td></tr>
<tr><td>29</td><td>Connecticut</td><td>71.02</td><td>7</td><td>Louisiana</td><td>91.80</td></tr>
<tr><td>48</td><td>Delaware</td><td>47.24</td><td>8</td><td>Indiana</td><td>91.77</td></tr>
<tr><td>35</td><td>Florida</td><td>65.95</td><td>9</td><td>Virginia</td><td>90.78</td></tr>
<tr><td>18</td><td>Georgia</td><td>85.61</td><td>10</td><td>Arizona</td><td>90.21</td></tr>
<tr><td>14</td><td>Hawaii</td><td>88.70</td><td>11</td><td>Minnesota</td><td>90.19</td></tr>
<tr><td>19</td><td>Idaho</td><td>85.41</td><td>12</td><td>Rhode Island</td><td>89.75</td></tr>
<tr><td>5</td><td>Illinois</td><td>95.16</td><td>13</td><td>Utah</td><td>89.55</td></tr>
<tr><td>8</td><td>Indiana</td><td>91.77</td><td>14</td><td>Hawaii</td><td>88.70</td></tr>
<tr><td>16</td><td>Iowa</td><td>87.63</td><td>15</td><td>Missouri</td><td>88.26</td></tr>
<tr><td>4</td><td>Kansas</td><td>95.31</td><td>16</td><td>Iowa</td><td>87.63</td></tr>
<tr><td>39</td><td>Kentucky</td><td>61.28</td><td>17</td><td>Maryland</td><td>87.21</td></tr>
<tr><td>7</td><td>Louisiana</td><td>91.80</td><td>18</td><td>Georgia</td><td>85.61</td></tr>
<tr><td>42</td><td>Maine</td><td>57.53</td><td>19</td><td>Idaho</td><td>85.41</td></tr>
<tr><td>17</td><td>Maryland</td><td>87.21</td><td>20</td><td>Texas</td><td>84.40</td></tr>
<tr><td>50</td><td>Massachusetts</td><td>30.72</td><td>21</td><td>New York</td><td>84.03</td></tr>
<tr><td>23</td><td>Michigan</td><td>82.31</td><td>22</td><td>Tennessee</td><td>83.71</td></tr>
<tr><td>11</td><td>Minnesota</td><td>90.19</td><td>23</td><td>Michigan</td><td>82.31</td></tr>
<tr><td>47</td><td>Mississippi</td><td>49.97</td><td>24</td><td>New Jersey</td><td>81.40</td></tr>
<tr><td>15</td><td>Missouri</td><td>88.26</td><td>25</td><td>Montana</td><td>79.50</td></tr>
<tr><td>25</td><td>Montana</td><td>79.50</td><td>26</td><td>Pennsylvania</td><td>76.60</td></tr>
<tr><td>41</td><td>Nebraska</td><td>58.76</td><td>27</td><td>Arkansas</td><td>73.35</td></tr>
<tr><td>44</td><td>Nevada</td><td>53.40</td><td>28</td><td>West Virginia</td><td>72.77</td></tr>
<tr><td>36</td><td>New Hampshire</td><td>65.18</td><td>29</td><td>Connecticut</td><td>71.02</td></tr>
<tr><td>24</td><td>New Jersey</td><td>81.40</td><td>30</td><td>North Dakota</td><td>68.48</td></tr>
<tr><td>32</td><td>New Mexico</td><td>66.46</td><td>31</td><td>South Carolina</td><td>68.18</td></tr>
<tr><td>21</td><td>New York</td><td>84.03</td><td>32</td><td>New Mexico</td><td>66.46</td></tr>
<tr><td>1</td><td>North Carolina</td><td>97.40</td><td>33</td><td>Alabama</td><td>66.40</td></tr>
<tr><td>30</td><td>North Dakota</td><td>68.48</td><td>34</td><td>South Dakota</td><td>66.13</td></tr>
<tr><td>49</td><td>Ohio</td><td>44.42</td><td>35</td><td>Florida</td><td>65.95</td></tr>
<tr><td>46</td><td>Oklahoma</td><td>50.06</td><td>36</td><td>New Hampshire</td><td>65.18</td></tr>
<tr><td>2</td><td>Oregon</td><td>96.89</td><td>37</td><td>Vermont</td><td>63.43</td></tr>
<tr><td>26</td><td>Pennsylvania</td><td>76.60</td><td>38</td><td>Colorado</td><td>63.00</td></tr>
<tr><td>12</td><td>Rhode Island</td><td>89.75</td><td>39</td><td>Kentucky</td><td>61.28</td></tr>
<tr><td>31</td><td>South Carolina</td><td>68.18</td><td>40</td><td>Washington</td><td>60.62</td></tr>
<tr><td>34</td><td>South Dakota</td><td>66.13</td><td>41</td><td>Nebraska</td><td>58.76</td></tr>
<tr><td>22</td><td>Tennessee</td><td>83.71</td><td>42</td><td>Maine</td><td>57.53</td></tr>
<tr><td>20</td><td>Texas</td><td>84.40</td><td>43</td><td>Wyoming</td><td>57.47</td></tr>
<tr><td>13</td><td>Utah</td><td>89.55</td><td>44</td><td>Nevada</td><td>53.40</td></tr>
<tr><td>37</td><td>Vermont</td><td>63.43</td><td>45</td><td>Alaska</td><td>52.85</td></tr>
<tr><td>9</td><td>Virginia</td><td>90.78</td><td>46</td><td>Oklahoma</td><td>50.06</td></tr>
<tr><td>40</td><td>Washington</td><td>60.62</td><td>47</td><td>Mississippi</td><td>49.97</td></tr>
<tr><td>28</td><td>West Virginia</td><td>72.77</td><td>48</td><td>Delaware</td><td>47.24</td></tr>
<tr><td>3</td><td>Wisconsin</td><td>96.18</td><td>49</td><td>Ohio</td><td>44.42</td></tr>
<tr><td>43</td><td>Wyoming</td><td>57.47</td><td>50</td><td>Massachusetts</td><td>30.72</td></tr>
<tr><td></td><td></td><td></td><td></td><td>District of Columbia</td><td>28.02</td></tr>
</table>

Source: Morgan Quitno Corporation using data from U.S. Department of Justice, Bureau of Justice Statistics
"Correctional Populations in the United States, 1992" (February 1995, NCJ 146413)
*Released on parole, probation, supervised mandatory release or other conditions.

State Prisoners Released on Parole in 1992

National Total = 170,095 Prisoners

ALPHA ORDER

RANK	STATE	PRISONERS	% of USA
16	Alabama	2,871	1.69%
43	Alaska	166	0.10%
28	Arizona	995	0.58%
19	Arkansas	2,324	1.37%
50	California	0	0.00%
20	Colorado	2,209	1.30%
38	Connecticut	274	0.16%
42	Delaware	183	0.11%
41	Florida	190	0.11%
6	Georgia	9,139	5.37%
31	Hawaii	634	0.37%
36	Idaho	407	0.24%
46	Illinois	37	0.02%
48	Indiana	4	0.00%
22	Iowa	1,669	0.98%
18	Kansas	2,436	1.43%
17	Kentucky	2,545	1.50%
21	Louisiana	1,956	1.15%
49	Maine	2	0.00%
14	Maryland	3,907	2.30%
25	Massachusetts	1,400	0.82%
5	Michigan	9,219	5.42%
47	Minnesota	16	0.01%
26	Mississippi	1,357	0.80%
10	Missouri	5,756	3.38%
34	Montana	430	0.25%
30	Nebraska	812	0.48%
23	Nevada	1,604	0.94%
37	New Hampshire	387	0.23%
4	New Jersey	10,540	6.20%
27	New Mexico	1,151	0.68%
3	New York	20,343	11.96%
1	North Carolina	22,528	13.24%
45	North Dakota	117	0.07%
9	Ohio	5,926	3.48%
29	Oklahoma	951	0.56%
11	Oregon	4,700	2.76%
7	Pennsylvania	6,498	3.82%
35	Rhode Island	424	0.25%
13	South Carolina	3,917	2.30%
33	South Dakota	444	0.26%
12	Tennessee	4,011	2.36%
2	Texas	22,130	13.01%
24	Utah	1,422	0.84%
40	Vermont	195	0.11%
8	Virginia	6,208	3.65%
32	Washington	538	0.32%
39	West Virginia	259	0.15%
15	Wisconsin	2,875	1.69%
44	Wyoming	163	0.10%

RANK ORDER

RANK	STATE	PRISONERS	% of USA
1	North Carolina	22,528	13.24%
2	Texas	22,130	13.01%
3	New York	20,343	11.96%
4	New Jersey	10,540	6.20%
5	Michigan	9,219	5.42%
6	Georgia	9,139	5.37%
7	Pennsylvania	6,498	3.82%
8	Virginia	6,208	3.65%
9	Ohio	5,926	3.48%
10	Missouri	5,756	3.38%
11	Oregon	4,700	2.76%
12	Tennessee	4,011	2.36%
13	South Carolina	3,917	2.30%
14	Maryland	3,907	2.30%
15	Wisconsin	2,875	1.69%
16	Alabama	2,871	1.69%
17	Kentucky	2,545	1.50%
18	Kansas	2,436	1.43%
19	Arkansas	2,324	1.37%
20	Colorado	2,209	1.30%
21	Louisiana	1,956	1.15%
22	Iowa	1,669	0.98%
23	Nevada	1,604	0.94%
24	Utah	1,422	0.84%
25	Massachusetts	1,400	0.82%
26	Mississippi	1,357	0.80%
27	New Mexico	1,151	0.68%
28	Arizona	995	0.58%
29	Oklahoma	951	0.56%
30	Nebraska	812	0.48%
31	Hawaii	634	0.37%
32	Washington	538	0.32%
33	South Dakota	444	0.26%
34	Montana	430	0.25%
35	Rhode Island	424	0.25%
36	Idaho	407	0.24%
37	New Hampshire	387	0.23%
38	Connecticut	274	0.16%
39	West Virginia	259	0.15%
40	Vermont	195	0.11%
41	Florida	190	0.11%
42	Delaware	183	0.11%
43	Alaska	166	0.10%
44	Wyoming	163	0.10%
45	North Dakota	117	0.07%
46	Illinois	37	0.02%
47	Minnesota	16	0.01%
48	Indiana	4	0.00%
49	Maine	2	0.00%
50	California	0	0.00%
	District of Columbia	1,826	1.07%

Source: U.S. Department of Justice, Bureau of Justice Statistics
"Correctional Populations in the United States, 1992" (February 1995, NCJ 146413)

State Prisoners Released on Probation in 1992

National Total = 23,096 Prisoners

ALPHA ORDER

RANK	STATE	PRISONERS	% of USA
3	Alabama	2,229	9.65%
17	Alaska	398	1.72%
20	Arizona	171	0.74%
31	Arkansas	0	0.00%
31	California	0	0.00%
21	Colorado	156	0.68%
31	Connecticut	0	0.00%
31	Delaware	0	0.00%
4	Florida	1,643	7.11%
30	Georgia	16	0.07%
14	Hawaii	574	2.49%
12	Idaho	703	3.04%
31	Illinois	0	0.00%
2	Indiana	2,888	12.50%
19	Iowa	234	1.01%
13	Kansas	597	2.58%
11	Kentucky	707	3.06%
16	Louisiana	432	1.87%
15	Maine	486	2.10%
31	Maryland	0	0.00%
31	Massachusetts	0	0.00%
31	Michigan	0	0.00%
31	Minnesota	0	0.00%
10	Mississippi	933	4.04%
6	Missouri	1,438	6.23%
22	Montana	109	0.47%
31	Nebraska	0	0.00%
31	Nevada	0	0.00%
25	New Hampshire	51	0.22%
31	New Jersey	0	0.00%
31	New Mexico	0	0.00%
31	New York	0	0.00%
29	North Carolina	26	0.11%
23	North Dakota	103	0.45%
1	Ohio	3,322	14.38%
5	Oklahoma	1,621	7.02%
31	Oregon	0	0.00%
31	Pennsylvania	0	0.00%
18	Rhode Island	355	1.54%
7	South Carolina	1,354	5.86%
26	South Dakota	46	0.20%
8	Tennessee	1,242	5.38%
9	Texas	1,101	4.77%
31	Utah	0	0.00%
28	Vermont	27	0.12%
31	Virginia	0	0.00%
31	Washington	0	0.00%
27	West Virginia	43	0.19%
31	Wisconsin	0	0.00%
24	Wyoming	91	0.39%

RANK ORDER

RANK	STATE	PRISONERS	% of USA
1	Ohio	3,322	14.38%
2	Indiana	2,888	12.50%
3	Alabama	2,229	9.65%
4	Florida	1,643	7.11%
5	Oklahoma	1,621	7.02%
6	Missouri	1,438	6.23%
7	South Carolina	1,354	5.86%
8	Tennessee	1,242	5.38%
9	Texas	1,101	4.77%
10	Mississippi	933	4.04%
11	Kentucky	707	3.06%
12	Idaho	703	3.04%
13	Kansas	597	2.58%
14	Hawaii	574	2.49%
15	Maine	486	2.10%
16	Louisiana	432	1.87%
17	Alaska	398	1.72%
18	Rhode Island	355	1.54%
19	Iowa	234	1.01%
20	Arizona	171	0.74%
21	Colorado	156	0.68%
22	Montana	109	0.47%
23	North Dakota	103	0.45%
24	Wyoming	91	0.39%
25	New Hampshire	51	0.22%
26	South Dakota	46	0.20%
27	West Virginia	43	0.19%
28	Vermont	27	0.12%
29	North Carolina	26	0.11%
30	Georgia	16	0.07%
31	Arkansas	0	0.00%
31	California	0	0.00%
31	Connecticut	0	0.00%
31	Delaware	0	0.00%
31	Illinois	0	0.00%
31	Maryland	0	0.00%
31	Massachusetts	0	0.00%
31	Michigan	0	0.00%
31	Minnesota	0	0.00%
31	Nebraska	0	0.00%
31	Nevada	0	0.00%
31	New Jersey	0	0.00%
31	New Mexico	0	0.00%
31	New York	0	0.00%
31	Oregon	0	0.00%
31	Pennsylvania	0	0.00%
31	Utah	0	0.00%
31	Virginia	0	0.00%
31	Washington	0	0.00%
31	Wisconsin	0	0.00%
	District of Columbia	0	0.00%

Source: U.S. Department of Justice, Bureau of Justice Statistics
"Correctional Populations in the United States, 1992" (February 1995, NCJ 146413)

State Prisoners Released on Supervised Mandatory Release in 1992

National Total = 126,836 Prisoners

ALPHA ORDER

RANK	STATE	PRISONERS	% of USA
16	Alabama	0	0.00%
15	Alaska	168	0.13%
14	Arizona	231	0.18%
16	Arkansas	0	0.00%
1	California	81,142	63.97%
16	Colorado	0	0.00%
16	Connecticut	0	0.00%
13	Delaware	331	0.26%
16	Florida	0	0.00%
16	Georgia	0	0.00%
16	Hawaii	0	0.00%
16	Idaho	0	0.00%
2	Illinois	16,525	13.03%
7	Indiana	2,896	2.28%
16	Iowa	0	0.00%
16	Kansas	0	0.00%
16	Kentucky	0	0.00%
3	Louisiana	6,410	5.05%
16	Maine	0	0.00%
6	Maryland	3,192	2.52%
16	Massachusetts	0	0.00%
16	Michigan	0	0.00%
10	Minnesota	1,800	1.42%
16	Mississippi	0	0.00%
11	Missouri	720	0.57%
16	Montana	0	0.00%
16	Nebraska	0	0.00%
16	Nevada	0	0.00%
16	New Hampshire	0	0.00%
16	New Jersey	0	0.00%
16	New Mexico	0	0.00%
5	New York	3,313	2.61%
16	North Carolina	0	0.00%
16	North Dakota	0	0.00%
16	Ohio	0	0.00%
16	Oklahoma	0	0.00%
16	Oregon	0	0.00%
16	Pennsylvania	0	0.00%
16	Rhode Island	0	0.00%
16	South Carolina	0	0.00%
16	South Dakota	0	0.00%
16	Tennessee	0	0.00%
8	Texas	2,414	1.90%
16	Utah	0	0.00%
16	Vermont	0	0.00%
4	Virginia	4,600	3.63%
9	Washington	2,294	1.81%
16	West Virginia	0	0.00%
12	Wisconsin	620	0.49%
16	Wyoming	0	0.00%

RANK ORDER

RANK	STATE	PRISONERS	% of USA
1	California	81,142	63.97%
2	Illinois	16,525	13.03%
3	Louisiana	6,410	5.05%
4	Virginia	4,600	3.63%
5	New York	3,313	2.61%
6	Maryland	3,192	2.52%
7	Indiana	2,896	2.28%
8	Texas	2,414	1.90%
9	Washington	2,294	1.81%
10	Minnesota	1,800	1.42%
11	Missouri	720	0.57%
12	Wisconsin	620	0.49%
13	Delaware	331	0.26%
14	Arizona	231	0.18%
15	Alaska	168	0.13%
16	Alabama	0	0.00%
16	Arkansas	0	0.00%
16	Colorado	0	0.00%
16	Connecticut	0	0.00%
16	Florida	0	0.00%
16	Georgia	0	0.00%
16	Hawaii	0	0.00%
16	Idaho	0	0.00%
16	Iowa	0	0.00%
16	Kansas	0	0.00%
16	Kentucky	0	0.00%
16	Maine	0	0.00%
16	Massachusetts	0	0.00%
16	Michigan	0	0.00%
16	Mississippi	0	0.00%
16	Montana	0	0.00%
16	Nebraska	0	0.00%
16	Nevada	0	0.00%
16	New Hampshire	0	0.00%
16	New Jersey	0	0.00%
16	New Mexico	0	0.00%
16	North Carolina	0	0.00%
16	North Dakota	0	0.00%
16	Ohio	0	0.00%
16	Oklahoma	0	0.00%
16	Oregon	0	0.00%
16	Pennsylvania	0	0.00%
16	Rhode Island	0	0.00%
16	South Carolina	0	0.00%
16	South Dakota	0	0.00%
16	Tennessee	0	0.00%
16	Utah	0	0.00%
16	Vermont	0	0.00%
16	West Virginia	0	0.00%
16	Wyoming	0	0.00%
	District of Columbia	180	0.14%

Source: U.S. Department of Justice, Bureau of Justice Statistics
"Correctional Populations in the United States, 1992" (February 1995, NCJ 146413)

State Prisoners Released Unconditionally in 1992

National Total = 58,425 Prisoners

<table>
<tr><td colspan="4">ALPHA ORDER</td><td colspan="4">RANK ORDER</td></tr>
<tr><th>RANK</th><th>STATE</th><th>PRISONERS</th><th>% of USA</th><th>RANK</th><th>STATE</th><th>PRISONERS</th><th>% of USA</th></tr>
<tr><td>6</td><td>Alabama</td><td>2,107</td><td>3.61%</td><td>1</td><td>Ohio</td><td>11,182</td><td>19.14%</td></tr>
<tr><td>24</td><td>Alaska</td><td>600</td><td>1.03%</td><td>2</td><td>Florida</td><td>10,393</td><td>17.79%</td></tr>
<tr><td>29</td><td>Arizona</td><td>397</td><td>0.68%</td><td>3</td><td>Oklahoma</td><td>2,414</td><td>4.13%</td></tr>
<tr><td>17</td><td>Arkansas</td><td>905</td><td>1.55%</td><td>4</td><td>South Carolina</td><td>2,252</td><td>3.85%</td></tr>
<tr><td>14</td><td>California</td><td>1,290</td><td>2.21%</td><td>5</td><td>Mississippi</td><td>2,208</td><td>3.78%</td></tr>
<tr><td>16</td><td>Colorado</td><td>959</td><td>1.64%</td><td>6</td><td>Alabama</td><td>2,107</td><td>3.61%</td></tr>
<tr><td>8</td><td>Connecticut</td><td>2,044</td><td>3.50%</td><td>7</td><td>New Jersey</td><td>2,078</td><td>3.56%</td></tr>
<tr><td>33</td><td>Delaware</td><td>324</td><td>0.55%</td><td>8</td><td>Connecticut</td><td>2,044</td><td>3.50%</td></tr>
<tr><td>2</td><td>Florida</td><td>10,393</td><td>17.79%</td><td>9</td><td>Kentucky</td><td>1,807</td><td>3.09%</td></tr>
<tr><td>12</td><td>Georgia</td><td>1,391</td><td>2.38%</td><td>10</td><td>Massachusetts</td><td>1,690</td><td>2.89%</td></tr>
<tr><td>43</td><td>Hawaii</td><td>104</td><td>0.18%</td><td>11</td><td>Washington</td><td>1,616</td><td>2.77%</td></tr>
<tr><td>38</td><td>Idaho</td><td>156</td><td>0.27%</td><td>12</td><td>Georgia</td><td>1,391</td><td>2.38%</td></tr>
<tr><td>31</td><td>Illinois</td><td>352</td><td>0.60%</td><td>13</td><td>Nevada</td><td>1,324</td><td>2.27%</td></tr>
<tr><td>28</td><td>Indiana</td><td>470</td><td>0.80%</td><td>14</td><td>California</td><td>1,290</td><td>2.21%</td></tr>
<tr><td>34</td><td>Iowa</td><td>265</td><td>0.45%</td><td>15</td><td>Virginia</td><td>1,008</td><td>1.73%</td></tr>
<tr><td>41</td><td>Kansas</td><td>118</td><td>0.20%</td><td>16</td><td>Colorado</td><td>959</td><td>1.64%</td></tr>
<tr><td>9</td><td>Kentucky</td><td>1,807</td><td>3.09%</td><td>17</td><td>Arkansas</td><td>905</td><td>1.55%</td></tr>
<tr><td>26</td><td>Louisiana</td><td>530</td><td>0.91%</td><td>18</td><td>Maryland</td><td>882</td><td>1.51%</td></tr>
<tr><td>32</td><td>Maine</td><td>333</td><td>0.57%</td><td>19</td><td>Tennessee</td><td>797</td><td>1.36%</td></tr>
<tr><td>18</td><td>Maryland</td><td>882</td><td>1.51%</td><td>20</td><td>Pennsylvania</td><td>784</td><td>1.34%</td></tr>
<tr><td>10</td><td>Massachusetts</td><td>1,690</td><td>2.89%</td><td>21</td><td>New York</td><td>694</td><td>1.19%</td></tr>
<tr><td>23</td><td>Michigan</td><td>611</td><td>1.05%</td><td>22</td><td>New Mexico</td><td>633</td><td>1.08%</td></tr>
<tr><td>37</td><td>Minnesota</td><td>220</td><td>0.38%</td><td>23</td><td>Michigan</td><td>611</td><td>1.05%</td></tr>
<tr><td>5</td><td>Mississippi</td><td>2,208</td><td>3.78%</td><td>24</td><td>Alaska</td><td>600</td><td>1.03%</td></tr>
<tr><td>27</td><td>Missouri</td><td>526</td><td>0.90%</td><td>25</td><td>Nebraska</td><td>551</td><td>0.94%</td></tr>
<tr><td>46</td><td>Montana</td><td>92</td><td>0.16%</td><td>26</td><td>Louisiana</td><td>530</td><td>0.91%</td></tr>
<tr><td>25</td><td>Nebraska</td><td>551</td><td>0.94%</td><td>27</td><td>Missouri</td><td>526</td><td>0.90%</td></tr>
<tr><td>13</td><td>Nevada</td><td>1,324</td><td>2.27%</td><td>28</td><td>Indiana</td><td>470</td><td>0.80%</td></tr>
<tr><td>42</td><td>New Hampshire</td><td>116</td><td>0.20%</td><td>29</td><td>Arizona</td><td>397</td><td>0.68%</td></tr>
<tr><td>7</td><td>New Jersey</td><td>2,078</td><td>3.56%</td><td>30</td><td>North Carolina</td><td>365</td><td>0.62%</td></tr>
<tr><td>22</td><td>New Mexico</td><td>633</td><td>1.08%</td><td>31</td><td>Illinois</td><td>352</td><td>0.60%</td></tr>
<tr><td>21</td><td>New York</td><td>694</td><td>1.19%</td><td>32</td><td>Maine</td><td>333</td><td>0.57%</td></tr>
<tr><td>30</td><td>North Carolina</td><td>365</td><td>0.62%</td><td>33</td><td>Delaware</td><td>324</td><td>0.55%</td></tr>
<tr><td>46</td><td>North Dakota</td><td>92</td><td>0.16%</td><td>34</td><td>Iowa</td><td>265</td><td>0.45%</td></tr>
<tr><td>1</td><td>Ohio</td><td>11,182</td><td>19.14%</td><td>35</td><td>Texas</td><td>234</td><td>0.40%</td></tr>
<tr><td>3</td><td>Oklahoma</td><td>2,414</td><td>4.13%</td><td>36</td><td>South Dakota</td><td>226</td><td>0.39%</td></tr>
<tr><td>49</td><td>Oregon</td><td>39</td><td>0.07%</td><td>37</td><td>Minnesota</td><td>220</td><td>0.38%</td></tr>
<tr><td>20</td><td>Pennsylvania</td><td>784</td><td>1.34%</td><td>38</td><td>Idaho</td><td>156</td><td>0.27%</td></tr>
<tr><td>50</td><td>Rhode Island</td><td>15</td><td>0.03%</td><td>39</td><td>Wyoming</td><td>150</td><td>0.26%</td></tr>
<tr><td>4</td><td>South Carolina</td><td>2,252</td><td>3.85%</td><td>40</td><td>Utah</td><td>138</td><td>0.24%</td></tr>
<tr><td>36</td><td>South Dakota</td><td>226</td><td>0.39%</td><td>41</td><td>Kansas</td><td>118</td><td>0.20%</td></tr>
<tr><td>19</td><td>Tennessee</td><td>797</td><td>1.36%</td><td>42</td><td>New Hampshire</td><td>116</td><td>0.20%</td></tr>
<tr><td>35</td><td>Texas</td><td>234</td><td>0.40%</td><td>43</td><td>Hawaii</td><td>104</td><td>0.18%</td></tr>
<tr><td>40</td><td>Utah</td><td>138</td><td>0.24%</td><td>44</td><td>Wisconsin</td><td>101</td><td>0.17%</td></tr>
<tr><td>45</td><td>Vermont</td><td>98</td><td>0.17%</td><td>45</td><td>Vermont</td><td>98</td><td>0.17%</td></tr>
<tr><td>15</td><td>Virginia</td><td>1,008</td><td>1.73%</td><td>46</td><td>Montana</td><td>92</td><td>0.16%</td></tr>
<tr><td>11</td><td>Washington</td><td>1,616</td><td>2.77%</td><td>46</td><td>North Dakota</td><td>92</td><td>0.16%</td></tr>
<tr><td>48</td><td>West Virginia</td><td>82</td><td>0.14%</td><td>48</td><td>West Virginia</td><td>82</td><td>0.14%</td></tr>
<tr><td>44</td><td>Wisconsin</td><td>101</td><td>0.17%</td><td>49</td><td>Oregon</td><td>39</td><td>0.07%</td></tr>
<tr><td>39</td><td>Wyoming</td><td>150</td><td>0.26%</td><td>50</td><td>Rhode Island</td><td>15</td><td>0.03%</td></tr>
<tr><td></td><td></td><td></td><td></td><td></td><td>District of Columbia</td><td>662</td><td>1.13%</td></tr>
</table>

Source: U.S. Department of Justice, Bureau of Justice Statistics
"Correctional Populations in the United States, 1992" (February 1995, NCJ 146413)

State Prisoners Released Unconditionally as a Percent of All Releases in 1992

National Percent = 13.07% of Released Prisoners

ALPHA ORDER

RANK ORDER

RANK	STATE	PERCENT		RANK	STATE	PERCENT
19	Alabama	27.43		1	Ohio	53.71
4	Alaska	43.26		2	Mississippi	48.18
38	Arizona	5.93		3	Nevada	44.07
21	Arkansas	21.93		4	Alaska	43.26
48	California	1.47		5	Oklahoma	42.00
20	Colorado	25.55		6	Nebraska	39.87
22	Connecticut	21.36		7	Maine	37.12
15	Delaware	29.78		8	Massachusetts	37.08
12	Florida	31.62		9	Washington	34.58
30	Georgia	9.54		10	Kentucky	34.05
36	Hawaii	7.53		11	Wyoming	33.94
28	Idaho	11.62		12	Florida	31.62
45	Illinois	2.02		13	South Dakota	30.50
37	Indiana	7.45		14	New Mexico	29.90
32	Iowa	8.93		15	Delaware	29.78
42	Kansas	3.30		16	South Carolina	29.06
10	Kentucky	34.05		17	Vermont	28.00
40	Louisiana	5.52		18	North Dakota	27.88
7	Maine	37.12		19	Alabama	27.43
29	Maryland	10.84		20	Colorado	25.55
8	Massachusetts	37.08		21	Arkansas	21.93
41	Michigan	5.45		22	Connecticut	21.36
34	Minnesota	8.57		23	West Virginia	19.76
2	Mississippi	48.18		24	New Hampshire	17.26
39	Missouri	5.87		25	New Jersey	15.59
26	Montana	13.57		26	Montana	13.57
6	Nebraska	39.87		27	Tennessee	12.47
3	Nevada	44.07		28	Idaho	11.62
24	New Hampshire	17.26		29	Maryland	10.84
25	New Jersey	15.59		30	Georgia	9.54
14	New Mexico	29.90		31	Pennsylvania	9.24
44	New York	2.47		32	Iowa	8.93
47	North Carolina	1.58		33	Utah	8.69
18	North Dakota	27.88		34	Minnesota	8.57
1	Ohio	53.71		35	Virginia	8.47
5	Oklahoma	42.00		36	Hawaii	7.53
49	Oregon	0.80		37	Indiana	7.45
31	Pennsylvania	9.24		38	Arizona	5.93
46	Rhode Island	1.73		39	Missouri	5.87
16	South Carolina	29.06		40	Louisiana	5.52
13	South Dakota	30.50		41	Michigan	5.45
27	Tennessee	12.47		42	Kansas	3.30
50	Texas	0.77		43	Wisconsin	2.78
33	Utah	8.69		44	New York	2.47
17	Vermont	28.00		45	Illinois	2.02
35	Virginia	8.47		46	Rhode Island	1.73
9	Washington	34.58		47	North Carolina	1.58
23	West Virginia	19.76		48	California	1.47
43	Wisconsin	2.78		49	Oregon	0.80
11	Wyoming	33.94		50	Texas	0.77
					District of Columbia	9.25

Source: Morgan Quitno Corporation using data from U.S. Department of Justice, Bureau of Justice Statistics
"Correctional Populations in the United States, 1992" (February 1995, NCJ 146413)

State Prisoners Released on Appeal or Bond in 1992

National Total = 1,203 Prisoners

<table>
<tr><td colspan="4"><u>ALPHA ORDER</u></td><td colspan="4"><u>RANK ORDER</u></td></tr>
<tr><td>RANK</td><td>STATE</td><td>PRISONERS</td><td>% of USA</td><td>RANK</td><td>STATE</td><td>PRISONERS</td><td>% of USA</td></tr>
<tr><td>6</td><td>Alabama</td><td>94</td><td>7.81%</td><td>1</td><td>Connecticut</td><td>239</td><td>19.87%</td></tr>
<tr><td>13</td><td>Alaska</td><td>24</td><td>2.00%</td><td>2</td><td>New York</td><td>151</td><td>12.55%</td></tr>
<tr><td>32</td><td>Arizona</td><td>0</td><td>0.00%</td><td>3</td><td>Michigan</td><td>132</td><td>10.97%</td></tr>
<tr><td>4</td><td>Arkansas</td><td>127</td><td>10.56%</td><td>4</td><td>Arkansas</td><td>127</td><td>10.56%</td></tr>
<tr><td>NA</td><td>California*</td><td>NA</td><td>NA</td><td>5</td><td>New Jersey</td><td>95</td><td>7.90%</td></tr>
<tr><td>17</td><td>Colorado</td><td>11</td><td>0.91%</td><td>6</td><td>Alabama</td><td>94</td><td>7.81%</td></tr>
<tr><td>1</td><td>Connecticut</td><td>239</td><td>19.87%</td><td>7</td><td>Louisiana</td><td>57</td><td>4.74%</td></tr>
<tr><td>32</td><td>Delaware</td><td>0</td><td>0.00%</td><td>8</td><td>Ohio</td><td>42</td><td>3.49%</td></tr>
<tr><td>NA</td><td>Florida*</td><td>NA</td><td>NA</td><td>9</td><td>Washington</td><td>33</td><td>2.74%</td></tr>
<tr><td>NA</td><td>Georgia*</td><td>NA</td><td>NA</td><td>10</td><td>Pennsylvania</td><td>29</td><td>2.41%</td></tr>
<tr><td>32</td><td>Hawaii</td><td>0</td><td>0.00%</td><td>11</td><td>Iowa</td><td>26</td><td>2.16%</td></tr>
<tr><td>28</td><td>Idaho</td><td>2</td><td>0.17%</td><td>12</td><td>Missouri</td><td>25</td><td>2.08%</td></tr>
<tr><td>14</td><td>Illinois</td><td>21</td><td>1.75%</td><td>13</td><td>Alaska</td><td>24</td><td>2.00%</td></tr>
<tr><td>NA</td><td>Indiana*</td><td>NA</td><td>NA</td><td>14</td><td>Illinois</td><td>21</td><td>1.75%</td></tr>
<tr><td>11</td><td>Iowa</td><td>26</td><td>2.16%</td><td>15</td><td>South Carolina</td><td>16</td><td>1.33%</td></tr>
<tr><td>19</td><td>Kansas</td><td>8</td><td>0.67%</td><td>15</td><td>Virginia</td><td>16</td><td>1.33%</td></tr>
<tr><td>NA</td><td>Kentucky*</td><td>NA</td><td>NA</td><td>17</td><td>Colorado</td><td>11</td><td>0.91%</td></tr>
<tr><td>7</td><td>Louisiana</td><td>57</td><td>4.74%</td><td>17</td><td>Utah</td><td>11</td><td>0.91%</td></tr>
<tr><td>20</td><td>Maine</td><td>7</td><td>0.58%</td><td>19</td><td>Kansas</td><td>8</td><td>0.67%</td></tr>
<tr><td>NA</td><td>Maryland*</td><td>NA</td><td>NA</td><td>20</td><td>Maine</td><td>7</td><td>0.58%</td></tr>
<tr><td>NA</td><td>Massachusetts*</td><td>NA</td><td>NA</td><td>20</td><td>Rhode Island</td><td>7</td><td>0.58%</td></tr>
<tr><td>3</td><td>Michigan</td><td>132</td><td>10.97%</td><td>22</td><td>New Hampshire</td><td>6</td><td>0.50%</td></tr>
<tr><td>32</td><td>Minnesota</td><td>0</td><td>0.00%</td><td>23</td><td>New Mexico</td><td>5</td><td>0.42%</td></tr>
<tr><td>NA</td><td>Mississippi*</td><td>NA</td><td>NA</td><td>24</td><td>Oklahoma</td><td>4</td><td>0.33%</td></tr>
<tr><td>12</td><td>Missouri</td><td>25</td><td>2.08%</td><td>24</td><td>Wyoming</td><td>4</td><td>0.33%</td></tr>
<tr><td>26</td><td>Montana</td><td>3</td><td>0.25%</td><td>26</td><td>Montana</td><td>3</td><td>0.25%</td></tr>
<tr><td>NA</td><td>Nebraska*</td><td>NA</td><td>NA</td><td>26</td><td>Nevada</td><td>3</td><td>0.25%</td></tr>
<tr><td>26</td><td>Nevada</td><td>3</td><td>0.25%</td><td>28</td><td>Idaho</td><td>2</td><td>0.17%</td></tr>
<tr><td>22</td><td>New Hampshire</td><td>6</td><td>0.50%</td><td>28</td><td>North Dakota</td><td>2</td><td>0.17%</td></tr>
<tr><td>5</td><td>New Jersey</td><td>95</td><td>7.90%</td><td>28</td><td>Oregon</td><td>2</td><td>0.17%</td></tr>
<tr><td>23</td><td>New Mexico</td><td>5</td><td>0.42%</td><td>31</td><td>South Dakota</td><td>1</td><td>0.08%</td></tr>
<tr><td>2</td><td>New York</td><td>151</td><td>12.55%</td><td>32</td><td>Arizona</td><td>0</td><td>0.00%</td></tr>
<tr><td>32</td><td>North Carolina</td><td>0</td><td>0.00%</td><td>32</td><td>Delaware</td><td>0</td><td>0.00%</td></tr>
<tr><td>28</td><td>North Dakota</td><td>2</td><td>0.17%</td><td>32</td><td>Hawaii</td><td>0</td><td>0.00%</td></tr>
<tr><td>8</td><td>Ohio</td><td>42</td><td>3.49%</td><td>32</td><td>Minnesota</td><td>0</td><td>0.00%</td></tr>
<tr><td>24</td><td>Oklahoma</td><td>4</td><td>0.33%</td><td>32</td><td>North Carolina</td><td>0</td><td>0.00%</td></tr>
<tr><td>28</td><td>Oregon</td><td>2</td><td>0.17%</td><td>32</td><td>West Virginia</td><td>0</td><td>0.00%</td></tr>
<tr><td>10</td><td>Pennsylvania</td><td>29</td><td>2.41%</td><td>NA</td><td>California*</td><td>NA</td><td>NA</td></tr>
<tr><td>20</td><td>Rhode Island</td><td>7</td><td>0.58%</td><td>NA</td><td>Florida*</td><td>NA</td><td>NA</td></tr>
<tr><td>15</td><td>South Carolina</td><td>16</td><td>1.33%</td><td>NA</td><td>Georgia*</td><td>NA</td><td>NA</td></tr>
<tr><td>31</td><td>South Dakota</td><td>1</td><td>0.08%</td><td>NA</td><td>Indiana*</td><td>NA</td><td>NA</td></tr>
<tr><td>NA</td><td>Tennessee*</td><td>NA</td><td>NA</td><td>NA</td><td>Kentucky*</td><td>NA</td><td>NA</td></tr>
<tr><td>NA</td><td>Texas*</td><td>NA</td><td>NA</td><td>NA</td><td>Maryland*</td><td>NA</td><td>NA</td></tr>
<tr><td>17</td><td>Utah</td><td>11</td><td>0.91%</td><td>NA</td><td>Massachusetts*</td><td>NA</td><td>NA</td></tr>
<tr><td>NA</td><td>Vermont*</td><td>NA</td><td>NA</td><td>NA</td><td>Mississippi*</td><td>NA</td><td>NA</td></tr>
<tr><td>15</td><td>Virginia</td><td>16</td><td>1.33%</td><td>NA</td><td>Nebraska*</td><td>NA</td><td>NA</td></tr>
<tr><td>9</td><td>Washington</td><td>33</td><td>2.74%</td><td>NA</td><td>Tennessee*</td><td>NA</td><td>NA</td></tr>
<tr><td>32</td><td>West Virginia</td><td>0</td><td>0.00%</td><td>NA</td><td>Texas*</td><td>NA</td><td>NA</td></tr>
<tr><td>NA</td><td>Wisconsin*</td><td>NA</td><td>NA</td><td>NA</td><td>Vermont*</td><td>NA</td><td>NA</td></tr>
<tr><td>24</td><td>Wyoming</td><td>4</td><td>0.33%</td><td>NA</td><td>Wisconsin*</td><td>NA</td><td>NA</td></tr>
<tr><td></td><td></td><td></td><td></td><td></td><td>District of Columbia*</td><td>NA</td><td>NA</td></tr>
</table>

Source: U.S. Department of Justice, Bureau of Justice Statistics
   "Correctional Populations in the United States, 1992" (February 1995, NCJ 146413)
*Not available.

State Prisoners Escaped in 1992

National Total = 10,706 Prisoners*

ALPHA ORDER					RANK ORDER			
RANK	STATE	PRISONERS	% of USA		RANK	STATE	PRISONERS	% of USA
10	Alabama	199	1.86%		1	New York	2,629	24.56%
45	Alaska	8	0.07%		2	California	1,218	11.38%
16	Arizona	127	1.19%		3	Michigan	1,070	9.99%
47	Arkansas	5	0.05%		4	Missouri	453	4.23%
2	California	1,218	11.38%		5	Oklahoma	400	3.74%
8	Colorado	209	1.95%		6	Connecticut	326	3.05%
6	Connecticut	326	3.05%		7	Illinois	274	2.56%
21	Delaware	92	0.86%		8	Colorado	209	1.95%
12	Florida	177	1.65%		9	North Carolina	200	1.87%
15	Georgia	131	1.22%		10	Alabama	199	1.86%
47	Hawaii	5	0.05%		11	New Jersey	189	1.77%
46	Idaho	6	0.06%		12	Florida	177	1.65%
7	Illinois	274	2.56%		13	Washington	174	1.63%
37	Indiana	12	0.11%		14	South Carolina	138	1.29%
37	Iowa	12	0.11%		15	Georgia	131	1.22%
30	Kansas	31	0.29%		16	Arizona	127	1.19%
17	Kentucky	126	1.18%		17	Kentucky	126	1.18%
22	Louisiana	79	0.74%		18	Maryland	111	1.04%
43	Maine	9	0.08%		19	Tennessee	103	0.96%
18	Maryland	111	1.04%		20	Oregon	96	0.90%
24	Massachusetts	67	0.63%		21	Delaware	92	0.86%
3	Michigan	1,070	9.99%		22	Louisiana	79	0.74%
32	Minnesota	26	0.24%		23	Pennsylvania	77	0.72%
34	Mississippi	21	0.20%		24	Massachusetts	67	0.63%
4	Missouri	453	4.23%		25	Texas	62	0.58%
28	Montana	39	0.36%		26	Nevada	55	0.51%
41	Nebraska	10	0.09%		27	Rhode Island	41	0.38%
26	Nevada	55	0.51%		28	Montana	39	0.36%
39	New Hampshire	11	0.10%		29	New Mexico	34	0.32%
11	New Jersey	189	1.77%		30	Kansas	31	0.29%
29	New Mexico	34	0.32%		31	Vermont	29	0.27%
1	New York	2,629	24.56%		32	Minnesota	26	0.24%
9	North Carolina	200	1.87%		33	West Virginia	22	0.21%
41	North Dakota	10	0.09%		34	Mississippi	21	0.20%
43	Ohio	9	0.08%		35	Wyoming	18	0.17%
5	Oklahoma	400	3.74%		36	South Dakota	15	0.14%
20	Oregon	96	0.90%		37	Indiana	12	0.11%
23	Pennsylvania	77	0.72%		37	Iowa	12	0.11%
27	Rhode Island	41	0.38%		39	New Hampshire	11	0.10%
14	South Carolina	138	1.29%		39	Utah	11	0.10%
36	South Dakota	15	0.14%		41	Nebraska	10	0.09%
19	Tennessee	103	0.96%		41	North Dakota	10	0.09%
25	Texas	62	0.58%		43	Maine	9	0.08%
39	Utah	11	0.10%		43	Ohio	9	0.08%
31	Vermont	29	0.27%		45	Alaska	8	0.07%
49	Virginia	4	0.04%		46	Idaho	6	0.06%
13	Washington	174	1.63%		47	Arkansas	5	0.05%
33	West Virginia	22	0.21%		47	Hawaii	5	0.05%
NA	Wisconsin*	NA	NA		49	Virginia	4	0.04%
35	Wyoming	18	0.17%		NA	Wisconsin**	NA	NA
						District of Columbia	1,536	14.35%

Source: U.S. Department of Justice, Bureau of Justice Statistics
    "Correctional Populations in the United States, 1992" (February 1995, NCJ 146413)
*Includes AWOLs.
**Not available.

State Prisoner Deaths in 1992

National Total = 2,088 Prisoners

ALPHA ORDER					RANK ORDER			

RANK	STATE	PRISONERS	% of USA		RANK	STATE	PRISONERS	% of USA
13	Alabama	58	2.78%		1	New York	310	14.85%
47	Alaska	3	0.14%		2	Texas	152	7.28%
16	Arizona	42	2.01%		3	California	137	6.56%
26	Arkansas	19	0.91%		3	Florida	137	6.56%
3	California	137	6.56%		5	New Jersey	116	5.56%
30	Colorado	14	0.67%		6	Connecticut	84	4.02%
6	Connecticut	84	4.02%		7	Ohio	82	3.93%
32	Delaware	13	0.62%		7	Pennsylvania	82	3.93%
3	Florida	137	6.56%		9	Georgia	80	3.83%
9	Georgia	80	3.83%		10	Michigan	74	3.54%
38	Hawaii	6	0.29%		11	Illinois	62	2.97%
36	Idaho	7	0.34%		12	South Carolina	60	2.87%
11	Illinois	62	2.97%		13	Alabama	58	2.78%
19	Indiana	37	1.77%		14	Virginia	54	2.59%
38	Iowa	6	0.29%		15	Oklahoma	48	2.30%
33	Kansas	11	0.53%		16	Arizona	42	2.01%
25	Kentucky	22	1.05%		16	Louisiana	42	2.01%
16	Louisiana	42	2.01%		18	Maryland	41	1.96%
38	Maine	6	0.29%		19	Indiana	37	1.77%
18	Maryland	41	1.96%		19	North Carolina	37	1.77%
24	Massachusetts	28	1.34%		21	Mississippi	33	1.58%
10	Michigan	74	3.54%		21	Tennessee	33	1.58%
38	Minnesota	6	0.29%		23	Missouri	30	1.44%
21	Mississippi	33	1.58%		24	Massachusetts	28	1.34%
23	Missouri	30	1.44%		25	Kentucky	22	1.05%
45	Montana	4	0.19%		26	Arkansas	19	0.91%
36	Nebraska	7	0.34%		27	Washington	17	0.81%
29	Nevada	15	0.72%		27	Wisconsin	17	0.81%
43	New Hampshire	5	0.24%		29	Nevada	15	0.72%
5	New Jersey	116	5.56%		30	Colorado	14	0.67%
34	New Mexico	9	0.43%		30	Oregon	14	0.67%
1	New York	310	14.85%		32	Delaware	13	0.62%
19	North Carolina	37	1.77%		33	Kansas	11	0.53%
50	North Dakota	0	0.00%		34	New Mexico	9	0.43%
7	Ohio	82	3.93%		34	West Virginia	9	0.43%
15	Oklahoma	48	2.30%		36	Idaho	7	0.34%
30	Oregon	14	0.67%		36	Nebraska	7	0.34%
7	Pennsylvania	82	3.93%		38	Hawaii	6	0.29%
47	Rhode Island	3	0.14%		38	Iowa	6	0.29%
12	South Carolina	60	2.87%		38	Maine	6	0.29%
45	South Dakota	4	0.19%		38	Minnesota	6	0.29%
21	Tennessee	33	1.58%		38	Utah	6	0.29%
2	Texas	152	7.28%		43	New Hampshire	5	0.24%
38	Utah	6	0.29%		43	Wyoming	5	0.24%
49	Vermont	1	0.05%		45	Montana	4	0.19%
14	Virginia	54	2.59%		45	South Dakota	4	0.19%
27	Washington	17	0.81%		47	Alaska	3	0.14%
34	West Virginia	9	0.43%		47	Rhode Island	3	0.14%
27	Wisconsin	17	0.81%		49	Vermont	1	0.05%
43	Wyoming	5	0.24%		50	North Dakota	0	0.00%
						District of Columbia*	NA	NA

Source: U.S. Department of Justice, Bureau of Justice Statistics
"Correctional Populations in the United States, 1992" (February 1995, NCJ 146413)
*Not available.

State Prisoner Deaths by Illness or Other Natural Causes in 1992

National Total = 957 Deaths*

ALPHA ORDER

RANK	STATE	DEATHS	% of USA
NA	Alabama**	NA	NA
44	Alaska	0	0.00%
14	Arizona	30	3.13%
23	Arkansas	12	1.25%
2	California	67	7.00%
30	Colorado	6	0.63%
NA	Connecticut**	NA	NA
30	Delaware	6	0.63%
5	Florida	60	6.27%
12	Georgia	32	3.34%
35	Hawaii	4	0.42%
33	Idaho	5	0.52%
11	Illinois	33	3.45%
9	Indiana	34	3.55%
35	Iowa	4	0.42%
29	Kansas	7	0.73%
21	Kentucky	16	1.67%
8	Louisiana	35	3.66%
35	Maine	4	0.42%
19	Maryland	22	2.30%
27	Massachusetts	9	0.94%
1	Michigan	69	7.21%
33	Minnesota	5	0.52%
14	Mississippi	30	3.13%
20	Missouri	20	2.09%
40	Montana	3	0.31%
30	Nebraska	6	0.63%
26	Nevada	10	1.04%
40	New Hampshire	3	0.31%
7	New Jersey	37	3.87%
NA	New Mexico**	NA	NA
4	New York	66	6.90%
18	North Carolina	23	2.40%
44	North Dakota	0	0.00%
2	Ohio	67	7.00%
13	Oklahoma	31	3.24%
24	Oregon	11	1.15%
6	Pennsylvania	58	6.06%
43	Rhode Island	1	0.10%
9	South Carolina	34	3.55%
40	South Dakota	3	0.31%
17	Tennessee	24	2.51%
NA	Texas**	NA	NA
35	Utah	4	0.42%
44	Vermont	0	0.00%
14	Virginia	30	3.13%
22	Washington	13	1.36%
28	West Virginia	8	0.84%
24	Wisconsin	11	1.15%
35	Wyoming	4	0.42%

RANK ORDER

RANK	STATE	DEATHS	% of USA
1	Michigan	69	7.21%
2	California	67	7.00%
2	Ohio	67	7.00%
4	New York	66	6.90%
5	Florida	60	6.27%
6	Pennsylvania	58	6.06%
7	New Jersey	37	3.87%
8	Louisiana	35	3.66%
9	Indiana	34	3.55%
9	South Carolina	34	3.55%
11	Illinois	33	3.45%
12	Georgia	32	3.34%
13	Oklahoma	31	3.24%
14	Arizona	30	3.13%
14	Mississippi	30	3.13%
14	Virginia	30	3.13%
17	Tennessee	24	2.51%
18	North Carolina	23	2.40%
19	Maryland	22	2.30%
20	Missouri	20	2.09%
21	Kentucky	16	1.67%
22	Washington	13	1.36%
23	Arkansas	12	1.25%
24	Oregon	11	1.15%
24	Wisconsin	11	1.15%
26	Nevada	10	1.04%
27	Massachusetts	9	0.94%
28	West Virginia	8	0.84%
29	Kansas	7	0.73%
30	Colorado	6	0.63%
30	Delaware	6	0.63%
30	Nebraska	6	0.63%
33	Idaho	5	0.52%
33	Minnesota	5	0.52%
35	Hawaii	4	0.42%
35	Iowa	4	0.42%
35	Maine	4	0.42%
35	Utah	4	0.42%
35	Wyoming	4	0.42%
40	Montana	3	0.31%
40	New Hampshire	3	0.31%
40	South Dakota	3	0.31%
43	Rhode Island	1	0.10%
44	Alaska	0	0.00%
44	North Dakota	0	0.00%
44	Vermont	0	0.00%
NA	Alabama**	NA	NA
NA	Connecticut**	NA	NA
NA	New Mexico**	NA	NA
NA	Texas**	NA	NA
	District of Columbia**	NA	NA

Source: U.S. Department of Justice, Bureau of Justice Statistics
"Correctional Populations in the United States, 1992" (February 1995, NCJ 146413)
*Excludes AIDS.
**Not available.

Deaths of State Prisoners by Illness or Other Natural Causes
As a Percent of All Prison Deaths in 1992
National Percent = 45.83% of Deaths*

ALPHA ORDER

RANK	STATE	PERCENT
NA	Alabama**	NA
44	Alaska	0.00
16	Arizona	71.43
28	Arkansas	63.16
35	California	48.91
38	Colorado	42.86
NA	Connecticut**	NA
36	Delaware	46.15
37	Florida	43.80
39	Georgia	40.00
19	Hawaii	66.67
16	Idaho	71.43
34	Illinois	53.23
2	Indiana	91.89
19	Iowa	66.67
27	Kansas	63.64
14	Kentucky	72.73
6	Louisiana	83.33
19	Maine	66.67
33	Maryland	53.66
41	Massachusetts	32.14
1	Michigan	93.24
6	Minnesota	83.33
3	Mississippi	90.91
19	Missouri	66.67
12	Montana	75.00
5	Nebraska	85.71
19	Nevada	66.67
30	New Hampshire	60.00
42	New Jersey	31.90
NA	New Mexico**	NA
43	New York	21.29
29	North Carolina	62.16
44	North Dakota	0.00
8	Ohio	81.71
26	Oklahoma	64.58
10	Oregon	78.57
18	Pennsylvania	70.73
40	Rhode Island	33.33
31	South Carolina	56.67
12	South Dakota	75.00
14	Tennessee	72.73
NA	Texas**	NA
19	Utah	66.67
44	Vermont	0.00
32	Virginia	55.56
11	Washington	76.47
4	West Virginia	88.89
25	Wisconsin	64.71
9	Wyoming	80.00

RANK ORDER

RANK	STATE	PERCENT
1	Michigan	93.24
2	Indiana	91.89
3	Mississippi	90.91
4	West Virginia	88.89
5	Nebraska	85.71
6	Louisiana	83.33
6	Minnesota	83.33
8	Ohio	81.71
9	Wyoming	80.00
10	Oregon	78.57
11	Washington	76.47
12	Montana	75.00
12	South Dakota	75.00
14	Kentucky	72.73
14	Tennessee	72.73
16	Arizona	71.43
16	Idaho	71.43
18	Pennsylvania	70.73
19	Hawaii	66.67
19	Iowa	66.67
19	Maine	66.67
19	Missouri	66.67
19	Nevada	66.67
19	Utah	66.67
25	Wisconsin	64.71
26	Oklahoma	64.58
27	Kansas	63.64
28	Arkansas	63.16
29	North Carolina	62.16
30	New Hampshire	60.00
31	South Carolina	56.67
32	Virginia	55.56
33	Maryland	53.66
34	Illinois	53.23
35	California	48.91
36	Delaware	46.15
37	Florida	43.80
38	Colorado	42.86
39	Georgia	40.00
40	Rhode Island	33.33
41	Massachusetts	32.14
42	New Jersey	31.90
43	New York	21.29
44	Alaska	0.00
44	North Dakota	0.00
44	Vermont	0.00
NA	Alabama**	NA
NA	Connecticut**	NA
NA	New Mexico**	NA
NA	Texas**	NA
	District of Columbia**	NA

Source: Morgan Quitno Corporation using data from U.S. Department of Justice, Bureau of Justice Statistics
"Correctional Populations in the United States, 1992" (February 1995, NCJ 146413)

*Excludes AIDS.

**Not available.

Deaths of State Prisoners by AIDS in 1992

National Total = 648 Deaths

<u>ALPHA ORDER</u>

RANK	STATE	DEATHS	% of USA
NA	Alabama*	NA	NA
31	Alaska	0	0.00%
31	Arizona	0	0.00%
20	Arkansas	2	0.31%
5	California	41	6.33%
23	Colorado	1	0.15%
6	Connecticut	34	5.25%
16	Delaware	4	0.62%
2	Florida	67	10.34%
6	Georgia	34	5.25%
31	Hawaii	0	0.00%
23	Idaho	1	0.15%
11	Illinois	14	2.16%
NA	Indiana*	NA	NA
31	Iowa	0	0.00%
23	Kansas	1	0.15%
17	Kentucky	3	0.46%
NA	Louisiana*	NA	NA
31	Maine	0	0.00%
12	Maryland	13	2.01%
10	Massachusetts	15	2.31%
NA	Michigan*	NA	NA
31	Minnesota	0	0.00%
NA	Mississippi*	NA	NA
17	Missouri	3	0.46%
23	Montana	1	0.15%
23	Nebraska	1	0.15%
23	Nevada	1	0.15%
20	New Hampshire	2	0.31%
3	New Jersey	65	10.03%
31	New Mexico	0	0.00%
1	New York	210	32.41%
14	North Carolina	11	1.70%
31	North Dakota	0	0.00%
14	Ohio	11	1.70%
20	Oklahoma	2	0.31%
23	Oregon	1	0.15%
12	Pennsylvania	13	2.01%
31	Rhode Island	0	0.00%
8	South Carolina	21	3.24%
NA	South Dakota*	NA	NA
17	Tennessee	3	0.46%
4	Texas	54	8.33%
31	Utah	0	0.00%
31	Vermont	0	0.00%
9	Virginia	18	2.78%
31	Washington	0	0.00%
31	West Virginia	0	0.00%
23	Wisconsin	1	0.15%
31	Wyoming	0	0.00%

<u>RANK ORDER</u>

RANK	STATE	DEATHS	% of USA
1	New York	210	32.41%
2	Florida	67	10.34%
3	New Jersey	65	10.03%
4	Texas	54	8.33%
5	California	41	6.33%
6	Connecticut	34	5.25%
6	Georgia	34	5.25%
8	South Carolina	21	3.24%
9	Virginia	18	2.78%
10	Massachusetts	15	2.31%
11	Illinois	14	2.16%
12	Maryland	13	2.01%
12	Pennsylvania	13	2.01%
14	North Carolina	11	1.70%
14	Ohio	11	1.70%
16	Delaware	4	0.62%
17	Kentucky	3	0.46%
17	Missouri	3	0.46%
17	Tennessee	3	0.46%
20	Arkansas	2	0.31%
20	New Hampshire	2	0.31%
20	Oklahoma	2	0.31%
23	Colorado	1	0.15%
23	Idaho	1	0.15%
23	Kansas	1	0.15%
23	Montana	1	0.15%
23	Nebraska	1	0.15%
23	Nevada	1	0.15%
23	Oregon	1	0.15%
23	Wisconsin	1	0.15%
31	Alaska	0	0.00%
31	Arizona	0	0.00%
31	Hawaii	0	0.00%
31	Iowa	0	0.00%
31	Maine	0	0.00%
31	Minnesota	0	0.00%
31	New Mexico	0	0.00%
31	North Dakota	0	0.00%
31	Rhode Island	0	0.00%
31	Utah	0	0.00%
31	Vermont	0	0.00%
31	Washington	0	0.00%
31	West Virginia	0	0.00%
31	Wyoming	0	0.00%
NA	Alabama*	NA	NA
NA	Indiana*	NA	NA
NA	Louisiana*	NA	NA
NA	Michigan*	NA	NA
NA	Mississippi*	NA	NA
NA	South Dakota*	NA	NA
	District of Columbia*	NA	NA

Source: U.S. Department of Justice, Bureau of Justice Statistics
"Correctional Populations in the United States, 1992" (February 1995, NCJ 146413)
Not available.

Deaths of State Prisoners by AIDS as a Percent of All Prison Deaths in 1992

National Percent = 31.03% of Deaths

<table>
<tr><td colspan="3">ALPHA ORDER</td><td colspan="3">RANK ORDER</td></tr>
<tr><th>RANK</th><th>STATE</th><th>PERCENT</th><th>RANK</th><th>STATE</th><th>PERCENT</th></tr>
<tr><td>NA</td><td>Alabama*</td><td>NA</td><td>1</td><td>New York</td><td>67.74</td></tr>
<tr><td>31</td><td>Alaska</td><td>0.00</td><td>2</td><td>New Jersey</td><td>56.03</td></tr>
<tr><td>31</td><td>Arizona</td><td>0.00</td><td>3</td><td>Massachusetts</td><td>53.57</td></tr>
<tr><td>22</td><td>Arkansas</td><td>10.53</td><td>4</td><td>Florida</td><td>48.91</td></tr>
<tr><td>13</td><td>California</td><td>29.93</td><td>5</td><td>Georgia</td><td>42.50</td></tr>
<tr><td>26</td><td>Colorado</td><td>7.14</td><td>6</td><td>Connecticut</td><td>40.48</td></tr>
<tr><td>6</td><td>Connecticut</td><td>40.48</td><td>7</td><td>New Hampshire</td><td>40.00</td></tr>
<tr><td>12</td><td>Delaware</td><td>30.77</td><td>8</td><td>Texas</td><td>35.53</td></tr>
<tr><td>4</td><td>Florida</td><td>48.91</td><td>9</td><td>South Carolina</td><td>35.00</td></tr>
<tr><td>5</td><td>Georgia</td><td>42.50</td><td>10</td><td>Virginia</td><td>33.33</td></tr>
<tr><td>31</td><td>Hawaii</td><td>0.00</td><td>11</td><td>Maryland</td><td>31.71</td></tr>
<tr><td>18</td><td>Idaho</td><td>14.29</td><td>12</td><td>Delaware</td><td>30.77</td></tr>
<tr><td>16</td><td>Illinois</td><td>22.58</td><td>13</td><td>California</td><td>29.93</td></tr>
<tr><td>NA</td><td>Indiana*</td><td>NA</td><td>14</td><td>North Carolina</td><td>29.73</td></tr>
<tr><td>31</td><td>Iowa</td><td>0.00</td><td>15</td><td>Montana</td><td>25.00</td></tr>
<tr><td>24</td><td>Kansas</td><td>9.09</td><td>16</td><td>Illinois</td><td>22.58</td></tr>
<tr><td>20</td><td>Kentucky</td><td>13.64</td><td>17</td><td>Pennsylvania</td><td>15.85</td></tr>
<tr><td>NA</td><td>Louisiana*</td><td>NA</td><td>18</td><td>Idaho</td><td>14.29</td></tr>
<tr><td>31</td><td>Maine</td><td>0.00</td><td>18</td><td>Nebraska</td><td>14.29</td></tr>
<tr><td>11</td><td>Maryland</td><td>31.71</td><td>20</td><td>Kentucky</td><td>13.64</td></tr>
<tr><td>3</td><td>Massachusetts</td><td>53.57</td><td>21</td><td>Ohio</td><td>13.41</td></tr>
<tr><td>NA</td><td>Michigan*</td><td>NA</td><td>22</td><td>Arkansas</td><td>10.53</td></tr>
<tr><td>31</td><td>Minnesota</td><td>0.00</td><td>23</td><td>Missouri</td><td>10.00</td></tr>
<tr><td>NA</td><td>Mississippi*</td><td>NA</td><td>24</td><td>Kansas</td><td>9.09</td></tr>
<tr><td>23</td><td>Missouri</td><td>10.00</td><td>24</td><td>Tennessee</td><td>9.09</td></tr>
<tr><td>15</td><td>Montana</td><td>25.00</td><td>26</td><td>Colorado</td><td>7.14</td></tr>
<tr><td>18</td><td>Nebraska</td><td>14.29</td><td>26</td><td>Oregon</td><td>7.14</td></tr>
<tr><td>28</td><td>Nevada</td><td>6.67</td><td>28</td><td>Nevada</td><td>6.67</td></tr>
<tr><td>7</td><td>New Hampshire</td><td>40.00</td><td>29</td><td>Wisconsin</td><td>5.88</td></tr>
<tr><td>2</td><td>New Jersey</td><td>56.03</td><td>30</td><td>Oklahoma</td><td>4.17</td></tr>
<tr><td>31</td><td>New Mexico</td><td>0.00</td><td>31</td><td>Alaska</td><td>0.00</td></tr>
<tr><td>1</td><td>New York</td><td>67.74</td><td>31</td><td>Arizona</td><td>0.00</td></tr>
<tr><td>14</td><td>North Carolina</td><td>29.73</td><td>31</td><td>Hawaii</td><td>0.00</td></tr>
<tr><td>31</td><td>North Dakota</td><td>0.00</td><td>31</td><td>Iowa</td><td>0.00</td></tr>
<tr><td>21</td><td>Ohio</td><td>13.41</td><td>31</td><td>Maine</td><td>0.00</td></tr>
<tr><td>30</td><td>Oklahoma</td><td>4.17</td><td>31</td><td>Minnesota</td><td>0.00</td></tr>
<tr><td>26</td><td>Oregon</td><td>7.14</td><td>31</td><td>New Mexico</td><td>0.00</td></tr>
<tr><td>17</td><td>Pennsylvania</td><td>15.85</td><td>31</td><td>North Dakota</td><td>0.00</td></tr>
<tr><td>31</td><td>Rhode Island</td><td>0.00</td><td>31</td><td>Rhode Island</td><td>0.00</td></tr>
<tr><td>9</td><td>South Carolina</td><td>35.00</td><td>31</td><td>Utah</td><td>0.00</td></tr>
<tr><td>NA</td><td>South Dakota*</td><td>NA</td><td>31</td><td>Vermont</td><td>0.00</td></tr>
<tr><td>24</td><td>Tennessee</td><td>9.09</td><td>31</td><td>Washington</td><td>0.00</td></tr>
<tr><td>8</td><td>Texas</td><td>35.53</td><td>31</td><td>West Virginia</td><td>0.00</td></tr>
<tr><td>31</td><td>Utah</td><td>0.00</td><td>31</td><td>Wyoming</td><td>0.00</td></tr>
<tr><td>31</td><td>Vermont</td><td>0.00</td><td>NA</td><td>Alabama*</td><td>NA</td></tr>
<tr><td>10</td><td>Virginia</td><td>33.33</td><td>NA</td><td>Indiana*</td><td>NA</td></tr>
<tr><td>31</td><td>Washington</td><td>0.00</td><td>NA</td><td>Louisiana*</td><td>NA</td></tr>
<tr><td>31</td><td>West Virginia</td><td>0.00</td><td>NA</td><td>Michigan*</td><td>NA</td></tr>
<tr><td>29</td><td>Wisconsin</td><td>5.88</td><td>NA</td><td>Mississippi*</td><td>NA</td></tr>
<tr><td>31</td><td>Wyoming</td><td>0.00</td><td>NA</td><td>South Dakota*</td><td>NA</td></tr>
<tr><td></td><td></td><td></td><td></td><td>District of Columbia*</td><td>NA</td></tr>
</table>

Source: Morgan Quitno Corporation using data from U.S. Department of Justice, Bureau of Justice Statistics
  "Correctional Populations in the United States, 1992" (February 1995, NCJ 146413)
*Not available.

State Prisoners Known to be Positive for HIV Infection/AIDS in 1991

National Total = 16,849 Inmates*

ALPHA ORDER

RANK	STATE	INMATES	% of USA
14	Alabama	178	1.06%
43	Alaska	9	0.05%
24	Arizona	84	0.50%
27	Arkansas	68	0.40%
5	California	714	4.24%
25	Colorado	82	0.49%
7	Connecticut	574	3.41%
23	Delaware	85	0.50%
2	Florida	1,105	6.56%
3	Georgia	807	4.79%
35	Hawaii	19	0.11%
41	Idaho	10	0.06%
13	Illinois	299	1.77%
28	Indiana	62	0.37%
35	Iowa	19	0.11%
39	Kansas	13	0.08%
33	Kentucky	27	0.16%
21	Louisiana	100	0.59%
48	Maine	1	0.01%
9	Maryland	478	2.84%
8	Massachusetts	484	2.87%
10	Michigan	390	2.31%
38	Minnesota	14	0.08%
20	Mississippi	106	0.63%
18	Missouri	127	0.75%
44	Montana	7	0.04%
40	Nebraska	11	0.07%
19	Nevada	117	0.69%
37	New Hampshire	18	0.11%
4	New Jersey	756	4.49%
41	New Mexico	10	0.06%
1	New York	8,000	47.48%
15	North Carolina	170	1.01%
48	North Dakota	1	0.01%
16	Ohio	152	0.90%
26	Oklahoma	74	0.44%
34	Oregon	24	0.14%
12	Pennsylvania	313	1.86%
22	Rhode Island	98	0.58%
11	South Carolina	316	1.88%
NA	South Dakota**	NA	NA
32	Tennessee	28	0.17%
6	Texas	615	3.65%
31	Utah	35	0.21%
47	Vermont	3	0.02%
16	Virginia	152	0.90%
29	Washington	42	0.25%
46	West Virginia	5	0.03%
30	Wisconsin	40	0.24%
44	Wyoming	7	0.04%

RANK ORDER

RANK	STATE	INMATES	% of USA
1	New York	8,000	47.48%
2	Florida	1,105	6.56%
3	Georgia	807	4.79%
4	New Jersey	756	4.49%
5	California	714	4.24%
6	Texas	615	3.65%
7	Connecticut	574	3.41%
8	Massachusetts	484	2.87%
9	Maryland	478	2.84%
10	Michigan	390	2.31%
11	South Carolina	316	1.88%
12	Pennsylvania	313	1.86%
13	Illinois	299	1.77%
14	Alabama	178	1.06%
15	North Carolina	170	1.01%
16	Ohio	152	0.90%
16	Virginia	152	0.90%
18	Missouri	127	0.75%
19	Nevada	117	0.69%
20	Mississippi	106	0.63%
21	Louisiana	100	0.59%
22	Rhode Island	98	0.58%
23	Delaware	85	0.50%
24	Arizona	84	0.50%
25	Colorado	82	0.49%
26	Oklahoma	74	0.44%
27	Arkansas	68	0.40%
28	Indiana	62	0.37%
29	Washington	42	0.25%
30	Wisconsin	40	0.24%
31	Utah	35	0.21%
32	Tennessee	28	0.17%
33	Kentucky	27	0.16%
34	Oregon	24	0.14%
35	Hawaii	19	0.11%
35	Iowa	19	0.11%
37	New Hampshire	18	0.11%
38	Minnesota	14	0.08%
39	Kansas	13	0.08%
40	Nebraska	11	0.07%
41	Idaho	10	0.06%
41	New Mexico	10	0.06%
43	Alaska	9	0.05%
44	Montana	7	0.04%
44	Wyoming	7	0.04%
46	West Virginia	5	0.03%
47	Vermont	3	0.02%
48	Maine	1	0.01%
48	North Dakota	1	0.01%
NA	South Dakota**	NA	NA
	District of Columbia**	NA	NA

Source: U.S. Department of Justice, Bureau of Justice Statistics
"HIV in U.S. Prisons and Jails" (Special Report, September 1993, NCJ-143292)
*Does not include 630 positive federal inmates.
**Not available.

State Prisoners Known to be Positive for HIV infection/AIDS
As a Percent of Total Prison Population in 1991
National Percent = 2.3% of State Prisoners*

ALPHA ORDER

RANK ORDER

RANK	STATE	PERCENT		RANK	STATE	PERCENT
17	Alabama	1.1		1	New York	13.8
37	Alaska	0.4		2	Connecticut	5.4
30	Arizona	0.5		3	Massachusetts	5.3
21	Arkansas	0.9		4	New Jersey	4.0
26	California	0.7		5	Rhode Island	3.5
19	Colorado	1.0		6	Georgia	3.4
2	Connecticut	5.4		7	Delaware	2.6
7	Delaware	2.6		8	Maryland	2.5
9	Florida	2.4		9	Florida	2.4
6	Georgia	3.4		10	Nevada	2.0
24	Hawaii	0.8		10	South Carolina	2.0
30	Idaho	0.5		12	Mississippi	1.3
19	Illinois	1.0		12	Pennsylvania	1.3
30	Indiana	0.5		12	Utah	1.3
30	Iowa	0.5		15	New Hampshire	1.2
47	Kansas	0.2		15	Texas	1.2
42	Kentucky	0.3		17	Alabama	1.1
26	Louisiana	0.7		17	Michigan	1.1
49	Maine	0.1		19	Colorado	1.0
8	Maryland	2.5		19	Illinois	1.0
3	Massachusetts	5.3		21	Arkansas	0.9
17	Michigan	1.1		21	North Carolina	0.9
37	Minnesota	0.4		21	Virginia	0.9
12	Mississippi	1.3		24	Hawaii	0.8
24	Missouri	0.8		24	Missouri	0.8
30	Montana	0.5		26	California	0.7
37	Nebraska	0.4		26	Louisiana	0.7
10	Nevada	2.0		26	Oklahoma	0.7
15	New Hampshire	1.2		29	Wyoming	0.6
4	New Jersey	4.0		30	Arizona	0.5
42	New Mexico	0.3		30	Idaho	0.5
1	New York	13.8		30	Indiana	0.5
21	North Carolina	0.9		30	Iowa	0.5
47	North Dakota	0.2		30	Montana	0.5
37	Ohio	0.4		30	Washington	0.5
26	Oklahoma	0.7		30	Wisconsin	0.5
37	Oregon	0.4		37	Alaska	0.4
12	Pennsylvania	1.3		37	Minnesota	0.4
5	Rhode Island	3.5		37	Nebraska	0.4
10	South Carolina	2.0		37	Ohio	0.4
NA	South Dakota**	NA		37	Oregon	0.4
42	Tennessee	0.3		42	Kentucky	0.3
15	Texas	1.2		42	New Mexico	0.3
12	Utah	1.3		42	Tennessee	0.3
42	Vermont	0.3		42	Vermont	0.3
21	Virginia	0.9		42	West Virginia	0.3
30	Washington	0.5		47	Kansas	0.2
42	West Virginia	0.3		47	North Dakota	0.2
30	Wisconsin	0.5		49	Maine	0.1
29	Wyoming	0.6		NA	South Dakota**	NA
					District of Columbia**	NA

Source: U.S. Department of Justice, Bureau of Justice Statistics
  "HIV in U.S. Prisons and Jails" (Special Report, September 1993, NCJ-143292)
*Federal rate is 1.0%, combined state and federal rate is 2.2%.
**Not available.

State Prisoner Deaths by Suicide in 1992

National Total = 103 Suicides

ALPHA ORDER					RANK ORDER			
RANK	**STATE**		**SUICIDES**	**% of USA**	**RANK**	**STATE**	**SUICIDES**	**% of USA**
NA	Alabama*		NA	NA	1	California	13	12.62%
9	Alaska		3	2.91%	2	New York	9	8.74%
3	Arizona		8	7.77%	3	Arizona	8	7.77%
27	Arkansas		1	0.97%	4	Florida	6	5.83%
1	California		13	12.62%	5	Massachusetts	4	3.88%
16	Colorado		2	1.94%	5	Michigan	4	3.88%
NA	Connecticut*		NA	NA	5	Oklahoma	4	3.88%
16	Delaware		2	1.94%	5	Pennsylvania	4	3.88%
4	Florida		6	5.83%	9	Alaska	3	2.91%
9	Georgia		3	2.91%	9	Georgia	3	2.91%
27	Hawaii		1	0.97%	9	Illinois	3	2.91%
27	Idaho		1	0.97%	9	Missouri	3	2.91%
9	Illinois		3	2.91%	9	Nevada	3	2.91%
16	Indiana		2	1.94%	9	Washington	3	2.91%
35	Iowa		0	0.00%	9	Wisconsin	3	2.91%
35	Kansas		0	0.00%	16	Colorado	2	1.94%
16	Kentucky		2	1.94%	16	Delaware	2	1.94%
NA	Louisiana*		NA	NA	16	Indiana	2	1.94%
16	Maine		2	1.94%	16	Kentucky	2	1.94%
27	Maryland		1	0.97%	16	Maine	2	1.94%
5	Massachusetts		4	3.88%	16	North Carolina	2	1.94%
5	Michigan		4	3.88%	16	Ohio	2	1.94%
27	Minnesota		1	0.97%	16	Oregon	2	1.94%
27	Mississippi		1	0.97%	16	South Carolina	2	1.94%
9	Missouri		3	2.91%	16	Tennessee	2	1.94%
35	Montana		0	0.00%	16	Virginia	2	1.94%
35	Nebraska		0	0.00%	27	Arkansas	1	0.97%
9	Nevada		3	2.91%	27	Hawaii	1	0.97%
35	New Hampshire		0	0.00%	27	Idaho	1	0.97%
27	New Jersey		1	0.97%	27	Maryland	1	0.97%
NA	New Mexico*		NA	NA	27	Minnesota	1	0.97%
2	New York		9	8.74%	27	Mississippi	1	0.97%
16	North Carolina		2	1.94%	27	New Jersey	1	0.97%
35	North Dakota		0	0.00%	27	Utah	1	0.97%
16	Ohio		2	1.94%	35	Iowa	0	0.00%
5	Oklahoma		4	3.88%	35	Kansas	0	0.00%
16	Oregon		2	1.94%	35	Montana	0	0.00%
5	Pennsylvania		4	3.88%	35	Nebraska	0	0.00%
35	Rhode Island		0	0.00%	35	New Hampshire	0	0.00%
16	South Carolina		2	1.94%	35	North Dakota	0	0.00%
35	South Dakota		0	0.00%	35	Rhode Island	0	0.00%
16	Tennessee		2	1.94%	35	South Dakota	0	0.00%
NA	Texas*		NA	NA	35	Vermont	0	0.00%
27	Utah		1	0.97%	35	West Virginia	0	0.00%
35	Vermont		0	0.00%	35	Wyoming	0	0.00%
16	Virginia		2	1.94%	NA	Alabama*	NA	NA
9	Washington		3	2.91%	NA	Connecticut*	NA	NA
35	West Virginia		0	0.00%	NA	Louisiana*	NA	NA
9	Wisconsin		3	2.91%	NA	New Mexico*	NA	NA
35	Wyoming		0	0.00%	NA	Texas*	NA	NA
						District of Columbia*	NA	NA

Source: U.S. Department of Justice, Bureau of Justice Statistics
"Correctional Populations in the United States, 1992" (February 1995, NCJ 146413)
*Not available.

Deaths of State Prisoners by Suicide as a Percent of All Prison Deaths in 1992

National Percent = 4.93% of Deaths

ALPHA ORDER				RANK ORDER		
RANK	STATE	PERCENT		RANK	STATE	PERCENT
NA	Alabama*	NA		1	Alaska	100.00
1	Alaska	100.00		2	Maine	33.33
4	Arizona	19.05		3	Nevada	20.00
23	Arkansas	5.26		4	Arizona	19.05
16	California	9.49		5	Washington	17.65
11	Colorado	14.29		5	Wisconsin	17.65
NA	Connecticut*	NA		7	Hawaii	16.67
10	Delaware	15.38		7	Minnesota	16.67
26	Florida	4.38		7	Utah	16.67
27	Georgia	3.75		10	Delaware	15.38
7	Hawaii	16.67		11	Colorado	14.29
11	Idaho	14.29		11	Idaho	14.29
25	Illinois	4.84		11	Massachusetts	14.29
20	Indiana	5.41		11	Oregon	14.29
35	Iowa	0.00		15	Missouri	10.00
35	Kansas	0.00		16	California	9.49
17	Kentucky	9.09		17	Kentucky	9.09
NA	Louisiana*	NA		18	Oklahoma	8.33
2	Maine	33.33		19	Tennessee	6.06
32	Maryland	2.44		20	Indiana	5.41
11	Massachusetts	14.29		20	Michigan	5.41
20	Michigan	5.41		20	North Carolina	5.41
7	Minnesota	16.67		23	Arkansas	5.26
30	Mississippi	3.03		24	Pennsylvania	4.88
15	Missouri	10.00		25	Illinois	4.84
35	Montana	0.00		26	Florida	4.38
35	Nebraska	0.00		27	Georgia	3.75
3	Nevada	20.00		28	Virginia	3.70
35	New Hampshire	0.00		29	South Carolina	3.33
34	New Jersey	0.86		30	Mississippi	3.03
NA	New Mexico*	NA		31	New York	2.90
31	New York	2.90		32	Maryland	2.44
20	North Carolina	5.41		32	Ohio	2.44
35	North Dakota	0.00		34	New Jersey	0.86
32	Ohio	2.44		35	Iowa	0.00
18	Oklahoma	8.33		35	Kansas	0.00
11	Oregon	14.29		35	Montana	0.00
24	Pennsylvania	4.88		35	Nebraska	0.00
35	Rhode Island	0.00		35	New Hampshire	0.00
29	South Carolina	3.33		35	North Dakota	0.00
35	South Dakota	0.00		35	Rhode Island	0.00
19	Tennessee	6.06		35	South Dakota	0.00
NA	Texas*	NA		35	Vermont	0.00
7	Utah	16.67		35	West Virginia	0.00
35	Vermont	0.00		35	Wyoming	0.00
28	Virginia	3.70		NA	Alabama*	NA
5	Washington	17.65		NA	Connecticut*	NA
35	West Virginia	0.00		NA	Louisiana*	NA
5	Wisconsin	17.65		NA	New Mexico*	NA
35	Wyoming	0.00		NA	Texas*	NA
					District of Columbia*	NA

Source: Morgan Quitno Corporation using data from U.S. Department of Justice, Bureau of Justice Statistics
"Correctional Populations in the United States, 1992" (February 1995, NCJ 146413)
*Not available.

Adults on State Probation in 1993

National Total = 2,800,350 Adults*

<u>ALPHA ORDER</u>

RANK	STATE	ADULTS	% of USA
24	Alabama	33,721	1.20%
48	Alaska	3,214	0.11%
22	Arizona	36,815	1.31%
30	Arkansas	17,527	0.63%
2	California	280,749	10.03%
23	Colorado	35,494	1.27%
16	Connecticut	50,904	1.82%
32	Delaware	15,571	0.56%
3	Florida	199,275	7.12%
5	Georgia	145,230	5.19%
36	Hawaii	10,100	0.36%
44	Idaho	4,749	0.17%
15	Illinois	73,550	2.63%
12	Indiana	82,804	2.96%
34	Iowa	14,505	0.52%
28	Kansas	24,083	0.86%
35	Kentucky	11,458	0.41%
26	Louisiana	32,434	1.16%
39	Maine	8,650	0.31%
13	Maryland	80,208	2.86%
17	Massachusetts	47,150	1.68%
6	Michigan	139,682	4.99%
14	Minnesota	74,186	2.65%
37	Mississippi	9,943	0.36%
25	Missouri	32,916	1.18%
46	Montana	4,107	0.15%
33	Nebraska	14,594	0.52%
38	Nevada	8,826	0.32%
45	New Hampshire	4,122	0.15%
8	New Jersey	109,576	3.91%
40	New Mexico	7,673	0.27%
4	New York	156,617	5.59%
11	North Carolina	86,212	3.08%
50	North Dakota	1,954	0.07%
9	Ohio	98,211	3.51%
27	Oklahoma	25,689	0.92%
21	Oregon	37,902	1.35%
10	Pennsylvania	88,180	3.15%
31	Rhode Island	16,604	0.59%
20	South Carolina	38,855	1.39%
47	South Dakota	3,781	0.14%
19	Tennessee	40,463	1.44%
1	Texas	378,523	13.52%
41	Utah	7,325	0.26%
42	Vermont	6,058	0.22%
29	Virginia	23,619	0.84%
7	Washington	114,018	4.07%
43	West Virginia	6,006	0.21%
18	Wisconsin	43,125	1.54%
49	Wyoming	2,958	0.11%

<u>RANK ORDER</u>

RANK	STATE	ADULTS	% of USA
1	Texas	378,523	13.52%
2	California	280,749	10.03%
3	Florida	199,275	7.12%
4	New York	156,617	5.59%
5	Georgia	145,230	5.19%
6	Michigan	139,682	4.99%
7	Washington	114,018	4.07%
8	New Jersey	109,576	3.91%
9	Ohio	98,211	3.51%
10	Pennsylvania	88,180	3.15%
11	North Carolina	86,212	3.08%
12	Indiana	82,804	2.96%
13	Maryland	80,208	2.86%
14	Minnesota	74,186	2.65%
15	Illinois	73,550	2.63%
16	Connecticut	50,904	1.82%
17	Massachusetts	47,150	1.68%
18	Wisconsin	43,125	1.54%
19	Tennessee	40,463	1.44%
20	South Carolina	38,855	1.39%
21	Oregon	37,902	1.35%
22	Arizona	36,815	1.31%
23	Colorado	35,494	1.27%
24	Alabama	33,721	1.20%
25	Missouri	32,916	1.18%
26	Louisiana	32,434	1.16%
27	Oklahoma	25,689	0.92%
28	Kansas	24,083	0.86%
29	Virginia	23,619	0.84%
30	Arkansas	17,527	0.63%
31	Rhode Island	16,604	0.59%
32	Delaware	15,571	0.56%
33	Nebraska	14,594	0.52%
34	Iowa	14,505	0.52%
35	Kentucky	11,458	0.41%
36	Hawaii	10,100	0.36%
37	Mississippi	9,943	0.36%
38	Nevada	8,826	0.32%
39	Maine	8,650	0.31%
40	New Mexico	7,673	0.27%
41	Utah	7,325	0.26%
42	Vermont	6,058	0.22%
43	West Virginia	6,006	0.21%
44	Idaho	4,749	0.17%
45	New Hampshire	4,122	0.15%
46	Montana	4,107	0.15%
47	South Dakota	3,781	0.14%
48	Alaska	3,214	0.11%
49	Wyoming	2,958	0.11%
50	North Dakota	1,954	0.07%
	District of Columbia	10,434	0.37%

Source: U.S. Department of Justice, Bureau of Justice Statistics
   "Probation and Parole Populations Reach New Highs" (Press Release, September 11, 1994)
*As of December 31, 1993. Does not include 43,095 on federal probation.

Rate of Adults on State Probation in 1993

National Rate = 1,468 Adults on Probation per 100,000 Adult Population*

ALPHA ORDER				RANK ORDER		
RANK	STATE	RATE		RANK	STATE	RATE
27	Alabama	1,064		1	Delaware	2,955
38	Alaska	784		2	Washington	2,952
19	Arizona	1,285		3	Texas	2,946
31	Arkansas	980		4	Georgia	2,861
21	California	1,241		5	Minnesota	2,256
17	Colorado	1,351		6	Rhode Island	2,170
8	Connecticut	2,035		7	Maryland	2,154
1	Delaware	2,955		8	Connecticut	2,035
11	Florida	1,896		9	Michigan	2,003
4	Georgia	2,861		10	Indiana	1,951
24	Hawaii	1,157		11	Florida	1,896
43	Idaho	620		12	New Jersey	1,831
35	Illinois	852		13	Oregon	1,685
10	Indiana	1,951		14	North Carolina	1,645
40	Iowa	697		15	South Carolina	1,444
18	Kansas	1,304		16	Vermont	1,402
50	Kentucky	407		17	Colorado	1,351
28	Louisiana	1,063		18	Kansas	1,304
33	Maine	928		19	Arizona	1,285
7	Maryland	2,154		20	Nebraska	1,249
30	Massachusetts	1,021		21	California	1,241
9	Michigan	2,003		22	Ohio	1,193
5	Minnesota	2,256		23	Wisconsin	1,167
45	Mississippi	527		24	Hawaii	1,157
37	Missouri	850		25	New York	1,141
41	Montana	677		26	Oklahoma	1,088
20	Nebraska	1,249		27	Alabama	1,064
36	Nevada	851		28	Louisiana	1,063
46	New Hampshire	490		29	Tennessee	1,056
12	New Jersey	1,831		30	Massachusetts	1,021
42	New Mexico	676		31	Arkansas	980
25	New York	1,141		32	Pennsylvania	961
14	North Carolina	1,645		33	Maine	928
49	North Dakota	422		34	Wyoming	891
22	Ohio	1,193		35	Illinois	852
26	Oklahoma	1,088		36	Nevada	851
13	Oregon	1,685		37	Missouri	850
32	Pennsylvania	961		38	Alaska	784
6	Rhode Island	2,170		39	South Dakota	746
15	South Carolina	1,444		40	Iowa	697
39	South Dakota	746		41	Montana	677
29	Tennessee	1,056		42	New Mexico	676
3	Texas	2,946		43	Idaho	620
44	Utah	613		44	Utah	613
16	Vermont	1,402		45	Mississippi	527
47	Virginia	482		46	New Hampshire	490
2	Washington	2,952		47	Virginia	482
48	West Virginia	433		48	West Virginia	433
23	Wisconsin	1,167		49	North Dakota	422
34	Wyoming	891		50	Kentucky	407
					District of Columbia	2,254

Source: U.S. Department of Justice, Bureau of Justice Statistics
   "Probation and Parole Populations Reach New Highs" (Press Release, September 11, 1994)
*As of December 31, 1993. Federal rate is 23 adults on probation per 100,000 adult population.

Adults on State Parole in 1993

National Total = 627,314 Adults*

ALPHA ORDER					RANK ORDER			
RANK	STATE	ADULTS	% of USA		RANK	STATE	ADULTS	% of USA
17	Alabama	7,284	1.16%		1	Texas	116,021	18.49%
42	Alaska	685	0.11%		2	California	87,018	13.87%
24	Arizona	4,017	0.64%		3	Pennsylvania	72,100	11.49%
25	Arkansas	3,940	0.63%		4	New York	52,186	8.32%
2	California	87,018	13.87%		5	New Jersey	35,775	5.70%
29	Colorado	2,731	0.44%		6	Illinois	24,177	3.85%
44	Connecticut	624	0.10%		7	Georgia	20,790	3.31%
38	Delaware	914	0.15%		8	Florida	17,326	2.76%
8	Florida	17,326	2.76%		9	North Carolina	17,284	2.76%
7	Georgia	20,790	3.31%		10	Louisiana	14,463	2.31%
35	Hawaii	1,604	0.26%		11	Michigan	14,015	2.23%
39	Idaho	837	0.13%		12	Maryland	13,858	2.21%
6	Illinois	24,177	3.85%		13	Oregon	13,687	2.18%
28	Indiana	2,891	0.46%		14	Missouri	13,643	2.17%
34	Iowa	1,887	0.30%		15	Tennessee	11,819	1.88%
18	Kansas	7,141	1.14%		16	Virginia	11,504	1.83%
23	Kentucky	4,144	0.66%		17	Alabama	7,284	1.16%
10	Louisiana	14,463	2.31%		18	Kansas	7,141	1.14%
50	Maine	34	0.01%		19	Ohio	6,997	1.12%
12	Maryland	13,858	2.21%		20	Wisconsin	6,615	1.05%
22	Massachusetts	4,370	0.70%		21	South Carolina	5,671	0.90%
11	Michigan	14,015	2.23%		22	Massachusetts	4,370	0.70%
32	Minnesota	2,094	0.33%		23	Kentucky	4,144	0.66%
33	Mississippi	2,003	0.32%		24	Arizona	4,017	0.64%
14	Missouri	13,643	2.17%		25	Arkansas	3,940	0.63%
41	Montana	708	0.11%		26	Washington	3,720	0.59%
40	Nebraska	815	0.13%		27	Nevada	3,398	0.54%
27	Nevada	3,398	0.54%		28	Indiana	2,891	0.46%
44	New Hampshire	624	0.10%		29	Colorado	2,731	0.44%
5	New Jersey	35,775	5.70%		30	Oklahoma	2,503	0.40%
36	New Mexico	1,281	0.20%		31	Utah	2,213	0.35%
4	New York	52,186	8.32%		32	Minnesota	2,094	0.33%
9	North Carolina	17,284	2.76%		33	Mississippi	2,003	0.32%
49	North Dakota	91	0.01%		34	Iowa	1,887	0.30%
19	Ohio	6,997	1.12%		35	Hawaii	1,604	0.26%
30	Oklahoma	2,503	0.40%		36	New Mexico	1,281	0.20%
13	Oregon	13,687	2.18%		37	West Virginia	1,073	0.17%
3	Pennsylvania	72,100	11.49%		38	Delaware	914	0.15%
47	Rhode Island	538	0.09%		39	Idaho	837	0.13%
21	South Carolina	5,671	0.90%		40	Nebraska	815	0.13%
43	South Dakota	676	0.11%		41	Montana	708	0.11%
15	Tennessee	11,819	1.88%		42	Alaska	685	0.11%
1	Texas	116,021	18.49%		43	South Dakota	676	0.11%
31	Utah	2,213	0.35%		44	Connecticut	624	0.10%
46	Vermont	555	0.09%		44	New Hampshire	624	0.10%
16	Virginia	11,504	1.83%		46	Vermont	555	0.09%
26	Washington	3,720	0.59%		47	Rhode Island	538	0.09%
37	West Virginia	1,073	0.17%		48	Wyoming	379	0.06%
20	Wisconsin	6,615	1.05%		49	North Dakota	91	0.01%
48	Wyoming	379	0.06%		50	Maine	34	0.01%
					District of Columbia		6,591	1.05%

Source: U.S. Department of Justice, Bureau of Justice Statistics
"Probation and Parole Populations Reach New Highs" (Press Release, September 11, 1994)
*As of December 31, 1993. Does not include 44,156 adults on federal parole.

Rate of Adults on State Parole in 1993

National Rate = 329 Adults on Parole per 100,000 Population*

ALPHA ORDER				RANK ORDER		
RANK	**STATE**	**RATE**		**RANK**	**STATE**	**RATE**
17	Alabama	234		1	Texas	903
25	Alaska	167		2	Pennsylvania	786
28	Arizona	140		3	Oregon	608
18	Arkansas	220		4	New Jersey	598
8	California	385		5	Louisiana	474
37	Colorado	104		6	Georgia	410
48	Connecticut	25		7	Kansas	387
24	Delaware	174		8	California	385
26	Florida	165		9	New York	380
6	Georgia	410		10	Maryland	372
22	Hawaii	184		11	Missouri	352
34	Idaho	109		12	North Carolina	330
15	Illinois	280		13	Nevada	328
46	Indiana	68		14	Tennessee	309
40	Iowa	91		15	Illinois	280
7	Kansas	387		16	Virginia	235
27	Kentucky	147		17	Alabama	234
5	Louisiana	474		18	Arkansas	220
50	Maine	4		19	South Carolina	211
10	Maryland	372		20	Michigan	201
39	Massachusetts	95		21	Utah	185
20	Michigan	201		22	Hawaii	184
47	Minnesota	64		23	Wisconsin	179
35	Mississippi	106		24	Delaware	174
11	Missouri	352		25	Alaska	167
31	Montana	117		26	Florida	165
44	Nebraska	70		27	Kentucky	147
13	Nevada	328		28	Arizona	140
43	New Hampshire	74		29	South Dakota	133
4	New Jersey	598		30	Vermont	128
33	New Mexico	113		31	Montana	117
9	New York	380		32	Wyoming	114
12	North Carolina	330		33	New Mexico	113
49	North Dakota	20		34	Idaho	109
41	Ohio	85		35	Mississippi	106
35	Oklahoma	106		35	Oklahoma	106
3	Oregon	608		37	Colorado	104
2	Pennsylvania	786		38	Washington	96
44	Rhode Island	70		39	Massachusetts	95
19	South Carolina	211		40	Iowa	91
29	South Dakota	133		41	Ohio	85
14	Tennessee	309		42	West Virginia	77
1	Texas	903		43	New Hampshire	74
21	Utah	185		44	Nebraska	70
30	Vermont	128		44	Rhode Island	70
16	Virginia	235		46	Indiana	68
38	Washington	96		47	Minnesota	64
42	West Virginia	77		48	Connecticut	25
23	Wisconsin	179		49	North Dakota	20
32	Wyoming	114		50	Maine	4
					District of Columbia	1,424

Source: U.S. Department of Justice, Bureau of Justice Statistics
"Probation and Parole Populations Reach New Highs" (Press Release, September 11, 1994)
As of December 31, 1993. Federal rate is 23 adults on parole per 100,000 adult population.

State and Local Government Employees in Corrections in 1992

National Total = 533,569 Employees*

ALPHA ORDER

RANK	STATE	EMPLOYEES	% of USA
25	Alabama	5,869	1.10%
45	Alaska	1,273	0.24%
15	Arizona	10,123	1.90%
31	Arkansas	3,805	0.71%
1	California	60,854	11.41%
24	Colorado	6,183	1.16%
28	Connecticut	5,418	1.02%
41	Delaware	1,675	0.31%
4	Florida	41,785	7.83%
7	Georgia	18,796	3.52%
38	Hawaii	2,026	0.38%
42	Idaho	1,654	0.31%
5	Illinois	19,614	3.68%
18	Indiana	9,408	1.76%
36	Iowa	2,781	0.52%
30	Kansas	4,890	0.92%
23	Kentucky	6,807	1.28%
16	Louisiana	9,801	1.84%
39	Maine	1,868	0.35%
13	Maryland	10,921	2.05%
17	Massachusetts	9,630	1.80%
6	Michigan	19,403	3.64%
27	Minnesota	5,533	1.04%
34	Mississippi	3,525	0.66%
21	Missouri	8,610	1.61%
46	Montana	1,265	0.24%
37	Nebraska	2,550	0.48%
33	Nevada	3,571	0.67%
44	New Hampshire	1,376	0.26%
9	New Jersey	18,158	3.40%
32	New Mexico	3,736	0.70%
2	New York	58,988	11.06%
11	North Carolina	15,099	2.83%
50	North Dakota	674	0.13%
10	Ohio	16,722	3.13%
26	Oklahoma	5,641	1.06%
29	Oregon	5,370	1.01%
8	Pennsylvania	18,653	3.50%
40	Rhode Island	1,821	0.34%
20	South Carolina	8,651	1.62%
47	South Dakota	820	0.15%
14	Tennessee	10,579	1.98%
3	Texas	46,440	8.70%
35	Utah	2,815	0.53%
49	Vermont	697	0.13%
12	Virginia	13,988	2.62%
19	Washington	9,121	1.71%
43	West Virginia	1,414	0.27%
22	Wisconsin	7,329	1.37%
48	Wyoming	779	0.15%

RANK ORDER

RANK	STATE	EMPLOYEES	% of USA
1	California	60,854	11.41%
2	New York	58,988	11.06%
3	Texas	46,440	8.70%
4	Florida	41,785	7.83%
5	Illinois	19,614	3.68%
6	Michigan	19,403	3.64%
7	Georgia	18,796	3.52%
8	Pennsylvania	18,653	3.50%
9	New Jersey	18,158	3.40%
10	Ohio	16,722	3.13%
11	North Carolina	15,099	2.83%
12	Virginia	13,988	2.62%
13	Maryland	10,921	2.05%
14	Tennessee	10,579	1.98%
15	Arizona	10,123	1.90%
16	Louisiana	9,801	1.84%
17	Massachusetts	9,630	1.80%
18	Indiana	9,408	1.76%
19	Washington	9,121	1.71%
20	South Carolina	8,651	1.62%
21	Missouri	8,610	1.61%
22	Wisconsin	7,329	1.37%
23	Kentucky	6,807	1.28%
24	Colorado	6,183	1.16%
25	Alabama	5,869	1.10%
26	Oklahoma	5,641	1.06%
27	Minnesota	5,533	1.04%
28	Connecticut	5,418	1.02%
29	Oregon	5,370	1.01%
30	Kansas	4,890	0.92%
31	Arkansas	3,805	0.71%
32	New Mexico	3,736	0.70%
33	Nevada	3,571	0.67%
34	Mississippi	3,525	0.66%
35	Utah	2,815	0.53%
36	Iowa	2,781	0.52%
37	Nebraska	2,550	0.48%
38	Hawaii	2,026	0.38%
39	Maine	1,868	0.35%
40	Rhode Island	1,821	0.34%
41	Delaware	1,675	0.31%
42	Idaho	1,654	0.31%
43	West Virginia	1,414	0.27%
44	New Hampshire	1,376	0.26%
45	Alaska	1,273	0.24%
46	Montana	1,265	0.24%
47	South Dakota	820	0.15%
48	Wyoming	779	0.15%
49	Vermont	697	0.13%
50	North Dakota	674	0.13%
	District of Columbia	5,060	0.95%

Source: U.S. Bureau of the Census
"Public Employment: 1992" (September 1994, GE/92-1)
*Full-time equivalent as of October 1992.

State and Local Government Employees in Corrections
As a Percent of All State and Local Government Employees in 1992
National Percent = 3.99% of Employees*

ALPHA ORDER

RANK	STATE	EMPLOYEES
41	Alabama	2.49
37	Alaska	2.77
4	Arizona	5.08
34	Arkansas	2.96
11	California	4.26
26	Colorado	3.34
20	Connecticut	3.58
8	Delaware	4.44
1	Florida	6.29
5	Georgia	4.73
29	Hawaii	3.14
38	Idaho	2.75
23	Illinois	3.46
28	Indiana	3.16
49	Iowa	1.79
30	Kansas	3.11
23	Kentucky	3.46
16	Louisiana	3.93
35	Maine	2.87
7	Maryland	4.56
22	Massachusetts	3.47
12	Michigan	4.21
43	Minnesota	2.31
45	Mississippi	2.27
21	Missouri	3.48
42	Montana	2.33
40	Nebraska	2.56
2	Nevada	5.41
39	New Hampshire	2.66
9	New Jersey	4.35
19	New Mexico	3.65
3	New York	5.12
14	North Carolina	4.09
48	North Dakota	1.80
31	Ohio	3.10
33	Oklahoma	3.00
23	Oregon	3.46
18	Pennsylvania	3.66
17	Rhode Island	3.82
10	South Carolina	4.29
47	South Dakota	2.09
13	Tennessee	4.17
6	Texas	4.70
32	Utah	3.03
44	Vermont	2.28
15	Virginia	4.05
27	Washington	3.31
50	West Virginia	1.53
36	Wisconsin	2.80
46	Wyoming	2.13

RANK ORDER

RANK	STATE	EMPLOYEES
1	Florida	6.29
2	Nevada	5.41
3	New York	5.12
4	Arizona	5.08
5	Georgia	4.73
6	Texas	4.70
7	Maryland	4.56
8	Delaware	4.44
9	New Jersey	4.35
10	South Carolina	4.29
11	California	4.26
12	Michigan	4.21
13	Tennessee	4.17
14	North Carolina	4.09
15	Virginia	4.05
16	Louisiana	3.93
17	Rhode Island	3.82
18	Pennsylvania	3.66
19	New Mexico	3.65
20	Connecticut	3.58
21	Missouri	3.48
22	Massachusetts	3.47
23	Illinois	3.46
23	Kentucky	3.46
23	Oregon	3.46
26	Colorado	3.34
27	Washington	3.31
28	Indiana	3.16
29	Hawaii	3.14
30	Kansas	3.11
31	Ohio	3.10
32	Utah	3.03
33	Oklahoma	3.00
34	Arkansas	2.96
35	Maine	2.87
36	Wisconsin	2.80
37	Alaska	2.77
38	Idaho	2.75
39	New Hampshire	2.66
40	Nebraska	2.56
41	Alabama	2.49
42	Montana	2.33
43	Minnesota	2.31
44	Vermont	2.28
45	Mississippi	2.27
46	Wyoming	2.13
47	South Dakota	2.09
48	North Dakota	1.80
49	Iowa	1.79
50	West Virginia	1.53
	District of Columbia	9.26

Source: Morgan Quitno Corporation using data from U.S. Bureau of the Census
  "Public Employment: 1992" (September 1994, GE/92-1)
*Full-time equivalent as of October 1992.

State Government Employees in Corrections in 1992

National Total = 344,793 Employees*

ALPHA ORDER					RANK ORDER			
RANK	STATE	EMPLOYEES	% of USA		RANK	STATE	EMPLOYEES	% of USA
26	Alabama	3,911	1.13%		1	California	34,870	10.11%
42	Alaska	1,216	0.35%		2	New York	33,083	9.60%
19	Arizona	6,232	1.81%		3	Texas	29,397	8.53%
30	Arkansas	2,812	0.82%		4	Florida	29,080	8.43%
1	California	34,870	10.11%		5	Michigan	14,965	4.34%
28	Colorado	3,448	1.00%		6	Georgia	14,040	4.07%
22	Connecticut	5,418	1.57%		7	North Carolina	12,367	3.59%
40	Delaware	1,675	0.49%		8	Illinois	11,806	3.42%
4	Florida	29,080	8.43%		9	Ohio	10,794	3.13%
6	Georgia	14,040	4.07%		10	New Jersey	9,791	2.84%
37	Hawaii	2,026	0.59%		11	Virginia	8,836	2.56%
43	Idaho	1,139	0.33%		12	Maryland	8,812	2.56%
8	Illinois	11,806	3.42%		13	Pennsylvania	8,688	2.52%
16	Indiana	6,470	1.88%		14	South Carolina	7,321	2.12%
36	Iowa	2,092	0.61%		15	Louisiana	6,617	1.92%
27	Kansas	3,558	1.03%		16	Indiana	6,470	1.88%
24	Kentucky	5,093	1.48%		17	Tennessee	6,409	1.86%
15	Louisiana	6,617	1.92%		18	Missouri	6,280	1.82%
41	Maine	1,251	0.36%		19	Arizona	6,232	1.81%
12	Maryland	8,812	2.56%		20	Washington	6,095	1.77%
23	Massachusetts	5,311	1.54%		21	Wisconsin	5,422	1.57%
5	Michigan	14,965	4.34%		22	Connecticut	5,418	1.57%
33	Minnesota	2,455	0.71%		23	Massachusetts	5,311	1.54%
29	Mississippi	2,965	0.86%		24	Kentucky	5,093	1.48%
18	Missouri	6,280	1.82%		25	Oklahoma	4,823	1.40%
44	Montana	943	0.27%		26	Alabama	3,911	1.13%
39	Nebraska	1,751	0.51%		27	Kansas	3,558	1.03%
34	Nevada	2,252	0.65%		28	Colorado	3,448	1.00%
45	New Hampshire	900	0.26%		29	Mississippi	2,965	0.86%
10	New Jersey	9,791	2.84%		30	Arkansas	2,812	0.82%
32	New Mexico	2,628	0.76%		31	Oregon	2,709	0.79%
2	New York	33,083	9.60%		32	New Mexico	2,628	0.76%
7	North Carolina	12,367	3.59%		33	Minnesota	2,455	0.71%
49	North Dakota	487	0.14%		34	Nevada	2,252	0.65%
9	Ohio	10,794	3.13%		35	Utah	2,194	0.64%
25	Oklahoma	4,823	1.40%		36	Iowa	2,092	0.61%
31	Oregon	2,709	0.79%		37	Hawaii	2,026	0.59%
13	Pennsylvania	8,688	2.52%		38	Rhode Island	1,821	0.53%
38	Rhode Island	1,821	0.53%		39	Nebraska	1,751	0.51%
14	South Carolina	7,321	2.12%		40	Delaware	1,675	0.49%
48	South Dakota	582	0.17%		41	Maine	1,251	0.36%
17	Tennessee	6,409	1.86%		42	Alaska	1,216	0.35%
3	Texas	29,397	8.53%		43	Idaho	1,139	0.33%
35	Utah	2,194	0.64%		44	Montana	943	0.27%
47	Vermont	697	0.20%		45	New Hampshire	900	0.26%
11	Virginia	8,836	2.56%		46	West Virginia	786	0.23%
20	Washington	6,095	1.77%		47	Vermont	697	0.20%
46	West Virginia	786	0.23%		48	South Dakota	582	0.17%
21	Wisconsin	5,422	1.57%		49	North Dakota	487	0.14%
50	Wyoming	475	0.14%		50	Wyoming	475	0.14%
					District of Columbia**		NA	NA

Source: U.S. Bureau of the Census
 "Public Employment: 1992" (September 1994, GE/92-1)
*Full-time equivalent as of October 1992.
**Not applicable.

State Government Employees in Corrections
As a Percent of All State Government Employees in 1992
National Percent = 8.94% of Employees*

ALPHA ORDER

RANK	STATE	PERCENT
43	Alabama	4.82
42	Alaska	5.02
6	Arizona	11.53
34	Arkansas	6.03
9	California	10.83
27	Colorado	6.51
11	Connecticut	10.00
18	Delaware	8.30
1	Florida	17.68
3	Georgia	12.27
47	Hawaii	4.00
36	Idaho	5.62
14	Illinois	8.64
25	Indiana	6.80
44	Iowa	4.42
23	Kansas	7.43
26	Kentucky	6.68
22	Louisiana	7.45
35	Maine	5.68
10	Maryland	10.74
28	Massachusetts	6.25
8	Michigan	10.86
48	Minnesota	3.65
28	Mississippi	6.25
15	Missouri	8.48
38	Montana	5.52
32	Nebraska	6.09
5	Nevada	11.76
38	New Hampshire	5.52
16	New Jersey	8.46
30	New Mexico	6.23
2	New York	12.37
7	North Carolina	11.34
49	North Dakota	2.96
19	Ohio	7.69
24	Oklahoma	7.19
40	Oregon	5.45
33	Pennsylvania	6.06
13	Rhode Island	9.16
12	South Carolina	9.42
45	South Dakota	4.31
17	Tennessee	8.44
4	Texas	12.26
37	Utah	5.54
41	Vermont	5.39
20	Virginia	7.63
31	Washington	6.22
50	West Virginia	2.34
21	Wisconsin	7.46
46	Wyoming	4.21

RANK ORDER

RANK	STATE	PERCENT
1	Florida	17.68
2	New York	12.37
3	Georgia	12.27
4	Texas	12.26
5	Nevada	11.76
6	Arizona	11.53
7	North Carolina	11.34
8	Michigan	10.86
9	California	10.83
10	Maryland	10.74
11	Connecticut	10.00
12	South Carolina	9.42
13	Rhode Island	9.16
14	Illinois	8.64
15	Missouri	8.48
16	New Jersey	8.46
17	Tennessee	8.44
18	Delaware	8.30
19	Ohio	7.69
20	Virginia	7.63
21	Wisconsin	7.46
22	Louisiana	7.45
23	Kansas	7.43
24	Oklahoma	7.19
25	Indiana	6.80
26	Kentucky	6.68
27	Colorado	6.51
28	Massachusetts	6.25
28	Mississippi	6.25
30	New Mexico	6.23
31	Washington	6.22
32	Nebraska	6.09
33	Pennsylvania	6.06
34	Arkansas	6.03
35	Maine	5.68
36	Idaho	5.62
37	Utah	5.54
38	Montana	5.52
38	New Hampshire	5.52
40	Oregon	5.45
41	Vermont	5.39
42	Alaska	5.02
43	Alabama	4.82
44	Iowa	4.42
45	South Dakota	4.31
46	Wyoming	4.21
47	Hawaii	4.00
48	Minnesota	3.65
49	North Dakota	2.96
50	West Virginia	2.34

| | District of Columbia** | NA |

Source: Morgan Quitno Corporation using data from U.S. Bureau of the Census
  "Public Employment: 1992" (September 1994, GE/92-1)
*Full-time equivalent as of October 1992.

State Correctional Officers in Adult Systems in 1993

National Total = 182,643 Officers*

ALPHA ORDER					RANK ORDER			
RANK	STATE	OFFICERS	% of USA		RANK	STATE	OFFICERS	% of USA
22	Alabama	2,435	1.33%		1	New York	20,818	11.40%
40	Alaska	779	0.43%		2	California	17,127	9.38%
15	Arizona	3,927	2.15%		3	Texas	15,131	8.28%
28	Arkansas	1,729	0.95%		4	Florida	12,252	6.71%
2	California	17,127	9.38%		5	Michigan	8,157	4.47%
25	Colorado	1,975	1.08%		6	North Carolina	7,564	4.14%
18	Connecticut	3,389	1.86%		7	Illinois	7,194	3.94%
38	Delaware	912	0.50%		8	Georgia	6,566	3.59%
4	Florida	12,252	6.71%		9	New Jersey	5,655	3.10%
8	Georgia	6,566	3.59%		10	Ohio	5,372	2.94%
37	Hawaii	956	0.52%		11	Virginia	5,008	2.74%
39	Idaho	838	0.46%		12	Pennsylvania	4,806	2.63%
7	Illinois	7,194	3.94%		13	Maryland	4,798	2.63%
16	Indiana	3,640	1.99%		14	Louisiana	4,478	2.45%
32	Iowa	1,162	0.64%		15	Arizona	3,927	2.15%
27	Kansas	1,769	0.97%		16	Indiana	3,640	1.99%
30	Kentucky	1,342	0.73%		17	South Carolina	3,552	1.94%
14	Louisiana	4,478	2.45%		18	Connecticut	3,389	1.86%
42	Maine	685	0.38%		19	Massachusetts	3,349	1.83%
13	Maryland	4,798	2.63%		20	Tennessee	2,965	1.62%
19	Massachusetts	3,349	1.83%		21	Missouri	2,773	1.52%
5	Michigan	8,157	4.47%		22	Alabama	2,435	1.33%
33	Minnesota	1,131	0.62%		23	Washington	2,348	1.29%
26	Mississippi	1,834	1.00%		24	Wisconsin	2,156	1.18%
21	Missouri	2,773	1.52%		25	Colorado	1,975	1.08%
48	Montana	290	0.16%		26	Mississippi	1,834	1.00%
43	Nebraska	557	0.30%		27	Kansas	1,769	0.97%
35	Nevada	1,059	0.58%		28	Arkansas	1,729	0.95%
45	New Hampshire	413	0.23%		29	Oklahoma	1,578	0.86%
9	New Jersey	5,655	3.10%		30	Kentucky	1,342	0.73%
31	New Mexico	1,181	0.65%		31	New Mexico	1,181	0.65%
1	New York	20,818	11.40%		32	Iowa	1,162	0.64%
6	North Carolina	7,564	4.14%		33	Minnesota	1,131	0.62%
50	North Dakota	123	0.07%		34	Oregon	1,090	0.60%
10	Ohio	5,372	2.94%		35	Nevada	1,059	0.58%
29	Oklahoma	1,578	0.86%		36	Rhode Island	1,035	0.57%
34	Oregon	1,090	0.60%		37	Hawaii	956	0.52%
12	Pennsylvania	4,806	2.63%		38	Delaware	912	0.50%
36	Rhode Island	1,035	0.57%		39	Idaho	838	0.46%
17	South Carolina	3,552	1.94%		40	Alaska	779	0.43%
47	South Dakota	313	0.17%		41	Utah	717	0.39%
20	Tennessee	2,965	1.62%		42	Maine	685	0.38%
3	Texas	15,131	8.28%		43	Nebraska	557	0.30%
41	Utah	717	0.39%		44	West Virginia	445	0.24%
46	Vermont	345	0.19%		45	New Hampshire	413	0.23%
11	Virginia	5,008	2.74%		46	Vermont	345	0.19%
23	Washington	2,348	1.29%		47	South Dakota	313	0.17%
44	West Virginia	445	0.24%		48	Montana	290	0.16%
24	Wisconsin	2,156	1.18%		49	Wyoming	240	0.13%
49	Wyoming	240	0.13%		50	North Dakota	123	0.07%
					District of Columbia		2,685	1.47%

Source: American Correctional Association (Laurel, MD)
"1994 Directory of Juvenile and Adult Correctional Departments, Institutions, Agencies and Paroling Authorities (1994)
*As of June 30, 1993. Total does not include 9,437 federal correctional officers.

Male Correctional Officers in Adult Systems in 1993

National Total = 151,645 Male Officers*

ALPHA ORDER					RANK ORDER			
RANK	STATE	OFFICERS	% of USA		RANK	STATE	OFFICERS	% of USA
22	Alabama	1,895	1.25%		1	New York	19,242	12.69%
40	Alaska	632	0.42%		2	California	13,877	9.15%
15	Arizona	3,348	2.21%		3	Texas	11,701	7.72%
27	Arkansas	1,414	0.93%		4	Florida	9,354	6.17%
2	California	13,877	9.15%		5	North Carolina	6,653	4.39%
25	Colorado	1,611	1.06%		6	Michigan	6,542	4.31%
17	Connecticut	2,900	1.91%		7	Illinois	6,281	4.14%
38	Delaware	782	0.52%		8	Georgia	5,498	3.63%
4	Florida	9,354	6.17%		9	New Jersey	4,952	3.27%
8	Georgia	5,498	3.63%		10	Ohio	4,419	2.91%
37	Hawaii	830	0.55%		11	Pennsylvania	4,391	2.90%
39	Idaho	726	0.48%		12	Virginia	4,023	2.65%
7	Illinois	6,281	4.14%		13	Maryland	3,769	2.49%
18	Indiana	2,867	1.89%		14	Louisiana	3,500	2.31%
32	Iowa	996	0.66%		15	Arizona	3,348	2.21%
26	Kansas	1,484	0.98%		16	Massachusetts	2,986	1.97%
29	Kentucky	1,093	0.72%		17	Connecticut	2,900	1.91%
14	Louisiana	3,500	2.31%		18	Indiana	2,867	1.89%
41	Maine	617	0.41%		19	South Carolina	2,602	1.72%
13	Maryland	3,769	2.49%		20	Tennessee	2,394	1.58%
16	Massachusetts	2,986	1.97%		21	Missouri	2,381	1.57%
6	Michigan	6,542	4.31%		22	Alabama	1,895	1.25%
34	Minnesota	945	0.62%		22	Washington	1,895	1.25%
30	Mississippi	1,086	0.72%		24	Wisconsin	1,815	1.20%
21	Missouri	2,381	1.57%		25	Colorado	1,611	1.06%
46	Montana	251	0.17%		26	Kansas	1,484	0.98%
42	Nebraska	453	0.30%		27	Arkansas	1,414	0.93%
36	Nevada	900	0.59%		28	Oklahoma	1,392	0.92%
44	New Hampshire	371	0.24%		29	Kentucky	1,093	0.72%
9	New Jersey	4,952	3.27%		30	Mississippi	1,086	0.72%
31	New Mexico	1,077	0.71%		31	New Mexico	1,077	0.71%
1	New York	19,242	12.69%		32	Iowa	996	0.66%
5	North Carolina	6,653	4.39%		33	Rhode Island	951	0.63%
48	North Dakota	90	0.06%		34	Minnesota	945	0.62%
10	Ohio	4,419	2.91%		35	Oregon	910	0.60%
28	Oklahoma	1,392	0.92%		36	Nevada	900	0.59%
35	Oregon	910	0.60%		37	Hawaii	830	0.55%
11	Pennsylvania	4,391	2.90%		38	Delaware	782	0.52%
33	Rhode Island	951	0.63%		39	Idaho	726	0.48%
19	South Carolina	2,602	1.72%		40	Alaska	632	0.42%
45	South Dakota	255	0.17%		41	Maine	617	0.41%
20	Tennessee	2,394	1.58%		42	Nebraska	453	0.30%
3	Texas	11,701	7.72%		43	West Virginia	394	0.26%
NA	Utah**	NA	NA		44	New Hampshire	371	0.24%
NA	Vermont**	NA	NA		45	South Dakota	255	0.17%
12	Virginia	4,023	2.65%		46	Montana	251	0.17%
22	Washington	1,895	1.25%		47	Wyoming	191	0.13%
43	West Virginia	394	0.26%		48	North Dakota	90	0.06%
24	Wisconsin	1,815	1.20%		NA	Utah**	NA	NA
47	Wyoming	191	0.13%		NA	Vermont**	NA	NA
						District of Columbia	1,884	1.24%

Source: American Correctional Association (Laurel, MD)

"1994 Directory of Juvenile and Adult Correctional Departments, Institutions, Agencies and Paroling Authorities (1994)
As of June 30, 1993. Total does not include 8,366 male federal correctional officers.
**Sex of officers not available.*

Female Correctional Officers in Adult Systems in 1993

National Total = 30,998 Female Officers*

ALPHA ORDER					RANK ORDER			
RANK	STATE	OFFICERS	% of USA		RANK	STATE	OFFICERS	% of USA
19	Alabama	540	1.74%		1	Texas	3,430	11.07%
35	Alaska	147	0.47%		2	California	3,250	10.48%
17	Arizona	579	1.87%		3	Florida	2,898	9.35%
27	Arkansas	315	1.02%		4	Michigan	1,615	5.21%
2	California	3,250	10.48%		5	New York	1,576	5.08%
24	Colorado	364	1.17%		6	Georgia	1,068	3.45%
20	Connecticut	489	1.58%		7	Maryland	1,029	3.32%
36	Delaware	130	0.42%		8	Virginia	985	3.18%
3	Florida	2,898	9.35%		9	Louisiana	978	3.16%
6	Georgia	1,068	3.45%		10	Ohio	953	3.07%
37	Hawaii	126	0.41%		11	South Carolina	950	3.06%
38	Idaho	112	0.36%		12	Illinois	913	2.95%
12	Illinois	913	2.95%		13	North Carolina	911	2.94%
14	Indiana	773	2.49%		14	Indiana	773	2.49%
33	Iowa	166	0.54%		15	Mississippi	748	2.41%
28	Kansas	285	0.92%		16	New Jersey	703	2.27%
29	Kentucky	249	0.80%		17	Arizona	579	1.87%
9	Louisiana	978	3.16%		18	Tennessee	571	1.84%
42	Maine	68	0.22%		19	Alabama	540	1.74%
7	Maryland	1,029	3.32%		20	Connecticut	489	1.58%
25	Massachusetts	363	1.17%		21	Washington	453	1.46%
4	Michigan	1,615	5.21%		22	Pennsylvania	415	1.34%
30	Minnesota	186	0.60%		23	Missouri	392	1.26%
15	Mississippi	748	2.41%		24	Colorado	364	1.17%
23	Missouri	392	1.26%		25	Massachusetts	363	1.17%
47	Montana	39	0.13%		26	Wisconsin	341	1.10%
39	Nebraska	104	0.34%		27	Arkansas	315	1.02%
34	Nevada	159	0.51%		28	Kansas	285	0.92%
46	New Hampshire	42	0.14%		29	Kentucky	249	0.80%
16	New Jersey	703	2.27%		30	Minnesota	186	0.60%
39	New Mexico	104	0.34%		30	Oklahoma	186	0.60%
5	New York	1,576	5.08%		32	Oregon	180	0.58%
13	North Carolina	911	2.94%		33	Iowa	166	0.54%
48	North Dakota	33	0.11%		34	Nevada	159	0.51%
10	Ohio	953	3.07%		35	Alaska	147	0.47%
30	Oklahoma	186	0.60%		36	Delaware	130	0.42%
32	Oregon	180	0.58%		37	Hawaii	126	0.41%
22	Pennsylvania	415	1.34%		38	Idaho	112	0.36%
41	Rhode Island	84	0.27%		39	Nebraska	104	0.34%
11	South Carolina	950	3.06%		39	New Mexico	104	0.34%
43	South Dakota	58	0.19%		41	Rhode Island	84	0.27%
18	Tennessee	571	1.84%		42	Maine	68	0.22%
1	Texas	3,430	11.07%		43	South Dakota	58	0.19%
NA	Utah**	NA	NA		44	West Virginia	51	0.16%
NA	Vermont**	NA	NA		45	Wyoming	49	0.16%
8	Virginia	985	3.18%		46	New Hampshire	42	0.14%
21	Washington	453	1.46%		47	Montana	39	0.13%
44	West Virginia	51	0.16%		48	North Dakota	33	0.11%
26	Wisconsin	341	1.10%		NA	Utah**	NA	NA
45	Wyoming	49	0.16%		NA	Vermont**	NA	NA
						District of Columbia	801	2.58%

Source: American Correctional Association (Laurel, MD)
    "1994 Directory of Juvenile and Adult Correctional Departments, Institutions, Agencies and Paroling Authorities (1994)
*As of June 30, 1993. Total does not include 1,071 female federal correctional officers.
**Sex of officers not available.

State Prisoners per Correctional Officer in 1993

National Rate = 4.20 Prisoners per Officer*

ALPHA ORDER

RANK	STATE	RATE
8	Alabama	6.20
41	Alaska	3.00
19	Arizona	4.50
14	Arkansas	5.00
2	California	12.00
24	Colorado	4.30
2	Connecticut	12.00
28	Delaware	4.19
16	Florida	4.85
24	Georgia	4.30
48	Hawaii	2.50
19	Idaho	4.50
29	Illinois	4.00
32	Indiana	3.66
1	Iowa	12.23
34	Kansas	3.58
6	Kentucky	7.48
33	Louisiana	3.60
50	Maine	2.20
14	Maryland	5.00
41	Massachusetts	3.00
19	Michigan	4.50
35	Minnesota	3.50
11	Mississippi	5.75
7	Missouri	6.60
36	Montana	3.41
17	Nebraska	4.60
38	Nevada	3.40
27	New Hampshire	4.20
40	New Jersey	3.10
41	New Mexico	3.00
41	New York	3.00
38	North Carolina	3.40
29	North Dakota	4.00
4	Ohio	8.30
5	Oklahoma	7.50
9	Oregon	5.87
13	Pennsylvania	5.15
48	Rhode Island	2.50
17	South Carolina	4.60
26	South Dakota	4.21
41	Tennessee	3.00
23	Texas	4.31
10	Utah	5.80
47	Vermont	2.90
36	Virginia	3.41
22	Washington	4.40
41	West Virginia	3.00
29	Wisconsin	4.00
12	Wyoming	5.65

RANK ORDER

RANK	STATE	RATE
1	Iowa	12.23
2	California	12.00
2	Connecticut	12.00
4	Ohio	8.30
5	Oklahoma	7.50
6	Kentucky	7.48
7	Missouri	6.60
8	Alabama	6.20
9	Oregon	5.87
10	Utah	5.80
11	Mississippi	5.75
12	Wyoming	5.65
13	Pennsylvania	5.15
14	Arkansas	5.00
14	Maryland	5.00
16	Florida	4.85
17	Nebraska	4.60
17	South Carolina	4.60
19	Arizona	4.50
19	Idaho	4.50
19	Michigan	4.50
22	Washington	4.40
23	Texas	4.31
24	Colorado	4.30
24	Georgia	4.30
26	South Dakota	4.21
27	New Hampshire	4.20
28	Delaware	4.19
29	Illinois	4.00
29	North Dakota	4.00
29	Wisconsin	4.00
32	Indiana	3.66
33	Louisiana	3.60
34	Kansas	3.58
35	Minnesota	3.50
36	Montana	3.41
36	Virginia	3.41
38	Nevada	3.40
38	North Carolina	3.40
40	New Jersey	3.10
41	Alaska	3.00
41	Massachusetts	3.00
41	New Mexico	3.00
41	New York	3.00
41	Tennessee	3.00
41	West Virginia	3.00
47	Vermont	2.90
48	Hawaii	2.50
48	Rhode Island	2.50
50	Maine	2.20
	District of Columbia	3.73

Source: American Correctional Association (Laurel, MD)
"1994 Directory of Juvenile and Adult Correctional Departments, Institutions, Agencies and Paroling Authorities (1994)
*As of June 30, 1993. National rate does not include federal or District of Columbia prisoner to officer rate.

Turnover Rate of Correctional Officers in Adult Systems in 1993

National Rate = 10.90%*

ALPHA ORDER			RANK ORDER		
RANK	STATE	TURNOVER RATE	RANK	STATE	TURNOVER RATE
44	Alabama	4.17	1	Arizona	20.00
18	Alaska	13.00	1	Arkansas	20.00
1	Arizona	20.00	1	Georgia	20.00
1	Arkansas	20.00	1	Vermont	20.00
30	California	9.00	5	South Carolina	18.30
40	Colorado	4.50	6	Louisiana	18.00
21	Connecticut	11.00	7	Massachusetts	17.00
43	Delaware	4.20	7	Wyoming	17.00
33	Florida	7.78	9	Nebraska	16.69
1	Georgia	20.00	10	Indiana	16.26
37	Hawaii	5.00	11	Maryland	16.00
23	Idaho	10.53	12	Maine	15.00
40	Illinois	4.50	12	Missouri	15.00
10	Indiana	16.26	14	Virginia	14.90
32	Iowa	8.54	15	Tennessee	14.40
16	Kansas	13.22	16	Kansas	13.22
NA	Kentucky**	NA	17	New Mexico	13.20
6	Louisiana	18.00	18	Alaska	13.00
12	Maine	15.00	18	South Dakota	13.00
11	Maryland	16.00	20	Ohio	12.80
7	Massachusetts	17.00	21	Connecticut	11.00
48	Michigan	2.70	22	Nevada	10.90
29	Minnesota	9.60	23	Idaho	10.53
36	Mississippi	5.40	24	North Carolina	10.51
12	Missouri	15.00	25	Montana	10.00
25	Montana	10.00	25	New Hampshire	10.00
9	Nebraska	16.69	25	West Virginia	10.00
22	Nevada	10.90	25	Wisconsin	10.00
25	New Hampshire	10.00	29	Minnesota	9.60
39	New Jersey	4.89	30	California	9.00
17	New Mexico	13.20	30	Oregon	9.00
49	New York	2.50	32	Iowa	8.54
24	North Carolina	10.51	33	Florida	7.78
45	North Dakota	4.00	34	Texas	6.50
20	Ohio	12.80	35	Washington	6.00
45	Oklahoma	4.00	36	Mississippi	5.40
30	Oregon	9.00	37	Hawaii	5.00
47	Pennsylvania	3.30	37	Rhode Island	5.00
37	Rhode Island	5.00	39	New Jersey	4.89
5	South Carolina	18.30	40	Colorado	4.50
18	South Dakota	13.00	40	Illinois	4.50
15	Tennessee	14.40	40	Utah	4.50
34	Texas	6.50	43	Delaware	4.20
40	Utah	4.50	44	Alabama	4.17
1	Vermont	20.00	45	North Dakota	4.00
14	Virginia	14.90	45	Oklahoma	4.00
35	Washington	6.00	47	Pennsylvania	3.30
25	West Virginia	10.00	48	Michigan	2.70
25	Wisconsin	10.00	49	New York	2.50
7	Wyoming	17.00	NA	Kentucky**	NA
			District of Columbia		2.50

Source: American Correctional Association (Laurel, MD)
        "1994 Directory of Juvenile and Adult Correctional Departments, Institutions, Agencies and Paroling Authorities (1994)
*As of June 30, 1993. National rate does not include federal or District of Columbia turnover rate.
**Not available.

Average Annual Salary of State Corrections Officers in 1992

National Average = $24,239*

	ALPHA ORDER				RANK ORDER	
RANK	STATE	SALARY		RANK	STATE	SALARY
14	Alabama	$25,240		1	Alaska	$41,215
1	Alaska	41,215		2	California	38,604
26	Arizona	20,250		3	New Jersey	34,984
45	Arkansas	16,458		4	New York	29,128
2	California	38,604		5	Connecticut	29,000
11	Colorado	26,220		6	Oregon	28,944
5	Connecticut	29,000		7	Michigan	28,870
35	Delaware	18,902		8	Pennsylvania	28,479
34	Florida	18,987		9	Nevada	27,622
28	Georgia	20,171		10	Minnesota	27,000
17	Hawaii	24,701		11	Colorado	26,220
25	Idaho	20,363		12	Iowa	25,800
13	Illinois	25,440		13	Illinois	25,440
NA	Indiana**	NA		14	Alabama	25,240
12	Iowa	25,800		15	Washington	25,098
18	Kansas	24,144		16	Massachusetts	25,000
40	Kentucky	17,796		17	Hawaii	24,701
27	Louisiana	20,184		18	Kansas	24,144
31	Maine	19,427		19	Rhode Island	24,136
NA	Maryland**	NA		20	New Hampshire	23,897
16	Massachusetts	25,000		21	Texas	23,385
7	Michigan	28,870		22	Ohio	23,046
10	Minnesota	27,000		23	Vermont	21,653
37	Mississippi	18,000		24	Virginia	21,534
36	Missouri	18,015		25	Idaho	20,363
41	Montana	17,506		26	Arizona	20,250
30	Nebraska	19,902		27	Louisiana	20,184
9	Nevada	27,622		28	Georgia	20,171
20	New Hampshire	23,897		29	Wisconsin	20,006
3	New Jersey	34,984		30	Nebraska	19,902
42	New Mexico	17,325		31	Maine	19,427
4	New York	29,128		32	North Carolina	19,236
32	North Carolina	19,236		33	Oklahoma	19,038
46	North Dakota	16,000		34	Florida	18,987
22	Ohio	23,046		35	Delaware	18,902
33	Oklahoma	19,038		36	Missouri	18,015
6	Oregon	28,944		37	Mississippi	18,000
8	Pennsylvania	28,479		37	Tennessee	18,000
19	Rhode Island	24,136		37	West Virginia	18,000
44	South Carolina	16,498		40	Kentucky	17,796
47	South Dakota	15,548		41	Montana	17,506
37	Tennessee	18,000		42	New Mexico	17,325
21	Texas	23,385		43	Wyoming	17,249
NA	Utah**	NA		44	South Carolina	16,498
23	Vermont	21,653		45	Arkansas	16,458
24	Virginia	21,534		46	North Dakota	16,000
15	Washington	25,098		47	South Dakota	15,548
37	West Virginia	18,000		NA	Indiana**	NA
29	Wisconsin	20,006		NA	Maryland**	NA
43	Wyoming	17,249		NA	Utah**	NA
				District of Columbia		35,027

Source: Corrections Compendium (Lincoln, NE) (October 1992)

*The national average was calculated by Morgan Quitno Corporation by using a weighted average of the 48 state averages.
**Not available.

Inmates in Local Jails in 1992

National Total = 408,951 Inmates*

ALPHA ORDER					RANK ORDER			
RANK	STATE	INMATES	% of USA		RANK	STATE	INMATES	% of USA
23	Alabama	5,620	1.37%		1	California	69,305	16.95%
NA	Alaska**	NA	NA		2	Texas	44,800	10.95%
21	Arizona	5,709	1.40%		3	Florida	32,469	7.94%
33	Arkansas	2,149	0.53%		4	New York	30,335	7.42%
1	California	69,305	16.95%		5	Georgia	19,762	4.83%
20	Colorado	6,215	1.52%		6	Pennsylvania	16,839	4.12%
NA	Connecticut**	NA	NA		7	Louisiana	13,415	3.28%
NA	Delaware**	NA	NA		8	Virginia	12,977	3.17%
3	Florida	32,469	7.94%		9	New Jersey	12,333	3.02%
5	Georgia	19,762	4.83%		10	Tennessee	11,729	2.87%
NA	Hawaii**	NA	NA		11	Illinois	11,217	2.74%
38	Idaho	1,213	0.30%		12	Ohio	11,085	2.71%
11	Illinois	11,217	2.74%		13	Michigan	11,039	2.70%
17	Indiana	6,753	1.65%		14	Maryland	8,866	2.17%
37	Iowa	1,338	0.33%		15	Washington	6,870	1.68%
30	Kansas	2,622	0.64%		16	Massachusetts	6,865	1.68%
22	Kentucky	5,661	1.38%		17	Indiana	6,753	1.65%
7	Louisiana	13,415	3.28%		18	Wisconsin	6,696	1.64%
40	Maine	698	0.17%		19	North Carolina	6,512	1.59%
14	Maryland	8,866	2.17%		20	Colorado	6,215	1.52%
16	Massachusetts	6,865	1.68%		21	Arizona	5,709	1.40%
13	Michigan	11,039	2.70%		22	Kentucky	5,661	1.38%
28	Minnesota	3,323	0.81%		23	Alabama	5,620	1.37%
27	Mississippi	3,776	0.92%		24	South Carolina	4,520	1.11%
25	Missouri	4,510	1.10%		25	Missouri	4,510	1.10%
41	Montana	675	0.17%		26	Oregon	3,816	0.93%
35	Nebraska	1,759	0.43%		27	Mississippi	3,776	0.92%
31	Nevada	2,621	0.64%		28	Minnesota	3,323	0.81%
39	New Hampshire	1,027	0.25%		29	Oklahoma	3,189	0.78%
9	New Jersey	12,333	3.02%		30	Kansas	2,622	0.64%
32	New Mexico	2,257	0.55%		31	Nevada	2,621	0.64%
4	New York	30,335	7.42%		32	New Mexico	2,257	0.55%
19	North Carolina	6,512	1.59%		33	Arkansas	2,149	0.53%
44	North Dakota	352	0.09%		34	Utah	1,875	0.46%
12	Ohio	11,085	2.71%		35	Nebraska	1,759	0.43%
29	Oklahoma	3,189	0.78%		36	West Virginia	1,631	0.40%
26	Oregon	3,816	0.93%		37	Iowa	1,338	0.33%
6	Pennsylvania	16,839	4.12%		38	Idaho	1,213	0.30%
NA	Rhode Island**	NA	NA		39	New Hampshire	1,027	0.25%
24	South Carolina	4,520	1.11%		40	Maine	698	0.17%
42	South Dakota	530	0.13%		41	Montana	675	0.17%
10	Tennessee	11,729	2.87%		42	South Dakota	530	0.13%
2	Texas	44,800	10.95%		43	Wyoming	498	0.12%
34	Utah	1,875	0.46%		44	North Dakota	352	0.09%
NA	Vermont**	NA	NA		NA	Alaska**	NA	NA
8	Virginia	12,977	3.17%		NA	Connecticut**	NA	NA
15	Washington	6,870	1.68%		NA	Delaware**	NA	NA
36	West Virginia	1,631	0.40%		NA	Hawaii**	NA	NA
18	Wisconsin	6,696	1.64%		NA	Rhode Island**	NA	NA
43	Wyoming	498	0.12%		NA	Vermont**	NA	NA
					District of Columbia**		NA	NA

Source: American Correctional Association (Laurel, MD)
  "1993–1995 National Jail and Adult Detention Directory"
As of December 31, 1992. Based on a survey mailed to the 50 states.
**These states have combined state and local jail systems and are excluded from this count.*

Jails and Detention Centers in 1992

National Total = 3,016 Jails*

ALPHA ORDER				RANK ORDER			
RANK	STATE	JAILS	% of USA	RANK	STATE	JAILS	% of USA
19	Alabama	73	2.42%	1	Texas	255	8.45%
NA	Alaska**	NA	NA	2	Georgia	176	5.84%
39	Arizona	22	0.73%	3	California	131	4.34%
24	Arkansas	68	2.25%	4	Missouri	108	3.58%
3	California	131	4.34%	5	Tennessee	104	3.45%
26	Colorado	56	1.86%	6	North Carolina	102	3.38%
NA	Connecticut**	NA	NA	7	Virginia	96	3.18%
NA	Delaware**	NA	NA	8	Iowa	95	3.15%
11	Florida	91	3.02%	8	Kansas	95	3.15%
2	Georgia	176	5.84%	10	Illinois	93	3.08%
NA	Hawaii**	NA	NA	11	Florida	91	3.02%
30	Idaho	37	1.23%	12	Indiana	90	2.98%
10	Illinois	93	3.08%	12	Kentucky	90	2.98%
12	Indiana	90	2.98%	12	Ohio	90	2.98%
8	Iowa	95	3.15%	15	Mississippi	85	2.82%
8	Kansas	95	3.15%	16	Michigan	84	2.79%
12	Kentucky	90	2.98%	17	New York	83	2.75%
23	Louisiana	72	2.39%	18	Oklahoma	77	2.55%
43	Maine	16	0.53%	19	Alabama	73	2.42%
33	Maryland	30	0.99%	19	Minnesota	73	2.42%
42	Massachusetts	17	0.56%	19	Pennsylvania	73	2.42%
16	Michigan	84	2.79%	19	Wisconsin	73	2.42%
19	Minnesota	73	2.42%	23	Louisiana	72	2.39%
15	Mississippi	85	2.82%	24	Arkansas	68	2.25%
4	Missouri	108	3.58%	25	Nebraska	67	2.22%
28	Montana	45	1.49%	26	Colorado	56	1.86%
25	Nebraska	67	2.22%	27	South Carolina	52	1.72%
41	Nevada	18	0.60%	28	Montana	45	1.49%
44	New Hampshire	10	0.33%	29	West Virginia	43	1.43%
35	New Jersey	26	0.86%	30	Idaho	37	1.23%
34	New Mexico	29	0.96%	30	Oregon	37	1.23%
17	New York	83	2.75%	30	Washington	37	1.23%
6	North Carolina	102	3.38%	33	Maryland	30	0.99%
38	North Dakota	24	0.80%	34	New Mexico	29	0.96%
12	Ohio	90	2.98%	35	New Jersey	26	0.86%
18	Oklahoma	77	2.55%	35	Utah	26	0.86%
30	Oregon	37	1.23%	37	South Dakota	25	0.83%
19	Pennsylvania	73	2.42%	38	North Dakota	24	0.80%
NA	Rhode Island**	NA	NA	39	Arizona	22	0.73%
27	South Carolina	52	1.72%	39	Wyoming	22	0.73%
37	South Dakota	25	0.83%	41	Nevada	18	0.60%
5	Tennessee	104	3.45%	42	Massachusetts	17	0.56%
1	Texas	255	8.45%	43	Maine	16	0.53%
35	Utah	26	0.86%	44	New Hampshire	10	0.33%
NA	Vermont**	NA	NA	NA	Alaska**	NA	NA
7	Virginia	96	3.18%	NA	Connecticut**	NA	NA
30	Washington	37	1.23%	NA	Delaware**	NA	NA
29	West Virginia	43	1.43%	NA	Hawaii**	NA	NA
19	Wisconsin	73	2.42%	NA	Rhode Island**	NA	NA
39	Wyoming	22	0.73%	NA	Vermont**	NA	NA
				District of Columbia**		NA	NA

Source: American Correctional Association (Laurel, MD)
  "1993-1995 National Jail and Adult Detention Directory"
*As of December 31, 1992. Based on a survey mailed to the 50 states.
**These states have combined state and local jail systems and are excluded from this count.

Inmates in Local Jails in 1988

National Total = 343,569 Inmates*

ALPHA ORDER					RANK ORDER			
RANK	**STATE**		**INMATES**	**% of USA**	**RANK**	**STATE**	**INMATES**	**% of USA**
21	Alabama		4,819	1.40%	1	California	64,216	18.69%
45	Alaska		27	0.01%	2	Texas	29,439	8.57%
15	Arizona		6,006	1.75%	3	Florida	28,236	8.22%
32	Arkansas		1,994	0.58%	4	New York	25,928	7.55%
1	California		64,216	18.69%	5	Georgia	17,482	5.09%
20	Colorado		4,882	1.42%	6	Pennsylvania	13,649	3.97%
NA	Connecticut**		NA	NA	7	Louisiana	11,222	3.27%
NA	Delaware**		NA	NA	8	New Jersey	11,124	3.24%
3	Florida		28,236	8.22%	9	Tennessee	10,858	3.16%
5	Georgia		17,482	5.09%	10	Illinois	9,891	2.88%
NA	Hawaii**		NA	NA	11	Michigan	9,404	2.74%
38	Idaho		810	0.24%	12	Virginia	9,372	2.73%
10	Illinois		9,891	2.88%	13	Ohio	9,160	2.67%
19	Indiana		5,235	1.52%	14	Maryland	7,486	2.18%
37	Iowa		1,036	0.30%	15	Arizona	6,006	1.75%
33	Kansas		1,906	0.55%	16	Washington	5,934	1.73%
22	Kentucky		4,695	1.37%	17	North Carolina	5,469	1.59%
7	Louisiana		11,222	3.27%	18	Massachusetts	5,454	1.59%
40	Maine		669	0.19%	19	Indiana	5,235	1.52%
14	Maryland		7,486	2.18%	20	Colorado	4,882	1.42%
18	Massachusetts		5,454	1.59%	21	Alabama	4,819	1.40%
11	Michigan		9,404	2.74%	22	Kentucky	4,695	1.37%
27	Minnesota		3,227	0.94%	23	Wisconsin	4,667	1.36%
25	Mississippi		3,501	1.02%	24	Missouri	4,154	1.21%
24	Missouri		4,154	1.21%	25	Mississippi	3,501	1.02%
41	Montana		616	0.18%	26	South Carolina	3,497	1.02%
36	Nebraska		1,156	0.34%	27	Minnesota	3,227	0.94%
30	Nevada		2,343	0.68%	28	Oregon	2,819	0.82%
39	New Hampshire		789	0.23%	29	Oklahoma	2,595	0.76%
8	New Jersey		11,124	3.24%	30	Nevada	2,343	0.68%
31	New Mexico		2,188	0.64%	31	New Mexico	2,188	0.64%
4	New York		25,928	7.55%	32	Arkansas	1,994	0.58%
17	North Carolina		5,469	1.59%	33	Kansas	1,906	0.55%
44	North Dakota		288	0.08%	34	West Virginia	1,393	0.41%
13	Ohio		9,160	2.67%	35	Utah	1,261	0.37%
29	Oklahoma		2,595	0.76%	36	Nebraska	1,156	0.34%
28	Oregon		2,819	0.82%	37	Iowa	1,036	0.30%
6	Pennsylvania		13,649	3.97%	38	Idaho	810	0.24%
NA	Rhode Island**		NA	NA	39	New Hampshire	789	0.23%
26	South Carolina		3,497	1.02%	40	Maine	669	0.19%
42	South Dakota		522	0.15%	41	Montana	616	0.18%
9	Tennessee		10,858	3.16%	42	South Dakota	522	0.15%
2	Texas		29,439	8.57%	43	Wyoming	457	0.13%
35	Utah		1,261	0.37%	44	North Dakota	288	0.08%
NA	Vermont**		NA	NA	45	Alaska	27	0.01%
12	Virginia		9,372	2.73%	NA	Connecticut**	NA	NA
16	Washington		5,934	1.73%	NA	Delaware**	NA	NA
34	West Virginia		1,393	0.41%	NA	Hawaii**	NA	NA
23	Wisconsin		4,667	1.36%	NA	Rhode Island**	NA	NA
43	Wyoming		457	0.13%	NA	Vermont**	NA	NA
						District of Columbia	1,693	0.49%

Source: U.S. Department of Justice, Bureau of Justice Statistics
  "Census of Local Jails, 1988" (1991, NCJ-127992)
*As of June 30, 1988. National total does not include data from states not reporting.
**Not reported.

Male Inmates in Local Jails in 1988

National Total = 313,158 Male Inmates*

RANK	STATE	INMATES	% of USA
20	Alabama	4,469	1.43%
45	Alaska	25	0.01%
15	Arizona	5,496	1.76%
32	Arkansas	1,861	0.59%
1	California	56,570	18.06%
21	Colorado	4,439	1.42%
NA	Connecticut**	NA	NA
NA	Delaware**	NA	NA
3	Florida	25,460	8.13%
5	Georgia	16,364	5.23%
NA	Hawaii**	NA	NA
38	Idaho	766	0.24%
10	Illinois	9,333	2.98%
19	Indiana	4,870	1.56%
37	Iowa	958	0.31%
33	Kansas	1,772	0.57%
22	Kentucky	4,304	1.37%
7	Louisiana	10,397	3.32%
40	Maine	642	0.21%
14	Maryland	6,897	2.20%
16	Massachusetts	5,430	1.73%
11	Michigan	8,687	2.77%
27	Minnesota	3,034	0.97%
25	Mississippi	3,298	1.05%
24	Missouri	3,845	1.23%
41	Montana	547	0.17%
36	Nebraska	1,044	0.33%
30	Nevada	2,078	0.66%
39	New Hampshire	749	0.24%
9	New Jersey	10,241	3.27%
31	New Mexico	2,015	0.64%
4	New York	23,240	7.42%
18	North Carolina	5,063	1.62%
44	North Dakota	262	0.08%
13	Ohio	8,355	2.67%
29	Oklahoma	2,318	0.74%
28	Oregon	2,590	0.83%
6	Pennsylvania	12,663	4.04%
NA	Rhode Island**	NA	NA
26	South Carolina	3,259	1.04%
42	South Dakota	478	0.15%
8	Tennessee	10,244	3.27%
2	Texas	26,753	8.54%
35	Utah	1,165	0.37%
NA	Vermont**	NA	NA
12	Virginia	8,544	2.73%
17	Washington	5,423	1.73%
34	West Virginia	1,310	0.42%
23	Wisconsin	4,289	1.37%
43	Wyoming	402	0.13%

RANK	STATE	INMATES	% of USA
1	California	56,570	18.06%
2	Texas	26,753	8.54%
3	Florida	25,460	8.13%
4	New York	23,240	7.42%
5	Georgia	16,364	5.23%
6	Pennsylvania	12,663	4.04%
7	Louisiana	10,397	3.32%
8	Tennessee	10,244	3.27%
9	New Jersey	10,241	3.27%
10	Illinois	9,333	2.98%
11	Michigan	8,687	2.77%
12	Virginia	8,544	2.73%
13	Ohio	8,355	2.67%
14	Maryland	6,897	2.20%
15	Arizona	5,496	1.76%
16	Massachusetts	5,430	1.73%
17	Washington	5,423	1.73%
18	North Carolina	5,063	1.62%
19	Indiana	4,870	1.56%
20	Alabama	4,469	1.43%
21	Colorado	4,439	1.42%
22	Kentucky	4,304	1.37%
23	Wisconsin	4,289	1.37%
24	Missouri	3,845	1.23%
25	Mississippi	3,298	1.05%
26	South Carolina	3,259	1.04%
27	Minnesota	3,034	0.97%
28	Oregon	2,590	0.83%
29	Oklahoma	2,318	0.74%
30	Nevada	2,078	0.66%
31	New Mexico	2,015	0.64%
32	Arkansas	1,861	0.59%
33	Kansas	1,772	0.57%
34	West Virginia	1,310	0.42%
35	Utah	1,165	0.37%
36	Nebraska	1,044	0.33%
37	Iowa	958	0.31%
38	Idaho	766	0.24%
39	New Hampshire	749	0.24%
40	Maine	642	0.21%
41	Montana	547	0.17%
42	South Dakota	478	0.15%
43	Wyoming	402	0.13%
44	North Dakota	262	0.08%
45	Alaska	25	0.01%
NA	Connecticut**	NA	NA
NA	Delaware**	NA	NA
NA	Hawaii**	NA	NA
NA	Rhode Island**	NA	NA
NA	Vermont**	NA	NA
	District of Columbia	1,209	0.39%

Source: U.S. Department of Justice, Bureau of Justice Statistics
  "Census of Local Jails, 1988" (1991, NCJ-127992)
*As of June 30, 1988. National total does not include data from states not reporting.
**Not reported.

Female Inmates in Local Jails in 1988

National Total = 30,411 Female Inmates*

<u>ALPHA ORDER</u>

RANK	STATE	INMATES	% of USA
22	Alabama	350	1.15%
45	Alaska	2	0.01%
16	Arizona	510	1.68%
32	Arkansas	133	0.44%
1	California	7,646	25.14%
17	Colorado	443	1.46%
NA	Connecticut**	NA	NA
NA	Delaware**	NA	NA
2	Florida	2,776	9.13%
5	Georgia	1,118	3.68%
NA	Hawaii**	NA	NA
39	Idaho	44	0.14%
14	Illinois	558	1.83%
21	Indiana	365	1.20%
36	Iowa	78	0.26%
31	Kansas	134	0.44%
19	Kentucky	391	1.29%
9	Louisiana	825	2.71%
42	Maine	27	0.09%
13	Maryland	589	1.94%
44	Massachusetts	24	0.08%
11	Michigan	717	2.36%
29	Minnesota	193	0.63%
28	Mississippi	203	0.67%
23	Missouri	309	1.02%
37	Montana	69	0.23%
33	Nebraska	112	0.37%
25	Nevada	265	0.87%
41	New Hampshire	40	0.13%
7	New Jersey	883	2.90%
30	New Mexico	173	0.57%
3	New York	2,688	8.84%
18	North Carolina	406	1.34%
43	North Dakota	26	0.09%
10	Ohio	805	2.65%
24	Oklahoma	277	0.91%
27	Oregon	229	0.75%
6	Pennsylvania	986	3.24%
NA	Rhode Island**	NA	NA
26	South Carolina	238	0.78%
39	South Dakota	44	0.14%
12	Tennessee	614	2.02%
4	Texas	2,686	8.83%
34	Utah	96	0.32%
NA	Vermont**	NA	NA
8	Virginia	828	2.72%
15	Washington	511	1.68%
35	West Virginia	83	0.27%
20	Wisconsin	378	1.24%
38	Wyoming	55	0.18%

<u>RANK ORDER</u>

RANK	STATE	INMATES	% of USA
1	California	7,646	25.14%
2	Florida	2,776	9.13%
3	New York	2,688	8.84%
4	Texas	2,686	8.83%
5	Georgia	1,118	3.68%
6	Pennsylvania	986	3.24%
7	New Jersey	883	2.90%
8	Virginia	828	2.72%
9	Louisiana	825	2.71%
10	Ohio	805	2.65%
11	Michigan	717	2.36%
12	Tennessee	614	2.02%
13	Maryland	589	1.94%
14	Illinois	558	1.83%
15	Washington	511	1.68%
16	Arizona	510	1.68%
17	Colorado	443	1.46%
18	North Carolina	406	1.34%
19	Kentucky	391	1.29%
20	Wisconsin	378	1.24%
21	Indiana	365	1.20%
22	Alabama	350	1.15%
23	Missouri	309	1.02%
24	Oklahoma	277	0.91%
25	Nevada	265	0.87%
26	South Carolina	238	0.78%
27	Oregon	229	0.75%
28	Mississippi	203	0.67%
29	Minnesota	193	0.63%
30	New Mexico	173	0.57%
31	Kansas	134	0.44%
32	Arkansas	133	0.44%
33	Nebraska	112	0.37%
34	Utah	96	0.32%
35	West Virginia	83	0.27%
36	Iowa	78	0.26%
37	Montana	69	0.23%
38	Wyoming	55	0.18%
39	Idaho	44	0.14%
39	South Dakota	44	0.14%
41	New Hampshire	40	0.13%
42	Maine	27	0.09%
43	North Dakota	26	0.09%
44	Massachusetts	24	0.08%
45	Alaska	2	0.01%
NA	Connecticut**	NA	NA
NA	Delaware**	NA	NA
NA	Hawaii**	NA	NA
NA	Rhode Island**	NA	NA
NA	Vermont**	NA	NA

District of Columbia — 484 — 1.59%

Source: U.S. Department of Justice, Bureau of Justice Statistics
   "Census of Local Jails, 1988" (1991, NCJ-127992)
*As of June 30, 1988. National total does not include data from states not reporting.
**Not reported.

White Inmates in Local Jails in 1988

National Total = 148,893 White Inmates*

RANK	STATE	INMATES	% of USA
24	Alabama	2,312	1.55%
45	Alaska	14	0.01%
13	Arizona	3,391	2.28%
32	Arkansas	1,136	0.76%
1	California	22,992	15.44%
20	Colorado	2,773	1.86%
NA	Connecticut**	NA	NA
NA	Delaware**	NA	NA
2	Florida	11,547	7.76%
4	Georgia	7,022	4.72%
NA	Hawaii**	NA	NA
40	Idaho	622	0.42%
15	Illinois	3,272	2.20%
14	Indiana	3,387	2.27%
35	Iowa	816	0.55%
30	Kansas	1,298	0.87%
12	Kentucky	3,511	2.36%
16	Louisiana	3,254	2.19%
38	Maine	647	0.43%
21	Maryland	2,699	1.81%
17	Massachusetts	3,075	2.07%
7	Michigan	5,660	3.80%
22	Minnesota	2,385	1.60%
34	Mississippi	1,006	0.68%
23	Missouri	2,339	1.57%
41	Montana	447	0.30%
35	Nebraska	816	0.55%
27	Nevada	1,529	1.03%
37	New Hampshire	734	0.49%
18	New Jersey	3,069	2.06%
39	New Mexico	635	0.43%
6	New York	6,821	4.58%
25	North Carolina	2,271	1.53%
44	North Dakota	194	0.13%
9	Ohio	5,267	3.54%
28	Oklahoma	1,522	1.02%
26	Oregon	2,240	1.50%
5	Pennsylvania	6,978	4.69%
NA	Rhode Island**	NA	NA
29	South Carolina	1,337	0.90%
43	South Dakota	358	0.24%
8	Tennessee	5,589	3.75%
3	Texas	10,513	7.06%
33	Utah	1,061	0.71%
NA	Vermont**	NA	NA
11	Virginia	3,806	2.56%
10	Washington	3,819	2.56%
31	West Virginia	1,198	0.80%
19	Wisconsin	3,001	2.02%
42	Wyoming	360	0.24%

RANK	STATE	INMATES	% of USA
1	California	22,992	15.44%
2	Florida	11,547	7.76%
3	Texas	10,513	7.06%
4	Georgia	7,022	4.72%
5	Pennsylvania	6,978	4.69%
6	New York	6,821	4.58%
7	Michigan	5,660	3.80%
8	Tennessee	5,589	3.75%
9	Ohio	5,267	3.54%
10	Washington	3,819	2.56%
11	Virginia	3,806	2.56%
12	Kentucky	3,511	2.36%
13	Arizona	3,391	2.28%
14	Indiana	3,387	2.27%
15	Illinois	3,272	2.20%
16	Louisiana	3,254	2.19%
17	Massachusetts	3,075	2.07%
18	New Jersey	3,069	2.06%
19	Wisconsin	3,001	2.02%
20	Colorado	2,773	1.86%
21	Maryland	2,699	1.81%
22	Minnesota	2,385	1.60%
23	Missouri	2,339	1.57%
24	Alabama	2,312	1.55%
25	North Carolina	2,271	1.53%
26	Oregon	2,240	1.50%
27	Nevada	1,529	1.03%
28	Oklahoma	1,522	1.02%
29	South Carolina	1,337	0.90%
30	Kansas	1,298	0.87%
31	West Virginia	1,198	0.80%
32	Arkansas	1,136	0.76%
33	Utah	1,061	0.71%
34	Mississippi	1,006	0.68%
35	Iowa	816	0.55%
35	Nebraska	816	0.55%
37	New Hampshire	734	0.49%
38	Maine	647	0.43%
39	New Mexico	635	0.43%
40	Idaho	622	0.42%
41	Montana	447	0.30%
42	Wyoming	360	0.24%
43	South Dakota	358	0.24%
44	North Dakota	194	0.13%
45	Alaska	14	0.01%
NA	Connecticut**	NA	NA
NA	Delaware**	NA	NA
NA	Hawaii**	NA	NA
NA	Rhode Island**	NA	NA
NA	Vermont**	NA	NA
	District of Columbia	170	0.11%

Source: U.S. Department of Justice, Bureau of Justice Statistics
"Census of Local Jails, 1988" (1991, NCJ-127992)
*As of June 30, 1988. National total does not include data from states not reporting.
**Not reported.

White Inmates in Local Jails as a Percent of All Inmates in 1988

National Percent = 43.34% of Inmates*

ALPHA ORDER				RANK ORDER		
RANK	STATE	PERCENT		RANK	STATE	PERCENT
31	Alabama	47.98		1	Maine	96.71
28	Alaska	51.85		2	New Hampshire	93.03
25	Arizona	56.46		3	West Virginia	86.00
23	Arkansas	56.97		4	Utah	84.14
38	California	35.80		5	Oregon	79.46
24	Colorado	56.80		6	Wyoming	78.77
NA	Connecticut**	NA		7	Iowa	78.76
NA	Delaware**	NA		8	Idaho	76.79
33	Florida	40.89		9	Kentucky	74.78
35	Georgia	40.17		10	Minnesota	73.91
NA	Hawaii**	NA		11	Montana	72.56
8	Idaho	76.79		12	Nebraska	70.59
40	Illinois	33.08		13	South Dakota	68.58
17	Indiana	64.70		14	Kansas	68.10
7	Iowa	78.76		15	North Dakota	67.36
14	Kansas	68.10		16	Nevada	65.26
9	Kentucky	74.78		17	Indiana	64.70
42	Louisiana	29.00		18	Washington	64.36
1	Maine	96.71		19	Wisconsin	64.30
37	Maryland	36.05		20	Michigan	60.19
26	Massachusetts	56.38		21	Oklahoma	58.65
20	Michigan	60.19		22	Ohio	57.50
10	Minnesota	73.91		23	Arkansas	56.97
43	Mississippi	28.73		24	Colorado	56.80
27	Missouri	56.31		25	Arizona	56.46
11	Montana	72.56		26	Massachusetts	56.38
12	Nebraska	70.59		27	Missouri	56.31
16	Nevada	65.26		28	Alaska	51.85
2	New Hampshire	93.03		29	Tennessee	51.47
44	New Jersey	27.59		30	Pennsylvania	51.12
41	New Mexico	29.02		31	Alabama	47.98
45	New York	26.31		32	North Carolina	41.52
32	North Carolina	41.52		33	Florida	40.89
15	North Dakota	67.36		34	Virginia	40.61
22	Ohio	57.50		35	Georgia	40.17
21	Oklahoma	58.65		36	South Carolina	38.23
5	Oregon	79.46		37	Maryland	36.05
30	Pennsylvania	51.12		38	California	35.80
NA	Rhode Island**	NA		39	Texas	35.71
36	South Carolina	38.23		40	Illinois	33.08
13	South Dakota	68.58		41	New Mexico	29.02
29	Tennessee	51.47		42	Louisiana	29.00
39	Texas	35.71		43	Mississippi	28.73
4	Utah	84.14		44	New Jersey	27.59
NA	Vermont**	NA		45	New York	26.31
34	Virginia	40.61		NA	Connecticut**	NA
18	Washington	64.36		NA	Delaware**	NA
3	West Virginia	86.00		NA	Hawaii**	NA
19	Wisconsin	64.30		NA	Rhode Island**	NA
6	Wyoming	78.77		NA	Vermont**	NA
					District of Columbia	10.04

Source: Morgan Quitno Corporation using data from U.S. Department of Justice, Bureau of Justice Statistics "Census of Local Jails, 1988" (1991, NCJ-127992)

*As of June 30, 1988. National total does not include data from states not reporting.

**Not reported.

Black Inmates in Local Jails in 1988

National Total = 139,289 Black Inmates*

RANK	STATE	INMATES	% of USA
16	Alabama	2,489	1.79%
45	Alaska	1	0.00%
26	Arizona	850	0.61%
27	Arkansas	808	0.58%
1	California	17,495	12.56%
25	Colorado	929	0.67%
NA	Connecticut**	NA	NA
NA	Delaware**	NA	NA
2	Florida	14,324	10.28%
5	Georgia	10,277	7.38%
NA	Hawaii**	NA	NA
41	Idaho	12	0.01%
8	Illinois	5,810	4.17%
19	Indiana	1,819	1.31%
35	Iowa	169	0.12%
31	Kansas	480	0.34%
23	Kentucky	1,158	0.83%
6	Louisiana	7,509	5.39%
39	Maine	16	0.01%
12	Maryland	4,649	3.34%
22	Massachusetts	1,233	0.89%
14	Michigan	3,433	2.46%
30	Minnesota	551	0.40%
17	Mississippi	2,433	1.75%
20	Missouri	1,747	1.25%
39	Montana	16	0.01%
33	Nebraska	231	0.17%
29	Nevada	707	0.51%
38	New Hampshire	37	0.03%
7	New Jersey	5,980	4.29%
36	New Mexico	157	0.11%
3	New York	12,755	9.16%
15	North Carolina	3,105	2.23%
44	North Dakota	5	0.00%
13	Ohio	3,713	2.67%
28	Oklahoma	757	0.54%
32	Oregon	294	0.21%
9	Pennsylvania	5,642	4.05%
NA	Rhode Island**	NA	NA
18	South Carolina	2,129	1.53%
42	South Dakota	10	0.01%
11	Tennessee	5,178	3.72%
4	Texas	10,740	7.71%
37	Utah	61	0.04%
NA	Vermont**	NA	NA
10	Virginia	5,422	3.89%
24	Washington	1,098	0.79%
34	West Virginia	185	0.13%
21	Wisconsin	1,342	0.96%
42	Wyoming	10	0.01%

RANK	STATE	INMATES	% of USA
1	California	17,495	12.56%
2	Florida	14,324	10.28%
3	New York	12,755	9.16%
4	Texas	10,740	7.71%
5	Georgia	10,277	7.38%
6	Louisiana	7,509	5.39%
7	New Jersey	5,980	4.29%
8	Illinois	5,810	4.17%
9	Pennsylvania	5,642	4.05%
10	Virginia	5,422	3.89%
11	Tennessee	5,178	3.72%
12	Maryland	4,649	3.34%
13	Ohio	3,713	2.67%
14	Michigan	3,433	2.46%
15	North Carolina	3,105	2.23%
16	Alabama	2,489	1.79%
17	Mississippi	2,433	1.75%
18	South Carolina	2,129	1.53%
19	Indiana	1,819	1.31%
20	Missouri	1,747	1.25%
21	Wisconsin	1,342	0.96%
22	Massachusetts	1,233	0.89%
23	Kentucky	1,158	0.83%
24	Washington	1,098	0.79%
25	Colorado	929	0.67%
26	Arizona	850	0.61%
27	Arkansas	808	0.58%
28	Oklahoma	757	0.54%
29	Nevada	707	0.51%
30	Minnesota	551	0.40%
31	Kansas	480	0.34%
32	Oregon	294	0.21%
33	Nebraska	231	0.17%
34	West Virginia	185	0.13%
35	Iowa	169	0.12%
36	New Mexico	157	0.11%
37	Utah	61	0.04%
38	New Hampshire	37	0.03%
39	Maine	16	0.01%
39	Montana	16	0.01%
41	Idaho	12	0.01%
42	South Dakota	10	0.01%
42	Wyoming	10	0.01%
44	North Dakota	5	0.00%
45	Alaska	1	0.00%
NA	Connecticut**	NA	NA
NA	Delaware**	NA	NA
NA	Hawaii**	NA	NA
NA	Rhode Island**	NA	NA
NA	Vermont**	NA	NA
	District of Columbia	1,523	1.09%

Source: U.S. Department of Justice, Bureau of Justice Statistics
  "Census of Local Jails, 1988" (1991, NCJ-127992)
*As of June 30, 1988. National total does not include data from states not reporting.
**Not reported.

Black Inmates in Local Jails as a Percent of All Inmates in 1988

National Percent = 40.54% of Inmates*

ALPHA ORDER				RANK ORDER		
RANK	STATE	PERCENT		RANK	STATE	PERCENT
10	Alabama	51.65		1	Mississippi	69.49
39	Alaska	3.70		2	Louisiana	66.91
33	Arizona	14.15		3	Maryland	62.10
17	Arkansas	40.52		4	South Carolina	60.88
24	California	27.24		5	Georgia	58.79
29	Colorado	19.03		6	Illinois	58.74
NA	Connecticut**	NA		7	Virginia	57.85
NA	Delaware**	NA		8	North Carolina	56.77
11	Florida	50.73		9	New Jersey	53.76
5	Georgia	58.79		10	Alabama	51.65
NA	Hawaii**	NA		11	Florida	50.73
45	Idaho	1.48		12	New York	49.19
6	Illinois	58.74		13	Tennessee	47.69
20	Indiana	34.75		14	Missouri	42.06
32	Iowa	16.31		15	Pennsylvania	41.34
25	Kansas	25.18		16	Ohio	40.53
26	Kentucky	24.66		17	Arkansas	40.52
2	Louisiana	66.91		18	Michigan	36.51
41	Maine	2.39		19	Texas	36.48
3	Maryland	62.10		20	Indiana	34.75
27	Massachusetts	22.61		21	Nevada	30.17
18	Michigan	36.51		22	Oklahoma	29.17
31	Minnesota	17.07		23	Wisconsin	28.76
1	Mississippi	69.49		24	California	27.24
14	Missouri	42.06		25	Kansas	25.18
40	Montana	2.60		26	Kentucky	24.66
28	Nebraska	19.98		27	Massachusetts	22.61
21	Nevada	30.17		28	Nebraska	19.98
38	New Hampshire	4.69		29	Colorado	19.03
9	New Jersey	53.76		30	Washington	18.50
36	New Mexico	7.18		31	Minnesota	17.07
12	New York	49.19		32	Iowa	16.31
8	North Carolina	56.77		33	Arizona	14.15
44	North Dakota	1.74		34	West Virginia	13.28
16	Ohio	40.53		35	Oregon	10.43
22	Oklahoma	29.17		36	New Mexico	7.18
35	Oregon	10.43		37	Utah	4.84
15	Pennsylvania	41.34		38	New Hampshire	4.69
NA	Rhode Island**	NA		39	Alaska	3.70
4	South Carolina	60.88		40	Montana	2.60
43	South Dakota	1.92		41	Maine	2.39
13	Tennessee	47.69		42	Wyoming	2.19
19	Texas	36.48		43	South Dakota	1.92
37	Utah	4.84		44	North Dakota	1.74
NA	Vermont**	NA		45	Idaho	1.48
7	Virginia	57.85		NA	Connecticut**	NA
30	Washington	18.50		NA	Delaware**	NA
34	West Virginia	13.28		NA	Hawaii**	NA
23	Wisconsin	28.76		NA	Rhode Island**	NA
42	Wyoming	2.19		NA	Vermont**	NA

District of Columbia   89.96

Source: Morgan Quitno Corporation using data from U.S. Department of Justice, Bureau of Justice Statistics
"Census of Local Jails, 1988" (1991, NCJ-127992)

*As of June 30, 1988. National total does not include data from states not reporting.

**Not reported.

Hispanic Inmates in Local Jails in 1988

National Total = 51,455 Hispanic Inmates*

RANK	STATE	INMATES	% of USA
40	Alabama	16	0.03%
45	Alaska	1	0.00%
6	Arizona	1,502	2.92%
32	Arkansas	44	0.09%
1	California	22,400	43.53%
8	Colorado	1,130	2.20%
NA	Connecticut**	NA	NA
NA	Delaware**	NA	NA
4	Florida	2,320	4.51%
17	Georgia	178	0.35%
NA	Hawaii**	NA	NA
19	Idaho	139	0.27%
11	Illinois	788	1.53%
36	Indiana	26	0.05%
33	Iowa	30	0.06%
22	Kansas	114	0.22%
36	Kentucky	26	0.05%
13	Louisiana	424	0.82%
44	Maine	2	0.00%
24	Maryland	107	0.21%
9	Massachusetts	1,115	2.17%
14	Michigan	266	0.52%
25	Minnesota	85	0.17%
28	Mississippi	60	0.12%
28	Missouri	60	0.12%
38	Montana	20	0.04%
31	Nebraska	54	0.10%
26	Nevada	70	0.14%
39	New Hampshire	18	0.03%
5	New Jersey	2,055	3.99%
7	New Mexico	1,182	2.30%
3	New York	6,213	12.07%
30	North Carolina	57	0.11%
42	North Dakota	6	0.01%
18	Ohio	153	0.30%
21	Oklahoma	125	0.24%
15	Oregon	214	0.42%
10	Pennsylvania	985	1.91%
NA	Rhode Island**	NA	NA
33	South Carolina	30	0.06%
43	South Dakota	4	0.01%
33	Tennessee	30	0.06%
2	Texas	8,151	15.84%
23	Utah	111	0.22%
NA	Vermont**	NA	NA
20	Virginia	137	0.27%
12	Washington	720	1.40%
41	West Virginia	9	0.02%
15	Wisconsin	214	0.42%
27	Wyoming	64	0.12%

RANK	STATE	INMATES	% of USA
1	California	22,400	43.53%
2	Texas	8,151	15.84%
3	New York	6,213	12.07%
4	Florida	2,320	4.51%
5	New Jersey	2,055	3.99%
6	Arizona	1,502	2.92%
7	New Mexico	1,182	2.30%
8	Colorado	1,130	2.20%
9	Massachusetts	1,115	2.17%
10	Pennsylvania	985	1.91%
11	Illinois	788	1.53%
12	Washington	720	1.40%
13	Louisiana	424	0.82%
14	Michigan	266	0.52%
15	Oregon	214	0.42%
15	Wisconsin	214	0.42%
17	Georgia	178	0.35%
18	Ohio	153	0.30%
19	Idaho	139	0.27%
20	Virginia	137	0.27%
21	Oklahoma	125	0.24%
22	Kansas	114	0.22%
23	Utah	111	0.22%
24	Maryland	107	0.21%
25	Minnesota	85	0.17%
26	Nevada	70	0.14%
27	Wyoming	64	0.12%
28	Mississippi	60	0.12%
28	Missouri	60	0.12%
30	North Carolina	57	0.11%
31	Nebraska	54	0.10%
32	Arkansas	44	0.09%
33	Iowa	30	0.06%
33	South Carolina	30	0.06%
33	Tennessee	30	0.06%
36	Indiana	26	0.05%
36	Kentucky	26	0.05%
38	Montana	20	0.04%
39	New Hampshire	18	0.03%
40	Alabama	16	0.03%
41	West Virginia	9	0.02%
42	North Dakota	6	0.01%
43	South Dakota	4	0.01%
44	Maine	2	0.00%
45	Alaska	1	0.00%
NA	Connecticut**	NA	NA
NA	Delaware**	NA	NA
NA	Hawaii**	NA	NA
NA	Rhode Island**	NA	NA
NA	Vermont**	NA	NA
	District of Columbia	0	0.00%

Source: U.S. Department of Justice, Bureau of Justice Statistics
"Census of Local Jails, 1988" (1991, NCJ-127992)
*As of June 30, 1988. National total does not include data from states not reporting.
**Not reported.

Hispanic Inmates in Local Jails as a Percent of All Inmates in 1988

National Percent = 14.98% of Inmates*

ALPHA ORDER				RANK ORDER		
RANK	STATE	PERCENT		RANK	STATE	PERCENT
43	Alabama	0.33		1	New Mexico	54.02
22	Alaska	3.70		2	California	34.88
4	Arizona	25.01		3	Texas	27.69
29	Arkansas	2.21		4	Arizona	25.01
2	California	34.88		5	New York	23.96
6	Colorado	23.15		6	Colorado	23.15
NA	Connecticut**	NA		7	Massachusetts	20.44
NA	Delaware**	NA		8	New Jersey	18.47
13	Florida	8.22		9	Idaho	17.16
37	Georgia	1.02		10	Wyoming	14.00
NA	Hawaii**	NA		11	Washington	12.13
9	Idaho	17.16		12	Utah	8.80
14	Illinois	7.97		13	Florida	8.22
42	Indiana	0.50		14	Illinois	7.97
25	Iowa	2.90		15	Oregon	7.59
17	Kansas	5.98		16	Pennsylvania	7.22
41	Kentucky	0.55		17	Kansas	5.98
21	Louisiana	3.78		18	Oklahoma	4.82
44	Maine	0.30		19	Nebraska	4.67
35	Maryland	1.43		20	Wisconsin	4.59
7	Massachusetts	20.44		21	Louisiana	3.78
26	Michigan	2.83		22	Alaska	3.70
27	Minnesota	2.63		23	Montana	3.25
31	Mississippi	1.71		24	Nevada	2.99
34	Missouri	1.44		25	Iowa	2.90
23	Montana	3.25		26	Michigan	2.83
19	Nebraska	4.67		27	Minnesota	2.63
24	Nevada	2.99		28	New Hampshire	2.28
28	New Hampshire	2.28		29	Arkansas	2.21
8	New Jersey	18.47		30	North Dakota	2.08
1	New Mexico	54.02		31	Mississippi	1.71
5	New York	23.96		32	Ohio	1.67
36	North Carolina	1.04		33	Virginia	1.46
30	North Dakota	2.08		34	Missouri	1.44
32	Ohio	1.67		35	Maryland	1.43
18	Oklahoma	4.82		36	North Carolina	1.04
15	Oregon	7.59		37	Georgia	1.02
16	Pennsylvania	7.22		38	South Carolina	0.86
NA	Rhode Island**	NA		39	South Dakota	0.77
38	South Carolina	0.86		40	West Virginia	0.65
39	South Dakota	0.77		41	Kentucky	0.55
45	Tennessee	0.28		42	Indiana	0.50
3	Texas	27.69		43	Alabama	0.33
12	Utah	8.80		44	Maine	0.30
NA	Vermont**	NA		45	Tennessee	0.28
33	Virginia	1.46		NA	Connecticut**	NA
11	Washington	12.13		NA	Delaware**	NA
40	West Virginia	0.65		NA	Hawaii**	NA
20	Wisconsin	4.59		NA	Rhode Island**	NA
10	Wyoming	14.00		NA	Vermont**	NA

	District of Columbia	0.00

Source: Morgan Quitno Corporation using data from U.S. Department of Justice, Bureau of Justice Statistics "Census of Local Jails, 1988" (1991, NCJ-127992)

*As of June 30, 1988. National total does not include data from states not reporting.

**Not reported.

Juvenile Offenders in Custody in 1993

National Total = 36,374 Juveniles*

<table>
<tr><td colspan="4">ALPHA ORDER</td><td colspan="4">RANK ORDER</td></tr>
<tr><th>RANK</th><th>STATE</th><th>JUVENILES</th><th>% of USA</th><th>RANK</th><th>STATE</th><th>JUVENILES</th><th>% of USA</th></tr>
<tr><td>NA</td><td>Alabama**</td><td>NA</td><td>NA</td><td>1</td><td>California</td><td>7,694</td><td>21.15%</td></tr>
<tr><td>NA</td><td>Alaska**</td><td>NA</td><td>NA</td><td>2</td><td>New York</td><td>3,349</td><td>9.21%</td></tr>
<tr><td>22</td><td>Arizona</td><td>537</td><td>1.48%</td><td>3</td><td>Ohio</td><td>2,123</td><td>5.84%</td></tr>
<tr><td>35</td><td>Arkansas</td><td>200</td><td>0.55%</td><td>4</td><td>Texas</td><td>1,967</td><td>5.41%</td></tr>
<tr><td>1</td><td>California</td><td>7,694</td><td>21.15%</td><td>5</td><td>Massachusetts</td><td>1,747</td><td>4.80%</td></tr>
<tr><td>9</td><td>Colorado</td><td>1,005</td><td>2.76%</td><td>6</td><td>Illinois</td><td>1,403</td><td>3.86%</td></tr>
<tr><td>32</td><td>Connecticut</td><td>237</td><td>0.65%</td><td>7</td><td>Florida</td><td>1,272</td><td>3.50%</td></tr>
<tr><td>NA</td><td>Delaware**</td><td>NA</td><td>NA</td><td>8</td><td>South Carolina</td><td>1,174</td><td>3.23%</td></tr>
<tr><td>7</td><td>Florida</td><td>1,272</td><td>3.50%</td><td>9</td><td>Colorado</td><td>1,005</td><td>2.76%</td></tr>
<tr><td>13</td><td>Georgia</td><td>742</td><td>2.04%</td><td>10</td><td>Louisiana</td><td>981</td><td>2.70%</td></tr>
<tr><td>43</td><td>Hawaii</td><td>62</td><td>0.17%</td><td>11</td><td>North Carolina</td><td>862</td><td>2.37%</td></tr>
<tr><td>NA</td><td>Idaho**</td><td>NA</td><td>NA</td><td>12</td><td>Indiana</td><td>812</td><td>2.23%</td></tr>
<tr><td>6</td><td>Illinois</td><td>1,403</td><td>3.86%</td><td>13</td><td>Georgia</td><td>742</td><td>2.04%</td></tr>
<tr><td>12</td><td>Indiana</td><td>812</td><td>2.23%</td><td>14</td><td>Wisconsin</td><td>740</td><td>2.03%</td></tr>
<tr><td>34</td><td>Iowa</td><td>210</td><td>0.58%</td><td>15</td><td>Michigan</td><td>689</td><td>1.89%</td></tr>
<tr><td>27</td><td>Kansas</td><td>385</td><td>1.06%</td><td>16</td><td>Maryland</td><td>639</td><td>1.76%</td></tr>
<tr><td>18</td><td>Kentucky</td><td>576</td><td>1.58%</td><td>17</td><td>Tennessee</td><td>617</td><td>1.70%</td></tr>
<tr><td>10</td><td>Louisiana</td><td>981</td><td>2.70%</td><td>18</td><td>Kentucky</td><td>576</td><td>1.58%</td></tr>
<tr><td>33</td><td>Maine</td><td>234</td><td>0.64%</td><td>19</td><td>Pennsylvania</td><td>572</td><td>1.57%</td></tr>
<tr><td>16</td><td>Maryland</td><td>639</td><td>1.76%</td><td>20</td><td>New Jersey</td><td>560</td><td>1.54%</td></tr>
<tr><td>5</td><td>Massachusetts</td><td>1,747</td><td>4.80%</td><td>21</td><td>Oregon</td><td>552</td><td>1.52%</td></tr>
<tr><td>15</td><td>Michigan</td><td>689</td><td>1.89%</td><td>22</td><td>Arizona</td><td>537</td><td>1.48%</td></tr>
<tr><td>39</td><td>Minnesota</td><td>165</td><td>0.45%</td><td>23</td><td>Utah</td><td>474</td><td>1.30%</td></tr>
<tr><td>26</td><td>Mississippi</td><td>451</td><td>1.24%</td><td>24</td><td>Missouri</td><td>470</td><td>1.29%</td></tr>
<tr><td>24</td><td>Missouri</td><td>470</td><td>1.29%</td><td>25</td><td>Oklahoma</td><td>467</td><td>1.28%</td></tr>
<tr><td>42</td><td>Montana</td><td>105</td><td>0.29%</td><td>26</td><td>Mississippi</td><td>451</td><td>1.24%</td></tr>
<tr><td>30</td><td>Nebraska</td><td>262</td><td>0.72%</td><td>27</td><td>Kansas</td><td>385</td><td>1.06%</td></tr>
<tr><td>29</td><td>Nevada</td><td>267</td><td>0.73%</td><td>28</td><td>New Mexico</td><td>308</td><td>0.85%</td></tr>
<tr><td>36</td><td>New Hampshire</td><td>183</td><td>0.50%</td><td>29</td><td>Nevada</td><td>267</td><td>0.73%</td></tr>
<tr><td>20</td><td>New Jersey</td><td>560</td><td>1.54%</td><td>30</td><td>Nebraska</td><td>262</td><td>0.72%</td></tr>
<tr><td>28</td><td>New Mexico</td><td>308</td><td>0.85%</td><td>31</td><td>North Dakota</td><td>251</td><td>0.69%</td></tr>
<tr><td>2</td><td>New York</td><td>3,349</td><td>9.21%</td><td>32</td><td>Connecticut</td><td>237</td><td>0.65%</td></tr>
<tr><td>11</td><td>North Carolina</td><td>862</td><td>2.37%</td><td>33</td><td>Maine</td><td>234</td><td>0.64%</td></tr>
<tr><td>31</td><td>North Dakota</td><td>251</td><td>0.69%</td><td>34</td><td>Iowa</td><td>210</td><td>0.58%</td></tr>
<tr><td>3</td><td>Ohio</td><td>2,123</td><td>5.84%</td><td>35</td><td>Arkansas</td><td>200</td><td>0.55%</td></tr>
<tr><td>25</td><td>Oklahoma</td><td>467</td><td>1.28%</td><td>36</td><td>New Hampshire</td><td>183</td><td>0.50%</td></tr>
<tr><td>21</td><td>Oregon</td><td>552</td><td>1.52%</td><td>37</td><td>South Dakota</td><td>182</td><td>0.50%</td></tr>
<tr><td>19</td><td>Pennsylvania</td><td>572</td><td>1.57%</td><td>38</td><td>Wyoming</td><td>171</td><td>0.47%</td></tr>
<tr><td>40</td><td>Rhode Island</td><td>160</td><td>0.44%</td><td>39</td><td>Minnesota</td><td>165</td><td>0.45%</td></tr>
<tr><td>8</td><td>South Carolina</td><td>1,174</td><td>3.23%</td><td>40</td><td>Rhode Island</td><td>160</td><td>0.44%</td></tr>
<tr><td>37</td><td>South Dakota</td><td>182</td><td>0.50%</td><td>41</td><td>West Virginia</td><td>109</td><td>0.30%</td></tr>
<tr><td>17</td><td>Tennessee</td><td>617</td><td>1.70%</td><td>42</td><td>Montana</td><td>105</td><td>0.29%</td></tr>
<tr><td>4</td><td>Texas</td><td>1,967</td><td>5.41%</td><td>43</td><td>Hawaii</td><td>62</td><td>0.17%</td></tr>
<tr><td>23</td><td>Utah</td><td>474</td><td>1.30%</td><td>44</td><td>Vermont</td><td>28</td><td>0.08%</td></tr>
<tr><td>44</td><td>Vermont</td><td>28</td><td>0.08%</td><td>NA</td><td>Alabama**</td><td>NA</td><td>NA</td></tr>
<tr><td>NA</td><td>Virginia**</td><td>NA</td><td>NA</td><td>NA</td><td>Alaska**</td><td>NA</td><td>NA</td></tr>
<tr><td>NA</td><td>Washington**</td><td>NA</td><td>NA</td><td>NA</td><td>Delaware**</td><td>NA</td><td>NA</td></tr>
<tr><td>41</td><td>West Virginia</td><td>109</td><td>0.30%</td><td>NA</td><td>Idaho**</td><td>NA</td><td>NA</td></tr>
<tr><td>14</td><td>Wisconsin</td><td>740</td><td>2.03%</td><td>NA</td><td>Virginia**</td><td>NA</td><td>NA</td></tr>
<tr><td>38</td><td>Wyoming</td><td>171</td><td>0.47%</td><td>NA</td><td>Washington**</td><td>NA</td><td>NA</td></tr>
<tr><td></td><td></td><td></td><td></td><td colspan="2">District of Columbia</td><td>380</td><td>1.04%</td></tr>
</table>

Source: Contact Publications (Lincoln, NE)
"Corrections Compendium" (December 1993)
*National total is only for states shown. This information was collected through a survey mailed to the departments of juvenile corrections in the 50 states, the District of Columbia and the Federal Bureau of Prisons. Alabama and Alaska were unable to participate and Delaware, Idaho, Virginia and Washington did not respond.
**Not available.

Juvenile Custody Rate in 1993

National Rate = 58 Juveniles per 100,000 Juveniles*

ALPHA ORDER				RANK ORDER		
RANK	**STATE**	**RATE**		**RANK**	**STATE**	**RATE**
NA	Alabama**	NA		1	North Dakota	146
NA	Alaska**	NA		2	Massachusetts	125
27	Arizona	50		3	Wyoming	124
35	Arkansas	31		4	South Carolina	123
6	California	90		5	Colorado	107
5	Colorado	107		6	California	90
35	Connecticut	31		7	South Dakota	88
NA	Delaware**	NA		8	Louisiana	79
31	Florida	40		9	Maine	76
31	Georgia	40		9	Nevada	76
41	Hawaii	21		11	New York	75
NA	Idaho**	NA		12	Ohio	74
29	Illinois	46		13	Oregon	71
22	Indiana	55		13	Utah	71
38	Iowa	29		15	Rhode Island	68
21	Kansas	56		16	New Hampshire	65
19	Kentucky	59		17	New Mexico	64
8	Louisiana	79		18	Nebraska	60
9	Maine	76		19	Kentucky	59
25	Maryland	51		19	Mississippi	59
2	Massachusetts	125		21	Kansas	56
39	Michigan	27		22	Indiana	55
44	Minnesota	13		22	Wisconsin	55
19	Mississippi	59		24	Oklahoma	54
34	Missouri	34		25	Maryland	51
30	Montana	45		25	North Carolina	51
18	Nebraska	60		27	Arizona	50
9	Nevada	76		28	Tennessee	49
16	New Hampshire	65		29	Illinois	46
37	New Jersey	30		30	Montana	45
17	New Mexico	64		31	Florida	40
11	New York	75		31	Georgia	40
25	North Carolina	51		33	Texas	38
1	North Dakota	146		34	Missouri	34
12	Ohio	74		35	Arkansas	31
24	Oklahoma	54		35	Connecticut	31
13	Oregon	71		37	New Jersey	30
42	Pennsylvania	20		38	Iowa	29
15	Rhode Island	68		39	Michigan	27
4	South Carolina	123		40	West Virginia	25
7	South Dakota	88		41	Hawaii	21
28	Tennessee	49		42	Pennsylvania	20
33	Texas	38		43	Vermont	19
13	Utah	71		44	Minnesota	13
43	Vermont	19		NA	Alabama**	NA
NA	Virginia**	NA		NA	Alaska**	NA
NA	Washington**	NA		NA	Delaware**	NA
40	West Virginia	25		NA	Idaho**	NA
22	Wisconsin	55		NA	Virginia**	NA
3	Wyoming	124		NA	Washington**	NA

District of Columbia   330

Source: Morgan Quitno Corporation using data from Contact Publications (Lincoln, NE)
"Corrections Compendium" (December 1993)

National rate is only for states shown. This information was collected through a survey mailed to the departments of juvenile corrections in the 50 states, the District of Columbia and the Federal Bureau of Prisons. Alabama and Alaska were unable to participate and Delaware, Idaho, Virginia and Washington did not respond.

**Not available.

162

Juveniles Admitted to Public Juvenile Facilities in 1990

National Total = 683,636 Juveniles

ALPHA ORDER					RANK ORDER			

RANK	STATE	JUVENILES	% of USA		RANK	STATE	JUVENILES	% of USA
21	Alabama	10,217	1.49%		1	California	170,462	24.93%
41	Alaska	1,482	0.22%		2	Ohio	48,035	7.03%
13	Arizona	15,857	2.32%		3	Florida	40,276	5.89%
33	Arkansas	4,555	0.67%		4	Texas	38,398	5.62%
1	California	170,462	24.93%		5	Washington	23,166	3.39%
17	Colorado	13,691	2.00%		6	Illinois	22,412	3.28%
36	Connecticut	2,960	0.43%		7	Tennessee	21,349	3.12%
42	Delaware	1,424	0.21%		8	Nevada	19,665	2.88%
3	Florida	40,276	5.89%		9	Michigan	17,816	2.61%
11	Georgia	17,343	2.54%		10	Virginia	17,411	2.55%
40	Hawaii	1,555	0.23%		11	Georgia	17,343	2.54%
43	Idaho	1,235	0.18%		12	Indiana	16,363	2.39%
6	Illinois	22,412	3.28%		13	Arizona	15,857	2.32%
12	Indiana	16,363	2.39%		14	Pennsylvania	15,249	2.23%
34	Iowa	3,861	0.56%		15	New Jersey	15,130	2.21%
30	Kansas	5,921	0.87%		16	New York	15,109	2.21%
31	Kentucky	5,526	0.81%		17	Colorado	13,691	2.00%
27	Louisiana	6,307	0.92%		18	Missouri	10,945	1.60%
47	Maine	572	0.08%		19	Minnesota	10,878	1.59%
22	Maryland	9,482	1.39%		20	Oregon	10,354	1.51%
35	Massachusetts	3,254	0.48%		21	Alabama	10,217	1.49%
9	Michigan	17,816	2.61%		22	Maryland	9,482	1.39%
19	Minnesota	10,878	1.59%		23	Wisconsin	9,269	1.36%
28	Mississippi	6,190	0.91%		24	Utah	8,559	1.25%
18	Missouri	10,945	1.60%		25	New Mexico	7,115	1.04%
44	Montana	1,084	0.16%		26	North Carolina	6,977	1.02%
37	Nebraska	2,911	0.43%		27	Louisiana	6,307	0.92%
8	Nevada	19,665	2.88%		28	Mississippi	6,190	0.91%
48	New Hampshire	516	0.08%		29	Oklahoma	5,963	0.87%
15	New Jersey	15,130	2.21%		30	Kansas	5,921	0.87%
25	New Mexico	7,115	1.04%		31	Kentucky	5,526	0.81%
16	New York	15,109	2.21%		32	South Carolina	4,742	0.69%
26	North Carolina	6,977	1.02%		33	Arkansas	4,555	0.67%
45	North Dakota	664	0.10%		34	Iowa	3,861	0.56%
2	Ohio	48,035	7.03%		35	Massachusetts	3,254	0.48%
29	Oklahoma	5,963	0.87%		36	Connecticut	2,960	0.43%
20	Oregon	10,354	1.51%		37	Nebraska	2,911	0.43%
14	Pennsylvania	15,249	2.23%		38	South Dakota	2,837	0.41%
46	Rhode Island	589	0.09%		39	West Virginia	1,611	0.24%
32	South Carolina	4,742	0.69%		40	Hawaii	1,555	0.23%
38	South Dakota	2,837	0.41%		41	Alaska	1,482	0.22%
7	Tennessee	21,349	3.12%		42	Delaware	1,424	0.21%
4	Texas	38,398	5.62%		43	Idaho	1,235	0.18%
24	Utah	8,559	1.25%		44	Montana	1,084	0.16%
50	Vermont	308	0.05%		45	North Dakota	664	0.10%
10	Virginia	17,411	2.55%		46	Rhode Island	589	0.09%
5	Washington	23,166	3.39%		47	Maine	572	0.08%
39	West Virginia	1,611	0.24%		48	New Hampshire	516	0.08%
23	Wisconsin	9,269	1.36%		49	Wyoming	353	0.05%
49	Wyoming	353	0.05%		50	Vermont	308	0.05%
						District of Columbia	5,688	0.83%

Source: U.S. Department of Justice, Bureau of Justice Statistics
"Sourcebook of Criminal Justice Statistics 1993" (September 1994, NCJ-148211)

Juveniles Discharged from Public Juvenile Facilities in 1990

National Total = 674,597 Juveniles

ALPHA ORDER

RANK	STATE	JUVENILES	% of USA
20	Alabama	10,322	1.53%
41	Alaska	1,472	0.22%
13	Arizona	15,520	2.30%
33	Arkansas	4,521	0.67%
1	California	168,252	24.94%
17	Colorado	13,593	2.01%
36	Connecticut	2,948	0.44%
42	Delaware	1,432	0.21%
3	Florida	40,133	5.95%
10	Georgia	17,382	2.58%
40	Hawaii	1,562	0.23%
43	Idaho	1,221	0.18%
6	Illinois	22,443	3.33%
12	Indiana	15,933	2.36%
34	Iowa	3,872	0.57%
29	Kansas	5,851	0.87%
31	Kentucky	5,445	0.81%
30	Louisiana	5,814	0.86%
48	Maine	386	0.06%
22	Maryland	9,494	1.41%
35	Massachusetts	3,229	0.48%
9	Michigan	17,550	2.60%
18	Minnesota	10,814	1.60%
27	Mississippi	6,206	0.92%
19	Missouri	10,779	1.60%
44	Montana	966	0.14%
37	Nebraska	2,937	0.44%
8	Nevada	19,585	2.90%
47	New Hampshire	562	0.08%
16	New Jersey	14,611	2.17%
25	New Mexico	6,984	1.04%
15	New York	14,791	2.19%
26	North Carolina	6,736	1.00%
46	North Dakota	580	0.09%
2	Ohio	47,264	7.01%
28	Oklahoma	5,943	0.88%
21	Oregon	10,204	1.51%
14	Pennsylvania	14,909	2.21%
45	Rhode Island	607	0.09%
32	South Carolina	4,543	0.67%
38	South Dakota	2,842	0.42%
7	Tennessee	21,447	3.18%
4	Texas	37,816	5.61%
24	Utah	8,402	1.25%
50	Vermont	308	0.05%
11	Virginia	16,894	2.50%
5	Washington	22,683	3.36%
39	West Virginia	1,597	0.24%
23	Wisconsin	9,124	1.35%
49	Wyoming	344	0.05%

RANK ORDER

RANK	STATE	JUVENILES	% of USA
1	California	168,252	24.94%
2	Ohio	47,264	7.01%
3	Florida	40,133	5.95%
4	Texas	37,816	5.61%
5	Washington	22,683	3.36%
6	Illinois	22,443	3.33%
7	Tennessee	21,447	3.18%
8	Nevada	19,585	2.90%
9	Michigan	17,550	2.60%
10	Georgia	17,382	2.58%
11	Virginia	16,894	2.50%
12	Indiana	15,933	2.36%
13	Arizona	15,520	2.30%
14	Pennsylvania	14,909	2.21%
15	New York	14,791	2.19%
16	New Jersey	14,611	2.17%
17	Colorado	13,593	2.01%
18	Minnesota	10,814	1.60%
19	Missouri	10,779	1.60%
20	Alabama	10,322	1.53%
21	Oregon	10,204	1.51%
22	Maryland	9,494	1.41%
23	Wisconsin	9,124	1.35%
24	Utah	8,402	1.25%
25	New Mexico	6,984	1.04%
26	North Carolina	6,736	1.00%
27	Mississippi	6,206	0.92%
28	Oklahoma	5,943	0.88%
29	Kansas	5,851	0.87%
30	Louisiana	5,814	0.86%
31	Kentucky	5,445	0.81%
32	South Carolina	4,543	0.67%
33	Arkansas	4,521	0.67%
34	Iowa	3,872	0.57%
35	Massachusetts	3,229	0.48%
36	Connecticut	2,948	0.44%
37	Nebraska	2,937	0.44%
38	South Dakota	2,842	0.42%
39	West Virginia	1,597	0.24%
40	Hawaii	1,562	0.23%
41	Alaska	1,472	0.22%
42	Delaware	1,432	0.21%
43	Idaho	1,221	0.18%
44	Montana	966	0.14%
45	Rhode Island	607	0.09%
46	North Dakota	580	0.09%
47	New Hampshire	562	0.08%
48	Maine	386	0.06%
49	Wyoming	344	0.05%
50	Vermont	308	0.05%
	District of Columbia	5,744	0.85%

Source: U.S. Department of Justice, Bureau of Justice Statistics
"Sourcebook of Criminal Justice Statistics 1993" (September 1994, NCJ-148211)

Public Juvenile Facilities Administered by State and Local Governments in 1991

National Total = 1,076 Facilities

ALPHA ORDER				
RANK	STATE		FACILITIES	% of USA
16	Alabama		22	2.04%
38	Alaska		5	0.46%
21	Arizona		16	1.49%
31	Arkansas		10	0.93%
1	California		106	9.85%
32	Colorado		9	0.84%
40	Connecticut		4	0.37%
42	Delaware		3	0.28%
7	Florida		51	4.74%
14	Georgia		28	2.60%
45	Hawaii		2	0.19%
42	Idaho		3	0.28%
18	Illinois		20	1.86%
12	Indiana		33	3.07%
27	Iowa		12	1.12%
27	Kansas		12	1.12%
11	Kentucky		34	3.16%
23	Louisiana		15	1.39%
49	Maine		1	0.09%
23	Maryland		15	1.39%
32	Massachusetts		9	0.84%
8	Michigan		46	4.28%
19	Minnesota		19	1.77%
35	Mississippi		8	0.74%
9	Missouri		42	3.90%
38	Montana		5	0.46%
40	Nebraska		4	0.37%
32	Nevada		9	0.84%
45	New Hampshire		2	0.19%
6	New Jersey		53	4.93%
26	New Mexico		14	1.30%
2	New York		78	7.25%
15	North Carolina		24	2.23%
42	North Dakota		3	0.28%
3	Ohio		64	5.95%
21	Oklahoma		16	1.49%
23	Oregon		15	1.39%
10	Pennsylvania		35	3.25%
45	Rhode Island		2	0.19%
29	South Carolina		11	1.02%
36	South Dakota		6	0.56%
16	Tennessee		22	2.04%
5	Texas		56	5.20%
20	Utah		17	1.58%
49	Vermont		1	0.09%
4	Virginia		61	5.67%
13	Washington		30	2.79%
36	West Virginia		6	0.56%
29	Wisconsin		11	1.02%
45	Wyoming		2	0.19%

RANK ORDER				
RANK	STATE		FACILITIES	% of USA
1	California		106	9.85%
2	New York		78	7.25%
3	Ohio		64	5.95%
4	Virginia		61	5.67%
5	Texas		56	5.20%
6	New Jersey		53	4.93%
7	Florida		51	4.74%
8	Michigan		46	4.28%
9	Missouri		42	3.90%
10	Pennsylvania		35	3.25%
11	Kentucky		34	3.16%
12	Indiana		33	3.07%
13	Washington		30	2.79%
14	Georgia		28	2.60%
15	North Carolina		24	2.23%
16	Alabama		22	2.04%
16	Tennessee		22	2.04%
18	Illinois		20	1.86%
19	Minnesota		19	1.77%
20	Utah		17	1.58%
21	Arizona		16	1.49%
21	Oklahoma		16	1.49%
23	Louisiana		15	1.39%
23	Maryland		15	1.39%
23	Oregon		15	1.39%
26	New Mexico		14	1.30%
27	Iowa		12	1.12%
27	Kansas		12	1.12%
29	South Carolina		11	1.02%
29	Wisconsin		11	1.02%
31	Arkansas		10	0.93%
32	Colorado		9	0.84%
32	Massachusetts		9	0.84%
32	Nevada		9	0.84%
35	Mississippi		8	0.74%
36	South Dakota		6	0.56%
36	West Virginia		6	0.56%
38	Alaska		5	0.46%
38	Montana		5	0.46%
40	Connecticut		4	0.37%
40	Nebraska		4	0.37%
42	Delaware		3	0.28%
42	Idaho		3	0.28%
42	North Dakota		3	0.28%
45	Hawaii		2	0.19%
45	New Hampshire		2	0.19%
45	Rhode Island		2	0.19%
45	Wyoming		2	0.19%
49	Maine		1	0.09%
49	Vermont		1	0.09%
	District of Columbia		4	0.37%

Source: U.S. Department of Justice, Bureau of Justice Statistics
"Sourcebook of Criminal Justice Statistics 1993" (September 1994, NCJ-148211)

Boot Camp and Shock Incarceration Camps Participants in 1993

National Total = 5,937 Participants*

<table>
<tr><th colspan="4">ALPHA ORDER</th><th colspan="4">RANK ORDER</th></tr>
<tr><th>RANK</th><th>STATE</th><th>PARTICIPANTS</th><th>% of USA</th><th>RANK</th><th>STATE</th><th>PARTICIPANTS</th><th>% of USA</th></tr>
<tr><td>14</td><td>Alabama</td><td>113</td><td>1.90%</td><td>1</td><td>New York</td><td>1,492</td><td>25.13%</td></tr>
<tr><td>NA</td><td>Alaska**</td><td>NA</td><td>NA</td><td>2</td><td>Georgia</td><td>1,273</td><td>21.44%</td></tr>
<tr><td>11</td><td>Arizona</td><td>131</td><td>2.21%</td><td>3</td><td>Illinois</td><td>405</td><td>6.82%</td></tr>
<tr><td>8</td><td>Arkansas</td><td>150</td><td>2.53%</td><td>4</td><td>Oklahoma</td><td>368</td><td>6.20%</td></tr>
<tr><td>10</td><td>California</td><td>133</td><td>2.24%</td><td>5</td><td>Texas</td><td>301</td><td>5.07%</td></tr>
<tr><td>13</td><td>Colorado</td><td>114</td><td>1.92%</td><td>6</td><td>Michigan</td><td>300</td><td>5.05%</td></tr>
<tr><td>NA</td><td>Connecticut**</td><td>NA</td><td>NA</td><td>7</td><td>Mississippi</td><td>238</td><td>4.01%</td></tr>
<tr><td>NA</td><td>Delaware**</td><td>NA</td><td>NA</td><td>8</td><td>Arkansas</td><td>150</td><td>2.53%</td></tr>
<tr><td>16</td><td>Florida</td><td>97</td><td>1.63%</td><td>9</td><td>Massachusetts</td><td>137</td><td>2.31%</td></tr>
<tr><td>2</td><td>Georgia</td><td>1,273</td><td>21.44%</td><td>10</td><td>California</td><td>133</td><td>2.24%</td></tr>
<tr><td>NA</td><td>Hawaii**</td><td>NA</td><td>NA</td><td>11</td><td>Arizona</td><td>131</td><td>2.21%</td></tr>
<tr><td>NA</td><td>Idaho**</td><td>NA</td><td>NA</td><td>12</td><td>Louisiana</td><td>120</td><td>2.02%</td></tr>
<tr><td>3</td><td>Illinois</td><td>405</td><td>6.82%</td><td>13</td><td>Colorado</td><td>114</td><td>1.92%</td></tr>
<tr><td>NA</td><td>Indiana**</td><td>NA</td><td>NA</td><td>14</td><td>Alabama</td><td>113</td><td>1.90%</td></tr>
<tr><td>NA</td><td>Iowa**</td><td>NA</td><td>NA</td><td>15</td><td>Tennessee</td><td>100</td><td>1.68%</td></tr>
<tr><td>18</td><td>Kansas</td><td>78</td><td>1.31%</td><td>16</td><td>Florida</td><td>97</td><td>1.63%</td></tr>
<tr><td>25</td><td>Kentucky</td><td>20</td><td>0.34%</td><td>17</td><td>North Carolina</td><td>84</td><td>1.41%</td></tr>
<tr><td>12</td><td>Louisiana</td><td>120</td><td>2.02%</td><td>18</td><td>Kansas</td><td>78</td><td>1.31%</td></tr>
<tr><td>NA</td><td>Maine**</td><td>NA</td><td>NA</td><td>19</td><td>Nevada</td><td>77</td><td>1.30%</td></tr>
<tr><td>NA</td><td>Maryland**</td><td>NA</td><td>NA</td><td>20</td><td>Virginia</td><td>54</td><td>0.91%</td></tr>
<tr><td>9</td><td>Massachusetts</td><td>137</td><td>2.31%</td><td>21</td><td>Pennsylvania</td><td>48</td><td>0.81%</td></tr>
<tr><td>6</td><td>Michigan</td><td>300</td><td>5.05%</td><td>22</td><td>Minnesota</td><td>38</td><td>0.64%</td></tr>
<tr><td>22</td><td>Minnesota</td><td>38</td><td>0.64%</td><td>22</td><td>Wisconsin</td><td>38</td><td>0.64%</td></tr>
<tr><td>7</td><td>Mississippi</td><td>238</td><td>4.01%</td><td>24</td><td>New Hampshire</td><td>28</td><td>0.47%</td></tr>
<tr><td>NA</td><td>Missouri**</td><td>NA</td><td>NA</td><td>25</td><td>Kentucky</td><td>20</td><td>0.34%</td></tr>
<tr><td>NA</td><td>Montana**</td><td>NA</td><td>NA</td><td>NA</td><td>Alaska**</td><td>NA</td><td>NA</td></tr>
<tr><td>NA</td><td>Nebraska**</td><td>NA</td><td>NA</td><td>NA</td><td>Connecticut**</td><td>NA</td><td>NA</td></tr>
<tr><td>19</td><td>Nevada</td><td>77</td><td>1.30%</td><td>NA</td><td>Delaware**</td><td>NA</td><td>NA</td></tr>
<tr><td>24</td><td>New Hampshire</td><td>28</td><td>0.47%</td><td>NA</td><td>Hawaii**</td><td>NA</td><td>NA</td></tr>
<tr><td>NA</td><td>New Jersey**</td><td>NA</td><td>NA</td><td>NA</td><td>Idaho**</td><td>NA</td><td>NA</td></tr>
<tr><td>NA</td><td>New Mexico**</td><td>NA</td><td>NA</td><td>NA</td><td>Indiana**</td><td>NA</td><td>NA</td></tr>
<tr><td>1</td><td>New York</td><td>1,492</td><td>25.13%</td><td>NA</td><td>Iowa**</td><td>NA</td><td>NA</td></tr>
<tr><td>17</td><td>North Carolina</td><td>84</td><td>1.41%</td><td>NA</td><td>Maine**</td><td>NA</td><td>NA</td></tr>
<tr><td>NA</td><td>North Dakota**</td><td>NA</td><td>NA</td><td>NA</td><td>Maryland**</td><td>NA</td><td>NA</td></tr>
<tr><td>NA</td><td>Ohio**</td><td>NA</td><td>NA</td><td>NA</td><td>Missouri**</td><td>NA</td><td>NA</td></tr>
<tr><td>4</td><td>Oklahoma</td><td>368</td><td>6.20%</td><td>NA</td><td>Montana**</td><td>NA</td><td>NA</td></tr>
<tr><td>NA</td><td>Oregon**</td><td>NA</td><td>NA</td><td>NA</td><td>Nebraska**</td><td>NA</td><td>NA</td></tr>
<tr><td>21</td><td>Pennsylvania</td><td>48</td><td>0.81%</td><td>NA</td><td>New Jersey**</td><td>NA</td><td>NA</td></tr>
<tr><td>NA</td><td>Rhode Island**</td><td>NA</td><td>NA</td><td>NA</td><td>New Mexico**</td><td>NA</td><td>NA</td></tr>
<tr><td>NA</td><td>South Carolina**</td><td>NA</td><td>NA</td><td>NA</td><td>North Dakota**</td><td>NA</td><td>NA</td></tr>
<tr><td>NA</td><td>South Dakota**</td><td>NA</td><td>NA</td><td>NA</td><td>Ohio**</td><td>NA</td><td>NA</td></tr>
<tr><td>15</td><td>Tennessee</td><td>100</td><td>1.68%</td><td>NA</td><td>Oregon**</td><td>NA</td><td>NA</td></tr>
<tr><td>5</td><td>Texas</td><td>301</td><td>5.07%</td><td>NA</td><td>Rhode Island**</td><td>NA</td><td>NA</td></tr>
<tr><td>NA</td><td>Utah**</td><td>NA</td><td>NA</td><td>NA</td><td>South Carolina**</td><td>NA</td><td>NA</td></tr>
<tr><td>NA</td><td>Vermont**</td><td>NA</td><td>NA</td><td>NA</td><td>South Dakota**</td><td>NA</td><td>NA</td></tr>
<tr><td>20</td><td>Virginia</td><td>54</td><td>0.91%</td><td>NA</td><td>Utah**</td><td>NA</td><td>NA</td></tr>
<tr><td>NA</td><td>Washington**</td><td>NA</td><td>NA</td><td>NA</td><td>Vermont**</td><td>NA</td><td>NA</td></tr>
<tr><td>NA</td><td>West Virginia**</td><td>NA</td><td>NA</td><td>NA</td><td>Washington**</td><td>NA</td><td>NA</td></tr>
<tr><td>22</td><td>Wisconsin</td><td>38</td><td>0.64%</td><td>NA</td><td>West Virginia**</td><td>NA</td><td>NA</td></tr>
<tr><td>NA</td><td>Wyoming**</td><td>NA</td><td>NA</td><td>NA</td><td>Wyoming**</td><td>NA</td><td>NA</td></tr>
<tr><td></td><td></td><td></td><td></td><td></td><td>District of Columbia**</td><td>NA</td><td>NA</td></tr>
</table>

Source: Contact Publications (Lincoln, NE)
    "Corrections Compendium" (September 1993)

*National total is only for states shown. This information was collected through a survey mailed to the departments of juvenile corrections in the 50 states, the District of Columbia and the Federal Bureau of Prisons.
**Either no program or did not respond to survey.

III. DRUGS AND ALCOHOL

Alcohol and Other Drug Treatment Units in 1992

National Total = 6,765 Units*

ALPHA ORDER

RANK	STATE	UNITS	% of USA
32	Alabama	52	0.78%
21	Alaska	80	1.20%
21	Arizona	80	1.20%
43	Arkansas	24	0.36%
2	California	711	10.66%
19	Colorado	95	1.42%
14	Connecticut	127	1.90%
44	Delaware	23	0.34%
18	Florida	108	1.62%
31	Georgia	55	0.82%
46	Hawaii	21	0.31%
35	Idaho	47	0.70%
10	Illinois	242	3.63%
17	Indiana	109	1.63%
41	Iowa	31	0.46%
23	Kansas	72	1.08%
13	Kentucky	153	2.29%
25	Louisiana	69	1.03%
32	Maine	52	0.78%
7	Maryland	300	4.50%
6	Massachusetts	334	5.01%
3	Michigan	374	5.61%
9	Minnesota	257	3.85%
23	Mississippi	72	1.08%
19	Missouri	95	1.42%
41	Montana	31	0.46%
15	Nebraska	126	1.89%
27	Nevada	65	0.97%
40	New Hampshire	34	0.51%
12	New Jersey	179	2.68%
35	New Mexico	47	0.70%
1	New York	798	11.97%
37	North Carolina	44	0.66%
47	North Dakota	8	0.12%
8	Ohio	273	4.09%
28	Oklahoma	63	0.94%
NA	Oregon**	NA	NA
4	Pennsylvania	364	5.46%
34	Rhode Island	51	0.76%
39	South Carolina	40	0.60%
38	South Dakota	43	0.64%
29	Tennessee	62	0.93%
5	Texas	362	5.43%
26	Utah	67	1.00%
45	Vermont	22	0.33%
11	Virginia	182	2.73%
16	Washington	121	1.81%
30	West Virginia	60	0.90%
NA	Wisconsin**	NA	NA
NA	Wyoming**	NA	NA

RANK ORDER

RANK	STATE	UNITS	% of USA
1	New York	798	11.97%
2	California	711	10.66%
3	Michigan	374	5.61%
4	Pennsylvania	364	5.46%
5	Texas	362	5.43%
6	Massachusetts	334	5.01%
7	Maryland	300	4.50%
8	Ohio	273	4.09%
9	Minnesota	257	3.85%
10	Illinois	242	3.63%
11	Virginia	182	2.73%
12	New Jersey	179	2.68%
13	Kentucky	153	2.29%
14	Connecticut	127	1.90%
15	Nebraska	126	1.89%
16	Washington	121	1.81%
17	Indiana	109	1.63%
18	Florida	108	1.62%
19	Colorado	95	1.42%
19	Missouri	95	1.42%
21	Alaska	80	1.20%
21	Arizona	80	1.20%
23	Kansas	72	1.08%
23	Mississippi	72	1.08%
25	Louisiana	69	1.03%
26	Utah	67	1.00%
27	Nevada	65	0.97%
28	Oklahoma	63	0.94%
29	Tennessee	62	0.93%
30	West Virginia	60	0.90%
31	Georgia	55	0.82%
32	Alabama	52	0.78%
32	Maine	52	0.78%
34	Rhode Island	51	0.76%
35	Idaho	47	0.70%
35	New Mexico	47	0.70%
37	North Carolina	44	0.66%
38	South Dakota	43	0.64%
39	South Carolina	40	0.60%
40	New Hampshire	34	0.51%
41	Iowa	31	0.46%
41	Montana	31	0.46%
43	Arkansas	24	0.36%
44	Delaware	23	0.34%
45	Vermont	22	0.33%
46	Hawaii	21	0.31%
47	North Dakota	8	0.12%
NA	Oregon**	NA	NA
NA	Wisconsin**	NA	NA
NA	Wyoming**	NA	NA
	District of Columbia	43	0.64%

Source: U.S. Department of Health and Human Services, Substance Abuse and Mental Health Services Administration
"State Resources and Services Related to Alcohol and Other Drug Problems-Fiscal Year 1992" (SMA 94-2092 (1994))
*Does not include 97 units in U.S. territories. Data are only from treatment units that received at least some funds administered by a state's alcohol/drug agency in fiscal year 1992.
**Not available.

Alcohol and Other Drug Treatment Admissions in 1992

National Total = 1,769,197 Admissions*

<u>ALPHA ORDER</u>

RANK	STATE	ADMISSIONS	% of USA
29	Alabama	15,907	0.90%
31	Alaska	14,266	0.81%
24	Arizona	25,692	1.45%
32	Arkansas	13,468	0.76%
2	California	134,433	7.60%
10	Colorado	64,279	3.63%
20	Connecticut	32,183	1.82%
44	Delaware	5,899	0.33%
4	Florida	97,427	5.51%
12	Georgia	58,838	3.33%
47	Hawaii	4,431	0.25%
42	Idaho	7,497	0.42%
6	Illinois	81,875	4.63%
25	Indiana	23,911	1.35%
26	Iowa	22,468	1.27%
27	Kansas	17,988	1.02%
19	Kentucky	33,628	1.90%
23	Louisiana	25,956	1.47%
39	Maine	8,187	0.46%
17	Maryland	35,529	2.01%
5	Massachusetts	84,324	4.77%
7	Michigan	75,996	4.30%
11	Minnesota	60,138	3.40%
38	Mississippi	11,159	0.63%
18	Missouri	34,013	1.92%
41	Montana	7,749	0.44%
22	Nebraska	26,534	1.50%
40	Nevada	7,873	0.45%
45	New Hampshire	5,808	0.33%
13	New Jersey	52,912	2.99%
34	New Mexico	12,679	0.72%
1	New York	148,445	8.39%
15	North Carolina	43,142	2.44%
46	North Dakota	4,577	0.26%
8	Ohio	68,484	3.87%
28	Oklahoma	17,234	0.97%
NA	Oregon**	NA	NA
9	Pennsylvania	65,438	3.70%
36	Rhode Island	12,173	0.69%
21	South Carolina	28,144	1.59%
35	South Dakota	12,410	0.70%
33	Tennessee	13,097	0.74%
14	Texas	50,134	2.83%
30	Utah	15,512	0.88%
43	Vermont	6,121	0.35%
16	Virginia	36,640	2.07%
NA	Washington**	NA	NA
37	West Virginia	11,703	0.66%
3	Wisconsin	121,283	6.86%
NA	Wyoming**	NA	NA

<u>RANK ORDER</u>

RANK	STATE	ADMISSIONS	% of USA
1	New York	148,445	8.39%
2	California	134,433	7.60%
3	Wisconsin	121,283	6.86%
4	Florida	97,427	5.51%
5	Massachusetts	84,324	4.77%
6	Illinois	81,875	4.63%
7	Michigan	75,996	4.30%
8	Ohio	68,484	3.87%
9	Pennsylvania	65,438	3.70%
10	Colorado	64,279	3.63%
11	Minnesota	60,138	3.40%
12	Georgia	58,838	3.33%
13	New Jersey	52,912	2.99%
14	Texas	50,134	2.83%
15	North Carolina	43,142	2.44%
16	Virginia	36,640	2.07%
17	Maryland	35,529	2.01%
18	Missouri	34,013	1.92%
19	Kentucky	33,628	1.90%
20	Connecticut	32,183	1.82%
21	South Carolina	28,144	1.59%
22	Nebraska	26,534	1.50%
23	Louisiana	25,956	1.47%
24	Arizona	25,692	1.45%
25	Indiana	23,911	1.35%
26	Iowa	22,468	1.27%
27	Kansas	17,988	1.02%
28	Oklahoma	17,234	0.97%
29	Alabama	15,907	0.90%
30	Utah	15,512	0.88%
31	Alaska	14,266	0.81%
32	Arkansas	13,468	0.76%
33	Tennessee	13,097	0.74%
34	New Mexico	12,679	0.72%
35	South Dakota	12,410	0.70%
36	Rhode Island	12,173	0.69%
37	West Virginia	11,703	0.66%
38	Mississippi	11,159	0.63%
39	Maine	8,187	0.46%
40	Nevada	7,873	0.45%
41	Montana	7,749	0.44%
42	Idaho	7,497	0.42%
43	Vermont	6,121	0.35%
44	Delaware	5,899	0.33%
45	New Hampshire	5,808	0.33%
46	North Dakota	4,577	0.26%
47	Hawaii	4,431	0.25%
NA	Oregon**	NA	NA
NA	Washington**	NA	NA
NA	Wyoming**	NA	NA
	District of Columbia	11,613	0.66%

Source: U.S. Department of Health and Human Services, Substance Abuse and Mental Health Services Administration
   "State Resources and Services Related to Alcohol and Other Drug Problems-Fiscal Year 1992" (SMA 94-2092 (1994))
*Does not include 23,725 admissions in U.S. territories. Data are only from treatment units that received at least some funds administered by a state's alcohol/drug agency in fiscal year 1992.
**Not available.

Male Admissions in Alcohol and Other Drug Treatment Programs in 1992

National Total = 1,270,115 Admissions*

ALPHA ORDER

RANK	STATE	ADMISSIONS	% of USA
30	Alabama	12,081	0.95%
32	Alaska	10,265	0.81%
25	Arizona	14,580	1.15%
31	Arkansas	10,823	0.85%
2	California	89,227	7.03%
8	Colorado	52,052	4.10%
22	Connecticut	18,839	1.48%
44	Delaware	4,426	0.35%
4	Florida	71,094	5.60%
12	Georgia	43,189	3.40%
47	Hawaii	3,048	0.24%
41	Idaho	5,358	0.42%
6	Illinois	57,315	4.51%
23	Indiana	17,505	1.38%
24	Iowa	17,160	1.35%
27	Kansas	13,702	1.08%
17	Kentucky	25,555	2.01%
21	Louisiana	20,197	1.59%
39	Maine	6,199	0.49%
16	Maryland	25,607	2.02%
5	Massachusetts	61,033	4.81%
7	Michigan	52,117	4.10%
10	Minnesota	47,160	3.71%
37	Mississippi	8,692	0.68%
18	Missouri	24,251	1.91%
40	Montana	5,595	0.44%
20	Nebraska	20,519	1.62%
45	Nevada	4,001	0.32%
43	New Hampshire	4,429	0.35%
13	New Jersey	38,125	3.00%
34	New Mexico	9,561	0.75%
1	New York	111,585	8.79%
15	North Carolina	32,829	2.58%
46	North Dakota	3,258	0.26%
11	Ohio	45,802	3.61%
28	Oklahoma	12,700	1.00%
NA	Oregon**	NA	NA
9	Pennsylvania	47,523	3.74%
38	Rhode Island	8,550	0.67%
19	South Carolina	21,319	1.68%
36	South Dakota	8,789	0.69%
35	Tennessee	9,484	0.75%
14	Texas	36,955	2.91%
29	Utah	12,370	0.97%
42	Vermont	4,570	0.36%
26	Virginia	14,168	1.12%
NA	Washington**	NA	NA
33	West Virginia	9,653	0.76%
3	Wisconsin	88,897	7.00%
NA	Wyoming**	NA	NA

RANK ORDER

RANK	STATE	ADMISSIONS	% of USA
1	New York	111,585	8.79%
2	California	89,227	7.03%
3	Wisconsin	88,897	7.00%
4	Florida	71,094	5.60%
5	Massachusetts	61,033	4.81%
6	Illinois	57,315	4.51%
7	Michigan	52,117	4.10%
8	Colorado	52,052	4.10%
9	Pennsylvania	47,523	3.74%
10	Minnesota	47,160	3.71%
11	Ohio	45,802	3.61%
12	Georgia	43,189	3.40%
13	New Jersey	38,125	3.00%
14	Texas	36,955	2.91%
15	North Carolina	32,829	2.58%
16	Maryland	25,607	2.02%
17	Kentucky	25,555	2.01%
18	Missouri	24,251	1.91%
19	South Carolina	21,319	1.68%
20	Nebraska	20,519	1.62%
21	Louisiana	20,197	1.59%
22	Connecticut	18,839	1.48%
23	Indiana	17,505	1.38%
24	Iowa	17,160	1.35%
25	Arizona	14,580	1.15%
26	Virginia	14,168	1.12%
27	Kansas	13,702	1.08%
28	Oklahoma	12,700	1.00%
29	Utah	12,370	0.97%
30	Alabama	12,081	0.95%
31	Arkansas	10,823	0.85%
32	Alaska	10,265	0.81%
33	West Virginia	9,653	0.76%
34	New Mexico	9,561	0.75%
35	Tennessee	9,484	0.75%
36	South Dakota	8,789	0.69%
37	Mississippi	8,692	0.68%
38	Rhode Island	8,550	0.67%
39	Maine	6,199	0.49%
40	Montana	5,595	0.44%
41	Idaho	5,358	0.42%
42	Vermont	4,570	0.36%
43	New Hampshire	4,429	0.35%
44	Delaware	4,426	0.35%
45	Nevada	4,001	0.32%
46	North Dakota	3,258	0.26%
47	Hawaii	3,048	0.24%
NA	Oregon**	NA	NA
NA	Washington**	NA	NA
NA	Wyoming**	NA	NA
	District of Columbia	7,958	0.63%

Source: U.S. Department of Health and Human Services, Substance Abuse and Mental Health Services Administration
   "State Resources and Services Related to Alcohol and Other Drug Problems-Fiscal Year 1992" (SMA 94-2092 (1994))
*Does not include 21,422 admissions in U.S. territories. Data are only from treatment units that received at least some
funds administered by a state's alcohol/drug agency in fiscal year 1992. An additional 11,436 admissions were not
reported by sex.
**Not available.   169

Male Admissions in Alcohol and Other Drug Treatment Programs
As a Percent of All Admissions in 1992
National Percent = 71.79% Males*

ALPHA ORDER

RANK	STATE	PERCENT
14	Alabama	75.95
33	Alaska	71.95
45	Arizona	56.75
3	Arkansas	80.36
43	California	66.37
2	Colorado	80.98
44	Connecticut	58.54
19	Delaware	75.03
26	Florida	72.97
23	Georgia	73.40
40	Hawaii	68.79
34	Idaho	71.47
39	Illinois	70.00
25	Indiana	73.21
9	Iowa	76.38
11	Kansas	76.17
13	Kentucky	75.99
7	Louisiana	77.81
16	Maine	75.72
31	Maryland	72.07
29	Massachusetts	72.38
41	Michigan	68.58
5	Minnesota	78.42
6	Mississippi	77.89
35	Missouri	71.30
30	Montana	72.20
8	Nebraska	77.33
46	Nevada	50.82
10	New Hampshire	76.26
32	New Jersey	72.05
17	New Mexico	75.41
18	New York	75.17
12	North Carolina	76.10
36	North Dakota	71.18
42	Ohio	66.88
22	Oklahoma	73.69
NA	Oregon**	NA
27	Pennsylvania	72.62
38	Rhode Island	70.24
15	South Carolina	75.75
37	South Dakota	70.82
28	Tennessee	72.41
21	Texas	73.71
4	Utah	79.74
20	Vermont	74.66
47	Virginia	38.67
NA	Washington**	NA
1	West Virginia	82.48
24	Wisconsin	73.30
NA	Wyoming**	NA

RANK ORDER

RANK	STATE	PERCENT
1	West Virginia	82.48
2	Colorado	80.98
3	Arkansas	80.36
4	Utah	79.74
5	Minnesota	78.42
6	Mississippi	77.89
7	Louisiana	77.81
8	Nebraska	77.33
9	Iowa	76.38
10	New Hampshire	76.26
11	Kansas	76.17
12	North Carolina	76.10
13	Kentucky	75.99
14	Alabama	75.95
15	South Carolina	75.75
16	Maine	75.72
17	New Mexico	75.41
18	New York	75.17
19	Delaware	75.03
20	Vermont	74.66
21	Texas	73.71
22	Oklahoma	73.69
23	Georgia	73.40
24	Wisconsin	73.30
25	Indiana	73.21
26	Florida	72.97
27	Pennsylvania	72.62
28	Tennessee	72.41
29	Massachusetts	72.38
30	Montana	72.20
31	Maryland	72.07
32	New Jersey	72.05
33	Alaska	71.95
34	Idaho	71.47
35	Missouri	71.30
36	North Dakota	71.18
37	South Dakota	70.82
38	Rhode Island	70.24
39	Illinois	70.00
40	Hawaii	68.79
41	Michigan	68.58
42	Ohio	66.88
43	California	66.37
44	Connecticut	58.54
45	Arizona	56.75
46	Nevada	50.82
47	Virginia	38.67
NA	Oregon**	NA
NA	Washington**	NA
NA	Wyoming**	NA

District of Columbia   68.53

Source: Morgan Quitno Corporation using data from U.S. Department of Health and Human Services, Substance Abuse and Mental Health Services Administration

"State Resources and Services Related to Alcohol and Other Drug Problems-Fiscal Year 1992" (SMA 94-2092 (1994))
*Does not include admissions in U.S. territories. Data are only from treatment units that received at least some funds administered by a state's alcohol/drug agency in fiscal year 1992. An additional 11,436 admissions were not reported by sex. **Not available.

Female Admissions to Alcohol and Other Drug Treatment Programs in 1992

National Total = 482,558 Female Admissions*

ALPHA ORDER

RANK	STATE	ADMISSIONS	% of USA
30	Alabama	3,826	0.79%
29	Alaska	4,001	0.83%
24	Arizona	5,712	1.18%
36	Arkansas	2,645	0.55%
1	California	45,206	9.37%
15	Colorado	12,227	2.53%
26	Connecticut	5,255	1.09%
44	Delaware	1,437	0.30%
4	Florida	26,278	5.45%
11	Georgia	15,649	3.24%
45	Hawaii	1,383	0.29%
40	Idaho	2,075	0.43%
5	Illinois	24,560	5.09%
20	Indiana	6,406	1.33%
25	Iowa	5,308	1.10%
28	Kansas	4,286	0.89%
19	Kentucky	8,073	1.67%
22	Louisiana	5,759	1.19%
42	Maine	1,988	0.41%
17	Maryland	9,910	2.05%
7	Massachusetts	23,291	4.83%
6	Michigan	23,879	4.95%
14	Minnesota	12,823	2.66%
37	Mississippi	2,467	0.51%
18	Missouri	9,762	2.02%
39	Montana	2,141	0.44%
21	Nebraska	6,015	1.25%
38	Nevada	2,372	0.49%
46	New Hampshire	1,379	0.29%
12	New Jersey	14,787	3.06%
34	New Mexico	3,118	0.65%
2	New York	36,860	7.64%
16	North Carolina	10,313	2.14%
47	North Dakota	1,310	0.27%
8	Ohio	22,682	4.70%
27	Oklahoma	4,534	0.94%
NA	Oregon**	NA	NA
10	Pennsylvania	17,915	3.71%
31	Rhode Island	3,623	0.75%
23	South Carolina	5,733	1.19%
32	South Dakota	3,621	0.75%
33	Tennessee	3,613	0.75%
13	Texas	13,179	2.73%
35	Utah	3,046	0.63%
43	Vermont	1,551	0.32%
9	Virginia	22,472	4.66%
NA	Washington**	NA	NA
41	West Virginia	2,047	0.42%
3	Wisconsin	32,386	6.71%
NA	Wyoming**	NA	NA

RANK ORDER

RANK	STATE	ADMISSIONS	% of USA
1	California	45,206	9.37%
2	New York	36,860	7.64%
3	Wisconsin	32,386	6.71%
4	Florida	26,278	5.45%
5	Illinois	24,560	5.09%
6	Michigan	23,879	4.95%
7	Massachusetts	23,291	4.83%
8	Ohio	22,682	4.70%
9	Virginia	22,472	4.66%
10	Pennsylvania	17,915	3.71%
11	Georgia	15,649	3.24%
12	New Jersey	14,787	3.06%
13	Texas	13,179	2.73%
14	Minnesota	12,823	2.66%
15	Colorado	12,227	2.53%
16	North Carolina	10,313	2.14%
17	Maryland	9,910	2.05%
18	Missouri	9,762	2.02%
19	Kentucky	8,073	1.67%
20	Indiana	6,406	1.33%
21	Nebraska	6,015	1.25%
22	Louisiana	5,759	1.19%
23	South Carolina	5,733	1.19%
24	Arizona	5,712	1.18%
25	Iowa	5,308	1.10%
26	Connecticut	5,255	1.09%
27	Oklahoma	4,534	0.94%
28	Kansas	4,286	0.89%
29	Alaska	4,001	0.83%
30	Alabama	3,826	0.79%
31	Rhode Island	3,623	0.75%
32	South Dakota	3,621	0.75%
33	Tennessee	3,613	0.75%
34	New Mexico	3,118	0.65%
35	Utah	3,046	0.63%
36	Arkansas	2,645	0.55%
37	Mississippi	2,467	0.51%
38	Nevada	2,372	0.49%
39	Montana	2,141	0.44%
40	Idaho	2,075	0.43%
41	West Virginia	2,047	0.42%
42	Maine	1,988	0.41%
43	Vermont	1,551	0.32%
44	Delaware	1,437	0.30%
45	Hawaii	1,383	0.29%
46	New Hampshire	1,379	0.29%
47	North Dakota	1,310	0.27%
NA	Oregon**	NA	NA
NA	Washington**	NA	NA
NA	Wyoming**	NA	NA
	District of Columbia	3,655	0.76%

Source: U.S. Department of Health and Human Services, Substance Abuse and Mental Health Services Administration
"State Resources and Services Related to Alcohol and Other Drug Problems-Fiscal Year 1992" (SMA 94-2092 (1994))
Does not include 2,298 admissions in U.S. territories. Data are only from treatment units that received at least some
funds administered by a state's alcohol/drug agency in fiscal year 1992. An additional 11,436 admissions were not
reported by sex.
***Not available.*   171

Female Admissions in Alcohol and Other Drug Treatment Programs
As a Percent of All Admissions in 1992
National Percent = 27.28% Female*

ALPHA ORDER

RANK	STATE	PERCENT
31	Alabama	24.05
12	Alaska	28.05
38	Arizona	22.23
43	Arkansas	19.64
2	California	33.63
45	Colorado	19.02
47	Connecticut	16.33
29	Delaware	24.36
20	Florida	26.97
23	Georgia	26.60
5	Hawaii	31.21
15	Idaho	27.68
7	Illinois	30.00
21	Indiana	26.79
36	Iowa	23.62
34	Kansas	23.83
32	Kentucky	24.01
39	Louisiana	22.19
30	Maine	24.28
14	Maryland	27.89
17	Massachusetts	27.62
4	Michigan	31.42
41	Minnesota	21.32
40	Mississippi	22.11
10	Missouri	28.70
16	Montana	27.63
37	Nebraska	22.67
6	Nevada	30.13
35	New Hampshire	23.74
13	New Jersey	27.95
28	New Mexico	24.59
27	New York	24.83
33	North Carolina	23.90
11	North Dakota	28.62
3	Ohio	33.12
24	Oklahoma	26.31
NA	Oregon**	NA
19	Pennsylvania	27.38
8	Rhode Island	29.76
42	South Carolina	20.37
9	South Dakota	29.18
18	Tennessee	27.59
25	Texas	26.29
43	Utah	19.64
26	Vermont	25.34
1	Virginia	61.33
NA	Washington**	NA
46	West Virginia	17.49
22	Wisconsin	26.70
NA	Wyoming**	NA

RANK ORDER

RANK	STATE	PERCENT
1	Virginia	61.33
2	California	33.63
3	Ohio	33.12
4	Michigan	31.42
5	Hawaii	31.21
6	Nevada	30.13
7	Illinois	30.00
8	Rhode Island	29.76
9	South Dakota	29.18
10	Missouri	28.70
11	North Dakota	28.62
12	Alaska	28.05
13	New Jersey	27.95
14	Maryland	27.89
15	Idaho	27.68
16	Montana	27.63
17	Massachusetts	27.62
18	Tennessee	27.59
19	Pennsylvania	27.38
20	Florida	26.97
21	Indiana	26.79
22	Wisconsin	26.70
23	Georgia	26.60
24	Oklahoma	26.31
25	Texas	26.29
26	Vermont	25.34
27	New York	24.83
28	New Mexico	24.59
29	Delaware	24.36
30	Maine	24.28
31	Alabama	24.05
32	Kentucky	24.01
33	North Carolina	23.90
34	Kansas	23.83
35	New Hampshire	23.74
36	Iowa	23.62
37	Nebraska	22.67
38	Arizona	22.23
39	Louisiana	22.19
40	Mississippi	22.11
41	Minnesota	21.32
42	South Carolina	20.37
43	Arkansas	19.64
43	Utah	19.64
45	Colorado	19.02
46	West Virginia	17.49
47	Connecticut	16.33
NA	Oregon**	NA
NA	Washington**	NA
NA	Wyoming**	NA

District of Columbia   31.47

Source: Morgan Quitno Corporation using data from U.S. Department of Health and Human Services, Substance Abuse and Mental Health Services Administration

"State Resources and Services Related to Alcohol and Other Drug Problems–Fiscal Year 1992" (SMA 94-2092 (1994))
*Does not include admissions in U.S. territories. Data are only from treatment units that received at least some funds administered by a state's alcohol/drug agency in fiscal year 1992. An additional 11,436 admissions were not reported by sex. **Not available.

White Admissions to Alcohol and Other Drug Treatment Programs in 1992

National Total = 1,063,315 White Admissions*

<table>
<tr><td colspan="4">ALPHA ORDER</td><td colspan="4">RANK ORDER</td></tr>
<tr><td>RANK</td><td>STATE</td><td>ADMISSIONS</td><td>% of USA</td><td>RANK</td><td>STATE</td><td>ADMISSIONS</td><td>% of USA</td></tr>
<tr><td>31</td><td>Alabama</td><td>9,690</td><td>0.91%</td><td>1</td><td>Wisconsin</td><td>103,428</td><td>9.73%</td></tr>
<tr><td>37</td><td>Alaska</td><td>6,633</td><td>0.62%</td><td>2</td><td>New York</td><td>76,186</td><td>7.16%</td></tr>
<tr><td>28</td><td>Arizona</td><td>11,672</td><td>1.10%</td><td>3</td><td>California</td><td>72,256</td><td>6.80%</td></tr>
<tr><td>34</td><td>Arkansas</td><td>8,741</td><td>0.82%</td><td>4</td><td>Massachusetts</td><td>57,779</td><td>5.43%</td></tr>
<tr><td>3</td><td>California</td><td>72,256</td><td>6.80%</td><td>5</td><td>Michigan</td><td>51,077</td><td>4.80%</td></tr>
<tr><td>8</td><td>Colorado</td><td>38,857</td><td>3.65%</td><td>6</td><td>Ohio</td><td>47,079</td><td>4.43%</td></tr>
<tr><td>25</td><td>Connecticut</td><td>13,104</td><td>1.23%</td><td>7</td><td>Minnesota</td><td>42,208</td><td>3.97%</td></tr>
<tr><td>46</td><td>Delaware</td><td>3,199</td><td>0.30%</td><td>8</td><td>Colorado</td><td>38,857</td><td>3.65%</td></tr>
<tr><td>11</td><td>Florida</td><td>34,875</td><td>3.28%</td><td>9</td><td>Pennsylvania</td><td>38,828</td><td>3.65%</td></tr>
<tr><td>12</td><td>Georgia</td><td>30,668</td><td>2.88%</td><td>10</td><td>Illinois</td><td>38,819</td><td>3.65%</td></tr>
<tr><td>47</td><td>Hawaii</td><td>1,779</td><td>0.17%</td><td>11</td><td>Florida</td><td>34,875</td><td>3.28%</td></tr>
<tr><td>38</td><td>Idaho</td><td>6,507</td><td>0.61%</td><td>12</td><td>Georgia</td><td>30,668</td><td>2.88%</td></tr>
<tr><td>10</td><td>Illinois</td><td>38,819</td><td>3.65%</td><td>13</td><td>Kentucky</td><td>29,952</td><td>2.82%</td></tr>
<tr><td>22</td><td>Indiana</td><td>16,591</td><td>1.56%</td><td>14</td><td>New Jersey</td><td>25,583</td><td>2.41%</td></tr>
<tr><td>19</td><td>Iowa</td><td>20,385</td><td>1.92%</td><td>15</td><td>North Carolina</td><td>24,564</td><td>2.31%</td></tr>
<tr><td>24</td><td>Kansas</td><td>13,130</td><td>1.23%</td><td>16</td><td>Missouri</td><td>24,067</td><td>2.26%</td></tr>
<tr><td>13</td><td>Kentucky</td><td>29,952</td><td>2.82%</td><td>17</td><td>Texas</td><td>21,979</td><td>2.07%</td></tr>
<tr><td>27</td><td>Louisiana</td><td>12,001</td><td>1.13%</td><td>18</td><td>Virginia</td><td>21,300</td><td>2.00%</td></tr>
<tr><td>35</td><td>Maine</td><td>7,963</td><td>0.75%</td><td>19</td><td>Iowa</td><td>20,385</td><td>1.92%</td></tr>
<tr><td>21</td><td>Maryland</td><td>17,927</td><td>1.69%</td><td>20</td><td>Nebraska</td><td>19,739</td><td>1.86%</td></tr>
<tr><td>4</td><td>Massachusetts</td><td>57,779</td><td>5.43%</td><td>21</td><td>Maryland</td><td>17,927</td><td>1.69%</td></tr>
<tr><td>5</td><td>Michigan</td><td>51,077</td><td>4.80%</td><td>22</td><td>Indiana</td><td>16,591</td><td>1.56%</td></tr>
<tr><td>7</td><td>Minnesota</td><td>42,208</td><td>3.97%</td><td>23</td><td>South Carolina</td><td>16,499</td><td>1.55%</td></tr>
<tr><td>43</td><td>Mississippi</td><td>5,403</td><td>0.51%</td><td>24</td><td>Kansas</td><td>13,130</td><td>1.23%</td></tr>
<tr><td>16</td><td>Missouri</td><td>24,067</td><td>2.26%</td><td>25</td><td>Connecticut</td><td>13,104</td><td>1.23%</td></tr>
<tr><td>39</td><td>Montana</td><td>5,934</td><td>0.56%</td><td>26</td><td>Oklahoma</td><td>12,114</td><td>1.14%</td></tr>
<tr><td>20</td><td>Nebraska</td><td>19,739</td><td>1.86%</td><td>27</td><td>Louisiana</td><td>12,001</td><td>1.13%</td></tr>
<tr><td>44</td><td>Nevada</td><td>4,771</td><td>0.45%</td><td>28</td><td>Arizona</td><td>11,672</td><td>1.10%</td></tr>
<tr><td>42</td><td>New Hampshire</td><td>5,589</td><td>0.53%</td><td>29</td><td>Utah</td><td>11,172</td><td>1.05%</td></tr>
<tr><td>14</td><td>New Jersey</td><td>25,583</td><td>2.41%</td><td>30</td><td>West Virginia</td><td>10,959</td><td>1.03%</td></tr>
<tr><td>41</td><td>New Mexico</td><td>5,627</td><td>0.53%</td><td>31</td><td>Alabama</td><td>9,690</td><td>0.91%</td></tr>
<tr><td>2</td><td>New York</td><td>76,186</td><td>7.16%</td><td>32</td><td>Rhode Island</td><td>9,605</td><td>0.90%</td></tr>
<tr><td>15</td><td>North Carolina</td><td>24,564</td><td>2.31%</td><td>33</td><td>Tennessee</td><td>9,586</td><td>0.90%</td></tr>
<tr><td>45</td><td>North Dakota</td><td>3,543</td><td>0.33%</td><td>34</td><td>Arkansas</td><td>8,741</td><td>0.82%</td></tr>
<tr><td>6</td><td>Ohio</td><td>47,079</td><td>4.43%</td><td>35</td><td>Maine</td><td>7,963</td><td>0.75%</td></tr>
<tr><td>26</td><td>Oklahoma</td><td>12,114</td><td>1.14%</td><td>36</td><td>South Dakota</td><td>7,611</td><td>0.72%</td></tr>
<tr><td>NA</td><td>Oregon**</td><td>NA</td><td>NA</td><td>37</td><td>Alaska</td><td>6,633</td><td>0.62%</td></tr>
<tr><td>9</td><td>Pennsylvania</td><td>38,828</td><td>3.65%</td><td>38</td><td>Idaho</td><td>6,507</td><td>0.61%</td></tr>
<tr><td>32</td><td>Rhode Island</td><td>9,605</td><td>0.90%</td><td>39</td><td>Montana</td><td>5,934</td><td>0.56%</td></tr>
<tr><td>23</td><td>South Carolina</td><td>16,499</td><td>1.55%</td><td>40</td><td>Vermont</td><td>5,775</td><td>0.54%</td></tr>
<tr><td>36</td><td>South Dakota</td><td>7,611</td><td>0.72%</td><td>41</td><td>New Mexico</td><td>5,627</td><td>0.53%</td></tr>
<tr><td>33</td><td>Tennessee</td><td>9,586</td><td>0.90%</td><td>42</td><td>New Hampshire</td><td>5,589</td><td>0.53%</td></tr>
<tr><td>17</td><td>Texas</td><td>21,979</td><td>2.07%</td><td>43</td><td>Mississippi</td><td>5,403</td><td>0.51%</td></tr>
<tr><td>29</td><td>Utah</td><td>11,172</td><td>1.05%</td><td>44</td><td>Nevada</td><td>4,771</td><td>0.45%</td></tr>
<tr><td>40</td><td>Vermont</td><td>5,775</td><td>0.54%</td><td>45</td><td>North Dakota</td><td>3,543</td><td>0.33%</td></tr>
<tr><td>18</td><td>Virginia</td><td>21,300</td><td>2.00%</td><td>46</td><td>Delaware</td><td>3,199</td><td>0.30%</td></tr>
<tr><td>NA</td><td>Washington**</td><td>NA</td><td>NA</td><td>47</td><td>Hawaii</td><td>1,779</td><td>0.17%</td></tr>
<tr><td>30</td><td>West Virginia</td><td>10,959</td><td>1.03%</td><td>NA</td><td>Oregon**</td><td>NA</td><td>NA</td></tr>
<tr><td>1</td><td>Wisconsin</td><td>103,428</td><td>9.73%</td><td>NA</td><td>Washington**</td><td>NA</td><td>NA</td></tr>
<tr><td>NA</td><td>Wyoming**</td><td>NA</td><td>NA</td><td>NA</td><td>Wyoming**</td><td>NA</td><td>NA</td></tr>
<tr><td></td><td></td><td></td><td></td><td colspan="2">District of Columbia</td><td>561</td><td>0.05%</td></tr>
</table>

Source: U.S. Department of Health and Human Services, Substance Abuse and Mental Health Services Administration
"State Resources and Services Related to Alcohol and Other Drug Problems-Fiscal Year 1992" (SMA 94-2092 (1994))
*Does not include 44 white admissions in U.S. territories. Data are only from treatment units that received at least some
funds administered by a state's alcohol/drug agency in fiscal year 1992.
**Not available.

White Admissions to Alcohol and Other Drug Treatment Programs
As a Percent of All Admissions in 1992
National Percent = 60.10% of Admissions*

ALPHA ORDER				RANK ORDER		
RANK	STATE	PERCENT		RANK	STATE	PERCENT
25	Alabama	60.92		1	Maine	97.26
40	Alaska	46.50		2	New Hampshire	96.23
42	Arizona	45.43		3	Vermont	94.35
23	Arkansas	64.90		4	West Virginia	93.64
33	California	53.75		5	Iowa	90.73
27	Colorado	60.45		6	Kentucky	89.07
45	Connecticut	40.72		7	Idaho	86.79
32	Delaware	54.23		8	Wisconsin	85.28
47	Florida	35.80		9	Rhode Island	78.90
34	Georgia	52.12		10	North Dakota	77.41
46	Hawaii	40.15		11	Montana	76.58
7	Idaho	86.79		12	Nebraska	74.39
39	Illinois	47.41		13	Tennessee	73.19
19	Indiana	69.39		14	Kansas	72.99
5	Iowa	90.73		15	Utah	72.02
14	Kansas	72.99		16	Missouri	70.76
6	Kentucky	89.07		17	Oklahoma	70.29
41	Louisiana	46.24		18	Minnesota	70.19
1	Maine	97.26		19	Indiana	69.39
36	Maryland	50.46		20	Ohio	68.74
21	Massachusetts	68.52		21	Massachusetts	68.52
22	Michigan	67.21		22	Michigan	67.21
18	Minnesota	70.19		23	Arkansas	64.90
37	Mississippi	48.42		24	South Dakota	61.33
16	Missouri	70.76		25	Alabama	60.92
11	Montana	76.58		26	Nevada	60.60
12	Nebraska	74.39		27	Colorado	60.45
26	Nevada	60.60		28	Pennsylvania	59.34
2	New Hampshire	96.23		29	South Carolina	58.62
38	New Jersey	48.35		30	Virginia	58.13
43	New Mexico	44.38		31	North Carolina	56.94
35	New York	51.32		32	Delaware	54.23
31	North Carolina	56.94		33	California	53.75
10	North Dakota	77.41		34	Georgia	52.12
20	Ohio	68.74		35	New York	51.32
17	Oklahoma	70.29		36	Maryland	50.46
NA	Oregon**	NA		37	Mississippi	48.42
28	Pennsylvania	59.34		38	New Jersey	48.35
9	Rhode Island	78.90		39	Illinois	47.41
29	South Carolina	58.62		40	Alaska	46.50
24	South Dakota	61.33		41	Louisiana	46.24
13	Tennessee	73.19		42	Arizona	45.43
44	Texas	43.84		43	New Mexico	44.38
15	Utah	72.02		44	Texas	43.84
3	Vermont	94.35		45	Connecticut	40.72
30	Virginia	58.13		46	Hawaii	40.15
NA	Washington**	NA		47	Florida	35.80
4	West Virginia	93.64		NA	Oregon**	NA
8	Wisconsin	85.28		NA	Washington**	NA
NA	Wyoming**	NA		NA	Wyoming**	NA

District of Columbia 4.83

Source: Morgan Quitno Corporation using data from U.S. Department of Health and Human Services, Substance Abuse and Mental Health Services Administration

"State Resources and Services Related to Alcohol and Other Drug Problems-Fiscal Year 1992" (SMA 94-2092 (1994))
*Does not include admissions in U.S. territories. Data are only from treatment units that received at least some funds administered by a state's alcohol/drug agency in fiscal year 1992.
**Not available.

Black Admissions to Alcohol and Other Drug Treatment Programs in 1992

National Total = 436,985 Black Admissions*

ALPHA ORDER

RANK	STATE	ADMISSIONS	% of USA
20	Alabama	6,165	1.41%
37	Alaska	524	0.12%
32	Arizona	1,545	0.35%
24	Arkansas	4,586	1.05%
3	California	28,054	6.42%
23	Colorado	5,241	1.20%
19	Connecticut	7,004	1.60%
30	Delaware	2,580	0.59%
10	Florida	17,361	3.97%
4	Georgia	27,806	6.36%
41	Hawaii	140	0.03%
44	Idaho	57	0.01%
2	Illinois	35,977	8.23%
29	Indiana	2,705	0.62%
34	Iowa	1,158	0.26%
28	Kansas	2,749	0.63%
25	Kentucky	3,312	0.76%
14	Louisiana	13,855	3.17%
45	Maine	54	0.01%
11	Maryland	17,001	3.89%
13	Massachusetts	14,164	3.24%
6	Michigan	21,058	4.82%
21	Minnesota	5,776	1.32%
22	Mississippi	5,727	1.31%
18	Missouri	9,438	2.16%
46	Montana	48	0.01%
31	Nebraska	2,021	0.46%
35	Nevada	810	0.19%
40	New Hampshire	154	0.04%
7	New Jersey	19,747	4.52%
39	New Mexico	259	0.06%
1	New York	50,814	11.63%
9	North Carolina	17,604	4.03%
47	North Dakota	22	0.01%
8	Ohio	19,220	4.40%
27	Oklahoma	2,803	0.64%
NA	Oregon**	NA	NA
5	Pennsylvania	23,421	5.36%
33	Rhode Island	1,518	0.35%
17	South Carolina	11,053	2.53%
42	South Dakota	121	0.03%
26	Tennessee	3,306	0.76%
12	Texas	15,369	3.52%
38	Utah	508	0.12%
43	Vermont	97	0.02%
16	Virginia	11,643	2.66%
NA	Washington**	NA	NA
36	West Virginia	650	0.15%
15	Wisconsin	11,666	2.67%
NA	Wyoming**	NA	NA

RANK ORDER

RANK	STATE	ADMISSIONS	% of USA
1	New York	50,814	11.63%
2	Illinois	35,977	8.23%
3	California	28,054	6.42%
4	Georgia	27,806	6.36%
5	Pennsylvania	23,421	5.36%
6	Michigan	21,058	4.82%
7	New Jersey	19,747	4.52%
8	Ohio	19,220	4.40%
9	North Carolina	17,604	4.03%
10	Florida	17,361	3.97%
11	Maryland	17,001	3.89%
12	Texas	15,369	3.52%
13	Massachusetts	14,164	3.24%
14	Louisiana	13,855	3.17%
15	Wisconsin	11,666	2.67%
16	Virginia	11,643	2.66%
17	South Carolina	11,053	2.53%
18	Missouri	9,438	2.16%
19	Connecticut	7,004	1.60%
20	Alabama	6,165	1.41%
21	Minnesota	5,776	1.32%
22	Mississippi	5,727	1.31%
23	Colorado	5,241	1.20%
24	Arkansas	4,586	1.05%
25	Kentucky	3,312	0.76%
26	Tennessee	3,306	0.76%
27	Oklahoma	2,803	0.64%
28	Kansas	2,749	0.63%
29	Indiana	2,705	0.62%
30	Delaware	2,580	0.59%
31	Nebraska	2,021	0.46%
32	Arizona	1,545	0.35%
33	Rhode Island	1,518	0.35%
34	Iowa	1,158	0.26%
35	Nevada	810	0.19%
36	West Virginia	650	0.15%
37	Alaska	524	0.12%
38	Utah	508	0.12%
39	New Mexico	259	0.06%
40	New Hampshire	154	0.04%
41	Hawaii	140	0.03%
42	South Dakota	121	0.03%
43	Vermont	97	0.02%
44	Idaho	57	0.01%
45	Maine	54	0.01%
46	Montana	48	0.01%
47	North Dakota	22	0.01%
NA	Oregon**	NA	NA
NA	Washington**	NA	NA
NA	Wyoming**	NA	NA
	District of Columbia	10,094	2.31%

*Source: U.S. Department of Health and Human Services, Substance Abuse and Mental Health Services Administration
"State Resources and Services Related to Alcohol and Other Drug Problems-Fiscal Year 1992" (SMA 94-2092 (1994))*
*There were no black admissions in U.S. territories. Data are only from treatment units that received at least some funds administered by a state's alcohol/drug agency in fiscal year 1992.
**Not available.

Black Admissions to Alcohol and Other Drug Treatment Programs
As a Percent of All Admissions in 1992
National Percent = 24.70% of Admissions*

ALPHA ORDER			RANK ORDER		
RANK	STATE	PERCENT	RANK	STATE	PERCENT
9	Alabama	38.76	1	Louisiana	53.38
37	Alaska	3.67	2	Mississippi	51.32
34	Arizona	6.01	3	Maryland	47.85
13	Arkansas	34.05	4	Georgia	47.26
21	California	20.87	5	Illinois	43.94
32	Colorado	8.15	6	Delaware	43.74
20	Connecticut	21.76	7	North Carolina	40.80
6	Delaware	43.74	8	South Carolina	39.27
22	Florida	17.82	9	Alabama	38.76
4	Georgia	47.26	10	New Jersey	37.32
39	Hawaii	3.16	11	Pennsylvania	35.79
44	Idaho	0.76	12	New York	34.23
5	Illinois	43.94	13	Arkansas	34.05
27	Indiana	11.31	14	Virginia	31.78
36	Iowa	5.15	15	Texas	30.66
25	Kansas	15.28	16	Ohio	28.06
29	Kentucky	9.85	17	Missouri	27.75
1	Louisiana	53.38	18	Michigan	27.71
45	Maine	0.66	19	Tennessee	25.24
3	Maryland	47.85	20	Connecticut	21.76
23	Massachusetts	16.80	21	California	20.87
18	Michigan	27.71	22	Florida	17.82
31	Minnesota	9.60	23	Massachusetts	16.80
2	Mississippi	51.32	24	Oklahoma	16.26
17	Missouri	27.75	25	Kansas	15.28
46	Montana	0.62	26	Rhode Island	12.47
33	Nebraska	7.62	27	Indiana	11.31
28	Nevada	10.29	28	Nevada	10.29
40	New Hampshire	2.65	29	Kentucky	9.85
10	New Jersey	37.32	30	Wisconsin	9.62
41	New Mexico	2.04	31	Minnesota	9.60
12	New York	34.23	32	Colorado	8.15
7	North Carolina	40.80	33	Nebraska	7.62
47	North Dakota	0.48	34	Arizona	6.01
16	Ohio	28.06	35	West Virginia	5.55
24	Oklahoma	16.26	36	Iowa	5.15
NA	Oregon**	NA	37	Alaska	3.67
11	Pennsylvania	35.79	38	Utah	3.27
26	Rhode Island	12.47	39	Hawaii	3.16
8	South Carolina	39.27	40	New Hampshire	2.65
43	South Dakota	0.98	41	New Mexico	2.04
19	Tennessee	25.24	42	Vermont	1.58
15	Texas	30.66	43	South Dakota	0.98
38	Utah	3.27	44	Idaho	0.76
42	Vermont	1.58	45	Maine	0.66
14	Virginia	31.78	46	Montana	0.62
NA	Washington**	NA	47	North Dakota	0.48
35	West Virginia	5.55	NA	Oregon**	NA
30	Wisconsin	9.62	NA	Washington**	NA
NA	Wyoming**	NA	NA	Wyoming**	NA

District of Columbia   86.92

Source: Morgan Quitno Corporation using data from U.S. Department of Health and Human Services, Substance Abuse and Mental Health Services Administration

"State Resources and Services Related to Alcohol and Other Drug Problems-Fiscal Year 1992" (SMA 94-2092 (1994))

*There were no black admissions in U.S. territories. Data are only from treatment units that received at least some funds administered by a state's alcohol/drug agency in fiscal year 1992.

**Not available.

Hispanic Admissions to Alcohol and Other Drug Treatment Programs in 1992

National Total = 134,150 Hispanic Admissions*

ALPHA ORDER					RANK ORDER			
RANK	STATE	ADMISSIONS	% of USA		RANK	STATE	ADMISSIONS	% of USA
NA	Alabama**	NA	NA		1	California	28,744	21.43%
29	Alaska	206	0.15%		2	New York	17,615	13.13%
9	Arizona	4,252	3.17%		3	Colorado	16,471	12.28%
35	Arkansas	69	0.05%		4	Texas	12,316	9.18%
1	California	28,744	21.43%		5	Massachusetts	8,100	6.04%
3	Colorado	16,471	12.28%		6	New Jersey	7,056	5.26%
11	Connecticut	3,848	2.87%		7	Florida	6,590	4.91%
37	Delaware	56	0.04%		8	Illinois	5,400	4.03%
7	Florida	6,590	4.91%		9	Arizona	4,252	3.17%
30	Georgia	175	0.13%		10	New Mexico	4,097	3.05%
27	Hawaii	214	0.16%		11	Connecticut	3,848	2.87%
22	Idaho	478	0.36%		12	Pennsylvania	3,005	2.24%
8	Illinois	5,400	4.03%		13	Wisconsin	2,724	2.03%
32	Indiana	151	0.11%		14	Michigan	2,137	1.59%
21	Iowa	510	0.38%		15	Minnesota	2,105	1.57%
18	Kansas	1,064	0.79%		16	Utah	1,524	1.14%
40	Kentucky	1	0.00%		17	Ohio	1,199	0.89%
NA	Louisiana**	NA	NA		18	Kansas	1,064	0.79%
41	Maine	0	0.00%		19	Virginia	897	0.67%
25	Maryland	329	0.25%		20	Rhode Island	661	0.49%
5	Massachusetts	8,100	6.04%		21	Iowa	510	0.38%
14	Michigan	2,137	1.59%		22	Idaho	478	0.36%
15	Minnesota	2,105	1.57%		23	Nevada	426	0.32%
41	Mississippi	0	0.00%		24	Oklahoma	400	0.30%
31	Missouri	169	0.13%		25	Maryland	329	0.25%
33	Montana	139	0.10%		26	South Carolina	307	0.23%
41	Nebraska	0	0.00%		27	Hawaii	214	0.16%
23	Nevada	426	0.32%		28	North Carolina	212	0.16%
38	New Hampshire	24	0.02%		29	Alaska	206	0.15%
6	New Jersey	7,056	5.26%		30	Georgia	175	0.13%
10	New Mexico	4,097	3.05%		31	Missouri	169	0.13%
2	New York	17,615	13.13%		32	Indiana	151	0.11%
28	North Carolina	212	0.16%		33	Montana	139	0.10%
41	North Dakota	0	0.00%		34	Tennessee	130	0.10%
17	Ohio	1,199	0.89%		35	Arkansas	69	0.05%
24	Oklahoma	400	0.30%		36	West Virginia	57	0.04%
NA	Oregon**	NA	NA		37	Delaware	56	0.04%
12	Pennsylvania	3,005	2.24%		38	New Hampshire	24	0.02%
20	Rhode Island	661	0.49%		39	Vermont	20	0.01%
26	South Carolina	307	0.23%		40	Kentucky	1	0.00%
41	South Dakota	0	0.00%		41	Maine	0	0.00%
34	Tennessee	130	0.10%		41	Mississippi	0	0.00%
4	Texas	12,316	9.18%		41	Nebraska	0	0.00%
16	Utah	1,524	1.14%		41	North Dakota	0	0.00%
39	Vermont	20	0.01%		41	South Dakota	0	0.00%
19	Virginia	897	0.67%		NA	Alabama**	NA	NA
NA	Washington**	NA	NA		NA	Louisiana**	NA	NA
36	West Virginia	57	0.04%		NA	Oregon**	NA	NA
13	Wisconsin	2,724	2.03%		NA	Washington**	NA	NA
NA	Wyoming**	NA	NA		NA	Wyoming**	NA	NA
					District of Columbia		272	0.20%

Source: U.S. Department of Health and Human Services, Substance Abuse and Mental Health Services Administration
"State Resources and Services Related to Alcohol and Other Drug Problems–Fiscal Year 1992" (SMA 94-2092 (1994))
Does not include 23,597 Hispanic admissions in U.S. territories. Data are only from treatment units that received at least some funds administered by a state's alcohol/drug agency in fiscal year 1992.
**Not available.*

Hispanic Admissions to Alcohol and Other Drug Treatment Programs
As a Percent of All Admissions in 1992
National Percent = 7.58% of Admissions*

ALPHA ORDER			RANK ORDER		
RANK	STATE	PERCENT	RANK	STATE	PERCENT
NA	Alabama**	NA	1	New Mexico	32.31
27	Alaska	1.44	2	Colorado	25.62
5	Arizona	16.55	3	Texas	24.57
33	Arkansas	0.51	4	California	21.38
4	California	21.38	5	Arizona	16.55
2	Colorado	25.62	6	New Jersey	13.34
7	Connecticut	11.96	7	Connecticut	11.96
30	Delaware	0.95	8	New York	11.87
11	Florida	6.76	9	Utah	9.82
39	Georgia	0.30	10	Massachusetts	9.61
17	Hawaii	4.83	11	Florida	6.76
13	Idaho	6.38	12	Illinois	6.60
12	Illinois	6.60	13	Idaho	6.38
32	Indiana	0.63	14	Kansas	5.92
23	Iowa	2.27	15	Rhode Island	5.43
14	Kansas	5.92	16	Nevada	5.41
40	Kentucky	0.00	17	Hawaii	4.83
NA	Louisiana**	NA	18	Pennsylvania	4.59
40	Maine	0.00	19	Minnesota	3.50
31	Maryland	0.93	20	Michigan	2.81
10	Massachusetts	9.61	21	Virginia	2.45
20	Michigan	2.81	22	Oklahoma	2.32
19	Minnesota	3.50	23	Iowa	2.27
40	Mississippi	0.00	24	Wisconsin	2.25
34	Missouri	0.50	25	Montana	1.79
25	Montana	1.79	26	Ohio	1.75
40	Nebraska	0.00	27	Alaska	1.44
16	Nevada	5.41	28	South Carolina	1.09
37	New Hampshire	0.41	29	Tennessee	0.99
6	New Jersey	13.34	30	Delaware	0.95
1	New Mexico	32.31	31	Maryland	0.93
8	New York	11.87	32	Indiana	0.63
35	North Carolina	0.49	33	Arkansas	0.51
40	North Dakota	0.00	34	Missouri	0.50
26	Ohio	1.75	35	North Carolina	0.49
22	Oklahoma	2.32	35	West Virginia	0.49
NA	Oregon**	NA	37	New Hampshire	0.41
18	Pennsylvania	4.59	38	Vermont	0.33
15	Rhode Island	5.43	39	Georgia	0.30
28	South Carolina	1.09	40	Kentucky	0.00
40	South Dakota	0.00	40	Maine	0.00
29	Tennessee	0.99	40	Mississippi	0.00
3	Texas	24.57	40	Nebraska	0.00
9	Utah	9.82	40	North Dakota	0.00
38	Vermont	0.33	40	South Dakota	0.00
21	Virginia	2.45	NA	Alabama**	NA
NA	Washington**	NA	NA	Louisiana**	NA
35	West Virginia	0.49	NA	Oregon**	NA
24	Wisconsin	2.25	NA	Washington**	NA
NA	Wyoming**	NA	NA	Wyoming**	NA

District of Columbia   2.34

Source: Morgan Quitno Corporation using data from U.S. Department of Health and Human Services, Substance Abuse and Mental Health Services Administration

"State Resources and Services Related to Alcohol and Other Drug Problems-Fiscal Year 1992" (SMA 94-2092 (1994))
Does not include admissions in U.S. territories. Data are only from treatment units that received at least some funds administered by a state's alcohol/drug agency in fiscal year 1992.
**Not available.*

Admissions of Juveniles in Alcohol and Other Drug Treatment Programs in 1992

National Total = 97,773 Juvenile Admissions*

ALPHA ORDER					RANK ORDER			
RANK	STATE	ADMISSIONS	% of USA		RANK	STATE	ADMISSIONS	% of USA
38	Alabama	473	0.48%		1	Illinois	9,476	9.69%
23	Alaska	1,375	1.41%		2	Ohio	8,800	9.00%
34	Arizona	659	0.67%		3	California	7,205	7.37%
32	Arkansas	843	0.86%		4	Wisconsin	5,696	5.83%
3	California	7,205	7.37%		5	New York	5,531	5.66%
10	Colorado	2,932	3.00%		6	Michigan	5,399	5.52%
39	Connecticut	335	0.34%		7	Florida	5,368	5.49%
45	Delaware	29	0.03%		8	Pennsylvania	4,374	4.47%
7	Florida	5,368	5.49%		9	Maryland	3,831	3.92%
18	Georgia	1,654	1.69%		10	Colorado	2,932	3.00%
21	Hawaii	1,427	1.46%		11	Missouri	2,824	2.89%
17	Idaho	1,669	1.71%		12	Kentucky	2,635	2.70%
1	Illinois	9,476	9.69%		13	New Jersey	2,453	2.51%
30	Indiana	891	0.91%		14	Minnesota	2,086	2.13%
16	Iowa	1,941	1.99%		15	Massachusetts	1,970	2.01%
28	Kansas	1,011	1.03%		16	Iowa	1,941	1.99%
12	Kentucky	2,635	2.70%		17	Idaho	1,669	1.71%
24	Louisiana	1,316	1.35%		18	Georgia	1,654	1.69%
37	Maine	475	0.49%		19	South Dakota	1,641	1.68%
9	Maryland	3,831	3.92%		20	Utah	1,446	1.48%
15	Massachusetts	1,970	2.01%		21	Hawaii	1,427	1.46%
6	Michigan	5,399	5.52%		22	North Carolina	1,396	1.43%
14	Minnesota	2,086	2.13%		23	Alaska	1,375	1.41%
43	Mississippi	191	0.20%		24	Louisiana	1,316	1.35%
11	Missouri	2,824	2.89%		25	South Carolina	1,228	1.26%
35	Montana	594	0.61%		26	Nebraska	1,214	1.24%
26	Nebraska	1,214	1.24%		27	New Mexico	1,122	1.15%
NA	Nevada**	NA	NA		28	Kansas	1,011	1.03%
40	New Hampshire	283	0.29%		29	Tennessee	1,009	1.03%
13	New Jersey	2,453	2.51%		30	Indiana	891	0.91%
27	New Mexico	1,122	1.15%		31	Oklahoma	872	0.89%
5	New York	5,531	5.66%		32	Arkansas	843	0.86%
22	North Carolina	1,396	1.43%		33	West Virginia	768	0.79%
42	North Dakota	216	0.22%		34	Arizona	659	0.67%
2	Ohio	8,800	9.00%		35	Montana	594	0.61%
31	Oklahoma	872	0.89%		36	Rhode Island	563	0.58%
NA	Oregon**	NA	NA		37	Maine	475	0.49%
8	Pennsylvania	4,374	4.47%		38	Alabama	473	0.48%
36	Rhode Island	563	0.58%		39	Connecticut	335	0.34%
25	South Carolina	1,228	1.26%		40	New Hampshire	283	0.29%
19	South Dakota	1,641	1.68%		41	Vermont	268	0.27%
29	Tennessee	1,009	1.03%		42	North Dakota	216	0.22%
44	Texas	181	0.19%		43	Mississippi	191	0.20%
20	Utah	1,446	1.48%		44	Texas	181	0.19%
41	Vermont	268	0.27%		45	Delaware	29	0.03%
NA	Virginia**	NA	NA		NA	Nevada**	NA	NA
NA	Washington**	NA	NA		NA	Oregon**	NA	NA
33	West Virginia	768	0.79%		NA	Virginia**	NA	NA
4	Wisconsin	5,696	5.83%		NA	Washington**	NA	NA
NA	Wyoming**	NA	NA		NA	Wyoming**	NA	NA
						District of Columbia	103	0.11%

Source: U.S. Department of Health and Human Services, Substance Abuse and Mental Health Services Administration
"State Resources and Services Related to Alcohol and Other Drug Problems-Fiscal Year 1992" (SMA 94-2092 (1994))
*Youths 17 years old and younger. Does not include 1,392 admissions of juveniles in U.S. territories. Data are only from treatment units that received at least some funds administered by a state's alcohol/drug agency in fiscal year 1992.
**Not available.

Admissions of Juveniles to Alcohol and Other Drug Treatment Programs
As a Percent of All Admissions in 1992
National Percent = 5.53% of Admissions*

ALPHA ORDER				RANK ORDER		
RANK	STATE	PERCENT		RANK	STATE	PERCENT
38	Alabama	2.97		1	Hawaii	32.20
7	Alaska	9.64		2	Idaho	22.26
40	Arizona	2.57		3	South Dakota	13.22
18	Arkansas	6.26		4	Ohio	12.85
22	California	5.36		5	Illinois	11.57
31	Colorado	4.56		6	Maryland	10.78
43	Connecticut	1.04		7	Alaska	9.64
44	Delaware	0.49		8	Utah	9.32
21	Florida	5.51		9	New Mexico	8.85
39	Georgia	2.81		10	Iowa	8.64
1	Hawaii	32.20		11	Missouri	8.30
2	Idaho	22.26		12	Kentucky	7.84
5	Illinois	11.57		13	Tennessee	7.70
34	Indiana	3.73		14	Montana	7.67
10	Iowa	8.64		15	Michigan	7.10
20	Kansas	5.62		16	Pennsylvania	6.68
12	Kentucky	7.84		17	West Virginia	6.56
23	Louisiana	5.07		18	Arkansas	6.26
19	Maine	5.80		19	Maine	5.80
6	Maryland	10.78		20	Kansas	5.62
41	Massachusetts	2.34		21	Florida	5.51
15	Michigan	7.10		22	California	5.36
36	Minnesota	3.47		23	Louisiana	5.07
42	Mississippi	1.71		24	Oklahoma	5.06
11	Missouri	8.30		25	New Hampshire	4.87
14	Montana	7.67		26	North Dakota	4.72
30	Nebraska	4.58		27	Wisconsin	4.70
NA	Nevada**	NA		28	New Jersey	4.64
25	New Hampshire	4.87		29	Rhode Island	4.62
28	New Jersey	4.64		30	Nebraska	4.58
9	New Mexico	8.85		31	Colorado	4.56
34	New York	3.73		32	Vermont	4.38
37	North Carolina	3.24		33	South Carolina	4.36
26	North Dakota	4.72		34	Indiana	3.73
4	Ohio	12.85		34	New York	3.73
24	Oklahoma	5.06		36	Minnesota	3.47
NA	Oregon**	NA		37	North Carolina	3.24
16	Pennsylvania	6.68		38	Alabama	2.97
29	Rhode Island	4.62		39	Georgia	2.81
33	South Carolina	4.36		40	Arizona	2.57
3	South Dakota	13.22		41	Massachusetts	2.34
13	Tennessee	7.70		42	Mississippi	1.71
45	Texas	0.36		43	Connecticut	1.04
8	Utah	9.32		44	Delaware	0.49
32	Vermont	4.38		45	Texas	0.36
NA	Virginia**	NA		NA	Nevada**	NA
NA	Washington**	NA		NA	Oregon**	NA
17	West Virginia	6.56		NA	Virginia**	NA
27	Wisconsin	4.70		NA	Washington**	NA
NA	Wyoming**	NA		NA	Wyoming**	NA
				District of Columbia		0.89

Source: Morgan Quitno Corporation using data from U.S. Department of Health and Human Services, Substance Abuse and Mental Health Services Administration

"State Resources and Services Related to Alcohol and Other Drug Problems-Fiscal Year 1992" (SMA 94-2092 (1994))
*Youths 17 years old and younger. Does not include admissions in U.S. territories. Data are only from treatment units that received at least some funds administered by a state's alcohol/drug agency in fiscal year 1992.
**Not available.

Expenditures for State-Supported Alcohol and Other Drug Abuse Services in 1992

National Total = $3,336,499,798*

ALPHA ORDER			
RANK	STATE	EXPENDITURES	% of USA
31	Alabama	$21,400,303	0.64%
24	Alaska	35,243,453	1.06%
23	Arizona	36,149,518	1.08%
41	Arkansas	10,311,013	0.31%
2	California	506,900,529	15.19%
20	Colorado	43,832,743	1.31%
12	Connecticut	85,351,749	2.56%
44	Delaware	7,415,490	0.22%
3	Florida	145,965,113	4.37%
17	Georgia	50,397,337	1.51%
34	Hawaii	15,108,760	0.45%
46	Idaho	5,624,563	0.17%
5	Illinois	139,105,700	4.17%
19	Indiana	44,815,570	1.34%
25	Iowa	30,619,844	0.92%
37	Kansas	13,151,043	0.39%
29	Kentucky	24,032,251	0.72%
26	Louisiana	29,771,888	0.89%
43	Maine	8,914,559	0.27%
11	Maryland	85,568,083	2.56%
10	Massachusetts	96,399,899	2.89%
8	Michigan	108,599,931	3.25%
16	Minnesota	55,121,779	1.65%
40	Mississippi	11,022,779	0.33%
22	Missouri	41,867,342	1.25%
36	Montana	13,327,163	0.40%
38	Nebraska	13,095,972	0.39%
42	Nevada	9,265,538	0.28%
48	New Hampshire	4,939,133	0.15%
13	New Jersey	83,648,000	2.51%
33	New Mexico	17,428,868	0.52%
1	New York	668,355,640	20.03%
18	North Carolina	46,465,208	1.39%
47	North Dakota	5,310,276	0.16%
6	Ohio	126,266,651	3.78%
30	Oklahoma	22,694,435	0.68%
NA	Oregon**	NA	NA
4	Pennsylvania	139,966,322	4.20%
32	Rhode Island	19,889,000	0.60%
21	South Carolina	41,881,097	1.26%
39	South Dakota	11,145,677	0.33%
27	Tennessee	27,465,208	0.82%
9	Texas	107,389,227	3.22%
28	Utah	25,497,429	0.76%
45	Vermont	7,150,366	0.21%
14	Virginia	61,703,760	1.85%
15	Washington	58,782,932	1.76%
35	West Virginia	14,227,863	0.43%
7	Wisconsin	124,757,796	3.74%
NA	Wyoming**	NA	NA

RANK ORDER			
RANK	STATE	EXPENDITURES	% of USA
1	New York	$668,355,640	20.03%
2	California	506,900,529	15.19%
3	Florida	145,965,113	4.37%
4	Pennsylvania	139,966,322	4.20%
5	Illinois	139,105,700	4.17%
6	Ohio	126,266,651	3.78%
7	Wisconsin	124,757,796	3.74%
8	Michigan	108,599,931	3.25%
9	Texas	107,389,227	3.22%
10	Massachusetts	96,399,899	2.89%
11	Maryland	85,568,083	2.56%
12	Connecticut	85,351,749	2.56%
13	New Jersey	83,648,000	2.51%
14	Virginia	61,703,760	1.85%
15	Washington	58,782,932	1.76%
16	Minnesota	55,121,779	1.65%
17	Georgia	50,397,337	1.51%
18	North Carolina	46,465,208	1.39%
19	Indiana	44,815,570	1.34%
20	Colorado	43,832,743	1.31%
21	South Carolina	41,881,097	1.26%
22	Missouri	41,867,342	1.25%
23	Arizona	36,149,518	1.08%
24	Alaska	35,243,453	1.06%
25	Iowa	30,619,844	0.92%
26	Louisiana	29,771,888	0.89%
27	Tennessee	27,465,208	0.82%
28	Utah	25,497,429	0.76%
29	Kentucky	24,032,251	0.72%
30	Oklahoma	22,694,435	0.68%
31	Alabama	21,400,303	0.64%
32	Rhode Island	19,889,000	0.60%
33	New Mexico	17,428,868	0.52%
34	Hawaii	15,108,760	0.45%
35	West Virginia	14,227,863	0.43%
36	Montana	13,327,163	0.40%
37	Kansas	13,151,043	0.39%
38	Nebraska	13,095,972	0.39%
39	South Dakota	11,145,677	0.33%
40	Mississippi	11,022,779	0.33%
41	Arkansas	10,311,013	0.31%
42	Nevada	9,265,538	0.28%
43	Maine	8,914,559	0.27%
44	Delaware	7,415,490	0.22%
45	Vermont	7,150,366	0.21%
46	Idaho	5,624,563	0.17%
47	North Dakota	5,310,276	0.16%
48	New Hampshire	4,939,133	0.15%
NA	Oregon**	NA	NA
NA	Wyoming**	NA	NA
	District of Columbia	33,154,998	0.99%

Source: U.S. Department of Health and Human Services, Substance Abuse and Mental Health Services Administration
"State Resources and Services Related to Alcohol and Other Drug Problems-Fiscal Year 1992" (SMA 94-2092 (1994))
Funds for treatment and prevention programs as well as "other" costs (e.g. administration, capital construction and research.) Total does not include $51,189,659 in Puerto Rico and $688,105 in Guam.
**Not available.*

Per Capita Expenditures for State-Supported Alcohol and Other Drug Abuse Services in 1992
National Per Capita = $13.08*

ALPHA ORDER

RANK	STATE	PER CAPITA
45	Alabama	$5.17
1	Alaska	59.94
28	Arizona	9.43
47	Arkansas	4.31
7	California	16.41
13	Colorado	12.65
3	Connecticut	26.03
25	Delaware	10.73
24	Florida	10.83
34	Georgia	7.44
12	Hawaii	13.07
43	Idaho	5.28
16	Illinois	11.98
32	Indiana	7.92
23	Iowa	10.92
44	Kansas	5.23
40	Kentucky	6.40
37	Louisiana	6.96
35	Maine	7.21
6	Maryland	17.40
9	Massachusetts	16.09
19	Michigan	11.51
15	Minnesota	12.34
48	Mississippi	4.22
31	Missouri	8.07
8	Montana	16.21
30	Nebraska	8.18
38	Nevada	6.94
46	New Hampshire	4.43
26	New Jersey	10.70
22	New Mexico	11.02
2	New York	36.91
39	North Carolina	6.80
29	North Dakota	8.38
20	Ohio	11.46
36	Oklahoma	7.08
NA	Oregon**	NA
17	Pennsylvania	11.67
5	Rhode Island	19.87
18	South Carolina	11.62
10	South Dakota	15.74
42	Tennessee	5.47
41	Texas	6.07
11	Utah	14.08
14	Vermont	12.52
27	Virginia	9.65
21	Washington	11.43
33	West Virginia	7.87
4	Wisconsin	24.99
NA	Wyoming**	NA

RANK ORDER

RANK	STATE	PER CAPITA
1	Alaska	$59.94
2	New York	36.91
3	Connecticut	26.03
4	Wisconsin	24.99
5	Rhode Island	19.87
6	Maryland	17.40
7	California	16.41
8	Montana	16.21
9	Massachusetts	16.09
10	South Dakota	15.74
11	Utah	14.08
12	Hawaii	13.07
13	Colorado	12.65
14	Vermont	12.52
15	Minnesota	12.34
16	Illinois	11.98
17	Pennsylvania	11.67
18	South Carolina	11.62
19	Michigan	11.51
20	Ohio	11.46
21	Washington	11.43
22	New Mexico	11.02
23	Iowa	10.92
24	Florida	10.83
25	Delaware	10.73
26	New Jersey	10.70
27	Virginia	9.65
28	Arizona	9.43
29	North Dakota	8.38
30	Nebraska	8.18
31	Missouri	8.07
32	Indiana	7.92
33	West Virginia	7.87
34	Georgia	7.44
35	Maine	7.21
36	Oklahoma	7.08
37	Louisiana	6.96
38	Nevada	6.94
39	North Carolina	6.80
40	Kentucky	6.40
41	Texas	6.07
42	Tennessee	5.47
43	Idaho	5.28
44	Kansas	5.23
45	Alabama	5.17
46	New Hampshire	4.43
47	Arkansas	4.31
48	Mississippi	4.22
NA	Oregon**	NA
NA	Wyoming**	NA
	District of Columbia	56.68

Source: Morgan Quitno Corporation using data from U.S. Department of Health and Human Services, Substance Abuse and Mental Health Services Administration

"State Resources and Services Related to Alcohol and Other Drug Problems-Fiscal Year 1992" (SMA 94-2092 (1994))

*Funds for treatment and prevention programs as well as "other" costs (e.g. administration, capital construction and research.) National per capita does not include expenditures in Puerto Rico and Guam.

**Not available.

Expenditures for State-Supported Alcohol and Other Drug Abuse Treatment Programs in 1992
National Total = $2,579,368,311*

ALPHA ORDER

RANK	STATE	EXPENDITURES	% of USA
31	Alabama	$15,778,775	0.61%
25	Alaska	25,604,478	0.99%
22	Arizona	32,034,441	1.24%
41	Arkansas	7,662,398	0.30%
2	California	370,248,710	14.35%
20	Colorado	34,339,783	1.33%
10	Connecticut	72,486,649	2.81%
44	Delaware	6,497,266	0.25%
3	Florida	127,850,816	4.96%
17	Georgia	46,906,048	1.82%
34	Hawaii	12,509,017	0.48%
47	Idaho	4,051,717	0.16%
4	Illinois	109,449,300	4.24%
18	Indiana	36,920,106	1.43%
26	Iowa	24,298,070	0.94%
37	Kansas	10,433,861	0.40%
29	Kentucky	18,613,571	0.72%
24	Louisiana	26,439,066	1.03%
42	Maine	6,963,526	0.27%
11	Maryland	69,601,308	2.70%
7	Massachusetts	86,697,595	3.36%
9	Michigan	78,860,965	3.06%
16	Minnesota	48,864,773	1.89%
40	Mississippi	7,679,031	0.30%
19	Missouri	34,642,066	1.34%
36	Montana	10,755,848	0.42%
38	Nebraska	10,180,974	0.39%
43	Nevada	6,615,554	0.26%
48	New Hampshire	3,601,611	0.14%
13	New Jersey	60,970,000	2.36%
33	New Mexico	13,201,428	0.51%
1	New York	531,321,190	20.60%
21	North Carolina	33,211,598	1.29%
45	North Dakota	4,908,430	0.19%
6	Ohio	90,917,407	3.52%
28	Oklahoma	18,881,075	0.73%
NA	Oregon**	NA	NA
5	Pennsylvania	96,678,584	3.75%
32	Rhode Island	13,915,000	0.54%
23	South Carolina	27,396,429	1.06%
39	South Dakota	9,356,095	0.36%
27	Tennessee	19,788,254	0.77%
12	Texas	64,808,131	2.51%
30	Utah	17,887,367	0.69%
46	Vermont	4,400,920	0.17%
14	Virginia	52,648,330	2.04%
15	Washington	49,571,033	1.92%
35	West Virginia	10,806,870	0.42%
8	Wisconsin	85,724,830	3.32%
NA	Wyoming**	NA	NA

RANK ORDER

RANK	STATE	EXPENDITURES	% of USA
1	New York	$531,321,190	20.60%
2	California	370,248,710	14.35%
3	Florida	127,850,816	4.96%
4	Illinois	109,449,300	4.24%
5	Pennsylvania	96,678,584	3.75%
6	Ohio	90,917,407	3.52%
7	Massachusetts	86,697,595	3.36%
8	Wisconsin	85,724,830	3.32%
9	Michigan	78,860,965	3.06%
10	Connecticut	72,486,649	2.81%
11	Maryland	69,601,308	2.70%
12	Texas	64,808,131	2.51%
13	New Jersey	60,970,000	2.36%
14	Virginia	52,648,330	2.04%
15	Washington	49,571,033	1.92%
16	Minnesota	48,864,773	1.89%
17	Georgia	46,906,048	1.82%
18	Indiana	36,920,106	1.43%
19	Missouri	34,642,066	1.34%
20	Colorado	34,339,783	1.33%
21	North Carolina	33,211,598	1.29%
22	Arizona	32,034,441	1.24%
23	South Carolina	27,396,429	1.06%
24	Louisiana	26,439,066	1.03%
25	Alaska	25,604,478	0.99%
26	Iowa	24,298,070	0.94%
27	Tennessee	19,788,254	0.77%
28	Oklahoma	18,881,075	0.73%
29	Kentucky	18,613,571	0.72%
30	Utah	17,887,367	0.69%
31	Alabama	15,778,775	0.61%
32	Rhode Island	13,915,000	0.54%
33	New Mexico	13,201,428	0.51%
34	Hawaii	12,509,017	0.48%
35	West Virginia	10,806,870	0.42%
36	Montana	10,755,848	0.42%
37	Kansas	10,433,861	0.40%
38	Nebraska	10,180,974	0.39%
39	South Dakota	9,356,095	0.36%
40	Mississippi	7,679,031	0.30%
41	Arkansas	7,662,398	0.30%
42	Maine	6,963,526	0.27%
43	Nevada	6,615,554	0.26%
44	Delaware	6,497,266	0.25%
45	North Dakota	4,908,430	0.19%
46	Vermont	4,400,920	0.17%
47	Idaho	4,051,717	0.16%
48	New Hampshire	3,601,611	0.14%
NA	Oregon**	NA	NA
NA	Wyoming**	NA	NA
	District of Columbia	26,388,017	1.02%

Source: U.S. Department of Health and Human Services, Substance Abuse and Mental Health Services Administration "State Resources and Services Related to Alcohol and Other Drug Problems-Fiscal Year 1992" (SMA 94-2092 (1994))
*Total does not include $32,071,632 in Puerto Rico and $475,636 in Guam.
**Not available.

Expenditures per Alcohol and Other Drug Treatment Admission in 1992

National Rate = $1,458 per Admission*

ALPHA ORDER				RANK ORDER		
RANK	STATE	RATE		RANK	STATE	RATE
29	Alabama	$992		1	New York	$3,579
6	Alaska	1,795		2	Hawaii	2,823
16	Arizona	1,247		3	California	2,754
43	Arkansas	569		4	Connecticut	2,252
3	California	2,754		5	Maryland	1,959
46	Colorado	534		6	Alaska	1,795
4	Connecticut	2,252		7	Indiana	1,544
20	Delaware	1,101		8	Tennessee	1,511
14	Florida	1,312		9	Pennsylvania	1,477
35	Georgia	797		10	Virginia	1,437
2	Hawaii	2,823		11	Montana	1,388
45	Idaho	540		12	Illinois	1,337
12	Illinois	1,337		13	Ohio	1,328
7	Indiana	1,544		14	Florida	1,312
22	Iowa	1,081		15	Texas	1,293
42	Kansas	580		16	Arizona	1,247
44	Kentucky	554		17	Utah	1,153
27	Louisiana	1,019		18	New Jersey	1,152
32	Maine	851		19	Rhode Island	1,143
5	Maryland	1,959		20	Delaware	1,101
26	Massachusetts	1,028		21	Oklahoma	1,096
25	Michigan	1,038		22	Iowa	1,081
34	Minnesota	813		23	North Dakota	1,072
40	Mississippi	688		24	New Mexico	1,041
28	Missouri	1,018		25	Michigan	1,038
11	Montana	1,388		26	Massachusetts	1,028
47	Nebraska	384		27	Louisiana	1,019
33	Nevada	840		28	Missouri	1,018
41	New Hampshire	620		29	Alabama	992
18	New Jersey	1,152		30	South Carolina	973
24	New Mexico	1,041		31	West Virginia	923
1	New York	3,579		32	Maine	851
36	North Carolina	770		33	Nevada	840
23	North Dakota	1,072		34	Minnesota	813
13	Ohio	1,328		35	Georgia	797
21	Oklahoma	1,096		36	North Carolina	770
NA	Oregon**	NA		37	South Dakota	754
9	Pennsylvania	1,477		38	Vermont	719
19	Rhode Island	1,143		39	Wisconsin	707
30	South Carolina	973		40	Mississippi	688
37	South Dakota	754		41	New Hampshire	620
8	Tennessee	1,511		42	Kansas	580
15	Texas	1,293		43	Arkansas	569
17	Utah	1,153		44	Kentucky	554
38	Vermont	719		45	Idaho	540
10	Virginia	1,437		46	Colorado	534
NA	Washington**	NA		47	Nebraska	384
31	West Virginia	923		NA	Oregon**	NA
39	Wisconsin	707		NA	Washington**	NA
NA	Wyoming**	NA		NA	Wyoming**	NA

District of Columbia 2,272

Source: Morgan Quitno Corporation using data from U.S. Department of Health and Human Services, Substance Abuse
and Mental Health Services Administration
"State Resources and Services Related to Alcohol and Other Drug Problems-Fiscal Year 1992" (SMA 94-2092 (1994))
*Does not include admissions in U.S. territories. Data are only from treatment units that received at least some funds
administered by a state's alcohol/drug agency in fiscal year 1992.
**Not available.

Per Capita Expenditures for State–Supported Alcohol and Other Drug Abuse Treatment Programs in 1992
National Per Capita = $10.11*

<table>
<tr><td colspan="3"><u>ALPHA ORDER</u></td><td colspan="3"><u>RANK ORDER</u></td></tr>
<tr><td>RANK</td><td>STATE</td><td>PER CAPITA</td><td>RANK</td><td>STATE</td><td>PER CAPITA</td></tr>
<tr><td>43</td><td>Alabama</td><td>$3.81</td><td>1</td><td>Alaska</td><td>$43.55</td></tr>
<tr><td>1</td><td>Alaska</td><td>43.55</td><td>2</td><td>New York</td><td>29.34</td></tr>
<tr><td>20</td><td>Arizona</td><td>8.36</td><td>3</td><td>Connecticut</td><td>22.11</td></tr>
<tr><td>47</td><td>Arkansas</td><td>3.20</td><td>4</td><td>Wisconsin</td><td>17.17</td></tr>
<tr><td>10</td><td>California</td><td>11.98</td><td>5</td><td>Massachusetts</td><td>14.47</td></tr>
<tr><td>13</td><td>Colorado</td><td>9.91</td><td>6</td><td>Maryland</td><td>14.16</td></tr>
<tr><td>3</td><td>Connecticut</td><td>22.11</td><td>7</td><td>Rhode Island</td><td>13.90</td></tr>
<tr><td>18</td><td>Delaware</td><td>9.40</td><td>8</td><td>South Dakota</td><td>13.21</td></tr>
<tr><td>16</td><td>Florida</td><td>9.48</td><td>9</td><td>Montana</td><td>13.08</td></tr>
<tr><td>30</td><td>Georgia</td><td>6.93</td><td>10</td><td>California</td><td>11.98</td></tr>
<tr><td>12</td><td>Hawaii</td><td>10.82</td><td>11</td><td>Minnesota</td><td>10.94</td></tr>
<tr><td>44</td><td>Idaho</td><td>3.80</td><td>12</td><td>Hawaii</td><td>10.82</td></tr>
<tr><td>17</td><td>Illinois</td><td>9.42</td><td>13</td><td>Colorado</td><td>9.91</td></tr>
<tr><td>32</td><td>Indiana</td><td>6.53</td><td>14</td><td>Utah</td><td>9.88</td></tr>
<tr><td>19</td><td>Iowa</td><td>8.67</td><td>15</td><td>Washington</td><td>9.64</td></tr>
<tr><td>41</td><td>Kansas</td><td>4.15</td><td>16</td><td>Florida</td><td>9.48</td></tr>
<tr><td>38</td><td>Kentucky</td><td>4.96</td><td>17</td><td>Illinois</td><td>9.42</td></tr>
<tr><td>34</td><td>Louisiana</td><td>6.18</td><td>18</td><td>Delaware</td><td>9.40</td></tr>
<tr><td>37</td><td>Maine</td><td>5.63</td><td>19</td><td>Iowa</td><td>8.67</td></tr>
<tr><td>6</td><td>Maryland</td><td>14.16</td><td>20</td><td>Arizona</td><td>8.36</td></tr>
<tr><td>5</td><td>Massachusetts</td><td>14.47</td><td>20</td><td>Michigan</td><td>8.36</td></tr>
<tr><td>20</td><td>Michigan</td><td>8.36</td><td>22</td><td>New Mexico</td><td>8.34</td></tr>
<tr><td>11</td><td>Minnesota</td><td>10.94</td><td>23</td><td>Ohio</td><td>8.25</td></tr>
<tr><td>48</td><td>Mississippi</td><td>2.94</td><td>24</td><td>Virginia</td><td>8.23</td></tr>
<tr><td>31</td><td>Missouri</td><td>6.67</td><td>25</td><td>Pennsylvania</td><td>8.06</td></tr>
<tr><td>9</td><td>Montana</td><td>13.08</td><td>26</td><td>New Jersey</td><td>7.80</td></tr>
<tr><td>33</td><td>Nebraska</td><td>6.36</td><td>27</td><td>North Dakota</td><td>7.74</td></tr>
<tr><td>39</td><td>Nevada</td><td>4.95</td><td>28</td><td>Vermont</td><td>7.71</td></tr>
<tr><td>46</td><td>New Hampshire</td><td>3.23</td><td>29</td><td>South Carolina</td><td>7.60</td></tr>
<tr><td>26</td><td>New Jersey</td><td>7.80</td><td>30</td><td>Georgia</td><td>6.93</td></tr>
<tr><td>22</td><td>New Mexico</td><td>8.34</td><td>31</td><td>Missouri</td><td>6.67</td></tr>
<tr><td>2</td><td>New York</td><td>29.34</td><td>32</td><td>Indiana</td><td>6.53</td></tr>
<tr><td>40</td><td>North Carolina</td><td>4.86</td><td>33</td><td>Nebraska</td><td>6.36</td></tr>
<tr><td>27</td><td>North Dakota</td><td>7.74</td><td>34</td><td>Louisiana</td><td>6.18</td></tr>
<tr><td>23</td><td>Ohio</td><td>8.25</td><td>35</td><td>West Virginia</td><td>5.97</td></tr>
<tr><td>36</td><td>Oklahoma</td><td>5.89</td><td>36</td><td>Oklahoma</td><td>5.89</td></tr>
<tr><td>NA</td><td>Oregon**</td><td>NA</td><td>37</td><td>Maine</td><td>5.63</td></tr>
<tr><td>25</td><td>Pennsylvania</td><td>8.06</td><td>38</td><td>Kentucky</td><td>4.96</td></tr>
<tr><td>7</td><td>Rhode Island</td><td>13.90</td><td>39</td><td>Nevada</td><td>4.95</td></tr>
<tr><td>29</td><td>South Carolina</td><td>7.60</td><td>40</td><td>North Carolina</td><td>4.86</td></tr>
<tr><td>8</td><td>South Dakota</td><td>13.21</td><td>41</td><td>Kansas</td><td>4.15</td></tr>
<tr><td>42</td><td>Tennessee</td><td>3.94</td><td>42</td><td>Tennessee</td><td>3.94</td></tr>
<tr><td>45</td><td>Texas</td><td>3.66</td><td>43</td><td>Alabama</td><td>3.81</td></tr>
<tr><td>14</td><td>Utah</td><td>9.88</td><td>44</td><td>Idaho</td><td>3.80</td></tr>
<tr><td>28</td><td>Vermont</td><td>7.71</td><td>45</td><td>Texas</td><td>3.66</td></tr>
<tr><td>24</td><td>Virginia</td><td>8.23</td><td>46</td><td>New Hampshire</td><td>3.23</td></tr>
<tr><td>15</td><td>Washington</td><td>9.64</td><td>47</td><td>Arkansas</td><td>3.20</td></tr>
<tr><td>35</td><td>West Virginia</td><td>5.97</td><td>48</td><td>Mississippi</td><td>2.94</td></tr>
<tr><td>4</td><td>Wisconsin</td><td>17.17</td><td>NA</td><td>Oregon**</td><td>NA</td></tr>
<tr><td>NA</td><td>Wyoming**</td><td>NA</td><td>NA</td><td>Wyoming**</td><td>NA</td></tr>
</table>

District of Columbia   45.11

Source: Morgan Quitno Corporation using data from U.S. Department of Health and Human Services, Substance Abuse and Mental Health Services Administration

"State Resources and Services Related to Alcohol and Other Drug Problems-Fiscal Year 1992" (SMA 94-2092 (1994))

*National per capita does not include expenditures in Puerto Rico and Guam.

**Not available.

Expenditures for State-Supported Alcohol and
Other Drug Abuse Prevention Programs in 1992
National Total = $509,998,743*

RANK	STATE	EXPENDITURES	% of USA
30	Alabama	$2,883,956	0.57%
15	Alaska	8,012,275	1.57%
28	Arizona	3,697,077	0.72%
36	Arkansas	2,056,287	0.40%
2	California	67,994,653	13.33%
18	Colorado	6,984,107	1.37%
16	Connecticut	7,312,695	1.43%
47	Delaware	668,723	0.13%
10	Florida	15,961,123	3.13%
29	Georgia	3,491,289	0.68%
39	Hawaii	1,505,499	0.30%
45	Idaho	893,360	0.18%
8	Illinois	19,157,700	3.76%
19	Indiana	6,901,561	1.35%
24	Iowa	5,459,598	1.07%
32	Kansas	2,717,182	0.53%
25	Kentucky	4,486,036	0.88%
34	Louisiana	2,400,877	0.47%
44	Maine	1,002,352	0.20%
13	Maryland	9,091,552	1.78%
17	Massachusetts	7,148,304	1.40%
7	Michigan	19,647,887	3.85%
26	Minnesota	4,445,906	0.87%
40	Mississippi	1,362,302	0.27%
23	Missouri	5,538,004	1.09%
37	Montana	2,033,853	0.40%
33	Nebraska	2,511,651	0.49%
38	Nevada	1,656,115	0.32%
46	New Hampshire	864,735	0.17%
9	New Jersey	18,868,000	3.70%
41	New Mexico	1,348,938	0.26%
1	New York	93,242,426	18.28%
12	North Carolina	9,867,155	1.93%
48	North Dakota	400,596	0.08%
4	Ohio	30,569,088	5.99%
31	Oklahoma	2,873,474	0.56%
NA	Oregon**	NA	NA
5	Pennsylvania	29,213,067	5.73%
21	Rhode Island	5,877,000	1.15%
11	South Carolina	13,343,875	2.62%
43	South Dakota	1,038,991	0.20%
22	Tennessee	5,628,153	1.10%
3	Texas	33,684,118	6.60%
20	Utah	5,924,381	1.16%
35	Vermont	2,251,131	0.44%
14	Virginia	8,727,377	1.71%
27	Washington	4,179,739	0.82%
42	West Virginia	1,081,826	0.21%
6	Wisconsin	20,171,258	3.96%
NA	Wyoming**	NA	NA

RANK	STATE	EXPENDITURES	% of USA
1	New York	$93,242,426	18.28%
2	California	67,994,653	13.33%
3	Texas	33,684,118	6.60%
4	Ohio	30,569,088	5.99%
5	Pennsylvania	29,213,067	5.73%
6	Wisconsin	20,171,258	3.96%
7	Michigan	19,647,887	3.85%
8	Illinois	19,157,700	3.76%
9	New Jersey	18,868,000	3.70%
10	Florida	15,961,123	3.13%
11	South Carolina	13,343,875	2.62%
12	North Carolina	9,867,155	1.93%
13	Maryland	9,091,552	1.78%
14	Virginia	8,727,377	1.71%
15	Alaska	8,012,275	1.57%
16	Connecticut	7,312,695	1.43%
17	Massachusetts	7,148,304	1.40%
18	Colorado	6,984,107	1.37%
19	Indiana	6,901,561	1.35%
20	Utah	5,924,381	1.16%
21	Rhode Island	5,877,000	1.15%
22	Tennessee	5,628,153	1.10%
23	Missouri	5,538,004	1.09%
24	Iowa	5,459,598	1.07%
25	Kentucky	4,486,036	0.88%
26	Minnesota	4,445,906	0.87%
27	Washington	4,179,739	0.82%
28	Arizona	3,697,077	0.72%
29	Georgia	3,491,289	0.68%
30	Alabama	2,883,956	0.57%
31	Oklahoma	2,873,474	0.56%
32	Kansas	2,717,182	0.53%
33	Nebraska	2,511,651	0.49%
34	Louisiana	2,400,877	0.47%
35	Vermont	2,251,131	0.44%
36	Arkansas	2,056,287	0.40%
37	Montana	2,033,853	0.40%
38	Nevada	1,656,115	0.32%
39	Hawaii	1,505,499	0.30%
40	Mississippi	1,362,302	0.27%
41	New Mexico	1,348,938	0.26%
42	West Virginia	1,081,826	0.21%
43	South Dakota	1,038,991	0.20%
44	Maine	1,002,352	0.20%
45	Idaho	893,360	0.18%
46	New Hampshire	864,735	0.17%
47	Delaware	668,723	0.13%
48	North Dakota	400,596	0.08%
NA	Oregon**	NA	NA
NA	Wyoming**	NA	NA
	District of Columbia	3,821,491	0.75%

Source: U.S. Department of Health and Human Services, Substance Abuse and Mental Health Services Administration
"State Resources and Services Related to Alcohol and Other Drug Problems-Fiscal Year 1992" (SMA 94-2092 (1994))
Total does not include $9,849,673 in Puerto Rico and $195,530 in Guam.
**Not available.*

Per Capita Expenditures for State-Supported Alcohol and Other Drug Abuse Prevention Programs in 1992
National Per Capita = $2.00*

<table>
<tr><td colspan="3">ALPHA ORDER</td><td colspan="3">RANK ORDER</td></tr>
<tr><td>RANK</td><td>STATE</td><td>PER CAPITA</td><td>RANK</td><td>STATE</td><td>PER CAPITA</td></tr>
<tr><td>43</td><td>Alabama</td><td>$0.70</td><td>1</td><td>Alaska</td><td>$13.63</td></tr>
<tr><td>1</td><td>Alaska</td><td>13.63</td><td>2</td><td>Rhode Island</td><td>5.87</td></tr>
<tr><td>35</td><td>Arizona</td><td>0.96</td><td>3</td><td>New York</td><td>5.15</td></tr>
<tr><td>37</td><td>Arkansas</td><td>0.86</td><td>4</td><td>Wisconsin</td><td>4.04</td></tr>
<tr><td>13</td><td>California</td><td>2.20</td><td>5</td><td>Vermont</td><td>3.94</td></tr>
<tr><td>15</td><td>Colorado</td><td>2.02</td><td>6</td><td>South Carolina</td><td>3.70</td></tr>
<tr><td>12</td><td>Connecticut</td><td>2.23</td><td>7</td><td>Utah</td><td>3.27</td></tr>
<tr><td>34</td><td>Delaware</td><td>0.97</td><td>8</td><td>Ohio</td><td>2.77</td></tr>
<tr><td>29</td><td>Florida</td><td>1.18</td><td>9</td><td>Montana</td><td>2.47</td></tr>
<tr><td>47</td><td>Georgia</td><td>0.52</td><td>10</td><td>Pennsylvania</td><td>2.44</td></tr>
<tr><td>24</td><td>Hawaii</td><td>1.30</td><td>11</td><td>New Jersey</td><td>2.41</td></tr>
<tr><td>39</td><td>Idaho</td><td>0.84</td><td>12</td><td>Connecticut</td><td>2.23</td></tr>
<tr><td>19</td><td>Illinois</td><td>1.65</td><td>13</td><td>California</td><td>2.20</td></tr>
<tr><td>26</td><td>Indiana</td><td>1.22</td><td>14</td><td>Michigan</td><td>2.08</td></tr>
<tr><td>16</td><td>Iowa</td><td>1.95</td><td>15</td><td>Colorado</td><td>2.02</td></tr>
<tr><td>31</td><td>Kansas</td><td>1.08</td><td>16</td><td>Iowa</td><td>1.95</td></tr>
<tr><td>27</td><td>Kentucky</td><td>1.20</td><td>17</td><td>Texas</td><td>1.90</td></tr>
<tr><td>46</td><td>Louisiana</td><td>0.56</td><td>18</td><td>Maryland</td><td>1.85</td></tr>
<tr><td>40</td><td>Maine</td><td>0.81</td><td>19</td><td>Illinois</td><td>1.65</td></tr>
<tr><td>18</td><td>Maryland</td><td>1.85</td><td>20</td><td>Nebraska</td><td>1.57</td></tr>
<tr><td>28</td><td>Massachusetts</td><td>1.19</td><td>21</td><td>South Dakota</td><td>1.47</td></tr>
<tr><td>14</td><td>Michigan</td><td>2.08</td><td>22</td><td>North Carolina</td><td>1.44</td></tr>
<tr><td>33</td><td>Minnesota</td><td>1.00</td><td>23</td><td>Virginia</td><td>1.36</td></tr>
<tr><td>47</td><td>Mississippi</td><td>0.52</td><td>24</td><td>Hawaii</td><td>1.30</td></tr>
<tr><td>32</td><td>Missouri</td><td>1.07</td><td>25</td><td>Nevada</td><td>1.24</td></tr>
<tr><td>9</td><td>Montana</td><td>2.47</td><td>26</td><td>Indiana</td><td>1.22</td></tr>
<tr><td>20</td><td>Nebraska</td><td>1.57</td><td>27</td><td>Kentucky</td><td>1.20</td></tr>
<tr><td>25</td><td>Nevada</td><td>1.24</td><td>28</td><td>Massachusetts</td><td>1.19</td></tr>
<tr><td>42</td><td>New Hampshire</td><td>0.78</td><td>29</td><td>Florida</td><td>1.18</td></tr>
<tr><td>11</td><td>New Jersey</td><td>2.41</td><td>30</td><td>Tennessee</td><td>1.12</td></tr>
<tr><td>38</td><td>New Mexico</td><td>0.85</td><td>31</td><td>Kansas</td><td>1.08</td></tr>
<tr><td>3</td><td>New York</td><td>5.15</td><td>32</td><td>Missouri</td><td>1.07</td></tr>
<tr><td>22</td><td>North Carolina</td><td>1.44</td><td>33</td><td>Minnesota</td><td>1.00</td></tr>
<tr><td>44</td><td>North Dakota</td><td>0.63</td><td>34</td><td>Delaware</td><td>0.97</td></tr>
<tr><td>8</td><td>Ohio</td><td>2.77</td><td>35</td><td>Arizona</td><td>0.96</td></tr>
<tr><td>36</td><td>Oklahoma</td><td>0.90</td><td>36</td><td>Oklahoma</td><td>0.90</td></tr>
<tr><td>NA</td><td>Oregon**</td><td>NA</td><td>37</td><td>Arkansas</td><td>0.86</td></tr>
<tr><td>10</td><td>Pennsylvania</td><td>2.44</td><td>38</td><td>New Mexico</td><td>0.85</td></tr>
<tr><td>2</td><td>Rhode Island</td><td>5.87</td><td>39</td><td>Idaho</td><td>0.84</td></tr>
<tr><td>6</td><td>South Carolina</td><td>3.70</td><td>40</td><td>Maine</td><td>0.81</td></tr>
<tr><td>21</td><td>South Dakota</td><td>1.47</td><td>40</td><td>Washington</td><td>0.81</td></tr>
<tr><td>30</td><td>Tennessee</td><td>1.12</td><td>42</td><td>New Hampshire</td><td>0.78</td></tr>
<tr><td>17</td><td>Texas</td><td>1.90</td><td>43</td><td>Alabama</td><td>0.70</td></tr>
<tr><td>7</td><td>Utah</td><td>3.27</td><td>44</td><td>North Dakota</td><td>0.63</td></tr>
<tr><td>5</td><td>Vermont</td><td>3.94</td><td>45</td><td>West Virginia</td><td>0.60</td></tr>
<tr><td>23</td><td>Virginia</td><td>1.36</td><td>46</td><td>Louisiana</td><td>0.56</td></tr>
<tr><td>40</td><td>Washington</td><td>0.81</td><td>47</td><td>Georgia</td><td>0.52</td></tr>
<tr><td>45</td><td>West Virginia</td><td>0.60</td><td>47</td><td>Mississippi</td><td>0.52</td></tr>
<tr><td>4</td><td>Wisconsin</td><td>4.04</td><td>NA</td><td>Oregon**</td><td>NA</td></tr>
<tr><td>NA</td><td>Wyoming**</td><td>NA</td><td>NA</td><td>Wyoming**</td><td>NA</td></tr>
<tr><td></td><td></td><td></td><td></td><td>District of Columbia</td><td>6.53</td></tr>
</table>

Source: Morgan Quitno Corporation using data from U.S. Department of Health and Human Services, Substance Abuse and Mental Health Services Administration
"State Resources and Services Related to Alcohol and Other Drug Problems-Fiscal Year 1992" (SMA 94-2092 (1994))
*National per capita does not include expenditures in Puerto Rico and Guam.
**Not available.

IV. FINANCE

State and Local Government Expenditures for Justice Activities in 1992

National Total = $79,502,478,000*

<table>
<tr><td colspan="4">ALPHA ORDER</td><td colspan="4">RANK ORDER</td></tr>
<tr><td>RANK</td><td>STATE</td><td>EXPENDITURES</td><td>% of USA</td><td>RANK</td><td>STATE</td><td>EXPENDITURES</td><td>% of USA</td></tr>
<tr><td>27</td><td>Alabama</td><td>$824,974,000</td><td>1.04%</td><td>1</td><td>California</td><td>$14,031,698,000</td><td>17.65%</td></tr>
<tr><td>36</td><td>Alaska</td><td>365,943,000</td><td>0.46%</td><td>2</td><td>New York</td><td>8,999,947,000</td><td>11.32%</td></tr>
<tr><td>17</td><td>Arizona</td><td>1,404,385,000</td><td>1.77%</td><td>3</td><td>Florida</td><td>5,152,905,000</td><td>6.48%</td></tr>
<tr><td>37</td><td>Arkansas</td><td>365,641,000</td><td>0.46%</td><td>4</td><td>Texas</td><td>4,595,617,000</td><td>5.78%</td></tr>
<tr><td>1</td><td>California</td><td>14,031,698,000</td><td>17.65%</td><td>5</td><td>Illinois</td><td>3,255,123,000</td><td>4.09%</td></tr>
<tr><td>22</td><td>Colorado</td><td>1,050,659,000</td><td>1.32%</td><td>6</td><td>Michigan</td><td>2,985,090,000</td><td>3.75%</td></tr>
<tr><td>20</td><td>Connecticut</td><td>1,090,612,000</td><td>1.37%</td><td>7</td><td>Pennsylvania</td><td>2,943,759,000</td><td>3.70%</td></tr>
<tr><td>42</td><td>Delaware</td><td>258,909,000</td><td>0.33%</td><td>8</td><td>New Jersey</td><td>2,887,203,000</td><td>3.63%</td></tr>
<tr><td>3</td><td>Florida</td><td>5,152,905,000</td><td>6.48%</td><td>9</td><td>Ohio</td><td>2,882,897,000</td><td>3.63%</td></tr>
<tr><td>10</td><td>Georgia</td><td>1,806,160,000</td><td>2.27%</td><td>10</td><td>Georgia</td><td>1,806,160,000</td><td>2.27%</td></tr>
<tr><td>34</td><td>Hawaii</td><td>406,794,000</td><td>0.51%</td><td>11</td><td>Massachusetts</td><td>1,780,609,000</td><td>2.24%</td></tr>
<tr><td>44</td><td>Idaho</td><td>234,113,000</td><td>0.29%</td><td>12</td><td>Maryland</td><td>1,709,356,000</td><td>2.15%</td></tr>
<tr><td>5</td><td>Illinois</td><td>3,255,123,000</td><td>4.09%</td><td>13</td><td>Virginia</td><td>1,697,987,000</td><td>2.14%</td></tr>
<tr><td>23</td><td>Indiana</td><td>1,025,668,000</td><td>1.29%</td><td>14</td><td>Washington</td><td>1,679,415,000</td><td>2.11%</td></tr>
<tr><td>33</td><td>Iowa</td><td>451,868,000</td><td>0.57%</td><td>15</td><td>North Carolina</td><td>1,609,322,000</td><td>2.02%</td></tr>
<tr><td>31</td><td>Kansas</td><td>603,593,000</td><td>0.76%</td><td>16</td><td>Wisconsin</td><td>1,466,677,000</td><td>1.84%</td></tr>
<tr><td>28</td><td>Kentucky</td><td>722,382,000</td><td>0.91%</td><td>17</td><td>Arizona</td><td>1,404,385,000</td><td>1.77%</td></tr>
<tr><td>19</td><td>Louisiana</td><td>1,095,766,000</td><td>1.38%</td><td>18</td><td>Tennessee</td><td>1,135,415,000</td><td>1.43%</td></tr>
<tr><td>43</td><td>Maine</td><td>248,347,000</td><td>0.31%</td><td>19</td><td>Louisiana</td><td>1,095,766,000</td><td>1.38%</td></tr>
<tr><td>12</td><td>Maryland</td><td>1,709,356,000</td><td>2.15%</td><td>20</td><td>Connecticut</td><td>1,090,612,000</td><td>1.37%</td></tr>
<tr><td>11</td><td>Massachusetts</td><td>1,780,609,000</td><td>2.24%</td><td>21</td><td>Minnesota</td><td>1,078,098,000</td><td>1.36%</td></tr>
<tr><td>6</td><td>Michigan</td><td>2,985,090,000</td><td>3.75%</td><td>22</td><td>Colorado</td><td>1,050,659,000</td><td>1.32%</td></tr>
<tr><td>21</td><td>Minnesota</td><td>1,078,098,000</td><td>1.36%</td><td>23</td><td>Indiana</td><td>1,025,668,000</td><td>1.29%</td></tr>
<tr><td>38</td><td>Mississippi</td><td>356,028,000</td><td>0.45%</td><td>24</td><td>Missouri</td><td>1,020,275,000</td><td>1.28%</td></tr>
<tr><td>24</td><td>Missouri</td><td>1,020,275,000</td><td>1.28%</td><td>25</td><td>South Carolina</td><td>868,865,000</td><td>1.09%</td></tr>
<tr><td>46</td><td>Montana</td><td>172,622,000</td><td>0.22%</td><td>26</td><td>Oregon</td><td>851,264,000</td><td>1.07%</td></tr>
<tr><td>39</td><td>Nebraska</td><td>310,157,000</td><td>0.39%</td><td>27</td><td>Alabama</td><td>824,974,000</td><td>1.04%</td></tr>
<tr><td>30</td><td>Nevada</td><td>607,049,000</td><td>0.76%</td><td>28</td><td>Kentucky</td><td>722,382,000</td><td>0.91%</td></tr>
<tr><td>41</td><td>New Hampshire</td><td>269,256,000</td><td>0.34%</td><td>29</td><td>Oklahoma</td><td>622,651,000</td><td>0.78%</td></tr>
<tr><td>8</td><td>New Jersey</td><td>2,887,203,000</td><td>3.63%</td><td>30</td><td>Nevada</td><td>607,049,000</td><td>0.76%</td></tr>
<tr><td>32</td><td>New Mexico</td><td>462,872,000</td><td>0.58%</td><td>31</td><td>Kansas</td><td>603,593,000</td><td>0.76%</td></tr>
<tr><td>2</td><td>New York</td><td>8,999,947,000</td><td>11.32%</td><td>32</td><td>New Mexico</td><td>462,872,000</td><td>0.58%</td></tr>
<tr><td>15</td><td>North Carolina</td><td>1,609,322,000</td><td>2.02%</td><td>33</td><td>Iowa</td><td>451,868,000</td><td>0.57%</td></tr>
<tr><td>50</td><td>North Dakota</td><td>98,183,000</td><td>0.12%</td><td>34</td><td>Hawaii</td><td>406,794,000</td><td>0.51%</td></tr>
<tr><td>9</td><td>Ohio</td><td>2,882,897,000</td><td>3.63%</td><td>35</td><td>Utah</td><td>396,298,000</td><td>0.50%</td></tr>
<tr><td>29</td><td>Oklahoma</td><td>622,651,000</td><td>0.78%</td><td>36</td><td>Alaska</td><td>365,943,000</td><td>0.46%</td></tr>
<tr><td>26</td><td>Oregon</td><td>851,264,000</td><td>1.07%</td><td>37</td><td>Arkansas</td><td>365,641,000</td><td>0.46%</td></tr>
<tr><td>7</td><td>Pennsylvania</td><td>2,943,759,000</td><td>3.70%</td><td>38</td><td>Mississippi</td><td>356,028,000</td><td>0.45%</td></tr>
<tr><td>40</td><td>Rhode Island</td><td>302,615,000</td><td>0.38%</td><td>39</td><td>Nebraska</td><td>310,157,000</td><td>0.39%</td></tr>
<tr><td>25</td><td>South Carolina</td><td>868,865,000</td><td>1.09%</td><td>40</td><td>Rhode Island</td><td>302,615,000</td><td>0.38%</td></tr>
<tr><td>48</td><td>South Dakota</td><td>120,592,000</td><td>0.15%</td><td>41</td><td>New Hampshire</td><td>269,256,000</td><td>0.34%</td></tr>
<tr><td>18</td><td>Tennessee</td><td>1,135,415,000</td><td>1.43%</td><td>42</td><td>Delaware</td><td>258,909,000</td><td>0.33%</td></tr>
<tr><td>4</td><td>Texas</td><td>4,595,617,000</td><td>5.78%</td><td>43</td><td>Maine</td><td>248,347,000</td><td>0.31%</td></tr>
<tr><td>35</td><td>Utah</td><td>396,298,000</td><td>0.50%</td><td>44</td><td>Idaho</td><td>234,113,000</td><td>0.29%</td></tr>
<tr><td>49</td><td>Vermont</td><td>118,017,000</td><td>0.15%</td><td>45</td><td>West Virginia</td><td>211,503,000</td><td>0.27%</td></tr>
<tr><td>13</td><td>Virginia</td><td>1,697,987,000</td><td>2.14%</td><td>46</td><td>Montana</td><td>172,622,000</td><td>0.22%</td></tr>
<tr><td>14</td><td>Washington</td><td>1,679,415,000</td><td>2.11%</td><td>47</td><td>Wyoming</td><td>148,259,000</td><td>0.19%</td></tr>
<tr><td>45</td><td>West Virginia</td><td>211,503,000</td><td>0.27%</td><td>48</td><td>South Dakota</td><td>120,592,000</td><td>0.15%</td></tr>
<tr><td>16</td><td>Wisconsin</td><td>1,466,677,000</td><td>1.84%</td><td>49</td><td>Vermont</td><td>118,017,000</td><td>0.15%</td></tr>
<tr><td>47</td><td>Wyoming</td><td>148,259,000</td><td>0.19%</td><td>50</td><td>North Dakota</td><td>98,183,000</td><td>0.12%</td></tr>
<tr><td></td><td></td><td></td><td></td><td colspan="2">District of Columbia</td><td>719,040,000</td><td>0.90%</td></tr>
</table>

Source: Morgan Quitno Corporation using data from U.S. Bureau of the Census
"Government Finances: 1991-92 (Preliminary Report)" (August 1994, GF/92-5P)
*Direct expenditures. Preliminary data. Includes Police Protection, Corrections and Judicial and Legal Services.

Per Capita State and Local Government Expenditures for Justice Activities in 1992

National Per Capita = $311.68*

ALPHA ORDER				RANK ORDER		
RANK	STATE	PER CAPITA		RANK	STATE	PER CAPITA
39	Alabama	$199.37		1	Alaska	$622.35
1	Alaska	622.35		2	New York	496.99
8	Arizona	366.49		3	Nevada	454.38
48	Arkansas	152.73		4	California	454.17
4	California	454.17		5	Florida	382.18
15	Colorado	303.22		6	Delaware	374.69
11	Connecticut	332.61		7	New Jersey	369.21
6	Delaware	374.69		8	Arizona	366.49
5	Florida	382.18		9	Hawaii	351.90
22	Georgia	266.67		10	Maryland	347.64
9	Hawaii	351.90		11	Connecticut	332.61
34	Idaho	219.62		12	Washington	326.54
21	Illinois	280.30		13	Wyoming	318.84
44	Indiana	181.28		14	Michigan	316.42
46	Iowa	161.21		15	Colorado	303.22
31	Kansas	240.00		16	Rhode Island	302.31
43	Kentucky	192.43		17	Massachusetts	297.11
26	Louisiana	256.08		18	Wisconsin	293.75
38	Maine	200.93		19	New Mexico	292.59
10	Maryland	347.64		20	Oregon	286.43
17	Massachusetts	297.11		21	Illinois	280.30
14	Michigan	316.42		22	Georgia	266.67
29	Minnesota	241.29		23	Virginia	265.56
49	Mississippi	136.15		24	Ohio	261.58
40	Missouri	196.55		25	Texas	259.89
36	Montana	210.00		26	Louisiana	256.08
42	Nebraska	193.73		27	Pennsylvania	245.42
3	Nevada	454.38		28	New Hampshire	241.49
28	New Hampshire	241.49		29	Minnesota	241.29
7	New Jersey	369.21		30	South Carolina	241.15
19	New Mexico	292.59		31	Kansas	240.00
2	New York	496.99		32	North Carolina	235.42
32	North Carolina	235.42		33	Tennessee	225.95
47	North Dakota	154.86		34	Idaho	219.62
24	Ohio	261.58		35	Utah	218.83
41	Oklahoma	194.27		36	Montana	210.00
20	Oregon	286.43		37	Vermont	206.68
27	Pennsylvania	245.42		38	Maine	200.93
16	Rhode Island	302.31		39	Alabama	199.37
30	South Carolina	241.15		40	Missouri	196.55
45	South Dakota	170.33		41	Oklahoma	194.27
33	Tennessee	225.95		42	Nebraska	193.73
25	Texas	259.89		43	Kentucky	192.43
35	Utah	218.83		44	Indiana	181.28
37	Vermont	206.68		45	South Dakota	170.33
23	Virginia	265.56		46	Iowa	161.21
12	Washington	326.54		47	North Dakota	154.86
50	West Virginia	116.92		48	Arkansas	152.73
18	Wisconsin	293.75		49	Mississippi	136.15
13	Wyoming	318.84		50	West Virginia	116.92
					District of Columbia	1,229.13

Source: Morgan Quitno Corporation using data from U.S. Bureau of the Census
"Government Finances: 1991-92 (Preliminary Report)" (August 1994, GF/92-5P)
*Direct expenditures. Preliminary data. Includes Police Protection, Corrections and Judicial and Legal Services.

State and Local Government Expenditures for Justice Activities
As a Percent of All Direct Expenditures in 1992
National Percent = 6.93% of Direct Expenditures*

ALPHA ORDER			RANK ORDER		
RANK	STATE	PERCENT	RANK	STATE	PERCENT
34	Alabama	5.47	1	Florida	9.52
32	Alaska	5.55	2	Nevada	9.48
3	Arizona	8.83	3	Arizona	8.83
41	Arkansas	4.99	4	California	8.76
4	California	8.76	5	Maryland	8.29
13	Colorado	6.95	6	Delaware	7.91
19	Connecticut	6.33	7	New York	7.26
6	Delaware	7.91	8	Michigan	7.22
1	Florida	9.52	8	Virginia	7.22
14	Georgia	6.93	10	Texas	7.08
25	Hawaii	6.10	11	New Mexico	7.02
17	Idaho	6.42	12	Illinois	6.96
12	Illinois	6.96	13	Colorado	6.95
40	Indiana	5.16	14	Georgia	6.93
48	Iowa	4.07	15	New Jersey	6.82
21	Kansas	6.28	16	Wisconsin	6.69
38	Kentucky	5.33	17	Idaho	6.42
23	Louisiana	6.22	18	North Carolina	6.34
44	Maine	4.75	19	Connecticut	6.33
5	Maryland	8.29	19	Ohio	6.33
30	Massachusetts	5.84	21	Kansas	6.28
8	Michigan	7.22	22	South Carolina	6.23
43	Minnesota	4.76	23	Louisiana	6.22
46	Mississippi	4.22	24	Oregon	6.19
27	Missouri	6.00	25	Hawaii	6.10
39	Montana	5.19	26	Washington	6.07
47	Nebraska	4.19	27	Missouri	6.00
2	Nevada	9.48	28	Rhode Island	5.90
29	New Hampshire	5.89	29	New Hampshire	5.89
15	New Jersey	6.82	30	Massachusetts	5.84
11	New Mexico	7.02	31	Tennessee	5.75
7	New York	7.26	32	Alaska	5.55
18	North Carolina	6.34	33	Pennsylvania	5.54
49	North Dakota	3.64	34	Alabama	5.47
19	Ohio	6.33	35	Utah	5.45
37	Oklahoma	5.36	36	Wyoming	5.43
24	Oregon	6.19	37	Oklahoma	5.36
33	Pennsylvania	5.54	38	Kentucky	5.33
28	Rhode Island	5.90	39	Montana	5.19
22	South Carolina	6.23	40	Indiana	5.16
42	South Dakota	4.92	41	Arkansas	4.99
31	Tennessee	5.75	42	South Dakota	4.92
10	Texas	7.08	43	Minnesota	4.76
35	Utah	5.45	44	Maine	4.75
45	Vermont	4.57	45	Vermont	4.57
8	Virginia	7.22	46	Mississippi	4.22
26	Washington	6.07	47	Nebraska	4.19
50	West Virginia	3.10	48	Iowa	4.07
16	Wisconsin	6.69	49	North Dakota	3.64
36	Wyoming	5.43	50	West Virginia	3.10
				District of Columbia	12.35

Source: Morgan Quitno Corporation using data from U.S. Bureau of the Census
"Government Finances: 1991–92 (Preliminary Report)" (August 1994, GF/92-5P)
*Direct expenditures. Preliminary data. Includes Police Protection, Corrections and Judicial and Legal Services.

State Government Expenditures for Justice Activities in 1992

National Total = $29,495,331,000*

ALPHA ORDER

RANK	STATE	EXPENDITURES	% of USA
27	Alabama	$374,706,000	1.27%
31	Alaska	275,482,000	0.93%
17	Arizona	480,231,000	1.63%
38	Arkansas	167,611,000	0.57%
1	California	3,964,910,000	13.44%
22	Colorado	419,302,000	1.42%
16	Connecticut	680,846,000	2.31%
34	Delaware	189,849,000	0.64%
3	Florida	1,708,610,000	5.79%
13	Georgia	727,823,000	2.47%
33	Hawaii	213,148,000	0.72%
44	Idaho	105,230,000	0.36%
8	Illinois	990,517,000	3.36%
20	Indiana	439,735,000	1.49%
39	Iowa	160,953,000	0.55%
30	Kansas	294,778,000	1.00%
24	Kentucky	403,534,000	1.37%
23	Louisiana	414,581,000	1.41%
42	Maine	129,604,000	0.44%
12	Maryland	895,355,000	3.04%
10	Massachusetts	910,721,000	3.09%
5	Michigan	1,193,575,000	4.05%
29	Minnesota	310,691,000	1.05%
40	Mississippi	143,811,000	0.49%
25	Missouri	388,063,000	1.32%
47	Montana	81,574,000	0.28%
41	Nebraska	130,810,000	0.44%
37	Nevada	176,248,000	0.60%
43	New Hampshire	129,058,000	0.44%
6	New Jersey	1,045,482,000	3.54%
32	New Mexico	250,240,000	0.85%
2	New York	3,081,218,000	10.45%
9	North Carolina	921,737,000	3.13%
50	North Dakota	40,641,000	0.14%
11	Ohio	908,026,000	3.08%
28	Oklahoma	314,028,000	1.06%
26	Oregon	378,021,000	1.28%
7	Pennsylvania	1,025,969,000	3.48%
35	Rhode Island	188,308,000	0.64%
21	South Carolina	419,599,000	1.42%
49	South Dakota	58,515,000	0.20%
19	Tennessee	461,771,000	1.57%
4	Texas	1,605,124,000	5.44%
36	Utah	183,831,000	0.62%
46	Vermont	88,506,000	0.30%
15	Virginia	692,704,000	2.35%
14	Washington	704,910,000	2.39%
45	West Virginia	100,188,000	0.34%
18	Wisconsin	465,818,000	1.58%
48	Wyoming	59,339,000	0.20%

RANK ORDER

RANK	STATE	EXPENDITURES	% of USA
1	California	$3,964,910,000	13.44%
2	New York	3,081,218,000	10.45%
3	Florida	1,708,610,000	5.79%
4	Texas	1,605,124,000	5.44%
5	Michigan	1,193,575,000	4.05%
6	New Jersey	1,045,482,000	3.54%
7	Pennsylvania	1,025,969,000	3.48%
8	Illinois	990,517,000	3.36%
9	North Carolina	921,737,000	3.13%
10	Massachusetts	910,721,000	3.09%
11	Ohio	908,026,000	3.08%
12	Maryland	895,355,000	3.04%
13	Georgia	727,823,000	2.47%
14	Washington	704,910,000	2.39%
15	Virginia	692,704,000	2.35%
16	Connecticut	680,846,000	2.31%
17	Arizona	480,231,000	1.63%
18	Wisconsin	465,818,000	1.58%
19	Tennessee	461,771,000	1.57%
20	Indiana	439,735,000	1.49%
21	South Carolina	419,599,000	1.42%
22	Colorado	419,302,000	1.42%
23	Louisiana	414,581,000	1.41%
24	Kentucky	403,534,000	1.37%
25	Missouri	388,063,000	1.32%
26	Oregon	378,021,000	1.28%
27	Alabama	374,706,000	1.27%
28	Oklahoma	314,028,000	1.06%
29	Minnesota	310,691,000	1.05%
30	Kansas	294,778,000	1.00%
31	Alaska	275,482,000	0.93%
32	New Mexico	250,240,000	0.85%
33	Hawaii	213,148,000	0.72%
34	Delaware	189,849,000	0.64%
35	Rhode Island	188,308,000	0.64%
36	Utah	183,831,000	0.62%
37	Nevada	176,248,000	0.60%
38	Arkansas	167,611,000	0.57%
39	Iowa	160,953,000	0.55%
40	Mississippi	143,811,000	0.49%
41	Nebraska	130,810,000	0.44%
42	Maine	129,604,000	0.44%
43	New Hampshire	129,058,000	0.44%
44	Idaho	105,230,000	0.36%
45	West Virginia	100,188,000	0.34%
46	Vermont	88,506,000	0.30%
47	Montana	81,574,000	0.28%
48	Wyoming	59,339,000	0.20%
49	South Dakota	58,515,000	0.20%
50	North Dakota	40,641,000	0.14%
	District of Columbia**	NA	NA

Source: Morgan Quitno Corporation using data from U.S. Bureau of the Census
"Government Finances: 1991-92 (Preliminary Report)" (August 1994, GF/92-5P)
*Direct expenditures. Preliminary data. Includes Police Protection, Corrections and Judicial and Legal Services.
**Not applicable.

Per Capita State Government Expenditures for Justice Activities in 1992

National Per Capita = $115.63*

<table>
<tr><td colspan="3">ALPHA ORDER</td><td colspan="3">RANK ORDER</td></tr>
<tr><th>RANK</th><th>STATE</th><th>PER CAPITA</th><th>RANK</th><th>STATE</th><th>PER CAPITA</th></tr>
<tr><td>37</td><td>Alabama</td><td>$90.55</td><td>1</td><td>Alaska</td><td>$468.51</td></tr>
<tr><td>1</td><td>Alaska</td><td>468.51</td><td>2</td><td>Delaware</td><td>274.75</td></tr>
<tr><td>20</td><td>Arizona</td><td>125.32</td><td>3</td><td>Connecticut</td><td>207.64</td></tr>
<tr><td>45</td><td>Arkansas</td><td>70.01</td><td>4</td><td>Rhode Island</td><td>188.12</td></tr>
<tr><td>15</td><td>California</td><td>128.34</td><td>5</td><td>Hawaii</td><td>184.38</td></tr>
<tr><td>21</td><td>Colorado</td><td>121.01</td><td>6</td><td>Maryland</td><td>182.09</td></tr>
<tr><td>3</td><td>Connecticut</td><td>207.64</td><td>7</td><td>New York</td><td>170.15</td></tr>
<tr><td>2</td><td>Delaware</td><td>274.75</td><td>8</td><td>New Mexico</td><td>158.18</td></tr>
<tr><td>18</td><td>Florida</td><td>126.72</td><td>9</td><td>Vermont</td><td>155.00</td></tr>
<tr><td>27</td><td>Georgia</td><td>107.46</td><td>10</td><td>Massachusetts</td><td>151.96</td></tr>
<tr><td>5</td><td>Hawaii</td><td>184.38</td><td>11</td><td>Washington</td><td>137.06</td></tr>
<tr><td>31</td><td>Idaho</td><td>98.71</td><td>12</td><td>North Carolina</td><td>134.84</td></tr>
<tr><td>39</td><td>Illinois</td><td>85.29</td><td>13</td><td>New Jersey</td><td>133.69</td></tr>
<tr><td>43</td><td>Indiana</td><td>77.72</td><td>14</td><td>Nevada</td><td>131.92</td></tr>
<tr><td>48</td><td>Iowa</td><td>57.42</td><td>15</td><td>California</td><td>128.34</td></tr>
<tr><td>22</td><td>Kansas</td><td>117.21</td><td>16</td><td>Wyoming</td><td>127.61</td></tr>
<tr><td>26</td><td>Kentucky</td><td>107.49</td><td>17</td><td>Oregon</td><td>127.19</td></tr>
<tr><td>33</td><td>Louisiana</td><td>96.89</td><td>18</td><td>Florida</td><td>126.72</td></tr>
<tr><td>28</td><td>Maine</td><td>104.86</td><td>19</td><td>Michigan</td><td>126.52</td></tr>
<tr><td>6</td><td>Maryland</td><td>182.09</td><td>20</td><td>Arizona</td><td>125.32</td></tr>
<tr><td>10</td><td>Massachusetts</td><td>151.96</td><td>21</td><td>Colorado</td><td>121.01</td></tr>
<tr><td>19</td><td>Michigan</td><td>126.52</td><td>22</td><td>Kansas</td><td>117.21</td></tr>
<tr><td>46</td><td>Minnesota</td><td>69.54</td><td>23</td><td>South Carolina</td><td>116.46</td></tr>
<tr><td>50</td><td>Mississippi</td><td>54.99</td><td>24</td><td>New Hampshire</td><td>115.75</td></tr>
<tr><td>44</td><td>Missouri</td><td>74.76</td><td>25</td><td>Virginia</td><td>108.34</td></tr>
<tr><td>30</td><td>Montana</td><td>99.24</td><td>26</td><td>Kentucky</td><td>107.49</td></tr>
<tr><td>42</td><td>Nebraska</td><td>81.71</td><td>27</td><td>Georgia</td><td>107.46</td></tr>
<tr><td>14</td><td>Nevada</td><td>131.92</td><td>28</td><td>Maine</td><td>104.86</td></tr>
<tr><td>24</td><td>New Hampshire</td><td>115.75</td><td>29</td><td>Utah</td><td>101.51</td></tr>
<tr><td>13</td><td>New Jersey</td><td>133.69</td><td>30</td><td>Montana</td><td>99.24</td></tr>
<tr><td>8</td><td>New Mexico</td><td>158.18</td><td>31</td><td>Idaho</td><td>98.71</td></tr>
<tr><td>7</td><td>New York</td><td>170.15</td><td>32</td><td>Oklahoma</td><td>97.98</td></tr>
<tr><td>12</td><td>North Carolina</td><td>134.84</td><td>33</td><td>Louisiana</td><td>96.89</td></tr>
<tr><td>47</td><td>North Dakota</td><td>64.10</td><td>34</td><td>Wisconsin</td><td>93.29</td></tr>
<tr><td>41</td><td>Ohio</td><td>82.39</td><td>35</td><td>Tennessee</td><td>91.89</td></tr>
<tr><td>32</td><td>Oklahoma</td><td>97.98</td><td>36</td><td>Texas</td><td>90.77</td></tr>
<tr><td>17</td><td>Oregon</td><td>127.19</td><td>37</td><td>Alabama</td><td>90.55</td></tr>
<tr><td>38</td><td>Pennsylvania</td><td>85.53</td><td>38</td><td>Pennsylvania</td><td>85.53</td></tr>
<tr><td>4</td><td>Rhode Island</td><td>188.12</td><td>39</td><td>Illinois</td><td>85.29</td></tr>
<tr><td>23</td><td>South Carolina</td><td>116.46</td><td>40</td><td>South Dakota</td><td>82.65</td></tr>
<tr><td>40</td><td>South Dakota</td><td>82.65</td><td>41</td><td>Ohio</td><td>82.39</td></tr>
<tr><td>35</td><td>Tennessee</td><td>91.89</td><td>42</td><td>Nebraska</td><td>81.71</td></tr>
<tr><td>36</td><td>Texas</td><td>90.77</td><td>43</td><td>Indiana</td><td>77.72</td></tr>
<tr><td>29</td><td>Utah</td><td>101.51</td><td>44</td><td>Missouri</td><td>74.76</td></tr>
<tr><td>9</td><td>Vermont</td><td>155.00</td><td>45</td><td>Arkansas</td><td>70.01</td></tr>
<tr><td>25</td><td>Virginia</td><td>108.34</td><td>46</td><td>Minnesota</td><td>69.54</td></tr>
<tr><td>11</td><td>Washington</td><td>137.06</td><td>47</td><td>North Dakota</td><td>64.10</td></tr>
<tr><td>49</td><td>West Virginia</td><td>55.38</td><td>48</td><td>Iowa</td><td>57.42</td></tr>
<tr><td>34</td><td>Wisconsin</td><td>93.29</td><td>49</td><td>West Virginia</td><td>55.38</td></tr>
<tr><td>16</td><td>Wyoming</td><td>127.61</td><td>50</td><td>Mississippi</td><td>54.99</td></tr>
<tr><td></td><td></td><td></td><td></td><td>District of Columbia**</td><td>NA</td></tr>
</table>

Source: Morgan Quitno Corporation using data from U.S. Bureau of the Census
"Government Finances: 1991-92 (Preliminary Report)" (August 1994, GF/92-5P)
*Direct expenditures. Preliminary data. Includes Police Protection, Corrections and Judicial and Legal Services.
**Not applicable.

State Government Expenditures for Justice Activities
As a Percent of All Direct Expenditures in 1992
National Percent = 5.91% of Direct Expenditures*

ALPHA ORDER

RANK ORDER

RANK	STATE	PERCENT		RANK	STATE	PERCENT
34	Alabama	4.99		1	Florida	9.15
13	Alaska	6.55		2	Delaware	9.11
5	Arizona	7.87		3	North Carolina	8.76
42	Arkansas	4.18		4	Maryland	8.57
10	California	7.04		5	Arizona	7.87
6	Colorado	7.59		6	Colorado	7.59
8	Connecticut	7.14		7	Kansas	7.30
2	Delaware	9.11		8	Connecticut	7.14
1	Florida	9.15		9	Georgia	7.05
9	Georgia	7.05		10	California	7.04
43	Hawaii	4.12		11	New Mexico	7.02
19	Idaho	5.76		12	Virginia	6.64
35	Illinois	4.92		13	Alaska	6.55
30	Indiana	5.08		14	Nevada	6.48
48	Iowa	3.26		15	Michigan	6.43
7	Kansas	7.30		15	Texas	6.43
29	Kentucky	5.20		17	New York	6.36
39	Louisiana	4.54		18	Oregon	5.94
41	Maine	4.31		19	Idaho	5.76
4	Maryland	8.57		20	Vermont	5.75
23	Massachusetts	5.58		21	Tennessee	5.69
15	Michigan	6.43		22	South Carolina	5.67
47	Minnesota	3.53		23	Massachusetts	5.58
46	Mississippi	3.60		24	Washington	5.51
31	Missouri	5.06		25	Utah	5.50
40	Montana	4.41		26	Rhode Island	5.43
31	Nebraska	5.06		27	Wisconsin	5.32
14	Nevada	6.48		28	Oklahoma	5.22
33	New Hampshire	5.01		29	Kentucky	5.20
36	New Jersey	4.87		30	Indiana	5.08
11	New Mexico	7.02		31	Missouri	5.06
17	New York	6.36		31	Nebraska	5.06
3	North Carolina	8.76		33	New Hampshire	5.01
49	North Dakota	2.54		34	Alabama	4.99
44	Ohio	4.05		35	Illinois	4.92
28	Oklahoma	5.22		36	New Jersey	4.87
18	Oregon	5.94		37	Wyoming	4.65
45	Pennsylvania	3.87		38	South Dakota	4.56
26	Rhode Island	5.43		39	Louisiana	4.54
22	South Carolina	5.67		40	Montana	4.41
38	South Dakota	4.56		41	Maine	4.31
21	Tennessee	5.69		42	Arkansas	4.18
15	Texas	6.43		43	Hawaii	4.12
25	Utah	5.50		44	Ohio	4.05
20	Vermont	5.75		45	Pennsylvania	3.87
12	Virginia	6.64		46	Mississippi	3.60
24	Washington	5.51		47	Minnesota	3.53
50	West Virginia	2.44		48	Iowa	3.26
27	Wisconsin	5.32		49	North Dakota	2.54
37	Wyoming	4.65		50	West Virginia	2.44
					District of Columbia**	NA

Source: Morgan Quitno Corporation using data from U.S. Bureau of the Census
  "Government Finances: 1991-92 (Preliminary Report)" (August 1994, GF/92-5P)
*Direct expenditures. Preliminary data. Includes Police Protection, Corrections and Judicial and Legal Services.
**Not applicable.

Local Government Expenditures for Justice Activities in 1992

National Total = $50,007,147,000*

ALPHA ORDER

RANK	STATE	EXPENDITURES	% of USA
25	Alabama	$450,268,000	0.90%
45	Alaska	90,461,000	0.18%
14	Arizona	924,154,000	1.85%
36	Arkansas	198,030,000	0.40%
1	California	10,066,788,000	20.13%
22	Colorado	631,357,000	1.26%
28	Connecticut	409,766,000	0.82%
47	Delaware	69,060,000	0.14%
3	Florida	3,444,295,000	6.89%
10	Georgia	1,078,337,000	2.16%
37	Hawaii	193,646,000	0.39%
40	Idaho	128,883,000	0.26%
5	Illinois	2,264,606,000	4.53%
23	Indiana	585,933,000	1.17%
32	Iowa	290,915,000	0.58%
30	Kansas	308,815,000	0.62%
29	Kentucky	318,848,000	0.64%
19	Louisiana	681,185,000	1.36%
41	Maine	118,743,000	0.24%
16	Maryland	814,001,000	1.63%
15	Massachusetts	869,888,000	1.74%
9	Michigan	1,791,515,000	3.58%
17	Minnesota	767,407,000	1.53%
35	Mississippi	212,217,000	0.42%
21	Missouri	632,212,000	1.26%
44	Montana	91,048,000	0.18%
38	Nebraska	179,347,000	0.36%
27	Nevada	430,801,000	0.86%
39	New Hampshire	140,198,000	0.28%
8	New Jersey	1,841,721,000	3.68%
33	New Mexico	212,632,000	0.43%
2	New York	5,918,729,000	11.84%
18	North Carolina	687,585,000	1.37%
49	North Dakota	57,542,000	0.12%
6	Ohio	1,974,871,000	3.95%
31	Oklahoma	308,623,000	0.62%
24	Oregon	473,243,000	0.95%
7	Pennsylvania	1,917,790,000	3.84%
42	Rhode Island	114,307,000	0.23%
26	South Carolina	449,266,000	0.90%
48	South Dakota	62,077,000	0.12%
20	Tennessee	673,644,000	1.35%
4	Texas	2,990,493,000	5.98%
34	Utah	212,467,000	0.42%
50	Vermont	29,511,000	0.06%
11	Virginia	1,005,283,000	2.01%
13	Washington	974,505,000	1.95%
43	West Virginia	111,315,000	0.22%
12	Wisconsin	1,000,859,000	2.00%
46	Wyoming	88,920,000	0.18%

RANK ORDER

RANK	STATE	EXPENDITURES	% of USA
1	California	$10,066,788,000	20.13%
2	New York	5,918,729,000	11.84%
3	Florida	3,444,295,000	6.89%
4	Texas	2,990,493,000	5.98%
5	Illinois	2,264,606,000	4.53%
6	Ohio	1,974,871,000	3.95%
7	Pennsylvania	1,917,790,000	3.84%
8	New Jersey	1,841,721,000	3.68%
9	Michigan	1,791,515,000	3.58%
10	Georgia	1,078,337,000	2.16%
11	Virginia	1,005,283,000	2.01%
12	Wisconsin	1,000,859,000	2.00%
13	Washington	974,505,000	1.95%
14	Arizona	924,154,000	1.85%
15	Massachusetts	869,888,000	1.74%
16	Maryland	814,001,000	1.63%
17	Minnesota	767,407,000	1.53%
18	North Carolina	687,585,000	1.37%
19	Louisiana	681,185,000	1.36%
20	Tennessee	673,644,000	1.35%
21	Missouri	632,212,000	1.26%
22	Colorado	631,357,000	1.26%
23	Indiana	585,933,000	1.17%
24	Oregon	473,243,000	0.95%
25	Alabama	450,268,000	0.90%
26	South Carolina	449,266,000	0.90%
27	Nevada	430,801,000	0.86%
28	Connecticut	409,766,000	0.82%
29	Kentucky	318,848,000	0.64%
30	Kansas	308,815,000	0.62%
31	Oklahoma	308,623,000	0.62%
32	Iowa	290,915,000	0.58%
33	New Mexico	212,632,000	0.43%
34	Utah	212,467,000	0.42%
35	Mississippi	212,217,000	0.42%
36	Arkansas	198,030,000	0.40%
37	Hawaii	193,646,000	0.39%
38	Nebraska	179,347,000	0.36%
39	New Hampshire	140,198,000	0.28%
40	Idaho	128,883,000	0.26%
41	Maine	118,743,000	0.24%
42	Rhode Island	114,307,000	0.23%
43	West Virginia	111,315,000	0.22%
44	Montana	91,048,000	0.18%
45	Alaska	90,461,000	0.18%
46	Wyoming	88,920,000	0.18%
47	Delaware	69,060,000	0.14%
48	South Dakota	62,077,000	0.12%
49	North Dakota	57,542,000	0.12%
50	Vermont	29,511,000	0.06%
	District of Columbia	719,040,000	1.44%

Source: Morgan Quitno Corporation using data from U.S. Bureau of the Census
"Government Finances: 1991-92 (Preliminary Report)" (August 1994, GF/92-5P)
*Direct expenditures. Preliminary data. Includes Police Protection, Corrections and Judicial and Legal Services.

Per Capita Local Government Expenditures for Justice Activities in 1992

National Per Capita = $196.05*

ALPHA ORDER				RANK ORDER		
RANK	STATE	PER CAPITA		RANK	STATE	PER CAPITA
37	Alabama	$108.81		1	New York	$326.84
23	Alaska	153.85		2	California	325.84
5	Arizona	241.17		3	Nevada	322.46
47	Arkansas	82.72		4	Florida	255.45
2	California	325.84		5	Arizona	241.17
12	Colorado	182.21		6	New Jersey	235.51
28	Connecticut	124.97		7	Wisconsin	200.45
41	Delaware	99.94		8	Illinois	195.01
4	Florida	255.45		9	Wyoming	191.23
20	Georgia	159.21		10	Michigan	189.90
16	Hawaii	167.51		11	Washington	189.48
32	Idaho	120.90		12	Colorado	182.21
8	Illinois	195.01		13	Ohio	179.19
39	Indiana	103.56		14	Minnesota	171.76
38	Iowa	103.79		15	Texas	169.12
30	Kansas	122.79		16	Hawaii	167.51
46	Kentucky	84.94		17	Maryland	165.55
21	Louisiana	159.19		18	Pennsylvania	159.88
43	Maine	96.07		19	Oregon	159.23
17	Maryland	165.55		20	Georgia	159.21
24	Massachusetts	145.15		21	Louisiana	159.19
10	Michigan	189.90		22	Virginia	157.22
14	Minnesota	171.76		23	Alaska	153.85
48	Mississippi	81.15		24	Massachusetts	145.15
31	Missouri	121.79		25	New Mexico	134.41
36	Montana	110.76		26	Tennessee	134.06
35	Nebraska	112.02		27	New Hampshire	125.74
3	Nevada	322.46		28	Connecticut	124.97
27	New Hampshire	125.74		29	South Carolina	124.69
6	New Jersey	235.51		30	Kansas	122.79
25	New Mexico	134.41		31	Missouri	121.79
1	New York	326.84		32	Idaho	120.90
40	North Carolina	100.58		33	Utah	117.32
44	North Dakota	90.76		34	Rhode Island	114.19
13	Ohio	179.19		35	Nebraska	112.02
42	Oklahoma	96.29		36	Montana	110.76
19	Oregon	159.23		37	Alabama	108.81
18	Pennsylvania	159.88		38	Iowa	103.79
34	Rhode Island	114.19		39	Indiana	103.56
29	South Carolina	124.69		40	North Carolina	100.58
45	South Dakota	87.68		41	Delaware	99.94
26	Tennessee	134.06		42	Oklahoma	96.29
15	Texas	169.12		43	Maine	96.07
33	Utah	117.32		44	North Dakota	90.76
50	Vermont	51.68		45	South Dakota	87.68
22	Virginia	157.22		46	Kentucky	84.94
11	Washington	189.48		47	Arkansas	82.72
49	West Virginia	61.53		48	Mississippi	81.15
7	Wisconsin	200.45		49	West Virginia	61.53
9	Wyoming	191.23		50	Vermont	51.68
					District of Columbia	1,229.13

Source: Morgan Quitno Corporation using data from U.S. Bureau of the Census
"Government Finances: 1991-92 (Preliminary Report)" (August 1994, GF/92-5P)
*Direct expenditures. Preliminary data. Includes Police Protection, Corrections and Judicial and Legal Services.

Local Government Expenditures for Justice Activities
As a Percent of All Direct Expenditures in 1992
National Percent = 7.72% of Direct Expenditures*

RANK	STATE	PERCENT
31	Alabama	5.94
48	Alaska	3.80
5	Arizona	9.42
30	Arkansas	5.98
4	California	9.69
24	Colorado	6.58
40	Connecticut	5.32
32	Delaware	5.81
3	Florida	9.71
22	Georgia	6.85
1	Hawaii	12.91
17	Idaho	7.09
8	Illinois	8.50
42	Indiana	5.23
45	Iowa	4.73
34	Kansas	5.55
37	Kentucky	5.49
9	Louisiana	8.04
39	Maine	5.35
10	Maryland	8.01
28	Massachusetts	6.15
11	Michigan	7.86
35	Minnesota	5.54
44	Mississippi	4.79
23	Missouri	6.78
27	Montana	6.17
49	Nebraska	3.72
2	Nevada	11.70
18	New Hampshire	7.04
6	New Jersey	8.82
19	New Mexico	7.03
12	New York	7.84
46	North Carolina	4.63
43	North Dakota	5.22
7	Ohio	8.53
36	Oklahoma	5.50
26	Oregon	6.41
16	Pennsylvania	7.20
20	Rhode Island	6.87
21	South Carolina	6.86
40	South Dakota	5.32
33	Tennessee	5.79
15	Texas	7.49
38	Utah	5.41
50	Vermont	2.83
13	Virginia	7.68
25	Washington	6.55
47	West Virginia	4.11
14	Wisconsin	7.59
29	Wyoming	6.10

RANK	STATE	PERCENT
1	Hawaii	12.91
2	Nevada	11.70
3	Florida	9.71
4	California	9.69
5	Arizona	9.42
6	New Jersey	8.82
7	Ohio	8.53
8	Illinois	8.50
9	Louisiana	8.04
10	Maryland	8.01
11	Michigan	7.86
12	New York	7.84
13	Virginia	7.68
14	Wisconsin	7.59
15	Texas	7.49
16	Pennsylvania	7.20
17	Idaho	7.09
18	New Hampshire	7.04
19	New Mexico	7.03
20	Rhode Island	6.87
21	South Carolina	6.86
22	Georgia	6.85
23	Missouri	6.78
24	Colorado	6.58
25	Washington	6.55
26	Oregon	6.41
27	Montana	6.17
28	Massachusetts	6.15
29	Wyoming	6.10
30	Arkansas	5.98
31	Alabama	5.94
32	Delaware	5.81
33	Tennessee	5.79
34	Kansas	5.55
35	Minnesota	5.54
36	Oklahoma	5.50
37	Kentucky	5.49
38	Utah	5.41
39	Maine	5.35
40	Connecticut	5.32
40	South Dakota	5.32
42	Indiana	5.23
43	North Dakota	5.22
44	Mississippi	4.79
45	Iowa	4.73
46	North Carolina	4.63
47	West Virginia	4.11
48	Alaska	3.80
49	Nebraska	3.72
50	Vermont	2.83

	District of Columbia	12.35

Source: Morgan Quitno Corporation using data from U.S. Bureau of the Census
"Government Finances: 1991–92 (Preliminary Report)" (August 1994, GF/92–5P)
*Direct expenditures. Preliminary data. Includes Police Protection, Corrections and Judicial and Legal Services.

State and Local Government Expenditures for Police Protection in 1992

National Total = $34,544,772,000*

ALPHA ORDER

RANK	STATE	EXPENDITURES	% of USA
25	Alabama	$391,563,000	1.13%
40	Alaska	127,419,000	0.37%
17	Arizona	600,255,000	1.74%
36	Arkansas	167,349,000	0.48%
1	California	5,888,852,000	17.05%
23	Colorado	461,787,000	1.34%
22	Connecticut	465,936,000	1.35%
44	Delaware	97,689,000	0.28%
3	Florida	2,291,399,000	6.63%
12	Georgia	711,132,000	2.06%
37	Hawaii	166,251,000	0.48%
42	Idaho	112,088,000	0.32%
5	Illinois	1,721,852,000	4.98%
24	Indiana	429,115,000	1.24%
31	Iowa	262,372,000	0.76%
30	Kansas	269,072,000	0.78%
28	Kentucky	300,800,000	0.87%
18	Louisiana	543,103,000	1.57%
43	Maine	98,782,000	0.29%
13	Maryland	705,963,000	2.04%
10	Massachusetts	786,885,000	2.28%
8	Michigan	1,260,337,000	3.65%
20	Minnesota	509,920,000	1.48%
34	Mississippi	187,445,000	0.54%
19	Missouri	529,734,000	1.53%
46	Montana	73,646,000	0.21%
38	Nebraska	141,766,000	0.41%
32	Nevada	253,580,000	0.73%
41	New Hampshire	127,109,000	0.37%
7	New Jersey	1,324,992,000	3.84%
33	New Mexico	213,040,000	0.62%
2	New York	3,714,111,000	10.75%
14	North Carolina	701,642,000	2.03%
50	North Dakota	42,394,000	0.12%
6	Ohio	1,331,925,000	3.86%
29	Oklahoma	292,785,000	0.85%
26	Oregon	358,850,000	1.04%
9	Pennsylvania	1,231,598,000	3.57%
39	Rhode Island	129,221,000	0.37%
27	South Carolina	328,740,000	0.95%
48	South Dakota	56,233,000	0.16%
21	Tennessee	469,585,000	1.36%
4	Texas	1,945,118,000	5.63%
35	Utah	174,693,000	0.51%
49	Vermont	54,725,000	0.16%
11	Virginia	733,980,000	2.12%
16	Washington	627,034,000	1.82%
45	West Virginia	92,983,000	0.27%
15	Wisconsin	696,349,000	2.02%
47	Wyoming	68,824,000	0.20%

RANK ORDER

RANK	STATE	EXPENDITURES	% of USA
1	California	$5,888,852,000	17.05%
2	New York	3,714,111,000	10.75%
3	Florida	2,291,399,000	6.63%
4	Texas	1,945,118,000	5.63%
5	Illinois	1,721,852,000	4.98%
6	Ohio	1,331,925,000	3.86%
7	New Jersey	1,324,992,000	3.84%
8	Michigan	1,260,337,000	3.65%
9	Pennsylvania	1,231,598,000	3.57%
10	Massachusetts	786,885,000	2.28%
11	Virginia	733,980,000	2.12%
12	Georgia	711,132,000	2.06%
13	Maryland	705,963,000	2.04%
14	North Carolina	701,642,000	2.03%
15	Wisconsin	696,349,000	2.02%
16	Washington	627,034,000	1.82%
17	Arizona	600,255,000	1.74%
18	Louisiana	543,103,000	1.57%
19	Missouri	529,734,000	1.53%
20	Minnesota	509,920,000	1.48%
21	Tennessee	469,585,000	1.36%
22	Connecticut	465,936,000	1.35%
23	Colorado	461,787,000	1.34%
24	Indiana	429,115,000	1.24%
25	Alabama	391,563,000	1.13%
26	Oregon	358,850,000	1.04%
27	South Carolina	328,740,000	0.95%
28	Kentucky	300,800,000	0.87%
29	Oklahoma	292,785,000	0.85%
30	Kansas	269,072,000	0.78%
31	Iowa	262,372,000	0.76%
32	Nevada	253,580,000	0.73%
33	New Mexico	213,040,000	0.62%
34	Mississippi	187,445,000	0.54%
35	Utah	174,693,000	0.51%
36	Arkansas	167,349,000	0.48%
37	Hawaii	166,251,000	0.48%
38	Nebraska	141,766,000	0.41%
39	Rhode Island	129,221,000	0.37%
40	Alaska	127,419,000	0.37%
41	New Hampshire	127,109,000	0.37%
42	Idaho	112,088,000	0.32%
43	Maine	98,782,000	0.29%
44	Delaware	97,689,000	0.28%
45	West Virginia	92,983,000	0.27%
46	Montana	73,646,000	0.21%
47	Wyoming	68,824,000	0.20%
48	South Dakota	56,233,000	0.16%
49	Vermont	54,725,000	0.16%
50	North Dakota	42,394,000	0.12%
	District of Columbia	272,749,000	0.79%

Source: U.S. Bureau of the Census
   "Government Finances: 1991–92 (Preliminary Report)" (August 1994, GF/92–5P)
*Direct expenditures. Preliminary data.

Per Capita State and Local Government Expenditures for Police Protection in 1992

National Per Capita = $135.43*

<u>ALPHA ORDER</u>

RANK	STATE	PER CAPITA
36	Alabama	$94.63
1	Alaska	216.70
7	Arizona	156.64
48	Arkansas	69.90
3	California	190.61
17	Colorado	133.27
12	Connecticut	142.10
13	Delaware	141.37
5	Florida	169.95
30	Georgia	105.00
10	Hawaii	143.82
29	Idaho	105.15
8	Illinois	148.27
46	Indiana	75.84
37	Iowa	93.60
28	Kansas	106.99
43	Kentucky	80.13
20	Louisiana	126.92
44	Maine	79.92
11	Maryland	143.58
18	Massachusetts	131.30
16	Michigan	133.60
25	Minnesota	114.13
47	Mississippi	71.68
33	Missouri	102.05
41	Montana	89.59
42	Nebraska	88.55
4	Nevada	189.81
26	New Hampshire	114.00
6	New Jersey	169.44
15	New Mexico	134.66
2	New York	205.10
32	North Carolina	102.64
49	North Dakota	66.87
22	Ohio	120.85
39	Oklahoma	91.35
23	Oregon	120.74
31	Pennsylvania	102.68
19	Rhode Island	129.09
40	South Carolina	91.24
45	South Dakota	79.43
38	Tennessee	93.45
27	Texas	110.00
34	Utah	96.46
35	Vermont	95.84
24	Virginia	114.79
21	Washington	121.92
50	West Virginia	51.40
14	Wisconsin	139.47
9	Wyoming	148.01

<u>RANK ORDER</u>

RANK	STATE	PER CAPITA
1	Alaska	$216.70
2	New York	205.10
3	California	190.61
4	Nevada	189.81
5	Florida	169.95
6	New Jersey	169.44
7	Arizona	156.64
8	Illinois	148.27
9	Wyoming	148.01
10	Hawaii	143.82
11	Maryland	143.58
12	Connecticut	142.10
13	Delaware	141.37
14	Wisconsin	139.47
15	New Mexico	134.66
16	Michigan	133.60
17	Colorado	133.27
18	Massachusetts	131.30
19	Rhode Island	129.09
20	Louisiana	126.92
21	Washington	121.92
22	Ohio	120.85
23	Oregon	120.74
24	Virginia	114.79
25	Minnesota	114.13
26	New Hampshire	114.00
27	Texas	110.00
28	Kansas	106.99
29	Idaho	105.15
30	Georgia	105.00
31	Pennsylvania	102.68
32	North Carolina	102.64
33	Missouri	102.05
34	Utah	96.46
35	Vermont	95.84
36	Alabama	94.63
37	Iowa	93.60
38	Tennessee	93.45
39	Oklahoma	91.35
40	South Carolina	91.24
41	Montana	89.59
42	Nebraska	88.55
43	Kentucky	80.13
44	Maine	79.92
45	South Dakota	79.43
46	Indiana	75.84
47	Mississippi	71.68
48	Arkansas	69.90
49	North Dakota	66.87
50	West Virginia	51.40
	District of Columbia	466.24

Source: Morgan Quitno Corporation using data from U.S. Bureau of the Census
"Government Finances: 1991–92 (Preliminary Report)" (August 1994, GF/92-5P)
*Direct expenditures. Preliminary data.

State and Local Government Expenditures for Police Protection
As a Percent of All Direct Expenditures in 1992
National Percent = 3.01% of Direct Expenditures

ALPHA ORDER

RANK ORDER

RANK	STATE	PERCENT		RANK	STATE	PERCENT
26	Alabama	2.59		1	Florida	4.23
46	Alaska	1.93		2	Nevada	3.96
3	Arizona	3.77		3	Arizona	3.77
37	Arkansas	2.29		4	Illinois	3.68
5	California	3.67		5	California	3.67
14	Colorado	3.06		6	Maryland	3.43
24	Connecticut	2.70		7	New Mexico	3.23
18	Delaware	2.99		8	Wisconsin	3.17
1	Florida	4.23		9	New Jersey	3.13
23	Georgia	2.73		10	Missouri	3.12
31	Hawaii	2.49		10	Virginia	3.12
13	Idaho	3.07		12	Louisiana	3.08
4	Illinois	3.68		13	Idaho	3.07
44	Indiana	2.16		14	Colorado	3.06
34	Iowa	2.37		15	Michigan	3.05
20	Kansas	2.80		16	New York	3.00
41	Kentucky	2.22		16	Texas	3.00
12	Louisiana	3.08		18	Delaware	2.99
48	Maine	1.89		19	Ohio	2.92
6	Maryland	3.43		20	Kansas	2.80
27	Massachusetts	2.58		21	New Hampshire	2.78
15	Michigan	3.05		22	North Carolina	2.77
40	Minnesota	2.25		23	Georgia	2.73
41	Mississippi	2.22		24	Connecticut	2.70
10	Missouri	3.12		25	Oregon	2.61
43	Montana	2.21		26	Alabama	2.59
47	Nebraska	1.91		27	Massachusetts	2.58
2	Nevada	3.96		28	Oklahoma	2.52
21	New Hampshire	2.78		28	Rhode Island	2.52
9	New Jersey	3.13		28	Wyoming	2.52
7	New Mexico	3.23		31	Hawaii	2.49
16	New York	3.00		32	Utah	2.40
22	North Carolina	2.77		33	Tennessee	2.38
49	North Dakota	1.57		34	Iowa	2.37
19	Ohio	2.92		35	South Carolina	2.36
28	Oklahoma	2.52		36	Pennsylvania	2.32
25	Oregon	2.61		37	Arkansas	2.29
36	Pennsylvania	2.32		37	South Dakota	2.29
28	Rhode Island	2.52		39	Washington	2.27
35	South Carolina	2.36		40	Minnesota	2.25
37	South Dakota	2.29		41	Kentucky	2.22
33	Tennessee	2.38		41	Mississippi	2.22
16	Texas	3.00		43	Montana	2.21
32	Utah	2.40		44	Indiana	2.16
45	Vermont	2.12		45	Vermont	2.12
10	Virginia	3.12		46	Alaska	1.93
39	Washington	2.27		47	Nebraska	1.91
50	West Virginia	1.36		48	Maine	1.89
8	Wisconsin	3.17		49	North Dakota	1.57
28	Wyoming	2.52		50	West Virginia	1.36

District of Columbia   4.68

Source: Morgan Quitno Corporation using data from U.S. Bureau of the Census
   "Government Finances: 1991-92 (Preliminary Report)" (August 1994, GF/92-5P)
*Preliminary data.

State Government Expenditures for Police Protection in 1992

National Total = $4,863,131,000*

ALPHA ORDER

RANK	STATE	EXPENDITURES	% of USA
24	Alabama	$66,322,000	1.36%
30	Alaska	46,393,000	0.95%
15	Arizona	100,441,000	2.07%
33	Arkansas	36,939,000	0.76%
1	California	760,957,000	15.65%
29	Colorado	47,853,000	0.98%
21	Connecticut	79,484,000	1.63%
35	Delaware	35,884,000	0.74%
4	Florida	222,411,000	4.57%
16	Georgia	99,188,000	2.04%
50	Hawaii	3,616,000	0.07%
40	Idaho	26,978,000	0.55%
6	Illinois	213,878,000	4.40%
19	Indiana	88,348,000	1.82%
31	Iowa	44,233,000	0.91%
36	Kansas	34,108,000	0.70%
18	Kentucky	90,850,000	1.87%
17	Louisiana	94,276,000	1.94%
42	Maine	25,720,000	0.53%
11	Maryland	143,488,000	2.95%
13	Massachusetts	114,547,000	2.36%
8	Michigan	197,408,000	4.06%
26	Minnesota	59,459,000	1.22%
34	Mississippi	36,393,000	0.75%
22	Missouri	72,974,000	1.50%
46	Montana	16,849,000	0.35%
38	Nebraska	30,136,000	0.62%
39	Nevada	28,413,000	0.58%
44	New Hampshire	23,578,000	0.48%
7	New Jersey	203,716,000	4.19%
28	New Mexico	47,984,000	0.99%
3	New York	274,563,000	5.65%
9	North Carolina	148,706,000	3.06%
49	North Dakota	8,018,000	0.16%
10	Ohio	147,729,000	3.04%
32	Oklahoma	43,770,000	0.90%
23	Oregon	71,087,000	1.46%
2	Pennsylvania	300,102,000	6.17%
45	Rhode Island	21,637,000	0.44%
20	South Carolina	81,519,000	1.68%
47	South Dakota	13,474,000	0.28%
25	Tennessee	61,529,000	1.27%
5	Texas	215,192,000	4.42%
37	Utah	31,485,000	0.65%
41	Vermont	26,848,000	0.55%
12	Virginia	130,112,000	2.68%
14	Washington	108,037,000	2.22%
43	West Virginia	23,850,000	0.49%
27	Wisconsin	50,780,000	1.04%
48	Wyoming	11,869,000	0.24%

RANK ORDER

RANK	STATE	EXPENDITURES	% of USA
1	California	$760,957,000	15.65%
2	Pennsylvania	300,102,000	6.17%
3	New York	274,563,000	5.65%
4	Florida	222,411,000	4.57%
5	Texas	215,192,000	4.42%
6	Illinois	213,878,000	4.40%
7	New Jersey	203,716,000	4.19%
8	Michigan	197,408,000	4.06%
9	North Carolina	148,706,000	3.06%
10	Ohio	147,729,000	3.04%
11	Maryland	143,488,000	2.95%
12	Virginia	130,112,000	2.68%
13	Massachusetts	114,547,000	2.36%
14	Washington	108,037,000	2.22%
15	Arizona	100,441,000	2.07%
16	Georgia	99,188,000	2.04%
17	Louisiana	94,276,000	1.94%
18	Kentucky	90,850,000	1.87%
19	Indiana	88,348,000	1.82%
20	South Carolina	81,519,000	1.68%
21	Connecticut	79,484,000	1.63%
22	Missouri	72,974,000	1.50%
23	Oregon	71,087,000	1.46%
24	Alabama	66,322,000	1.36%
25	Tennessee	61,529,000	1.27%
26	Minnesota	59,459,000	1.22%
27	Wisconsin	50,780,000	1.04%
28	New Mexico	47,984,000	0.99%
29	Colorado	47,853,000	0.98%
30	Alaska	46,393,000	0.95%
31	Iowa	44,233,000	0.91%
32	Oklahoma	43,770,000	0.90%
33	Arkansas	36,939,000	0.76%
34	Mississippi	36,393,000	0.75%
35	Delaware	35,884,000	0.74%
36	Kansas	34,108,000	0.70%
37	Utah	31,485,000	0.65%
38	Nebraska	30,136,000	0.62%
39	Nevada	28,413,000	0.58%
40	Idaho	26,978,000	0.55%
41	Vermont	26,848,000	0.55%
42	Maine	25,720,000	0.53%
43	West Virginia	23,850,000	0.49%
44	New Hampshire	23,578,000	0.48%
45	Rhode Island	21,637,000	0.44%
46	Montana	16,849,000	0.35%
47	South Dakota	13,474,000	0.28%
48	Wyoming	11,869,000	0.24%
49	North Dakota	8,018,000	0.16%
50	Hawaii	3,616,000	0.07%
	District of Columbia**	NA	NA

Source: U.S. Bureau of the Census
   "Government Finances: 1991-92 (Preliminary Report)" (August 1994, GF/92-5P)
*Direct expenditures. Preliminary data.
**Not applicable.

Per Capita State Government Expenditures for Police Protection in 1992

National Per Capita = $19.07*

ALPHA ORDER			RANK ORDER		
RANK	STATE	PER CAPITA	RANK	STATE	PER CAPITA
32	Alabama	$16.03	1	Alaska	$78.90
1	Alaska	78.90	2	Delaware	51.93
6	Arizona	26.21	3	Vermont	47.02
35	Arkansas	15.43	4	New Mexico	30.33
11	California	24.63	5	Maryland	29.18
40	Colorado	13.81	6	Arizona	26.21
12	Connecticut	24.24	7	New Jersey	26.05
2	Delaware	51.93	8	Wyoming	25.52
31	Florida	16.50	9	Idaho	25.31
37	Georgia	14.64	10	Pennsylvania	25.02
50	Hawaii	3.13	11	California	24.63
9	Idaho	25.31	12	Connecticut	24.24
29	Illinois	18.42	13	Kentucky	24.20
34	Indiana	15.61	14	Oregon	23.92
33	Iowa	15.78	15	South Carolina	22.63
42	Kansas	13.56	16	Louisiana	22.03
13	Kentucky	24.20	17	North Carolina	21.75
16	Louisiana	22.03	18	Rhode Island	21.62
23	Maine	20.81	19	Nevada	21.27
5	Maryland	29.18	20	New Hampshire	21.15
26	Massachusetts	19.11	21	Washington	21.01
22	Michigan	20.93	22	Michigan	20.93
44	Minnesota	13.31	23	Maine	20.81
39	Mississippi	13.92	24	Montana	20.50
38	Missouri	14.06	25	Virginia	20.35
24	Montana	20.50	26	Massachusetts	19.11
28	Nebraska	18.82	27	South Dakota	19.03
19	Nevada	21.27	28	Nebraska	18.82
20	New Hampshire	21.15	29	Illinois	18.42
7	New Jersey	26.05	30	Utah	17.39
4	New Mexico	30.33	31	Florida	16.50
36	New York	15.16	32	Alabama	16.03
17	North Carolina	21.75	33	Iowa	15.78
46	North Dakota	12.65	34	Indiana	15.61
43	Ohio	13.40	35	Arkansas	15.43
41	Oklahoma	13.66	36	New York	15.16
14	Oregon	23.92	37	Georgia	14.64
10	Pennsylvania	25.02	38	Missouri	14.06
18	Rhode Island	21.62	39	Mississippi	13.92
15	South Carolina	22.63	40	Colorado	13.81
27	South Dakota	19.03	41	Oklahoma	13.66
47	Tennessee	12.24	42	Kansas	13.56
48	Texas	12.17	43	Ohio	13.40
30	Utah	17.39	44	Minnesota	13.31
3	Vermont	47.02	45	West Virginia	13.18
25	Virginia	20.35	46	North Dakota	12.65
21	Washington	21.01	47	Tennessee	12.24
45	West Virginia	13.18	48	Texas	12.17
49	Wisconsin	10.17	49	Wisconsin	10.17
8	Wyoming	25.52	50	Hawaii	3.13
				District of Columbia**	NA

Source: Morgan Quitno Corporation using data from U.S. Bureau of the Census
    "Government Finances: 1991-92 (Preliminary Report)" (August 1994, GF/92-5P)
*Direct expenditures. Preliminary data.
**Not applicable.

State Government Expenditures for Police Protection
As a Percent of All Direct Expenditures in 1992
National Percent = 0.97% of Direct Expenditures*

ALPHA ORDER

RANK	STATE	PERCENT
33	Alabama	0.88
15	Alaska	1.10
3	Arizona	1.65
28	Arkansas	0.92
7	California	1.35
34	Colorado	0.87
39	Connecticut	0.83
2	Delaware	1.72
10	Florida	1.19
23	Georgia	0.96
50	Hawaii	0.07
4	Idaho	1.48
17	Illinois	1.06
22	Indiana	1.02
32	Iowa	0.90
37	Kansas	0.84
11	Kentucky	1.17
21	Louisiana	1.03
36	Maine	0.85
6	Maryland	1.37
42	Massachusetts	0.70
17	Michigan	1.06
43	Minnesota	0.68
29	Mississippi	0.91
24	Missouri	0.95
29	Montana	0.91
11	Nebraska	1.17
19	Nevada	1.05
29	New Hampshire	0.91
24	New Jersey	0.95
7	New Mexico	1.35
48	New York	0.57
5	North Carolina	1.41
49	North Dakota	0.50
44	Ohio	0.66
41	Oklahoma	0.73
14	Oregon	1.12
13	Pennsylvania	1.13
45	Rhode Island	0.62
15	South Carolina	1.10
19	South Dakota	1.05
40	Tennessee	0.76
35	Texas	0.86
26	Utah	0.94
1	Vermont	1.75
9	Virginia	1.25
37	Washington	0.84
46	West Virginia	0.58
46	Wisconsin	0.58
27	Wyoming	0.93

RANK ORDER

RANK	STATE	PERCENT
1	Vermont	1.75
2	Delaware	1.72
3	Arizona	1.65
4	Idaho	1.48
5	North Carolina	1.41
6	Maryland	1.37
7	California	1.35
7	New Mexico	1.35
9	Virginia	1.25
10	Florida	1.19
11	Kentucky	1.17
11	Nebraska	1.17
13	Pennsylvania	1.13
14	Oregon	1.12
15	Alaska	1.10
15	South Carolina	1.10
17	Illinois	1.06
17	Michigan	1.06
19	Nevada	1.05
19	South Dakota	1.05
21	Louisiana	1.03
22	Indiana	1.02
23	Georgia	0.96
24	Missouri	0.95
24	New Jersey	0.95
26	Utah	0.94
27	Wyoming	0.93
28	Arkansas	0.92
29	Mississippi	0.91
29	Montana	0.91
29	New Hampshire	0.91
32	Iowa	0.90
33	Alabama	0.88
34	Colorado	0.87
35	Texas	0.86
36	Maine	0.85
37	Kansas	0.84
37	Washington	0.84
39	Connecticut	0.83
40	Tennessee	0.76
41	Oklahoma	0.73
42	Massachusetts	0.70
43	Minnesota	0.68
44	Ohio	0.66
45	Rhode Island	0.62
46	West Virginia	0.58
46	Wisconsin	0.58
48	New York	0.57
49	North Dakota	0.50
50	Hawaii	0.07

District of Columbia**	NA

Source: Morgan Quitno Corporation using data from U.S. Bureau of the Census
"Government Finances: 1991-92 (Preliminary Report)" (August 1994, GF/92-5P)
*Preliminary data.
**Not applicable.

Local Government Expenditures for Police Protection in 1992

National Total = $29,681,641,000*

ALPHA ORDER					RANK ORDER			

ALPHA ORDER

RANK	STATE	EXPENDITURES	% of USA
25	Alabama	$325,241,000	1.10%
42	Alaska	81,026,000	0.27%
17	Arizona	499,814,000	1.68%
37	Arkansas	130,410,000	0.44%
1	California	5,127,895,000	17.28%
21	Colorado	413,934,000	1.39%
23	Connecticut	386,452,000	1.30%
45	Delaware	61,805,000	0.21%
3	Florida	2,068,988,000	6.97%
12	Georgia	611,944,000	2.06%
34	Hawaii	162,635,000	0.55%
41	Idaho	85,110,000	0.29%
5	Illinois	1,507,974,000	5.08%
24	Indiana	340,767,000	1.15%
31	Iowa	218,139,000	0.73%
29	Kansas	234,964,000	0.79%
32	Kentucky	209,950,000	0.71%
20	Louisiana	448,827,000	1.51%
43	Maine	73,062,000	0.25%
14	Maryland	562,475,000	1.90%
10	Massachusetts	672,338,000	2.27%
8	Michigan	1,062,929,000	3.58%
19	Minnesota	450,461,000	1.52%
35	Mississippi	151,052,000	0.51%
18	Missouri	456,760,000	1.54%
47	Montana	56,797,000	0.19%
38	Nebraska	111,630,000	0.38%
30	Nevada	225,167,000	0.76%
40	New Hampshire	103,531,000	0.35%
7	New Jersey	1,121,276,000	3.78%
33	New Mexico	165,056,000	0.56%
2	New York	3,439,548,000	11.59%
15	North Carolina	552,936,000	1.86%
49	North Dakota	34,376,000	0.12%
6	Ohio	1,184,196,000	3.99%
27	Oklahoma	249,015,000	0.84%
26	Oregon	287,763,000	0.97%
9	Pennsylvania	931,496,000	3.14%
39	Rhode Island	107,584,000	0.36%
28	South Carolina	247,221,000	0.83%
48	South Dakota	42,759,000	0.14%
22	Tennessee	408,056,000	1.37%
4	Texas	1,729,926,000	5.83%
36	Utah	143,208,000	0.48%
50	Vermont	27,877,000	0.09%
13	Virginia	603,868,000	2.03%
16	Washington	518,997,000	1.75%
44	West Virginia	69,133,000	0.23%
11	Wisconsin	645,569,000	2.17%
46	Wyoming	56,955,000	0.19%

RANK ORDER

RANK	STATE	EXPENDITURES	% of USA
1	California	$5,127,895,000	17.28%
2	New York	3,439,548,000	11.59%
3	Florida	2,068,988,000	6.97%
4	Texas	1,729,926,000	5.83%
5	Illinois	1,507,974,000	5.08%
6	Ohio	1,184,196,000	3.99%
7	New Jersey	1,121,276,000	3.78%
8	Michigan	1,062,929,000	3.58%
9	Pennsylvania	931,496,000	3.14%
10	Massachusetts	672,338,000	2.27%
11	Wisconsin	645,569,000	2.17%
12	Georgia	611,944,000	2.06%
13	Virginia	603,868,000	2.03%
14	Maryland	562,475,000	1.90%
15	North Carolina	552,936,000	1.86%
16	Washington	518,997,000	1.75%
17	Arizona	499,814,000	1.68%
18	Missouri	456,760,000	1.54%
19	Minnesota	450,461,000	1.52%
20	Louisiana	448,827,000	1.51%
21	Colorado	413,934,000	1.39%
22	Tennessee	408,056,000	1.37%
23	Connecticut	386,452,000	1.30%
24	Indiana	340,767,000	1.15%
25	Alabama	325,241,000	1.10%
26	Oregon	287,763,000	0.97%
27	Oklahoma	249,015,000	0.84%
28	South Carolina	247,221,000	0.83%
29	Kansas	234,964,000	0.79%
30	Nevada	225,167,000	0.76%
31	Iowa	218,139,000	0.73%
32	Kentucky	209,950,000	0.71%
33	New Mexico	165,056,000	0.56%
34	Hawaii	162,635,000	0.55%
35	Mississippi	151,052,000	0.51%
36	Utah	143,208,000	0.48%
37	Arkansas	130,410,000	0.44%
38	Nebraska	111,630,000	0.38%
39	Rhode Island	107,584,000	0.36%
40	New Hampshire	103,531,000	0.35%
41	Idaho	85,110,000	0.29%
42	Alaska	81,026,000	0.27%
43	Maine	73,062,000	0.25%
44	West Virginia	69,133,000	0.23%
45	Delaware	61,805,000	0.21%
46	Wyoming	56,955,000	0.19%
47	Montana	56,797,000	0.19%
48	South Dakota	42,759,000	0.14%
49	North Dakota	34,376,000	0.12%
50	Vermont	27,877,000	0.09%
	District of Columbia	272,749,000	0.92%

Source: U.S. Bureau of the Census
"Government Finances: 1991–92 (Preliminary Report)" (August 1994, GF/92-5P)
*Direct expenditures. Preliminary data.

Per Capita Local Government Expenditures for Police Protection in 1992

National Per Capita = $116.36*

ALPHA ORDER

RANK ORDER

RANK	STATE	PER CAPITA	RANK	STATE	PER CAPITA
35	Alabama	$78.60	1	New York	$189.94
7	Alaska	137.80	2	Nevada	168.54
8	Arizona	130.43	3	California	165.98
47	Arkansas	54.47	4	Florida	153.45
3	California	165.98	5	New Jersey	143.39
12	Colorado	119.46	6	Hawaii	140.69
13	Connecticut	117.86	7	Alaska	137.80
29	Delaware	89.44	8	Arizona	130.43
4	Florida	153.45	9	Illinois	129.85
28	Georgia	90.35	10	Wisconsin	129.29
6	Hawaii	140.69	11	Wyoming	122.48
33	Idaho	79.84	12	Colorado	119.46
9	Illinois	129.85	13	Connecticut	117.86
43	Indiana	60.23	14	Maryland	114.39
36	Iowa	77.82	15	Michigan	112.67
26	Kansas	93.43	16	Massachusetts	112.19
46	Kentucky	55.93	17	Rhode Island	107.48
19	Louisiana	104.89	18	Ohio	107.45
44	Maine	59.11	19	Louisiana	104.89
14	Maryland	114.39	20	New Mexico	104.33
16	Massachusetts	112.19	21	Washington	100.91
15	Michigan	112.67	22	Minnesota	100.82
22	Minnesota	100.82	23	Texas	97.83
45	Mississippi	57.76	24	Oregon	96.82
30	Missouri	87.99	25	Virginia	94.44
40	Montana	69.10	26	Kansas	93.43
39	Nebraska	69.73	27	New Hampshire	92.85
2	Nevada	168.54	28	Georgia	90.35
27	New Hampshire	92.85	29	Delaware	89.44
5	New Jersey	143.39	30	Missouri	87.99
20	New Mexico	104.33	31	Tennessee	81.21
1	New York	189.94	32	North Carolina	80.89
32	North Carolina	80.89	33	Idaho	79.84
48	North Dakota	54.22	34	Utah	79.08
18	Ohio	107.45	35	Alabama	78.60
37	Oklahoma	77.70	36	Iowa	77.82
24	Oregon	96.82	37	Oklahoma	77.70
38	Pennsylvania	77.66	38	Pennsylvania	77.66
17	Rhode Island	107.48	39	Nebraska	69.73
41	South Carolina	68.62	40	Montana	69.10
42	South Dakota	60.39	41	South Carolina	68.62
31	Tennessee	81.21	42	South Dakota	60.39
23	Texas	97.83	43	Indiana	60.23
34	Utah	79.08	44	Maine	59.11
49	Vermont	48.82	45	Mississippi	57.76
25	Virginia	94.44	46	Kentucky	55.93
21	Washington	100.91	47	Arkansas	54.47
50	West Virginia	38.22	48	North Dakota	54.22
10	Wisconsin	129.29	49	Vermont	48.82
11	Wyoming	122.48	50	West Virginia	38.22

District of Columbia   466.24

Source: Morgan Quitno Corporation using data from U.S. Bureau of the Census
"Government Finances: 1991–92 (Preliminary Report)" (August 1994, GF/92-5P)
Direct expenditures. Preliminary data.

Local Government Expenditures for Police Protection
As a Percent of All Direct Expenditures in 1992
National Percent = 4.58% of Direct Expenditures*

<table>
<tr><th colspan="3">ALPHA ORDER</th><th colspan="3">RANK ORDER</th></tr>
<tr><th>RANK</th><th>STATE</th><th>PERCENT</th><th>RANK</th><th>STATE</th><th>PERCENT</th></tr>
<tr><td>26</td><td>Alabama</td><td>4.29</td><td>1</td><td>Hawaii</td><td>10.84</td></tr>
<tr><td>43</td><td>Alaska</td><td>3.40</td><td>2</td><td>Rhode Island</td><td>6.47</td></tr>
<tr><td>13</td><td>Arizona</td><td>5.09</td><td>3</td><td>Nevada</td><td>6.12</td></tr>
<tr><td>28</td><td>Arkansas</td><td>3.94</td><td>4</td><td>Florida</td><td>5.84</td></tr>
<tr><td>15</td><td>California</td><td>4.93</td><td>5</td><td>Illinois</td><td>5.66</td></tr>
<tr><td>25</td><td>Colorado</td><td>4.32</td><td>6</td><td>Maryland</td><td>5.53</td></tr>
<tr><td>14</td><td>Connecticut</td><td>5.02</td><td>7</td><td>New Mexico</td><td>5.46</td></tr>
<tr><td>10</td><td>Delaware</td><td>5.20</td><td>8</td><td>New Jersey</td><td>5.37</td></tr>
<tr><td>4</td><td>Florida</td><td>5.84</td><td>9</td><td>Louisiana</td><td>5.30</td></tr>
<tr><td>31</td><td>Georgia</td><td>3.89</td><td>10</td><td>Delaware</td><td>5.20</td></tr>
<tr><td>1</td><td>Hawaii</td><td>10.84</td><td>10</td><td>New Hampshire</td><td>5.20</td></tr>
<tr><td>19</td><td>Idaho</td><td>4.68</td><td>12</td><td>Ohio</td><td>5.12</td></tr>
<tr><td>5</td><td>Illinois</td><td>5.66</td><td>13</td><td>Arizona</td><td>5.09</td></tr>
<tr><td>47</td><td>Indiana</td><td>3.04</td><td>14</td><td>Connecticut</td><td>5.02</td></tr>
<tr><td>38</td><td>Iowa</td><td>3.55</td><td>15</td><td>California</td><td>4.93</td></tr>
<tr><td>27</td><td>Kansas</td><td>4.22</td><td>16</td><td>Missouri</td><td>4.90</td></tr>
<tr><td>37</td><td>Kentucky</td><td>3.62</td><td>16</td><td>Wisconsin</td><td>4.90</td></tr>
<tr><td>9</td><td>Louisiana</td><td>5.30</td><td>18</td><td>Massachusetts</td><td>4.75</td></tr>
<tr><td>44</td><td>Maine</td><td>3.29</td><td>19</td><td>Idaho</td><td>4.68</td></tr>
<tr><td>6</td><td>Maryland</td><td>5.53</td><td>20</td><td>Michigan</td><td>4.66</td></tr>
<tr><td>18</td><td>Massachusetts</td><td>4.75</td><td>21</td><td>Virginia</td><td>4.61</td></tr>
<tr><td>20</td><td>Michigan</td><td>4.66</td><td>22</td><td>New York</td><td>4.56</td></tr>
<tr><td>45</td><td>Minnesota</td><td>3.25</td><td>23</td><td>Oklahoma</td><td>4.44</td></tr>
<tr><td>42</td><td>Mississippi</td><td>3.41</td><td>24</td><td>Texas</td><td>4.33</td></tr>
<tr><td>16</td><td>Missouri</td><td>4.90</td><td>25</td><td>Colorado</td><td>4.32</td></tr>
<tr><td>32</td><td>Montana</td><td>3.85</td><td>26</td><td>Alabama</td><td>4.29</td></tr>
<tr><td>50</td><td>Nebraska</td><td>2.31</td><td>27</td><td>Kansas</td><td>4.22</td></tr>
<tr><td>3</td><td>Nevada</td><td>6.12</td><td>28</td><td>Arkansas</td><td>3.94</td></tr>
<tr><td>10</td><td>New Hampshire</td><td>5.20</td><td>29</td><td>Wyoming</td><td>3.91</td></tr>
<tr><td>8</td><td>New Jersey</td><td>5.37</td><td>30</td><td>Oregon</td><td>3.90</td></tr>
<tr><td>7</td><td>New Mexico</td><td>5.46</td><td>31</td><td>Georgia</td><td>3.89</td></tr>
<tr><td>22</td><td>New York</td><td>4.56</td><td>32</td><td>Montana</td><td>3.85</td></tr>
<tr><td>34</td><td>North Carolina</td><td>3.72</td><td>33</td><td>South Carolina</td><td>3.78</td></tr>
<tr><td>46</td><td>North Dakota</td><td>3.12</td><td>34</td><td>North Carolina</td><td>3.72</td></tr>
<tr><td>12</td><td>Ohio</td><td>5.12</td><td>35</td><td>South Dakota</td><td>3.67</td></tr>
<tr><td>23</td><td>Oklahoma</td><td>4.44</td><td>36</td><td>Utah</td><td>3.65</td></tr>
<tr><td>30</td><td>Oregon</td><td>3.90</td><td>37</td><td>Kentucky</td><td>3.62</td></tr>
<tr><td>40</td><td>Pennsylvania</td><td>3.50</td><td>38</td><td>Iowa</td><td>3.55</td></tr>
<tr><td>2</td><td>Rhode Island</td><td>6.47</td><td>39</td><td>Tennessee</td><td>3.51</td></tr>
<tr><td>33</td><td>South Carolina</td><td>3.78</td><td>40</td><td>Pennsylvania</td><td>3.50</td></tr>
<tr><td>35</td><td>South Dakota</td><td>3.67</td><td>41</td><td>Washington</td><td>3.49</td></tr>
<tr><td>39</td><td>Tennessee</td><td>3.51</td><td>42</td><td>Mississippi</td><td>3.41</td></tr>
<tr><td>24</td><td>Texas</td><td>4.33</td><td>43</td><td>Alaska</td><td>3.40</td></tr>
<tr><td>36</td><td>Utah</td><td>3.65</td><td>44</td><td>Maine</td><td>3.29</td></tr>
<tr><td>48</td><td>Vermont</td><td>2.67</td><td>45</td><td>Minnesota</td><td>3.25</td></tr>
<tr><td>21</td><td>Virginia</td><td>4.61</td><td>46</td><td>North Dakota</td><td>3.12</td></tr>
<tr><td>41</td><td>Washington</td><td>3.49</td><td>47</td><td>Indiana</td><td>3.04</td></tr>
<tr><td>49</td><td>West Virginia</td><td>2.55</td><td>48</td><td>Vermont</td><td>2.67</td></tr>
<tr><td>16</td><td>Wisconsin</td><td>4.90</td><td>49</td><td>West Virginia</td><td>2.55</td></tr>
<tr><td>29</td><td>Wyoming</td><td>3.91</td><td>50</td><td>Nebraska</td><td>2.31</td></tr>
<tr><td></td><td></td><td></td><td></td><td>District of Columbia</td><td>4.68</td></tr>
</table>

Source: Morgan Quitno Corporation using data from U.S. Bureau of the Census
  "Government Finances: 1991-92 (Preliminary Report)" (August 1994, GF/92-5P)
*Preliminary data.

State and Local Government Expenditures for Corrections in 1992

National Total = $28,605,642,000*

<table>
<tr><td colspan="4">ALPHA ORDER</td><td colspan="4">RANK ORDER</td></tr>
<tr><td>RANK</td><td>STATE</td><td>EXPENDITURES</td><td>% of USA</td><td>RANK</td><td>STATE</td><td>EXPENDITURES</td><td>% of USA</td></tr>
<tr><td>28</td><td>Alabama</td><td>$245,404,000</td><td>0.86%</td><td>1</td><td>California</td><td>$4,953,217,000</td><td>17.32%</td></tr>
<tr><td>34</td><td>Alaska</td><td>132,186,000</td><td>0.46%</td><td>2</td><td>New York</td><td>3,464,465,000</td><td>12.11%</td></tr>
<tr><td>17</td><td>Arizona</td><td>484,196,000</td><td>1.69%</td><td>3</td><td>Florida</td><td>1,883,641,000</td><td>6.58%</td></tr>
<tr><td>35</td><td>Arkansas</td><td>130,677,000</td><td>0.46%</td><td>4</td><td>Texas</td><td>1,828,736,000</td><td>6.39%</td></tr>
<tr><td>1</td><td>California</td><td>4,953,217,000</td><td>17.32%</td><td>5</td><td>Michigan</td><td>1,120,302,000</td><td>3.92%</td></tr>
<tr><td>22</td><td>Colorado</td><td>387,878,000</td><td>1.36%</td><td>6</td><td>Pennsylvania</td><td>1,042,026,000</td><td>3.64%</td></tr>
<tr><td>19</td><td>Connecticut</td><td>420,815,000</td><td>1.47%</td><td>7</td><td>Illinois</td><td>935,022,000</td><td>3.27%</td></tr>
<tr><td>36</td><td>Delaware</td><td>109,140,000</td><td>0.38%</td><td>8</td><td>New Jersey</td><td>924,289,000</td><td>3.23%</td></tr>
<tr><td>3</td><td>Florida</td><td>1,883,641,000</td><td>6.58%</td><td>9</td><td>Ohio</td><td>899,486,000</td><td>3.14%</td></tr>
<tr><td>10</td><td>Georgia</td><td>800,837,000</td><td>2.80%</td><td>10</td><td>Georgia</td><td>800,837,000</td><td>2.80%</td></tr>
<tr><td>39</td><td>Hawaii</td><td>104,655,000</td><td>0.37%</td><td>11</td><td>Washington</td><td>730,646,000</td><td>2.55%</td></tr>
<tr><td>42</td><td>Idaho</td><td>71,571,000</td><td>0.25%</td><td>12</td><td>Virginia</td><td>671,499,000</td><td>2.35%</td></tr>
<tr><td>7</td><td>Illinois</td><td>935,022,000</td><td>3.27%</td><td>13</td><td>Maryland</td><td>664,307,000</td><td>2.32%</td></tr>
<tr><td>21</td><td>Indiana</td><td>399,414,000</td><td>1.40%</td><td>14</td><td>North Carolina</td><td>648,727,000</td><td>2.27%</td></tr>
<tr><td>47</td><td>Iowa</td><td>41,148,000</td><td>0.14%</td><td>15</td><td>Massachusetts</td><td>647,645,000</td><td>2.26%</td></tr>
<tr><td>31</td><td>Kansas</td><td>208,570,000</td><td>0.73%</td><td>16</td><td>Wisconsin</td><td>484,630,000</td><td>1.69%</td></tr>
<tr><td>27</td><td>Kentucky</td><td>264,224,000</td><td>0.92%</td><td>17</td><td>Arizona</td><td>484,196,000</td><td>1.69%</td></tr>
<tr><td>23</td><td>Louisiana</td><td>349,474,000</td><td>1.22%</td><td>18</td><td>Tennessee</td><td>456,239,000</td><td>1.59%</td></tr>
<tr><td>38</td><td>Maine</td><td>105,692,000</td><td>0.37%</td><td>19</td><td>Connecticut</td><td>420,815,000</td><td>1.47%</td></tr>
<tr><td>13</td><td>Maryland</td><td>664,307,000</td><td>2.32%</td><td>20</td><td>South Carolina</td><td>416,257,000</td><td>1.46%</td></tr>
<tr><td>15</td><td>Massachusetts</td><td>647,645,000</td><td>2.26%</td><td>21</td><td>Indiana</td><td>399,414,000</td><td>1.40%</td></tr>
<tr><td>5</td><td>Michigan</td><td>1,120,302,000</td><td>3.92%</td><td>22</td><td>Colorado</td><td>387,878,000</td><td>1.36%</td></tr>
<tr><td>25</td><td>Minnesota</td><td>298,146,000</td><td>1.04%</td><td>23</td><td>Louisiana</td><td>349,474,000</td><td>1.22%</td></tr>
<tr><td>40</td><td>Mississippi</td><td>103,250,000</td><td>0.36%</td><td>24</td><td>Oregon</td><td>302,925,000</td><td>1.06%</td></tr>
<tr><td>26</td><td>Missouri</td><td>281,495,000</td><td>0.98%</td><td>25</td><td>Minnesota</td><td>298,146,000</td><td>1.04%</td></tr>
<tr><td>45</td><td>Montana</td><td>45,344,000</td><td>0.16%</td><td>26</td><td>Missouri</td><td>281,495,000</td><td>0.98%</td></tr>
<tr><td>37</td><td>Nebraska</td><td>106,719,000</td><td>0.37%</td><td>27</td><td>Kentucky</td><td>264,224,000</td><td>0.92%</td></tr>
<tr><td>29</td><td>Nevada</td><td>233,190,000</td><td>0.82%</td><td>28</td><td>Alabama</td><td>245,404,000</td><td>0.86%</td></tr>
<tr><td>43</td><td>New Hampshire</td><td>70,978,000</td><td>0.25%</td><td>29</td><td>Nevada</td><td>233,190,000</td><td>0.82%</td></tr>
<tr><td>8</td><td>New Jersey</td><td>924,289,000</td><td>3.23%</td><td>30</td><td>Oklahoma</td><td>217,430,000</td><td>0.76%</td></tr>
<tr><td>32</td><td>New Mexico</td><td>165,679,000</td><td>0.58%</td><td>31</td><td>Kansas</td><td>208,570,000</td><td>0.73%</td></tr>
<tr><td>2</td><td>New York</td><td>3,464,465,000</td><td>12.11%</td><td>32</td><td>New Mexico</td><td>165,679,000</td><td>0.58%</td></tr>
<tr><td>14</td><td>North Carolina</td><td>648,727,000</td><td>2.27%</td><td>33</td><td>Utah</td><td>135,064,000</td><td>0.47%</td></tr>
<tr><td>50</td><td>North Dakota</td><td>26,903,000</td><td>0.09%</td><td>34</td><td>Alaska</td><td>132,186,000</td><td>0.46%</td></tr>
<tr><td>9</td><td>Ohio</td><td>899,486,000</td><td>3.14%</td><td>35</td><td>Arkansas</td><td>130,677,000</td><td>0.46%</td></tr>
<tr><td>30</td><td>Oklahoma</td><td>217,430,000</td><td>0.76%</td><td>36</td><td>Delaware</td><td>109,140,000</td><td>0.38%</td></tr>
<tr><td>24</td><td>Oregon</td><td>302,925,000</td><td>1.06%</td><td>37</td><td>Nebraska</td><td>106,719,000</td><td>0.37%</td></tr>
<tr><td>6</td><td>Pennsylvania</td><td>1,042,026,000</td><td>3.64%</td><td>38</td><td>Maine</td><td>105,692,000</td><td>0.37%</td></tr>
<tr><td>41</td><td>Rhode Island</td><td>101,022,000</td><td>0.35%</td><td>39</td><td>Hawaii</td><td>104,655,000</td><td>0.37%</td></tr>
<tr><td>20</td><td>South Carolina</td><td>416,257,000</td><td>1.46%</td><td>40</td><td>Mississippi</td><td>103,250,000</td><td>0.36%</td></tr>
<tr><td>48</td><td>South Dakota</td><td>38,899,000</td><td>0.14%</td><td>41</td><td>Rhode Island</td><td>101,022,000</td><td>0.35%</td></tr>
<tr><td>18</td><td>Tennessee</td><td>456,239,000</td><td>1.59%</td><td>42</td><td>Idaho</td><td>71,571,000</td><td>0.25%</td></tr>
<tr><td>4</td><td>Texas</td><td>1,828,736,000</td><td>6.39%</td><td>43</td><td>New Hampshire</td><td>70,978,000</td><td>0.25%</td></tr>
<tr><td>33</td><td>Utah</td><td>135,064,000</td><td>0.47%</td><td>44</td><td>West Virginia</td><td>57,545,000</td><td>0.20%</td></tr>
<tr><td>49</td><td>Vermont</td><td>33,748,000</td><td>0.12%</td><td>45</td><td>Montana</td><td>45,344,000</td><td>0.16%</td></tr>
<tr><td>12</td><td>Virginia</td><td>671,499,000</td><td>2.35%</td><td>46</td><td>Wyoming</td><td>41,974,000</td><td>0.15%</td></tr>
<tr><td>11</td><td>Washington</td><td>730,646,000</td><td>2.55%</td><td>47</td><td>Iowa</td><td>41,148,000</td><td>0.14%</td></tr>
<tr><td>44</td><td>West Virginia</td><td>57,545,000</td><td>0.20%</td><td>48</td><td>South Dakota</td><td>38,899,000</td><td>0.14%</td></tr>
<tr><td>16</td><td>Wisconsin</td><td>484,630,000</td><td>1.69%</td><td>49</td><td>Vermont</td><td>33,748,000</td><td>0.12%</td></tr>
<tr><td>46</td><td>Wyoming</td><td>41,974,000</td><td>0.15%</td><td>50</td><td>North Dakota</td><td>26,903,000</td><td>0.09%</td></tr>
<tr><td></td><td></td><td></td><td></td><td></td><td>District of Columbia</td><td>318,316,000</td><td>1.11%</td></tr>
</table>

Source: U.S. Bureau of the Census
  "Government Finances: 1991-92 (Preliminary Report)" (August 1994, GF/92-5P)
Direct expenditures. Preliminary data.

Per Capita State and Local Government Expenditures for Corrections in 1992

National Per Capita = $112.14*

ALPHA ORDER

RANK	STATE	PER CAPITA
41	Alabama	$59.30
1	Alaska	224.81
10	Arizona	126.36
45	Arkansas	54.59
4	California	160.32
15	Colorado	111.94
9	Connecticut	128.34
5	Delaware	157.95
7	Florida	139.70
12	Georgia	118.24
25	Hawaii	90.53
37	Idaho	67.14
32	Illinois	80.52
34	Indiana	70.59
50	Iowa	14.68
29	Kansas	82.93
35	Kentucky	70.38
30	Louisiana	81.67
28	Maine	85.51
8	Maryland	135.10
16	Massachusetts	108.07
11	Michigan	118.75
38	Minnesota	66.73
48	Mississippi	39.48
46	Missouri	54.23
43	Montana	55.16
39	Nebraska	66.66
3	Nevada	174.54
40	New Hampshire	63.66
13	New Jersey	118.20
18	New Mexico	104.73
2	New York	191.31
23	North Carolina	94.90
47	North Dakota	42.43
31	Ohio	81.62
36	Oklahoma	67.84
20	Oregon	101.93
27	Pennsylvania	86.87
21	Rhode Island	100.92
14	South Carolina	115.53
44	South Dakota	54.94
24	Tennessee	90.79
19	Texas	103.42
33	Utah	74.58
42	Vermont	59.10
17	Virginia	105.02
6	Washington	142.07
49	West Virginia	31.81
22	Wisconsin	97.06
26	Wyoming	90.27

RANK ORDER

RANK	STATE	PER CAPITA
1	Alaska	$224.81
2	New York	191.31
3	Nevada	174.54
4	California	160.32
5	Delaware	157.95
6	Washington	142.07
7	Florida	139.70
8	Maryland	135.10
9	Connecticut	128.34
10	Arizona	126.36
11	Michigan	118.75
12	Georgia	118.24
13	New Jersey	118.20
14	South Carolina	115.53
15	Colorado	111.94
16	Massachusetts	108.07
17	Virginia	105.02
18	New Mexico	104.73
19	Texas	103.42
20	Oregon	101.93
21	Rhode Island	100.92
22	Wisconsin	97.06
23	North Carolina	94.90
24	Tennessee	90.79
25	Hawaii	90.53
26	Wyoming	90.27
27	Pennsylvania	86.87
28	Maine	85.51
29	Kansas	82.93
30	Louisiana	81.67
31	Ohio	81.62
32	Illinois	80.52
33	Utah	74.58
34	Indiana	70.59
35	Kentucky	70.38
36	Oklahoma	67.84
37	Idaho	67.14
38	Minnesota	66.73
39	Nebraska	66.66
40	New Hampshire	63.66
41	Alabama	59.30
42	Vermont	59.10
43	Montana	55.16
44	South Dakota	54.94
45	Arkansas	54.59
46	Missouri	54.23
47	North Dakota	42.43
48	Mississippi	39.48
49	West Virginia	31.81
50	Iowa	14.68
	District of Columbia	544.13

Source: Morgan Quitno Corporation using data from U.S. Bureau of the Census
"Government Finances: 1991-92 (Preliminary Report)" (August 1994, GF/92-5P)
*Direct expenditures. Preliminary data.

State and Local Government Expenditures for Corrections
As a Percent of All Direct Expenditures in 1992
National Percent = 2.49% of Direct Expenditures*

ALPHA ORDER

RANK	STATE	PERCENT
38	Alabama	1.63
25	Alaska	2.01
7	Arizona	3.04
36	Arkansas	1.78
5	California	3.09
14	Colorado	2.57
17	Connecticut	2.44
3	Delaware	3.34
2	Florida	3.48
6	Georgia	3.07
40	Hawaii	1.57
31	Idaho	1.96
27	Illinois	2.00
25	Indiana	2.01
50	Iowa	0.37
22	Kansas	2.17
33	Kentucky	1.95
28	Louisiana	1.98
24	Maine	2.02
4	Maryland	3.22
23	Massachusetts	2.13
12	Michigan	2.71
45	Minnesota	1.32
47	Mississippi	1.23
37	Missouri	1.66
44	Montana	1.36
43	Nebraska	1.44
1	Nevada	3.64
41	New Hampshire	1.55
21	New Jersey	2.18
16	New Mexico	2.51
11	New York	2.80
15	North Carolina	2.56
48	North Dakota	1.00
29	Ohio	1.97
34	Oklahoma	1.87
20	Oregon	2.20
31	Pennsylvania	1.96
29	Rhode Island	1.97
8	South Carolina	2.98
39	South Dakota	1.59
18	Tennessee	2.31
10	Texas	2.82
35	Utah	1.86
46	Vermont	1.31
9	Virginia	2.85
13	Washington	2.64
49	West Virginia	0.84
19	Wisconsin	2.21
42	Wyoming	1.54

RANK ORDER

RANK	STATE	PERCENT
1	Nevada	3.64
2	Florida	3.48
3	Delaware	3.34
4	Maryland	3.22
5	California	3.09
6	Georgia	3.07
7	Arizona	3.04
8	South Carolina	2.98
9	Virginia	2.85
10	Texas	2.82
11	New York	2.80
12	Michigan	2.71
13	Washington	2.64
14	Colorado	2.57
15	North Carolina	2.56
16	New Mexico	2.51
17	Connecticut	2.44
18	Tennessee	2.31
19	Wisconsin	2.21
20	Oregon	2.20
21	New Jersey	2.18
22	Kansas	2.17
23	Massachusetts	2.13
24	Maine	2.02
25	Alaska	2.01
25	Indiana	2.01
27	Illinois	2.00
28	Louisiana	1.98
29	Ohio	1.97
29	Rhode Island	1.97
31	Idaho	1.96
31	Pennsylvania	1.96
33	Kentucky	1.95
34	Oklahoma	1.87
35	Utah	1.86
36	Arkansas	1.78
37	Missouri	1.66
38	Alabama	1.63
39	South Dakota	1.59
40	Hawaii	1.57
41	New Hampshire	1.55
42	Wyoming	1.54
43	Nebraska	1.44
44	Montana	1.36
45	Minnesota	1.32
46	Vermont	1.31
47	Mississippi	1.23
48	North Dakota	1.00
49	West Virginia	0.84
50	Iowa	0.37

| | District of Columbia | 5.47 |

Source: Morgan Quitno Corporation using data from U.S. Bureau of the Census
   "Government Finances: 1991-92 (Preliminary Report)" (August 1994, GF/92-5P)
*Preliminary data.

State Government Expenditures for Corrections in 1992

National Total = $18,306,035,000*

ALPHA ORDER

RANK	STATE	EXPENDITURES	% of USA
28	Alabama	$178,595,000	0.98%
31	Alaska	130,904,000	0.72%
18	Arizona	314,497,000	1.72%
36	Arkansas	103,169,000	0.56%
1	California	2,900,302,000	15.84%
22	Colorado	261,678,000	1.43%
15	Connecticut	420,815,000	2.30%
34	Delaware	109,140,000	0.60%
4	Florida	1,036,611,000	5.66%
9	Georgia	579,334,000	3.16%
35	Hawaii	104,655,000	0.57%
42	Idaho	52,764,000	0.29%
7	Illinois	592,882,000	3.24%
19	Indiana	301,275,000	1.65%
50	Iowa	9,869,000	0.05%
27	Kansas	179,103,000	0.98%
26	Kentucky	181,074,000	0.99%
23	Louisiana	234,446,000	1.28%
41	Maine	67,339,000	0.37%
11	Maryland	545,585,000	2.98%
14	Massachusetts	494,016,000	2.70%
5	Michigan	847,008,000	4.63%
30	Minnesota	163,206,000	0.89%
39	Mississippi	85,149,000	0.47%
24	Missouri	201,052,000	1.10%
44	Montana	37,479,000	0.20%
40	Nebraska	73,336,000	0.40%
33	Nevada	126,800,000	0.69%
43	New Hampshire	45,428,000	0.25%
8	New Jersey	590,599,000	3.23%
32	New Mexico	127,490,000	0.70%
2	New York	1,735,889,000	9.48%
13	North Carolina	540,383,000	2.95%
49	North Dakota	16,081,000	0.09%
6	Ohio	648,887,000	3.54%
25	Oklahoma	195,712,000	1.07%
29	Oregon	175,066,000	0.96%
10	Pennsylvania	552,462,000	3.02%
37	Rhode Island	101,022,000	0.55%
20	South Carolina	297,225,000	1.62%
47	South Dakota	29,893,000	0.16%
17	Tennessee	317,298,000	1.73%
3	Texas	1,162,612,000	6.35%
38	Utah	96,951,000	0.53%
46	Vermont	33,644,000	0.18%
16	Virginia	413,269,000	2.26%
12	Washington	544,770,000	2.98%
45	West Virginia	36,491,000	0.20%
21	Wisconsin	288,869,000	1.58%
48	Wyoming	23,911,000	0.13%

RANK ORDER

RANK	STATE	EXPENDITURES	% of USA
1	California	$2,900,302,000	15.84%
2	New York	1,735,889,000	9.48%
3	Texas	1,162,612,000	6.35%
4	Florida	1,036,611,000	5.66%
5	Michigan	847,008,000	4.63%
6	Ohio	648,887,000	3.54%
7	Illinois	592,882,000	3.24%
8	New Jersey	590,599,000	3.23%
9	Georgia	579,334,000	3.16%
10	Pennsylvania	552,462,000	3.02%
11	Maryland	545,585,000	2.98%
12	Washington	544,770,000	2.98%
13	North Carolina	540,383,000	2.95%
14	Massachusetts	494,016,000	2.70%
15	Connecticut	420,815,000	2.30%
16	Virginia	413,269,000	2.26%
17	Tennessee	317,298,000	1.73%
18	Arizona	314,497,000	1.72%
19	Indiana	301,275,000	1.65%
20	South Carolina	297,225,000	1.62%
21	Wisconsin	288,869,000	1.58%
22	Colorado	261,678,000	1.43%
23	Louisiana	234,446,000	1.28%
24	Missouri	201,052,000	1.10%
25	Oklahoma	195,712,000	1.07%
26	Kentucky	181,074,000	0.99%
27	Kansas	179,103,000	0.98%
28	Alabama	178,595,000	0.98%
29	Oregon	175,066,000	0.96%
30	Minnesota	163,206,000	0.89%
31	Alaska	130,904,000	0.72%
32	New Mexico	127,490,000	0.70%
33	Nevada	126,800,000	0.69%
34	Delaware	109,140,000	0.60%
35	Hawaii	104,655,000	0.57%
36	Arkansas	103,169,000	0.56%
37	Rhode Island	101,022,000	0.55%
38	Utah	96,951,000	0.53%
39	Mississippi	85,149,000	0.47%
40	Nebraska	73,336,000	0.40%
41	Maine	67,339,000	0.37%
42	Idaho	52,764,000	0.29%
43	New Hampshire	45,428,000	0.25%
44	Montana	37,479,000	0.20%
45	West Virginia	36,491,000	0.20%
46	Vermont	33,644,000	0.18%
47	South Dakota	29,893,000	0.16%
48	Wyoming	23,911,000	0.13%
49	North Dakota	16,081,000	0.09%
50	Iowa	9,869,000	0.05%
	District of Columbia**	NA	NA

Source: U.S. Bureau of the Census
  "Government Finances: 1991-92 (Preliminary Report)" (August 1994, GF/92-5P)
*Direct expenditures. Preliminary data.
**Not applicable.

Per Capita State Government Expenditures for Corrections in 1992

National Per Capita = $71.77*

ALPHA ORDER

RANK	STATE	PER CAPITA
41	Alabama	$43.16
1	Alaska	222.63
15	Arizona	82.07
42	Arkansas	43.09
9	California	93.88
19	Colorado	75.52
3	Connecticut	128.34
2	Delaware	157.95
18	Florida	76.88
12	Georgia	85.54
10	Hawaii	90.53
36	Idaho	49.50
35	Illinois	51.05
33	Indiana	53.25
50	Iowa	3.52
21	Kansas	71.21
37	Kentucky	48.23
30	Louisiana	54.79
31	Maine	54.48
4	Maryland	110.96
14	Massachusetts	82.43
11	Michigan	89.78
46	Minnesota	36.53
47	Mississippi	32.56
45	Missouri	38.73
40	Montana	45.59
39	Nebraska	45.81
8	Nevada	94.91
44	New Hampshire	40.74
19	New Jersey	75.52
16	New Mexico	80.59
7	New York	95.86
17	North Carolina	79.05
48	North Dakota	25.36
28	Ohio	58.88
25	Oklahoma	61.06
27	Oregon	58.91
38	Pennsylvania	46.06
6	Rhode Island	100.92
13	South Carolina	82.49
43	South Dakota	42.22
24	Tennessee	63.14
22	Texas	65.75
32	Utah	53.53
26	Vermont	58.92
23	Virginia	64.63
5	Washington	105.92
49	West Virginia	20.17
29	Wisconsin	57.85
34	Wyoming	51.42

RANK ORDER

RANK	STATE	PER CAPITA
1	Alaska	$222.63
2	Delaware	157.95
3	Connecticut	128.34
4	Maryland	110.96
5	Washington	105.92
6	Rhode Island	100.92
7	New York	95.86
8	Nevada	94.91
9	California	93.88
10	Hawaii	90.53
11	Michigan	89.78
12	Georgia	85.54
13	South Carolina	82.49
14	Massachusetts	82.43
15	Arizona	82.07
16	New Mexico	80.59
17	North Carolina	79.05
18	Florida	76.88
19	Colorado	75.52
19	New Jersey	75.52
21	Kansas	71.21
22	Texas	65.75
23	Virginia	64.63
24	Tennessee	63.14
25	Oklahoma	61.06
26	Vermont	58.92
27	Oregon	58.91
28	Ohio	58.88
29	Wisconsin	57.85
30	Louisiana	54.79
31	Maine	54.48
32	Utah	53.53
33	Indiana	53.25
34	Wyoming	51.42
35	Illinois	51.05
36	Idaho	49.50
37	Kentucky	48.23
38	Pennsylvania	46.06
39	Nebraska	45.81
40	Montana	45.59
41	Alabama	43.16
42	Arkansas	43.09
43	South Dakota	42.22
44	New Hampshire	40.74
45	Missouri	38.73
46	Minnesota	36.53
47	Mississippi	32.56
48	North Dakota	25.36
49	West Virginia	20.17
50	Iowa	3.52
	District of Columbia**	NA

Source: Morgan Quitno Corporation using data from U.S. Bureau of the Census
   "Government Finances: 1991–92 (Preliminary Report)" (August 1994, GF/92-5P)
*Direct expenditures. Preliminary data.
**Not applicable.

State Government Expenditures for Corrections
As a Percent of All Direct Expenditures in 1992
National Percent = 3.67% of Direct Expenditures*

ALPHA ORDER

RANK ORDER

RANK	STATE	PERCENT	RANK	STATE	PERCENT
36	Alabama	2.38	1	Georgia	5.61
23	Alaska	3.11	2	Florida	5.55
5	Arizona	5.16	3	Delaware	5.24
34	Arkansas	2.57	4	Maryland	5.22
6	California	5.15	5	Arizona	5.16
8	Colorado	4.74	6	California	5.15
13	Connecticut	4.41	7	North Carolina	5.14
3	Delaware	5.24	8	Colorado	4.74
2	Florida	5.55	9	Nevada	4.66
1	Georgia	5.61	10	Texas	4.65
44	Hawaii	2.02	11	Michigan	4.57
28	Idaho	2.89	12	Kansas	4.43
25	Illinois	2.95	13	Connecticut	4.41
20	Indiana	3.48	14	Washington	4.26
50	Iowa	0.20	15	South Carolina	4.02
12	Kansas	4.43	16	Virginia	3.96
37	Kentucky	2.33	17	Tennessee	3.91
34	Louisiana	2.57	18	New Mexico	3.58
39	Maine	2.24	18	New York	3.58
4	Maryland	5.22	20	Indiana	3.48
24	Massachusetts	3.03	21	Wisconsin	3.30
11	Michigan	4.57	22	Oklahoma	3.25
46	Minnesota	1.86	23	Alaska	3.11
41	Mississippi	2.13	24	Massachusetts	3.03
33	Missouri	2.62	25	Illinois	2.95
43	Montana	2.03	26	Rhode Island	2.91
30	Nebraska	2.84	27	Utah	2.90
9	Nevada	4.66	28	Idaho	2.89
47	New Hampshire	1.76	28	Ohio	2.89
31	New Jersey	2.75	30	Nebraska	2.84
18	New Mexico	3.58	31	New Jersey	2.75
18	New York	3.58	31	Oregon	2.75
7	North Carolina	5.14	33	Missouri	2.62
48	North Dakota	1.01	34	Arkansas	2.57
28	Ohio	2.89	34	Louisiana	2.57
22	Oklahoma	3.25	36	Alabama	2.38
31	Oregon	2.75	37	Kentucky	2.33
42	Pennsylvania	2.09	37	South Dakota	2.33
26	Rhode Island	2.91	39	Maine	2.24
15	South Carolina	4.02	40	Vermont	2.19
37	South Dakota	2.33	41	Mississippi	2.13
17	Tennessee	3.91	42	Pennsylvania	2.09
10	Texas	4.65	43	Montana	2.03
27	Utah	2.90	44	Hawaii	2.02
40	Vermont	2.19	45	Wyoming	1.88
16	Virginia	3.96	46	Minnesota	1.86
14	Washington	4.26	47	New Hampshire	1.76
49	West Virginia	0.89	48	North Dakota	1.01
21	Wisconsin	3.30	49	West Virginia	0.89
45	Wyoming	1.88	50	Iowa	0.20

District of Columbia**   NA

Source: Morgan Quitno Corporation using data from U.S. Bureau of the Census
"Government Finances: 1991-92 (Preliminary Report)" (August 1994, GF/92-5P)

*Preliminary data.

**Not applicable.

Local Government Expenditures for Corrections in 1992

National Total = $10,299,607,000*

ALPHA ORDER

RANK	STATE	EXPENDITURES	% of USA
28	Alabama	$66,809,000	0.65%
45	Alaska	1,282,000	0.01%
14	Arizona	169,699,000	1.65%
35	Arkansas	27,508,000	0.27%
1	California	2,052,915,000	19.93%
19	Colorado	126,200,000	1.23%
47	Connecticut	0	0.00%
47	Delaware	0	0.00%
3	Florida	847,030,000	8.22%
11	Georgia	221,503,000	2.15%
47	Hawaii	0	0.00%
39	Idaho	18,807,000	0.18%
6	Illinois	342,140,000	3.32%
25	Indiana	98,139,000	0.95%
33	Iowa	31,279,000	0.30%
34	Kansas	29,467,000	0.29%
26	Kentucky	83,150,000	0.81%
22	Louisiana	115,028,000	1.12%
29	Maine	38,353,000	0.37%
21	Maryland	118,722,000	1.15%
15	Massachusetts	153,629,000	1.49%
8	Michigan	273,294,000	2.65%
17	Minnesota	134,940,000	1.31%
40	Mississippi	18,101,000	0.18%
27	Missouri	80,443,000	0.78%
44	Montana	7,865,000	0.08%
32	Nebraska	33,383,000	0.32%
24	Nevada	106,390,000	1.03%
36	New Hampshire	25,550,000	0.25%
7	New Jersey	333,690,000	3.24%
30	New Mexico	38,189,000	0.37%
2	New York	1,728,576,000	16.78%
23	North Carolina	108,344,000	1.05%
42	North Dakota	10,822,000	0.11%
10	Ohio	250,599,000	2.43%
37	Oklahoma	21,718,000	0.21%
18	Oregon	127,859,000	1.24%
5	Pennsylvania	489,564,000	4.75%
47	Rhode Island	0	0.00%
20	South Carolina	119,032,000	1.16%
43	South Dakota	9,006,000	0.09%
16	Tennessee	138,941,000	1.35%
4	Texas	666,124,000	6.47%
31	Utah	38,113,000	0.37%
46	Vermont	104,000	0.00%
9	Virginia	258,230,000	2.51%
13	Washington	185,876,000	1.80%
38	West Virginia	21,054,000	0.20%
12	Wisconsin	195,761,000	1.90%
41	Wyoming	18,063,000	0.18%

RANK ORDER

RANK	STATE	EXPENDITURES	% of USA
1	California	$2,052,915,000	19.93%
2	New York	1,728,576,000	16.78%
3	Florida	847,030,000	8.22%
4	Texas	666,124,000	6.47%
5	Pennsylvania	489,564,000	4.75%
6	Illinois	342,140,000	3.32%
7	New Jersey	333,690,000	3.24%
8	Michigan	273,294,000	2.65%
9	Virginia	258,230,000	2.51%
10	Ohio	250,599,000	2.43%
11	Georgia	221,503,000	2.15%
12	Wisconsin	195,761,000	1.90%
13	Washington	185,876,000	1.80%
14	Arizona	169,699,000	1.65%
15	Massachusetts	153,629,000	1.49%
16	Tennessee	138,941,000	1.35%
17	Minnesota	134,940,000	1.31%
18	Oregon	127,859,000	1.24%
19	Colorado	126,200,000	1.23%
20	South Carolina	119,032,000	1.16%
21	Maryland	118,722,000	1.15%
22	Louisiana	115,028,000	1.12%
23	North Carolina	108,344,000	1.05%
24	Nevada	106,390,000	1.03%
25	Indiana	98,139,000	0.95%
26	Kentucky	83,150,000	0.81%
27	Missouri	80,443,000	0.78%
28	Alabama	66,809,000	0.65%
29	Maine	38,353,000	0.37%
30	New Mexico	38,189,000	0.37%
31	Utah	38,113,000	0.37%
32	Nebraska	33,383,000	0.32%
33	Iowa	31,279,000	0.30%
34	Kansas	29,467,000	0.29%
35	Arkansas	27,508,000	0.27%
36	New Hampshire	25,550,000	0.25%
37	Oklahoma	21,718,000	0.21%
38	West Virginia	21,054,000	0.20%
39	Idaho	18,807,000	0.18%
40	Mississippi	18,101,000	0.18%
41	Wyoming	18,063,000	0.18%
42	North Dakota	10,822,000	0.11%
43	South Dakota	9,006,000	0.09%
44	Montana	7,865,000	0.08%
45	Alaska	1,282,000	0.01%
46	Vermont	104,000	0.00%
47	Connecticut	0	0.00%
47	Delaware	0	0.00%
47	Hawaii	0	0.00%
47	Rhode Island	0	0.00%
	District of Columbia	318,316,000	3.09%

Source: U.S. Bureau of the Census

"Government Finances: 1991–92 (Preliminary Report)" (August 1994, GF/92-5P)

*Direct expenditures. Preliminary data.

Per Capita Local Government Expenditures for Corrections in 1992

National Per Capita = $40.38*

<table>
<tr><th colspan="3">ALPHA ORDER</th><th colspan="3">RANK ORDER</th></tr>
<tr><th>RANK</th><th>STATE</th><th>PER CAPITA</th><th>RANK</th><th>STATE</th><th>PER CAPITA</th></tr>
<tr><td>34</td><td>Alabama</td><td>$16.15</td><td>1</td><td>New York</td><td>$95.45</td></tr>
<tr><td>45</td><td>Alaska</td><td>2.18</td><td>2</td><td>Nevada</td><td>79.63</td></tr>
<tr><td>5</td><td>Arizona</td><td>44.28</td><td>3</td><td>California</td><td>66.45</td></tr>
<tr><td>40</td><td>Arkansas</td><td>11.49</td><td>4</td><td>Florida</td><td>62.82</td></tr>
<tr><td>3</td><td>California</td><td>66.45</td><td>5</td><td>Arizona</td><td>44.28</td></tr>
<tr><td>13</td><td>Colorado</td><td>36.42</td><td>6</td><td>Oregon</td><td>43.02</td></tr>
<tr><td>47</td><td>Connecticut</td><td>0.00</td><td>7</td><td>New Jersey</td><td>42.67</td></tr>
<tr><td>47</td><td>Delaware</td><td>0.00</td><td>8</td><td>Pennsylvania</td><td>40.81</td></tr>
<tr><td>4</td><td>Florida</td><td>62.82</td><td>9</td><td>Virginia</td><td>40.39</td></tr>
<tr><td>16</td><td>Georgia</td><td>32.70</td><td>10</td><td>Wisconsin</td><td>39.21</td></tr>
<tr><td>47</td><td>Hawaii</td><td>0.00</td><td>11</td><td>Wyoming</td><td>38.85</td></tr>
<tr><td>31</td><td>Idaho</td><td>17.64</td><td>12</td><td>Texas</td><td>37.67</td></tr>
<tr><td>19</td><td>Illinois</td><td>29.46</td><td>13</td><td>Colorado</td><td>36.42</td></tr>
<tr><td>32</td><td>Indiana</td><td>17.35</td><td>14</td><td>Washington</td><td>36.14</td></tr>
<tr><td>41</td><td>Iowa</td><td>11.16</td><td>15</td><td>South Carolina</td><td>33.04</td></tr>
<tr><td>38</td><td>Kansas</td><td>11.72</td><td>16</td><td>Georgia</td><td>32.70</td></tr>
<tr><td>28</td><td>Kentucky</td><td>22.15</td><td>17</td><td>Maine</td><td>31.03</td></tr>
<tr><td>22</td><td>Louisiana</td><td>26.88</td><td>18</td><td>Minnesota</td><td>30.20</td></tr>
<tr><td>17</td><td>Maine</td><td>31.03</td><td>19</td><td>Illinois</td><td>29.46</td></tr>
<tr><td>24</td><td>Maryland</td><td>24.15</td><td>20</td><td>Michigan</td><td>28.97</td></tr>
<tr><td>23</td><td>Massachusetts</td><td>25.63</td><td>21</td><td>Tennessee</td><td>27.65</td></tr>
<tr><td>20</td><td>Michigan</td><td>28.97</td><td>22</td><td>Louisiana</td><td>26.88</td></tr>
<tr><td>18</td><td>Minnesota</td><td>30.20</td><td>23</td><td>Massachusetts</td><td>25.63</td></tr>
<tr><td>43</td><td>Mississippi</td><td>6.92</td><td>24</td><td>Maryland</td><td>24.15</td></tr>
<tr><td>36</td><td>Missouri</td><td>15.50</td><td>25</td><td>New Mexico</td><td>24.14</td></tr>
<tr><td>42</td><td>Montana</td><td>9.57</td><td>26</td><td>New Hampshire</td><td>22.91</td></tr>
<tr><td>30</td><td>Nebraska</td><td>20.85</td><td>27</td><td>Ohio</td><td>22.74</td></tr>
<tr><td>2</td><td>Nevada</td><td>79.63</td><td>28</td><td>Kentucky</td><td>22.15</td></tr>
<tr><td>26</td><td>New Hampshire</td><td>22.91</td><td>29</td><td>Utah</td><td>21.05</td></tr>
<tr><td>7</td><td>New Jersey</td><td>42.67</td><td>30</td><td>Nebraska</td><td>20.85</td></tr>
<tr><td>25</td><td>New Mexico</td><td>24.14</td><td>31</td><td>Idaho</td><td>17.64</td></tr>
<tr><td>1</td><td>New York</td><td>95.45</td><td>32</td><td>Indiana</td><td>17.35</td></tr>
<tr><td>35</td><td>North Carolina</td><td>15.85</td><td>33</td><td>North Dakota</td><td>17.07</td></tr>
<tr><td>33</td><td>North Dakota</td><td>17.07</td><td>34</td><td>Alabama</td><td>16.15</td></tr>
<tr><td>27</td><td>Ohio</td><td>22.74</td><td>35</td><td>North Carolina</td><td>15.85</td></tr>
<tr><td>44</td><td>Oklahoma</td><td>6.78</td><td>36</td><td>Missouri</td><td>15.50</td></tr>
<tr><td>6</td><td>Oregon</td><td>43.02</td><td>37</td><td>South Dakota</td><td>12.72</td></tr>
<tr><td>8</td><td>Pennsylvania</td><td>40.81</td><td>38</td><td>Kansas</td><td>11.72</td></tr>
<tr><td>47</td><td>Rhode Island</td><td>0.00</td><td>39</td><td>West Virginia</td><td>11.64</td></tr>
<tr><td>15</td><td>South Carolina</td><td>33.04</td><td>40</td><td>Arkansas</td><td>11.49</td></tr>
<tr><td>37</td><td>South Dakota</td><td>12.72</td><td>41</td><td>Iowa</td><td>11.16</td></tr>
<tr><td>21</td><td>Tennessee</td><td>27.65</td><td>42</td><td>Montana</td><td>9.57</td></tr>
<tr><td>12</td><td>Texas</td><td>37.67</td><td>43</td><td>Mississippi</td><td>6.92</td></tr>
<tr><td>29</td><td>Utah</td><td>21.05</td><td>44</td><td>Oklahoma</td><td>6.78</td></tr>
<tr><td>46</td><td>Vermont</td><td>0.18</td><td>45</td><td>Alaska</td><td>2.18</td></tr>
<tr><td>9</td><td>Virginia</td><td>40.39</td><td>46</td><td>Vermont</td><td>0.18</td></tr>
<tr><td>14</td><td>Washington</td><td>36.14</td><td>47</td><td>Connecticut</td><td>0.00</td></tr>
<tr><td>39</td><td>West Virginia</td><td>11.64</td><td>47</td><td>Delaware</td><td>0.00</td></tr>
<tr><td>10</td><td>Wisconsin</td><td>39.21</td><td>47</td><td>Hawaii</td><td>0.00</td></tr>
<tr><td>11</td><td>Wyoming</td><td>38.85</td><td>47</td><td>Rhode Island</td><td>0.00</td></tr>
<tr><td></td><td></td><td></td><td></td><td>District of Columbia</td><td>544.13</td></tr>
</table>

Source: Morgan Quitno Corporation using data from U.S. Bureau of the Census
"Government Finances: 1991–92 (Preliminary Report)" (August 1994, GF/92–5P)
*Direct expenditures. Preliminary data.

Local Government Expenditures for Corrections
As a Percent of All Direct Expenditures in 1992
National Percent = 1.59% of Direct Expenditures*

ALPHA ORDER

RANK	STATE	PERCENT
32	Alabama	0.88
45	Alaska	0.05
8	Arizona	1.73
35	Arkansas	0.83
4	California	1.98
17	Colorado	1.32
47	Connecticut	0.00
47	Delaware	0.00
2	Florida	2.39
15	Georgia	1.41
47	Hawaii	0.00
28	Idaho	1.03
18	Illinois	1.28
32	Indiana	0.88
42	Iowa	0.51
40	Kansas	0.53
14	Kentucky	1.43
16	Louisiana	1.36
8	Maine	1.73
25	Maryland	1.17
26	Massachusetts	1.09
23	Michigan	1.20
30	Minnesota	0.97
43	Mississippi	0.41
34	Missouri	0.86
40	Montana	0.53
39	Nebraska	0.69
1	Nevada	2.89
18	New Hampshire	1.28
12	New Jersey	1.60
20	New Mexico	1.26
3	New York	2.29
38	North Carolina	0.73
29	North Dakota	0.98
27	Ohio	1.08
44	Oklahoma	0.39
8	Oregon	1.73
6	Pennsylvania	1.84
47	Rhode Island	0.00
7	South Carolina	1.82
37	South Dakota	0.77
24	Tennessee	1.19
11	Texas	1.67
30	Utah	0.97
46	Vermont	0.01
5	Virginia	1.97
21	Washington	1.25
36	West Virginia	0.78
13	Wisconsin	1.48
22	Wyoming	1.24

RANK ORDER

RANK	STATE	PERCENT
1	Nevada	2.89
2	Florida	2.39
3	New York	2.29
4	California	1.98
5	Virginia	1.97
6	Pennsylvania	1.84
7	South Carolina	1.82
8	Arizona	1.73
8	Maine	1.73
8	Oregon	1.73
11	Texas	1.67
12	New Jersey	1.60
13	Wisconsin	1.48
14	Kentucky	1.43
15	Georgia	1.41
16	Louisiana	1.36
17	Colorado	1.32
18	Illinois	1.28
18	New Hampshire	1.28
20	New Mexico	1.26
21	Washington	1.25
22	Wyoming	1.24
23	Michigan	1.20
24	Tennessee	1.19
25	Maryland	1.17
26	Massachusetts	1.09
27	Ohio	1.08
28	Idaho	1.03
29	North Dakota	0.98
30	Minnesota	0.97
30	Utah	0.97
32	Alabama	0.88
32	Indiana	0.88
34	Missouri	0.86
35	Arkansas	0.83
36	West Virginia	0.78
37	South Dakota	0.77
38	North Carolina	0.73
39	Nebraska	0.69
40	Kansas	0.53
40	Montana	0.53
42	Iowa	0.51
43	Mississippi	0.41
44	Oklahoma	0.39
45	Alaska	0.05
46	Vermont	0.01
47	Connecticut	0.00
47	Delaware	0.00
47	Hawaii	0.00
47	Rhode Island	0.00

District of Columbia	5.47

Source: Morgan Quitno Corporation using data from U.S. Bureau of the Census
"Government Finances: 1991-92 (Preliminary Report)" (August 1994, GF/92-5P)
*Preliminary data.

State and Local Government Expenditures for Judicial and Legal Services in 1992

National Total = $16,352,064,000*

ALPHA ORDER

RANK	STATE	EXPENDITURES	% of USA
26	Alabama	$188,007,000	1.15%
34	Alaska	106,338,000	0.65%
13	Arizona	319,934,000	1.96%
39	Arkansas	67,615,000	0.41%
1	California	3,189,629,000	19.51%
23	Colorado	200,994,000	1.23%
21	Connecticut	203,861,000	1.25%
44	Delaware	52,080,000	0.32%
3	Florida	977,865,000	5.98%
14	Georgia	294,191,000	1.80%
29	Hawaii	135,888,000	0.83%
45	Idaho	50,454,000	0.31%
9	Illinois	598,249,000	3.66%
24	Indiana	197,139,000	1.21%
28	Iowa	148,348,000	0.91%
30	Kansas	125,951,000	0.77%
27	Kentucky	157,358,000	0.96%
22	Louisiana	203,189,000	1.24%
46	Maine	43,873,000	0.27%
11	Maryland	339,086,000	2.07%
10	Massachusetts	346,079,000	2.12%
8	Michigan	604,451,000	3.70%
17	Minnesota	270,032,000	1.65%
40	Mississippi	65,333,000	0.40%
20	Missouri	209,046,000	1.28%
43	Montana	53,632,000	0.33%
41	Nebraska	61,672,000	0.38%
32	Nevada	120,279,000	0.74%
38	New Hampshire	71,169,000	0.44%
7	New Jersey	637,922,000	3.90%
36	New Mexico	84,153,000	0.51%
2	New York	1,821,371,000	11.14%
18	North Carolina	258,953,000	1.58%
49	North Dakota	28,886,000	0.18%
6	Ohio	651,486,000	3.98%
33	Oklahoma	112,436,000	0.69%
25	Oregon	189,489,000	1.16%
5	Pennsylvania	670,135,000	4.10%
37	Rhode Island	72,372,000	0.44%
31	South Carolina	123,868,000	0.76%
50	South Dakota	25,460,000	0.16%
19	Tennessee	209,591,000	1.28%
4	Texas	821,763,000	5.03%
35	Utah	86,541,000	0.53%
48	Vermont	29,544,000	0.18%
15	Virginia	292,508,000	1.79%
12	Washington	321,735,000	1.97%
42	West Virginia	60,975,000	0.37%
16	Wisconsin	285,698,000	1.75%
47	Wyoming	37,461,000	0.23%

RANK ORDER

RANK	STATE	EXPENDITURES	% of USA
1	California	$3,189,629,000	19.51%
2	New York	1,821,371,000	11.14%
3	Florida	977,865,000	5.98%
4	Texas	821,763,000	5.03%
5	Pennsylvania	670,135,000	4.10%
6	Ohio	651,486,000	3.98%
7	New Jersey	637,922,000	3.90%
8	Michigan	604,451,000	3.70%
9	Illinois	598,249,000	3.66%
10	Massachusetts	346,079,000	2.12%
11	Maryland	339,086,000	2.07%
12	Washington	321,735,000	1.97%
13	Arizona	319,934,000	1.96%
14	Georgia	294,191,000	1.80%
15	Virginia	292,508,000	1.79%
16	Wisconsin	285,698,000	1.75%
17	Minnesota	270,032,000	1.65%
18	North Carolina	258,953,000	1.58%
19	Tennessee	209,591,000	1.28%
20	Missouri	209,046,000	1.28%
21	Connecticut	203,861,000	1.25%
22	Louisiana	203,189,000	1.24%
23	Colorado	200,994,000	1.23%
24	Indiana	197,139,000	1.21%
25	Oregon	189,489,000	1.16%
26	Alabama	188,007,000	1.15%
27	Kentucky	157,358,000	0.96%
28	Iowa	148,348,000	0.91%
29	Hawaii	135,888,000	0.83%
30	Kansas	125,951,000	0.77%
31	South Carolina	123,868,000	0.76%
32	Nevada	120,279,000	0.74%
33	Oklahoma	112,436,000	0.69%
34	Alaska	106,338,000	0.65%
35	Utah	86,541,000	0.53%
36	New Mexico	84,153,000	0.51%
37	Rhode Island	72,372,000	0.44%
38	New Hampshire	71,169,000	0.44%
39	Arkansas	67,615,000	0.41%
40	Mississippi	65,333,000	0.40%
41	Nebraska	61,672,000	0.38%
42	West Virginia	60,975,000	0.37%
43	Montana	53,632,000	0.33%
44	Delaware	52,080,000	0.32%
45	Idaho	50,454,000	0.31%
46	Maine	43,873,000	0.27%
47	Wyoming	37,461,000	0.23%
48	Vermont	29,544,000	0.18%
49	North Dakota	28,886,000	0.18%
50	South Dakota	25,460,000	0.16%
	District of Columbia	127,975,000	0.78%

Source: U.S. Bureau of the Census
"Government Finances: 1991-92 (Preliminary Report)" (August 1994, GF/92-5P)
*Direct expenditures. Preliminary data. Includes Courts, Prosecution and Legal Services and Public Defense.

Per Capita State and Local Government Expenditures
For Judicial and Legal Services in 1992
National Per Capita = $64.11*

<u>ALPHA ORDER</u>

RANK	STATE	PER CAPITA
36	Alabama	$45.43
1	Alaska	180.85
6	Arizona	83.49
49	Arkansas	28.24
3	California	103.24
21	Colorado	58.01
18	Connecticut	62.17
9	Delaware	75.37
10	Florida	72.53
37	Georgia	43.44
2	Hawaii	117.55
32	Idaho	47.33
28	Illinois	51.52
46	Indiana	34.84
26	Iowa	52.92
29	Kansas	50.08
38	Kentucky	41.92
31	Louisiana	47.49
44	Maine	35.50
12	Maryland	68.96
22	Massachusetts	57.75
14	Michigan	64.07
19	Minnesota	60.44
50	Mississippi	24.98
40	Missouri	40.27
13	Montana	65.25
41	Nebraska	38.52
5	Nevada	90.03
15	New Hampshire	63.83
7	New Jersey	81.58
25	New Mexico	53.19
4	New York	100.58
42	North Carolina	37.88
35	North Dakota	45.56
20	Ohio	59.11
45	Oklahoma	35.08
16	Oregon	63.76
24	Pennsylvania	55.87
11	Rhode Island	72.30
47	South Carolina	34.38
43	South Dakota	35.96
39	Tennessee	41.71
33	Texas	46.47
30	Utah	47.79
27	Vermont	51.74
34	Virginia	45.75
17	Washington	62.56
48	West Virginia	33.71
23	Wisconsin	57.22
8	Wyoming	80.56

<u>RANK ORDER</u>

RANK	STATE	PER CAPITA
1	Alaska	$180.85
2	Hawaii	117.55
3	California	103.24
4	New York	100.58
5	Nevada	90.03
6	Arizona	83.49
7	New Jersey	81.58
8	Wyoming	80.56
9	Delaware	75.37
10	Florida	72.53
11	Rhode Island	72.30
12	Maryland	68.96
13	Montana	65.25
14	Michigan	64.07
15	New Hampshire	63.83
16	Oregon	63.76
17	Washington	62.56
18	Connecticut	62.17
19	Minnesota	60.44
20	Ohio	59.11
21	Colorado	58.01
22	Massachusetts	57.75
23	Wisconsin	57.22
24	Pennsylvania	55.87
25	New Mexico	53.19
26	Iowa	52.92
27	Vermont	51.74
28	Illinois	51.52
29	Kansas	50.08
30	Utah	47.79
31	Louisiana	47.49
32	Idaho	47.33
33	Texas	46.47
34	Virginia	45.75
35	North Dakota	45.56
36	Alabama	45.43
37	Georgia	43.44
38	Kentucky	41.92
39	Tennessee	41.71
40	Missouri	40.27
41	Nebraska	38.52
42	North Carolina	37.88
43	South Dakota	35.96
44	Maine	35.50
45	Oklahoma	35.08
46	Indiana	34.84
47	South Carolina	34.38
48	West Virginia	33.71
49	Arkansas	28.24
50	Mississippi	24.98
	District of Columbia	218.76

*Source: Morgan Quitno Corporation using data from U.S. Bureau of the Census
"Government Finances: 1991-92 (Preliminary Report)" (August 1994, GF/92-5P)*
Direct expenditures. Preliminary data. Includes Courts, Prosecution and Legal Services and Public Defense.

State and Local Government Expenditures for Judicial and Legal Services
As a Percent of All Direct Expenditures in 1992
National Percent = 1.43% of Direct Expenditures*

ALPHA ORDER

RANK	STATE	PERCENT
27	Alabama	1.25
7	Alaska	1.61
2	Arizona	2.01
45	Arkansas	0.92
3	California	1.99
20	Colorado	1.33
32	Connecticut	1.18
9	Delaware	1.59
5	Florida	1.81
38	Georgia	1.13
1	Hawaii	2.04
16	Idaho	1.38
23	Illinois	1.28
43	Indiana	0.99
19	Iowa	1.34
21	Kansas	1.31
33	Kentucky	1.16
35	Louisiana	1.15
48	Maine	0.84
6	Maryland	1.65
36	Massachusetts	1.14
13	Michigan	1.46
30	Minnesota	1.19
50	Mississippi	0.78
29	Missouri	1.23
7	Montana	1.61
49	Nebraska	0.83
4	Nevada	1.88
10	New Hampshire	1.56
11	New Jersey	1.51
23	New Mexico	1.28
12	New York	1.47
42	North Carolina	1.02
39	North Dakota	1.07
14	Ohio	1.43
44	Oklahoma	0.97
16	Oregon	1.38
26	Pennsylvania	1.26
15	Rhode Island	1.41
46	South Carolina	0.89
41	South Dakota	1.04
40	Tennessee	1.06
25	Texas	1.27
30	Utah	1.19
36	Vermont	1.14
28	Virginia	1.24
33	Washington	1.16
46	West Virginia	0.89
22	Wisconsin	1.30
18	Wyoming	1.37

RANK ORDER

RANK	STATE	PERCENT
1	Hawaii	2.04
2	Arizona	2.01
3	California	1.99
4	Nevada	1.88
5	Florida	1.81
6	Maryland	1.65
7	Alaska	1.61
7	Montana	1.61
9	Delaware	1.59
10	New Hampshire	1.56
11	New Jersey	1.51
12	New York	1.47
13	Michigan	1.46
14	Ohio	1.43
15	Rhode Island	1.41
16	Idaho	1.38
16	Oregon	1.38
18	Wyoming	1.37
19	Iowa	1.34
20	Colorado	1.33
21	Kansas	1.31
22	Wisconsin	1.30
23	Illinois	1.28
23	New Mexico	1.28
25	Texas	1.27
26	Pennsylvania	1.26
27	Alabama	1.25
28	Virginia	1.24
29	Missouri	1.23
30	Minnesota	1.19
30	Utah	1.19
32	Connecticut	1.18
33	Kentucky	1.16
33	Washington	1.16
35	Louisiana	1.15
36	Massachusetts	1.14
36	Vermont	1.14
38	Georgia	1.13
39	North Dakota	1.07
40	Tennessee	1.06
41	South Dakota	1.04
42	North Carolina	1.02
43	Indiana	0.99
44	Oklahoma	0.97
45	Arkansas	0.92
46	South Carolina	0.89
46	West Virginia	0.89
48	Maine	0.84
49	Nebraska	0.83
50	Mississippi	0.78
	District of Columbia	2.20

Source: Morgan Quitno Corporation using data from U.S. Bureau of the Census
"Government Finances: 1991-92 (Preliminary Report)" (August 1994, GF/92-5P)
*Preliminary data. Includes Courts, Prosecution and Legal Services and Public Defense.

State Government Expenditures for Judicial and Legal Services in 1992

National Total = $6,326,165,000*

ALPHA ORDER

RANK	STATE	EXPENDITURES	% of USA
16	Alabama	$129,789,000	2.05%
23	Alaska	98,185,000	1.55%
31	Arizona	65,293,000	1.03%
42	Arkansas	27,503,000	0.43%
3	California	303,651,000	4.80%
20	Colorado	109,771,000	1.74%
10	Connecticut	180,547,000	2.85%
37	Delaware	44,825,000	0.71%
2	Florida	449,588,000	7.11%
36	Georgia	49,301,000	0.78%
22	Hawaii	104,877,000	1.66%
45	Idaho	25,488,000	0.40%
9	Illinois	183,757,000	2.90%
35	Indiana	50,112,000	0.79%
21	Iowa	106,851,000	1.69%
27	Kansas	81,567,000	1.29%
15	Kentucky	131,610,000	2.08%
25	Louisiana	85,859,000	1.36%
40	Maine	36,545,000	0.58%
8	Maryland	206,282,000	3.26%
4	Massachusetts	302,158,000	4.78%
13	Michigan	149,159,000	2.36%
24	Minnesota	88,026,000	1.39%
47	Mississippi	22,269,000	0.35%
18	Missouri	114,037,000	1.80%
44	Montana	27,246,000	0.43%
43	Nebraska	27,338,000	0.43%
48	Nevada	21,035,000	0.33%
32	New Hampshire	60,052,000	0.95%
5	New Jersey	251,167,000	3.97%
28	New Mexico	74,766,000	1.18%
1	New York	1,070,766,000	16.93%
6	North Carolina	232,648,000	3.68%
49	North Dakota	16,542,000	0.26%
19	Ohio	111,410,000	1.76%
29	Oklahoma	74,546,000	1.18%
14	Oregon	131,868,000	2.08%
11	Pennsylvania	173,405,000	2.74%
30	Rhode Island	65,649,000	1.04%
38	South Carolina	40,855,000	0.65%
50	South Dakota	15,148,000	0.24%
26	Tennessee	82,944,000	1.31%
7	Texas	227,320,000	3.59%
33	Utah	55,395,000	0.88%
41	Vermont	28,014,000	0.44%
12	Virginia	149,323,000	2.36%
34	Washington	52,103,000	0.82%
39	West Virginia	39,847,000	0.63%
17	Wisconsin	126,169,000	1.99%
46	Wyoming	23,559,000	0.37%

RANK ORDER

RANK	STATE	EXPENDITURES	% of USA
1	New York	$1,070,766,000	16.93%
2	Florida	449,588,000	7.11%
3	California	303,651,000	4.80%
4	Massachusetts	302,158,000	4.78%
5	New Jersey	251,167,000	3.97%
6	North Carolina	232,648,000	3.68%
7	Texas	227,320,000	3.59%
8	Maryland	206,282,000	3.26%
9	Illinois	183,757,000	2.90%
10	Connecticut	180,547,000	2.85%
11	Pennsylvania	173,405,000	2.74%
12	Virginia	149,323,000	2.36%
13	Michigan	149,159,000	2.36%
14	Oregon	131,868,000	2.08%
15	Kentucky	131,610,000	2.08%
16	Alabama	129,789,000	2.05%
17	Wisconsin	126,169,000	1.99%
18	Missouri	114,037,000	1.80%
19	Ohio	111,410,000	1.76%
20	Colorado	109,771,000	1.74%
21	Iowa	106,851,000	1.69%
22	Hawaii	104,877,000	1.66%
23	Alaska	98,185,000	1.55%
24	Minnesota	88,026,000	1.39%
25	Louisiana	85,859,000	1.36%
26	Tennessee	82,944,000	1.31%
27	Kansas	81,567,000	1.29%
28	New Mexico	74,766,000	1.18%
29	Oklahoma	74,546,000	1.18%
30	Rhode Island	65,649,000	1.04%
31	Arizona	65,293,000	1.03%
32	New Hampshire	60,052,000	0.95%
33	Utah	55,395,000	0.88%
34	Washington	52,103,000	0.82%
35	Indiana	50,112,000	0.79%
36	Georgia	49,301,000	0.78%
37	Delaware	44,825,000	0.71%
38	South Carolina	40,855,000	0.65%
39	West Virginia	39,847,000	0.63%
40	Maine	36,545,000	0.58%
41	Vermont	28,014,000	0.44%
42	Arkansas	27,503,000	0.43%
43	Nebraska	27,338,000	0.43%
44	Montana	27,246,000	0.43%
45	Idaho	25,488,000	0.40%
46	Wyoming	23,559,000	0.37%
47	Mississippi	22,269,000	0.35%
48	Nevada	21,035,000	0.33%
49	North Dakota	16,542,000	0.26%
50	South Dakota	15,148,000	0.24%
	District of Columbia**	NA	NA

Source: U.S. Bureau of the Census

"Government Finances: 1991-92 (Preliminary Report)" (August 1994, GF/92-5P)

*Direct expenditures. Preliminary data. Includes Courts, Prosecution and Legal Services and Public Defense.

**Not applicable.

Per Capita State Government Expenditures for Judicial and Legal Services in 1992

National Per Capita = $24.80*

<u>ALPHA ORDER</u>

RANK	STATE	PER CAPITA
22	Alabama	$31.37
1	Alaska	166.98
36	Arizona	17.04
43	Arkansas	11.49
47	California	9.83
21	Colorado	31.68
6	Connecticut	55.06
4	Delaware	64.87
17	Florida	33.34
50	Georgia	7.28
2	Hawaii	90.72
27	Idaho	23.91
38	Illinois	15.82
48	Indiana	8.86
14	Iowa	38.12
19	Kansas	32.43
15	Kentucky	35.06
33	Louisiana	20.07
24	Maine	29.57
13	Maryland	41.95
9	Massachusetts	50.42
39	Michigan	15.81
34	Minnesota	19.70
49	Mississippi	8.52
31	Missouri	21.97
18	Montana	33.15
35	Nebraska	17.08
40	Nevada	15.74
7	New Hampshire	53.86
20	New Jersey	32.12
11	New Mexico	47.26
5	New York	59.13
16	North Carolina	34.03
25	North Dakota	26.09
46	Ohio	10.11
29	Oklahoma	23.26
12	Oregon	44.37
41	Pennsylvania	14.46
3	Rhode Island	65.58
44	South Carolina	11.34
32	South Dakota	21.40
37	Tennessee	16.51
42	Texas	12.86
23	Utah	30.59
10	Vermont	49.06
28	Virginia	23.35
45	Washington	10.13
30	West Virginia	22.03
26	Wisconsin	25.27
8	Wyoming	50.66

<u>RANK ORDER</u>

RANK	STATE	PER CAPITA
1	Alaska	$166.98
2	Hawaii	90.72
3	Rhode Island	65.58
4	Delaware	64.87
5	New York	59.13
6	Connecticut	55.06
7	New Hampshire	53.86
8	Wyoming	50.66
9	Massachusetts	50.42
10	Vermont	49.06
11	New Mexico	47.26
12	Oregon	44.37
13	Maryland	41.95
14	Iowa	38.12
15	Kentucky	35.06
16	North Carolina	34.03
17	Florida	33.34
18	Montana	33.15
19	Kansas	32.43
20	New Jersey	32.12
21	Colorado	31.68
22	Alabama	31.37
23	Utah	30.59
24	Maine	29.57
25	North Dakota	26.09
26	Wisconsin	25.27
27	Idaho	23.91
28	Virginia	23.35
29	Oklahoma	23.26
30	West Virginia	22.03
31	Missouri	21.97
32	South Dakota	21.40
33	Louisiana	20.07
34	Minnesota	19.70
35	Nebraska	17.08
36	Arizona	17.04
37	Tennessee	16.51
38	Illinois	15.82
39	Michigan	15.81
40	Nevada	15.74
41	Pennsylvania	14.46
42	Texas	12.86
43	Arkansas	11.49
44	South Carolina	11.34
45	Washington	10.13
46	Ohio	10.11
47	California	9.83
48	Indiana	8.86
49	Mississippi	8.52
50	Georgia	7.28
	District of Columbia**	NA

Source: Morgan Quitno Corporation using data from U.S. Bureau of the Census
   "Government Finances: 1991-92 (Preliminary Report)" (August 1994, GF/92-5P)
*Direct expenditures. Preliminary data. Includes Courts, Prosecution and Legal Services and Public Defense.
**Not applicable.

State Government Expenditures for Judicial and Legal Services
As a Percent of All Direct Expenditures in 1992
National Percent = 1.27% of Direct Expenditures*

ALPHA ORDER

RANK ORDER

RANK	STATE	PERCENT
19	Alabama	1.73
2	Alaska	2.33
31	Arizona	1.07
42	Arkansas	0.69
47	California	0.54
12	Colorado	1.99
14	Connecticut	1.89
7	Delaware	2.15
1	Florida	2.41
49	Georgia	0.48
10	Hawaii	2.03
26	Idaho	1.39
38	Illinois	0.91
44	Indiana	0.58
6	Iowa	2.16
11	Kansas	2.02
20	Kentucky	1.70
37	Louisiana	0.94
28	Maine	1.21
13	Maryland	1.97
16	Massachusetts	1.85
40	Michigan	0.80
35	Minnesota	1.00
45	Mississippi	0.56
22	Missouri	1.49
23	Montana	1.47
32	Nebraska	1.06
41	Nevada	0.77
2	New Hampshire	2.33
30	New Jersey	1.17
8	New Mexico	2.10
4	New York	2.21
4	North Carolina	2.21
33	North Dakota	1.04
48	Ohio	0.50
27	Oklahoma	1.24
9	Oregon	2.07
43	Pennsylvania	0.65
14	Rhode Island	1.89
46	South Carolina	0.55
29	South Dakota	1.18
34	Tennessee	1.02
38	Texas	0.91
21	Utah	1.66
18	Vermont	1.82
25	Virginia	1.43
50	Washington	0.41
36	West Virginia	0.97
24	Wisconsin	1.44
16	Wyoming	1.85

RANK	STATE	PERCENT
1	Florida	2.41
2	Alaska	2.33
2	New Hampshire	2.33
4	New York	2.21
4	North Carolina	2.21
6	Iowa	2.16
7	Delaware	2.15
8	New Mexico	2.10
9	Oregon	2.07
10	Hawaii	2.03
11	Kansas	2.02
12	Colorado	1.99
13	Maryland	1.97
14	Connecticut	1.89
14	Rhode Island	1.89
16	Massachusetts	1.85
16	Wyoming	1.85
18	Vermont	1.82
19	Alabama	1.73
20	Kentucky	1.70
21	Utah	1.66
22	Missouri	1.49
23	Montana	1.47
24	Wisconsin	1.44
25	Virginia	1.43
26	Idaho	1.39
27	Oklahoma	1.24
28	Maine	1.21
29	South Dakota	1.18
30	New Jersey	1.17
31	Arizona	1.07
32	Nebraska	1.06
33	North Dakota	1.04
34	Tennessee	1.02
35	Minnesota	1.00
36	West Virginia	0.97
37	Louisiana	0.94
38	Illinois	0.91
38	Texas	0.91
40	Michigan	0.80
41	Nevada	0.77
42	Arkansas	0.69
43	Pennsylvania	0.65
44	Indiana	0.58
45	Mississippi	0.56
46	South Carolina	0.55
47	California	0.54
48	Ohio	0.50
49	Georgia	0.48
50	Washington	0.41

District of Columbia**   NA

Source: Morgan Quitno Corporation using data from U.S. Bureau of the Census
   "Government Finances: 1991–92 (Preliminary Report)" (August 1994, GF/92-5P)
*Preliminary data. Includes Courts, Prosecution and Legal Services and Public Defense.
**Not applicable.

Local Government Expenditures for Judicial and Legal Services in 1992

National Total = $10,025,899,000*

RANK	STATE	EXPENDITURES	% of USA
24	Alabama	$58,218,000	0.58%
46	Alaska	8,153,000	0.08%
11	Arizona	254,641,000	2.54%
30	Arkansas	40,112,000	0.40%
1	California	2,885,978,000	28.79%
22	Colorado	91,223,000	0.91%
39	Connecticut	23,314,000	0.23%
48	Delaware	7,255,000	0.07%
5	Florida	528,277,000	5.27%
12	Georgia	244,890,000	2.44%
34	Hawaii	31,011,000	0.31%
38	Idaho	24,966,000	0.25%
8	Illinois	414,492,000	4.13%
15	Indiana	147,027,000	1.47%
29	Iowa	41,497,000	0.41%
26	Kansas	44,384,000	0.44%
37	Kentucky	25,748,000	0.26%
19	Louisiana	117,330,000	1.17%
47	Maine	7,328,000	0.07%
17	Maryland	132,804,000	1.32%
27	Massachusetts	43,921,000	0.44%
7	Michigan	455,292,000	4.54%
13	Minnesota	182,006,000	1.82%
28	Mississippi	43,064,000	0.43%
21	Missouri	95,009,000	0.95%
35	Montana	26,386,000	0.26%
32	Nebraska	34,334,000	0.34%
20	Nevada	99,244,000	0.99%
43	New Hampshire	11,117,000	0.11%
9	New Jersey	386,755,000	3.86%
45	New Mexico	9,387,000	0.09%
2	New York	750,605,000	7.49%
36	North Carolina	26,305,000	0.26%
42	North Dakota	12,344,000	0.12%
4	Ohio	540,076,000	5.39%
31	Oklahoma	37,890,000	0.38%
25	Oregon	57,621,000	0.57%
6	Pennsylvania	496,730,000	4.95%
49	Rhode Island	6,723,000	0.07%
23	South Carolina	83,013,000	0.83%
44	South Dakota	10,312,000	0.10%
18	Tennessee	126,647,000	1.26%
3	Texas	594,443,000	5.93%
33	Utah	31,146,000	0.31%
50	Vermont	1,530,000	0.02%
16	Virginia	143,185,000	1.43%
10	Washington	269,632,000	2.69%
40	West Virginia	21,128,000	0.21%
14	Wisconsin	159,529,000	1.59%
41	Wyoming	13,902,000	0.14%

RANK	STATE	EXPENDITURES	% of USA
1	California	$2,885,978,000	28.79%
2	New York	750,605,000	7.49%
3	Texas	594,443,000	5.93%
4	Ohio	540,076,000	5.39%
5	Florida	528,277,000	5.27%
6	Pennsylvania	496,730,000	4.95%
7	Michigan	455,292,000	4.54%
8	Illinois	414,492,000	4.13%
9	New Jersey	386,755,000	3.86%
10	Washington	269,632,000	2.69%
11	Arizona	254,641,000	2.54%
12	Georgia	244,890,000	2.44%
13	Minnesota	182,006,000	1.82%
14	Wisconsin	159,529,000	1.59%
15	Indiana	147,027,000	1.47%
16	Virginia	143,185,000	1.43%
17	Maryland	132,804,000	1.32%
18	Tennessee	126,647,000	1.26%
19	Louisiana	117,330,000	1.17%
20	Nevada	99,244,000	0.99%
21	Missouri	95,009,000	0.95%
22	Colorado	91,223,000	0.91%
23	South Carolina	83,013,000	0.83%
24	Alabama	58,218,000	0.58%
25	Oregon	57,621,000	0.57%
26	Kansas	44,384,000	0.44%
27	Massachusetts	43,921,000	0.44%
28	Mississippi	43,064,000	0.43%
29	Iowa	41,497,000	0.41%
30	Arkansas	40,112,000	0.40%
31	Oklahoma	37,890,000	0.38%
32	Nebraska	34,334,000	0.34%
33	Utah	31,146,000	0.31%
34	Hawaii	31,011,000	0.31%
35	Montana	26,386,000	0.26%
36	North Carolina	26,305,000	0.26%
37	Kentucky	25,748,000	0.26%
38	Idaho	24,966,000	0.25%
39	Connecticut	23,314,000	0.23%
40	West Virginia	21,128,000	0.21%
41	Wyoming	13,902,000	0.14%
42	North Dakota	12,344,000	0.12%
43	New Hampshire	11,117,000	0.11%
44	South Dakota	10,312,000	0.10%
45	New Mexico	9,387,000	0.09%
46	Alaska	8,153,000	0.08%
47	Maine	7,328,000	0.07%
48	Delaware	7,255,000	0.07%
49	Rhode Island	6,723,000	0.07%
50	Vermont	1,530,000	0.02%
	District of Columbia	127,975,000	1.28%

Source: U.S. Bureau of the Census
"Government Finances: 1991-92 (Preliminary Report)" (August 1994, GF/92-5P)
*Direct expenditures. Preliminary data. Includes Courts, Prosecution and Legal Services and Public Defense.

Per Capita Local Government Expenditures for Judicial and Legal Services in 1992

National Per Capita = $39.31*

ALPHA ORDER			RANK ORDER		
RANK	STATE	PER CAPITA	RANK	STATE	PER CAPITA
37	Alabama	$14.07	1	California	$93.41
38	Alaska	13.87	2	Nevada	74.28
3	Arizona	66.45	3	Arizona	66.45
33	Arkansas	16.76	4	Washington	52.43
1	California	93.41	5	New Jersey	49.46
21	Colorado	26.33	6	Ohio	49.00
44	Connecticut	7.11	7	Michigan	48.26
41	Delaware	10.50	8	New York	41.45
11	Florida	39.18	9	Pennsylvania	41.41
12	Georgia	36.16	10	Minnesota	40.74
20	Hawaii	26.83	11	Florida	39.18
24	Idaho	23.42	12	Georgia	36.16
13	Illinois	35.69	13	Illinois	35.69
22	Indiana	25.99	14	Texas	33.62
35	Iowa	14.80	15	Montana	32.10
31	Kansas	17.65	16	Wisconsin	31.95
45	Kentucky	6.86	17	Wyoming	29.90
18	Louisiana	27.42	18	Louisiana	27.42
47	Maine	5.93	19	Maryland	27.01
19	Maryland	27.01	20	Hawaii	26.83
43	Massachusetts	7.33	21	Colorado	26.33
7	Michigan	48.26	22	Indiana	25.99
10	Minnesota	40.74	23	Tennessee	25.20
34	Mississippi	16.47	24	Idaho	23.42
30	Missouri	18.30	25	South Carolina	23.04
15	Montana	32.10	26	Virginia	22.39
27	Nebraska	21.45	27	Nebraska	21.45
2	Nevada	74.28	28	North Dakota	19.47
42	New Hampshire	9.97	29	Oregon	19.39
5	New Jersey	49.46	30	Missouri	18.30
47	New Mexico	5.93	31	Kansas	17.65
8	New York	41.45	32	Utah	17.20
49	North Carolina	3.85	33	Arkansas	16.76
28	North Dakota	19.47	34	Mississippi	16.47
6	Ohio	49.00	35	Iowa	14.80
39	Oklahoma	11.82	36	South Dakota	14.56
29	Oregon	19.39	37	Alabama	14.07
9	Pennsylvania	41.41	38	Alaska	13.87
46	Rhode Island	6.72	39	Oklahoma	11.82
25	South Carolina	23.04	40	West Virginia	11.68
36	South Dakota	14.56	41	Delaware	10.50
23	Tennessee	25.20	42	New Hampshire	9.97
14	Texas	33.62	43	Massachusetts	7.33
32	Utah	17.20	44	Connecticut	7.11
50	Vermont	2.68	45	Kentucky	6.86
26	Virginia	22.39	46	Rhode Island	6.72
4	Washington	52.43	47	Maine	5.93
40	West Virginia	11.68	47	New Mexico	5.93
16	Wisconsin	31.95	49	North Carolina	3.85
17	Wyoming	29.90	50	Vermont	2.68

	District of Columbia	218.76

Source: Morgan Quitno Corporation using data from U.S. Bureau of the Census
"Government Finances: 1991-92 (Preliminary Report)" (August 1994, GF/92-5P)
*Direct expenditures. Preliminary data. Includes Courts, Prosecution and Legal Services and Public Defense.

Local Government Expenditures for Judicial and Legal Services
As a Percent of All Direct Expenditures in 1992
National Percent = 1.55% of Direct Expenditures*

ALPHA ORDER

RANK	STATE	PERCENT
36	Alabama	0.77
44	Alaska	0.34
3	Arizona	2.60
21	Arkansas	1.21
1	California	2.78
29	Colorado	0.95
48	Connecticut	0.30
40	Delaware	0.61
13	Florida	1.49
12	Georgia	1.55
5	Hawaii	2.07
16	Idaho	1.37
11	Illinois	1.56
17	Indiana	1.31
39	Iowa	0.67
32	Kansas	0.80
42	Kentucky	0.44
15	Louisiana	1.38
45	Maine	0.33
17	Maryland	1.31
46	Massachusetts	0.31
6	Michigan	2.00
17	Minnesota	1.31
28	Mississippi	0.97
26	Missouri	1.02
10	Montana	1.79
37	Nebraska	0.71
2	Nevada	2.70
41	New Hampshire	0.56
8	New Jersey	1.85
46	New Mexico	0.31
27	New York	0.99
49	North Carolina	0.18
23	North Dakota	1.12
4	Ohio	2.33
38	Oklahoma	0.68
34	Oregon	0.78
7	Pennsylvania	1.87
43	Rhode Island	0.40
20	South Carolina	1.27
31	South Dakota	0.88
24	Tennessee	1.09
13	Texas	1.49
33	Utah	0.79
50	Vermont	0.15
24	Virginia	1.09
9	Washington	1.81
34	West Virginia	0.78
21	Wisconsin	1.21
29	Wyoming	0.95

RANK ORDER

RANK	STATE	PERCENT
1	California	2.78
2	Nevada	2.70
3	Arizona	2.60
4	Ohio	2.33
5	Hawaii	2.07
6	Michigan	2.00
7	Pennsylvania	1.87
8	New Jersey	1.85
9	Washington	1.81
10	Montana	1.79
11	Illinois	1.56
12	Georgia	1.55
13	Florida	1.49
13	Texas	1.49
15	Louisiana	1.38
16	Idaho	1.37
17	Indiana	1.31
17	Maryland	1.31
17	Minnesota	1.31
20	South Carolina	1.27
21	Arkansas	1.21
21	Wisconsin	1.21
23	North Dakota	1.12
24	Tennessee	1.09
24	Virginia	1.09
26	Missouri	1.02
27	New York	0.99
28	Mississippi	0.97
29	Colorado	0.95
29	Wyoming	0.95
31	South Dakota	0.88
32	Kansas	0.80
33	Utah	0.79
34	Oregon	0.78
34	West Virginia	0.78
36	Alabama	0.77
37	Nebraska	0.71
38	Oklahoma	0.68
39	Iowa	0.67
40	Delaware	0.61
41	New Hampshire	0.56
42	Kentucky	0.44
43	Rhode Island	0.40
44	Alaska	0.34
45	Maine	0.33
46	Massachusetts	0.31
46	New Mexico	0.31
48	Connecticut	0.30
49	North Carolina	0.18
50	Vermont	0.15

| District of Columbia | | 2.20 |

Source: Morgan Quitno Corporation using data from U.S. Bureau of the Census
"Government Finances: 1991-92 (Preliminary Report)" (August 1994, GF/92-5P)
*Preliminary data. Includes Courts, Prosecution and Legal Services and Public Defense.

State and Local Government Judicial and Legal Payroll in 1992

National Total = $832,108,000*

ALPHA ORDER					RANK ORDER			

RANK	STATE	PAYROLL	% of USA
25	Alabama	$9,508,000	1.14%
35	Alaska	4,423,000	0.53%
12	Arizona	17,024,000	2.05%
40	Arkansas	3,418,000	0.41%
1	California	133,094,000	15.99%
19	Colorado	12,953,000	1.56%
23	Connecticut	10,709,000	1.29%
39	Delaware	3,450,000	0.41%
3	Florida	48,121,000	5.78%
13	Georgia	16,311,000	1.96%
28	Hawaii	7,932,000	0.95%
43	Idaho	2,776,000	0.33%
6	Illinois	34,995,000	4.21%
24	Indiana	10,016,000	1.20%
29	Iowa	7,599,000	0.91%
31	Kansas	6,630,000	0.80%
27	Kentucky	8,737,000	1.05%
21	Louisiana	11,300,000	1.36%
45	Maine	1,893,000	0.23%
10	Maryland	18,067,000	2.17%
14	Massachusetts	15,867,000	1.91%
9	Michigan	28,990,000	3.48%
17	Minnesota	13,450,000	1.62%
36	Mississippi	4,300,000	0.52%
20	Missouri	11,513,000	1.38%
47	Montana	1,674,000	0.20%
38	Nebraska	3,644,000	0.44%
32	Nevada	6,612,000	0.79%
44	New Hampshire	2,296,000	0.28%
4	New Jersey	46,455,000	5.58%
34	New Mexico	4,729,000	0.57%
2	New York	96,616,000	11.61%
16	North Carolina	14,009,000	1.68%
48	North Dakota	1,645,000	0.20%
7	Ohio	34,683,000	4.17%
30	Oklahoma	6,664,000	0.80%
26	Oregon	9,088,000	1.09%
8	Pennsylvania	34,513,000	4.15%
41	Rhode Island	3,122,000	0.38%
33	South Carolina	5,813,000	0.70%
46	South Dakota	1,715,000	0.21%
22	Tennessee	10,756,000	1.29%
5	Texas	43,180,000	5.19%
37	Utah	4,288,000	0.52%
50	Vermont	1,460,000	0.18%
15	Virginia	14,796,000	1.78%
11	Washington	17,601,000	2.12%
42	West Virginia	3,111,000	0.37%
18	Wisconsin	13,072,000	1.57%
49	Wyoming	1,574,000	0.19%

RANK	STATE	PAYROLL	% of USA
1	California	$133,094,000	15.99%
2	New York	96,616,000	11.61%
3	Florida	48,121,000	5.78%
4	New Jersey	46,455,000	5.58%
5	Texas	43,180,000	5.19%
6	Illinois	34,995,000	4.21%
7	Ohio	34,683,000	4.17%
8	Pennsylvania	34,513,000	4.15%
9	Michigan	28,990,000	3.48%
10	Maryland	18,067,000	2.17%
11	Washington	17,601,000	2.12%
12	Arizona	17,024,000	2.05%
13	Georgia	16,311,000	1.96%
14	Massachusetts	15,867,000	1.91%
15	Virginia	14,796,000	1.78%
16	North Carolina	14,009,000	1.68%
17	Minnesota	13,450,000	1.62%
18	Wisconsin	13,072,000	1.57%
19	Colorado	12,953,000	1.56%
20	Missouri	11,513,000	1.38%
21	Louisiana	11,300,000	1.36%
22	Tennessee	10,756,000	1.29%
23	Connecticut	10,709,000	1.29%
24	Indiana	10,016,000	1.20%
25	Alabama	9,508,000	1.14%
26	Oregon	9,088,000	1.09%
27	Kentucky	8,737,000	1.05%
28	Hawaii	7,932,000	0.95%
29	Iowa	7,599,000	0.91%
30	Oklahoma	6,664,000	0.80%
31	Kansas	6,630,000	0.80%
32	Nevada	6,612,000	0.79%
33	South Carolina	5,813,000	0.70%
34	New Mexico	4,729,000	0.57%
35	Alaska	4,423,000	0.53%
36	Mississippi	4,300,000	0.52%
37	Utah	4,288,000	0.52%
38	Nebraska	3,644,000	0.44%
39	Delaware	3,450,000	0.41%
40	Arkansas	3,418,000	0.41%
41	Rhode Island	3,122,000	0.38%
42	West Virginia	3,111,000	0.37%
43	Idaho	2,776,000	0.33%
44	New Hampshire	2,296,000	0.28%
45	Maine	1,893,000	0.23%
46	South Dakota	1,715,000	0.21%
47	Montana	1,674,000	0.20%
48	North Dakota	1,645,000	0.20%
49	Wyoming	1,574,000	0.19%
50	Vermont	1,460,000	0.18%
	District of Columbia	5,914,000	0.71%

Source: U.S. Bureau of the Census
   "Public Employment: 1992" (September 1994, GE/92-1)
*Includes court and court related activities (except probation and parole which are part of corrections), court activities of
sheriff's offices, prosecuting attorneys' and public defenders' offices, legal departments and attorneys providing
governmentwide legal service.

State and Local Government Police Protection Payroll in 1992

National Total = $2,061,157,000*

RANK	STATE	PAYROLL	% of USA
24	Alabama	$23,009,000	1.12%
42	Alaska	6,225,000	0.30%
18	Arizona	32,647,000	1.58%
35	Arkansas	10,006,000	0.49%
1	California	326,715,000	15.85%
23	Colorado	26,053,000	1.26%
19	Connecticut	31,041,000	1.51%
45	Delaware	5,503,000	0.27%
3	Florida	127,130,000	6.17%
13	Georgia	39,849,000	1.93%
33	Hawaii	11,857,000	0.58%
43	Idaho	6,172,000	0.30%
4	Illinois	120,889,000	5.87%
20	Indiana	27,941,000	1.36%
31	Iowa	15,168,000	0.74%
30	Kansas	15,687,000	0.76%
29	Kentucky	16,189,000	0.79%
25	Louisiana	22,383,000	1.09%
41	Maine	6,719,000	0.33%
11	Maryland	43,439,000	2.11%
10	Massachusetts	55,287,000	2.68%
9	Michigan	63,433,000	3.08%
21	Minnesota	27,538,000	1.34%
34	Mississippi	10,345,000	0.50%
17	Missouri	33,626,000	1.63%
46	Montana	4,137,000	0.20%
36	Nebraska	9,551,000	0.46%
32	Nevada	14,535,000	0.71%
40	New Hampshire	8,007,000	0.39%
6	New Jersey	101,253,000	4.91%
37	New Mexico	9,420,000	0.46%
2	New York	254,441,000	12.34%
14	North Carolina	38,070,000	1.85%
50	North Dakota	2,702,000	0.13%
8	Ohio	72,250,000	3.51%
27	Oklahoma	18,103,000	0.88%
26	Oregon	19,653,000	0.95%
7	Pennsylvania	82,363,000	4.00%
39	Rhode Island	8,102,000	0.39%
28	South Carolina	17,574,000	0.85%
49	South Dakota	3,000,000	0.15%
22	Tennessee	26,083,000	1.27%
5	Texas	117,654,000	5.71%
38	Utah	9,010,000	0.44%
48	Vermont	3,266,000	0.16%
12	Virginia	40,527,000	1.97%
15	Washington	35,917,000	1.74%
44	West Virginia	5,848,000	0.28%
16	Wisconsin	34,881,000	1.69%
47	Wyoming	3,325,000	0.16%

RANK	STATE	PAYROLL	% of USA
1	California	$326,715,000	15.85%
2	New York	254,441,000	12.34%
3	Florida	127,130,000	6.17%
4	Illinois	120,889,000	5.87%
5	Texas	117,654,000	5.71%
6	New Jersey	101,253,000	4.91%
7	Pennsylvania	82,363,000	4.00%
8	Ohio	72,250,000	3.51%
9	Michigan	63,433,000	3.08%
10	Massachusetts	55,287,000	2.68%
11	Maryland	43,439,000	2.11%
12	Virginia	40,527,000	1.97%
13	Georgia	39,849,000	1.93%
14	North Carolina	38,070,000	1.85%
15	Washington	35,917,000	1.74%
16	Wisconsin	34,881,000	1.69%
17	Missouri	33,626,000	1.63%
18	Arizona	32,647,000	1.58%
19	Connecticut	31,041,000	1.51%
20	Indiana	27,941,000	1.36%
21	Minnesota	27,538,000	1.34%
22	Tennessee	26,083,000	1.27%
23	Colorado	26,053,000	1.26%
24	Alabama	23,009,000	1.12%
25	Louisiana	22,383,000	1.09%
26	Oregon	19,653,000	0.95%
27	Oklahoma	18,103,000	0.88%
28	South Carolina	17,574,000	0.85%
29	Kentucky	16,189,000	0.79%
30	Kansas	15,687,000	0.76%
31	Iowa	15,168,000	0.74%
32	Nevada	14,535,000	0.71%
33	Hawaii	11,857,000	0.58%
34	Mississippi	10,345,000	0.50%
35	Arkansas	10,006,000	0.49%
36	Nebraska	9,551,000	0.46%
37	New Mexico	9,420,000	0.46%
38	Utah	9,010,000	0.44%
39	Rhode Island	8,102,000	0.39%
40	New Hampshire	8,007,000	0.39%
41	Maine	6,719,000	0.33%
42	Alaska	6,225,000	0.30%
43	Idaho	6,172,000	0.30%
44	West Virginia	5,848,000	0.28%
45	Delaware	5,503,000	0.27%
46	Montana	4,137,000	0.20%
47	Wyoming	3,325,000	0.16%
48	Vermont	3,266,000	0.16%
49	South Dakota	3,000,000	0.15%
50	North Dakota	2,702,000	0.13%
	District of Columbia	16,635,000	0.81%

Source: U.S. Bureau of the Census
"Public Employment: 1992" (September 1994, GE/92-1)
*All activities concerned with the enforcement of law and order, including coroner's offices, police training academies, investigation bureaus and local jails.

State and Local Government Corrections Payroll in 1992

National Total = $1,307,814,000*

ALPHA ORDER

RANK	STATE	PAYROLL	% of USA
28	Alabama	$11,992,000	0.92%
39	Alaska	4,672,000	0.36%
16	Arizona	20,516,000	1.57%
34	Arkansas	6,124,000	0.47%
1	California	205,551,000	15.72%
22	Colorado	16,041,000	1.23%
18	Connecticut	18,123,000	1.39%
42	Delaware	3,685,000	0.28%
4	Florida	85,184,000	6.51%
11	Georgia	28,857,000	2.21%
40	Hawaii	4,581,000	0.35%
44	Idaho	3,242,000	0.25%
7	Illinois	47,493,000	3.63%
21	Indiana	16,862,000	1.29%
33	Iowa	6,714,000	0.51%
29	Kansas	10,861,000	0.83%
27	Kentucky	12,154,000	0.93%
19	Louisiana	18,092,000	1.38%
41	Maine	3,983,000	0.30%
13	Maryland	27,579,000	2.11%
14	Massachusetts	25,706,000	1.97%
5	Michigan	57,333,000	4.38%
23	Minnesota	15,430,000	1.18%
37	Mississippi	5,236,000	0.40%
25	Missouri	14,761,000	1.13%
45	Montana	2,464,000	0.19%
38	Nebraska	4,781,000	0.37%
30	Nevada	10,324,000	0.79%
43	New Hampshire	3,452,000	0.26%
6	New Jersey	52,508,000	4.01%
32	New Mexico	7,085,000	0.54%
2	New York	192,737,000	14.74%
10	North Carolina	29,753,000	2.28%
50	North Dakota	1,249,000	0.10%
9	Ohio	39,925,000	3.05%
31	Oklahoma	9,605,000	0.73%
26	Oregon	13,810,000	1.06%
8	Pennsylvania	43,444,000	3.32%
35	Rhode Island	5,973,000	0.46%
24	South Carolina	15,220,000	1.16%
48	South Dakota	1,436,000	0.11%
17	Tennessee	19,496,000	1.49%
3	Texas	89,725,000	6.86%
36	Utah	5,792,000	0.44%
47	Vermont	1,643,000	0.13%
12	Virginia	27,844,000	2.13%
15	Washington	23,257,000	1.78%
46	West Virginia	1,932,000	0.15%
20	Wisconsin	17,361,000	1.33%
49	Wyoming	1,344,000	0.10%

RANK ORDER

RANK	STATE	PAYROLL	% of USA
1	California	$205,551,000	15.72%
2	New York	192,737,000	14.74%
3	Texas	89,725,000	6.86%
4	Florida	85,184,000	6.51%
5	Michigan	57,333,000	4.38%
6	New Jersey	52,508,000	4.01%
7	Illinois	47,493,000	3.63%
8	Pennsylvania	43,444,000	3.32%
9	Ohio	39,925,000	3.05%
10	North Carolina	29,753,000	2.28%
11	Georgia	28,857,000	2.21%
12	Virginia	27,844,000	2.13%
13	Maryland	27,579,000	2.11%
14	Massachusetts	25,706,000	1.97%
15	Washington	23,257,000	1.78%
16	Arizona	20,516,000	1.57%
17	Tennessee	19,496,000	1.49%
18	Connecticut	18,123,000	1.39%
19	Louisiana	18,092,000	1.38%
20	Wisconsin	17,361,000	1.33%
21	Indiana	16,862,000	1.29%
22	Colorado	16,041,000	1.23%
23	Minnesota	15,430,000	1.18%
24	South Carolina	15,220,000	1.16%
25	Missouri	14,761,000	1.13%
26	Oregon	13,810,000	1.06%
27	Kentucky	12,154,000	0.93%
28	Alabama	11,992,000	0.92%
29	Kansas	10,861,000	0.83%
30	Nevada	10,324,000	0.79%
31	Oklahoma	9,605,000	0.73%
32	New Mexico	7,085,000	0.54%
33	Iowa	6,714,000	0.51%
34	Arkansas	6,124,000	0.47%
35	Rhode Island	5,973,000	0.46%
36	Utah	5,792,000	0.44%
37	Mississippi	5,236,000	0.40%
38	Nebraska	4,781,000	0.37%
39	Alaska	4,672,000	0.36%
40	Hawaii	4,581,000	0.35%
41	Maine	3,983,000	0.30%
42	Delaware	3,685,000	0.28%
43	New Hampshire	3,452,000	0.26%
44	Idaho	3,242,000	0.25%
45	Montana	2,464,000	0.19%
46	West Virginia	1,932,000	0.15%
47	Vermont	1,643,000	0.13%
48	South Dakota	1,436,000	0.11%
49	Wyoming	1,344,000	0.10%
50	North Dakota	1,249,000	0.10%
	District of Columbia	14,884,000	1.14%

Source: U.S. Bureau of the Census
"Public Employment: 1992" (September 1994, GE/92-1)
*All activities pertaining to the confinement and correction of adults and minors accused or convicted of criminal offenses. Includes any pardon, probation or parole activity.

Base Salary for Justices of States' Highest Courts in 1994

National Average = $94,368

ALPHA ORDER

RANK	STATE	SALARY
10	Alabama	$107,125
12	Alaska	104,472
31	Arizona	91,728
24	Arkansas	95,216
1	California	127,267
38	Colorado	84,000
11	Connecticut	106,553
7	Delaware	108,300
13	Florida	103,457
6	Georgia	109,459
27	Hawaii	93,780
45	Idaho	79,183
4	Illinois	112,124
43	Indiana	81,000
29	Iowa	92,100
35	Kansas	86,577
40	Kentucky	83,752
28	Louisiana	93,400
42	Maine	83,616
15	Maryland	102,000
33	Massachusetts	90,450
5	Michigan	111,941
26	Minnesota	94,395
32	Mississippi	90,800
22	Missouri	95,897
50	Montana	64,452
34	Nebraska	88,157
36	Nevada	85,000
23	New Hampshire	95,623
3	New Jersey	115,000
44	New Mexico	79,567
2	New York	122,500
21	North Carolina	96,000
49	North Dakota	71,555
16	Ohio	101,150
39	Oklahoma	83,871
41	Oregon	83,700
8	Pennsylvania	108,045
17	Rhode Island	99,431
20	South Carolina	97,040
46	South Dakota	74,241
18	Tennessee	99,240
25	Texas	94,685
30	Utah	92,000
47	Vermont	73,890
14	Virginia	102,700
9	Washington	107,200
48	West Virginia	72,000
19	Wisconsin	97,756
36	Wyoming	85,000

RANK ORDER

RANK	STATE	SALARY
1	California	$127,267
2	New York	122,500
3	New Jersey	115,000
4	Illinois	112,124
5	Michigan	111,941
6	Georgia	109,459
7	Delaware	108,300
8	Pennsylvania	108,045
9	Washington	107,200
10	Alabama	107,125
11	Connecticut	106,553
12	Alaska	104,472
13	Florida	103,457
14	Virginia	102,700
15	Maryland	102,000
16	Ohio	101,150
17	Rhode Island	99,431
18	Tennessee	99,240
19	Wisconsin	97,756
20	South Carolina	97,040
21	North Carolina	96,000
22	Missouri	95,897
23	New Hampshire	95,623
24	Arkansas	95,216
25	Texas	94,685
26	Minnesota	94,395
27	Hawaii	93,780
28	Louisiana	93,400
29	Iowa	92,100
30	Utah	92,000
31	Arizona	91,728
32	Mississippi	90,800
33	Massachusetts	90,450
34	Nebraska	88,157
35	Kansas	86,577
36	Nevada	85,000
36	Wyoming	85,000
38	Colorado	84,000
39	Oklahoma	83,871
40	Kentucky	83,752
41	Oregon	83,700
42	Maine	83,616
43	Indiana	81,000
44	New Mexico	79,567
45	Idaho	79,183
46	South Dakota	74,241
47	Vermont	73,890
48	West Virginia	72,000
49	North Dakota	71,555
50	Montana	64,452
	District of Columbia	141,700

Source: National Center for State Courts
"Survey of Judicial Salaries" (July 1994, Volume 20, Number 2)

Base Salary of Judges of Intermediate Appellate Courts in 1994

National Average = $93,164

ALPHA ORDER			RANK ORDER		
RANK	STATE	SALARY	RANK	STATE	SALARY
6	Alabama	$106,125	1	California	$119,314
11	Alaska	98,688	2	New York	114,875
24	Arizona	89,544	3	Georgia	108,765
17	Arkansas	92,205	4	New Jersey	108,000
1	California	119,314	5	Michigan	107,463
34	Colorado	79,500	6	Alabama	106,125
10	Connecticut	99,077	7	Illinois	105,528
NA	Delaware*	NA	8	Pennsylvania	104,444
12	Florida	98,284	9	Washington	101,900
3	Georgia	108,765	10	Connecticut	99,077
22	Hawaii	89,780	11	Alaska	98,688
36	Idaho	78,183	12	Florida	98,284
7	Illinois	105,528	13	Virginia	97,565
37	Indiana	76,500	14	Maryland	95,300
26	Iowa	88,500	15	Tennessee	94,620
31	Kansas	83,487	16	Ohio	94,200
33	Kentucky	80,333	17	Arkansas	92,205
27	Louisiana	88,400	18	South Carolina	92,190
NA	Maine*	NA	19	Wisconsin	92,041
14	Maryland	95,300	20	North Carolina	92,000
30	Massachusetts	83,708	21	Texas	89,952
5	Michigan	107,463	22	Hawaii	89,780
25	Minnesota	88,945	23	Missouri	89,558
NA	Mississippi*	NA	24	Arizona	89,544
23	Missouri	89,558	25	Minnesota	88,945
NA	Montana*	NA	26	Iowa	88,500
29	Nebraska	83,749	27	Louisiana	88,400
NA	Nevada*	NA	28	Utah	87,850
NA	New Hampshire*	NA	29	Nebraska	83,749
4	New Jersey	108,000	30	Massachusetts	83,708
38	New Mexico	75,589	31	Kansas	83,487
2	New York	114,875	32	Oregon	81,700
20	North Carolina	92,000	33	Kentucky	80,333
NA	North Dakota*	NA	34	Colorado	79,500
16	Ohio	94,200	35	Oklahoma	78,660
35	Oklahoma	78,660	36	Idaho	78,183
32	Oregon	81,700	37	Indiana	76,500
8	Pennsylvania	104,444	38	New Mexico	75,589
NA	Rhode Island*	NA	NA	Delaware*	NA
18	South Carolina	92,190	NA	Maine*	NA
NA	South Dakota*	NA	NA	Mississippi*	NA
15	Tennessee	94,620	NA	Montana*	NA
21	Texas	89,952	NA	Nevada*	NA
28	Utah	87,850	NA	New Hampshire*	NA
NA	Vermont*	NA	NA	North Dakota*	NA
13	Virginia	97,565	NA	Rhode Island*	NA
9	Washington	101,900	NA	South Dakota*	NA
NA	West Virginia*	NA	NA	Vermont*	NA
19	Wisconsin	92,041	NA	West Virginia*	NA
NA	Wyoming*	NA	NA	Wyoming*	NA
				District of Columbia*	NA

Source: National Center for State Courts
"Survey of Judicial Salaries" (July 1994, Volume 20, Number 2)
*No intermediate court.

Base Salaries of Judges of General Trial Courts in 1994

National Average = $84,542

ALPHA ORDER

RANK	STATE	SALARY
42	Alabama	$72,500
7	Alaska	96,600
19	Arizona	87,360
18	Arkansas	89,188
2	California	104,262
40	Colorado	75,000
10	Connecticut	94,647
3	Delaware	102,900
11	Florida	93,111
34	Georgia	78,564
21	Hawaii	86,780
41	Idaho	74,214
6	Illinois	96,837
50	Indiana	61,740
24	Iowa	84,200
39	Kansas	75,266
36	Kentucky	76,916
27	Louisiana	83,400
32	Maine	79,073
14	Maryland	91,700
31	Massachusetts	80,360
5	Michigan	98,844
26	Minnesota	83,494
30	Mississippi	81,200
28	Missouri	82,967
49	Montana	63,178
29	Nebraska	81,546
33	Nevada	79,000
16	New Hampshire	89,646
4	New Jersey	100,000
43	New Mexico	71,810
1	New York	108,500
20	North Carolina	87,000
47	North Dakota	65,970
38	Ohio	76,150
44	Oklahoma	71,330
37	Oregon	76,200
12	Pennsylvania	92,610
17	Rhode Island	89,521
13	South Carolina	92,190
46	South Dakota	69,333
15	Tennessee	90,540
23	Texas	85,217
25	Utah	83,650
45	Vermont	70,188
9	Virginia	95,340
7	Washington	96,600
48	West Virginia	65,000
22	Wisconsin	86,289
35	Wyoming	77,000

RANK ORDER

RANK	STATE	SALARY
1	New York	$108,500
2	California	104,262
3	Delaware	102,900
4	New Jersey	100,000
5	Michigan	98,844
6	Illinois	96,837
7	Alaska	96,600
7	Washington	96,600
9	Virginia	95,340
10	Connecticut	94,647
11	Florida	93,111
12	Pennsylvania	92,610
13	South Carolina	92,190
14	Maryland	91,700
15	Tennessee	90,540
16	New Hampshire	89,646
17	Rhode Island	89,521
18	Arkansas	89,188
19	Arizona	87,360
20	North Carolina	87,000
21	Hawaii	86,780
22	Wisconsin	86,289
23	Texas	85,217
24	Iowa	84,200
25	Utah	83,650
26	Minnesota	83,494
27	Louisiana	83,400
28	Missouri	82,967
29	Nebraska	81,546
30	Mississippi	81,200
31	Massachusetts	80,360
32	Maine	79,073
33	Nevada	79,000
34	Georgia	78,564
35	Wyoming	77,000
36	Kentucky	76,916
37	Oregon	76,200
38	Ohio	76,150
39	Kansas	75,266
40	Colorado	75,000
41	Idaho	74,214
42	Alabama	72,500
43	New Mexico	71,810
44	Oklahoma	71,330
45	Vermont	70,188
46	South Dakota	69,333
47	North Dakota	65,970
48	West Virginia	65,000
49	Montana	63,178
50	Indiana	61,740
	District of Columbia	133,600

Source: National Center for State Courts
"Survey of Judicial Salaries" (July 1994, Volume 20, Number 2)

V. LAW ENFORCEMENT

Federal Law Enforcement Officers in 1993

National Total = 68,825 Officers

ALPHA ORDER

RANK	STATE	OFFICERS	% of USA
20	Alabama	888	1.29%
41	Alaska	234	0.34%
7	Arizona	2,103	3.06%
42	Arkansas	227	0.33%
1	California	9,006	13.09%
14	Colorado	1,084	1.58%
30	Connecticut	451	0.66%
49	Delaware	81	0.12%
4	Florida	4,362	6.34%
8	Georgia	1,866	2.71%
28	Hawaii	483	0.70%
43	Idaho	178	0.26%
6	Illinois	2,365	3.44%
27	Indiana	585	0.85%
46	Iowa	123	0.18%
31	Kansas	441	0.64%
21	Kentucky	829	1.20%
12	Louisiana	1,254	1.82%
36	Maine	303	0.44%
19	Maryland	892	1.30%
17	Massachusetts	989	1.44%
10	Michigan	1,523	2.21%
22	Minnesota	734	1.07%
40	Mississippi	236	0.34%
16	Missouri	1,014	1.47%
35	Montana	306	0.44%
44	Nebraska	172	0.25%
33	Nevada	344	0.50%
50	New Hampshire	55	0.08%
9	New Jersey	1,755	2.55%
24	New Mexico	633	0.92%
3	New York	6,305	9.16%
23	North Carolina	721	1.05%
38	North Dakota	251	0.36%
18	Ohio	903	1.31%
25	Oklahoma	608	0.88%
26	Oregon	596	0.87%
5	Pennsylvania	2,820	4.10%
47	Rhode Island	114	0.17%
29	South Carolina	461	0.67%
45	South Dakota	158	0.23%
13	Tennessee	1,211	1.76%
2	Texas	7,761	11.28%
39	Utah	249	0.36%
37	Vermont	269	0.39%
11	Virginia	1,274	1.85%
15	Washington	1,058	1.54%
33	West Virginia	344	0.50%
32	Wisconsin	410	0.60%
48	Wyoming	93	0.14%

RANK ORDER

RANK	STATE	OFFICERS	% of USA
1	California	9,006	13.09%
2	Texas	7,761	11.28%
3	New York	6,305	9.16%
4	Florida	4,362	6.34%
5	Pennsylvania	2,820	4.10%
6	Illinois	2,365	3.44%
7	Arizona	2,103	3.06%
8	Georgia	1,866	2.71%
9	New Jersey	1,755	2.55%
10	Michigan	1,523	2.21%
11	Virginia	1,274	1.85%
12	Louisiana	1,254	1.82%
13	Tennessee	1,211	1.76%
14	Colorado	1,084	1.58%
15	Washington	1,058	1.54%
16	Missouri	1,014	1.47%
17	Massachusetts	989	1.44%
18	Ohio	903	1.31%
19	Maryland	892	1.30%
20	Alabama	888	1.29%
21	Kentucky	829	1.20%
22	Minnesota	734	1.07%
23	North Carolina	721	1.05%
24	New Mexico	633	0.92%
25	Oklahoma	608	0.88%
26	Oregon	596	0.87%
27	Indiana	585	0.85%
28	Hawaii	483	0.70%
29	South Carolina	461	0.67%
30	Connecticut	451	0.66%
31	Kansas	441	0.64%
32	Wisconsin	410	0.60%
33	Nevada	344	0.50%
33	West Virginia	344	0.50%
35	Montana	306	0.44%
36	Maine	303	0.44%
37	Vermont	269	0.39%
38	North Dakota	251	0.36%
39	Utah	249	0.36%
40	Mississippi	236	0.34%
41	Alaska	234	0.34%
42	Arkansas	227	0.33%
43	Idaho	178	0.26%
44	Nebraska	172	0.25%
45	South Dakota	158	0.23%
46	Iowa	123	0.18%
47	Rhode Island	114	0.17%
48	Wyoming	93	0.14%
49	Delaware	81	0.12%
50	New Hampshire	55	0.08%
	District of Columbia	6,133	8.91%

Source: U.S. Department of Justice, Bureau of Justice Statistics
 "Federal Law Enforcement Officers, 1993" (NCJ-151166, December 1994)
Full-time officers authorized to carry firearms and make arrests. National total includes 1,570 officers whose state was not available. Includes F.B.I., Customs Service, Immigration and Naturalization Serv, I.R.S., Postal Inspection, Drug Enf. Admn, Secret Service, Nat'l Park Service, Bur of Alcohol, Tobacco and Firearms, Capitol Police, U.S. Courts, Fed Bureau of Prisons, Tenn Valley Auth, and U.S. Forest Service. 230

Rate of Federal Law Enforcement Officers in 1993

National Rate = 2.7 Officers per 10,000 Population*

ALPHA ORDER			RANK ORDER		
RANK	STATE	RATE	RANK	STATE	RATE
22	Alabama	2.1	1	Arizona	5.3
6	Alaska	3.9	2	Vermont	4.7
1	Arizona	5.3	3	Texas	4.3
45	Arkansas	0.9	4	Hawaii	4.1
12	California	2.9	5	North Dakota	4.0
11	Colorado	3.0	6	Alaska	3.9
37	Connecticut	1.4	6	New Mexico	3.9
40	Delaware	1.2	8	Montana	3.6
10	Florida	3.2	9	New York	3.5
14	Georgia	2.7	10	Florida	3.2
4	Hawaii	4.1	11	Colorado	3.0
33	Idaho	1.6	12	California	2.9
23	Illinois	2.0	12	Louisiana	2.9
43	Indiana	1.0	14	Georgia	2.7
50	Iowa	0.4	15	Nevada	2.5
32	Kansas	1.7	16	Maine	2.4
19	Kentucky	2.2	16	Tennessee	2.4
12	Louisiana	2.9	18	Pennsylvania	2.3
16	Maine	2.4	19	Kentucky	2.2
31	Maryland	1.8	19	New Jersey	2.2
33	Massachusetts	1.6	19	South Dakota	2.2
33	Michigan	1.6	22	Alabama	2.1
33	Minnesota	1.6	23	Illinois	2.0
45	Mississippi	0.9	23	Oregon	2.0
28	Missouri	1.9	23	Virginia	2.0
8	Montana	3.6	23	Washington	2.0
41	Nebraska	1.1	23	Wyoming	2.0
15	Nevada	2.5	28	Missouri	1.9
49	New Hampshire	0.5	28	Oklahoma	1.9
19	New Jersey	2.2	28	West Virginia	1.9
6	New Mexico	3.9	31	Maryland	1.8
9	New York	3.5	32	Kansas	1.7
43	North Carolina	1.0	33	Idaho	1.6
5	North Dakota	4.0	33	Massachusetts	1.6
47	Ohio	0.8	33	Michigan	1.6
28	Oklahoma	1.9	33	Minnesota	1.6
23	Oregon	2.0	37	Connecticut	1.4
18	Pennsylvania	2.3	38	South Carolina	1.3
41	Rhode Island	1.1	38	Utah	1.3
38	South Carolina	1.3	40	Delaware	1.2
19	South Dakota	2.2	41	Nebraska	1.1
16	Tennessee	2.4	41	Rhode Island	1.1
3	Texas	4.3	43	Indiana	1.0
38	Utah	1.3	43	North Carolina	1.0
2	Vermont	4.7	45	Arkansas	0.9
23	Virginia	2.0	45	Mississippi	0.9
23	Washington	2.0	47	Ohio	0.8
28	West Virginia	1.9	47	Wisconsin	0.8
47	Wisconsin	0.8	49	New Hampshire	0.5
23	Wyoming	2.0	50	Iowa	0.4
				District of Columbia	106.1

Source: U.S. Department of Justice, Bureau of Justice Statistics
   "Federal Law Enforcement Officers, 1993" (NCJ-151166, December 1994)
Full-time officers authorized to carry firearms and make arrests. National total includes officers whose state was not available. Includes F.B.I., Customs Service, Immigration and Naturalization Serv, I.R.S., Postal Inspection, Drug Enf. Admn, Secret Service, Nat'l Park Service, Bur of Alcohol, Tobacco and Firearms, Capitol Police, U.S. Courts, Fed Bureau of Prisons, Tenn Valley Auth, and U.S. Forest Service.   231

Law Enforcement Agencies in 1992

National Total = 17,358 Agencies*

ALPHA ORDER

RANK	STATE	AGENCIES	% of USA
18	Alabama	377	2.17%
46	Alaska	48	0.28%
43	Arizona	102	0.59%
26	Arkansas	277	1.60%
11	California	493	2.84%
32	Colorado	218	1.26%
37	Connecticut	133	0.77%
48	Delaware	42	0.24%
20	Florida	371	2.14%
8	Georgia	540	3.11%
50	Hawaii	6	0.03%
42	Idaho	112	0.65%
4	Illinois	894	5.15%
14	Indiana	448	2.58%
15	Iowa	427	2.46%
22	Kansas	345	1.99%
18	Kentucky	377	2.17%
21	Louisiana	348	2.00%
35	Maine	142	0.82%
39	Maryland	124	0.71%
17	Massachusetts	388	2.24%
6	Michigan	578	3.33%
13	Minnesota	456	2.63%
25	Mississippi	297	1.71%
5	Missouri	594	3.42%
40	Montana	119	0.69%
29	Nebraska	247	1.42%
49	Nevada	35	0.20%
30	New Hampshire	228	1.31%
9	New Jersey	534	3.08%
41	New Mexico	115	0.66%
6	New York	578	3.33%
12	North Carolina	458	2.64%
36	North Dakota	134	0.77%
3	Ohio	908	5.23%
16	Oklahoma	410	2.36%
33	Oregon	183	1.05%
2	Pennsylvania	1,167	6.72%
46	Rhode Island	48	0.28%
27	South Carolina	255	1.47%
34	South Dakota	171	0.99%
24	Tennessee	326	1.88%
1	Texas	1,712	9.86%
38	Utah	127	0.73%
45	Vermont	73	0.42%
23	Virginia	327	1.88%
28	Washington	252	1.45%
30	West Virginia	228	1.31%
10	Wisconsin	506	2.92%
44	Wyoming	77	0.44%

RANK ORDER

RANK	STATE	AGENCIES	% of USA
1	Texas	1,712	9.86%
2	Pennsylvania	1,167	6.72%
3	Ohio	908	5.23%
4	Illinois	894	5.15%
5	Missouri	594	3.42%
6	Michigan	578	3.33%
6	New York	578	3.33%
8	Georgia	540	3.11%
9	New Jersey	534	3.08%
10	Wisconsin	506	2.92%
11	California	493	2.84%
12	North Carolina	458	2.64%
13	Minnesota	456	2.63%
14	Indiana	448	2.58%
15	Iowa	427	2.46%
16	Oklahoma	410	2.36%
17	Massachusetts	388	2.24%
18	Alabama	377	2.17%
18	Kentucky	377	2.17%
20	Florida	371	2.14%
21	Louisiana	348	2.00%
22	Kansas	345	1.99%
23	Virginia	327	1.88%
24	Tennessee	326	1.88%
25	Mississippi	297	1.71%
26	Arkansas	277	1.60%
27	South Carolina	255	1.47%
28	Washington	252	1.45%
29	Nebraska	247	1.42%
30	New Hampshire	228	1.31%
30	West Virginia	228	1.31%
32	Colorado	218	1.26%
33	Oregon	183	1.05%
34	South Dakota	171	0.99%
35	Maine	142	0.82%
36	North Dakota	134	0.77%
37	Connecticut	133	0.77%
38	Utah	127	0.73%
39	Maryland	124	0.71%
40	Montana	119	0.69%
41	New Mexico	115	0.66%
42	Idaho	112	0.65%
43	Arizona	102	0.59%
44	Wyoming	77	0.44%
45	Vermont	73	0.42%
46	Alaska	48	0.28%
46	Rhode Island	48	0.28%
48	Delaware	42	0.24%
49	Nevada	35	0.20%
50	Hawaii	6	0.03%
	District of Columbia	3	0.02%

Source: U.S. Department of Justice, Bureau of Justice Statistics
"Census of State and Local Law Enforcement Agencies, 1992" (Bulletin, July 1993, NCJ-142972)
*Includes state and local police, sheriffs' departments and special police agencies.

Population per Law Enforcement Agency in 1992

National Rate = 14,695 Population per Agency *

ALPHA ORDER

RANK ORDER

RANK	STATE	RATE
29	Alabama	10,971
27	Alaska	12,229
5	Arizona	37,569
39	Arkansas	8,661
2	California	62,611
15	Colorado	15,917
8	Connecticut	24,669
12	Delaware	16,405
6	Florida	36,356
25	Georgia	12,502
1	Hawaii	193,333
35	Idaho	9,527
23	Illinois	13,010
24	Indiana	12,638
45	Iowa	6,585
43	Kansas	7,313
32	Kentucky	9,960
26	Louisiana	12,319
38	Maine	8,697
3	Maryland	39,581
16	Massachusetts	15,459
13	Michigan	16,327
34	Minnesota	9,825
36	Mississippi	8,801
37	Missouri	8,742
44	Montana	6,924
46	Nebraska	6,502
4	Nevada	37,914
48	New Hampshire	4,873
19	New Jersey	14,586
22	New Mexico	13,748
7	New York	31,348
18	North Carolina	14,941
49	North Dakota	4,746
28	Ohio	12,132
41	Oklahoma	7,834
14	Oregon	16,268
31	Pennsylvania	10,290
9	Rhode Island	20,938
21	South Carolina	14,129
50	South Dakota	4,158
17	Tennessee	15,411
30	Texas	10,313
20	Utah	14,276
42	Vermont	7,808
11	Virginia	19,502
10	Washington	20,381
40	West Virginia	7,947
33	Wisconsin	9,895
47	Wyoming	6,052

RANK	STATE	RATE
1	Hawaii	193,333
2	California	62,611
3	Maryland	39,581
4	Nevada	37,914
5	Arizona	37,569
6	Florida	36,356
7	New York	31,348
8	Connecticut	24,669
9	Rhode Island	20,938
10	Washington	20,381
11	Virginia	19,502
12	Delaware	16,405
13	Michigan	16,327
14	Oregon	16,268
15	Colorado	15,917
16	Massachusetts	15,459
17	Tennessee	15,411
18	North Carolina	14,941
19	New Jersey	14,586
20	Utah	14,276
21	South Carolina	14,129
22	New Mexico	13,748
23	Illinois	13,010
24	Indiana	12,638
25	Georgia	12,502
26	Louisiana	12,319
27	Alaska	12,229
28	Ohio	12,132
29	Alabama	10,971
30	Texas	10,313
31	Pennsylvania	10,290
32	Kentucky	9,960
33	Wisconsin	9,895
34	Minnesota	9,825
35	Idaho	9,527
36	Mississippi	8,801
37	Missouri	8,742
38	Maine	8,697
39	Arkansas	8,661
40	West Virginia	7,947
41	Oklahoma	7,834
42	Vermont	7,808
43	Kansas	7,313
44	Montana	6,924
45	Iowa	6,585
46	Nebraska	6,502
47	Wyoming	6,052
48	New Hampshire	4,873
49	North Dakota	4,746
50	South Dakota	4,158

District of Columbia 196,333

Source: Morgan Quitno Corporation using data from U.S. Department of Justice, Bureau of Justice Statistics
"Census of State and Local Law Enforcement Agencies, 1992" (Bulletin, July 1993, NCJ-142972)
*Includes state and local police, sheriffs' departments and special police agencies.

Law Enforcement Agencies per 1,000 Square Miles in 1992

National Rate = 4.58 Agencies per 1,000 Square Miles*

ALPHA ORDER

RANK ORDER

RANK	STATE	RATE	RANK	STATE	RATE
24	Alabama	7.19	1	New Jersey	61.22
50	Alaska	0.07	2	Massachusetts	36.76
45	Arizona	0.89	3	Rhode Island	31.07
32	Arkansas	5.21	4	Pennsylvania	25.34
37	California	3.01	5	New Hampshire	24.38
39	Colorado	2.09	6	Connecticut	23.99
6	Connecticut	23.99	7	Ohio	20.26
8	Delaware	16.87	8	Delaware	16.87
30	Florida	5.64	9	Illinois	15.44
15	Georgia	9.08	10	Indiana	12.30
48	Hawaii	0.55	11	New York	10.61
43	Idaho	1.34	12	Maryland	9.99
9	Illinois	15.44	13	West Virginia	9.41
10	Indiana	12.30	14	Kentucky	9.33
22	Iowa	7.59	15	Georgia	9.08
33	Kansas	4.19	16	Missouri	8.52
14	Kentucky	9.33	17	North Carolina	8.51
25	Louisiana	6.71	18	South Carolina	7.97
34	Maine	4.01	19	Tennessee	7.74
12	Maryland	9.99	20	Wisconsin	7.72
2	Massachusetts	36.76	21	Virginia	7.65
28	Michigan	5.97	22	Iowa	7.59
31	Minnesota	5.24	22	Vermont	7.59
27	Mississippi	6.13	24	Alabama	7.19
16	Missouri	8.52	25	Louisiana	6.71
46	Montana	0.81	26	Texas	6.37
36	Nebraska	3.19	27	Mississippi	6.13
49	Nevada	0.32	28	Michigan	5.97
5	New Hampshire	24.38	29	Oklahoma	5.87
1	New Jersey	61.22	30	Florida	5.64
44	New Mexico	0.95	31	Minnesota	5.24
11	New York	10.61	32	Arkansas	5.21
17	North Carolina	8.51	33	Kansas	4.19
40	North Dakota	1.90	34	Maine	4.01
7	Ohio	20.26	35	Washington	3.53
29	Oklahoma	5.87	36	Nebraska	3.19
41	Oregon	1.86	37	California	3.01
4	Pennsylvania	25.34	38	South Dakota	2.22
3	Rhode Island	31.07	39	Colorado	2.09
18	South Carolina	7.97	40	North Dakota	1.90
38	South Dakota	2.22	41	Oregon	1.86
19	Tennessee	7.74	42	Utah	1.50
26	Texas	6.37	43	Idaho	1.34
42	Utah	1.50	44	New Mexico	0.95
22	Vermont	7.59	45	Arizona	0.89
21	Virginia	7.65	46	Montana	0.81
35	Washington	3.53	47	Wyoming	0.79
13	West Virginia	9.41	48	Hawaii	0.55
20	Wisconsin	7.72	49	Nevada	0.32
47	Wyoming	0.79	50	Alaska	0.07

District of Columbia**   NA

Source: Morgan Quitno Corporation using data from U.S. Department of Justice, Bureau of Justice Statistics
"Census of State and Local Law Enforcement Agencies, 1992" (Bulletin, July 1993, NCJ-142972)
*Includes state and local police, sheriffs' departments and special police agencies.
**The District of Columbia has three agencies for its 68 square miles.

Full–Time Sworn Officers in Law Enforcement Agencies in 1992

National Total = 603,954 Officers*

<table>
<tr><td colspan="4">ALPHA ORDER</td><td colspan="4">RANK ORDER</td></tr>
<tr><td>RANK</td><td>STATE</td><td>OFFICERS</td><td>% of USA</td><td>RANK</td><td>STATE</td><td>OFFICERS</td><td>% of USA</td></tr>
<tr><td>20</td><td>Alabama</td><td>8,771</td><td>1.45%</td><td>1</td><td>New York</td><td>68,208</td><td>11.29%</td></tr>
<tr><td>49</td><td>Alaska</td><td>1,057</td><td>0.18%</td><td>2</td><td>California</td><td>65,797</td><td>10.89%</td></tr>
<tr><td>23</td><td>Arizona</td><td>7,900</td><td>1.31%</td><td>3</td><td>Texas</td><td>41,349</td><td>6.85%</td></tr>
<tr><td>33</td><td>Arkansas</td><td>4,475</td><td>0.74%</td><td>4</td><td>Illinois</td><td>35,674</td><td>5.91%</td></tr>
<tr><td>2</td><td>California</td><td>65,797</td><td>10.89%</td><td>5</td><td>Florida</td><td>32,879</td><td>5.44%</td></tr>
<tr><td>21</td><td>Colorado</td><td>8,726</td><td>1.44%</td><td>6</td><td>New Jersey</td><td>26,688</td><td>4.42%</td></tr>
<tr><td>25</td><td>Connecticut</td><td>7,639</td><td>1.26%</td><td>7</td><td>Pennsylvania</td><td>23,700</td><td>3.92%</td></tr>
<tr><td>44</td><td>Delaware</td><td>1,572</td><td>0.26%</td><td>8</td><td>Ohio</td><td>20,929</td><td>3.47%</td></tr>
<tr><td>5</td><td>Florida</td><td>32,879</td><td>5.44%</td><td>9</td><td>Michigan</td><td>19,642</td><td>3.25%</td></tr>
<tr><td>10</td><td>Georgia</td><td>16,792</td><td>2.78%</td><td>10</td><td>Georgia</td><td>16,792</td><td>2.78%</td></tr>
<tr><td>38</td><td>Hawaii</td><td>2,783</td><td>0.46%</td><td>11</td><td>Virginia</td><td>16,365</td><td>2.71%</td></tr>
<tr><td>42</td><td>Idaho</td><td>2,157</td><td>0.36%</td><td>12</td><td>Massachusetts</td><td>16,014</td><td>2.65%</td></tr>
<tr><td>4</td><td>Illinois</td><td>35,674</td><td>5.91%</td><td>13</td><td>Louisiana</td><td>15,049</td><td>2.49%</td></tr>
<tr><td>19</td><td>Indiana</td><td>10,038</td><td>1.66%</td><td>14</td><td>North Carolina</td><td>14,586</td><td>2.42%</td></tr>
<tr><td>31</td><td>Iowa</td><td>4,703</td><td>0.78%</td><td>15</td><td>Maryland</td><td>12,601</td><td>2.09%</td></tr>
<tr><td>29</td><td>Kansas</td><td>5,631</td><td>0.93%</td><td>16</td><td>Wisconsin</td><td>11,594</td><td>1.92%</td></tr>
<tr><td>28</td><td>Kentucky</td><td>6,085</td><td>1.01%</td><td>17</td><td>Missouri</td><td>11,266</td><td>1.87%</td></tr>
<tr><td>13</td><td>Louisiana</td><td>15,049</td><td>2.49%</td><td>18</td><td>Tennessee</td><td>10,379</td><td>1.72%</td></tr>
<tr><td>41</td><td>Maine</td><td>2,267</td><td>0.38%</td><td>19</td><td>Indiana</td><td>10,038</td><td>1.66%</td></tr>
<tr><td>15</td><td>Maryland</td><td>12,601</td><td>2.09%</td><td>20</td><td>Alabama</td><td>8,771</td><td>1.45%</td></tr>
<tr><td>12</td><td>Massachusetts</td><td>16,014</td><td>2.65%</td><td>21</td><td>Colorado</td><td>8,726</td><td>1.44%</td></tr>
<tr><td>9</td><td>Michigan</td><td>19,642</td><td>3.25%</td><td>22</td><td>Washington</td><td>8,192</td><td>1.36%</td></tr>
<tr><td>26</td><td>Minnesota</td><td>7,365</td><td>1.22%</td><td>23</td><td>Arizona</td><td>7,900</td><td>1.31%</td></tr>
<tr><td>32</td><td>Mississippi</td><td>4,675</td><td>0.77%</td><td>24</td><td>South Carolina</td><td>7,752</td><td>1.28%</td></tr>
<tr><td>17</td><td>Missouri</td><td>11,266</td><td>1.87%</td><td>25</td><td>Connecticut</td><td>7,639</td><td>1.26%</td></tr>
<tr><td>45</td><td>Montana</td><td>1,410</td><td>0.23%</td><td>26</td><td>Minnesota</td><td>7,365</td><td>1.22%</td></tr>
<tr><td>35</td><td>Nebraska</td><td>3,084</td><td>0.51%</td><td>27</td><td>Oklahoma</td><td>6,458</td><td>1.07%</td></tr>
<tr><td>36</td><td>Nevada</td><td>3,052</td><td>0.51%</td><td>28</td><td>Kentucky</td><td>6,085</td><td>1.01%</td></tr>
<tr><td>43</td><td>New Hampshire</td><td>2,139</td><td>0.35%</td><td>29</td><td>Kansas</td><td>5,631</td><td>0.93%</td></tr>
<tr><td>6</td><td>New Jersey</td><td>26,688</td><td>4.42%</td><td>30</td><td>Oregon</td><td>5,495</td><td>0.91%</td></tr>
<tr><td>34</td><td>New Mexico</td><td>3,420</td><td>0.57%</td><td>31</td><td>Iowa</td><td>4,703</td><td>0.78%</td></tr>
<tr><td>1</td><td>New York</td><td>68,208</td><td>11.29%</td><td>32</td><td>Mississippi</td><td>4,675</td><td>0.77%</td></tr>
<tr><td>14</td><td>North Carolina</td><td>14,586</td><td>2.42%</td><td>33</td><td>Arkansas</td><td>4,475</td><td>0.74%</td></tr>
<tr><td>48</td><td>North Dakota</td><td>1,060</td><td>0.18%</td><td>34</td><td>New Mexico</td><td>3,420</td><td>0.57%</td></tr>
<tr><td>8</td><td>Ohio</td><td>20,929</td><td>3.47%</td><td>35</td><td>Nebraska</td><td>3,084</td><td>0.51%</td></tr>
<tr><td>27</td><td>Oklahoma</td><td>6,458</td><td>1.07%</td><td>36</td><td>Nevada</td><td>3,052</td><td>0.51%</td></tr>
<tr><td>30</td><td>Oregon</td><td>5,495</td><td>0.91%</td><td>37</td><td>Utah</td><td>2,979</td><td>0.49%</td></tr>
<tr><td>7</td><td>Pennsylvania</td><td>23,700</td><td>3.92%</td><td>38</td><td>Hawaii</td><td>2,783</td><td>0.46%</td></tr>
<tr><td>40</td><td>Rhode Island</td><td>2,389</td><td>0.40%</td><td>39</td><td>West Virginia</td><td>2,622</td><td>0.43%</td></tr>
<tr><td>24</td><td>South Carolina</td><td>7,752</td><td>1.28%</td><td>40</td><td>Rhode Island</td><td>2,389</td><td>0.40%</td></tr>
<tr><td>47</td><td>South Dakota</td><td>1,145</td><td>0.19%</td><td>41</td><td>Maine</td><td>2,267</td><td>0.38%</td></tr>
<tr><td>18</td><td>Tennessee</td><td>10,379</td><td>1.72%</td><td>42</td><td>Idaho</td><td>2,157</td><td>0.36%</td></tr>
<tr><td>3</td><td>Texas</td><td>41,349</td><td>6.85%</td><td>43</td><td>New Hampshire</td><td>2,139</td><td>0.35%</td></tr>
<tr><td>37</td><td>Utah</td><td>2,979</td><td>0.49%</td><td>44</td><td>Delaware</td><td>1,572</td><td>0.26%</td></tr>
<tr><td>50</td><td>Vermont</td><td>978</td><td>0.16%</td><td>45</td><td>Montana</td><td>1,410</td><td>0.23%</td></tr>
<tr><td>11</td><td>Virginia</td><td>16,365</td><td>2.71%</td><td>46</td><td>Wyoming</td><td>1,210</td><td>0.20%</td></tr>
<tr><td>22</td><td>Washington</td><td>8,192</td><td>1.36%</td><td>47</td><td>South Dakota</td><td>1,145</td><td>0.19%</td></tr>
<tr><td>39</td><td>West Virginia</td><td>2,622</td><td>0.43%</td><td>48</td><td>North Dakota</td><td>1,060</td><td>0.18%</td></tr>
<tr><td>16</td><td>Wisconsin</td><td>11,594</td><td>1.92%</td><td>49</td><td>Alaska</td><td>1,057</td><td>0.18%</td></tr>
<tr><td>46</td><td>Wyoming</td><td>1,210</td><td>0.20%</td><td>50</td><td>Vermont</td><td>978</td><td>0.16%</td></tr>
<tr><td></td><td></td><td></td><td></td><td></td><td>District of Columbia</td><td>5,213</td><td>0.86%</td></tr>
</table>

Source: U.S. Department of Justice, Bureau of Justice Statistics
"Census of State and Local Law Enforcement Agencies, 1992" (Bulletin, July 1993, NCJ-142972)
*Includes state and local police, sheriffs' departments and special police agencies.

Percent of Full-Time Law Enforcement Agency Employees
Who are Sworn Officers: 1992
National Rate = 71.81% of Employees are Sworn Officers*

ALPHA ORDER

RANK ORDER

RANK	STATE	PERCENT		RANK	STATE	PERCENT
29	Alabama	70.07		1	Louisiana	86.64
44	Alaska	64.26		2	Pennsylvania	83.67
50	Arizona	59.65		3	Rhode Island	82.64
40	Arkansas	65.59		4	Connecticut	82.35
41	California	65.42		5	New Jersey	81.40
31	Colorado	69.48		6	New York	80.08
4	Connecticut	82.35		7	Hawaii	80.02
8	Delaware	78.36		8	Delaware	78.36
48	Florida	60.87		9	Illinois	77.23
33	Georgia	68.49		10	South Carolina	76.76
7	Hawaii	80.02		11	Kentucky	76.55
20	Idaho	73.82		12	Virginia	76.28
9	Illinois	77.23		13	Wisconsin	75.88
36	Indiana	67.21		14	Massachusetts	75.61
15	Iowa	75.16		15	Iowa	75.16
27	Kansas	71.90		16	Maryland	74.69
11	Kentucky	76.55		17	Michigan	74.47
1	Louisiana	86.64		18	North Carolina	74.29
34	Maine	68.43		19	New Hampshire	73.91
16	Maryland	74.69		20	Idaho	73.82
14	Massachusetts	75.61		21	Vermont	73.59
17	Michigan	74.47		22	Nebraska	73.53
25	Minnesota	72.41		23	Missouri	73.30
30	Mississippi	69.89		24	North Dakota	73.15
23	Missouri	73.30		25	Minnesota	72.41
38	Montana	66.48		26	South Dakota	71.92
22	Nebraska	73.53		27	Kansas	71.90
47	Nevada	61.13		28	Ohio	70.43
19	New Hampshire	73.91		29	Alabama	70.07
5	New Jersey	81.40		30	Mississippi	69.89
32	New Mexico	68.99		31	Colorado	69.48
6	New York	80.08		32	New Mexico	68.99
18	North Carolina	74.29		33	Georgia	68.49
24	North Dakota	73.15		34	Maine	68.43
28	Ohio	70.43		35	Oklahoma	67.59
35	Oklahoma	67.59		36	Indiana	67.21
39	Oregon	66.13		37	West Virginia	67.02
2	Pennsylvania	83.67		38	Montana	66.48
3	Rhode Island	82.64		39	Oregon	66.13
10	South Carolina	76.76		40	Arkansas	65.59
26	South Dakota	71.92		41	California	65.42
45	Tennessee	63.48		42	Texas	64.36
42	Texas	64.36		43	Washington	64.34
46	Utah	61.64		44	Alaska	64.26
21	Vermont	73.59		45	Tennessee	63.48
12	Virginia	76.28		46	Utah	61.64
43	Washington	64.34		47	Nevada	61.13
37	West Virginia	67.02		48	Florida	60.87
13	Wisconsin	75.88		49	Wyoming	60.02
49	Wyoming	60.02		50	Arizona	59.65

District of Columbia 84.43

Source: Morgan Quitno Corporation using data from U.S. Department of Justice, Bureau of Justice Statistics
"Census of State and Local Law Enforcement Agencies, 1992" (Bulletin, July 1993, NCJ-142972)
*Includes state and local police, sheriffs' departments and special police agencies.

Rate of Full-Time Sworn Officers in Law Enforcement Agencies in 1992

National Rate = 23.68 Officers per 10,000 Population*

ALPHA ORDER				RANK ORDER		
RANK	STATE	RATE		RANK	STATE	RATE
25	Alabama	21.21		1	New York	37.64
38	Alaska	18.01		2	Louisiana	35.10
28	Arizona	20.62		3	New Jersey	34.26
35	Arkansas	18.65		4	Illinois	30.67
23	California	21.32		5	Massachusetts	26.70
9	Colorado	25.15		6	Wyoming	25.97
15	Connecticut	23.28		7	Maryland	25.67
18	Delaware	22.82		8	Virginia	25.66
11	Florida	24.38		9	Colorado	25.15
10	Georgia	24.87		10	Georgia	24.87
12	Hawaii	23.99		11	Florida	24.38
29	Idaho	20.22		12	Hawaii	23.99
4	Illinois	30.67		13	Rhode Island	23.77
40	Indiana	17.73		14	Texas	23.42
43	Iowa	16.72		15	Connecticut	23.28
19	Kansas	22.32		16	Wisconsin	23.16
47	Kentucky	16.21		17	Nevada	23.00
2	Louisiana	35.10		18	Delaware	22.82
37	Maine	18.36		19	Kansas	22.32
7	Maryland	25.67		20	Missouri	21.69
5	Massachusetts	26.70		21	New Mexico	21.63
26	Michigan	20.81		22	South Carolina	21.52
45	Minnesota	16.44		23	California	21.32
39	Mississippi	17.88		23	North Carolina	21.32
20	Missouri	21.69		25	Alabama	21.21
42	Montana	17.11		26	Michigan	20.81
33	Nebraska	19.20		27	Tennessee	20.66
17	Nevada	23.00		28	Arizona	20.62
32	New Hampshire	19.25		29	Idaho	20.22
3	New Jersey	34.26		30	Oklahoma	20.11
21	New Mexico	21.63		31	Pennsylvania	19.74
1	New York	37.64		32	New Hampshire	19.25
23	North Carolina	21.32		33	Nebraska	19.20
44	North Dakota	16.67		34	Ohio	19.00
34	Ohio	19.00		35	Arkansas	18.65
30	Oklahoma	20.11		36	Oregon	18.46
36	Oregon	18.46		37	Maine	18.36
31	Pennsylvania	19.74		38	Alaska	18.01
13	Rhode Island	23.77		39	Mississippi	17.88
22	South Carolina	21.52		40	Indiana	17.73
48	South Dakota	16.10		41	Vermont	17.16
27	Tennessee	20.66		42	Montana	17.11
14	Texas	23.42		43	Iowa	16.72
46	Utah	16.43		44	North Dakota	16.67
41	Vermont	17.16		45	Minnesota	16.44
8	Virginia	25.66		46	Utah	16.43
49	Washington	15.95		47	Kentucky	16.21
50	West Virginia	14.47		48	South Dakota	16.10
16	Wisconsin	23.16		49	Washington	15.95
6	Wyoming	25.97		50	West Virginia	14.47
					District of Columbia	88.51

Source: Morgan Quitno Corporation using data from U.S. Department of Justice, Bureau of Justice Statistics
"Census of State and Local Law Enforcement Agencies, 1992" (Bulletin, July 1993, NCJ-142972)
*Includes state and local police, sheriffs' departments and special police agencies.

Full–Time Sworn Law Enforcement Officers per 1,000 Square Miles in 1992

National Rate = 159 Officers per 1,000 Square Miles*

ALPHA ORDER

RANK	STATE	RATE
24	Alabama	167
50	Alaska	2
37	Arizona	69
34	Arkansas	84
12	California	402
34	Colorado	84
4	Connecticut	1,378
7	Delaware	632
10	Florida	500
15	Georgia	282
18	Hawaii	255
45	Idaho	26
8	Illinois	616
16	Indiana	276
34	Iowa	84
38	Kansas	68
27	Kentucky	151
14	Louisiana	290
39	Maine	64
6	Maryland	1,016
3	Massachusetts	1,517
22	Michigan	203
33	Minnesota	85
31	Mississippi	97
25	Missouri	162
49	Montana	10
41	Nebraska	40
43	Nevada	28
21	New Hampshire	229
1	New Jersey	3,060
43	New Mexico	28
5	New York	1,252
17	North Carolina	271
46	North Dakota	15
11	Ohio	467
32	Oklahoma	92
40	Oregon	56
9	Pennsylvania	515
2	Rhode Island	1,546
20	South Carolina	242
46	South Dakota	15
19	Tennessee	246
26	Texas	154
42	Utah	35
30	Vermont	102
13	Virginia	383
28	Washington	115
29	West Virginia	108
23	Wisconsin	177
48	Wyoming	12

RANK ORDER

RANK	STATE	RATE
1	New Jersey	3,060
2	Rhode Island	1,546
3	Massachusetts	1,517
4	Connecticut	1,378
5	New York	1,252
6	Maryland	1,016
7	Delaware	632
8	Illinois	616
9	Pennsylvania	515
10	Florida	500
11	Ohio	467
12	California	402
13	Virginia	383
14	Louisiana	290
15	Georgia	282
16	Indiana	276
17	North Carolina	271
18	Hawaii	255
19	Tennessee	246
20	South Carolina	242
21	New Hampshire	229
22	Michigan	203
23	Wisconsin	177
24	Alabama	167
25	Missouri	162
26	Texas	154
27	Kentucky	151
28	Washington	115
29	West Virginia	108
30	Vermont	102
31	Mississippi	97
32	Oklahoma	92
33	Minnesota	85
34	Arkansas	84
34	Colorado	84
34	Iowa	84
37	Arizona	69
38	Kansas	68
39	Maine	64
40	Oregon	56
41	Nebraska	40
42	Utah	35
43	Nevada	28
43	New Mexico	28
45	Idaho	26
46	North Dakota	15
46	South Dakota	15
48	Wyoming	12
49	Montana	10
50	Alaska	2

District of Columbia**   NA

Source: Morgan Quitno Corporation using data from U.S. Department of Justice, Bureau of Justice Statistics
"Census of State and Local Law Enforcement Agencies, 1992" (Bulletin, July 1993, NCJ–142972)
*Includes state and local police, sheriffs' departments and special police agencies.
**The District of Columbia has 5,213 sworn officers for its 68 square miles.

Full-Time Employees in Law Enforcement Agencies in 1992

National Total = 841,099 Employees*

ALPHA ORDER

RANK	STATE	EMPLOYEES	% of USA
23	Alabama	12,517	1.49%
47	Alaska	1,645	0.20%
20	Arizona	13,243	1.57%
31	Arkansas	6,823	0.81%
1	California	100,582	11.96%
22	Colorado	12,559	1.49%
27	Connecticut	9,276	1.10%
46	Delaware	2,006	0.24%
4	Florida	54,011	6.42%
10	Georgia	24,516	2.91%
39	Hawaii	3,478	0.41%
41	Idaho	2,922	0.35%
5	Illinois	46,189	5.49%
19	Indiana	14,935	1.78%
33	Iowa	6,257	0.74%
30	Kansas	7,832	0.93%
29	Kentucky	7,949	0.95%
14	Louisiana	17,370	2.07%
40	Maine	3,313	0.39%
15	Maryland	16,871	2.01%
12	Massachusetts	21,181	2.52%
9	Michigan	26,375	3.14%
24	Minnesota	10,171	1.21%
32	Mississippi	6,689	0.80%
17	Missouri	15,370	1.83%
44	Montana	2,121	0.25%
37	Nebraska	4,194	0.50%
34	Nevada	4,993	0.59%
42	New Hampshire	2,894	0.34%
6	New Jersey	32,785	3.90%
35	New Mexico	4,957	0.59%
2	New York	85,177	10.13%
13	North Carolina	19,633	2.33%
49	North Dakota	1,449	0.17%
7	Ohio	29,718	3.53%
26	Oklahoma	9,554	1.14%
28	Oregon	8,310	0.99%
8	Pennsylvania	28,326	3.37%
43	Rhode Island	2,891	0.34%
25	South Carolina	10,099	1.20%
48	South Dakota	1,592	0.19%
16	Tennessee	16,349	1.94%
3	Texas	64,247	7.64%
36	Utah	4,833	0.57%
50	Vermont	1,329	0.16%
11	Virginia	21,454	2.55%
21	Washington	12,733	1.51%
38	West Virginia	3,912	0.47%
18	Wisconsin	15,279	1.82%
45	Wyoming	2,016	0.24%

RANK ORDER

RANK	STATE	EMPLOYEES	% of USA
1	California	100,582	11.96%
2	New York	85,177	10.13%
3	Texas	64,247	7.64%
4	Florida	54,011	6.42%
5	Illinois	46,189	5.49%
6	New Jersey	32,785	3.90%
7	Ohio	29,718	3.53%
8	Pennsylvania	28,326	3.37%
9	Michigan	26,375	3.14%
10	Georgia	24,516	2.91%
11	Virginia	21,454	2.55%
12	Massachusetts	21,181	2.52%
13	North Carolina	19,633	2.33%
14	Louisiana	17,370	2.07%
15	Maryland	16,871	2.01%
16	Tennessee	16,349	1.94%
17	Missouri	15,370	1.83%
18	Wisconsin	15,279	1.82%
19	Indiana	14,935	1.78%
20	Arizona	13,243	1.57%
21	Washington	12,733	1.51%
22	Colorado	12,559	1.49%
23	Alabama	12,517	1.49%
24	Minnesota	10,171	1.21%
25	South Carolina	10,099	1.20%
26	Oklahoma	9,554	1.14%
27	Connecticut	9,276	1.10%
28	Oregon	8,310	0.99%
29	Kentucky	7,949	0.95%
30	Kansas	7,832	0.93%
31	Arkansas	6,823	0.81%
32	Mississippi	6,689	0.80%
33	Iowa	6,257	0.74%
34	Nevada	4,993	0.59%
35	New Mexico	4,957	0.59%
36	Utah	4,833	0.57%
37	Nebraska	4,194	0.50%
38	West Virginia	3,912	0.47%
39	Hawaii	3,478	0.41%
40	Maine	3,313	0.39%
41	Idaho	2,922	0.35%
42	New Hampshire	2,894	0.34%
43	Rhode Island	2,891	0.34%
44	Montana	2,121	0.25%
45	Wyoming	2,016	0.24%
46	Delaware	2,006	0.24%
47	Alaska	1,645	0.20%
48	South Dakota	1,592	0.19%
49	North Dakota	1,449	0.17%
50	Vermont	1,329	0.16%
	District of Columbia	6,174	0.73%

Source: U.S. Department of Justice, Bureau of Justice Statistics
"Census of State and Local Law Enforcement Agencies, 1992" (Bulletin, July 1993, NCJ-142972)
*Includes state and local police, sheriffs' departments and special police agencies.

Full–Time Employees in Law Enforcement Agencies per 10,000 Population in 1992

National Rate = 32.97 Employees per 10,000 Population*

<u>ALPHA ORDER</u>

RANK	STATE	RATE
20	Alabama	30.26
30	Alaska	28.02
12	Arizona	34.56
27	Arkansas	28.44
15	California	32.59
10	Colorado	36.19
28	Connecticut	28.27
24	Delaware	29.11
5	Florida	40.04
9	Georgia	36.31
21	Hawaii	29.98
33	Idaho	27.39
6	Illinois	39.71
37	Indiana	26.38
48	Iowa	22.25
18	Kansas	31.04
50	Kentucky	21.17
4	Louisiana	40.52
35	Maine	26.83
13	Maryland	34.37
11	Massachusetts	35.31
31	Michigan	27.95
46	Minnesota	22.70
41	Mississippi	25.59
23	Missouri	29.60
40	Montana	25.74
38	Nebraska	26.11
7	Nevada	37.63
39	New Hampshire	26.05
3	New Jersey	42.09
17	New Mexico	31.35
1	New York	47.01
26	North Carolina	28.69
45	North Dakota	22.78
34	Ohio	26.98
22	Oklahoma	29.74
32	Oregon	27.91
43	Pennsylvania	23.59
25	Rhode Island	28.77
29	South Carolina	28.03
47	South Dakota	22.39
16	Tennessee	32.54
8	Texas	36.39
36	Utah	26.66
44	Vermont	23.32
14	Virginia	33.64
42	Washington	24.79
49	West Virginia	21.59
19	Wisconsin	30.52
2	Wyoming	43.26

<u>RANK ORDER</u>

RANK	STATE	RATE
1	New York	47.01
2	Wyoming	43.26
3	New Jersey	42.09
4	Louisiana	40.52
5	Florida	40.04
6	Illinois	39.71
7	Nevada	37.63
8	Texas	36.39
9	Georgia	36.31
10	Colorado	36.19
11	Massachusetts	35.31
12	Arizona	34.56
13	Maryland	34.37
14	Virginia	33.64
15	California	32.59
16	Tennessee	32.54
17	New Mexico	31.35
18	Kansas	31.04
19	Wisconsin	30.52
20	Alabama	30.26
21	Hawaii	29.98
22	Oklahoma	29.74
23	Missouri	29.60
24	Delaware	29.11
25	Rhode Island	28.77
26	North Carolina	28.69
27	Arkansas	28.44
28	Connecticut	28.27
29	South Carolina	28.03
30	Alaska	28.02
31	Michigan	27.95
32	Oregon	27.91
33	Idaho	27.39
34	Ohio	26.98
35	Maine	26.83
36	Utah	26.66
37	Indiana	26.38
38	Nebraska	26.11
39	New Hampshire	26.05
40	Montana	25.74
41	Mississippi	25.59
42	Washington	24.79
43	Pennsylvania	23.59
44	Vermont	23.32
45	North Dakota	22.78
46	Minnesota	22.70
47	South Dakota	22.39
48	Iowa	22.25
49	West Virginia	21.59
50	Kentucky	21.17

	District of Columbia	104.82

Source: Morgan Quitno Corporation using data from U.S. Department of Justice, Bureau of Justice Statistics
"Census of State and Local Law Enforcement Agencies, 1992" (Bulletin, July 1993, NCJ-142972)
*Includes state and local police, sheriffs' departments and special police agencies.

Full-Time Sworn Officers in State Police Departments in 1992

National Total = 52,980 Officers*

ALPHA ORDER					RANK ORDER			

RANK	STATE	OFFICERS	% of USA
26	Alabama	629	1.19%
42	Alaska	260	0.49%
15	Arizona	1,100	2.08%
34	Arkansas	484	0.91%
1	California	6,062	11.44%
33	Colorado	493	0.93%
19	Connecticut	905	1.71%
28	Delaware	505	0.95%
11	Florida	1,605	3.03%
24	Georgia	777	1.47%
50	Hawaii	0	0.00%
45	Idaho	192	0.36%
8	Illinois	1,977	3.73%
16	Indiana	1,097	2.07%
37	Iowa	410	0.77%
27	Kansas	604	1.14%
18	Kentucky	960	1.81%
25	Louisiana	714	1.35%
39	Maine	332	0.63%
9	Maryland	1,700	3.21%
6	Massachusetts	2,070	3.91%
7	Michigan	2,019	3.81%
30	Minnesota	501	0.95%
31	Mississippi	499	0.94%
21	Missouri	883	1.67%
44	Montana	200	0.38%
29	Nebraska	502	0.95%
40	Nevada	306	0.58%
43	New Hampshire	250	0.47%
5	New Jersey	2,572	4.85%
36	New Mexico	425	0.80%
3	New York	4,013	7.57%
13	North Carolina	1,260	2.38%
49	North Dakota	125	0.24%
12	Ohio	1,292	2.44%
22	Oklahoma	786	1.48%
19	Oregon	905	1.71%
2	Pennsylvania	4,075	7.69%
46	Rhode Island	165	0.31%
14	South Carolina	1,193	2.25%
48	South Dakota	151	0.29%
23	Tennessee	782	1.48%
4	Texas	2,789	5.26%
38	Utah	365	0.69%
41	Vermont	285	0.54%
10	Virginia	1,606	3.03%
17	Washington	1,032	1.95%
35	West Virginia	468	0.88%
32	Wisconsin	498	0.94%
47	Wyoming	157	0.30%

RANK	STATE	OFFICERS	% of USA
1	California	6,062	11.44%
2	Pennsylvania	4,075	7.69%
3	New York	4,013	7.57%
4	Texas	2,789	5.26%
5	New Jersey	2,572	4.85%
6	Massachusetts	2,070	3.91%
7	Michigan	2,019	3.81%
8	Illinois	1,977	3.73%
9	Maryland	1,700	3.21%
10	Virginia	1,606	3.03%
11	Florida	1,605	3.03%
12	Ohio	1,292	2.44%
13	North Carolina	1,260	2.38%
14	South Carolina	1,193	2.25%
15	Arizona	1,100	2.08%
16	Indiana	1,097	2.07%
17	Washington	1,032	1.95%
18	Kentucky	960	1.81%
19	Connecticut	905	1.71%
19	Oregon	905	1.71%
21	Missouri	883	1.67%
22	Oklahoma	786	1.48%
23	Tennessee	782	1.48%
24	Georgia	777	1.47%
25	Louisiana	714	1.35%
26	Alabama	629	1.19%
27	Kansas	604	1.14%
28	Delaware	505	0.95%
29	Nebraska	502	0.95%
30	Minnesota	501	0.95%
31	Mississippi	499	0.94%
32	Wisconsin	498	0.94%
33	Colorado	493	0.93%
34	Arkansas	484	0.91%
35	West Virginia	468	0.88%
36	New Mexico	425	0.80%
37	Iowa	410	0.77%
38	Utah	365	0.69%
39	Maine	332	0.63%
40	Nevada	306	0.58%
41	Vermont	285	0.54%
42	Alaska	260	0.49%
43	New Hampshire	250	0.47%
44	Montana	200	0.38%
45	Idaho	192	0.36%
46	Rhode Island	165	0.31%
47	Wyoming	157	0.30%
48	South Dakota	151	0.29%
49	North Dakota	125	0.24%
50	Hawaii	0	0.00%
	District of Columbia	0	0.00%

Source: U.S. Department of Justice, Bureau of Justice Statistics
"Census of State and Local Law Enforcement Agencies, 1992" (Bulletin, July 1993, NCJ-142972)
All states except Hawaii and the District of Columbia have a state police department.

Percent of Full–Time State Police Department Employees Who are Sworn Officers: 1992

National Rate = 67.43% of Employees*

RANK	STATE	PERCENT		RANK	STATE	PERCENT
47	Alabama	49.10		1	South Carolina	100.00
39	Alaska	59.23		2	Utah	92.41
30	Arizona	68.28		3	South Dakota	89.35
24	Arkansas	71.28		4	Iowa	89.32
31	California	68.16		5	New York	85.67
23	Colorado	71.66		6	Rhode Island	81.28
29	Connecticut	68.51		7	Massachusetts	80.26
19	Delaware	73.51		8	Oregon	79.04
14	Florida	76.21		9	North Carolina	78.65
49	Georgia	40.89		10	Nebraska	78.07
NA	Hawaii**	NA		11	Pennsylvania	77.89
15	Idaho	75.59		12	New Mexico	76.99
37	Illinois	59.91		13	Montana	76.34
35	Indiana	62.87		14	Florida	76.21
4	Iowa	89.32		15	Idaho	75.59
17	Kansas	73.57		16	Wisconsin	74.89
40	Kentucky	58.04		17	Kansas	73.57
28	Louisiana	68.52		18	New Hampshire	73.53
22	Maine	72.17		19	Delaware	73.51
25	Maryland	70.83		20	Virginia	72.80
7	Massachusetts	80.26		21	New Jersey	72.45
26	Michigan	69.31		22	Maine	72.17
27	Minnesota	69.29		23	Colorado	71.66
38	Mississippi	59.55		24	Arkansas	71.28
48	Missouri	48.17		25	Maryland	70.83
13	Montana	76.34		26	Michigan	69.31
10	Nebraska	78.07		27	Minnesota	69.29
33	Nevada	66.67		28	Louisiana	68.52
18	New Hampshire	73.53		29	Connecticut	68.51
21	New Jersey	72.45		30	Arizona	68.28
12	New Mexico	76.99		31	California	68.16
5	New York	85.67		32	Vermont	66.90
9	North Carolina	78.65		33	Nevada	66.67
36	North Dakota	62.81		34	West Virginia	63.76
42	Ohio	55.03		35	Indiana	62.87
41	Oklahoma	55.90		36	North Dakota	62.81
8	Oregon	79.04		37	Illinois	59.91
11	Pennsylvania	77.89		38	Mississippi	59.55
6	Rhode Island	81.28		39	Alaska	59.23
1	South Carolina	100.00		40	Kentucky	58.04
3	South Dakota	89.35		41	Oklahoma	55.90
44	Tennessee	50.68		42	Ohio	55.03
45	Texas	49.76		43	Wyoming	50.97
2	Utah	92.41		44	Tennessee	50.68
32	Vermont	66.90		45	Texas	49.76
20	Virginia	72.80		45	Washington	49.76
45	Washington	49.76		47	Alabama	49.10
34	West Virginia	63.76		48	Missouri	48.17
16	Wisconsin	74.89		49	Georgia	40.89
43	Wyoming	50.97		NA	Hawaii**	NA
					District of Columbia**	NA

ALPHA ORDER

RANK ORDER

Source: Morgan Quitno Corporation using data from U.S. Department of Justice, Bureau of Justice Statistics
"Census of State and Local Law Enforcement Agencies, 1992" (Bulletin, July 1993, NCJ-142972)
*All states except Hawaii and the District of Columbia have a state police department.
**Not available.

242

Rate of Full-Time Sworn Officers in State Police Departments in 1992

National Rate = 2.08 Officers per 10,000 Population*

ALPHA ORDER				RANK ORDER		
RANK	STATE	RATE		RANK	STATE	RATE
42	Alabama	1.52		1	Delaware	7.33
3	Alaska	4.43		2	Vermont	5.00
12	Arizona	2.87		3	Alaska	4.43
27	Arkansas	2.02		4	Maryland	3.46
31	California	1.96		5	Massachusetts	3.45
44	Colorado	1.42		6	Pennsylvania	3.39
13	Connecticut	2.76		7	Wyoming	3.37
1	Delaware	7.33		8	South Carolina	3.31
45	Florida	1.19		9	New Jersey	3.30
47	Georgia	1.15		10	Nebraska	3.13
50	Hawaii	0.00		11	Oregon	3.04
35	Idaho	1.80		12	Arizona	2.87
36	Illinois	1.70		13	Connecticut	2.76
32	Indiana	1.94		14	Maine	2.69
43	Iowa	1.46		14	New Mexico	2.69
21	Kansas	2.39		16	West Virginia	2.58
17	Kentucky	2.56		17	Kentucky	2.56
38	Louisiana	1.67		18	Virginia	2.52
14	Maine	2.69		19	Oklahoma	2.45
4	Maryland	3.46		20	Montana	2.43
5	Massachusetts	3.45		21	Kansas	2.39
25	Michigan	2.14		22	Nevada	2.31
48	Minnesota	1.12		23	New Hampshire	2.25
33	Mississippi	1.91		24	New York	2.21
36	Missouri	1.70		25	Michigan	2.14
20	Montana	2.43		26	South Dakota	2.12
10	Nebraska	3.13		27	Arkansas	2.02
22	Nevada	2.31		28	Utah	2.01
23	New Hampshire	2.25		28	Washington	2.01
9	New Jersey	3.30		30	North Dakota	1.97
14	New Mexico	2.69		31	California	1.96
24	New York	2.21		32	Indiana	1.94
34	North Carolina	1.84		33	Mississippi	1.91
30	North Dakota	1.97		34	North Carolina	1.84
46	Ohio	1.17		35	Idaho	1.80
19	Oklahoma	2.45		36	Illinois	1.70
11	Oregon	3.04		36	Missouri	1.70
6	Pennsylvania	3.39		38	Louisiana	1.67
39	Rhode Island	1.64		39	Rhode Island	1.64
8	South Carolina	3.31		40	Texas	1.58
26	South Dakota	2.12		41	Tennessee	1.56
41	Tennessee	1.56		42	Alabama	1.52
40	Texas	1.58		43	Iowa	1.46
28	Utah	2.01		44	Colorado	1.42
2	Vermont	5.00		45	Florida	1.19
18	Virginia	2.52		46	Ohio	1.17
28	Washington	2.01		47	Georgia	1.15
16	West Virginia	2.58		48	Minnesota	1.12
49	Wisconsin	0.99		49	Wisconsin	0.99
7	Wyoming	3.37		50	Hawaii	0.00
					District of Columbia	0.00

Source: Morgan Quitno Corporation using data from U.S. Department of Justice, Bureau of Justice Statistics
"Census of State and Local Law Enforcement Agencies, 1992" (Bulletin, July 1993, NCJ-142972)
*All states except Hawaii and the District of Columbia have a state police department.

State Government Law Enforcement Officers in 1993

National Total = 60,711 Officers*

ALPHA ORDER

RANK	STATE	OFFICERS	% of USA
22	Alabama	804	1.32%
41	Alaska	356	0.59%
20	Arizona	916	1.51%
34	Arkansas	480	0.79%
1	California	6,397	10.54%
27	Colorado	676	1.11%
19	Connecticut	964	1.59%
28	Delaware	637	1.05%
4	Florida	2,832	4.66%
13	Georgia	1,800	2.96%
50	Hawaii	0	0.00%
45	Idaho	222	0.37%
10	Illinois	2,097	3.45%
17	Indiana	1,040	1.71%
30	Iowa	584	0.96%
31	Kansas	577	0.95%
15	Kentucky	1,599	2.63%
25	Louisiana	719	1.18%
39	Maine	389	0.64%
8	Maryland	2,473	4.07%
9	Massachusetts	2,285	3.76%
12	Michigan	1,938	3.19%
35	Minnesota	479	0.79%
36	Mississippi	469	0.77%
21	Missouri	866	1.43%
37	Montana	455	0.75%
33	Nebraska	482	0.79%
42	Nevada	321	0.53%
44	New Hampshire	252	0.42%
6	New Jersey	2,607	4.29%
38	New Mexico	425	0.70%
3	New York	4,263	7.02%
5	North Carolina	2,625	4.32%
49	North Dakota	121	0.20%
16	Ohio	1,426	2.35%
26	Oklahoma	717	1.18%
23	Oregon	791	1.30%
2	Pennsylvania	4,359	7.18%
46	Rhode Island	180	0.30%
14	South Carolina	1,772	2.92%
47	South Dakota	157	0.26%
24	Tennessee	742	1.22%
7	Texas	2,491	4.10%
40	Utah	369	0.61%
43	Vermont	269	0.44%
11	Virginia	2,039	3.36%
18	Washington	983	1.62%
29	West Virginia	602	0.99%
32	Wisconsin	543	0.89%
48	Wyoming	143	0.24%

RANK ORDER

RANK	STATE	OFFICERS	% of USA
1	California	6,397	10.54%
2	Pennsylvania	4,359	7.18%
3	New York	4,263	7.02%
4	Florida	2,832	4.66%
5	North Carolina	2,625	4.32%
6	New Jersey	2,607	4.29%
7	Texas	2,491	4.10%
8	Maryland	2,473	4.07%
9	Massachusetts	2,285	3.76%
10	Illinois	2,097	3.45%
11	Virginia	2,039	3.36%
12	Michigan	1,938	3.19%
13	Georgia	1,800	2.96%
14	South Carolina	1,772	2.92%
15	Kentucky	1,599	2.63%
16	Ohio	1,426	2.35%
17	Indiana	1,040	1.71%
18	Washington	983	1.62%
19	Connecticut	964	1.59%
20	Arizona	916	1.51%
21	Missouri	866	1.43%
22	Alabama	804	1.32%
23	Oregon	791	1.30%
24	Tennessee	742	1.22%
25	Louisiana	719	1.18%
26	Oklahoma	717	1.18%
27	Colorado	676	1.11%
28	Delaware	637	1.05%
29	West Virginia	602	0.99%
30	Iowa	584	0.96%
31	Kansas	577	0.95%
32	Wisconsin	543	0.89%
33	Nebraska	482	0.79%
34	Arkansas	480	0.79%
35	Minnesota	479	0.79%
36	Mississippi	469	0.77%
37	Montana	455	0.75%
38	New Mexico	425	0.70%
39	Maine	389	0.64%
40	Utah	369	0.61%
41	Alaska	356	0.59%
42	Nevada	321	0.53%
43	Vermont	269	0.44%
44	New Hampshire	252	0.42%
45	Idaho	222	0.37%
46	Rhode Island	180	0.30%
47	South Dakota	157	0.26%
48	Wyoming	143	0.24%
49	North Dakota	121	0.20%
50	Hawaii	0	0.00%
	District of Columbia	0	0.00%

Source: U.S. Department of Justice, Federal Bureau of Investigation
"Crime in the United States 1993" (Uniform Crime Reports, December 4, 1994)
*Full-time employees. Includes state police agencies and other agencies with law enforcement powers. Hawaii and the District of Columbia do not have a state police agency.

Male State Government Law Enforcement Officers in 1993

National Total = 57,132 Male Officers*

ALPHA ORDER					RANK ORDER			
RANK	STATE	OFFICERS	% of USA		RANK	STATE	OFFICERS	% of USA
22	Alabama	787	1.38%		1	California	5,831	10.21%
41	Alaska	337	0.59%		2	Pennsylvania	4,190	7.33%
20	Arizona	864	1.51%		3	New York	3,961	6.93%
34	Arkansas	461	0.81%		4	Florida	2,573	4.50%
1	California	5,831	10.21%		5	New Jersey	2,545	4.45%
27	Colorado	636	1.11%		6	North Carolina	2,502	4.38%
19	Connecticut	908	1.59%		7	Texas	2,426	4.25%
28	Delaware	595	1.04%		8	Maryland	2,233	3.91%
4	Florida	2,573	4.50%		9	Massachusetts	2,084	3.65%
13	Georgia	1,668	2.92%		10	Virginia	1,960	3.43%
50	Hawaii	0	0.00%		11	Illinois	1,921	3.36%
45	Idaho	212	0.37%		12	Michigan	1,749	3.06%
11	Illinois	1,921	3.36%		13	Georgia	1,668	2.92%
17	Indiana	995	1.74%		14	South Carolina	1,664	2.91%
30	Iowa	557	0.97%		15	Kentucky	1,558	2.73%
31	Kansas	538	0.94%		16	Ohio	1,342	2.35%
15	Kentucky	1,558	2.73%		17	Indiana	995	1.74%
25	Louisiana	711	1.24%		18	Washington	943	1.65%
39	Maine	374	0.65%		19	Connecticut	908	1.59%
8	Maryland	2,233	3.91%		20	Arizona	864	1.51%
9	Massachusetts	2,084	3.65%		21	Missouri	851	1.49%
12	Michigan	1,749	3.06%		22	Alabama	787	1.38%
36	Minnesota	460	0.81%		23	Oregon	752	1.32%
34	Mississippi	461	0.81%		24	Tennessee	720	1.26%
21	Missouri	851	1.49%		25	Louisiana	711	1.24%
37	Montana	418	0.73%		25	Oklahoma	711	1.24%
33	Nebraska	462	0.81%		27	Colorado	636	1.11%
42	Nevada	299	0.52%		28	Delaware	595	1.04%
44	New Hampshire	231	0.40%		29	West Virginia	588	1.03%
5	New Jersey	2,545	4.45%		30	Iowa	557	0.97%
38	New Mexico	415	0.73%		31	Kansas	538	0.94%
3	New York	3,961	6.93%		32	Wisconsin	470	0.82%
6	North Carolina	2,502	4.38%		33	Nebraska	462	0.81%
49	North Dakota	119	0.21%		34	Arkansas	461	0.81%
16	Ohio	1,342	2.35%		34	Mississippi	461	0.81%
25	Oklahoma	711	1.24%		36	Minnesota	460	0.81%
23	Oregon	752	1.32%		37	Montana	418	0.73%
2	Pennsylvania	4,190	7.33%		38	New Mexico	415	0.73%
46	Rhode Island	167	0.29%		39	Maine	374	0.65%
14	South Carolina	1,664	2.91%		40	Utah	350	0.61%
47	South Dakota	155	0.27%		41	Alaska	337	0.59%
24	Tennessee	720	1.26%		42	Nevada	299	0.52%
7	Texas	2,426	4.25%		43	Vermont	259	0.45%
40	Utah	350	0.61%		44	New Hampshire	231	0.40%
43	Vermont	259	0.45%		45	Idaho	212	0.37%
10	Virginia	1,960	3.43%		46	Rhode Island	167	0.29%
18	Washington	943	1.65%		47	South Dakota	155	0.27%
29	West Virginia	588	1.03%		48	Wyoming	141	0.25%
32	Wisconsin	470	0.82%		49	North Dakota	119	0.21%
48	Wyoming	141	0.25%		50	Hawaii	0	0.00%
						District of Columbia	0	0.00%

Source: U.S. Department of Justice, Federal Bureau of Investigation
"Crime in the United States 1993" (Uniform Crime Reports, December 4, 1994)
*Full-time employees. Includes state police agencies and other agencies with law enforcement powers. Hawaii and the District of Columbia do not have a state police agency.

Female State Government Law Enforcement Officers in 1993

National Total = 3,579 Female Officers*

ALPHA ORDER					RANK ORDER			
RANK	STATE	OFFICERS	% of USA		RANK	STATE	OFFICERS	% of USA
36	Alabama	17	0.47%		1	California	566	15.81%
32	Alaska	19	0.53%		2	New York	302	8.44%
18	Arizona	52	1.45%		3	Florida	259	7.24%
32	Arkansas	19	0.53%		4	Maryland	240	6.71%
1	California	566	15.81%		5	Massachusetts	201	5.62%
22	Colorado	40	1.12%		6	Michigan	189	5.28%
17	Connecticut	56	1.56%		7	Illinois	176	4.92%
20	Delaware	42	1.17%		8	Pennsylvania	169	4.72%
3	Florida	259	7.24%		9	Georgia	132	3.69%
9	Georgia	132	3.69%		10	North Carolina	123	3.44%
50	Hawaii	0	0.00%		11	South Carolina	108	3.02%
41	Idaho	10	0.28%		12	Ohio	84	2.35%
7	Illinois	176	4.92%		13	Virginia	79	2.21%
19	Indiana	45	1.26%		14	Wisconsin	73	2.04%
27	Iowa	27	0.75%		15	Texas	65	1.82%
24	Kansas	39	1.09%		16	New Jersey	62	1.73%
21	Kentucky	41	1.15%		17	Connecticut	56	1.56%
44	Louisiana	8	0.22%		18	Arizona	52	1.45%
37	Maine	15	0.42%		19	Indiana	45	1.26%
4	Maryland	240	6.71%		20	Delaware	42	1.17%
5	Massachusetts	201	5.62%		21	Kentucky	41	1.15%
6	Michigan	189	5.28%		22	Colorado	40	1.12%
32	Minnesota	19	0.53%		22	Washington	40	1.12%
44	Mississippi	8	0.22%		24	Kansas	39	1.09%
37	Missouri	15	0.42%		24	Oregon	39	1.09%
26	Montana	37	1.03%		26	Montana	37	1.03%
31	Nebraska	20	0.56%		27	Iowa	27	0.75%
28	Nevada	22	0.61%		28	Nevada	22	0.61%
30	New Hampshire	21	0.59%		28	Tennessee	22	0.61%
16	New Jersey	62	1.73%		30	New Hampshire	21	0.59%
41	New Mexico	10	0.28%		31	Nebraska	20	0.56%
2	New York	302	8.44%		32	Alaska	19	0.53%
10	North Carolina	123	3.44%		32	Arkansas	19	0.53%
47	North Dakota	2	0.06%		32	Minnesota	19	0.53%
12	Ohio	84	2.35%		32	Utah	19	0.53%
46	Oklahoma	6	0.17%		36	Alabama	17	0.47%
24	Oregon	39	1.09%		37	Maine	15	0.42%
8	Pennsylvania	169	4.72%		37	Missouri	15	0.42%
40	Rhode Island	13	0.36%		39	West Virginia	14	0.39%
11	South Carolina	108	3.02%		40	Rhode Island	13	0.36%
47	South Dakota	2	0.06%		41	Idaho	10	0.28%
28	Tennessee	22	0.61%		41	New Mexico	10	0.28%
15	Texas	65	1.82%		41	Vermont	10	0.28%
32	Utah	19	0.53%		44	Louisiana	8	0.22%
41	Vermont	10	0.28%		44	Mississippi	8	0.22%
13	Virginia	79	2.21%		46	Oklahoma	6	0.17%
22	Washington	40	1.12%		47	North Dakota	2	0.06%
39	West Virginia	14	0.39%		47	South Dakota	2	0.06%
14	Wisconsin	73	2.04%		47	Wyoming	2	0.06%
47	Wyoming	2	0.06%		50	Hawaii	0	0.00%
						District of Columbia	0	0.00%

Source: U.S. Department of Justice, Federal Bureau of Investigation
   "Crime in the United States 1993" (Uniform Crime Reports, December 4, 1994)
*Full-time employees. Includes state police agencies and other agencies with law enforcement powers. Hawaii and the District of Columbia do not have a state police agency.

Female State Government Law Enforcement Officers as a Percent of All Officers: 1993

National Percent = 5.90% of Officers*

ALPHA ORDER				RANK ORDER		
RANK	STATE	PERCENT		RANK	STATE	PERCENT
42	Alabama	2.11		1	Wisconsin	13.44
21	Alaska	5.34		2	Michigan	9.75
20	Arizona	5.68		3	Maryland	9.70
31	Arkansas	3.96		4	Florida	9.15
5	California	8.85		5	California	8.85
17	Colorado	5.92		6	Massachusetts	8.80
19	Connecticut	5.81		7	Illinois	8.39
15	Delaware	6.59		8	New Hampshire	8.33
4	Florida	9.15		9	Montana	8.13
10	Georgia	7.33		10	Georgia	7.33
NA	Hawaii**	NA		11	Rhode Island	7.22
26	Idaho	4.50		12	New York	7.08
7	Illinois	8.39		13	Nevada	6.85
27	Indiana	4.33		14	Kansas	6.76
25	Iowa	4.62		15	Delaware	6.59
14	Kansas	6.76		16	South Carolina	6.09
38	Kentucky	2.56		17	Colorado	5.92
48	Louisiana	1.11		18	Ohio	5.89
34	Maine	3.86		19	Connecticut	5.81
3	Maryland	9.70		20	Arizona	5.68
6	Massachusetts	8.80		21	Alaska	5.34
2	Michigan	9.75		22	Utah	5.15
30	Minnesota	3.97		23	Oregon	4.93
44	Mississippi	1.71		24	North Carolina	4.69
43	Missouri	1.73		25	Iowa	4.62
9	Montana	8.13		26	Idaho	4.50
28	Nebraska	4.15		27	Indiana	4.33
13	Nevada	6.85		28	Nebraska	4.15
8	New Hampshire	8.33		29	Washington	4.07
39	New Jersey	2.38		30	Minnesota	3.97
40	New Mexico	2.35		31	Arkansas	3.96
12	New York	7.08		32	Pennsylvania	3.88
24	North Carolina	4.69		33	Virginia	3.87
45	North Dakota	1.65		34	Maine	3.86
18	Ohio	5.89		35	Vermont	3.72
49	Oklahoma	0.84		36	Tennessee	2.96
23	Oregon	4.93		37	Texas	2.61
32	Pennsylvania	3.88		38	Kentucky	2.56
11	Rhode Island	7.22		39	New Jersey	2.38
16	South Carolina	6.09		40	New Mexico	2.35
47	South Dakota	1.27		41	West Virginia	2.33
36	Tennessee	2.96		42	Alabama	2.11
37	Texas	2.61		43	Missouri	1.73
22	Utah	5.15		44	Mississippi	1.71
35	Vermont	3.72		45	North Dakota	1.65
33	Virginia	3.87		46	Wyoming	1.40
29	Washington	4.07		47	South Dakota	1.27
41	West Virginia	2.33		48	Louisiana	1.11
1	Wisconsin	13.44		49	Oklahoma	0.84
46	Wyoming	1.40		NA	Hawaii**	NA
					District of Columbia**	NA

Source: Morgan Quitno Corporation using data from U.S. Department of Justice, Federal Bureau of Investigation
"Crime in the United States 1993" (Uniform Crime Reports, December 4, 1994)
*Full-time employees. Includes state police agencies and other agencies with law enforcement powers.
**Not applicable. Hawaii and the District of Columbia do not have a state police agency.

Local Police Departments in 1992

National Total = 12,502 Departments*

ALPHA ORDER

RANK	STATE	DEPARTMENTS	% of USA
18	Alabama	285	2.28%
46	Alaska	43	0.34%
40	Arizona	75	0.60%
28	Arkansas	185	1.48%
12	California	341	2.73%
32	Colorado	140	1.12%
35	Connecticut	108	0.86%
48	Delaware	33	0.26%
18	Florida	285	2.28%
11	Georgia	343	2.74%
50	Hawaii	4	0.03%
42	Idaho	66	0.53%
3	Illinois	748	5.98%
14	Indiana	336	2.69%
16	Iowa	321	2.57%
22	Kansas	221	1.77%
21	Kentucky	240	1.92%
20	Louisiana	256	2.05%
34	Maine	119	0.95%
38	Maryland	78	0.62%
12	Massachusetts	341	2.73%
6	Michigan	474	3.79%
10	Minnesota	359	2.87%
26	Mississippi	189	1.51%
7	Missouri	463	3.70%
43	Montana	59	0.47%
31	Nebraska	149	1.19%
49	Nevada	14	0.11%
23	New Hampshire	214	1.71%
5	New Jersey	488	3.90%
41	New Mexico	72	0.58%
7	New York	463	3.70%
15	North Carolina	332	2.66%
39	North Dakota	76	0.61%
2	Ohio	776	6.21%
17	Oklahoma	312	2.50%
33	Oregon	137	1.10%
1	Pennsylvania	1,049	8.39%
47	Rhode Island	39	0.31%
27	South Carolina	188	1.50%
36	South Dakota	102	0.82%
24	Tennessee	211	1.69%
4	Texas	632	5.06%
37	Utah	84	0.67%
44	Vermont	57	0.46%
29	Virginia	167	1.34%
25	Washington	202	1.62%
30	West Virginia	158	1.26%
9	Wisconsin	417	3.34%
45	Wyoming	50	0.40%

RANK ORDER

RANK	STATE	DEPARTMENTS	% of USA
1	Pennsylvania	1,049	8.39%
2	Ohio	776	6.21%
3	Illinois	748	5.98%
4	Texas	632	5.06%
5	New Jersey	488	3.90%
6	Michigan	474	3.79%
7	Missouri	463	3.70%
7	New York	463	3.70%
9	Wisconsin	417	3.34%
10	Minnesota	359	2.87%
11	Georgia	343	2.74%
12	California	341	2.73%
12	Massachusetts	341	2.73%
14	Indiana	336	2.69%
15	North Carolina	332	2.66%
16	Iowa	321	2.57%
17	Oklahoma	312	2.50%
18	Alabama	285	2.28%
18	Florida	285	2.28%
20	Louisiana	256	2.05%
21	Kentucky	240	1.92%
22	Kansas	221	1.77%
23	New Hampshire	214	1.71%
24	Tennessee	211	1.69%
25	Washington	202	1.62%
26	Mississippi	189	1.51%
27	South Carolina	188	1.50%
28	Arkansas	185	1.48%
29	Virginia	167	1.34%
30	West Virginia	158	1.26%
31	Nebraska	149	1.19%
32	Colorado	140	1.12%
33	Oregon	137	1.10%
34	Maine	119	0.95%
35	Connecticut	108	0.86%
36	South Dakota	102	0.82%
37	Utah	84	0.67%
38	Maryland	78	0.62%
39	North Dakota	76	0.61%
40	Arizona	75	0.60%
41	New Mexico	72	0.58%
42	Idaho	66	0.53%
43	Montana	59	0.47%
44	Vermont	57	0.46%
45	Wyoming	50	0.40%
46	Alaska	43	0.34%
47	Rhode Island	39	0.31%
48	Delaware	33	0.26%
49	Nevada	14	0.11%
50	Hawaii	4	0.03%
	District of Columbia	1	0.01%

Source: U.S. Department of Justice, Bureau of Justice Statistics
"Census of State and Local Law Enforcement Agencies, 1992" (Bulletin, July 1993, NCJ-142972)
*Includes consolidated police-sheriffs' departments.

Full-Time Officers in Local Police Departments in 1992

National Total = 373,061 Officers*

<table>
<tr><th colspan="4">ALPHA ORDER</th><th colspan="4">RANK ORDER</th></tr>
<tr><th>RANK</th><th>STATE</th><th>OFFICERS</th><th>% of USA</th><th>RANK</th><th>STATE</th><th>OFFICERS</th><th>% of USA</th></tr>
<tr><td>20</td><td>Alabama</td><td>5,640</td><td>1.51%</td><td>1</td><td>New York</td><td>45,822</td><td>12.28%</td></tr>
<tr><td>45</td><td>Alaska</td><td>677</td><td>0.18%</td><td>2</td><td>California</td><td>33,191</td><td>8.90%</td></tr>
<tr><td>22</td><td>Arizona</td><td>5,209</td><td>1.40%</td><td>3</td><td>Illinois</td><td>24,988</td><td>6.70%</td></tr>
<tr><td>34</td><td>Arkansas</td><td>2,494</td><td>0.67%</td><td>4</td><td>Texas</td><td>24,576</td><td>6.59%</td></tr>
<tr><td>2</td><td>California</td><td>33,191</td><td>8.90%</td><td>5</td><td>New Jersey</td><td>19,221</td><td>5.15%</td></tr>
<tr><td>23</td><td>Colorado</td><td>4,787</td><td>1.28%</td><td>6</td><td>Florida</td><td>18,037</td><td>4.83%</td></tr>
<tr><td>18</td><td>Connecticut</td><td>6,068</td><td>1.63%</td><td>7</td><td>Pennsylvania</td><td>17,256</td><td>4.63%</td></tr>
<tr><td>44</td><td>Delaware</td><td>887</td><td>0.24%</td><td>8</td><td>Ohio</td><td>14,668</td><td>3.93%</td></tr>
<tr><td>6</td><td>Florida</td><td>18,037</td><td>4.83%</td><td>9</td><td>Michigan</td><td>13,027</td><td>3.49%</td></tr>
<tr><td>11</td><td>Georgia</td><td>9,404</td><td>2.52%</td><td>10</td><td>Massachusetts</td><td>12,087</td><td>3.24%</td></tr>
<tr><td>33</td><td>Hawaii</td><td>2,690</td><td>0.72%</td><td>11</td><td>Georgia</td><td>9,404</td><td>2.52%</td></tr>
<tr><td>43</td><td>Idaho</td><td>921</td><td>0.25%</td><td>12</td><td>Maryland</td><td>8,273</td><td>2.22%</td></tr>
<tr><td>3</td><td>Illinois</td><td>24,988</td><td>6.70%</td><td>13</td><td>Virginia</td><td>8,205</td><td>2.20%</td></tr>
<tr><td>19</td><td>Indiana</td><td>5,992</td><td>1.61%</td><td>14</td><td>North Carolina</td><td>8,023</td><td>2.15%</td></tr>
<tr><td>30</td><td>Iowa</td><td>2,863</td><td>0.77%</td><td>15</td><td>Missouri</td><td>7,921</td><td>2.12%</td></tr>
<tr><td>29</td><td>Kansas</td><td>3,189</td><td>0.85%</td><td>16</td><td>Wisconsin</td><td>7,184</td><td>1.93%</td></tr>
<tr><td>27</td><td>Kentucky</td><td>3,804</td><td>1.02%</td><td>17</td><td>Tennessee</td><td>6,214</td><td>1.67%</td></tr>
<tr><td>21</td><td>Louisiana</td><td>5,548</td><td>1.49%</td><td>18</td><td>Connecticut</td><td>6,068</td><td>1.63%</td></tr>
<tr><td>41</td><td>Maine</td><td>1,399</td><td>0.38%</td><td>19</td><td>Indiana</td><td>5,992</td><td>1.61%</td></tr>
<tr><td>12</td><td>Maryland</td><td>8,273</td><td>2.22%</td><td>20</td><td>Alabama</td><td>5,640</td><td>1.51%</td></tr>
<tr><td>10</td><td>Massachusetts</td><td>12,087</td><td>3.24%</td><td>21</td><td>Louisiana</td><td>5,548</td><td>1.49%</td></tr>
<tr><td>9</td><td>Michigan</td><td>13,027</td><td>3.49%</td><td>22</td><td>Arizona</td><td>5,209</td><td>1.40%</td></tr>
<tr><td>25</td><td>Minnesota</td><td>4,580</td><td>1.23%</td><td>23</td><td>Colorado</td><td>4,787</td><td>1.28%</td></tr>
<tr><td>32</td><td>Mississippi</td><td>2,745</td><td>0.74%</td><td>24</td><td>Washington</td><td>4,704</td><td>1.26%</td></tr>
<tr><td>15</td><td>Missouri</td><td>7,921</td><td>2.12%</td><td>25</td><td>Minnesota</td><td>4,580</td><td>1.23%</td></tr>
<tr><td>49</td><td>Montana</td><td>568</td><td>0.15%</td><td>26</td><td>Oklahoma</td><td>4,529</td><td>1.21%</td></tr>
<tr><td>38</td><td>Nebraska</td><td>1,720</td><td>0.46%</td><td>27</td><td>Kentucky</td><td>3,804</td><td>1.02%</td></tr>
<tr><td>37</td><td>Nevada</td><td>1,795</td><td>0.48%</td><td>28</td><td>South Carolina</td><td>3,481</td><td>0.93%</td></tr>
<tr><td>39</td><td>New Hampshire</td><td>1,717</td><td>0.46%</td><td>29</td><td>Kansas</td><td>3,189</td><td>0.85%</td></tr>
<tr><td>5</td><td>New Jersey</td><td>19,221</td><td>5.15%</td><td>30</td><td>Iowa</td><td>2,863</td><td>0.77%</td></tr>
<tr><td>35</td><td>New Mexico</td><td>2,092</td><td>0.56%</td><td>31</td><td>Oregon</td><td>2,782</td><td>0.75%</td></tr>
<tr><td>1</td><td>New York</td><td>45,822</td><td>12.28%</td><td>32</td><td>Mississippi</td><td>2,745</td><td>0.74%</td></tr>
<tr><td>14</td><td>North Carolina</td><td>8,023</td><td>2.15%</td><td>33</td><td>Hawaii</td><td>2,690</td><td>0.72%</td></tr>
<tr><td>50</td><td>North Dakota</td><td>538</td><td>0.14%</td><td>34</td><td>Arkansas</td><td>2,494</td><td>0.67%</td></tr>
<tr><td>8</td><td>Ohio</td><td>14,668</td><td>3.93%</td><td>35</td><td>New Mexico</td><td>2,092</td><td>0.56%</td></tr>
<tr><td>26</td><td>Oklahoma</td><td>4,529</td><td>1.21%</td><td>36</td><td>Rhode Island</td><td>2,024</td><td>0.54%</td></tr>
<tr><td>31</td><td>Oregon</td><td>2,782</td><td>0.75%</td><td>37</td><td>Nevada</td><td>1,795</td><td>0.48%</td></tr>
<tr><td>7</td><td>Pennsylvania</td><td>17,256</td><td>4.63%</td><td>38</td><td>Nebraska</td><td>1,720</td><td>0.46%</td></tr>
<tr><td>36</td><td>Rhode Island</td><td>2,024</td><td>0.54%</td><td>39</td><td>New Hampshire</td><td>1,717</td><td>0.46%</td></tr>
<tr><td>28</td><td>South Carolina</td><td>3,481</td><td>0.93%</td><td>40</td><td>Utah</td><td>1,546</td><td>0.41%</td></tr>
<tr><td>46</td><td>South Dakota</td><td>648</td><td>0.17%</td><td>41</td><td>Maine</td><td>1,399</td><td>0.38%</td></tr>
<tr><td>17</td><td>Tennessee</td><td>6,214</td><td>1.67%</td><td>42</td><td>West Virginia</td><td>1,260</td><td>0.34%</td></tr>
<tr><td>4</td><td>Texas</td><td>24,576</td><td>6.59%</td><td>43</td><td>Idaho</td><td>921</td><td>0.25%</td></tr>
<tr><td>40</td><td>Utah</td><td>1,546</td><td>0.41%</td><td>44</td><td>Delaware</td><td>887</td><td>0.24%</td></tr>
<tr><td>47</td><td>Vermont</td><td>594</td><td>0.16%</td><td>45</td><td>Alaska</td><td>677</td><td>0.18%</td></tr>
<tr><td>13</td><td>Virginia</td><td>8,205</td><td>2.20%</td><td>46</td><td>South Dakota</td><td>648</td><td>0.17%</td></tr>
<tr><td>24</td><td>Washington</td><td>4,704</td><td>1.26%</td><td>47</td><td>Vermont</td><td>594</td><td>0.16%</td></tr>
<tr><td>42</td><td>West Virginia</td><td>1,260</td><td>0.34%</td><td>48</td><td>Wyoming</td><td>584</td><td>0.16%</td></tr>
<tr><td>16</td><td>Wisconsin</td><td>7,184</td><td>1.93%</td><td>49</td><td>Montana</td><td>568</td><td>0.15%</td></tr>
<tr><td>48</td><td>Wyoming</td><td>584</td><td>0.16%</td><td>50</td><td>North Dakota</td><td>538</td><td>0.14%</td></tr>
<tr><td></td><td></td><td></td><td></td><td></td><td>District of Columbia</td><td>4,889</td><td>1.31%</td></tr>
</table>

Source: U.S. Department of Justice, Bureau of Justice Statistics
  "Census of State and Local Law Enforcement Agencies, 1992" (Bulletin, July 1993, NCJ-142972)
*Includes consolidated police-sheriffs' departments.

Percent of Full–Time Local Police Department Employees Who Are Sworn Officers: 1992

National Percent = 78.33% of Employees*

<table>
<tr><td colspan="3">ALPHA ORDER</td><td colspan="3">RANK ORDER</td></tr>
<tr><td>RANK</td><td>STATE</td><td>PERCENT</td><td>RANK</td><td>STATE</td><td>PERCENT</td></tr>
<tr><td>31</td><td>Alabama</td><td>77.31</td><td>1</td><td>Pennsylvania</td><td>86.68</td></tr>
<tr><td>49</td><td>Alaska</td><td>63.21</td><td>2</td><td>Massachusetts</td><td>85.02</td></tr>
<tr><td>44</td><td>Arizona</td><td>72.57</td><td>3</td><td>Delaware</td><td>84.72</td></tr>
<tr><td>32</td><td>Arkansas</td><td>76.46</td><td>4</td><td>New Jersey</td><td>84.33</td></tr>
<tr><td>46</td><td>California</td><td>70.70</td><td>5</td><td>Connecticut</td><td>83.86</td></tr>
<tr><td>42</td><td>Colorado</td><td>74.27</td><td>6</td><td>Michigan</td><td>83.31</td></tr>
<tr><td>5</td><td>Connecticut</td><td>83.86</td><td>7</td><td>Minnesota</td><td>83.18</td></tr>
<tr><td>3</td><td>Delaware</td><td>84.72</td><td>8</td><td>West Virginia</td><td>82.51</td></tr>
<tr><td>47</td><td>Florida</td><td>70.46</td><td>9</td><td>Rhode Island</td><td>82.41</td></tr>
<tr><td>40</td><td>Georgia</td><td>75.09</td><td>10</td><td>Iowa</td><td>82.36</td></tr>
<tr><td>25</td><td>Hawaii</td><td>79.49</td><td>11</td><td>Utah</td><td>82.15</td></tr>
<tr><td>23</td><td>Idaho</td><td>80.02</td><td>12</td><td>Louisiana</td><td>82.07</td></tr>
<tr><td>18</td><td>Illinois</td><td>80.68</td><td>13</td><td>North Carolina</td><td>81.83</td></tr>
<tr><td>33</td><td>Indiana</td><td>76.20</td><td>14</td><td>Ohio</td><td>81.78</td></tr>
<tr><td>10</td><td>Iowa</td><td>82.36</td><td>15</td><td>Wisconsin</td><td>81.68</td></tr>
<tr><td>36</td><td>Kansas</td><td>75.66</td><td>16</td><td>Maryland</td><td>81.46</td></tr>
<tr><td>20</td><td>Kentucky</td><td>80.58</td><td>17</td><td>New York</td><td>81.24</td></tr>
<tr><td>12</td><td>Louisiana</td><td>82.07</td><td>18</td><td>Illinois</td><td>80.68</td></tr>
<tr><td>26</td><td>Maine</td><td>79.22</td><td>19</td><td>South Dakota</td><td>80.60</td></tr>
<tr><td>16</td><td>Maryland</td><td>81.46</td><td>20</td><td>Kentucky</td><td>80.58</td></tr>
<tr><td>2</td><td>Massachusetts</td><td>85.02</td><td>21</td><td>South Carolina</td><td>80.52</td></tr>
<tr><td>6</td><td>Michigan</td><td>83.31</td><td>22</td><td>Nebraska</td><td>80.11</td></tr>
<tr><td>7</td><td>Minnesota</td><td>83.18</td><td>23</td><td>Idaho</td><td>80.02</td></tr>
<tr><td>37</td><td>Mississippi</td><td>75.56</td><td>24</td><td>North Dakota</td><td>79.82</td></tr>
<tr><td>33</td><td>Missouri</td><td>76.20</td><td>25</td><td>Hawaii</td><td>79.49</td></tr>
<tr><td>30</td><td>Montana</td><td>77.49</td><td>26</td><td>Maine</td><td>79.22</td></tr>
<tr><td>22</td><td>Nebraska</td><td>80.11</td><td>27</td><td>Vermont</td><td>78.99</td></tr>
<tr><td>50</td><td>Nevada</td><td>56.54</td><td>28</td><td>New Hampshire</td><td>78.37</td></tr>
<tr><td>28</td><td>New Hampshire</td><td>78.37</td><td>29</td><td>Virginia</td><td>77.93</td></tr>
<tr><td>4</td><td>New Jersey</td><td>84.33</td><td>30</td><td>Montana</td><td>77.49</td></tr>
<tr><td>48</td><td>New Mexico</td><td>69.66</td><td>31</td><td>Alabama</td><td>77.31</td></tr>
<tr><td>17</td><td>New York</td><td>81.24</td><td>32</td><td>Arkansas</td><td>76.46</td></tr>
<tr><td>13</td><td>North Carolina</td><td>81.83</td><td>33</td><td>Indiana</td><td>76.20</td></tr>
<tr><td>24</td><td>North Dakota</td><td>79.82</td><td>33</td><td>Missouri</td><td>76.20</td></tr>
<tr><td>14</td><td>Ohio</td><td>81.78</td><td>35</td><td>Tennessee</td><td>75.74</td></tr>
<tr><td>39</td><td>Oklahoma</td><td>75.13</td><td>36</td><td>Kansas</td><td>75.66</td></tr>
<tr><td>45</td><td>Oregon</td><td>71.65</td><td>37</td><td>Mississippi</td><td>75.56</td></tr>
<tr><td>1</td><td>Pennsylvania</td><td>86.68</td><td>38</td><td>Washington</td><td>75.31</td></tr>
<tr><td>9</td><td>Rhode Island</td><td>82.41</td><td>39</td><td>Oklahoma</td><td>75.13</td></tr>
<tr><td>21</td><td>South Carolina</td><td>80.52</td><td>40</td><td>Georgia</td><td>75.09</td></tr>
<tr><td>19</td><td>South Dakota</td><td>80.60</td><td>41</td><td>Texas</td><td>74.34</td></tr>
<tr><td>35</td><td>Tennessee</td><td>75.74</td><td>42</td><td>Colorado</td><td>74.27</td></tr>
<tr><td>41</td><td>Texas</td><td>74.34</td><td>43</td><td>Wyoming</td><td>73.09</td></tr>
<tr><td>11</td><td>Utah</td><td>82.15</td><td>44</td><td>Arizona</td><td>72.57</td></tr>
<tr><td>27</td><td>Vermont</td><td>78.99</td><td>45</td><td>Oregon</td><td>71.65</td></tr>
<tr><td>29</td><td>Virginia</td><td>77.93</td><td>46</td><td>California</td><td>70.70</td></tr>
<tr><td>38</td><td>Washington</td><td>75.31</td><td>47</td><td>Florida</td><td>70.46</td></tr>
<tr><td>8</td><td>West Virginia</td><td>82.51</td><td>48</td><td>New Mexico</td><td>69.66</td></tr>
<tr><td>15</td><td>Wisconsin</td><td>81.68</td><td>49</td><td>Alaska</td><td>63.21</td></tr>
<tr><td>43</td><td>Wyoming</td><td>73.09</td><td>50</td><td>Nevada</td><td>56.54</td></tr>
</table>

District of Columbia   85.03

Source: Morgan Quitno Corporation using data from U.S. Department of Justice, Bureau of Justice Statistics
"Census of State and Local Law Enforcement Agencies, 1992" (Bulletin, July 1993, NCJ-142972)
*Includes consolidated police-sheriffs' departments.

Rate of Full-Time Officers in Local Police Departments in 1992

National Rate = 14.63 Officers per 10,000 Population*

ALPHA ORDER

RANK	STATE	RATE
18	Alabama	13.64
31	Alaska	11.53
19	Arizona	13.59
38	Arkansas	10.40
33	California	10.75
16	Colorado	13.80
7	Connecticut	18.49
25	Delaware	12.87
21	Florida	13.37
14	Georgia	13.93
3	Hawaii	23.19
46	Idaho	8.63
4	Illinois	21.48
35	Indiana	10.58
40	Iowa	10.18
27	Kansas	12.64
41	Kentucky	10.13
24	Louisiana	12.94
32	Maine	11.33
8	Maryland	16.86
5	Massachusetts	20.15
16	Michigan	13.80
39	Minnesota	10.22
36	Mississippi	10.50
10	Missouri	15.25
50	Montana	6.89
34	Nebraska	10.71
20	Nevada	13.53
9	New Hampshire	15.45
2	New Jersey	24.68
23	New Mexico	13.23
1	New York	25.29
30	North Carolina	11.72
48	North Dakota	8.46
22	Ohio	13.32
13	Oklahoma	14.10
43	Oregon	9.34
11	Pennsylvania	14.37
6	Rhode Island	20.14
42	South Carolina	9.66
45	South Dakota	9.11
29	Tennessee	12.37
15	Texas	13.92
47	Utah	8.53
37	Vermont	10.42
25	Virginia	12.87
44	Washington	9.16
49	West Virginia	6.95
12	Wisconsin	14.35
28	Wyoming	12.53

RANK ORDER

RANK	STATE	RATE
1	New York	25.29
2	New Jersey	24.68
3	Hawaii	23.19
4	Illinois	21.48
5	Massachusetts	20.15
6	Rhode Island	20.14
7	Connecticut	18.49
8	Maryland	16.86
9	New Hampshire	15.45
10	Missouri	15.25
11	Pennsylvania	14.37
12	Wisconsin	14.35
13	Oklahoma	14.10
14	Georgia	13.93
15	Texas	13.92
16	Colorado	13.80
16	Michigan	13.80
18	Alabama	13.64
19	Arizona	13.59
20	Nevada	13.53
21	Florida	13.37
22	Ohio	13.32
23	New Mexico	13.23
24	Louisiana	12.94
25	Delaware	12.87
25	Virginia	12.87
27	Kansas	12.64
28	Wyoming	12.53
29	Tennessee	12.37
30	North Carolina	11.72
31	Alaska	11.53
32	Maine	11.33
33	California	10.75
34	Nebraska	10.71
35	Indiana	10.58
36	Mississippi	10.50
37	Vermont	10.42
38	Arkansas	10.40
39	Minnesota	10.22
40	Iowa	10.18
41	Kentucky	10.13
42	South Carolina	9.66
43	Oregon	9.34
44	Washington	9.16
45	South Dakota	9.11
46	Idaho	8.63
47	Utah	8.53
48	North Dakota	8.46
49	West Virginia	6.95
50	Montana	6.89
	District of Columbia	83.01

Source: Morgan Quitno Corporation using data from U.S. Department of Justice, Bureau of Justice Statistics
"Census of State and Local Law Enforcement Agencies, 1992" (Bulletin, July 1993, NCJ-142972)
*Includes consolidated police-sheriffs' departments.

Full–Time Employees in Local Police Departments in 1992

National Total = 476,261 Employees*

ALPHA ORDER					RANK ORDER			
RANK	STATE	EMPLOYEES	% of USA		RANK	STATE	EMPLOYEES	% of USA
19	Alabama	7,295	1.53%		1	New York	56,406	11.84%
44	Alaska	1,071	0.22%		2	California	46,947	9.86%
21	Arizona	7,178	1.51%		3	Texas	33,059	6.94%
34	Arkansas	3,262	0.68%		4	Illinois	30,971	6.50%
2	California	46,947	9.86%		5	Florida	25,598	5.37%
23	Colorado	6,445	1.35%		6	New Jersey	22,793	4.79%
20	Connecticut	7,236	1.52%		7	Pennsylvania	19,907	4.18%
45	Delaware	1,047	0.22%		8	Ohio	17,936	3.77%
5	Florida	25,598	5.37%		9	Michigan	15,636	3.28%
11	Georgia	12,524	2.63%		10	Massachusetts	14,217	2.99%
33	Hawaii	3,384	0.71%		11	Georgia	12,524	2.63%
43	Idaho	1,151	0.24%		12	Virginia	10,529	2.21%
4	Illinois	30,971	6.50%		13	Missouri	10,395	2.18%
18	Indiana	7,864	1.65%		14	Maryland	10,156	2.13%
32	Iowa	3,476	0.73%		15	North Carolina	9,805	2.06%
29	Kansas	4,215	0.89%		16	Wisconsin	8,795	1.85%
27	Kentucky	4,721	0.99%		17	Tennessee	8,204	1.72%
22	Louisiana	6,760	1.42%		18	Indiana	7,864	1.65%
41	Maine	1,766	0.37%		19	Alabama	7,295	1.53%
14	Maryland	10,156	2.13%		20	Connecticut	7,236	1.52%
10	Massachusetts	14,217	2.99%		21	Arizona	7,178	1.51%
9	Michigan	15,636	3.28%		22	Louisiana	6,760	1.42%
26	Minnesota	5,506	1.16%		23	Colorado	6,445	1.35%
31	Mississippi	3,633	0.76%		24	Washington	6,246	1.31%
13	Missouri	10,395	2.18%		25	Oklahoma	6,028	1.27%
49	Montana	733	0.15%		26	Minnesota	5,506	1.16%
39	Nebraska	2,147	0.45%		27	Kentucky	4,721	0.99%
35	Nevada	3,175	0.67%		28	South Carolina	4,323	0.91%
38	New Hampshire	2,191	0.46%		29	Kansas	4,215	0.89%
6	New Jersey	22,793	4.79%		30	Oregon	3,883	0.82%
36	New Mexico	3,003	0.63%		31	Mississippi	3,633	0.76%
1	New York	56,406	11.84%		32	Iowa	3,476	0.73%
15	North Carolina	9,805	2.06%		33	Hawaii	3,384	0.71%
50	North Dakota	674	0.14%		34	Arkansas	3,262	0.68%
8	Ohio	17,936	3.77%		35	Nevada	3,175	0.67%
25	Oklahoma	6,028	1.27%		36	New Mexico	3,003	0.63%
30	Oregon	3,883	0.82%		37	Rhode Island	2,456	0.52%
7	Pennsylvania	19,907	4.18%		38	New Hampshire	2,191	0.46%
37	Rhode Island	2,456	0.52%		39	Nebraska	2,147	0.45%
28	South Carolina	4,323	0.91%		40	Utah	1,882	0.40%
46	South Dakota	804	0.17%		41	Maine	1,766	0.37%
17	Tennessee	8,204	1.72%		42	West Virginia	1,527	0.32%
3	Texas	33,059	6.94%		43	Idaho	1,151	0.24%
40	Utah	1,882	0.40%		44	Alaska	1,071	0.22%
48	Vermont	752	0.16%		45	Delaware	1,047	0.22%
12	Virginia	10,529	2.21%		46	South Dakota	804	0.17%
24	Washington	6,246	1.31%		47	Wyoming	799	0.17%
42	West Virginia	1,527	0.32%		48	Vermont	752	0.16%
16	Wisconsin	8,795	1.85%		49	Montana	733	0.15%
47	Wyoming	799	0.17%		50	North Dakota	674	0.14%
						District of Columbia	5,750	1.21%

Source: U.S. Department of Justice, Bureau of Justice Statistics
  "Census of State and Local Law Enforcement Agencies, 1992" (Bulletin, July 1993, NCJ-142972)
*Includes consolidated police–sheriffs' departments.

Sheriffs' Departments in 1992

National Total = 3,086 Departments*

ALPHA ORDER				RANK ORDER			
RANK	**STATE**	**DEPARTMENTS**	**% of USA**	**RANK**	**STATE**	**DEPARTMENTS**	**% of USA**
20	Alabama	67	2.17%	1	Texas	255	8.26%
49	Alaska	0	0.00%	2	Georgia	159	5.15%
42	Arizona	15	0.49%	3	Virginia	125	4.05%
18	Arkansas	75	2.43%	4	Kentucky	120	3.89%
26	California	58	1.88%	5	Missouri	114	3.69%
25	Colorado	63	2.04%	6	Kansas	105	3.40%
46	Connecticut	8	0.26%	7	Illinois	102	3.31%
48	Delaware	3	0.10%	8	North Carolina	100	3.24%
23	Florida	65	2.11%	9	Iowa	99	3.21%
2	Georgia	159	5.15%	10	Tennessee	95	3.08%
49	Hawaii	0	0.00%	11	Nebraska	93	3.01%
32	Idaho	44	1.43%	12	Indiana	91	2.95%
7	Illinois	102	3.31%	13	Ohio	88	2.85%
12	Indiana	91	2.95%	14	Minnesota	87	2.82%
9	Iowa	99	3.21%	15	Michigan	83	2.69%
6	Kansas	105	3.40%	16	Mississippi	82	2.66%
4	Kentucky	120	3.89%	17	Oklahoma	77	2.50%
24	Louisiana	64	2.07%	18	Arkansas	75	2.43%
40	Maine	16	0.52%	19	Wisconsin	72	2.33%
37	Maryland	24	0.78%	20	Alabama	67	2.17%
43	Massachusetts	14	0.45%	21	Pennsylvania	66	2.14%
15	Michigan	83	2.69%	21	South Dakota	66	2.14%
14	Minnesota	87	2.82%	23	Florida	65	2.11%
16	Mississippi	82	2.66%	24	Louisiana	64	2.07%
5	Missouri	114	3.69%	25	Colorado	63	2.04%
28	Montana	55	1.78%	26	California	58	1.88%
11	Nebraska	93	3.01%	27	New York	57	1.85%
40	Nevada	16	0.52%	28	Montana	55	1.78%
45	New Hampshire	10	0.32%	28	West Virginia	55	1.78%
39	New Jersey	21	0.68%	30	North Dakota	53	1.72%
35	New Mexico	33	1.07%	31	South Carolina	46	1.49%
27	New York	57	1.85%	32	Idaho	44	1.43%
8	North Carolina	100	3.24%	33	Washington	39	1.26%
30	North Dakota	53	1.72%	34	Oregon	36	1.17%
13	Ohio	88	2.85%	35	New Mexico	33	1.07%
17	Oklahoma	77	2.50%	36	Utah	29	0.94%
34	Oregon	36	1.17%	37	Maryland	24	0.78%
21	Pennsylvania	66	2.14%	38	Wyoming	23	0.75%
47	Rhode Island	4	0.13%	39	New Jersey	21	0.68%
31	South Carolina	46	1.49%	40	Maine	16	0.52%
21	South Dakota	66	2.14%	40	Nevada	16	0.52%
10	Tennessee	95	3.08%	42	Arizona	15	0.49%
1	Texas	255	8.26%	43	Massachusetts	14	0.45%
36	Utah	29	0.94%	43	Vermont	14	0.45%
43	Vermont	14	0.45%	45	New Hampshire	10	0.32%
3	Virginia	125	4.05%	46	Connecticut	8	0.26%
33	Washington	39	1.26%	47	Rhode Island	4	0.13%
28	West Virginia	55	1.78%	48	Delaware	3	0.10%
19	Wisconsin	72	2.33%	49	Alaska	0	0.00%
38	Wyoming	23	0.75%	49	Hawaii	0	0.00%
					District of Columbia	0	0.00%

Source: U.S. Department of Justice, Bureau of Justice Statistics
  "Census of State and Local Law Enforcement Agencies, 1992" (Bulletin, July 1993, NCJ-142972)
*Sheriffs' departments generally operate at the county level.

Full–Time Sworn Officers in Sheriffs' Departments in 1992

National Total = 136,542 Officers*

ALPHA ORDER				RANK ORDER			
RANK	STATE	OFFICERS	% of USA	RANK	STATE	OFFICERS	% of USA
20	Alabama	1,902	1.39%	1	California	22,552	16.52%
49	Alaska	0	0.00%	2	Florida	11,805	8.65%
24	Arizona	1,427	1.05%	3	Texas	9,876	7.23%
30	Arkansas	1,054	0.77%	4	Louisiana	8,217	6.02%
1	California	22,552	16.52%	5	Illinois	7,845	5.75%
14	Colorado	3,042	2.23%	6	Georgia	5,852	4.29%
41	Connecticut	418	0.31%	7	Virginia	5,590	4.09%
48	Delaware	22	0.02%	8	New York	5,039	3.69%
2	Florida	11,805	8.65%	9	North Carolina	4,596	3.37%
6	Georgia	5,852	4.29%	10	Michigan	3,954	2.90%
49	Hawaii	0	0.00%	11	Ohio	3,870	2.83%
32	Idaho	1,032	0.76%	12	New Jersey	3,833	2.81%
5	Illinois	7,845	5.75%	13	Wisconsin	3,309	2.42%
17	Indiana	2,389	1.75%	14	Colorado	3,042	2.23%
27	Iowa	1,217	0.89%	15	Tennessee	2,866	2.10%
23	Kansas	1,546	1.13%	16	South Carolina	2,494	1.83%
31	Kentucky	1,041	0.76%	17	Indiana	2,389	1.75%
4	Louisiana	8,217	6.02%	18	Washington	2,228	1.63%
42	Maine	367	0.27%	19	Missouri	2,071	1.52%
25	Maryland	1,348	0.99%	20	Alabama	1,902	1.39%
26	Massachusetts	1,264	0.93%	21	Minnesota	1,887	1.38%
10	Michigan	3,954	2.90%	22	Oregon	1,691	1.24%
21	Minnesota	1,887	1.38%	23	Kansas	1,546	1.13%
28	Mississippi	1,107	0.81%	24	Arizona	1,427	1.05%
19	Missouri	2,071	1.52%	25	Maryland	1,348	0.99%
39	Montana	595	0.44%	26	Massachusetts	1,264	0.93%
37	Nebraska	769	0.56%	27	Iowa	1,217	0.89%
35	Nevada	808	0.59%	28	Mississippi	1,107	0.81%
46	New Hampshire	104	0.08%	29	Pennsylvania	1,076	0.79%
12	New Jersey	3,833	2.81%	30	Arkansas	1,054	0.77%
36	New Mexico	792	0.58%	31	Kentucky	1,041	0.76%
8	New York	5,039	3.69%	32	Idaho	1,032	0.76%
9	North Carolina	4,596	3.37%	33	Oklahoma	842	0.62%
43	North Dakota	348	0.25%	34	Utah	818	0.60%
11	Ohio	3,870	2.83%	35	Nevada	808	0.59%
33	Oklahoma	842	0.62%	36	New Mexico	792	0.58%
22	Oregon	1,691	1.24%	37	Nebraska	769	0.56%
29	Pennsylvania	1,076	0.79%	38	West Virginia	651	0.48%
45	Rhode Island	124	0.09%	39	Montana	595	0.44%
16	South Carolina	2,494	1.83%	40	Wyoming	448	0.33%
44	South Dakota	338	0.25%	41	Connecticut	418	0.31%
15	Tennessee	2,866	2.10%	42	Maine	367	0.27%
3	Texas	9,876	7.23%	43	North Dakota	348	0.25%
34	Utah	818	0.60%	44	South Dakota	338	0.25%
47	Vermont	78	0.06%	45	Rhode Island	124	0.09%
7	Virginia	5,590	4.09%	46	New Hampshire	104	0.08%
18	Washington	2,228	1.63%	47	Vermont	78	0.06%
38	West Virginia	651	0.48%	48	Delaware	22	0.02%
13	Wisconsin	3,309	2.42%	49	Alaska	0	0.00%
40	Wyoming	448	0.33%	49	Hawaii	0	0.00%
					District of Columbia	0	0.00%

Source: U.S. Department of Justice, Bureau of Justice Statistics
   "Census of State and Local Law Enforcement Agencies, 1992" (Bulletin, July 1993, NCJ–142972)
*Sheriffs' departments generally operate at the county level.

Full–Time Employees in Sheriffs' Departments in 1992

National Total = 225,342 Employees*

ALPHA ORDER

RANK	STATE	EMPLOYEES	% of USA
22	Alabama	3,172	1.41%
49	Alaska	0	0.00%
17	Arizona	4,196	1.86%
28	Arkansas	1,849	0.82%
1	California	36,243	16.08%
16	Colorado	4,513	2.00%
44	Connecticut	425	0.19%
48	Delaware	40	0.02%
2	Florida	24,426	10.84%
7	Georgia	8,381	3.72%
49	Hawaii	0	0.00%
32	Idaho	1,502	0.67%
4	Illinois	10,817	4.80%
15	Indiana	4,601	2.04%
27	Iowa	2,058	0.91%
26	Kansas	2,397	1.06%
38	Kentucky	1,141	0.51%
6	Louisiana	8,889	3.94%
40	Maine	896	0.40%
25	Maryland	2,546	1.13%
19	Massachusetts	3,615	1.60%
10	Michigan	6,861	3.04%
20	Minnesota	3,466	1.54%
29	Mississippi	1,768	0.78%
24	Missouri	2,619	1.16%
39	Montana	1,034	0.46%
35	Nebraska	1,303	0.58%
37	Nevada	1,142	0.51%
45	New Hampshire	158	0.07%
14	New Jersey	4,706	2.09%
36	New Mexico	1,241	0.55%
5	New York	9,284	4.12%
9	North Carolina	7,109	3.15%
43	North Dakota	503	0.22%
8	Ohio	7,522	3.34%
30	Oklahoma	1,736	0.77%
23	Oregon	3,107	1.38%
33	Pennsylvania	1,453	0.64%
46	Rhode Island	125	0.06%
21	South Carolina	3,423	1.52%
42	South Dakota	603	0.27%
12	Tennessee	5,927	2.63%
3	Texas	19,077	8.47%
31	Utah	1,709	0.76%
47	Vermont	119	0.05%
11	Virginia	6,550	2.91%
18	Washington	4,090	1.82%
34	West Virginia	1,373	0.61%
13	Wisconsin	4,752	2.11%
41	Wyoming	875	0.39%

RANK ORDER

RANK	STATE	EMPLOYEES	% of USA
1	California	36,243	16.08%
2	Florida	24,426	10.84%
3	Texas	19,077	8.47%
4	Illinois	10,817	4.80%
5	New York	9,284	4.12%
6	Louisiana	8,889	3.94%
7	Georgia	8,381	3.72%
8	Ohio	7,522	3.34%
9	North Carolina	7,109	3.15%
10	Michigan	6,861	3.04%
11	Virginia	6,550	2.91%
12	Tennessee	5,927	2.63%
13	Wisconsin	4,752	2.11%
14	New Jersey	4,706	2.09%
15	Indiana	4,601	2.04%
16	Colorado	4,513	2.00%
17	Arizona	4,196	1.86%
18	Washington	4,090	1.82%
19	Massachusetts	3,615	1.60%
20	Minnesota	3,466	1.54%
21	South Carolina	3,423	1.52%
22	Alabama	3,172	1.41%
23	Oregon	3,107	1.38%
24	Missouri	2,619	1.16%
25	Maryland	2,546	1.13%
26	Kansas	2,397	1.06%
27	Iowa	2,058	0.91%
28	Arkansas	1,849	0.82%
29	Mississippi	1,768	0.78%
30	Oklahoma	1,736	0.77%
31	Utah	1,709	0.76%
32	Idaho	1,502	0.67%
33	Pennsylvania	1,453	0.64%
34	West Virginia	1,373	0.61%
35	Nebraska	1,303	0.58%
36	New Mexico	1,241	0.55%
37	Nevada	1,142	0.51%
38	Kentucky	1,141	0.51%
39	Montana	1,034	0.46%
40	Maine	896	0.40%
41	Wyoming	875	0.39%
42	South Dakota	603	0.27%
43	North Dakota	503	0.22%
44	Connecticut	425	0.19%
45	New Hampshire	158	0.07%
46	Rhode Island	125	0.06%
47	Vermont	119	0.05%
48	Delaware	40	0.02%
49	Alaska	0	0.00%
49	Hawaii	0	0.00%
	District of Columbia	0	0.00%

Source: U.S. Department of Justice, Bureau of Justice Statistics
"Census of State and Local Law Enforcement Agencies, 1992" (Bulletin, July 1993, NCJ–142972)
*Sheriffs' departments generally operate at the county level.

Special Police Agencies in 1992

National Total = 1,721 Agencies*

ALPHA ORDER

RANK	STATE	AGENCIES	% of USA
13	Alabama	24	1.39%
39	Alaska	4	0.23%
31	Arizona	11	0.64%
23	Arkansas	16	0.93%
2	California	93	5.40%
28	Colorado	14	0.81%
23	Connecticut	16	0.93%
38	Delaware	5	0.29%
16	Florida	20	1.16%
7	Georgia	37	2.15%
47	Hawaii	2	0.12%
49	Idaho	1	0.06%
5	Illinois	43	2.50%
16	Indiana	20	1.16%
36	Iowa	6	0.35%
22	Kansas	18	1.05%
23	Kentucky	16	0.93%
10	Louisiana	27	1.57%
36	Maine	6	0.35%
15	Maryland	21	1.22%
9	Massachusetts	32	1.86%
16	Michigan	20	1.16%
33	Minnesota	9	0.52%
11	Mississippi	25	1.45%
23	Missouri	16	0.93%
39	Montana	4	0.23%
39	Nebraska	4	0.23%
39	Nevada	4	0.23%
45	New Hampshire	3	0.17%
13	New Jersey	24	1.39%
33	New Mexico	9	0.52%
3	New York	57	3.31%
11	North Carolina	25	1.45%
39	North Dakota	4	0.23%
5	Ohio	43	2.50%
16	Oklahoma	20	1.16%
33	Oregon	9	0.52%
4	Pennsylvania	51	2.96%
39	Rhode Island	4	0.23%
16	South Carolina	20	1.16%
47	South Dakota	2	0.12%
21	Tennessee	19	1.10%
1	Texas**	824	47.88%
30	Utah	13	0.76%
49	Vermont	1	0.06%
8	Virginia	34	1.98%
32	Washington	10	0.58%
28	West Virginia	14	0.81%
23	Wisconsin	16	0.93%
45	Wyoming	3	0.17%

RANK ORDER

RANK	STATE	AGENCIES	% of USA
1	Texas**	824	47.88%
2	California	93	5.40%
3	New York	57	3.31%
4	Pennsylvania	51	2.96%
5	Illinois	43	2.50%
5	Ohio	43	2.50%
7	Georgia	37	2.15%
8	Virginia	34	1.98%
9	Massachusetts	32	1.86%
10	Louisiana	27	1.57%
11	Mississippi	25	1.45%
11	North Carolina	25	1.45%
13	Alabama	24	1.39%
13	New Jersey	24	1.39%
15	Maryland	21	1.22%
16	Florida	20	1.16%
16	Indiana	20	1.16%
16	Michigan	20	1.16%
16	Oklahoma	20	1.16%
16	South Carolina	20	1.16%
21	Tennessee	19	1.10%
22	Kansas	18	1.05%
23	Arkansas	16	0.93%
23	Connecticut	16	0.93%
23	Kentucky	16	0.93%
23	Missouri	16	0.93%
23	Wisconsin	16	0.93%
28	Colorado	14	0.81%
28	West Virginia	14	0.81%
30	Utah	13	0.76%
31	Arizona	11	0.64%
32	Washington	10	0.58%
33	Minnesota	9	0.52%
33	New Mexico	9	0.52%
33	Oregon	9	0.52%
36	Iowa	6	0.35%
36	Maine	6	0.35%
38	Delaware	5	0.29%
39	Alaska	4	0.23%
39	Montana	4	0.23%
39	Nebraska	4	0.23%
39	Nevada	4	0.23%
39	North Dakota	4	0.23%
39	Rhode Island	4	0.23%
45	New Hampshire	3	0.17%
45	Wyoming	3	0.17%
47	Hawaii	2	0.12%
47	South Dakota	2	0.12%
49	Idaho	1	0.06%
49	Vermont	1	0.06%
	District of Columbia	2	0.12%

Source: U.S. Department of Justice, Bureau of Justice Statistics
   "Census of State and Local Law Enforcement Agencies, 1992" (Bulletin, July 1993, NCJ–142972)
*Agencies with special jurisdictions or special enforcement responsibilities.
**Texas' total includes 751 county constable offices.

Full–Time Sworn Officers in Special Police Departments in 1992

National Total = 41,371 Officers*

ALPHA ORDER

RANK	STATE	OFFICERS	% of USA
15	Alabama	600	1.45%
38	Alaska	120	0.29%
35	Arizona	164	0.40%
21	Arkansas	443	1.07%
3	California	3,992	9.65%
22	Colorado	404	0.98%
30	Connecticut	248	0.60%
36	Delaware	158	0.38%
4	Florida	1,432	3.46%
11	Georgia	759	1.83%
41	Hawaii	93	0.22%
49	Idaho	12	0.03%
10	Illinois	864	2.09%
19	Indiana	560	1.35%
33	Iowa	213	0.51%
27	Kansas	292	0.71%
28	Kentucky	280	0.68%
18	Louisiana	570	1.38%
34	Maine	169	0.41%
6	Maryland	1,280	3.09%
16	Massachusetts	593	1.43%
13	Michigan	642	1.55%
23	Minnesota	397	0.96%
25	Mississippi	324	0.78%
24	Missouri	391	0.95%
46	Montana	47	0.11%
41	Nebraska	93	0.22%
37	Nevada	143	0.35%
44	New Hampshire	68	0.16%
8	New Jersey	1,062	2.57%
40	New Mexico	111	0.27%
1	New York	13,334	32.23%
12	North Carolina	707	1.71%
45	North Dakota	49	0.12%
7	Ohio	1,099	2.66%
26	Oklahoma	301	0.73%
39	Oregon	117	0.28%
5	Pennsylvania	1,293	3.13%
43	Rhode Island	76	0.18%
17	South Carolina	584	1.41%
50	South Dakota	8	0.02%
20	Tennessee	517	1.25%
2	Texas**	4,108	9.93%
29	Utah	250	0.60%
47	Vermont	21	0.05%
9	Virginia	964	2.33%
32	Washington	228	0.55%
31	West Virginia	243	0.59%
14	Wisconsin	603	1.46%
47	Wyoming	21	0.05%

RANK ORDER

RANK	STATE	OFFICERS	% of USA
1	New York	13,334	32.23%
2	Texas**	4,108	9.93%
3	California	3,992	9.65%
4	Florida	1,432	3.46%
5	Pennsylvania	1,293	3.13%
6	Maryland	1,280	3.09%
7	Ohio	1,099	2.66%
8	New Jersey	1,062	2.57%
9	Virginia	964	2.33%
10	Illinois	864	2.09%
11	Georgia	759	1.83%
12	North Carolina	707	1.71%
13	Michigan	642	1.55%
14	Wisconsin	603	1.46%
15	Alabama	600	1.45%
16	Massachusetts	593	1.43%
17	South Carolina	584	1.41%
18	Louisiana	570	1.38%
19	Indiana	560	1.35%
20	Tennessee	517	1.25%
21	Arkansas	443	1.07%
22	Colorado	404	0.98%
23	Minnesota	397	0.96%
24	Missouri	391	0.95%
25	Mississippi	324	0.78%
26	Oklahoma	301	0.73%
27	Kansas	292	0.71%
28	Kentucky	280	0.68%
29	Utah	250	0.60%
30	Connecticut	248	0.60%
31	West Virginia	243	0.59%
32	Washington	228	0.55%
33	Iowa	213	0.51%
34	Maine	169	0.41%
35	Arizona	164	0.40%
36	Delaware	158	0.38%
37	Nevada	143	0.35%
38	Alaska	120	0.29%
39	Oregon	117	0.28%
40	New Mexico	111	0.27%
41	Hawaii	93	0.22%
41	Nebraska	93	0.22%
43	Rhode Island	76	0.18%
44	New Hampshire	68	0.16%
45	North Dakota	49	0.12%
46	Montana	47	0.11%
47	Vermont	21	0.05%
47	Wyoming	21	0.05%
49	Idaho	12	0.03%
50	South Dakota	8	0.02%
	District of Columbia	324	0.78%

Source: U.S. Department of Justice, Bureau of Justice Statistics
  "Census of State and Local Law Enforcement Agencies, 1992" (Bulletin, July 1993, NCJ–142972)
*Agencies with special jurisdictions or special enforcement responsibilities.
**Texas' total includes 751 county constable offices with 1,723 sworn constable office employees..

Percent of Full-Time Special Police Department Employees Who Are Officers: 1992

National Percent = 67.90% of Employees*

ALPHA ORDER			RANK ORDER		
RANK	STATE	PERCENT	RANK	STATE	PERCENT
14	Alabama	78.02	1	Hawaii	98.94
4	Alaska	88.89	2	Nebraska	92.08
34	Arizona	63.57	3	New York	90.08
48	Arkansas	42.88	4	Alaska	88.89
44	California	46.98	5	Maine	88.48
47	Colorado	44.25	6	West Virginia	87.41
7	Connecticut	84.35	7	Connecticut	84.35
27	Delaware	68.10	8	Louisiana	83.95
18	Florida	76.13	9	Minnesota	83.40
46	Georgia	44.36	10	Iowa	80.68
1	Hawaii	98.94	11	Idaho	80.00
11	Idaho	80.00	12	Illinois	78.47
12	Illinois	78.47	13	Oklahoma	78.39
15	Indiana	77.24	14	Alabama	78.02
10	Iowa	80.68	15	Indiana	77.24
21	Kansas	73.18	16	Massachusetts	77.01
33	Kentucky	64.67	17	Tennessee	76.59
8	Louisiana	83.95	18	Florida	76.13
5	Maine	88.48	19	Missouri	74.76
22	Maryland	72.36	20	Pennsylvania	74.57
16	Massachusetts	77.01	21	Kansas	73.18
30	Michigan	66.53	22	Maryland	72.36
9	Minnesota	83.40	23	Mississippi	72.00
23	Mississippi	72.00	24	Rhode Island	71.03
19	Missouri	74.76	25	Washington	70.59
41	Montana	51.09	26	New Mexico	68.94
2	Nebraska	92.08	27	Delaware	68.10
31	Nevada	65.90	28	North Dakota	67.12
49	New Hampshire	33.17	29	Oregon	66.86
38	New Jersey	61.18	30	Michigan	66.53
26	New Mexico	68.94	31	Nevada	65.90
3	New York	90.08	32	Vermont	65.63
35	North Carolina	63.29	33	Kentucky	64.67
28	North Dakota	67.12	34	Arizona	63.57
39	Ohio	57.48	35	North Carolina	63.29
13	Oklahoma	78.39	36	Texas**	63.14
29	Oregon	66.86	37	Wyoming	61.76
20	Pennsylvania	74.57	38	New Jersey	61.18
24	Rhode Island	71.03	39	Ohio	57.48
42	South Carolina	50.34	40	Wisconsin	56.51
43	South Dakota	50.00	41	Montana	51.09
17	Tennessee	76.59	42	South Carolina	50.34
36	Texas**	63.14	43	South Dakota	50.00
50	Utah	29.52	44	California	46.98
32	Vermont	65.63	45	Virginia	44.44
45	Virginia	44.44	46	Georgia	44.36
25	Washington	70.59	47	Colorado	44.25
6	West Virginia	87.41	48	Arkansas	42.88
40	Wisconsin	56.51	49	New Hampshire	33.17
37	Wyoming	61.76	50	Utah	29.52

District of Columbia   76.42

Source: Morgan Quitno Corporation using data from U.S. Department of Justice, Bureau of Justice Statistics
   "Census of State and Local Law Enforcement Agencies, 1992" (Bulletin, July 1993, NCJ-142972)
*Agencies with special jurisdictions or special enforcement responsibilities.
**Texas' total includes 751 county constable offices with 1,723 sworn constable office employees..

Rate of Full–Time Sworn Officers in Special Police Departments in 1992

National Rate = 1.62 Officers per 10,000 Population*

ALPHA ORDER				RANK ORDER		
RANK	STATE	RATE		RANK	STATE	RATE
9	Alabama	1.45		1	New York	7.36
5	Alaska	2.04		2	Maryland	2.61
46	Arizona	0.43		3	Texas**	2.33
6	Arkansas	1.85		4	Delaware	2.29
15	California	1.29		5	Alaska	2.04
18	Colorado	1.16		6	Arkansas	1.85
33	Connecticut	0.76		7	South Carolina	1.62
4	Delaware	2.29		8	Virginia	1.51
23	Florida	1.06		9	Alabama	1.45
20	Georgia	1.12		10	Utah	1.38
31	Hawaii	0.80		11	Maine	1.37
49	Idaho	0.11		12	New Jersey	1.36
38	Illinois	0.74		13	West Virginia	1.34
27	Indiana	0.99		14	Louisiana	1.33
33	Iowa	0.76		15	California	1.29
18	Kansas	1.16		16	Mississippi	1.24
36	Kentucky	0.75		17	Wisconsin	1.20
14	Louisiana	1.33		18	Colorado	1.16
11	Maine	1.37		18	Kansas	1.16
2	Maryland	2.61		20	Georgia	1.12
27	Massachusetts	0.99		21	Nevada	1.08
40	Michigan	0.68		21	Pennsylvania	1.08
30	Minnesota	0.89		23	Florida	1.06
16	Mississippi	1.24		24	North Carolina	1.03
36	Missouri	0.75		24	Tennessee	1.03
43	Montana	0.57		26	Ohio	1.00
42	Nebraska	0.58		27	Indiana	0.99
21	Nevada	1.08		27	Massachusetts	0.99
41	New Hampshire	0.61		29	Oklahoma	0.94
12	New Jersey	1.36		30	Minnesota	0.89
39	New Mexico	0.70		31	Hawaii	0.80
1	New York	7.36		32	North Dakota	0.77
24	North Carolina	1.03		33	Connecticut	0.76
32	North Dakota	0.77		33	Iowa	0.76
26	Ohio	1.00		33	Rhode Island	0.76
29	Oklahoma	0.94		36	Kentucky	0.75
47	Oregon	0.39		36	Missouri	0.75
21	Pennsylvania	1.08		38	Illinois	0.74
33	Rhode Island	0.76		39	New Mexico	0.70
7	South Carolina	1.62		40	Michigan	0.68
49	South Dakota	0.11		41	New Hampshire	0.61
24	Tennessee	1.03		42	Nebraska	0.58
3	Texas**	2.33		43	Montana	0.57
10	Utah	1.38		44	Wyoming	0.45
48	Vermont	0.37		45	Washington	0.44
8	Virginia	1.51		46	Arizona	0.43
45	Washington	0.44		47	Oregon	0.39
13	West Virginia	1.34		48	Vermont	0.37
17	Wisconsin	1.20		49	Idaho	0.11
44	Wyoming	0.45		49	South Dakota	0.11
					District of Columbia	5.50

Source: Morgan Quitno Corporation using data from U.S. Department of Justice, Bureau of Justice Statistics
"Census of State and Local Law Enforcement Agencies, 1992" (Bulletin, July 1993, NCJ-142972)
*Agencies with special jurisdictions or special enforcement responsibilities.
**Texas' total includes 751 county constable offices with 1,723 sworn constable office employees..

Full–Time Employees in Special Police Departments in 1992

National Total = 60,926 Employees*

ALPHA ORDER

RANK	STATE	EMPLOYEES	% of USA
20	Alabama	769	1.26%
41	Alaska	135	0.22%
34	Arizona	258	0.42%
15	Arkansas	1,033	1.70%
2	California	8,498	13.95%
17	Colorado	913	1.50%
31	Connecticut	294	0.48%
35	Delaware	232	0.38%
6	Florida	1,881	3.09%
10	Georgia	1,711	2.81%
44	Hawaii	94	0.15%
50	Idaho	15	0.02%
13	Illinois	1,101	1.81%
21	Indiana	725	1.19%
33	Iowa	264	0.43%
28	Kansas	399	0.65%
27	Kentucky	433	0.71%
22	Louisiana	679	1.11%
38	Maine	191	0.31%
7	Maryland	1,769	2.90%
19	Massachusetts	770	1.26%
16	Michigan	965	1.58%
25	Minnesota	476	0.78%
26	Mississippi	450	0.74%
24	Missouri	523	0.86%
45	Montana	92	0.15%
43	Nebraska	101	0.17%
36	Nevada	217	0.36%
37	New Hampshire	205	0.34%
8	New Jersey	1,736	2.85%
40	New Mexico	161	0.26%
1	New York	14,803	24.30%
12	North Carolina	1,117	1.83%
46	North Dakota	73	0.12%
5	Ohio	1,912	3.14%
29	Oklahoma	384	0.63%
39	Oregon	175	0.29%
9	Pennsylvania	1,734	2.85%
42	Rhode Island	107	0.18%
11	South Carolina	1,160	1.90%
49	South Dakota	16	0.03%
23	Tennessee	675	1.11%
3	Texas**	6,506	10.68%
18	Utah	847	1.39%
48	Vermont	32	0.05%
4	Virginia	2,169	3.56%
30	Washington	323	0.53%
32	West Virginia	278	0.46%
14	Wisconsin	1,067	1.75%
47	Wyoming	34	0.06%

RANK ORDER

RANK	STATE	EMPLOYEES	% of USA
1	New York	14,803	24.30%
2	California	8,498	13.95%
3	Texas**	6,506	10.68%
4	Virginia	2,169	3.56%
5	Ohio	1,912	3.14%
6	Florida	1,881	3.09%
7	Maryland	1,769	2.90%
8	New Jersey	1,736	2.85%
9	Pennsylvania	1,734	2.85%
10	Georgia	1,711	2.81%
11	South Carolina	1,160	1.90%
12	North Carolina	1,117	1.83%
13	Illinois	1,101	1.81%
14	Wisconsin	1,067	1.75%
15	Arkansas	1,033	1.70%
16	Michigan	965	1.58%
17	Colorado	913	1.50%
18	Utah	847	1.39%
19	Massachusetts	770	1.26%
20	Alabama	769	1.26%
21	Indiana	725	1.19%
22	Louisiana	679	1.11%
23	Tennessee	675	1.11%
24	Missouri	523	0.86%
25	Minnesota	476	0.78%
26	Mississippi	450	0.74%
27	Kentucky	433	0.71%
28	Kansas	399	0.65%
29	Oklahoma	384	0.63%
30	Washington	323	0.53%
31	Connecticut	294	0.48%
32	West Virginia	278	0.46%
33	Iowa	264	0.43%
34	Arizona	258	0.42%
35	Delaware	232	0.38%
36	Nevada	217	0.36%
37	New Hampshire	205	0.34%
38	Maine	191	0.31%
39	Oregon	175	0.29%
40	New Mexico	161	0.26%
41	Alaska	135	0.22%
42	Rhode Island	107	0.18%
43	Nebraska	101	0.17%
44	Hawaii	94	0.15%
45	Montana	92	0.15%
46	North Dakota	73	0.12%
47	Wyoming	34	0.06%
48	Vermont	32	0.05%
49	South Dakota	16	0.03%
50	Idaho	15	0.02%
	District of Columbia	424	0.70%

Source: U.S. Department of Justice, Bureau of Justice Statistics
  "Census of State and Local Law Enforcement Agencies, 1992" (Bulletin, July 1993, NCJ-142972)
*Agencies with special jurisdictions or special enforcement responsibilities.
**Texas' total includes 751 county constable offices with 1,723 sworn constable office employees..

Law Enforcement Officers Feloniously Killed in 1993

National Total = 62 Officers*

<table>
<tr><td colspan="4">ALPHA ORDER</td><td colspan="4">RANK ORDER</td></tr>
<tr><td>RANK</td><td>STATE</td><td>OFFICERS</td><td>% of USA</td><td>RANK</td><td>STATE</td><td>OFFICERS</td><td>% of USA</td></tr>
<tr><td>10</td><td>Alabama</td><td>1</td><td>1.61%</td><td>1</td><td>Texas</td><td>11</td><td>17.74%</td></tr>
<tr><td>29</td><td>Alaska</td><td>0</td><td>0.00%</td><td>2</td><td>California</td><td>8</td><td>12.90%</td></tr>
<tr><td>10</td><td>Arizona</td><td>1</td><td>1.61%</td><td>3</td><td>Indiana</td><td>4</td><td>6.45%</td></tr>
<tr><td>29</td><td>Arkansas</td><td>0</td><td>0.00%</td><td>3</td><td>North Carolina</td><td>4</td><td>6.45%</td></tr>
<tr><td>2</td><td>California</td><td>8</td><td>12.90%</td><td>3</td><td>Pennsylvania</td><td>4</td><td>6.45%</td></tr>
<tr><td>29</td><td>Colorado</td><td>0</td><td>0.00%</td><td>6</td><td>Florida</td><td>3</td><td>4.84%</td></tr>
<tr><td>29</td><td>Connecticut</td><td>0</td><td>0.00%</td><td>6</td><td>New York</td><td>3</td><td>4.84%</td></tr>
<tr><td>29</td><td>Delaware</td><td>0</td><td>0.00%</td><td>8</td><td>Louisiana</td><td>2</td><td>3.23%</td></tr>
<tr><td>6</td><td>Florida</td><td>3</td><td>4.84%</td><td>8</td><td>Ohio</td><td>2</td><td>3.23%</td></tr>
<tr><td>10</td><td>Georgia</td><td>1</td><td>1.61%</td><td>10</td><td>Alabama</td><td>1</td><td>1.61%</td></tr>
<tr><td>29</td><td>Hawaii</td><td>0</td><td>0.00%</td><td>10</td><td>Arizona</td><td>1</td><td>1.61%</td></tr>
<tr><td>29</td><td>Idaho</td><td>0</td><td>0.00%</td><td>10</td><td>Georgia</td><td>1</td><td>1.61%</td></tr>
<tr><td>10</td><td>Illinois</td><td>1</td><td>1.61%</td><td>10</td><td>Illinois</td><td>1</td><td>1.61%</td></tr>
<tr><td>3</td><td>Indiana</td><td>4</td><td>6.45%</td><td>10</td><td>Kentucky</td><td>1</td><td>1.61%</td></tr>
<tr><td>29</td><td>Iowa</td><td>0</td><td>0.00%</td><td>10</td><td>Maryland</td><td>1</td><td>1.61%</td></tr>
<tr><td>29</td><td>Kansas</td><td>0</td><td>0.00%</td><td>10</td><td>Massachusetts</td><td>1</td><td>1.61%</td></tr>
<tr><td>10</td><td>Kentucky</td><td>1</td><td>1.61%</td><td>10</td><td>Michigan</td><td>1</td><td>1.61%</td></tr>
<tr><td>8</td><td>Louisiana</td><td>2</td><td>3.23%</td><td>10</td><td>Minnesota</td><td>1</td><td>1.61%</td></tr>
<tr><td>29</td><td>Maine</td><td>0</td><td>0.00%</td><td>10</td><td>Mississippi</td><td>1</td><td>1.61%</td></tr>
<tr><td>10</td><td>Maryland</td><td>1</td><td>1.61%</td><td>10</td><td>Nebraska</td><td>1</td><td>1.61%</td></tr>
<tr><td>10</td><td>Massachusetts</td><td>1</td><td>1.61%</td><td>10</td><td>Nevada</td><td>1</td><td>1.61%</td></tr>
<tr><td>10</td><td>Michigan</td><td>1</td><td>1.61%</td><td>10</td><td>New Jersey</td><td>1</td><td>1.61%</td></tr>
<tr><td>10</td><td>Minnesota</td><td>1</td><td>1.61%</td><td>10</td><td>North Dakota</td><td>1</td><td>1.61%</td></tr>
<tr><td>10</td><td>Mississippi</td><td>1</td><td>1.61%</td><td>10</td><td>Oklahoma</td><td>1</td><td>1.61%</td></tr>
<tr><td>29</td><td>Missouri</td><td>0</td><td>0.00%</td><td>10</td><td>South Carolina</td><td>1</td><td>1.61%</td></tr>
<tr><td>29</td><td>Montana</td><td>0</td><td>0.00%</td><td>10</td><td>Utah</td><td>1</td><td>1.61%</td></tr>
<tr><td>10</td><td>Nebraska</td><td>1</td><td>1.61%</td><td>10</td><td>Virginia</td><td>1</td><td>1.61%</td></tr>
<tr><td>10</td><td>Nevada</td><td>1</td><td>1.61%</td><td>10</td><td>West Virginia</td><td>1</td><td>1.61%</td></tr>
<tr><td>29</td><td>New Hampshire</td><td>0</td><td>0.00%</td><td>29</td><td>Alaska</td><td>0</td><td>0.00%</td></tr>
<tr><td>10</td><td>New Jersey</td><td>1</td><td>1.61%</td><td>29</td><td>Arkansas</td><td>0</td><td>0.00%</td></tr>
<tr><td>29</td><td>New Mexico</td><td>0</td><td>0.00%</td><td>29</td><td>Colorado</td><td>0</td><td>0.00%</td></tr>
<tr><td>6</td><td>New York</td><td>3</td><td>4.84%</td><td>29</td><td>Connecticut</td><td>0</td><td>0.00%</td></tr>
<tr><td>3</td><td>North Carolina</td><td>4</td><td>6.45%</td><td>29</td><td>Delaware</td><td>0</td><td>0.00%</td></tr>
<tr><td>10</td><td>North Dakota</td><td>1</td><td>1.61%</td><td>29</td><td>Hawaii</td><td>0</td><td>0.00%</td></tr>
<tr><td>8</td><td>Ohio</td><td>2</td><td>3.23%</td><td>29</td><td>Idaho</td><td>0</td><td>0.00%</td></tr>
<tr><td>10</td><td>Oklahoma</td><td>1</td><td>1.61%</td><td>29</td><td>Iowa</td><td>0</td><td>0.00%</td></tr>
<tr><td>29</td><td>Oregon</td><td>0</td><td>0.00%</td><td>29</td><td>Kansas</td><td>0</td><td>0.00%</td></tr>
<tr><td>3</td><td>Pennsylvania</td><td>4</td><td>6.45%</td><td>29</td><td>Maine</td><td>0</td><td>0.00%</td></tr>
<tr><td>29</td><td>Rhode Island</td><td>0</td><td>0.00%</td><td>29</td><td>Missouri</td><td>0</td><td>0.00%</td></tr>
<tr><td>10</td><td>South Carolina</td><td>1</td><td>1.61%</td><td>29</td><td>Montana</td><td>0</td><td>0.00%</td></tr>
<tr><td>29</td><td>South Dakota</td><td>0</td><td>0.00%</td><td>29</td><td>New Hampshire</td><td>0</td><td>0.00%</td></tr>
<tr><td>29</td><td>Tennessee</td><td>0</td><td>0.00%</td><td>29</td><td>New Mexico</td><td>0</td><td>0.00%</td></tr>
<tr><td>1</td><td>Texas</td><td>11</td><td>17.74%</td><td>29</td><td>Oregon</td><td>0</td><td>0.00%</td></tr>
<tr><td>10</td><td>Utah</td><td>1</td><td>1.61%</td><td>29</td><td>Rhode Island</td><td>0</td><td>0.00%</td></tr>
<tr><td>29</td><td>Vermont</td><td>0</td><td>0.00%</td><td>29</td><td>South Dakota</td><td>0</td><td>0.00%</td></tr>
<tr><td>10</td><td>Virginia</td><td>1</td><td>1.61%</td><td>29</td><td>Tennessee</td><td>0</td><td>0.00%</td></tr>
<tr><td>29</td><td>Washington</td><td>0</td><td>0.00%</td><td>29</td><td>Vermont</td><td>0</td><td>0.00%</td></tr>
<tr><td>10</td><td>West Virginia</td><td>1</td><td>1.61%</td><td>29</td><td>Washington</td><td>0</td><td>0.00%</td></tr>
<tr><td>29</td><td>Wisconsin</td><td>0</td><td>0.00%</td><td>29</td><td>Wisconsin</td><td>0</td><td>0.00%</td></tr>
<tr><td>29</td><td>Wyoming</td><td>0</td><td>0.00%</td><td>29</td><td>Wyoming</td><td>0</td><td>0.00%</td></tr>
<tr><td></td><td></td><td></td><td></td><td></td><td>District of Columbia</td><td>2</td><td>3.23%</td></tr>
</table>

Source: U.S. Department of Justice, Federal Bureau of Investigation
unpublished data

*Preliminary data. Total does not include eight officers killed in Puerto Rico in 1993.

Law Enforcement Officers Feloniously Killed: 1984 to 1993

National Total = 653 Officers*

ALPHA ORDER

RANK	STATE	OFFICERS	% of USA
17	Alabama	14	2.14%
30	Alaska	6	0.92%
12	Arizona	17	2.60%
19	Arkansas	12	1.84%
2	California	56	8.58%
25	Colorado	9	1.38%
36	Connecticut	3	0.46%
46	Delaware	0	0.00%
3	Florida	48	7.35%
5	Georgia	30	4.59%
36	Hawaii	3	0.46%
40	Idaho	2	0.31%
6	Illinois	28	4.29%
19	Indiana	12	1.84%
40	Iowa	2	0.31%
32	Kansas	5	0.77%
14	Kentucky	16	2.45%
10	Louisiana	19	2.91%
40	Maine	2	0.31%
21	Maryland	10	1.53%
21	Massachusetts	10	1.53%
7	Michigan	26	3.98%
27	Minnesota	8	1.23%
8	Mississippi	24	3.68%
14	Missouri	16	2.45%
32	Montana	5	0.77%
36	Nebraska	3	0.46%
34	Nevada	4	0.61%
46	New Hampshire	0	0.00%
21	New Jersey	10	1.53%
30	New Mexico	6	0.92%
4	New York	40	6.13%
10	North Carolina	19	2.91%
44	North Dakota	1	0.15%
17	Ohio	14	2.14%
25	Oklahoma	9	1.38%
36	Oregon	3	0.46%
9	Pennsylvania	21	3.22%
46	Rhode Island	0	0.00%
14	South Carolina	16	2.45%
44	South Dakota	1	0.15%
21	Tennessee	10	1.53%
1	Texas	70	10.72%
40	Utah	2	0.31%
46	Vermont	0	0.00%
12	Virginia	17	2.60%
29	Washington	7	1.07%
34	West Virginia	4	0.61%
27	Wisconsin	8	1.23%
46	Wyoming	0	0.00%

RANK ORDER

RANK	STATE	OFFICERS	% of USA
1	Texas	70	10.72%
2	California	56	8.58%
3	Florida	48	7.35%
4	New York	40	6.13%
5	Georgia	30	4.59%
6	Illinois	28	4.29%
7	Michigan	26	3.98%
8	Mississippi	24	3.68%
9	Pennsylvania	21	3.22%
10	Louisiana	19	2.91%
10	North Carolina	19	2.91%
12	Arizona	17	2.60%
12	Virginia	17	2.60%
14	Kentucky	16	2.45%
14	Missouri	16	2.45%
14	South Carolina	16	2.45%
17	Alabama	14	2.14%
17	Ohio	14	2.14%
19	Arkansas	12	1.84%
19	Indiana	12	1.84%
21	Maryland	10	1.53%
21	Massachusetts	10	1.53%
21	New Jersey	10	1.53%
21	Tennessee	10	1.53%
25	Colorado	9	1.38%
25	Oklahoma	9	1.38%
27	Minnesota	8	1.23%
27	Wisconsin	8	1.23%
29	Washington	7	1.07%
30	Alaska	6	0.92%
30	New Mexico	6	0.92%
32	Kansas	5	0.77%
32	Montana	5	0.77%
34	Nevada	4	0.61%
34	West Virginia	4	0.61%
36	Connecticut	3	0.46%
36	Hawaii	3	0.46%
36	Nebraska	3	0.46%
36	Oregon	3	0.46%
40	Idaho	2	0.31%
40	Iowa	2	0.31%
40	Maine	2	0.31%
40	Utah	2	0.31%
44	North Dakota	1	0.15%
44	South Dakota	1	0.15%
46	Delaware	0	0.00%
46	New Hampshire	0	0.00%
46	Rhode Island	0	0.00%
46	Vermont	0	0.00%
46	Wyoming	0	0.00%
	District of Columbia	5	0.77%

Source: U.S. Department of Justice, Federal Bureau of Investigation
    unpublished data

*Preliminary data. Total does not include 51 officers killed in U.S. Territories or abroad. Of this total, 48 officers were killed

U.S. District Judgeships in 1993

National Total = 649 Judges*

ALPHA ORDER			
RANK	STATE	JUDGES	% of USA
12	Alabama	14	2.16%
41	Alaska	3	0.46%
25	Arizona	8	1.23%
25	Arkansas	8	1.23%
1	California	56	8.63%
29	Colorado	7	1.08%
25	Connecticut	8	1.23%
37	Delaware	4	0.62%
5	Florida	31	4.78%
10	Georgia	18	2.77%
37	Hawaii	4	0.62%
48	Idaho	2	0.31%
6	Illinois	30	4.62%
20	Indiana	10	1.54%
34	Iowa	5	0.77%
31	Kansas	6	0.92%
22	Kentucky	9	1.39%
7	Louisiana	22	3.39%
41	Maine	3	0.46%
20	Maryland	10	1.54%
16	Massachusetts	13	2.00%
8	Michigan	20	3.08%
29	Minnesota	7	1.08%
22	Mississippi	9	1.39%
12	Missouri	14	2.16%
41	Montana	3	0.46%
37	Nebraska	4	0.62%
37	Nevada	4	0.62%
41	New Hampshire	3	0.46%
11	New Jersey	17	2.62%
34	New Mexico	5	0.77%
2	New York	52	8.01%
17	North Carolina	11	1.69%
48	North Dakota	2	0.31%
8	Ohio	20	3.08%
17	Oklahoma	11	1.69%
31	Oregon	6	0.92%
4	Pennsylvania	39	6.01%
41	Rhode Island	3	0.46%
22	South Carolina	9	1.39%
41	South Dakota	3	0.46%
12	Tennessee	14	2.16%
3	Texas	47	7.24%
34	Utah	5	0.77%
48	Vermont	2	0.31%
12	Virginia	14	2.16%
17	Washington	11	1.69%
25	West Virginia	8	1.23%
31	Wisconsin	6	0.92%
41	Wyoming	3	0.46%

RANK ORDER			
RANK	STATE	JUDGES	% of USA
1	California	56	8.63%
2	New York	52	8.01%
3	Texas	47	7.24%
4	Pennsylvania	39	6.01%
5	Florida	31	4.78%
6	Illinois	30	4.62%
7	Louisiana	22	3.39%
8	Michigan	20	3.08%
8	Ohio	20	3.08%
10	Georgia	18	2.77%
11	New Jersey	17	2.62%
12	Alabama	14	2.16%
12	Missouri	14	2.16%
12	Tennessee	14	2.16%
12	Virginia	14	2.16%
16	Massachusetts	13	2.00%
17	North Carolina	11	1.69%
17	Oklahoma	11	1.69%
17	Washington	11	1.69%
20	Indiana	10	1.54%
20	Maryland	10	1.54%
22	Kentucky	9	1.39%
22	Mississippi	9	1.39%
22	South Carolina	9	1.39%
25	Arizona	8	1.23%
25	Arkansas	8	1.23%
25	Connecticut	8	1.23%
25	West Virginia	8	1.23%
29	Colorado	7	1.08%
29	Minnesota	7	1.08%
31	Kansas	6	0.92%
31	Oregon	6	0.92%
31	Wisconsin	6	0.92%
34	Iowa	5	0.77%
34	New Mexico	5	0.77%
34	Utah	5	0.77%
37	Delaware	4	0.62%
37	Hawaii	4	0.62%
37	Nebraska	4	0.62%
37	Nevada	4	0.62%
41	Alaska	3	0.46%
41	Maine	3	0.46%
41	Montana	3	0.46%
41	New Hampshire	3	0.46%
41	Rhode Island	3	0.46%
41	South Dakota	3	0.46%
41	Wyoming	3	0.46%
48	Idaho	2	0.31%
48	North Dakota	2	0.31%
48	Vermont	2	0.31%
	District of Columbia	15	2.31%

Source: Administrative Office of the United States Courts
"1993 Federal Court Management Statistics" (March 1994)
*Total includes 11 judgeships in U.S. territories.

Rate of U.S. District Judges in 1993

National Rate = 0.25 Judges per 100,000 Population*

ALPHA ORDER			RANK ORDER		
RANK	STATE	RATE	RANK	STATE	RATE
12	Alabama	0.33	1	Wyoming	0.64
4	Alaska	0.50	2	Delaware	0.57
39	Arizona	0.20	3	Louisiana	0.51
12	Arkansas	0.33	4	Alaska	0.50
43	California	0.18	5	West Virginia	0.44
39	Colorado	0.20	6	South Dakota	0.42
29	Connecticut	0.24	7	Montana	0.36
2	Delaware	0.57	8	Vermont	0.35
33	Florida	0.23	9	Hawaii	0.34
24	Georgia	0.26	9	Mississippi	0.34
9	Hawaii	0.34	9	Oklahoma	0.34
43	Idaho	0.18	12	Alabama	0.33
24	Illinois	0.26	12	Arkansas	0.33
43	Indiana	0.18	14	Pennsylvania	0.32
43	Iowa	0.18	15	New Mexico	0.31
29	Kansas	0.24	15	North Dakota	0.31
29	Kentucky	0.24	17	Rhode Island	0.30
3	Louisiana	0.51	18	Nevada	0.29
29	Maine	0.24	18	New York	0.29
39	Maryland	0.20	20	Missouri	0.27
34	Massachusetts	0.22	20	New Hampshire	0.27
37	Michigan	0.21	20	Tennessee	0.27
49	Minnesota	0.15	20	Utah	0.27
9	Mississippi	0.34	24	Georgia	0.26
20	Missouri	0.27	24	Illinois	0.26
7	Montana	0.36	24	Texas	0.26
27	Nebraska	0.25	27	Nebraska	0.25
18	Nevada	0.29	27	South Carolina	0.25
20	New Hampshire	0.27	29	Connecticut	0.24
34	New Jersey	0.22	29	Kansas	0.24
15	New Mexico	0.31	29	Kentucky	0.24
18	New York	0.29	29	Maine	0.24
48	North Carolina	0.16	33	Florida	0.23
15	North Dakota	0.31	34	Massachusetts	0.22
43	Ohio	0.18	34	New Jersey	0.22
9	Oklahoma	0.34	34	Virginia	0.22
39	Oregon	0.20	37	Michigan	0.21
14	Pennsylvania	0.32	37	Washington	0.21
17	Rhode Island	0.30	39	Arizona	0.20
27	South Carolina	0.25	39	Colorado	0.20
6	South Dakota	0.42	39	Maryland	0.20
20	Tennessee	0.27	39	Oregon	0.20
24	Texas	0.26	43	California	0.18
20	Utah	0.27	43	Idaho	0.18
8	Vermont	0.35	43	Indiana	0.18
34	Virginia	0.22	43	Iowa	0.18
37	Washington	0.21	43	Ohio	0.18
5	West Virginia	0.44	48	North Carolina	0.16
50	Wisconsin	0.12	49	Minnesota	0.15
1	Wyoming	0.64	50	Wisconsin	0.12
				District of Columbia	2.60

Source: Morgan Quitno Corporation using data from Administrative Office of the United States Courts
"1993 Federal Court Management Statistics" (March 1994)
*Total excludes judgeships and population in U.S. territories.

Felony Criminal Cases Filed in U.S. District Court in 1993

National Total = 33,391 Felony Criminal Cases*

ALPHA ORDER

RANK	STATE	CASES	% of USA
15	Alabama	703	2.11%
44	Alaska	96	0.29%
10	Arizona	901	2.70%
31	Arkansas	320	0.96%
1	California	3,386	10.14%
29	Colorado	351	1.05%
35	Connecticut	265	0.79%
49	Delaware	72	0.22%
4	Florida	2,151	6.44%
13	Georgia	784	2.35%
41	Hawaii	149	0.45%
50	Idaho	60	0.18%
7	Illinois	1,059	3.17%
27	Indiana	389	1.16%
38	Iowa	222	0.66%
36	Kansas	243	0.73%
22	Kentucky	456	1.37%
18	Louisiana	602	1.80%
43	Maine	119	0.36%
28	Maryland	352	1.05%
31	Massachusetts	320	0.96%
9	Michigan	915	2.74%
33	Minnesota	305	0.91%
25	Mississippi	419	1.25%
16	Missouri	608	1.82%
37	Montana	225	0.67%
40	Nebraska	178	0.53%
25	Nevada	419	1.25%
48	New Hampshire	77	0.23%
17	New Jersey	604	1.81%
19	New Mexico	587	1.76%
3	New York	2,764	8.28%
8	North Carolina	987	2.96%
42	North Dakota	126	0.38%
11	Ohio	880	2.64%
23	Oklahoma	452	1.35%
21	Oregon	471	1.41%
5	Pennsylvania	1,118	3.35%
45	Rhode Island	88	0.26%
20	South Carolina	492	1.47%
39	South Dakota	211	0.63%
12	Tennessee	852	2.55%
2	Texas	3,277	9.81%
34	Utah	286	0.86%
47	Vermont	83	0.25%
6	Virginia	1,062	3.18%
14	Washington	711	2.13%
24	West Virginia	451	1.35%
30	Wisconsin	326	0.98%
46	Wyoming	86	0.26%

RANK ORDER

RANK	STATE	CASES	% of USA
1	California	3,386	10.14%
2	Texas	3,277	9.81%
3	New York	2,764	8.28%
4	Florida	2,151	6.44%
5	Pennsylvania	1,118	3.35%
6	Virginia	1,062	3.18%
7	Illinois	1,059	3.17%
8	North Carolina	987	2.96%
9	Michigan	915	2.74%
10	Arizona	901	2.70%
11	Ohio	880	2.64%
12	Tennessee	852	2.55%
13	Georgia	784	2.35%
14	Washington	711	2.13%
15	Alabama	703	2.11%
16	Missouri	608	1.82%
17	New Jersey	604	1.81%
18	Louisiana	602	1.80%
19	New Mexico	587	1.76%
20	South Carolina	492	1.47%
21	Oregon	471	1.41%
22	Kentucky	456	1.37%
23	Oklahoma	452	1.35%
24	West Virginia	451	1.35%
25	Mississippi	419	1.25%
25	Nevada	419	1.25%
27	Indiana	389	1.16%
28	Maryland	352	1.05%
29	Colorado	351	1.05%
30	Wisconsin	326	0.98%
31	Arkansas	320	0.96%
31	Massachusetts	320	0.96%
33	Minnesota	305	0.91%
34	Utah	286	0.86%
35	Connecticut	265	0.79%
36	Kansas	243	0.73%
37	Montana	225	0.67%
38	Iowa	222	0.66%
39	South Dakota	211	0.63%
40	Nebraska	178	0.53%
41	Hawaii	149	0.45%
42	North Dakota	126	0.38%
43	Maine	119	0.36%
44	Alaska	96	0.29%
45	Rhode Island	88	0.26%
46	Wyoming	86	0.26%
47	Vermont	83	0.25%
48	New Hampshire	77	0.23%
49	Delaware	72	0.22%
50	Idaho	60	0.18%
	District of Columbia	442	1.32%

Source: Administrative Office of the United States Courts
"1993 Federal Court Management Statistics" (March 1994)
*Total includes 889 cases filed in U.S. territories. Does not include transfers from one district to another.

Felony Criminal Cases Filed per U.S. District Judge in 1993

National Rate = 51 Felony Criminal Cases per Judge*

ALPHA ORDER			RANK ORDER		
RANK	STATE	RATE	RANK	STATE	RATE
21	Alabama	50	1	New Mexico	117
42	Alaska	32	2	Arizona	113
2	Arizona	113	3	Nevada	105
34	Arkansas	40	4	North Carolina	90
14	California	60	5	Oregon	79
21	Colorado	50	6	Virginia	76
41	Connecticut	33	7	Montana	75
50	Delaware	18	8	South Dakota	70
10	Florida	69	8	Texas	70
26	Georgia	44	10	Florida	69
37	Hawaii	37	11	Washington	65
43	Idaho	30	12	North Dakota	63
39	Illinois	35	13	Tennessee	61
36	Indiana	39	14	California	60
26	Iowa	44	15	Utah	57
32	Kansas	41	16	West Virginia	56
20	Kentucky	51	17	South Carolina	55
47	Louisiana	27	18	Wisconsin	54
34	Maine	40	19	New York	53
39	Maryland	35	20	Kentucky	51
49	Massachusetts	25	21	Alabama	50
24	Michigan	46	21	Colorado	50
26	Minnesota	44	23	Mississippi	47
23	Mississippi	47	24	Michigan	46
30	Missouri	43	25	Nebraska	45
7	Montana	75	26	Georgia	44
25	Nebraska	45	26	Iowa	44
3	Nevada	105	26	Minnesota	44
48	New Hampshire	26	26	Ohio	44
38	New Jersey	36	30	Missouri	43
1	New Mexico	117	31	Vermont	42
19	New York	53	32	Kansas	41
4	North Carolina	90	32	Oklahoma	41
12	North Dakota	63	34	Arkansas	40
26	Ohio	44	34	Maine	40
32	Oklahoma	41	36	Indiana	39
5	Oregon	79	37	Hawaii	37
44	Pennsylvania	29	38	New Jersey	36
44	Rhode Island	29	39	Illinois	35
17	South Carolina	55	39	Maryland	35
8	South Dakota	70	41	Connecticut	33
13	Tennessee	61	42	Alaska	32
8	Texas	70	43	Idaho	30
15	Utah	57	44	Pennsylvania	29
31	Vermont	42	44	Rhode Island	29
6	Virginia	76	44	Wyoming	29
11	Washington	65	47	Louisiana	27
16	West Virginia	56	48	New Hampshire	26
18	Wisconsin	54	49	Massachusetts	25
44	Wyoming	29	50	Delaware	18
				District of Columbia	29

Source: Morgan Quitno Corporation using data from Administrative Office of the United States Courts
"1993 Federal Court Management Statistics" (March 1994)
*National rate includes cases filed in U.S. territories. Does not include transfers from one district to another.

Median Length of Federal Criminal Cases in 1993

National Median = 6.3 Months*

<table>
<tr><td colspan="3"><u>ALPHA ORDER</u></td><td colspan="3"><u>RANK ORDER</u></td></tr>
<tr><td>RANK</td><td>STATE</td><td>MONTHS</td><td>RANK</td><td>STATE</td><td>MONTHS</td></tr>
<tr><td>46</td><td>Alabama</td><td>4.4</td><td>1</td><td>Vermont</td><td>11.8</td></tr>
<tr><td>37</td><td>Alaska</td><td>5.7</td><td>2</td><td>Massachusetts</td><td>9.9</td></tr>
<tr><td>24</td><td>Arizona</td><td>6.6</td><td>3</td><td>Hawaii</td><td>8.4</td></tr>
<tr><td>39</td><td>Arkansas</td><td>5.5</td><td>3</td><td>New Jersey</td><td>8.4</td></tr>
<tr><td>28</td><td>California</td><td>6.4</td><td>5</td><td>Nebraska</td><td>8.1</td></tr>
<tr><td>44</td><td>Colorado</td><td>5.1</td><td>5</td><td>South Carolina</td><td>8.1</td></tr>
<tr><td>30</td><td>Connecticut</td><td>6.3</td><td>7</td><td>Idaho</td><td>8.0</td></tr>
<tr><td>46</td><td>Delaware</td><td>4.4</td><td>7</td><td>Nevada</td><td>8.0</td></tr>
<tr><td>20</td><td>Florida</td><td>6.8</td><td>9</td><td>Georgia</td><td>7.9</td></tr>
<tr><td>9</td><td>Georgia</td><td>7.9</td><td>9</td><td>Tennessee</td><td>7.9</td></tr>
<tr><td>3</td><td>Hawaii</td><td>8.4</td><td>11</td><td>New York</td><td>7.8</td></tr>
<tr><td>7</td><td>Idaho</td><td>8.0</td><td>12</td><td>New Hampshire</td><td>7.5</td></tr>
<tr><td>15</td><td>Illinois</td><td>7.1</td><td>13</td><td>Michigan</td><td>7.4</td></tr>
<tr><td>31</td><td>Indiana</td><td>6.2</td><td>14</td><td>Maine</td><td>7.2</td></tr>
<tr><td>28</td><td>Iowa</td><td>6.4</td><td>15</td><td>Illinois</td><td>7.1</td></tr>
<tr><td>35</td><td>Kansas</td><td>5.9</td><td>15</td><td>Missouri</td><td>7.1</td></tr>
<tr><td>25</td><td>Kentucky</td><td>6.5</td><td>17</td><td>Maryland</td><td>7.0</td></tr>
<tr><td>42</td><td>Louisiana</td><td>5.4</td><td>17</td><td>North Carolina</td><td>7.0</td></tr>
<tr><td>14</td><td>Maine</td><td>7.2</td><td>17</td><td>Utah</td><td>7.0</td></tr>
<tr><td>17</td><td>Maryland</td><td>7.0</td><td>20</td><td>Florida</td><td>6.8</td></tr>
<tr><td>2</td><td>Massachusetts</td><td>9.9</td><td>20</td><td>Pennsylvania</td><td>6.8</td></tr>
<tr><td>13</td><td>Michigan</td><td>7.4</td><td>20</td><td>Rhode Island</td><td>6.8</td></tr>
<tr><td>33</td><td>Minnesota</td><td>6.0</td><td>23</td><td>Wyoming</td><td>6.7</td></tr>
<tr><td>39</td><td>Mississippi</td><td>5.5</td><td>24</td><td>Arizona</td><td>6.6</td></tr>
<tr><td>15</td><td>Missouri</td><td>7.1</td><td>25</td><td>Kentucky</td><td>6.5</td></tr>
<tr><td>43</td><td>Montana</td><td>5.3</td><td>25</td><td>Oregon</td><td>6.5</td></tr>
<tr><td>5</td><td>Nebraska</td><td>8.1</td><td>25</td><td>West Virginia</td><td>6.5</td></tr>
<tr><td>7</td><td>Nevada</td><td>8.0</td><td>28</td><td>California</td><td>6.4</td></tr>
<tr><td>12</td><td>New Hampshire</td><td>7.5</td><td>28</td><td>Iowa</td><td>6.4</td></tr>
<tr><td>3</td><td>New Jersey</td><td>8.4</td><td>30</td><td>Connecticut</td><td>6.3</td></tr>
<tr><td>31</td><td>New Mexico</td><td>6.2</td><td>31</td><td>Indiana</td><td>6.2</td></tr>
<tr><td>11</td><td>New York</td><td>7.8</td><td>31</td><td>New Mexico</td><td>6.2</td></tr>
<tr><td>17</td><td>North Carolina</td><td>7.0</td><td>33</td><td>Minnesota</td><td>6.0</td></tr>
<tr><td>49</td><td>North Dakota</td><td>4.0</td><td>33</td><td>Ohio</td><td>6.0</td></tr>
<tr><td>33</td><td>Ohio</td><td>6.0</td><td>35</td><td>Kansas</td><td>5.9</td></tr>
<tr><td>49</td><td>Oklahoma</td><td>4.0</td><td>36</td><td>Virginia</td><td>5.8</td></tr>
<tr><td>25</td><td>Oregon</td><td>6.5</td><td>37</td><td>Alaska</td><td>5.7</td></tr>
<tr><td>20</td><td>Pennsylvania</td><td>6.8</td><td>37</td><td>South Dakota</td><td>5.7</td></tr>
<tr><td>20</td><td>Rhode Island</td><td>6.8</td><td>39</td><td>Arkansas</td><td>5.5</td></tr>
<tr><td>5</td><td>South Carolina</td><td>8.1</td><td>39</td><td>Mississippi</td><td>5.5</td></tr>
<tr><td>37</td><td>South Dakota</td><td>5.7</td><td>39</td><td>Wisconsin</td><td>5.5</td></tr>
<tr><td>9</td><td>Tennessee</td><td>7.9</td><td>42</td><td>Louisiana</td><td>5.4</td></tr>
<tr><td>44</td><td>Texas</td><td>5.1</td><td>43</td><td>Montana</td><td>5.3</td></tr>
<tr><td>17</td><td>Utah</td><td>7.0</td><td>44</td><td>Colorado</td><td>5.1</td></tr>
<tr><td>1</td><td>Vermont</td><td>11.8</td><td>44</td><td>Texas</td><td>5.1</td></tr>
<tr><td>36</td><td>Virginia</td><td>5.8</td><td>46</td><td>Alabama</td><td>4.4</td></tr>
<tr><td>48</td><td>Washington</td><td>4.1</td><td>46</td><td>Delaware</td><td>4.4</td></tr>
<tr><td>25</td><td>West Virginia</td><td>6.5</td><td>48</td><td>Washington</td><td>4.1</td></tr>
<tr><td>39</td><td>Wisconsin</td><td>5.5</td><td>49</td><td>North Dakota</td><td>4.0</td></tr>
<tr><td>23</td><td>Wyoming</td><td>6.7</td><td>49</td><td>Oklahoma</td><td>4.0</td></tr>
<tr><td></td><td></td><td></td><td></td><td>District of Columbia</td><td>6.8</td></tr>
</table>

Source: Administrative Office of the United States Courts
  "1993 Federal Court Management Statistics" (March 1994)
*Felony criminal cases. National rate includes cases filed in U.S. territories. Does not include transfers from one district to another.

State and Local Justice System Employment in 1992

National Total = 1,551,884 Employees*

ALPHA ORDER

RANK	STATE	EMPLOYEES	% of USA
23	Alabama	20,322	1.31%
46	Alaska	4,040	0.26%
17	Arizona	27,770	1.79%
33	Arkansas	10,882	0.70%
1	California	184,196	11.87%
24	Colorado	20,081	1.29%
27	Connecticut	17,959	1.16%
44	Delaware	4,952	0.32%
4	Florida	106,017	6.83%
10	Georgia	44,539	2.87%
36	Hawaii	8,173	0.53%
41	Idaho	5,587	0.36%
5	Illinois	74,763	4.82%
18	Indiana	27,663	1.78%
31	Iowa	11,660	0.75%
30	Kansas	14,680	0.95%
26	Kentucky	18,787	1.21%
19	Louisiana	27,606	1.78%
42	Maine	5,544	0.36%
14	Maryland	31,582	2.04%
13	Massachusetts	32,372	2.09%
9	Michigan	51,043	3.29%
25	Minnesota	19,234	1.24%
32	Mississippi	11,631	0.75%
15	Missouri	28,664	1.85%
45	Montana	4,053	0.26%
38	Nebraska	8,005	0.52%
35	Nevada	10,030	0.65%
43	New Hampshire	5,324	0.34%
6	New Jersey	64,941	4.18%
34	New Mexico	10,240	0.66%
2	New York	154,357	9.95%
11	North Carolina	38,362	2.47%
49	North Dakota	2,715	0.17%
8	Ohio	60,467	3.90%
28	Oklahoma	17,265	1.11%
29	Oregon	15,483	1.00%
7	Pennsylvania	62,620	4.04%
40	Rhode Island	5,855	0.38%
22	South Carolina	20,505	1.32%
47	South Dakota	3,089	0.20%
16	Tennessee	27,810	1.79%
3	Texas	113,336	7.30%
37	Utah	8,166	0.53%
50	Vermont	2,479	0.16%
12	Virginia	34,794	2.24%
20	Washington	26,222	1.69%
39	West Virginia	6,062	0.39%
21	Wisconsin	24,985	1.61%
48	Wyoming	3,036	0.20%

RANK ORDER

RANK	STATE	EMPLOYEES	% of USA
1	California	184,196	11.87%
2	New York	154,357	9.95%
3	Texas	113,336	7.30%
4	Florida	106,017	6.83%
5	Illinois	74,763	4.82%
6	New Jersey	64,941	4.18%
7	Pennsylvania	62,620	4.04%
8	Ohio	60,467	3.90%
9	Michigan	51,043	3.29%
10	Georgia	44,539	2.87%
11	North Carolina	38,362	2.47%
12	Virginia	34,794	2.24%
13	Massachusetts	32,372	2.09%
14	Maryland	31,582	2.04%
15	Missouri	28,664	1.85%
16	Tennessee	27,810	1.79%
17	Arizona	27,770	1.79%
18	Indiana	27,663	1.78%
19	Louisiana	27,606	1.78%
20	Washington	26,222	1.69%
21	Wisconsin	24,985	1.61%
22	South Carolina	20,505	1.32%
23	Alabama	20,322	1.31%
24	Colorado	20,081	1.29%
25	Minnesota	19,234	1.24%
26	Kentucky	18,787	1.21%
27	Connecticut	17,959	1.16%
28	Oklahoma	17,265	1.11%
29	Oregon	15,483	1.00%
30	Kansas	14,680	0.95%
31	Iowa	11,660	0.75%
32	Mississippi	11,631	0.75%
33	Arkansas	10,882	0.70%
34	New Mexico	10,240	0.66%
35	Nevada	10,030	0.65%
36	Hawaii	8,173	0.53%
37	Utah	8,166	0.53%
38	Nebraska	8,005	0.52%
39	West Virginia	6,062	0.39%
40	Rhode Island	5,855	0.38%
41	Idaho	5,587	0.36%
42	Maine	5,544	0.36%
43	New Hampshire	5,324	0.34%
44	Delaware	4,952	0.32%
45	Montana	4,053	0.26%
46	Alaska	4,040	0.26%
47	South Dakota	3,089	0.20%
48	Wyoming	3,036	0.20%
49	North Dakota	2,715	0.17%
50	Vermont	2,479	0.16%
	District of Columbia	11,936	0.77%

Source: Morgan Quitno Corporation using data from U.S. Bureau of the Census
"Public Employment: 1992" (GE/92-1, September 1994)
*Full-time equivalent. Includes police, courts, prosecution, public defense and corrections.

Rate of State and Local Justice System Employees in 1992

National Rate = 60.8 Employees per 10,000 Population*

ALPHA ORDER			RANK ORDER		
RANK	STATE	RATE	RANK	STATE	RATE
37	Alabama	49.2	1	New York	85.2
8	Alaska	68.8	2	New Jersey	83.4
5	Arizona	72.5	3	Florida	78.6
41	Arkansas	45.4	4	Nevada	75.5
16	California	59.7	5	Arizona	72.5
19	Colorado	57.9	6	Delaware	71.8
25	Connecticut	54.7	7	Hawaii	70.5
6	Delaware	71.8	8	Alaska	68.8
3	Florida	78.6	9	Georgia	66.0
9	Georgia	66.0	10	Wyoming	65.1
7	Hawaii	70.5	11	New Mexico	64.7
30	Idaho	52.3	12	Louisiana	64.5
14	Illinois	64.3	13	Maryland	64.4
39	Indiana	48.8	14	Illinois	64.3
49	Iowa	41.5	15	Texas	64.2
17	Kansas	58.2	16	California	59.7
34	Kentucky	50.0	17	Kansas	58.2
12	Louisiana	64.5	17	Rhode Island	58.2
43	Maine	44.9	19	Colorado	57.9
13	Maryland	64.4	20	South Carolina	56.9
28	Massachusetts	54.0	21	North Carolina	56.1
27	Michigan	54.2	22	Tennessee	55.4
47	Minnesota	43.0	23	Missouri	55.3
44	Mississippi	44.5	24	Ohio	54.9
23	Missouri	55.3	25	Connecticut	54.7
37	Montana	49.2	26	Virginia	54.5
35	Nebraska	49.9	27	Michigan	54.2
4	Nevada	75.5	28	Massachusetts	54.0
40	New Hampshire	48.0	29	Oklahoma	53.8
2	New Jersey	83.4	30	Idaho	52.3
11	New Mexico	64.7	31	Pennsylvania	52.1
1	New York	85.2	32	Oregon	52.0
21	North Carolina	56.1	33	Washington	51.1
48	North Dakota	42.7	34	Kentucky	50.0
24	Ohio	54.9	35	Nebraska	49.9
29	Oklahoma	53.8	35	Wisconsin	49.9
32	Oregon	52.0	37	Alabama	49.2
31	Pennsylvania	52.1	37	Montana	49.2
17	Rhode Island	58.2	39	Indiana	48.8
20	South Carolina	56.9	40	New Hampshire	48.0
46	South Dakota	43.4	41	Arkansas	45.4
22	Tennessee	55.4	42	Utah	45.0
15	Texas	64.2	43	Maine	44.9
42	Utah	45.0	44	Mississippi	44.5
45	Vermont	43.5	45	Vermont	43.5
26	Virginia	54.5	46	South Dakota	43.4
33	Washington	51.1	47	Minnesota	43.0
50	West Virginia	33.5	48	North Dakota	42.7
35	Wisconsin	49.9	49	Iowa	41.5
10	Wyoming	65.1	50	West Virginia	33.5
				District of Columbia	202.6

Source: Morgan Quitno Corporation using data from U.S. Bureau of the Census
"Public Employment: 1992" (GE/92-1, September 1994)
*Full-time equivalent. Includes police, courts, prosecution, public defense and corrections.

State and Local Judicial and Legal System Employment in 1992

National Total = 303,607 Employees*

ALPHA ORDER

RANK	STATE	EMPLOYEES	% of USA
25	Alabama	3,874	1.28%
42	Alaska	1,170	0.39%
11	Arizona	6,467	2.13%
36	Arkansas	1,703	0.56%
1	California	37,875	12.48%
22	Colorado	4,441	1.46%
27	Connecticut	3,292	1.08%
40	Delaware	1,331	0.44%
3	Florida	18,915	6.23%
10	Georgia	7,063	2.33%
32	Hawaii	2,711	0.89%
41	Idaho	1,197	0.39%
8	Illinois	14,474	4.77%
19	Indiana	5,035	1.66%
31	Iowa	2,805	0.92%
28	Kansas	2,903	0.96%
24	Kentucky	4,327	1.43%
16	Louisiana	5,553	1.83%
47	Maine	740	0.24%
12	Maryland	6,041	1.99%
14	Massachusetts	5,637	1.86%
9	Michigan	10,350	3.41%
23	Minnesota	4,335	1.43%
33	Mississippi	2,123	0.70%
18	Missouri	5,174	1.70%
45	Montana	783	0.26%
39	Nebraska	1,519	0.50%
34	Nevada	2,090	0.69%
44	New Hampshire	917	0.30%
6	New Jersey	15,880	5.23%
35	New Mexico	1,961	0.65%
2	New York	27,514	9.06%
15	North Carolina	5,601	1.84%
48	North Dakota	704	0.23%
5	Ohio	16,114	5.31%
30	Oklahoma	2,820	0.93%
26	Oregon	3,489	1.15%
7	Pennsylvania	15,064	4.96%
43	Rhode Island	1,030	0.34%
29	South Carolina	2,854	0.94%
46	South Dakota	747	0.25%
20	Tennessee	4,668	1.54%
4	Texas	18,202	6.00%
38	Utah	1,618	0.53%
50	Vermont	540	0.18%
17	Virginia	5,411	1.78%
13	Washington	5,834	1.92%
37	West Virginia	1,628	0.54%
21	Wisconsin	4,601	1.52%
49	Wyoming	690	0.23%

RANK ORDER

RANK	STATE	EMPLOYEES	% of USA
1	California	37,875	12.48%
2	New York	27,514	9.06%
3	Florida	18,915	6.23%
4	Texas	18,202	6.00%
5	Ohio	16,114	5.31%
6	New Jersey	15,880	5.23%
7	Pennsylvania	15,064	4.96%
8	Illinois	14,474	4.77%
9	Michigan	10,350	3.41%
10	Georgia	7,063	2.33%
11	Arizona	6,467	2.13%
12	Maryland	6,041	1.99%
13	Washington	5,834	1.92%
14	Massachusetts	5,637	1.86%
15	North Carolina	5,601	1.84%
16	Louisiana	5,553	1.83%
17	Virginia	5,411	1.78%
18	Missouri	5,174	1.70%
19	Indiana	5,035	1.66%
20	Tennessee	4,668	1.54%
21	Wisconsin	4,601	1.52%
22	Colorado	4,441	1.46%
23	Minnesota	4,335	1.43%
24	Kentucky	4,327	1.43%
25	Alabama	3,874	1.28%
26	Oregon	3,489	1.15%
27	Connecticut	3,292	1.08%
28	Kansas	2,903	0.96%
29	South Carolina	2,854	0.94%
30	Oklahoma	2,820	0.93%
31	Iowa	2,805	0.92%
32	Hawaii	2,711	0.89%
33	Mississippi	2,123	0.70%
34	Nevada	2,090	0.69%
35	New Mexico	1,961	0.65%
36	Arkansas	1,703	0.56%
37	West Virginia	1,628	0.54%
38	Utah	1,618	0.53%
39	Nebraska	1,519	0.50%
40	Delaware	1,331	0.44%
41	Idaho	1,197	0.39%
42	Alaska	1,170	0.39%
43	Rhode Island	1,030	0.34%
44	New Hampshire	917	0.30%
45	Montana	783	0.26%
46	South Dakota	747	0.25%
47	Maine	740	0.24%
48	North Dakota	704	0.23%
49	Wyoming	690	0.23%
50	Vermont	540	0.18%
	District of Columbia	1,792	0.59%

Source: U.S. Bureau of the Census
"Public Employment: 1992" (GE/92-1, September 1994)
*Full-time equivalent. Includes courts, prosecution and public defense.

Rate of State and Local Judicial and Legal System Employment in 1992

National Rate = 11.9 Employees per 10,000 Population*

ALPHA ORDER

RANK	STATE	RATE
36	Alabama	9.4
3	Alaska	19.9
5	Arizona	16.9
49	Arkansas	7.1
16	California	12.3
12	Colorado	12.8
29	Connecticut	10.0
4	Delaware	19.3
10	Florida	14.0
25	Georgia	10.5
1	Hawaii	23.4
22	Idaho	11.2
14	Illinois	12.4
41	Indiana	8.9
29	Iowa	10.0
19	Kansas	11.5
19	Kentucky	11.5
11	Louisiana	13.0
50	Maine	6.0
16	Maryland	12.3
36	Massachusetts	9.4
24	Michigan	11.0
32	Minnesota	9.7
47	Mississippi	8.1
29	Missouri	10.0
33	Montana	9.5
33	Nebraska	9.5
6	Nevada	15.7
45	New Hampshire	8.3
2	New Jersey	20.4
14	New Mexico	12.4
7	New York	15.2
46	North Carolina	8.2
23	North Dakota	11.1
9	Ohio	14.6
43	Oklahoma	8.8
18	Oregon	11.7
13	Pennsylvania	12.5
28	Rhode Island	10.2
48	South Carolina	7.9
25	South Dakota	10.5
38	Tennessee	9.3
27	Texas	10.3
41	Utah	8.9
33	Vermont	9.5
44	Virginia	8.5
21	Washington	11.4
40	West Virginia	9.0
39	Wisconsin	9.2
8	Wyoming	14.8

RANK ORDER

RANK	STATE	RATE
1	Hawaii	23.4
2	New Jersey	20.4
3	Alaska	19.9
4	Delaware	19.3
5	Arizona	16.9
6	Nevada	15.7
7	New York	15.2
8	Wyoming	14.8
9	Ohio	14.6
10	Florida	14.0
11	Louisiana	13.0
12	Colorado	12.8
13	Pennsylvania	12.5
14	Illinois	12.4
14	New Mexico	12.4
16	California	12.3
16	Maryland	12.3
18	Oregon	11.7
19	Kansas	11.5
19	Kentucky	11.5
21	Washington	11.4
22	Idaho	11.2
23	North Dakota	11.1
24	Michigan	11.0
25	Georgia	10.5
25	South Dakota	10.5
27	Texas	10.3
28	Rhode Island	10.2
29	Connecticut	10.0
29	Iowa	10.0
29	Missouri	10.0
32	Minnesota	9.7
33	Montana	9.5
33	Nebraska	9.5
33	Vermont	9.5
36	Alabama	9.4
36	Massachusetts	9.4
38	Tennessee	9.3
39	Wisconsin	9.2
40	West Virginia	9.0
41	Indiana	8.9
41	Utah	8.9
43	Oklahoma	8.8
44	Virginia	8.5
45	New Hampshire	8.3
46	North Carolina	8.2
47	Mississippi	8.1
48	South Carolina	7.9
49	Arkansas	7.1
50	Maine	6.0

District of Columbia	30.4

Source: U.S. Bureau of the Census
   "Public Employment: 1992" (GE/92-1, September 1994)
*Full-time equivalent. Includes courts, prosecution and public defense.

Authorized Wiretaps: 1991 Through 1993

National Total = 1,605 Authorized Wiretaps*

ALPHA ORDER

RANK	STATE	WIRETAPS	% of USA
NA	Alabama**	NA	NA
NA	Alaska**	NA	NA
10	Arizona	21	1.31%
NA	Arkansas**	NA	NA
18	California	6	0.37%
16	Colorado	9	0.56%
7	Connecticut	31	1.93%
22	Delaware	3	0.19%
4	Florida	195	12.15%
6	Georgia	43	2.68%
30	Hawaii	0	0.00%
30	Idaho	0	0.00%
30	Illinois	0	0.00%
22	Indiana	3	0.19%
30	Iowa	0	0.00%
13	Kansas	10	0.62%
NA	Kentucky**	NA	NA
29	Louisiana	1	0.06%
NA	Maine**	NA	NA
5	Maryland	58	3.61%
8	Massachusetts	27	1.68%
NA	Michigan**	NA	NA
13	Minnesota	10	0.62%
26	Mississippi	2	0.12%
30	Missouri	0	0.00%
NA	Montana**	NA	NA
13	Nebraska	10	0.62%
11	Nevada	20	1.25%
26	New Hampshire	2	0.12%
2	New Jersey	330	20.56%
17	New Mexico	8	0.50%
1	New York	537	33.46%
NA	North Carolina**	NA	NA
30	North Dakota	0	0.00%
30	Ohio	0	0.00%
20	Oklahoma	5	0.31%
26	Oregon	2	0.12%
3	Pennsylvania	214	13.33%
18	Rhode Island	6	0.37%
NA	South Carolina**	NA	NA
30	South Dakota	0	0.00%
NA	Tennessee**	NA	NA
9	Texas	24	1.50%
12	Utah	18	1.12%
NA	Vermont**	NA	NA
21	Virginia	4	0.25%
NA	Washington**	NA	NA
NA	West Virginia**	NA	NA
22	Wisconsin	3	0.19%
22	Wyoming	3	0.19%

RANK ORDER

RANK	STATE	WIRETAPS	% of USA
1	New York	537	33.46%
2	New Jersey	330	20.56%
3	Pennsylvania	214	13.33%
4	Florida	195	12.15%
5	Maryland	58	3.61%
6	Georgia	43	2.68%
7	Connecticut	31	1.93%
8	Massachusetts	27	1.68%
9	Texas	24	1.50%
10	Arizona	21	1.31%
11	Nevada	20	1.25%
12	Utah	18	1.12%
13	Kansas	10	0.62%
13	Minnesota	10	0.62%
13	Nebraska	10	0.62%
16	Colorado	9	0.56%
17	New Mexico	8	0.50%
18	California	6	0.37%
18	Rhode Island	6	0.37%
20	Oklahoma	5	0.31%
21	Virginia	4	0.25%
22	Delaware	3	0.19%
22	Indiana	3	0.19%
22	Wisconsin	3	0.19%
22	Wyoming	3	0.19%
26	Mississippi	2	0.12%
26	New Hampshire	2	0.12%
26	Oregon	2	0.12%
29	Louisiana	1	0.06%
30	Hawaii	0	0.00%
30	Idaho	0	0.00%
30	Illinois	0	0.00%
30	Iowa	0	0.00%
30	Missouri	0	0.00%
30	North Dakota	0	0.00%
30	Ohio	0	0.00%
30	South Dakota	0	0.00%
NA	Alabama**	NA	NA
NA	Alaska**	NA	NA
NA	Arkansas**	NA	NA
NA	Kentucky**	NA	NA
NA	Maine**	NA	NA
NA	Michigan**	NA	NA
NA	Montana**	NA	NA
NA	North Carolina**	NA	NA
NA	South Carolina**	NA	NA
NA	Tennessee**	NA	NA
NA	Vermont**	NA	NA
NA	Washington**	NA	NA
NA	West Virginia**	NA	NA
	District of Columbia	0	0.00%

Source: Administrative Office of the United States Courts
"Wiretap Reports 1991, 1992 and 1993"
Total does not include 1,046 wiretaps authorized under federal statute.
**No statute authorizing wiretaps.*

VI. OFFENSES

VI. OFFENSES (continued)

Urban/Rural Crime

VI. OFFENSES (continued)

390 Urban Robbery Rate in 1993
391 Percent of Robberies Occurring in Urban Areas in 1993
392 Robbery in Rural Areas in 1993
393 Rural Robbery Rate in 1993
394 Percent of Robberies Occurring in Rural Areas in 1993
395 Aggravated Assault in Urban Areas in 1993
396 Urban Aggravated Assault Rate in 1993
397 Percent of Aggravated Assaults Occurring in Urban Areas in 1993
398 Aggravated Assault in Rural Areas in 1993
399 Rural Aggravated Assault Rate in 1993
400 Percent of Aggravated Assaults Occurring in Rural Areas in 1993
401 Property Crime in Urban Areas in 1993
402 Urban Property Crime Rate in 1993
403 Percent of Property Crimes Occurring in Urban Areas in 1993
404 Property Crime in Rural Areas in 1993
405 Rural Property Crime Rate in 1993
406 Percent of Property Crime Occurring in Rural Areas in 1993
407 Burglary in Urban Areas in 1993
408 Urban Burglary Rate in 1993
409 Percent of Burglaries Occurring in Urban Areas in 1993
410 Burglary in Rural Areas in 1993
411 Rural Burglary Rate in 1993
412 Percent of Burglaries Occurring in Rural Areas in 1993
413 Larceny and Theft in Urban Areas in 1993
414 Urban Larceny and Theft Rate in 1993
415 Percent of Larcenies and Thefts Occurring in Urban Areas in 1993
416 Larceny and Theft in Rural Areas in 1993
417 Rural Larceny and Theft Rate in 1993
418 Percent of Larcenies and Thefts Occurring in Rural Areas in 1993
419 Motor Vehicle Theft in Urban Areas in 1993
420 Urban Motor Vehicle Theft Rate in 1993
421 Percent of Motor Vehicle Thefts Occurring in Urban Areas in 1993
422 Motor Vehicle Theft in Rural Areas in 1993
423 Rural Motor Vehicle Theft Rate in 1993
424 Percent of Motor Vehicle Thefts Occurring in Rural Areas in 1993
425 Crimes Reported at Universities and Colleges in 1993
426 Crimes Reported at Universities and Colleges as a Percent of All Crimes in 1993
427 Violent Crimes Reported at Universities and Colleges in 1993
428 Violent Crimes Reported at Universities and Colleges As a Percent of All Violent Crimes in 1993
429 Property Crimes Reported at Universities and Colleges in 1993
430 Property Crimes Reported at Universities and Colleges As a Percent of All Property Crimes in 1993

1989 Crimes

431 Crimes in 1989
432 Percent Change in Number of Crimes: 1989 to 1993
433 Crime Rate in 1989
434 Percent Change in Crime Rate: 1989 to 1993
435 Violent Crimes in 1989
436 Percent Change in Number of Violent Crimes: 1989 to 1993
437 Violent Crime Rate in 1989
438 Percent Change in Violent Crime Rate: 1989 to 1993
439 Murders in 1989
440 Percent Change in Number of Murders: 1989 to 1993
441 Murder Rate in 1989
442 Percent Change in Murder Rate: 1989 to 1993
443 Rapes in 1989
444 Percent Change in Number of Rapes: 1989 to 1993
445 Rape Rate in 1989

VI. OFFENSES (continued)

Crimes in 1993

National Total = 14,140,952 Crimes*

ALPHA ORDER

RANK	STATE	CRIMES	% of USA
22	Alabama	204,274	1.44%
45	Alaska	33,352	0.24%
16	Arizona	292,513	2.07%
32	Arkansas	116,612	0.82%
1	California	2,015,265	14.25%
25	Colorado	197,085	1.39%
28	Connecticut	152,392	1.08%
44	Delaware	34,105	0.24%
3	Florida	1,142,338	8.08%
8	Georgia	428,367	3.03%
37	Hawaii	73,566	0.52%
41	Idaho	42,258	0.30%
5	Illinois	657,129	4.65%
20	Indiana	255,090	1.80%
33	Iowa	108,239	0.77%
29	Kansas	125,924	0.89%
30	Kentucky	123,509	0.87%
15	Louisiana	294,061	2.08%
43	Maine	39,077	0.28%
13	Maryland	303,187	2.14%
14	Massachusetts	294,224	2.08%
6	Michigan	516,788	3.65%
24	Minnesota	198,125	1.40%
31	Mississippi	116,775	0.83%
19	Missouri	266,694	1.89%
42	Montana	40,188	0.28%
38	Nebraska	66,162	0.47%
36	Nevada	85,842	0.61%
46	New Hampshire	32,681	0.23%
11	New Jersey	378,257	2.67%
34	New Mexico	101,260	0.72%
4	New York	1,010,176	7.14%
10	North Carolina	392,555	2.78%
50	North Dakota	17,909	0.13%
7	Ohio	497,465	3.52%
27	Oklahoma	171,058	1.21%
26	Oregon	174,812	1.24%
9	Pennsylvania	394,136	2.79%
40	Rhode Island	44,990	0.32%
21	South Carolina	215,060	1.52%
48	South Dakota	21,151	0.15%
17	Tennessee	267,164	1.89%
2	Texas	1,161,031	8.21%
35	Utah	97,415	0.69%
47	Vermont	22,881	0.16%
18	Virginia	267,135	1.89%
12	Washington	312,793	2.21%
39	West Virginia	46,093	0.33%
23	Wisconsin	204,244	1.44%
49	Wyoming	19,566	0.14%

RANK ORDER

RANK	STATE	CRIMES	% of USA
1	California	2,015,265	14.25%
2	Texas	1,161,031	8.21%
3	Florida	1,142,338	8.08%
4	New York	1,010,176	7.14%
5	Illinois	657,129	4.65%
6	Michigan	516,788	3.65%
7	Ohio	497,465	3.52%
8	Georgia	428,367	3.03%
9	Pennsylvania	394,136	2.79%
10	North Carolina	392,555	2.78%
11	New Jersey	378,257	2.67%
12	Washington	312,793	2.21%
13	Maryland	303,187	2.14%
14	Massachusetts	294,224	2.08%
15	Louisiana	294,061	2.08%
16	Arizona	292,513	2.07%
17	Tennessee	267,164	1.89%
18	Virginia	267,135	1.89%
19	Missouri	266,694	1.89%
20	Indiana	255,090	1.80%
21	South Carolina	215,060	1.52%
22	Alabama	204,274	1.44%
23	Wisconsin	204,244	1.44%
24	Minnesota	198,125	1.40%
25	Colorado	197,085	1.39%
26	Oregon	174,812	1.24%
27	Oklahoma	171,058	1.21%
28	Connecticut	152,392	1.08%
29	Kansas	125,924	0.89%
30	Kentucky	123,509	0.87%
31	Mississippi	116,775	0.83%
32	Arkansas	116,612	0.82%
33	Iowa	108,239	0.77%
34	New Mexico	101,260	0.72%
35	Utah	97,415	0.69%
36	Nevada	85,842	0.61%
37	Hawaii	73,566	0.52%
38	Nebraska	66,162	0.47%
39	West Virginia	46,093	0.33%
40	Rhode Island	44,990	0.32%
41	Idaho	42,258	0.30%
42	Montana	40,188	0.28%
43	Maine	39,077	0.28%
44	Delaware	34,105	0.24%
45	Alaska	33,352	0.24%
46	New Hampshire	32,681	0.23%
47	Vermont	22,881	0.16%
48	South Dakota	21,151	0.15%
49	Wyoming	19,566	0.14%
50	North Dakota	17,909	0.13%
	District of Columbia	67,979	0.48%

Source: U.S. Department of Justice, Federal Bureau of Investigation
    "Crime in the United States 1993" (Uniform Crime Reports, December 4, 1994)
*Includes murder, rape, robbery, aggravated assault, burglary, larceny-theft and motor vehicle theft.

Average Time Between Crimes in 1993

National Rate = A Crime Occurs Every 2 Seconds*

ALPHA ORDER			RANK ORDER		

RANK	STATE	MINUTES.SECONDS	RANK	STATE	MINUTES.SECONDS
28	Alabama	2.34	1	North Dakota	29.21
6	Alaska	15.46	2	Wyoming	26.52
35	Arizona	1.48	3	South Dakota	24.51
19	Arkansas	4.31	4	Vermont	22.58
50	California	0.16	5	New Hampshire	16.05
26	Colorado	2.40	6	Alaska	15.46
23	Connecticut	3.27	7	Delaware	15.25
7	Delaware	15.25	8	Maine	13.27
48	Florida	0.28	9	Montana	13.05
43	Georgia	1.14	10	Idaho	12.26
14	Hawaii	7.08	11	Rhode Island	11.41
10	Idaho	12.26	12	West Virginia	11.24
46	Illinois	0.48	13	Nebraska	7.56
31	Indiana	2.04	14	Hawaii	7.08
18	Iowa	4.52	15	Nevada	6.07
22	Kansas	4.10	16	Utah	5.24
21	Kentucky	4.16	17	New Mexico	5.11
36	Louisiana	1.47	18	Iowa	4.52
8	Maine	13.27	19	Arkansas	4.31
38	Maryland	1.44	20	Mississippi	4.30
36	Massachusetts	1.47	21	Kentucky	4.16
45	Michigan	1.01	22	Kansas	4.10
27	Minnesota	2.39	23	Connecticut	3.27
20	Mississippi	4.30	24	Oklahoma	3.04
32	Missouri	1.58	25	Oregon	3.01
9	Montana	13.05	26	Colorado	2.40
13	Nebraska	7.56	27	Minnesota	2.39
15	Nevada	6.07	28	Alabama	2.34
5	New Hampshire	16.05	28	Wisconsin	2.34
40	New Jersey	1.23	30	South Carolina	2.26
17	New Mexico	5.11	31	Indiana	2.04
47	New York	0.31	32	Missouri	1.58
41	North Carolina	1.20	32	Tennessee	1.58
1	North Dakota	29.21	32	Virginia	1.58
44	Ohio	1.04	35	Arizona	1.48
24	Oklahoma	3.04	36	Louisiana	1.47
25	Oregon	3.01	36	Massachusetts	1.47
41	Pennsylvania	1.20	38	Maryland	1.44
11	Rhode Island	11.41	39	Washington	1.41
30	South Carolina	2.26	40	New Jersey	1.23
3	South Dakota	24.51	41	North Carolina	1.20
32	Tennessee	1.58	41	Pennsylvania	1.20
49	Texas	0.27	43	Georgia	1.14
16	Utah	5.24	44	Ohio	1.04
4	Vermont	22.58	45	Michigan	1.01
32	Virginia	1.58	46	Illinois	0.48
39	Washington	1.41	47	New York	0.31
12	West Virginia	11.24	48	Florida	0.28
28	Wisconsin	2.34	49	Texas	0.27
2	Wyoming	26.52	50	California	0.16

District of Columbia 7.44

Source: Morgan Quitno Corporation using data from U.S. Department of Justice, Federal Bureau of Investigation
"Crime in the United States 1993" (Uniform Crime Reports, December 4, 1994)
*Includes murder, rape, robbery, aggravated assault, burglary, larceny-theft and motor vehicle theft.

Crimes per Square Mile in 1993

National Rate = 3.73 Crimes per Square Mile*

<table>
<tr><td colspan="3"><u>ALPHA ORDER</u></td><td colspan="3"><u>RANK ORDER</u></td></tr>
<tr><th>RANK</th><th>STATE</th><th>RATE</th><th>RANK</th><th>STATE</th><th>RATE</th></tr>
<tr><td>24</td><td>Alabama</td><td>3.90</td><td>1</td><td>New Jersey</td><td>43.37</td></tr>
<tr><td>50</td><td>Alaska</td><td>0.05</td><td>2</td><td>Rhode Island</td><td>29.12</td></tr>
<tr><td>29</td><td>Arizona</td><td>2.57</td><td>3</td><td>Massachusetts</td><td>27.88</td></tr>
<tr><td>34</td><td>Arkansas</td><td>2.19</td><td>4</td><td>Connecticut</td><td>27.49</td></tr>
<tr><td>9</td><td>California</td><td>12.31</td><td>5</td><td>Maryland</td><td>24.44</td></tr>
<tr><td>37</td><td>Colorado</td><td>1.89</td><td>6</td><td>New York</td><td>18.52</td></tr>
<tr><td>4</td><td>Connecticut</td><td>27.49</td><td>7</td><td>Florida</td><td>17.37</td></tr>
<tr><td>8</td><td>Delaware</td><td>13.70</td><td>8</td><td>Delaware</td><td>13.70</td></tr>
<tr><td>7</td><td>Florida</td><td>17.37</td><td>9</td><td>California</td><td>12.31</td></tr>
<tr><td>14</td><td>Georgia</td><td>7.21</td><td>10</td><td>Illinois</td><td>11.35</td></tr>
<tr><td>16</td><td>Hawaii</td><td>6.73</td><td>11</td><td>Ohio</td><td>11.10</td></tr>
<tr><td>45</td><td>Idaho</td><td>0.51</td><td>12</td><td>Pennsylvania</td><td>8.56</td></tr>
<tr><td>10</td><td>Illinois</td><td>11.35</td><td>13</td><td>North Carolina</td><td>7.29</td></tr>
<tr><td>15</td><td>Indiana</td><td>7.00</td><td>14</td><td>Georgia</td><td>7.21</td></tr>
<tr><td>35</td><td>Iowa</td><td>1.92</td><td>15</td><td>Indiana</td><td>7.00</td></tr>
<tr><td>39</td><td>Kansas</td><td>1.53</td><td>16</td><td>Hawaii</td><td>6.73</td></tr>
<tr><td>28</td><td>Kentucky</td><td>3.06</td><td>17</td><td>South Carolina</td><td>6.72</td></tr>
<tr><td>20</td><td>Louisiana</td><td>5.67</td><td>18</td><td>Tennessee</td><td>6.34</td></tr>
<tr><td>41</td><td>Maine</td><td>1.10</td><td>19</td><td>Virginia</td><td>6.24</td></tr>
<tr><td>5</td><td>Maryland</td><td>24.44</td><td>20</td><td>Louisiana</td><td>5.67</td></tr>
<tr><td>3</td><td>Massachusetts</td><td>27.88</td><td>21</td><td>Michigan</td><td>5.34</td></tr>
<tr><td>21</td><td>Michigan</td><td>5.34</td><td>22</td><td>Washington</td><td>4.39</td></tr>
<tr><td>33</td><td>Minnesota</td><td>2.28</td><td>23</td><td>Texas</td><td>4.32</td></tr>
<tr><td>31</td><td>Mississippi</td><td>2.41</td><td>24</td><td>Alabama</td><td>3.90</td></tr>
<tr><td>25</td><td>Missouri</td><td>3.83</td><td>25</td><td>Missouri</td><td>3.83</td></tr>
<tr><td>46</td><td>Montana</td><td>0.27</td><td>26</td><td>New Hampshire</td><td>3.49</td></tr>
<tr><td>42</td><td>Nebraska</td><td>0.86</td><td>27</td><td>Wisconsin</td><td>3.12</td></tr>
<tr><td>44</td><td>Nevada</td><td>0.78</td><td>28</td><td>Kentucky</td><td>3.06</td></tr>
<tr><td>26</td><td>New Hampshire</td><td>3.49</td><td>29</td><td>Arizona</td><td>2.57</td></tr>
<tr><td>1</td><td>New Jersey</td><td>43.37</td><td>30</td><td>Oklahoma</td><td>2.45</td></tr>
<tr><td>43</td><td>New Mexico</td><td>0.83</td><td>31</td><td>Mississippi</td><td>2.41</td></tr>
<tr><td>6</td><td>New York</td><td>18.52</td><td>32</td><td>Vermont</td><td>2.38</td></tr>
<tr><td>13</td><td>North Carolina</td><td>7.29</td><td>33</td><td>Minnesota</td><td>2.28</td></tr>
<tr><td>48</td><td>North Dakota</td><td>0.25</td><td>34</td><td>Arkansas</td><td>2.19</td></tr>
<tr><td>11</td><td>Ohio</td><td>11.10</td><td>35</td><td>Iowa</td><td>1.92</td></tr>
<tr><td>30</td><td>Oklahoma</td><td>2.45</td><td>36</td><td>West Virginia</td><td>1.90</td></tr>
<tr><td>38</td><td>Oregon</td><td>1.78</td><td>37</td><td>Colorado</td><td>1.89</td></tr>
<tr><td>12</td><td>Pennsylvania</td><td>8.56</td><td>38</td><td>Oregon</td><td>1.78</td></tr>
<tr><td>2</td><td>Rhode Island</td><td>29.12</td><td>39</td><td>Kansas</td><td>1.53</td></tr>
<tr><td>17</td><td>South Carolina</td><td>6.72</td><td>40</td><td>Utah</td><td>1.15</td></tr>
<tr><td>46</td><td>South Dakota</td><td>0.27</td><td>41</td><td>Maine</td><td>1.10</td></tr>
<tr><td>18</td><td>Tennessee</td><td>6.34</td><td>42</td><td>Nebraska</td><td>0.86</td></tr>
<tr><td>23</td><td>Texas</td><td>4.32</td><td>43</td><td>New Mexico</td><td>0.83</td></tr>
<tr><td>40</td><td>Utah</td><td>1.15</td><td>44</td><td>Nevada</td><td>0.78</td></tr>
<tr><td>32</td><td>Vermont</td><td>2.38</td><td>45</td><td>Idaho</td><td>0.51</td></tr>
<tr><td>19</td><td>Virginia</td><td>6.24</td><td>46</td><td>Montana</td><td>0.27</td></tr>
<tr><td>22</td><td>Washington</td><td>4.39</td><td>46</td><td>South Dakota</td><td>0.27</td></tr>
<tr><td>36</td><td>West Virginia</td><td>1.90</td><td>48</td><td>North Dakota</td><td>0.25</td></tr>
<tr><td>27</td><td>Wisconsin</td><td>3.12</td><td>49</td><td>Wyoming</td><td>0.20</td></tr>
<tr><td>49</td><td>Wyoming</td><td>0.20</td><td>50</td><td>Alaska</td><td>0.05</td></tr>
<tr><td></td><td></td><td></td><td></td><td>District of Columbia</td><td>999.69</td></tr>
</table>

Source: Morgan Quitno Corporation using data from U.S. Department of Justice, Federal Bureau of Investigation
"Crime in the United States 1993" (Uniform Crime Reports, December 4, 1994)
*Includes murder, rape, robbery, aggravated assault, burglary, larceny–theft and motor vehicle theft.

Percent Change in Number of Crimes: 1992 to 1993

National Percent Change = 2.1% Decrease*

<table>
<tr><td colspan="3"><u>ALPHA ORDER</u></td><td colspan="3"><u>RANK ORDER</u></td></tr>
<tr><td>RANK</td><td>STATE</td><td>PERCENT CHANGE</td><td>RANK</td><td>STATE</td><td>PERCENT CHANGE</td></tr>
<tr><td>43</td><td>Alabama</td><td>(6.2)</td><td>1</td><td>Vermont</td><td>17.7</td></tr>
<tr><td>11</td><td>Alaska</td><td>2.0</td><td>2</td><td>Arizona</td><td>8.6</td></tr>
<tr><td>2</td><td>Arizona</td><td>8.6</td><td>3</td><td>Montana</td><td>6.1</td></tr>
<tr><td>9</td><td>Arkansas</td><td>2.1</td><td>4</td><td>Louisiana</td><td>4.8</td></tr>
<tr><td>28</td><td>California</td><td>(2.3)</td><td>5</td><td>Mississippi</td><td>4.3</td></tr>
<tr><td>38</td><td>Colorado</td><td>(4.7)</td><td>5</td><td>Nevada</td><td>4.3</td></tr>
<tr><td>46</td><td>Connecticut</td><td>(8.1)</td><td>7</td><td>Hawaii</td><td>3.8</td></tr>
<tr><td>9</td><td>Delaware</td><td>2.1</td><td>8</td><td>Tennessee</td><td>3.5</td></tr>
<tr><td>12</td><td>Florida</td><td>1.3</td><td>9</td><td>Arkansas</td><td>2.1</td></tr>
<tr><td>19</td><td>Georgia</td><td>(0.9)</td><td>9</td><td>Delaware</td><td>2.1</td></tr>
<tr><td>7</td><td>Hawaii</td><td>3.8</td><td>11</td><td>Alaska</td><td>2.0</td></tr>
<tr><td>19</td><td>Idaho</td><td>(0.9)</td><td>12</td><td>Florida</td><td>1.3</td></tr>
<tr><td>25</td><td>Illinois</td><td>(2.0)</td><td>12</td><td>South Carolina</td><td>1.3</td></tr>
<tr><td>35</td><td>Indiana</td><td>(3.9)</td><td>14</td><td>Oregon</td><td>0.9</td></tr>
<tr><td>31</td><td>Iowa</td><td>(2.7)</td><td>15</td><td>Missouri</td><td>0.8</td></tr>
<tr><td>43</td><td>Kansas</td><td>(6.2)</td><td>16</td><td>New Mexico</td><td>(0.5)</td></tr>
<tr><td>21</td><td>Kentucky</td><td>(1.0)</td><td>17</td><td>Maryland</td><td>(0.8)</td></tr>
<tr><td>4</td><td>Louisiana</td><td>4.8</td><td>17</td><td>South Dakota</td><td>(0.8)</td></tr>
<tr><td>48</td><td>Maine</td><td>(10.2)</td><td>19</td><td>Georgia</td><td>(0.9)</td></tr>
<tr><td>17</td><td>Maryland</td><td>(0.8)</td><td>19</td><td>Idaho</td><td>(0.9)</td></tr>
<tr><td>24</td><td>Massachusetts</td><td>(1.9)</td><td>21</td><td>Kentucky</td><td>(1.0)</td></tr>
<tr><td>NA</td><td>Michigan**</td><td>NA</td><td>22</td><td>North Carolina</td><td>(1.1)</td></tr>
<tr><td>NA</td><td>Minnesota**</td><td>NA</td><td>23</td><td>Washington</td><td>(1.3)</td></tr>
<tr><td>5</td><td>Mississippi</td><td>4.3</td><td>24</td><td>Massachusetts</td><td>(1.9)</td></tr>
<tr><td>15</td><td>Missouri</td><td>0.8</td><td>25</td><td>Illinois</td><td>(2.0)</td></tr>
<tr><td>3</td><td>Montana</td><td>6.1</td><td>25</td><td>Oklahoma</td><td>(2.0)</td></tr>
<tr><td>38</td><td>Nebraska</td><td>(4.7)</td><td>27</td><td>Rhode Island</td><td>(2.2)</td></tr>
<tr><td>5</td><td>Nevada</td><td>4.3</td><td>28</td><td>California</td><td>(2.3)</td></tr>
<tr><td>37</td><td>New Hampshire</td><td>(4.5)</td><td>29</td><td>Virginia</td><td>(2.5)</td></tr>
<tr><td>36</td><td>New Jersey</td><td>(4.1)</td><td>29</td><td>West Virginia</td><td>(2.5)</td></tr>
<tr><td>16</td><td>New Mexico</td><td>(0.5)</td><td>31</td><td>Iowa</td><td>(2.7)</td></tr>
<tr><td>40</td><td>New York</td><td>(4.8)</td><td>32</td><td>North Dakota</td><td>(3.0)</td></tr>
<tr><td>22</td><td>North Carolina</td><td>(1.1)</td><td>33</td><td>Ohio</td><td>(3.2)</td></tr>
<tr><td>32</td><td>North Dakota</td><td>(3.0)</td><td>34</td><td>Pennsylvania</td><td>(3.3)</td></tr>
<tr><td>33</td><td>Ohio</td><td>(3.2)</td><td>35</td><td>Indiana</td><td>(3.9)</td></tr>
<tr><td>25</td><td>Oklahoma</td><td>(2.0)</td><td>36</td><td>New Jersey</td><td>(4.1)</td></tr>
<tr><td>14</td><td>Oregon</td><td>0.9</td><td>37</td><td>New Hampshire</td><td>(4.5)</td></tr>
<tr><td>34</td><td>Pennsylvania</td><td>(3.3)</td><td>38</td><td>Colorado</td><td>(4.7)</td></tr>
<tr><td>27</td><td>Rhode Island</td><td>(2.2)</td><td>38</td><td>Nebraska</td><td>(4.7)</td></tr>
<tr><td>12</td><td>South Carolina</td><td>1.3</td><td>40</td><td>New York</td><td>(4.8)</td></tr>
<tr><td>17</td><td>South Dakota</td><td>(0.8)</td><td>41</td><td>Utah</td><td>(5.0)</td></tr>
<tr><td>8</td><td>Tennessee</td><td>3.5</td><td>42</td><td>Wisconsin</td><td>(5.6)</td></tr>
<tr><td>45</td><td>Texas</td><td>(6.8)</td><td>43</td><td>Alabama</td><td>(6.2)</td></tr>
<tr><td>41</td><td>Utah</td><td>(5.0)</td><td>43</td><td>Kansas</td><td>(6.2)</td></tr>
<tr><td>1</td><td>Vermont</td><td>17.7</td><td>45</td><td>Texas</td><td>(6.8)</td></tr>
<tr><td>29</td><td>Virginia</td><td>(2.5)</td><td>46</td><td>Connecticut</td><td>(8.1)</td></tr>
<tr><td>23</td><td>Washington</td><td>(1.3)</td><td>47</td><td>Wyoming</td><td>(8.2)</td></tr>
<tr><td>29</td><td>West Virginia</td><td>(2.5)</td><td>48</td><td>Maine</td><td>(10.2)</td></tr>
<tr><td>42</td><td>Wisconsin</td><td>(5.6)</td><td>NA</td><td>Michigan**</td><td>NA</td></tr>
<tr><td>47</td><td>Wyoming</td><td>(8.2)</td><td>NA</td><td>Minnesota**</td><td>NA</td></tr>
<tr><td colspan="3"></td><td></td><td>District of Columbia</td><td>1.2</td></tr>
</table>

Source: U.S. Department of Justice, Federal Bureau of Investigation

"Crime in the United States 1993" (Uniform Crime Reports, December 4, 1994)

*Includes murder, rape, robbery, aggravated assault, burglary, larceny-theft and motor vehicle theft.

**Not available.

Crime Rate in 1993

National Rate = 5,482.9 Crimes per 100,000 Population*

ALPHA ORDER				RANK ORDER		
RANK	STATE	RATE		RANK	STATE	RATE
26	Alabama	4,878.8		1	Florida	8,351.0
16	Alaska	5,567.9		2	Arizona	7,431.7
2	Arizona	7,431.7		3	Louisiana	6,846.6
28	Arkansas	4,810.7		4	California	6,456.9
4	California	6,456.9		5	Texas	6,439.1
18	Colorado	5,526.8		6	Hawaii	6,277.0
31	Connecticut	4,650.4		7	New Mexico	6,266.1
27	Delaware	4,872.1		8	Georgia	6,193.0
1	Florida	8,351.0		9	Nevada	6,180.1
8	Georgia	6,193.0		10	Maryland	6,106.5
6	Hawaii	6,277.0		11	Washington	5,952.3
43	Idaho	3,845.1		12	South Carolina	5,903.4
15	Illinois	5,617.9		13	Oregon	5,765.6
34	Indiana	4,465.1		14	North Carolina	5,652.3
42	Iowa	3,846.4		15	Illinois	5,617.9
24	Kansas	4,975.3		16	Alaska	5,567.9
45	Kentucky	3,259.7		17	New York	5,551.3
3	Louisiana	6,846.6		18	Colorado	5,526.8
46	Maine	3,153.9		19	Michigan	5,452.5
10	Maryland	6,106.5		20	Oklahoma	5,294.3
25	Massachusetts	4,893.9		21	Tennessee	5,239.5
19	Michigan	5,452.5		22	Utah	5,237.4
36	Minnesota	4,386.2		23	Missouri	5,095.4
35	Mississippi	4,418.3		24	Kansas	4,975.3
23	Missouri	5,095.4		25	Massachusetts	4,893.9
30	Montana	4,790.0		26	Alabama	4,878.8
38	Nebraska	4,117.1		27	Delaware	4,872.1
9	Nevada	6,180.1		28	Arkansas	4,810.7
48	New Hampshire	2,905.0		29	New Jersey	4,800.8
29	New Jersey	4,800.8		30	Montana	4,790.0
7	New Mexico	6,266.1		31	Connecticut	4,650.4
17	New York	5,551.3		32	Rhode Island	4,499.0
14	North Carolina	5,652.3		33	Ohio	4,485.3
49	North Dakota	2,820.3		34	Indiana	4,465.1
33	Ohio	4,485.3		35	Mississippi	4,418.3
20	Oklahoma	5,294.3		36	Minnesota	4,386.2
13	Oregon	5,765.6		37	Wyoming	4,163.0
44	Pennsylvania	3,271.4		38	Nebraska	4,117.1
32	Rhode Island	4,499.0		39	Virginia	4,115.5
12	South Carolina	5,903.4		40	Wisconsin	4,054.1
47	South Dakota	2,958.2		41	Vermont	3,972.4
21	Tennessee	5,239.5		42	Iowa	3,846.4
5	Texas	6,439.1		43	Idaho	3,845.1
22	Utah	5,237.4		44	Pennsylvania	3,271.4
41	Vermont	3,972.4		45	Kentucky	3,259.7
39	Virginia	4,115.5		46	Maine	3,153.9
11	Washington	5,952.3		47	South Dakota	2,958.2
50	West Virginia	2,532.6		48	New Hampshire	2,905.0
40	Wisconsin	4,054.1		49	North Dakota	2,820.3
37	Wyoming	4,163.0		50	West Virginia	2,532.6
					District of Columbia	11,761.1

Source: U.S. Department of Justice, Federal Bureau of Investigation
  "Crime in the United States 1993" (Uniform Crime Reports, December 4, 1994)
*Includes murder, rape, robbery, aggravated assault, burglary, larceny-theft and motor vehicle theft.

Percent Change in Crime Rate: 1992 to 1993

National Percent Change = 3.1% Decrease*

ALPHA ORDER				RANK ORDER		
RANK	STATE	PERCENT CHANGE		RANK	STATE	PERCENT CHANGE
43	Alabama	(7.4)		1	Vermont	16.5
11	Alaska	0.0		2	Arizona	5.7
2	Arizona	5.7		3	Louisiana	4.6
8	Arkansas	1.0		4	Montana	4.2
28	California	(3.3)		5	Mississippi	3.2
42	Colorado	(7.2)		6	Hawaii	2.7
45	Connecticut	(8.0)		7	Tennessee	2.0
9	Delaware	0.5		8	Arkansas	1.0
13	Florida	(0.1)		9	Delaware	0.5
28	Georgia	(3.3)		10	South Carolina	0.2
6	Hawaii	2.7		11	Alaska	0.0
32	Idaho	(3.8)		11	Missouri	0.0
22	Illinois	(2.6)		13	Florida	(0.1)
35	Indiana	(4.7)		14	Nevada	(0.4)
25	Iowa	(2.8)		15	Oregon	(1.0)
41	Kansas	(6.5)		16	South Dakota	(1.4)
18	Kentucky	(1.9)		17	Rhode Island	(1.7)
3	Louisiana	4.6		18	Kentucky	(1.9)
48	Maine	(10.5)		18	Maryland	(1.9)
18	Maryland	(1.9)		20	Massachusetts	(2.2)
20	Massachusetts	(2.2)		21	Oklahoma	(2.5)
NA	Michigan**	NA		22	Illinois	(2.6)
NA	Minnesota**	NA		22	New Mexico	(2.6)
5	Mississippi	3.2		22	North Carolina	(2.6)
11	Missouri	0.0		25	Iowa	(2.8)
4	Montana	4.2		26	North Dakota	(2.9)
36	Nebraska	(4.8)		27	West Virginia	(3.0)
14	Nevada	(0.4)		28	California	(3.3)
39	New Hampshire	(5.7)		28	Georgia	(3.3)
37	New Jersey	(5.2)		30	Pennsylvania	(3.6)
22	New Mexico	(2.6)		30	Washington	(3.6)
37	New York	(5.2)		32	Idaho	(3.8)
22	North Carolina	(2.6)		33	Ohio	(3.9)
26	North Dakota	(2.9)		34	Virginia	(4.3)
33	Ohio	(3.9)		35	Indiana	(4.7)
21	Oklahoma	(2.5)		36	Nebraska	(4.8)
15	Oregon	(1.0)		37	New Jersey	(5.2)
30	Pennsylvania	(3.6)		37	New York	(5.2)
17	Rhode Island	(1.7)		39	New Hampshire	(5.7)
10	South Carolina	0.2		40	Wisconsin	(6.1)
16	South Dakota	(1.4)		41	Kansas	(6.5)
7	Tennessee	2.0		42	Colorado	(7.2)
46	Texas	(8.8)		43	Alabama	(7.4)
43	Utah	(7.4)		43	Utah	(7.4)
1	Vermont	16.5		45	Connecticut	(8.0)
34	Virginia	(4.3)		46	Texas	(8.8)
30	Washington	(3.6)		47	Wyoming	(9.0)
27	West Virginia	(3.0)		48	Maine	(10.5)
40	Wisconsin	(6.1)		NA	Michigan**	NA
47	Wyoming	(9.0)		NA	Minnesota**	NA

District of Columbia   3.1

Source: U.S. Department of Justice, Federal Bureau of Investigation

   "Crime in the United States 1993" (Uniform Crime Reports, December 4, 1994)

*Includes murder, rape, robbery, aggravated assault, burglary, larceny-theft and motor vehicle theft.

**Not available.

Violent Crimes in 1993

National Total = 1,924,188 Violent Crimes*

ALPHA ORDER					RANK ORDER			
RANK	STATE	CRIMES	% of USA		RANK	STATE	CRIMES	% of USA
18	Alabama	32,676	1.70%		1	California	336,381	17.48%
39	Alaska	4,557	0.24%		2	New York	195,352	10.15%
19	Arizona	28,142	1.46%		3	Florida	164,975	8.57%
30	Arkansas	14,381	0.75%		4	Texas	137,419	7.14%
1	California	336,381	17.48%		5	Illinois	112,260	5.83%
24	Colorado	20,229	1.05%		6	Michigan	75,021	3.90%
28	Connecticut	14,949	0.78%		7	Ohio	55,915	2.91%
38	Delaware	4,801	0.25%		8	Pennsylvania	50,295	2.61%
3	Florida	164,975	8.57%		9	Georgia	50,019	2.60%
9	Georgia	50,019	2.60%		10	Maryland	49,540	2.57%
43	Hawaii	3,061	0.16%		11	New Jersey	49,390	2.57%
42	Idaho	3,097	0.16%		12	Massachusetts	48,393	2.51%
5	Illinois	112,260	5.83%		13	North Carolina	47,178	2.45%
20	Indiana	27,941	1.45%		14	Louisiana	45,600	2.37%
35	Iowa	9,159	0.48%		15	Tennessee	39,047	2.03%
32	Kansas	12,564	0.65%		16	Missouri	38,963	2.02%
25	Kentucky	17,530	0.91%		17	South Carolina	37,281	1.94%
14	Louisiana	45,600	2.37%		18	Alabama	32,676	1.70%
44	Maine	1,558	0.08%		19	Arizona	28,142	1.46%
10	Maryland	49,540	2.57%		20	Indiana	27,941	1.45%
12	Massachusetts	48,393	2.51%		21	Washington	27,040	1.41%
6	Michigan	75,021	3.90%		22	Virginia	24,160	1.26%
29	Minnesota	14,778	0.77%		23	Oklahoma	20,512	1.07%
34	Mississippi	11,467	0.60%		24	Colorado	20,229	1.05%
16	Missouri	38,963	2.02%		25	Kentucky	17,530	0.91%
47	Montana	1,489	0.08%		26	Oregon	15,254	0.79%
37	Nebraska	5,450	0.28%		27	New Mexico	15,024	0.78%
33	Nevada	12,157	0.63%		28	Connecticut	14,949	0.78%
45	New Hampshire	1,550	0.08%		29	Minnesota	14,778	0.77%
11	New Jersey	49,390	2.57%		30	Arkansas	14,381	0.75%
27	New Mexico	15,024	0.78%		31	Wisconsin	13,321	0.69%
2	New York	195,352	10.15%		32	Kansas	12,564	0.65%
13	North Carolina	47,178	2.45%		33	Nevada	12,157	0.63%
50	North Dakota	522	0.03%		34	Mississippi	11,467	0.60%
7	Ohio	55,915	2.91%		35	Iowa	9,159	0.48%
23	Oklahoma	20,512	1.07%		36	Utah	5,599	0.29%
26	Oregon	15,254	0.79%		37	Nebraska	5,450	0.28%
8	Pennsylvania	50,295	2.61%		38	Delaware	4,801	0.25%
40	Rhode Island	4,017	0.21%		39	Alaska	4,557	0.24%
17	South Carolina	37,281	1.94%		40	Rhode Island	4,017	0.21%
46	South Dakota	1,490	0.08%		41	West Virginia	3,793	0.20%
15	Tennessee	39,047	2.03%		42	Idaho	3,097	0.16%
4	Texas	137,419	7.14%		43	Hawaii	3,061	0.16%
36	Utah	5,599	0.29%		44	Maine	1,558	0.08%
49	Vermont	658	0.03%		45	New Hampshire	1,550	0.08%
22	Virginia	24,160	1.26%		46	South Dakota	1,490	0.08%
21	Washington	27,040	1.41%		47	Montana	1,489	0.08%
41	West Virginia	3,793	0.20%		48	Wyoming	1,345	0.07%
31	Wisconsin	13,321	0.69%		49	Vermont	658	0.03%
48	Wyoming	1,345	0.07%		50	North Dakota	522	0.03%
						District of Columbia	16,888	0.88%

Source: U.S. Department of Justice, Federal Bureau of Investigation
"Crime in the United States 1993" (Uniform Crime Reports, December 4, 1994)
*Violent crimes are offenses of murder, rape, robbery and aggravated assault.

Average Time Between Violent Crimes in 1993

National Rate = A Violent Crime Occurs Every 16 Seconds*

ALPHA ORDER				RANK ORDER		
RANK	STATE	MINUTES.SECONDS		RANK	STATE	MINUTES.SECONDS
33	Alabama	16.05		1	North Dakota	1,006.54
12	Alaska	115.20		2	Vermont	798.47
32	Arizona	18.41		3	Wyoming	390.47
21	Arkansas	36.33		4	Montana	352.59
50	California	1.34		5	South Dakota	352.45
27	Colorado	25.59		6	New Hampshire	339.06
23	Connecticut	35.10		7	Maine	337.22
13	Delaware	109.29		8	Hawaii	171.43
48	Florida	3.11		9	Idaho	169.43
42	Georgia	10.31		10	West Virginia	138.34
8	Hawaii	171.43		11	Rhode Island	130.50
9	Idaho	169.43		12	Alaska	115.20
46	Illinois	4.41		13	Delaware	109.29
31	Indiana	18.49		14	Nebraska	96.26
16	Iowa	57.23		15	Utah	93.52
19	Kansas	41.50		16	Iowa	57.23
26	Kentucky	29.59		17	Mississippi	45.50
37	Louisiana	11.32		18	Nevada	43.14
7	Maine	337.22		19	Kansas	41.50
41	Maryland	10.37		20	Wisconsin	39.28
39	Massachusetts	10.52		21	Arkansas	36.33
45	Michigan	7.01		22	Minnesota	35.34
22	Minnesota	35.34		23	Connecticut	35.10
17	Mississippi	45.50		24	New Mexico	34.59
35	Missouri	13.29		25	Oregon	34.28
4	Montana	352.59		26	Kentucky	29.59
14	Nebraska	96.26		27	Colorado	25.59
18	Nevada	43.14		28	Oklahoma	25.37
6	New Hampshire	339.06		29	Virginia	21.46
40	New Jersey	10.38		30	Washington	19.26
24	New Mexico	34.59		31	Indiana	18.49
49	New York	2.41		32	Arizona	18.41
38	North Carolina	11.08		33	Alabama	16.05
1	North Dakota	1,006.54		34	South Carolina	14.06
44	Ohio	9.24		35	Missouri	13.29
28	Oklahoma	25.37		36	Tennessee	13.28
25	Oregon	34.28		37	Louisiana	11.32
43	Pennsylvania	10.27		38	North Carolina	11.08
11	Rhode Island	130.50		39	Massachusetts	10.52
34	South Carolina	14.06		40	New Jersey	10.38
5	South Dakota	352.45		41	Maryland	10.37
36	Tennessee	13.28		42	Georgia	10.31
47	Texas	3.49		43	Pennsylvania	10.27
15	Utah	93.52		44	Ohio	9.24
2	Vermont	798.47		45	Michigan	7.01
29	Virginia	21.46		46	Illinois	4.41
30	Washington	19.26		47	Texas	3.49
10	West Virginia	138.34		48	Florida	3.11
20	Wisconsin	39.28		49	New York	2.41
3	Wyoming	390.47		50	California	1.34

District of Columbia 31.07

Source: Morgan Quitno Corporation using data from U.S. Department of Justice, Federal Bureau of Investigation
"Crime in the United States 1993" (Uniform Crime Reports, December 4, 1994)
*Violent crimes are offenses of murder, rape, robbery and aggravated assault.

Violent Crimes per Square Mile in 1993

National Rate = 0.51 Violent Crimes per Square Mile*

ALPHA ORDER				RANK ORDER		
RANK	STATE	RATE		RANK	STATE	RATE
20	Alabama	0.62		1	New Jersey	5.66
47	Alaska	0.01		2	Massachusetts	4.58
29	Arizona	0.25		3	Maryland	3.99
28	Arkansas	0.27		4	New York	3.58
8	California	2.05		5	Connecticut	2.70
32	Colorado	0.19		6	Rhode Island	2.60
5	Connecticut	2.70		7	Florida	2.51
10	Delaware	1.93		8	California	2.05
7	Florida	2.51		9	Illinois	1.94
17	Georgia	0.84		10	Delaware	1.93
27	Hawaii	0.28		11	Ohio	1.25
44	Idaho	0.04		12	South Carolina	1.16
9	Illinois	1.94		13	Pennsylvania	1.09
19	Indiana	0.77		14	Tennessee	0.93
35	Iowa	0.16		15	Louisiana	0.88
38	Kansas	0.15		15	North Carolina	0.88
24	Kentucky	0.43		17	Georgia	0.84
15	Louisiana	0.88		18	Michigan	0.78
44	Maine	0.04		19	Indiana	0.77
3	Maryland	3.99		20	Alabama	0.62
2	Massachusetts	4.58		21	Missouri	0.56
18	Michigan	0.78		21	Virginia	0.56
33	Minnesota	0.17		23	Texas	0.51
30	Mississippi	0.24		24	Kentucky	0.43
21	Missouri	0.56		25	Washington	0.38
47	Montana	0.01		26	Oklahoma	0.29
41	Nebraska	0.07		27	Hawaii	0.28
40	Nevada	0.11		28	Arkansas	0.27
33	New Hampshire	0.17		29	Arizona	0.25
1	New Jersey	5.66		30	Mississippi	0.24
39	New Mexico	0.12		31	Wisconsin	0.20
4	New York	3.58		32	Colorado	0.19
15	North Carolina	0.88		33	Minnesota	0.17
47	North Dakota	0.01		33	New Hampshire	0.17
11	Ohio	1.25		35	Iowa	0.16
26	Oklahoma	0.29		35	Oregon	0.16
35	Oregon	0.16		35	West Virginia	0.16
13	Pennsylvania	1.09		38	Kansas	0.15
6	Rhode Island	2.60		39	New Mexico	0.12
12	South Carolina	1.16		40	Nevada	0.11
46	South Dakota	0.02		41	Nebraska	0.07
14	Tennessee	0.93		41	Utah	0.07
23	Texas	0.51		41	Vermont	0.07
41	Utah	0.07		44	Idaho	0.04
41	Vermont	0.07		44	Maine	0.04
21	Virginia	0.56		46	South Dakota	0.02
25	Washington	0.38		47	Alaska	0.01
35	West Virginia	0.16		47	Montana	0.01
31	Wisconsin	0.20		47	North Dakota	0.01
47	Wyoming	0.01		47	Wyoming	0.01

	District of Columbia	248.35

Source: Morgan Quitno Corporation using data from U.S. Department of Justice, Federal Bureau of Investigation
"Crime in the United States 1993" (Uniform Crime Reports, December 4, 1994)
*Violent crimes are offenses of murder, rape, robbery and aggravated assault.

Percent Change in Number of Violent Crimes: 1992 to 1993

National Percent Change = 0.4% Decrease*

ALPHA ORDER				RANK ORDER		
RANK	STATE	PERCENT CHANGE		RANK	STATE	PERCENT CHANGE
46	Alabama	(9.4)		1	Nevada	31.5
2	Alaska	17.5		2	Alaska	17.5
7	Arizona	9.5		3	Iowa	17.2
15	Arkansas	4.0		4	Delaware	12.2
38	California	(2.7)		5	New Hampshire	11.0
29	Colorado	0.7		6	South Carolina	9.6
45	Connecticut	(8.0)		7	Arizona	9.5
4	Delaware	12.2		8	Louisiana	8.0
21	Florida	1.3		9	South Dakota	7.7
26	Georgia	1.1		10	Mississippi	6.5
19	Hawaii	2.1		11	Montana	6.4
17	Idaho	3.1		12	Utah	6.3
32	Illinois	(1.2)		13	Vermont	5.4
39	Indiana	(3.0)		14	Tennessee	4.2
3	Iowa	17.2		15	Arkansas	4.0
36	Kansas	(2.5)		16	Massachusetts	3.6
48	Kentucky	(12.8)		17	Idaho	3.1
8	Louisiana	8.0		18	Oklahoma	2.5
43	Maine	(3.6)		19	Hawaii	2.1
28	Maryland	0.9		20	New Mexico	1.6
16	Massachusetts	3.6		21	Florida	1.3
NA	Michigan**	NA		21	Missouri	1.3
NA	Minnesota**	NA		21	New Jersey	1.3
10	Mississippi	6.5		21	Rhode Island	1.3
21	Missouri	1.3		25	North Carolina	1.2
11	Montana	6.4		26	Georgia	1.1
37	Nebraska	(2.6)		26	Virginia	1.1
1	Nevada	31.5		28	Maryland	0.9
5	New Hampshire	11.0		29	Colorado	0.7
21	New Jersey	1.3		30	Oregon	0.4
20	New Mexico	1.6		31	West Virginia	(1.0)
44	New York	(3.9)		32	Illinois	(1.2)
25	North Carolina	1.2		33	North Dakota	(1.5)
33	North Dakota	(1.5)		33	Washington	(1.5)
40	Ohio	(3.5)		35	Pennsylvania	(1.9)
18	Oklahoma	2.5		36	Kansas	(2.5)
30	Oregon	0.4		37	Nebraska	(2.6)
35	Pennsylvania	(1.9)		38	California	(2.7)
21	Rhode Island	1.3		39	Indiana	(3.0)
6	South Carolina	9.6		40	Ohio	(3.5)
9	South Dakota	7.7		40	Texas	(3.5)
14	Tennessee	4.2		40	Wisconsin	(3.5)
40	Texas	(3.5)		43	Maine	(3.6)
12	Utah	6.3		44	New York	(3.9)
13	Vermont	5.4		45	Connecticut	(8.0)
26	Virginia	1.1		46	Alabama	(9.4)
33	Washington	(1.5)		47	Wyoming	(9.7)
31	West Virginia	(1.0)		48	Kentucky	(12.8)
40	Wisconsin	(3.5)		NA	Michigan**	NA
47	Wyoming	(9.7)		NA	Minnesota**	NA
					District of Columbia	1.2

Source: U.S. Department of Justice, Federal Bureau of Investigation
   "Crime in the United States 1993" (Uniform Crime Reports, December 4, 1994)
*Violent crimes are offenses of murder, rape, robbery and aggravated assault.
**Not available.

Violent Crime Rate in 1993

National Rate = 746.1 Violent Crimes per 100,000 Population*

<u>ALPHA ORDER</u>

RANK	STATE	RATE
12	Alabama	780.4
15	Alaska	760.8
18	Arizona	715.0
23	Arkansas	593.3
2	California	1,077.8
24	Colorado	567.3
31	Connecticut	456.2
19	Delaware	685.9
1	Florida	1,206.0
17	Georgia	723.1
43	Hawaii	261.2
41	Idaho	281.8
7	Illinois	959.7
29	Indiana	489.1
38	Iowa	325.5
28	Kansas	496.4
30	Kentucky	462.7
4	Louisiana	1,061.7
48	Maine	125.7
6	Maryland	997.8
10	Massachusetts	804.9
11	Michigan	791.5
37	Minnesota	327.2
32	Mississippi	433.9
16	Missouri	744.4
46	Montana	177.5
36	Nebraska	339.1
9	Nevada	875.2
47	New Hampshire	137.8
22	New Jersey	626.9
8	New Mexico	929.7
3	New York	1,073.5
20	North Carolina	679.3
50	North Dakota	82.2
26	Ohio	504.1
21	Oklahoma	634.8
27	Oregon	503.1
33	Pennsylvania	417.5
34	Rhode Island	401.7
5	South Carolina	1,023.4
44	South Dakota	208.4
13	Tennessee	765.8
14	Texas	762.1
39	Utah	301.0
49	Vermont	114.2
35	Virginia	372.2
25	Washington	514.6
44	West Virginia	208.4
42	Wisconsin	264.4
40	Wyoming	286.2

<u>RANK ORDER</u>

RANK	STATE	RATE
1	Florida	1,206.0
2	California	1,077.8
3	New York	1,073.5
4	Louisiana	1,061.7
5	South Carolina	1,023.4
6	Maryland	997.8
7	Illinois	959.7
8	New Mexico	929.7
9	Nevada	875.2
10	Massachusetts	804.9
11	Michigan	791.5
12	Alabama	780.4
13	Tennessee	765.8
14	Texas	762.1
15	Alaska	760.8
16	Missouri	744.4
17	Georgia	723.1
18	Arizona	715.0
19	Delaware	685.9
20	North Carolina	679.3
21	Oklahoma	634.8
22	New Jersey	626.9
23	Arkansas	593.3
24	Colorado	567.3
25	Washington	514.6
26	Ohio	504.1
27	Oregon	503.1
28	Kansas	496.4
29	Indiana	489.1
30	Kentucky	462.7
31	Connecticut	456.2
32	Mississippi	433.9
33	Pennsylvania	417.5
34	Rhode Island	401.7
35	Virginia	372.2
36	Nebraska	339.1
37	Minnesota	327.2
38	Iowa	325.5
39	Utah	301.0
40	Wyoming	286.2
41	Idaho	281.8
42	Wisconsin	264.4
43	Hawaii	261.2
44	South Dakota	208.4
44	West Virginia	208.4
46	Montana	177.5
47	New Hampshire	137.8
48	Maine	125.7
49	Vermont	114.2
50	North Dakota	82.2

District of Columbia — 2,921.8

Source: U.S. Department of Justice, Federal Bureau of Investigation
"Crime in the United States 1993" (Uniform Crime Reports, December 4, 1994)
*Violent crimes are offenses of murder, rape, robbery and aggravated assault.

Percent Change in Violent Crime Rate: 1992 to 1993

National Percent Change = 1.5% Decrease*

ALPHA ORDER				RANK ORDER		
RANK	STATE	PERCENT CHANGE		RANK	STATE	PERCENT CHANGE
47	Alabama	(10.5)		1	Nevada	25.6
3	Alaska	15.2		2	Iowa	17.1
9	Arizona	6.6		3	Alaska	15.2
15	Arkansas	2.9		4	Delaware	10.4
37	California	(3.7)		5	New Hampshire	9.6
33	Colorado	(2.0)		6	South Carolina	8.4
45	Connecticut	(7.9)		7	Louisiana	7.8
4	Delaware	10.4		8	South Dakota	7.1
23	Florida	(0.1)		9	Arizona	6.6
29	Georgia	(1.4)		10	Mississippi	5.4
19	Hawaii	1.1		11	Montana	4.5
22	Idaho	0.1		12	Vermont	4.3
32	Illinois	(1.8)		13	Utah	3.6
39	Indiana	(3.8)		14	Massachusetts	3.3
2	Iowa	17.1		15	Arkansas	2.9
36	Kansas	(2.8)		16	Tennessee	2.6
48	Kentucky	(13.6)		17	Oklahoma	1.9
7	Louisiana	7.8		18	Rhode Island	1.8
40	Maine	(4.0)		19	Hawaii	1.1
24	Maryland	(0.2)		20	Missouri	0.5
14	Massachusetts	3.3		21	New Jersey	0.2
NA	Michigan**	NA		22	Idaho	0.1
NA	Minnesota**	NA		23	Florida	(0.1)
10	Mississippi	5.4		24	Maryland	(0.2)
20	Missouri	0.5		24	North Carolina	(0.2)
11	Montana	4.5		26	New Mexico	(0.6)
35	Nebraska	(2.7)		27	Virginia	(0.7)
1	Nevada	25.6		28	North Dakota	(1.3)
5	New Hampshire	9.6		29	Georgia	(1.4)
21	New Jersey	0.2		29	Oregon	(1.4)
26	New Mexico	(0.6)		31	West Virginia	(1.5)
43	New York	(4.3)		32	Illinois	(1.8)
24	North Carolina	(0.2)		33	Colorado	(2.0)
28	North Dakota	(1.3)		34	Pennsylvania	(2.2)
41	Ohio	(4.1)		35	Nebraska	(2.7)
17	Oklahoma	1.9		36	Kansas	(2.8)
29	Oregon	(1.4)		37	California	(3.7)
34	Pennsylvania	(2.2)		37	Washington	(3.7)
18	Rhode Island	1.8		39	Indiana	(3.8)
6	South Carolina	8.4		40	Maine	(4.0)
8	South Dakota	7.1		41	Ohio	(4.1)
16	Tennessee	2.6		41	Wisconsin	(4.1)
44	Texas	(5.5)		43	New York	(4.3)
13	Utah	3.6		44	Texas	(5.5)
12	Vermont	4.3		45	Connecticut	(7.9)
27	Virginia	(0.7)		46	Wyoming	(10.4)
37	Washington	(3.7)		47	Alabama	(10.5)
31	West Virginia	(1.5)		48	Kentucky	(13.6)
41	Wisconsin	(4.1)		NA	Michigan**	NA
46	Wyoming	(10.4)		NA	Minnesota**	NA
					District of Columbia	3.1

Source: U.S. Department of Justice, Federal Bureau of Investigation
    "Crime in the United States 1993" (Uniform Crime Reports, December 4, 1994)
*Violent crimes are offenses of murder, rape, robbery and aggravated assault.
**Not available.

Violent Crimes with Firearms in 1993

National Total = 509,728 Violent Crimes*

ALPHA ORDER					RANK ORDER			
RANK	STATE	CRIMES	% of USA		RANK	STATE	CRIMES	% of USA
25	Alabama	3,923	0.77%		1	California	99,752	19.57%
34	Alaska	1,022	0.20%		2	New York	56,128	11.01%
15	Arizona	9,983	1.96%		3	Texas	45,548	8.94%
23	Arkansas	4,776	0.94%		4	Florida	44,905	8.81%
1	California	99,752	19.57%		5	Michigan	25,130	4.93%
21	Colorado	5,533	1.09%		6	Maryland	18,794	3.69%
26	Connecticut	3,722	0.73%		7	Georgia	16,574	3.25%
40	Delaware	244	0.05%		8	North Carolina	15,712	3.08%
4	Florida	44,905	8.81%		9	Louisiana	15,424	3.03%
7	Georgia	16,574	3.25%		10	Missouri	15,104	2.96%
39	Hawaii	322	0.06%		11	Ohio	14,483	2.84%
36	Idaho	705	0.14%		12	Pennsylvania	13,077	2.57%
NA	Illinois**	NA	NA		13	New Jersey	12,347	2.42%
20	Indiana	5,715	1.12%		14	Tennessee	12,065	2.37%
37	Iowa	677	0.13%		15	Arizona	9,983	1.96%
NA	Kansas**	NA	NA		16	South Carolina	9,899	1.94%
27	Kentucky	3,660	0.72%		17	Virginia	7,270	1.43%
9	Louisiana	15,424	3.03%		18	Washington	6,792	1.33%
45	Maine	118	0.02%		19	Oklahoma	5,777	1.13%
6	Maryland	18,794	3.69%		20	Indiana	5,715	1.12%
22	Massachusetts	5,001	0.98%		21	Colorado	5,533	1.09%
5	Michigan	25,130	4.93%		22	Massachusetts	5,001	0.98%
29	Minnesota	3,411	0.67%		23	Arkansas	4,776	0.94%
31	Mississippi	2,908	0.57%		24	Wisconsin	4,533	0.89%
10	Missouri	15,104	2.96%		25	Alabama	3,923	0.77%
NA	Montana**	NA	NA		26	Connecticut	3,722	0.73%
42	Nebraska	197	0.04%		27	Kentucky	3,660	0.72%
30	Nevada	3,294	0.65%		28	Oregon	3,550	0.70%
44	New Hampshire	127	0.02%		29	Minnesota	3,411	0.67%
13	New Jersey	12,347	2.42%		30	Nevada	3,294	0.65%
32	New Mexico	2,819	0.55%		31	Mississippi	2,908	0.57%
2	New York	56,128	11.01%		32	New Mexico	2,819	0.55%
8	North Carolina	15,712	3.08%		33	Utah	1,037	0.20%
47	North Dakota	29	0.01%		34	Alaska	1,022	0.20%
11	Ohio	14,483	2.84%		35	West Virginia	796	0.16%
19	Oklahoma	5,777	1.13%		36	Idaho	705	0.14%
28	Oregon	3,550	0.70%		37	Iowa	677	0.13%
12	Pennsylvania	13,077	2.57%		38	Rhode Island	610	0.12%
38	Rhode Island	610	0.12%		39	Hawaii	322	0.06%
16	South Carolina	9,899	1.94%		40	Delaware	244	0.05%
41	South Dakota	211	0.04%		41	South Dakota	211	0.04%
14	Tennessee	12,065	2.37%		42	Nebraska	197	0.04%
3	Texas	45,548	8.94%		43	Wyoming	160	0.03%
33	Utah	1,037	0.20%		44	New Hampshire	127	0.02%
46	Vermont	58	0.01%		45	Maine	118	0.02%
17	Virginia	7,270	1.43%		46	Vermont	58	0.01%
18	Washington	6,792	1.33%		47	North Dakota	29	0.01%
35	West Virginia	796	0.16%		NA	Illinois**	NA	NA
24	Wisconsin	4,533	0.89%		NA	Kansas**	NA	NA
43	Wyoming	160	0.03%		NA	Montana**	NA	NA
						District of Columbia	5,641	1.11%

Source: Morgan Quitno Corporation using data from U.S. Department of Justice, Federal Bureau of Investigation
   "Crime in the United States 1993" (Uniform Crime Reports, December 4, 1994)
*Includes murder, robbery and aggravated assault. National total reflects only those violent crimes for which the type of we
was known and reported. Includes only those states shown separately.
**Not available.

Violent Crime Rate with Firearms in 1993

National Rate = 209.9 Violent Crimes per 100,000 Population*

<u>ALPHA ORDER</u>

RANK	STATE	RATE
30	Alabama	93.7
18	Alaska	170.6
9	Arizona	253.6
15	Arkansas	197.0
4	California	319.6
20	Colorado	155.2
24	Connecticut	113.6
38	Delaware	34.9
3	Florida	328.3
11	Georgia	239.6
41	Hawaii	27.5
34	Idaho	64.1
NA	Illinois**	NA
28	Indiana	100.0
42	Iowa	24.1
NA	Kansas**	NA
29	Kentucky	96.6
2	Louisiana	359.1
46	Maine	9.5
1	Maryland	378.5
32	Massachusetts	83.2
8	Michigan	265.1
33	Minnesota	75.5
26	Mississippi	110.0
6	Missouri	288.6
NA	Montana**	NA
43	Nebraska	12.3
12	Nevada	237.1
44	New Hampshire	11.3
19	New Jersey	156.7
17	New Mexico	174.4
5	New York	308.4
14	North Carolina	226.2
47	North Dakota	4.6
21	Ohio	130.6
16	Oklahoma	178.8
23	Oregon	117.1
27	Pennsylvania	108.5
35	Rhode Island	61.0
7	South Carolina	271.7
40	South Dakota	29.5
13	Tennessee	236.6
10	Texas	252.6
36	Utah	55.8
45	Vermont	10.1
25	Virginia	112.0
22	Washington	129.2
37	West Virginia	43.7
31	Wisconsin	90.0
39	Wyoming	34.0

<u>RANK ORDER</u>

RANK	STATE	RATE
1	Maryland	378.5
2	Louisiana	359.1
3	Florida	328.3
4	California	319.6
5	New York	308.4
6	Missouri	288.6
7	South Carolina	271.7
8	Michigan	265.1
9	Arizona	253.6
10	Texas	252.6
11	Georgia	239.6
12	Nevada	237.1
13	Tennessee	236.6
14	North Carolina	226.2
15	Arkansas	197.0
16	Oklahoma	178.8
17	New Mexico	174.4
18	Alaska	170.6
19	New Jersey	156.7
20	Colorado	155.2
21	Ohio	130.6
22	Washington	129.2
23	Oregon	117.1
24	Connecticut	113.6
25	Virginia	112.0
26	Mississippi	110.0
27	Pennsylvania	108.5
28	Indiana	100.0
29	Kentucky	96.6
30	Alabama	93.7
31	Wisconsin	90.0
32	Massachusetts	83.2
33	Minnesota	75.5
34	Idaho	64.1
35	Rhode Island	61.0
36	Utah	55.8
37	West Virginia	43.7
38	Delaware	34.9
39	Wyoming	34.0
40	South Dakota	29.5
41	Hawaii	27.5
42	Iowa	24.1
43	Nebraska	12.3
44	New Hampshire	11.3
45	Vermont	10.1
46	Maine	9.5
47	North Dakota	4.6
NA	Illinois**	NA
NA	Kansas**	NA
NA	Montana**	NA

District of Columbia 976.0

Source: Morgan Quitno Corporation using data from U.S. Department of Justice, Federal Bureau of Investigation
"Crime in the United States 1993" (Uniform Crime Reports, December 4, 1994)
*Includes murder, robbery and aggravated assault. Rate reflects only those violent crimes for which the type of weapon was known and reported. National rate based on population of reporting states.
**Not available.

Percent of Violent Crimes Involving Firearms in 1993

National Percent = 31.86% of Violent Crimes*

ALPHA ORDER

RANK	STATE	PERCENT
41	Alabama	14.27
28	Alaska	26.27
6	Arizona	38.92
10	Arkansas	36.05
20	California	30.77
18	Colorado	31.22
28	Connecticut	26.27
37	Delaware	20.17
22	Florida	30.19
5	Georgia	39.32
44	Hawaii	12.08
17	Idaho	31.56
NA	Illinois**	NA
25	Indiana	28.22
40	Iowa	15.13
NA	Kansas**	NA
27	Kentucky	27.92
1	Louisiana	47.16
47	Maine	9.86
4	Maryland	39.70
43	Massachusetts	12.61
7	Michigan	38.22
32	Minnesota	25.98
2	Mississippi	46.09
3	Missouri	43.51
NA	Montana**	NA
45	Nebraska	10.19
13	Nevada	35.34
42	New Hampshire	13.69
31	New Jersey	26.17
19	New Mexico	30.83
23	New York	29.84
11	North Carolina	36.03
46	North Dakota	10.07
14	Ohio	34.61
21	Oklahoma	30.62
30	Oregon	26.25
16	Pennsylvania	32.66
38	Rhode Island	17.00
26	South Carolina	28.21
36	South Dakota	21.18
9	Tennessee	36.49
12	Texas	35.87
35	Utah	22.16
33	Vermont	25.89
15	Virginia	32.93
24	Washington	29.30
34	West Virginia	23.25
8	Wisconsin	37.75
39	Wyoming	16.56

RANK ORDER

RANK	STATE	PERCENT
1	Louisiana	47.16
2	Mississippi	46.09
3	Missouri	43.51
4	Maryland	39.70
5	Georgia	39.32
6	Arizona	38.92
7	Michigan	38.22
8	Wisconsin	37.75
9	Tennessee	36.49
10	Arkansas	36.05
11	North Carolina	36.03
12	Texas	35.87
13	Nevada	35.34
14	Ohio	34.61
15	Virginia	32.93
16	Pennsylvania	32.66
17	Idaho	31.56
18	Colorado	31.22
19	New Mexico	30.83
20	California	30.77
21	Oklahoma	30.62
22	Florida	30.19
23	New York	29.84
24	Washington	29.30
25	Indiana	28.22
26	South Carolina	28.21
27	Kentucky	27.92
28	Alaska	26.27
28	Connecticut	26.27
30	Oregon	26.25
31	New Jersey	26.17
32	Minnesota	25.98
33	Vermont	25.89
34	West Virginia	23.25
35	Utah	22.16
36	South Dakota	21.18
37	Delaware	20.17
38	Rhode Island	17.00
39	Wyoming	16.56
40	Iowa	15.13
41	Alabama	14.27
42	New Hampshire	13.69
43	Massachusetts	12.61
44	Hawaii	12.08
45	Nebraska	10.19
46	North Dakota	10.07
47	Maine	9.86
NA	Illinois**	NA
NA	Kansas**	NA
NA	Montana**	NA

District of Columbia   34.13

Source: Morgan Quitno Corporation using data from U.S. Department of Justice, Federal Bureau of Investigation
"Crime in the United States 1993" (Uniform Crime Reports, December 4, 1994)
*Of the 1,599,979 violent crimes in 1993 for which supplemental data were received by the F.B.I. There were an additional 324,209 violent crimes for which the type of weapon was not reported to the F.B.I. Violent crimes are offenses of murder, robbery and aggravated assault. Weapons used in forcible rape are not tracked.
**Not available.

Murders in 1993

National Total = 24,526 Murders*

ALPHA ORDER				RANK ORDER			
RANK	STATE	MURDERS	% of USA	RANK	STATE	MURDERS	% of USA
16	Alabama	484	1.97%	1	California	4,096	16.70%
39	Alaska	54	0.22%	2	New York	2,420	9.87%
21	Arizona	339	1.38%	3	Texas	2,147	8.75%
25	Arkansas	247	1.01%	4	Illinois	1,332	5.43%
1	California	4,096	16.70%	5	Florida	1,224	4.99%
28	Colorado	206	0.84%	6	Michigan	933	3.80%
28	Connecticut	206	0.84%	7	Louisiana	874	3.56%
42	Delaware	35	0.14%	8	Pennsylvania	823	3.36%
5	Florida	1,224	4.99%	9	Georgia	789	3.22%
9	Georgia	789	3.22%	10	North Carolina	785	3.20%
40	Hawaii	45	0.18%	11	Ohio	667	2.72%
43	Idaho	32	0.13%	12	Maryland	632	2.58%
4	Illinois	1,332	5.43%	13	Missouri	590	2.41%
17	Indiana	430	1.75%	14	Virginia	539	2.20%
36	Iowa	66	0.27%	15	Tennessee	521	2.12%
30	Kansas	161	0.66%	16	Alabama	484	1.97%
24	Kentucky	249	1.02%	17	Indiana	430	1.75%
7	Louisiana	874	3.56%	18	New Jersey	418	1.70%
48	Maine	20	0.08%	19	South Carolina	377	1.54%
12	Maryland	632	2.58%	20	Mississippi	357	1.46%
26	Massachusetts	233	0.95%	21	Arizona	339	1.38%
6	Michigan	933	3.80%	22	Oklahoma	273	1.11%
31	Minnesota	155	0.63%	23	Washington	271	1.10%
20	Mississippi	357	1.46%	24	Kentucky	249	1.02%
13	Missouri	590	2.41%	25	Arkansas	247	1.01%
44	Montana	25	0.10%	26	Massachusetts	233	0.95%
37	Nebraska	63	0.26%	27	Wisconsin	222	0.91%
32	Nevada	144	0.59%	28	Colorado	206	0.84%
46	New Hampshire	23	0.09%	28	Connecticut	206	0.84%
18	New Jersey	418	1.70%	30	Kansas	161	0.66%
34	New Mexico	130	0.53%	31	Minnesota	155	0.63%
2	New York	2,420	9.87%	32	Nevada	144	0.59%
10	North Carolina	785	3.20%	33	Oregon	140	0.57%
50	North Dakota	11	0.04%	34	New Mexico	130	0.53%
11	Ohio	667	2.72%	35	West Virginia	126	0.51%
22	Oklahoma	273	1.11%	36	Iowa	66	0.27%
33	Oregon	140	0.57%	37	Nebraska	63	0.26%
8	Pennsylvania	823	3.36%	38	Utah	58	0.24%
41	Rhode Island	39	0.16%	39	Alaska	54	0.22%
19	South Carolina	377	1.54%	40	Hawaii	45	0.18%
45	South Dakota	24	0.10%	41	Rhode Island	39	0.16%
15	Tennessee	521	2.12%	42	Delaware	35	0.14%
3	Texas	2,147	8.75%	43	Idaho	32	0.13%
38	Utah	58	0.24%	44	Montana	25	0.10%
47	Vermont	21	0.09%	45	South Dakota	24	0.10%
14	Virginia	539	2.20%	46	New Hampshire	23	0.09%
23	Washington	271	1.10%	47	Vermont	21	0.09%
35	West Virginia	126	0.51%	48	Maine	20	0.08%
27	Wisconsin	222	0.91%	49	Wyoming	16	0.07%
49	Wyoming	16	0.07%	50	North Dakota	11	0.04%
					District of Columbia	454	1.85%

Source: U.S. Department of Justice, Federal Bureau of Investigation
    "Crime in the United States 1993" (Uniform Crime Reports, December 4, 1994)
*Includes nonnegligent manslaughter.

Average Time Between Murders in 1993

National Rate = A Murder Occurs Every 21 Minutes*

<table>
<tr><td colspan="3">ALPHA ORDER</td><td colspan="3">RANK ORDER</td></tr>
<tr><td>RANK</td><td>STATE</td><td>HOURS.MINUTES</td><td>RANK</td><td>STATE</td><td>HOURS.MINUTES</td></tr>
<tr><td>35</td><td>Alabama</td><td>18.06</td><td>1</td><td>North Dakota</td><td>796.22</td></tr>
<tr><td>12</td><td>Alaska</td><td>162.13</td><td>2</td><td>Wyoming</td><td>547.30</td></tr>
<tr><td>30</td><td>Arizona</td><td>25.50</td><td>3</td><td>Maine</td><td>438.00</td></tr>
<tr><td>26</td><td>Arkansas</td><td>35.28</td><td>4</td><td>Vermont</td><td>417.08</td></tr>
<tr><td>50</td><td>California</td><td>2.08</td><td>5</td><td>New Hampshire</td><td>380.52</td></tr>
<tr><td>22</td><td>Colorado</td><td>42.31</td><td>6</td><td>South Dakota</td><td>365.00</td></tr>
<tr><td>22</td><td>Connecticut</td><td>42.31</td><td>7</td><td>Montana</td><td>350.24</td></tr>
<tr><td>9</td><td>Delaware</td><td>250.17</td><td>8</td><td>Idaho</td><td>273.45</td></tr>
<tr><td>46</td><td>Florida</td><td>7.10</td><td>9</td><td>Delaware</td><td>250.17</td></tr>
<tr><td>42</td><td>Georgia</td><td>11.06</td><td>10</td><td>Rhode Island</td><td>224.37</td></tr>
<tr><td>11</td><td>Hawaii</td><td>194.40</td><td>11</td><td>Hawaii</td><td>194.40</td></tr>
<tr><td>8</td><td>Idaho</td><td>273.45</td><td>12</td><td>Alaska</td><td>162.13</td></tr>
<tr><td>47</td><td>Illinois</td><td>6.35</td><td>13</td><td>Utah</td><td>151.02</td></tr>
<tr><td>34</td><td>Indiana</td><td>20.22</td><td>14</td><td>Nebraska</td><td>139.03</td></tr>
<tr><td>15</td><td>Iowa</td><td>132.44</td><td>15</td><td>Iowa</td><td>132.44</td></tr>
<tr><td>21</td><td>Kansas</td><td>54.25</td><td>16</td><td>West Virginia</td><td>69.31</td></tr>
<tr><td>27</td><td>Kentucky</td><td>35.11</td><td>17</td><td>New Mexico</td><td>67.23</td></tr>
<tr><td>44</td><td>Louisiana</td><td>10.01</td><td>18</td><td>Oregon</td><td>62.34</td></tr>
<tr><td>3</td><td>Maine</td><td>438.00</td><td>19</td><td>Nevada</td><td>60.50</td></tr>
<tr><td>39</td><td>Maryland</td><td>13.52</td><td>20</td><td>Minnesota</td><td>56.31</td></tr>
<tr><td>25</td><td>Massachusetts</td><td>37.36</td><td>21</td><td>Kansas</td><td>54.25</td></tr>
<tr><td>45</td><td>Michigan</td><td>9.23</td><td>22</td><td>Colorado</td><td>42.31</td></tr>
<tr><td>20</td><td>Minnesota</td><td>56.31</td><td>22</td><td>Connecticut</td><td>42.31</td></tr>
<tr><td>31</td><td>Mississippi</td><td>24.32</td><td>24</td><td>Wisconsin</td><td>39.28</td></tr>
<tr><td>38</td><td>Missouri</td><td>14.51</td><td>25</td><td>Massachusetts</td><td>37.36</td></tr>
<tr><td>7</td><td>Montana</td><td>350.24</td><td>26</td><td>Arkansas</td><td>35.28</td></tr>
<tr><td>14</td><td>Nebraska</td><td>139.03</td><td>27</td><td>Kentucky</td><td>35.11</td></tr>
<tr><td>19</td><td>Nevada</td><td>60.50</td><td>28</td><td>Washington</td><td>32.19</td></tr>
<tr><td>5</td><td>New Hampshire</td><td>380.52</td><td>29</td><td>Oklahoma</td><td>32.05</td></tr>
<tr><td>33</td><td>New Jersey</td><td>20.58</td><td>30</td><td>Arizona</td><td>25.50</td></tr>
<tr><td>17</td><td>New Mexico</td><td>67.23</td><td>31</td><td>Mississippi</td><td>24.32</td></tr>
<tr><td>49</td><td>New York</td><td>3.37</td><td>32</td><td>South Carolina</td><td>23.14</td></tr>
<tr><td>41</td><td>North Carolina</td><td>11.10</td><td>33</td><td>New Jersey</td><td>20.58</td></tr>
<tr><td>1</td><td>North Dakota</td><td>796.22</td><td>34</td><td>Indiana</td><td>20.22</td></tr>
<tr><td>40</td><td>Ohio</td><td>13.08</td><td>35</td><td>Alabama</td><td>18.06</td></tr>
<tr><td>29</td><td>Oklahoma</td><td>32.05</td><td>36</td><td>Tennessee</td><td>16.49</td></tr>
<tr><td>18</td><td>Oregon</td><td>62.34</td><td>37</td><td>Virginia</td><td>16.15</td></tr>
<tr><td>43</td><td>Pennsylvania</td><td>10.38</td><td>38</td><td>Missouri</td><td>14.51</td></tr>
<tr><td>10</td><td>Rhode Island</td><td>224.37</td><td>39</td><td>Maryland</td><td>13.52</td></tr>
<tr><td>32</td><td>South Carolina</td><td>23.14</td><td>40</td><td>Ohio</td><td>13.08</td></tr>
<tr><td>6</td><td>South Dakota</td><td>365.00</td><td>41</td><td>North Carolina</td><td>11.10</td></tr>
<tr><td>36</td><td>Tennessee</td><td>16.49</td><td>42</td><td>Georgia</td><td>11.06</td></tr>
<tr><td>48</td><td>Texas</td><td>4.05</td><td>43</td><td>Pennsylvania</td><td>10.38</td></tr>
<tr><td>13</td><td>Utah</td><td>151.02</td><td>44</td><td>Louisiana</td><td>10.01</td></tr>
<tr><td>4</td><td>Vermont</td><td>417.08</td><td>45</td><td>Michigan</td><td>9.23</td></tr>
<tr><td>37</td><td>Virginia</td><td>16.15</td><td>46</td><td>Florida</td><td>7.10</td></tr>
<tr><td>28</td><td>Washington</td><td>32.19</td><td>47</td><td>Illinois</td><td>6.35</td></tr>
<tr><td>16</td><td>West Virginia</td><td>69.31</td><td>48</td><td>Texas</td><td>4.05</td></tr>
<tr><td>24</td><td>Wisconsin</td><td>39.28</td><td>49</td><td>New York</td><td>3.37</td></tr>
<tr><td>2</td><td>Wyoming</td><td>547.30</td><td>50</td><td>California</td><td>2.08</td></tr>
<tr><td></td><td></td><td></td><td></td><td>District of Columbia</td><td>19.18</td></tr>
</table>

Source: Morgan Quitno Corporation using data from U.S. Department of Justice, Federal Bureau of Investigation
   "Crime in the United States 1993" (Uniform Crime Reports, December 4, 1994)
*Includes nonnegligent manslaughter.

Percent Change in Number of Murders: 1992 to 1993

National Percent Change = 3.2% Increase*

ALPHA ORDER				RANK ORDER		
RANK	STATE	PERCENT CHANGE		RANK	STATE	PERCENT CHANGE
23	Alabama	6.4		1	South Dakota	500.0
7	Alaska	22.7		2	Vermont	75.0
15	Arizona	8.7		3	Iowa	50.0
41	Arkansas	(4.6)		4	Oklahoma	30.0
27	California	4.5		5	New Hampshire	27.8
41	Colorado	(4.6)		6	Connecticut	24.1
6	Connecticut	24.1		7	Alaska	22.7
13	Delaware	9.4		8	Louisiana	17.0
31	Florida	1.3		9	Kentucky	15.3
22	Georgia	6.5		10	Mississippi	11.6
20	Hawaii	7.1		11	Pennsylvania	10.3
50	Idaho	(13.5)		12	West Virginia	9.6
34	Illinois	0.8		13	Delaware	9.4
45	Indiana	(7.3)		14	Massachusetts	8.9
3	Iowa	50.0		15	Arizona	8.7
21	Kansas	6.6		16	North Carolina	8.6
9	Kentucky	15.3		17	Rhode Island	8.3
8	Louisiana	17.0		18	Missouri	7.9
43	Maine	(4.8)		19	Utah	7.4
24	Maryland	6.0		20	Hawaii	7.1
14	Massachusetts	8.9		21	Kansas	6.6
37	Michigan	(0.5)		22	Georgia	6.5
29	Minnesota	3.3		23	Alabama	6.4
10	Mississippi	11.6		24	Maryland	6.0
18	Missouri	7.9		25	New Jersey	5.3
28	Montana	4.2		26	Washington	5.0
46	Nebraska	(7.4)		27	California	4.5
38	Nevada	(0.7)		28	Montana	4.2
5	New Hampshire	27.8		29	Minnesota	3.3
25	New Jersey	5.3		30	Wisconsin	1.8
47	New Mexico	(7.8)		31	Florida	1.3
33	New York	1.0		32	South Carolina	1.1
16	North Carolina	8.6		33	New York	1.0
49	North Dakota	(8.3)		34	Illinois	0.8
48	Ohio	(7.9)		35	Oregon	0.7
4	Oklahoma	30.0		36	Tennessee	0.2
35	Oregon	0.7		37	Michigan	(0.5)
11	Pennsylvania	10.3		38	Nevada	(0.7)
17	Rhode Island	8.3		39	Texas	(4.1)
32	South Carolina	1.1		40	Virginia	(4.4)
1	South Dakota	500.0		41	Arkansas	(4.6)
36	Tennessee	0.2		41	Colorado	(4.6)
39	Texas	(4.1)		43	Maine	(4.8)
19	Utah	7.4		44	Wyoming	(5.9)
2	Vermont	75.0		45	Indiana	(7.3)
40	Virginia	(4.4)		46	Nebraska	(7.4)
26	Washington	5.0		47	New Mexico	(7.8)
12	West Virginia	9.6		48	Ohio	(7.9)
30	Wisconsin	1.8		49	North Dakota	(8.3)
44	Wyoming	(5.9)		50	Idaho	(13.5)

District of Columbia	2.5

Source: U.S. Department of Justice, Federal Bureau of Investigation
"Crime in the United States 1993" (Uniform Crime Reports, December 4, 1994)
*Includes nonnegligent manslaughter.

Murder Rate in 1993

National Rate = 9.5 Murders per 100,000 Population*

ALPHA ORDER				RANK ORDER		
RANK	STATE	RATE		RANK	STATE	RATE
7	Alabama	11.6		1	Louisiana	20.3
17	Alaska	9.0		2	Mississippi	13.5
19	Arizona	8.6		3	New York	13.3
14	Arkansas	10.2		4	California	13.1
4	California	13.1		5	Maryland	12.7
30	Colorado	5.8		6	Texas	11.9
28	Connecticut	6.3		7	Alabama	11.6
33	Delaware	5.0		8	Georgia	11.4
18	Florida	8.9		8	Illinois	11.4
8	Georgia	11.4		10	Missouri	11.3
39	Hawaii	3.8		10	North Carolina	11.3
46	Idaho	2.9		12	Nevada	10.4
8	Illinois	11.4		13	South Carolina	10.3
23	Indiana	7.5		14	Arkansas	10.2
47	Iowa	2.3		14	Tennessee	10.2
27	Kansas	6.4		16	Michigan	9.8
26	Kentucky	6.6		17	Alaska	9.0
1	Louisiana	20.3		18	Florida	8.9
50	Maine	1.6		19	Arizona	8.6
5	Maryland	12.7		20	Oklahoma	8.4
36	Massachusetts	3.9		21	Virginia	8.3
16	Michigan	9.8		22	New Mexico	8.0
41	Minnesota	3.4		23	Indiana	7.5
2	Mississippi	13.5		24	West Virginia	6.9
10	Missouri	11.3		25	Pennsylvania	6.8
45	Montana	3.0		26	Kentucky	6.6
36	Nebraska	3.9		27	Kansas	6.4
12	Nevada	10.4		28	Connecticut	6.3
48	New Hampshire	2.0		29	Ohio	6.0
31	New Jersey	5.3		30	Colorado	5.8
22	New Mexico	8.0		31	New Jersey	5.3
3	New York	13.3		32	Washington	5.2
10	North Carolina	11.3		33	Delaware	5.0
49	North Dakota	1.7		34	Oregon	4.6
29	Ohio	6.0		35	Wisconsin	4.4
20	Oklahoma	8.4		36	Massachusetts	3.9
34	Oregon	4.6		36	Nebraska	3.9
25	Pennsylvania	6.8		36	Rhode Island	3.9
36	Rhode Island	3.9		39	Hawaii	3.8
13	South Carolina	10.3		40	Vermont	3.6
41	South Dakota	3.4		41	Minnesota	3.4
14	Tennessee	10.2		41	South Dakota	3.4
6	Texas	11.9		41	Wyoming	3.4
44	Utah	3.1		44	Utah	3.1
40	Vermont	3.6		45	Montana	3.0
21	Virginia	8.3		46	Idaho	2.9
32	Washington	5.2		47	Iowa	2.3
24	West Virginia	6.9		48	New Hampshire	2.0
35	Wisconsin	4.4		49	North Dakota	1.7
41	Wyoming	3.4		50	Maine	1.6
					District of Columbia	78.5

Source: U.S. Department of Justice, Federal Bureau of Investigation
"Crime in the United States 1993" (Uniform Crime Reports, December 4, 1994)
*Includes nonnegligent manslaughter.

Percent Change in Murder Rate: 1992 to 1993

National Percent Change = 2.2% Increase*

ALPHA ORDER				RANK ORDER		
RANK	STATE	PERCENT CHANGE		RANK	STATE	PERCENT CHANGE
21	Alabama	5.5		1	South Dakota	466.7
7	Alaska	20.0		2	Vermont	71.4
19	Arizona	6.2		3	Iowa	43.8
39	Arkansas	(5.6)		4	Oklahoma	29.2
28	California	3.1		5	New Hampshire	25.0
44	Colorado	(6.5)		6	Connecticut	23.5
6	Connecticut	23.5		7	Alaska	20.0
13	Delaware	8.7		8	Louisiana	16.7
35	Florida	(1.1)		9	Kentucky	13.8
25	Georgia	3.6		10	Mississippi	10.7
20	Hawaii	5.6		11	Pennsylvania	9.7
50	Idaho	(17.1)		12	West Virginia	9.5
31	Illinois	0.0		13	Delaware	8.7
46	Indiana	(8.5)		14	Massachusetts	8.3
3	Iowa	43.8		14	Rhode Island	8.3
17	Kansas	6.7		16	Missouri	7.6
9	Kentucky	13.8		17	Kansas	6.7
8	Louisiana	16.7		18	North Carolina	6.6
42	Maine	(5.9)		19	Arizona	6.2
22	Maryland	5.0		20	Hawaii	5.6
14	Massachusetts	8.3		21	Alabama	5.5
33	Michigan	(1.0)		22	Maryland	5.0
29	Minnesota	3.0		23	Washington	4.0
10	Mississippi	10.7		24	New Jersey	3.9
16	Missouri	7.6		25	Georgia	3.6
26	Montana	3.4		26	Montana	3.4
45	Nebraska	(7.1)		27	Utah	3.3
38	Nevada	(4.6)		28	California	3.1
5	New Hampshire	25.0		29	Minnesota	3.0
24	New Jersey	3.9		30	New York	0.8
48	New Mexico	(10.1)		31	Illinois	0.0
30	New York	0.8		31	Wisconsin	0.0
18	North Carolina	6.6		33	Michigan	(1.0)
49	North Dakota	(10.5)		33	South Carolina	(1.0)
47	Ohio	(9.1)		35	Florida	(1.1)
4	Oklahoma	29.2		36	Tennessee	(1.9)
37	Oregon	(2.1)		37	Oregon	(2.1)
11	Pennsylvania	9.7		38	Nevada	(4.6)
14	Rhode Island	8.3		39	Arkansas	(5.6)
33	South Carolina	(1.0)		39	Wyoming	(5.6)
1	South Dakota	466.7		41	Virginia	(5.7)
36	Tennessee	(1.9)		42	Maine	(5.9)
43	Texas	(6.3)		43	Texas	(6.3)
27	Utah	3.3		44	Colorado	(6.5)
2	Vermont	71.4		45	Nebraska	(7.1)
41	Virginia	(5.7)		46	Indiana	(8.5)
23	Washington	4.0		47	Ohio	(9.1)
12	West Virginia	9.5		48	New Mexico	(10.1)
31	Wisconsin	0.0		49	North Dakota	(10.5)
39	Wyoming	(5.6)		50	Idaho	(17.1)

District of Columbia	4.4

Source: U.S. Department of Justice, Federal Bureau of Investigation
"Crime in the United States 1993" (Uniform Crime Reports, December 4, 1994)
*Includes nonnegligent manslaughter.

Murders with Firearms in 1993

National Total = 15,367 Murders with Firearms*

ALPHA ORDER

RANK	STATE	MURDERS	%
15	Alabama	284	1.85%
34	Alaska	27	0.18%
18	Arizona	230	1.50%
20	Arkansas	175	1.14%
1	California	3,007	19.57%
26	Colorado	132	0.86%
25	Connecticut	139	0.90%
41	Delaware	12	0.08%
4	Florida	753	4.90%
8	Georgia	506	3.29%
39	Hawaii	16	0.10%
38	Idaho	17	0.11%
NA	Illinois**	NA	NA
17	Indiana	260	1.69%
37	Iowa	18	0.12%
NA	Kansas**	NA	NA
22	Kentucky	161	1.05%
6	Louisiana	586	3.81%
46	Maine	5	0.03%
10	Maryland	458	2.98%
28	Massachusetts	110	0.72%
5	Michigan	681	4.43%
32	Minnesota	69	0.45%
22	Mississippi	161	1.05%
12	Missouri	410	2.67%
NA	Montana**	NA	NA
40	Nebraska	13	0.08%
30	Nevada	84	0.55%
42	New Hampshire	10	0.07%
19	New Jersey	213	1.39%
33	New Mexico	49	0.32%
2	New York	1,739	11.32%
9	North Carolina	493	3.21%
46	North Dakota	5	0.03%
11	Ohio	431	2.80%
21	Oklahoma	170	1.11%
31	Oregon	76	0.49%
7	Pennsylvania	573	3.73%
36	Rhode Island	21	0.14%
16	South Carolina	264	1.72%
42	South Dakota	10	0.07%
14	Tennessee	322	2.10%
3	Texas	1,535	9.99%
35	Utah	23	0.15%
45	Vermont	8	0.05%
13	Virginia	394	2.56%
24	Washington	155	1.01%
29	West Virginia	85	0.55%
27	Wisconsin	117	0.76%
42	Wyoming	10	0.07%

RANK ORDER

RANK	STATE	MURDERS	%
1	California	3,007	19.57%
2	New York	1,739	11.32%
3	Texas	1,535	9.99%
4	Florida	753	4.90%
5	Michigan	681	4.43%
6	Louisiana	586	3.81%
7	Pennsylvania	573	3.73%
8	Georgia	506	3.29%
9	North Carolina	493	3.21%
10	Maryland	458	2.98%
11	Ohio	431	2.80%
12	Missouri	410	2.67%
13	Virginia	394	2.56%
14	Tennessee	322	2.10%
15	Alabama	284	1.85%
16	South Carolina	264	1.72%
17	Indiana	260	1.69%
18	Arizona	230	1.50%
19	New Jersey	213	1.39%
20	Arkansas	175	1.14%
21	Oklahoma	170	1.11%
22	Kentucky	161	1.05%
22	Mississippi	161	1.05%
24	Washington	155	1.01%
25	Connecticut	139	0.90%
26	Colorado	132	0.86%
27	Wisconsin	117	0.76%
28	Massachusetts	110	0.72%
29	West Virginia	85	0.55%
30	Nevada	84	0.55%
31	Oregon	76	0.49%
32	Minnesota	69	0.45%
33	New Mexico	49	0.32%
34	Alaska	27	0.18%
35	Utah	23	0.15%
36	Rhode Island	21	0.14%
37	Iowa	18	0.12%
38	Idaho	17	0.11%
39	Hawaii	16	0.10%
40	Nebraska	13	0.08%
41	Delaware	12	0.08%
42	New Hampshire	10	0.07%
42	South Dakota	10	0.07%
42	Wyoming	10	0.07%
45	Vermont	8	0.05%
46	Maine	5	0.03%
46	North Dakota	5	0.03%
NA	Illinois**	NA	NA
NA	Kansas**	NA	NA
NA	Montana**	NA	NA
	District of Columbia	350	2.28%

Source: U.S. Department of Justice, Federal Bureau of Investigation
"Crime in the United States 1993" (Uniform Crime Reports, December 4, 1994)
Of the 22,081 murders in 1993 for which supplemental data were received by the F.B.I. There were an additional 2,445 murders for which the type of murder weapon was not reported to the F.B.I. Includes nonnegligent manslaughter.
**Not available.*

Murder Rate with Firearms in 1993

National Rate = 6.33 Murders per 100,000 Population*

ALPHA ORDER

RANK ORDER

RANK	STATE	RATE	RANK	STATE	RATE
12	Alabama	6.78	1	Louisiana	13.64
23	Alaska	4.51	2	California	9.63
17	Arizona	5.84	3	New York	9.56
9	Arkansas	7.22	4	Maryland	9.22
2	California	9.63	5	Texas	8.51
27	Colorado	3.70	6	Missouri	7.83
25	Connecticut	4.24	7	Georgia	7.32
36	Delaware	1.71	8	South Carolina	7.25
18	Florida	5.50	9	Arkansas	7.22
7	Georgia	7.32	10	Michigan	7.19
41	Hawaii	1.37	11	North Carolina	7.10
37	Idaho	1.55	12	Alabama	6.78
NA	Illinois**	NA	13	Tennessee	6.31
22	Indiana	4.55	14	Mississippi	6.09
46	Iowa	0.64	15	Virginia	6.07
NA	Kansas**	NA	16	Nevada	6.05
24	Kentucky	4.25	17	Arizona	5.84
1	Louisiana	13.64	18	Florida	5.50
47	Maine	0.40	19	Oklahoma	5.26
4	Maryland	9.22	20	Pennsylvania	4.76
35	Massachusetts	1.83	21	West Virginia	4.67
10	Michigan	7.19	22	Indiana	4.55
38	Minnesota	1.53	23	Alaska	4.51
14	Mississippi	6.09	24	Kentucky	4.25
6	Missouri	7.83	25	Connecticut	4.24
NA	Montana**	NA	26	Ohio	3.89
44	Nebraska	0.81	27	Colorado	3.70
16	Nevada	6.05	28	New Mexico	3.03
43	New Hampshire	0.89	29	Washington	2.95
30	New Jersey	2.70	30	New Jersey	2.70
28	New Mexico	3.03	31	Oregon	2.51
3	New York	9.56	32	Wisconsin	2.32
11	North Carolina	7.10	33	Wyoming	2.13
45	North Dakota	0.79	34	Rhode Island	2.10
26	Ohio	3.89	35	Massachusetts	1.83
19	Oklahoma	5.26	36	Delaware	1.71
31	Oregon	2.51	37	Idaho	1.55
20	Pennsylvania	4.76	38	Minnesota	1.53
34	Rhode Island	2.10	39	South Dakota	1.40
8	South Carolina	7.25	40	Vermont	1.39
39	South Dakota	1.40	41	Hawaii	1.37
13	Tennessee	6.31	42	Utah	1.24
5	Texas	8.51	43	New Hampshire	0.89
42	Utah	1.24	44	Nebraska	0.81
40	Vermont	1.39	45	North Dakota	0.79
15	Virginia	6.07	46	Iowa	0.64
29	Washington	2.95	47	Maine	0.40
21	West Virginia	4.67	NA	Illinois**	NA
32	Wisconsin	2.32	NA	Kansas**	NA
33	Wyoming	2.13	NA	Montana**	NA

	District of Columbia	60.55

Source: Morgan Quitno Corporation using data from U.S. Department of Justice, Federal Bureau of Investigation
"Crime in the United States 1993" (Uniform Crime Reports, December 4, 1994)

*Of the 22,081 murders in 1993 for which supplemental data were received by the F.B.I. There were an additional 2,445 murders for which the type of murder weapon was not reported to the F.B.I. Includes nonnegligent manslaughter. National rate based on population for reporting states.

**Not available.

296

Percent of Murders Involving Firearms in 1993

National Percent = 69.59% of Murders*

<table>
<tr><td colspan="3"><u>ALPHA ORDER</u></td><td colspan="3"><u>RANK ORDER</u></td></tr>
<tr><td>RANK</td><td>STATE</td><td>PERCENT</td><td>RANK</td><td>STATE</td><td>PERCENT</td></tr>
<tr><td>29</td><td>Alabama</td><td>60.04</td><td>1</td><td>Louisiana</td><td>81.28</td></tr>
<tr><td>41</td><td>Alaska</td><td>50.00</td><td>2</td><td>Missouri</td><td>75.09</td></tr>
<tr><td>17</td><td>Arizona</td><td>69.70</td><td>3</td><td>Michigan</td><td>73.86</td></tr>
<tr><td>11</td><td>Arkansas</td><td>71.72</td><td>4</td><td>Mississippi</td><td>73.85</td></tr>
<tr><td>5</td><td>California</td><td>73.45</td><td>5</td><td>California</td><td>73.45</td></tr>
<tr><td>24</td><td>Colorado</td><td>64.08</td><td>6</td><td>Virginia</td><td>73.10</td></tr>
<tr><td>20</td><td>Connecticut</td><td>67.48</td><td>7</td><td>Indiana</td><td>72.83</td></tr>
<tr><td>30</td><td>Delaware</td><td>60.00</td><td>8</td><td>Maryland</td><td>72.47</td></tr>
<tr><td>28</td><td>Florida</td><td>61.57</td><td>9</td><td>New York</td><td>72.01</td></tr>
<tr><td>21</td><td>Georgia</td><td>67.47</td><td>10</td><td>Ohio</td><td>71.95</td></tr>
<tr><td>47</td><td>Hawaii</td><td>37.21</td><td>11</td><td>Arkansas</td><td>71.72</td></tr>
<tr><td>33</td><td>Idaho</td><td>54.84</td><td>12</td><td>Texas</td><td>71.66</td></tr>
<tr><td>NA</td><td>Illinois**</td><td>NA</td><td>13</td><td>Tennessee</td><td>71.56</td></tr>
<tr><td>7</td><td>Indiana</td><td>72.83</td><td>14</td><td>Maine</td><td>71.43</td></tr>
<tr><td>45</td><td>Iowa</td><td>40.00</td><td>15</td><td>Pennsylvania</td><td>71.27</td></tr>
<tr><td>NA</td><td>Kansas**</td><td>NA</td><td>16</td><td>South Carolina</td><td>70.40</td></tr>
<tr><td>18</td><td>Kentucky</td><td>68.22</td><td>17</td><td>Arizona</td><td>69.70</td></tr>
<tr><td>1</td><td>Louisiana</td><td>81.28</td><td>18</td><td>Kentucky</td><td>68.22</td></tr>
<tr><td>14</td><td>Maine</td><td>71.43</td><td>19</td><td>West Virginia</td><td>68.00</td></tr>
<tr><td>8</td><td>Maryland</td><td>72.47</td><td>20</td><td>Connecticut</td><td>67.48</td></tr>
<tr><td>38</td><td>Massachusetts</td><td>52.38</td><td>21</td><td>Georgia</td><td>67.47</td></tr>
<tr><td>3</td><td>Michigan</td><td>73.86</td><td>22</td><td>Vermont</td><td>66.67</td></tr>
<tr><td>37</td><td>Minnesota</td><td>52.67</td><td>23</td><td>Nevada</td><td>65.12</td></tr>
<tr><td>4</td><td>Mississippi</td><td>73.85</td><td>24</td><td>Colorado</td><td>64.08</td></tr>
<tr><td>2</td><td>Missouri</td><td>75.09</td><td>25</td><td>North Carolina</td><td>63.94</td></tr>
<tr><td>NA</td><td>Montana**</td><td>NA</td><td>26</td><td>Oklahoma</td><td>62.50</td></tr>
<tr><td>43</td><td>Nebraska</td><td>46.43</td><td>26</td><td>Wyoming</td><td>62.50</td></tr>
<tr><td>23</td><td>Nevada</td><td>65.12</td><td>28</td><td>Florida</td><td>61.57</td></tr>
<tr><td>41</td><td>New Hampshire</td><td>50.00</td><td>29</td><td>Alabama</td><td>60.04</td></tr>
<tr><td>40</td><td>New Jersey</td><td>50.96</td><td>30</td><td>Delaware</td><td>60.00</td></tr>
<tr><td>39</td><td>New Mexico</td><td>51.58</td><td>31</td><td>Washington</td><td>58.71</td></tr>
<tr><td>9</td><td>New York</td><td>72.01</td><td>32</td><td>South Dakota</td><td>55.56</td></tr>
<tr><td>25</td><td>North Carolina</td><td>63.94</td><td>33</td><td>Idaho</td><td>54.84</td></tr>
<tr><td>44</td><td>North Dakota</td><td>45.45</td><td>34</td><td>Rhode Island</td><td>53.85</td></tr>
<tr><td>10</td><td>Ohio</td><td>71.95</td><td>35</td><td>Oregon</td><td>53.15</td></tr>
<tr><td>26</td><td>Oklahoma</td><td>62.50</td><td>36</td><td>Wisconsin</td><td>52.70</td></tr>
<tr><td>35</td><td>Oregon</td><td>53.15</td><td>37</td><td>Minnesota</td><td>52.67</td></tr>
<tr><td>15</td><td>Pennsylvania</td><td>71.27</td><td>38</td><td>Massachusetts</td><td>52.38</td></tr>
<tr><td>34</td><td>Rhode Island</td><td>53.85</td><td>39</td><td>New Mexico</td><td>51.58</td></tr>
<tr><td>16</td><td>South Carolina</td><td>70.40</td><td>40</td><td>New Jersey</td><td>50.96</td></tr>
<tr><td>32</td><td>South Dakota</td><td>55.56</td><td>41</td><td>Alaska</td><td>50.00</td></tr>
<tr><td>13</td><td>Tennessee</td><td>71.56</td><td>41</td><td>New Hampshire</td><td>50.00</td></tr>
<tr><td>12</td><td>Texas</td><td>71.66</td><td>43</td><td>Nebraska</td><td>46.43</td></tr>
<tr><td>46</td><td>Utah</td><td>39.66</td><td>44</td><td>North Dakota</td><td>45.45</td></tr>
<tr><td>22</td><td>Vermont</td><td>66.67</td><td>45</td><td>Iowa</td><td>40.00</td></tr>
<tr><td>6</td><td>Virginia</td><td>73.10</td><td>46</td><td>Utah</td><td>39.66</td></tr>
<tr><td>31</td><td>Washington</td><td>58.71</td><td>47</td><td>Hawaii</td><td>37.21</td></tr>
<tr><td>19</td><td>West Virginia</td><td>68.00</td><td>NA</td><td>Illinois**</td><td>NA</td></tr>
<tr><td>36</td><td>Wisconsin</td><td>52.70</td><td>NA</td><td>Kansas**</td><td>NA</td></tr>
<tr><td>26</td><td>Wyoming</td><td>62.50</td><td>NA</td><td>Montana**</td><td>NA</td></tr>
<tr><td></td><td></td><td></td><td></td><td>District of Columbia</td><td>83.93</td></tr>
</table>

Source: Morgan Quitno Corporation using data from U.S. Department of Justice, Federal Bureau of Investigation
"Crime in the United States 1993" (Uniform Crime Reports, December 4, 1994)
*Of the 22,081 murders in 1993 for which supplemental data were received by the F.B.I. There were an additional 2,445 murders for which the type of murder weapon was not reported to the F.B.I. Includes nonnegligent manslaughter.
**Not available.

Murders with Handguns in 1993

National Total = 12,519 Murders with Handguns*

ALPHA ORDER

RANK	STATE	MURDERS	%
15	Alabama	234	1.87%
34	Alaska	20	0.16%
19	Arizona	168	1.34%
23	Arkansas	125	1.00%
1	California	2,609	20.84%
26	Colorado	111	0.89%
24	Connecticut	117	0.93%
39	Delaware	10	0.08%
5	Florida	486	3.88%
7	Georgia	435	3.47%
38	Hawaii	12	0.10%
37	Idaho	14	0.11%
NA	Illinois**	NA	NA
16	Indiana	225	1.80%
39	Iowa	10	0.08%
NA	Kansas**	NA	NA
25	Kentucky	115	0.92%
4	Louisiana	520	4.15%
46	Maine	4	0.03%
8	Maryland	427	3.41%
29	Massachusetts	60	0.48%
9	Michigan	379	3.03%
32	Minnesota	51	0.41%
20	Mississippi	141	1.13%
13	Missouri	324	2.59%
NA	Montana**	NA	NA
42	Nebraska	7	0.06%
28	Nevada	79	0.63%
44	New Hampshire	5	0.04%
18	New Jersey	182	1.45%
33	New Mexico	39	0.31%
2	New York	1,604	12.81%
11	North Carolina	368	2.94%
47	North Dakota	3	0.02%
10	Ohio	375	3.00%
21	Oklahoma	131	1.05%
30	Oregon	57	0.46%
5	Pennsylvania	486	3.88%
36	Rhode Island	16	0.13%
17	South Carolina	213	1.70%
41	South Dakota	8	0.06%
14	Tennessee	271	2.16%
3	Texas	1,107	8.84%
35	Utah	17	0.14%
44	Vermont	5	0.04%
12	Virginia	325	2.60%
22	Washington	127	1.01%
31	West Virginia	53	0.42%
27	Wisconsin	88	0.70%
43	Wyoming	6	0.05%

RANK ORDER

RANK	STATE	MURDERS	%
1	California	2,609	20.84%
2	New York	1,604	12.81%
3	Texas	1,107	8.84%
4	Louisiana	520	4.15%
5	Florida	486	3.88%
5	Pennsylvania	486	3.88%
7	Georgia	435	3.47%
8	Maryland	427	3.41%
9	Michigan	379	3.03%
10	Ohio	375	3.00%
11	North Carolina	368	2.94%
12	Virginia	325	2.60%
13	Missouri	324	2.59%
14	Tennessee	271	2.16%
15	Alabama	234	1.87%
16	Indiana	225	1.80%
17	South Carolina	213	1.70%
18	New Jersey	182	1.45%
19	Arizona	168	1.34%
20	Mississippi	141	1.13%
21	Oklahoma	131	1.05%
22	Washington	127	1.01%
23	Arkansas	125	1.00%
24	Connecticut	117	0.93%
25	Kentucky	115	0.92%
26	Colorado	111	0.89%
27	Wisconsin	88	0.70%
28	Nevada	79	0.63%
29	Massachusetts	60	0.48%
30	Oregon	57	0.46%
31	West Virginia	53	0.42%
32	Minnesota	51	0.41%
33	New Mexico	39	0.31%
34	Alaska	20	0.16%
35	Utah	17	0.14%
36	Rhode Island	16	0.13%
37	Idaho	14	0.11%
38	Hawaii	12	0.10%
39	Delaware	10	0.08%
39	Iowa	10	0.08%
41	South Dakota	8	0.06%
42	Nebraska	7	0.06%
43	Wyoming	6	0.05%
44	New Hampshire	5	0.04%
44	Vermont	5	0.04%
46	Maine	4	0.03%
47	North Dakota	3	0.02%
NA	Illinois**	NA	NA
NA	Kansas**	NA	NA
NA	Montana**	NA	NA
	District of Columbia	350	2.80%

Source: U.S. Department of Justice, Federal Bureau of Investigation
  "Crime in the United States 1993" (Uniform Crime Reports, December 4, 1994)
*Of the 22,081 murders in 1993 for which supplemental data were received by the F.B.I. There were an additional 2,445 murders for which the type of murder weapon was not reported to the F.B.I. Includes nonnegligent manslaughter.
**Not available.

Murder Rate with Handguns in 1993

National Rate = 5.16 Murders per 100,000 Population*

<u>ALPHA ORDER</u>

RANK	STATE	RATE
10	Alabama	5.59
24	Alaska	3.34
16	Arizona	4.27
14	Arkansas	5.16
4	California	8.36
25	Colorado	3.11
21	Connecticut	3.57
34	Delaware	1.43
22	Florida	3.55
5	Georgia	6.29
39	Hawaii	1.02
36	Idaho	1.27
NA	Illinois**	NA
20	Indiana	3.94
46	Iowa	0.36
NA	Kansas**	NA
26	Kentucky	3.04
1	Louisiana	12.11
47	Maine	0.32
3	Maryland	8.60
40	Massachusetts	1.00
19	Michigan	4.00
37	Minnesota	1.13
11	Mississippi	5.33
6	Missouri	6.19
NA	Montana**	NA
44	Nebraska	0.44
9	Nevada	5.69
44	New Hampshire	0.44
30	New Jersey	2.31
29	New Mexico	2.41
2	New York	8.81
13	North Carolina	5.30
43	North Dakota	0.47
23	Ohio	3.38
17	Oklahoma	4.05
31	Oregon	1.88
18	Pennsylvania	4.03
33	Rhode Island	1.60
8	South Carolina	5.85
38	South Dakota	1.12
12	Tennessee	5.31
7	Texas	6.14
41	Utah	0.91
42	Vermont	0.87
15	Virginia	5.01
28	Washington	2.42
27	West Virginia	2.91
32	Wisconsin	1.75
35	Wyoming	1.28

<u>RANK ORDER</u>

RANK	STATE	RATE
1	Louisiana	12.11
2	New York	8.81
3	Maryland	8.60
4	California	8.36
5	Georgia	6.29
6	Missouri	6.19
7	Texas	6.14
8	South Carolina	5.85
9	Nevada	5.69
10	Alabama	5.59
11	Mississippi	5.33
12	Tennessee	5.31
13	North Carolina	5.30
14	Arkansas	5.16
15	Virginia	5.01
16	Arizona	4.27
17	Oklahoma	4.05
18	Pennsylvania	4.03
19	Michigan	4.00
20	Indiana	3.94
21	Connecticut	3.57
22	Florida	3.55
23	Ohio	3.38
24	Alaska	3.34
25	Colorado	3.11
26	Kentucky	3.04
27	West Virginia	2.91
28	Washington	2.42
29	New Mexico	2.41
30	New Jersey	2.31
31	Oregon	1.88
32	Wisconsin	1.75
33	Rhode Island	1.60
34	Delaware	1.43
35	Wyoming	1.28
36	Idaho	1.27
37	Minnesota	1.13
38	South Dakota	1.12
39	Hawaii	1.02
40	Massachusetts	1.00
41	Utah	0.91
42	Vermont	0.87
43	North Dakota	0.47
44	Nebraska	0.44
44	New Hampshire	0.44
46	Iowa	0.36
47	Maine	0.32
NA	Illinois**	NA
NA	Kansas**	NA
NA	Montana**	NA

District of Columbia   60.55

Source: Morgan Quitno Corporation using data from U.S. Department of Justice, Federal Bureau of Investigation
"Crime in the United States 1993" (Uniform Crime Reports, December 4, 1994)
*Of the 22,081 murders in 1993 for which supplemental data were received by the F.B.I. There were an additional 2,445 murders for which the type of murder weapon was not reported to the F.B.I. Includes nonnegligent manslaughter. National rate based on population for reporting states.
**Not available.   299

Percent of Murders Involving Handguns in 1993

National Percent = 56.70% of Murders*

ALPHA ORDER

ALPHA ORDER

RANK	STATE	PERCENT
22	Alabama	49.47
40	Alaska	37.04
20	Arizona	50.91
19	Arkansas	51.23
5	California	63.73
17	Colorado	53.88
15	Connecticut	56.80
21	Delaware	50.00
36	Florida	39.74
13	Georgia	58.00
43	Hawaii	27.91
27	Idaho	45.16
NA	Illinois**	NA
6	Indiana	63.03
47	Iowa	22.22
NA	Kansas**	NA
23	Kentucky	48.73
1	Louisiana	72.12
14	Maine	57.14
2	Maryland	67.56
42	Massachusetts	28.57
32	Michigan	41.11
38	Minnesota	38.93
4	Mississippi	64.68
12	Missouri	59.34
NA	Montana**	NA
45	Nebraska	25.00
8	Nevada	61.24
45	New Hampshire	25.00
29	New Jersey	43.54
33	New Mexico	41.05
3	New York	66.42
26	North Carolina	47.73
44	North Dakota	27.27
7	Ohio	62.60
24	Oklahoma	48.16
35	Oregon	39.86
9	Pennsylvania	60.45
34	Rhode Island	41.03
15	South Carolina	56.80
28	South Dakota	44.44
11	Tennessee	60.22
18	Texas	51.68
41	Utah	29.31
31	Vermont	41.67
10	Virginia	60.30
25	Washington	48.11
30	West Virginia	42.40
37	Wisconsin	39.64
39	Wyoming	37.50

RANK ORDER

RANK	STATE	PERCENT
1	Louisiana	72.12
2	Maryland	67.56
3	New York	66.42
4	Mississippi	64.68
5	California	63.73
6	Indiana	63.03
7	Ohio	62.60
8	Nevada	61.24
9	Pennsylvania	60.45
10	Virginia	60.30
11	Tennessee	60.22
12	Missouri	59.34
13	Georgia	58.00
14	Maine	57.14
15	Connecticut	56.80
15	South Carolina	56.80
17	Colorado	53.88
18	Texas	51.68
19	Arkansas	51.23
20	Arizona	50.91
21	Delaware	50.00
22	Alabama	49.47
23	Kentucky	48.73
24	Oklahoma	48.16
25	Washington	48.11
26	North Carolina	47.73
27	Idaho	45.16
28	South Dakota	44.44
29	New Jersey	43.54
30	West Virginia	42.40
31	Vermont	41.67
32	Michigan	41.11
33	New Mexico	41.05
34	Rhode Island	41.03
35	Oregon	39.86
36	Florida	39.74
37	Wisconsin	39.64
38	Minnesota	38.93
39	Wyoming	37.50
40	Alaska	37.04
41	Utah	29.31
42	Massachusetts	28.57
43	Hawaii	27.91
44	North Dakota	27.27
45	Nebraska	25.00
45	New Hampshire	25.00
47	Iowa	22.22
NA	Illinois**	NA
NA	Kansas**	NA
NA	Montana**	NA

District of Columbia 83.93

Source: Morgan Quitno Corporation using data from U.S. Department of Justice, Federal Bureau of Investigation
"Crime in the United States 1993" (Uniform Crime Reports, December 4, 1994)
*Of the 22,081 murders in 1993 for which supplemental data were received by the F.B.I. There were an additional 2,445 murders for which the type of murder weapon was not reported to the F.B.I. Includes nonnegligent manslaughter.
**Not available.

Murders with Rifles in 1993

National Total = 738 Murders with Rifles*

ALPHA ORDER

RANK	STATE	MURDERS	%
16	Alabama	14	1.90%
28	Alaska	5	0.68%
14	Arizona	15	2.03%
11	Arkansas	17	2.30%
1	California	154	20.87%
28	Colorado	5	0.68%
28	Connecticut	5	0.68%
42	Delaware	1	0.14%
7	Florida	24	3.25%
7	Georgia	24	3.25%
36	Hawaii	2	0.27%
33	Idaho	3	0.41%
NA	Illinois**	NA	NA
16	Indiana	14	1.90%
42	Iowa	1	0.14%
NA	Kansas**	NA	NA
22	Kentucky	10	1.36%
5	Louisiana	39	5.28%
45	Maine	0	0.00%
36	Maryland	2	0.27%
33	Massachusetts	3	0.41%
3	Michigan	49	6.64%
24	Minnesota	8	1.08%
24	Mississippi	8	1.08%
6	Missouri	26	3.52%
NA	Montana**	NA	NA
42	Nebraska	1	0.14%
36	Nevada	2	0.27%
45	New Hampshire	0	0.00%
23	New Jersey	9	1.22%
28	New Mexico	5	0.68%
13	New York	16	2.17%
3	North Carolina	49	6.64%
45	North Dakota	0	0.00%
20	Ohio	12	1.63%
9	Oklahoma	22	2.98%
26	Oregon	7	0.95%
16	Pennsylvania	14	1.90%
36	Rhode Island	2	0.27%
10	South Carolina	18	2.44%
36	South Dakota	2	0.27%
19	Tennessee	13	1.76%
2	Texas	77	10.43%
33	Utah	3	0.41%
36	Vermont	2	0.27%
11	Virginia	17	2.30%
14	Washington	15	2.03%
20	West Virginia	12	1.63%
26	Wisconsin	7	0.95%
32	Wyoming	4	0.54%

RANK ORDER

RANK	STATE	MURDERS	%
1	California	154	20.87%
2	Texas	77	10.43%
3	Michigan	49	6.64%
3	North Carolina	49	6.64%
5	Louisiana	39	5.28%
6	Missouri	26	3.52%
7	Florida	24	3.25%
7	Georgia	24	3.25%
9	Oklahoma	22	2.98%
10	South Carolina	18	2.44%
11	Arkansas	17	2.30%
11	Virginia	17	2.30%
13	New York	16	2.17%
14	Arizona	15	2.03%
14	Washington	15	2.03%
16	Alabama	14	1.90%
16	Indiana	14	1.90%
16	Pennsylvania	14	1.90%
19	Tennessee	13	1.76%
20	Ohio	12	1.63%
20	West Virginia	12	1.63%
22	Kentucky	10	1.36%
23	New Jersey	9	1.22%
24	Minnesota	8	1.08%
24	Mississippi	8	1.08%
26	Oregon	7	0.95%
26	Wisconsin	7	0.95%
28	Alaska	5	0.68%
28	Colorado	5	0.68%
28	Connecticut	5	0.68%
28	New Mexico	5	0.68%
32	Wyoming	4	0.54%
33	Idaho	3	0.41%
33	Massachusetts	3	0.41%
33	Utah	3	0.41%
36	Hawaii	2	0.27%
36	Maryland	2	0.27%
36	Nevada	2	0.27%
36	Rhode Island	2	0.27%
36	South Dakota	2	0.27%
36	Vermont	2	0.27%
42	Delaware	1	0.14%
42	Iowa	1	0.14%
42	Nebraska	1	0.14%
45	Maine	0	0.00%
45	New Hampshire	0	0.00%
45	North Dakota	0	0.00%
NA	Illinois**	NA	NA
NA	Kansas**	NA	NA
NA	Montana**	NA	NA
	District of Columbia	0	0.00%

Source: U.S. Department of Justice, Federal Bureau of Investigation
"Crime in the United States 1993" (Uniform Crime Reports, December 4, 1994)
*Of the 22,081 murders in 1993 for which supplemental data were received by the F.B.I. There were an additional 2,445 murders for which the type of murder weapon was not reported to the F.B.I. Includes nonnegligent manslaughter.
**Not available.

Percent of Murders Involving Rifles in 1993

National Percent = 3.34% of Murders*

ALPHA ORDER			RANK ORDER		
RANK	**STATE**	**PERCENT**	**RANK**	**STATE**	**PERCENT**
32	Alabama	2.96	1	Wyoming	25.00
6	Alaska	9.26	2	Vermont	16.67
22	Arizona	4.55	3	South Dakota	11.11
8	Arkansas	6.97	4	Idaho	9.68
25	California	3.76	5	West Virginia	9.60
34	Colorado	2.43	6	Alaska	9.26
34	Connecticut	2.43	7	Oklahoma	8.09
17	Delaware	5.00	8	Arkansas	6.97
39	Florida	1.96	9	North Carolina	6.36
29	Georgia	3.20	10	Minnesota	6.11
21	Hawaii	4.65	11	Washington	5.68
4	Idaho	9.68	12	Louisiana	5.41
NA	Illinois**	NA	13	Michigan	5.31
24	Indiana	3.92	14	New Mexico	5.26
36	Iowa	2.22	15	Utah	5.17
NA	Kansas**	NA	16	Rhode Island	5.13
23	Kentucky	4.24	17	Delaware	5.00
12	Louisiana	5.41	18	Oregon	4.90
45	Maine	0.00	19	South Carolina	4.80
44	Maryland	0.32	20	Missouri	4.76
42	Massachusetts	1.43	21	Hawaii	4.65
13	Michigan	5.31	22	Arizona	4.55
10	Minnesota	6.11	23	Kentucky	4.24
26	Mississippi	3.67	24	Indiana	3.92
20	Missouri	4.76	25	California	3.76
NA	Montana**	NA	26	Mississippi	3.67
28	Nebraska	3.57	27	Texas	3.59
41	Nevada	1.55	28	Nebraska	3.57
45	New Hampshire	0.00	29	Georgia	3.20
37	New Jersey	2.15	30	Virginia	3.15
14	New Mexico	5.26	30	Wisconsin	3.15
43	New York	0.66	32	Alabama	2.96
9	North Carolina	6.36	33	Tennessee	2.89
45	North Dakota	0.00	34	Colorado	2.43
38	Ohio	2.00	34	Connecticut	2.43
7	Oklahoma	8.09	36	Iowa	2.22
18	Oregon	4.90	37	New Jersey	2.15
40	Pennsylvania	1.74	38	Ohio	2.00
16	Rhode Island	5.13	39	Florida	1.96
19	South Carolina	4.80	40	Pennsylvania	1.74
3	South Dakota	11.11	41	Nevada	1.55
33	Tennessee	2.89	42	Massachusetts	1.43
27	Texas	3.59	43	New York	0.66
15	Utah	5.17	44	Maryland	0.32
2	Vermont	16.67	45	Maine	0.00
30	Virginia	3.15	45	New Hampshire	0.00
11	Washington	5.68	45	North Dakota	0.00
5	West Virginia	9.60	NA	Illinois**	NA
30	Wisconsin	3.15	NA	Kansas**	NA
1	Wyoming	25.00	NA	Montana**	NA
				District of Columbia	0.00

Source: Morgan Quitno Corporation using data from U.S. Department of Justice, Federal Bureau of Investigation "Crime in the United States 1993" (Uniform Crime Reports, December 4, 1994)

*Of the 22,081 murders in 1993 for which supplemental data were received by the F.B.I. There were an additional 2,445 murders for which the type of murder weapon was not reported to the F.B.I. Includes nonnegligent manslaughter.

**Not available.

Murders with Shotguns in 1993

National Total = 1,033 Murders with Shotguns*

<u>ALPHA ORDER</u>

RANK	STATE	MURDERS	%
8	Alabama	35	3.39%
38	Alaska	1	0.10%
22	Arizona	15	1.45%
18	Arkansas	20	1.94%
1	California	167	16.17%
29	Colorado	6	0.58%
34	Connecticut	2	0.19%
38	Delaware	1	0.10%
7	Florida	36	3.48%
10	Georgia	32	3.10%
34	Hawaii	2	0.19%
44	Idaho	0	0.00%
NA	Illinois**	NA	NA
19	Indiana	17	1.65%
32	Iowa	3	0.29%
NA	Kansas**	NA	NA
14	Kentucky	24	2.32%
17	Louisiana	21	2.03%
44	Maine	0	0.00%
16	Maryland	22	2.13%
34	Massachusetts	2	0.19%
4	Michigan	70	6.78%
25	Minnesota	10	0.97%
27	Mississippi	8	0.77%
12	Missouri	28	2.71%
NA	Montana**	NA	NA
30	Nebraska	5	0.48%
32	Nevada	3	0.29%
34	New Hampshire	2	0.19%
22	New Jersey	15	1.45%
30	New Mexico	5	0.48%
5	New York	50	4.84%
3	North Carolina	71	6.87%
38	North Dakota	1	0.10%
12	Ohio	28	2.71%
21	Oklahoma	16	1.55%
27	Oregon	8	0.77%
8	Pennsylvania	35	3.39%
38	Rhode Island	1	0.10%
14	South Carolina	24	2.32%
44	South Dakota	0	0.00%
10	Tennessee	32	3.10%
2	Texas	133	12.88%
38	Utah	1	0.10%
38	Vermont	1	0.10%
6	Virginia	41	3.97%
25	Washington	10	0.97%
19	West Virginia	17	1.65%
24	Wisconsin	12	1.16%
44	Wyoming	0	0.00%

<u>RANK ORDER</u>

RANK	STATE	MURDERS	%
1	California	167	16.17%
2	Texas	133	12.88%
3	North Carolina	71	6.87%
4	Michigan	70	6.78%
5	New York	50	4.84%
6	Virginia	41	3.97%
7	Florida	36	3.48%
8	Alabama	35	3.39%
8	Pennsylvania	35	3.39%
10	Georgia	32	3.10%
10	Tennessee	32	3.10%
12	Missouri	28	2.71%
12	Ohio	28	2.71%
14	Kentucky	24	2.32%
14	South Carolina	24	2.32%
16	Maryland	22	2.13%
17	Louisiana	21	2.03%
18	Arkansas	20	1.94%
19	Indiana	17	1.65%
19	West Virginia	17	1.65%
21	Oklahoma	16	1.55%
22	Arizona	15	1.45%
22	New Jersey	15	1.45%
24	Wisconsin	12	1.16%
25	Minnesota	10	0.97%
25	Washington	10	0.97%
27	Mississippi	8	0.77%
27	Oregon	8	0.77%
29	Colorado	6	0.58%
30	Nebraska	5	0.48%
30	New Mexico	5	0.48%
32	Iowa	3	0.29%
32	Nevada	3	0.29%
34	Connecticut	2	0.19%
34	Hawaii	2	0.19%
34	Massachusetts	2	0.19%
34	New Hampshire	2	0.19%
38	Alaska	1	0.10%
38	Delaware	1	0.10%
38	North Dakota	1	0.10%
38	Rhode Island	1	0.10%
38	Utah	1	0.10%
38	Vermont	1	0.10%
44	Idaho	0	0.00%
44	Maine	0	0.00%
44	South Dakota	0	0.00%
44	Wyoming	0	0.00%
NA	Illinois**	NA	NA
NA	Kansas**	NA	NA
NA	Montana**	NA	NA
	District of Columbia	0	0.00%

Source: Morgan Quitno Corporation using data from U.S. Department of Justice, Federal Bureau of Investigation "Crime in the United States 1993" (Uniform Crime Reports, December 4, 1994)
Of the 22,081 murders in 1993 for which supplemental data were received by the F.B.I. There were an additional 2,445 murders for which the type of murder weapon was not reported to the F.B.I. Includes nonnegligent manslaughter.
**Not available.*

303

Percent of Murders Involving Shotguns in 1993

National Percent = 4.68% of Murders*

<table>
<tr><td colspan="3">ALPHA ORDER</td><td colspan="3">RANK ORDER</td></tr>
<tr><td>RANK</td><td>STATE</td><td>PERCENT</td><td>RANK</td><td>STATE</td><td>PERCENT</td></tr>
<tr><td>12</td><td>Alabama</td><td>7.40</td><td>1</td><td>Nebraska</td><td>17.86</td></tr>
<tr><td>40</td><td>Alaska</td><td>1.85</td><td>2</td><td>West Virginia</td><td>13.60</td></tr>
<tr><td>26</td><td>Arizona</td><td>4.55</td><td>3</td><td>Kentucky</td><td>10.17</td></tr>
<tr><td>8</td><td>Arkansas</td><td>8.20</td><td>4</td><td>New Hampshire</td><td>10.00</td></tr>
<tr><td>29</td><td>California</td><td>4.08</td><td>5</td><td>North Carolina</td><td>9.21</td></tr>
<tr><td>35</td><td>Colorado</td><td>2.91</td><td>6</td><td>North Dakota</td><td>9.09</td></tr>
<tr><td>42</td><td>Connecticut</td><td>0.97</td><td>7</td><td>Vermont</td><td>8.33</td></tr>
<tr><td>22</td><td>Delaware</td><td>5.00</td><td>8</td><td>Arkansas</td><td>8.20</td></tr>
<tr><td>34</td><td>Florida</td><td>2.94</td><td>9</td><td>Minnesota</td><td>7.63</td></tr>
<tr><td>28</td><td>Georgia</td><td>4.27</td><td>10</td><td>Virginia</td><td>7.61</td></tr>
<tr><td>25</td><td>Hawaii</td><td>4.65</td><td>11</td><td>Michigan</td><td>7.59</td></tr>
<tr><td>44</td><td>Idaho</td><td>0.00</td><td>12</td><td>Alabama</td><td>7.40</td></tr>
<tr><td>NA</td><td>Illinois**</td><td>NA</td><td>13</td><td>Tennessee</td><td>7.11</td></tr>
<tr><td>23</td><td>Indiana</td><td>4.76</td><td>14</td><td>Iowa</td><td>6.67</td></tr>
<tr><td>14</td><td>Iowa</td><td>6.67</td><td>15</td><td>South Carolina</td><td>6.40</td></tr>
<tr><td>NA</td><td>Kansas**</td><td>NA</td><td>16</td><td>Texas</td><td>6.21</td></tr>
<tr><td>3</td><td>Kentucky</td><td>10.17</td><td>17</td><td>Oklahoma</td><td>5.88</td></tr>
<tr><td>35</td><td>Louisiana</td><td>2.91</td><td>18</td><td>Oregon</td><td>5.59</td></tr>
<tr><td>44</td><td>Maine</td><td>0.00</td><td>19</td><td>Wisconsin</td><td>5.41</td></tr>
<tr><td>33</td><td>Maryland</td><td>3.48</td><td>20</td><td>New Mexico</td><td>5.26</td></tr>
<tr><td>43</td><td>Massachusetts</td><td>0.95</td><td>21</td><td>Missouri</td><td>5.13</td></tr>
<tr><td>11</td><td>Michigan</td><td>7.59</td><td>22</td><td>Delaware</td><td>5.00</td></tr>
<tr><td>9</td><td>Minnesota</td><td>7.63</td><td>23</td><td>Indiana</td><td>4.76</td></tr>
<tr><td>31</td><td>Mississippi</td><td>3.67</td><td>24</td><td>Ohio</td><td>4.67</td></tr>
<tr><td>21</td><td>Missouri</td><td>5.13</td><td>25</td><td>Hawaii</td><td>4.65</td></tr>
<tr><td>NA</td><td>Montana**</td><td>NA</td><td>26</td><td>Arizona</td><td>4.55</td></tr>
<tr><td>1</td><td>Nebraska</td><td>17.86</td><td>27</td><td>Pennsylvania</td><td>4.35</td></tr>
<tr><td>38</td><td>Nevada</td><td>2.33</td><td>28</td><td>Georgia</td><td>4.27</td></tr>
<tr><td>4</td><td>New Hampshire</td><td>10.00</td><td>29</td><td>California</td><td>4.08</td></tr>
<tr><td>32</td><td>New Jersey</td><td>3.59</td><td>30</td><td>Washington</td><td>3.79</td></tr>
<tr><td>20</td><td>New Mexico</td><td>5.26</td><td>31</td><td>Mississippi</td><td>3.67</td></tr>
<tr><td>39</td><td>New York</td><td>2.07</td><td>32</td><td>New Jersey</td><td>3.59</td></tr>
<tr><td>5</td><td>North Carolina</td><td>9.21</td><td>33</td><td>Maryland</td><td>3.48</td></tr>
<tr><td>6</td><td>North Dakota</td><td>9.09</td><td>34</td><td>Florida</td><td>2.94</td></tr>
<tr><td>24</td><td>Ohio</td><td>4.67</td><td>35</td><td>Colorado</td><td>2.91</td></tr>
<tr><td>17</td><td>Oklahoma</td><td>5.88</td><td>35</td><td>Louisiana</td><td>2.91</td></tr>
<tr><td>18</td><td>Oregon</td><td>5.59</td><td>37</td><td>Rhode Island</td><td>2.56</td></tr>
<tr><td>27</td><td>Pennsylvania</td><td>4.35</td><td>38</td><td>Nevada</td><td>2.33</td></tr>
<tr><td>37</td><td>Rhode Island</td><td>2.56</td><td>39</td><td>New York</td><td>2.07</td></tr>
<tr><td>15</td><td>South Carolina</td><td>6.40</td><td>40</td><td>Alaska</td><td>1.85</td></tr>
<tr><td>44</td><td>South Dakota</td><td>0.00</td><td>41</td><td>Utah</td><td>1.72</td></tr>
<tr><td>13</td><td>Tennessee</td><td>7.11</td><td>42</td><td>Connecticut</td><td>0.97</td></tr>
<tr><td>16</td><td>Texas</td><td>6.21</td><td>43</td><td>Massachusetts</td><td>0.95</td></tr>
<tr><td>41</td><td>Utah</td><td>1.72</td><td>44</td><td>Idaho</td><td>0.00</td></tr>
<tr><td>7</td><td>Vermont</td><td>8.33</td><td>44</td><td>Maine</td><td>0.00</td></tr>
<tr><td>10</td><td>Virginia</td><td>7.61</td><td>44</td><td>South Dakota</td><td>0.00</td></tr>
<tr><td>30</td><td>Washington</td><td>3.79</td><td>44</td><td>Wyoming</td><td>0.00</td></tr>
<tr><td>2</td><td>West Virginia</td><td>13.60</td><td>NA</td><td>Illinois**</td><td>NA</td></tr>
<tr><td>19</td><td>Wisconsin</td><td>5.41</td><td>NA</td><td>Kansas**</td><td>NA</td></tr>
<tr><td>44</td><td>Wyoming</td><td>0.00</td><td>NA</td><td>Montana**</td><td>NA</td></tr>
<tr><td></td><td></td><td></td><td></td><td>District of Columbia</td><td>0.00</td></tr>
</table>

Source: Morgan Quitno Corporation using data from U.S. Department of Justice, Federal Bureau of Investigation
"Crime in the United States 1993" (Uniform Crime Reports, December 4, 1994)
*Of the 22,081 murders in 1993 for which supplemental data were received by the F.B.I. There were an additional 2,445 murders for which the type of murder weapon was not reported to the F.B.I. Includes nonnegligent manslaughter.
**Not available.

Murders with Knives or Cutting Instruments in 1993

National Total = 2,817 Murders with Knives or Cutting Instruments*

<table>
<tr><td colspan="4">ALPHA ORDER</td><td colspan="4">RANK ORDER</td></tr>
<tr><td>RANK</td><td>STATE</td><td>MURDERS</td><td>%</td><td>RANK</td><td>STATE</td><td>MURDERS</td><td>%</td></tr>
<tr><td>12</td><td>Alabama</td><td>66</td><td>2.34%</td><td>1</td><td>California</td><td>473</td><td>16.79%</td></tr>
<tr><td>37</td><td>Alaska</td><td>11</td><td>0.39%</td><td>2</td><td>New York</td><td>310</td><td>11.00%</td></tr>
<tr><td>19</td><td>Arizona</td><td>45</td><td>1.60%</td><td>3</td><td>Texas</td><td>281</td><td>9.98%</td></tr>
<tr><td>29</td><td>Arkansas</td><td>26</td><td>0.92%</td><td>4</td><td>Florida</td><td>143</td><td>5.08%</td></tr>
<tr><td>1</td><td>California</td><td>473</td><td>16.79%</td><td>5</td><td>Georgia</td><td>114</td><td>4.05%</td></tr>
<tr><td>23</td><td>Colorado</td><td>32</td><td>1.14%</td><td>6</td><td>North Carolina</td><td>107</td><td>3.80%</td></tr>
<tr><td>28</td><td>Connecticut</td><td>28</td><td>0.99%</td><td>7</td><td>New Jersey</td><td>93</td><td>3.30%</td></tr>
<tr><td>41</td><td>Delaware</td><td>4</td><td>0.14%</td><td>7</td><td>Pennsylvania</td><td>93</td><td>3.30%</td></tr>
<tr><td>4</td><td>Florida</td><td>143</td><td>5.08%</td><td>9</td><td>Michigan</td><td>90</td><td>3.19%</td></tr>
<tr><td>5</td><td>Georgia</td><td>114</td><td>4.05%</td><td>10</td><td>Maryland</td><td>80</td><td>2.84%</td></tr>
<tr><td>35</td><td>Hawaii</td><td>12</td><td>0.43%</td><td>11</td><td>Virginia</td><td>71</td><td>2.52%</td></tr>
<tr><td>38</td><td>Idaho</td><td>7</td><td>0.25%</td><td>12</td><td>Alabama</td><td>66</td><td>2.34%</td></tr>
<tr><td>NA</td><td>Illinois**</td><td>NA</td><td>NA</td><td>13</td><td>Ohio</td><td>62</td><td>2.20%</td></tr>
<tr><td>22</td><td>Indiana</td><td>35</td><td>1.24%</td><td>14</td><td>Tennessee</td><td>58</td><td>2.06%</td></tr>
<tr><td>33</td><td>Iowa</td><td>13</td><td>0.46%</td><td>15</td><td>Massachusetts</td><td>57</td><td>2.02%</td></tr>
<tr><td>NA</td><td>Kansas**</td><td>NA</td><td>NA</td><td>15</td><td>Missouri</td><td>57</td><td>2.02%</td></tr>
<tr><td>31</td><td>Kentucky</td><td>17</td><td>0.60%</td><td>17</td><td>South Carolina</td><td>53</td><td>1.88%</td></tr>
<tr><td>18</td><td>Louisiana</td><td>52</td><td>1.85%</td><td>18</td><td>Louisiana</td><td>52</td><td>1.85%</td></tr>
<tr><td>46</td><td>Maine</td><td>0</td><td>0.00%</td><td>19</td><td>Arizona</td><td>45</td><td>1.60%</td></tr>
<tr><td>10</td><td>Maryland</td><td>80</td><td>2.84%</td><td>19</td><td>Washington</td><td>45</td><td>1.60%</td></tr>
<tr><td>15</td><td>Massachusetts</td><td>57</td><td>2.02%</td><td>21</td><td>Oklahoma</td><td>39</td><td>1.38%</td></tr>
<tr><td>9</td><td>Michigan</td><td>90</td><td>3.19%</td><td>22</td><td>Indiana</td><td>35</td><td>1.24%</td></tr>
<tr><td>26</td><td>Minnesota</td><td>29</td><td>1.03%</td><td>23</td><td>Colorado</td><td>32</td><td>1.14%</td></tr>
<tr><td>23</td><td>Mississippi</td><td>32</td><td>1.14%</td><td>23</td><td>Mississippi</td><td>32</td><td>1.14%</td></tr>
<tr><td>15</td><td>Missouri</td><td>57</td><td>2.02%</td><td>25</td><td>Oregon</td><td>31</td><td>1.10%</td></tr>
<tr><td>NA</td><td>Montana**</td><td>NA</td><td>NA</td><td>26</td><td>Minnesota</td><td>29</td><td>1.03%</td></tr>
<tr><td>42</td><td>Nebraska</td><td>3</td><td>0.11%</td><td>26</td><td>Wisconsin</td><td>29</td><td>1.03%</td></tr>
<tr><td>31</td><td>Nevada</td><td>17</td><td>0.60%</td><td>28</td><td>Connecticut</td><td>28</td><td>0.99%</td></tr>
<tr><td>38</td><td>New Hampshire</td><td>7</td><td>0.25%</td><td>29</td><td>Arkansas</td><td>26</td><td>0.92%</td></tr>
<tr><td>7</td><td>New Jersey</td><td>93</td><td>3.30%</td><td>29</td><td>New Mexico</td><td>26</td><td>0.92%</td></tr>
<tr><td>29</td><td>New Mexico</td><td>26</td><td>0.92%</td><td>31</td><td>Kentucky</td><td>17</td><td>0.60%</td></tr>
<tr><td>2</td><td>New York</td><td>310</td><td>11.00%</td><td>31</td><td>Nevada</td><td>17</td><td>0.60%</td></tr>
<tr><td>6</td><td>North Carolina</td><td>107</td><td>3.80%</td><td>33</td><td>Iowa</td><td>13</td><td>0.46%</td></tr>
<tr><td>43</td><td>North Dakota</td><td>2</td><td>0.07%</td><td>33</td><td>Utah</td><td>13</td><td>0.46%</td></tr>
<tr><td>13</td><td>Ohio</td><td>62</td><td>2.20%</td><td>35</td><td>Hawaii</td><td>12</td><td>0.43%</td></tr>
<tr><td>21</td><td>Oklahoma</td><td>39</td><td>1.38%</td><td>35</td><td>West Virginia</td><td>12</td><td>0.43%</td></tr>
<tr><td>25</td><td>Oregon</td><td>31</td><td>1.10%</td><td>37</td><td>Alaska</td><td>11</td><td>0.39%</td></tr>
<tr><td>7</td><td>Pennsylvania</td><td>93</td><td>3.30%</td><td>38</td><td>Idaho</td><td>7</td><td>0.25%</td></tr>
<tr><td>38</td><td>Rhode Island</td><td>7</td><td>0.25%</td><td>38</td><td>New Hampshire</td><td>7</td><td>0.25%</td></tr>
<tr><td>17</td><td>South Carolina</td><td>53</td><td>1.88%</td><td>38</td><td>Rhode Island</td><td>7</td><td>0.25%</td></tr>
<tr><td>46</td><td>South Dakota</td><td>0</td><td>0.00%</td><td>41</td><td>Delaware</td><td>4</td><td>0.14%</td></tr>
<tr><td>14</td><td>Tennessee</td><td>58</td><td>2.06%</td><td>42</td><td>Nebraska</td><td>3</td><td>0.11%</td></tr>
<tr><td>3</td><td>Texas</td><td>281</td><td>9.98%</td><td>43</td><td>North Dakota</td><td>2</td><td>0.07%</td></tr>
<tr><td>33</td><td>Utah</td><td>13</td><td>0.46%</td><td>43</td><td>Wyoming</td><td>2</td><td>0.07%</td></tr>
<tr><td>45</td><td>Vermont</td><td>1</td><td>0.04%</td><td>45</td><td>Vermont</td><td>1</td><td>0.04%</td></tr>
<tr><td>11</td><td>Virginia</td><td>71</td><td>2.52%</td><td>46</td><td>Maine</td><td>0</td><td>0.00%</td></tr>
<tr><td>19</td><td>Washington</td><td>45</td><td>1.60%</td><td>46</td><td>South Dakota</td><td>0</td><td>0.00%</td></tr>
<tr><td>35</td><td>West Virginia</td><td>12</td><td>0.43%</td><td>NA</td><td>Illinois**</td><td>NA</td><td>NA</td></tr>
<tr><td>26</td><td>Wisconsin</td><td>29</td><td>1.03%</td><td>NA</td><td>Kansas**</td><td>NA</td><td>NA</td></tr>
<tr><td>43</td><td>Wyoming</td><td>2</td><td>0.07%</td><td>NA</td><td>Montana**</td><td>NA</td><td>NA</td></tr>
<tr><td></td><td></td><td></td><td></td><td></td><td>District of Columbia</td><td>32</td><td>1.14%</td></tr>
</table>

Source: U.S. Department of Justice, Federal Bureau of Investigation
  "Crime in the United States 1993" (Uniform Crime Reports, December 4, 1994)
*Of the 22,081 murders in 1993 for which supplemental data were received by the F.B.I. There were an additional 2,445 murders for which the type of murder weapon was not reported to the F.B.I. Includes nonnegligent manslaughter.
**Not available.

Percent of Murders Involving Knives or Cutting Instruments in 1993

National Percent = 12.76% of Murders*

ALPHA ORDER			RANK ORDER		
RANK	**STATE**	**PERCENT**	**RANK**	**STATE**	**PERCENT**
21	Alabama	13.95	1	New Hampshire	35.00
11	Alaska	20.37	2	Iowa	28.89
23	Arizona	13.64	3	Hawaii	27.91
37	Arkansas	10.66	4	New Mexico	27.37
35	California	11.55	5	Massachusetts	27.14
16	Colorado	15.53	6	Idaho	22.58
24	Connecticut	13.59	7	Utah	22.41
12	Delaware	20.00	8	New Jersey	22.25
33	Florida	11.69	9	Minnesota	22.14
17	Georgia	15.20	10	Oregon	21.68
3	Hawaii	27.91	11	Alaska	20.37
6	Idaho	22.58	12	Delaware	20.00
NA	Illinois**	NA	13	North Dakota	18.18
40	Indiana	9.80	14	Rhode Island	17.95
2	Iowa	28.89	15	Washington	17.05
NA	Kansas**	NA	16	Colorado	15.53
45	Kentucky	7.20	17	Georgia	15.20
44	Louisiana	7.21	18	Mississippi	14.68
46	Maine	0.00	19	Oklahoma	14.34
31	Maryland	12.66	20	South Carolina	14.13
5	Massachusetts	27.14	21	Alabama	13.95
41	Michigan	9.76	22	North Carolina	13.88
9	Minnesota	22.14	23	Arizona	13.64
18	Mississippi	14.68	24	Connecticut	13.59
38	Missouri	10.44	25	Nevada	13.18
NA	Montana**	NA	26	Virginia	13.17
36	Nebraska	10.71	27	Texas	13.12
25	Nevada	13.18	28	Wisconsin	13.06
1	New Hampshire	35.00	29	Tennessee	12.89
8	New Jersey	22.25	30	New York	12.84
4	New Mexico	27.37	31	Maryland	12.66
30	New York	12.84	32	Wyoming	12.50
22	North Carolina	13.88	33	Florida	11.69
13	North Dakota	18.18	34	Pennsylvania	11.57
39	Ohio	10.35	35	California	11.55
19	Oklahoma	14.34	36	Nebraska	10.71
10	Oregon	21.68	37	Arkansas	10.66
34	Pennsylvania	11.57	38	Missouri	10.44
14	Rhode Island	17.95	39	Ohio	10.35
20	South Carolina	14.13	40	Indiana	9.80
46	South Dakota	0.00	41	Michigan	9.76
29	Tennessee	12.89	42	West Virginia	9.60
27	Texas	13.12	43	Vermont	8.33
7	Utah	22.41	44	Louisiana	7.21
43	Vermont	8.33	45	Kentucky	7.20
26	Virginia	13.17	46	Maine	0.00
15	Washington	17.05	46	South Dakota	0.00
42	West Virginia	9.60	NA	Illinois**	NA
28	Wisconsin	13.06	NA	Kansas**	NA
32	Wyoming	12.50	NA	Montana**	NA
				District of Columbia	7.67

Source: Morgan Quitno Corporation using data from U.S. Department of Justice, Federal Bureau of Investigation
     "Crime in the United States 1993" (Uniform Crime Reports, December 4, 1994)
Of the 22,081 murders in 1993 for which supplemental data were received by the F.B.I. There were an additional 2,445 murders for which the type of murder weapon was not reported to the F.B.I. Includes nonnegligent manslaughter.
**Not available.*

Murders by Hands, Fists or Feet in 1993

National Total = 1,100 Murders by Hands, Fists or Feet*

ALPHA ORDER

RANK	STATE	MURDERS	%
19	Alabama	18	1.64%
41	Alaska	2	0.18%
16	Arizona	22	2.00%
26	Arkansas	12	1.09%
1	California	138	12.55%
26	Colorado	12	1.09%
35	Connecticut	9	0.82%
41	Delaware	2	0.18%
4	Florida	57	5.18%
10	Georgia	36	3.27%
30	Hawaii	10	0.91%
39	Idaho	3	0.27%
NA	Illinois**	NA	NA
21	Indiana	16	1.45%
36	Iowa	5	0.45%
NA	Kansas**	NA	NA
30	Kentucky	10	0.91%
12	Louisiana	28	2.55%
46	Maine	0	0.00%
11	Maryland	29	2.64%
30	Massachusetts	10	0.91%
9	Michigan	39	3.55%
21·	Minnesota	16	1.45%
28	Mississippi	11	1.00%
15	Missouri	23	2.09%
NA	Montana**	NA	NA
37	Nebraska	4	0.36%
19	Nevada	18	1.64%
44	New Hampshire	1	0.09%
8	New Jersey	44	4.00%
28	New Mexico	11	1.00%
2	New York	104	9.45%
7	North Carolina	45	4.09%
44	North Dakota	1	0.09%
6	Ohio	48	4.36%
24	Oklahoma	15	1.36%
30	Oregon	10	0.91%
5	Pennsylvania	56	5.09%
41	Rhode Island	2	0.18%
17	South Carolina	21	1.91%
37	South Dakota	4	0.36%
17	Tennessee	21	1.91%
3	Texas	92	8.36%
21	Utah	16	1.45%
46	Vermont	0	0.00%
13	Virginia	26	2.36%
24	Washington	15	1.36%
30	West Virginia	10	0.91%
14	Wisconsin	25	2.27%
39	Wyoming	3	0.27%

RANK ORDER

RANK	STATE	MURDERS	%
1	California	138	12.55%
2	New York	104	9.45%
3	Texas	92	8.36%
4	Florida	57	5.18%
5	Pennsylvania	56	5.09%
6	Ohio	48	4.36%
7	North Carolina	45	4.09%
8	New Jersey	44	4.00%
9	Michigan	39	3.55%
10	Georgia	36	3.27%
11	Maryland	29	2.64%
12	Louisiana	28	2.55%
13	Virginia	26	2.36%
14	Wisconsin	25	2.27%
15	Missouri	23	2.09%
16	Arizona	22	2.00%
17	South Carolina	21	1.91%
17	Tennessee	21	1.91%
19	Alabama	18	1.64%
19	Nevada	18	1.64%
21	Indiana	16	1.45%
21	Minnesota	16	1.45%
21	Utah	16	1.45%
24	Oklahoma	15	1.36%
24	Washington	15	1.36%
26	Arkansas	12	1.09%
26	Colorado	12	1.09%
28	Mississippi	11	1.00%
28	New Mexico	11	1.00%
30	Hawaii	10	0.91%
30	Kentucky	10	0.91%
30	Massachusetts	10	0.91%
30	Oregon	10	0.91%
30	West Virginia	10	0.91%
35	Connecticut	9	0.82%
36	Iowa	5	0.45%
37	Nebraska	4	0.36%
37	South Dakota	4	0.36%
39	Idaho	3	0.27%
39	Wyoming	3	0.27%
41	Alaska	2	0.18%
41	Delaware	2	0.18%
41	Rhode Island	2	0.18%
44	New Hampshire	1	0.09%
44	North Dakota	1	0.09%
46	Maine	0	0.00%
46	Vermont	0	0.00%
NA	Illinois**	NA	NA
NA	Kansas**	NA	NA
NA	Montana**	NA	NA
	District of Columbia	0	0.00%

Source: U.S. Department of Justice, Federal Bureau of Investigation
"Crime in the United States 1993" (Uniform Crime Reports, December 4, 1994)
*Of the 22,081 murders in 1993 for which supplemental data were received by the F.B.I. There were an additional 2,445 murders for which the type of murder weapon was not reported to the F.B.I. Includes nonnegligent manslaughter.
**Not available.

Percent of Murders Involving Hands, Fists or Feet in 1993

National Percent = 4.98% of Murders*

ALPHA ORDER				RANK ORDER		
RANK	STATE	PERCENT		RANK	STATE	PERCENT
43	Alabama	3.81		1	Utah	27.59
44	Alaska	3.70		2	Hawaii	23.26
19	Arizona	6.67		3	South Dakota	22.22
28	Arkansas	4.92		4	Wyoming	18.75
45	California	3.37		5	Nebraska	14.29
21	Colorado	5.83		6	Nevada	13.95
36	Connecticut	4.37		7	Minnesota	12.21
12	Delaware	10.00		8	New Mexico	11.58
33	Florida	4.66		9	Wisconsin	11.26
30	Georgia	4.80		10	Iowa	11.11
2	Hawaii	23.26		11	New Jersey	10.53
13	Idaho	9.68		12	Delaware	10.00
NA	Illinois**	NA		13	Idaho	9.68
35	Indiana	4.48		14	North Dakota	9.09
10	Iowa	11.11		15	Ohio	8.01
NA	Kansas**	NA		16	West Virginia	8.00
39	Kentucky	4.24		17	Oregon	6.99
42	Louisiana	3.88		18	Pennsylvania	6.97
46	Maine	0.00		19	Arizona	6.67
34	Maryland	4.59		20	North Carolina	5.84
31	Massachusetts	4.76		21	Colorado	5.83
40	Michigan	4.23		22	Washington	5.68
7	Minnesota	12.21		23	South Carolina	5.60
26	Mississippi	5.05		24	Oklahoma	5.51
41	Missouri	4.21		25	Rhode Island	5.13
NA	Montana**	NA		26	Mississippi	5.05
5	Nebraska	14.29		27	New Hampshire	5.00
6	Nevada	13.95		28	Arkansas	4.92
27	New Hampshire	5.00		29	Virginia	4.82
11	New Jersey	10.53		30	Georgia	4.80
8	New Mexico	11.58		31	Massachusetts	4.76
37	New York	4.31		32	Tennessee	4.67
20	North Carolina	5.84		33	Florida	4.66
14	North Dakota	9.09		34	Maryland	4.59
15	Ohio	8.01		35	Indiana	4.48
24	Oklahoma	5.51		36	Connecticut	4.37
17	Oregon	6.99		37	New York	4.31
18	Pennsylvania	6.97		38	Texas	4.30
25	Rhode Island	5.13		39	Kentucky	4.24
23	South Carolina	5.60		40	Michigan	4.23
3	South Dakota	22.22		41	Missouri	4.21
32	Tennessee	4.67		42	Louisiana	3.88
38	Texas	4.30		43	Alabama	3.81
1	Utah	27.59		44	Alaska	3.70
46	Vermont	0.00		45	California	3.37
29	Virginia	4.82		46	Maine	0.00
22	Washington	5.68		46	Vermont	0.00
16	West Virginia	8.00		NA	Illinois**	NA
9	Wisconsin	11.26		NA	Kansas**	NA
4	Wyoming	18.75		NA	Montana**	NA
					District of Columbia	0.00

Source: Morgan Quitno Corporation using data from U.S. Department of Justice, Federal Bureau of Investigation
   "Crime in the United States 1993" (Uniform Crime Reports, December 4, 1994)
*Of the 22,081 murders in 1993 for which supplemental data were received by the F.B.I. There were an additional 2,445 murders for which the type of murder weapon was not reported to the F.B.I. Includes nonnegligent manslaughter.
**Not available.

Rapes in 1993

National Total = 104,806 Rapes*

ALPHA ORDER					RANK ORDER			
RANK	STATE	RAPES	% of USA		RANK	STATE	RAPES	% of USA
26	Alabama	1,471	1.40%		1	California	11,766	11.23%
38	Alaska	502	0.48%		2	Texas	9,922	9.47%
25	Arizona	1,488	1.42%		3	Florida	7,359	7.02%
30	Arkansas	1,028	0.98%		4	Michigan	6,740	6.43%
1	California	11,766	11.23%		5	Ohio	5,444	5.19%
21	Colorado	1,633	1.56%		6	New York	5,008	4.78%
35	Connecticut	800	0.76%		7	Illinois	4,046	3.86%
37	Delaware	539	0.51%		8	Washington	3,384	3.23%
3	Florida	7,359	7.02%		9	Pennsylvania	3,195	3.05%
11	Georgia	2,448	2.34%		10	Tennessee	2,544	2.43%
41	Hawaii	394	0.38%		11	Georgia	2,448	2.34%
42	Idaho	388	0.37%		12	North Carolina	2,379	2.27%
7	Illinois	4,046	3.86%		13	Indiana	2,234	2.13%
13	Indiana	2,234	2.13%		14	New Jersey	2,215	2.11%
36	Iowa	686	0.65%		15	Maryland	2,185	2.08%
31	Kansas	1,016	0.97%		16	Virginia	2,083	1.99%
27	Kentucky	1,301	1.24%		17	Massachusetts	2,006	1.91%
20	Louisiana	1,817	1.73%		18	South Carolina	1,905	1.82%
44	Maine	329	0.31%		19	Missouri	1,894	1.81%
15	Maryland	2,185	2.08%		20	Louisiana	1,817	1.73%
17	Massachusetts	2,006	1.91%		21	Colorado	1,633	1.56%
4	Michigan	6,740	6.43%		22	Oklahoma	1,592	1.52%
23	Minnesota	1,588	1.52%		23	Minnesota	1,588	1.52%
29	Mississippi	1,125	1.07%		24	Oregon	1,554	1.48%
19	Missouri	1,894	1.81%		25	Arizona	1,488	1.42%
47	Montana	234	0.22%		26	Alabama	1,471	1.40%
40	Nebraska	447	0.43%		27	Kentucky	1,301	1.24%
32	Nevada	846	0.81%		28	Wisconsin	1,269	1.21%
39	New Hampshire	499	0.48%		29	Mississippi	1,125	1.07%
14	New Jersey	2,215	2.11%		30	Arkansas	1,028	0.98%
33	New Mexico	842	0.80%		31	Kansas	1,016	0.97%
6	New York	5,008	4.78%		32	Nevada	846	0.81%
12	North Carolina	2,379	2.27%		33	New Mexico	842	0.80%
50	North Dakota	149	0.14%		34	Utah	829	0.79%
5	Ohio	5,444	5.19%		35	Connecticut	800	0.76%
22	Oklahoma	1,592	1.52%		36	Iowa	686	0.65%
24	Oregon	1,554	1.48%		37	Delaware	539	0.51%
9	Pennsylvania	3,195	3.05%		38	Alaska	502	0.48%
46	Rhode Island	286	0.27%		39	New Hampshire	499	0.48%
18	South Carolina	1,905	1.82%		40	Nebraska	447	0.43%
45	South Dakota	318	0.30%		41	Hawaii	394	0.38%
10	Tennessee	2,544	2.43%		42	Idaho	388	0.37%
2	Texas	9,922	9.47%		43	West Virginia	365	0.35%
34	Utah	829	0.79%		44	Maine	329	0.31%
48	Vermont	229	0.22%		45	South Dakota	318	0.30%
16	Virginia	2,083	1.99%		46	Rhode Island	286	0.27%
8	Washington	3,384	3.23%		47	Montana	234	0.22%
43	West Virginia	365	0.35%		48	Vermont	229	0.22%
28	Wisconsin	1,269	1.21%		49	Wyoming	161	0.15%
49	Wyoming	161	0.15%		50	North Dakota	149	0.14%
						District of Columbia	324	0.31%

Source: U.S. Department of Justice, Federal Bureau of Investigation
  "Crime in the United States 1993" (Uniform Crime Reports, December 4, 1994)
*Forcible rape is the carnal knowledge of a female forcibly and against her will. Assaults or attempts to commit rape by force or threat of force are included. However, statutory rape without force and other sex offenses are excluded.

Average Time Between Rapes in 1993

National Rate = A Rape Occurs every 5 Minutes*

ALPHA ORDER

RANK	STATE	HOURS.MINUTES
25	Alabama	5.58
13	Alaska	17.27
26	Arizona	5.53
21	Arkansas	8.31
50	California	0.44
30	Colorado	5.22
16	Connecticut	10.57
14	Delaware	16.15
48	Florida	1.11
40	Georgia	3.35
10	Hawaii	22.14
9	Idaho	22.35
44	Illinois	2.10
38	Indiana	3.55
15	Iowa	12.46
20	Kansas	8.37
24	Kentucky	6.44
31	Louisiana	4.49
7	Maine	26.38
36	Maryland	4.01
34	Massachusetts	4.22
47	Michigan	1.18
28	Minnesota	5.31
22	Mississippi	7.47
32	Missouri	4.38
4	Montana	37.26
11	Nebraska	19.36
19	Nevada	10.21
12	New Hampshire	17.34
37	New Jersey	3.57
18	New Mexico	10.24
45	New York	1.45
39	North Carolina	3.41
1	North Dakota	58.47
46	Ohio	1.37
29	Oklahoma	5.30
27	Oregon	5.38
42	Pennsylvania	2.44
5	Rhode Island	30.38
33	South Carolina	4.36
6	South Dakota	27.33
41	Tennessee	3.26
49	Texas	0.53
17	Utah	10.34
3	Vermont	38.15
35	Virginia	4.13
43	Washington	2.35
8	West Virginia	24.00
23	Wisconsin	6.54
2	Wyoming	54.25

RANK ORDER

RANK	STATE	HOURS.MINUTES
1	North Dakota	58.47
2	Wyoming	54.25
3	Vermont	38.15
4	Montana	37.26
5	Rhode Island	30.38
6	South Dakota	27.33
7	Maine	26.38
8	West Virginia	24.00
9	Idaho	22.35
10	Hawaii	22.14
11	Nebraska	19.36
12	New Hampshire	17.34
13	Alaska	17.27
14	Delaware	16.15
15	Iowa	12.46
16	Connecticut	10.57
17	Utah	10.34
18	New Mexico	10.24
19	Nevada	10.21
20	Kansas	8.37
21	Arkansas	8.31
22	Mississippi	7.47
23	Wisconsin	6.54
24	Kentucky	6.44
25	Alabama	5.58
26	Arizona	5.53
27	Oregon	5.38
28	Minnesota	5.31
29	Oklahoma	5.30
30	Colorado	5.22
31	Louisiana	4.49
32	Missouri	4.38
33	South Carolina	4.36
34	Massachusetts	4.22
35	Virginia	4.13
36	Maryland	4.01
37	New Jersey	3.57
38	Indiana	3.55
39	North Carolina	3.41
40	Georgia	3.35
41	Tennessee	3.26
42	Pennsylvania	2.44
43	Washington	2.35
44	Illinois	2.10
45	New York	1.45
46	Ohio	1.37
47	Michigan	1.18
48	Florida	1.11
49	Texas	0.53
50	California	0.44

District of Columbia	27.02

Source: Morgan Quitno Corporation using data from U.S. Department of Justice, Federal Bureau of Investigation "Crime in the United States 1993" (Uniform Crime Reports, December 4, 1994)

Forcible rape is the carnal knowledge of a female forcibly and against her will. Assaults or attempts to commit rape by force or threat of force are included. However, statutory rape without force and other sex offenses are excluded.

Percent Change in Number of Rapes: 1992 to 1993

National Percent Change = 3.9% Decrease*

ALPHA ORDER				RANK ORDER		
RANK	STATE	PERCENT CHANGE		RANK	STATE	PERCENT CHANGE
46	Alabama	(13.7)		1	Vermont	61.3
44	Alaska	(13.3)		2	Iowa	29.9
41	Arizona	(9.7)		3	New Hampshire	17.7
10	Arkansas	3.8		4	Idaho	14.5
35	California	(7.8)		5	Maine	11.9
19	Colorado	(0.5)		6	Montana	11.4
40	Connecticut	(9.5)		7	Kentucky	7.6
39	Delaware	(8.8)		8	Tennessee	7.0
14	Florida	0.7		9	Texas	5.1
48	Georgia	(19.9)		10	Arkansas	3.8
42	Hawaii	(10.5)		11	Virginia	3.7
4	Idaho	14.5		12	Oklahoma	2.3
30	Illinois	(6.2)		13	Nevada	1.6
31	Indiana	(6.8)		14	Florida	0.7
2	Iowa	29.9		14	North Dakota	0.7
22	Kansas	(2.5)		14	Utah	0.7
7	Kentucky	7.6		17	Louisiana	0.2
17	Louisiana	0.2		18	Missouri	(0.1)
5	Maine	11.9		19	Colorado	(0.5)
28	Maryland	(4.1)		20	Wyoming	(1.2)
33	Massachusetts	(7.4)		21	Oregon	(1.6)
NA	Michigan**	NA		22	Kansas	(2.5)
NA	Minnesota**	NA		23	New York	(2.8)
25	Mississippi	(3.5)		24	North Carolina	(3.1)
18	Missouri	(0.1)		25	Mississippi	(3.5)
6	Montana	11.4		25	Wisconsin	(3.5)
43	Nebraska	(11.3)		27	Pennsylvania	(3.9)
13	Nevada	1.6		28	Maryland	(4.1)
3	New Hampshire	17.7		29	Ohio	(5.1)
33	New Jersey	(7.4)		30	Illinois	(6.2)
47	New Mexico	(14.9)		31	Indiana	(6.8)
23	New York	(2.8)		32	West Virginia	(7.1)
24	North Carolina	(3.1)		33	Massachusetts	(7.4)
14	North Dakota	0.7		33	New Jersey	(7.4)
29	Ohio	(5.1)		35	California	(7.8)
12	Oklahoma	2.3		36	Rhode Island	(8.0)
21	Oregon	(1.6)		37	South Carolina	(8.1)
27	Pennsylvania	(3.9)		38	Washington	(8.5)
36	Rhode Island	(8.0)		39	Delaware	(8.8)
37	South Carolina	(8.1)		40	Connecticut	(9.5)
45	South Dakota	(13.6)		41	Arizona	(9.7)
8	Tennessee	7.0		42	Hawaii	(10.5)
9	Texas	5.1		43	Nebraska	(11.3)
14	Utah	0.7		44	Alaska	(13.3)
1	Vermont	61.3		45	South Dakota	(13.6)
11	Virginia	3.7		46	Alabama	(13.7)
38	Washington	(8.5)		47	New Mexico	(14.9)
32	West Virginia	(7.1)		48	Georgia	(19.9)
25	Wisconsin	(3.5)		NA	Michigan**	NA
20	Wyoming	(1.2)		NA	Minnesota**	NA
					District of Columbia	50.7

Source: U.S. Department of Justice, Federal Bureau of Investigation
"Crime in the United States 1993" (Uniform Crime Reports, December 4, 1994)
Forcible rape is the carnal knowledge of a female forcibly and against her will. Assaults or attempts to commit rape by force or threat of force are included. However, statutory rape without force and other sex offenses are excluded.
**Not available.*

311

Rape Rate in 1993

National Rate = 40.6 Rapes per 100,000 Population*

ALPHA ORDER

RANK	STATE	RATE
31	Alabama	35.1
1	Alaska	83.8
25	Arizona	37.8
20	Arkansas	42.4
26	California	37.7
14	Colorado	45.8
47	Connecticut	24.4
2	Delaware	77.0
7	Florida	53.8
28	Georgia	35.4
36	Hawaii	33.6
29	Idaho	35.3
32	Illinois	34.6
24	Indiana	39.1
47	Iowa	24.4
22	Kansas	40.1
33	Kentucky	34.3
21	Louisiana	42.3
44	Maine	26.6
18	Maryland	44.0
37	Massachusetts	33.4
3	Michigan	71.1
30	Minnesota	35.2
19	Mississippi	42.6
27	Missouri	36.2
41	Montana	27.9
42	Nebraska	27.8
5	Nevada	60.9
17	New Hampshire	44.4
40	New Jersey	28.1
9	New Mexico	52.1
43	New York	27.5
33	North Carolina	34.3
49	North Dakota	23.5
13	Ohio	49.1
12	Oklahoma	49.3
10	Oregon	51.3
45	Pennsylvania	26.5
39	Rhode Island	28.6
8	South Carolina	52.3
16	South Dakota	44.5
11	Tennessee	49.9
6	Texas	55.0
15	Utah	44.6
23	Vermont	39.8
38	Virginia	32.1
4	Washington	64.4
50	West Virginia	20.1
46	Wisconsin	25.2
33	Wyoming	34.3

RANK ORDER

RANK	STATE	RATE
1	Alaska	83.8
2	Delaware	77.0
3	Michigan	71.1
4	Washington	64.4
5	Nevada	60.9
6	Texas	55.0
7	Florida	53.8
8	South Carolina	52.3
9	New Mexico	52.1
10	Oregon	51.3
11	Tennessee	49.9
12	Oklahoma	49.3
13	Ohio	49.1
14	Colorado	45.8
15	Utah	44.6
16	South Dakota	44.5
17	New Hampshire	44.4
18	Maryland	44.0
19	Mississippi	42.6
20	Arkansas	42.4
21	Louisiana	42.3
22	Kansas	40.1
23	Vermont	39.8
24	Indiana	39.1
25	Arizona	37.8
26	California	37.7
27	Missouri	36.2
28	Georgia	35.4
29	Idaho	35.3
30	Minnesota	35.2
31	Alabama	35.1
32	Illinois	34.6
33	Kentucky	34.3
33	North Carolina	34.3
33	Wyoming	34.3
36	Hawaii	33.6
37	Massachusetts	33.4
38	Virginia	32.1
39	Rhode Island	28.6
40	New Jersey	28.1
41	Montana	27.9
42	Nebraska	27.8
43	New York	27.5
44	Maine	26.6
45	Pennsylvania	26.5
46	Wisconsin	25.2
47	Connecticut	24.4
47	Iowa	24.4
49	North Dakota	23.5
50	West Virginia	20.1
	District of Columbia	56.1

Source: U.S. Department of Justice, Federal Bureau of Investigation
"Crime in the United States 1993" (Uniform Crime Reports, December 4, 1994)
*Forcible rape is the carnal knowledge of a female forcibly and against her will. Assaults or attempts to commit rape by force or threat of force are included. However, statutory rape without force and other sex offenses are excluded.

Percent Change in Rape Rate: 1992 to 1993

National Percent Change = 5.1% Decrease*

<u>ALPHA ORDER</u>

RANK	STATE	PERCENT CHANGE
45	Alabama	(14.8)
46	Alaska	(15.0)
43	Arizona	(12.1)
10	Arkansas	2.7
36	California	(8.7)
21	Colorado	(3.2)
38	Connecticut	(9.3)
39	Delaware	(10.3)
15	Florida	(0.7)
48	Georgia	(21.9)
41	Hawaii	(11.3)
5	Idaho	11.0
30	Illinois	(6.7)
34	Indiana	(7.8)
2	Iowa	29.8
19	Kansas	(2.9)
7	Kentucky	6.5
14	Louisiana	0.0
4	Maine	11.8
28	Maryland	(5.2)
33	Massachusetts	(7.5)
NA	Michigan**	NA
NA	Minnesota**	NA
26	Mississippi	(4.5)
16	Missouri	(0.8)
6	Montana	9.4
42	Nebraska	(11.5)
20	Nevada	(3.0)
3	New Hampshire	16.2
35	New Jersey	(8.5)
47	New Mexico	(16.8)
21	New York	(3.2)
26	North Carolina	(4.5)
13	North Dakota	0.9
29	Ohio	(5.8)
11	Oklahoma	1.9
23	Oregon	(3.4)
25	Pennsylvania	(4.3)
31	Rhode Island	(7.4)
37	South Carolina	(9.0)
44	South Dakota	(14.1)
8	Tennessee	5.5
9	Texas	3.0
17	Utah	(1.8)
1	Vermont	59.8
11	Virginia	1.9
40	Washington	(10.6)
31	West Virginia	(7.4)
24	Wisconsin	(4.2)
18	Wyoming	(2.0)

<u>RANK ORDER</u>

RANK	STATE	PERCENT CHANGE
1	Vermont	59.8
2	Iowa	29.8
3	New Hampshire	16.2
4	Maine	11.8
5	Idaho	11.0
6	Montana	9.4
7	Kentucky	6.5
8	Tennessee	5.5
9	Texas	3.0
10	Arkansas	2.7
11	Oklahoma	1.9
11	Virginia	1.9
13	North Dakota	0.9
14	Louisiana	0.0
15	Florida	(0.7)
16	Missouri	(0.8)
17	Utah	(1.8)
18	Wyoming	(2.0)
19	Kansas	(2.9)
20	Nevada	(3.0)
21	Colorado	(3.2)
21	New York	(3.2)
23	Oregon	(3.4)
24	Wisconsin	(4.2)
25	Pennsylvania	(4.3)
26	Mississippi	(4.5)
26	North Carolina	(4.5)
28	Maryland	(5.2)
29	Ohio	(5.8)
30	Illinois	(6.7)
31	Rhode Island	(7.4)
31	West Virginia	(7.4)
33	Massachusetts	(7.5)
34	Indiana	(7.8)
35	New Jersey	(8.5)
36	California	(8.7)
37	South Carolina	(9.0)
38	Connecticut	(9.3)
39	Delaware	(10.3)
40	Washington	(10.6)
41	Hawaii	(11.3)
42	Nebraska	(11.5)
43	Arizona	(12.1)
44	South Dakota	(14.1)
45	Alabama	(14.8)
46	Alaska	(15.0)
47	New Mexico	(16.8)
48	Georgia	(21.9)
NA	Michigan**	NA
NA	Minnesota**	NA
	District of Columbia	53.7

Source: U.S. Department of Justice, Federal Bureau of Investigation
   "Crime in the United States 1993" (Uniform Crime Reports, December 4, 1994)
Forcible rape is the carnal knowledge of a female forcibly and against her will. Assaults or attempts to commit rape by force or threat of force are included. However, statutory rape without force and other sex offenses are excluded.
**Not available.*

313

Rape Rate per 100,000 Female Population in 1993

National Rate = 80.26 Rapes per 100,000 Females*

ALPHA ORDER			RANK ORDER		
RANK	**STATE**	**RATE**	**RANK**	**STATE**	**RATE**
33	Alabama	68.36	1	Alaska	181.23
1	Alaska	181.23	2	Delaware	152.26
24	Arizona	76.74	3	Michigan	138.97
19	Arkansas	82.77	4	Washington	130.91
26	California	76.35	5	Nevada	129.95
14	Colorado	93.31	6	Texas	110.80
48	Connecticut	47.31	7	Florida	105.82
2	Delaware	152.26	8	New Mexico	104.99
7	Florida	105.82	9	Oregon	102.85
28	Georgia	70.53	10	South Carolina	102.58
32	Hawaii	69.00	11	Tennessee	97.73
27	Idaho	72.52	12	Oklahoma	96.72
34	Illinois	67.73	13	Ohio	95.48
25	Indiana	76.69	14	Colorado	93.31
47	Iowa	47.41	15	Utah	90.90
22	Kansas	79.19	16	South Dakota	88.09
36	Kentucky	67.24	17	New Hampshire	88.01
21	Louisiana	81.77	18	Maryland	86.57
44	Maine	51.97	19	Arkansas	82.77
18	Maryland	86.57	20	Mississippi	82.48
37	Massachusetts	64.42	21	Louisiana	81.77
3	Michigan	138.97	22	Kansas	79.19
30	Minnesota	69.65	23	Vermont	78.97
20	Mississippi	82.48	24	Arizona	76.74
29	Missouri	70.49	25	Indiana	76.69
39	Montana	56.39	26	California	76.35
42	Nebraska	54.38	27	Idaho	72.52
5	Nevada	129.95	28	Georgia	70.53
17	New Hampshire	88.01	29	Missouri	70.49
40	New Jersey	55.06	30	Minnesota	69.65
8	New Mexico	104.99	31	Wyoming	69.40
43	New York	53.17	32	Hawaii	69.00
35	North Carolina	67.57	33	Alabama	68.36
49	North Dakota	46.71	34	Illinois	67.73
13	Ohio	95.48	35	North Carolina	67.57
12	Oklahoma	96.72	36	Kentucky	67.24
9	Oregon	102.85	37	Massachusetts	64.42
45	Pennsylvania	51.15	38	Virginia	64.09
41	Rhode Island	54.79	39	Montana	56.39
10	South Carolina	102.58	40	New Jersey	55.06
16	South Dakota	88.09	41	Rhode Island	54.79
11	Tennessee	97.73	42	Nebraska	54.38
6	Texas	110.80	43	New York	53.17
15	Utah	90.90	44	Maine	51.97
23	Vermont	78.97	45	Pennsylvania	51.15
38	Virginia	64.09	46	Wisconsin	49.71
4	Washington	130.91	47	Iowa	47.41
50	West Virginia	38.83	48	Connecticut	47.31
46	Wisconsin	49.71	49	North Dakota	46.71
31	Wyoming	69.40	50	West Virginia	38.83

District of Columbia 103.51

Source: Morgan Quitno Corporation using data from U.S. Department of Justice, Federal Bureau of Investigation "Crime in the United States 1993" (Uniform Crime Reports, December 4, 1994)

*Rates were determined using 1992 female population figures. Forcible rape is the carnal knowledge of a female forcibly and against her will. Assaults or attempts to commit rape by force or threat of force are included. However, statutory rape without force and other sex offenses are excluded.

Robberies in 1993

National Total = 659,757 Robberies*

ALPHA ORDER

RANK ORDER

RANK	STATE	ROBBERIES	% of USA	RANK	STATE	ROBBERIES	% of USA
21	Alabama	6,677	1.01%	1	California	126,436	19.16%
42	Alaska	733	0.11%	2	New York	102,122	15.48%
23	Arizona	6,412	0.97%	3	Florida	48,913	7.41%
33	Arkansas	3,027	0.46%	4	Illinois	44,584	6.76%
1	California	126,436	19.16%	5	Texas	40,469	6.13%
27	Colorado	4,160	0.63%	6	New Jersey	23,319	3.53%
22	Connecticut	6,447	0.98%	7	Michigan	22,601	3.43%
36	Delaware	1,307	0.20%	8	Maryland	21,582	3.27%
3	Florida	48,913	7.41%	9	Pennsylvania	21,563	3.27%
11	Georgia	17,154	2.60%	10	Ohio	21,373	3.24%
37	Hawaii	1,214	0.18%	11	Georgia	17,154	2.60%
46	Idaho	186	0.03%	12	North Carolina	13,364	2.03%
4	Illinois	44,584	6.76%	13	Missouri	12,654	1.92%
19	Indiana	6,845	1.04%	14	Louisiana	12,182	1.85%
35	Iowa	1,517	0.23%	15	Tennessee	11,224	1.70%
32	Kansas	3,128	0.47%	16	Massachusetts	10,563	1.60%
31	Kentucky	3,425	0.52%	17	Virginia	9,216	1.40%
14	Louisiana	12,182	1.85%	18	Washington	7,204	1.09%
45	Maine	264	0.04%	19	Indiana	6,845	1.04%
8	Maryland	21,582	3.27%	20	South Carolina	6,825	1.03%
16	Massachusetts	10,563	1.60%	21	Alabama	6,677	1.01%
7	Michigan	22,601	3.43%	22	Connecticut	6,447	0.98%
25	Minnesota	5,092	0.77%	23	Arizona	6,412	0.97%
30	Mississippi	3,683	0.56%	24	Wisconsin	5,714	0.87%
13	Missouri	12,654	1.92%	25	Minnesota	5,092	0.77%
44	Montana	272	0.04%	26	Nevada	4,724	0.72%
40	Nebraska	890	0.13%	27	Colorado	4,160	0.63%
26	Nevada	4,724	0.72%	28	Oklahoma	3,935	0.60%
43	New Hampshire	307	0.05%	29	Oregon	3,930	0.60%
6	New Jersey	23,319	3.53%	30	Mississippi	3,683	0.56%
34	New Mexico	2,237	0.34%	31	Kentucky	3,425	0.52%
2	New York	102,122	15.48%	32	Kansas	3,128	0.47%
12	North Carolina	13,364	2.03%	33	Arkansas	3,027	0.46%
49	North Dakota	53	0.01%	34	New Mexico	2,237	0.34%
10	Ohio	21,373	3.24%	35	Iowa	1,517	0.23%
28	Oklahoma	3,935	0.60%	36	Delaware	1,307	0.20%
29	Oregon	3,930	0.60%	37	Hawaii	1,214	0.18%
9	Pennsylvania	21,563	3.27%	38	Utah	1,090	0.17%
39	Rhode Island	1,011	0.15%	39	Rhode Island	1,011	0.15%
20	South Carolina	6,825	1.03%	40	Nebraska	890	0.13%
47	South Dakota	107	0.02%	41	West Virginia	782	0.12%
15	Tennessee	11,224	1.70%	42	Alaska	733	0.11%
5	Texas	40,469	6.13%	43	New Hampshire	307	0.05%
38	Utah	1,090	0.17%	44	Montana	272	0.04%
50	Vermont	52	0.01%	45	Maine	264	0.04%
17	Virginia	9,216	1.40%	46	Idaho	186	0.03%
18	Washington	7,204	1.09%	47	South Dakota	107	0.02%
41	West Virginia	782	0.12%	48	Wyoming	81	0.01%
24	Wisconsin	5,714	0.87%	49	North Dakota	53	0.01%
48	Wyoming	81	0.01%	50	Vermont	52	0.01%
					District of Columbia	7,107	1.08%

Source: U.S. Department of Justice, Federal Bureau of Investigation
"Crime in the United States 1993" (Uniform Crime Reports, December 4, 1994)
*Robbery is the taking or attempting to take anything of value by force or threat of force.

Average Time Between Robberies in 1993

National Rate = A Robbery Occurs Every 48 Seconds*

ALPHA ORDER				RANK ORDER		
RANK	STATE	HOURS.MINUTES		RANK	STATE	HOURS.MINUTES
30	Alabama	1.19		1	Vermont	168.28
9	Alaska	11.57		2	North Dakota	165.17
28	Arizona	1.22		3	Wyoming	108.09
18	Arkansas	2.53		4	South Dakota	81.52
50	California	0.04		5	Idaho	47.06
24	Colorado	2.07		6	Maine	33.11
28	Connecticut	1.22		7	Montana	32.13
15	Delaware	6.42		8	New Hampshire	28.32
48	Florida	0.11		9	Alaska	11.57
40	Georgia	0.31		10	West Virginia	11.12
14	Hawaii	7.13		11	Nebraska	9.50
5	Idaho	47.06		12	Rhode Island	8.40
47	Illinois	0.12		13	Utah	8.02
31	Indiana	1.17		14	Hawaii	7.13
16	Iowa	5.46		15	Delaware	6.42
19	Kansas	2.48		16	Iowa	5.46
20	Kentucky	2.34		17	New Mexico	3.55
37	Louisiana	0.43		18	Arkansas	2.53
6	Maine	33.11		19	Kansas	2.48
41	Maryland	0.25		20	Kentucky	2.34
35	Massachusetts	0.50		21	Mississippi	2.23
44	Michigan	0.23		22	Oklahoma	2.14
26	Minnesota	1.43		22	Oregon	2.14
21	Mississippi	2.23		24	Colorado	2.07
38	Missouri	0.41		25	Nevada	1.51
7	Montana	32.13		26	Minnesota	1.43
11	Nebraska	9.50		27	Wisconsin	1.32
25	Nevada	1.51		28	Arizona	1.22
8	New Hampshire	28.32		28	Connecticut	1.22
44	New Jersey	0.23		30	Alabama	1.19
17	New Mexico	3.55		31	Indiana	1.17
49	New York	0.05		31	South Carolina	1.17
39	North Carolina	0.40		33	Washington	1.13
2	North Dakota	165.17		34	Virginia	0.57
41	Ohio	0.25		35	Massachusetts	0.50
22	Oklahoma	2.14		36	Tennessee	0.47
22	Oregon	2.14		37	Louisiana	0.43
41	Pennsylvania	0.25		38	Missouri	0.41
12	Rhode Island	8.40		39	North Carolina	0.40
31	South Carolina	1.17		40	Georgia	0.31
4	South Dakota	81.52		41	Maryland	0.25
36	Tennessee	0.47		41	Ohio	0.25
46	Texas	0.13		41	Pennsylvania	0.25
13	Utah	8.02		44	Michigan	0.23
1	Vermont	168.28		44	New Jersey	0.23
34	Virginia	0.57		46	Texas	0.13
33	Washington	1.13		47	Illinois	0.12
10	West Virginia	11.12		48	Florida	0.11
27	Wisconsin	1.32		49	New York	0.05
3	Wyoming	108.09		50	California	0.04

District of Columbia   1.14

Source: Morgan Quitno Corporation using data from U.S. Department of Justice, Federal Bureau of Investigation
"Crime in the United States 1993" (Uniform Crime Reports, December 4, 1994)
*Robbery is the taking or attempting to take anything of value by force or threat of force.

Percent Change in Number of Robberies: 1992 to 1993

National Percent Change = 1.9% Decrease*

ALPHA ORDER				RANK ORDER		
RANK	STATE	PERCENT CHANGE		RANK	STATE	PERCENT CHANGE
33	Alabama	(2.1)		1	Iowa	36.3
4	Alaska	14.5		2	Delaware	25.4
7	Arizona	9.3		3	Montana	22.5
26	Arkansas	0.5		4	Alaska	14.5
36	California	(3.4)		5	Mississippi	13.2
28	Colorado	(0.5)		6	South Carolina	11.0
42	Connecticut	(6.8)		7	Arizona	9.3
2	Delaware	25.4		8	Michigan	8.1
31	Florida	(1.1)		9	Utah	7.5
24	Georgia	1.7		10	Missouri	7.4
14	Hawaii	5.5		10	Nevada	7.4
50	Idaho	(18.8)		12	Rhode Island	6.4
43	Illinois	(7.1)		13	North Dakota	6.0
31	Indiana	(1.1)		14	Hawaii	5.5
1	Iowa	36.3		15	New Jersey	5.0
38	Kansas	(4.5)		16	Virginia	4.9
18	Kentucky	4.6		17	Louisiana	4.7
17	Louisiana	4.7		18	Kentucky	4.6
44	Maine	(8.3)		19	North Carolina	4.5
21	Maryland	2.5		20	Minnesota	3.8
38	Massachusetts	(4.5)		21	Maryland	2.5
8	Michigan	8.1		22	Tennessee	2.4
20	Minnesota	3.8		23	Vermont	2.0
5	Mississippi	13.2		24	Georgia	1.7
10	Missouri	7.4		25	New Mexico	1.6
3	Montana	22.5		26	Arkansas	0.5
34	Nebraska	(2.3)		27	Washington	0.4
10	Nevada	7.4		28	Colorado	(0.5)
49	New Hampshire	(16.3)		29	Pennsylvania	(0.6)
15	New Jersey	5.0		30	West Virginia	(0.8)
25	New Mexico	1.6		31	Florida	(1.1)
41	New York	(5.6)		31	Indiana	(1.1)
19	North Carolina	4.5		33	Alabama	(2.1)
13	North Dakota	6.0		34	Nebraska	(2.3)
35	Ohio	(2.5)		35	Ohio	(2.5)
46	Oklahoma	(10.1)		36	California	(3.4)
48	Oregon	(12.8)		37	Wyoming	(3.6)
29	Pennsylvania	(0.6)		38	Kansas	(4.5)
12	Rhode Island	6.4		38	Massachusetts	(4.5)
6	South Carolina	11.0		40	Wisconsin	(4.7)
47	South Dakota	(10.8)		41	New York	(5.6)
22	Tennessee	2.4		42	Connecticut	(6.8)
45	Texas	(9.2)		43	Illinois	(7.1)
9	Utah	7.5		44	Maine	(8.3)
23	Vermont	2.0		45	Texas	(9.2)
16	Virginia	4.9		46	Oklahoma	(10.1)
27	Washington	0.4		47	South Dakota	(10.8)
30	West Virginia	(0.8)		48	Oregon	(12.8)
40	Wisconsin	(4.7)		49	New Hampshire	(16.3)
37	Wyoming	(3.6)		50	Idaho	(18.8)
					District of Columbia	(4.7)

Source: U.S. Department of Justice, Federal Bureau of Investigation
  "Crime in the United States 1993" (Uniform Crime Reports, December 4, 1994)
*Robbery is the taking or attempting to take anything of value by force or threat of force.

Robbery Rate in 1993

National Rate = 255.8 Robberies per 100,000 Population*

ALPHA ORDER				RANK ORDER		

RANK	STATE	RATE		RANK	STATE	RATE
22	Alabama	159.5		1	New York	561.2
30	Alaska	122.4		2	Maryland	434.7
21	Arizona	162.9		3	California	405.1
28	Arkansas	124.9		4	Illinois	381.2
3	California	405.1		5	Florida	357.6
33	Colorado	116.7		6	Nevada	340.1
14	Connecticut	196.7		7	New Jersey	296.0
18	Delaware	186.7		8	Louisiana	283.6
5	Florida	357.6		9	Georgia	248.0
9	Georgia	248.0		10	Missouri	241.8
36	Hawaii	103.6		11	Michigan	238.5
47	Idaho	16.9		12	Texas	224.4
4	Illinois	381.2		13	Tennessee	220.1
32	Indiana	119.8		14	Connecticut	196.7
41	Iowa	53.9		15	Ohio	192.7
29	Kansas	123.6		16	North Carolina	192.4
38	Kentucky	90.4		17	South Carolina	187.3
8	Louisiana	283.6		18	Delaware	186.7
45	Maine	21.3		19	Pennsylvania	179.0
2	Maryland	434.7		20	Massachusetts	175.7
20	Massachusetts	175.7		21	Arizona	162.9
11	Michigan	238.5		22	Alabama	159.5
35	Minnesota	112.7		23	Virginia	142.0
24	Mississippi	139.3		24	Mississippi	139.3
10	Missouri	241.8		25	New Mexico	138.4
43	Montana	32.4		26	Washington	137.1
40	Nebraska	55.4		27	Oregon	129.6
6	Nevada	340.1		28	Arkansas	124.9
44	New Hampshire	27.3		29	Kansas	123.6
7	New Jersey	296.0		30	Alaska	122.4
25	New Mexico	138.4		31	Oklahoma	121.8
1	New York	561.2		32	Indiana	119.8
16	North Carolina	192.4		33	Colorado	116.7
50	North Dakota	8.3		34	Wisconsin	113.4
15	Ohio	192.7		35	Minnesota	112.7
31	Oklahoma	121.8		36	Hawaii	103.6
27	Oregon	129.6		37	Rhode Island	101.1
19	Pennsylvania	179.0		38	Kentucky	90.4
37	Rhode Island	101.1		39	Utah	58.6
17	South Carolina	187.3		40	Nebraska	55.4
48	South Dakota	15.0		41	Iowa	53.9
13	Tennessee	220.1		42	West Virginia	43.0
12	Texas	224.4		43	Montana	32.4
39	Utah	58.6		44	New Hampshire	27.3
49	Vermont	9.0		45	Maine	21.3
23	Virginia	142.0		46	Wyoming	17.2
26	Washington	137.1		47	Idaho	16.9
42	West Virginia	43.0		48	South Dakota	15.0
34	Wisconsin	113.4		49	Vermont	9.0
46	Wyoming	17.2		50	North Dakota	8.3

District of Columbia   1,229.6

Source: U.S. Department of Justice, Federal Bureau of Investigation
"Crime in the United States 1993" (Uniform Crime Reports, December 4, 1994)
*Robbery is the taking or attempting to take anything of value by force or threat of force.

Percent Change in Robbery Rate: 1992 to 1993

National Percent Change = 3.0% Decrease*

ALPHA ORDER

RANK	STATE	PERCENT CHANGE
35	Alabama	(3.3)
4	Alaska	12.3
10	Arizona	6.4
24	Arkansas	(0.5)
37	California	(4.5)
33	Colorado	(3.2)
42	Connecticut	(6.7)
2	Delaware	23.5
32	Florida	(2.5)
26	Georgia	(0.7)
14	Hawaii	4.4
50	Idaho	(21.4)
43	Illinois	(7.6)
30	Indiana	(2.0)
1	Iowa	36.1
39	Kansas	(4.8)
16	Kentucky	3.7
13	Louisiana	4.5
44	Maine	(8.6)
21	Maryland	1.3
38	Massachusetts	(4.7)
7	Michigan	7.7
19	Minnesota	2.9
5	Mississippi	11.9
9	Missouri	6.6
3	Montana	20.4
31	Nebraska	(2.3)
20	Nevada	2.7
49	New Hampshire	(17.3)
15	New Jersey	3.8
25	New Mexico	(0.6)
41	New York	(6.0)
17	North Carolina	3.0
11	North Dakota	5.1
33	Ohio	(3.2)
45	Oklahoma	(10.6)
48	Oregon	(14.4)
27	Pennsylvania	(0.9)
8	Rhode Island	7.0
6	South Carolina	9.8
47	South Dakota	(11.2)
23	Tennessee	0.9
46	Texas	(11.1)
12	Utah	4.8
22	Vermont	1.1
17	Virginia	3.0
29	Washington	(1.9)
28	West Virginia	(1.1)
40	Wisconsin	(5.3)
36	Wyoming	(4.4)

RANK ORDER

RANK	STATE	PERCENT CHANGE
1	Iowa	36.1
2	Delaware	23.5
3	Montana	20.4
4	Alaska	12.3
5	Mississippi	11.9
6	South Carolina	9.8
7	Michigan	7.7
8	Rhode Island	7.0
9	Missouri	6.6
10	Arizona	6.4
11	North Dakota	5.1
12	Utah	4.8
13	Louisiana	4.5
14	Hawaii	4.4
15	New Jersey	3.8
16	Kentucky	3.7
17	North Carolina	3.0
17	Virginia	3.0
19	Minnesota	2.9
20	Nevada	2.7
21	Maryland	1.3
22	Vermont	1.1
23	Tennessee	0.9
24	Arkansas	(0.5)
25	New Mexico	(0.6)
26	Georgia	(0.7)
27	Pennsylvania	(0.9)
28	West Virginia	(1.1)
29	Washington	(1.9)
30	Indiana	(2.0)
31	Nebraska	(2.3)
32	Florida	(2.5)
33	Colorado	(3.2)
33	Ohio	(3.2)
35	Alabama	(3.3)
36	Wyoming	(4.4)
37	California	(4.5)
38	Massachusetts	(4.7)
39	Kansas	(4.8)
40	Wisconsin	(5.3)
41	New York	(6.0)
42	Connecticut	(6.7)
43	Illinois	(7.6)
44	Maine	(8.6)
45	Oklahoma	(10.6)
46	Texas	(11.1)
47	South Dakota	(11.2)
48	Oregon	(14.4)
49	New Hampshire	(17.3)
50	Idaho	(21.4)
	District of Columbia	(2.9)

Source: U.S. Department of Justice, Federal Bureau of Investigation
   "Crime in the United States 1993" (Uniform Crime Reports, December 4, 1994)
*Robbery is the taking or attempting to take anything of value by force or threat of force.

Robberies with Firearms in 1993

National Total = 249,495 Robberies with Firearms*

ALPHA ORDER

RANK	STATE	ROBBERIES	%
31	Alabama	1,046	0.42%
35	Alaska	266	0.11%
18	Arizona	2,594	1.04%
25	Arkansas	1,460	0.59%
1	California	51,890	20.80%
26	Colorado	1,429	0.57%
20	Connecticut	2,518	1.01%
41	Delaware	46	0.02%
4	Florida	18,580	7.45%
7	Georgia	8,401	3.37%
37	Hawaii	131	0.05%
43	Idaho	44	0.02%
NA	Illinois**	NA	NA
17	Indiana	2,797	1.12%
38	Iowa	129	0.05%
NA	Kansas**	NA	NA
30	Kentucky	1,159	0.46%
11	Louisiana	6,862	2.75%
39	Maine	66	0.03%
5	Maryland	12,125	4.86%
22	Massachusetts	2,298	0.92%
6	Michigan	11,909	4.77%
28	Minnesota	1,266	0.51%
27	Mississippi	1,284	0.51%
12	Missouri	6,144	2.46%
46	Montana	17	0.01%
40	Nebraska	54	0.02%
23	Nevada	2,180	0.87%
42	New Hampshire	45	0.02%
9	New Jersey	8,091	3.24%
32	New Mexico	808	0.32%
2	New York	37,650	15.09%
13	North Carolina	5,806	2.33%
47	North Dakota	6	0.00%
10	Ohio	7,822	3.14%
24	Oklahoma	1,608	0.64%
29	Oregon	1,237	0.50%
8	Pennsylvania	8,373	3.36%
36	Rhode Island	249	0.10%
19	South Carolina	2,538	1.02%
44	South Dakota	25	0.01%
14	Tennessee	5,733	2.30%
3	Texas	19,257	7.72%
33	Utah	350	0.14%
48	Vermont	2	0.00%
15	Virginia	4,429	1.78%
21	Washington	2,315	0.93%
34	West Virginia	284	0.11%
16	Wisconsin	3,026	1.21%
44	Wyoming	25	0.01%

RANK ORDER

RANK	STATE	ROBBERIES	%
1	California	51,890	20.80%
2	New York	37,650	15.09%
3	Texas	19,257	7.72%
4	Florida	18,580	7.45%
5	Maryland	12,125	4.86%
6	Michigan	11,909	4.77%
7	Georgia	8,401	3.37%
8	Pennsylvania	8,373	3.36%
9	New Jersey	8,091	3.24%
10	Ohio	7,822	3.14%
11	Louisiana	6,862	2.75%
12	Missouri	6,144	2.46%
13	North Carolina	5,806	2.33%
14	Tennessee	5,733	2.30%
15	Virginia	4,429	1.78%
16	Wisconsin	3,026	1.21%
17	Indiana	2,797	1.12%
18	Arizona	2,594	1.04%
19	South Carolina	2,538	1.02%
20	Connecticut	2,518	1.01%
21	Washington	2,315	0.93%
22	Massachusetts	2,298	0.92%
23	Nevada	2,180	0.87%
24	Oklahoma	1,608	0.64%
25	Arkansas	1,460	0.59%
26	Colorado	1,429	0.57%
27	Mississippi	1,284	0.51%
28	Minnesota	1,266	0.51%
29	Oregon	1,237	0.50%
30	Kentucky	1,159	0.46%
31	Alabama	1,046	0.42%
32	New Mexico	808	0.32%
33	Utah	350	0.14%
34	West Virginia	284	0.11%
35	Alaska	266	0.11%
36	Rhode Island	249	0.10%
37	Hawaii	131	0.05%
38	Iowa	129	0.05%
39	Maine	66	0.03%
40	Nebraska	54	0.02%
41	Delaware	46	0.02%
42	New Hampshire	45	0.02%
43	Idaho	44	0.02%
44	South Dakota	25	0.01%
44	Wyoming	25	0.01%
46	Montana	17	0.01%
47	North Dakota	6	0.00%
48	Vermont	2	0.00%
NA	Illinois**	NA	NA
NA	Kansas**	NA	NA
	District of Columbia	3,121	1.25%

Source: U.S. Department of Justice, Federal Bureau of Investigation
"Crime in the United States 1993" (Uniform Crime Reports, December 4, 1994)
Of the 588,706 robberies in 1993 for which supplemental data were received by the F.B.I. There were an additional 71,051 robberies for which the type of weapon was not reported to the F.B.I. Robbery is the taking or attempting to take anything of value by force or threat of force.
**Not available.*

320

Robbery Rate with Firearms in 1993

National Rate = 102.39 Robberies per 100,000 Population*

ALPHA ORDER

RANK	STATE	RATE
33	Alabama	24.98
26	Alaska	44.41
19	Arizona	65.90
20	Arkansas	60.23
3	California	166.26
29	Colorado	40.07
14	Connecticut	76.84
38	Delaware	6.57
6	Florida	135.83
8	Georgia	121.45
37	Hawaii	11.18
42	Idaho	4.00
NA	Illinois**	NA
24	Indiana	48.96
41	Iowa	4.58
NA	Kansas**	NA
31	Kentucky	30.59
4	Louisiana	159.77
39	Maine	5.33
1	Maryland	244.21
30	Massachusetts	38.22
7	Michigan	125.65
32	Minnesota	28.03
25	Mississippi	48.58
9	Missouri	117.39
46	Montana	2.03
45	Nebraska	3.36
5	Nevada	156.95
42	New Hampshire	4.00
12	New Jersey	102.69
22	New Mexico	50.00
2	New York	206.90
13	North Carolina	83.60
47	North Dakota	0.94
15	Ohio	70.53
23	Oklahoma	49.77
28	Oregon	40.80
17	Pennsylvania	69.50
34	Rhode Island	24.90
16	South Carolina	69.67
44	South Dakota	3.50
10	Tennessee	112.43
11	Texas	106.80
35	Utah	18.82
48	Vermont	0.35
18	Virginia	68.23
27	Washington	44.05
36	West Virginia	15.60
21	Wisconsin	60.06
40	Wyoming	5.32

RANK ORDER

RANK	STATE	RATE
1	Maryland	244.21
2	New York	206.90
3	California	166.26
4	Louisiana	159.77
5	Nevada	156.95
6	Florida	135.83
7	Michigan	125.65
8	Georgia	121.45
9	Missouri	117.39
10	Tennessee	112.43
11	Texas	106.80
12	New Jersey	102.69
13	North Carolina	83.60
14	Connecticut	76.84
15	Ohio	70.53
16	South Carolina	69.67
17	Pennsylvania	69.50
18	Virginia	68.23
19	Arizona	65.90
20	Arkansas	60.23
21	Wisconsin	60.06
22	New Mexico	50.00
23	Oklahoma	49.77
24	Indiana	48.96
25	Mississippi	48.58
26	Alaska	44.41
27	Washington	44.05
28	Oregon	40.80
29	Colorado	40.07
30	Massachusetts	38.22
31	Kentucky	30.59
32	Minnesota	28.03
33	Alabama	24.98
34	Rhode Island	24.90
35	Utah	18.82
36	West Virginia	15.60
37	Hawaii	11.18
38	Delaware	6.57
39	Maine	5.33
40	Wyoming	5.32
41	Iowa	4.58
42	Idaho	4.00
42	New Hampshire	4.00
44	South Dakota	3.50
45	Nebraska	3.36
46	Montana	2.03
47	North Dakota	0.94
48	Vermont	0.35
NA	Illinois**	NA
NA	Kansas**	NA

District of Columbia   539.97

Source: Morgan Quitno Corporation using data from U.S. Department of Justice, Federal Bureau of Investigation
"Crime in the United States 1993" (Uniform Crime Reports, December 4, 1994)
*Of the 588,706 robberies in 1993 for which supplemental data were received by the F.B.I. There were an additional 71,051 robberies for which the type of weapon was not reported to the F.B.I. Robbery is the taking or attempting to take anything of value by force or threat of force. National rate based on population of reporting states.
**Not available.

Percent of Robberies Involving Firearms in 1993

National Percent = 42.38% of Robberies*

ALPHA ORDER				RANK ORDER		
RANK	STATE	PERCENT		RANK	STATE	PERCENT
36	Alabama	26.94		1	Louisiana	63.75
27	Alaska	37.31		2	Maryland	56.19
20	Arizona	41.39		3	Michigan	54.06
11	Arkansas	48.39		4	Georgia	53.55
21	California	41.08		5	Tennessee	53.20
30	Colorado	35.15		6	Wisconsin	53.00
24	Connecticut	39.01		7	Nevada	50.92
42	Delaware	22.01		8	Mississippi	50.25
23	Florida	39.94		9	Montana	50.00
4	Georgia	53.55		10	Missouri	49.91
47	Hawaii	10.79		11	Arkansas	48.39
33	Idaho	32.12		12	Virginia	48.06
NA	Illinois**	NA		13	Texas	47.70
14	Indiana	46.62		14	Indiana	46.62
44	Iowa	20.77		15	New Mexico	45.60
NA	Kansas**	NA		16	North Carolina	44.29
25	Kentucky	38.56		17	Wyoming	43.86
1	Louisiana	63.75		18	Pennsylvania	42.80
38	Maine	25.10		19	Ohio	42.09
2	Maryland	56.19		20	Arizona	41.39
41	Massachusetts	24.64		21	California	41.08
3	Michigan	54.06		22	Oklahoma	40.88
39	Minnesota	24.90		23	Florida	39.94
8	Mississippi	50.25		24	Connecticut	39.01
10	Missouri	49.91		25	Kentucky	38.56
9	Montana	50.00		26	South Carolina	37.41
43	Nebraska	21.43		27	Alaska	37.31
7	Nevada	50.92		28	New York	37.09
45	New Hampshire	15.85		29	West Virginia	36.36
31	New Jersey	34.70		30	Colorado	35.15
15	New Mexico	45.60		31	New Jersey	34.70
28	New York	37.09		32	Washington	32.72
16	North Carolina	44.29		33	Idaho	32.12
46	North Dakota	12.00		34	Utah	32.11
19	Ohio	42.09		35	Oregon	31.75
22	Oklahoma	40.88		36	Alabama	26.94
35	Oregon	31.75		37	South Dakota	25.77
18	Pennsylvania	42.80		38	Maine	25.10
40	Rhode Island	24.73		39	Minnesota	24.90
26	South Carolina	37.41		40	Rhode Island	24.73
37	South Dakota	25.77		41	Massachusetts	24.64
5	Tennessee	53.20		42	Delaware	22.01
13	Texas	47.70		43	Nebraska	21.43
34	Utah	32.11		44	Iowa	20.77
48	Vermont	8.70		45	New Hampshire	15.85
12	Virginia	48.06		46	North Dakota	12.00
32	Washington	32.72		47	Hawaii	10.79
29	West Virginia	36.36		48	Vermont	8.70
6	Wisconsin	53.00		NA	Illinois**	NA
17	Wyoming	43.86		NA	Kansas**	NA

District of Columbia 43.91

Source: Morgan Quitno Corporation using data from U.S. Department of Justice, Federal Bureau of Investigation "Crime in the United States 1993" (Uniform Crime Reports, December 4, 1994)

*Of the 588,706 robberies in 1993 for which supplemental data were received by the F.B.I. There were an additional 71,051 robberies for which the type of weapon was not reported to the F.B.I. Robbery is the taking or attempting to take anything of value by force or threat of force.

**Not available.

322

Robberies with Knives or Cutting Instruments in 1993

National Total = 58,756 Robberies with Knives or Cutting Instruments*

ALPHA ORDER

RANK	STATE	ROBBERIES	%
13	Alabama	933	1.59%
37	Alaska	74	0.13%
21	Arizona	585	1.00%
31	Arkansas	232	0.39%
2	California	12,791	21.77%
25	Colorado	435	0.74%
19	Connecticut	658	1.12%
43	Delaware	17	0.03%
4	Florida	3,371	5.74%
12	Georgia	1,015	1.73%
35	Hawaii	93	0.16%
42	Idaho	28	0.05%
NA	Illinois**	NA	NA
22	Indiana	522	0.89%
36	Iowa	91	0.15%
NA	Kansas**	NA	NA
28	Kentucky	338	0.58%
20	Louisiana	648	1.10%
40	Maine	29	0.05%
7	Maryland	1,566	2.67%
6	Massachusetts	1,921	3.27%
9	Michigan	1,370	2.33%
26	Minnesota	433	0.74%
32	Mississippi	167	0.28%
14	Missouri	848	1.44%
44	Montana	7	0.01%
40	Nebraska	29	0.05%
27	Nevada	385	0.66%
39	New Hampshire	40	0.07%
5	New Jersey	2,397	4.08%
30	New Mexico	252	0.43%
1	New York	15,079	25.66%
11	North Carolina	1,107	1.88%
47	North Dakota	6	0.01%
10	Ohio	1,122	1.91%
29	Oklahoma	306	0.52%
24	Oregon	449	0.76%
8	Pennsylvania	1,527	2.60%
33	Rhode Island	122	0.21%
16	South Carolina	718	1.22%
44	South Dakota	7	0.01%
15	Tennessee	765	1.30%
3	Texas	3,724	6.34%
34	Utah	97	0.17%
48	Vermont	5	0.01%
17	Virginia	711	1.21%
18	Washington	686	1.17%
38	West Virginia	64	0.11%
23	Wisconsin	458	0.78%
44	Wyoming	7	0.01%

RANK ORDER

RANK	STATE	ROBBERIES	%
1	New York	15,079	25.66%
2	California	12,791	21.77%
3	Texas	3,724	6.34%
4	Florida	3,371	5.74%
5	New Jersey	2,397	4.08%
6	Massachusetts	1,921	3.27%
7	Maryland	1,566	2.67%
8	Pennsylvania	1,527	2.60%
9	Michigan	1,370	2.33%
10	Ohio	1,122	1.91%
11	North Carolina	1,107	1.88%
12	Georgia	1,015	1.73%
13	Alabama	933	1.59%
14	Missouri	848	1.44%
15	Tennessee	765	1.30%
16	South Carolina	718	1.22%
17	Virginia	711	1.21%
18	Washington	686	1.17%
19	Connecticut	658	1.12%
20	Louisiana	648	1.10%
21	Arizona	585	1.00%
22	Indiana	522	0.89%
23	Wisconsin	458	0.78%
24	Oregon	449	0.76%
25	Colorado	435	0.74%
26	Minnesota	433	0.74%
27	Nevada	385	0.66%
28	Kentucky	338	0.58%
29	Oklahoma	306	0.52%
30	New Mexico	252	0.43%
31	Arkansas	232	0.39%
32	Mississippi	167	0.28%
33	Rhode Island	122	0.21%
34	Utah	97	0.17%
35	Hawaii	93	0.16%
36	Iowa	91	0.15%
37	Alaska	74	0.13%
38	West Virginia	64	0.11%
39	New Hampshire	40	0.07%
40	Maine	29	0.05%
40	Nebraska	29	0.05%
42	Idaho	28	0.05%
43	Delaware	17	0.03%
44	Montana	7	0.01%
44	South Dakota	7	0.01%
44	Wyoming	7	0.01%
47	North Dakota	6	0.01%
48	Vermont	5	0.01%
NA	Illinois**	NA	NA
NA	Kansas**	NA	NA
	District of Columbia	521	0.89%

Source: U.S. Department of Justice, Federal Bureau of Investigation
   "Crime in the United States 1993" (Uniform Crime Reports, December 4, 1994)
*Of the 588,706 robberies in 1993 for which supplemental data were received by the F.B.I. There were an additional
71,051 robberies for which the type of weapon was not reported to the F.B.I. Robbery is the taking or attempting to take
anything of value by force or threat of force.
**Not available.   323

Percent of Robberies Involving Knives or Cutting Instruments in 1993

National Percent = 9.98% of Robberies*

ALPHA ORDER				RANK ORDER		
RANK	STATE	PERCENT		RANK	STATE	PERCENT
1	Alabama	24.03		1	Alabama	24.03
19	Alaska	10.38		2	Vermont	21.74
24	Arizona	9.33		3	Massachusetts	20.59
37	Arkansas	7.69		3	Montana	20.59
22	California	10.13		5	Idaho	20.44
17	Colorado	10.70		6	New York	14.86
21	Connecticut	10.20		7	Iowa	14.65
32	Delaware	8.13		8	New Mexico	14.22
40	Florida	7.25		9	New Hampshire	14.08
45	Georgia	6.47		10	Wyoming	12.28
38	Hawaii	7.66		11	Rhode Island	12.12
5	Idaho	20.44		12	North Dakota	12.00
NA	Illinois**	NA		13	Oregon	11.52
28	Indiana	8.70		14	Nebraska	11.51
7	Iowa	14.65		15	Kentucky	11.24
NA	Kansas**	NA		16	Maine	11.03
15	Kentucky	11.24		17	Colorado	10.70
48	Louisiana	6.02		18	South Carolina	10.58
16	Maine	11.03		19	Alaska	10.38
39	Maryland	7.26		20	New Jersey	10.28
3	Massachusetts	20.59		21	Connecticut	10.20
46	Michigan	6.22		22	California	10.13
29	Minnesota	8.52		23	Washington	9.69
44	Mississippi	6.54		24	Arizona	9.33
43	Missouri	6.89		25	Texas	9.22
3	Montana	20.59		26	Nevada	8.99
14	Nebraska	11.51		27	Utah	8.90
26	Nevada	8.99		28	Indiana	8.70
9	New Hampshire	14.08		29	Minnesota	8.52
20	New Jersey	10.28		30	North Carolina	8.44
8	New Mexico	14.22		31	West Virginia	8.19
6	New York	14.86		32	Delaware	8.13
30	North Carolina	8.44		33	Wisconsin	8.02
12	North Dakota	12.00		34	Pennsylvania	7.81
47	Ohio	6.04		35	Oklahoma	7.78
35	Oklahoma	7.78		36	Virginia	7.71
13	Oregon	11.52		37	Arkansas	7.69
34	Pennsylvania	7.81		38	Hawaii	7.66
11	Rhode Island	12.12		39	Maryland	7.26
18	South Carolina	10.58		40	Florida	7.25
41	South Dakota	7.22		41	South Dakota	7.22
42	Tennessee	7.10		42	Tennessee	7.10
25	Texas	9.22		43	Missouri	6.89
27	Utah	8.90		44	Mississippi	6.54
2	Vermont	21.74		45	Georgia	6.47
36	Virginia	7.71		46	Michigan	6.22
23	Washington	9.69		47	Ohio	6.04
31	West Virginia	8.19		48	Louisiana	6.02
33	Wisconsin	8.02		NA	Illinois**	NA
10	Wyoming	12.28		NA	Kansas**	NA
					District of Columbia	7.33

Source: Morgan Quitno Corporation using data from U.S. Department of Justice, Federal Bureau of Investigation
"Crime in the United States 1993" (Uniform Crime Reports, December 4, 1994)
*Of the 588,706 robberies in 1993 for which supplemental data were received by the F.B.I. There were an additional
71,051 robberies for which the type of weapon was not reported to the F.B.I. Robbery is the taking or attempting to take
anything of value by force or threat of force.
**Not available.

Robberies with Blunt Objects and Other Dangerous Weapons in 1993

National Total = 55,667 Robberies with Blunt Objects and Other Dangerous Weapons*

<u>ALPHA ORDER</u>

RANK	STATE	ROBBERIES	%
12	Alabama	919	1.65%
36	Alaska	57	0.10%
20	Arizona	540	0.97%
30	Arkansas	233	0.42%
1	California	15,178	27.27%
22	Colorado	468	0.84%
21	Connecticut	531	0.95%
43	Delaware	17	0.03%
4	Florida	3,290	5.91%
6	Georgia	2,029	3.64%
39	Hawaii	25	0.04%
44	Idaho	16	0.03%
NA	Illinois**	NA	NA
24	Indiana	388	0.70%
34	Iowa	100	0.18%
NA	Kansas**	NA	NA
27	Kentucky	283	0.51%
15	Louisiana	770	1.38%
40	Maine	18	0.03%
10	Maryland	1,279	2.30%
13	Massachusetts	912	1.64%
5	Michigan	3,163	5.68%
23	Minnesota	423	0.76%
31	Mississippi	169	0.30%
14	Missouri	863	1.55%
48	Montana	1	0.00%
40	Nebraska	18	0.03%
29	Nevada	242	0.43%
40	New Hampshire	18	0.03%
7	New Jersey	1,783	3.20%
32	New Mexico	168	0.30%
2	New York	9,949	17.87%
9	North Carolina	1,299	2.33%
38	North Dakota	30	0.05%
8	Ohio	1,694	3.04%
28	Oklahoma	266	0.48%
25	Oregon	351	0.63%
11	Pennsylvania	1,035	1.86%
35	Rhode Island	86	0.15%
17	South Carolina	747	1.34%
46	South Dakota	8	0.01%
18	Tennessee	695	1.25%
3	Texas	3,440	6.18%
33	Utah	133	0.24%
45	Vermont	10	0.02%
16	Virginia	759	1.36%
19	Washington	621	1.12%
37	West Virginia	48	0.09%
26	Wisconsin	297	0.53%
47	Wyoming	6	0.01%

<u>RANK ORDER</u>

RANK	STATE	ROBBERIES	%
1	California	15,178	27.27%
2	New York	9,949	17.87%
3	Texas	3,440	6.18%
4	Florida	3,290	5.91%
5	Michigan	3,163	5.68%
6	Georgia	2,029	3.64%
7	New Jersey	1,783	3.20%
8	Ohio	1,694	3.04%
9	North Carolina	1,299	2.33%
10	Maryland	1,279	2.30%
11	Pennsylvania	1,035	1.86%
12	Alabama	919	1.65%
13	Massachusetts	912	1.64%
14	Missouri	863	1.55%
15	Louisiana	770	1.38%
16	Virginia	759	1.36%
17	South Carolina	747	1.34%
18	Tennessee	695	1.25%
19	Washington	621	1.12%
20	Arizona	540	0.97%
21	Connecticut	531	0.95%
22	Colorado	468	0.84%
23	Minnesota	423	0.76%
24	Indiana	388	0.70%
25	Oregon	351	0.63%
26	Wisconsin	297	0.53%
27	Kentucky	283	0.51%
28	Oklahoma	266	0.48%
29	Nevada	242	0.43%
30	Arkansas	233	0.42%
31	Mississippi	169	0.30%
32	New Mexico	168	0.30%
33	Utah	133	0.24%
34	Iowa	100	0.18%
35	Rhode Island	86	0.15%
36	Alaska	57	0.10%
37	West Virginia	48	0.09%
38	North Dakota	30	0.05%
39	Hawaii	25	0.04%
40	Maine	18	0.03%
40	Nebraska	18	0.03%
40	New Hampshire	18	0.03%
43	Delaware	17	0.03%
44	Idaho	16	0.03%
45	Vermont	10	0.02%
46	South Dakota	8	0.01%
47	Wyoming	6	0.01%
48	Montana	1	0.00%
NA	Illinois**	NA	NA
NA	Kansas**	NA	NA
	District of Columbia	292	0.52%

Source: U.S. Department of Justice, Federal Bureau of Investigation
   "Crime in the United States 1993" (Uniform Crime Reports, December 4, 1994)
*Of the 588,706 robberies in 1993 for which supplemental data were received by the F.B.I. There were an additional
71,051 robberies for which the type of weapon was not reported to the F.B.I. Robbery is the taking or attempting to take
anything of value by force or threat of force.
**Not available.

Percent of Robberies Involving Blunt Objects and Other Dangerous Weapons in 1993

National Percent = 9.46% of Robberies*

<table>
<tr><td colspan="3"><u>ALPHA ORDER</u></td><td colspan="3"><u>RANK ORDER</u></td></tr>
<tr><th>RANK</th><th>STATE</th><th>PERCENT</th><th>RANK</th><th>STATE</th><th>PERCENT</th></tr>
<tr><td>3</td><td>Alabama</td><td>23.67</td><td>1</td><td>North Dakota</td><td>60.00</td></tr>
<tr><td>29</td><td>Alaska</td><td>7.99</td><td>2</td><td>Vermont</td><td>43.48</td></tr>
<tr><td>21</td><td>Arizona</td><td>8.62</td><td>3</td><td>Alabama</td><td>23.67</td></tr>
<tr><td>30</td><td>Arkansas</td><td>7.72</td><td>4</td><td>Iowa</td><td>16.10</td></tr>
<tr><td>8</td><td>California</td><td>12.02</td><td>5</td><td>Michigan</td><td>14.36</td></tr>
<tr><td>10</td><td>Colorado</td><td>11.51</td><td>6</td><td>Georgia</td><td>12.93</td></tr>
<tr><td>27</td><td>Connecticut</td><td>8.23</td><td>7</td><td>Utah</td><td>12.20</td></tr>
<tr><td>28</td><td>Delaware</td><td>8.13</td><td>8</td><td>California</td><td>12.02</td></tr>
<tr><td>34</td><td>Florida</td><td>7.07</td><td>9</td><td>Idaho</td><td>11.68</td></tr>
<tr><td>6</td><td>Georgia</td><td>12.93</td><td>10</td><td>Colorado</td><td>11.51</td></tr>
<tr><td>48</td><td>Hawaii</td><td>2.06</td><td>11</td><td>South Carolina</td><td>11.01</td></tr>
<tr><td>9</td><td>Idaho</td><td>11.68</td><td>12</td><td>Wyoming</td><td>10.53</td></tr>
<tr><td>NA</td><td>Illinois**</td><td>NA</td><td>13</td><td>North Carolina</td><td>9.91</td></tr>
<tr><td>39</td><td>Indiana</td><td>6.47</td><td>14</td><td>New York</td><td>9.80</td></tr>
<tr><td>4</td><td>Iowa</td><td>16.10</td><td>15</td><td>Massachusetts</td><td>9.78</td></tr>
<tr><td>NA</td><td>Kansas**</td><td>NA</td><td>16</td><td>New Mexico</td><td>9.48</td></tr>
<tr><td>17</td><td>Kentucky</td><td>9.41</td><td>17</td><td>Kentucky</td><td>9.41</td></tr>
<tr><td>32</td><td>Louisiana</td><td>7.15</td><td>18</td><td>Ohio</td><td>9.11</td></tr>
<tr><td>36</td><td>Maine</td><td>6.84</td><td>19</td><td>Oregon</td><td>9.01</td></tr>
<tr><td>43</td><td>Maryland</td><td>5.93</td><td>20</td><td>Washington</td><td>8.78</td></tr>
<tr><td>15</td><td>Massachusetts</td><td>9.78</td><td>21</td><td>Arizona</td><td>8.62</td></tr>
<tr><td>5</td><td>Michigan</td><td>14.36</td><td>22</td><td>Rhode Island</td><td>8.54</td></tr>
<tr><td>24</td><td>Minnesota</td><td>8.32</td><td>23</td><td>Texas</td><td>8.52</td></tr>
<tr><td>38</td><td>Mississippi</td><td>6.61</td><td>24</td><td>Minnesota</td><td>8.32</td></tr>
<tr><td>35</td><td>Missouri</td><td>7.01</td><td>25</td><td>South Dakota</td><td>8.25</td></tr>
<tr><td>47</td><td>Montana</td><td>2.94</td><td>26</td><td>Virginia</td><td>8.24</td></tr>
<tr><td>33</td><td>Nebraska</td><td>7.14</td><td>27</td><td>Connecticut</td><td>8.23</td></tr>
<tr><td>44</td><td>Nevada</td><td>5.65</td><td>28</td><td>Delaware</td><td>8.13</td></tr>
<tr><td>41</td><td>New Hampshire</td><td>6.34</td><td>29</td><td>Alaska</td><td>7.99</td></tr>
<tr><td>31</td><td>New Jersey</td><td>7.65</td><td>30</td><td>Arkansas</td><td>7.72</td></tr>
<tr><td>16</td><td>New Mexico</td><td>9.48</td><td>31</td><td>New Jersey</td><td>7.65</td></tr>
<tr><td>14</td><td>New York</td><td>9.80</td><td>32</td><td>Louisiana</td><td>7.15</td></tr>
<tr><td>13</td><td>North Carolina</td><td>9.91</td><td>33</td><td>Nebraska</td><td>7.14</td></tr>
<tr><td>1</td><td>North Dakota</td><td>60.00</td><td>34</td><td>Florida</td><td>7.07</td></tr>
<tr><td>18</td><td>Ohio</td><td>9.11</td><td>35</td><td>Missouri</td><td>7.01</td></tr>
<tr><td>37</td><td>Oklahoma</td><td>6.76</td><td>36</td><td>Maine</td><td>6.84</td></tr>
<tr><td>19</td><td>Oregon</td><td>9.01</td><td>37</td><td>Oklahoma</td><td>6.76</td></tr>
<tr><td>45</td><td>Pennsylvania</td><td>5.29</td><td>38</td><td>Mississippi</td><td>6.61</td></tr>
<tr><td>22</td><td>Rhode Island</td><td>8.54</td><td>39</td><td>Indiana</td><td>6.47</td></tr>
<tr><td>11</td><td>South Carolina</td><td>11.01</td><td>40</td><td>Tennessee</td><td>6.45</td></tr>
<tr><td>25</td><td>South Dakota</td><td>8.25</td><td>41</td><td>New Hampshire</td><td>6.34</td></tr>
<tr><td>40</td><td>Tennessee</td><td>6.45</td><td>42</td><td>West Virginia</td><td>6.15</td></tr>
<tr><td>23</td><td>Texas</td><td>8.52</td><td>43</td><td>Maryland</td><td>5.93</td></tr>
<tr><td>7</td><td>Utah</td><td>12.20</td><td>44</td><td>Nevada</td><td>5.65</td></tr>
<tr><td>2</td><td>Vermont</td><td>43.48</td><td>45</td><td>Pennsylvania</td><td>5.29</td></tr>
<tr><td>26</td><td>Virginia</td><td>8.24</td><td>46</td><td>Wisconsin</td><td>5.20</td></tr>
<tr><td>20</td><td>Washington</td><td>8.78</td><td>47</td><td>Montana</td><td>2.94</td></tr>
<tr><td>42</td><td>West Virginia</td><td>6.15</td><td>48</td><td>Hawaii</td><td>2.06</td></tr>
<tr><td>46</td><td>Wisconsin</td><td>5.20</td><td>NA</td><td>Illinois**</td><td>NA</td></tr>
<tr><td>12</td><td>Wyoming</td><td>10.53</td><td>NA</td><td>Kansas**</td><td>NA</td></tr>
<tr><td></td><td></td><td></td><td></td><td>District of Columbia</td><td>4.11</td></tr>
</table>

Source: Morgan Quitno Corporation using data from U.S. Department of Justice, Federal Bureau of Investigation
   "Crime in the United States 1993" (Uniform Crime Reports, December 4, 1994)
*Of the 588,706 robberies in 1993 for which supplemental data were received by the F.B.I. There were an additional 71,051 robberies for which the type of weapon was not reported to the F.B.I. Robbery is the taking or attempting to take anything of value by force or threat of force.
**Not available.

Robberies Committed Hands, Fists or Feet in 1993

National Total = 224,788 Robberies Committed with Hands, Fists or Feet*

ALPHA ORDER					RANK ORDER			
RANK	STATE	ROBBERIES	% of USA		RANK	STATE	ROBBERIES	% of USA
30	Alabama	985	0.44%		1	California	46,455	20.67%
37	Alaska	316	0.14%		2	New York	38,827	17.27%
20	Arizona	2,548	1.13%		3	Florida	21,282	9.47%
29	Arkansas	1,092	0.49%		4	Texas	13,954	6.21%
1	California	46,455	20.67%		5	New Jersey	11,048	4.91%
26	Colorado	1,733	0.77%		6	Pennsylvania	8,627	3.84%
19	Connecticut	2,747	1.22%		7	Ohio	7,947	3.54%
42	Delaware	129	0.06%		8	Maryland	6,610	2.94%
3	Florida	21,282	9.47%		9	Michigan	5,586	2.49%
12	Georgia	4,244	1.89%		10	North Carolina	4,898	2.18%
31	Hawaii	965	0.43%		11	Missouri	4,455	1.98%
44	Idaho	49	0.02%		12	Georgia	4,244	1.89%
NA	Illinois**	NA	NA		13	Massachusetts	4,197	1.87%
22	Indiana	2,292	1.02%		14	Tennessee	3,583	1.59%
38	Iowa	301	0.13%		15	Washington	3,454	1.54%
NA	Kansas**	NA	NA		16	Virginia	3,317	1.48%
28	Kentucky	1,226	0.55%		17	Minnesota	2,963	1.32%
21	Louisiana	2,484	1.11%		18	South Carolina	2,782	1.24%
41	Maine	150	0.07%		19	Connecticut	2,747	1.22%
8	Maryland	6,610	2.94%		20	Arizona	2,548	1.13%
13	Massachusetts	4,197	1.87%		21	Louisiana	2,484	1.11%
9	Michigan	5,586	2.49%		22	Indiana	2,292	1.02%
17	Minnesota	2,963	1.32%		23	Wisconsin	1,928	0.86%
32	Mississippi	935	0.42%		24	Oregon	1,859	0.83%
11	Missouri	4,455	1.98%		25	Oklahoma	1,753	0.78%
46	Montana	9	0.00%		26	Colorado	1,733	0.77%
40	Nebraska	151	0.07%		27	Nevada	1,474	0.66%
27	Nevada	1,474	0.66%		28	Kentucky	1,226	0.55%
39	New Hampshire	181	0.08%		29	Arkansas	1,092	0.49%
5	New Jersey	11,048	4.91%		30	Alabama	985	0.44%
34	New Mexico	544	0.24%		31	Hawaii	965	0.43%
2	New York	38,827	17.27%		32	Mississippi	935	0.42%
10	North Carolina	4,898	2.18%		33	Rhode Island	550	0.24%
47	North Dakota	8	0.00%		34	New Mexico	544	0.24%
7	Ohio	7,947	3.54%		35	Utah	510	0.23%
25	Oklahoma	1,753	0.78%		36	West Virginia	385	0.17%
24	Oregon	1,859	0.83%		37	Alaska	316	0.14%
6	Pennsylvania	8,627	3.84%		38	Iowa	301	0.13%
33	Rhode Island	550	0.24%		39	New Hampshire	181	0.08%
18	South Carolina	2,782	1.24%		40	Nebraska	151	0.07%
43	South Dakota	57	0.03%		41	Maine	150	0.07%
14	Tennessee	3,583	1.59%		42	Delaware	129	0.06%
4	Texas	13,954	6.21%		43	South Dakota	57	0.03%
35	Utah	510	0.23%		44	Idaho	49	0.02%
48	Vermont	6	0.00%		45	Wyoming	19	0.01%
16	Virginia	3,317	1.48%		46	Montana	9	0.00%
15	Washington	3,454	1.54%		47	North Dakota	8	0.00%
36	West Virginia	385	0.17%		48	Vermont	6	0.00%
23	Wisconsin	1,928	0.86%		NA	Illinois**	NA	NA
45	Wyoming	19	0.01%		NA	Kansas**	NA	NA
						District of Columbia	3,173	1.41%

Source: U.S. Department of Justice, Federal Bureau of Investigation
"Crime in the United States 1993" (Uniform Crime Reports, December 4, 1994)
*Of the 588,706 robberies in 1993 for which supplemental data were received by the F.B.I. There were an additional
71,051 robberies for which the type of weapon was not reported to the F.B.I. Robbery is the taking or attempting to take
anything of value by force or threat of force. Also called strong-armed robberies.
**Not available.

Percent of Robberies Committed with Hands, Fists or Feet in 1993

National Percent = 38.18% of Robberies Committed with Hands, Fists or Feet*

<u>ALPHA ORDER</u>

RANK	STATE	PERCENT
45	Alabama	25.37
18	Alaska	44.32
25	Arizona	40.66
31	Arkansas	36.19
29	California	36.78
21	Colorado	42.63
22	Connecticut	42.56
3	Delaware	61.72
15	Florida	45.75
42	Georgia	27.05
1	Hawaii	79.49
34	Idaho	35.77
NA	Illinois**	NA
27	Indiana	38.21
11	Iowa	48.47
NA	Kansas**	NA
24	Kentucky	40.79
47	Louisiana	23.08
7	Maine	57.03
41	Maryland	30.63
16	Massachusetts	44.99
46	Michigan	25.36
6	Minnesota	58.27
30	Mississippi	36.59
31	Missouri	36.19
43	Montana	26.47
4	Nebraska	59.92
36	Nevada	34.43
2	New Hampshire	63.73
13	New Jersey	47.38
40	New Mexico	30.70
26	New York	38.25
28	North Carolina	37.36
48	North Dakota	16.00
20	Ohio	42.76
17	Oklahoma	44.57
12	Oregon	47.72
19	Pennsylvania	44.10
8	Rhode Island	54.62
23	South Carolina	41.00
5	South Dakota	58.76
39	Tennessee	33.25
35	Texas	34.56
14	Utah	46.79
44	Vermont	26.09
33	Virginia	35.99
10	Washington	48.81
9	West Virginia	49.30
37	Wisconsin	33.77
38	Wyoming	33.33

<u>RANK ORDER</u>

RANK	STATE	PERCENT
1	Hawaii	79.49
2	New Hampshire	63.73
3	Delaware	61.72
4	Nebraska	59.92
5	South Dakota	58.76
6	Minnesota	58.27
7	Maine	57.03
8	Rhode Island	54.62
9	West Virginia	49.30
10	Washington	48.81
11	Iowa	48.47
12	Oregon	47.72
13	New Jersey	47.38
14	Utah	46.79
15	Florida	45.75
16	Massachusetts	44.99
17	Oklahoma	44.57
18	Alaska	44.32
19	Pennsylvania	44.10
20	Ohio	42.76
21	Colorado	42.63
22	Connecticut	42.56
23	South Carolina	41.00
24	Kentucky	40.79
25	Arizona	40.66
26	New York	38.25
27	Indiana	38.21
28	North Carolina	37.36
29	California	36.78
30	Mississippi	36.59
31	Arkansas	36.19
31	Missouri	36.19
33	Virginia	35.99
34	Idaho	35.77
35	Texas	34.56
36	Nevada	34.43
37	Wisconsin	33.77
38	Wyoming	33.33
39	Tennessee	33.25
40	New Mexico	30.70
41	Maryland	30.63
42	Georgia	27.05
43	Montana	26.47
44	Vermont	26.09
45	Alabama	25.37
46	Michigan	25.36
47	Louisiana	23.08
48	North Dakota	16.00
NA	Illinois**	NA
NA	Kansas**	NA

District of Columbia   44.65

Source: Morgan Quitno Corporation using data from U.S. Department of Justice, Federal Bureau of Investigation "Crime in the United States 1993" (Uniform Crime Reports, December 4, 1994)

Of the 588,706 robberies in 1993 for which supplemental data were received by the F.B.I. There were an additional 71,051 robberies for which the type of weapon was not reported to the F.B.I. Robbery is the taking or attempting to take anything of value by force or threat of force. Also called strong-armed robberies.

**Not available.*

328

Bank Robberies in 1993

National Total = 8,538 Robberies*

<table>
<tr><td colspan="4">ALPHA ORDER</td><td></td><td colspan="4">RANK ORDER</td></tr>
<tr><td>RANK</td><td>STATE</td><td>ROBBERIES</td><td>% of USA</td><td></td><td>RANK</td><td>STATE</td><td>ROBBERIES</td><td>% of USA</td></tr>
<tr><td>29</td><td>Alabama</td><td>47</td><td>0.55%</td><td></td><td>1</td><td>California</td><td>3,024</td><td>35.42%</td></tr>
<tr><td>43</td><td>Alaska</td><td>8</td><td>0.09%</td><td></td><td>2</td><td>Florida</td><td>683</td><td>8.00%</td></tr>
<tr><td>7</td><td>Arizona</td><td>239</td><td>2.80%</td><td></td><td>3</td><td>New York</td><td>668</td><td>7.82%</td></tr>
<tr><td>34</td><td>Arkansas</td><td>29</td><td>0.34%</td><td></td><td>4</td><td>Maryland</td><td>322</td><td>3.77%</td></tr>
<tr><td>1</td><td>California</td><td>3,024</td><td>35.42%</td><td></td><td>5</td><td>Washington</td><td>265</td><td>3.10%</td></tr>
<tr><td>22</td><td>Colorado</td><td>85</td><td>1.00%</td><td></td><td>6</td><td>Ohio</td><td>264</td><td>3.09%</td></tr>
<tr><td>26</td><td>Connecticut</td><td>62</td><td>0.73%</td><td></td><td>7</td><td>Arizona</td><td>239</td><td>2.80%</td></tr>
<tr><td>39</td><td>Delaware</td><td>16</td><td>0.19%</td><td></td><td>8</td><td>Oregon</td><td>231</td><td>2.71%</td></tr>
<tr><td>2</td><td>Florida</td><td>683</td><td>8.00%</td><td></td><td>9</td><td>North Carolina</td><td>227</td><td>2.66%</td></tr>
<tr><td>12</td><td>Georgia</td><td>184</td><td>2.16%</td><td></td><td>10</td><td>Michigan</td><td>219</td><td>2.57%</td></tr>
<tr><td>27</td><td>Hawaii</td><td>55</td><td>0.64%</td><td></td><td>11</td><td>Pennsylvania</td><td>197</td><td>2.31%</td></tr>
<tr><td>42</td><td>Idaho</td><td>9</td><td>0.11%</td><td></td><td>12</td><td>Georgia</td><td>184</td><td>2.16%</td></tr>
<tr><td>16</td><td>Illinois</td><td>132</td><td>1.55%</td><td></td><td>13</td><td>Texas</td><td>181</td><td>2.12%</td></tr>
<tr><td>20</td><td>Indiana</td><td>96</td><td>1.12%</td><td></td><td>14</td><td>Massachusetts</td><td>149</td><td>1.75%</td></tr>
<tr><td>38</td><td>Iowa</td><td>18</td><td>0.21%</td><td></td><td>15</td><td>Virginia</td><td>134</td><td>1.57%</td></tr>
<tr><td>34</td><td>Kansas</td><td>29</td><td>0.34%</td><td></td><td>16</td><td>Illinois</td><td>132</td><td>1.55%</td></tr>
<tr><td>30</td><td>Kentucky</td><td>46</td><td>0.54%</td><td></td><td>17</td><td>Nevada</td><td>128</td><td>1.50%</td></tr>
<tr><td>25</td><td>Louisiana</td><td>64</td><td>0.75%</td><td></td><td>18</td><td>Tennessee</td><td>106</td><td>1.24%</td></tr>
<tr><td>41</td><td>Maine</td><td>10</td><td>0.12%</td><td></td><td>19</td><td>New Jersey</td><td>103</td><td>1.21%</td></tr>
<tr><td>4</td><td>Maryland</td><td>322</td><td>3.77%</td><td></td><td>20</td><td>Indiana</td><td>96</td><td>1.12%</td></tr>
<tr><td>14</td><td>Massachusetts</td><td>149</td><td>1.75%</td><td></td><td>21</td><td>Wisconsin</td><td>87</td><td>1.02%</td></tr>
<tr><td>10</td><td>Michigan</td><td>219</td><td>2.57%</td><td></td><td>22</td><td>Colorado</td><td>85</td><td>1.00%</td></tr>
<tr><td>24</td><td>Minnesota</td><td>67</td><td>0.78%</td><td></td><td>22</td><td>South Carolina</td><td>85</td><td>1.00%</td></tr>
<tr><td>31</td><td>Mississippi</td><td>39</td><td>0.46%</td><td></td><td>24</td><td>Minnesota</td><td>67</td><td>0.78%</td></tr>
<tr><td>28</td><td>Missouri</td><td>53</td><td>0.62%</td><td></td><td>25</td><td>Louisiana</td><td>64</td><td>0.75%</td></tr>
<tr><td>50</td><td>Montana</td><td>0</td><td>0.00%</td><td></td><td>26</td><td>Connecticut</td><td>62</td><td>0.73%</td></tr>
<tr><td>37</td><td>Nebraska</td><td>21</td><td>0.25%</td><td></td><td>27</td><td>Hawaii</td><td>55</td><td>0.64%</td></tr>
<tr><td>17</td><td>Nevada</td><td>128</td><td>1.50%</td><td></td><td>28</td><td>Missouri</td><td>53</td><td>0.62%</td></tr>
<tr><td>45</td><td>New Hampshire</td><td>4</td><td>0.05%</td><td></td><td>29</td><td>Alabama</td><td>47</td><td>0.55%</td></tr>
<tr><td>19</td><td>New Jersey</td><td>103</td><td>1.21%</td><td></td><td>30</td><td>Kentucky</td><td>46</td><td>0.54%</td></tr>
<tr><td>33</td><td>New Mexico</td><td>32</td><td>0.37%</td><td></td><td>31</td><td>Mississippi</td><td>39</td><td>0.46%</td></tr>
<tr><td>3</td><td>New York</td><td>668</td><td>7.82%</td><td></td><td>32</td><td>Utah</td><td>36</td><td>0.42%</td></tr>
<tr><td>9</td><td>North Carolina</td><td>227</td><td>2.66%</td><td></td><td>33</td><td>New Mexico</td><td>32</td><td>0.37%</td></tr>
<tr><td>48</td><td>North Dakota</td><td>2</td><td>0.02%</td><td></td><td>34</td><td>Arkansas</td><td>29</td><td>0.34%</td></tr>
<tr><td>6</td><td>Ohio</td><td>264</td><td>3.09%</td><td></td><td>34</td><td>Kansas</td><td>29</td><td>0.34%</td></tr>
<tr><td>36</td><td>Oklahoma</td><td>28</td><td>0.33%</td><td></td><td>36</td><td>Oklahoma</td><td>28</td><td>0.33%</td></tr>
<tr><td>8</td><td>Oregon</td><td>231</td><td>2.71%</td><td></td><td>37</td><td>Nebraska</td><td>21</td><td>0.25%</td></tr>
<tr><td>11</td><td>Pennsylvania</td><td>197</td><td>2.31%</td><td></td><td>38</td><td>Iowa</td><td>18</td><td>0.21%</td></tr>
<tr><td>40</td><td>Rhode Island</td><td>14</td><td>0.16%</td><td></td><td>39</td><td>Delaware</td><td>16</td><td>0.19%</td></tr>
<tr><td>22</td><td>South Carolina</td><td>85</td><td>1.00%</td><td></td><td>40</td><td>Rhode Island</td><td>14</td><td>0.16%</td></tr>
<tr><td>45</td><td>South Dakota</td><td>4</td><td>0.05%</td><td></td><td>41</td><td>Maine</td><td>10</td><td>0.12%</td></tr>
<tr><td>18</td><td>Tennessee</td><td>106</td><td>1.24%</td><td></td><td>42</td><td>Idaho</td><td>9</td><td>0.11%</td></tr>
<tr><td>13</td><td>Texas</td><td>181</td><td>2.12%</td><td></td><td>43</td><td>Alaska</td><td>8</td><td>0.09%</td></tr>
<tr><td>32</td><td>Utah</td><td>36</td><td>0.42%</td><td></td><td>44</td><td>West Virginia</td><td>5</td><td>0.06%</td></tr>
<tr><td>47</td><td>Vermont</td><td>3</td><td>0.04%</td><td></td><td>45</td><td>New Hampshire</td><td>4</td><td>0.05%</td></tr>
<tr><td>15</td><td>Virginia</td><td>134</td><td>1.57%</td><td></td><td>45</td><td>South Dakota</td><td>4</td><td>0.05%</td></tr>
<tr><td>5</td><td>Washington</td><td>265</td><td>3.10%</td><td></td><td>47</td><td>Vermont</td><td>3</td><td>0.04%</td></tr>
<tr><td>44</td><td>West Virginia</td><td>5</td><td>0.06%</td><td></td><td>48</td><td>North Dakota</td><td>2</td><td>0.02%</td></tr>
<tr><td>21</td><td>Wisconsin</td><td>87</td><td>1.02%</td><td></td><td>49</td><td>Wyoming</td><td>1</td><td>0.01%</td></tr>
<tr><td>49</td><td>Wyoming</td><td>1</td><td>0.01%</td><td></td><td>50</td><td>Montana</td><td>0</td><td>0.00%</td></tr>
<tr><td></td><td></td><td></td><td></td><td></td><td></td><td>District of Columbia</td><td>27</td><td>0.32%</td></tr>
</table>

Source: U.S. Department of Justice, Federal Bureau of Investigation
   "Bank Crime Statistics, Federally Insured Financial Institutions, January 1, 1993 – December 31, 1993"
*Does not include 38 robberies in Puerto Rico and 2 in the Virgin Islands. In addition, there were 309 bank burglaries, 78 bank larcenies and 39 extortions. Of these 8,966 bank crimes, loot valued at $89,392,771 was taken in 8,291 cases. Of this, $32,317,009 was recovered.

Aggravated Assaults in 1993

National Total = 1,135,099 Aggravated Assaults*

RANK	STATE	ASSAULTS	% of USA
16	Alabama	24,044	2.12%
38	Alaska	3,268	0.29%
19	Arizona	19,903	1.75%
27	Arkansas	10,079	0.89%
1	California	194,083	17.10%
23	Colorado	14,230	1.25%
31	Connecticut	7,496	0.66%
39	Delaware	2,920	0.26%
2	Florida	107,479	9.47%
10	Georgia	29,628	2.61%
43	Hawaii	1,408	0.12%
42	Idaho	2,491	0.22%
5	Illinois	62,298	5.49%
20	Indiana	18,432	1.62%
32	Iowa	6,890	0.61%
29	Kansas	8,259	0.73%
24	Kentucky	12,555	1.11%
8	Louisiana	30,727	2.71%
47	Maine	945	0.08%
13	Maryland	25,141	2.21%
7	Massachusetts	35,591	3.14%
6	Michigan	44,747	3.94%
30	Minnesota	7,943	0.70%
34	Mississippi	6,302	0.56%
17	Missouri	23,825	2.10%
46	Montana	958	0.08%
36	Nebraska	4,050	0.36%
33	Nevada	6,443	0.57%
48	New Hampshire	721	0.06%
18	New Jersey	23,438	2.06%
26	New Mexico	11,815	1.04%
3	New York	85,802	7.56%
9	North Carolina	30,650	2.70%
50	North Dakota	309	0.03%
11	Ohio	28,431	2.50%
22	Oklahoma	14,712	1.30%
28	Oregon	9,630	0.85%
15	Pennsylvania	24,714	2.18%
40	Rhode Island	2,681	0.24%
12	South Carolina	28,174	2.48%
45	South Dakota	1,041	0.09%
14	Tennessee	24,758	2.18%
4	Texas	84,881	7.48%
37	Utah	3,622	0.32%
49	Vermont	356	0.03%
25	Virginia	12,322	1.09%
21	Washington	16,181	1.43%
41	West Virginia	2,520	0.22%
35	Wisconsin	6,116	0.54%
44	Wyoming	1,087	0.10%

RANK	STATE	ASSAULTS	% of USA
1	California	194,083	17.10%
2	Florida	107,479	9.47%
3	New York	85,802	7.56%
4	Texas	84,881	7.48%
5	Illinois	62,298	5.49%
6	Michigan	44,747	3.94%
7	Massachusetts	35,591	3.14%
8	Louisiana	30,727	2.71%
9	North Carolina	30,650	2.70%
10	Georgia	29,628	2.61%
11	Ohio	28,431	2.50%
12	South Carolina	28,174	2.48%
13	Maryland	25,141	2.21%
14	Tennessee	24,758	2.18%
15	Pennsylvania	24,714	2.18%
16	Alabama	24,044	2.12%
17	Missouri	23,825	2.10%
18	New Jersey	23,438	2.06%
19	Arizona	19,903	1.75%
20	Indiana	18,432	1.62%
21	Washington	16,181	1.43%
22	Oklahoma	14,712	1.30%
23	Colorado	14,230	1.25%
24	Kentucky	12,555	1.11%
25	Virginia	12,322	1.09%
26	New Mexico	11,815	1.04%
27	Arkansas	10,079	0.89%
28	Oregon	9,630	0.85%
29	Kansas	8,259	0.73%
30	Minnesota	7,943	0.70%
31	Connecticut	7,496	0.66%
32	Iowa	6,890	0.61%
33	Nevada	6,443	0.57%
34	Mississippi	6,302	0.56%
35	Wisconsin	6,116	0.54%
36	Nebraska	4,050	0.36%
37	Utah	3,622	0.32%
38	Alaska	3,268	0.29%
39	Delaware	2,920	0.26%
40	Rhode Island	2,681	0.24%
41	West Virginia	2,520	0.22%
42	Idaho	2,491	0.22%
43	Hawaii	1,408	0.12%
44	Wyoming	1,087	0.10%
45	South Dakota	1,041	0.09%
46	Montana	958	0.08%
47	Maine	945	0.08%
48	New Hampshire	721	0.06%
49	Vermont	356	0.03%
50	North Dakota	309	0.03%
	District of Columbia	9,003	0.79%

Source: U.S. Department of Justice, Federal Bureau of Investigation
"Crime in the United States 1993" (Uniform Crime Reports, December 4, 1994)
*Aggravated assault is an attack for the purpose of inflicting severe bodily injury.

Average Time Between Aggravated Assaults in 1993

National Rate = An Aggravated Assault Occurs Every 28 Seconds*

ALPHA ORDER		
RANK	STATE	MINUTES.SECONDS
35	Alabama	21.52
13	Alaska	160.50
32	Arizona	26.25
24	Arkansas	52.09
50	California	2.43
28	Colorado	36.56
20	Connecticut	70.07
12	Delaware	180.00
49	Florida	4.53
41	Georgia	17.44
8	Hawaii	373.18
9	Idaho	211.00
46	Illinois	8.26
31	Indiana	28.31
19	Iowa	76.17
22	Kansas	63.38
27	Kentucky	41.52
43	Louisiana	17.07
4	Maine	556.11
38	Maryland	20.55
44	Massachusetts	14.46
45	Michigan	11.45
21	Minnesota	66.10
17	Mississippi	83.24
34	Missouri	22.04
5	Montana	548.38
15	Nebraska	129.47
18	Nevada	81.35
3	New Hampshire	728.59
33	New Jersey	22.26
25	New Mexico	44.29
48	New York	6.08
42	North Carolina	17.09
1	North Dakota	1,700.58
40	Ohio	18.29
29	Oklahoma	35.44
23	Oregon	54.35
36	Pennsylvania	21.16
11	Rhode Island	196.03
39	South Carolina	18.40
6	South Dakota	504.54
37	Tennessee	21.14
47	Texas	6.11
14	Utah	145.07
2	Vermont	1,476.24
26	Virginia	42.40
30	Washington	32.29
10	West Virginia	208.34
16	Wisconsin	85.56
7	Wyoming	483.32

RANK ORDER		
RANK	STATE	MINUTES.SECONDS
1	North Dakota	1,700.58
2	Vermont	1,476.24
3	New Hampshire	728.59
4	Maine	556.11
5	Montana	548.38
6	South Dakota	504.54
7	Wyoming	483.32
8	Hawaii	373.18
9	Idaho	211.00
10	West Virginia	208.34
11	Rhode Island	196.03
12	Delaware	180.00
13	Alaska	160.50
14	Utah	145.07
15	Nebraska	129.47
16	Wisconsin	85.56
17	Mississippi	83.24
18	Nevada	81.35
19	Iowa	76.17
20	Connecticut	70.07
21	Minnesota	66.10
22	Kansas	63.38
23	Oregon	54.35
24	Arkansas	52.09
25	New Mexico	44.29
26	Virginia	42.40
27	Kentucky	41.52
28	Colorado	36.56
29	Oklahoma	35.44
30	Washington	32.29
31	Indiana	28.31
32	Arizona	26.25
33	New Jersey	22.26
34	Missouri	22.04
35	Alabama	21.52
36	Pennsylvania	21.16
37	Tennessee	21.14
38	Maryland	20.55
39	South Carolina	18.40
40	Ohio	18.29
41	Georgia	17.44
42	North Carolina	17.09
43	Louisiana	17.07
44	Massachusetts	14.46
45	Michigan	11.45
46	Illinois	8.26
47	Texas	6.11
48	New York	6.08
49	Florida	4.53
50	California	2.43
	District of Columbia	58.23

Source: Morgan Quitno Corporation using data from U.S. Department of Justice, Federal Bureau of Investigation
"Crime in the United States 1993" (Uniform Crime Reports, December 4, 1994)
*Aggravated assault is an attack for the purpose of inflicting severe bodily injury.

Percent Change in Number of Aggravated Assaults: 1992 to 1993

National Percent Change = 0.7% Increase*

ALPHA ORDER

RANK	STATE	PERCENT CHANGE
47	Alabama	(11.2)
2	Alaska	25.0
7	Arizona	11.3
14	Arkansas	5.3
37	California	(2.0)
25	Colorado	1.3
46	Connecticut	(9.5)
6	Delaware	11.7
23	Florida	2.5
22	Georgia	2.8
20	Hawaii	3.2
17	Idaho	3.9
18	Illinois	3.7
40	Indiana	(3.0)
5	Iowa	12.4
36	Kansas	(1.9)
50	Kentucky	(18.5)
9	Louisiana	9.7
45	Maine	(6.7)
28	Maryland	(0.1)
12	Massachusetts	6.9
19	Michigan	3.4
43	Minnesota	(3.7)
16	Mississippi	4.6
33	Missouri	(1.6)
24	Montana	1.5
33	Nebraska	(1.6)
1	Nevada	66.4
3	New Hampshire	22.6
31	New Jersey	(1.3)
20	New Mexico	3.2
38	New York	(2.1)
27	North Carolina	0.1
42	North Dakota	(3.4)
44	Ohio	(3.8)
13	Oklahoma	6.1
10	Oregon	7.4
41	Pennsylvania	(3.1)
26	Rhode Island	0.5
8	South Carolina	10.8
4	South Dakota	16.8
15	Tennessee	4.8
32	Texas	(1.4)
11	Utah	7.3
49	Vermont	(15.0)
35	Virginia	(1.8)
30	Washington	(0.9)
29	West Virginia	(0.7)
39	Wisconsin	(2.5)
48	Wyoming	(11.3)

RANK ORDER

RANK	STATE	PERCENT CHANGE
1	Nevada	66.4
2	Alaska	25.0
3	New Hampshire	22.6
4	South Dakota	16.8
5	Iowa	12.4
6	Delaware	11.7
7	Arizona	11.3
8	South Carolina	10.8
9	Louisiana	9.7
10	Oregon	7.4
11	Utah	7.3
12	Massachusetts	6.9
13	Oklahoma	6.1
14	Arkansas	5.3
15	Tennessee	4.8
16	Mississippi	4.6
17	Idaho	3.9
18	Illinois	3.7
19	Michigan	3.4
20	Hawaii	3.2
20	New Mexico	3.2
22	Georgia	2.8
23	Florida	2.5
24	Montana	1.5
25	Colorado	1.3
26	Rhode Island	0.5
27	North Carolina	0.1
28	Maryland	(0.1)
29	West Virginia	(0.7)
30	Washington	(0.9)
31	New Jersey	(1.3)
32	Texas	(1.4)
33	Missouri	(1.6)
33	Nebraska	(1.6)
35	Virginia	(1.8)
36	Kansas	(1.9)
37	California	(2.0)
38	New York	(2.1)
39	Wisconsin	(2.5)
40	Indiana	(3.0)
41	Pennsylvania	(3.1)
42	North Dakota	(3.4)
43	Minnesota	(3.7)
44	Ohio	(3.8)
45	Maine	(6.7)
46	Connecticut	(9.5)
47	Alabama	(11.2)
48	Wyoming	(11.3)
49	Vermont	(15.0)
50	Kentucky	(18.5)

	District of Columbia	5.1

Source: U.S. Department of Justice, Federal Bureau of Investigation
   "Crime in the United States 1993" (Uniform Crime Reports, December 4, 1994)
*Aggravated assault is an attack for the purpose of inflicting severe bodily injury.

Aggravated Assault Rate in 1993

National Rate = 440.1 Aggravated Assaults per 100,000 Population*

ALPHA ORDER

RANK	STATE	RATE
7	Alabama	574.3
8	Alaska	545.6
11	Arizona	505.7
22	Arkansas	415.8
5	California	621.8
23	Colorado	399.0
36	Connecticut	228.7
21	Delaware	417.1
1	Florida	785.7
20	Georgia	428.3
45	Hawaii	120.1
37	Idaho	226.7
9	Illinois	532.6
26	Indiana	322.6
33	Iowa	244.8
25	Kansas	326.3
24	Kentucky	331.4
4	Louisiana	715.4
47	Maine	76.3
10	Maryland	506.4
6	Massachusetts	592.0
13	Michigan	472.1
41	Minnesota	175.8
34	Mississippi	238.4
18	Missouri	455.2
46	Montana	114.2
32	Nebraska	252.0
16	Nevada	463.9
48	New Hampshire	64.1
29	New Jersey	297.5
3	New Mexico	731.1
14	New York	471.5
19	North Carolina	441.3
50	North Dakota	48.7
31	Ohio	256.3
17	Oklahoma	455.3
27	Oregon	317.6
38	Pennsylvania	205.1
30	Rhode Island	268.1
2	South Carolina	773.4
42	South Dakota	145.6
12	Tennessee	485.5
15	Texas	470.8
39	Utah	194.7
49	Vermont	61.8
40	Virginia	189.8
28	Washington	307.9
43	West Virginia	138.5
44	Wisconsin	121.4
35	Wyoming	231.3

RANK ORDER

RANK	STATE	RATE
1	Florida	785.7
2	South Carolina	773.4
3	New Mexico	731.1
4	Louisiana	715.4
5	California	621.8
6	Massachusetts	592.0
7	Alabama	574.3
8	Alaska	545.6
9	Illinois	532.6
10	Maryland	506.4
11	Arizona	505.7
12	Tennessee	485.5
13	Michigan	472.1
14	New York	471.5
15	Texas	470.8
16	Nevada	463.9
17	Oklahoma	455.3
18	Missouri	455.2
19	North Carolina	441.3
20	Georgia	428.3
21	Delaware	417.1
22	Arkansas	415.8
23	Colorado	399.0
24	Kentucky	331.4
25	Kansas	326.3
26	Indiana	322.6
27	Oregon	317.6
28	Washington	307.9
29	New Jersey	297.5
30	Rhode Island	268.1
31	Ohio	256.3
32	Nebraska	252.0
33	Iowa	244.8
34	Mississippi	238.4
35	Wyoming	231.3
36	Connecticut	228.7
37	Idaho	226.7
38	Pennsylvania	205.1
39	Utah	194.7
40	Virginia	189.8
41	Minnesota	175.8
42	South Dakota	145.6
43	West Virginia	138.5
44	Wisconsin	121.4
45	Hawaii	120.1
46	Montana	114.2
47	Maine	76.3
48	New Hampshire	64.1
49	Vermont	61.8
50	North Dakota	48.7

District of Columbia — 1,557.6

Source: U.S. Department of Justice, Federal Bureau of Investigation
"Crime in the United States 1993" (Uniform Crime Reports, December 4, 1994)
*Aggravated assault is an attack for the purpose of inflicting severe bodily injury.

Percent Change in Rate of Aggravated Assaults: 1992 to 1993

National Percent Change = 0.4% Decrease*

ALPHA ORDER				RANK ORDER		
RANK	STATE	PERCENT CHANGE		RANK	STATE	PERCENT CHANGE
48	Alabama	(12.3)		1	Nevada	59.0
2	Alaska	22.5		2	Alaska	22.5
9	Arizona	8.4		3	New Hampshire	21.2
14	Arkansas	4.2		4	South Dakota	16.2
35	California	(3.1)		5	Iowa	12.3
29	Colorado	(1.5)		6	Delaware	9.9
46	Connecticut	(9.4)		7	Louisiana	9.5
6	Delaware	9.9		7	South Carolina	9.5
20	Florida	1.1		9	Arizona	8.4
24	Georgia	0.3		10	Massachusetts	6.7
19	Hawaii	2.0		11	Oklahoma	5.5
23	Idaho	0.9		11	Oregon	5.5
17	Illinois	3.1		13	Utah	4.6
42	Indiana	(3.9)		14	Arkansas	4.2
5	Iowa	12.3		15	Mississippi	3.5
31	Kansas	(2.2)		16	Tennessee	3.2
50	Kentucky	(19.2)		17	Illinois	3.1
7	Louisiana	9.5		18	Michigan	2.9
45	Maine	(7.0)		19	Hawaii	2.0
27	Maryland	(1.2)		20	Florida	1.1
10	Massachusetts	6.7		21	New Mexico	1.0
18	Michigan	2.9		21	Rhode Island	1.0
44	Minnesota	(4.5)		23	Idaho	0.9
15	Mississippi	3.5		24	Georgia	0.3
32	Missouri	(2.4)		25	Montana	(0.3)
25	Montana	(0.3)		26	West Virginia	(1.1)
30	Nebraska	(1.6)		27	Maryland	(1.2)
1	Nevada	59.0		28	North Carolina	(1.4)
3	New Hampshire	21.2		29	Colorado	(1.5)
32	New Jersey	(2.4)		30	Nebraska	(1.6)
21	New Mexico	1.0		31	Kansas	(2.2)
34	New York	(2.5)		32	Missouri	(2.4)
28	North Carolina	(1.4)		32	New Jersey	(2.4)
38	North Dakota	(3.2)		34	New York	(2.5)
43	Ohio	(4.4)		35	California	(3.1)
11	Oklahoma	5.5		35	Washington	(3.1)
11	Oregon	5.5		35	Wisconsin	(3.1)
39	Pennsylvania	(3.4)		38	North Dakota	(3.2)
21	Rhode Island	1.0		39	Pennsylvania	(3.4)
7	South Carolina	9.5		40	Texas	(3.5)
4	South Dakota	16.2		41	Virginia	(3.6)
16	Tennessee	3.2		42	Indiana	(3.9)
40	Texas	(3.5)		43	Ohio	(4.4)
13	Utah	4.6		44	Minnesota	(4.5)
49	Vermont	(15.9)		45	Maine	(7.0)
41	Virginia	(3.6)		46	Connecticut	(9.4)
35	Washington	(3.1)		47	Wyoming	(12.0)
26	West Virginia	(1.1)		48	Alabama	(12.3)
35	Wisconsin	(3.1)		49	Vermont	(15.9)
47	Wyoming	(12.0)		50	Kentucky	(19.2)

District of Columbia   7.1

Source: U.S. Department of Justice, Federal Bureau of Investigation
"Crime in the United States 1993" (Uniform Crime Reports, December 4, 1994)
*Aggravated assault is an attack for the purpose of inflicting severe bodily injury.

Aggravated Assaults with Firearms in 1993

National Total = 244,866 Aggravated Assaults with Firearms*

ALPHA ORDER					RANK ORDER			

<table>
<tr><th colspan="2">ALPHA ORDER</th><th></th><th></th><th></th><th colspan="2">RANK ORDER</th><th></th><th></th></tr>
<tr><th>RANK</th><th>STATE</th><th>ASSAULTS</th><th>% of USA</th><th></th><th>RANK</th><th>STATE</th><th>ASSAULTS</th><th>% of USA</th></tr>
<tr><td>22</td><td>Alabama</td><td>2,593</td><td>1.06%</td><td></td><td>1</td><td>California</td><td>44,855</td><td>18.32%</td></tr>
<tr><td>33</td><td>Alaska</td><td>729</td><td>0.30%</td><td></td><td>2</td><td>Florida</td><td>25,572</td><td>10.44%</td></tr>
<tr><td>10</td><td>Arizona</td><td>7,159</td><td>2.92%</td><td></td><td>3</td><td>Texas</td><td>24,756</td><td>10.11%</td></tr>
<tr><td>20</td><td>Arkansas</td><td>3,141</td><td>1.28%</td><td></td><td>4</td><td>New York</td><td>16,739</td><td>6.84%</td></tr>
<tr><td>1</td><td>California</td><td>44,855</td><td>18.32%</td><td></td><td>5</td><td>Michigan</td><td>12,540</td><td>5.12%</td></tr>
<tr><td>19</td><td>Colorado</td><td>3,972</td><td>1.62%</td><td></td><td>6</td><td>North Carolina</td><td>9,413</td><td>3.84%</td></tr>
<tr><td>31</td><td>Connecticut</td><td>1,065</td><td>0.43%</td><td></td><td>7</td><td>Missouri</td><td>8,550</td><td>3.49%</td></tr>
<tr><td>39</td><td>Delaware</td><td>186</td><td>0.08%</td><td></td><td>8</td><td>Louisiana</td><td>7,976</td><td>3.26%</td></tr>
<tr><td>2</td><td>Florida</td><td>25,572</td><td>10.44%</td><td></td><td>9</td><td>Georgia</td><td>7,667</td><td>3.13%</td></tr>
<tr><td>9</td><td>Georgia</td><td>7,667</td><td>3.13%</td><td></td><td>10</td><td>Arizona</td><td>7,159</td><td>2.92%</td></tr>
<tr><td>41</td><td>Hawaii</td><td>175</td><td>0.07%</td><td></td><td>11</td><td>South Carolina</td><td>7,097</td><td>2.90%</td></tr>
<tr><td>35</td><td>Idaho</td><td>644</td><td>0.26%</td><td></td><td>12</td><td>Ohio</td><td>6,230</td><td>2.54%</td></tr>
<tr><td>NA</td><td>Illinois**</td><td>NA</td><td>NA</td><td></td><td>13</td><td>Maryland</td><td>6,211</td><td>2.54%</td></tr>
<tr><td>21</td><td>Indiana</td><td>2,658</td><td>1.09%</td><td></td><td>14</td><td>Tennessee</td><td>6,010</td><td>2.45%</td></tr>
<tr><td>36</td><td>Iowa</td><td>530</td><td>0.22%</td><td></td><td>15</td><td>Washington</td><td>4,322</td><td>1.77%</td></tr>
<tr><td>NA</td><td>Kansas**</td><td>NA</td><td>NA</td><td></td><td>16</td><td>Pennsylvania</td><td>4,131</td><td>1.69%</td></tr>
<tr><td>25</td><td>Kentucky</td><td>2,340</td><td>0.96%</td><td></td><td>17</td><td>New Jersey</td><td>4,043</td><td>1.65%</td></tr>
<tr><td>8</td><td>Louisiana</td><td>7,976</td><td>3.26%</td><td></td><td>18</td><td>Oklahoma</td><td>3,999</td><td>1.63%</td></tr>
<tr><td>47</td><td>Maine</td><td>47</td><td>0.02%</td><td></td><td>19</td><td>Colorado</td><td>3,972</td><td>1.62%</td></tr>
<tr><td>13</td><td>Maryland</td><td>6,211</td><td>2.54%</td><td></td><td>20</td><td>Arkansas</td><td>3,141</td><td>1.28%</td></tr>
<tr><td>22</td><td>Massachusetts</td><td>2,593</td><td>1.06%</td><td></td><td>21</td><td>Indiana</td><td>2,658</td><td>1.09%</td></tr>
<tr><td>5</td><td>Michigan</td><td>12,540</td><td>5.12%</td><td></td><td>22</td><td>Alabama</td><td>2,593</td><td>1.06%</td></tr>
<tr><td>27</td><td>Minnesota</td><td>2,076</td><td>0.85%</td><td></td><td>22</td><td>Massachusetts</td><td>2,593</td><td>1.06%</td></tr>
<tr><td>29</td><td>Mississippi</td><td>1,463</td><td>0.60%</td><td></td><td>24</td><td>Virginia</td><td>2,447</td><td>1.00%</td></tr>
<tr><td>7</td><td>Missouri</td><td>8,550</td><td>3.49%</td><td></td><td>25</td><td>Kentucky</td><td>2,340</td><td>0.96%</td></tr>
<tr><td>42</td><td>Montana</td><td>148</td><td>0.06%</td><td></td><td>26</td><td>Oregon</td><td>2,237</td><td>0.91%</td></tr>
<tr><td>43</td><td>Nebraska</td><td>130</td><td>0.05%</td><td></td><td>27</td><td>Minnesota</td><td>2,076</td><td>0.85%</td></tr>
<tr><td>32</td><td>Nevada</td><td>1,030</td><td>0.42%</td><td></td><td>28</td><td>New Mexico</td><td>1,962</td><td>0.80%</td></tr>
<tr><td>45</td><td>New Hampshire</td><td>72</td><td>0.03%</td><td></td><td>29</td><td>Mississippi</td><td>1,463</td><td>0.60%</td></tr>
<tr><td>17</td><td>New Jersey</td><td>4,043</td><td>1.65%</td><td></td><td>30</td><td>Wisconsin</td><td>1,390</td><td>0.57%</td></tr>
<tr><td>28</td><td>New Mexico</td><td>1,962</td><td>0.80%</td><td></td><td>31</td><td>Connecticut</td><td>1,065</td><td>0.43%</td></tr>
<tr><td>4</td><td>New York</td><td>16,739</td><td>6.84%</td><td></td><td>32</td><td>Nevada</td><td>1,030</td><td>0.42%</td></tr>
<tr><td>6</td><td>North Carolina</td><td>9,413</td><td>3.84%</td><td></td><td>33</td><td>Alaska</td><td>729</td><td>0.30%</td></tr>
<tr><td>48</td><td>North Dakota</td><td>18</td><td>0.01%</td><td></td><td>34</td><td>Utah</td><td>664</td><td>0.27%</td></tr>
<tr><td>12</td><td>Ohio</td><td>6,230</td><td>2.54%</td><td></td><td>35</td><td>Idaho</td><td>644</td><td>0.26%</td></tr>
<tr><td>18</td><td>Oklahoma</td><td>3,999</td><td>1.63%</td><td></td><td>36</td><td>Iowa</td><td>530</td><td>0.22%</td></tr>
<tr><td>26</td><td>Oregon</td><td>2,237</td><td>0.91%</td><td></td><td>37</td><td>West Virginia</td><td>427</td><td>0.17%</td></tr>
<tr><td>16</td><td>Pennsylvania</td><td>4,131</td><td>1.69%</td><td></td><td>38</td><td>Rhode Island</td><td>340</td><td>0.14%</td></tr>
<tr><td>38</td><td>Rhode Island</td><td>340</td><td>0.14%</td><td></td><td>39</td><td>Delaware</td><td>186</td><td>0.08%</td></tr>
<tr><td>11</td><td>South Carolina</td><td>7,097</td><td>2.90%</td><td></td><td>40</td><td>South Dakota</td><td>176</td><td>0.07%</td></tr>
<tr><td>40</td><td>South Dakota</td><td>176</td><td>0.07%</td><td></td><td>41</td><td>Hawaii</td><td>175</td><td>0.07%</td></tr>
<tr><td>14</td><td>Tennessee</td><td>6,010</td><td>2.45%</td><td></td><td>42</td><td>Montana</td><td>148</td><td>0.06%</td></tr>
<tr><td>3</td><td>Texas</td><td>24,756</td><td>10.11%</td><td></td><td>43</td><td>Nebraska</td><td>130</td><td>0.05%</td></tr>
<tr><td>34</td><td>Utah</td><td>664</td><td>0.27%</td><td></td><td>44</td><td>Wyoming</td><td>125</td><td>0.05%</td></tr>
<tr><td>46</td><td>Vermont</td><td>48</td><td>0.02%</td><td></td><td>45</td><td>New Hampshire</td><td>72</td><td>0.03%</td></tr>
<tr><td>24</td><td>Virginia</td><td>2,447</td><td>1.00%</td><td></td><td>46</td><td>Vermont</td><td>48</td><td>0.02%</td></tr>
<tr><td>15</td><td>Washington</td><td>4,322</td><td>1.77%</td><td></td><td>47</td><td>Maine</td><td>47</td><td>0.02%</td></tr>
<tr><td>37</td><td>West Virginia</td><td>427</td><td>0.17%</td><td></td><td>48</td><td>North Dakota</td><td>18</td><td>0.01%</td></tr>
<tr><td>30</td><td>Wisconsin</td><td>1,390</td><td>0.57%</td><td></td><td>NA</td><td>Illinois**</td><td>NA</td><td>NA</td></tr>
<tr><td>44</td><td>Wyoming</td><td>125</td><td>0.05%</td><td></td><td>NA</td><td>Kansas**</td><td>NA</td><td>NA</td></tr>
<tr><td></td><td></td><td></td><td></td><td></td><td></td><td>District of Columbia</td><td>2,170</td><td>0.89%</td></tr>
</table>

Source: U.S. Department of Justice, Federal Bureau of Investigation
   "Crime in the United States 1993" (Uniform Crime Reports, December 4, 1994)
*Of the 989,192 aggravated assaults in 1993 for which supplemental data were received by the F.B.I. There were an additional 145,907 aggravated assaults for which the type of weapon was not reported to the F.B.I. Aggravated assault is an attack for the purpose of inflicting severe bodily injury.
**Not available.

335

Aggravated Assault Rate with Firearms in 1993

National Rate = 100.83 Aggravated Assaults per 100,000 Population*

ALPHA ORDER			RANK ORDER		
RANK	STATE	RATE	RANK	STATE	RATE
22	Alabama	61.93	1	South Carolina	194.81
13	Alaska	121.70	2	Florida	186.94
4	Arizona	181.89	3	Louisiana	185.70
10	Arkansas	129.58	4	Arizona	181.89
6	California	143.72	5	Missouri	163.35
16	Colorado	111.39	6	California	143.72
35	Connecticut	32.50	7	Texas	137.30
38	Delaware	26.57	8	North Carolina	135.54
2	Florida	186.94	9	Michigan	132.31
17	Georgia	110.84	10	Arkansas	129.58
43	Hawaii	14.93	11	Maryland	125.10
24	Idaho	58.60	12	Oklahoma	123.77
NA	Illinois**	NA	13	Alaska	121.70
28	Indiana	46.53	14	New Mexico	121.41
41	Iowa	18.83	15	Tennessee	117.87
NA	Kansas**	NA	16	Colorado	111.39
23	Kentucky	61.76	17	Georgia	110.84
3	Louisiana	185.70	18	New York	91.99
47	Maine	3.79	19	Washington	82.25
11	Maryland	125.10	20	Nevada	74.15
30	Massachusetts	43.13	21	Oregon	73.78
9	Michigan	132.31	22	Alabama	61.93
29	Minnesota	45.96	23	Kentucky	61.76
26	Mississippi	55.35	24	Idaho	58.60
5	Missouri	163.35	25	Ohio	56.17
42	Montana	17.64	26	Mississippi	55.35
45	Nebraska	8.09	27	New Jersey	51.31
20	Nevada	74.15	28	Indiana	46.53
46	New Hampshire	6.40	29	Minnesota	45.96
27	New Jersey	51.31	30	Massachusetts	43.13
14	New Mexico	121.41	31	Virginia	37.70
18	New York	91.99	32	Utah	35.70
8	North Carolina	135.54	33	Pennsylvania	34.29
48	North Dakota	2.83	34	Rhode Island	34.00
25	Ohio	56.17	35	Connecticut	32.50
12	Oklahoma	123.77	36	Wisconsin	27.59
21	Oregon	73.78	37	Wyoming	26.60
33	Pennsylvania	34.29	38	Delaware	26.57
34	Rhode Island	34.00	39	South Dakota	24.62
1	South Carolina	194.81	40	West Virginia	23.46
39	South Dakota	24.62	41	Iowa	18.83
15	Tennessee	117.87	42	Montana	17.64
7	Texas	137.30	43	Hawaii	14.93
32	Utah	35.70	44	Vermont	8.33
44	Vermont	8.33	45	Nebraska	8.09
31	Virginia	37.70	46	New Hampshire	6.40
19	Washington	82.25	47	Maine	3.79
40	West Virginia	23.46	48	North Dakota	2.83
36	Wisconsin	27.59	NA	Illinois**	NA
37	Wyoming	26.60	NA	Kansas**	NA

District of Columbia 375.43

Source: Morgan Quitno Corporation using data from U.S. Department of Justice, Federal Bureau of Investigation
"Crime in the United States 1993" (Uniform Crime Reports, December 4, 1994)
*Of the 989,192 aggravated assaults in 1993 for which supplemental data were received by the F.B.I. There were an
additional 145,907 aggravated assaults for which the type of weapon was not reported to the F.B.I. Aggravated assault is
an attack for the purpose of inflicting severe bodily injury. National rate based on population of reporting states.
**Not available.

Percent of Aggravated Assaults Involving Firearms in 1993

National Percent = 24.75% of Aggravated Assaults*

<table>
<tr><th colspan="3">ALPHA ORDER</th><th colspan="3">RANK ORDER</th></tr>
<tr><th>RANK</th><th>STATE</th><th>PERCENT</th><th>RANK</th><th>STATE</th><th>PERCENT</th></tr>
<tr><td>44</td><td>Alabama</td><td>11.20</td><td>1</td><td>Mississippi</td><td>41.36</td></tr>
<tr><td>25</td><td>Alaska</td><td>23.34</td><td>2</td><td>Missouri</td><td>39.11</td></tr>
<tr><td>4</td><td>Arizona</td><td>37.58</td><td>3</td><td>Montana</td><td>38.85</td></tr>
<tr><td>7</td><td>Arkansas</td><td>31.44</td><td>4</td><td>Arizona</td><td>37.58</td></tr>
<tr><td>26</td><td>California</td><td>23.15</td><td>4</td><td>Louisiana</td><td>37.58</td></tr>
<tr><td>10</td><td>Colorado</td><td>29.53</td><td>6</td><td>North Carolina</td><td>31.67</td></tr>
<tr><td>38</td><td>Connecticut</td><td>14.19</td><td>7</td><td>Arkansas</td><td>31.44</td></tr>
<tr><td>34</td><td>Delaware</td><td>18.96</td><td>8</td><td>Idaho</td><td>31.17</td></tr>
<tr><td>21</td><td>Florida</td><td>25.32</td><td>9</td><td>Georgia</td><td>29.82</td></tr>
<tr><td>9</td><td>Georgia</td><td>29.82</td><td>10</td><td>Colorado</td><td>29.53</td></tr>
<tr><td>42</td><td>Hawaii</td><td>12.43</td><td>11</td><td>Texas</td><td>29.31</td></tr>
<tr><td>8</td><td>Idaho</td><td>31.17</td><td>12</td><td>Michigan</td><td>29.30</td></tr>
<tr><td>NA</td><td>Illinois**</td><td>NA</td><td>13</td><td>Tennessee</td><td>27.52</td></tr>
<tr><td>33</td><td>Indiana</td><td>19.13</td><td>14</td><td>Ohio</td><td>27.49</td></tr>
<tr><td>40</td><td>Iowa</td><td>13.91</td><td>15</td><td>Washington</td><td>27.29</td></tr>
<tr><td>NA</td><td>Kansas**</td><td>NA</td><td>16</td><td>Oklahoma</td><td>27.27</td></tr>
<tr><td>23</td><td>Kentucky</td><td>23.71</td><td>17</td><td>New Mexico</td><td>26.97</td></tr>
<tr><td>4</td><td>Louisiana</td><td>37.58</td><td>18</td><td>Minnesota</td><td>26.23</td></tr>
<tr><td>48</td><td>Maine</td><td>5.07</td><td>19</td><td>South Carolina</td><td>25.41</td></tr>
<tr><td>22</td><td>Maryland</td><td>24.71</td><td>20</td><td>Vermont</td><td>25.40</td></tr>
<tr><td>45</td><td>Massachusetts</td><td>8.61</td><td>21</td><td>Florida</td><td>25.32</td></tr>
<tr><td>12</td><td>Michigan</td><td>29.30</td><td>22</td><td>Maryland</td><td>24.71</td></tr>
<tr><td>18</td><td>Minnesota</td><td>26.23</td><td>23</td><td>Kentucky</td><td>23.71</td></tr>
<tr><td>1</td><td>Mississippi</td><td>41.36</td><td>24</td><td>Oregon</td><td>23.59</td></tr>
<tr><td>2</td><td>Missouri</td><td>39.11</td><td>25</td><td>Alaska</td><td>23.34</td></tr>
<tr><td>3</td><td>Montana</td><td>38.85</td><td>26</td><td>California</td><td>23.15</td></tr>
<tr><td>47</td><td>Nebraska</td><td>7.86</td><td>27</td><td>Wisconsin</td><td>22.88</td></tr>
<tr><td>29</td><td>Nevada</td><td>20.97</td><td>28</td><td>Pennsylvania</td><td>21.00</td></tr>
<tr><td>43</td><td>New Hampshire</td><td>11.54</td><td>29</td><td>Nevada</td><td>20.97</td></tr>
<tr><td>36</td><td>New Jersey</td><td>17.25</td><td>30</td><td>South Dakota</td><td>19.98</td></tr>
<tr><td>17</td><td>New Mexico</td><td>26.97</td><td>31</td><td>New York</td><td>19.89</td></tr>
<tr><td>31</td><td>New York</td><td>19.89</td><td>32</td><td>Virginia</td><td>19.86</td></tr>
<tr><td>6</td><td>North Carolina</td><td>31.67</td><td>33</td><td>Indiana</td><td>19.13</td></tr>
<tr><td>46</td><td>North Dakota</td><td>7.93</td><td>34</td><td>Delaware</td><td>18.96</td></tr>
<tr><td>14</td><td>Ohio</td><td>27.49</td><td>35</td><td>Utah</td><td>18.80</td></tr>
<tr><td>16</td><td>Oklahoma</td><td>27.27</td><td>36</td><td>New Jersey</td><td>17.25</td></tr>
<tr><td>24</td><td>Oregon</td><td>23.59</td><td>37</td><td>West Virginia</td><td>16.96</td></tr>
<tr><td>28</td><td>Pennsylvania</td><td>21.00</td><td>38</td><td>Connecticut</td><td>14.19</td></tr>
<tr><td>41</td><td>Rhode Island</td><td>13.38</td><td>39</td><td>Wyoming</td><td>14.00</td></tr>
<tr><td>19</td><td>South Carolina</td><td>25.41</td><td>40</td><td>Iowa</td><td>13.91</td></tr>
<tr><td>30</td><td>South Dakota</td><td>19.98</td><td>41</td><td>Rhode Island</td><td>13.38</td></tr>
<tr><td>13</td><td>Tennessee</td><td>27.52</td><td>42</td><td>Hawaii</td><td>12.43</td></tr>
<tr><td>11</td><td>Texas</td><td>29.31</td><td>43</td><td>New Hampshire</td><td>11.54</td></tr>
<tr><td>35</td><td>Utah</td><td>18.80</td><td>44</td><td>Alabama</td><td>11.20</td></tr>
<tr><td>20</td><td>Vermont</td><td>25.40</td><td>45</td><td>Massachusetts</td><td>8.61</td></tr>
<tr><td>32</td><td>Virginia</td><td>19.86</td><td>46</td><td>North Dakota</td><td>7.93</td></tr>
<tr><td>15</td><td>Washington</td><td>27.29</td><td>47</td><td>Nebraska</td><td>7.86</td></tr>
<tr><td>37</td><td>West Virginia</td><td>16.96</td><td>48</td><td>Maine</td><td>5.07</td></tr>
<tr><td>27</td><td>Wisconsin</td><td>22.88</td><td>NA</td><td>Illinois**</td><td>NA</td></tr>
<tr><td>39</td><td>Wyoming</td><td>14.00</td><td>NA</td><td>Kansas**</td><td>NA</td></tr>
<tr><td></td><td></td><td></td><td></td><td>District of Columbia</td><td>24.10</td></tr>
</table>

Source: Morgan Quitno Corporation using data from U.S. Department of Justice, Federal Bureau of Investigation
"Crime in the United States 1993" (Uniform Crime Reports, December 4, 1994)

*Of the 989,192 aggravated assaults in 1993 for which supplemental data were received by the F.B.I. There were an additional 145,907 aggravated assaults for which the type of weapon was not reported to the F.B.I. Aggravated assault is an attack for the purpose of inflicting severe bodily injury.

**Not available.

Aggravated Assaults with Knives or Cutting Instruments in 1993

National Total = 171,934 Aggravated Assaults with Knives or Cutting Instruments*

ALPHA ORDER

RANK	STATE	ASSAULTS	% of USA
22	Alabama	2,084	1.21%
33	Alaska	670	0.39%
17	Arizona	2,940	1.71%
26	Arkansas	1,434	0.83%
1	California	24,312	14.14%
20	Colorado	2,266	1.32%
28	Connecticut	1,224	0.71%
40	Delaware	263	0.15%
3	Florida	18,887	10.99%
9	Georgia	5,338	3.10%
44	Hawaii	144	0.08%
38	Idaho	415	0.24%
NA	Illinois**	NA	NA
24	Indiana	1,776	1.03%
31	Iowa	679	0.39%
NA	Kansas**	NA	NA
27	Kentucky	1,314	0.76%
13	Louisiana	3,753	2.18%
42	Maine	157	0.09%
10	Maryland	5,183	3.01%
11	Massachusetts	5,010	2.91%
5	Michigan	7,277	4.23%
23	Minnesota	2,044	1.19%
34	Mississippi	645	0.38%
15	Missouri	3,233	1.88%
46	Montana	52	0.03%
39	Nebraska	318	0.18%
32	Nevada	678	0.39%
45	New Hampshire	105	0.06%
8	New Jersey	5,398	3.14%
29	New Mexico	1,152	0.67%
2	New York	20,312	11.81%
7	North Carolina	5,651	3.29%
48	North Dakota	33	0.02%
12	Ohio	3,954	2.30%
21	Oklahoma	2,101	1.22%
25	Oregon	1,541	0.90%
16	Pennsylvania	3,041	1.77%
37	Rhode Island	465	0.27%
6	South Carolina	6,291	3.66%
41	South Dakota	211	0.12%
14	Tennessee	3,732	2.17%
4	Texas	16,168	9.40%
35	Utah	623	0.36%
47	Vermont	35	0.02%
18	Virginia	2,767	1.61%
19	Washington	2,546	1.48%
36	West Virginia	492	0.29%
30	Wisconsin	937	0.54%
43	Wyoming	154	0.09%

RANK ORDER

RANK	STATE	ASSAULTS	% of USA
1	California	24,312	14.14%
2	New York	20,312	11.81%
3	Florida	18,887	10.99%
4	Texas	16,168	9.40%
5	Michigan	7,277	4.23%
6	South Carolina	6,291	3.66%
7	North Carolina	5,651	3.29%
8	New Jersey	5,398	3.14%
9	Georgia	5,338	3.10%
10	Maryland	5,183	3.01%
11	Massachusetts	5,010	2.91%
12	Ohio	3,954	2.30%
13	Louisiana	3,753	2.18%
14	Tennessee	3,732	2.17%
15	Missouri	3,233	1.88%
16	Pennsylvania	3,041	1.77%
17	Arizona	2,940	1.71%
18	Virginia	2,767	1.61%
19	Washington	2,546	1.48%
20	Colorado	2,266	1.32%
21	Oklahoma	2,101	1.22%
22	Alabama	2,084	1.21%
23	Minnesota	2,044	1.19%
24	Indiana	1,776	1.03%
25	Oregon	1,541	0.90%
26	Arkansas	1,434	0.83%
27	Kentucky	1,314	0.76%
28	Connecticut	1,224	0.71%
29	New Mexico	1,152	0.67%
30	Wisconsin	937	0.54%
31	Iowa	679	0.39%
32	Nevada	678	0.39%
33	Alaska	670	0.39%
34	Mississippi	645	0.38%
35	Utah	623	0.36%
36	West Virginia	492	0.29%
37	Rhode Island	465	0.27%
38	Idaho	415	0.24%
39	Nebraska	318	0.18%
40	Delaware	263	0.15%
41	South Dakota	211	0.12%
42	Maine	157	0.09%
43	Wyoming	154	0.09%
44	Hawaii	144	0.08%
45	New Hampshire	105	0.06%
46	Montana	52	0.03%
47	Vermont	35	0.02%
48	North Dakota	33	0.02%
NA	Illinois**	NA	NA
NA	Kansas**	NA	NA
	District of Columbia	2,129	1.24%

Source: U.S. Department of Justice, Federal Bureau of Investigation
  "Crime in the United States 1993" (Uniform Crime Reports, December 4, 1994)
*Of the 989,192 aggravated assaults in 1993 for which supplemental data were received by the F.B.I. There were an additional 145,907 aggravated assaults for which the type of weapon was not reported to the F.B.I. Aggravated assault is an attack for the purpose of inflicting severe bodily injury.
**Not available.

338

Percent of Aggravated Assaults Involving Knives or Cutting Instruments in 1993

National Percent = 17.38% of Aggravated Assaults*

ALPHA ORDER

RANK ORDER

RANK	STATE	PERCENT
48	Alabama	9.00
8	Alaska	21.45
36	Arizona	15.43
40	Arkansas	14.36
46	California	12.55
28	Colorado	16.85
31	Connecticut	16.30
1	Delaware	26.81
16	Florida	18.70
9	Georgia	20.76
47	Hawaii	10.23
11	Idaho	20.09
NA	Illinois**	NA
45	Indiana	12.78
20	Iowa	17.82
NA	Kansas**	NA
44	Kentucky	13.32
21	Louisiana	17.68
27	Maine	16.94
10	Maryland	20.62
30	Massachusetts	16.63
26	Michigan	17.00
2	Minnesota	25.82
19	Mississippi	18.24
38	Missouri	14.79
43	Montana	13.65
13	Nebraska	19.23
42	Nevada	13.80
29	New Hampshire	16.83
5	New Jersey	23.03
34	New Mexico	15.83
3	New York	24.13
15	North Carolina	19.01
39	North Dakota	14.54
23	Ohio	17.45
41	Oklahoma	14.33
32	Oregon	16.25
35	Pennsylvania	15.46
18	Rhode Island	18.29
6	South Carolina	22.52
4	South Dakota	23.95
25	Tennessee	17.09
14	Texas	19.14
22	Utah	17.64
17	Vermont	18.52
7	Virginia	22.46
33	Washington	16.08
12	West Virginia	19.55
37	Wisconsin	15.42
24	Wyoming	17.25

RANK	STATE	PERCENT
1	Delaware	26.81
2	Minnesota	25.82
3	New York	24.13
4	South Dakota	23.95
5	New Jersey	23.03
6	South Carolina	22.52
7	Virginia	22.46
8	Alaska	21.45
9	Georgia	20.76
10	Maryland	20.62
11	Idaho	20.09
12	West Virginia	19.55
13	Nebraska	19.23
14	Texas	19.14
15	North Carolina	19.01
16	Florida	18.70
17	Vermont	18.52
18	Rhode Island	18.29
19	Mississippi	18.24
20	Iowa	17.82
21	Louisiana	17.68
22	Utah	17.64
23	Ohio	17.45
24	Wyoming	17.25
25	Tennessee	17.09
26	Michigan	17.00
27	Maine	16.94
28	Colorado	16.85
29	New Hampshire	16.83
30	Massachusetts	16.63
31	Connecticut	16.30
32	Oregon	16.25
33	Washington	16.08
34	New Mexico	15.83
35	Pennsylvania	15.46
36	Arizona	15.43
37	Wisconsin	15.42
38	Missouri	14.79
39	North Dakota	14.54
40	Arkansas	14.36
41	Oklahoma	14.33
42	Nevada	13.80
43	Montana	13.65
44	Kentucky	13.32
45	Indiana	12.78
46	California	12.55
47	Hawaii	10.23
48	Alabama	9.00
NA	Illinois**	NA
NA	Kansas**	NA

District of Columbia   23.65

Source: Morgan Quitno Corporation using data from U.S. Department of Justice, Federal Bureau of Investigation
    "Crime in the United States 1993" (Uniform Crime Reports, December 4, 1994)
*Of the 989,192 aggravated assaults in 1993 for which supplemental data were received by the F.B.I. There were an
additional 145,907 aggravated assaults for which the type of weapon was not reported to the F.B.I. Aggravated assault is
an attack for the purpose of inflicting severe bodily injury.
**Not available.   339

Aggravated Assaults with Blunt Objects and Other Dangerous Weapons in 1993

National Total = 301,592 Aggravated Assaults*

RANK	STATE	ASSAULTS	% of USA
29	Alabama	2,132	0.71%
37	Alaska	685	0.23%
16	Arizona	4,970	1.65%
28	Arkansas	2,250	0.75%
1	California	52,174	17.30%
20	Colorado	4,107	1.36%
26	Connecticut	2,701	0.90%
40	Delaware	383	0.13%
2	Florida	41,111	13.63%
10	Georgia	8,032	2.66%
41	Hawaii	300	0.10%
39	Idaho	465	0.15%
NA	Illinois**	NA	NA
22	Indiana	3,362	1.11%
33	Iowa	957	0.32%
NA	Kansas**	NA	NA
24	Kentucky	3,171	1.05%
15	Louisiana	5,783	1.92%
42	Maine	252	0.08%
8	Maryland	9,746	3.23%
7	Massachusetts	10,218	3.39%
5	Michigan	17,329	5.75%
27	Minnesota	2,264	0.75%
36	Mississippi	696	0.23%
13	Missouri	6,364	2.11%
47	Montana	59	0.02%
35	Nebraska	772	0.26%
30	Nevada	1,643	0.54%
45	New Hampshire	119	0.04%
11	New Jersey	7,382	2.45%
25	New Mexico	2,795	0.93%
3	New York	28,388	9.41%
9	North Carolina	8,088	2.68%
46	North Dakota	100	0.03%
14	Ohio	6,120	2.03%
19	Oklahoma	4,142	1.37%
23	Oregon	3,227	1.07%
18	Pennsylvania	4,580	1.52%
34	Rhode Island	871	0.29%
6	South Carolina	10,729	3.56%
44	South Dakota	160	0.05%
12	Tennessee	6,812	2.26%
4	Texas	20,933	6.94%
31	Utah	1,267	0.42%
48	Vermont	53	0.02%
21	Virginia	3,436	1.14%
17	Washington	4,850	1.61%
38	West Virginia	561	0.19%
32	Wisconsin	1,009	0.33%
43	Wyoming	196	0.06%

RANK	STATE	ASSAULTS	% of USA
1	California	52,174	17.30%
2	Florida	41,111	13.63%
3	New York	28,388	9.41%
4	Texas	20,933	6.94%
5	Michigan	17,329	5.75%
6	South Carolina	10,729	3.56%
7	Massachusetts	10,218	3.39%
8	Maryland	9,746	3.23%
9	North Carolina	8,088	2.68%
10	Georgia	8,032	2.66%
11	New Jersey	7,382	2.45%
12	Tennessee	6,812	2.26%
13	Missouri	6,364	2.11%
14	Ohio	6,120	2.03%
15	Louisiana	5,783	1.92%
16	Arizona	4,970	1.65%
17	Washington	4,850	1.61%
18	Pennsylvania	4,580	1.52%
19	Oklahoma	4,142	1.37%
20	Colorado	4,107	1.36%
21	Virginia	3,436	1.14%
22	Indiana	3,362	1.11%
23	Oregon	3,227	1.07%
24	Kentucky	3,171	1.05%
25	New Mexico	2,795	0.93%
26	Connecticut	2,701	0.90%
27	Minnesota	2,264	0.75%
28	Arkansas	2,250	0.75%
29	Alabama	2,132	0.71%
30	Nevada	1,643	0.54%
31	Utah	1,267	0.42%
32	Wisconsin	1,009	0.33%
33	Iowa	957	0.32%
34	Rhode Island	871	0.29%
35	Nebraska	772	0.26%
36	Mississippi	696	0.23%
37	Alaska	685	0.23%
38	West Virginia	561	0.19%
39	Idaho	465	0.15%
40	Delaware	383	0.13%
41	Hawaii	300	0.10%
42	Maine	252	0.08%
43	Wyoming	196	0.06%
44	South Dakota	160	0.05%
45	New Hampshire	119	0.04%
46	North Dakota	100	0.03%
47	Montana	59	0.02%
48	Vermont	53	0.02%
NA	Illinois**	NA	NA
NA	Kansas**	NA	NA
	District of Columbia	3,848	1.28%

Source: U.S. Department of Justice, Federal Bureau of Investigation
"Crime in the United States 1993" (Uniform Crime Reports, December 4, 1994)
*Of the 989,192 aggravated assaults in 1993 for which supplemental data were received by the F.B.I. There were an additional 145,907 aggravated assaults for which the type of weapon was not reported to the F.B.I. Aggravated assault is an attack for the purpose of inflicting severe bodily injury.
**Not available.

Percent of Aggravated Assaults Involving Blunt and Other Dangerous Weapons in 1993

National Percent = 30.49% of Aggravated Assaults*

ALPHA ORDER				RANK ORDER		
RANK	**STATE**	**PERCENT**		**RANK**	**STATE**	**PERCENT**
48	Alabama	9.21		1	Nebraska	46.67
41	Alaska	21.93		2	North Dakota	44.05
32	Arizona	26.09		3	Florida	40.71
37	Arkansas	22.52		4	Michigan	40.49
31	California	26.93		5	Delaware	39.04
21	Colorado	30.53		6	Maryland	38.78
9	Connecticut	35.98		7	New Mexico	38.41
5	Delaware	39.04		7	South Carolina	38.41
3	Florida	40.71		9	Connecticut	35.98
18	Georgia	31.24		10	Utah	35.87
42	Hawaii	21.31		11	Rhode Island	34.26
38	Idaho	22.51		12	Oregon	34.03
NA	Illinois**	NA		13	Massachusetts	33.92
35	Indiana	24.19		14	New York	33.73
33	Iowa	25.12		15	Nevada	33.45
NA	Kansas**	NA		16	Kentucky	32.13
16	Kentucky	32.13		17	New Jersey	31.50
27	Louisiana	27.25		18	Georgia	31.24
29	Maine	27.18		19	Tennessee	31.19
6	Maryland	38.78		20	Washington	30.62
13	Massachusetts	33.92		21	Colorado	30.53
4	Michigan	40.49		22	Missouri	29.11
23	Minnesota	28.60		23	Minnesota	28.60
43	Mississippi	19.68		24	Oklahoma	28.25
22	Missouri	29.11		25	Vermont	28.04
47	Montana	15.49		26	Virginia	27.89
1	Nebraska	46.67		27	Louisiana	27.25
15	Nevada	33.45		28	North Carolina	27.21
44	New Hampshire	19.07		29	Maine	27.18
17	New Jersey	31.50		30	Ohio	27.01
7	New Mexico	38.41		31	California	26.93
14	New York	33.73		32	Arizona	26.09
28	North Carolina	27.21		33	Iowa	25.12
2	North Dakota	44.05		34	Texas	24.78
30	Ohio	27.01		35	Indiana	24.19
24	Oklahoma	28.25		36	Pennsylvania	23.28
12	Oregon	34.03		37	Arkansas	22.52
36	Pennsylvania	23.28		38	Idaho	22.51
11	Rhode Island	34.26		39	West Virginia	22.29
7	South Carolina	38.41		40	Wyoming	21.95
45	South Dakota	18.16		41	Alaska	21.93
19	Tennessee	31.19		42	Hawaii	21.31
34	Texas	24.78		43	Mississippi	19.68
10	Utah	35.87		44	New Hampshire	19.07
25	Vermont	28.04		45	South Dakota	18.16
26	Virginia	27.89		46	Wisconsin	16.61
20	Washington	30.62		47	Montana	15.49
39	West Virginia	22.29		48	Alabama	9.21
46	Wisconsin	16.61		NA	Illinois**	NA
40	Wyoming	21.95		NA	Kansas**	NA
					District of Columbia	42.74

Source: Morgan Quitno Corporation using data from U.S. Department of Justice, Federal Bureau of Investigation
"Crime in the United States 1993" (Uniform Crime Reports, December 4, 1994)
*Of the 989,192 aggravated assaults in 1993 for which supplemental data were received by the F.B.I. There were an additional 145,907 aggravated assaults for which the type of weapon was not reported to the F.B.I. Aggravated assault is an attack for the purpose of inflicting severe bodily injury.
**Not available.

341

Aggravated Assaults Committed with Hands, Fists or Feet in 1993

National Total = 270,800 Aggravated Assaults Committed with Hands, Fists or Feet*

<table>
<tr><td colspan="4">ALPHA ORDER</td><td colspan="4">RANK ORDER</td></tr>
<tr><th>RANK</th><th>STATE</th><th>ASSAULTS</th><th>% of USA</th><th>RANK</th><th>STATE</th><th>ASSAULTS</th><th>% of USA</th></tr>
<tr><td>4</td><td>Alabama</td><td>16,335</td><td>6.03%</td><td>1</td><td>California</td><td>72,432</td><td>26.75%</td></tr>
<tr><td>33</td><td>Alaska</td><td>1,040</td><td>0.38%</td><td>2</td><td>Texas</td><td>22,617</td><td>8.35%</td></tr>
<tr><td>18</td><td>Arizona</td><td>3,983</td><td>1.47%</td><td>3</td><td>New York</td><td>18,730</td><td>6.92%</td></tr>
<tr><td>23</td><td>Arkansas</td><td>3,164</td><td>1.17%</td><td>4</td><td>Alabama</td><td>16,335</td><td>6.03%</td></tr>
<tr><td>1</td><td>California</td><td>72,432</td><td>26.75%</td><td>5</td><td>Florida</td><td>15,407</td><td>5.69%</td></tr>
<tr><td>24</td><td>Colorado</td><td>3,106</td><td>1.15%</td><td>6</td><td>Massachusetts</td><td>12,301</td><td>4.54%</td></tr>
<tr><td>27</td><td>Connecticut</td><td>2,517</td><td>0.93%</td><td>7</td><td>Pennsylvania</td><td>7,920</td><td>2.92%</td></tr>
<tr><td>45</td><td>Delaware</td><td>149</td><td>0.06%</td><td>8</td><td>New Jersey</td><td>6,615</td><td>2.44%</td></tr>
<tr><td>5</td><td>Florida</td><td>15,407</td><td>5.69%</td><td>9</td><td>North Carolina</td><td>6,572</td><td>2.43%</td></tr>
<tr><td>14</td><td>Georgia</td><td>4,673</td><td>1.73%</td><td>10</td><td>Ohio</td><td>6,356</td><td>2.35%</td></tr>
<tr><td>37</td><td>Hawaii</td><td>789</td><td>0.29%</td><td>11</td><td>Indiana</td><td>6,100</td><td>2.25%</td></tr>
<tr><td>39</td><td>Idaho</td><td>542</td><td>0.20%</td><td>12</td><td>Michigan</td><td>5,654</td><td>2.09%</td></tr>
<tr><td>NA</td><td>Illinois**</td><td>NA</td><td>NA</td><td>13</td><td>Tennessee</td><td>5,285</td><td>1.95%</td></tr>
<tr><td>11</td><td>Indiana</td><td>6,100</td><td>2.25%</td><td>14</td><td>Georgia</td><td>4,673</td><td>1.73%</td></tr>
<tr><td>29</td><td>Iowa</td><td>1,644</td><td>0.61%</td><td>15</td><td>Oklahoma</td><td>4,420</td><td>1.63%</td></tr>
<tr><td>NA</td><td>Kansas**</td><td>NA</td><td>NA</td><td>16</td><td>Washington</td><td>4,119</td><td>1.52%</td></tr>
<tr><td>25</td><td>Kentucky</td><td>3,043</td><td>1.12%</td><td>17</td><td>Maryland</td><td>3,993</td><td>1.47%</td></tr>
<tr><td>21</td><td>Louisiana</td><td>3,710</td><td>1.37%</td><td>18</td><td>Arizona</td><td>3,983</td><td>1.47%</td></tr>
<tr><td>40</td><td>Maine</td><td>471</td><td>0.17%</td><td>19</td><td>South Carolina</td><td>3,814</td><td>1.41%</td></tr>
<tr><td>17</td><td>Maryland</td><td>3,993</td><td>1.47%</td><td>20</td><td>Missouri</td><td>3,714</td><td>1.37%</td></tr>
<tr><td>6</td><td>Massachusetts</td><td>12,301</td><td>4.54%</td><td>21</td><td>Louisiana</td><td>3,710</td><td>1.37%</td></tr>
<tr><td>12</td><td>Michigan</td><td>5,654</td><td>2.09%</td><td>22</td><td>Virginia</td><td>3,672</td><td>1.36%</td></tr>
<tr><td>31</td><td>Minnesota</td><td>1,531</td><td>0.57%</td><td>23</td><td>Arkansas</td><td>3,164</td><td>1.17%</td></tr>
<tr><td>38</td><td>Mississippi</td><td>733</td><td>0.27%</td><td>24</td><td>Colorado</td><td>3,106</td><td>1.15%</td></tr>
<tr><td>20</td><td>Missouri</td><td>3,714</td><td>1.37%</td><td>25</td><td>Kentucky</td><td>3,043</td><td>1.12%</td></tr>
<tr><td>46</td><td>Montana</td><td>122</td><td>0.05%</td><td>26</td><td>Wisconsin</td><td>2,740</td><td>1.01%</td></tr>
<tr><td>41</td><td>Nebraska</td><td>434</td><td>0.16%</td><td>27</td><td>Connecticut</td><td>2,517</td><td>0.93%</td></tr>
<tr><td>30</td><td>Nevada</td><td>1,561</td><td>0.58%</td><td>28</td><td>Oregon</td><td>2,479</td><td>0.92%</td></tr>
<tr><td>44</td><td>New Hampshire</td><td>328</td><td>0.12%</td><td>29</td><td>Iowa</td><td>1,644</td><td>0.61%</td></tr>
<tr><td>8</td><td>New Jersey</td><td>6,615</td><td>2.44%</td><td>30</td><td>Nevada</td><td>1,561</td><td>0.58%</td></tr>
<tr><td>32</td><td>New Mexico</td><td>1,367</td><td>0.50%</td><td>31</td><td>Minnesota</td><td>1,531</td><td>0.57%</td></tr>
<tr><td>3</td><td>New York</td><td>18,730</td><td>6.92%</td><td>32</td><td>New Mexico</td><td>1,367</td><td>0.50%</td></tr>
<tr><td>9</td><td>North Carolina</td><td>6,572</td><td>2.43%</td><td>33</td><td>Alaska</td><td>1,040</td><td>0.38%</td></tr>
<tr><td>47</td><td>North Dakota</td><td>76</td><td>0.03%</td><td>34</td><td>West Virginia</td><td>1,037</td><td>0.38%</td></tr>
<tr><td>10</td><td>Ohio</td><td>6,356</td><td>2.35%</td><td>35</td><td>Utah</td><td>978</td><td>0.36%</td></tr>
<tr><td>15</td><td>Oklahoma</td><td>4,420</td><td>1.63%</td><td>36</td><td>Rhode Island</td><td>866</td><td>0.32%</td></tr>
<tr><td>28</td><td>Oregon</td><td>2,479</td><td>0.92%</td><td>37</td><td>Hawaii</td><td>789</td><td>0.29%</td></tr>
<tr><td>7</td><td>Pennsylvania</td><td>7,920</td><td>2.92%</td><td>38</td><td>Mississippi</td><td>733</td><td>0.27%</td></tr>
<tr><td>36</td><td>Rhode Island</td><td>866</td><td>0.32%</td><td>39</td><td>Idaho</td><td>542</td><td>0.20%</td></tr>
<tr><td>19</td><td>South Carolina</td><td>3,814</td><td>1.41%</td><td>40</td><td>Maine</td><td>471</td><td>0.17%</td></tr>
<tr><td>43</td><td>South Dakota</td><td>334</td><td>0.12%</td><td>41</td><td>Nebraska</td><td>434</td><td>0.16%</td></tr>
<tr><td>13</td><td>Tennessee</td><td>5,285</td><td>1.95%</td><td>42</td><td>Wyoming</td><td>418</td><td>0.15%</td></tr>
<tr><td>2</td><td>Texas</td><td>22,617</td><td>8.35%</td><td>43</td><td>South Dakota</td><td>334</td><td>0.12%</td></tr>
<tr><td>35</td><td>Utah</td><td>978</td><td>0.36%</td><td>44</td><td>New Hampshire</td><td>328</td><td>0.12%</td></tr>
<tr><td>48</td><td>Vermont</td><td>53</td><td>0.02%</td><td>45</td><td>Delaware</td><td>149</td><td>0.06%</td></tr>
<tr><td>22</td><td>Virginia</td><td>3,672</td><td>1.36%</td><td>46</td><td>Montana</td><td>122</td><td>0.05%</td></tr>
<tr><td>16</td><td>Washington</td><td>4,119</td><td>1.52%</td><td>47</td><td>North Dakota</td><td>76</td><td>0.03%</td></tr>
<tr><td>34</td><td>West Virginia</td><td>1,037</td><td>0.38%</td><td>48</td><td>Vermont</td><td>53</td><td>0.02%</td></tr>
<tr><td>26</td><td>Wisconsin</td><td>2,740</td><td>1.01%</td><td>NA</td><td>Illinois**</td><td>NA</td><td>NA</td></tr>
<tr><td>42</td><td>Wyoming</td><td>418</td><td>0.15%</td><td>NA</td><td>Kansas**</td><td>NA</td><td>NA</td></tr>
<tr><td></td><td></td><td></td><td></td><td></td><td>District of Columbia</td><td>856</td><td>0.32%</td></tr>
</table>

Source: U.S. Department of Justice, Federal Bureau of Investigation
    "Crime in the United States 1993" (Uniform Crime Reports, December 4, 1994)
*Of the 989,192 aggravated assaults in 1993 for which supplemental data were received by the F.B.I. There were an additional 145,907 aggravated assaults for which the type of weapon was not reported to the F.B.I. Aggravated assault is an attack for the purpose of inflicting severe bodily injury. Referred to as "personal weapons" by the F.B.I.
**Not available.

Percent of Aggravated Assaults Committed with Hands, Fists or Feet in 1993

National Percent = 27.38% of Aggravated Assaults*

ALPHA ORDER

RANK	STATE	PERCENT
1	Alabama	70.58
17	Alaska	33.29
37	Arizona	20.91
20	Arkansas	31.67
13	California	37.38
34	Colorado	23.09
15	Connecticut	33.53
46	Delaware	15.19
45	Florida	15.26
41	Georgia	18.18
2	Hawaii	56.04
30	Idaho	26.23
NA	Illinois**	NA
7	Indiana	43.90
8	Iowa	43.15
NA	Kansas**	NA
21	Kentucky	30.84
42	Louisiana	17.48
4	Maine	50.81
44	Maryland	15.89
10	Massachusetts	40.84
48	Michigan	13.21
39	Minnesota	19.34
38	Mississippi	20.72
43	Missouri	16.99
18	Montana	32.02
29	Nebraska	26.24
19	Nevada	31.78
3	New Hampshire	52.56
24	New Jersey	28.22
40	New Mexico	18.79
35	New York	22.25
36	North Carolina	22.11
16	North Dakota	33.48
25	Ohio	28.05
22	Oklahoma	30.15
31	Oregon	26.14
11	Pennsylvania	40.26
14	Rhode Island	34.07
47	South Carolina	13.66
12	South Dakota	37.91
33	Tennessee	24.20
28	Texas	26.77
27	Utah	27.69
26	Vermont	28.04
23	Virginia	29.80
32	Washington	26.01
9	West Virginia	41.20
6	Wisconsin	45.10
5	Wyoming	46.81

RANK ORDER

RANK	STATE	PERCENT
1	Alabama	70.58
2	Hawaii	56.04
3	New Hampshire	52.56
4	Maine	50.81
5	Wyoming	46.81
6	Wisconsin	45.10
7	Indiana	43.90
8	Iowa	43.15
9	West Virginia	41.20
10	Massachusetts	40.84
11	Pennsylvania	40.26
12	South Dakota	37.91
13	California	37.38
14	Rhode Island	34.07
15	Connecticut	33.53
16	North Dakota	33.48
17	Alaska	33.29
18	Montana	32.02
19	Nevada	31.78
20	Arkansas	31.67
21	Kentucky	30.84
22	Oklahoma	30.15
23	Virginia	29.80
24	New Jersey	28.22
25	Ohio	28.05
26	Vermont	28.04
27	Utah	27.69
28	Texas	26.77
29	Nebraska	26.24
30	Idaho	26.23
31	Oregon	26.14
32	Washington	26.01
33	Tennessee	24.20
34	Colorado	23.09
35	New York	22.25
36	North Carolina	22.11
37	Arizona	20.91
38	Mississippi	20.72
39	Minnesota	19.34
40	New Mexico	18.79
41	Georgia	18.18
42	Louisiana	17.48
43	Missouri	16.99
44	Maryland	15.89
45	Florida	15.26
46	Delaware	15.19
47	South Carolina	13.66
48	Michigan	13.21
NA	Illinois**	NA
NA	Kansas**	NA

District of Columbia   9.51

Source: Morgan Quitno Corporation using data from U.S. Department of Justice, Federal Bureau of Investigation
    "Crime in the United States 1993" (Uniform Crime Reports, December 4, 1994)
*Of the 989,192 aggravated assaults in 1993 for which supplemental data were received by the F.B.I. There were an
additional 145,907 aggravated assaults for which the type of weapon was not reported to the F.B.I. Aggravated assault is
an attack for the purpose of inflicting severe bodily injury. Referred to as "personal weapons" by the F.B.I.
**Not available.   343

Property Crimes in 1993

National Total = 12,216,764 Property Crimes*

ALPHA ORDER

RANK	STATE	CRIMES	% of USA
25	Alabama	171,598	1.40%
46	Alaska	28,795	0.24%
13	Arizona	264,371	2.16%
32	Arkansas	102,231	0.84%
1	California	1,678,884	13.74%
24	Colorado	176,856	1.45%
28	Connecticut	137,443	1.13%
45	Delaware	29,304	0.24%
3	Florida	977,363	8.00%
8	Georgia	378,348	3.10%
37	Hawaii	70,505	0.58%
41	Idaho	39,161	0.32%
5	Illinois	544,869	4.46%
20	Indiana	227,149	1.86%
33	Iowa	99,080	0.81%
29	Kansas	113,360	0.93%
30	Kentucky	105,979	0.87%
15	Louisiana	248,461	2.03%
43	Maine	37,519	0.31%
14	Maryland	253,647	2.08%
16	Massachusetts	245,831	2.01%
6	Michigan	441,767	3.62%
22	Minnesota	183,347	1.50%
31	Mississippi	105,308	0.86%
19	Missouri	227,731	1.86%
42	Montana	38,699	0.32%
38	Nebraska	60,712	0.50%
36	Nevada	73,685	0.60%
44	New Hampshire	31,131	0.25%
11	New Jersey	328,867	2.69%
35	New Mexico	86,236	0.71%
4	New York	814,824	6.67%
9	North Carolina	345,377	2.83%
50	North Dakota	17,387	0.14%
7	Ohio	441,550	3.61%
27	Oklahoma	150,546	1.23%
26	Oregon	159,558	1.31%
10	Pennsylvania	343,841	2.81%
40	Rhode Island	40,973	0.34%
23	South Carolina	177,779	1.46%
48	South Dakota	19,661	0.16%
18	Tennessee	228,117	1.87%
2	Texas	1,023,612	8.38%
34	Utah	91,816	0.75%
47	Vermont	22,223	0.18%
17	Virginia	242,975	1.99%
12	Washington	285,753	2.34%
39	West Virginia	42,300	0.35%
21	Wisconsin	190,923	1.56%
49	Wyoming	18,221	0.15%

RANK ORDER

RANK	STATE	CRIMES	% of USA
1	California	1,678,884	13.74%
2	Texas	1,023,612	8.38%
3	Florida	977,363	8.00%
4	New York	814,824	6.67%
5	Illinois	544,869	4.46%
6	Michigan	441,767	3.62%
7	Ohio	441,550	3.61%
8	Georgia	378,348	3.10%
9	North Carolina	345,377	2.83%
10	Pennsylvania	343,841	2.81%
11	New Jersey	328,867	2.69%
12	Washington	285,753	2.34%
13	Arizona	264,371	2.16%
14	Maryland	253,647	2.08%
15	Louisiana	248,461	2.03%
16	Massachusetts	245,831	2.01%
17	Virginia	242,975	1.99%
18	Tennessee	228,117	1.87%
19	Missouri	227,731	1.86%
20	Indiana	227,149	1.86%
21	Wisconsin	190,923	1.56%
22	Minnesota	183,347	1.50%
23	South Carolina	177,779	1.46%
24	Colorado	176,856	1.45%
25	Alabama	171,598	1.40%
26	Oregon	159,558	1.31%
27	Oklahoma	150,546	1.23%
28	Connecticut	137,443	1.13%
29	Kansas	113,360	0.93%
30	Kentucky	105,979	0.87%
31	Mississippi	105,308	0.86%
32	Arkansas	102,231	0.84%
33	Iowa	99,080	0.81%
34	Utah	91,816	0.75%
35	New Mexico	86,236	0.71%
36	Nevada	73,685	0.60%
37	Hawaii	70,505	0.58%
38	Nebraska	60,712	0.50%
39	West Virginia	42,300	0.35%
40	Rhode Island	40,973	0.34%
41	Idaho	39,161	0.32%
42	Montana	38,699	0.32%
43	Maine	37,519	0.31%
44	New Hampshire	31,131	0.25%
45	Delaware	29,304	0.24%
46	Alaska	28,795	0.24%
47	Vermont	22,223	0.18%
48	South Dakota	19,661	0.16%
49	Wyoming	18,221	0.15%
50	North Dakota	17,387	0.14%
	District of Columbia	51,091	0.42%

Source: U.S. Department of Justice, Federal Bureau of Investigation
    "Crime in the United States 1993" (Uniform Crime Reports, December 4, 1994)
*Property crimes are offenses of burglary, larceny-theft and motor vehicle theft.

Average Time Between Property Crimes in 1993

National Rate = A Property Crime Occurs Every 3 Seconds*

<u>ALPHA ORDER</u>

RANK	STATE	MINUTES.SECONDS
26	Alabama	3.04
5	Alaska	18.15
38	Arizona	1.59
19	Arkansas	5.08
50	California	0.19
27	Colorado	2.58
23	Connecticut	3.49
6	Delaware	17.56
48	Florida	0.32
43	Georgia	1.23
14	Hawaii	7.27
10	Idaho	13.25
46	Illinois	0.58
31	Indiana	2.19
18	Iowa	5.18
22	Kansas	4.38
21	Kentucky	4.58
36	Louisiana	2.07
8	Maine	14.01
37	Maryland	2.04
35	Massachusetts	2.08
44	Michigan	1.11
29	Minnesota	2.52
20	Mississippi	4.59
31	Missouri	2.19
9	Montana	13.35
13	Nebraska	8.40
15	Nevada	7.08
7	New Hampshire	16.53
40	New Jersey	1.36
16	New Mexico	6.05
47	New York	0.39
42	North Carolina	1.31
1	North Dakota	30.14
44	Ohio	1.11
24	Oklahoma	3.29
25	Oregon	3.17
41	Pennsylvania	1.32
11	Rhode Island	12.50
27	South Carolina	2.58
3	South Dakota	26.44
33	Tennessee	2.18
49	Texas	0.31
17	Utah	5.43
4	Vermont	23.39
34	Virginia	2.10
39	Washington	1.50
12	West Virginia	12.26
30	Wisconsin	2.45
2	Wyoming	28.51

<u>RANK ORDER</u>

RANK	STATE	MINUTES.SECONDS
1	North Dakota	30.14
2	Wyoming	28.51
3	South Dakota	26.44
4	Vermont	23.39
5	Alaska	18.15
6	Delaware	17.56
7	New Hampshire	16.53
8	Maine	14.01
9	Montana	13.35
10	Idaho	13.25
11	Rhode Island	12.50
12	West Virginia	12.26
13	Nebraska	8.40
14	Hawaii	7.27
15	Nevada	7.08
16	New Mexico	6.05
17	Utah	5.43
18	Iowa	5.18
19	Arkansas	5.08
20	Mississippi	4.59
21	Kentucky	4.58
22	Kansas	4.38
23	Connecticut	3.49
24	Oklahoma	3.29
25	Oregon	3.17
26	Alabama	3.04
27	Colorado	2.58
27	South Carolina	2.58
29	Minnesota	2.52
30	Wisconsin	2.45
31	Indiana	2.19
31	Missouri	2.19
33	Tennessee	2.18
34	Virginia	2.10
35	Massachusetts	2.08
36	Louisiana	2.07
37	Maryland	2.04
38	Arizona	1.59
39	Washington	1.50
40	New Jersey	1.36
41	Pennsylvania	1.32
42	North Carolina	1.31
43	Georgia	1.23
44	Michigan	1.11
44	Ohio	1.11
46	Illinois	0.58
47	New York	0.39
48	Florida	0.32
49	Texas	0.31
50	California	0.19

District of Columbia 10.17

Source: Morgan Quitno Corporation using data from U.S. Department of Justice, Federal Bureau of Investigation
"Crime in the United States 1993" (Uniform Crime Reports, December 4, 1994)
*Property crimes are offenses of burglary, larceny-theft and motor vehicle theft.

Property Crimes per Square Mile in 1993

National Rate = 3.23 Property Crimes per Square Mile*

ALPHA ORDER			RANK ORDER		
RANK	STATE	RATE	RANK	STATE	RATE
25	Alabama	3.27	1	New Jersey	37.71
50	Alaska	0.04	2	Rhode Island	26.52
29	Arizona	2.32	3	Connecticut	24.79
34	Arkansas	1.92	4	Massachusetts	23.29
9	California	10.26	5	Maryland	20.44
37	Colorado	1.70	6	New York	14.94
3	Connecticut	24.79	7	Florida	14.86
8	Delaware	11.77	8	Delaware	11.77
7	Florida	14.86	9	California	10.26
15	Georgia	6.37	10	Ohio	9.85
13	Hawaii	6.45	11	Illinois	9.41
45	Idaho	0.47	12	Pennsylvania	7.47
11	Illinois	9.41	13	Hawaii	6.45
16	Indiana	6.24	14	North Carolina	6.42
35	Iowa	1.76	15	Georgia	6.37
39	Kansas	1.38	16	Indiana	6.24
28	Kentucky	2.62	17	Virginia	5.68
20	Louisiana	4.79	18	South Carolina	5.55
41	Maine	1.06	19	Tennessee	5.41
5	Maryland	20.44	20	Louisiana	4.79
4	Massachusetts	23.29	21	Michigan	4.57
21	Michigan	4.57	22	Washington	4.01
33	Minnesota	2.11	23	Texas	3.81
31	Mississippi	2.17	24	New Hampshire	3.33
25	Missouri	3.27	25	Alabama	3.27
46	Montana	0.26	25	Missouri	3.27
42	Nebraska	0.78	27	Wisconsin	2.91
44	Nevada	0.67	28	Kentucky	2.62
24	New Hampshire	3.33	29	Arizona	2.32
1	New Jersey	37.71	30	Vermont	2.31
43	New Mexico	0.71	31	Mississippi	2.17
6	New York	14.94	32	Oklahoma	2.15
14	North Carolina	6.42	33	Minnesota	2.11
47	North Dakota	0.25	34	Arkansas	1.92
10	Ohio	9.85	35	Iowa	1.76
32	Oklahoma	2.15	36	West Virginia	1.75
38	Oregon	1.62	37	Colorado	1.70
12	Pennsylvania	7.47	38	Oregon	1.62
2	Rhode Island	26.52	39	Kansas	1.38
18	South Carolina	5.55	40	Utah	1.08
47	South Dakota	0.25	41	Maine	1.06
19	Tennessee	5.41	42	Nebraska	0.78
23	Texas	3.81	43	New Mexico	0.71
40	Utah	1.08	44	Nevada	0.67
30	Vermont	2.31	45	Idaho	0.47
17	Virginia	5.68	46	Montana	0.26
22	Washington	4.01	47	North Dakota	0.25
36	West Virginia	1.75	47	South Dakota	0.25
27	Wisconsin	2.91	49	Wyoming	0.19
49	Wyoming	0.19	50	Alaska	0.04

District of Columbia	751.34

Source: Morgan Quitno Corporation using data from U.S. Department of Justice, Federal Bureau of Investigation
"Crime in the United States 1993" (Uniform Crime Reports, December 4, 1994)
*Property crimes are offenses of burglary, larceny-theft and motor vehicle theft.

Percent Change in Number of Property Crimes: 1992 to 1993

National Percent Change = 2.3% Decrease*

<u>ALPHA ORDER</u>

RANK	STATE	PERCENT CHANGE
43	Alabama	(5.6)
15	Alaska	(0.1)
2	Arizona	8.5
8	Arkansas	1.8
24	California	(2.2)
42	Colorado	(5.3)
48	Connecticut	(8.1)
14	Delaware	0.6
9	Florida	1.3
19	Georgia	(1.2)
6	Hawaii	3.8
19	Idaho	(1.2)
24	Illinois	(2.2)
36	Indiana	(4.0)
37	Iowa	(4.2)
46	Kansas	(6.6)
10	Kentucky	1.2
4	Louisiana	4.2
50	Maine	(10.5)
18	Maryland	(1.1)
30	Massachusetts	(3.0)
33	Michigan	(3.3)
35	Minnesota	(3.8)
5	Mississippi	4.1
13	Missouri	0.7
3	Montana	6.1
38	Nebraska	(4.9)
12	Nevada	0.8
41	New Hampshire	(5.2)
38	New Jersey	(4.9)
17	New Mexico	(0.8)
40	New York	(5.1)
22	North Carolina	(1.4)
31	North Dakota	(3.1)
32	Ohio	(3.2)
26	Oklahoma	(2.5)
11	Oregon	0.9
34	Pennsylvania	(3.5)
26	Rhode Island	(2.5)
16	South Carolina	(0.3)
22	South Dakota	(1.4)
7	Tennessee	3.4
47	Texas	(7.3)
44	Utah	(5.7)
1	Vermont	18.1
29	Virginia	(2.9)
21	Washington	(1.3)
28	West Virginia	(2.7)
44	Wisconsin	(5.7)
48	Wyoming	(8.1)

<u>RANK ORDER</u>

RANK	STATE	PERCENT CHANGE
1	Vermont	18.1
2	Arizona	8.5
3	Montana	6.1
4	Louisiana	4.2
5	Mississippi	4.1
6	Hawaii	3.8
7	Tennessee	3.4
8	Arkansas	1.8
9	Florida	1.3
10	Kentucky	1.2
11	Oregon	0.9
12	Nevada	0.8
13	Missouri	0.7
14	Delaware	0.6
15	Alaska	(0.1)
16	South Carolina	(0.3)
17	New Mexico	(0.8)
18	Maryland	(1.1)
19	Georgia	(1.2)
19	Idaho	(1.2)
21	Washington	(1.3)
22	North Carolina	(1.4)
22	South Dakota	(1.4)
24	California	(2.2)
24	Illinois	(2.2)
26	Oklahoma	(2.5)
26	Rhode Island	(2.5)
28	West Virginia	(2.7)
29	Virginia	(2.9)
30	Massachusetts	(3.0)
31	North Dakota	(3.1)
32	Ohio	(3.2)
33	Michigan	(3.3)
34	Pennsylvania	(3.5)
35	Minnesota	(3.8)
36	Indiana	(4.0)
37	Iowa	(4.2)
38	Nebraska	(4.9)
38	New Jersey	(4.9)
40	New York	(5.1)
41	New Hampshire	(5.2)
42	Colorado	(5.3)
43	Alabama	(5.6)
44	Utah	(5.7)
44	Wisconsin	(5.7)
46	Kansas	(6.6)
47	Texas	(7.3)
48	Connecticut	(8.1)
48	Wyoming	(8.1)
50	Maine	(10.5)

District of Columbia   1.2

Source: U.S. Department of Justice, Federal Bureau of Investigation
"Crime in the United States 1993" (Uniform Crime Reports, December 4, 1994)
*Property crimes are offenses of burglary, larceny-theft and motor vehicle theft.

Property Crime Rate in 1993

National Rate = 4,736.9 Property Crimes per 100,000 Population*

<u>ALPHA ORDER</u>

RANK	STATE	RATE
30	Alabama	4,098.4
17	Alaska	4,807.2
2	Arizona	6,716.7
26	Arkansas	4,217.5
8	California	5,379.1
14	Colorado	4,959.5
27	Connecticut	4,194.2
28	Delaware	4,186.3
1	Florida	7,145.0
6	Georgia	5,469.8
3	Hawaii	6,015.8
42	Idaho	3,563.3
20	Illinois	4,658.2
36	Indiana	3,976.0
43	Iowa	3,521.0
22	Kansas	4,478.8
46	Kentucky	2,797.0
4	Louisiana	5,784.9
44	Maine	3,028.2
12	Maryland	5,108.7
32	Massachusetts	4,089.0
18	Michigan	4,661.0
33	Minnesota	4,059.0
34	Mississippi	3,984.4
25	Missouri	4,351.0
21	Montana	4,612.5
40	Nebraska	3,778.0
10	Nevada	5,304.9
47	New Hampshire	2,767.2
29	New Jersey	4,174.0
9	New Mexico	5,336.4
23	New York	4,477.8
13	North Carolina	4,973.0
49	North Dakota	2,738.1
35	Ohio	3,981.2
19	Oklahoma	4,659.4
11	Oregon	5,262.5
45	Pennsylvania	2,853.9
31	Rhode Island	4,097.3
16	South Carolina	4,880.0
48	South Dakota	2,749.8
24	Tennessee	4,473.8
5	Texas	5,677.0
15	Utah	4,936.3
38	Vermont	3,858.2
41	Virginia	3,743.3
7	Washington	5,437.7
50	West Virginia	2,324.2
39	Wisconsin	3,789.7
37	Wyoming	3,876.8

<u>RANK ORDER</u>

RANK	STATE	RATE
1	Florida	7,145.0
2	Arizona	6,716.7
3	Hawaii	6,015.8
4	Louisiana	5,784.9
5	Texas	5,677.0
6	Georgia	5,469.8
7	Washington	5,437.7
8	California	5,379.1
9	New Mexico	5,336.4
10	Nevada	5,304.9
11	Oregon	5,262.5
12	Maryland	5,108.7
13	North Carolina	4,973.0
14	Colorado	4,959.5
15	Utah	4,936.3
16	South Carolina	4,880.0
17	Alaska	4,807.2
18	Michigan	4,661.0
19	Oklahoma	4,659.4
20	Illinois	4,658.2
21	Montana	4,612.5
22	Kansas	4,478.8
23	New York	4,477.8
24	Tennessee	4,473.8
25	Missouri	4,351.0
26	Arkansas	4,217.5
27	Connecticut	4,194.2
28	Delaware	4,186.3
29	New Jersey	4,174.0
30	Alabama	4,098.4
31	Rhode Island	4,097.3
32	Massachusetts	4,089.0
33	Minnesota	4,059.0
34	Mississippi	3,984.4
35	Ohio	3,981.2
36	Indiana	3,976.0
37	Wyoming	3,876.8
38	Vermont	3,858.2
39	Wisconsin	3,789.7
40	Nebraska	3,778.0
41	Virginia	3,743.3
42	Idaho	3,563.3
43	Iowa	3,521.0
44	Maine	3,028.2
45	Pennsylvania	2,853.9
46	Kentucky	2,797.0
47	New Hampshire	2,767.2
48	South Dakota	2,749.8
49	North Dakota	2,738.1
50	West Virginia	2,324.2

	District of Columbia	8,839.3

Source: U.S. Department of Justice, Federal Bureau of Investigation
  "Crime in the United States 1993" (Uniform Crime Reports, December 4, 1994)
*Property crimes are offenses of burglary, larceny-theft and motor vehicle theft.

Percent Change in Rate of Property Crime: 1992 to 1993

National Percent Change = 3.4% Decrease*

ALPHA ORDER

RANK ORDER

RANK	STATE	PERCENT CHANGE	RANK	STATE	PERCENT CHANGE
43	Alabama	(6.8)	1	Vermont	16.9
16	Alaska	(2.1)	2	Arizona	5.6
2	Arizona	5.6	3	Montana	4.2
8	Arkansas	0.8	4	Louisiana	4.0
26	California	(3.3)	5	Mississippi	2.9
45	Colorado	(7.8)	6	Hawaii	2.8
46	Connecticut	(8.0)	7	Tennessee	1.9
13	Delaware	(1.0)	8	Arkansas	0.8
10	Florida	(0.1)	9	Kentucky	0.3
27	Georgia	(3.6)	10	Florida	(0.1)
6	Hawaii	2.8	10	Missouri	(0.1)
33	Idaho	(4.1)	12	Oregon	(0.9)
19	Illinois	(2.7)	13	Delaware	(1.0)
37	Indiana	(4.8)	14	South Carolina	(1.4)
34	Iowa	(4.3)	15	South Dakota	(1.9)
44	Kansas	(6.9)	16	Alaska	(2.1)
9	Kentucky	0.3	16	Rhode Island	(2.1)
4	Louisiana	4.0	18	Maryland	(2.2)
50	Maine	(10.7)	19	Illinois	(2.7)
18	Maryland	(2.2)	20	North Carolina	(2.9)
25	Massachusetts	(3.2)	20	North Dakota	(2.9)
29	Michigan	(3.7)	22	New Mexico	(3.0)
35	Minnesota	(4.6)	23	Oklahoma	(3.1)
5	Mississippi	2.9	23	West Virginia	(3.1)
10	Missouri	(0.1)	25	Massachusetts	(3.2)
3	Montana	4.2	26	California	(3.3)
38	Nebraska	(5.0)	27	Georgia	(3.6)
29	Nevada	(3.7)	27	Washington	(3.6)
41	New Hampshire	(6.3)	29	Michigan	(3.7)
40	New Jersey	(6.0)	29	Nevada	(3.7)
22	New Mexico	(3.0)	31	Ohio	(3.8)
39	New York	(5.5)	31	Pennsylvania	(3.8)
20	North Carolina	(2.9)	33	Idaho	(4.1)
20	North Dakota	(2.9)	34	Iowa	(4.3)
31	Ohio	(3.8)	35	Minnesota	(4.6)
23	Oklahoma	(3.1)	35	Virginia	(4.6)
12	Oregon	(0.9)	37	Indiana	(4.8)
31	Pennsylvania	(3.8)	38	Nebraska	(5.0)
16	Rhode Island	(2.1)	39	New York	(5.5)
14	South Carolina	(1.4)	40	New Jersey	(6.0)
15	South Dakota	(1.9)	41	New Hampshire	(6.3)
7	Tennessee	1.9	41	Wisconsin	(6.3)
49	Texas	(9.2)	43	Alabama	(6.8)
46	Utah	(8.0)	44	Kansas	(6.9)
1	Vermont	16.9	45	Colorado	(7.8)
35	Virginia	(4.6)	46	Connecticut	(8.0)
27	Washington	(3.6)	46	Utah	(8.0)
23	West Virginia	(3.1)	48	Wyoming	(8.9)
41	Wisconsin	(6.3)	49	Texas	(9.2)
48	Wyoming	(8.9)	50	Maine	(10.7)

| | District of Columbia | 3.1 |

Source: U.S. Department of Justice, Federal Bureau of Investigation
"Crime in the United States 1993" (Uniform Crime Reports, December 4, 1994)
*Property crimes are offenses of burglary, larceny-theft and motor vehicle theft.

Burglaries in 1993

National Total = 2,834,808 Burglaries*

ALPHA ORDER					RANK ORDER			
RANK	STATE	BURGLARIES	% of USA		RANK	STATE	BURGLARIES	% of USA
21	Alabama	45,578	1.61%		1	California	414,182	14.61%
47	Alaska	4,893	0.17%		2	Florida	251,063	8.86%
15	Arizona	57,684	2.03%		3	Texas	233,913	8.25%
32	Arkansas	26,646	0.94%		4	New York	181,709	6.41%
1	California	414,182	14.61%		5	Illinois	118,788	4.19%
25	Colorado	36,011	1.27%		6	North Carolina	105,270	3.71%
28	Connecticut	32,052	1.13%		7	Ohio	97,394	3.44%
43	Delaware	6,244	0.22%		8	Michigan	93,143	3.29%
2	Florida	251,063	8.86%		9	Georgia	90,423	3.19%
9	Georgia	90,423	3.19%		10	New Jersey	76,738	2.71%
37	Hawaii	13,310	0.47%		11	Pennsylvania	70,125	2.47%
42	Idaho	7,350	0.26%		12	Tennessee	60,299	2.13%
5	Illinois	118,788	4.19%		13	Massachusetts	60,220	2.12%
19	Indiana	48,677	1.72%		14	Louisiana	58,768	2.07%
34	Iowa	20,562	0.73%		15	Arizona	57,684	2.03%
30	Kansas	28,655	1.01%		16	Maryland	56,246	1.98%
31	Kentucky	28,041	0.99%		17	Washington	56,083	1.98%
14	Louisiana	58,768	2.07%		18	Missouri	53,673	1.89%
41	Maine	8,909	0.31%		19	Indiana	48,677	1.72%
16	Maryland	56,246	1.98%		20	South Carolina	47,695	1.68%
13	Massachusetts	60,220	2.12%		21	Alabama	45,578	1.61%
8	Michigan	93,143	3.29%		22	Virginia	43,338	1.53%
24	Minnesota	38,147	1.35%		23	Oklahoma	39,903	1.41%
26	Mississippi	33,985	1.20%		24	Minnesota	38,147	1.35%
18	Missouri	53,673	1.89%		25	Colorado	36,011	1.27%
44	Montana	5,992	0.21%		26	Mississippi	33,985	1.20%
39	Nebraska	10,662	0.38%		27	Wisconsin	33,400	1.18%
35	Nevada	17,293	0.61%		28	Connecticut	32,052	1.13%
45	New Hampshire	5,795	0.20%		29	Oregon	31,072	1.10%
10	New Jersey	76,738	2.71%		30	Kansas	28,655	1.01%
33	New Mexico	22,966	0.81%		31	Kentucky	28,041	0.99%
4	New York	181,709	6.41%		32	Arkansas	26,646	0.94%
6	North Carolina	105,270	3.71%		33	New Mexico	22,966	0.81%
50	North Dakota	2,370	0.08%		34	Iowa	20,562	0.73%
7	Ohio	97,394	3.44%		35	Nevada	17,293	0.61%
23	Oklahoma	39,903	1.41%		36	Utah	14,708	0.52%
29	Oregon	31,072	1.10%		37	Hawaii	13,310	0.47%
11	Pennsylvania	70,125	2.47%		38	West Virginia	10,904	0.38%
40	Rhode Island	10,409	0.37%		39	Nebraska	10,662	0.38%
20	South Carolina	47,695	1.68%		40	Rhode Island	10,409	0.37%
48	South Dakota	3,927	0.14%		41	Maine	8,909	0.31%
12	Tennessee	60,299	2.13%		42	Idaho	7,350	0.26%
3	Texas	233,913	8.25%		43	Delaware	6,244	0.22%
36	Utah	14,708	0.52%		44	Montana	5,992	0.21%
46	Vermont	5,036	0.18%		45	New Hampshire	5,795	0.20%
22	Virginia	43,338	1.53%		46	Vermont	5,036	0.18%
17	Washington	56,083	1.98%		47	Alaska	4,893	0.17%
38	West Virginia	10,904	0.38%		48	South Dakota	3,927	0.14%
27	Wisconsin	33,400	1.18%		49	Wyoming	3,023	0.11%
49	Wyoming	3,023	0.11%		50	North Dakota	2,370	0.08%
					District of Columbia		11,534	0.41%

Source: U.S. Department of Justice, Federal Bureau of Investigation
   "Crime in the United States 1993" (Uniform Crime Reports, December 4, 1994)
*Burglary is the unlawful entry of a structure to commit a felony or theft. Attempts are included.

Average Time Between Burglaries in 1993

National Rate = A Burglary Occurs Every 11 Seconds*

ALPHA ORDER

RANK	STATE	MINUTES.SECONDS
30	Alabama	11.32
4	Alaska	107.25
36	Arizona	9.07
19	Arkansas	19.44
50	California	1.16
26	Colorado	14.36
23	Connecticut	16.24
8	Delaware	84.11
49	Florida	2.05
42	Georgia	5.49
14	Hawaii	39.29
9	Idaho	71.31
46	Illinois	4.25
32	Indiana	10.48
17	Iowa	25.34
21	Kansas	18.20
20	Kentucky	18.44
37	Louisiana	8.56
10	Maine	59.00
35	Maryland	9.20
38	Massachusetts	8.44
43	Michigan	5.38
27	Minnesota	13.47
25	Mississippi	15.28
33	Missouri	9.47
7	Montana	87.43
12	Nebraska	49.18
16	Nevada	30.23
6	New Hampshire	90.42
41	New Jersey	6.51
18	New Mexico	22.53
47	New York	2.53
45	North Carolina	4.59
1	North Dakota	221.46
44	Ohio	5.24
28	Oklahoma	13.10
22	Oregon	16.55
40	Pennsylvania	7.30
11	Rhode Island	50.29
31	South Carolina	11.01
3	South Dakota	133.50
39	Tennessee	8.43
48	Texas	2.15
15	Utah	35.44
5	Vermont	104.22
29	Virginia	12.08
34	Washington	9.22
13	West Virginia	48.12
24	Wisconsin	15.44
2	Wyoming	173.52

RANK ORDER

RANK	STATE	MINUTES.SECONDS
1	North Dakota	221.46
2	Wyoming	173.52
3	South Dakota	133.50
4	Alaska	107.25
5	Vermont	104.22
6	New Hampshire	90.42
7	Montana	87.43
8	Delaware	84.11
9	Idaho	71.31
10	Maine	59.00
11	Rhode Island	50.29
12	Nebraska	49.18
13	West Virginia	48.12
14	Hawaii	39.29
15	Utah	35.44
16	Nevada	30.23
17	Iowa	25.34
18	New Mexico	22.53
19	Arkansas	19.44
20	Kentucky	18.44
21	Kansas	18.20
22	Oregon	16.55
23	Connecticut	16.24
24	Wisconsin	15.44
25	Mississippi	15.28
26	Colorado	14.36
27	Minnesota	13.47
28	Oklahoma	13.10
29	Virginia	12.08
30	Alabama	11.32
31	South Carolina	11.01
32	Indiana	10.48
33	Missouri	9.47
34	Washington	9.22
35	Maryland	9.20
36	Arizona	9.07
37	Louisiana	8.56
38	Massachusetts	8.44
39	Tennessee	8.43
40	Pennsylvania	7.30
41	New Jersey	6.51
42	Georgia	5.49
43	Michigan	5.38
44	Ohio	5.24
45	North Carolina	4.59
46	Illinois	4.25
47	New York	2.53
48	Texas	2.15
49	Florida	2.05
50	California	1.16
	District of Columbia	45.34

Source: Morgan Quitno Corporation using data from U.S. Department of Justice, Federal Bureau of Investigation
"Crime in the United States 1993" (Uniform Crime Reports, December 4, 1994)
*Burglary is the unlawful entry of a structure to commit a felony or theft. Attempts are included.

Percent Change in Number of Burglaries: 1992 to 1993

National Percent Change = 4.9% Decrease *

ALPHA ORDER				RANK ORDER		
RANK	STATE	PERCENT CHANGE		RANK	STATE	PERCENT CHANGE
38	Alabama	(7.1)		1	Montana	12.9
30	Alaska	(5.4)		2	Vermont	7.0
3	Arizona	6.6		3	Arizona	6.6
7	Arkansas	1.6		4	Kentucky	2.4
17	California	(3.1)		5	Hawaii	2.3
26	Colorado	(4.9)		6	South Dakota	2.0
46	Connecticut	(11.9)		7	Arkansas	1.6
30	Delaware	(5.4)		7	New Jersey	1.6
14	Florida	(1.4)		9	Maryland	1.3
40	Georgia	(7.2)		9	Mississippi	1.3
5	Hawaii	2.3		11	Nevada	1.1
41	Idaho	(7.4)		12	Louisiana	0.3
27	Illinois	(5.2)		13	Rhode Island	(1.1)
45	Indiana	(9.7)		14	Florida	(1.4)
16	Iowa	(3.0)		15	Washington	(2.7)
47	Kansas	(12.2)		16	Iowa	(3.0)
4	Kentucky	2.4		17	California	(3.1)
12	Louisiana	0.3		18	Wyoming	(3.3)
48	Maine	(12.3)		19	West Virginia	(3.4)
9	Maryland	1.3		20	Wisconsin	(3.6)
35	Massachusetts	(6.4)		21	New Mexico	(3.9)
27	Michigan	(5.2)		22	South Carolina	(4.0)
24	Minnesota	(4.3)		23	Virginia	(4.2)
9	Mississippi	1.3		24	Minnesota	(4.3)
33	Missouri	(6.0)		25	North Dakota	(4.7)
1	Montana	12.9		26	Colorado	(4.9)
38	Nebraska	(7.1)		27	Illinois	(5.2)
11	Nevada	1.1		27	Michigan	(5.2)
50	New Hampshire	(16.1)		29	Tennessee	(5.3)
7	New Jersey	1.6		30	Alaska	(5.4)
21	New Mexico	(3.9)		30	Delaware	(5.4)
34	New York	(6.1)		32	Oregon	(5.7)
37	North Carolina	(6.9)		33	Missouri	(6.0)
25	North Dakota	(4.7)		34	New York	(6.1)
36	Ohio	(6.7)		35	Massachusetts	(6.4)
44	Oklahoma	(8.6)		36	Ohio	(6.7)
32	Oregon	(5.7)		37	North Carolina	(6.9)
42	Pennsylvania	(7.5)		38	Alabama	(7.1)
13	Rhode Island	(1.1)		38	Nebraska	(7.1)
22	South Carolina	(4.0)		40	Georgia	(7.2)
6	South Dakota	2.0		41	Idaho	(7.4)
29	Tennessee	(5.3)		42	Pennsylvania	(7.5)
49	Texas	(13.0)		43	Utah	(8.3)
43	Utah	(8.3)		44	Oklahoma	(8.6)
2	Vermont	7.0		45	Indiana	(9.7)
23	Virginia	(4.2)		46	Connecticut	(11.9)
15	Washington	(2.7)		47	Kansas	(12.2)
19	West Virginia	(3.4)		48	Maine	(12.3)
20	Wisconsin	(3.6)		49	Texas	(13.0)
18	Wyoming	(3.3)		50	New Hampshire	(16.1)
					District of Columbia	7.6

Source: U.S. Department of Justice, Federal Bureau of Investigation
"Crime in the United States 1993" (Uniform Crime Reports, December 4, 1994)
*Burglary is the unlawful entry of a structure to commit a felony or theft. Attempts are included.

352

Burglary Rate in 1993

National Rate = 1,099.2 Burglaries per 100,000 Population*

ALPHA ORDER

RANK	STATE	RATE
18	Alabama	1,088.6
35	Alaska	816.9
3	Arizona	1,465.5
17	Arkansas	1,099.3
6	California	1,327.0
24	Colorado	1,009.8
28	Connecticut	978.1
30	Delaware	892.0
1	Florida	1,835.4
8	Georgia	1,307.3
14	Hawaii	1,135.7
41	Idaho	668.8
23	Illinois	1,015.5
33	Indiana	852.0
38	Iowa	730.7
16	Kansas	1,132.2
37	Kentucky	740.1
5	Louisiana	1,368.3
39	Maine	719.0
15	Maryland	1,132.8
25	Massachusetts	1,001.7
27	Michigan	982.7
34	Minnesota	844.5
10	Mississippi	1,285.8
21	Missouri	1,025.5
40	Montana	714.2
43	Nebraska	663.5
11	Nevada	1,245.0
49	New Hampshire	515.1
29	New Jersey	974.0
4	New Mexico	1,421.2
26	New York	998.6
2	North Carolina	1,515.8
50	North Dakota	373.2
31	Ohio	878.1
12	Oklahoma	1,235.0
22	Oregon	1,024.8
47	Pennsylvania	582.0
20	Rhode Island	1,040.9
7	South Carolina	1,309.2
48	South Dakota	549.2
13	Tennessee	1,182.6
9	Texas	1,297.3
36	Utah	790.8
32	Vermont	874.3
42	Virginia	667.7
19	Washington	1,067.2
46	West Virginia	599.1
44	Wisconsin	663.0
45	Wyoming	643.2

RANK ORDER

RANK	STATE	RATE
1	Florida	1,835.4
2	North Carolina	1,515.8
3	Arizona	1,465.5
4	New Mexico	1,421.2
5	Louisiana	1,368.3
6	California	1,327.0
7	South Carolina	1,309.2
8	Georgia	1,307.3
9	Texas	1,297.3
10	Mississippi	1,285.8
11	Nevada	1,245.0
12	Oklahoma	1,235.0
13	Tennessee	1,182.6
14	Hawaii	1,135.7
15	Maryland	1,132.8
16	Kansas	1,132.2
17	Arkansas	1,099.3
18	Alabama	1,088.6
19	Washington	1,067.2
20	Rhode Island	1,040.9
21	Missouri	1,025.5
22	Oregon	1,024.8
23	Illinois	1,015.5
24	Colorado	1,009.8
25	Massachusetts	1,001.7
26	New York	998.6
27	Michigan	982.7
28	Connecticut	978.1
29	New Jersey	974.0
30	Delaware	892.0
31	Ohio	878.1
32	Vermont	874.3
33	Indiana	852.0
34	Minnesota	844.5
35	Alaska	816.9
36	Utah	790.8
37	Kentucky	740.1
38	Iowa	730.7
39	Maine	719.0
40	Montana	714.2
41	Idaho	668.8
42	Virginia	667.7
43	Nebraska	663.5
44	Wisconsin	663.0
45	Wyoming	643.2
46	West Virginia	599.1
47	Pennsylvania	582.0
48	South Dakota	549.2
49	New Hampshire	515.1
50	North Dakota	373.2
	District of Columbia	1,995.5

Source: U.S. Department of Justice, Federal Bureau of Investigation
"Crime in the United States 1993" (Uniform Crime Reports, December 4, 1994)
*Burglary is the unlawful entry of a structure to commit a felony or theft. Attempts are included.

Percent Change in Rate of Burglaries: 1992 to 1993

National Percent Change = 5.9% Decrease*

<u>ALPHA ORDER</u>

RANK	STATE	PERCENT CHANGE
39	Alabama	(8.2)
33	Alaska	(7.2)
3	Arizona	3.8
7	Arkansas	0.6
18	California	(4.2)
36	Colorado	(7.4)
46	Connecticut	(11.8)
32	Delaware	(6.9)
13	Florida	(2.8)
42	Georgia	(9.4)
6	Hawaii	1.3
43	Idaho	(10.1)
25	Illinois	(5.7)
44	Indiana	(10.5)
14	Iowa	(3.1)
47	Kansas	(12.5)
4	Kentucky	1.5
10	Louisiana	0.1
48	Maine	(12.6)
10	Maryland	0.1
29	Massachusetts	(6.6)
24	Michigan	(5.6)
23	Minnesota	(5.1)
9	Mississippi	0.2
31	Missouri	(6.8)
1	Montana	10.9
33	Nebraska	(7.2)
15	Nevada	(3.4)
50	New Hampshire	(17.2)
8	New Jersey	0.5
27	New Mexico	(6.0)
28	New York	(6.5)
40	North Carolina	(8.3)
20	North Dakota	(4.6)
35	Ohio	(7.3)
41	Oklahoma	(9.2)
36	Oregon	(7.4)
38	Pennsylvania	(7.8)
12	Rhode Island	(0.6)
22	South Carolina	(5.0)
5	South Dakota	1.4
30	Tennessee	(6.7)
49	Texas	(14.8)
45	Utah	(10.6)
2	Vermont	5.9
26	Virginia	(5.8)
21	Washington	(4.9)
16	West Virginia	(3.8)
18	Wisconsin	(4.2)
17	Wyoming	(4.1)

<u>RANK ORDER</u>

RANK	STATE	PERCENT CHANGE
1	Montana	10.9
2	Vermont	5.9
3	Arizona	3.8
4	Kentucky	1.5
5	South Dakota	1.4
6	Hawaii	1.3
7	Arkansas	0.6
8	New Jersey	0.5
9	Mississippi	0.2
10	Louisiana	0.1
10	Maryland	0.1
12	Rhode Island	(0.6)
13	Florida	(2.8)
14	Iowa	(3.1)
15	Nevada	(3.4)
16	West Virginia	(3.8)
17	Wyoming	(4.1)
18	California	(4.2)
18	Wisconsin	(4.2)
20	North Dakota	(4.6)
21	Washington	(4.9)
22	South Carolina	(5.0)
23	Minnesota	(5.1)
24	Michigan	(5.6)
25	Illinois	(5.7)
26	Virginia	(5.8)
27	New Mexico	(6.0)
28	New York	(6.5)
29	Massachusetts	(6.6)
30	Tennessee	(6.7)
31	Missouri	(6.8)
32	Delaware	(6.9)
33	Alaska	(7.2)
33	Nebraska	(7.2)
35	Ohio	(7.3)
36	Colorado	(7.4)
36	Oregon	(7.4)
38	Pennsylvania	(7.8)
39	Alabama	(8.2)
40	North Carolina	(8.3)
41	Oklahoma	(9.2)
42	Georgia	(9.4)
43	Idaho	(10.1)
44	Indiana	(10.5)
45	Utah	(10.6)
46	Connecticut	(11.8)
47	Kansas	(12.5)
48	Maine	(12.6)
49	Texas	(14.8)
50	New Hampshire	(17.2)

	District of Columbia	9.6

Source: U.S. Department of Justice, Federal Bureau of Investigation
    "Crime in the United States 1993" (Uniform Crime Reports, December 4, 1994)
Burglary is the unlawful entry of a structure to commit a felony or theft. Attempts are included.

Larceny and Theft in 1993

National Total = 7,820,909 Larcenies and Thefts*

ALPHA ORDER

RANK	STATE	LARCENIES	% of USA
25	Alabama	111,878	1.43%
45	Alaska	21,201	0.27%
14	Arizona	172,689	2.21%
33	Arkansas	67,767	0.87%
1	California	945,407	12.09%
23	Colorado	124,787	1.60%
28	Connecticut	85,876	1.10%
46	Delaware	20,853	0.27%
3	Florida	603,784	7.72%
8	Georgia	246,849	3.16%
36	Hawaii	51,912	0.66%
40	Idaho	29,795	0.38%
5	Illinois	360,730	4.61%
17	Indiana	154,016	1.97%
30	Iowa	73,148	0.94%
29	Kansas	76,538	0.98%
32	Kentucky	69,745	0.89%
16	Louisiana	163,334	2.09%
42	Maine	26,945	0.34%
15	Maryland	163,471	2.09%
21	Massachusetts	136,548	1.75%
7	Michigan	290,333	3.71%
22	Minnesota	129,727	1.66%
34	Mississippi	62,467	0.80%
18	Missouri	145,392	1.86%
39	Montana	30,641	0.39%
37	Nebraska	46,811	0.60%
38	Nevada	46,137	0.59%
44	New Hampshire	23,153	0.30%
12	New Jersey	195,876	2.50%
35	New Mexico	56,723	0.73%
4	New York	481,166	6.15%
10	North Carolina	220,071	2.81%
50	North Dakota	14,073	0.18%
6	Ohio	295,880	3.78%
27	Oklahoma	95,111	1.22%
26	Oregon	110,878	1.42%
9	Pennsylvania	220,683	2.82%
43	Rhode Island	24,101	0.31%
24	South Carolina	117,553	1.50%
48	South Dakota	14,915	0.19%
20	Tennessee	137,683	1.76%
2	Texas	664,862	8.50%
31	Utah	72,603	0.93%
47	Vermont	16,423	0.21%
13	Virginia	181,104	2.32%
11	Washington	205,701	2.63%
41	West Virginia	28,456	0.36%
19	Wisconsin	139,148	1.78%
49	Wyoming	14,470	0.19%

RANK ORDER

RANK	STATE	LARCENIES	% of USA
1	California	945,407	12.09%
2	Texas	664,862	8.50%
3	Florida	603,784	7.72%
4	New York	481,166	6.15%
5	Illinois	360,730	4.61%
6	Ohio	295,880	3.78%
7	Michigan	290,333	3.71%
8	Georgia	246,849	3.16%
9	Pennsylvania	220,683	2.82%
10	North Carolina	220,071	2.81%
11	Washington	205,701	2.63%
12	New Jersey	195,876	2.50%
13	Virginia	181,104	2.32%
14	Arizona	172,689	2.21%
15	Maryland	163,471	2.09%
16	Louisiana	163,334	2.09%
17	Indiana	154,016	1.97%
18	Missouri	145,392	1.86%
19	Wisconsin	139,148	1.78%
20	Tennessee	137,683	1.76%
21	Massachusetts	136,548	1.75%
22	Minnesota	129,727	1.66%
23	Colorado	124,787	1.60%
24	South Carolina	117,553	1.50%
25	Alabama	111,878	1.43%
26	Oregon	110,878	1.42%
27	Oklahoma	95,111	1.22%
28	Connecticut	85,876	1.10%
29	Kansas	76,538	0.98%
30	Iowa	73,148	0.94%
31	Utah	72,603	0.93%
32	Kentucky	69,745	0.89%
33	Arkansas	67,767	0.87%
34	Mississippi	62,467	0.80%
35	New Mexico	56,723	0.73%
36	Hawaii	51,912	0.66%
37	Nebraska	46,811	0.60%
38	Nevada	46,137	0.59%
39	Montana	30,641	0.39%
40	Idaho	29,795	0.38%
41	West Virginia	28,456	0.36%
42	Maine	26,945	0.34%
43	Rhode Island	24,101	0.31%
44	New Hampshire	23,153	0.30%
45	Alaska	21,201	0.27%
46	Delaware	20,853	0.27%
47	Vermont	16,423	0.21%
48	South Dakota	14,915	0.19%
49	Wyoming	14,470	0.19%
50	North Dakota	14,073	0.18%
	District of Columbia	31,495	0.40%

Source: U.S. Department of Justice, Federal Bureau of Investigation
"Crime in the United States 1993" (Uniform Crime Reports, December 4, 1994)
*Larceny and theft is the unlawful taking of property without use of force, violence or fraud. Attempts are included. Motor vehicle thefts are excluded.

Average Time Between Larcenies–Thefts in 1993

National Rate = A Larceny–Theft Occurs Every 4 Seconds*

<table>
<tr><td colspan="3">ALPHA ORDER</td><td colspan="3">RANK ORDER</td></tr>
<tr><td>RANK</td><td>STATE</td><td>MINUTES.SECONDS</td><td>RANK</td><td>STATE</td><td>MINUTES.SECONDS</td></tr>
<tr><td>26</td><td>Alabama</td><td>4.42</td><td>1</td><td>North Dakota</td><td>37.21</td></tr>
<tr><td>6</td><td>Alaska</td><td>24.47</td><td>2</td><td>Wyoming</td><td>36.19</td></tr>
<tr><td>37</td><td>Arizona</td><td>3.02</td><td>3</td><td>South Dakota</td><td>35.14</td></tr>
<tr><td>18</td><td>Arkansas</td><td>7.46</td><td>4</td><td>Vermont</td><td>32.00</td></tr>
<tr><td>50</td><td>California</td><td>0.34</td><td>5</td><td>Delaware</td><td>25.13</td></tr>
<tr><td>28</td><td>Colorado</td><td>4.13</td><td>6</td><td>Alaska</td><td>24.47</td></tr>
<tr><td>23</td><td>Connecticut</td><td>6.07</td><td>7</td><td>New Hampshire</td><td>22.42</td></tr>
<tr><td>5</td><td>Delaware</td><td>25.13</td><td>8</td><td>Rhode Island</td><td>21.49</td></tr>
<tr><td>48</td><td>Florida</td><td>0.52</td><td>9</td><td>Maine</td><td>19.31</td></tr>
<tr><td>43</td><td>Georgia</td><td>2.08</td><td>10</td><td>West Virginia</td><td>18.28</td></tr>
<tr><td>15</td><td>Hawaii</td><td>10.07</td><td>11</td><td>Idaho</td><td>17.38</td></tr>
<tr><td>11</td><td>Idaho</td><td>17.38</td><td>12</td><td>Montana</td><td>17.09</td></tr>
<tr><td>46</td><td>Illinois</td><td>1.28</td><td>13</td><td>Nevada</td><td>11.23</td></tr>
<tr><td>34</td><td>Indiana</td><td>3.25</td><td>14</td><td>Nebraska</td><td>11.14</td></tr>
<tr><td>21</td><td>Iowa</td><td>7.11</td><td>15</td><td>Hawaii</td><td>10.07</td></tr>
<tr><td>22</td><td>Kansas</td><td>6.52</td><td>16</td><td>New Mexico</td><td>9.16</td></tr>
<tr><td>19</td><td>Kentucky</td><td>7.32</td><td>17</td><td>Mississippi</td><td>8.25</td></tr>
<tr><td>35</td><td>Louisiana</td><td>3.13</td><td>18</td><td>Arkansas</td><td>7.46</td></tr>
<tr><td>9</td><td>Maine</td><td>19.31</td><td>19</td><td>Kentucky</td><td>7.32</td></tr>
<tr><td>35</td><td>Maryland</td><td>3.13</td><td>20</td><td>Utah</td><td>7.14</td></tr>
<tr><td>30</td><td>Massachusetts</td><td>3.51</td><td>21</td><td>Iowa</td><td>7.11</td></tr>
<tr><td>44</td><td>Michigan</td><td>1.49</td><td>22</td><td>Kansas</td><td>6.52</td></tr>
<tr><td>29</td><td>Minnesota</td><td>4.03</td><td>23</td><td>Connecticut</td><td>6.07</td></tr>
<tr><td>17</td><td>Mississippi</td><td>8.25</td><td>24</td><td>Oklahoma</td><td>5.32</td></tr>
<tr><td>33</td><td>Missouri</td><td>3.37</td><td>25</td><td>Oregon</td><td>4.44</td></tr>
<tr><td>12</td><td>Montana</td><td>17.09</td><td>26</td><td>Alabama</td><td>4.42</td></tr>
<tr><td>14</td><td>Nebraska</td><td>11.14</td><td>27</td><td>South Carolina</td><td>4.28</td></tr>
<tr><td>13</td><td>Nevada</td><td>11.23</td><td>28</td><td>Colorado</td><td>4.13</td></tr>
<tr><td>7</td><td>New Hampshire</td><td>22.42</td><td>29</td><td>Minnesota</td><td>4.03</td></tr>
<tr><td>39</td><td>New Jersey</td><td>2.41</td><td>30</td><td>Massachusetts</td><td>3.51</td></tr>
<tr><td>16</td><td>New Mexico</td><td>9.16</td><td>31</td><td>Tennessee</td><td>3.49</td></tr>
<tr><td>47</td><td>New York</td><td>1.05</td><td>32</td><td>Wisconsin</td><td>3.47</td></tr>
<tr><td>41</td><td>North Carolina</td><td>2.23</td><td>33</td><td>Missouri</td><td>3.37</td></tr>
<tr><td>1</td><td>North Dakota</td><td>37.21</td><td>34</td><td>Indiana</td><td>3.25</td></tr>
<tr><td>45</td><td>Ohio</td><td>1.47</td><td>35</td><td>Louisiana</td><td>3.13</td></tr>
<tr><td>24</td><td>Oklahoma</td><td>5.32</td><td>35</td><td>Maryland</td><td>3.13</td></tr>
<tr><td>25</td><td>Oregon</td><td>4.44</td><td>37</td><td>Arizona</td><td>3.02</td></tr>
<tr><td>41</td><td>Pennsylvania</td><td>2.23</td><td>38</td><td>Virginia</td><td>2.54</td></tr>
<tr><td>8</td><td>Rhode Island</td><td>21.49</td><td>39</td><td>New Jersey</td><td>2.41</td></tr>
<tr><td>27</td><td>South Carolina</td><td>4.28</td><td>40</td><td>Washington</td><td>2.34</td></tr>
<tr><td>3</td><td>South Dakota</td><td>35.14</td><td>41</td><td>North Carolina</td><td>2.23</td></tr>
<tr><td>31</td><td>Tennessee</td><td>3.49</td><td>41</td><td>Pennsylvania</td><td>2.23</td></tr>
<tr><td>49</td><td>Texas</td><td>0.47</td><td>43</td><td>Georgia</td><td>2.08</td></tr>
<tr><td>20</td><td>Utah</td><td>7.14</td><td>44</td><td>Michigan</td><td>1.49</td></tr>
<tr><td>4</td><td>Vermont</td><td>32.00</td><td>45</td><td>Ohio</td><td>1.47</td></tr>
<tr><td>38</td><td>Virginia</td><td>2.54</td><td>46</td><td>Illinois</td><td>1.28</td></tr>
<tr><td>40</td><td>Washington</td><td>2.34</td><td>47</td><td>New York</td><td>1.05</td></tr>
<tr><td>10</td><td>West Virginia</td><td>18.28</td><td>48</td><td>Florida</td><td>0.52</td></tr>
<tr><td>32</td><td>Wisconsin</td><td>3.47</td><td>49</td><td>Texas</td><td>0.47</td></tr>
<tr><td>2</td><td>Wyoming</td><td>36.19</td><td>50</td><td>California</td><td>0.34</td></tr>
<tr><td></td><td></td><td></td><td></td><td>District of Columbia</td><td>16.41</td></tr>
</table>

Source: Morgan Quitno Corporation using data from U.S. Department of Justice, Federal Bureau of Investigation
  "Crime in the United States 1993" (Uniform Crime Reports, December 4, 1994)

*Larceny and theft is the unlawful taking of property without use of force, violence or fraud. Attempts are included. Motor vehicle thefts are excluded.

Percent Change in Number of Larcenies and Thefts: 1992 to 1993

National Percent Change = 1.2% Decrease*

ALPHA ORDER				RANK ORDER		

RANK	STATE	PERCENT CHANGE		RANK	STATE	PERCENT CHANGE
44	Alabama	(5.0)		1	Vermont	21.6
8	Alaska	2.3		2	Arizona	9.3
2	Arizona	9.3		3	Tennessee	7.6
9	Arkansas	2.2		4	Louisiana	6.8
29	California	(2.4)		5	Mississippi	6.1
43	Colorado	(4.9)		6	Montana	4.8
40	Connecticut	(4.0)		7	Hawaii	2.7
10	Delaware	2.1		8	Alaska	2.3
15	Florida	1.0		9	Arkansas	2.2
20	Georgia	0.1		10	Delaware	2.1
7	Hawaii	2.7		11	Missouri	1.5
22	Idaho	(0.8)		11	Oregon	1.5
18	Illinois	0.3		13	South Carolina	1.2
28	Indiana	(2.0)		14	North Carolina	1.1
48	Iowa	(6.0)		15	Florida	1.0
44	Kansas	(5.0)		15	Oklahoma	1.0
17	Kentucky	0.8		17	Kentucky	0.8
4	Louisiana	6.8		18	Illinois	0.3
50	Maine	(10.1)		19	Rhode Island	0.2
24	Maryland	(1.1)		20	Georgia	0.1
37	Massachusetts	(3.6)		21	New Mexico	(0.6)
36	Michigan	(3.1)		22	Idaho	(0.8)
39	Minnesota	(3.7)		23	Washington	(1.0)
5	Mississippi	6.1		24	Maryland	(1.1)
11	Missouri	1.5		25	Nevada	(1.2)
6	Montana	4.8		26	Ohio	(1.3)
41	Nebraska	(4.7)		27	Pennsylvania	(1.5)
25	Nevada	(1.2)		28	Indiana	(2.0)
31	New Hampshire	(2.5)		29	California	(2.4)
46	New Jersey	(5.2)		29	Virginia	(2.4)
21	New Mexico	(0.6)		31	New Hampshire	(2.5)
33	New York	(2.9)		31	West Virginia	(2.5)
14	North Carolina	1.1		33	New York	(2.9)
33	North Dakota	(2.9)		33	North Dakota	(2.9)
26	Ohio	(1.3)		35	South Dakota	(3.0)
15	Oklahoma	1.0		36	Michigan	(3.1)
11	Oregon	1.5		37	Massachusetts	(3.6)
27	Pennsylvania	(1.5)		37	Texas	(3.6)
19	Rhode Island	0.2		39	Minnesota	(3.7)
13	South Carolina	1.2		40	Connecticut	(4.0)
35	South Dakota	(3.0)		41	Nebraska	(4.7)
3	Tennessee	7.6		42	Wisconsin	(4.8)
37	Texas	(3.6)		43	Colorado	(4.9)
47	Utah	(5.7)		44	Alabama	(5.0)
1	Vermont	21.6		44	Kansas	(5.0)
29	Virginia	(2.4)		46	New Jersey	(5.2)
23	Washington	(1.0)		47	Utah	(5.7)
31	West Virginia	(2.5)		48	Iowa	(6.0)
42	Wisconsin	(4.8)		49	Wyoming	(9.6)
49	Wyoming	(9.6)		50	Maine	(10.1)

District of Columbia   2.7

Source: U.S. Department of Justice, Federal Bureau of Investigation
    "Crime in the United States 1993" (Uniform Crime Reports, December 4, 1994)
*Larceny and theft is the unlawful taking of property without use of force, violence or fraud. Attempts are included. Motor vehicle thefts are excluded.

Larceny and Theft Rate in 1993

National Rate = 3,032.4 Larcenies and Thefts per 100,000 Population*

ALPHA ORDER			RANK ORDER		
RANK	STATE	RATE	RANK	STATE	RATE
35	Alabama	2,672.0	1	Hawaii	4,429.4
11	Alaska	3,539.4	2	Florida	4,413.9
3	Arizona	4,387.4	3	Arizona	4,387.4
28	Arkansas	2,795.7	4	Washington	3,914.4
21	California	3,029.1	5	Utah	3,903.4
13	Colorado	3,499.4	6	Louisiana	3,802.9
38	Connecticut	2,620.6	7	Texas	3,687.3
23	Delaware	2,979.0	8	Oregon	3,656.9
2	Florida	4,413.9	9	Montana	3,652.1
10	Georgia	3,568.7	10	Georgia	3,568.7
1	Hawaii	4,429.4	11	Alaska	3,539.4
32	Idaho	2,711.1	12	New Mexico	3,510.1
18	Illinois	3,084.0	13	Colorado	3,499.4
34	Indiana	2,695.9	14	Nevada	3,321.6
39	Iowa	2,599.4	15	Maryland	3,292.5
22	Kansas	3,024.0	16	South Carolina	3,226.8
48	Kentucky	1,840.7	17	North Carolina	3,168.8
6	Louisiana	3,802.9	18	Illinois	3,084.0
45	Maine	2,174.7	19	Wyoming	3,078.7
15	Maryland	3,292.5	20	Michigan	3,063.2
43	Massachusetts	2,271.3	21	California	3,029.1
20	Michigan	3,063.2	22	Kansas	3,024.0
26	Minnesota	2,872.0	23	Delaware	2,979.0
42	Mississippi	2,363.5	24	Oklahoma	2,943.7
30	Missouri	2,777.8	25	Nebraska	2,912.9
9	Montana	3,652.1	26	Minnesota	2,872.0
25	Nebraska	2,912.9	27	Vermont	2,851.2
14	Nevada	3,321.6	28	Arkansas	2,795.7
47	New Hampshire	2,058.0	29	Virginia	2,790.1
40	New Jersey	2,486.1	30	Missouri	2,777.8
12	New Mexico	3,510.1	31	Wisconsin	2,762.0
37	New York	2,644.2	32	Idaho	2,711.1
17	North Carolina	3,168.8	33	Tennessee	2,700.2
44	North Dakota	2,216.2	34	Indiana	2,695.9
36	Ohio	2,667.7	35	Alabama	2,672.0
24	Oklahoma	2,943.7	36	Ohio	2,667.7
8	Oregon	3,656.9	37	New York	2,644.2
49	Pennsylvania	1,831.7	38	Connecticut	2,620.6
41	Rhode Island	2,410.1	39	Iowa	2,599.4
16	South Carolina	3,226.8	40	New Jersey	2,486.1
46	South Dakota	2,086.0	41	Rhode Island	2,410.1
33	Tennessee	2,700.2	42	Mississippi	2,363.5
7	Texas	3,687.3	43	Massachusetts	2,271.3
5	Utah	3,903.4	44	North Dakota	2,216.2
27	Vermont	2,851.2	45	Maine	2,174.7
29	Virginia	2,790.1	46	South Dakota	2,086.0
4	Washington	3,914.4	47	New Hampshire	2,058.0
50	West Virginia	1,563.5	48	Kentucky	1,840.7
31	Wisconsin	2,762.0	49	Pennsylvania	1,831.7
19	Wyoming	3,078.7	50	West Virginia	1,563.5
				District of Columbia	5,449.0

Source: U.S. Department of Justice, Federal Bureau of Investigation
    "Crime in the United States 1993" (Uniform Crime Reports, December 4, 1994)
*Larceny and theft is the unlawful taking of property without use of force, violence or fraud. Attempts are included. Motor vehicle thefts are excluded.

Percent Change in Rate of Larceny and Theft: 1992 to 1993

National Percent Change = 2.3% Decrease*

ALPHA ORDER				RANK ORDER		
RANK	STATE	PERCENT CHANGE		RANK	STATE	PERCENT CHANGE
45	Alabama	(6.2)		1	Vermont	20.3
13	Alaska	0.2		2	Louisiana	6.6
3	Arizona	6.4		3	Arizona	6.4
8	Arkansas	1.2		4	Tennessee	6.0
30	California	(3.5)		5	Mississippi	5.0
47	Colorado	(7.4)		6	Montana	2.9
36	Connecticut	(3.9)		7	Hawaii	1.7
11	Delaware	0.5		8	Arkansas	1.2
19	Florida	(0.5)		9	Missouri	0.7
23	Georgia	(2.3)		9	Rhode Island	0.7
7	Hawaii	1.7		11	Delaware	0.5
33	Idaho	(3.6)		12	Oklahoma	0.4
16	Illinois	(0.3)		13	Alaska	0.2
26	Indiana	(2.9)		14	South Carolina	0.1
44	Iowa	(6.0)		15	Kentucky	(0.1)
40	Kansas	(5.3)		16	Illinois	(0.3)
15	Kentucky	(0.1)		17	North Carolina	(0.4)
2	Louisiana	6.6		17	Oregon	(0.4)
50	Maine	(10.4)		19	Florida	(0.5)
22	Maryland	(2.2)		20	Pennsylvania	(1.9)
35	Massachusetts	(3.8)		21	Ohio	(2.0)
30	Michigan	(3.5)		22	Maryland	(2.2)
38	Minnesota	(4.5)		23	Georgia	(2.3)
5	Mississippi	5.0		24	New Mexico	(2.8)
9	Missouri	0.7		24	North Dakota	(2.8)
6	Montana	2.9		26	Indiana	(2.9)
39	Nebraska	(4.8)		27	West Virginia	(3.0)
42	Nevada	(5.6)		28	Washington	(3.2)
34	New Hampshire	(3.7)		29	New York	(3.3)
46	New Jersey	(6.3)		30	California	(3.5)
24	New Mexico	(2.8)		30	Michigan	(3.5)
29	New York	(3.3)		30	South Dakota	(3.5)
17	North Carolina	(0.4)		33	Idaho	(3.6)
24	North Dakota	(2.8)		34	New Hampshire	(3.7)
21	Ohio	(2.0)		35	Massachusetts	(3.8)
12	Oklahoma	0.4		36	Connecticut	(3.9)
17	Oregon	(0.4)		37	Virginia	(4.1)
20	Pennsylvania	(1.9)		38	Minnesota	(4.5)
9	Rhode Island	0.7		39	Nebraska	(4.8)
14	South Carolina	0.1		40	Kansas	(5.3)
30	South Dakota	(3.5)		41	Wisconsin	(5.4)
4	Tennessee	6.0		42	Nevada	(5.6)
42	Texas	(5.6)		42	Texas	(5.6)
48	Utah	(8.0)		44	Iowa	(6.0)
1	Vermont	20.3		45	Alabama	(6.2)
37	Virginia	(4.1)		46	New Jersey	(6.3)
28	Washington	(3.2)		47	Colorado	(7.4)
27	West Virginia	(3.0)		48	Utah	(8.0)
41	Wisconsin	(5.4)		49	Wyoming	(10.3)
49	Wyoming	(10.3)		50	Maine	(10.4)
					District of Columbia	4.7

Source: U.S. Department of Justice, Federal Bureau of Investigation
   "Crime in the United States 1993" (Uniform Crime Reports, December 4, 1994)
Larceny and theft is the unlawful taking of property without use of force, violence or fraud. Attempts are included. Motor vehicle thefts are excluded.

Motor Vehicle Thefts in 1993

National Total = 1,561,047 Motor Vehicle Thefts*

ALPHA ORDER

RANK	STATE	THEFTS	% of USA
27	Alabama	14,142	0.91%
41	Alaska	2,701	0.17%
12	Arizona	33,998	2.18%
33	Arkansas	7,818	0.50%
1	California	319,295	20.45%
24	Colorado	16,058	1.03%
20	Connecticut	19,515	1.25%
42	Delaware	2,207	0.14%
4	Florida	122,516	7.85%
11	Georgia	41,076	2.63%
37	Hawaii	5,283	0.34%
45	Idaho	2,016	0.13%
5	Illinois	65,351	4.19%
17	Indiana	24,456	1.57%
36	Iowa	5,370	0.34%
32	Kansas	8,167	0.52%
31	Kentucky	8,193	0.52%
16	Louisiana	26,359	1.69%
46	Maine	1,665	0.11%
13	Maryland	33,930	2.17%
9	Massachusetts	49,063	3.14%
6	Michigan	58,291	3.73%
26	Minnesota	15,473	0.99%
30	Mississippi	8,856	0.57%
15	Missouri	28,666	1.84%
44	Montana	2,066	0.13%
39	Nebraska	3,239	0.21%
29	Nevada	10,255	0.66%
43	New Hampshire	2,183	0.14%
7	New Jersey	56,253	3.60%
34	New Mexico	6,547	0.42%
2	New York	151,949	9.73%
19	North Carolina	20,036	1.28%
47	North Dakota	944	0.06%
10	Ohio	48,276	3.09%
25	Oklahoma	15,532	0.99%
23	Oregon	17,608	1.13%
8	Pennsylvania	53,033	3.40%
35	Rhode Island	6,463	0.41%
28	South Carolina	12,531	0.80%
48	South Dakota	819	0.05%
14	Tennessee	30,135	1.93%
3	Texas	124,837	8.00%
38	Utah	4,505	0.29%
49	Vermont	764	0.05%
21	Virginia	18,533	1.19%
18	Washington	23,969	1.54%
40	West Virginia	2,940	0.19%
22	Wisconsin	18,375	1.18%
50	Wyoming	728	0.05%

RANK ORDER

RANK	STATE	THEFTS	% of USA
1	California	319,295	20.45%
2	New York	151,949	9.73%
3	Texas	124,837	8.00%
4	Florida	122,516	7.85%
5	Illinois	65,351	4.19%
6	Michigan	58,291	3.73%
7	New Jersey	56,253	3.60%
8	Pennsylvania	53,033	3.40%
9	Massachusetts	49,063	3.14%
10	Ohio	48,276	3.09%
11	Georgia	41,076	2.63%
12	Arizona	33,998	2.18%
13	Maryland	33,930	2.17%
14	Tennessee	30,135	1.93%
15	Missouri	28,666	1.84%
16	Louisiana	26,359	1.69%
17	Indiana	24,456	1.57%
18	Washington	23,969	1.54%
19	North Carolina	20,036	1.28%
20	Connecticut	19,515	1.25%
21	Virginia	18,533	1.19%
22	Wisconsin	18,375	1.18%
23	Oregon	17,608	1.13%
24	Colorado	16,058	1.03%
25	Oklahoma	15,532	0.99%
26	Minnesota	15,473	0.99%
27	Alabama	14,142	0.91%
28	South Carolina	12,531	0.80%
29	Nevada	10,255	0.66%
30	Mississippi	8,856	0.57%
31	Kentucky	8,193	0.52%
32	Kansas	8,167	0.52%
33	Arkansas	7,818	0.50%
34	New Mexico	6,547	0.42%
35	Rhode Island	6,463	0.41%
36	Iowa	5,370	0.34%
37	Hawaii	5,283	0.34%
38	Utah	4,505	0.29%
39	Nebraska	3,239	0.21%
40	West Virginia	2,940	0.19%
41	Alaska	2,701	0.17%
42	Delaware	2,207	0.14%
43	New Hampshire	2,183	0.14%
44	Montana	2,066	0.13%
45	Idaho	2,016	0.13%
46	Maine	1,665	0.11%
47	North Dakota	944	0.06%
48	South Dakota	819	0.05%
49	Vermont	764	0.05%
50	Wyoming	728	0.05%
	District of Columbia	8,062	0.52%

Source: U.S. Department of Justice, Federal Bureau of Investigation
"Crime in the United States 1993" (Uniform Crime Reports, December 4, 1994)
Includes the theft or attempted theft of a self-propelled vehicle. Excludes motorboats, construction equipment, airplanes and farming equipment.

Average Time Between Motor Vehicle Thefts in 1993

National Rate = A Motor Vehicle Theft Occurs Every 20 Seconds*

ALPHA ORDER				RANK ORDER		
RANK	STATE	MINUTES.SECONDS		RANK	STATE	MINUTES.SECONDS
24	Alabama	37.10		1	Wyoming	721.59
10	Alaska	194.35		2	Vermont	687.58
39	Arizona	15.28		3	South Dakota	641.46
18	Arkansas	67.14		4	North Dakota	556.47
50	California	1.39		5	Maine	315.41
27	Colorado	32.44		6	Idaho	260.43
31	Connecticut	26.56		7	Montana	254.24
9	Delaware	238.09		8	New Hampshire	240.46
47	Florida	4.17		9	Delaware	238.09
40	Georgia	12.48		10	Alaska	194.35
14	Hawaii	99.29		11	West Virginia	178.47
6	Idaho	260.43		12	Nebraska	162.16
46	Illinois	8.02		13	Utah	116.40
34	Indiana	21.29		14	Hawaii	99.29
15	Iowa	97.53		15	Iowa	97.53
19	Kansas	64.22		16	Rhode Island	81.19
20	Kentucky	64.09		17	New Mexico	80.17
35	Louisiana	19.56		18	Arkansas	67.14
5	Maine	315.41		19	Kansas	64.22
38	Maryland	15.29		20	Kentucky	64.09
42	Massachusetts	10.43		21	Mississippi	59.21
45	Michigan	9.01		22	Nevada	51.15
25	Minnesota	33.58		23	South Carolina	41.56
21	Mississippi	59.21		24	Alabama	37.10
36	Missouri	18.20		25	Minnesota	33.58
7	Montana	254.24		26	Oklahoma	33.50
12	Nebraska	162.16		27	Colorado	32.44
22	Nevada	51.15		28	Oregon	29.51
8	New Hampshire	240.46		29	Wisconsin	28.36
44	New Jersey	9.20		30	Virginia	28.22
17	New Mexico	80.17		31	Connecticut	26.56
49	New York	3.28		32	North Carolina	26.14
32	North Carolina	26.14		33	Washington	21.56
4	North Dakota	556.47		34	Indiana	21.29
41	Ohio	10.53		35	Louisiana	19.56
26	Oklahoma	33.50		36	Missouri	18.20
28	Oregon	29.51		37	Tennessee	17.26
43	Pennsylvania	9.55		38	Maryland	15.29
16	Rhode Island	81.19		39	Arizona	15.28
23	South Carolina	41.56		40	Georgia	12.48
3	South Dakota	641.46		41	Ohio	10.53
37	Tennessee	17.26		42	Massachusetts	10.43
48	Texas	4.13		43	Pennsylvania	9.55
13	Utah	116.40		44	New Jersey	9.20
2	Vermont	687.58		45	Michigan	9.01
30	Virginia	28.22		46	Illinois	8.02
33	Washington	21.56		47	Florida	4.17
11	West Virginia	178.47		48	Texas	4.13
29	Wisconsin	28.36		49	New York	3.28
1	Wyoming	721.59		50	California	1.39
					District of Columbia	65.11

Source: Morgan Quitno Corporation using data from U.S. Department of Justice, Federal Bureau of Investigation
"Crime in the United States 1993" (Uniform Crime Reports, December 4, 1994)
*Includes the theft or attempted theft of a self-propelled vehicle. Excludes motorboats, construction equipment, airplanes and farming equipment.

Percent Change in Number of Motor Vehicle Thefts: 1992 to 1993

National Percent Change = 3.1% Decrease*

ALPHA ORDER			RANK ORDER		
RANK	STATE	PERCENT CHANGE	RANK	STATE	PERCENT CHANGE
37	Alabama	(5.6)	1	Vermont	27.3
42	Alaska	(7.4)	2	Hawaii	21.4
11	Arizona	8.0	3	Idaho	20.1
29	Arkansas	(1.0)	4	Iowa	20.0
26	California	(0.3)	5	South Dakota	13.9
43	Colorado	(9.1)	6	Missouri	11.0
50	Connecticut	(17.7)	7	Oregon	10.9
14	Delaware	4.6	8	Nevada	10.8
9	Florida	9.7	9	Florida	9.7
13	Georgia	5.6	10	New Mexico	9.6
2	Hawaii	21.4	11	Arizona	8.0
3	Idaho	20.1	12	Montana	7.4
44	Illinois	(9.2)	13	Georgia	5.6
34	Indiana	(4.1)	14	Delaware	4.6
4	Iowa	20.0	15	Utah	4.5
25	Kansas	0.0	16	Tennessee	4.1
20	Kentucky	0.8	17	Wyoming	3.9
32	Louisiana	(2.1)	18	Massachusetts	3.5
39	Maine	(6.4)	19	North Carolina	2.2
35	Maryland	(4.8)	20	Kentucky	0.8
18	Massachusetts	3.5	20	New Hampshire	0.8
31	Michigan	(1.3)	22	Mississippi	0.7
33	Minnesota	(2.8)	22	South Carolina	0.7
22	Mississippi	0.7	24	Nebraska	0.4
6	Missouri	11.0	25	Kansas	0.0
12	Montana	7.4	26	California	(0.3)
24	Nebraska	0.4	27	North Dakota	(0.6)
8	Nevada	10.8	28	West Virginia	(0.9)
20	New Hampshire	0.8	29	Arkansas	(1.0)
46	New Jersey	(11.4)	29	Washington	(1.0)
10	New Mexico	9.6	31	Michigan	(1.3)
45	New York	(10.0)	32	Louisiana	(2.1)
19	North Carolina	2.2	33	Minnesota	(2.8)
27	North Dakota	(0.6)	34	Indiana	(4.1)
41	Ohio	(7.0)	35	Maryland	(4.8)
39	Oklahoma	(6.4)	36	Virginia	(4.9)
7	Oregon	10.9	37	Alabama	(5.6)
37	Pennsylvania	(5.6)	37	Pennsylvania	(5.6)
47	Rhode Island	(13.4)	39	Maine	(6.4)
22	South Carolina	0.7	39	Oklahoma	(6.4)
5	South Dakota	13.9	41	Ohio	(7.0)
16	Tennessee	4.1	42	Alaska	(7.4)
48	Texas	(13.9)	43	Colorado	(9.1)
15	Utah	4.5	44	Illinois	(9.2)
1	Vermont	27.3	45	New York	(10.0)
36	Virginia	(4.9)	46	New Jersey	(11.4)
29	Washington	(1.0)	47	Rhode Island	(13.4)
28	West Virginia	(0.9)	48	Texas	(13.9)
49	Wisconsin	(15.0)	49	Wisconsin	(15.0)
17	Wyoming	3.9	50	Connecticut	(17.7)
				District of Columbia	(11.6)

Source: U.S. Department of Justice, Federal Bureau of Investigation
"Crime in the United States 1993" (Uniform Crime Reports, December 4, 1994)
*Includes the theft or attempted theft of a self-propelled vehicle. Excludes motorboats, construction equipment, airplanes and farming equipment.

Motor Vehicle Theft Rate in 1993

National Rate = 605.3 Motor Vehicle Thefts per 100,000 Population*

ALPHA ORDER				RANK ORDER		
RANK	STATE	RATE		RANK	STATE	RATE
31	Alabama	337.8		1	California	1,023.0
21	Alaska	450.9		2	Florida	895.7
3	Arizona	863.8		3	Arizona	863.8
34	Arkansas	322.5		4	New York	835.0
1	California	1,023.0		5	Massachusetts	816.1
23	Colorado	450.3		6	Nevada	738.3
13	Connecticut	595.5		7	New Jersey	714.0
35	Delaware	315.3		8	Texas	692.3
2	Florida	895.7		9	Maryland	683.4
14	Georgia	593.8		10	Rhode Island	646.3
22	Hawaii	450.8		11	Michigan	615.0
44	Idaho	183.4		12	Louisiana	613.7
17	Illinois	558.7		13	Connecticut	595.5
26	Indiana	428.1		14	Georgia	593.8
43	Iowa	190.8		15	Tennessee	591.0
33	Kansas	322.7		16	Oregon	580.7
40	Kentucky	216.2		17	Illinois	558.7
12	Louisiana	613.7		18	Missouri	547.7
48	Maine	134.4		19	Oklahoma	480.7
9	Maryland	683.4		20	Washington	456.1
5	Massachusetts	816.1		21	Alaska	450.9
11	Michigan	615.0		22	Hawaii	450.8
30	Minnesota	342.6		23	Colorado	450.3
32	Mississippi	335.1		24	Pennsylvania	440.2
18	Missouri	547.7		25	Ohio	435.3
38	Montana	246.2		26	Indiana	428.1
41	Nebraska	201.6		27	New Mexico	405.1
6	Nevada	738.3		28	Wisconsin	364.7
42	New Hampshire	194.0		29	South Carolina	344.0
7	New Jersey	714.0		30	Minnesota	342.6
27	New Mexico	405.1		31	Alabama	337.8
4	New York	835.0		32	Mississippi	335.1
36	North Carolina	288.5		33	Kansas	322.7
47	North Dakota	148.7		34	Arkansas	322.5
25	Ohio	435.3		35	Delaware	315.3
19	Oklahoma	480.7		36	North Carolina	288.5
16	Oregon	580.7		37	Virginia	285.5
24	Pennsylvania	440.2		38	Montana	246.2
10	Rhode Island	646.3		39	Utah	242.2
29	South Carolina	344.0		40	Kentucky	216.2
50	South Dakota	114.5		41	Nebraska	201.6
15	Tennessee	591.0		42	New Hampshire	194.0
8	Texas	692.3		43	Iowa	190.8
39	Utah	242.2		44	Idaho	183.4
49	Vermont	132.6		45	West Virginia	161.5
37	Virginia	285.5		46	Wyoming	154.9
20	Washington	456.1		47	North Dakota	148.7
45	West Virginia	161.5		48	Maine	134.4
28	Wisconsin	364.7		49	Vermont	132.6
46	Wyoming	154.9		50	South Dakota	114.5
					District of Columbia	1,394.8

Source: U.S. Department of Justice, Federal Bureau of Investigation
"Crime in the United States 1993" (Uniform Crime Reports, December 4, 1994)
*Includes the theft or attempted theft of a self-propelled vehicle. Excludes motorboats, construction equipment, airplanes and farming equipment.

Percent Change in Rate of Motor Vehicle Thefts: 1992 to 1993

National Percent Change = 4.1% Decrease*

ALPHA ORDER

RANK	STATE	PERCENT CHANGE
39	Alabama	(6.8)
42	Alaska	(9.3)
12	Arizona	5.1
30	Arkansas	(2.1)
27	California	(1.4)
45	Colorado	(11.5)
50	Connecticut	(17.6)
14	Delaware	3.0
8	Florida	8.2
14	Georgia	3.0
2	Hawaii	20.2
4	Idaho	16.5
43	Illinois	(9.7)
34	Indiana	(4.9)
3	Iowa	19.9
22	Kansas	(0.3)
21	Kentucky	(0.1)
31	Louisiana	(2.3)
38	Maine	(6.7)
35	Maryland	(5.9)
13	Massachusetts	3.2
29	Michigan	(1.7)
33	Minnesota	(3.5)
23	Mississippi	(0.4)
6	Missouri	10.1
11	Montana	5.5
20	Nebraska	0.4
10	Nevada	5.9
25	New Hampshire	(0.5)
46	New Jersey	(12.5)
9	New Mexico	7.2
44	New York	(10.4)
19	North Carolina	0.7
25	North Dakota	(0.5)
41	Ohio	(7.6)
40	Oklahoma	(7.0)
7	Oregon	8.8
35	Pennsylvania	(5.9)
47	Rhode Island	(13.0)
23	South Carolina	(0.4)
5	South Dakota	13.3
17	Tennessee	2.6
49	Texas	(15.7)
18	Utah	1.8
1	Vermont	25.9
37	Virginia	(6.6)
32	Washington	(3.3)
27	West Virginia	(1.4)
48	Wisconsin	(15.5)
14	Wyoming	3.0

RANK ORDER

RANK	STATE	PERCENT CHANGE
1	Vermont	25.9
2	Hawaii	20.2
3	Iowa	19.9
4	Idaho	16.5
5	South Dakota	13.3
6	Missouri	10.1
7	Oregon	8.8
8	Florida	8.2
9	New Mexico	7.2
10	Nevada	5.9
11	Montana	5.5
12	Arizona	5.1
13	Massachusetts	3.2
14	Delaware	3.0
14	Georgia	3.0
14	Wyoming	3.0
17	Tennessee	2.6
18	Utah	1.8
19	North Carolina	0.7
20	Nebraska	0.4
21	Kentucky	(0.1)
22	Kansas	(0.3)
23	Mississippi	(0.4)
23	South Carolina	(0.4)
25	New Hampshire	(0.5)
25	North Dakota	(0.5)
27	California	(1.4)
27	West Virginia	(1.4)
29	Michigan	(1.7)
30	Arkansas	(2.1)
31	Louisiana	(2.3)
32	Washington	(3.3)
33	Minnesota	(3.5)
34	Indiana	(4.9)
35	Maryland	(5.9)
35	Pennsylvania	(5.9)
37	Virginia	(6.6)
38	Maine	(6.7)
39	Alabama	(6.8)
40	Oklahoma	(7.0)
41	Ohio	(7.6)
42	Alaska	(9.3)
43	Illinois	(9.7)
44	New York	(10.4)
45	Colorado	(11.5)
46	New Jersey	(12.5)
47	Rhode Island	(13.0)
48	Wisconsin	(15.5)
49	Texas	(15.7)
50	Connecticut	(17.6)

| | District of Columbia | (9.9) |

Source: U.S. Department of Justice, Federal Bureau of Investigation
    "Crime in the United States 1993" (Uniform Crime Reports, December 4, 1994)
*Includes the theft or attempted theft of a self-propelled vehicle. Excludes motorboats, construction equipment, airplanes and farming equipment.

Crime in Urban Areas in 1993

National Total = 13,515,670 Crimes*

<table>
<tr><td colspan="4"><u>ALPHA ORDER</u></td><td colspan="4"><u>RANK ORDER</u></td></tr>
<tr><th>RANK</th><th>STATE</th><th>CRIMES</th><th>% of USA</th><th>RANK</th><th>STATE</th><th>CRIMES</th><th>% of USA</th></tr>
<tr><td>19</td><td>Alabama</td><td>194,621</td><td>1.44%</td><td>1</td><td>California</td><td>1,995,866</td><td>14.77%</td></tr>
<tr><td>43</td><td>Alaska</td><td>26,358</td><td>0.20%</td><td>2</td><td>Texas</td><td>1,128,286</td><td>8.35%</td></tr>
<tr><td>13</td><td>Arizona</td><td>286,406</td><td>2.12%</td><td>3</td><td>Florida</td><td>1,113,191</td><td>8.24%</td></tr>
<tr><td>28</td><td>Arkansas</td><td>104,281</td><td>0.77%</td><td>4</td><td>New York</td><td>990,643</td><td>7.33%</td></tr>
<tr><td>1</td><td>California</td><td>1,995,866</td><td>14.77%</td><td>5</td><td>Ohio</td><td>479,752</td><td>3.55%</td></tr>
<tr><td>21</td><td>Colorado</td><td>187,061</td><td>1.38%</td><td>6</td><td>Georgia</td><td>393,410</td><td>2.91%</td></tr>
<tr><td>25</td><td>Connecticut</td><td>149,128</td><td>1.10%</td><td>7</td><td>Pennsylvania</td><td>378,360</td><td>2.80%</td></tr>
<tr><td>41</td><td>Delaware</td><td>31,161</td><td>0.23%</td><td>8</td><td>New Jersey</td><td>378,257</td><td>2.80%</td></tr>
<tr><td>3</td><td>Florida</td><td>1,113,191</td><td>8.24%</td><td>9</td><td>North Carolina</td><td>352,925</td><td>2.61%</td></tr>
<tr><td>6</td><td>Georgia</td><td>393,410</td><td>2.91%</td><td>10</td><td>Washington</td><td>299,173</td><td>2.21%</td></tr>
<tr><td>35</td><td>Hawaii</td><td>59,113</td><td>0.44%</td><td>11</td><td>Maryland</td><td>296,432</td><td>2.19%</td></tr>
<tr><td>38</td><td>Idaho</td><td>34,939</td><td>0.26%</td><td>12</td><td>Massachusetts</td><td>294,100</td><td>2.18%</td></tr>
<tr><td>NA</td><td>Illinois**</td><td>NA</td><td>NA</td><td>13</td><td>Arizona</td><td>286,406</td><td>2.12%</td></tr>
<tr><td>18</td><td>Indiana</td><td>237,602</td><td>1.76%</td><td>14</td><td>Louisiana</td><td>277,103</td><td>2.05%</td></tr>
<tr><td>30</td><td>Iowa</td><td>97,690</td><td>0.72%</td><td>15</td><td>Missouri</td><td>253,792</td><td>1.88%</td></tr>
<tr><td>26</td><td>Kansas</td><td>118,274</td><td>0.88%</td><td>16</td><td>Virginia</td><td>251,632</td><td>1.86%</td></tr>
<tr><td>27</td><td>Kentucky</td><td>105,650</td><td>0.78%</td><td>17</td><td>Tennessee</td><td>248,627</td><td>1.84%</td></tr>
<tr><td>14</td><td>Louisiana</td><td>277,103</td><td>2.05%</td><td>18</td><td>Indiana</td><td>237,602</td><td>1.76%</td></tr>
<tr><td>39</td><td>Maine</td><td>32,810</td><td>0.24%</td><td>19</td><td>Alabama</td><td>194,621</td><td>1.44%</td></tr>
<tr><td>11</td><td>Maryland</td><td>296,432</td><td>2.19%</td><td>20</td><td>Wisconsin</td><td>187,631</td><td>1.39%</td></tr>
<tr><td>12</td><td>Massachusetts</td><td>294,100</td><td>2.18%</td><td>21</td><td>Colorado</td><td>187,061</td><td>1.38%</td></tr>
<tr><td>NA</td><td>Michigan**</td><td>NA</td><td>NA</td><td>22</td><td>South Carolina</td><td>185,178</td><td>1.37%</td></tr>
<tr><td>NA</td><td>Minnesota**</td><td>NA</td><td>NA</td><td>23</td><td>Oregon</td><td>162,811</td><td>1.20%</td></tr>
<tr><td>29</td><td>Mississippi</td><td>101,432</td><td>0.75%</td><td>24</td><td>Oklahoma</td><td>160,561</td><td>1.19%</td></tr>
<tr><td>15</td><td>Missouri</td><td>253,792</td><td>1.88%</td><td>25</td><td>Connecticut</td><td>149,128</td><td>1.10%</td></tr>
<tr><td>42</td><td>Montana</td><td>29,003</td><td>0.21%</td><td>26</td><td>Kansas</td><td>118,274</td><td>0.88%</td></tr>
<tr><td>34</td><td>Nebraska</td><td>60,577</td><td>0.45%</td><td>27</td><td>Kentucky</td><td>105,650</td><td>0.78%</td></tr>
<tr><td>33</td><td>Nevada</td><td>79,717</td><td>0.59%</td><td>28</td><td>Arkansas</td><td>104,281</td><td>0.77%</td></tr>
<tr><td>40</td><td>New Hampshire</td><td>31,760</td><td>0.23%</td><td>29</td><td>Mississippi</td><td>101,432</td><td>0.75%</td></tr>
<tr><td>8</td><td>New Jersey</td><td>378,257</td><td>2.80%</td><td>30</td><td>Iowa</td><td>97,690</td><td>0.72%</td></tr>
<tr><td>31</td><td>New Mexico</td><td>96,074</td><td>0.71%</td><td>31</td><td>New Mexico</td><td>96,074</td><td>0.71%</td></tr>
<tr><td>4</td><td>New York</td><td>990,643</td><td>7.33%</td><td>32</td><td>Utah</td><td>93,202</td><td>0.69%</td></tr>
<tr><td>9</td><td>North Carolina</td><td>352,925</td><td>2.61%</td><td>33</td><td>Nevada</td><td>79,717</td><td>0.59%</td></tr>
<tr><td>47</td><td>North Dakota</td><td>15,710</td><td>0.12%</td><td>34</td><td>Nebraska</td><td>60,577</td><td>0.45%</td></tr>
<tr><td>5</td><td>Ohio</td><td>479,752</td><td>3.55%</td><td>35</td><td>Hawaii</td><td>59,113</td><td>0.44%</td></tr>
<tr><td>24</td><td>Oklahoma</td><td>160,561</td><td>1.19%</td><td>36</td><td>Rhode Island</td><td>44,969</td><td>0.33%</td></tr>
<tr><td>23</td><td>Oregon</td><td>162,811</td><td>1.20%</td><td>37</td><td>West Virginia</td><td>35,676</td><td>0.26%</td></tr>
<tr><td>7</td><td>Pennsylvania</td><td>378,360</td><td>2.80%</td><td>38</td><td>Idaho</td><td>34,939</td><td>0.26%</td></tr>
<tr><td>36</td><td>Rhode Island</td><td>44,969</td><td>0.33%</td><td>39</td><td>Maine</td><td>32,810</td><td>0.24%</td></tr>
<tr><td>22</td><td>South Carolina</td><td>185,178</td><td>1.37%</td><td>40</td><td>New Hampshire</td><td>31,760</td><td>0.23%</td></tr>
<tr><td>44</td><td>South Dakota</td><td>17,994</td><td>0.13%</td><td>41</td><td>Delaware</td><td>31,161</td><td>0.23%</td></tr>
<tr><td>17</td><td>Tennessee</td><td>248,627</td><td>1.84%</td><td>42</td><td>Montana</td><td>29,003</td><td>0.21%</td></tr>
<tr><td>2</td><td>Texas</td><td>1,128,286</td><td>8.35%</td><td>43</td><td>Alaska</td><td>26,358</td><td>0.20%</td></tr>
<tr><td>32</td><td>Utah</td><td>93,202</td><td>0.69%</td><td>44</td><td>South Dakota</td><td>17,994</td><td>0.13%</td></tr>
<tr><td>45</td><td>Vermont</td><td>17,435</td><td>0.13%</td><td>45</td><td>Vermont</td><td>17,435</td><td>0.13%</td></tr>
<tr><td>16</td><td>Virginia</td><td>251,632</td><td>1.86%</td><td>46</td><td>Wyoming</td><td>16,996</td><td>0.13%</td></tr>
<tr><td>10</td><td>Washington</td><td>299,173</td><td>2.21%</td><td>47</td><td>North Dakota</td><td>15,710</td><td>0.12%</td></tr>
<tr><td>37</td><td>West Virginia</td><td>35,676</td><td>0.26%</td><td>NA</td><td>Illinois**</td><td>NA</td><td>NA</td></tr>
<tr><td>20</td><td>Wisconsin</td><td>187,631</td><td>1.39%</td><td>NA</td><td>Michigan**</td><td>NA</td><td>NA</td></tr>
<tr><td>46</td><td>Wyoming</td><td>16,996</td><td>0.13%</td><td>NA</td><td>Minnesota**</td><td>NA</td><td>NA</td></tr>
<tr><td></td><td></td><td></td><td></td><td></td><td>District of Columbia</td><td>67,979</td><td>0.50%</td></tr>
</table>

Source: Morgan Quitno Corporation using data from U.S. Department of Justice, Federal Bureau of Investigation
"Crime in the United States 1993" (Uniform Crime Reports, December 4, 1994)
*Estimated totals for urban areas, defined by the F.B.I. as Metropolitan Statistical Areas and other cities outside such areas. National total includes those states listed as not available. Includes murder, rape, robbery, aggravated assault, burglary, larceny-theft and motor vehicle theft.
**Not available.

Urban Crime Rate in 1993

National Rate = 5,975.5 Crimes per 100,000 Population*

ALPHA ORDER

RANK	STATE	RATE
23	Alabama	5,725.7
15	Alaska	6,429.6
2	Arizona	7,881.4
13	Arkansas	6,479.1
11	California	6,523.7
22	Colorado	5,830.2
36	Connecticut	4,832.3
29	Delaware	5,094.8
1	Florida	8,604.5
6	Georgia	7,077.4
14	Hawaii	6,462.0
35	Idaho	4,882.2
NA	Illinois**	NA
28	Indiana	5,096.8
30	Iowa	5,088.6
25	Kansas	5,700.4
41	Kentucky	4,386.1
3	Louisiana	7,832.4
44	Maine	3,674.1
17	Maryland	6,308.4
34	Massachusetts	4,901.9
NA	Michigan**	NA
NA	Minnesota**	NA
8	Mississippi	6,788.4
19	Missouri	6,254.1
5	Montana	7,110.6
31	Nebraska	5,075.6
10	Nevada	6,538.7
47	New Hampshire	3,226.1
37	New Jersey	4,800.8
4	New Mexico	7,262.6
24	New York	5,713.1
9	North Carolina	6,653.0
43	North Dakota	3,843.4
33	Ohio	4,907.3
21	Oklahoma	6,162.8
16	Oregon	6,401.1
45	Pennsylvania	3,444.6
40	Rhode Island	4,496.9
12	South Carolina	6,480.7
42	South Dakota	4,238.1
20	Tennessee	6,231.2
7	Texas	6,863.6
26	Utah	5,619.2
27	Vermont	5,575.1
39	Virginia	4,623.1
18	Washington	6,271.1
46	West Virginia	3,434.6
38	Wisconsin	4,630.0
32	Wyoming	4,914.6

RANK ORDER

RANK	STATE	RATE
1	Florida	8,604.5
2	Arizona	7,881.4
3	Louisiana	7,832.4
4	New Mexico	7,262.6
5	Montana	7,110.6
6	Georgia	7,077.4
7	Texas	6,863.6
8	Mississippi	6,788.4
9	North Carolina	6,653.0
10	Nevada	6,538.7
11	California	6,523.7
12	South Carolina	6,480.7
13	Arkansas	6,479.1
14	Hawaii	6,462.0
15	Alaska	6,429.6
16	Oregon	6,401.1
17	Maryland	6,308.4
18	Washington	6,271.1
19	Missouri	6,254.1
20	Tennessee	6,231.2
21	Oklahoma	6,162.8
22	Colorado	5,830.2
23	Alabama	5,725.7
24	New York	5,713.1
25	Kansas	5,700.4
26	Utah	5,619.2
27	Vermont	5,575.1
28	Indiana	5,096.8
29	Delaware	5,094.8
30	Iowa	5,088.6
31	Nebraska	5,075.6
32	Wyoming	4,914.6
33	Ohio	4,907.3
34	Massachusetts	4,901.9
35	Idaho	4,882.2
36	Connecticut	4,832.3
37	New Jersey	4,800.8
38	Wisconsin	4,630.0
39	Virginia	4,623.1
40	Rhode Island	4,496.9
41	Kentucky	4,386.1
42	South Dakota	4,238.1
43	North Dakota	3,843.4
44	Maine	3,674.1
45	Pennsylvania	3,444.6
46	West Virginia	3,434.6
47	New Hampshire	3,226.1
NA	Illinois**	NA
NA	Michigan**	NA
NA	Minnesota**	NA

District of Columbia   11,761.1

Source: Morgan Quitno Corporation using data from U.S. Department of Justice, Federal Bureau of Investigation
"Crime in the United States 1993" (Uniform Crime Reports, December 4, 1994)
*Estimated rates for urban areas, defined by the F.B.I. as Metropolitan Statistical Areas and other cities outside such areas. National rate includes those states listed as not available. Includes murder, rape, robbery, aggravated assault, burglary, larceny-theft and motor vehicle theft.
**Not available.

Percent of Crimes Occurring in Urban Areas in 1993

National Percent = 95.58% of Crimes*

<table>
<tr><td colspan="3">ALPHA ORDER</td><td colspan="3">RANK ORDER</td></tr>
<tr><td>RANK</td><td>STATE</td><td>PERCENT</td><td>RANK</td><td>STATE</td><td>PERCENT</td></tr>
<tr><td>16</td><td>Alabama</td><td>95.27</td><td>1</td><td>New Jersey</td><td>100.00</td></tr>
<tr><td>44</td><td>Alaska</td><td>79.03</td><td>2</td><td>Massachusetts</td><td>99.96</td></tr>
<tr><td>6</td><td>Arizona</td><td>97.91</td><td>3</td><td>Rhode Island</td><td>99.95</td></tr>
<tr><td>34</td><td>Arkansas</td><td>89.43</td><td>4</td><td>California</td><td>99.04</td></tr>
<tr><td>4</td><td>California</td><td>99.04</td><td>5</td><td>New York</td><td>98.07</td></tr>
<tr><td>18</td><td>Colorado</td><td>94.91</td><td>6</td><td>Arizona</td><td>97.91</td></tr>
<tr><td>7</td><td>Connecticut</td><td>97.86</td><td>7</td><td>Connecticut</td><td>97.86</td></tr>
<tr><td>31</td><td>Delaware</td><td>91.37</td><td>8</td><td>Maryland</td><td>97.77</td></tr>
<tr><td>9</td><td>Florida</td><td>97.45</td><td>9</td><td>Florida</td><td>97.45</td></tr>
<tr><td>29</td><td>Georgia</td><td>91.84</td><td>10</td><td>New Hampshire</td><td>97.18</td></tr>
<tr><td>43</td><td>Hawaii</td><td>80.35</td><td>10</td><td>Texas</td><td>97.18</td></tr>
<tr><td>42</td><td>Idaho</td><td>82.68</td><td>12</td><td>Ohio</td><td>96.44</td></tr>
<tr><td>NA</td><td>Illinois**</td><td>NA</td><td>13</td><td>Pennsylvania</td><td>96.00</td></tr>
<tr><td>24</td><td>Indiana</td><td>93.14</td><td>14</td><td>Utah</td><td>95.68</td></tr>
<tr><td>32</td><td>Iowa</td><td>90.25</td><td>15</td><td>Washington</td><td>95.65</td></tr>
<tr><td>22</td><td>Kansas</td><td>93.92</td><td>16</td><td>Alabama</td><td>95.27</td></tr>
<tr><td>39</td><td>Kentucky</td><td>85.54</td><td>17</td><td>Missouri</td><td>95.16</td></tr>
<tr><td>20</td><td>Louisiana</td><td>94.23</td><td>18</td><td>Colorado</td><td>94.91</td></tr>
<tr><td>41</td><td>Maine</td><td>83.96</td><td>19</td><td>New Mexico</td><td>94.88</td></tr>
<tr><td>8</td><td>Maryland</td><td>97.77</td><td>20</td><td>Louisiana</td><td>94.23</td></tr>
<tr><td>2</td><td>Massachusetts</td><td>99.96</td><td>21</td><td>Virginia</td><td>94.20</td></tr>
<tr><td>NA</td><td>Michigan**</td><td>NA</td><td>22</td><td>Kansas</td><td>93.92</td></tr>
<tr><td>NA</td><td>Minnesota**</td><td>NA</td><td>23</td><td>Oklahoma</td><td>93.86</td></tr>
<tr><td>36</td><td>Mississippi</td><td>86.86</td><td>24</td><td>Indiana</td><td>93.14</td></tr>
<tr><td>17</td><td>Missouri</td><td>95.16</td><td>25</td><td>Oregon</td><td>93.13</td></tr>
<tr><td>47</td><td>Montana</td><td>72.17</td><td>26</td><td>Tennessee</td><td>93.06</td></tr>
<tr><td>30</td><td>Nebraska</td><td>91.56</td><td>27</td><td>Nevada</td><td>92.86</td></tr>
<tr><td>27</td><td>Nevada</td><td>92.86</td><td>28</td><td>Wisconsin</td><td>91.87</td></tr>
<tr><td>10</td><td>New Hampshire</td><td>97.18</td><td>29</td><td>Georgia</td><td>91.84</td></tr>
<tr><td>1</td><td>New Jersey</td><td>100.00</td><td>30</td><td>Nebraska</td><td>91.56</td></tr>
<tr><td>19</td><td>New Mexico</td><td>94.88</td><td>31</td><td>Delaware</td><td>91.37</td></tr>
<tr><td>5</td><td>New York</td><td>98.07</td><td>32</td><td>Iowa</td><td>90.25</td></tr>
<tr><td>33</td><td>North Carolina</td><td>89.90</td><td>33</td><td>North Carolina</td><td>89.90</td></tr>
<tr><td>35</td><td>North Dakota</td><td>87.72</td><td>34</td><td>Arkansas</td><td>89.43</td></tr>
<tr><td>12</td><td>Ohio</td><td>96.44</td><td>35</td><td>North Dakota</td><td>87.72</td></tr>
<tr><td>23</td><td>Oklahoma</td><td>93.86</td><td>36</td><td>Mississippi</td><td>86.86</td></tr>
<tr><td>25</td><td>Oregon</td><td>93.13</td><td>36</td><td>Wyoming</td><td>86.86</td></tr>
<tr><td>13</td><td>Pennsylvania</td><td>96.00</td><td>38</td><td>South Carolina</td><td>86.11</td></tr>
<tr><td>3</td><td>Rhode Island</td><td>99.95</td><td>39</td><td>Kentucky</td><td>85.54</td></tr>
<tr><td>38</td><td>South Carolina</td><td>86.11</td><td>40</td><td>South Dakota</td><td>85.07</td></tr>
<tr><td>40</td><td>South Dakota</td><td>85.07</td><td>41</td><td>Maine</td><td>83.96</td></tr>
<tr><td>26</td><td>Tennessee</td><td>93.06</td><td>42</td><td>Idaho</td><td>82.68</td></tr>
<tr><td>10</td><td>Texas</td><td>97.18</td><td>43</td><td>Hawaii</td><td>80.35</td></tr>
<tr><td>14</td><td>Utah</td><td>95.68</td><td>44</td><td>Alaska</td><td>79.03</td></tr>
<tr><td>46</td><td>Vermont</td><td>76.20</td><td>45</td><td>West Virginia</td><td>77.40</td></tr>
<tr><td>21</td><td>Virginia</td><td>94.20</td><td>46</td><td>Vermont</td><td>76.20</td></tr>
<tr><td>15</td><td>Washington</td><td>95.65</td><td>47</td><td>Montana</td><td>72.17</td></tr>
<tr><td>45</td><td>West Virginia</td><td>77.40</td><td>NA</td><td>Illinois**</td><td>NA</td></tr>
<tr><td>28</td><td>Wisconsin</td><td>91.87</td><td>NA</td><td>Michigan**</td><td>NA</td></tr>
<tr><td>36</td><td>Wyoming</td><td>86.86</td><td>NA</td><td>Minnesota**</td><td>NA</td></tr>
</table>

District of Columbia   100.00

Source: Morgan Quitno Corporation using data from U.S. Department of Justice, Federal Bureau of Investigation
"Crime in the United States 1993" (Uniform Crime Reports, December 4, 1994)
*Estimated percentages for urban areas, defined by the F.B.I. as Metropolitan Statistical Areas and other cities outside such areas. National percent includes those states listed as not available. Includes murder, rape, robbery, aggravated assault, burglary, larceny-theft and motor vehicle theft.
**Not available.

Crime in Rural Areas in 1993

National Total = 625,282 Crimes*

<table>
<tr><td colspan="4"><u>ALPHA ORDER</u></td><td colspan="4"><u>RANK ORDER</u></td></tr>
<tr><td>RANK</td><td>STATE</td><td>CRIMES</td><td>% of USA</td><td>RANK</td><td>STATE</td><td>CRIMES</td><td>% of USA</td></tr>
<tr><td>27</td><td>Alabama</td><td>9,653</td><td>1.54%</td><td>1</td><td>North Carolina</td><td>39,630</td><td>6.34%</td></tr>
<tr><td>30</td><td>Alaska</td><td>6,994</td><td>1.12%</td><td>2</td><td>Georgia</td><td>34,957</td><td>5.59%</td></tr>
<tr><td>34</td><td>Arizona</td><td>6,107</td><td>0.98%</td><td>3</td><td>Texas</td><td>32,745</td><td>5.24%</td></tr>
<tr><td>20</td><td>Arkansas</td><td>12,331</td><td>1.97%</td><td>4</td><td>South Carolina</td><td>29,882</td><td>4.78%</td></tr>
<tr><td>7</td><td>California</td><td>19,399</td><td>3.10%</td><td>5</td><td>Florida</td><td>29,147</td><td>4.66%</td></tr>
<tr><td>26</td><td>Colorado</td><td>10,024</td><td>1.60%</td><td>6</td><td>New York</td><td>19,533</td><td>3.12%</td></tr>
<tr><td>39</td><td>Connecticut</td><td>3,264</td><td>0.52%</td><td>7</td><td>California</td><td>19,399</td><td>3.10%</td></tr>
<tr><td>41</td><td>Delaware</td><td>2,944</td><td>0.47%</td><td>8</td><td>Tennessee</td><td>18,537</td><td>2.96%</td></tr>
<tr><td>5</td><td>Florida</td><td>29,147</td><td>4.66%</td><td>9</td><td>Kentucky</td><td>17,859</td><td>2.86%</td></tr>
<tr><td>2</td><td>Georgia</td><td>34,957</td><td>5.59%</td><td>10</td><td>Ohio</td><td>17,713</td><td>2.83%</td></tr>
<tr><td>17</td><td>Hawaii</td><td>14,453</td><td>2.31%</td><td>11</td><td>Indiana</td><td>17,488</td><td>2.80%</td></tr>
<tr><td>29</td><td>Idaho</td><td>7,319</td><td>1.17%</td><td>12</td><td>Louisiana</td><td>16,958</td><td>2.71%</td></tr>
<tr><td>NA</td><td>Illinois**</td><td>NA</td><td>NA</td><td>13</td><td>Wisconsin</td><td>16,613</td><td>2.66%</td></tr>
<tr><td>11</td><td>Indiana</td><td>17,488</td><td>2.80%</td><td>14</td><td>Pennsylvania</td><td>15,776</td><td>2.52%</td></tr>
<tr><td>23</td><td>Iowa</td><td>10,549</td><td>1.69%</td><td>15</td><td>Virginia</td><td>15,503</td><td>2.48%</td></tr>
<tr><td>28</td><td>Kansas</td><td>7,650</td><td>1.22%</td><td>16</td><td>Mississippi</td><td>15,343</td><td>2.45%</td></tr>
<tr><td>9</td><td>Kentucky</td><td>17,859</td><td>2.86%</td><td>17</td><td>Hawaii</td><td>14,453</td><td>2.31%</td></tr>
<tr><td>12</td><td>Louisiana</td><td>16,958</td><td>2.71%</td><td>18</td><td>Washington</td><td>13,620</td><td>2.18%</td></tr>
<tr><td>32</td><td>Maine</td><td>6,267</td><td>1.00%</td><td>19</td><td>Missouri</td><td>12,902</td><td>2.06%</td></tr>
<tr><td>31</td><td>Maryland</td><td>6,755</td><td>1.08%</td><td>20</td><td>Arkansas</td><td>12,331</td><td>1.97%</td></tr>
<tr><td>45</td><td>Massachusetts</td><td>124</td><td>0.02%</td><td>21</td><td>Oregon</td><td>12,001</td><td>1.92%</td></tr>
<tr><td>NA</td><td>Michigan**</td><td>NA</td><td>NA</td><td>22</td><td>Montana</td><td>11,185</td><td>1.79%</td></tr>
<tr><td>NA</td><td>Minnesota**</td><td>NA</td><td>NA</td><td>23</td><td>Iowa</td><td>10,549</td><td>1.69%</td></tr>
<tr><td>16</td><td>Mississippi</td><td>15,343</td><td>2.45%</td><td>24</td><td>Oklahoma</td><td>10,497</td><td>1.68%</td></tr>
<tr><td>19</td><td>Missouri</td><td>12,902</td><td>2.06%</td><td>25</td><td>West Virginia</td><td>10,417</td><td>1.67%</td></tr>
<tr><td>22</td><td>Montana</td><td>11,185</td><td>1.79%</td><td>26</td><td>Colorado</td><td>10,024</td><td>1.60%</td></tr>
<tr><td>35</td><td>Nebraska</td><td>5,585</td><td>0.89%</td><td>27</td><td>Alabama</td><td>9,653</td><td>1.54%</td></tr>
<tr><td>33</td><td>Nevada</td><td>6,125</td><td>0.98%</td><td>28</td><td>Kansas</td><td>7,650</td><td>1.22%</td></tr>
<tr><td>44</td><td>New Hampshire</td><td>921</td><td>0.15%</td><td>29</td><td>Idaho</td><td>7,319</td><td>1.17%</td></tr>
<tr><td>47</td><td>New Jersey</td><td>0</td><td>0.00%</td><td>30</td><td>Alaska</td><td>6,994</td><td>1.12%</td></tr>
<tr><td>37</td><td>New Mexico</td><td>5,186</td><td>0.83%</td><td>31</td><td>Maryland</td><td>6,755</td><td>1.08%</td></tr>
<tr><td>6</td><td>New York</td><td>19,533</td><td>3.12%</td><td>32</td><td>Maine</td><td>6,267</td><td>1.00%</td></tr>
<tr><td>1</td><td>North Carolina</td><td>39,630</td><td>6.34%</td><td>33</td><td>Nevada</td><td>6,125</td><td>0.98%</td></tr>
<tr><td>43</td><td>North Dakota</td><td>2,199</td><td>0.35%</td><td>34</td><td>Arizona</td><td>6,107</td><td>0.98%</td></tr>
<tr><td>10</td><td>Ohio</td><td>17,713</td><td>2.83%</td><td>35</td><td>Nebraska</td><td>5,585</td><td>0.89%</td></tr>
<tr><td>24</td><td>Oklahoma</td><td>10,497</td><td>1.68%</td><td>36</td><td>Vermont</td><td>5,446</td><td>0.87%</td></tr>
<tr><td>21</td><td>Oregon</td><td>12,001</td><td>1.92%</td><td>37</td><td>New Mexico</td><td>5,186</td><td>0.83%</td></tr>
<tr><td>14</td><td>Pennsylvania</td><td>15,776</td><td>2.52%</td><td>38</td><td>Utah</td><td>4,213</td><td>0.67%</td></tr>
<tr><td>46</td><td>Rhode Island</td><td>21</td><td>0.00%</td><td>39</td><td>Connecticut</td><td>3,264</td><td>0.52%</td></tr>
<tr><td>4</td><td>South Carolina</td><td>29,882</td><td>4.78%</td><td>40</td><td>South Dakota</td><td>3,157</td><td>0.50%</td></tr>
<tr><td>40</td><td>South Dakota</td><td>3,157</td><td>0.50%</td><td>41</td><td>Delaware</td><td>2,944</td><td>0.47%</td></tr>
<tr><td>8</td><td>Tennessee</td><td>18,537</td><td>2.96%</td><td>42</td><td>Wyoming</td><td>2,570</td><td>0.41%</td></tr>
<tr><td>3</td><td>Texas</td><td>32,745</td><td>5.24%</td><td>43</td><td>North Dakota</td><td>2,199</td><td>0.35%</td></tr>
<tr><td>38</td><td>Utah</td><td>4,213</td><td>0.67%</td><td>44</td><td>New Hampshire</td><td>921</td><td>0.15%</td></tr>
<tr><td>36</td><td>Vermont</td><td>5,446</td><td>0.87%</td><td>45</td><td>Massachusetts</td><td>124</td><td>0.02%</td></tr>
<tr><td>15</td><td>Virginia</td><td>15,503</td><td>2.48%</td><td>46</td><td>Rhode Island</td><td>21</td><td>0.00%</td></tr>
<tr><td>18</td><td>Washington</td><td>13,620</td><td>2.18%</td><td>47</td><td>New Jersey</td><td>0</td><td>0.00%</td></tr>
<tr><td>25</td><td>West Virginia</td><td>10,417</td><td>1.67%</td><td>NA</td><td>Illinois**</td><td>NA</td><td>NA</td></tr>
<tr><td>13</td><td>Wisconsin</td><td>16,613</td><td>2.66%</td><td>NA</td><td>Michigan**</td><td>NA</td><td>NA</td></tr>
<tr><td>42</td><td>Wyoming</td><td>2,570</td><td>0.41%</td><td>NA</td><td>Minnesota**</td><td>NA</td><td>NA</td></tr>
<tr><td colspan="4"></td><td colspan="2">District of Columbia</td><td>0</td><td>0.00%</td></tr>
</table>

Source: Morgan Quitno Corporation using data from U.S. Department of Justice, Federal Bureau of Investigation
    "Crime in the United States 1993" (Uniform Crime Reports, December 4, 1994)
*Estimated totals for rural areas, defined by the F.B.I. as other than Metropolitan Statistical Areas and other cities outside such areas. National total includes those states listed as not available. Includes murder, rape, robbery, aggravated assault, burglary, larceny-theft and motor vehicle theft.
**Not available.

Rural Crime Rate in 1993

National Rate = 1,971.1 Crimes per 100,000 Population*

<table>
<tr><td colspan="3">ALPHA ORDER</td><td colspan="3">RANK ORDER</td></tr>
<tr><td>RANK</td><td>STATE</td><td>RATE</td><td>RANK</td><td>STATE</td><td>RATE</td></tr>
<tr><td>39</td><td>Alabama</td><td>1,225.1</td><td>1</td><td>Hawaii</td><td>5,618.8</td></tr>
<tr><td>4</td><td>Alaska</td><td>3,699.5</td><td>2</td><td>Florida</td><td>3,930.1</td></tr>
<tr><td>21</td><td>Arizona</td><td>2,021.8</td><td>3</td><td>South Carolina</td><td>3,803.7</td></tr>
<tr><td>31</td><td>Arkansas</td><td>1,513.9</td><td>4</td><td>Alaska</td><td>3,699.5</td></tr>
<tr><td>7</td><td>California</td><td>3,144.7</td><td>5</td><td>Nevada</td><td>3,606.4</td></tr>
<tr><td>9</td><td>Colorado</td><td>2,803.7</td><td>6</td><td>Delaware</td><td>3,331.4</td></tr>
<tr><td>25</td><td>Connecticut</td><td>1,709.5</td><td>7</td><td>California</td><td>3,144.7</td></tr>
<tr><td>6</td><td>Delaware</td><td>3,331.4</td><td>8</td><td>Washington</td><td>2,812.1</td></tr>
<tr><td>2</td><td>Florida</td><td>3,930.1</td><td>9</td><td>Colorado</td><td>2,803.7</td></tr>
<tr><td>11</td><td>Georgia</td><td>2,573.5</td><td>10</td><td>Montana</td><td>2,594.4</td></tr>
<tr><td>1</td><td>Hawaii</td><td>5,618.8</td><td>11</td><td>Georgia</td><td>2,573.5</td></tr>
<tr><td>22</td><td>Idaho</td><td>1,909.2</td><td>12</td><td>Maryland</td><td>2,539.2</td></tr>
<tr><td>NA</td><td>Illinois**</td><td>NA</td><td>13</td><td>Oregon</td><td>2,456.7</td></tr>
<tr><td>30</td><td>Indiana</td><td>1,663.6</td><td>14</td><td>North Carolina</td><td>2,416.1</td></tr>
<tr><td>40</td><td>Iowa</td><td>1,179.7</td><td>15</td><td>New York</td><td>2,278.7</td></tr>
<tr><td>28</td><td>Kansas</td><td>1,677.0</td><td>16</td><td>Louisiana</td><td>2,239.8</td></tr>
<tr><td>38</td><td>Kentucky</td><td>1,293.9</td><td>17</td><td>Utah</td><td>2,092.2</td></tr>
<tr><td>16</td><td>Louisiana</td><td>2,239.8</td><td>18</td><td>Wyoming</td><td>2,069.7</td></tr>
<tr><td>23</td><td>Maine</td><td>1,811.3</td><td>19</td><td>Vermont</td><td>2,068.6</td></tr>
<tr><td>12</td><td>Maryland</td><td>2,539.2</td><td>20</td><td>Texas</td><td>2,056.4</td></tr>
<tr><td>43</td><td>Massachusetts</td><td>1,011.6</td><td>21</td><td>Arizona</td><td>2,021.8</td></tr>
<tr><td>NA</td><td>Michigan**</td><td>NA</td><td>22</td><td>Idaho</td><td>1,909.2</td></tr>
<tr><td>NA</td><td>Minnesota**</td><td>NA</td><td>23</td><td>Maine</td><td>1,811.3</td></tr>
<tr><td>36</td><td>Mississippi</td><td>1,335.6</td><td>24</td><td>New Mexico</td><td>1,769.1</td></tr>
<tr><td>41</td><td>Missouri</td><td>1,097.1</td><td>25</td><td>Connecticut</td><td>1,709.5</td></tr>
<tr><td>10</td><td>Montana</td><td>2,594.4</td><td>26</td><td>Wisconsin</td><td>1,685.7</td></tr>
<tr><td>34</td><td>Nebraska</td><td>1,350.6</td><td>27</td><td>Oklahoma</td><td>1,677.7</td></tr>
<tr><td>5</td><td>Nevada</td><td>3,606.4</td><td>28</td><td>Kansas</td><td>1,677.0</td></tr>
<tr><td>45</td><td>New Hampshire</td><td>655.4</td><td>29</td><td>Tennessee</td><td>1,671.6</td></tr>
<tr><td>NA</td><td>New Jersey**</td><td>NA</td><td>30</td><td>Indiana</td><td>1,663.6</td></tr>
<tr><td>24</td><td>New Mexico</td><td>1,769.1</td><td>31</td><td>Arkansas</td><td>1,513.9</td></tr>
<tr><td>15</td><td>New York</td><td>2,278.7</td><td>32</td><td>Pennsylvania</td><td>1,482.9</td></tr>
<tr><td>14</td><td>North Carolina</td><td>2,416.1</td><td>33</td><td>Virginia</td><td>1,479.2</td></tr>
<tr><td>44</td><td>North Dakota</td><td>972.0</td><td>34</td><td>Nebraska</td><td>1,350.6</td></tr>
<tr><td>35</td><td>Ohio</td><td>1,347.2</td><td>35</td><td>Ohio</td><td>1,347.2</td></tr>
<tr><td>27</td><td>Oklahoma</td><td>1,677.7</td><td>36</td><td>Mississippi</td><td>1,335.6</td></tr>
<tr><td>13</td><td>Oregon</td><td>2,456.7</td><td>37</td><td>West Virginia</td><td>1,333.3</td></tr>
<tr><td>32</td><td>Pennsylvania</td><td>1,482.9</td><td>38</td><td>Kentucky</td><td>1,293.9</td></tr>
<tr><td>46</td><td>Rhode Island</td><td>0.0</td><td>39</td><td>Alabama</td><td>1,225.1</td></tr>
<tr><td>3</td><td>South Carolina</td><td>3,803.7</td><td>40</td><td>Iowa</td><td>1,179.7</td></tr>
<tr><td>42</td><td>South Dakota</td><td>1,087.0</td><td>41</td><td>Missouri</td><td>1,097.1</td></tr>
<tr><td>29</td><td>Tennessee</td><td>1,671.6</td><td>42</td><td>South Dakota</td><td>1,087.0</td></tr>
<tr><td>20</td><td>Texas</td><td>2,056.4</td><td>43</td><td>Massachusetts</td><td>1,011.6</td></tr>
<tr><td>17</td><td>Utah</td><td>2,092.2</td><td>44</td><td>North Dakota</td><td>972.0</td></tr>
<tr><td>19</td><td>Vermont</td><td>2,068.6</td><td>45</td><td>New Hampshire</td><td>655.4</td></tr>
<tr><td>33</td><td>Virginia</td><td>1,479.2</td><td>46</td><td>Rhode Island</td><td>0.0</td></tr>
<tr><td>8</td><td>Washington</td><td>2,812.1</td><td>NA</td><td>Illinois**</td><td>NA</td></tr>
<tr><td>37</td><td>West Virginia</td><td>1,333.3</td><td>NA</td><td>Michigan**</td><td>NA</td></tr>
<tr><td>26</td><td>Wisconsin</td><td>1,685.7</td><td>NA</td><td>Minnesota**</td><td>NA</td></tr>
<tr><td>18</td><td>Wyoming</td><td>2,069.7</td><td>NA</td><td>New Jersey**</td><td>NA</td></tr>
<tr><td></td><td></td><td></td><td></td><td>District of Columbia**</td><td>NA</td></tr>
</table>

Source: U.S. Department of Justice, Federal Bureau of Investigation
   "Crime in the United States 1993" (Uniform Crime Reports, December 4, 1994)
*Estimated rates for rural areas, defined by the F.B.I. as other than Metropolitan Statistical Areas and other cities outside such areas. National rate includes those states listed as not available. Includes murder, rape, robbery, aggravated assault, burglary, larceny-theft and motor vehicle theft.
**Not available.   369

Percent of Crimes Occurring in Rural Areas in 1993

National Percent = 4.42% of Crimes*

<table>
<tr><td colspan="3"><u>ALPHA ORDER</u></td><td colspan="3"><u>RANK ORDER</u></td></tr>
<tr><td>RANK</td><td>STATE</td><td>PERCENT</td><td>RANK</td><td>STATE</td><td>PERCENT</td></tr>
<tr><td>32</td><td>Alabama</td><td>4.73</td><td>1</td><td>Montana</td><td>27.83</td></tr>
<tr><td>4</td><td>Alaska</td><td>20.97</td><td>2</td><td>Vermont</td><td>23.80</td></tr>
<tr><td>42</td><td>Arizona</td><td>2.09</td><td>3</td><td>West Virginia</td><td>22.60</td></tr>
<tr><td>14</td><td>Arkansas</td><td>10.57</td><td>4</td><td>Alaska</td><td>20.97</td></tr>
<tr><td>44</td><td>California</td><td>0.96</td><td>5</td><td>Hawaii</td><td>19.65</td></tr>
<tr><td>30</td><td>Colorado</td><td>5.09</td><td>6</td><td>Idaho</td><td>17.32</td></tr>
<tr><td>41</td><td>Connecticut</td><td>2.14</td><td>7</td><td>Maine</td><td>16.04</td></tr>
<tr><td>17</td><td>Delaware</td><td>8.63</td><td>8</td><td>South Dakota</td><td>14.93</td></tr>
<tr><td>39</td><td>Florida</td><td>2.55</td><td>9</td><td>Kentucky</td><td>14.46</td></tr>
<tr><td>19</td><td>Georgia</td><td>8.16</td><td>10</td><td>South Carolina</td><td>13.89</td></tr>
<tr><td>5</td><td>Hawaii</td><td>19.65</td><td>11</td><td>Mississippi</td><td>13.14</td></tr>
<tr><td>6</td><td>Idaho</td><td>17.32</td><td>11</td><td>Wyoming</td><td>13.14</td></tr>
<tr><td>NA</td><td>Illinois**</td><td>NA</td><td>13</td><td>North Dakota</td><td>12.28</td></tr>
<tr><td>24</td><td>Indiana</td><td>6.86</td><td>14</td><td>Arkansas</td><td>10.57</td></tr>
<tr><td>16</td><td>Iowa</td><td>9.75</td><td>15</td><td>North Carolina</td><td>10.10</td></tr>
<tr><td>26</td><td>Kansas</td><td>6.08</td><td>16</td><td>Iowa</td><td>9.75</td></tr>
<tr><td>9</td><td>Kentucky</td><td>14.46</td><td>17</td><td>Delaware</td><td>8.63</td></tr>
<tr><td>28</td><td>Louisiana</td><td>5.77</td><td>18</td><td>Nebraska</td><td>8.44</td></tr>
<tr><td>7</td><td>Maine</td><td>16.04</td><td>19</td><td>Georgia</td><td>8.16</td></tr>
<tr><td>40</td><td>Maryland</td><td>2.23</td><td>20</td><td>Wisconsin</td><td>8.13</td></tr>
<tr><td>46</td><td>Massachusetts</td><td>0.04</td><td>21</td><td>Nevada</td><td>7.14</td></tr>
<tr><td>NA</td><td>Michigan**</td><td>NA</td><td>22</td><td>Tennessee</td><td>6.94</td></tr>
<tr><td>NA</td><td>Minnesota**</td><td>NA</td><td>23</td><td>Oregon</td><td>6.87</td></tr>
<tr><td>11</td><td>Mississippi</td><td>13.14</td><td>24</td><td>Indiana</td><td>6.86</td></tr>
<tr><td>31</td><td>Missouri</td><td>4.84</td><td>25</td><td>Oklahoma</td><td>6.14</td></tr>
<tr><td>1</td><td>Montana</td><td>27.83</td><td>26</td><td>Kansas</td><td>6.08</td></tr>
<tr><td>18</td><td>Nebraska</td><td>8.44</td><td>27</td><td>Virginia</td><td>5.80</td></tr>
<tr><td>21</td><td>Nevada</td><td>7.14</td><td>28</td><td>Louisiana</td><td>5.77</td></tr>
<tr><td>37</td><td>New Hampshire</td><td>2.82</td><td>29</td><td>New Mexico</td><td>5.12</td></tr>
<tr><td>47</td><td>New Jersey</td><td>0.00</td><td>30</td><td>Colorado</td><td>5.09</td></tr>
<tr><td>29</td><td>New Mexico</td><td>5.12</td><td>31</td><td>Missouri</td><td>4.84</td></tr>
<tr><td>43</td><td>New York</td><td>1.93</td><td>32</td><td>Alabama</td><td>4.73</td></tr>
<tr><td>15</td><td>North Carolina</td><td>10.10</td><td>33</td><td>Washington</td><td>4.35</td></tr>
<tr><td>13</td><td>North Dakota</td><td>12.28</td><td>34</td><td>Utah</td><td>4.32</td></tr>
<tr><td>36</td><td>Ohio</td><td>3.56</td><td>35</td><td>Pennsylvania</td><td>4.00</td></tr>
<tr><td>25</td><td>Oklahoma</td><td>6.14</td><td>36</td><td>Ohio</td><td>3.56</td></tr>
<tr><td>23</td><td>Oregon</td><td>6.87</td><td>37</td><td>New Hampshire</td><td>2.82</td></tr>
<tr><td>35</td><td>Pennsylvania</td><td>4.00</td><td>37</td><td>Texas</td><td>2.82</td></tr>
<tr><td>45</td><td>Rhode Island</td><td>0.05</td><td>39</td><td>Florida</td><td>2.55</td></tr>
<tr><td>10</td><td>South Carolina</td><td>13.89</td><td>40</td><td>Maryland</td><td>2.23</td></tr>
<tr><td>8</td><td>South Dakota</td><td>14.93</td><td>41</td><td>Connecticut</td><td>2.14</td></tr>
<tr><td>22</td><td>Tennessee</td><td>6.94</td><td>42</td><td>Arizona</td><td>2.09</td></tr>
<tr><td>37</td><td>Texas</td><td>2.82</td><td>43</td><td>New York</td><td>1.93</td></tr>
<tr><td>34</td><td>Utah</td><td>4.32</td><td>44</td><td>California</td><td>0.96</td></tr>
<tr><td>2</td><td>Vermont</td><td>23.80</td><td>45</td><td>Rhode Island</td><td>0.05</td></tr>
<tr><td>27</td><td>Virginia</td><td>5.80</td><td>46</td><td>Massachusetts</td><td>0.04</td></tr>
<tr><td>33</td><td>Washington</td><td>4.35</td><td>47</td><td>New Jersey</td><td>0.00</td></tr>
<tr><td>3</td><td>West Virginia</td><td>22.60</td><td>NA</td><td>Illinois**</td><td>NA</td></tr>
<tr><td>20</td><td>Wisconsin</td><td>8.13</td><td>NA</td><td>Michigan**</td><td>NA</td></tr>
<tr><td>11</td><td>Wyoming</td><td>13.14</td><td>NA</td><td>Minnesota**</td><td>NA</td></tr>
<tr><td></td><td></td><td></td><td></td><td>District of Columbia</td><td>0.00</td></tr>
</table>

Source: Morgan Quitno Corporation using data from U.S. Department of Justice, Federal Bureau of Investigation
"Crime in the United States 1993" (Uniform Crime Reports, December 4, 1994)
*Estimated percentages for rural areas, defined by the F.B.I. as other than Metropolitan Statistical Areas and other cities outside such areas. National percent includes those states listed as not available. Includes murder, rape, robbery, aggravated assault, burglary, larceny-theft and motor vehicle theft.
**Not available.

Violent Crime in Urban Areas in 1993

National Total = 1,853,652 Violent Crimes*

<u>ALPHA ORDER</u>

RANK	STATE	CRIMES	% of USA
16	Alabama	31,176	1.68%
37	Alaska	3,462	0.19%
17	Arizona	27,361	1.48%
27	Arkansas	13,293	0.72%
1	California	333,943	18.02%
21	Colorado	19,483	1.05%
23	Connecticut	14,409	0.78%
35	Delaware	4,237	0.23%
3	Florida	160,619	8.67%
10	Georgia	45,858	2.47%
39	Hawaii	2,586	0.14%
40	Idaho	2,358	0.13%
NA	Illinois**	NA	NA
19	Indiana	25,704	1.39%
32	Iowa	8,648	0.47%
29	Kansas	11,833	0.64%
25	Kentucky	14,228	0.77%
12	Louisiana	42,172	2.28%
42	Maine	1,314	0.07%
8	Maryland	48,560	2.62%
9	Massachusetts	48,336	2.61%
NA	Michigan**	NA	NA
NA	Minnesota**	NA	NA
31	Mississippi	9,442	0.51%
13	Missouri	37,019	2.00%
45	Montana	827	0.04%
34	Nebraska	5,189	0.28%
30	Nevada	10,879	0.59%
41	New Hampshire	1,467	0.08%
6	New Jersey	49,390	2.66%
26	New Mexico	14,047	0.76%
2	New York	193,351	10.43%
11	North Carolina	43,030	2.32%
47	North Dakota	443	0.02%
5	Ohio	54,626	2.95%
22	Oklahoma	19,209	1.04%
24	Oregon	14,266	0.77%
7	Pennsylvania	48,979	2.64%
36	Rhode Island	4,016	0.22%
15	South Carolina	31,769	1.71%
43	South Dakota	1,241	0.07%
14	Tennessee	36,816	1.99%
4	Texas	132,951	7.17%
33	Utah	5,246	0.28%
46	Vermont	474	0.03%
20	Virginia	22,585	1.22%
18	Washington	26,139	1.41%
38	West Virginia	2,897	0.16%
28	Wisconsin	12,448	0.67%
44	Wyoming	1,034	0.06%

<u>RANK ORDER</u>

RANK	STATE	CRIMES	% of USA
1	California	333,943	18.02%
2	New York	193,351	10.43%
3	Florida	160,619	8.67%
4	Texas	132,951	7.17%
5	Ohio	54,626	2.95%
6	New Jersey	49,390	2.66%
7	Pennsylvania	48,979	2.64%
8	Maryland	48,560	2.62%
9	Massachusetts	48,336	2.61%
10	Georgia	45,858	2.47%
11	North Carolina	43,030	2.32%
12	Louisiana	42,172	2.28%
13	Missouri	37,019	2.00%
14	Tennessee	36,816	1.99%
15	South Carolina	31,769	1.71%
16	Alabama	31,176	1.68%
17	Arizona	27,361	1.48%
18	Washington	26,139	1.41%
19	Indiana	25,704	1.39%
20	Virginia	22,585	1.22%
21	Colorado	19,483	1.05%
22	Oklahoma	19,209	1.04%
23	Connecticut	14,409	0.78%
24	Oregon	14,266	0.77%
25	Kentucky	14,228	0.77%
26	New Mexico	14,047	0.76%
27	Arkansas	13,293	0.72%
28	Wisconsin	12,448	0.67%
29	Kansas	11,833	0.64%
30	Nevada	10,879	0.59%
31	Mississippi	9,442	0.51%
32	Iowa	8,648	0.47%
33	Utah	5,246	0.28%
34	Nebraska	5,189	0.28%
35	Delaware	4,237	0.23%
36	Rhode Island	4,016	0.22%
37	Alaska	3,462	0.19%
38	West Virginia	2,897	0.16%
39	Hawaii	2,586	0.14%
40	Idaho	2,358	0.13%
41	New Hampshire	1,467	0.08%
42	Maine	1,314	0.07%
43	South Dakota	1,241	0.07%
44	Wyoming	1,034	0.06%
45	Montana	827	0.04%
46	Vermont	474	0.03%
47	North Dakota	443	0.02%
NA	Illinois**	NA	NA
NA	Michigan**	NA	NA
NA	Minnesota**	NA	NA
	District of Columbia	16,888	0.91%

Source: U.S. Department of Justice, Federal Bureau of Investigation
   "Crime in the United States 1993" (Uniform Crime Reports, December 4, 1994)
*Estimated totals for urban areas, defined by the F.B.I. as Metropolitan Statistical Areas and other cities outside such areas. National total includes those states listed as not available. Violent crimes are offenses of murder, forcible rape, robbery and aggravated assault.
**Not available.

Urban Violent Crime Rate in 1993

National Urban Rate = 819.5 Violent Crimes per 100,000 Population*

<u>ALPHA ORDER</u>   <u>RANK ORDER</u>

RANK	STATE	RATE		RANK	STATE	RATE
9	Alabama	917.2		1	Florida	1,241.5
12	Alaska	844.5		2	Louisiana	1,192.0
18	Arizona	752.9		3	New York	1,115.1
13	Arkansas	825.9		4	South Carolina	1,111.8
5	California	1,091.5		5	California	1,091.5
23	Colorado	607.2		6	New Mexico	1,061.9
30	Connecticut	466.9		7	Maryland	1,033.4
20	Delaware	692.7		8	Tennessee	922.7
1	Florida	1,241.5		9	Alabama	917.2
14	Georgia	825.0		10	Missouri	912.2
41	Hawaii	282.7		11	Nevada	892.3
36	Idaho	329.5		12	Alaska	844.5
NA	Illinois**	NA		13	Arkansas	825.9
28	Indiana	551.4		14	Georgia	825.0
31	Iowa	450.5		15	North Carolina	811.2
25	Kansas	570.3		16	Texas	808.8
24	Kentucky	590.7		17	Massachusetts	805.6
2	Louisiana	1,192.0		18	Arizona	752.9
46	Maine	147.1		19	Oklahoma	737.3
7	Maryland	1,033.4		20	Delaware	692.7
17	Massachusetts	805.6		21	Mississippi	631.9
NA	Michigan**	NA		22	New Jersey	626.9
NA	Minnesota**	NA		23	Colorado	607.2
21	Mississippi	631.9		24	Kentucky	590.7
10	Missouri	912.2		25	Kansas	570.3
43	Montana	202.8		26	Oregon	560.9
33	Nebraska	434.8		27	Ohio	558.8
11	Nevada	892.3		28	Indiana	551.4
45	New Hampshire	149.0		29	Washington	547.9
22	New Jersey	626.9		30	Connecticut	466.9
6	New Mexico	1,061.9		31	Iowa	450.5
3	New York	1,115.1		32	Pennsylvania	445.9
15	North Carolina	811.2		33	Nebraska	434.8
47	North Dakota	108.4		34	Virginia	414.9
27	Ohio	558.8		35	Rhode Island	401.6
19	Oklahoma	737.3		36	Idaho	329.5
26	Oregon	560.9		37	Utah	316.3
32	Pennsylvania	445.9		38	Wisconsin	307.2
35	Rhode Island	401.6		39	Wyoming	299.0
4	South Carolina	1,111.8		40	South Dakota	292.3
40	South Dakota	292.3		41	Hawaii	282.7
8	Tennessee	922.7		42	West Virginia	278.9
16	Texas	808.8		43	Montana	202.8
37	Utah	316.3		44	Vermont	151.6
44	Vermont	151.6		45	New Hampshire	149.0
34	Virginia	414.9		46	Maine	147.1
29	Washington	547.9		47	North Dakota	108.4
42	West Virginia	278.9		NA	Illinois**	NA
38	Wisconsin	307.2		NA	Michigan**	NA
39	Wyoming	299.0		NA	Minnesota**	NA

District of Columbia   2,921.8

*Source: Morgan Quitno Corporation using data from U.S. Department of Justice, Federal Bureau of Investigation
"Crime in the United States 1993" (Uniform Crime Reports, December 4, 1994)*

*Estimated rates for urban areas, defined by the F.B.I. as Metropolitan Statistical Areas and other cities outside such
areas. National rate includes those states listed as not available. Violent crimes are offenses of murder, forcible rape,
robbery and aggravated assault.*

**Not available.

372

Percent of Violent Crime Occurring in Urban Areas in 1993

National Percent = 96.33% of Violent Crimes*

ALPHA ORDER				RANK ORDER		
RANK	STATE	PERCENT		RANK	STATE	PERCENT
15	Alabama	95.41		1	New Jersey	100.00
45	Alaska	75.97		2	Rhode Island	99.98
10	Arizona	97.22		3	Massachusetts	99.88
29	Arkansas	92.43		4	California	99.28
4	California	99.28		5	New York	98.98
14	Colorado	96.31		6	Maryland	98.02
13	Connecticut	96.39		7	Ohio	97.69
34	Delaware	88.25		8	Pennsylvania	97.38
9	Florida	97.36		9	Florida	97.36
31	Georgia	91.68		10	Arizona	97.22
37	Hawaii	84.48		11	Texas	96.75
44	Idaho	76.14		12	Washington	96.67
NA	Illinois**	NA		13	Connecticut	96.39
30	Indiana	91.99		14	Colorado	96.31
19	Iowa	94.42		15	Alabama	95.41
21	Kansas	94.18		16	Nebraska	95.21
41	Kentucky	81.16		17	Missouri	95.01
28	Louisiana	92.48		18	New Hampshire	94.65
38	Maine	84.34		19	Iowa	94.42
6	Maryland	98.02		20	Tennessee	94.29
3	Massachusetts	99.88		21	Kansas	94.18
NA	Michigan**	NA		22	Utah	93.70
NA	Minnesota**	NA		23	Oklahoma	93.65
40	Mississippi	82.34		24	Oregon	93.52
17	Missouri	95.01		25	New Mexico	93.50
47	Montana	55.54		26	Virginia	93.48
16	Nebraska	95.21		27	Wisconsin	93.45
33	Nevada	89.49		28	Louisiana	92.48
18	New Hampshire	94.65		29	Arkansas	92.43
1	New Jersey	100.00		30	Indiana	91.99
25	New Mexico	93.50		31	Georgia	91.68
5	New York	98.98		32	North Carolina	91.21
32	North Carolina	91.21		33	Nevada	89.49
36	North Dakota	84.87		34	Delaware	88.25
7	Ohio	97.69		35	South Carolina	85.21
23	Oklahoma	93.65		36	North Dakota	84.87
24	Oregon	93.52		37	Hawaii	84.48
8	Pennsylvania	97.38		38	Maine	84.34
2	Rhode Island	99.98		39	South Dakota	83.29
35	South Carolina	85.21		40	Mississippi	82.34
39	South Dakota	83.29		41	Kentucky	81.16
20	Tennessee	94.29		42	Wyoming	76.88
11	Texas	96.75		43	West Virginia	76.38
22	Utah	93.70		44	Idaho	76.14
46	Vermont	72.04		45	Alaska	75.97
26	Virginia	93.48		46	Vermont	72.04
12	Washington	96.67		47	Montana	55.54
43	West Virginia	76.38		NA	Illinois**	NA
27	Wisconsin	93.45		NA	Michigan**	NA
42	Wyoming	76.88		NA	Minnesota**	NA
					District of Columbia	100.00

Source: Morgan Quitno Corporation using data from U.S. Department of Justice, Federal Bureau of Investigation
   "Crime in the United States 1993" (Uniform Crime Reports, December 4, 1994)
Estimated percentages for urban areas, defined by the F.B.I. as Metropolitan Statistical Areas and other cities outside such areas. National percent includes those states listed as not available. Violent crimes are offenses of murder, forcible rape, robbery and aggravated assault.
**Not available.

Violent Crime in Rural Areas in 1993

National Total = 70,536 Violent Crimes*

ALPHA ORDER

RANK	STATE	CRIMES	% of USA
15	Alabama	1,500	2.13%
20	Alaska	1,095	1.55%
28	Arizona	781	1.11%
21	Arkansas	1,088	1.54%
8	California	2,438	3.46%
29	Colorado	746	1.06%
34	Connecticut	540	0.77%
33	Delaware	564	0.80%
3	Florida	4,356	6.18%
4	Georgia	4,161	5.90%
36	Hawaii	475	0.67%
30	Idaho	739	1.05%
NA	Illinois**	NA	NA
9	Indiana	2,237	3.17%
35	Iowa	511	0.72%
31	Kansas	731	1.04%
7	Kentucky	3,302	4.68%
6	Louisiana	3,428	4.86%
41	Maine	244	0.35%
23	Maryland	980	1.39%
45	Massachusetts	57	0.08%
NA	Michigan**	NA	NA
NA	Minnesota**	NA	NA
11	Mississippi	2,025	2.87%
13	Missouri	1,944	2.76%
32	Montana	662	0.94%
39	Nebraska	261	0.37%
19	Nevada	1,278	1.81%
43	New Hampshire	83	0.12%
47	New Jersey	0	0.00%
24	New Mexico	977	1.39%
12	New York	2,001	2.84%
5	North Carolina	4,148	5.88%
44	North Dakota	79	0.11%
18	Ohio	1,289	1.83%
17	Oklahoma	1,303	1.85%
22	Oregon	988	1.40%
16	Pennsylvania	1,316	1.87%
46	Rhode Island	1	0.00%
1	South Carolina	5,512	7.81%
40	South Dakota	249	0.35%
10	Tennessee	2,231	3.16%
2	Texas	4,468	6.33%
37	Utah	353	0.50%
42	Vermont	184	0.26%
14	Virginia	1,575	2.23%
25	Washington	901	1.28%
26	West Virginia	896	1.27%
27	Wisconsin	873	1.24%
38	Wyoming	311	0.44%

RANK ORDER

RANK	STATE	CRIMES	% of USA
1	South Carolina	5,512	7.81%
2	Texas	4,468	6.33%
3	Florida	4,356	6.18%
4	Georgia	4,161	5.90%
5	North Carolina	4,148	5.88%
6	Louisiana	3,428	4.86%
7	Kentucky	3,302	4.68%
8	California	2,438	3.46%
9	Indiana	2,237	3.17%
10	Tennessee	2,231	3.16%
11	Mississippi	2,025	2.87%
12	New York	2,001	2.84%
13	Missouri	1,944	2.76%
14	Virginia	1,575	2.23%
15	Alabama	1,500	2.13%
16	Pennsylvania	1,316	1.87%
17	Oklahoma	1,303	1.85%
18	Ohio	1,289	1.83%
19	Nevada	1,278	1.81%
20	Alaska	1,095	1.55%
21	Arkansas	1,088	1.54%
22	Oregon	988	1.40%
23	Maryland	980	1.39%
24	New Mexico	977	1.39%
25	Washington	901	1.28%
26	West Virginia	896	1.27%
27	Wisconsin	873	1.24%
28	Arizona	781	1.11%
29	Colorado	746	1.06%
30	Idaho	739	1.05%
31	Kansas	731	1.04%
32	Montana	662	0.94%
33	Delaware	564	0.80%
34	Connecticut	540	0.77%
35	Iowa	511	0.72%
36	Hawaii	475	0.67%
37	Utah	353	0.50%
38	Wyoming	311	0.44%
39	Nebraska	261	0.37%
40	South Dakota	249	0.35%
41	Maine	244	0.35%
42	Vermont	184	0.26%
43	New Hampshire	83	0.12%
44	North Dakota	79	0.11%
45	Massachusetts	57	0.08%
46	Rhode Island	1	0.00%
47	New Jersey	0	0.00%
NA	Illinois**	NA	NA
NA	Michigan**	NA	NA
NA	Minnesota**	NA	NA

District of Columbia	0	0.00%

Source: Morgan Quitno Corporation using data from U.S. Department of Justice, Federal Bureau of Investigation
"Crime in the United States 1993" (Uniform Crime Reports, December 4, 1994)
*Estimated totals for rural areas, defined by the F.B.I. as other than Metropolitan Statistical Areas and other cities outside such areas. National total includes those states listed as not available. Violent crimes are offenses of murder, forcible rape, robbery and aggravated assault.
**Not available.

Rural Violent Crime Rate in 1993

National Rural Rate = 222.4 Violent Crimes per 100,000 Population*

ALPHA ORDER			RANK ORDER		
RANK	STATE	RATE	RANK	STATE	RATE
25	Alabama	190.4	1	Nevada	752.5
5	Alaska	579.2	2	South Carolina	701.6
14	Arizona	258.6	3	Delaware	638.2
34	Arkansas	133.6	4	Florida	587.4
8	California	395.2	5	Alaska	579.2
20	Colorado	208.7	6	Massachusetts	465.0
12	Connecticut	282.8	7	Louisiana	452.8
3	Delaware	638.2	8	California	395.2
4	Florida	587.4	9	Maryland	368.4
11	Georgia	306.3	10	New Mexico	333.3
27	Hawaii	184.7	11	Georgia	306.3
24	Idaho	192.8	12	Connecticut	282.8
NA	Illinois**	NA	13	Texas	280.6
19	Indiana	212.8	14	Arizona	258.6
44	Iowa	57.1	15	North Carolina	252.9
31	Kansas	160.2	16	Wyoming	250.5
17	Kentucky	239.2	17	Kentucky	239.2
7	Louisiana	452.8	18	New York	233.4
40	Maine	70.5	19	Indiana	212.8
9	Maryland	368.4	20	Colorado	208.7
6	Massachusetts	465.0	21	Oklahoma	208.3
NA	Michigan**	NA	22	Oregon	202.3
NA	Minnesota**	NA	23	Tennessee	201.2
28	Mississippi	176.3	24	Idaho	192.8
30	Missouri	165.3	25	Alabama	190.4
32	Montana	153.6	26	Washington	186.0
42	Nebraska	63.1	27	Hawaii	184.7
1	Nevada	752.5	28	Mississippi	176.3
43	New Hampshire	59.1	29	Utah	175.3
46	New Jersey	0.0	30	Missouri	165.3
10	New Mexico	333.3	31	Kansas	160.2
18	New York	233.4	32	Montana	153.6
15	North Carolina	252.9	33	Virginia	150.3
45	North Dakota	34.9	34	Arkansas	133.6
37	Ohio	98.0	35	Pennsylvania	123.7
21	Oklahoma	208.3	36	West Virginia	114.7
22	Oregon	202.3	37	Ohio	98.0
35	Pennsylvania	123.7	38	Wisconsin	88.6
46	Rhode Island	0.0	39	South Dakota	85.7
2	South Carolina	701.6	40	Maine	70.5
39	South Dakota	85.7	41	Vermont	69.9
23	Tennessee	201.2	42	Nebraska	63.1
13	Texas	280.6	43	New Hampshire	59.1
29	Utah	175.3	44	Iowa	57.1
41	Vermont	69.9	45	North Dakota	34.9
33	Virginia	150.3	46	New Jersey	0.0
26	Washington	186.0	46	Rhode Island	0.0
36	West Virginia	114.7	NA	Illinois**	NA
38	Wisconsin	88.6	NA	Michigan**	NA
16	Wyoming	250.5	NA	Minnesota**	NA

District of Columbia   0.0

Source: Morgan Quitno Corporation using data from U.S. Department of Justice, Federal Bureau of Investigation
"Crime in the United States 1993" (Uniform Crime Reports, December 4, 1994)
*Estimated rates for rural areas, defined by the F.B.I. as other than Metropolitan Statistical Areas and other cities outside such areas. National rate includes those states listed as not available. Violent crimes are offenses of murder, forcible rape, robbery and aggravated assault.
**Not available.

Percent of Violent Crime Occurring in Rural Areas in 1993

National Percent = 3.67% of Violent Crimes*

<table>
<tr><td colspan="3"><u>ALPHA ORDER</u></td><td colspan="3"><u>RANK ORDER</u></td></tr>
<tr><th>RANK</th><th>STATE</th><th>PERCENT</th><th>RANK</th><th>STATE</th><th>PERCENT</th></tr>
<tr><td>33</td><td>Alabama</td><td>4.59</td><td>1</td><td>Montana</td><td>44.46</td></tr>
<tr><td>3</td><td>Alaska</td><td>24.03</td><td>2</td><td>Vermont</td><td>27.96</td></tr>
<tr><td>38</td><td>Arizona</td><td>2.78</td><td>3</td><td>Alaska</td><td>24.03</td></tr>
<tr><td>19</td><td>Arkansas</td><td>7.57</td><td>4</td><td>Idaho</td><td>23.86</td></tr>
<tr><td>44</td><td>California</td><td>0.72</td><td>5</td><td>West Virginia</td><td>23.62</td></tr>
<tr><td>34</td><td>Colorado</td><td>3.69</td><td>6</td><td>Wyoming</td><td>23.12</td></tr>
<tr><td>35</td><td>Connecticut</td><td>3.61</td><td>7</td><td>Kentucky</td><td>18.84</td></tr>
<tr><td>14</td><td>Delaware</td><td>11.75</td><td>8</td><td>Mississippi</td><td>17.66</td></tr>
<tr><td>39</td><td>Florida</td><td>2.64</td><td>9</td><td>South Dakota</td><td>16.71</td></tr>
<tr><td>17</td><td>Georgia</td><td>8.32</td><td>10</td><td>Maine</td><td>15.66</td></tr>
<tr><td>11</td><td>Hawaii</td><td>15.52</td><td>11</td><td>Hawaii</td><td>15.52</td></tr>
<tr><td>4</td><td>Idaho</td><td>23.86</td><td>12</td><td>North Dakota</td><td>15.13</td></tr>
<tr><td>NA</td><td>Illinois**</td><td>NA</td><td>13</td><td>South Carolina</td><td>14.79</td></tr>
<tr><td>18</td><td>Indiana</td><td>8.01</td><td>14</td><td>Delaware</td><td>11.75</td></tr>
<tr><td>29</td><td>Iowa</td><td>5.58</td><td>15</td><td>Nevada</td><td>10.51</td></tr>
<tr><td>27</td><td>Kansas</td><td>5.82</td><td>16</td><td>North Carolina</td><td>8.79</td></tr>
<tr><td>7</td><td>Kentucky</td><td>18.84</td><td>17</td><td>Georgia</td><td>8.32</td></tr>
<tr><td>20</td><td>Louisiana</td><td>7.52</td><td>18</td><td>Indiana</td><td>8.01</td></tr>
<tr><td>10</td><td>Maine</td><td>15.66</td><td>19</td><td>Arkansas</td><td>7.57</td></tr>
<tr><td>42</td><td>Maryland</td><td>1.98</td><td>20</td><td>Louisiana</td><td>7.52</td></tr>
<tr><td>45</td><td>Massachusetts</td><td>0.12</td><td>21</td><td>Wisconsin</td><td>6.55</td></tr>
<tr><td>NA</td><td>Michigan**</td><td>NA</td><td>22</td><td>Virginia</td><td>6.52</td></tr>
<tr><td>NA</td><td>Minnesota**</td><td>NA</td><td>23</td><td>New Mexico</td><td>6.50</td></tr>
<tr><td>8</td><td>Mississippi</td><td>17.66</td><td>24</td><td>Oregon</td><td>6.48</td></tr>
<tr><td>31</td><td>Missouri</td><td>4.99</td><td>25</td><td>Oklahoma</td><td>6.35</td></tr>
<tr><td>1</td><td>Montana</td><td>44.46</td><td>26</td><td>Utah</td><td>6.30</td></tr>
<tr><td>32</td><td>Nebraska</td><td>4.79</td><td>27</td><td>Kansas</td><td>5.82</td></tr>
<tr><td>15</td><td>Nevada</td><td>10.51</td><td>28</td><td>Tennessee</td><td>5.71</td></tr>
<tr><td>30</td><td>New Hampshire</td><td>5.35</td><td>29</td><td>Iowa</td><td>5.58</td></tr>
<tr><td>47</td><td>New Jersey</td><td>0.00</td><td>30</td><td>New Hampshire</td><td>5.35</td></tr>
<tr><td>23</td><td>New Mexico</td><td>6.50</td><td>31</td><td>Missouri</td><td>4.99</td></tr>
<tr><td>43</td><td>New York</td><td>1.02</td><td>32</td><td>Nebraska</td><td>4.79</td></tr>
<tr><td>16</td><td>North Carolina</td><td>8.79</td><td>33</td><td>Alabama</td><td>4.59</td></tr>
<tr><td>12</td><td>North Dakota</td><td>15.13</td><td>34</td><td>Colorado</td><td>3.69</td></tr>
<tr><td>41</td><td>Ohio</td><td>2.31</td><td>35</td><td>Connecticut</td><td>3.61</td></tr>
<tr><td>25</td><td>Oklahoma</td><td>6.35</td><td>36</td><td>Washington</td><td>3.33</td></tr>
<tr><td>24</td><td>Oregon</td><td>6.48</td><td>37</td><td>Texas</td><td>3.25</td></tr>
<tr><td>40</td><td>Pennsylvania</td><td>2.62</td><td>38</td><td>Arizona</td><td>2.78</td></tr>
<tr><td>46</td><td>Rhode Island</td><td>0.02</td><td>39</td><td>Florida</td><td>2.64</td></tr>
<tr><td>13</td><td>South Carolina</td><td>14.79</td><td>40</td><td>Pennsylvania</td><td>2.62</td></tr>
<tr><td>9</td><td>South Dakota</td><td>16.71</td><td>41</td><td>Ohio</td><td>2.31</td></tr>
<tr><td>28</td><td>Tennessee</td><td>5.71</td><td>42</td><td>Maryland</td><td>1.98</td></tr>
<tr><td>37</td><td>Texas</td><td>3.25</td><td>43</td><td>New York</td><td>1.02</td></tr>
<tr><td>26</td><td>Utah</td><td>6.30</td><td>44</td><td>California</td><td>0.72</td></tr>
<tr><td>2</td><td>Vermont</td><td>27.96</td><td>45</td><td>Massachusetts</td><td>0.12</td></tr>
<tr><td>22</td><td>Virginia</td><td>6.52</td><td>46</td><td>Rhode Island</td><td>0.02</td></tr>
<tr><td>36</td><td>Washington</td><td>3.33</td><td>47</td><td>New Jersey</td><td>0.00</td></tr>
<tr><td>5</td><td>West Virginia</td><td>23.62</td><td>NA</td><td>Illinois**</td><td>NA</td></tr>
<tr><td>21</td><td>Wisconsin</td><td>6.55</td><td>NA</td><td>Michigan**</td><td>NA</td></tr>
<tr><td>6</td><td>Wyoming</td><td>23.12</td><td>NA</td><td>Minnesota**</td><td>NA</td></tr>
<tr><td></td><td></td><td></td><td></td><td>District of Columbia</td><td>0.00</td></tr>
</table>

Source: Morgan Quitno Corporation using data from U.S. Department of Justice, Federal Bureau of Investigation "Crime in the United States 1993" (Uniform Crime Reports, December 4, 1994)

Estimated percentages for rural areas, defined by the F.B.I. as other than Metropolitan Statistical Areas and other cities outside such areas. National percent includes those states listed as not available. Violent crimes are offenses of murder, forcible rape, robbery and aggravated assault.

**Not available.

Murder in Urban Areas in 1993

National Total = 22,829 Murders*

<table>
<tr><td colspan="4"><u>ALPHA ORDER</u></td><td colspan="4"><u>RANK ORDER</u></td></tr>
<tr><td>RANK</td><td>STATE</td><td>MURDERS</td><td>% of USA</td><td>RANK</td><td>STATE</td><td>MURDERS</td><td>% of USA</td></tr>
<tr><td>15</td><td>Alabama</td><td>437</td><td>1.91%</td><td>1</td><td>California</td><td>4,050</td><td>17.74%</td></tr>
<tr><td>39</td><td>Alaska</td><td>38</td><td>0.17%</td><td>2</td><td>New York</td><td>2,390</td><td>10.47%</td></tr>
<tr><td>18</td><td>Arizona</td><td>326</td><td>1.43%</td><td>3</td><td>Texas</td><td>2,044</td><td>8.95%</td></tr>
<tr><td>24</td><td>Arkansas</td><td>212</td><td>0.93%</td><td>4</td><td>Florida</td><td>1,171</td><td>5.13%</td></tr>
<tr><td>1</td><td>California</td><td>4,050</td><td>17.74%</td><td>5</td><td>Michigan</td><td>908</td><td>3.98%</td></tr>
<tr><td>27</td><td>Colorado</td><td>189</td><td>0.83%</td><td>6</td><td>Louisiana</td><td>810</td><td>3.55%</td></tr>
<tr><td>26</td><td>Connecticut</td><td>203</td><td>0.89%</td><td>7</td><td>Pennsylvania</td><td>781</td><td>3.42%</td></tr>
<tr><td>41</td><td>Delaware</td><td>25</td><td>0.11%</td><td>8</td><td>Georgia</td><td>688</td><td>3.01%</td></tr>
<tr><td>4</td><td>Florida</td><td>1,171</td><td>5.13%</td><td>9</td><td>Ohio</td><td>642</td><td>2.81%</td></tr>
<tr><td>8</td><td>Georgia</td><td>688</td><td>3.01%</td><td>10</td><td>North Carolina</td><td>638</td><td>2.79%</td></tr>
<tr><td>40</td><td>Hawaii</td><td>33</td><td>0.14%</td><td>11</td><td>Maryland</td><td>621</td><td>2.72%</td></tr>
<tr><td>42</td><td>Idaho</td><td>21</td><td>0.09%</td><td>12</td><td>Missouri</td><td>536</td><td>2.35%</td></tr>
<tr><td>NA</td><td>Illinois**</td><td>NA</td><td>NA</td><td>13</td><td>Virginia</td><td>458</td><td>2.01%</td></tr>
<tr><td>17</td><td>Indiana</td><td>366</td><td>1.60%</td><td>14</td><td>Tennessee</td><td>454</td><td>1.99%</td></tr>
<tr><td>35</td><td>Iowa</td><td>61</td><td>0.27%</td><td>15</td><td>Alabama</td><td>437</td><td>1.91%</td></tr>
<tr><td>28</td><td>Kansas</td><td>153</td><td>0.67%</td><td>16</td><td>New Jersey</td><td>418</td><td>1.83%</td></tr>
<tr><td>33</td><td>Kentucky</td><td>114</td><td>0.50%</td><td>17</td><td>Indiana</td><td>366</td><td>1.60%</td></tr>
<tr><td>6</td><td>Louisiana</td><td>810</td><td>3.55%</td><td>18</td><td>Arizona</td><td>326</td><td>1.43%</td></tr>
<tr><td>47</td><td>Maine</td><td>8</td><td>0.04%</td><td>19</td><td>South Carolina</td><td>293</td><td>1.28%</td></tr>
<tr><td>11</td><td>Maryland</td><td>621</td><td>2.72%</td><td>20</td><td>Mississippi</td><td>267</td><td>1.17%</td></tr>
<tr><td>23</td><td>Massachusetts</td><td>233</td><td>1.02%</td><td>21</td><td>Washington</td><td>244</td><td>1.07%</td></tr>
<tr><td>5</td><td>Michigan</td><td>908</td><td>3.98%</td><td>22</td><td>Oklahoma</td><td>237</td><td>1.04%</td></tr>
<tr><td>30</td><td>Minnesota</td><td>136</td><td>0.60%</td><td>23</td><td>Massachusetts</td><td>233</td><td>1.02%</td></tr>
<tr><td>20</td><td>Mississippi</td><td>267</td><td>1.17%</td><td>24</td><td>Arkansas</td><td>212</td><td>0.93%</td></tr>
<tr><td>12</td><td>Missouri</td><td>536</td><td>2.35%</td><td>25</td><td>Wisconsin</td><td>209</td><td>0.92%</td></tr>
<tr><td>45</td><td>Montana</td><td>10</td><td>0.04%</td><td>26</td><td>Connecticut</td><td>203</td><td>0.89%</td></tr>
<tr><td>37</td><td>Nebraska</td><td>52</td><td>0.23%</td><td>27</td><td>Colorado</td><td>189</td><td>0.83%</td></tr>
<tr><td>29</td><td>Nevada</td><td>141</td><td>0.62%</td><td>28</td><td>Kansas</td><td>153</td><td>0.67%</td></tr>
<tr><td>43</td><td>New Hampshire</td><td>17</td><td>0.07%</td><td>29</td><td>Nevada</td><td>141</td><td>0.62%</td></tr>
<tr><td>16</td><td>New Jersey</td><td>418</td><td>1.83%</td><td>30</td><td>Minnesota</td><td>136</td><td>0.60%</td></tr>
<tr><td>31</td><td>New Mexico</td><td>120</td><td>0.53%</td><td>31</td><td>New Mexico</td><td>120</td><td>0.53%</td></tr>
<tr><td>2</td><td>New York</td><td>2,390</td><td>10.47%</td><td>32</td><td>Oregon</td><td>117</td><td>0.51%</td></tr>
<tr><td>10</td><td>North Carolina</td><td>638</td><td>2.79%</td><td>33</td><td>Kentucky</td><td>114</td><td>0.50%</td></tr>
<tr><td>49</td><td>North Dakota</td><td>4</td><td>0.02%</td><td>34</td><td>West Virginia</td><td>65</td><td>0.28%</td></tr>
<tr><td>9</td><td>Ohio</td><td>642</td><td>2.81%</td><td>35</td><td>Iowa</td><td>61</td><td>0.27%</td></tr>
<tr><td>22</td><td>Oklahoma</td><td>237</td><td>1.04%</td><td>36</td><td>Utah</td><td>55</td><td>0.24%</td></tr>
<tr><td>32</td><td>Oregon</td><td>117</td><td>0.51%</td><td>37</td><td>Nebraska</td><td>52</td><td>0.23%</td></tr>
<tr><td>7</td><td>Pennsylvania</td><td>781</td><td>3.42%</td><td>38</td><td>Rhode Island</td><td>39</td><td>0.17%</td></tr>
<tr><td>38</td><td>Rhode Island</td><td>39</td><td>0.17%</td><td>39</td><td>Alaska</td><td>38</td><td>0.17%</td></tr>
<tr><td>19</td><td>South Carolina</td><td>293</td><td>1.28%</td><td>40</td><td>Hawaii</td><td>33</td><td>0.14%</td></tr>
<tr><td>45</td><td>South Dakota</td><td>10</td><td>0.04%</td><td>41</td><td>Delaware</td><td>25</td><td>0.11%</td></tr>
<tr><td>14</td><td>Tennessee</td><td>454</td><td>1.99%</td><td>42</td><td>Idaho</td><td>21</td><td>0.09%</td></tr>
<tr><td>3</td><td>Texas</td><td>2,044</td><td>8.95%</td><td>43</td><td>New Hampshire</td><td>17</td><td>0.07%</td></tr>
<tr><td>36</td><td>Utah</td><td>55</td><td>0.24%</td><td>44</td><td>Vermont</td><td>11</td><td>0.05%</td></tr>
<tr><td>44</td><td>Vermont</td><td>11</td><td>0.05%</td><td>45</td><td>Montana</td><td>10</td><td>0.04%</td></tr>
<tr><td>13</td><td>Virginia</td><td>458</td><td>2.01%</td><td>45</td><td>South Dakota</td><td>10</td><td>0.04%</td></tr>
<tr><td>21</td><td>Washington</td><td>244</td><td>1.07%</td><td>47</td><td>Maine</td><td>8</td><td>0.04%</td></tr>
<tr><td>34</td><td>West Virginia</td><td>65</td><td>0.28%</td><td>48</td><td>Wyoming</td><td>6</td><td>0.03%</td></tr>
<tr><td>25</td><td>Wisconsin</td><td>209</td><td>0.92%</td><td>49</td><td>North Dakota</td><td>4</td><td>0.02%</td></tr>
<tr><td>48</td><td>Wyoming</td><td>6</td><td>0.03%</td><td>NA</td><td>Illinois**</td><td>NA</td><td>NA</td></tr>
<tr><td></td><td></td><td></td><td></td><td></td><td>District of Columbia</td><td>454</td><td>1.99%</td></tr>
</table>

Source: U.S. Department of Justice, Federal Bureau of Investigation
  "Crime in the United States 1993" (Uniform Crime Reports, December 4, 1994)
*Estimated totals for urban areas, defined by the F.B.I. as Metropolitan Statistical Areas and other cities outside such
areas. National total includes those states listed as not available. Includes nonnegligent manslaughter.
**Not available.

Urban Murder Rate in 1993

National Urban Rate = 10.1 Murders per 100,000 Population*

RANK	STATE (ALPHA ORDER)	RATE		RANK	STATE (RANK ORDER)	RATE
8	Alabama	12.9		1	Louisiana	22.9
16	Alaska	9.3		2	Mississippi	17.9
20	Arizona	9.0		3	New York	13.8
4	Arkansas	13.2		4	Arkansas	13.2
4	California	13.2		4	California	13.2
28	Colorado	5.9		4	Maryland	13.2
25	Connecticut	6.6		4	Missouri	13.2
35	Delaware	4.1		8	Alabama	12.9
17	Florida	9.1		9	Georgia	12.4
9	Georgia	12.4		9	Texas	12.4
39	Hawaii	3.6		11	North Carolina	12.0
43	Idaho	2.9		12	Nevada	11.6
NA	Illinois**	NA		13	Tennessee	11.4
22	Indiana	7.9		14	Michigan	10.7
42	Iowa	3.2		15	South Carolina	10.3
23	Kansas	7.4		16	Alaska	9.3
32	Kentucky	4.7		17	Florida	9.1
1	Louisiana	22.9		17	New Mexico	9.1
49	Maine	0.9		17	Oklahoma	9.1
4	Maryland	13.2		20	Arizona	9.0
36	Massachusetts	3.9		21	Virginia	8.4
14	Michigan	10.7		22	Indiana	7.9
38	Minnesota	3.7		23	Kansas	7.4
2	Mississippi	17.9		24	Pennsylvania	7.1
4	Missouri	13.2		25	Connecticut	6.6
44	Montana	2.5		25	Ohio	6.6
34	Nebraska	4.4		27	West Virginia	6.3
12	Nevada	11.6		28	Colorado	5.9
46	New Hampshire	1.7		29	New Jersey	5.3
29	New Jersey	5.3		30	Wisconsin	5.2
17	New Mexico	9.1		31	Washington	5.1
3	New York	13.8		32	Kentucky	4.7
11	North Carolina	12.0		33	Oregon	4.6
48	North Dakota	1.0		34	Nebraska	4.4
25	Ohio	6.6		35	Delaware	4.1
17	Oklahoma	9.1		36	Massachusetts	3.9
33	Oregon	4.6		36	Rhode Island	3.9
24	Pennsylvania	7.1		38	Minnesota	3.7
36	Rhode Island	3.9		39	Hawaii	3.6
15	South Carolina	10.3		40	Vermont	3.5
45	South Dakota	2.4		41	Utah	3.3
13	Tennessee	11.4		42	Iowa	3.2
9	Texas	12.4		43	Idaho	2.9
41	Utah	3.3		44	Montana	2.5
40	Vermont	3.5		45	South Dakota	2.4
21	Virginia	8.4		46	New Hampshire	1.7
31	Washington	5.1		46	Wyoming	1.7
27	West Virginia	6.3		48	North Dakota	1.0
30	Wisconsin	5.2		49	Maine	0.9
46	Wyoming	1.7		NA	Illinois**	NA

District of Columbia   78.5

Source: Morgan Quitno Corporation using data from U.S. Department of Justice, Federal Bureau of Investigation
"Crime in the United States 1993" (Uniform Crime Reports, December 4, 1994)
*Estimated rates for urban areas, defined by the F.B.I. as Metropolitan Statistical Areas and other cities outside such areas. National rate includes those states listed as not available. Includes nonnegligent manslaughter.
**Not available.

Percent of Murders Occurring in Urban Areas in 1993

National Percent = 93.08% of Murders*

ALPHA ORDER				RANK ORDER		
RANK	STATE	PERCENT		RANK	STATE	PERCENT
23	Alabama	90.29		1	Massachusetts	100.00
40	Alaska	70.37		1	New Jersey	100.00
11	Arizona	96.17		1	Rhode Island	100.00
29	Arkansas	85.83		4	California	98.88
4	California	98.88		5	New York	98.76
21	Colorado	91.75		6	Connecticut	98.54
6	Connecticut	98.54		7	Maryland	98.26
39	Delaware	71.43		8	Nevada	97.92
12	Florida	95.67		9	Michigan	97.32
26	Georgia	87.20		10	Ohio	96.25
38	Hawaii	73.33		11	Arizona	96.17
41	Idaho	65.63		12	Florida	95.67
NA	Illinois**	NA		13	Texas	95.20
30	Indiana	85.12		14	Kansas	95.03
19	Iowa	92.42		15	Pennsylvania	94.90
14	Kansas	95.03		16	Utah	94.83
44	Kentucky	45.78		17	Wisconsin	94.14
18	Louisiana	92.68		18	Louisiana	92.68
46	Maine	40.00		19	Iowa	92.42
7	Maryland	98.26		20	New Mexico	92.31
1	Massachusetts	100.00		21	Colorado	91.75
9	Michigan	97.32		22	Missouri	90.85
25	Minnesota	87.74		23	Alabama	90.29
36	Mississippi	74.79		24	Washington	90.04
22	Missouri	90.85		25	Minnesota	87.74
46	Montana	40.00		26	Georgia	87.20
33	Nebraska	82.54		27	Tennessee	87.14
8	Nevada	97.92		28	Oklahoma	86.81
37	New Hampshire	73.91		29	Arkansas	85.83
1	New Jersey	100.00		30	Indiana	85.12
20	New Mexico	92.31		31	Virginia	84.97
5	New York	98.76		32	Oregon	83.57
34	North Carolina	81.27		33	Nebraska	82.54
49	North Dakota	36.36		34	North Carolina	81.27
10	Ohio	96.25		35	South Carolina	77.72
28	Oklahoma	86.81		36	Mississippi	74.79
32	Oregon	83.57		37	New Hampshire	73.91
15	Pennsylvania	94.90		38	Hawaii	73.33
1	Rhode Island	100.00		39	Delaware	71.43
35	South Carolina	77.72		40	Alaska	70.37
45	South Dakota	41.67		41	Idaho	65.63
27	Tennessee	87.14		42	Vermont	52.38
13	Texas	95.20		43	West Virginia	51.59
16	Utah	94.83		44	Kentucky	45.78
42	Vermont	52.38		45	South Dakota	41.67
31	Virginia	84.97		46	Maine	40.00
24	Washington	90.04		46	Montana	40.00
43	West Virginia	51.59		48	Wyoming	37.50
17	Wisconsin	94.14		49	North Dakota	36.36
48	Wyoming	37.50		NA	Illinois**	NA
					District of Columbia	100.00

Source: Morgan Quitno Corporation using data from U.S. Department of Justice, Federal Bureau of Investigation
"Crime in the United States 1993" (Uniform Crime Reports, December 4, 1994)
*Estimated percentages for urban areas, defined by the F.B.I. as Metropolitan Statistical Areas and other cities outside such areas. National percent includes those states listed as not available. Includes nonnegligent manslaughter.
**Not available.

Murder in Rural Areas in 1993

National Total = 1,697 Murders*

<table>
<tr><td colspan="4">ALPHA ORDER</td><td colspan="4">RANK ORDER</td></tr>
<tr><td>RANK</td><td>STATE</td><td>MURDERS</td><td>% of USA</td><td>RANK</td><td>STATE</td><td>MURDERS</td><td>% of USA</td></tr>
<tr><td>14</td><td>Alabama</td><td>47</td><td>2.77%</td><td>1</td><td>North Carolina</td><td>147</td><td>8.66%</td></tr>
<tr><td>26</td><td>Alaska</td><td>16</td><td>0.94%</td><td>2</td><td>Kentucky</td><td>135</td><td>7.96%</td></tr>
<tr><td>29</td><td>Arizona</td><td>13</td><td>0.77%</td><td>3</td><td>Texas</td><td>103</td><td>6.07%</td></tr>
<tr><td>18</td><td>Arkansas</td><td>35</td><td>2.06%</td><td>4</td><td>Georgia</td><td>101</td><td>5.95%</td></tr>
<tr><td>15</td><td>California</td><td>46</td><td>2.71%</td><td>5</td><td>Mississippi</td><td>90</td><td>5.30%</td></tr>
<tr><td>25</td><td>Colorado</td><td>17</td><td>1.00%</td><td>6</td><td>South Carolina</td><td>84</td><td>4.95%</td></tr>
<tr><td>44</td><td>Connecticut</td><td>3</td><td>0.18%</td><td>7</td><td>Virginia</td><td>81</td><td>4.77%</td></tr>
<tr><td>36</td><td>Delaware</td><td>10</td><td>0.59%</td><td>8</td><td>Tennessee</td><td>67</td><td>3.95%</td></tr>
<tr><td>13</td><td>Florida</td><td>53</td><td>3.12%</td><td>9</td><td>Indiana</td><td>64</td><td>3.77%</td></tr>
<tr><td>4</td><td>Georgia</td><td>101</td><td>5.95%</td><td>9</td><td>Louisiana</td><td>64</td><td>3.77%</td></tr>
<tr><td>31</td><td>Hawaii</td><td>12</td><td>0.71%</td><td>11</td><td>West Virginia</td><td>61</td><td>3.59%</td></tr>
<tr><td>33</td><td>Idaho</td><td>11</td><td>0.65%</td><td>12</td><td>Missouri</td><td>54</td><td>3.18%</td></tr>
<tr><td>NA</td><td>Illinois**</td><td>NA</td><td>NA</td><td>13</td><td>Florida</td><td>53</td><td>3.12%</td></tr>
<tr><td>9</td><td>Indiana</td><td>64</td><td>3.77%</td><td>14</td><td>Alabama</td><td>47</td><td>2.77%</td></tr>
<tr><td>43</td><td>Iowa</td><td>5</td><td>0.29%</td><td>15</td><td>California</td><td>46</td><td>2.71%</td></tr>
<tr><td>40</td><td>Kansas</td><td>8</td><td>0.47%</td><td>16</td><td>Pennsylvania</td><td>42</td><td>2.47%</td></tr>
<tr><td>2</td><td>Kentucky</td><td>135</td><td>7.96%</td><td>17</td><td>Oklahoma</td><td>36</td><td>2.12%</td></tr>
<tr><td>9</td><td>Louisiana</td><td>64</td><td>3.77%</td><td>18</td><td>Arkansas</td><td>35</td><td>2.06%</td></tr>
<tr><td>31</td><td>Maine</td><td>12</td><td>0.71%</td><td>19</td><td>New York</td><td>30</td><td>1.77%</td></tr>
<tr><td>33</td><td>Maryland</td><td>11</td><td>0.65%</td><td>20</td><td>Washington</td><td>27</td><td>1.59%</td></tr>
<tr><td>47</td><td>Massachusetts</td><td>0</td><td>0.00%</td><td>21</td><td>Michigan</td><td>25</td><td>1.47%</td></tr>
<tr><td>21</td><td>Michigan</td><td>25</td><td>1.47%</td><td>21</td><td>Ohio</td><td>25</td><td>1.47%</td></tr>
<tr><td>24</td><td>Minnesota</td><td>19</td><td>1.12%</td><td>23</td><td>Oregon</td><td>23</td><td>1.36%</td></tr>
<tr><td>5</td><td>Mississippi</td><td>90</td><td>5.30%</td><td>24</td><td>Minnesota</td><td>19</td><td>1.12%</td></tr>
<tr><td>12</td><td>Missouri</td><td>54</td><td>3.18%</td><td>25</td><td>Colorado</td><td>17</td><td>1.00%</td></tr>
<tr><td>27</td><td>Montana</td><td>15</td><td>0.88%</td><td>26</td><td>Alaska</td><td>16</td><td>0.94%</td></tr>
<tr><td>33</td><td>Nebraska</td><td>11</td><td>0.65%</td><td>27</td><td>Montana</td><td>15</td><td>0.88%</td></tr>
<tr><td>44</td><td>Nevada</td><td>3</td><td>0.18%</td><td>28</td><td>South Dakota</td><td>14</td><td>0.82%</td></tr>
<tr><td>42</td><td>New Hampshire</td><td>6</td><td>0.35%</td><td>29</td><td>Arizona</td><td>13</td><td>0.77%</td></tr>
<tr><td>47</td><td>New Jersey</td><td>0</td><td>0.00%</td><td>29</td><td>Wisconsin</td><td>13</td><td>0.77%</td></tr>
<tr><td>36</td><td>New Mexico</td><td>10</td><td>0.59%</td><td>31</td><td>Hawaii</td><td>12</td><td>0.71%</td></tr>
<tr><td>19</td><td>New York</td><td>30</td><td>1.77%</td><td>31</td><td>Maine</td><td>12</td><td>0.71%</td></tr>
<tr><td>1</td><td>North Carolina</td><td>147</td><td>8.66%</td><td>33</td><td>Idaho</td><td>11</td><td>0.65%</td></tr>
<tr><td>41</td><td>North Dakota</td><td>7</td><td>0.41%</td><td>33</td><td>Maryland</td><td>11</td><td>0.65%</td></tr>
<tr><td>21</td><td>Ohio</td><td>25</td><td>1.47%</td><td>33</td><td>Nebraska</td><td>11</td><td>0.65%</td></tr>
<tr><td>17</td><td>Oklahoma</td><td>36</td><td>2.12%</td><td>36</td><td>Delaware</td><td>10</td><td>0.59%</td></tr>
<tr><td>23</td><td>Oregon</td><td>23</td><td>1.36%</td><td>36</td><td>New Mexico</td><td>10</td><td>0.59%</td></tr>
<tr><td>16</td><td>Pennsylvania</td><td>42</td><td>2.47%</td><td>36</td><td>Vermont</td><td>10</td><td>0.59%</td></tr>
<tr><td>47</td><td>Rhode Island</td><td>0</td><td>0.00%</td><td>36</td><td>Wyoming</td><td>10</td><td>0.59%</td></tr>
<tr><td>6</td><td>South Carolina</td><td>84</td><td>4.95%</td><td>40</td><td>Kansas</td><td>8</td><td>0.47%</td></tr>
<tr><td>28</td><td>South Dakota</td><td>14</td><td>0.82%</td><td>41</td><td>North Dakota</td><td>7</td><td>0.41%</td></tr>
<tr><td>8</td><td>Tennessee</td><td>67</td><td>3.95%</td><td>42</td><td>New Hampshire</td><td>6</td><td>0.35%</td></tr>
<tr><td>3</td><td>Texas</td><td>103</td><td>6.07%</td><td>43</td><td>Iowa</td><td>5</td><td>0.29%</td></tr>
<tr><td>44</td><td>Utah</td><td>3</td><td>0.18%</td><td>44</td><td>Connecticut</td><td>3</td><td>0.18%</td></tr>
<tr><td>36</td><td>Vermont</td><td>10</td><td>0.59%</td><td>44</td><td>Nevada</td><td>3</td><td>0.18%</td></tr>
<tr><td>7</td><td>Virginia</td><td>81</td><td>4.77%</td><td>44</td><td>Utah</td><td>3</td><td>0.18%</td></tr>
<tr><td>20</td><td>Washington</td><td>27</td><td>1.59%</td><td>47</td><td>Massachusetts</td><td>0</td><td>0.00%</td></tr>
<tr><td>11</td><td>West Virginia</td><td>61</td><td>3.59%</td><td>47</td><td>New Jersey</td><td>0</td><td>0.00%</td></tr>
<tr><td>29</td><td>Wisconsin</td><td>13</td><td>0.77%</td><td>47</td><td>Rhode Island</td><td>0</td><td>0.00%</td></tr>
<tr><td>36</td><td>Wyoming</td><td>10</td><td>0.59%</td><td>NA</td><td>Illinois**</td><td>NA</td><td>NA</td></tr>
<tr><td></td><td></td><td></td><td></td><td></td><td>District of Columbia</td><td>0</td><td>0.00%</td></tr>
</table>

Source: Morgan Quitno Corporation using data from U.S. Department of Justice, Federal Bureau of Investigation
"Crime in the United States 1993" (Uniform Crime Reports, December 4, 1994)
*Estimated totals for rural areas, defined by the F.B.I. as other than Metropolitan Statistical Areas and other cities outside such areas. National total includes those states listed as not available. Includes nonnegligent manslaughter.
**Not available.

Rural Murder Rate in 1993

National Rural Rate = 5.3 Murders per 100,000 Population*

ALPHA ORDER

RANK	STATE	RATE
16	Alabama	6.0
5	Alaska	8.5
25	Arizona	4.3
25	Arkansas	4.3
11	California	7.5
20	Colorado	4.8
43	Connecticut	1.6
1	Delaware	11.3
13	Florida	7.1
12	Georgia	7.4
22	Hawaii	4.7
36	Idaho	2.9
NA	Illinois**	NA
15	Indiana	6.1
46	Iowa	0.6
41	Kansas	1.8
3	Kentucky	9.8
5	Louisiana	8.5
31	Maine	3.5
28	Maryland	4.1
47	Massachusetts	0.0
38	Michigan	2.4
39	Minnesota	2.2
8	Mississippi	7.8
24	Missouri	4.6
31	Montana	3.5
37	Nebraska	2.7
41	Nevada	1.8
25	New Hampshire	4.3
47	New Jersey	0.0
34	New Mexico	3.4
31	New York	3.5
4	North Carolina	9.0
35	North Dakota	3.1
40	Ohio	1.9
18	Oklahoma	5.8
22	Oregon	4.7
29	Pennsylvania	3.9
47	Rhode Island	0.0
2	South Carolina	10.7
20	South Dakota	4.8
16	Tennessee	6.0
14	Texas	6.5
44	Utah	1.5
30	Vermont	3.8
10	Virginia	7.7
19	Washington	5.6
8	West Virginia	7.8
45	Wisconsin	1.3
7	Wyoming	8.1

RANK ORDER

RANK	STATE	RATE
1	Delaware	11.3
2	South Carolina	10.7
3	Kentucky	9.8
4	North Carolina	9.0
5	Alaska	8.5
5	Louisiana	8.5
7	Wyoming	8.1
8	Mississippi	7.8
8	West Virginia	7.8
10	Virginia	7.7
11	California	7.5
12	Georgia	7.4
13	Florida	7.1
14	Texas	6.5
15	Indiana	6.1
16	Alabama	6.0
16	Tennessee	6.0
18	Oklahoma	5.8
19	Washington	5.6
20	Colorado	4.8
20	South Dakota	4.8
22	Hawaii	4.7
22	Oregon	4.7
24	Missouri	4.6
25	Arizona	4.3
25	Arkansas	4.3
25	New Hampshire	4.3
28	Maryland	4.1
29	Pennsylvania	3.9
30	Vermont	3.8
31	Maine	3.5
31	Montana	3.5
31	New York	3.5
34	New Mexico	3.4
35	North Dakota	3.1
36	Idaho	2.9
37	Nebraska	2.7
38	Michigan	2.4
39	Minnesota	2.2
40	Ohio	1.9
41	Kansas	1.8
41	Nevada	1.8
43	Connecticut	1.6
44	Utah	1.5
45	Wisconsin	1.3
46	Iowa	0.6
47	Massachusetts	0.0
47	New Jersey	0.0
47	Rhode Island	0.0
NA	Illinois**	NA

District of Columbia 0.0

Source: Morgan Quitno Corporation using data from U.S. Department of Justice, Federal Bureau of Investigation
"Crime in the United States 1993" (Uniform Crime Reports, December 4, 1994)
*Estimated rates for rural areas, defined by the F.B.I. as other than Metropolitan Statistical Areas and other cities outside such areas. National rate includes those states listed as not available. Includes nonnegligent manslaughter.
**Not available.

Percent of Murders Occurring in Rural Areas in 1993

National Percent = 6.92% of Murders*

ALPHA ORDER				RANK ORDER		
RANK	**STATE**		**PERCENT**	**RANK**	**STATE**	**PERCENT**
27	Alabama		9.71	1	North Dakota	63.64
10	Alaska		29.63	2	Wyoming	62.50
39	Arizona		3.83	3	Maine	60.00
21	Arkansas		14.17	3	Montana	60.00
46	California		1.12	5	South Dakota	58.33
29	Colorado		8.25	6	Kentucky	54.22
44	Connecticut		1.46	7	West Virginia	48.41
11	Delaware		28.57	8	Vermont	47.62
38	Florida		4.33	9	Idaho	34.38
24	Georgia		12.80	10	Alaska	29.63
12	Hawaii		26.67	11	Delaware	28.57
9	Idaho		34.38	12	Hawaii	26.67
NA	Illinois**		NA	13	New Hampshire	26.09
20	Indiana		14.88	14	Mississippi	25.21
31	Iowa		7.58	15	South Carolina	22.28
36	Kansas		4.97	16	North Carolina	18.73
6	Kentucky		54.22	17	Nebraska	17.46
32	Louisiana		7.32	18	Oregon	16.43
3	Maine		60.00	19	Virginia	15.03
43	Maryland		1.74	20	Indiana	14.88
47	Massachusetts		0.00	21	Arkansas	14.17
41	Michigan		2.68	22	Oklahoma	13.19
25	Minnesota		12.26	23	Tennessee	12.86
14	Mississippi		25.21	24	Georgia	12.80
28	Missouri		9.15	25	Minnesota	12.26
3	Montana		60.00	26	Washington	9.96
17	Nebraska		17.46	27	Alabama	9.71
42	Nevada		2.08	28	Missouri	9.15
13	New Hampshire		26.09	29	Colorado	8.25
47	New Jersey		0.00	30	New Mexico	7.69
30	New Mexico		7.69	31	Iowa	7.58
45	New York		1.24	32	Louisiana	7.32
16	North Carolina		18.73	33	Wisconsin	5.86
1	North Dakota		63.64	34	Utah	5.17
40	Ohio		3.75	35	Pennsylvania	5.10
22	Oklahoma		13.19	36	Kansas	4.97
18	Oregon		16.43	37	Texas	4.80
35	Pennsylvania		5.10	38	Florida	4.33
47	Rhode Island		0.00	39	Arizona	3.83
15	South Carolina		22.28	40	Ohio	3.75
5	South Dakota		58.33	41	Michigan	2.68
23	Tennessee		12.86	42	Nevada	2.08
37	Texas		4.80	43	Maryland	1.74
34	Utah		5.17	44	Connecticut	1.46
8	Vermont		47.62	45	New York	1.24
19	Virginia		15.03	46	California	1.12
26	Washington		9.96	47	Massachusetts	0.00
7	West Virginia		48.41	47	New Jersey	0.00
33	Wisconsin		5.86	47	Rhode Island	0.00
2	Wyoming		62.50	NA	Illinois**	NA
					District of Columbia	0.00

Source: Morgan Quitno Corporation using data from U.S. Department of Justice, Federal Bureau of Investigation "Crime in the United States 1993" (Uniform Crime Reports, December 4, 1994)
*Estimated percentages for rural areas, defined by the F.B.I. as other than Metropolitan Statistical Areas and other cities outside such areas. National percent includes those states listed as not available. Includes nonnegligent manslaughter.
**Not available.

Rape in Urban Areas in 1993

National Total = 96,908 Rapes*

<table>
<tr><td colspan="4">ALPHA ORDER</td><td colspan="4">RANK ORDER</td></tr>
<tr><td>RANK</td><td>STATE</td><td>RAPES</td><td>% of USA</td><td>RANK</td><td>STATE</td><td>RAPES</td><td>% of USA</td></tr>
<tr><td>22</td><td>Alabama</td><td>1,377</td><td>1.42%</td><td>1</td><td>California</td><td>11,579</td><td>11.95%</td></tr>
<tr><td>37</td><td>Alaska</td><td>329</td><td>0.34%</td><td>2</td><td>Texas</td><td>9,530</td><td>9.83%</td></tr>
<tr><td>21</td><td>Arizona</td><td>1,431</td><td>1.48%</td><td>3</td><td>Florida</td><td>6,985</td><td>7.21%</td></tr>
<tr><td>26</td><td>Arkansas</td><td>865</td><td>0.89%</td><td>4</td><td>Ohio</td><td>5,240</td><td>5.41%</td></tr>
<tr><td>1</td><td>California</td><td>11,579</td><td>11.95%</td><td>5</td><td>New York</td><td>4,853</td><td>5.01%</td></tr>
<tr><td>19</td><td>Colorado</td><td>1,550</td><td>1.60%</td><td>6</td><td>Washington</td><td>3,147</td><td>3.25%</td></tr>
<tr><td>31</td><td>Connecticut</td><td>754</td><td>0.78%</td><td>7</td><td>Pennsylvania</td><td>2,969</td><td>3.06%</td></tr>
<tr><td>35</td><td>Delaware</td><td>435</td><td>0.45%</td><td>8</td><td>Tennessee</td><td>2,395</td><td>2.47%</td></tr>
<tr><td>3</td><td>Florida</td><td>6,985</td><td>7.21%</td><td>9</td><td>New Jersey</td><td>2,215</td><td>2.29%</td></tr>
<tr><td>10</td><td>Georgia</td><td>2,195</td><td>2.27%</td><td>10</td><td>Georgia</td><td>2,195</td><td>2.27%</td></tr>
<tr><td>38</td><td>Hawaii</td><td>302</td><td>0.31%</td><td>11</td><td>North Carolina</td><td>2,120</td><td>2.19%</td></tr>
<tr><td>39</td><td>Idaho</td><td>291</td><td>0.30%</td><td>12</td><td>Maryland</td><td>2,101</td><td>2.17%</td></tr>
<tr><td>NA</td><td>Illinois**</td><td>NA</td><td>NA</td><td>13</td><td>Indiana</td><td>2,068</td><td>2.13%</td></tr>
<tr><td>13</td><td>Indiana</td><td>2,068</td><td>2.13%</td><td>14</td><td>Massachusetts</td><td>2,004</td><td>2.07%</td></tr>
<tr><td>33</td><td>Iowa</td><td>632</td><td>0.65%</td><td>15</td><td>Virginia</td><td>1,881</td><td>1.94%</td></tr>
<tr><td>25</td><td>Kansas</td><td>944</td><td>0.97%</td><td>16</td><td>Missouri</td><td>1,742</td><td>1.80%</td></tr>
<tr><td>27</td><td>Kentucky</td><td>860</td><td>0.89%</td><td>17</td><td>Louisiana</td><td>1,610</td><td>1.66%</td></tr>
<tr><td>17</td><td>Louisiana</td><td>1,610</td><td>1.66%</td><td>18</td><td>South Carolina</td><td>1,579</td><td>1.63%</td></tr>
<tr><td>43</td><td>Maine</td><td>239</td><td>0.25%</td><td>19</td><td>Colorado</td><td>1,550</td><td>1.60%</td></tr>
<tr><td>12</td><td>Maryland</td><td>2,101</td><td>2.17%</td><td>20</td><td>Oklahoma</td><td>1,485</td><td>1.53%</td></tr>
<tr><td>14</td><td>Massachusetts</td><td>2,004</td><td>2.07%</td><td>21</td><td>Arizona</td><td>1,431</td><td>1.48%</td></tr>
<tr><td>NA</td><td>Michigan**</td><td>NA</td><td>NA</td><td>22</td><td>Alabama</td><td>1,377</td><td>1.42%</td></tr>
<tr><td>NA</td><td>Minnesota**</td><td>NA</td><td>NA</td><td>23</td><td>Oregon</td><td>1,317</td><td>1.36%</td></tr>
<tr><td>28</td><td>Mississippi</td><td>846</td><td>0.87%</td><td>24</td><td>Wisconsin</td><td>1,146</td><td>1.18%</td></tr>
<tr><td>16</td><td>Missouri</td><td>1,742</td><td>1.80%</td><td>25</td><td>Kansas</td><td>944</td><td>0.97%</td></tr>
<tr><td>47</td><td>Montana</td><td>119</td><td>0.12%</td><td>26</td><td>Arkansas</td><td>865</td><td>0.89%</td></tr>
<tr><td>36</td><td>Nebraska</td><td>401</td><td>0.41%</td><td>27</td><td>Kentucky</td><td>860</td><td>0.89%</td></tr>
<tr><td>29</td><td>Nevada</td><td>791</td><td>0.82%</td><td>28</td><td>Mississippi</td><td>846</td><td>0.87%</td></tr>
<tr><td>34</td><td>New Hampshire</td><td>472</td><td>0.49%</td><td>29</td><td>Nevada</td><td>791</td><td>0.82%</td></tr>
<tr><td>9</td><td>New Jersey</td><td>2,215</td><td>2.29%</td><td>30</td><td>Utah</td><td>768</td><td>0.79%</td></tr>
<tr><td>31</td><td>New Mexico</td><td>754</td><td>0.78%</td><td>31</td><td>Connecticut</td><td>754</td><td>0.78%</td></tr>
<tr><td>5</td><td>New York</td><td>4,853</td><td>5.01%</td><td>31</td><td>New Mexico</td><td>754</td><td>0.78%</td></tr>
<tr><td>11</td><td>North Carolina</td><td>2,120</td><td>2.19%</td><td>33</td><td>Iowa</td><td>632</td><td>0.65%</td></tr>
<tr><td>46</td><td>North Dakota</td><td>127</td><td>0.13%</td><td>34</td><td>New Hampshire</td><td>472</td><td>0.49%</td></tr>
<tr><td>4</td><td>Ohio</td><td>5,240</td><td>5.41%</td><td>35</td><td>Delaware</td><td>435</td><td>0.45%</td></tr>
<tr><td>20</td><td>Oklahoma</td><td>1,485</td><td>1.53%</td><td>36</td><td>Nebraska</td><td>401</td><td>0.41%</td></tr>
<tr><td>23</td><td>Oregon</td><td>1,317</td><td>1.36%</td><td>37</td><td>Alaska</td><td>329</td><td>0.34%</td></tr>
<tr><td>7</td><td>Pennsylvania</td><td>2,969</td><td>3.06%</td><td>38</td><td>Hawaii</td><td>302</td><td>0.31%</td></tr>
<tr><td>40</td><td>Rhode Island</td><td>286</td><td>0.30%</td><td>39</td><td>Idaho</td><td>291</td><td>0.30%</td></tr>
<tr><td>18</td><td>South Carolina</td><td>1,579</td><td>1.63%</td><td>40</td><td>Rhode Island</td><td>286</td><td>0.30%</td></tr>
<tr><td>42</td><td>South Dakota</td><td>270</td><td>0.28%</td><td>40</td><td>West Virginia</td><td>286</td><td>0.30%</td></tr>
<tr><td>8</td><td>Tennessee</td><td>2,395</td><td>2.47%</td><td>42</td><td>South Dakota</td><td>270</td><td>0.28%</td></tr>
<tr><td>2</td><td>Texas</td><td>9,530</td><td>9.83%</td><td>43</td><td>Maine</td><td>239</td><td>0.25%</td></tr>
<tr><td>30</td><td>Utah</td><td>768</td><td>0.79%</td><td>44</td><td>Vermont</td><td>168</td><td>0.17%</td></tr>
<tr><td>44</td><td>Vermont</td><td>168</td><td>0.17%</td><td>45</td><td>Wyoming</td><td>130</td><td>0.13%</td></tr>
<tr><td>15</td><td>Virginia</td><td>1,881</td><td>1.94%</td><td>46</td><td>North Dakota</td><td>127</td><td>0.13%</td></tr>
<tr><td>6</td><td>Washington</td><td>3,147</td><td>3.25%</td><td>47</td><td>Montana</td><td>119</td><td>0.12%</td></tr>
<tr><td>40</td><td>West Virginia</td><td>286</td><td>0.30%</td><td>NA</td><td>Illinois**</td><td>NA</td><td>NA</td></tr>
<tr><td>24</td><td>Wisconsin</td><td>1,146</td><td>1.18%</td><td>NA</td><td>Michigan**</td><td>NA</td><td>NA</td></tr>
<tr><td>45</td><td>Wyoming</td><td>130</td><td>0.13%</td><td>NA</td><td>Minnesota**</td><td>NA</td><td>NA</td></tr>
<tr><td colspan="4"></td><td colspan="2">District of Columbia</td><td>324</td><td>0.33%</td></tr>
</table>

Source: Morgan Quitno Corporation using data from U.S. Department of Justice, Federal Bureau of Investigation "Crime in the United States 1993" (Uniform Crime Reports, December 4, 1994)
*Estimated totals for urban areas, defined by the F.B.I. as Metropolitan Statistical Areas and other cities outside such areas. National total includes those states listed as not available. Forcible rape is the carnal knowledge of a female forcibly and against her will. Attempts are included. However, statutory rape without force and other sex offenses are excluded. **Not available.

Urban Rape Rate in 1993

National Urban Rate = 42.8 Rapes per 100,000 Population*

ALPHA ORDER				RANK ORDER		
RANK	STATE	RATE		RANK	STATE	RATE
26	Alabama	40.5		1	Alaska	80.3
1	Alaska	80.3		2	Delaware	71.1
29	Arizona	39.4		3	Washington	66.0
13	Arkansas	53.7		4	Nevada	64.9
30	California	37.8		5	South Dakota	63.6
17	Colorado	48.3		6	Tennessee	60.0
47	Connecticut	24.4		7	Texas	58.0
2	Delaware	71.1		8	New Mexico	57.0
12	Florida	54.0		8	Oklahoma	57.0
28	Georgia	39.5		10	Mississippi	56.6
36	Hawaii	33.0		11	South Carolina	55.3
25	Idaho	40.7		12	Florida	54.0
NA	Illinois**	NA		13	Arkansas	53.7
23	Indiana	44.4		13	Vermont	53.7
37	Iowa	32.9		15	Ohio	53.6
20	Kansas	45.5		16	Oregon	51.8
32	Kentucky	35.7		17	Colorado	48.3
20	Louisiana	45.5		18	New Hampshire	47.9
46	Maine	26.8		19	Utah	46.3
22	Maryland	44.7		20	Kansas	45.5
35	Massachusetts	33.4		20	Louisiana	45.5
NA	Michigan**	NA		22	Maryland	44.7
NA	Minnesota**	NA		23	Indiana	44.4
10	Mississippi	56.6		24	Missouri	42.9
24	Missouri	42.9		25	Idaho	40.7
39	Montana	29.2		26	Alabama	40.5
34	Nebraska	33.6		27	North Carolina	40.0
4	Nevada	64.9		28	Georgia	39.5
18	New Hampshire	47.9		29	Arizona	39.4
42	New Jersey	28.1		30	California	37.8
8	New Mexico	57.0		31	Wyoming	37.6
43	New York	28.0		32	Kentucky	35.7
27	North Carolina	40.0		33	Virginia	34.6
38	North Dakota	31.1		34	Nebraska	33.6
15	Ohio	53.6		35	Massachusetts	33.4
8	Oklahoma	57.0		36	Hawaii	33.0
16	Oregon	51.8		37	Iowa	32.9
45	Pennsylvania	27.0		38	North Dakota	31.1
40	Rhode Island	28.6		39	Montana	29.2
11	South Carolina	55.3		40	Rhode Island	28.6
5	South Dakota	63.6		41	Wisconsin	28.3
6	Tennessee	60.0		42	New Jersey	28.1
7	Texas	58.0		43	New York	28.0
19	Utah	46.3		44	West Virginia	27.5
13	Vermont	53.7		45	Pennsylvania	27.0
33	Virginia	34.6		46	Maine	26.8
3	Washington	66.0		47	Connecticut	24.4
44	West Virginia	27.5		NA	Illinois**	NA
41	Wisconsin	28.3		NA	Michigan**	NA
31	Wyoming	37.6		NA	Minnesota**	NA

District of Columbia 56.1

Source: Morgan Quitno Corporation using data from U.S. Department of Justice, Federal Bureau of Investigation
"Crime in the United States 1993" (Uniform Crime Reports, December 4, 1994)
*Estimated rates for urban areas, defined by the F.B.I. as Metropolitan Statistical Areas and other cities outside such
areas. National rate includes those states listed as not available. Forcible rape is the carnal knowledge of a female forcibly
and against her will. Attempts are included. However, statutory rape without force and other sex offenses are excluded.
**Not available.
384

Percent of Rapes Occurring in Urban Areas in 1993

National Percent = 92.46% of Rapes*

ALPHA ORDER

RANK	STATE	PERCENT
15	Alabama	93.61
46	Alaska	65.54
7	Arizona	96.17
35	Arkansas	84.14
4	California	98.41
10	Colorado	94.92
13	Connecticut	94.25
38	Delaware	80.71
10	Florida	94.92
28	Georgia	89.67
40	Hawaii	76.65
42	Idaho	75.00
NA	Illinois**	NA
22	Indiana	92.57
23	Iowa	92.13
20	Kansas	92.91
45	Kentucky	66.10
31	Louisiana	88.61
44	Maine	72.64
8	Maryland	96.16
3	Massachusetts	99.90
NA	Michigan**	NA
NA	Minnesota**	NA
41	Mississippi	75.20
24	Missouri	91.97
47	Montana	50.85
27	Nebraska	89.71
16	Nevada	93.50
12	New Hampshire	94.59
1	New Jersey	100.00
29	New Mexico	89.55
5	New York	96.90
30	North Carolina	89.11
32	North Dakota	85.23
6	Ohio	96.25
17	Oklahoma	93.28
34	Oregon	84.75
19	Pennsylvania	92.93
1	Rhode Island	100.00
36	South Carolina	82.89
33	South Dakota	84.91
14	Tennessee	94.14
9	Texas	96.05
21	Utah	92.64
43	Vermont	73.36
26	Virginia	90.30
18	Washington	93.00
39	West Virginia	78.36
25	Wisconsin	90.31
37	Wyoming	80.75

RANK ORDER

RANK	STATE	PERCENT
1	New Jersey	100.00
1	Rhode Island	100.00
3	Massachusetts	99.90
4	California	98.41
5	New York	96.90
6	Ohio	96.25
7	Arizona	96.17
8	Maryland	96.16
9	Texas	96.05
10	Colorado	94.92
10	Florida	94.92
12	New Hampshire	94.59
13	Connecticut	94.25
14	Tennessee	94.14
15	Alabama	93.61
16	Nevada	93.50
17	Oklahoma	93.28
18	Washington	93.00
19	Pennsylvania	92.93
20	Kansas	92.91
21	Utah	92.64
22	Indiana	92.57
23	Iowa	92.13
24	Missouri	91.97
25	Wisconsin	90.31
26	Virginia	90.30
27	Nebraska	89.71
28	Georgia	89.67
29	New Mexico	89.55
30	North Carolina	89.11
31	Louisiana	88.61
32	North Dakota	85.23
33	South Dakota	84.91
34	Oregon	84.75
35	Arkansas	84.14
36	South Carolina	82.89
37	Wyoming	80.75
38	Delaware	80.71
39	West Virginia	78.36
40	Hawaii	76.65
41	Mississippi	75.20
42	Idaho	75.00
43	Vermont	73.36
44	Maine	72.64
45	Kentucky	66.10
46	Alaska	65.54
47	Montana	50.85
NA	Illinois**	NA
NA	Michigan**	NA
NA	Minnesota**	NA
	District of Columbia	100.00

Source: Morgan Quitno Corporation using data from U.S. Department of Justice, Federal Bureau of Investigation
   "Crime in the United States 1993" (Uniform Crime Reports, December 4, 1994)
*Estimated percentages for urban areas, defined by the F.B.I. as Metropolitan Statistical Areas and other cities outside
such areas. National percent includes those states listed as not available. Forcible rape is the carnal knowledge of a
female forcibly and against her will. Attempts are included. However, statutory rape without force and other sex offenses
are excluded. **Not available.
385

Rape in Rural Areas in 1993

National Total = 7,898 Rapes*

ALPHA ORDER					RANK ORDER			
RANK	STATE	RAPES	% of USA		RANK	STATE	RAPES	% of USA
26	Alabama	94	1.19%		1	Kentucky	441	5.58%
15	Alaska	173	2.19%		2	Texas	392	4.96%
36	Arizona	57	0.72%		3	Florida	374	4.74%
17	Arkansas	163	2.06%		4	South Carolina	326	4.13%
14	California	187	2.37%		5	Mississippi	279	3.53%
31	Colorado	83	1.05%		6	North Carolina	259	3.28%
40	Connecticut	46	0.58%		7	Georgia	253	3.20%
24	Delaware	104	1.32%		8	Oregon	237	3.00%
3	Florida	374	4.74%		8	Washington	237	3.00%
7	Georgia	253	3.20%		10	Pennsylvania	226	2.86%
27	Hawaii	92	1.16%		11	Louisiana	207	2.62%
25	Idaho	97	1.23%		12	Ohio	204	2.58%
NA	Illinois**	NA	NA		13	Virginia	202	2.56%
16	Indiana	166	2.10%		14	California	187	2.37%
38	Iowa	54	0.68%		15	Alaska	173	2.19%
33	Kansas	72	0.91%		16	Indiana	166	2.10%
1	Kentucky	441	5.58%		17	Arkansas	163	2.06%
11	Louisiana	207	2.62%		18	New York	155	1.96%
28	Maine	90	1.14%		19	Missouri	152	1.92%
30	Maryland	84	1.06%		20	Tennessee	149	1.89%
45	Massachusetts	2	0.03%		21	Wisconsin	123	1.56%
NA	Michigan**	NA	NA		22	Montana	115	1.46%
NA	Minnesota**	NA	NA		23	Oklahoma	107	1.35%
5	Mississippi	279	3.53%		24	Delaware	104	1.32%
19	Missouri	152	1.92%		25	Idaho	97	1.23%
22	Montana	115	1.46%		26	Alabama	94	1.19%
40	Nebraska	46	0.58%		27	Hawaii	92	1.16%
37	Nevada	55	0.70%		28	Maine	90	1.14%
43	New Hampshire	27	0.34%		29	New Mexico	88	1.11%
46	New Jersey	0	0.00%		30	Maryland	84	1.06%
29	New Mexico	88	1.11%		31	Colorado	83	1.05%
18	New York	155	1.96%		32	West Virginia	79	1.00%
6	North Carolina	259	3.28%		33	Kansas	72	0.91%
44	North Dakota	22	0.28%		34	Utah	61	0.77%
12	Ohio	204	2.58%		34	Vermont	61	0.77%
23	Oklahoma	107	1.35%		36	Arizona	57	0.72%
8	Oregon	237	3.00%		37	Nevada	55	0.70%
10	Pennsylvania	226	2.86%		38	Iowa	54	0.68%
46	Rhode Island	0	0.00%		39	South Dakota	48	0.61%
4	South Carolina	326	4.13%		40	Connecticut	46	0.58%
39	South Dakota	48	0.61%		40	Nebraska	46	0.58%
20	Tennessee	149	1.89%		42	Wyoming	31	0.39%
2	Texas	392	4.96%		43	New Hampshire	27	0.34%
34	Utah	61	0.77%		44	North Dakota	22	0.28%
34	Vermont	61	0.77%		45	Massachusetts	2	0.03%
13	Virginia	202	2.56%		46	New Jersey	0	0.00%
8	Washington	237	3.00%		46	Rhode Island	0	0.00%
32	West Virginia	79	1.00%		NA	Illinois**	NA	NA
21	Wisconsin	123	1.56%		NA	Michigan**	NA	NA
42	Wyoming	31	0.39%		NA	Minnesota**	NA	NA
						District of Columbia	0	0.00%

Source: Morgan Quitno Corporation using data from U.S. Department of Justice, Federal Bureau of Investigation "Crime in the United States 1993" (Uniform Crime Reports, December 4, 1994)

*Estimated totals for rural areas, defined by the F.B.I. as other than Metropolitan Statistical Areas and other cities outside such areas. National total includes those states listed as not available. Forcible rape is the carnal knowledge of a female forcibly and against her will. Attempts are included. However, statutory rape without force and other sex offenses are excluded. **Not available.*

Rural Rape Rate in 1993

National Rural Rate = 24.9 Rapes per 100,000 Population*

<table>
<tr><td colspan="3">ALPHA ORDER</td><td colspan="3">RANK ORDER</td></tr>
<tr><td>RANK</td><td>STATE</td><td>RATE</td><td>RANK</td><td>STATE</td><td>RATE</td></tr>
<tr><td>41</td><td>Alabama</td><td>11.9</td><td>1</td><td>Delaware</td><td>117.7</td></tr>
<tr><td>2</td><td>Alaska</td><td>91.5</td><td>2</td><td>Alaska</td><td>91.5</td></tr>
<tr><td>28</td><td>Arizona</td><td>18.9</td><td>3</td><td>Florida</td><td>50.4</td></tr>
<tr><td>25</td><td>Arkansas</td><td>20.0</td><td>4</td><td>Washington</td><td>48.9</td></tr>
<tr><td>11</td><td>California</td><td>30.3</td><td>5</td><td>Oregon</td><td>48.5</td></tr>
<tr><td>22</td><td>Colorado</td><td>23.2</td><td>6</td><td>South Carolina</td><td>41.5</td></tr>
<tr><td>21</td><td>Connecticut</td><td>24.1</td><td>7</td><td>Hawaii</td><td>35.8</td></tr>
<tr><td>1</td><td>Delaware</td><td>117.7</td><td>8</td><td>Nevada</td><td>32.4</td></tr>
<tr><td>3</td><td>Florida</td><td>50.4</td><td>9</td><td>Kentucky</td><td>32.0</td></tr>
<tr><td>29</td><td>Georgia</td><td>18.6</td><td>10</td><td>Maryland</td><td>31.6</td></tr>
<tr><td>7</td><td>Hawaii</td><td>35.8</td><td>11</td><td>California</td><td>30.3</td></tr>
<tr><td>17</td><td>Idaho</td><td>25.3</td><td>11</td><td>Utah</td><td>30.3</td></tr>
<tr><td>NA</td><td>Illinois**</td><td>NA</td><td>13</td><td>New Mexico</td><td>30.0</td></tr>
<tr><td>34</td><td>Indiana</td><td>15.8</td><td>14</td><td>Louisiana</td><td>27.3</td></tr>
<tr><td>45</td><td>Iowa</td><td>6.0</td><td>15</td><td>Montana</td><td>26.7</td></tr>
<tr><td>34</td><td>Kansas</td><td>15.8</td><td>16</td><td>Maine</td><td>26.0</td></tr>
<tr><td>9</td><td>Kentucky</td><td>32.0</td><td>17</td><td>Idaho</td><td>25.3</td></tr>
<tr><td>14</td><td>Louisiana</td><td>27.3</td><td>18</td><td>Wyoming</td><td>25.0</td></tr>
<tr><td>16</td><td>Maine</td><td>26.0</td><td>19</td><td>Texas</td><td>24.6</td></tr>
<tr><td>10</td><td>Maryland</td><td>31.6</td><td>20</td><td>Mississippi</td><td>24.3</td></tr>
<tr><td>33</td><td>Massachusetts</td><td>16.3</td><td>21</td><td>Connecticut</td><td>24.1</td></tr>
<tr><td>NA</td><td>Michigan**</td><td>NA</td><td>22</td><td>Colorado</td><td>23.2</td></tr>
<tr><td>NA</td><td>Minnesota**</td><td>NA</td><td>22</td><td>Vermont</td><td>23.2</td></tr>
<tr><td>20</td><td>Mississippi</td><td>24.3</td><td>24</td><td>Pennsylvania</td><td>21.2</td></tr>
<tr><td>39</td><td>Missouri</td><td>12.9</td><td>25</td><td>Arkansas</td><td>20.0</td></tr>
<tr><td>15</td><td>Montana</td><td>26.7</td><td>26</td><td>Virginia</td><td>19.3</td></tr>
<tr><td>42</td><td>Nebraska</td><td>11.1</td><td>27</td><td>New Hampshire</td><td>19.2</td></tr>
<tr><td>8</td><td>Nevada</td><td>32.4</td><td>28</td><td>Arizona</td><td>18.9</td></tr>
<tr><td>27</td><td>New Hampshire</td><td>19.2</td><td>29</td><td>Georgia</td><td>18.6</td></tr>
<tr><td>46</td><td>New Jersey</td><td>0.0</td><td>30</td><td>New York</td><td>18.1</td></tr>
<tr><td>13</td><td>New Mexico</td><td>30.0</td><td>31</td><td>Oklahoma</td><td>17.1</td></tr>
<tr><td>30</td><td>New York</td><td>18.1</td><td>32</td><td>South Dakota</td><td>16.5</td></tr>
<tr><td>34</td><td>North Carolina</td><td>15.8</td><td>33</td><td>Massachusetts</td><td>16.3</td></tr>
<tr><td>44</td><td>North Dakota</td><td>9.7</td><td>34</td><td>Indiana</td><td>15.8</td></tr>
<tr><td>37</td><td>Ohio</td><td>15.5</td><td>34</td><td>Kansas</td><td>15.8</td></tr>
<tr><td>31</td><td>Oklahoma</td><td>17.1</td><td>34</td><td>North Carolina</td><td>15.8</td></tr>
<tr><td>5</td><td>Oregon</td><td>48.5</td><td>37</td><td>Ohio</td><td>15.5</td></tr>
<tr><td>24</td><td>Pennsylvania</td><td>21.2</td><td>38</td><td>Tennessee</td><td>13.4</td></tr>
<tr><td>46</td><td>Rhode Island</td><td>0.0</td><td>39</td><td>Missouri</td><td>12.9</td></tr>
<tr><td>6</td><td>South Carolina</td><td>41.5</td><td>40</td><td>Wisconsin</td><td>12.5</td></tr>
<tr><td>32</td><td>South Dakota</td><td>16.5</td><td>41</td><td>Alabama</td><td>11.9</td></tr>
<tr><td>38</td><td>Tennessee</td><td>13.4</td><td>42</td><td>Nebraska</td><td>11.1</td></tr>
<tr><td>19</td><td>Texas</td><td>24.6</td><td>43</td><td>West Virginia</td><td>10.1</td></tr>
<tr><td>11</td><td>Utah</td><td>30.3</td><td>44</td><td>North Dakota</td><td>9.7</td></tr>
<tr><td>22</td><td>Vermont</td><td>23.2</td><td>45</td><td>Iowa</td><td>6.0</td></tr>
<tr><td>26</td><td>Virginia</td><td>19.3</td><td>46</td><td>New Jersey</td><td>0.0</td></tr>
<tr><td>4</td><td>Washington</td><td>48.9</td><td>46</td><td>Rhode Island</td><td>0.0</td></tr>
<tr><td>43</td><td>West Virginia</td><td>10.1</td><td>NA</td><td>Illinois**</td><td>NA</td></tr>
<tr><td>40</td><td>Wisconsin</td><td>12.5</td><td>NA</td><td>Michigan**</td><td>NA</td></tr>
<tr><td>18</td><td>Wyoming</td><td>25.0</td><td>NA</td><td>Minnesota**</td><td>NA</td></tr>
<tr><td></td><td></td><td></td><td></td><td>District of Columbia</td><td>0.0</td></tr>
</table>

Source: Morgan Quitno Corporation using data from U.S. Department of Justice, Federal Bureau of Investigation
"Crime in the United States 1993" (Uniform Crime Reports, December 4, 1994)
*Estimated rates for rural areas, defined by the F.B.I. as other than Metropolitan Statistical Areas and other cities outside such areas. National rate includes those states listed as not available. Forcible rape is the carnal knowledge of a female forcibly and against her will. Attempts are included. However, statutory rape without force and other sex offenses are excluded. **Not available.

Percent of Rapes Occurring in Rural Areas in 1993

National Percent = 7.54% of Rapes*

ALPHA ORDER				RANK ORDER		
RANK	STATE	PERCENT		RANK	STATE	PERCENT
33	Alabama	6.39		1	Montana	49.15
2	Alaska	34.46		2	Alaska	34.46
41	Arizona	3.83		3	Kentucky	33.90
13	Arkansas	15.86		4	Maine	27.36
44	California	1.59		5	Vermont	26.64
37	Colorado	5.08		6	Idaho	25.00
35	Connecticut	5.75		7	Mississippi	24.80
10	Delaware	19.29		8	Hawaii	23.35
37	Florida	5.08		9	West Virginia	21.64
20	Georgia	10.33		10	Delaware	19.29
8	Hawaii	23.35		11	Wyoming	19.25
6	Idaho	25.00		12	South Carolina	17.11
NA	Illinois**	NA		13	Arkansas	15.86
26	Indiana	7.43		14	Oregon	15.25
25	Iowa	7.87		15	South Dakota	15.09
28	Kansas	7.09		16	North Dakota	14.77
3	Kentucky	33.90		17	Louisiana	11.39
17	Louisiana	11.39		18	North Carolina	10.89
4	Maine	27.36		19	New Mexico	10.45
40	Maryland	3.84		20	Georgia	10.33
45	Massachusetts	0.10		21	Nebraska	10.29
NA	Michigan**	NA		22	Virginia	9.70
NA	Minnesota**	NA		23	Wisconsin	9.69
7	Mississippi	24.80		24	Missouri	8.03
24	Missouri	8.03		25	Iowa	7.87
1	Montana	49.15		26	Indiana	7.43
21	Nebraska	10.29		27	Utah	7.36
32	Nevada	6.50		28	Kansas	7.09
36	New Hampshire	5.41		29	Pennsylvania	7.07
46	New Jersey	0.00		30	Washington	7.00
19	New Mexico	10.45		31	Oklahoma	6.72
43	New York	3.10		32	Nevada	6.50
18	North Carolina	10.89		33	Alabama	6.39
16	North Dakota	14.77		34	Tennessee	5.86
42	Ohio	3.75		35	Connecticut	5.75
31	Oklahoma	6.72		36	New Hampshire	5.41
14	Oregon	15.25		37	Colorado	5.08
29	Pennsylvania	7.07		37	Florida	5.08
46	Rhode Island	0.00		39	Texas	3.95
12	South Carolina	17.11		40	Maryland	3.84
15	South Dakota	15.09		41	Arizona	3.83
34	Tennessee	5.86		42	Ohio	3.75
39	Texas	3.95		43	New York	3.10
27	Utah	7.36		44	California	1.59
5	Vermont	26.64		45	Massachusetts	0.10
22	Virginia	9.70		46	New Jersey	0.00
30	Washington	7.00		46	Rhode Island	0.00
9	West Virginia	21.64		NA	Illinois**	NA
23	Wisconsin	9.69		NA	Michigan**	NA
11	Wyoming	19.25		NA	Minnesota**	NA
					District of Columbia	0.00

Source: Morgan Quitno Corporation using data from U.S. Department of Justice, Federal Bureau of Investigation
"Crime in the United States 1993" (Uniform Crime Reports, December 4, 1994)
*Estimated percentages for rural areas, defined by the F.B.I. as other than Metropolitan Statistical Areas and other cities outside such areas. National percent includes those states listed as not available. Forcible rape is the carnal knowledge of a female forcibly and against her will. Attempts are included. However, statutory rape without force and other sex offenses are excluded. **Not available.

Robbery in Urban Areas in 1993

National Total = 654,550 Robberies*

ALPHA ORDER					RANK ORDER			
RANK	STATE	ROBBERIES	% of USA		RANK	STATE	ROBBERIES	% of USA
19	Alabama	6,587	1.01%		1	California	126,261	19.29%
40	Alaska	704	0.11%		2	New York	102,048	15.59%
21	Arizona	6,372	0.97%		3	Florida	48,416	7.40%
32	Arkansas	2,928	0.45%		4	Texas	40,249	6.15%
1	California	126,261	19.29%		5	New Jersey	23,319	3.56%
26	Colorado	4,134	0.63%		6	Michigan	22,531	3.44%
20	Connecticut	6,408	0.98%		7	Maryland	21,479	3.28%
35	Delaware	1,255	0.19%		8	Pennsylvania	21,452	3.28%
3	Florida	48,416	7.40%		9	Ohio	21,288	3.25%
10	Georgia	16,696	2.55%		10	Georgia	16,696	2.55%
36	Hawaii	1,103	0.17%		11	North Carolina	12,934	1.98%
45	Idaho	170	0.03%		12	Missouri	12,586	1.92%
NA	Illinois**	NA	NA		13	Louisiana	11,944	1.82%
18	Indiana	6,716	1.03%		14	Tennessee	11,104	1.70%
34	Iowa	1,500	0.23%		15	Massachusetts	10,562	1.61%
31	Kansas	3,091	0.47%		16	Virginia	9,069	1.39%
30	Kentucky	3,256	0.50%		17	Washington	7,154	1.09%
13	Louisiana	11,944	1.82%		18	Indiana	6,716	1.03%
43	Maine	251	0.04%		19	Alabama	6,587	1.01%
7	Maryland	21,479	3.28%		20	Connecticut	6,408	0.98%
15	Massachusetts	10,562	1.61%		21	Arizona	6,372	0.97%
6	Michigan	22,531	3.44%		22	South Carolina	6,212	0.95%
24	Minnesota	5,059	0.77%		23	Wisconsin	5,669	0.87%
29	Mississippi	3,374	0.52%		24	Minnesota	5,059	0.77%
12	Missouri	12,586	1.92%		25	Nevada	4,671	0.71%
44	Montana	247	0.04%		26	Colorado	4,134	0.63%
39	Nebraska	875	0.13%		27	Oregon	3,873	0.59%
25	Nevada	4,671	0.71%		28	Oklahoma	3,861	0.59%
42	New Hampshire	303	0.05%		29	Mississippi	3,374	0.52%
5	New Jersey	23,319	3.56%		30	Kentucky	3,256	0.50%
33	New Mexico	2,178	0.33%		31	Kansas	3,091	0.47%
2	New York	102,048	15.59%		32	Arkansas	2,928	0.45%
11	North Carolina	12,934	1.98%		33	New Mexico	2,178	0.33%
48	North Dakota	49	0.01%		34	Iowa	1,500	0.23%
9	Ohio	21,288	3.25%		35	Delaware	1,255	0.19%
28	Oklahoma	3,861	0.59%		36	Hawaii	1,103	0.17%
27	Oregon	3,873	0.59%		37	Utah	1,078	0.16%
8	Pennsylvania	21,452	3.28%		38	Rhode Island	1,011	0.15%
38	Rhode Island	1,011	0.15%		39	Nebraska	875	0.13%
22	South Carolina	6,212	0.95%		40	Alaska	704	0.11%
46	South Dakota	99	0.02%		41	West Virginia	680	0.10%
14	Tennessee	11,104	1.70%		42	New Hampshire	303	0.05%
4	Texas	40,249	6.15%		43	Maine	251	0.04%
37	Utah	1,078	0.16%		44	Montana	247	0.04%
49	Vermont	48	0.01%		45	Idaho	170	0.03%
16	Virginia	9,069	1.39%		46	South Dakota	99	0.02%
17	Washington	7,154	1.09%		47	Wyoming	74	0.01%
41	West Virginia	680	0.10%		48	North Dakota	49	0.01%
23	Wisconsin	5,669	0.87%		49	Vermont	48	0.01%
47	Wyoming	74	0.01%		NA	Illinois**	NA	NA
						District of Columbia	7,107	1.09%

Source: Morgan Quitno Corporation using data from U.S. Department of Justice, Federal Bureau of Investigation
    "Crime in the United States 1993" (Uniform Crime Reports, December 4, 1994)
*Estimated totals for urban areas, defined by the F.B.I. as Metropolitan Statistical Areas and other cities outside such areas. National total includes those states listed as not available. Robbery is the taking or attempting to take anything of value by force or threat of force.
**Not available.

Urban Robbery Rate in 1993

National Urban Rate = 289.4 Robberies per 100,000 Population*

ALPHA ORDER

RANK	STATE	RATE
20	Alabama	193.8
24	Alaska	171.7
23	Arizona	175.3
21	Arkansas	181.9
3	California	412.7
35	Colorado	128.8
17	Connecticut	207.6
18	Delaware	205.2
5	Florida	374.2
8	Georgia	300.4
36	Hawaii	120.6
45	Idaho	23.8
NA	Illinois**	NA
31	Indiana	144.1
38	Iowa	78.1
29	Kansas	149.0
34	Kentucky	135.2
6	Louisiana	337.6
44	Maine	28.1
2	Maryland	457.1
22	Massachusetts	176.0
11	Michigan	266.7
33	Minnesota	138.6
14	Mississippi	225.8
7	Missouri	310.2
42	Montana	60.6
39	Nebraska	73.3
4	Nevada	383.1
43	New Hampshire	30.8
9	New Jersey	296.0
26	New Mexico	164.6
1	New York	588.5
13	North Carolina	243.8
49	North Dakota	12.0
15	Ohio	217.8
30	Oklahoma	148.2
27	Oregon	152.3
19	Pennsylvania	195.3
37	Rhode Island	101.1
16	South Carolina	217.4
46	South Dakota	23.3
10	Tennessee	278.3
12	Texas	244.8
41	Utah	65.0
48	Vermont	15.3
25	Virginia	166.6
28	Washington	150.0
40	West Virginia	65.5
32	Wisconsin	139.9
47	Wyoming	21.4

RANK ORDER

RANK	STATE	RATE
1	New York	588.5
2	Maryland	457.1
3	California	412.7
4	Nevada	383.1
5	Florida	374.2
6	Louisiana	337.6
7	Missouri	310.2
8	Georgia	300.4
9	New Jersey	296.0
10	Tennessee	278.3
11	Michigan	266.7
12	Texas	244.8
13	North Carolina	243.8
14	Mississippi	225.8
15	Ohio	217.8
16	South Carolina	217.4
17	Connecticut	207.6
18	Delaware	205.2
19	Pennsylvania	195.3
20	Alabama	193.8
21	Arkansas	181.9
22	Massachusetts	176.0
23	Arizona	175.3
24	Alaska	171.7
25	Virginia	166.6
26	New Mexico	164.6
27	Oregon	152.3
28	Washington	150.0
29	Kansas	149.0
30	Oklahoma	148.2
31	Indiana	144.1
32	Wisconsin	139.9
33	Minnesota	138.6
34	Kentucky	135.2
35	Colorado	128.8
36	Hawaii	120.6
37	Rhode Island	101.1
38	Iowa	78.1
39	Nebraska	73.3
40	West Virginia	65.5
41	Utah	65.0
42	Montana	60.6
43	New Hampshire	30.8
44	Maine	28.1
45	Idaho	23.8
46	South Dakota	23.3
47	Wyoming	21.4
48	Vermont	15.3
49	North Dakota	12.0
NA	Illinois**	NA

District of Columbia   1,229.6

Source: Morgan Quitno Corporation using data from U.S. Department of Justice, Federal Bureau of Investigation
"Crime in the United States 1993" (Uniform Crime Reports, December 4, 1994)
*Estimated rates for urban areas, defined by the F.B.I. as Metropolitan Statistical Areas and other cities outside such areas. National rate includes those states listed as not available. Robbery is the taking or attempting to take anything of value by force or threat of force.
**Not available.

Percent of Robberies Occurring in Urban Areas in 1993

National Percent = 99.21% of Robberies*

<table>
<tr><td colspan="3"><u>ALPHA ORDER</u></td><td colspan="3"><u>RANK ORDER</u></td></tr>
<tr><td>RANK</td><td>STATE</td><td>PERCENT</td><td>RANK</td><td>STATE</td><td>PERCENT</td></tr>
<tr><td>25</td><td>Alabama</td><td>98.65</td><td>1</td><td>New Jersey</td><td>100.00</td></tr>
<tr><td>36</td><td>Alaska</td><td>96.04</td><td>1</td><td>Rhode Island</td><td>100.00</td></tr>
<tr><td>13</td><td>Arizona</td><td>99.38</td><td>3</td><td>Massachusetts</td><td>99.99</td></tr>
<tr><td>35</td><td>Arkansas</td><td>96.73</td><td>4</td><td>New York</td><td>99.93</td></tr>
<tr><td>5</td><td>California</td><td>99.86</td><td>5</td><td>California</td><td>99.86</td></tr>
<tr><td>13</td><td>Colorado</td><td>99.38</td><td>6</td><td>Michigan</td><td>99.69</td></tr>
<tr><td>12</td><td>Connecticut</td><td>99.40</td><td>7</td><td>Ohio</td><td>99.60</td></tr>
<tr><td>37</td><td>Delaware</td><td>96.02</td><td>8</td><td>Maryland</td><td>99.52</td></tr>
<tr><td>18</td><td>Florida</td><td>98.98</td><td>9</td><td>Pennsylvania</td><td>99.49</td></tr>
<tr><td>33</td><td>Georgia</td><td>97.33</td><td>10</td><td>Missouri</td><td>99.46</td></tr>
<tr><td>47</td><td>Hawaii</td><td>90.86</td><td>10</td><td>Texas</td><td>99.46</td></tr>
<tr><td>44</td><td>Idaho</td><td>91.40</td><td>12</td><td>Connecticut</td><td>99.40</td></tr>
<tr><td>NA</td><td>Illinois**</td><td>NA</td><td>13</td><td>Arizona</td><td>99.38</td></tr>
<tr><td>29</td><td>Indiana</td><td>98.12</td><td>13</td><td>Colorado</td><td>99.38</td></tr>
<tr><td>21</td><td>Iowa</td><td>98.88</td><td>15</td><td>Minnesota</td><td>99.35</td></tr>
<tr><td>23</td><td>Kansas</td><td>98.82</td><td>16</td><td>Washington</td><td>99.31</td></tr>
<tr><td>39</td><td>Kentucky</td><td>95.07</td><td>17</td><td>Wisconsin</td><td>99.21</td></tr>
<tr><td>31</td><td>Louisiana</td><td>98.05</td><td>18</td><td>Florida</td><td>98.98</td></tr>
<tr><td>38</td><td>Maine</td><td>95.08</td><td>19</td><td>Tennessee</td><td>98.93</td></tr>
<tr><td>8</td><td>Maryland</td><td>99.52</td><td>20</td><td>Utah</td><td>98.90</td></tr>
<tr><td>3</td><td>Massachusetts</td><td>99.99</td><td>21</td><td>Iowa</td><td>98.88</td></tr>
<tr><td>6</td><td>Michigan</td><td>99.69</td><td>21</td><td>Nevada</td><td>98.88</td></tr>
<tr><td>15</td><td>Minnesota</td><td>99.35</td><td>23</td><td>Kansas</td><td>98.82</td></tr>
<tr><td>43</td><td>Mississippi</td><td>91.61</td><td>24</td><td>New Hampshire</td><td>98.70</td></tr>
<tr><td>10</td><td>Missouri</td><td>99.46</td><td>25</td><td>Alabama</td><td>98.65</td></tr>
<tr><td>48</td><td>Montana</td><td>90.81</td><td>26</td><td>Oregon</td><td>98.55</td></tr>
<tr><td>28</td><td>Nebraska</td><td>98.31</td><td>27</td><td>Virginia</td><td>98.40</td></tr>
<tr><td>21</td><td>Nevada</td><td>98.88</td><td>28</td><td>Nebraska</td><td>98.31</td></tr>
<tr><td>24</td><td>New Hampshire</td><td>98.70</td><td>29</td><td>Indiana</td><td>98.12</td></tr>
<tr><td>1</td><td>New Jersey</td><td>100.00</td><td>29</td><td>Oklahoma</td><td>98.12</td></tr>
<tr><td>32</td><td>New Mexico</td><td>97.36</td><td>31</td><td>Louisiana</td><td>98.05</td></tr>
<tr><td>4</td><td>New York</td><td>99.93</td><td>32</td><td>New Mexico</td><td>97.36</td></tr>
<tr><td>34</td><td>North Carolina</td><td>96.78</td><td>33</td><td>Georgia</td><td>97.33</td></tr>
<tr><td>41</td><td>North Dakota</td><td>92.45</td><td>34</td><td>North Carolina</td><td>96.78</td></tr>
<tr><td>7</td><td>Ohio</td><td>99.60</td><td>35</td><td>Arkansas</td><td>96.73</td></tr>
<tr><td>29</td><td>Oklahoma</td><td>98.12</td><td>36</td><td>Alaska</td><td>96.04</td></tr>
<tr><td>26</td><td>Oregon</td><td>98.55</td><td>37</td><td>Delaware</td><td>96.02</td></tr>
<tr><td>9</td><td>Pennsylvania</td><td>99.49</td><td>38</td><td>Maine</td><td>95.08</td></tr>
<tr><td>1</td><td>Rhode Island</td><td>100.00</td><td>39</td><td>Kentucky</td><td>95.07</td></tr>
<tr><td>46</td><td>South Carolina</td><td>91.02</td><td>40</td><td>South Dakota</td><td>92.52</td></tr>
<tr><td>40</td><td>South Dakota</td><td>92.52</td><td>41</td><td>North Dakota</td><td>92.45</td></tr>
<tr><td>19</td><td>Tennessee</td><td>98.93</td><td>42</td><td>Vermont</td><td>92.31</td></tr>
<tr><td>10</td><td>Texas</td><td>99.46</td><td>43</td><td>Mississippi</td><td>91.61</td></tr>
<tr><td>20</td><td>Utah</td><td>98.90</td><td>44</td><td>Idaho</td><td>91.40</td></tr>
<tr><td>42</td><td>Vermont</td><td>92.31</td><td>45</td><td>Wyoming</td><td>91.36</td></tr>
<tr><td>27</td><td>Virginia</td><td>98.40</td><td>46</td><td>South Carolina</td><td>91.02</td></tr>
<tr><td>16</td><td>Washington</td><td>99.31</td><td>47</td><td>Hawaii</td><td>90.86</td></tr>
<tr><td>49</td><td>West Virginia</td><td>86.96</td><td>48</td><td>Montana</td><td>90.81</td></tr>
<tr><td>17</td><td>Wisconsin</td><td>99.21</td><td>49</td><td>West Virginia</td><td>86.96</td></tr>
<tr><td>45</td><td>Wyoming</td><td>91.36</td><td>NA</td><td>Illinois**</td><td>NA</td></tr>
<tr><td></td><td></td><td></td><td></td><td>District of Columbia</td><td>100.00</td></tr>
</table>

Source: Morgan Quitno Corporation using data from U.S. Department of Justice, Federal Bureau of Investigation
   "Crime in the United States 1993" (Uniform Crime Reports, December 4, 1994)
*Estimated percentages for urban areas, defined by the F.B.I. as Metropolitan Statistical Areas and other cities outside such areas. National percent includes those states listed as not available. Robbery is the taking or attempting to take anything of value by force or threat of force.
**Not available.

Robbery in Rural Areas in 1993

National Total = 5,207 Robberies*

<table>
<tr><td colspan="4"><u>ALPHA ORDER</u></td><td colspan="4"><u>RANK ORDER</u></td></tr>
<tr><td>RANK</td><td>STATE</td><td>ROBBERIES</td><td>% of USA</td><td>RANK</td><td>STATE</td><td>ROBBERIES</td><td>% of USA</td></tr>
<tr><td>18</td><td>Alabama</td><td>90</td><td>1.73%</td><td>1</td><td>South Carolina</td><td>613</td><td>11.77%</td></tr>
<tr><td>34</td><td>Alaska</td><td>29</td><td>0.56%</td><td>2</td><td>Florida</td><td>497</td><td>9.54%</td></tr>
<tr><td>30</td><td>Arizona</td><td>40</td><td>0.77%</td><td>3</td><td>Georgia</td><td>458</td><td>8.80%</td></tr>
<tr><td>17</td><td>Arkansas</td><td>99</td><td>1.90%</td><td>4</td><td>North Carolina</td><td>430</td><td>8.26%</td></tr>
<tr><td>8</td><td>California</td><td>175</td><td>3.36%</td><td>5</td><td>Mississippi</td><td>309</td><td>5.93%</td></tr>
<tr><td>35</td><td>Colorado</td><td>26</td><td>0.50%</td><td>6</td><td>Louisiana</td><td>238</td><td>4.57%</td></tr>
<tr><td>31</td><td>Connecticut</td><td>39</td><td>0.75%</td><td>7</td><td>Texas</td><td>220</td><td>4.23%</td></tr>
<tr><td>27</td><td>Delaware</td><td>52</td><td>1.00%</td><td>8</td><td>California</td><td>175</td><td>3.36%</td></tr>
<tr><td>2</td><td>Florida</td><td>497</td><td>9.54%</td><td>9</td><td>Kentucky</td><td>169</td><td>3.25%</td></tr>
<tr><td>3</td><td>Georgia</td><td>458</td><td>8.80%</td><td>10</td><td>Virginia</td><td>147</td><td>2.82%</td></tr>
<tr><td>13</td><td>Hawaii</td><td>111</td><td>2.13%</td><td>11</td><td>Indiana</td><td>129</td><td>2.48%</td></tr>
<tr><td>38</td><td>Idaho</td><td>16</td><td>0.31%</td><td>12</td><td>Tennessee</td><td>120</td><td>2.30%</td></tr>
<tr><td>NA</td><td>Illinois**</td><td>NA</td><td>NA</td><td>13</td><td>Hawaii</td><td>111</td><td>2.13%</td></tr>
<tr><td>11</td><td>Indiana</td><td>129</td><td>2.48%</td><td>13</td><td>Pennsylvania</td><td>111</td><td>2.13%</td></tr>
<tr><td>37</td><td>Iowa</td><td>17</td><td>0.33%</td><td>15</td><td>Maryland</td><td>103</td><td>1.98%</td></tr>
<tr><td>32</td><td>Kansas</td><td>37</td><td>0.71%</td><td>16</td><td>West Virginia</td><td>102</td><td>1.96%</td></tr>
<tr><td>9</td><td>Kentucky</td><td>169</td><td>3.25%</td><td>17</td><td>Arkansas</td><td>99</td><td>1.90%</td></tr>
<tr><td>6</td><td>Louisiana</td><td>238</td><td>4.57%</td><td>18</td><td>Alabama</td><td>90</td><td>1.73%</td></tr>
<tr><td>40</td><td>Maine</td><td>13</td><td>0.25%</td><td>19</td><td>Ohio</td><td>85</td><td>1.63%</td></tr>
<tr><td>15</td><td>Maryland</td><td>103</td><td>1.98%</td><td>20</td><td>New York</td><td>74</td><td>1.42%</td></tr>
<tr><td>47</td><td>Massachusetts</td><td>1</td><td>0.02%</td><td>20</td><td>Oklahoma</td><td>74</td><td>1.42%</td></tr>
<tr><td>22</td><td>Michigan</td><td>70</td><td>1.34%</td><td>22</td><td>Michigan</td><td>70</td><td>1.34%</td></tr>
<tr><td>33</td><td>Minnesota</td><td>33</td><td>0.63%</td><td>23</td><td>Missouri</td><td>68</td><td>1.31%</td></tr>
<tr><td>5</td><td>Mississippi</td><td>309</td><td>5.93%</td><td>24</td><td>New Mexico</td><td>59</td><td>1.13%</td></tr>
<tr><td>23</td><td>Missouri</td><td>68</td><td>1.31%</td><td>25</td><td>Oregon</td><td>57</td><td>1.09%</td></tr>
<tr><td>36</td><td>Montana</td><td>25</td><td>0.48%</td><td>26</td><td>Nevada</td><td>53</td><td>1.02%</td></tr>
<tr><td>39</td><td>Nebraska</td><td>15</td><td>0.29%</td><td>27</td><td>Delaware</td><td>52</td><td>1.00%</td></tr>
<tr><td>26</td><td>Nevada</td><td>53</td><td>1.02%</td><td>28</td><td>Washington</td><td>50</td><td>0.96%</td></tr>
<tr><td>44</td><td>New Hampshire</td><td>4</td><td>0.08%</td><td>29</td><td>Wisconsin</td><td>45</td><td>0.86%</td></tr>
<tr><td>48</td><td>New Jersey</td><td>0</td><td>0.00%</td><td>30</td><td>Arizona</td><td>40</td><td>0.77%</td></tr>
<tr><td>24</td><td>New Mexico</td><td>59</td><td>1.13%</td><td>31</td><td>Connecticut</td><td>39</td><td>0.75%</td></tr>
<tr><td>20</td><td>New York</td><td>74</td><td>1.42%</td><td>32</td><td>Kansas</td><td>37</td><td>0.71%</td></tr>
<tr><td>4</td><td>North Carolina</td><td>430</td><td>8.26%</td><td>33</td><td>Minnesota</td><td>33</td><td>0.63%</td></tr>
<tr><td>44</td><td>North Dakota</td><td>4</td><td>0.08%</td><td>34</td><td>Alaska</td><td>29</td><td>0.56%</td></tr>
<tr><td>19</td><td>Ohio</td><td>85</td><td>1.63%</td><td>35</td><td>Colorado</td><td>26</td><td>0.50%</td></tr>
<tr><td>20</td><td>Oklahoma</td><td>74</td><td>1.42%</td><td>36</td><td>Montana</td><td>25</td><td>0.48%</td></tr>
<tr><td>25</td><td>Oregon</td><td>57</td><td>1.09%</td><td>37</td><td>Iowa</td><td>17</td><td>0.33%</td></tr>
<tr><td>13</td><td>Pennsylvania</td><td>111</td><td>2.13%</td><td>38</td><td>Idaho</td><td>16</td><td>0.31%</td></tr>
<tr><td>48</td><td>Rhode Island</td><td>0</td><td>0.00%</td><td>39</td><td>Nebraska</td><td>15</td><td>0.29%</td></tr>
<tr><td>1</td><td>South Carolina</td><td>613</td><td>11.77%</td><td>40</td><td>Maine</td><td>13</td><td>0.25%</td></tr>
<tr><td>42</td><td>South Dakota</td><td>8</td><td>0.15%</td><td>41</td><td>Utah</td><td>12</td><td>0.23%</td></tr>
<tr><td>12</td><td>Tennessee</td><td>120</td><td>2.30%</td><td>42</td><td>South Dakota</td><td>8</td><td>0.15%</td></tr>
<tr><td>7</td><td>Texas</td><td>220</td><td>4.23%</td><td>43</td><td>Wyoming</td><td>7</td><td>0.13%</td></tr>
<tr><td>41</td><td>Utah</td><td>12</td><td>0.23%</td><td>44</td><td>New Hampshire</td><td>4</td><td>0.08%</td></tr>
<tr><td>44</td><td>Vermont</td><td>4</td><td>0.08%</td><td>44</td><td>North Dakota</td><td>4</td><td>0.08%</td></tr>
<tr><td>10</td><td>Virginia</td><td>147</td><td>2.82%</td><td>44</td><td>Vermont</td><td>4</td><td>0.08%</td></tr>
<tr><td>28</td><td>Washington</td><td>50</td><td>0.96%</td><td>47</td><td>Massachusetts</td><td>1</td><td>0.02%</td></tr>
<tr><td>16</td><td>West Virginia</td><td>102</td><td>1.96%</td><td>48</td><td>New Jersey</td><td>0</td><td>0.00%</td></tr>
<tr><td>29</td><td>Wisconsin</td><td>45</td><td>0.86%</td><td>48</td><td>Rhode Island</td><td>0</td><td>0.00%</td></tr>
<tr><td>43</td><td>Wyoming</td><td>7</td><td>0.13%</td><td>NA</td><td>Illinois**</td><td>NA</td><td>NA</td></tr>
<tr><td></td><td></td><td></td><td></td><td></td><td>District of Columbia</td><td>0</td><td>0.00%</td></tr>
</table>

Source: Morgan Quitno Corporation using data from U.S. Department of Justice, Federal Bureau of Investigation
   "Crime in the United States 1993" (Uniform Crime Reports, December 4, 1994)
*Estimated totals for rural areas, defined by the F.B.I. as other than Metropolitan Statistical Areas and other cities outside
such areas. National total includes those states listed as not available. Robbery is the taking or attempting to take
anything of value by force or threat of force.
**Not available.

Rural Robbery Rate in 1993

National Rural Rate = 16.4 Robberies per 100,000 Population*

<table>
<tr><td colspan="3">ALPHA ORDER</td><td colspan="3">RANK ORDER</td></tr>
<tr><th>RANK</th><th>STATE</th><th>RATE</th><th>RANK</th><th>STATE</th><th>RATE</th></tr>
<tr><td>24</td><td>Alabama</td><td>11.4</td><td>1</td><td>South Carolina</td><td>78.0</td></tr>
<tr><td>14</td><td>Alaska</td><td>15.3</td><td>2</td><td>Florida</td><td>67.0</td></tr>
<tr><td>17</td><td>Arizona</td><td>13.2</td><td>3</td><td>Delaware</td><td>58.8</td></tr>
<tr><td>20</td><td>Arkansas</td><td>12.2</td><td>4</td><td>Hawaii</td><td>43.2</td></tr>
<tr><td>9</td><td>California</td><td>28.4</td><td>5</td><td>Maryland</td><td>38.7</td></tr>
<tr><td>31</td><td>Colorado</td><td>7.3</td><td>6</td><td>Georgia</td><td>33.7</td></tr>
<tr><td>12</td><td>Connecticut</td><td>20.4</td><td>7</td><td>Louisiana</td><td>31.4</td></tr>
<tr><td>3</td><td>Delaware</td><td>58.8</td><td>8</td><td>Nevada</td><td>31.2</td></tr>
<tr><td>2</td><td>Florida</td><td>67.0</td><td>9</td><td>California</td><td>28.4</td></tr>
<tr><td>6</td><td>Georgia</td><td>33.7</td><td>10</td><td>Mississippi</td><td>26.9</td></tr>
<tr><td>4</td><td>Hawaii</td><td>43.2</td><td>11</td><td>North Carolina</td><td>26.2</td></tr>
<tr><td>39</td><td>Idaho</td><td>4.2</td><td>12</td><td>Connecticut</td><td>20.4</td></tr>
<tr><td>NA</td><td>Illinois**</td><td>NA</td><td>13</td><td>New Mexico</td><td>20.1</td></tr>
<tr><td>19</td><td>Indiana</td><td>12.3</td><td>14</td><td>Alaska</td><td>15.3</td></tr>
<tr><td>45</td><td>Iowa</td><td>1.9</td><td>15</td><td>Virginia</td><td>14.0</td></tr>
<tr><td>30</td><td>Kansas</td><td>8.1</td><td>16</td><td>Texas</td><td>13.8</td></tr>
<tr><td>20</td><td>Kentucky</td><td>12.2</td><td>17</td><td>Arizona</td><td>13.2</td></tr>
<tr><td>7</td><td>Louisiana</td><td>31.4</td><td>18</td><td>West Virginia</td><td>13.1</td></tr>
<tr><td>40</td><td>Maine</td><td>3.8</td><td>19</td><td>Indiana</td><td>12.3</td></tr>
<tr><td>5</td><td>Maryland</td><td>38.7</td><td>20</td><td>Arkansas</td><td>12.2</td></tr>
<tr><td>29</td><td>Massachusetts</td><td>8.2</td><td>20</td><td>Kentucky</td><td>12.2</td></tr>
<tr><td>32</td><td>Michigan</td><td>6.8</td><td>22</td><td>Oklahoma</td><td>11.8</td></tr>
<tr><td>40</td><td>Minnesota</td><td>3.8</td><td>23</td><td>Oregon</td><td>11.7</td></tr>
<tr><td>10</td><td>Mississippi</td><td>26.9</td><td>24</td><td>Alabama</td><td>11.4</td></tr>
<tr><td>35</td><td>Missouri</td><td>5.8</td><td>25</td><td>Tennessee</td><td>10.8</td></tr>
<tr><td>35</td><td>Montana</td><td>5.8</td><td>26</td><td>Pennsylvania</td><td>10.4</td></tr>
<tr><td>42</td><td>Nebraska</td><td>3.6</td><td>27</td><td>Washington</td><td>10.3</td></tr>
<tr><td>8</td><td>Nevada</td><td>31.2</td><td>28</td><td>New York</td><td>8.6</td></tr>
<tr><td>43</td><td>New Hampshire</td><td>2.8</td><td>29</td><td>Massachusetts</td><td>8.2</td></tr>
<tr><td>48</td><td>New Jersey</td><td>0.0</td><td>30</td><td>Kansas</td><td>8.1</td></tr>
<tr><td>13</td><td>New Mexico</td><td>20.1</td><td>31</td><td>Colorado</td><td>7.3</td></tr>
<tr><td>28</td><td>New York</td><td>8.6</td><td>32</td><td>Michigan</td><td>6.8</td></tr>
<tr><td>11</td><td>North Carolina</td><td>26.2</td><td>33</td><td>Ohio</td><td>6.5</td></tr>
<tr><td>46</td><td>North Dakota</td><td>1.8</td><td>34</td><td>Utah</td><td>6.0</td></tr>
<tr><td>33</td><td>Ohio</td><td>6.5</td><td>35</td><td>Missouri</td><td>5.8</td></tr>
<tr><td>22</td><td>Oklahoma</td><td>11.8</td><td>35</td><td>Montana</td><td>5.8</td></tr>
<tr><td>23</td><td>Oregon</td><td>11.7</td><td>37</td><td>Wyoming</td><td>5.6</td></tr>
<tr><td>26</td><td>Pennsylvania</td><td>10.4</td><td>38</td><td>Wisconsin</td><td>4.6</td></tr>
<tr><td>48</td><td>Rhode Island</td><td>0.0</td><td>39</td><td>Idaho</td><td>4.2</td></tr>
<tr><td>1</td><td>South Carolina</td><td>78.0</td><td>40</td><td>Maine</td><td>3.8</td></tr>
<tr><td>43</td><td>South Dakota</td><td>2.8</td><td>40</td><td>Minnesota</td><td>3.8</td></tr>
<tr><td>25</td><td>Tennessee</td><td>10.8</td><td>42</td><td>Nebraska</td><td>3.6</td></tr>
<tr><td>16</td><td>Texas</td><td>13.8</td><td>43</td><td>New Hampshire</td><td>2.8</td></tr>
<tr><td>34</td><td>Utah</td><td>6.0</td><td>43</td><td>South Dakota</td><td>2.8</td></tr>
<tr><td>47</td><td>Vermont</td><td>1.5</td><td>45</td><td>Iowa</td><td>1.9</td></tr>
<tr><td>15</td><td>Virginia</td><td>14.0</td><td>46</td><td>North Dakota</td><td>1.8</td></tr>
<tr><td>27</td><td>Washington</td><td>10.3</td><td>47</td><td>Vermont</td><td>1.5</td></tr>
<tr><td>18</td><td>West Virginia</td><td>13.1</td><td>48</td><td>New Jersey</td><td>0.0</td></tr>
<tr><td>38</td><td>Wisconsin</td><td>4.6</td><td>48</td><td>Rhode Island</td><td>0.0</td></tr>
<tr><td>37</td><td>Wyoming</td><td>5.6</td><td>NA</td><td>Illinois**</td><td>NA</td></tr>
<tr><td></td><td></td><td></td><td></td><td>District of Columbia</td><td>0.0</td></tr>
</table>

Source: Morgan Quitno Corporation using data from U.S. Department of Justice, Federal Bureau of Investigation
    "Crime in the United States 1993" (Uniform Crime Reports, December 4, 1994)
*Estimated rates for rural areas, defined by the F.B.I. as other than Metropolitan Statistical Areas and other cities outside such areas. National rate includes those states listed as not available. Robbery is the taking or attempting to take anything of value by force or threat of force.
**Not available.

Percent of Robberies Occurring in Rural Areas in 1993

National Percent = 0.79% of Robberies*

ALPHA ORDER				RANK ORDER		
RANK	STATE	PERCENT		RANK	STATE	PERCENT
25	Alabama	1.35		1	West Virginia	13.04
14	Alaska	3.96		2	Montana	9.19
37	Arizona	0.62		3	Hawaii	9.14
15	Arkansas	3.27		4	South Carolina	8.98
45	California	0.14		5	Wyoming	8.64
36	Colorado	0.63		6	Idaho	8.60
38	Connecticut	0.60		7	Mississippi	8.39
13	Delaware	3.98		8	Vermont	7.69
32	Florida	1.02		9	North Dakota	7.55
17	Georgia	2.67		10	South Dakota	7.48
3	Hawaii	9.14		11	Kentucky	4.93
6	Idaho	8.60		12	Maine	4.92
NA	Illinois**	NA		13	Delaware	3.98
20	Indiana	1.88		14	Alaska	3.96
28	Iowa	1.12		15	Arkansas	3.27
27	Kansas	1.18		16	North Carolina	3.22
11	Kentucky	4.93		17	Georgia	2.67
19	Louisiana	1.95		18	New Mexico	2.64
12	Maine	4.92		19	Louisiana	1.95
42	Maryland	0.48		20	Indiana	1.88
47	Massachusetts	0.01		20	Oklahoma	1.88
44	Michigan	0.31		22	Nebraska	1.69
35	Minnesota	0.65		23	Virginia	1.60
7	Mississippi	8.39		24	Oregon	1.45
39	Missouri	0.54		25	Alabama	1.35
2	Montana	9.19		26	New Hampshire	1.30
22	Nebraska	1.69		27	Kansas	1.18
28	Nevada	1.12		28	Iowa	1.12
26	New Hampshire	1.30		28	Nevada	1.12
48	New Jersey	0.00		30	Utah	1.10
18	New Mexico	2.64		31	Tennessee	1.07
46	New York	0.07		32	Florida	1.02
16	North Carolina	3.22		33	Wisconsin	0.79
9	North Dakota	7.55		34	Washington	0.69
43	Ohio	0.40		35	Minnesota	0.65
20	Oklahoma	1.88		36	Colorado	0.63
24	Oregon	1.45		37	Arizona	0.62
41	Pennsylvania	0.51		38	Connecticut	0.60
48	Rhode Island	0.00		39	Missouri	0.54
4	South Carolina	8.98		39	Texas	0.54
10	South Dakota	7.48		41	Pennsylvania	0.51
31	Tennessee	1.07		42	Maryland	0.48
39	Texas	0.54		43	Ohio	0.40
30	Utah	1.10		44	Michigan	0.31
8	Vermont	7.69		45	California	0.14
23	Virginia	1.60		46	New York	0.07
34	Washington	0.69		47	Massachusetts	0.01
1	West Virginia	13.04		48	New Jersey	0.00
33	Wisconsin	0.79		48	Rhode Island	0.00
5	Wyoming	8.64		NA	Illinois**	NA
					District of Columbia	0.00

Source: Morgan Quitno Corporation using data from U.S. Department of Justice, Federal Bureau of Investigation
"Crime in the United States 1993" (Uniform Crime Reports, December 4, 1994)

*Estimated percentages for rural areas, defined by the F.B.I. as other than Metropolitan Statistical Areas and other cities outside such areas. National percent includes those states listed as not available. Robbery is the taking or attempting to take anything of value by force or threat of force.

**Not available.

Aggravated Assault in Urban Areas in 1993

National Total = 1,079,365 Aggravated Assaults*

<table>
<tr><td colspan="4">ALPHA ORDER</td><td colspan="4">RANK ORDER</td></tr>
<tr><td>RANK</td><td>STATE</td><td>ASSAULTS</td><td>% of USA</td><td>RANK</td><td>STATE</td><td>ASSAULTS</td><td>% of USA</td></tr>
<tr><td>16</td><td>Alabama</td><td>22,775</td><td>2.11%</td><td>1</td><td>California</td><td>192,053</td><td>17.79%</td></tr>
<tr><td>39</td><td>Alaska</td><td>2,391</td><td>0.22%</td><td>2</td><td>Florida</td><td>104,047</td><td>9.64%</td></tr>
<tr><td>18</td><td>Arizona</td><td>19,232</td><td>1.78%</td><td>3</td><td>New York</td><td>84,060</td><td>7.79%</td></tr>
<tr><td>26</td><td>Arkansas</td><td>9,288</td><td>0.86%</td><td>4</td><td>Texas</td><td>81,128</td><td>7.52%</td></tr>
<tr><td>1</td><td>California</td><td>192,053</td><td>17.79%</td><td>5</td><td>Michigan</td><td>43,181</td><td>4.00%</td></tr>
<tr><td>22</td><td>Colorado</td><td>13,610</td><td>1.26%</td><td>6</td><td>Massachusetts</td><td>35,537</td><td>3.29%</td></tr>
<tr><td>30</td><td>Connecticut</td><td>7,044</td><td>0.65%</td><td>7</td><td>Louisiana</td><td>27,808</td><td>2.58%</td></tr>
<tr><td>38</td><td>Delaware</td><td>2,522</td><td>0.23%</td><td>8</td><td>Ohio</td><td>27,456</td><td>2.54%</td></tr>
<tr><td>2</td><td>Florida</td><td>104,047</td><td>9.64%</td><td>9</td><td>North Carolina</td><td>27,338</td><td>2.53%</td></tr>
<tr><td>10</td><td>Georgia</td><td>26,279</td><td>2.43%</td><td>10</td><td>Georgia</td><td>26,279</td><td>2.43%</td></tr>
<tr><td>42</td><td>Hawaii</td><td>1,148</td><td>0.11%</td><td>11</td><td>Maryland</td><td>24,359</td><td>2.26%</td></tr>
<tr><td>40</td><td>Idaho</td><td>1,876</td><td>0.17%</td><td>12</td><td>Pennsylvania</td><td>23,777</td><td>2.20%</td></tr>
<tr><td>NA</td><td>Illinois**</td><td>NA</td><td>NA</td><td>13</td><td>South Carolina</td><td>23,685</td><td>2.19%</td></tr>
<tr><td>19</td><td>Indiana</td><td>16,554</td><td>1.53%</td><td>14</td><td>New Jersey</td><td>23,438</td><td>2.17%</td></tr>
<tr><td>31</td><td>Iowa</td><td>6,455</td><td>0.60%</td><td>15</td><td>Tennessee</td><td>22,863</td><td>2.12%</td></tr>
<tr><td>28</td><td>Kansas</td><td>7,645</td><td>0.71%</td><td>16</td><td>Alabama</td><td>22,775</td><td>2.11%</td></tr>
<tr><td>25</td><td>Kentucky</td><td>9,998</td><td>0.93%</td><td>17</td><td>Missouri</td><td>22,155</td><td>2.05%</td></tr>
<tr><td>7</td><td>Louisiana</td><td>27,808</td><td>2.58%</td><td>18</td><td>Arizona</td><td>19,232</td><td>1.78%</td></tr>
<tr><td>45</td><td>Maine</td><td>816</td><td>0.08%</td><td>19</td><td>Indiana</td><td>16,554</td><td>1.53%</td></tr>
<tr><td>11</td><td>Maryland</td><td>24,359</td><td>2.26%</td><td>20</td><td>Washington</td><td>15,594</td><td>1.44%</td></tr>
<tr><td>6</td><td>Massachusetts</td><td>35,537</td><td>3.29%</td><td>21</td><td>Oklahoma</td><td>13,626</td><td>1.26%</td></tr>
<tr><td>5</td><td>Michigan</td><td>43,181</td><td>4.00%</td><td>22</td><td>Colorado</td><td>13,610</td><td>1.26%</td></tr>
<tr><td>29</td><td>Minnesota</td><td>7,366</td><td>0.68%</td><td>23</td><td>Virginia</td><td>11,177</td><td>1.04%</td></tr>
<tr><td>34</td><td>Mississippi</td><td>4,955</td><td>0.46%</td><td>24</td><td>New Mexico</td><td>10,995</td><td>1.02%</td></tr>
<tr><td>17</td><td>Missouri</td><td>22,155</td><td>2.05%</td><td>25</td><td>Kentucky</td><td>9,998</td><td>0.93%</td></tr>
<tr><td>47</td><td>Montana</td><td>451</td><td>0.04%</td><td>26</td><td>Arkansas</td><td>9,288</td><td>0.86%</td></tr>
<tr><td>35</td><td>Nebraska</td><td>3,861</td><td>0.36%</td><td>27</td><td>Oregon</td><td>8,959</td><td>0.83%</td></tr>
<tr><td>33</td><td>Nevada</td><td>5,276</td><td>0.49%</td><td>28</td><td>Kansas</td><td>7,645</td><td>0.71%</td></tr>
<tr><td>46</td><td>New Hampshire</td><td>675</td><td>0.06%</td><td>29</td><td>Minnesota</td><td>7,366</td><td>0.68%</td></tr>
<tr><td>14</td><td>New Jersey</td><td>23,438</td><td>2.17%</td><td>30</td><td>Connecticut</td><td>7,044</td><td>0.65%</td></tr>
<tr><td>24</td><td>New Mexico</td><td>10,995</td><td>1.02%</td><td>31</td><td>Iowa</td><td>6,455</td><td>0.60%</td></tr>
<tr><td>3</td><td>New York</td><td>84,060</td><td>7.79%</td><td>32</td><td>Wisconsin</td><td>5,424</td><td>0.50%</td></tr>
<tr><td>9</td><td>North Carolina</td><td>27,338</td><td>2.53%</td><td>33</td><td>Nevada</td><td>5,276</td><td>0.49%</td></tr>
<tr><td>48</td><td>North Dakota</td><td>263</td><td>0.02%</td><td>34</td><td>Mississippi</td><td>4,955</td><td>0.46%</td></tr>
<tr><td>8</td><td>Ohio</td><td>27,456</td><td>2.54%</td><td>35</td><td>Nebraska</td><td>3,861</td><td>0.36%</td></tr>
<tr><td>21</td><td>Oklahoma</td><td>13,626</td><td>1.26%</td><td>36</td><td>Utah</td><td>3,345</td><td>0.31%</td></tr>
<tr><td>27</td><td>Oregon</td><td>8,959</td><td>0.83%</td><td>37</td><td>Rhode Island</td><td>2,680</td><td>0.25%</td></tr>
<tr><td>12</td><td>Pennsylvania</td><td>23,777</td><td>2.20%</td><td>38</td><td>Delaware</td><td>2,522</td><td>0.23%</td></tr>
<tr><td>37</td><td>Rhode Island</td><td>2,680</td><td>0.25%</td><td>39</td><td>Alaska</td><td>2,391</td><td>0.22%</td></tr>
<tr><td>13</td><td>South Carolina</td><td>23,685</td><td>2.19%</td><td>40</td><td>Idaho</td><td>1,876</td><td>0.17%</td></tr>
<tr><td>43</td><td>South Dakota</td><td>862</td><td>0.08%</td><td>41</td><td>West Virginia</td><td>1,866</td><td>0.17%</td></tr>
<tr><td>15</td><td>Tennessee</td><td>22,863</td><td>2.12%</td><td>42</td><td>Hawaii</td><td>1,148</td><td>0.11%</td></tr>
<tr><td>4</td><td>Texas</td><td>81,128</td><td>7.52%</td><td>43</td><td>South Dakota</td><td>862</td><td>0.08%</td></tr>
<tr><td>36</td><td>Utah</td><td>3,345</td><td>0.31%</td><td>44</td><td>Wyoming</td><td>824</td><td>0.08%</td></tr>
<tr><td>49</td><td>Vermont</td><td>247</td><td>0.02%</td><td>45</td><td>Maine</td><td>816</td><td>0.08%</td></tr>
<tr><td>23</td><td>Virginia</td><td>11,177</td><td>1.04%</td><td>46</td><td>New Hampshire</td><td>675</td><td>0.06%</td></tr>
<tr><td>20</td><td>Washington</td><td>15,594</td><td>1.44%</td><td>47</td><td>Montana</td><td>451</td><td>0.04%</td></tr>
<tr><td>41</td><td>West Virginia</td><td>1,866</td><td>0.17%</td><td>48</td><td>North Dakota</td><td>263</td><td>0.02%</td></tr>
<tr><td>32</td><td>Wisconsin</td><td>5,424</td><td>0.50%</td><td>49</td><td>Vermont</td><td>247</td><td>0.02%</td></tr>
<tr><td>44</td><td>Wyoming</td><td>824</td><td>0.08%</td><td>NA</td><td>Illinois**</td><td>NA</td><td>NA</td></tr>
<tr><td></td><td></td><td></td><td></td><td></td><td>District of Columbia</td><td>9,003</td><td>0.83%</td></tr>
</table>

Source: Morgan Quitno Corporation using data from U.S. Department of Justice, Federal Bureau of Investigation
"Crime in the United States 1993" (Uniform Crime Reports, December 4, 1994)
*Estimated totals for urban areas, defined by the F.B.I. as Metropolitan Statistical Areas and other cities outside such
areas. National total includes those states listed as not available. Aggravated assault is an attack for the purpose of
inflicting severe bodily injury.
**Not available.

Urban Aggravated Assault Rate in 1993

National Urban Rate = 477.2 Aggravated Assaults per 100,000 Population*

ALPHA ORDER

RANK	STATE	RATE
5	Alabama	670.0
8	Alaska	583.2
12	Arizona	529.2
9	Arkansas	577.1
6	California	627.7
21	Colorado	424.2
36	Connecticut	228.3
23	Delaware	412.3
3	Florida	804.2
19	Georgia	472.8
44	Hawaii	125.5
34	Idaho	262.1
NA	Illinois**	NA
25	Indiana	355.1
27	Iowa	336.2
24	Kansas	368.5
22	Kentucky	415.1
4	Louisiana	786.0
46	Maine	91.4
14	Maryland	518.4
7	Massachusetts	592.3
16	Michigan	511.2
40	Minnesota	201.8
28	Mississippi	331.6
11	Missouri	546.0
45	Montana	110.6
30	Nebraska	323.5
20	Nevada	432.8
48	New Hampshire	68.6
31	New Jersey	297.5
1	New Mexico	831.2
18	New York	484.8
15	North Carolina	515.4
49	North Dakota	64.3
32	Ohio	280.8
13	Oklahoma	523.0
26	Oregon	352.2
37	Pennsylvania	216.5
33	Rhode Island	268.0
2	South Carolina	828.9
39	South Dakota	203.0
10	Tennessee	573.0
17	Texas	493.5
41	Utah	201.7
47	Vermont	79.0
38	Virginia	205.3
29	Washington	326.9
42	West Virginia	179.6
43	Wisconsin	133.8
35	Wyoming	238.3

RANK ORDER

RANK	STATE	RATE
1	New Mexico	831.2
2	South Carolina	828.9
3	Florida	804.2
4	Louisiana	786.0
5	Alabama	670.0
6	California	627.7
7	Massachusetts	592.3
8	Alaska	583.2
9	Arkansas	577.1
10	Tennessee	573.0
11	Missouri	546.0
12	Arizona	529.2
13	Oklahoma	523.0
14	Maryland	518.4
15	North Carolina	515.4
16	Michigan	511.2
17	Texas	493.5
18	New York	484.8
19	Georgia	472.8
20	Nevada	432.8
21	Colorado	424.2
22	Kentucky	415.1
23	Delaware	412.3
24	Kansas	368.5
25	Indiana	355.1
26	Oregon	352.2
27	Iowa	336.2
28	Mississippi	331.6
29	Washington	326.9
30	Nebraska	323.5
31	New Jersey	297.5
32	Ohio	280.8
33	Rhode Island	268.0
34	Idaho	262.1
35	Wyoming	238.3
36	Connecticut	228.3
37	Pennsylvania	216.5
38	Virginia	205.3
39	South Dakota	203.0
40	Minnesota	201.8
41	Utah	201.7
42	West Virginia	179.6
43	Wisconsin	133.8
44	Hawaii	125.5
45	Montana	110.6
46	Maine	91.4
47	Vermont	79.0
48	New Hampshire	68.6
49	North Dakota	64.3
NA	Illinois**	NA

| | District of Columbia | 1,557.6 |

Source: Morgan Quitno Corporation using data from U.S. Department of Justice, Federal Bureau of Investigation
"Crime in the United States 1993" (Uniform Crime Reports, December 4, 1994)
*Estimated rates for urban areas, defined by the F.B.I. as Metropolitan Statistical Areas and other cities outside such areas. National rate includes those states listed as not available. Aggravated assault is an attack for the purpose of inflicting severe bodily injury.
**Not available.

Percent of Aggravated Assaults Occurring in Urban Areas in 1993

National Percent = 95.09% of Aggravated Assaults*

ALPHA ORDER				RANK ORDER		
RANK	**STATE**	**PERCENT**		**RANK**	**STATE**	**PERCENT**
16	Alabama	94.72		1	New Jersey	100.00
47	Alaska	73.16		2	Rhode Island	99.96
8	Arizona	96.63		3	Massachusetts	99.85
28	Arkansas	92.15		4	California	98.95
4	California	98.95		5	New York	97.97
13	Colorado	95.64		6	Maryland	96.89
17	Connecticut	93.97		7	Florida	96.81
35	Delaware	86.37		8	Arizona	96.63
7	Florida	96.81		9	Ohio	96.57
33	Georgia	88.70		10	Michigan	96.50
41	Hawaii	81.53		11	Washington	96.37
45	Idaho	75.31		12	Pennsylvania	96.21
NA	Illinois**	NA		13	Colorado	95.64
31	Indiana	89.81		14	Texas	95.58
18	Iowa	93.69		15	Nebraska	95.33
25	Kansas	92.57		16	Alabama	94.72
42	Kentucky	79.63		17	Connecticut	93.97
30	Louisiana	90.50		18	Iowa	93.69
36	Maine	86.35		19	New Hampshire	93.62
6	Maryland	96.89		20	New Mexico	93.06
3	Massachusetts	99.85		21	Oregon	93.03
10	Michigan	96.50		22	Missouri	92.99
23	Minnesota	92.74		23	Minnesota	92.74
43	Mississippi	78.63		24	Oklahoma	92.62
22	Missouri	92.99		25	Kansas	92.57
49	Montana	47.08		26	Tennessee	92.35
15	Nebraska	95.33		26	Utah	92.35
40	Nevada	81.89		28	Arkansas	92.15
19	New Hampshire	93.62		29	Virginia	90.71
1	New Jersey	100.00		30	Louisiana	90.50
20	New Mexico	93.06		31	Indiana	89.81
5	New York	97.97		32	North Carolina	89.19
32	North Carolina	89.19		33	Georgia	88.70
37	North Dakota	85.11		34	Wisconsin	88.69
9	Ohio	96.57		35	Delaware	86.37
24	Oklahoma	92.62		36	Maine	86.35
21	Oregon	93.03		37	North Dakota	85.11
12	Pennsylvania	96.21		38	South Carolina	84.07
2	Rhode Island	99.96		39	South Dakota	82.80
38	South Carolina	84.07		40	Nevada	81.89
39	South Dakota	82.80		41	Hawaii	81.53
26	Tennessee	92.35		42	Kentucky	79.63
14	Texas	95.58		43	Mississippi	78.63
26	Utah	92.35		44	Wyoming	75.80
48	Vermont	69.38		45	Idaho	75.31
29	Virginia	90.71		46	West Virginia	74.05
11	Washington	96.37		47	Alaska	73.16
46	West Virginia	74.05		48	Vermont	69.38
34	Wisconsin	88.69		49	Montana	47.08
44	Wyoming	75.80		NA	Illinois**	NA
					District of Columbia	100.00

Source: Morgan Quitno Corporation using data from U.S. Department of Justice, Federal Bureau of Investigation
"Crime in the United States 1993" (Uniform Crime Reports, December 4, 1994)
*Estimated percentages for urban areas, defined by the F.B.I. as Metropolitan Statistical Areas and other cities outside such areas. National percent includes those states listed as not available. Aggravated assault is an attack for the purpose of inflicting severe bodily injury.
**Not available.

Aggravated Assault in Rural Areas in 1993

National Total = 55,734 Aggravated Assaults*

ALPHA ORDER					RANK ORDER			
RANK	STATE	ASSAULTS	% of USA		RANK	STATE	ASSAULTS	% of USA
15	Alabama	1,269	2.28%		1	South Carolina	4,489	8.05%
21	Alaska	877	1.57%		2	Texas	3,753	6.73%
26	Arizona	671	1.20%		3	Florida	3,432	6.16%
23	Arkansas	791	1.42%		4	Georgia	3,349	6.01%
8	California	2,030	3.64%		5	North Carolina	3,312	5.94%
29	Colorado	620	1.11%		6	Louisiana	2,919	5.24%
35	Connecticut	452	0.81%		7	Kentucky	2,557	4.59%
37	Delaware	398	0.71%		8	California	2,030	3.64%
3	Florida	3,432	6.16%		9	Tennessee	1,895	3.40%
4	Georgia	3,349	6.01%		10	Indiana	1,878	3.37%
40	Hawaii	260	0.47%		11	New York	1,742	3.13%
30	Idaho	615	1.10%		12	Missouri	1,670	3.00%
NA	Illinois**	NA	NA		13	Michigan	1,566	2.81%
10	Indiana	1,878	3.37%		14	Mississippi	1,347	2.42%
36	Iowa	435	0.78%		15	Alabama	1,269	2.28%
31	Kansas	614	1.10%		16	Nevada	1,167	2.09%
7	Kentucky	2,557	4.59%		17	Virginia	1,145	2.05%
6	Louisiana	2,919	5.24%		18	Oklahoma	1,086	1.95%
43	Maine	129	0.23%		19	Ohio	975	1.75%
24	Maryland	782	1.40%		20	Pennsylvania	937	1.68%
45	Massachusetts	54	0.10%		21	Alaska	877	1.57%
13	Michigan	1,566	2.81%		22	New Mexico	820	1.47%
33	Minnesota	577	1.04%		23	Arkansas	791	1.42%
14	Mississippi	1,347	2.42%		24	Maryland	782	1.40%
12	Missouri	1,670	3.00%		25	Wisconsin	692	1.24%
34	Montana	507	0.91%		26	Arizona	671	1.20%
41	Nebraska	189	0.34%		26	Oregon	671	1.20%
16	Nevada	1,167	2.09%		28	West Virginia	654	1.17%
46	New Hampshire	46	0.08%		29	Colorado	620	1.11%
49	New Jersey	0	0.00%		30	Idaho	615	1.10%
22	New Mexico	820	1.47%		31	Kansas	614	1.10%
11	New York	1,742	3.13%		32	Washington	587	1.05%
5	North Carolina	3,312	5.94%		33	Minnesota	577	1.04%
46	North Dakota	46	0.08%		34	Montana	507	0.91%
19	Ohio	975	1.75%		35	Connecticut	452	0.81%
18	Oklahoma	1,086	1.95%		36	Iowa	435	0.78%
26	Oregon	671	1.20%		37	Delaware	398	0.71%
20	Pennsylvania	937	1.68%		38	Utah	277	0.50%
48	Rhode Island	1	0.00%		39	Wyoming	263	0.47%
1	South Carolina	4,489	8.05%		40	Hawaii	260	0.47%
42	South Dakota	179	0.32%		41	Nebraska	189	0.34%
9	Tennessee	1,895	3.40%		42	South Dakota	179	0.32%
2	Texas	3,753	6.73%		43	Maine	129	0.23%
38	Utah	277	0.50%		44	Vermont	109	0.20%
44	Vermont	109	0.20%		45	Massachusetts	54	0.10%
17	Virginia	1,145	2.05%		46	New Hampshire	46	0.08%
32	Washington	587	1.05%		46	North Dakota	46	0.08%
28	West Virginia	654	1.17%		48	Rhode Island	1	0.00%
25	Wisconsin	692	1.24%		49	New Jersey	0	0.00%
39	Wyoming	263	0.47%		NA	Illinois**	NA	NA
					District of Columbia		0	0.00%

Source: Morgan Quitno Corporation using data from U.S. Department of Justice, Federal Bureau of Investigation "Crime in the United States 1993" (Uniform Crime Reports, December 4, 1994)

*Estimated totals for rural areas, defined by the F.B.I. as other than Metropolitan Statistical Areas and other cities outside such areas. National total includes those states listed as not available. Aggravated assault is an attack for the purpose of inflicting severe bodily injury.

**Not available.

Rural Aggravated Assault Rate in 1993

National Rural Rate = 175.7 Aggravated Assaults per 100,000 Population*

<table>
<tr><td colspan="3">ALPHA ORDER</td><td colspan="3">RANK ORDER</td></tr>
<tr><th>RANK</th><th>STATE</th><th>RATE</th><th>RANK</th><th>STATE</th><th>RATE</th></tr>
<tr><td>23</td><td>Alabama</td><td>161.1</td><td>1</td><td>Nevada</td><td>687.1</td></tr>
<tr><td>3</td><td>Alaska</td><td>463.9</td><td>2</td><td>South Carolina</td><td>571.4</td></tr>
<tr><td>14</td><td>Arizona</td><td>222.1</td><td>3</td><td>Alaska</td><td>463.9</td></tr>
<tr><td>35</td><td>Arkansas</td><td>97.1</td><td>4</td><td>Florida</td><td>462.8</td></tr>
<tr><td>8</td><td>California</td><td>329.1</td><td>5</td><td>Delaware</td><td>450.4</td></tr>
<tr><td>21</td><td>Colorado</td><td>173.4</td><td>6</td><td>Massachusetts</td><td>440.5</td></tr>
<tr><td>12</td><td>Connecticut</td><td>236.7</td><td>7</td><td>Louisiana</td><td>385.5</td></tr>
<tr><td>5</td><td>Delaware</td><td>450.4</td><td>8</td><td>California</td><td>329.1</td></tr>
<tr><td>4</td><td>Florida</td><td>462.8</td><td>9</td><td>Maryland</td><td>294.0</td></tr>
<tr><td>11</td><td>Georgia</td><td>246.6</td><td>10</td><td>New Mexico</td><td>279.7</td></tr>
<tr><td>34</td><td>Hawaii</td><td>101.1</td><td>11</td><td>Georgia</td><td>246.6</td></tr>
<tr><td>24</td><td>Idaho</td><td>160.4</td><td>12</td><td>Connecticut</td><td>236.7</td></tr>
<tr><td>NA</td><td>Illinois**</td><td>NA</td><td>13</td><td>Texas</td><td>235.7</td></tr>
<tr><td>19</td><td>Indiana</td><td>178.7</td><td>14</td><td>Arizona</td><td>222.1</td></tr>
<tr><td>42</td><td>Iowa</td><td>48.6</td><td>15</td><td>Wyoming</td><td>211.8</td></tr>
<tr><td>29</td><td>Kansas</td><td>134.6</td><td>16</td><td>New York</td><td>203.2</td></tr>
<tr><td>18</td><td>Kentucky</td><td>185.3</td><td>17</td><td>North Carolina</td><td>201.9</td></tr>
<tr><td>7</td><td>Louisiana</td><td>385.5</td><td>18</td><td>Kentucky</td><td>185.3</td></tr>
<tr><td>45</td><td>Maine</td><td>37.3</td><td>19</td><td>Indiana</td><td>178.7</td></tr>
<tr><td>9</td><td>Maryland</td><td>294.0</td><td>20</td><td>Oklahoma</td><td>173.6</td></tr>
<tr><td>6</td><td>Massachusetts</td><td>440.5</td><td>21</td><td>Colorado</td><td>173.4</td></tr>
<tr><td>25</td><td>Michigan</td><td>151.9</td><td>22</td><td>Tennessee</td><td>170.9</td></tr>
<tr><td>40</td><td>Minnesota</td><td>66.6</td><td>23</td><td>Alabama</td><td>161.1</td></tr>
<tr><td>32</td><td>Mississippi</td><td>117.3</td><td>24</td><td>Idaho</td><td>160.4</td></tr>
<tr><td>26</td><td>Missouri</td><td>142.0</td><td>25</td><td>Michigan</td><td>151.9</td></tr>
<tr><td>31</td><td>Montana</td><td>117.6</td><td>26</td><td>Missouri</td><td>142.0</td></tr>
<tr><td>43</td><td>Nebraska</td><td>45.7</td><td>27</td><td>Utah</td><td>137.6</td></tr>
<tr><td>1</td><td>Nevada</td><td>687.1</td><td>28</td><td>Oregon</td><td>137.4</td></tr>
<tr><td>46</td><td>New Hampshire</td><td>32.7</td><td>29</td><td>Kansas</td><td>134.6</td></tr>
<tr><td>48</td><td>New Jersey</td><td>0.0</td><td>30</td><td>Washington</td><td>121.2</td></tr>
<tr><td>10</td><td>New Mexico</td><td>279.7</td><td>31</td><td>Montana</td><td>117.6</td></tr>
<tr><td>16</td><td>New York</td><td>203.2</td><td>32</td><td>Mississippi</td><td>117.3</td></tr>
<tr><td>17</td><td>North Carolina</td><td>201.9</td><td>33</td><td>Virginia</td><td>109.2</td></tr>
<tr><td>47</td><td>North Dakota</td><td>20.3</td><td>34</td><td>Hawaii</td><td>101.1</td></tr>
<tr><td>38</td><td>Ohio</td><td>74.2</td><td>35</td><td>Arkansas</td><td>97.1</td></tr>
<tr><td>20</td><td>Oklahoma</td><td>173.6</td><td>36</td><td>Pennsylvania</td><td>88.1</td></tr>
<tr><td>28</td><td>Oregon</td><td>137.4</td><td>37</td><td>West Virginia</td><td>83.7</td></tr>
<tr><td>36</td><td>Pennsylvania</td><td>88.1</td><td>38</td><td>Ohio</td><td>74.2</td></tr>
<tr><td>48</td><td>Rhode Island</td><td>0.0</td><td>39</td><td>Wisconsin</td><td>70.2</td></tr>
<tr><td>2</td><td>South Carolina</td><td>571.4</td><td>40</td><td>Minnesota</td><td>66.6</td></tr>
<tr><td>41</td><td>South Dakota</td><td>61.6</td><td>41</td><td>South Dakota</td><td>61.6</td></tr>
<tr><td>22</td><td>Tennessee</td><td>170.9</td><td>42</td><td>Iowa</td><td>48.6</td></tr>
<tr><td>13</td><td>Texas</td><td>235.7</td><td>43</td><td>Nebraska</td><td>45.7</td></tr>
<tr><td>27</td><td>Utah</td><td>137.6</td><td>44</td><td>Vermont</td><td>41.4</td></tr>
<tr><td>44</td><td>Vermont</td><td>41.4</td><td>45</td><td>Maine</td><td>37.3</td></tr>
<tr><td>33</td><td>Virginia</td><td>109.2</td><td>46</td><td>New Hampshire</td><td>32.7</td></tr>
<tr><td>30</td><td>Washington</td><td>121.2</td><td>47</td><td>North Dakota</td><td>20.3</td></tr>
<tr><td>37</td><td>West Virginia</td><td>83.7</td><td>48</td><td>New Jersey</td><td>0.0</td></tr>
<tr><td>39</td><td>Wisconsin</td><td>70.2</td><td>48</td><td>Rhode Island</td><td>0.0</td></tr>
<tr><td>15</td><td>Wyoming</td><td>211.8</td><td>NA</td><td>Illinois**</td><td>NA</td></tr>
<tr><td></td><td></td><td></td><td></td><td>District of Columbia</td><td>0.0</td></tr>
</table>

Source: Morgan Quitno Corporation using data from U.S. Department of Justice, Federal Bureau of Investigation
   "Crime in the United States 1993" (Uniform Crime Reports, December 4, 1994)
*Estimated rates for rural areas, defined by the F.B.I. as other than Metropolitan Statistical Areas and other cities outside such areas. National rate includes those states listed as not available. Aggravated assault is an attack for the purpose of inflicting severe bodily injury.
**Not available.

Percent of Aggravated Assaults Occurring in Rural Areas in 1993

National Percent = 4.91% of Aggravated Assaults*

ALPHA ORDER				RANK ORDER		
RANK	**STATE**	**PERCENT**		**RANK**	**STATE**	**PERCENT**
34	Alabama	5.28		1	Montana	52.92
3	Alaska	26.84		2	Vermont	30.62
42	Arizona	3.37		3	Alaska	26.84
22	Arkansas	7.85		4	West Virginia	25.95
46	California	1.05		5	Idaho	24.69
37	Colorado	4.36		6	Wyoming	24.20
33	Connecticut	6.03		7	Mississippi	21.37
15	Delaware	13.63		8	Kentucky	20.37
43	Florida	3.19		9	Hawaii	18.47
17	Georgia	11.30		10	Nevada	18.11
9	Hawaii	18.47		11	South Dakota	17.20
5	Idaho	24.69		12	South Carolina	15.93
NA	Illinois**	NA		13	North Dakota	14.89
19	Indiana	10.19		14	Maine	13.65
32	Iowa	6.31		15	Delaware	13.63
25	Kansas	7.43		16	Wisconsin	11.31
8	Kentucky	20.37		17	Georgia	11.30
20	Louisiana	9.50		18	North Carolina	10.81
14	Maine	13.65		19	Indiana	10.19
44	Maryland	3.11		20	Louisiana	9.50
47	Massachusetts	0.15		21	Virginia	9.29
40	Michigan	3.50		22	Arkansas	7.85
27	Minnesota	7.26		23	Tennessee	7.65
7	Mississippi	21.37		23	Utah	7.65
28	Missouri	7.01		25	Kansas	7.43
1	Montana	52.92		26	Oklahoma	7.38
35	Nebraska	4.67		27	Minnesota	7.26
10	Nevada	18.11		28	Missouri	7.01
31	New Hampshire	6.38		29	Oregon	6.97
49	New Jersey	0.00		30	New Mexico	6.94
30	New Mexico	6.94		31	New Hampshire	6.38
45	New York	2.03		32	Iowa	6.31
18	North Carolina	10.81		33	Connecticut	6.03
13	North Dakota	14.89		34	Alabama	5.28
41	Ohio	3.43		35	Nebraska	4.67
26	Oklahoma	7.38		36	Texas	4.42
29	Oregon	6.97		37	Colorado	4.36
38	Pennsylvania	3.79		38	Pennsylvania	3.79
48	Rhode Island	0.04		39	Washington	3.63
12	South Carolina	15.93		40	Michigan	3.50
11	South Dakota	17.20		41	Ohio	3.43
23	Tennessee	7.65		42	Arizona	3.37
36	Texas	4.42		43	Florida	3.19
23	Utah	7.65		44	Maryland	3.11
2	Vermont	30.62		45	New York	2.03
21	Virginia	9.29		46	California	1.05
39	Washington	3.63		47	Massachusetts	0.15
4	West Virginia	25.95		48	Rhode Island	0.04
16	Wisconsin	11.31		49	New Jersey	0.00
6	Wyoming	24.20		NA	Illinois**	NA
					District of Columbia	0.00

Source: Morgan Quitno Corporation using data from U.S. Department of Justice, Federal Bureau of Investigation
"Crime in the United States 1993" (Uniform Crime Reports, December 4, 1994)
*Estimated percentages for rural areas, defined by the F.B.I. as other than Metropolitan Statistical Areas and other cities outside such areas. National percent includes those states listed as not available. Aggravated assault is an attack for the purpose of inflicting severe bodily injury.
**Not available.

Property Crime in Urban Areas in 1993

National Total = 11,662,018 Property Crimes*

<table>
<tr><td colspan="4">ALPHA ORDER</td><td colspan="4">RANK ORDER</td></tr>
<tr><td>RANK</td><td>STATE</td><td>CRIMES</td><td>% of USA</td><td>RANK</td><td>STATE</td><td>CRIMES</td><td>% of USA</td></tr>
<tr><td>23</td><td>Alabama</td><td>163,445</td><td>1.40%</td><td>1</td><td>California</td><td>1,661,923</td><td>14.25%</td></tr>
<tr><td>45</td><td>Alaska</td><td>22,896</td><td>0.20%</td><td>2</td><td>Texas</td><td>995,335</td><td>8.53%</td></tr>
<tr><td>12</td><td>Arizona</td><td>259,045</td><td>2.22%</td><td>3</td><td>Florida</td><td>952,572</td><td>8.17%</td></tr>
<tr><td>31</td><td>Arkansas</td><td>90,988</td><td>0.78%</td><td>4</td><td>New York</td><td>797,292</td><td>6.84%</td></tr>
<tr><td>1</td><td>California</td><td>1,661,923</td><td>14.25%</td><td>5</td><td>Ohio</td><td>425,126</td><td>3.65%</td></tr>
<tr><td>21</td><td>Colorado</td><td>167,578</td><td>1.44%</td><td>6</td><td>Michigan</td><td>417,576</td><td>3.58%</td></tr>
<tr><td>27</td><td>Connecticut</td><td>134,719</td><td>1.16%</td><td>7</td><td>Georgia</td><td>347,552</td><td>2.98%</td></tr>
<tr><td>44</td><td>Delaware</td><td>26,924</td><td>0.23%</td><td>8</td><td>Pennsylvania</td><td>329,381</td><td>2.82%</td></tr>
<tr><td>3</td><td>Florida</td><td>952,572</td><td>8.17%</td><td>9</td><td>New Jersey</td><td>328,867</td><td>2.82%</td></tr>
<tr><td>7</td><td>Georgia</td><td>347,552</td><td>2.98%</td><td>10</td><td>North Carolina</td><td>309,895</td><td>2.66%</td></tr>
<tr><td>36</td><td>Hawaii</td><td>56,527</td><td>0.48%</td><td>11</td><td>Washington</td><td>273,034</td><td>2.34%</td></tr>
<tr><td>40</td><td>Idaho</td><td>32,581</td><td>0.28%</td><td>12</td><td>Arizona</td><td>259,045</td><td>2.22%</td></tr>
<tr><td>NA</td><td>Illinois**</td><td>NA</td><td>NA</td><td>13</td><td>Maryland</td><td>247,872</td><td>2.13%</td></tr>
<tr><td>18</td><td>Indiana</td><td>211,898</td><td>1.82%</td><td>14</td><td>Massachusetts</td><td>245,764</td><td>2.11%</td></tr>
<tr><td>32</td><td>Iowa</td><td>89,042</td><td>0.76%</td><td>15</td><td>Louisiana</td><td>234,931</td><td>2.01%</td></tr>
<tr><td>28</td><td>Kansas</td><td>106,441</td><td>0.91%</td><td>16</td><td>Virginia</td><td>229,047</td><td>1.96%</td></tr>
<tr><td>30</td><td>Kentucky</td><td>91,422</td><td>0.78%</td><td>17</td><td>Missouri</td><td>216,773</td><td>1.86%</td></tr>
<tr><td>15</td><td>Louisiana</td><td>234,931</td><td>2.01%</td><td>18</td><td>Indiana</td><td>211,898</td><td>1.82%</td></tr>
<tr><td>41</td><td>Maine</td><td>31,496</td><td>0.27%</td><td>19</td><td>Tennessee</td><td>211,811</td><td>1.82%</td></tr>
<tr><td>13</td><td>Maryland</td><td>247,872</td><td>2.13%</td><td>20</td><td>Wisconsin</td><td>175,183</td><td>1.50%</td></tr>
<tr><td>14</td><td>Massachusetts</td><td>245,764</td><td>2.11%</td><td>21</td><td>Colorado</td><td>167,578</td><td>1.44%</td></tr>
<tr><td>6</td><td>Michigan</td><td>417,576</td><td>3.58%</td><td>22</td><td>Minnesota</td><td>166,512</td><td>1.43%</td></tr>
<tr><td>22</td><td>Minnesota</td><td>166,512</td><td>1.43%</td><td>23</td><td>Alabama</td><td>163,445</td><td>1.40%</td></tr>
<tr><td>29</td><td>Mississippi</td><td>91,990</td><td>0.79%</td><td>24</td><td>South Carolina</td><td>153,409</td><td>1.32%</td></tr>
<tr><td>17</td><td>Missouri</td><td>216,773</td><td>1.86%</td><td>25</td><td>Oregon</td><td>148,545</td><td>1.27%</td></tr>
<tr><td>43</td><td>Montana</td><td>28,176</td><td>0.24%</td><td>26</td><td>Oklahoma</td><td>141,352</td><td>1.21%</td></tr>
<tr><td>37</td><td>Nebraska</td><td>55,388</td><td>0.47%</td><td>27</td><td>Connecticut</td><td>134,719</td><td>1.16%</td></tr>
<tr><td>35</td><td>Nevada</td><td>68,838</td><td>0.59%</td><td>28</td><td>Kansas</td><td>106,441</td><td>0.91%</td></tr>
<tr><td>42</td><td>New Hampshire</td><td>30,293</td><td>0.26%</td><td>29</td><td>Mississippi</td><td>91,990</td><td>0.79%</td></tr>
<tr><td>9</td><td>New Jersey</td><td>328,867</td><td>2.82%</td><td>30</td><td>Kentucky</td><td>91,422</td><td>0.78%</td></tr>
<tr><td>34</td><td>New Mexico</td><td>82,027</td><td>0.70%</td><td>31</td><td>Arkansas</td><td>90,988</td><td>0.78%</td></tr>
<tr><td>4</td><td>New York</td><td>797,292</td><td>6.84%</td><td>32</td><td>Iowa</td><td>89,042</td><td>0.76%</td></tr>
<tr><td>10</td><td>North Carolina</td><td>309,895</td><td>2.66%</td><td>33</td><td>Utah</td><td>87,956</td><td>0.75%</td></tr>
<tr><td>49</td><td>North Dakota</td><td>15,267</td><td>0.13%</td><td>34</td><td>New Mexico</td><td>82,027</td><td>0.70%</td></tr>
<tr><td>5</td><td>Ohio</td><td>425,126</td><td>3.65%</td><td>35</td><td>Nevada</td><td>68,838</td><td>0.59%</td></tr>
<tr><td>26</td><td>Oklahoma</td><td>141,352</td><td>1.21%</td><td>36</td><td>Hawaii</td><td>56,527</td><td>0.48%</td></tr>
<tr><td>25</td><td>Oregon</td><td>148,545</td><td>1.27%</td><td>37</td><td>Nebraska</td><td>55,388</td><td>0.47%</td></tr>
<tr><td>8</td><td>Pennsylvania</td><td>329,381</td><td>2.82%</td><td>38</td><td>Rhode Island</td><td>40,953</td><td>0.35%</td></tr>
<tr><td>38</td><td>Rhode Island</td><td>40,953</td><td>0.35%</td><td>39</td><td>West Virginia</td><td>32,779</td><td>0.28%</td></tr>
<tr><td>24</td><td>South Carolina</td><td>153,409</td><td>1.32%</td><td>40</td><td>Idaho</td><td>32,581</td><td>0.28%</td></tr>
<tr><td>47</td><td>South Dakota</td><td>16,753</td><td>0.14%</td><td>41</td><td>Maine</td><td>31,496</td><td>0.27%</td></tr>
<tr><td>19</td><td>Tennessee</td><td>211,811</td><td>1.82%</td><td>42</td><td>New Hampshire</td><td>30,293</td><td>0.26%</td></tr>
<tr><td>2</td><td>Texas</td><td>995,335</td><td>8.53%</td><td>43</td><td>Montana</td><td>28,176</td><td>0.24%</td></tr>
<tr><td>33</td><td>Utah</td><td>87,956</td><td>0.75%</td><td>44</td><td>Delaware</td><td>26,924</td><td>0.23%</td></tr>
<tr><td>46</td><td>Vermont</td><td>16,961</td><td>0.15%</td><td>45</td><td>Alaska</td><td>22,896</td><td>0.20%</td></tr>
<tr><td>16</td><td>Virginia</td><td>229,047</td><td>1.96%</td><td>46</td><td>Vermont</td><td>16,961</td><td>0.15%</td></tr>
<tr><td>11</td><td>Washington</td><td>273,034</td><td>2.34%</td><td>47</td><td>South Dakota</td><td>16,753</td><td>0.14%</td></tr>
<tr><td>39</td><td>West Virginia</td><td>32,779</td><td>0.28%</td><td>48</td><td>Wyoming</td><td>15,962</td><td>0.14%</td></tr>
<tr><td>20</td><td>Wisconsin</td><td>175,183</td><td>1.50%</td><td>49</td><td>North Dakota</td><td>15,267</td><td>0.13%</td></tr>
<tr><td>48</td><td>Wyoming</td><td>15,962</td><td>0.14%</td><td>NA</td><td>Illinois**</td><td>NA</td><td>NA</td></tr>
<tr><td></td><td></td><td></td><td></td><td></td><td>District of Columbia</td><td>51,091</td><td>0.44%</td></tr>
</table>

Source: Morgan Quitno Corporation using data from U.S. Department of Justice, Federal Bureau of Investigation
"Crime in the United States 1993" (Uniform Crime Reports, December 4, 1994)
*Estimated totals for urban areas, defined by the F.B.I. as Metropolitan Statistical Areas and other cities outside such areas. National total includes those states listed as not available. Property crimes are offenses of burglary, larceny-theft and motor vehicle theft.
**Not available.

Urban Property Crime Rate in 1993

National Urban Rate = 5,156.0 Property Crimes per 100,000 Population*

<table>
<tr><td colspan="3"><u>ALPHA ORDER</u></td><td colspan="3"><u>RANK ORDER</u></td></tr>
<tr><td>RANK</td><td>STATE</td><td>RATE</td><td>RANK</td><td>STATE</td><td>RATE</td></tr>
<tr><td>27</td><td>Alabama</td><td>4,808.5</td><td>1</td><td>Florida</td><td>7,363.0</td></tr>
<tr><td>15</td><td>Alaska</td><td>5,585.1</td><td>2</td><td>Arizona</td><td>7,128.5</td></tr>
<tr><td>2</td><td>Arizona</td><td>7,128.5</td><td>3</td><td>Montana</td><td>6,907.9</td></tr>
<tr><td>13</td><td>Arkansas</td><td>5,653.2</td><td>4</td><td>Louisiana</td><td>6,640.4</td></tr>
<tr><td>16</td><td>California</td><td>5,432.2</td><td>5</td><td>Georgia</td><td>6,252.4</td></tr>
<tr><td>24</td><td>Colorado</td><td>5,223.0</td><td>6</td><td>New Mexico</td><td>6,200.8</td></tr>
<tr><td>36</td><td>Connecticut</td><td>4,365.4</td><td>7</td><td>Hawaii</td><td>6,179.3</td></tr>
<tr><td>35</td><td>Delaware</td><td>4,402.0</td><td>8</td><td>Mississippi</td><td>6,156.4</td></tr>
<tr><td>1</td><td>Florida</td><td>7,363.0</td><td>9</td><td>Texas</td><td>6,054.8</td></tr>
<tr><td>5</td><td>Georgia</td><td>6,252.4</td><td>10</td><td>North Carolina</td><td>5,841.8</td></tr>
<tr><td>7</td><td>Hawaii</td><td>6,179.3</td><td>11</td><td>Oregon</td><td>5,840.2</td></tr>
<tr><td>33</td><td>Idaho</td><td>4,552.7</td><td>12</td><td>Washington</td><td>5,723.2</td></tr>
<tr><td>NA</td><td>Illinois**</td><td>NA</td><td>13</td><td>Arkansas</td><td>5,653.2</td></tr>
<tr><td>34</td><td>Indiana</td><td>4,545.4</td><td>14</td><td>Nevada</td><td>5,646.3</td></tr>
<tr><td>29</td><td>Iowa</td><td>4,638.1</td><td>15</td><td>Alaska</td><td>5,585.1</td></tr>
<tr><td>25</td><td>Kansas</td><td>5,130.1</td><td>16</td><td>California</td><td>5,432.2</td></tr>
<tr><td>44</td><td>Kentucky</td><td>3,795.4</td><td>17</td><td>Oklahoma</td><td>5,425.5</td></tr>
<tr><td>4</td><td>Louisiana</td><td>6,640.4</td><td>18</td><td>Vermont</td><td>5,423.5</td></tr>
<tr><td>46</td><td>Maine</td><td>3,527.0</td><td>19</td><td>South Carolina</td><td>5,368.8</td></tr>
<tr><td>23</td><td>Maryland</td><td>5,275.0</td><td>20</td><td>Missouri</td><td>5,341.9</td></tr>
<tr><td>41</td><td>Massachusetts</td><td>4,096.2</td><td>21</td><td>Tennessee</td><td>5,308.5</td></tr>
<tr><td>26</td><td>Michigan</td><td>4,943.5</td><td>22</td><td>Utah</td><td>5,302.9</td></tr>
<tr><td>32</td><td>Minnesota</td><td>4,561.2</td><td>23</td><td>Maryland</td><td>5,275.0</td></tr>
<tr><td>8</td><td>Mississippi</td><td>6,156.4</td><td>24</td><td>Colorado</td><td>5,223.0</td></tr>
<tr><td>20</td><td>Missouri</td><td>5,341.9</td><td>25</td><td>Kansas</td><td>5,130.1</td></tr>
<tr><td>3</td><td>Montana</td><td>6,907.9</td><td>26</td><td>Michigan</td><td>4,943.5</td></tr>
<tr><td>28</td><td>Nebraska</td><td>4,640.8</td><td>27</td><td>Alabama</td><td>4,808.5</td></tr>
<tr><td>14</td><td>Nevada</td><td>5,646.3</td><td>28</td><td>Nebraska</td><td>4,640.8</td></tr>
<tr><td>48</td><td>New Hampshire</td><td>3,077.1</td><td>29</td><td>Iowa</td><td>4,638.1</td></tr>
<tr><td>40</td><td>New Jersey</td><td>4,174.0</td><td>30</td><td>Wyoming</td><td>4,615.6</td></tr>
<tr><td>6</td><td>New Mexico</td><td>6,200.8</td><td>31</td><td>New York</td><td>4,598.1</td></tr>
<tr><td>31</td><td>New York</td><td>4,598.1</td><td>32</td><td>Minnesota</td><td>4,561.2</td></tr>
<tr><td>10</td><td>North Carolina</td><td>5,841.8</td><td>33</td><td>Idaho</td><td>4,552.7</td></tr>
<tr><td>45</td><td>North Dakota</td><td>3,735.0</td><td>34</td><td>Indiana</td><td>4,545.4</td></tr>
<tr><td>37</td><td>Ohio</td><td>4,348.6</td><td>35</td><td>Delaware</td><td>4,402.0</td></tr>
<tr><td>17</td><td>Oklahoma</td><td>5,425.5</td><td>36</td><td>Connecticut</td><td>4,365.4</td></tr>
<tr><td>11</td><td>Oregon</td><td>5,840.2</td><td>37</td><td>Ohio</td><td>4,348.6</td></tr>
<tr><td>49</td><td>Pennsylvania</td><td>2,998.7</td><td>38</td><td>Wisconsin</td><td>4,322.8</td></tr>
<tr><td>42</td><td>Rhode Island</td><td>4,095.3</td><td>39</td><td>Virginia</td><td>4,208.2</td></tr>
<tr><td>19</td><td>South Carolina</td><td>5,368.8</td><td>40</td><td>New Jersey</td><td>4,174.0</td></tr>
<tr><td>43</td><td>South Dakota</td><td>3,945.8</td><td>41</td><td>Massachusetts</td><td>4,096.2</td></tr>
<tr><td>21</td><td>Tennessee</td><td>5,308.5</td><td>42</td><td>Rhode Island</td><td>4,095.3</td></tr>
<tr><td>9</td><td>Texas</td><td>6,054.8</td><td>43</td><td>South Dakota</td><td>3,945.8</td></tr>
<tr><td>22</td><td>Utah</td><td>5,302.9</td><td>44</td><td>Kentucky</td><td>3,795.4</td></tr>
<tr><td>18</td><td>Vermont</td><td>5,423.5</td><td>45</td><td>North Dakota</td><td>3,735.0</td></tr>
<tr><td>39</td><td>Virginia</td><td>4,208.2</td><td>46</td><td>Maine</td><td>3,527.0</td></tr>
<tr><td>12</td><td>Washington</td><td>5,723.2</td><td>47</td><td>West Virginia</td><td>3,155.7</td></tr>
<tr><td>47</td><td>West Virginia</td><td>3,155.7</td><td>48</td><td>New Hampshire</td><td>3,077.1</td></tr>
<tr><td>38</td><td>Wisconsin</td><td>4,322.8</td><td>49</td><td>Pennsylvania</td><td>2,998.7</td></tr>
<tr><td>30</td><td>Wyoming</td><td>4,615.6</td><td>NA</td><td>Illinois**</td><td>NA</td></tr>
</table>

District of Columbia   8,839.3

Source: Morgan Quitno Corporation using data from U.S. Department of Justice, Federal Bureau of Investigation "Crime in the United States 1993" (Uniform Crime Reports, December 4, 1994)

*Estimated rates for urban areas, defined by the F.B.I. as Metropolitan Statistical Areas and other cities outside such areas. National rate includes those states listed as not available. Property crimes are offenses of burglary, larceny-theft and motor vehicle theft.

**Not available.

Percent of Property Crimes Occurring in Urban Areas in 1993

National Percent = 95.46% of Property Crimes*

ALPHA ORDER				RANK ORDER		
RANK	STATE	PERCENT		RANK	STATE	PERCENT
16	Alabama	95.25		1	New Jersey	100.00
46	Alaska	79.51		2	Massachusetts	99.97
6	Arizona	97.99		3	Rhode Island	99.95
36	Arkansas	89.00		4	California	98.99
4	California	98.99		5	Connecticut	98.02
19	Colorado	94.75		6	Arizona	97.99
5	Connecticut	98.02		7	New York	97.85
29	Delaware	91.88		8	Maryland	97.72
9	Florida	97.46		9	Florida	97.46
30	Georgia	91.86		10	New Hampshire	97.31
45	Hawaii	80.17		11	Texas	97.24
44	Idaho	83.20		12	Ohio	96.28
NA	Illinois**	NA		13	Utah	95.80
26	Indiana	93.29		14	Pennsylvania	95.79
34	Iowa	89.87		15	Washington	95.55
23	Kansas	93.90		16	Alabama	95.25
41	Kentucky	86.26		17	Missouri	95.19
20	Louisiana	94.55		18	New Mexico	95.12
43	Maine	83.95		19	Colorado	94.75
8	Maryland	97.72		20	Louisiana	94.55
2	Massachusetts	99.97		21	Michigan	94.52
21	Michigan	94.52		22	Virginia	94.27
33	Minnesota	90.82		23	Kansas	93.90
39	Mississippi	87.35		24	Oklahoma	93.89
17	Missouri	95.19		25	Nevada	93.42
49	Montana	72.81		26	Indiana	93.29
32	Nebraska	91.23		27	Oregon	93.10
25	Nevada	93.42		28	Tennessee	92.85
10	New Hampshire	97.31		29	Delaware	91.88
1	New Jersey	100.00		30	Georgia	91.86
18	New Mexico	95.12		31	Wisconsin	91.76
7	New York	97.85		32	Nebraska	91.23
35	North Carolina	89.73		33	Minnesota	90.82
37	North Dakota	87.81		34	Iowa	89.87
12	Ohio	96.28		35	North Carolina	89.73
24	Oklahoma	93.89		36	Arkansas	89.00
27	Oregon	93.10		37	North Dakota	87.81
14	Pennsylvania	95.79		38	Wyoming	87.60
3	Rhode Island	99.95		39	Mississippi	87.35
40	South Carolina	86.29		40	South Carolina	86.29
42	South Dakota	85.21		41	Kentucky	86.26
28	Tennessee	92.85		42	South Dakota	85.21
11	Texas	97.24		43	Maine	83.95
13	Utah	95.80		44	Idaho	83.20
48	Vermont	76.32		45	Hawaii	80.17
22	Virginia	94.27		46	Alaska	79.51
15	Washington	95.55		47	West Virginia	77.49
47	West Virginia	77.49		48	Vermont	76.32
31	Wisconsin	91.76		49	Montana	72.81
38	Wyoming	87.60		NA	Illinois**	NA
				District of Columbia		100.00

Source: Morgan Quitno Corporation using data from U.S. Department of Justice, Federal Bureau of Investigation
"Crime in the United States 1993" (Uniform Crime Reports, December 4, 1994)

*Estimated percentages for urban areas, defined by the F.B.I. as Metropolitan Statistical Areas and other cities outside such areas. National percent includes those states listed as not available. Property crimes are offenses of burglary, larceny-theft and motor vehicle theft.

**Not available.

Property Crime in Rural Areas in 1993

National Total = 554,746 Property Crimes*

ALPHA ORDER					RANK ORDER			

RANK	STATE	CRIMES	% of USA
29	Alabama	8,153	1.47%
33	Alaska	5,899	1.06%
35	Arizona	5,326	0.96%
21	Arkansas	11,243	2.03%
8	California	16,961	3.06%
27	Colorado	9,278	1.67%
42	Connecticut	2,724	0.49%
43	Delaware	2,380	0.43%
4	Florida	24,791	4.47%
2	Georgia	30,796	5.55%
16	Hawaii	13,978	2.52%
31	Idaho	6,580	1.19%
NA	Illinois**	NA	NA
13	Indiana	15,251	2.75%
25	Iowa	10,038	1.81%
30	Kansas	6,919	1.25%
14	Kentucky	14,557	2.62%
18	Louisiana	13,530	2.44%
32	Maine	6,023	1.09%
34	Maryland	5,775	1.04%
47	Massachusetts	67	0.01%
6	Michigan	24,191	4.36%
9	Minnesota	16,835	3.03%
19	Mississippi	13,318	2.40%
23	Missouri	10,958	1.98%
24	Montana	10,523	1.90%
36	Nebraska	5,324	0.96%
38	Nevada	4,847	0.87%
46	New Hampshire	838	0.15%
49	New Jersey	0	0.00%
39	New Mexico	4,209	0.76%
7	New York	17,532	3.16%
1	North Carolina	35,482	6.40%
45	North Dakota	2,120	0.38%
10	Ohio	16,424	2.96%
28	Oklahoma	9,194	1.66%
22	Oregon	11,013	1.99%
15	Pennsylvania	14,460	2.61%
48	Rhode Island	20	0.00%
5	South Carolina	24,370	4.39%
41	South Dakota	2,908	0.52%
11	Tennessee	16,306	2.94%
3	Texas	28,277	5.10%
40	Utah	3,860	0.70%
37	Vermont	5,262	0.95%
17	Virginia	13,928	2.51%
20	Washington	12,719	2.29%
26	West Virginia	9,521	1.72%
12	Wisconsin	15,740	2.84%
44	Wyoming	2,259	0.41%

RANK	STATE	CRIMES	% of USA
1	North Carolina	35,482	6.40%
2	Georgia	30,796	5.55%
3	Texas	28,277	5.10%
4	Florida	24,791	4.47%
5	South Carolina	24,370	4.39%
6	Michigan	24,191	4.36%
7	New York	17,532	3.16%
8	California	16,961	3.06%
9	Minnesota	16,835	3.03%
10	Ohio	16,424	2.96%
11	Tennessee	16,306	2.94%
12	Wisconsin	15,740	2.84%
13	Indiana	15,251	2.75%
14	Kentucky	14,557	2.62%
15	Pennsylvania	14,460	2.61%
16	Hawaii	13,978	2.52%
17	Virginia	13,928	2.51%
18	Louisiana	13,530	2.44%
19	Mississippi	13,318	2.40%
20	Washington	12,719	2.29%
21	Arkansas	11,243	2.03%
22	Oregon	11,013	1.99%
23	Missouri	10,958	1.98%
24	Montana	10,523	1.90%
25	Iowa	10,038	1.81%
26	West Virginia	9,521	1.72%
27	Colorado	9,278	1.67%
28	Oklahoma	9,194	1.66%
29	Alabama	8,153	1.47%
30	Kansas	6,919	1.25%
31	Idaho	6,580	1.19%
32	Maine	6,023	1.09%
33	Alaska	5,899	1.06%
34	Maryland	5,775	1.04%
35	Arizona	5,326	0.96%
36	Nebraska	5,324	0.96%
37	Vermont	5,262	0.95%
38	Nevada	4,847	0.87%
39	New Mexico	4,209	0.76%
40	Utah	3,860	0.70%
41	South Dakota	2,908	0.52%
42	Connecticut	2,724	0.49%
43	Delaware	2,380	0.43%
44	Wyoming	2,259	0.41%
45	North Dakota	2,120	0.38%
46	New Hampshire	838	0.15%
47	Massachusetts	67	0.01%
48	Rhode Island	20	0.00%
49	New Jersey	0	0.00%
NA	Illinois**	NA	NA
	District of Columbia	0	0.00%

Source: Morgan Quitno Corporation using data from U.S. Department of Justice, Federal Bureau of Investigation
"Crime in the United States 1993" (Uniform Crime Reports, December 4, 1994)

*Estimated totals for rural areas, defined by the F.B.I. as other than Metropolitan Statistical Areas and other cities outside such areas. National total includes those states listed as not available. Property crimes are offenses of burglary, larceny-theft and motor vehicle theft.

**Not available.

Rural Property Crime Rate in 1993

National Rural Rate = 1,749.0 Property Crimes per 100,000 Population*

ALPHA ORDER				RANK ORDER		
RANK	**STATE**	**RATE**		**RANK**	**STATE**	**RATE**
42	Alabama	1,034.7		1	Hawaii	5,434.2
3	Alaska	3,120.3		2	Florida	3,342.8
23	Arizona	1,763.2		3	Alaska	3,120.3
33	Arkansas	1,380.4		4	South Carolina	3,102.1
6	California	2,749.5		5	Nevada	2,853.9
9	Colorado	2,595.1		6	California	2,749.5
32	Connecticut	1,426.7		7	Delaware	2,693.2
7	Delaware	2,693.2		8	Washington	2,626.0
2	Florida	3,342.8		9	Colorado	2,595.1
12	Georgia	2,267.2		10	Montana	2,440.9
1	Hawaii	5,434.2		11	Michigan	2,346.3
25	Idaho	1,716.4		12	Georgia	2,267.2
NA	Illinois**	NA		13	Oregon	2,254.4
30	Indiana	1,450.8		14	Maryland	2,170.9
40	Iowa	1,122.6		15	North Carolina	2,163.2
27	Kansas	1,516.8		16	New York	2,045.2
41	Kentucky	1,054.7		17	Vermont	1,998.7
21	Louisiana	1,787.1		18	Minnesota	1,943.1
24	Maine	1,740.7		19	Utah	1,916.9
14	Maryland	2,170.9		20	Wyoming	1,819.3
47	Massachusetts	546.6		21	Louisiana	1,787.1
11	Michigan	2,346.3		22	Texas	1,775.8
18	Minnesota	1,943.1		23	Arizona	1,763.2
39	Mississippi	1,159.3		24	Maine	1,740.7
45	Missouri	931.8		25	Idaho	1,716.4
10	Montana	2,440.9		26	Wisconsin	1,597.1
36	Nebraska	1,287.5		27	Kansas	1,516.8
5	Nevada	2,853.9		28	Tennessee	1,470.4
46	New Hampshire	596.3		29	Oklahoma	1,469.5
48	New Jersey	0.0		30	Indiana	1,450.8
31	New Mexico	1,435.8		31	New Mexico	1,435.8
16	New York	2,045.2		32	Connecticut	1,426.7
15	North Carolina	2,163.2		33	Arkansas	1,380.4
44	North Dakota	937.0		34	Pennsylvania	1,359.2
37	Ohio	1,249.2		35	Virginia	1,328.9
29	Oklahoma	1,469.5		36	Nebraska	1,287.5
13	Oregon	2,254.4		37	Ohio	1,249.2
34	Pennsylvania	1,359.2		38	West Virginia	1,218.6
48	Rhode Island	0.0		39	Mississippi	1,159.3
4	South Carolina	3,102.1		40	Iowa	1,122.6
43	South Dakota	1,001.3		41	Kentucky	1,054.7
28	Tennessee	1,470.4		42	Alabama	1,034.7
22	Texas	1,775.8		43	South Dakota	1,001.3
19	Utah	1,916.9		44	North Dakota	937.0
17	Vermont	1,998.7		45	Missouri	931.8
35	Virginia	1,328.9		46	New Hampshire	596.3
8	Washington	2,626.0		47	Massachusetts	546.6
38	West Virginia	1,218.6		48	New Jersey	0.0
26	Wisconsin	1,597.1		48	Rhode Island	0.0
20	Wyoming	1,819.3		NA	Illinois**	NA
					District of Columbia	0.0

Source: Morgan Quitno Corporation using data from U.S. Department of Justice, Federal Bureau of Investigation
    "Crime in the United States 1993" (Uniform Crime Reports, December 4, 1994)
*Estimated rates for rural areas, defined by the F.B.I. as other than Metropolitan Statistical Areas and other cities outside
such areas. National rate includes those states listed as not available. Property crimes are offenses of burglary,
larceny-theft and motor vehicle theft.
**Not available.

Percent of Property Crime Occurring in Rural Areas in 1993

National Percent = 4.54% of Property Crimes*

<table>
<tr><td colspan="3"><u>ALPHA ORDER</u></td><td colspan="3"><u>RANK ORDER</u></td></tr>
<tr><td>RANK</td><td>STATE</td><td>PERCENT</td><td>RANK</td><td>STATE</td><td>PERCENT</td></tr>
<tr><td>34</td><td>Alabama</td><td>4.75</td><td>1</td><td>Montana</td><td>27.19</td></tr>
<tr><td>4</td><td>Alaska</td><td>20.49</td><td>2</td><td>Vermont</td><td>23.68</td></tr>
<tr><td>44</td><td>Arizona</td><td>2.01</td><td>3</td><td>West Virginia</td><td>22.51</td></tr>
<tr><td>14</td><td>Arkansas</td><td>11.00</td><td>4</td><td>Alaska</td><td>20.49</td></tr>
<tr><td>46</td><td>California</td><td>1.01</td><td>5</td><td>Hawaii</td><td>19.83</td></tr>
<tr><td>31</td><td>Colorado</td><td>5.25</td><td>6</td><td>Idaho</td><td>16.80</td></tr>
<tr><td>45</td><td>Connecticut</td><td>1.98</td><td>7</td><td>Maine</td><td>16.05</td></tr>
<tr><td>21</td><td>Delaware</td><td>8.12</td><td>8</td><td>South Dakota</td><td>14.79</td></tr>
<tr><td>41</td><td>Florida</td><td>2.54</td><td>9</td><td>Kentucky</td><td>13.74</td></tr>
<tr><td>20</td><td>Georgia</td><td>8.14</td><td>10</td><td>South Carolina</td><td>13.71</td></tr>
<tr><td>5</td><td>Hawaii</td><td>19.83</td><td>11</td><td>Mississippi</td><td>12.65</td></tr>
<tr><td>6</td><td>Idaho</td><td>16.80</td><td>12</td><td>Wyoming</td><td>12.40</td></tr>
<tr><td>NA</td><td>Illinois**</td><td>NA</td><td>13</td><td>North Dakota</td><td>12.19</td></tr>
<tr><td>24</td><td>Indiana</td><td>6.71</td><td>14</td><td>Arkansas</td><td>11.00</td></tr>
<tr><td>16</td><td>Iowa</td><td>10.13</td><td>15</td><td>North Carolina</td><td>10.27</td></tr>
<tr><td>27</td><td>Kansas</td><td>6.10</td><td>16</td><td>Iowa</td><td>10.13</td></tr>
<tr><td>9</td><td>Kentucky</td><td>13.74</td><td>17</td><td>Minnesota</td><td>9.18</td></tr>
<tr><td>30</td><td>Louisiana</td><td>5.45</td><td>18</td><td>Nebraska</td><td>8.77</td></tr>
<tr><td>7</td><td>Maine</td><td>16.05</td><td>19</td><td>Wisconsin</td><td>8.24</td></tr>
<tr><td>42</td><td>Maryland</td><td>2.28</td><td>20</td><td>Georgia</td><td>8.14</td></tr>
<tr><td>48</td><td>Massachusetts</td><td>0.03</td><td>21</td><td>Delaware</td><td>8.12</td></tr>
<tr><td>29</td><td>Michigan</td><td>5.48</td><td>22</td><td>Tennessee</td><td>7.15</td></tr>
<tr><td>17</td><td>Minnesota</td><td>9.18</td><td>23</td><td>Oregon</td><td>6.90</td></tr>
<tr><td>11</td><td>Mississippi</td><td>12.65</td><td>24</td><td>Indiana</td><td>6.71</td></tr>
<tr><td>33</td><td>Missouri</td><td>4.81</td><td>25</td><td>Nevada</td><td>6.58</td></tr>
<tr><td>1</td><td>Montana</td><td>27.19</td><td>26</td><td>Oklahoma</td><td>6.11</td></tr>
<tr><td>18</td><td>Nebraska</td><td>8.77</td><td>27</td><td>Kansas</td><td>6.10</td></tr>
<tr><td>25</td><td>Nevada</td><td>6.58</td><td>28</td><td>Virginia</td><td>5.73</td></tr>
<tr><td>40</td><td>New Hampshire</td><td>2.69</td><td>29</td><td>Michigan</td><td>5.48</td></tr>
<tr><td>49</td><td>New Jersey</td><td>0.00</td><td>30</td><td>Louisiana</td><td>5.45</td></tr>
<tr><td>32</td><td>New Mexico</td><td>4.88</td><td>31</td><td>Colorado</td><td>5.25</td></tr>
<tr><td>43</td><td>New York</td><td>2.15</td><td>32</td><td>New Mexico</td><td>4.88</td></tr>
<tr><td>15</td><td>North Carolina</td><td>10.27</td><td>33</td><td>Missouri</td><td>4.81</td></tr>
<tr><td>13</td><td>North Dakota</td><td>12.19</td><td>34</td><td>Alabama</td><td>4.75</td></tr>
<tr><td>38</td><td>Ohio</td><td>3.72</td><td>35</td><td>Washington</td><td>4.45</td></tr>
<tr><td>26</td><td>Oklahoma</td><td>6.11</td><td>36</td><td>Pennsylvania</td><td>4.21</td></tr>
<tr><td>23</td><td>Oregon</td><td>6.90</td><td>37</td><td>Utah</td><td>4.20</td></tr>
<tr><td>36</td><td>Pennsylvania</td><td>4.21</td><td>38</td><td>Ohio</td><td>3.72</td></tr>
<tr><td>47</td><td>Rhode Island</td><td>0.05</td><td>39</td><td>Texas</td><td>2.76</td></tr>
<tr><td>10</td><td>South Carolina</td><td>13.71</td><td>40</td><td>New Hampshire</td><td>2.69</td></tr>
<tr><td>8</td><td>South Dakota</td><td>14.79</td><td>41</td><td>Florida</td><td>2.54</td></tr>
<tr><td>22</td><td>Tennessee</td><td>7.15</td><td>42</td><td>Maryland</td><td>2.28</td></tr>
<tr><td>39</td><td>Texas</td><td>2.76</td><td>43</td><td>New York</td><td>2.15</td></tr>
<tr><td>37</td><td>Utah</td><td>4.20</td><td>44</td><td>Arizona</td><td>2.01</td></tr>
<tr><td>2</td><td>Vermont</td><td>23.68</td><td>45</td><td>Connecticut</td><td>1.98</td></tr>
<tr><td>28</td><td>Virginia</td><td>5.73</td><td>46</td><td>California</td><td>1.01</td></tr>
<tr><td>35</td><td>Washington</td><td>4.45</td><td>47</td><td>Rhode Island</td><td>0.05</td></tr>
<tr><td>3</td><td>West Virginia</td><td>22.51</td><td>48</td><td>Massachusetts</td><td>0.03</td></tr>
<tr><td>19</td><td>Wisconsin</td><td>8.24</td><td>49</td><td>New Jersey</td><td>0.00</td></tr>
<tr><td>12</td><td>Wyoming</td><td>12.40</td><td>NA</td><td>Illinois**</td><td>NA</td></tr>
<tr><td></td><td></td><td></td><td></td><td>District of Columbia</td><td>0.00</td></tr>
</table>

Source: Morgan Quitno Corporation using data from U.S. Department of Justice, Federal Bureau of Investigation "Crime in the United States 1993" (Uniform Crime Reports, December 4, 1994)

*Estimated percentages for rural areas, defined by the F.B.I. as other than Metropolitan Statistical Areas and other cities outside such areas. National percent includes those states listed as not available. Property crimes are offenses of burglary, larceny-theft and motor vehicle theft.

**Not available.

Burglary in Urban Areas in 1993

National Total = 2,633,906 Burglaries*

<table>
<tr><td colspan="4"><u>ALPHA ORDER</u></td><td colspan="4"><u>RANK ORDER</u></td></tr>
<tr><td>RANK</td><td>STATE</td><td>BURGLARIES</td><td>% of USA</td><td>RANK</td><td>STATE</td><td>BURGLARIES</td><td>% of USA</td></tr>
<tr><td>19</td><td>Alabama</td><td>41,702</td><td>1.58%</td><td>1</td><td>California</td><td>407,433</td><td>15.47%</td></tr>
<tr><td>45</td><td>Alaska</td><td>3,155</td><td>0.12%</td><td>2</td><td>Florida</td><td>241,832</td><td>9.18%</td></tr>
<tr><td>12</td><td>Arizona</td><td>55,729</td><td>2.12%</td><td>3</td><td>Texas</td><td>222,209</td><td>8.44%</td></tr>
<tr><td>30</td><td>Arkansas</td><td>22,464</td><td>0.85%</td><td>4</td><td>New York</td><td>175,337</td><td>6.66%</td></tr>
<tr><td>1</td><td>California</td><td>407,433</td><td>15.47%</td><td>5</td><td>Ohio</td><td>92,145</td><td>3.50%</td></tr>
<tr><td>23</td><td>Colorado</td><td>34,022</td><td>1.29%</td><td>6</td><td>North Carolina</td><td>89,381</td><td>3.39%</td></tr>
<tr><td>25</td><td>Connecticut</td><td>31,095</td><td>1.18%</td><td>7</td><td>Michigan</td><td>84,119</td><td>3.19%</td></tr>
<tr><td>43</td><td>Delaware</td><td>5,278</td><td>0.20%</td><td>8</td><td>Georgia</td><td>79,381</td><td>3.01%</td></tr>
<tr><td>2</td><td>Florida</td><td>241,832</td><td>9.18%</td><td>9</td><td>New Jersey</td><td>76,738</td><td>2.91%</td></tr>
<tr><td>8</td><td>Georgia</td><td>79,381</td><td>3.01%</td><td>10</td><td>Pennsylvania</td><td>64,061</td><td>2.43%</td></tr>
<tr><td>37</td><td>Hawaii</td><td>9,935</td><td>0.38%</td><td>11</td><td>Massachusetts</td><td>60,206</td><td>2.29%</td></tr>
<tr><td>41</td><td>Idaho</td><td>5,596</td><td>0.21%</td><td>12</td><td>Arizona</td><td>55,729</td><td>2.12%</td></tr>
<tr><td>NA</td><td>Illinois**</td><td>NA</td><td>NA</td><td>13</td><td>Louisiana</td><td>54,766</td><td>2.08%</td></tr>
<tr><td>18</td><td>Indiana</td><td>43,799</td><td>1.66%</td><td>14</td><td>Maryland</td><td>54,330</td><td>2.06%</td></tr>
<tr><td>33</td><td>Iowa</td><td>17,388</td><td>0.66%</td><td>15</td><td>Tennessee</td><td>52,821</td><td>2.01%</td></tr>
<tr><td>29</td><td>Kansas</td><td>26,061</td><td>0.99%</td><td>16</td><td>Washington</td><td>52,006</td><td>1.97%</td></tr>
<tr><td>31</td><td>Kentucky</td><td>21,990</td><td>0.83%</td><td>17</td><td>Missouri</td><td>48,841</td><td>1.85%</td></tr>
<tr><td>13</td><td>Louisiana</td><td>54,766</td><td>2.08%</td><td>18</td><td>Indiana</td><td>43,799</td><td>1.66%</td></tr>
<tr><td>40</td><td>Maine</td><td>6,340</td><td>0.24%</td><td>19</td><td>Alabama</td><td>41,702</td><td>1.58%</td></tr>
<tr><td>14</td><td>Maryland</td><td>54,330</td><td>2.06%</td><td>20</td><td>South Carolina</td><td>39,237</td><td>1.49%</td></tr>
<tr><td>11</td><td>Massachusetts</td><td>60,206</td><td>2.29%</td><td>21</td><td>Virginia</td><td>38,985</td><td>1.48%</td></tr>
<tr><td>7</td><td>Michigan</td><td>84,119</td><td>3.19%</td><td>22</td><td>Oklahoma</td><td>36,061</td><td>1.37%</td></tr>
<tr><td>24</td><td>Minnesota</td><td>32,540</td><td>1.24%</td><td>23</td><td>Colorado</td><td>34,022</td><td>1.29%</td></tr>
<tr><td>27</td><td>Mississippi</td><td>27,617</td><td>1.05%</td><td>24</td><td>Minnesota</td><td>32,540</td><td>1.24%</td></tr>
<tr><td>17</td><td>Missouri</td><td>48,841</td><td>1.85%</td><td>25</td><td>Connecticut</td><td>31,095</td><td>1.18%</td></tr>
<tr><td>44</td><td>Montana</td><td>4,003</td><td>0.15%</td><td>26</td><td>Wisconsin</td><td>27,719</td><td>1.05%</td></tr>
<tr><td>38</td><td>Nebraska</td><td>9,286</td><td>0.35%</td><td>27</td><td>Mississippi</td><td>27,617</td><td>1.05%</td></tr>
<tr><td>34</td><td>Nevada</td><td>16,092</td><td>0.61%</td><td>28</td><td>Oregon</td><td>27,553</td><td>1.05%</td></tr>
<tr><td>42</td><td>New Hampshire</td><td>5,490</td><td>0.21%</td><td>29</td><td>Kansas</td><td>26,061</td><td>0.99%</td></tr>
<tr><td>9</td><td>New Jersey</td><td>76,738</td><td>2.91%</td><td>30</td><td>Arkansas</td><td>22,464</td><td>0.85%</td></tr>
<tr><td>32</td><td>New Mexico</td><td>21,195</td><td>0.80%</td><td>31</td><td>Kentucky</td><td>21,990</td><td>0.83%</td></tr>
<tr><td>4</td><td>New York</td><td>175,337</td><td>6.66%</td><td>32</td><td>New Mexico</td><td>21,195</td><td>0.80%</td></tr>
<tr><td>6</td><td>North Carolina</td><td>89,381</td><td>3.39%</td><td>33</td><td>Iowa</td><td>17,388</td><td>0.66%</td></tr>
<tr><td>49</td><td>North Dakota</td><td>1,802</td><td>0.07%</td><td>34</td><td>Nevada</td><td>16,092</td><td>0.61%</td></tr>
<tr><td>5</td><td>Ohio</td><td>92,145</td><td>3.50%</td><td>35</td><td>Utah</td><td>13,819</td><td>0.52%</td></tr>
<tr><td>22</td><td>Oklahoma</td><td>36,061</td><td>1.37%</td><td>36</td><td>Rhode Island</td><td>10,407</td><td>0.40%</td></tr>
<tr><td>28</td><td>Oregon</td><td>27,553</td><td>1.05%</td><td>37</td><td>Hawaii</td><td>9,935</td><td>0.38%</td></tr>
<tr><td>10</td><td>Pennsylvania</td><td>64,061</td><td>2.43%</td><td>38</td><td>Nebraska</td><td>9,286</td><td>0.35%</td></tr>
<tr><td>36</td><td>Rhode Island</td><td>10,407</td><td>0.40%</td><td>39</td><td>West Virginia</td><td>7,561</td><td>0.29%</td></tr>
<tr><td>20</td><td>South Carolina</td><td>39,237</td><td>1.49%</td><td>40</td><td>Maine</td><td>6,340</td><td>0.24%</td></tr>
<tr><td>46</td><td>South Dakota</td><td>3,030</td><td>0.12%</td><td>41</td><td>Idaho</td><td>5,596</td><td>0.21%</td></tr>
<tr><td>15</td><td>Tennessee</td><td>52,821</td><td>2.01%</td><td>42</td><td>New Hampshire</td><td>5,490</td><td>0.21%</td></tr>
<tr><td>3</td><td>Texas</td><td>222,209</td><td>8.44%</td><td>43</td><td>Delaware</td><td>5,278</td><td>0.20%</td></tr>
<tr><td>35</td><td>Utah</td><td>13,819</td><td>0.52%</td><td>44</td><td>Montana</td><td>4,003</td><td>0.15%</td></tr>
<tr><td>47</td><td>Vermont</td><td>2,904</td><td>0.11%</td><td>45</td><td>Alaska</td><td>3,155</td><td>0.12%</td></tr>
<tr><td>21</td><td>Virginia</td><td>38,985</td><td>1.48%</td><td>46</td><td>South Dakota</td><td>3,030</td><td>0.12%</td></tr>
<tr><td>16</td><td>Washington</td><td>52,006</td><td>1.97%</td><td>47</td><td>Vermont</td><td>2,904</td><td>0.11%</td></tr>
<tr><td>39</td><td>West Virginia</td><td>7,561</td><td>0.29%</td><td>48</td><td>Wyoming</td><td>2,474</td><td>0.09%</td></tr>
<tr><td>26</td><td>Wisconsin</td><td>27,719</td><td>1.05%</td><td>49</td><td>North Dakota</td><td>1,802</td><td>0.07%</td></tr>
<tr><td>48</td><td>Wyoming</td><td>2,474</td><td>0.09%</td><td>NA</td><td>Illinois**</td><td>NA</td><td>NA</td></tr>
<tr><td></td><td></td><td></td><td></td><td></td><td>District of Columbia</td><td>11,534</td><td>0.44%</td></tr>
</table>

Source: Morgan Quitno Corporation using data from U.S. Department of Justice, Federal Bureau of Investigation
  "Crime in the United States 1993" (Uniform Crime Reports, December 4, 1994)
*Estimated totals for urban areas, defined by the F.B.I. as Metropolitan Statistical Areas and other cities outside such
areas. National total includes those states listed as not available. Burglary is the unlawful entry of a structure to commit a
felony or theft. Attempts are included.
**Not available.

Urban Burglary Rate in 1993

National Urban Rate = 1,164.5 Burglaries per 100,000 Population*

ALPHA ORDER			RANK ORDER		
RANK	**STATE**	**RATE**	**RANK**	**STATE**	**RATE**
16	Alabama	1,226.9	1	Florida	1,869.3
40	Alaska	769.6	2	Mississippi	1,848.3
6	Arizona	1,533.6	3	North Carolina	1,684.9
8	Arkansas	1,395.7	4	New Mexico	1,602.2
12	California	1,331.7	5	Louisiana	1,548.0
22	Colorado	1,060.4	6	Arizona	1,533.6
25	Connecticut	1,007.6	7	Georgia	1,428.1
36	Delaware	862.9	8	Arkansas	1,395.7
1	Florida	1,869.3	9	Oklahoma	1,384.1
7	Georgia	1,428.1	10	South Carolina	1,373.2
20	Hawaii	1,086.1	11	Texas	1,351.7
38	Idaho	782.0	12	California	1,331.7
NA	Illinois**	NA	13	Tennessee	1,323.8
31	Indiana	939.5	14	Nevada	1,319.9
34	Iowa	905.7	15	Kansas	1,256.1
15	Kansas	1,256.1	16	Alabama	1,226.9
33	Kentucky	912.9	17	Missouri	1,203.6
5	Louisiana	1,548.0	18	Maryland	1,156.2
45	Maine	710.0	19	Washington	1,090.1
18	Maryland	1,156.2	20	Hawaii	1,086.1
26	Massachusetts	1,003.5	21	Oregon	1,083.3
27	Michigan	995.9	22	Colorado	1,060.4
35	Minnesota	891.4	23	Rhode Island	1,040.7
2	Mississippi	1,848.3	24	New York	1,011.2
17	Missouri	1,203.6	25	Connecticut	1,007.6
28	Montana	981.4	26	Massachusetts	1,003.5
39	Nebraska	778.1	27	Michigan	995.9
14	Nevada	1,319.9	28	Montana	981.4
48	New Hampshire	557.7	29	New Jersey	974.0
29	New Jersey	974.0	30	Ohio	942.5
4	New Mexico	1,602.2	31	Indiana	939.5
24	New York	1,011.2	32	Vermont	928.6
3	North Carolina	1,684.9	33	Kentucky	912.9
49	North Dakota	440.9	34	Iowa	905.7
30	Ohio	942.5	35	Minnesota	891.4
9	Oklahoma	1,384.1	36	Delaware	862.9
21	Oregon	1,083.3	37	Utah	833.2
47	Pennsylvania	583.2	38	Idaho	782.0
23	Rhode Island	1,040.7	39	Nebraska	778.1
10	South Carolina	1,373.2	40	Alaska	769.6
44	South Dakota	713.6	41	West Virginia	727.9
13	Tennessee	1,323.8	42	Virginia	716.2
11	Texas	1,351.7	43	Wyoming	715.4
37	Utah	833.2	44	South Dakota	713.6
32	Vermont	928.6	45	Maine	710.0
42	Virginia	716.2	46	Wisconsin	684.0
19	Washington	1,090.1	47	Pennsylvania	583.2
41	West Virginia	727.9	48	New Hampshire	557.7
46	Wisconsin	684.0	49	North Dakota	440.9
43	Wyoming	715.4	NA	Illinois**	NA

District of Columbia   1,995.5

Source: Morgan Quitno Corporation using data from U.S. Department of Justice, Federal Bureau of Investigation
"Crime in the United States 1993" (Uniform Crime Reports, December 4, 1994)

Estimated rates for urban areas, defined by the F.B.I. as Metropolitan Statistical Areas and other cities outside such areas. National rate includes those states listed as not available. Burglary is the unlawful entry of a structure to commit a felony or theft. Attempts are included.

**Not available.

Percent of Burglaries Occurring in Urban Areas in 1993

National Percent = 92.91% of Burglaries*

ALPHA ORDER				RANK ORDER		
RANK	STATE	PERCENT		RANK	STATE	PERCENT
19	Alabama	91.50		1	New Jersey	100.00
48	Alaska	64.48		2	Massachusetts	99.98
6	Arizona	96.61		2	Rhode Island	99.98
35	Arkansas	84.31		4	California	98.37
4	California	98.37		5	Connecticut	97.01
13	Colorado	94.48		6	Arizona	96.61
5	Connecticut	97.01		7	Maryland	96.59
34	Delaware	84.53		8	New York	96.49
9	Florida	96.32		9	Florida	96.32
28	Georgia	87.79		10	Texas	95.00
44	Hawaii	74.64		11	New Hampshire	94.74
42	Idaho	76.14		12	Ohio	94.61
NA	Illinois**	NA		13	Colorado	94.48
25	Indiana	89.98		14	Utah	93.96
33	Iowa	84.56		15	Louisiana	93.19
22	Kansas	90.95		16	Nevada	93.05
40	Kentucky	78.42		17	Washington	92.73
15	Louisiana	93.19		18	New Mexico	92.29
45	Maine	71.16		19	Alabama	91.50
7	Maryland	96.59		20	Pennsylvania	91.35
2	Massachusetts	99.98		21	Missouri	91.00
24	Michigan	90.31		22	Kansas	90.95
31	Minnesota	85.30		23	Oklahoma	90.37
39	Mississippi	81.26		24	Michigan	90.31
21	Missouri	91.00		25	Indiana	89.98
47	Montana	66.81		26	Virginia	89.96
30	Nebraska	87.09		27	Oregon	88.67
16	Nevada	93.05		28	Georgia	87.79
11	New Hampshire	94.74		29	Tennessee	87.60
1	New Jersey	100.00		30	Nebraska	87.09
18	New Mexico	92.29		31	Minnesota	85.30
8	New York	96.49		32	North Carolina	84.91
32	North Carolina	84.91		33	Iowa	84.56
43	North Dakota	76.03		34	Delaware	84.53
12	Ohio	94.61		35	Arkansas	84.31
23	Oklahoma	90.37		36	Wisconsin	82.99
27	Oregon	88.67		37	South Carolina	82.27
20	Pennsylvania	91.35		38	Wyoming	81.84
2	Rhode Island	99.98		39	Mississippi	81.26
37	South Carolina	82.27		40	Kentucky	78.42
41	South Dakota	77.16		41	South Dakota	77.16
29	Tennessee	87.60		42	Idaho	76.14
10	Texas	95.00		43	North Dakota	76.03
14	Utah	93.96		44	Hawaii	74.64
49	Vermont	57.66		45	Maine	71.16
26	Virginia	89.96		46	West Virginia	69.34
17	Washington	92.73		47	Montana	66.81
46	West Virginia	69.34		48	Alaska	64.48
36	Wisconsin	82.99		49	Vermont	57.66
38	Wyoming	81.84		NA	Illinois**	NA
				District of Columbia		100.00

Source: Morgan Quitno Corporation using data from U.S. Department of Justice, Federal Bureau of Investigation
  "Crime in the United States 1993" (Uniform Crime Reports, December 4, 1994)
*Estimated percentages for urban areas, defined by the F.B.I. as Metropolitan Statistical Areas and other cities outside such areas. National percent includes those states listed as not available. Burglary is the unlawful entry of a structure to commit a felony or theft. Attempts are included.
**Not available.   409

Burglary in Rural Areas in 1993

National Total = 200,902 Burglaries*

ALPHA ORDER

RANK	STATE	BURGLARIES	% of USA
22	Alabama	3,876	1.93%
37	Alaska	1,738	0.87%
33	Arizona	1,955	0.97%
19	Arkansas	4,182	2.08%
8	California	6,749	3.36%
31	Colorado	1,989	0.99%
41	Connecticut	957	0.48%
40	Delaware	966	0.48%
4	Florida	9,231	4.59%
3	Georgia	11,042	5.50%
25	Hawaii	3,375	1.68%
36	Idaho	1,754	0.87%
NA	Illinois**	NA	NA
16	Indiana	4,878	2.43%
27	Iowa	3,174	1.58%
28	Kansas	2,594	1.29%
12	Kentucky	6,051	3.01%
21	Louisiana	4,002	1.99%
29	Maine	2,569	1.28%
34	Maryland	1,916	0.95%
47	Massachusetts	14	0.01%
5	Michigan	9,024	4.49%
14	Minnesota	5,607	2.79%
10	Mississippi	6,368	3.17%
17	Missouri	4,832	2.41%
31	Montana	1,989	0.99%
38	Nebraska	1,376	0.68%
39	Nevada	1,201	0.60%
46	New Hampshire	305	0.15%
49	New Jersey	0	0.00%
35	New Mexico	1,771	0.88%
9	New York	6,372	3.17%
1	North Carolina	15,889	7.91%
44	North Dakota	568	0.28%
15	Ohio	5,249	2.61%
23	Oklahoma	3,842	1.91%
24	Oregon	3,519	1.75%
11	Pennsylvania	6,064	3.02%
48	Rhode Island	2	0.00%
6	South Carolina	8,458	4.21%
42	South Dakota	897	0.45%
7	Tennessee	7,478	3.72%
2	Texas	11,704	5.83%
43	Utah	889	0.44%
30	Vermont	2,132	1.06%
18	Virginia	4,353	2.17%
20	Washington	4,077	2.03%
26	West Virginia	3,343	1.66%
13	Wisconsin	5,681	2.83%
45	Wyoming	549	0.27%

RANK ORDER

RANK	STATE	BURGLARIES	% of USA
1	North Carolina	15,889	7.91%
2	Texas	11,704	5.83%
3	Georgia	11,042	5.50%
4	Florida	9,231	4.59%
5	Michigan	9,024	4.49%
6	South Carolina	8,458	4.21%
7	Tennessee	7,478	3.72%
8	California	6,749	3.36%
9	New York	6,372	3.17%
10	Mississippi	6,368	3.17%
11	Pennsylvania	6,064	3.02%
12	Kentucky	6,051	3.01%
13	Wisconsin	5,681	2.83%
14	Minnesota	5,607	2.79%
15	Ohio	5,249	2.61%
16	Indiana	4,878	2.43%
17	Missouri	4,832	2.41%
18	Virginia	4,353	2.17%
19	Arkansas	4,182	2.08%
20	Washington	4,077	2.03%
21	Louisiana	4,002	1.99%
22	Alabama	3,876	1.93%
23	Oklahoma	3,842	1.91%
24	Oregon	3,519	1.75%
25	Hawaii	3,375	1.68%
26	West Virginia	3,343	1.66%
27	Iowa	3,174	1.58%
28	Kansas	2,594	1.29%
29	Maine	2,569	1.28%
30	Vermont	2,132	1.06%
31	Colorado	1,989	0.99%
31	Montana	1,989	0.99%
33	Arizona	1,955	0.97%
34	Maryland	1,916	0.95%
35	New Mexico	1,771	0.88%
36	Idaho	1,754	0.87%
37	Alaska	1,738	0.87%
38	Nebraska	1,376	0.68%
39	Nevada	1,201	0.60%
40	Delaware	966	0.48%
41	Connecticut	957	0.48%
42	South Dakota	897	0.45%
43	Utah	889	0.44%
44	North Dakota	568	0.28%
45	Wyoming	549	0.27%
46	New Hampshire	305	0.15%
47	Massachusetts	14	0.01%
48	Rhode Island	2	0.00%
49	New Jersey	0	0.00%
NA	Illinois**	NA	NA
	District of Columbia	0	0.00%

Source: Morgan Quitno Corporation using data from U.S. Department of Justice, Federal Bureau of Investigation
"Crime in the United States 1993" (Uniform Crime Reports, December 4, 1994)

*Estimated totals for rural areas, defined by the F.B.I. as other than Metropolitan Statistical Areas and other cities outside such areas. National total includes those states listed as not available. Burglary is the unlawful entry of a structure to commit a felony or theft. Attempts are included.

**Not available.

Rural Burglary Rate in 1993

National Rural Rate = 633.4 Burglaries per 100,000 Population*

ALPHA ORDER				RANK ORDER		
RANK	STATE	RATE		RANK	STATE	RATE
31	Alabama	491.9		1	Hawaii	1,312.1
7	Alaska	919.3		2	Florida	1,244.7
19	Arizona	647.2		3	California	1,094.1
29	Arkansas	513.4		4	Delaware	1,093.1
3	California	1,094.1		5	South Carolina	1,076.6
26	Colorado	556.3		6	North Carolina	968.7
30	Connecticut	501.2		7	Alaska	919.3
4	Delaware	1,093.1		8	Michigan	875.2
2	Florida	1,244.7		9	Washington	841.8
10	Georgia	812.9		10	Georgia	812.9
1	Hawaii	1,312.1		11	Vermont	809.8
34	Idaho	457.5		12	New York	743.3
NA	Illinois**	NA		13	Maine	742.5
32	Indiana	464.0		14	Texas	735.0
42	Iowa	354.9		15	Oregon	720.4
25	Kansas	568.6		16	Maryland	720.2
37	Kentucky	438.4		17	Nevada	707.1
28	Louisiana	528.6		18	Tennessee	674.3
13	Maine	742.5		19	Arizona	647.2
16	Maryland	720.2		19	Minnesota	647.2
47	Massachusetts	114.2		21	Oklahoma	614.1
8	Michigan	875.2		22	New Mexico	604.1
19	Minnesota	647.2		23	Wisconsin	576.5
27	Mississippi	554.3		24	Pennsylvania	570.0
40	Missouri	410.9		25	Kansas	568.6
33	Montana	461.4		26	Colorado	556.3
43	Nebraska	332.8		27	Mississippi	554.3
17	Nevada	707.1		28	Louisiana	528.6
46	New Hampshire	217.0		29	Arkansas	513.4
48	New Jersey	0.0		30	Connecticut	501.2
22	New Mexico	604.1		31	Alabama	491.9
12	New York	743.3		32	Indiana	464.0
6	North Carolina	968.7		33	Montana	461.4
45	North Dakota	251.1		34	Idaho	457.5
41	Ohio	399.2		35	Wyoming	442.1
21	Oklahoma	614.1		36	Utah	441.5
15	Oregon	720.4		37	Kentucky	438.4
24	Pennsylvania	570.0		38	West Virginia	427.9
48	Rhode Island	0.0		39	Virginia	415.3
5	South Carolina	1,076.6		40	Missouri	410.9
44	South Dakota	308.9		41	Ohio	399.2
18	Tennessee	674.3		42	Iowa	354.9
14	Texas	735.0		43	Nebraska	332.8
36	Utah	441.5		44	South Dakota	308.9
11	Vermont	809.8		45	North Dakota	251.1
39	Virginia	415.3		46	New Hampshire	217.0
9	Washington	841.8		47	Massachusetts	114.2
38	West Virginia	427.9		48	New Jersey	0.0
23	Wisconsin	576.5		48	Rhode Island	0.0
35	Wyoming	442.1		NA	Illinois**	NA
					District of Columbia	0.0

Source: Morgan Quitno Corporation using data from U.S. Department of Justice, Federal Bureau of Investigation
"Crime in the United States 1993" (Uniform Crime Reports, December 4, 1994)
*Estimated rates for rural areas, defined by the F.B.I. as other than Metropolitan Statistical Areas and other cities outside
such areas. National rate includes those states listed as not available. Burglary is the unlawful entry of a structure to
commit a felony or theft. Attempts are included.
**Not available.   411

Percent of Burglaries Occurring in Rural Areas in 1993

National Percent = 7.09% of Burglaries*

	ALPHA ORDER			RANK ORDER	
RANK	STATE	PERCENT	RANK	STATE	PERCENT
31	Alabama	8.50	1	Vermont	42.34
2	Alaska	35.52	2	Alaska	35.52
44	Arizona	3.39	3	Montana	33.19
15	Arkansas	15.69	4	West Virginia	30.66
46	California	1.63	5	Maine	28.84
37	Colorado	5.52	6	Hawaii	25.36
45	Connecticut	2.99	7	North Dakota	23.97
16	Delaware	15.47	8	Idaho	23.86
41	Florida	3.68	9	South Dakota	22.84
22	Georgia	12.21	10	Kentucky	21.58
6	Hawaii	25.36	11	Mississippi	18.74
8	Idaho	23.86	12	Wyoming	18.16
NA	Illinois**	NA	13	South Carolina	17.73
25	Indiana	10.02	14	Wisconsin	17.01
17	Iowa	15.44	15	Arkansas	15.69
28	Kansas	9.05	16	Delaware	15.47
10	Kentucky	21.58	17	Iowa	15.44
35	Louisiana	6.81	18	North Carolina	15.09
5	Maine	28.84	19	Minnesota	14.70
43	Maryland	3.41	20	Nebraska	12.91
47	Massachusetts	0.02	21	Tennessee	12.40
26	Michigan	9.69	22	Georgia	12.21
19	Minnesota	14.70	23	Oregon	11.33
11	Mississippi	18.74	24	Virginia	10.04
29	Missouri	9.00	25	Indiana	10.02
3	Montana	33.19	26	Michigan	9.69
20	Nebraska	12.91	27	Oklahoma	9.63
34	Nevada	6.95	28	Kansas	9.05
39	New Hampshire	5.26	29	Missouri	9.00
49	New Jersey	0.00	30	Pennsylvania	8.65
32	New Mexico	7.71	31	Alabama	8.50
42	New York	3.51	32	New Mexico	7.71
18	North Carolina	15.09	33	Washington	7.27
7	North Dakota	23.97	34	Nevada	6.95
38	Ohio	5.39	35	Louisiana	6.81
27	Oklahoma	9.63	36	Utah	6.04
23	Oregon	11.33	37	Colorado	5.52
30	Pennsylvania	8.65	38	Ohio	5.39
47	Rhode Island	0.02	39	New Hampshire	5.26
13	South Carolina	17.73	40	Texas	5.00
9	South Dakota	22.84	41	Florida	3.68
21	Tennessee	12.40	42	New York	3.51
40	Texas	5.00	43	Maryland	3.41
36	Utah	6.04	44	Arizona	3.39
1	Vermont	42.34	45	Connecticut	2.99
24	Virginia	10.04	46	California	1.63
33	Washington	7.27	47	Massachusetts	0.02
4	West Virginia	30.66	47	Rhode Island	0.02
14	Wisconsin	17.01	49	New Jersey	0.00
12	Wyoming	18.16	NA	Illinois**	NA
				District of Columbia	0.00

Source: Morgan Quitno Corporation using data from U.S. Department of Justice, Federal Bureau of Investigation
"Crime in the United States 1993" (Uniform Crime Reports, December 4, 1994)
*Estimated percentages for rural areas, defined by the F.B.I. as other than Metropolitan Statistical Areas and other cities outside such areas. National percent includes those states listed as not available. Burglary is the unlawful entry of a structure to commit a felony or theft. Attempts are included.
**Not available.

Larceny and Theft in Urban Areas in 1993

National Total = 7,501,916 Larcenies and Thefts*

ALPHA ORDER

RANK	STATE	THEFTS	% of USA
23	Alabama	108,150	1.44%
45	Alaska	17,555	0.23%
13	Arizona	169,702	2.26%
32	Arkansas	61,529	0.82%
1	California	936,390	12.48%
22	Colorado	117,911	1.57%
27	Connecticut	84,367	1.12%
44	Delaware	19,503	0.26%
3	Florida	589,840	7.86%
7	Georgia	229,376	3.06%
37	Hawaii	42,038	0.56%
38	Idaho	25,461	0.34%
NA	Illinois**	NA	NA
16	Indiana	144,734	1.93%
30	Iowa	66,797	0.89%
28	Kansas	72,527	0.97%
31	Kentucky	62,551	0.83%
15	Louisiana	154,243	2.06%
40	Maine	23,797	0.32%
14	Maryland	159,899	2.13%
18	Massachusetts	136,511	1.82%
6	Michigan	276,271	3.68%
21	Minnesota	119,753	1.60%
33	Mississippi	56,265	0.75%
17	Missouri	139,900	1.86%
42	Montana	22,816	0.30%
35	Nebraska	43,083	0.57%
36	Nevada	42,722	0.57%
43	New Hampshire	22,656	0.30%
11	New Jersey	195,876	2.61%
34	New Mexico	54,589	0.73%
4	New York	470,596	6.27%
9	North Carolina	202,778	2.70%
49	North Dakota	12,663	0.17%
5	Ohio	285,590	3.81%
26	Oklahoma	90,434	1.21%
24	Oregon	104,268	1.39%
8	Pennsylvania	213,496	2.85%
39	Rhode Island	24,083	0.32%
25	South Carolina	103,273	1.38%
47	South Dakota	13,056	0.17%
19	Tennessee	130,396	1.74%
2	Texas	649,795	8.66%
29	Utah	69,815	0.93%
46	Vermont	13,523	0.18%
12	Virginia	172,410	2.30%
10	Washington	197,758	2.64%
41	West Virginia	23,202	0.31%
20	Wisconsin	129,991	1.73%
48	Wyoming	12,865	0.17%

RANK ORDER

RANK	STATE	THEFTS	% of USA
1	California	936,390	12.48%
2	Texas	649,795	8.66%
3	Florida	589,840	7.86%
4	New York	470,596	6.27%
5	Ohio	285,590	3.81%
6	Michigan	276,271	3.68%
7	Georgia	229,376	3.06%
8	Pennsylvania	213,496	2.85%
9	North Carolina	202,778	2.70%
10	Washington	197,758	2.64%
11	New Jersey	195,876	2.61%
12	Virginia	172,410	2.30%
13	Arizona	169,702	2.26%
14	Maryland	159,899	2.13%
15	Louisiana	154,243	2.06%
16	Indiana	144,734	1.93%
17	Missouri	139,900	1.86%
18	Massachusetts	136,511	1.82%
19	Tennessee	130,396	1.74%
20	Wisconsin	129,991	1.73%
21	Minnesota	119,753	1.60%
22	Colorado	117,911	1.57%
23	Alabama	108,150	1.44%
24	Oregon	104,268	1.39%
25	South Carolina	103,273	1.38%
26	Oklahoma	90,434	1.21%
27	Connecticut	84,367	1.12%
28	Kansas	72,527	0.97%
29	Utah	69,815	0.93%
30	Iowa	66,797	0.89%
31	Kentucky	62,551	0.83%
32	Arkansas	61,529	0.82%
33	Mississippi	56,265	0.75%
34	New Mexico	54,589	0.73%
35	Nebraska	43,083	0.57%
36	Nevada	42,722	0.57%
37	Hawaii	42,038	0.56%
38	Idaho	25,461	0.34%
39	Rhode Island	24,083	0.32%
40	Maine	23,797	0.32%
41	West Virginia	23,202	0.31%
42	Montana	22,816	0.30%
43	New Hampshire	22,656	0.30%
44	Delaware	19,503	0.26%
45	Alaska	17,555	0.23%
46	Vermont	13,523	0.18%
47	South Dakota	13,056	0.17%
48	Wyoming	12,865	0.17%
49	North Dakota	12,663	0.17%
NA	Illinois**	NA	NA
	District of Columbia	31,495	0.42%

Source: Morgan Quitno Corporation using data from U.S. Department of Justice, Federal Bureau of Investigation
"Crime in the United States 1993" (Uniform Crime Reports, December 4, 1994)
*Estimated totals for urban areas, defined by the F.B.I. as Metropolitan Statistical Areas and other cities outside such areas. National total includes those states listed as not available. Larceny and theft is the unlawful taking of property without use of force, violence or fraud. Attempts are included. Motor vehicle thefts are excluded.
**Not available.

Urban Larceny and Theft Rate in 1993

National Urban Rate = 3,316.7 Larcenies and Thefts per 100,000 Population*

ALPHA ORDER

RANK	STATE	RATE
33	Alabama	3,181.8
7	Alaska	4,282.3
2	Arizona	4,669.9
14	Arkansas	3,822.9
38	California	3,060.7
18	Colorado	3,675.0
40	Connecticut	2,733.8
32	Delaware	3,188.7
4	Florida	4,559.2
11	Georgia	4,126.5
3	Hawaii	4,595.4
21	Idaho	3,557.8
NA	Illinois**	NA
35	Indiana	3,104.7
24	Iowa	3,479.4
23	Kansas	3,495.6
43	Kentucky	2,596.8
5	Louisiana	4,359.7
42	Maine	2,664.8
27	Maryland	3,402.8
47	Massachusetts	2,275.3
29	Michigan	3,270.7
28	Minnesota	3,280.3
16	Mississippi	3,765.5
26	Missouri	3,447.5
1	Montana	5,593.8
20	Nebraska	3,609.8
22	Nevada	3,504.2
46	New Hampshire	2,301.3
44	New Jersey	2,486.1
10	New Mexico	4,126.6
41	New York	2,714.0
15	North Carolina	3,822.6
36	North Dakota	3,097.9
39	Ohio	2,921.3
25	Oklahoma	3,471.1
12	Oregon	4,099.4
49	Pennsylvania	1,943.7
45	Rhode Island	2,408.3
19	South Carolina	3,614.2
37	South Dakota	3,075.1
30	Tennessee	3,268.0
13	Texas	3,952.8
8	Utah	4,209.2
6	Vermont	4,324.2
34	Virginia	3,167.6
9	Washington	4,145.3
48	West Virginia	2,233.7
31	Wisconsin	3,207.7
17	Wyoming	3,720.0

RANK ORDER

RANK	STATE	RATE
1	Montana	5,593.8
2	Arizona	4,669.9
3	Hawaii	4,595.4
4	Florida	4,559.2
5	Louisiana	4,359.7
6	Vermont	4,324.2
7	Alaska	4,282.3
8	Utah	4,209.2
9	Washington	4,145.3
10	New Mexico	4,126.6
11	Georgia	4,126.5
12	Oregon	4,099.4
13	Texas	3,952.8
14	Arkansas	3,822.9
15	North Carolina	3,822.6
16	Mississippi	3,765.5
17	Wyoming	3,720.0
18	Colorado	3,675.0
19	South Carolina	3,614.2
20	Nebraska	3,609.8
21	Idaho	3,557.8
22	Nevada	3,504.2
23	Kansas	3,495.6
24	Iowa	3,479.4
25	Oklahoma	3,471.1
26	Missouri	3,447.5
27	Maryland	3,402.8
28	Minnesota	3,280.3
29	Michigan	3,270.7
30	Tennessee	3,268.0
31	Wisconsin	3,207.7
32	Delaware	3,188.7
33	Alabama	3,181.8
34	Virginia	3,167.6
35	Indiana	3,104.7
36	North Dakota	3,097.9
37	South Dakota	3,075.1
38	California	3,060.7
39	Ohio	2,921.3
40	Connecticut	2,733.8
41	New York	2,714.0
42	Maine	2,664.8
43	Kentucky	2,596.8
44	New Jersey	2,486.1
45	Rhode Island	2,408.3
46	New Hampshire	2,301.3
47	Massachusetts	2,275.3
48	West Virginia	2,233.7
49	Pennsylvania	1,943.7
NA	Illinois**	NA

District of Columbia — 5,449.0

Source: Morgan Quitno Corporation using data from U.S. Department of Justice, Federal Bureau of Investigation
"Crime in the United States 1993" (Uniform Crime Reports, December 4, 1994)

*Estimated rates for urban areas, defined by the F.B.I. as Metropolitan Statistical Areas and other cities outside such areas. National rate includes those states listed as not available. Larceny and theft is the unlawful taking of property without use of force, violence or fraud. Attempts are included. Motor vehicle thefts are excluded.

**Not available.

Percent of Larcenies and Thefts Occurring in Urban Areas in 1993

National Percent = 95.92% of Larcenies and Thefts*

ALPHA ORDER				RANK ORDER		
RANK	STATE	PERCENT		RANK	STATE	PERCENT
13	Alabama	96.67		1	New Jersey	100.00
45	Alaska	82.80		2	Massachusetts	99.97
5	Arizona	98.27		3	Rhode Island	99.93
36	Arkansas	90.79		4	California	99.05
4	California	99.05		5	Arizona	98.27
24	Colorado	94.49		6	Connecticut	98.24
6	Connecticut	98.24		7	New Hampshire	97.85
28	Delaware	93.53		8	Maryland	97.81
11	Florida	97.69		9	New York	97.80
30	Georgia	92.92		10	Texas	97.73
48	Hawaii	80.98		11	Florida	97.69
44	Idaho	85.45		12	Pennsylvania	96.74
NA	Illinois**	NA		13	Alabama	96.67
27	Indiana	93.97		14	Ohio	96.52
35	Iowa	91.32		15	New Mexico	96.24
22	Kansas	94.76		16	Missouri	96.22
39	Kentucky	89.69		17	Utah	96.16
25	Louisiana	94.43		18	Washington	96.14
41	Maine	88.32		19	Virginia	95.20
8	Maryland	97.81		20	Michigan	95.16
2	Massachusetts	99.97		21	Oklahoma	95.08
20	Michigan	95.16		22	Kansas	94.76
32	Minnesota	92.31		23	Tennessee	94.71
37	Mississippi	90.07		24	Colorado	94.49
16	Missouri	96.22		25	Louisiana	94.43
49	Montana	74.46		26	Oregon	94.04
34	Nebraska	92.04		27	Indiana	93.97
31	Nevada	92.60		28	Delaware	93.53
7	New Hampshire	97.85		29	Wisconsin	93.42
1	New Jersey	100.00		30	Georgia	92.92
15	New Mexico	96.24		31	Nevada	92.60
9	New York	97.80		32	Minnesota	92.31
33	North Carolina	92.14		33	North Carolina	92.14
38	North Dakota	89.98		34	Nebraska	92.04
14	Ohio	96.52		35	Iowa	91.32
21	Oklahoma	95.08		36	Arkansas	90.79
26	Oregon	94.04		37	Mississippi	90.07
12	Pennsylvania	96.74		38	North Dakota	89.98
3	Rhode Island	99.93		39	Kentucky	89.69
42	South Carolina	87.85		40	Wyoming	88.91
43	South Dakota	87.54		41	Maine	88.32
23	Tennessee	94.71		42	South Carolina	87.85
10	Texas	97.73		43	South Dakota	87.54
17	Utah	96.16		44	Idaho	85.45
46	Vermont	82.34		45	Alaska	82.80
19	Virginia	95.20		46	Vermont	82.34
18	Washington	96.14		47	West Virginia	81.54
47	West Virginia	81.54		48	Hawaii	80.98
29	Wisconsin	93.42		49	Montana	74.46
40	Wyoming	88.91		NA	Illinois**	NA
					District of Columbia	100.00

Source: Morgan Quitno Corporation using data from U.S. Department of Justice, Federal Bureau of Investigation
  "Crime in the United States 1993" (Uniform Crime Reports, December 4, 1994)
*Estimated percentages for urban areas, defined by the F.B.I. as Metropolitan Statistical Areas and other cities outside such areas. National percent includes those states listed as not available. Larceny and theft is the unlawful taking of property without use of force, violence or fraud. Attempts are included. Motor vehicle thefts are excluded.
**Not available.

Larceny and Theft in Rural Areas in 1993

National Total = 318,993 Larcenies and Thefts*

<table>
<tr><td colspan="4"><u>ALPHA ORDER</u></td><td colspan="4"><u>RANK ORDER</u></td></tr>
<tr><td>RANK</td><td>STATE</td><td>THEFTS</td><td>% of USA</td><td>RANK</td><td>STATE</td><td>THEFTS</td><td>% of USA</td></tr>
<tr><td>31</td><td>Alabama</td><td>3,728</td><td>1.17%</td><td>1</td><td>Georgia</td><td>17,473</td><td>5.48%</td></tr>
<tr><td>33</td><td>Alaska</td><td>3,646</td><td>1.14%</td><td>2</td><td>North Carolina</td><td>17,293</td><td>5.42%</td></tr>
<tr><td>37</td><td>Arizona</td><td>2,987</td><td>0.94%</td><td>3</td><td>Texas</td><td>15,067</td><td>4.72%</td></tr>
<tr><td>24</td><td>Arkansas</td><td>6,238</td><td>1.96%</td><td>4</td><td>South Carolina</td><td>14,280</td><td>4.48%</td></tr>
<tr><td>14</td><td>California</td><td>9,017</td><td>2.83%</td><td>5</td><td>Michigan</td><td>14,062</td><td>4.41%</td></tr>
<tr><td>21</td><td>Colorado</td><td>6,876</td><td>2.16%</td><td>6</td><td>Florida</td><td>13,944</td><td>4.37%</td></tr>
<tr><td>43</td><td>Connecticut</td><td>1,509</td><td>0.47%</td><td>7</td><td>New York</td><td>10,570</td><td>3.31%</td></tr>
<tr><td>45</td><td>Delaware</td><td>1,350</td><td>0.42%</td><td>8</td><td>Ohio</td><td>10,290</td><td>3.23%</td></tr>
<tr><td>6</td><td>Florida</td><td>13,944</td><td>4.37%</td><td>9</td><td>Minnesota</td><td>9,974</td><td>3.13%</td></tr>
<tr><td>1</td><td>Georgia</td><td>17,473</td><td>5.48%</td><td>10</td><td>Hawaii</td><td>9,874</td><td>3.10%</td></tr>
<tr><td>10</td><td>Hawaii</td><td>9,874</td><td>3.10%</td><td>11</td><td>Indiana</td><td>9,282</td><td>2.91%</td></tr>
<tr><td>29</td><td>Idaho</td><td>4,334</td><td>1.36%</td><td>12</td><td>Wisconsin</td><td>9,157</td><td>2.87%</td></tr>
<tr><td>NA</td><td>Illinois**</td><td>NA</td><td>NA</td><td>13</td><td>Louisiana</td><td>9,091</td><td>2.85%</td></tr>
<tr><td>11</td><td>Indiana</td><td>9,282</td><td>2.91%</td><td>14</td><td>California</td><td>9,017</td><td>2.83%</td></tr>
<tr><td>23</td><td>Iowa</td><td>6,351</td><td>1.99%</td><td>15</td><td>Virginia</td><td>8,694</td><td>2.73%</td></tr>
<tr><td>30</td><td>Kansas</td><td>4,011</td><td>1.26%</td><td>16</td><td>Washington</td><td>7,943</td><td>2.49%</td></tr>
<tr><td>19</td><td>Kentucky</td><td>7,194</td><td>2.26%</td><td>17</td><td>Montana</td><td>7,825</td><td>2.45%</td></tr>
<tr><td>13</td><td>Louisiana</td><td>9,091</td><td>2.85%</td><td>18</td><td>Tennessee</td><td>7,287</td><td>2.28%</td></tr>
<tr><td>36</td><td>Maine</td><td>3,148</td><td>0.99%</td><td>19</td><td>Kentucky</td><td>7,194</td><td>2.26%</td></tr>
<tr><td>34</td><td>Maryland</td><td>3,572</td><td>1.12%</td><td>20</td><td>Pennsylvania</td><td>7,187</td><td>2.25%</td></tr>
<tr><td>47</td><td>Massachusetts</td><td>37</td><td>0.01%</td><td>21</td><td>Colorado</td><td>6,876</td><td>2.16%</td></tr>
<tr><td>5</td><td>Michigan</td><td>14,062</td><td>4.41%</td><td>22</td><td>Oregon</td><td>6,610</td><td>2.07%</td></tr>
<tr><td>9</td><td>Minnesota</td><td>9,974</td><td>3.13%</td><td>23</td><td>Iowa</td><td>6,351</td><td>1.99%</td></tr>
<tr><td>25</td><td>Mississippi</td><td>6,202</td><td>1.94%</td><td>24</td><td>Arkansas</td><td>6,238</td><td>1.96%</td></tr>
<tr><td>26</td><td>Missouri</td><td>5,492</td><td>1.72%</td><td>25</td><td>Mississippi</td><td>6,202</td><td>1.94%</td></tr>
<tr><td>17</td><td>Montana</td><td>7,825</td><td>2.45%</td><td>26</td><td>Missouri</td><td>5,492</td><td>1.72%</td></tr>
<tr><td>31</td><td>Nebraska</td><td>3,728</td><td>1.17%</td><td>27</td><td>West Virginia</td><td>5,254</td><td>1.65%</td></tr>
<tr><td>35</td><td>Nevada</td><td>3,415</td><td>1.07%</td><td>28</td><td>Oklahoma</td><td>4,677</td><td>1.47%</td></tr>
<tr><td>46</td><td>New Hampshire</td><td>497</td><td>0.16%</td><td>29</td><td>Idaho</td><td>4,334</td><td>1.36%</td></tr>
<tr><td>49</td><td>New Jersey</td><td>0</td><td>0.00%</td><td>30</td><td>Kansas</td><td>4,011</td><td>1.26%</td></tr>
<tr><td>40</td><td>New Mexico</td><td>2,134</td><td>0.67%</td><td>31</td><td>Alabama</td><td>3,728</td><td>1.17%</td></tr>
<tr><td>7</td><td>New York</td><td>10,570</td><td>3.31%</td><td>31</td><td>Nebraska</td><td>3,728</td><td>1.17%</td></tr>
<tr><td>2</td><td>North Carolina</td><td>17,293</td><td>5.42%</td><td>33</td><td>Alaska</td><td>3,646</td><td>1.14%</td></tr>
<tr><td>44</td><td>North Dakota</td><td>1,410</td><td>0.44%</td><td>34</td><td>Maryland</td><td>3,572</td><td>1.12%</td></tr>
<tr><td>8</td><td>Ohio</td><td>10,290</td><td>3.23%</td><td>35</td><td>Nevada</td><td>3,415</td><td>1.07%</td></tr>
<tr><td>28</td><td>Oklahoma</td><td>4,677</td><td>1.47%</td><td>36</td><td>Maine</td><td>3,148</td><td>0.99%</td></tr>
<tr><td>22</td><td>Oregon</td><td>6,610</td><td>2.07%</td><td>37</td><td>Arizona</td><td>2,987</td><td>0.94%</td></tr>
<tr><td>20</td><td>Pennsylvania</td><td>7,187</td><td>2.25%</td><td>38</td><td>Vermont</td><td>2,900</td><td>0.91%</td></tr>
<tr><td>48</td><td>Rhode Island</td><td>18</td><td>0.01%</td><td>39</td><td>Utah</td><td>2,788</td><td>0.87%</td></tr>
<tr><td>4</td><td>South Carolina</td><td>14,280</td><td>4.48%</td><td>40</td><td>New Mexico</td><td>2,134</td><td>0.67%</td></tr>
<tr><td>41</td><td>South Dakota</td><td>1,859</td><td>0.58%</td><td>41</td><td>South Dakota</td><td>1,859</td><td>0.58%</td></tr>
<tr><td>18</td><td>Tennessee</td><td>7,287</td><td>2.28%</td><td>42</td><td>Wyoming</td><td>1,605</td><td>0.50%</td></tr>
<tr><td>3</td><td>Texas</td><td>15,067</td><td>4.72%</td><td>43</td><td>Connecticut</td><td>1,509</td><td>0.47%</td></tr>
<tr><td>39</td><td>Utah</td><td>2,788</td><td>0.87%</td><td>44</td><td>North Dakota</td><td>1,410</td><td>0.44%</td></tr>
<tr><td>38</td><td>Vermont</td><td>2,900</td><td>0.91%</td><td>45</td><td>Delaware</td><td>1,350</td><td>0.42%</td></tr>
<tr><td>15</td><td>Virginia</td><td>8,694</td><td>2.73%</td><td>46</td><td>New Hampshire</td><td>497</td><td>0.16%</td></tr>
<tr><td>16</td><td>Washington</td><td>7,943</td><td>2.49%</td><td>47</td><td>Massachusetts</td><td>37</td><td>0.01%</td></tr>
<tr><td>27</td><td>West Virginia</td><td>5,254</td><td>1.65%</td><td>48</td><td>Rhode Island</td><td>18</td><td>0.01%</td></tr>
<tr><td>12</td><td>Wisconsin</td><td>9,157</td><td>2.87%</td><td>49</td><td>New Jersey</td><td>0</td><td>0.00%</td></tr>
<tr><td>42</td><td>Wyoming</td><td>1,605</td><td>0.50%</td><td>NA</td><td>Illinois**</td><td>NA</td><td>NA</td></tr>
<tr><td></td><td></td><td></td><td></td><td></td><td>District of Columbia</td><td>0</td><td>0.00%</td></tr>
</table>

Source: Morgan Quitno Corporation using data from U.S. Department of Justice, Federal Bureau of Investigation "Crime in the United States 1993" (Uniform Crime Reports, December 4, 1994)

Estimated totals for rural areas, defined by the F.B.I. as other than Metropolitan Statistical Areas and other cities outside such areas. National total includes those states listed as not available. Larceny and theft is the unlawful taking of property without use of force, violence or fraud. Attempts are included. Motor vehicle thefts are excluded.

**Not available.*

Rural Larceny and Theft Rate in 1993

National Rural Rate = 1,005.7 Larcenies and Thefts per 100,000 Population*

ALPHA ORDER

RANK	STATE	RATE
44	Alabama	473.1
3	Alaska	1,928.5
23	Arizona	988.9
33	Arkansas	765.9
10	California	1,461.7
4	Colorado	1,923.2
31	Connecticut	790.3
9	Delaware	1,527.6
5	Florida	1,880.2
16	Georgia	1,286.3
1	Hawaii	3,838.7
20	Idaho	1,130.5
NA	Illinois**	NA
28	Indiana	883.0
36	Iowa	710.2
29	Kansas	879.3
43	Kentucky	521.2
18	Louisiana	1,200.8
26	Maine	909.8
14	Maryland	1,342.7
47	Massachusetts	301.8
12	Michigan	1,363.9
19	Minnesota	1,151.2
42	Mississippi	539.9
45	Missouri	467.0
7	Montana	1,815.1
27	Nebraska	901.6
2	Nevada	2,010.7
46	New Hampshire	353.7
48	New Jersey	0.0
35	New Mexico	728.0
17	New York	1,233.1
22	North Carolina	1,054.3
41	North Dakota	623.2
32	Ohio	782.7
34	Oklahoma	747.5
13	Oregon	1,353.1
37	Pennsylvania	675.5
48	Rhode Island	0.0
6	South Carolina	1,817.7
40	South Dakota	640.1
39	Tennessee	657.1
24	Texas	946.2
11	Utah	1,384.5
21	Vermont	1,101.5
30	Virginia	829.5
8	Washington	1,640.0
38	West Virginia	672.5
25	Wisconsin	929.2
15	Wyoming	1,292.6

RANK ORDER

RANK	STATE	RATE
1	Hawaii	3,838.7
2	Nevada	2,010.7
3	Alaska	1,928.5
4	Colorado	1,923.2
5	Florida	1,880.2
6	South Carolina	1,817.7
7	Montana	1,815.1
8	Washington	1,640.0
9	Delaware	1,527.6
10	California	1,461.7
11	Utah	1,384.5
12	Michigan	1,363.9
13	Oregon	1,353.1
14	Maryland	1,342.7
15	Wyoming	1,292.6
16	Georgia	1,286.3
17	New York	1,233.1
18	Louisiana	1,200.8
19	Minnesota	1,151.2
20	Idaho	1,130.5
21	Vermont	1,101.5
22	North Carolina	1,054.3
23	Arizona	988.9
24	Texas	946.2
25	Wisconsin	929.2
26	Maine	909.8
27	Nebraska	901.6
28	Indiana	883.0
29	Kansas	879.3
30	Virginia	829.5
31	Connecticut	790.3
32	Ohio	782.7
33	Arkansas	765.9
34	Oklahoma	747.5
35	New Mexico	728.0
36	Iowa	710.2
37	Pennsylvania	675.5
38	West Virginia	672.5
39	Tennessee	657.1
40	South Dakota	640.1
41	North Dakota	623.2
42	Mississippi	539.9
43	Kentucky	521.2
44	Alabama	473.1
45	Missouri	467.0
46	New Hampshire	353.7
47	Massachusetts	301.8
48	New Jersey	0.0
48	Rhode Island	0.0
NA	Illinois**	NA

District of Columbia   0.0

Source: Morgan Quitno Corporation using data from U.S. Department of Justice, Federal Bureau of Investigation
"Crime in the United States 1993" (Uniform Crime Reports, December 4, 1994)
*Estimated rates for rural areas, defined by the F.B.I. as other than Metropolitan Statistical Areas and other cities outside such areas. National rate includes those states listed as not available. Motor vehicle theft includes the theft or attempted theft of a self-propelled vehicle. Excludes motorboats, construction equipment, airplanes and farming equipment.
**Not available.

Percent of Larcenies and Thefts Occurring in Rural Areas in 1993

National Percent = 4.08% of Larcenies and Thefts*

ALPHA ORDER				RANK ORDER		
RANK	STATE	PERCENT		RANK	STATE	PERCENT
37	Alabama	3.33		1	Montana	25.54
5	Alaska	17.20		2	Hawaii	19.02
45	Arizona	1.73		3	West Virginia	18.46
14	Arkansas	9.21		4	Vermont	17.66
46	California	0.95		5	Alaska	17.20
26	Colorado	5.51		6	Idaho	14.55
44	Connecticut	1.76		7	South Dakota	12.46
22	Delaware	6.47		8	South Carolina	12.15
39	Florida	2.31		9	Maine	11.68
20	Georgia	7.08		10	Wyoming	11.09
2	Hawaii	19.02		11	Kentucky	10.31
6	Idaho	14.55		12	North Dakota	10.02
NA	Illinois**	NA		13	Mississippi	9.93
23	Indiana	6.03		14	Arkansas	9.21
15	Iowa	8.68		15	Iowa	8.68
28	Kansas	5.24		16	Nebraska	7.96
11	Kentucky	10.31		17	North Carolina	7.86
25	Louisiana	5.57		18	Minnesota	7.69
9	Maine	11.68		19	Nevada	7.40
42	Maryland	2.19		20	Georgia	7.08
48	Massachusetts	0.03		21	Wisconsin	6.58
30	Michigan	4.84		22	Delaware	6.47
18	Minnesota	7.69		23	Indiana	6.03
13	Mississippi	9.93		24	Oregon	5.96
34	Missouri	3.78		25	Louisiana	5.57
1	Montana	25.54		26	Colorado	5.51
16	Nebraska	7.96		27	Tennessee	5.29
19	Nevada	7.40		28	Kansas	5.24
43	New Hampshire	2.15		29	Oklahoma	4.92
49	New Jersey	0.00		30	Michigan	4.84
35	New Mexico	3.76		31	Virginia	4.80
41	New York	2.20		32	Washington	3.86
17	North Carolina	7.86		33	Utah	3.84
12	North Dakota	10.02		34	Missouri	3.78
36	Ohio	3.48		35	New Mexico	3.76
29	Oklahoma	4.92		36	Ohio	3.48
24	Oregon	5.96		37	Alabama	3.33
38	Pennsylvania	3.26		38	Pennsylvania	3.26
47	Rhode Island	0.07		39	Florida	2.31
8	South Carolina	12.15		40	Texas	2.27
7	South Dakota	12.46		41	New York	2.20
27	Tennessee	5.29		42	Maryland	2.19
40	Texas	2.27		43	New Hampshire	2.15
33	Utah	3.84		44	Connecticut	1.76
4	Vermont	17.66		45	Arizona	1.73
31	Virginia	4.80		46	California	0.95
32	Washington	3.86		47	Rhode Island	0.07
3	West Virginia	18.46		48	Massachusetts	0.03
21	Wisconsin	6.58		49	New Jersey	0.00
10	Wyoming	11.09		NA	Illinois**	NA
					District of Columbia	0.00

Source: Morgan Quitno Corporation using data from U.S. Department of Justice, Federal Bureau of Investigation
  "Crime in the United States 1993" (Uniform Crime Reports, December 4, 1994)
*Estimated percentages for rural areas, defined by the F.B.I. as other than Metropolitan Statistical Areas and other cities
outside such areas. National percent includes those states listed as not available. Larceny and theft is the unlawful taking
of property without use of force, violence or fraud. Attempts are included. Motor vehicle thefts are excluded.
**Not available.

Motor Vehicle Theft in Urban Areas in 1993

National Total = 1,526,196 Motor Vehicle Thefts*

ALPHA ORDER

RANK	STATE	THEFTS	% of USA
26	Alabama	13,593	0.89%
39	Alaska	2,186	0.14%
12	Arizona	33,614	2.20%
31	Arkansas	6,995	0.46%
1	California	318,100	20.84%
23	Colorado	15,645	1.03%
18	Connecticut	19,257	1.26%
41	Delaware	2,143	0.14%
4	Florida	120,900	7.92%
10	Georgia	38,795	2.54%
36	Hawaii	4,554	0.30%
43	Idaho	1,524	0.10%
NA	Illinois**	NA	NA
16	Indiana	23,365	1.53%
35	Iowa	4,857	0.32%
30	Kansas	7,853	0.51%
32	Kentucky	6,881	0.45%
15	Louisiana	25,922	1.70%
44	Maine	1,359	0.09%
11	Maryland	33,643	2.20%
8	Massachusetts	49,047	3.21%
5	Michigan	57,186	3.75%
25	Minnesota	14,219	0.93%
29	Mississippi	8,108	0.53%
14	Missouri	28,032	1.84%
45	Montana	1,357	0.09%
38	Nebraska	3,019	0.20%
28	Nevada	10,024	0.66%
40	New Hampshire	2,147	0.14%
6	New Jersey	56,253	3.69%
34	New Mexico	6,243	0.41%
2	New York	151,359	9.92%
19	North Carolina	17,736	1.16%
46	North Dakota	802	0.05%
9	Ohio	47,391	3.11%
24	Oklahoma	14,857	0.97%
22	Oregon	16,724	1.10%
7	Pennsylvania	51,824	3.40%
33	Rhode Island	6,463	0.42%
27	South Carolina	10,899	0.71%
47	South Dakota	667	0.04%
13	Tennessee	28,594	1.87%
3	Texas	123,331	8.08%
37	Utah	4,322	0.28%
49	Vermont	534	0.03%
20	Virginia	17,652	1.16%
17	Washington	23,270	1.52%
42	West Virginia	2,016	0.13%
21	Wisconsin	17,473	1.14%
48	Wyoming	623	0.04%

RANK ORDER

RANK	STATE	THEFTS	% of USA
1	California	318,100	20.84%
2	New York	151,359	9.92%
3	Texas	123,331	8.08%
4	Florida	120,900	7.92%
5	Michigan	57,186	3.75%
6	New Jersey	56,253	3.69%
7	Pennsylvania	51,824	3.40%
8	Massachusetts	49,047	3.21%
9	Ohio	47,391	3.11%
10	Georgia	38,795	2.54%
11	Maryland	33,643	2.20%
12	Arizona	33,614	2.20%
13	Tennessee	28,594	1.87%
14	Missouri	28,032	1.84%
15	Louisiana	25,922	1.70%
16	Indiana	23,365	1.53%
17	Washington	23,270	1.52%
18	Connecticut	19,257	1.26%
19	North Carolina	17,736	1.16%
20	Virginia	17,652	1.16%
21	Wisconsin	17,473	1.14%
22	Oregon	16,724	1.10%
23	Colorado	15,645	1.03%
24	Oklahoma	14,857	0.97%
25	Minnesota	14,219	0.93%
26	Alabama	13,593	0.89%
27	South Carolina	10,899	0.71%
28	Nevada	10,024	0.66%
29	Mississippi	8,108	0.53%
30	Kansas	7,853	0.51%
31	Arkansas	6,995	0.46%
32	Kentucky	6,881	0.45%
33	Rhode Island	6,463	0.42%
34	New Mexico	6,243	0.41%
35	Iowa	4,857	0.32%
36	Hawaii	4,554	0.30%
37	Utah	4,322	0.28%
38	Nebraska	3,019	0.20%
39	Alaska	2,186	0.14%
40	New Hampshire	2,147	0.14%
41	Delaware	2,143	0.14%
42	West Virginia	2,016	0.13%
43	Idaho	1,524	0.10%
44	Maine	1,359	0.09%
45	Montana	1,357	0.09%
46	North Dakota	802	0.05%
47	South Dakota	667	0.04%
48	Wyoming	623	0.04%
49	Vermont	534	0.03%
NA	Illinois**	NA	NA

District of Columbia	8,062	0.53%

Source: Morgan Quitno Corporation using data from U.S. Department of Justice, Federal Bureau of Investigation
    "Crime in the United States 1993" (Uniform Crime Reports, December 4, 1994)
*Estimated totals for urban areas, defined by the F.B.I. as Metropolitan Statistical Areas and other cities outside such
areas. National total includes those states listed as not available. Motor vehicle theft includes the theft or attempted theft
of a self-propelled vehicle. Excludes motorboats, construction equipment, airplanes and farming equipment.
**Not available.

Urban Motor Vehicle Theft Rate in 1993

National Urban Rate = 674.8 Motor Vehicle Thefts per 100,000 Population*

ALPHA ORDER				RANK ORDER		
RANK	STATE	RATE		RANK	STATE	RATE
30	Alabama	399.9		1	California	1,039.7
20	Alaska	533.2		2	Florida	934.5
3	Arizona	925.0		3	Arizona	925.0
28	Arkansas	434.6		4	New York	872.9
1	California	1,039.7		5	Nevada	822.2
24	Colorado	487.6		6	Massachusetts	817.5
17	Connecticut	624.0		7	Texas	750.3
34	Delaware	350.4		8	Louisiana	732.7
2	Florida	934.5		9	Tennessee	716.6
12	Georgia	697.9		10	Maryland	716.0
22	Hawaii	497.8		11	New Jersey	714.0
43	Idaho	213.0		12	Georgia	697.9
NA	Illinois**	NA		13	Missouri	690.8
21	Indiana	501.2		14	Michigan	677.0
40	Iowa	253.0		15	Oregon	657.5
33	Kansas	378.5		16	Rhode Island	646.3
38	Kentucky	285.7		17	Connecticut	624.0
8	Louisiana	732.7		18	Oklahoma	570.3
49	Maine	152.2		19	Mississippi	542.6
10	Maryland	716.0		20	Alaska	533.2
6	Massachusetts	817.5		21	Indiana	501.2
14	Michigan	677.0		22	Hawaii	497.8
31	Minnesota	389.5		23	Washington	487.8
19	Mississippi	542.6		24	Colorado	487.6
13	Missouri	690.8		25	Ohio	484.8
36	Montana	332.7		26	New Mexico	471.9
40	Nebraska	253.0		27	Pennsylvania	471.8
5	Nevada	822.2		28	Arkansas	434.6
42	New Hampshire	218.1		29	Wisconsin	431.2
11	New Jersey	714.0		30	Alabama	399.9
26	New Mexico	471.9		31	Minnesota	389.5
4	New York	872.9		32	South Carolina	381.4
35	North Carolina	334.3		33	Kansas	378.5
44	North Dakota	196.2		34	Delaware	350.4
25	Ohio	484.8		35	North Carolina	334.3
18	Oklahoma	570.3		36	Montana	332.7
15	Oregon	657.5		37	Virginia	324.3
27	Pennsylvania	471.8		38	Kentucky	285.7
16	Rhode Island	646.3		39	Utah	260.6
32	South Carolina	381.4		40	Iowa	253.0
48	South Dakota	157.1		40	Nebraska	253.0
9	Tennessee	716.6		42	New Hampshire	218.1
7	Texas	750.3		43	Idaho	213.0
39	Utah	260.6		44	North Dakota	196.2
47	Vermont	170.8		45	West Virginia	194.1
37	Virginia	324.3		46	Wyoming	180.1
23	Washington	487.8		47	Vermont	170.8
45	West Virginia	194.1		48	South Dakota	157.1
29	Wisconsin	431.2		49	Maine	152.2
46	Wyoming	180.1		NA	Illinois**	NA

District of Columbia   1,394.8

Source: Morgan Quitno Corporation using data from U.S. Department of Justice, Federal Bureau of Investigation
"Crime in the United States 1993" (Uniform Crime Reports, December 4, 1994)
*Estimated rates for urban areas, defined by the F.B.I. as Metropolitan Statistical Areas and other cities outside such areas. National rate includes those states listed as not available. Motor vehicle theft includes the theft or attempted theft of a self-propelled vehicle. Excludes motorboats, construction equipment, airplanes and farming equipment.
**Not available.

Percent of Motor Vehicle Thefts Occurring in Urban Areas in 1993

National Percent = 97.77% of Motor Vehicle Thefts*

ALPHA ORDER

RANK	STATE	PERCENT
22	Alabama	96.12
45	Alaska	80.93
7	Arizona	98.87
36	Arkansas	89.47
4	California	99.63
18	Colorado	97.43
9	Connecticut	98.68
19	Delaware	97.10
9	Florida	98.68
31	Georgia	94.45
39	Hawaii	86.20
46	Idaho	75.60
NA	Illinois**	NA
25	Indiana	95.54
35	Iowa	90.45
21	Kansas	96.16
42	Kentucky	83.99
12	Louisiana	98.34
43	Maine	81.62
6	Maryland	99.15
3	Massachusetts	99.97
14	Michigan	98.10
33	Minnesota	91.90
34	Mississippi	91.55
15	Missouri	97.79
49	Montana	65.68
32	Nebraska	93.21
16	Nevada	97.75
11	New Hampshire	98.35
1	New Jersey	100.00
26	New Mexico	95.36
5	New York	99.61
37	North Carolina	88.52
41	North Dakota	84.96
13	Ohio	98.17
24	Oklahoma	95.65
29	Oregon	94.98
17	Pennsylvania	97.72
1	Rhode Island	100.00
38	South Carolina	86.98
44	South Dakota	81.44
30	Tennessee	94.89
8	Texas	98.79
23	Utah	95.94
47	Vermont	69.90
27	Virginia	95.25
20	Washington	97.08
48	West Virginia	68.57
28	Wisconsin	95.09
40	Wyoming	85.58

RANK ORDER

RANK	STATE	PERCENT
1	New Jersey	100.00
1	Rhode Island	100.00
3	Massachusetts	99.97
4	California	99.63
5	New York	99.61
6	Maryland	99.15
7	Arizona	98.87
8	Texas	98.79
9	Connecticut	98.68
9	Florida	98.68
11	New Hampshire	98.35
12	Louisiana	98.34
13	Ohio	98.17
14	Michigan	98.10
15	Missouri	97.79
16	Nevada	97.75
17	Pennsylvania	97.72
18	Colorado	97.43
19	Delaware	97.10
20	Washington	97.08
21	Kansas	96.16
22	Alabama	96.12
23	Utah	95.94
24	Oklahoma	95.65
25	Indiana	95.54
26	New Mexico	95.36
27	Virginia	95.25
28	Wisconsin	95.09
29	Oregon	94.98
30	Tennessee	94.89
31	Georgia	94.45
32	Nebraska	93.21
33	Minnesota	91.90
34	Mississippi	91.55
35	Iowa	90.45
36	Arkansas	89.47
37	North Carolina	88.52
38	South Carolina	86.98
39	Hawaii	86.20
40	Wyoming	85.58
41	North Dakota	84.96
42	Kentucky	83.99
43	Maine	81.62
44	South Dakota	81.44
45	Alaska	80.93
46	Idaho	75.60
47	Vermont	69.90
48	West Virginia	68.57
49	Montana	65.68
NA	Illinois**	NA

District of Columbia   100.00

Source: Morgan Quitno Corporation using data from U.S. Department of Justice, Federal Bureau of Investigation
    "Crime in the United States 1993" (Uniform Crime Reports, December 4, 1994)
*Estimated percentages for urban areas, defined by the F.B.I. as Metropolitan Statistical Areas and other cities outside
such areas. National percent includes those states listed as not available. Motor vehicle theft includes the theft or
attempted theft of a self-propelled vehicle. Excludes motorboats, construction equipment, airplanes and farming
equipment. **Not available.

Motor Vehicle Theft in Rural Areas in 1993

National Total = 34,851 Motor Vehicle Thefts*

ALPHA ORDER					RANK ORDER			
RANK	**STATE**	**THEFTS**	**% of USA**		**RANK**	**STATE**	**THEFTS**	**% of USA**
26	Alabama	549	1.58%		1	North Carolina	2,300	6.60%
27	Alaska	515	1.48%		2	Georgia	2,281	6.55%
32	Arizona	384	1.10%		3	South Carolina	1,632	4.68%
18	Arkansas	823	2.36%		4	Florida	1,616	4.64%
10	California	1,195	3.43%		5	Tennessee	1,541	4.42%
31	Colorado	413	1.19%		6	Texas	1,506	4.32%
37	Connecticut	258	0.74%		7	Kentucky	1,312	3.76%
45	Delaware	64	0.18%		8	Minnesota	1,254	3.60%
4	Florida	1,616	4.64%		9	Pennsylvania	1,209	3.47%
2	Georgia	2,281	6.55%		10	California	1,195	3.43%
20	Hawaii	729	2.09%		11	Michigan	1,105	3.17%
29	Idaho	492	1.41%		12	Indiana	1,091	3.13%
NA	Illinois**	NA	NA		13	West Virginia	924	2.65%
12	Indiana	1,091	3.13%		14	Wisconsin	902	2.59%
28	Iowa	513	1.47%		15	Ohio	885	2.54%
33	Kansas	314	0.90%		16	Oregon	884	2.54%
7	Kentucky	1,312	3.76%		17	Virginia	881	2.53%
30	Louisiana	437	1.25%		18	Arkansas	823	2.36%
34	Maine	306	0.88%		19	Mississippi	748	2.15%
36	Maryland	287	0.82%		20	Hawaii	729	2.09%
47	Massachusetts	16	0.05%		21	Montana	709	2.03%
11	Michigan	1,105	3.17%		22	Washington	699	2.01%
8	Minnesota	1,254	3.60%		23	Oklahoma	675	1.94%
19	Mississippi	748	2.15%		24	Missouri	634	1.82%
24	Missouri	634	1.82%		25	New York	590	1.69%
21	Montana	709	2.03%		26	Alabama	549	1.58%
40	Nebraska	220	0.63%		27	Alaska	515	1.48%
38	Nevada	231	0.66%		28	Iowa	513	1.47%
46	New Hampshire	36	0.10%		29	Idaho	492	1.41%
48	New Jersey	0	0.00%		30	Louisiana	437	1.25%
35	New Mexico	304	0.87%		31	Colorado	413	1.19%
25	New York	590	1.69%		32	Arizona	384	1.10%
1	North Carolina	2,300	6.60%		33	Kansas	314	0.90%
43	North Dakota	142	0.41%		34	Maine	306	0.88%
15	Ohio	885	2.54%		35	New Mexico	304	0.87%
23	Oklahoma	675	1.94%		36	Maryland	287	0.82%
16	Oregon	884	2.54%		37	Connecticut	258	0.74%
9	Pennsylvania	1,209	3.47%		38	Nevada	231	0.66%
48	Rhode Island	0	0.00%		39	Vermont	230	0.66%
3	South Carolina	1,632	4.68%		40	Nebraska	220	0.63%
42	South Dakota	152	0.44%		41	Utah	183	0.53%
5	Tennessee	1,541	4.42%		42	South Dakota	152	0.44%
6	Texas	1,506	4.32%		43	North Dakota	142	0.41%
41	Utah	183	0.53%		44	Wyoming	105	0.30%
39	Vermont	230	0.66%		45	Delaware	64	0.18%
17	Virginia	881	2.53%		46	New Hampshire	36	0.10%
22	Washington	699	2.01%		47	Massachusetts	16	0.05%
13	West Virginia	924	2.65%		48	New Jersey	0	0.00%
14	Wisconsin	902	2.59%		48	Rhode Island	0	0.00%
44	Wyoming	105	0.30%		NA	Illinois**	NA	NA
						District of Columbia	0	0.00%

Source: Morgan Quitno Corporation using data from U.S. Department of Justice, Federal Bureau of Investigation
    "Crime in the United States 1993" (Uniform Crime Reports, December 4, 1994)
*Estimated totals for rural areas, defined by the F.B.I. as other than Metropolitan Statistical Areas and other cities outside
such areas. National total includes those states listed as not available. Motor vehicle theft includes the theft or attempted
theft of a self-propelled vehicle. Excludes motorboats, construction equipment, airplanes and farming equipment.
**Not available.

Rural Motor Vehicle Theft Rate in 1993

National Rural Rate = 109.9 Motor Vehicle Thefts per 100,000 Population*

ALPHA ORDER				RANK ORDER		
RANK	STATE	RATE		RANK	STATE	RATE
36	Alabama	69.7		1	Hawaii	283.4
2	Alaska	272.4		2	Alaska	272.4
17	Arizona	127.1		3	Florida	217.9
26	Arkansas	101.0		4	South Carolina	207.7
5	California	193.7		5	California	193.7
19	Colorado	115.5		6	Oregon	181.0
14	Connecticut	135.1		7	Georgia	167.9
35	Delaware	72.4		8	Montana	164.5
3	Florida	217.9		9	Minnesota	144.7
7	Georgia	167.9		10	Washington	144.3
1	Hawaii	283.4		11	North Carolina	140.2
16	Idaho	128.3		12	Tennessee	139.0
NA	Illinois**	NA		13	Nevada	136.0
24	Indiana	103.8		14	Connecticut	135.1
43	Iowa	57.4		15	Massachusetts	130.5
37	Kansas	68.8		16	Idaho	128.3
27	Kentucky	95.1		17	Arizona	127.1
42	Louisiana	57.7		18	West Virginia	118.3
31	Maine	88.4		19	Colorado	115.5
21	Maryland	107.9		20	Pennsylvania	113.6
15	Massachusetts	130.5		21	Maryland	107.9
23	Michigan	107.2		21	Oklahoma	107.9
9	Minnesota	144.7		23	Michigan	107.2
40	Mississippi	65.1		24	Indiana	103.8
44	Missouri	53.9		25	New Mexico	103.7
8	Montana	164.5		26	Arkansas	101.0
45	Nebraska	53.2		27	Kentucky	95.1
13	Nevada	136.0		28	Texas	94.6
47	New Hampshire	25.6		29	Wisconsin	91.5
48	New Jersey	0.0		30	Utah	90.9
25	New Mexico	103.7		31	Maine	88.4
37	New York	68.8		32	Vermont	87.4
11	North Carolina	140.2		33	Wyoming	84.6
41	North Dakota	62.8		34	Virginia	84.1
39	Ohio	67.3		35	Delaware	72.4
21	Oklahoma	107.9		36	Alabama	69.7
6	Oregon	181.0		37	Kansas	68.8
20	Pennsylvania	113.6		37	New York	68.8
48	Rhode Island	0.0		39	Ohio	67.3
4	South Carolina	207.7		40	Mississippi	65.1
46	South Dakota	52.3		41	North Dakota	62.8
12	Tennessee	139.0		42	Louisiana	57.7
28	Texas	94.6		43	Iowa	57.4
30	Utah	90.9		44	Missouri	53.9
32	Vermont	87.4		45	Nebraska	53.2
34	Virginia	84.1		46	South Dakota	52.3
10	Washington	144.3		47	New Hampshire	25.6
18	West Virginia	118.3		48	New Jersey	0.0
29	Wisconsin	91.5		48	Rhode Island	0.0
33	Wyoming	84.6		NA	Illinois**	NA
					District of Columbia	0.0

Source: Morgan Quitno Corporation using data from U.S. Department of Justice, Federal Bureau of Investigation
"Crime in the United States 1993" (Uniform Crime Reports, December 4, 1994)

*Estimated rates for rural areas, defined by the F.B.I. as other than Metropolitan Statistical Areas and other cities outside such areas. National rate includes those states listed as not available. Motor vehicle theft includes the theft or attempted theft of a self-propelled vehicle. Excludes motorboats, construction equipment, airplanes and farming equipment.

**Not available.

Percent of Motor Vehicle Thefts Occurring in Rural Areas in 1993

National Percent = 2.23% of Motor Vehicle Thefts*

ALPHA ORDER				RANK ORDER		
RANK	STATE	PERCENT		RANK	STATE	PERCENT
28	Alabama	3.88		1	Montana	34.32
5	Alaska	19.07		2	West Virginia	31.43
43	Arizona	1.13		3	Vermont	30.10
14	Arkansas	10.53		4	Idaho	24.40
46	California	0.37		5	Alaska	19.07
32	Colorado	2.57		6	South Dakota	18.56
40	Connecticut	1.32		7	Maine	18.38
31	Delaware	2.90		8	Kentucky	16.01
40	Florida	1.32		9	North Dakota	15.04
19	Georgia	5.55		10	Wyoming	14.42
11	Hawaii	13.80		11	Hawaii	13.80
4	Idaho	24.40		12	South Carolina	13.02
NA	Illinois**	NA		13	North Carolina	11.48
25	Indiana	4.46		14	Arkansas	10.53
15	Iowa	9.55		15	Iowa	9.55
29	Kansas	3.84		16	Mississippi	8.45
8	Kentucky	16.01		17	Minnesota	8.10
38	Louisiana	1.66		18	Nebraska	6.79
7	Maine	18.38		19	Georgia	5.55
44	Maryland	0.85		20	Tennessee	5.11
47	Massachusetts	0.03		21	Oregon	5.02
36	Michigan	1.90		22	Wisconsin	4.91
17	Minnesota	8.10		23	Virginia	4.75
16	Mississippi	8.45		24	New Mexico	4.64
35	Missouri	2.21		25	Indiana	4.46
1	Montana	34.32		26	Oklahoma	4.35
18	Nebraska	6.79		27	Utah	4.06
34	Nevada	2.25		28	Alabama	3.88
39	New Hampshire	1.65		29	Kansas	3.84
48	New Jersey	0.00		30	Washington	2.92
24	New Mexico	4.64		31	Delaware	2.90
45	New York	0.39		32	Colorado	2.57
13	North Carolina	11.48		33	Pennsylvania	2.28
9	North Dakota	15.04		34	Nevada	2.25
37	Ohio	1.83		35	Missouri	2.21
26	Oklahoma	4.35		36	Michigan	1.90
21	Oregon	5.02		37	Ohio	1.83
33	Pennsylvania	2.28		38	Louisiana	1.66
48	Rhode Island	0.00		39	New Hampshire	1.65
12	South Carolina	13.02		40	Connecticut	1.32
6	South Dakota	18.56		40	Florida	1.32
20	Tennessee	5.11		42	Texas	1.21
42	Texas	1.21		43	Arizona	1.13
27	Utah	4.06		44	Maryland	0.85
3	Vermont	30.10		45	New York	0.39
23	Virginia	4.75		46	California	0.37
30	Washington	2.92		47	Massachusetts	0.03
2	West Virginia	31.43		48	New Jersey	0.00
22	Wisconsin	4.91		48	Rhode Island	0.00
10	Wyoming	14.42		NA	Illinois**	NA
					District of Columbia	0.00

Source: Morgan Quitno Corporation using data from U.S. Department of Justice, Federal Bureau of Investigation
"Crime in the United States 1993" (Uniform Crime Reports, December 4, 1994)
*Estimated percentages for rural areas, defined by the F.B.I. as other than Metropolitan Statistical Areas and other cities outside such areas. National percent includes those states listed as not available. Motor vehicle theft includes the theft or attempted theft of a self-propelled vehicle. Excludes motorboats, construction equipment, airplanes and farming equipment. **Not available.

Crimes Reported at Universities and Colleges in 1993

National Total = 123,436 Reported Crimes*

ALPHA ORDER					RANK ORDER			
RANK	STATE	CRIMES	% of USA		RANK	STATE	CRIMES	% of USA
22	Alabama	1,705	1.38%		1	California	18,833	15.26%
42	Alaska	157	0.13%		2	Texas	10,644	8.62%
13	Arizona	3,461	2.80%		3	New York	7,263	5.88%
30	Arkansas	829	0.67%		4	Ohio	6,021	4.88%
1	California	18,833	15.26%		5	North Carolina	5,767	4.67%
14	Colorado	2,516	2.04%		6	Virginia	4,741	3.84%
26	Connecticut	1,186	0.96%		7	Florida	4,499	3.64%
NA	Delaware**	NA	NA		8	Indiana	4,119	3.34%
7	Florida	4,499	3.64%		9	Georgia	4,089	3.31%
9	Georgia	4,089	3.31%		10	Massachusetts	3,929	3.18%
NA	Hawaii**	NA	NA		11	Maryland	3,863	3.13%
NA	Idaho**	NA	NA		12	New Jersey	3,721	3.01%
NA	Illinois**	NA	NA		13	Arizona	3,461	2.80%
8	Indiana	4,119	3.34%		14	Colorado	2,516	2.04%
32	Iowa	699	0.57%		15	Wisconsin	2,343	1.90%
NA	Kansas**	NA	NA		16	South Carolina	2,328	1.89%
19	Kentucky	2,127	1.72%		17	Pennsylvania	2,315	1.88%
18	Louisiana	2,268	1.84%		18	Louisiana	2,268	1.84%
35	Maine	501	0.41%		19	Kentucky	2,127	1.72%
11	Maryland	3,863	3.13%		20	Utah	2,099	1.70%
10	Massachusetts	3,929	3.18%		21	Washington	2,091	1.69%
NA	Michigan**	NA	NA		22	Alabama	1,705	1.38%
NA	Minnesota**	NA	NA		23	Tennessee	1,609	1.30%
28	Mississippi	1,040	0.84%		24	Oklahoma	1,467	1.19%
25	Missouri	1,292	1.05%		25	Missouri	1,292	1.05%
36	Montana	474	0.38%		26	Connecticut	1,186	0.96%
27	Nebraska	1,107	0.90%		27	Nebraska	1,107	0.90%
33	Nevada	696	0.56%		28	Mississippi	1,040	0.84%
37	New Hampshire	333	0.27%		29	Rhode Island	874	0.71%
12	New Jersey	3,721	3.01%		30	Arkansas	829	0.67%
34	New Mexico	692	0.56%		31	West Virginia	700	0.57%
3	New York	7,263	5.88%		32	Iowa	699	0.57%
5	North Carolina	5,767	4.67%		33	Nevada	696	0.56%
40	North Dakota	259	0.21%		34	New Mexico	692	0.56%
4	Ohio	6,021	4.88%		35	Maine	501	0.41%
24	Oklahoma	1,467	1.19%		36	Montana	474	0.38%
NA	Oregon**	NA	NA		37	New Hampshire	333	0.27%
17	Pennsylvania	2,315	1.88%		38	Vermont	326	0.26%
29	Rhode Island	874	0.71%		39	Wyoming	299	0.24%
16	South Carolina	2,328	1.89%		40	North Dakota	259	0.21%
41	South Dakota	222	0.18%		41	South Dakota	222	0.18%
23	Tennessee	1,609	1.30%		42	Alaska	157	0.13%
2	Texas	10,644	8.62%		NA	Delaware**	NA	NA
20	Utah	2,099	1.70%		NA	Hawaii**	NA	NA
38	Vermont	326	0.26%		NA	Idaho**	NA	NA
6	Virginia	4,741	3.84%		NA	Illinois**	NA	NA
21	Washington	2,091	1.69%		NA	Kansas**	NA	NA
31	West Virginia	700	0.57%		NA	Michigan**	NA	NA
15	Wisconsin	2,343	1.90%		NA	Minnesota**	NA	NA
39	Wyoming	299	0.24%		NA	Oregon**	NA	NA
						District of Columbia**	NA	NA

Source: U.S. Department of Justice, Federal Bureau of Investigation
  "Crime in the United States 1993" (Uniform Crime Reports, December 4, 1994)
*Includes murder, rape, robbery, aggravated assault, burglary, larceny-theft and motor vehicle theft. Total is only for states shown separately. Many states had incomplete reports.
**Not available.

Crimes Reported at Universities and Colleges as a Percent of All Crimes in 1993

National Percent = 1.01% of Reported Crimes*

ALPHA ORDER			RANK ORDER		
RANK	STATE	PERCENT	RANK	STATE	PERCENT
29	Alabama	0.83	1	Utah	2.15
41	Alaska	0.47	2	Rhode Island	1.94
17	Arizona	1.18	3	Virginia	1.77
34	Arkansas	0.71	4	Kentucky	1.72
25	California	0.93	5	Nebraska	1.67
13	Colorado	1.28	6	Indiana	1.61
31	Connecticut	0.78	7	Wyoming	1.53
NA	Delaware**	NA	8	West Virginia	1.52
42	Florida	0.39	9	North Carolina	1.47
24	Georgia	0.95	10	North Dakota	1.45
NA	Hawaii**	NA	11	Vermont	1.42
NA	Idaho**	NA	12	Massachusetts	1.34
NA	Illinois**	NA	13	Colorado	1.28
6	Indiana	1.61	13	Maine	1.28
37	Iowa	0.65	15	Maryland	1.27
NA	Kansas**	NA	16	Ohio	1.21
4	Kentucky	1.72	17	Arizona	1.18
32	Louisiana	0.77	17	Montana	1.18
13	Maine	1.28	19	Wisconsin	1.15
15	Maryland	1.27	20	South Carolina	1.08
12	Massachusetts	1.34	21	South Dakota	1.05
NA	Michigan**	NA	22	New Hampshire	1.02
NA	Minnesota**	NA	23	New Jersey	0.98
27	Mississippi	0.89	24	Georgia	0.95
40	Missouri	0.48	25	California	0.93
17	Montana	1.18	26	Texas	0.92
5	Nebraska	1.67	27	Mississippi	0.89
30	Nevada	0.81	28	Oklahoma	0.86
22	New Hampshire	1.02	29	Alabama	0.83
23	New Jersey	0.98	30	Nevada	0.81
35	New Mexico	0.68	31	Connecticut	0.78
33	New York	0.72	32	Louisiana	0.77
9	North Carolina	1.47	33	New York	0.72
10	North Dakota	1.45	34	Arkansas	0.71
16	Ohio	1.21	35	New Mexico	0.68
28	Oklahoma	0.86	36	Washington	0.67
NA	Oregon**	NA	37	Iowa	0.65
39	Pennsylvania	0.59	38	Tennessee	0.60
2	Rhode Island	1.94	39	Pennsylvania	0.59
20	South Carolina	1.08	40	Missouri	0.48
21	South Dakota	1.05	41	Alaska	0.47
38	Tennessee	0.60	42	Florida	0.39
26	Texas	0.92	NA	Delaware**	NA
1	Utah	2.15	NA	Hawaii**	NA
11	Vermont	1.42	NA	Idaho**	NA
3	Virginia	1.77	NA	Illinois**	NA
36	Washington	0.67	NA	Kansas**	NA
8	West Virginia	1.52	NA	Michigan**	NA
19	Wisconsin	1.15	NA	Minnesota**	NA
7	Wyoming	1.53	NA	Oregon**	NA
				District of Columbia**	NA

Source: Morgan Quitno Corporation using data from U.S. Department of Justice, Federal Bureau of Investigation
"Crime in the United States 1993" (Uniform Crime Reports, December 4, 1994)
Includes murder, rape, robbery, aggravated assault, burglary, larceny-theft and motor vehicle theft. National percent is only for states shown separately. Many states had incomplete reports.
**Not available.*

Violent Crimes Reported at Universities and Colleges in 1993

National Total = 3,150 Reported Violent Crimes*

ALPHA ORDER

RANK	STATE	CRIMES	% of USA
15	Alabama	76	2.41%
29	Alaska	22	0.70%
13	Arizona	103	3.27%
22	Arkansas	40	1.27%
1	California	428	13.59%
25	Colorado	37	1.17%
21	Connecticut	41	1.30%
NA	Delaware**	NA	NA
8	Florida	128	4.06%
11	Georgia	110	3.49%
NA	Hawaii**	NA	NA
NA	Idaho**	NA	NA
NA	Illinois**	NA	NA
13	Indiana	103	3.27%
32	Iowa	15	0.48%
NA	Kansas**	NA	NA
16	Kentucky	75	2.38%
12	Louisiana	108	3.43%
39	Maine	5	0.16%
7	Maryland	131	4.16%
10	Massachusetts	116	3.68%
NA	Michigan**	NA	NA
NA	Minnesota**	NA	NA
17	Mississippi	71	2.25%
29	Missouri	22	0.70%
35	Montana	12	0.38%
38	Nebraska	6	0.19%
32	Nevada	15	0.48%
37	New Hampshire	10	0.32%
4	New Jersey	191	6.06%
28	New Mexico	29	0.92%
9	New York	121	3.84%
3	North Carolina	217	6.89%
41	North Dakota	2	0.06%
6	Ohio	140	4.44%
27	Oklahoma	32	1.02%
NA	Oregon**	NA	NA
18	Pennsylvania	67	2.13%
34	Rhode Island	14	0.44%
19	South Carolina	63	2.00%
41	South Dakota	2	0.06%
23	Tennessee	39	1.24%
2	Texas	259	8.22%
26	Utah	34	1.08%
40	Vermont	4	0.13%
5	Virginia	150	4.76%
20	Washington	44	1.40%
31	West Virginia	18	0.57%
23	Wisconsin	39	1.24%
36	Wyoming	11	0.35%

RANK ORDER

RANK	STATE	CRIMES	% of USA
1	California	428	13.59%
2	Texas	259	8.22%
3	North Carolina	217	6.89%
4	New Jersey	191	6.06%
5	Virginia	150	4.76%
6	Ohio	140	4.44%
7	Maryland	131	4.16%
8	Florida	128	4.06%
9	New York	121	3.84%
10	Massachusetts	116	3.68%
11	Georgia	110	3.49%
12	Louisiana	108	3.43%
13	Arizona	103	3.27%
13	Indiana	103	3.27%
15	Alabama	76	2.41%
16	Kentucky	75	2.38%
17	Mississippi	71	2.25%
18	Pennsylvania	67	2.13%
19	South Carolina	63	2.00%
20	Washington	44	1.40%
21	Connecticut	41	1.30%
22	Arkansas	40	1.27%
23	Tennessee	39	1.24%
23	Wisconsin	39	1.24%
25	Colorado	37	1.17%
26	Utah	34	1.08%
27	Oklahoma	32	1.02%
28	New Mexico	29	0.92%
29	Alaska	22	0.70%
29	Missouri	22	0.70%
31	West Virginia	18	0.57%
32	Iowa	15	0.48%
32	Nevada	15	0.48%
34	Rhode Island	14	0.44%
35	Montana	12	0.38%
36	Wyoming	11	0.35%
37	New Hampshire	10	0.32%
38	Nebraska	6	0.19%
39	Maine	5	0.16%
40	Vermont	4	0.13%
41	North Dakota	2	0.06%
41	South Dakota	2	0.06%
NA	Delaware**	NA	NA
NA	Hawaii**	NA	NA
NA	Idaho**	NA	NA
NA	Illinois**	NA	NA
NA	Kansas**	NA	NA
NA	Michigan**	NA	NA
NA	Minnesota**	NA	NA
NA	Oregon**	NA	NA
	District of Columbia**	NA	NA

Source: U.S. Department of Justice, Federal Bureau of Investigation
"Crime in the United States 1993" (Uniform Crime Reports, December 4, 1994)
*Includes murder, rape, robbery and aggravated assault. Total is only for states shown separately. Many states had incomplete reports.
**Not available.

Violent Crimes Reported at Universities and Colleges
As a Percent of All Violent Crimes in 1993
National Percent = 0.19% of Violent Crimes*

ALPHA ORDER

ALPHA ORDER

RANK	STATE	PERCENT
25	Alabama	0.23
8	Alaska	0.48
14	Arizona	0.37
19	Arkansas	0.28
34	California	0.13
29	Colorado	0.18
20	Connecticut	0.27
NA	Delaware**	NA
40	Florida	0.08
26	Georgia	0.22
NA	Hawaii**	NA
NA	Idaho**	NA
NA	Illinois**	NA
14	Indiana	0.37
31	Iowa	0.16
NA	Kansas**	NA
11	Kentucky	0.43
23	Louisiana	0.24
17	Maine	0.32
21	Maryland	0.26
23	Massachusetts	0.24
NA	Michigan**	NA
NA	Minnesota**	NA
4	Mississippi	0.62
41	Missouri	0.06
2	Montana	0.81
38	Nebraska	0.11
37	Nevada	0.12
3	New Hampshire	0.65
12	New Jersey	0.39
27	New Mexico	0.19
41	New York	0.06
10	North Carolina	0.46
13	North Dakota	0.38
22	Ohio	0.25
31	Oklahoma	0.16
NA	Oregon**	NA
34	Pennsylvania	0.13
16	Rhode Island	0.35
30	South Carolina	0.17
34	South Dakota	0.13
39	Tennessee	0.10
27	Texas	0.19
6	Utah	0.61
6	Vermont	0.61
4	Virginia	0.62
31	Washington	0.16
9	West Virginia	0.47
18	Wisconsin	0.29
1	Wyoming	0.82

RANK ORDER

RANK	STATE	PERCENT
1	Wyoming	0.82
2	Montana	0.81
3	New Hampshire	0.65
4	Mississippi	0.62
4	Virginia	0.62
6	Utah	0.61
6	Vermont	0.61
8	Alaska	0.48
9	West Virginia	0.47
10	North Carolina	0.46
11	Kentucky	0.43
12	New Jersey	0.39
13	North Dakota	0.38
14	Arizona	0.37
14	Indiana	0.37
16	Rhode Island	0.35
17	Maine	0.32
18	Wisconsin	0.29
19	Arkansas	0.28
20	Connecticut	0.27
21	Maryland	0.26
22	Ohio	0.25
23	Louisiana	0.24
23	Massachusetts	0.24
25	Alabama	0.23
26	Georgia	0.22
27	New Mexico	0.19
27	Texas	0.19
29	Colorado	0.18
30	South Carolina	0.17
31	Iowa	0.16
31	Oklahoma	0.16
31	Washington	0.16
34	California	0.13
34	Pennsylvania	0.13
34	South Dakota	0.13
37	Nevada	0.12
38	Nebraska	0.11
39	Tennessee	0.10
40	Florida	0.08
41	Missouri	0.06
41	New York	0.06
NA	Delaware**	NA
NA	Hawaii**	NA
NA	Idaho**	NA
NA	Illinois**	NA
NA	Kansas**	NA
NA	Michigan**	NA
NA	Minnesota**	NA
NA	Oregon**	NA
	District of Columbia**	NA

Source: Morgan Quitno Corporation using data from U.S. Department of Justice, Federal Bureau of Investigation
    "Crime in the United States 1993" (Uniform Crime Reports, December 4, 1994)
*Includes murder, rape, robbery and aggravated assault. National percent is only for states shown separately. Many states had incomplete reports.
**Not available.

Property Crimes Reported at Universities and Colleges in 1993

National Reported Total = 120,286 Property Crimes*

ALPHA ORDER

RANK	STATE	CRIMES	% of USA
23	Alabama	1,629	1.35%
44	Alaska	135	0.11%
14	Arizona	3,358	2.79%
32	Arkansas	789	0.66%
1	California	18,405	15.30%
15	Colorado	2,479	2.06%
28	Connecticut	1,145	0.95%
NA	Delaware**	NA	NA
8	Florida	4,371	3.63%
10	Georgia	3,979	3.31%
NA	Hawaii**	NA	NA
NA	Idaho**	NA	NA
NA	Illinois**	NA	NA
9	Indiana	4,016	3.34%
33	Iowa	684	0.57%
NA	Kansas**	NA	NA
21	Kentucky	2,052	1.71%
19	Louisiana	2,160	1.80%
37	Maine	496	0.41%
12	Maryland	3,732	3.10%
11	Massachusetts	3,813	3.17%
4	Michigan	6,657	5.53%
26	Minnesota	1,275	1.06%
30	Mississippi	969	0.81%
27	Missouri	1,270	1.06%
38	Montana	462	0.38%
29	Nebraska	1,101	0.92%
35	Nevada	681	0.57%
39	New Hampshire	323	0.27%
13	New Jersey	3,530	2.93%
36	New Mexico	663	0.55%
3	New York	7,142	5.94%
6	North Carolina	5,550	4.61%
42	North Dakota	257	0.21%
5	Ohio	5,881	4.89%
25	Oklahoma	1,435	1.19%
NA	Oregon**	NA	NA
18	Pennsylvania	2,248	1.87%
31	Rhode Island	860	0.71%
17	South Carolina	2,265	1.88%
43	South Dakota	220	0.18%
24	Tennessee	1,570	1.31%
2	Texas	10,385	8.63%
20	Utah	2,065	1.72%
40	Vermont	322	0.27%
7	Virginia	4,591	3.82%
22	Washington	2,047	1.70%
34	West Virginia	682	0.57%
16	Wisconsin	2,304	1.92%
41	Wyoming	288	0.24%

RANK ORDER

RANK	STATE	CRIMES	% of USA
1	California	18,405	15.30%
2	Texas	10,385	8.63%
3	New York	7,142	5.94%
4	Michigan	6,657	5.53%
5	Ohio	5,881	4.89%
6	North Carolina	5,550	4.61%
7	Virginia	4,591	3.82%
8	Florida	4,371	3.63%
9	Indiana	4,016	3.34%
10	Georgia	3,979	3.31%
11	Massachusetts	3,813	3.17%
12	Maryland	3,732	3.10%
13	New Jersey	3,530	2.93%
14	Arizona	3,358	2.79%
15	Colorado	2,479	2.06%
16	Wisconsin	2,304	1.92%
17	South Carolina	2,265	1.88%
18	Pennsylvania	2,248	1.87%
19	Louisiana	2,160	1.80%
20	Utah	2,065	1.72%
21	Kentucky	2,052	1.71%
22	Washington	2,047	1.70%
23	Alabama	1,629	1.35%
24	Tennessee	1,570	1.31%
25	Oklahoma	1,435	1.19%
26	Minnesota	1,275	1.06%
27	Missouri	1,270	1.06%
28	Connecticut	1,145	0.95%
29	Nebraska	1,101	0.92%
30	Mississippi	969	0.81%
31	Rhode Island	860	0.71%
32	Arkansas	789	0.66%
33	Iowa	684	0.57%
34	West Virginia	682	0.57%
35	Nevada	681	0.57%
36	New Mexico	663	0.55%
37	Maine	496	0.41%
38	Montana	462	0.38%
39	New Hampshire	323	0.27%
40	Vermont	322	0.27%
41	Wyoming	288	0.24%
42	North Dakota	257	0.21%
43	South Dakota	220	0.18%
44	Alaska	135	0.11%
NA	Delaware**	NA	NA
NA	Hawaii**	NA	NA
NA	Idaho**	NA	NA
NA	Illinois**	NA	NA
NA	Kansas**	NA	NA
NA	Oregon**	NA	NA
	District of Columbia**	NA	NA

Source: U.S. Department of Justice, Federal Bureau of Investigation
   "Crime in the United States 1993" (Uniform Crime Reports, December 4, 1994)
*Includes burglary, larceny-theft and motor vehicle theft. Total is only for states shown separately. Many states had incomplete reports.
**Not available.

Property Crimes Reported at Universities and Colleges
As a Percent of All Property Crimes in 1993
National Percent = 1.07% of Property Crimes*

<u>ALPHA ORDER</u>

RANK	STATE	PERCENT
28	Alabama	0.95
43	Alaska	0.47
18	Arizona	1.27
35	Arkansas	0.77
23	California	1.10
15	Colorado	1.40
34	Connecticut	0.83
NA	Delaware**	NA
44	Florida	0.45
25	Georgia	1.05
NA	Hawaii**	NA
NA	Idaho**	NA
NA	Illinois**	NA
6	Indiana	1.77
39	Iowa	0.69
NA	Kansas**	NA
3	Kentucky	1.94
33	Louisiana	0.87
17	Maine	1.32
13	Maryland	1.47
10	Massachusetts	1.55
11	Michigan	1.51
38	Minnesota	0.70
30	Mississippi	0.92
42	Missouri	0.56
21	Montana	1.19
5	Nebraska	1.81
30	Nevada	0.92
26	New Hampshire	1.04
24	New Jersey	1.07
35	New Mexico	0.77
32	New York	0.88
7	North Carolina	1.61
12	North Dakota	1.48
16	Ohio	1.33
28	Oklahoma	0.95
NA	Oregon**	NA
41	Pennsylvania	0.65
2	Rhode Island	2.10
18	South Carolina	1.27
22	South Dakota	1.12
39	Tennessee	0.69
27	Texas	1.01
1	Utah	2.25
14	Vermont	1.45
4	Virginia	1.89
37	Washington	0.72
7	West Virginia	1.61
20	Wisconsin	1.21
9	Wyoming	1.58

<u>RANK ORDER</u>

RANK	STATE	PERCENT
1	Utah	2.25
2	Rhode Island	2.10
3	Kentucky	1.94
4	Virginia	1.89
5	Nebraska	1.81
6	Indiana	1.77
7	North Carolina	1.61
7	West Virginia	1.61
9	Wyoming	1.58
10	Massachusetts	1.55
11	Michigan	1.51
12	North Dakota	1.48
13	Maryland	1.47
14	Vermont	1.45
15	Colorado	1.40
16	Ohio	1.33
17	Maine	1.32
18	Arizona	1.27
18	South Carolina	1.27
20	Wisconsin	1.21
21	Montana	1.19
22	South Dakota	1.12
23	California	1.10
24	New Jersey	1.07
25	Georgia	1.05
26	New Hampshire	1.04
27	Texas	1.01
28	Alabama	0.95
28	Oklahoma	0.95
30	Mississippi	0.92
30	Nevada	0.92
32	New York	0.88
33	Louisiana	0.87
34	Connecticut	0.83
35	Arkansas	0.77
35	New Mexico	0.77
37	Washington	0.72
38	Minnesota	0.70
39	Iowa	0.69
39	Tennessee	0.69
41	Pennsylvania	0.65
42	Missouri	0.56
43	Alaska	0.47
44	Florida	0.45
NA	Delaware**	NA
NA	Hawaii**	NA
NA	Idaho**	NA
NA	Illinois**	NA
NA	Kansas**	NA
NA	Oregon**	NA
	District of Columbia**	NA

Source: Morgan Quitno Corporation using data from U.S. Department of Justice, Federal Bureau of Investigation "Crime in the United States 1993" (Uniform Crime Reports, December 4, 1994)

*Includes burglary, larceny-theft and motor vehicle theft. National percent is only for states shown separately. Many states had incomplete reports.
**Not available.

Crimes in 1989

National Total = 14,251,449 Crimes*

<table>
<tr><td colspan="4">ALPHA ORDER</td><td colspan="4">RANK ORDER</td></tr>
<tr><th>RANK</th><th>STATE</th><th>CRIMES</th><th>% of USA</th><th>RANK</th><th>STATE</th><th>CRIMES</th><th>% of USA</th></tr>
<tr><td>25</td><td>Alabama</td><td>190,573</td><td>1.34%</td><td>1</td><td>California</td><td>1,965,652</td><td>13.79%</td></tr>
<tr><td>46</td><td>Alaska</td><td>25,190</td><td>0.18%</td><td>2</td><td>Texas</td><td>1,346,866</td><td>9.45%</td></tr>
<tr><td>14</td><td>Arizona</td><td>286,604</td><td>2.01%</td><td>3</td><td>New York</td><td>1,129,638</td><td>7.93%</td></tr>
<tr><td>32</td><td>Arkansas</td><td>109,610</td><td>0.77%</td><td>4</td><td>Florida</td><td>1,115,617</td><td>7.83%</td></tr>
<tr><td>1</td><td>California</td><td>1,965,652</td><td>13.79%</td><td>5</td><td>Illinois</td><td>657,414</td><td>4.61%</td></tr>
<tr><td>22</td><td>Colorado</td><td>200,328</td><td>1.41%</td><td>6</td><td>Michigan</td><td>553,442</td><td>3.88%</td></tr>
<tr><td>28</td><td>Connecticut</td><td>170,695</td><td>1.20%</td><td>7</td><td>Ohio</td><td>516,252</td><td>3.62%</td></tr>
<tr><td>44</td><td>Delaware</td><td>32,743</td><td>0.23%</td><td>8</td><td>Georgia</td><td>455,225</td><td>3.19%</td></tr>
<tr><td>4</td><td>Florida</td><td>1,115,617</td><td>7.83%</td><td>9</td><td>New Jersey</td><td>407,643</td><td>2.86%</td></tr>
<tr><td>8</td><td>Georgia</td><td>455,225</td><td>3.19%</td><td>10</td><td>Pennsylvania</td><td>404,594</td><td>2.84%</td></tr>
<tr><td>36</td><td>Hawaii</td><td>69,727</td><td>0.49%</td><td>11</td><td>North Carolina</td><td>345,225</td><td>2.42%</td></tr>
<tr><td>42</td><td>Idaho</td><td>39,860</td><td>0.28%</td><td>12</td><td>Washington</td><td>313,932</td><td>2.20%</td></tr>
<tr><td>5</td><td>Illinois</td><td>657,414</td><td>4.61%</td><td>13</td><td>Massachusetts</td><td>303,692</td><td>2.13%</td></tr>
<tr><td>19</td><td>Indiana</td><td>248,327</td><td>1.74%</td><td>14</td><td>Arizona</td><td>286,604</td><td>2.01%</td></tr>
<tr><td>31</td><td>Iowa</td><td>115,912</td><td>0.81%</td><td>15</td><td>Louisiana</td><td>273,492</td><td>1.92%</td></tr>
<tr><td>29</td><td>Kansas</td><td>125,219</td><td>0.88%</td><td>16</td><td>Missouri</td><td>264,508</td><td>1.86%</td></tr>
<tr><td>30</td><td>Kentucky</td><td>123,630</td><td>0.87%</td><td>17</td><td>Maryland</td><td>261,107</td><td>1.83%</td></tr>
<tr><td>15</td><td>Louisiana</td><td>273,492</td><td>1.92%</td><td>18</td><td>Virginia</td><td>256,814</td><td>1.80%</td></tr>
<tr><td>41</td><td>Maine</td><td>43,792</td><td>0.31%</td><td>19</td><td>Indiana</td><td>248,327</td><td>1.74%</td></tr>
<tr><td>17</td><td>Maryland</td><td>261,107</td><td>1.83%</td><td>20</td><td>Tennessee</td><td>222,972</td><td>1.56%</td></tr>
<tr><td>13</td><td>Massachusetts</td><td>303,692</td><td>2.13%</td><td>21</td><td>Wisconsin</td><td>202,703</td><td>1.42%</td></tr>
<tr><td>6</td><td>Michigan</td><td>553,442</td><td>3.88%</td><td>22</td><td>Colorado</td><td>200,328</td><td>1.41%</td></tr>
<tr><td>24</td><td>Minnesota</td><td>190,801</td><td>1.34%</td><td>23</td><td>South Carolina</td><td>197,348</td><td>1.38%</td></tr>
<tr><td>35</td><td>Mississippi</td><td>92,136</td><td>0.65%</td><td>24</td><td>Minnesota</td><td>190,801</td><td>1.34%</td></tr>
<tr><td>16</td><td>Missouri</td><td>264,508</td><td>1.86%</td><td>25</td><td>Alabama</td><td>190,573</td><td>1.34%</td></tr>
<tr><td>45</td><td>Montana</td><td>32,220</td><td>0.23%</td><td>26</td><td>Oklahoma</td><td>177,405</td><td>1.24%</td></tr>
<tr><td>38</td><td>Nebraska</td><td>65,916</td><td>0.46%</td><td>27</td><td>Oregon</td><td>173,744</td><td>1.22%</td></tr>
<tr><td>37</td><td>Nevada</td><td>69,679</td><td>0.49%</td><td>28</td><td>Connecticut</td><td>170,695</td><td>1.20%</td></tr>
<tr><td>43</td><td>New Hampshire</td><td>39,810</td><td>0.28%</td><td>29</td><td>Kansas</td><td>125,219</td><td>0.88%</td></tr>
<tr><td>9</td><td>New Jersey</td><td>407,643</td><td>2.86%</td><td>30</td><td>Kentucky</td><td>123,630</td><td>0.87%</td></tr>
<tr><td>33</td><td>New Mexico</td><td>100,448</td><td>0.70%</td><td>31</td><td>Iowa</td><td>115,912</td><td>0.81%</td></tr>
<tr><td>3</td><td>New York</td><td>1,129,638</td><td>7.93%</td><td>32</td><td>Arkansas</td><td>109,610</td><td>0.77%</td></tr>
<tr><td>11</td><td>North Carolina</td><td>345,225</td><td>2.42%</td><td>33</td><td>New Mexico</td><td>100,448</td><td>0.70%</td></tr>
<tr><td>50</td><td>North Dakota</td><td>16,902</td><td>0.12%</td><td>34</td><td>Utah</td><td>96,994</td><td>0.68%</td></tr>
<tr><td>7</td><td>Ohio</td><td>516,252</td><td>3.62%</td><td>35</td><td>Mississippi</td><td>92,136</td><td>0.65%</td></tr>
<tr><td>26</td><td>Oklahoma</td><td>177,405</td><td>1.24%</td><td>36</td><td>Hawaii</td><td>69,727</td><td>0.49%</td></tr>
<tr><td>27</td><td>Oregon</td><td>173,744</td><td>1.22%</td><td>37</td><td>Nevada</td><td>69,679</td><td>0.49%</td></tr>
<tr><td>10</td><td>Pennsylvania</td><td>404,594</td><td>2.84%</td><td>38</td><td>Nebraska</td><td>65,916</td><td>0.46%</td></tr>
<tr><td>39</td><td>Rhode Island</td><td>52,144</td><td>0.37%</td><td>39</td><td>Rhode Island</td><td>52,144</td><td>0.37%</td></tr>
<tr><td>23</td><td>South Carolina</td><td>197,348</td><td>1.38%</td><td>40</td><td>West Virginia</td><td>43,878</td><td>0.31%</td></tr>
<tr><td>48</td><td>South Dakota</td><td>19,199</td><td>0.13%</td><td>41</td><td>Maine</td><td>43,792</td><td>0.31%</td></tr>
<tr><td>20</td><td>Tennessee</td><td>222,972</td><td>1.56%</td><td>42</td><td>Idaho</td><td>39,860</td><td>0.28%</td></tr>
<tr><td>2</td><td>Texas</td><td>1,346,866</td><td>9.45%</td><td>43</td><td>New Hampshire</td><td>39,810</td><td>0.28%</td></tr>
<tr><td>34</td><td>Utah</td><td>96,994</td><td>0.68%</td><td>44</td><td>Delaware</td><td>32,743</td><td>0.23%</td></tr>
<tr><td>47</td><td>Vermont</td><td>23,182</td><td>0.16%</td><td>45</td><td>Montana</td><td>32,220</td><td>0.23%</td></tr>
<tr><td>18</td><td>Virginia</td><td>256,814</td><td>1.80%</td><td>46</td><td>Alaska</td><td>25,190</td><td>0.18%</td></tr>
<tr><td>12</td><td>Washington</td><td>313,932</td><td>2.20%</td><td>47</td><td>Vermont</td><td>23,182</td><td>0.16%</td></tr>
<tr><td>40</td><td>West Virginia</td><td>43,878</td><td>0.31%</td><td>48</td><td>South Dakota</td><td>19,199</td><td>0.13%</td></tr>
<tr><td>21</td><td>Wisconsin</td><td>202,703</td><td>1.42%</td><td>49</td><td>Wyoming</td><td>18,473</td><td>0.13%</td></tr>
<tr><td>49</td><td>Wyoming</td><td>18,473</td><td>0.13%</td><td>50</td><td>North Dakota</td><td>16,902</td><td>0.12%</td></tr>
<tr><td></td><td></td><td></td><td></td><td></td><td>District of Columbia</td><td>62,172</td><td>0.44%</td></tr>
</table>

Source: U.S. Department of Justice, Federal Bureau of Investigation
   "Crime in the United States 1989" (Uniform Crime Reports, August 5, 1990)
*Includes murder, rape, robbery, aggravated assault, burglary, larceny-theft and motor vehicle theft.

Percent Change in Number of Crimes: 1989 to 1993

National Percent Change = 0.8% Decrease*

ALPHA ORDER

RANK ORDER

RANK	STATE	PERCENT CHANGE	RANK	STATE	PERCENT CHANGE
11	Alabama	7.2	1	Alaska	32.4
1	Alaska	32.4	2	Mississippi	26.7
24	Arizona	2.1	3	Montana	24.7
12	Arkansas	6.4	4	Nevada	23.2
22	California	2.5	5	Tennessee	19.8
36	Colorado	(1.6)	6	Maryland	16.1
46	Connecticut	(10.7)	7	North Carolina	13.7
18	Delaware	4.2	8	South Dakota	10.2
23	Florida	2.4	9	South Carolina	9.0
41	Georgia	(5.9)	10	Louisiana	7.5
16	Hawaii	5.5	11	Alabama	7.2
13	Idaho	6.0	12	Arkansas	6.4
32	Illinois	0.0	13	Idaho	6.0
21	Indiana	2.7	13	North Dakota	6.0
42	Iowa	(6.6)	15	Wyoming	5.9
28	Kansas	0.6	16	Hawaii	5.5
33	Kentucky	(0.1)	17	West Virginia	5.0
10	Louisiana	7.5	18	Delaware	4.2
47	Maine	(10.8)	19	Virginia	4.0
6	Maryland	16.1	20	Minnesota	3.8
38	Massachusetts	(3.1)	21	Indiana	2.7
42	Michigan	(6.6)	22	California	2.5
20	Minnesota	3.8	23	Florida	2.4
2	Mississippi	26.7	24	Arizona	2.1
25	Missouri	0.8	25	Missouri	0.8
3	Montana	24.7	25	New Mexico	0.8
30	Nebraska	0.4	25	Wisconsin	0.8
4	Nevada	23.2	28	Kansas	0.6
50	New Hampshire	(17.9)	28	Oregon	0.6
44	New Jersey	(7.2)	30	Nebraska	0.4
25	New Mexico	0.8	30	Utah	0.4
45	New York	(10.6)	32	Illinois	0.0
7	North Carolina	13.7	33	Kentucky	(0.1)
13	North Dakota	6.0	34	Washington	(0.4)
39	Ohio	(3.6)	35	Vermont	(1.3)
39	Oklahoma	(3.6)	36	Colorado	(1.6)
28	Oregon	0.6	37	Pennsylvania	(2.6)
37	Pennsylvania	(2.6)	38	Massachusetts	(3.1)
48	Rhode Island	(13.7)	39	Ohio	(3.6)
9	South Carolina	9.0	39	Oklahoma	(3.6)
8	South Dakota	10.2	41	Georgia	(5.9)
5	Tennessee	19.8	42	Iowa	(6.6)
49	Texas	(13.8)	42	Michigan	(6.6)
30	Utah	0.4	44	New Jersey	(7.2)
35	Vermont	(1.3)	45	New York	(10.6)
19	Virginia	4.0	46	Connecticut	(10.7)
34	Washington	(0.4)	47	Maine	(10.8)
17	West Virginia	5.0	48	Rhode Island	(13.7)
25	Wisconsin	0.8	49	Texas	(13.8)
15	Wyoming	5.9	50	New Hampshire	(17.9)

District of Columbia   9.3

Source: Morgan Quitno Corporation using data from U.S. Department of Justice, Federal Bureau of Investigation
"Crime in the United States" (Uniform Crime Reports, 1989 and 1993 editions)
*Includes murder, rape, robbery, aggravated assault, burglary, larceny-theft and motor vehicle theft.

Crime Rate in 1989

National Rate = 5,741.0 Crimes per 100,000 Population*

ALPHA ORDER

RANK ORDER

RANK	STATE	RATE
30	Alabama	4,627.8
28	Alaska	4,779.9
2	Arizona	8,059.7
31	Arkansas	4,555.7
5	California	6,763.4
13	Colorado	6,039.4
20	Connecticut	5,270.0
27	Delaware	4,865.2
1	Florida	8,804.5
4	Georgia	7,073.1
10	Hawaii	6,270.4
41	Idaho	3,931.0
16	Illinois	5,639.2
33	Indiana	4,440.0
39	Iowa	4,081.4
26	Kansas	4,982.8
47	Kentucky	3,317.1
11	Louisiana	6,241.3
44	Maine	3,583.6
18	Maryland	5,562.6
24	Massachusetts	5,136.0
14	Michigan	5,968.3
34	Minnesota	4,383.2
45	Mississippi	3,515.3
25	Missouri	5,127.1
40	Montana	3,997.5
37	Nebraska	4,091.6
9	Nevada	6,271.7
43	New Hampshire	3,596.2
21	New Jersey	5,269.4
7	New Mexico	6,573.8
8	New York	6,293.2
22	North Carolina	5,253.8
49	North Dakota	2,560.9
29	Ohio	4,733.2
19	Oklahoma	5,502.6
12	Oregon	6,161.1
46	Pennsylvania	3,360.4
23	Rhode Island	5,224.8
17	South Carolina	5,619.2
48	South Dakota	2,685.2
32	Tennessee	4,513.6
3	Texas	7,926.9
15	Utah	5,682.1
38	Vermont	4,088.5
35	Virginia	4,211.4
6	Washington	6,593.8
50	West Virginia	2,362.8
36	Wisconsin	4,164.8
42	Wyoming	3,889.1

RANK	STATE	RATE
1	Florida	8,804.5
2	Arizona	8,059.7
3	Texas	7,926.9
4	Georgia	7,073.1
5	California	6,763.4
6	Washington	6,593.8
7	New Mexico	6,573.8
8	New York	6,293.2
9	Nevada	6,271.7
10	Hawaii	6,270.4
11	Louisiana	6,241.3
12	Oregon	6,161.1
13	Colorado	6,039.4
14	Michigan	5,968.3
15	Utah	5,682.1
16	Illinois	5,639.2
17	South Carolina	5,619.2
18	Maryland	5,562.6
19	Oklahoma	5,502.6
20	Connecticut	5,270.0
21	New Jersey	5,269.4
22	North Carolina	5,253.8
23	Rhode Island	5,224.8
24	Massachusetts	5,136.0
25	Missouri	5,127.1
26	Kansas	4,982.8
27	Delaware	4,865.2
28	Alaska	4,779.9
29	Ohio	4,733.2
30	Alabama	4,627.8
31	Arkansas	4,555.7
32	Tennessee	4,513.6
33	Indiana	4,440.0
34	Minnesota	4,383.2
35	Virginia	4,211.4
36	Wisconsin	4,164.8
37	Nebraska	4,091.6
38	Vermont	4,088.5
39	Iowa	4,081.4
40	Montana	3,997.5
41	Idaho	3,931.0
42	Wyoming	3,889.1
43	New Hampshire	3,596.2
44	Maine	3,583.6
45	Mississippi	3,515.3
46	Pennsylvania	3,360.4
47	Kentucky	3,317.1
48	South Dakota	2,685.2
49	North Dakota	2,560.9
50	West Virginia	2,362.8
	District of Columbia	10,293.4

Source: U.S. Department of Justice, Federal Bureau of Investigation
"Crime in the United States 1989" (Uniform Crime Reports, August 5, 1990)
Includes murder, rape, robbery, aggravated assault, burglary, larceny-theft and motor vehicle theft.

Percent Change in Crime Rate: 1989 to 1993

National Percent Change = 4.5% Decrease*

<table>
<tr><td colspan="3">ALPHA ORDER</td><td colspan="3">RANK ORDER</td></tr>
<tr><td>RANK</td><td>STATE</td><td>PERCENT CHANGE</td><td>RANK</td><td>STATE</td><td>PERCENT CHANGE</td></tr>
<tr><td>13</td><td>Alabama</td><td>5.4</td><td>1</td><td>Mississippi</td><td>25.7</td></tr>
<tr><td>3</td><td>Alaska</td><td>16.5</td><td>2</td><td>Montana</td><td>19.8</td></tr>
<tr><td>38</td><td>Arizona</td><td>(7.8)</td><td>3</td><td>Alaska</td><td>16.5</td></tr>
<tr><td>12</td><td>Arkansas</td><td>5.6</td><td>4</td><td>Tennessee</td><td>16.1</td></tr>
<tr><td>31</td><td>California</td><td>(4.5)</td><td>5</td><td>South Dakota</td><td>10.2</td></tr>
<tr><td>40</td><td>Colorado</td><td>(8.5)</td><td>6</td><td>North Dakota</td><td>10.1</td></tr>
<tr><td>44</td><td>Connecticut</td><td>(11.8)</td><td>7</td><td>Maryland</td><td>9.8</td></tr>
<tr><td>17</td><td>Delaware</td><td>0.1</td><td>8</td><td>Louisiana</td><td>9.7</td></tr>
<tr><td>34</td><td>Florida</td><td>(5.2)</td><td>9</td><td>North Carolina</td><td>7.6</td></tr>
<tr><td>47</td><td>Georgia</td><td>(12.4)</td><td>10</td><td>West Virginia</td><td>7.2</td></tr>
<tr><td>17</td><td>Hawaii</td><td>0.1</td><td>11</td><td>Wyoming</td><td>7.0</td></tr>
<tr><td>25</td><td>Idaho</td><td>(2.2)</td><td>12</td><td>Arkansas</td><td>5.6</td></tr>
<tr><td>21</td><td>Illinois</td><td>(0.4)</td><td>13</td><td>Alabama</td><td>5.4</td></tr>
<tr><td>15</td><td>Indiana</td><td>0.6</td><td>14</td><td>South Carolina</td><td>5.1</td></tr>
<tr><td>36</td><td>Iowa</td><td>(5.8)</td><td>15</td><td>Indiana</td><td>0.6</td></tr>
<tr><td>20</td><td>Kansas</td><td>(0.2)</td><td>15</td><td>Nebraska</td><td>0.6</td></tr>
<tr><td>24</td><td>Kentucky</td><td>(1.7)</td><td>17</td><td>Delaware</td><td>0.1</td></tr>
<tr><td>8</td><td>Louisiana</td><td>9.7</td><td>17</td><td>Hawaii</td><td>0.1</td></tr>
<tr><td>46</td><td>Maine</td><td>(12.0)</td><td>17</td><td>Minnesota</td><td>0.1</td></tr>
<tr><td>7</td><td>Maryland</td><td>9.8</td><td>20</td><td>Kansas</td><td>(0.2)</td></tr>
<tr><td>32</td><td>Massachusetts</td><td>(4.7)</td><td>21</td><td>Illinois</td><td>(0.4)</td></tr>
<tr><td>41</td><td>Michigan</td><td>(8.6)</td><td>22</td><td>Missouri</td><td>(0.6)</td></tr>
<tr><td>17</td><td>Minnesota</td><td>0.1</td><td>23</td><td>Nevada</td><td>(1.5)</td></tr>
<tr><td>1</td><td>Mississippi</td><td>25.7</td><td>24</td><td>Kentucky</td><td>(1.7)</td></tr>
<tr><td>22</td><td>Missouri</td><td>(0.6)</td><td>25</td><td>Idaho</td><td>(2.2)</td></tr>
<tr><td>2</td><td>Montana</td><td>19.8</td><td>26</td><td>Virginia</td><td>(2.3)</td></tr>
<tr><td>15</td><td>Nebraska</td><td>0.6</td><td>27</td><td>Pennsylvania</td><td>(2.6)</td></tr>
<tr><td>23</td><td>Nevada</td><td>(1.5)</td><td>28</td><td>Wisconsin</td><td>(2.7)</td></tr>
<tr><td>50</td><td>New Hampshire</td><td>(19.2)</td><td>29</td><td>Vermont</td><td>(2.8)</td></tr>
<tr><td>42</td><td>New Jersey</td><td>(8.9)</td><td>30</td><td>Oklahoma</td><td>(3.8)</td></tr>
<tr><td>32</td><td>New Mexico</td><td>(4.7)</td><td>31</td><td>California</td><td>(4.5)</td></tr>
<tr><td>44</td><td>New York</td><td>(11.8)</td><td>32</td><td>Massachusetts</td><td>(4.7)</td></tr>
<tr><td>9</td><td>North Carolina</td><td>7.6</td><td>32</td><td>New Mexico</td><td>(4.7)</td></tr>
<tr><td>6</td><td>North Dakota</td><td>10.1</td><td>34</td><td>Florida</td><td>(5.2)</td></tr>
<tr><td>34</td><td>Ohio</td><td>(5.2)</td><td>34</td><td>Ohio</td><td>(5.2)</td></tr>
<tr><td>30</td><td>Oklahoma</td><td>(3.8)</td><td>36</td><td>Iowa</td><td>(5.8)</td></tr>
<tr><td>37</td><td>Oregon</td><td>(6.4)</td><td>37</td><td>Oregon</td><td>(6.4)</td></tr>
<tr><td>27</td><td>Pennsylvania</td><td>(2.6)</td><td>38</td><td>Arizona</td><td>(7.8)</td></tr>
<tr><td>48</td><td>Rhode Island</td><td>(13.9)</td><td>38</td><td>Utah</td><td>(7.8)</td></tr>
<tr><td>14</td><td>South Carolina</td><td>5.1</td><td>40</td><td>Colorado</td><td>(8.5)</td></tr>
<tr><td>5</td><td>South Dakota</td><td>10.2</td><td>41</td><td>Michigan</td><td>(8.6)</td></tr>
<tr><td>4</td><td>Tennessee</td><td>16.1</td><td>42</td><td>New Jersey</td><td>(8.9)</td></tr>
<tr><td>49</td><td>Texas</td><td>(18.8)</td><td>43</td><td>Washington</td><td>(9.7)</td></tr>
<tr><td>38</td><td>Utah</td><td>(7.8)</td><td>44</td><td>Connecticut</td><td>(11.8)</td></tr>
<tr><td>29</td><td>Vermont</td><td>(2.8)</td><td>44</td><td>New York</td><td>(11.8)</td></tr>
<tr><td>26</td><td>Virginia</td><td>(2.3)</td><td>46</td><td>Maine</td><td>(12.0)</td></tr>
<tr><td>43</td><td>Washington</td><td>(9.7)</td><td>47</td><td>Georgia</td><td>(12.4)</td></tr>
<tr><td>10</td><td>West Virginia</td><td>7.2</td><td>48</td><td>Rhode Island</td><td>(13.9)</td></tr>
<tr><td>28</td><td>Wisconsin</td><td>(2.7)</td><td>49</td><td>Texas</td><td>(18.8)</td></tr>
<tr><td>11</td><td>Wyoming</td><td>7.0</td><td>50</td><td>New Hampshire</td><td>(19.2)</td></tr>
</table>

District of Columbia   14.3

Source: Morgan Quitno Corporation using data from U.S. Department of Justice, Federal Bureau of Investigation
  "Crime in the United States" (Uniform Crime Reports, 1989 and 1993 editions)
*Includes murder, rape, robbery, aggravated assault, burglary, larceny-theft and motor vehicle theft.

Violent Crimes in 1989

National Total = 1,646,037 Violent Crimes*

ALPHA ORDER

RANK	STATE	CRIMES	% of USA
18	Alabama	24,329	1.48%
42	Alaska	2,623	0.16%
21	Arizona	21,320	1.30%
29	Arkansas	11,397	0.69%
1	California	284,136	17.26%
25	Colorado	15,636	0.95%
23	Connecticut	16,576	1.01%
39	Delaware	3,745	0.23%
3	Florida	140,575	8.54%
8	Georgia	47,357	2.88%
40	Hawaii	3,004	0.18%
43	Idaho	2,582	0.16%
5	Illinois	98,611	5.99%
19	Indiana	22,735	1.38%
34	Iowa	7,563	0.46%
32	Kansas	10,073	0.61%
27	Kentucky	13,302	0.81%
14	Louisiana	34,257	2.08%
45	Maine	1,676	0.10%
11	Maryland	40,152	2.44%
12	Massachusetts	39,912	2.42%
6	Michigan	65,760	4.00%
28	Minnesota	12,549	0.76%
33	Mississippi	8,156	0.50%
15	Missouri	32,634	1.98%
48	Montana	935	0.06%
36	Nebraska	4,503	0.27%
35	Nevada	6,947	0.42%
44	New Hampshire	1,865	0.11%
9	New Jersey	47,111	2.86%
31	New Mexico	10,755	0.65%
2	New York	203,042	12.34%
13	North Carolina	35,902	2.18%
50	North Dakota	417	0.03%
7	Ohio	51,109	3.10%
24	Oklahoma	15,847	0.96%
26	Oregon	14,625	0.89%
10	Pennsylvania	45,586	2.77%
38	Rhode Island	3,772	0.23%
16	South Carolina	28,576	1.74%
47	South Dakota	969	0.06%
17	Tennessee	27,118	1.65%
4	Texas	111,889	6.80%
37	Utah	4,417	0.27%
49	Vermont	753	0.05%
22	Virginia	19,057	1.16%
20	Washington	22,460	1.36%
41	West Virginia	2,724	0.17%
30	Wisconsin	10,834	0.66%
46	Wyoming	1,227	0.07%

RANK ORDER

RANK	STATE	CRIMES	% of USA
1	California	284,136	17.26%
2	New York	203,042	12.34%
3	Florida	140,575	8.54%
4	Texas	111,889	6.80%
5	Illinois	98,611	5.99%
6	Michigan	65,760	4.00%
7	Ohio	51,109	3.10%
8	Georgia	47,357	2.88%
9	New Jersey	47,111	2.86%
10	Pennsylvania	45,586	2.77%
11	Maryland	40,152	2.44%
12	Massachusetts	39,912	2.42%
13	North Carolina	35,902	2.18%
14	Louisiana	34,257	2.08%
15	Missouri	32,634	1.98%
16	South Carolina	28,576	1.74%
17	Tennessee	27,118	1.65%
18	Alabama	24,329	1.48%
19	Indiana	22,735	1.38%
20	Washington	22,460	1.36%
21	Arizona	21,320	1.30%
22	Virginia	19,057	1.16%
23	Connecticut	16,576	1.01%
24	Oklahoma	15,847	0.96%
25	Colorado	15,636	0.95%
26	Oregon	14,625	0.89%
27	Kentucky	13,302	0.81%
28	Minnesota	12,549	0.76%
29	Arkansas	11,397	0.69%
30	Wisconsin	10,834	0.66%
31	New Mexico	10,755	0.65%
32	Kansas	10,073	0.61%
33	Mississippi	8,156	0.50%
34	Iowa	7,563	0.46%
35	Nevada	6,947	0.42%
36	Nebraska	4,503	0.27%
37	Utah	4,417	0.27%
38	Rhode Island	3,772	0.23%
39	Delaware	3,745	0.23%
40	Hawaii	3,004	0.18%
41	West Virginia	2,724	0.17%
42	Alaska	2,623	0.16%
43	Idaho	2,582	0.16%
44	New Hampshire	1,865	0.11%
45	Maine	1,676	0.10%
46	Wyoming	1,227	0.07%
47	South Dakota	969	0.06%
48	Montana	935	0.06%
49	Vermont	753	0.05%
50	North Dakota	417	0.03%
	District of Columbia	12,937	0.79%

Source: U.S. Department of Justice, Federal Bureau of Investigation
"Crime in the United States 1989" (Uniform Crime Reports, August 5, 1990)
*Violent crimes are offenses of murder, rape, robbery and aggravated assault.

Percent Change in Number of Violent Crimes: 1989 to 1993

National Percent Change = 16.9% Increase*

ALPHA ORDER				RANK ORDER		
RANK	STATE	PERCENT CHANGE		RANK	STATE	PERCENT CHANGE
9	Alabama	34.3		1	Nevada	75.0
2	Alaska	73.7		2	Alaska	73.7
11	Arizona	32.0		3	Montana	59.3
20	Arkansas	26.2		4	South Dakota	53.8
33	California	18.4		5	Tennessee	44.0
15	Colorado	29.4		6	Mississippi	40.6
48	Connecticut	(9.8)		7	New Mexico	39.7
17	Delaware	28.2		8	West Virginia	39.2
35	Florida	17.4		9	Alabama	34.3
42	Georgia	5.6		10	Louisiana	33.1
45	Hawaii	1.9		11	Arizona	32.0
31	Idaho	19.9		12	Kentucky	31.8
37	Illinois	13.8		13	North Carolina	31.4
25	Indiana	22.9		14	South Carolina	30.5
28	Iowa	21.1		15	Colorado	29.4
22	Kansas	24.7		15	Oklahoma	29.4
12	Kentucky	31.8		17	Delaware	28.2
10	Louisiana	33.1		18	Utah	26.8
47	Maine	(7.0)		18	Virginia	26.8
23	Maryland	23.4		20	Arkansas	26.2
27	Massachusetts	21.2		21	North Dakota	25.2
36	Michigan	14.1		22	Kansas	24.7
34	Minnesota	17.8		23	Maryland	23.4
6	Mississippi	40.6		24	Wisconsin	23.0
32	Missouri	19.4		25	Indiana	22.9
3	Montana	59.3		26	Texas	22.8
29	Nebraska	21.0		27	Massachusetts	21.2
1	Nevada	75.0		28	Iowa	21.1
50	New Hampshire	(16.9)		29	Nebraska	21.0
43	New Jersey	4.8		30	Washington	20.4
7	New Mexico	39.7		31	Idaho	19.9
46	New York	(3.8)		32	Missouri	19.4
13	North Carolina	31.4		33	California	18.4
21	North Dakota	25.2		34	Minnesota	17.8
40	Ohio	9.4		35	Florida	17.4
15	Oklahoma	29.4		36	Michigan	14.1
44	Oregon	4.3		37	Illinois	13.8
38	Pennsylvania	10.3		38	Pennsylvania	10.3
41	Rhode Island	6.5		39	Wyoming	9.6
14	South Carolina	30.5		40	Ohio	9.4
4	South Dakota	53.8		41	Rhode Island	6.5
5	Tennessee	44.0		42	Georgia	5.6
26	Texas	22.8		43	New Jersey	4.8
18	Utah	26.8		44	Oregon	4.3
49	Vermont	(12.6)		45	Hawaii	1.9
18	Virginia	26.8		46	New York	(3.8)
30	Washington	20.4		47	Maine	(7.0)
8	West Virginia	39.2		48	Connecticut	(9.8)
24	Wisconsin	23.0		49	Vermont	(12.6)
39	Wyoming	9.6		50	New Hampshire	(16.9)

District of Columbia   30.5

*Source: Morgan Quitno Corporation using data from U.S. Department of Justice, Federal Bureau of Investigation
"Crime in the United States" (Uniform Crime Reports, 1989 and 1993 editions)*
Violent crimes are offenses of murder, rape, robbery and aggravated assault.

Violent Crime Rate in 1989

National Rate = 663.1 Violent Crimes per 100,000 Population*

ALPHA ORDER

RANK	STATE	RATE
17	Alabama	590.8
23	Alaska	497.7
16	Arizona	599.6
25	Arkansas	473.7
3	California	977.7
27	Colorado	471.4
22	Connecticut	511.8
18	Delaware	556.5
2	Florida	1,109.4
8	Georgia	735.8
38	Hawaii	270.1
42	Idaho	254.6
5	Illinois	845.9
29	Indiana	406.5
39	Iowa	266.3
30	Kansas	400.8
33	Kentucky	356.9
7	Louisiana	781.8
46	Maine	137.2
4	Maryland	855.4
11	Massachusetts	675.0
9	Michigan	709.2
36	Minnesota	288.3
35	Mississippi	311.2
13	Missouri	632.6
49	Montana	116.0
37	Nebraska	279.5
14	Nevada	625.3
44	New Hampshire	168.5
15	New Jersey	609.0
10	New Mexico	703.9
1	New York	1,131.2
20	North Carolina	546.4
50	North Dakota	63.2
28	Ohio	468.6
24	Oklahoma	491.5
21	Oregon	518.6
31	Pennsylvania	378.6
32	Rhode Island	378.0
6	South Carolina	813.7
47	South Dakota	135.5
19	Tennessee	548.9
12	Texas	658.5
40	Utah	258.8
48	Vermont	132.8
34	Virginia	312.5
26	Washington	471.7
45	West Virginia	146.7
43	Wisconsin	222.6
41	Wyoming	258.3

RANK ORDER

RANK	STATE	RATE
1	New York	1,131.2
2	Florida	1,109.4
3	California	977.7
4	Maryland	855.4
5	Illinois	845.9
6	South Carolina	813.7
7	Louisiana	781.8
8	Georgia	735.8
9	Michigan	709.2
10	New Mexico	703.9
11	Massachusetts	675.0
12	Texas	658.5
13	Missouri	632.6
14	Nevada	625.3
15	New Jersey	609.0
16	Arizona	599.6
17	Alabama	590.8
18	Delaware	556.5
19	Tennessee	548.9
20	North Carolina	546.4
21	Oregon	518.6
22	Connecticut	511.8
23	Alaska	497.7
24	Oklahoma	491.5
25	Arkansas	473.7
26	Washington	471.7
27	Colorado	471.4
28	Ohio	468.6
29	Indiana	406.5
30	Kansas	400.8
31	Pennsylvania	378.6
32	Rhode Island	378.0
33	Kentucky	356.9
34	Virginia	312.5
35	Mississippi	311.2
36	Minnesota	288.3
37	Nebraska	279.5
38	Hawaii	270.1
39	Iowa	266.3
40	Utah	258.8
41	Wyoming	258.3
42	Idaho	254.6
43	Wisconsin	222.6
44	New Hampshire	168.5
45	West Virginia	146.7
46	Maine	137.2
47	South Dakota	135.5
48	Vermont	132.8
49	Montana	116.0
50	North Dakota	63.2

| | District of Columbia | 2,141.9 |

Source: U.S. Department of Justice, Federal Bureau of Investigation
"Crime in the United States 1989" (Uniform Crime Reports, August 5, 1990)
Violent crimes are offenses of murder, rape, robbery and aggravated assault.

Percent Change in Violent Crime Rate: 1989 to 1993

National Percent Change = 12.5% Increase*

ALPHA ORDER

RANK ORDER

RANK	STATE	PERCENT CHANGE	RANK	STATE	PERCENT CHANGE
9	Alabama	32.1	1	South Dakota	53.8
3	Alaska	52.9	2	Montana	53.0
23	Arizona	19.2	3	Alaska	52.9
15	Arkansas	25.2	4	West Virginia	42.1
37	California	10.2	5	Nevada	40.0
21	Colorado	20.3	6	Tennessee	39.5
48	Connecticut	(10.9)	7	Mississippi	39.4
18	Delaware	23.3	8	Louisiana	35.8
39	Florida	8.7	9	Alabama	32.1
43	Georgia	(1.7)	9	New Mexico	32.1
45	Hawaii	(3.3)	11	North Dakota	30.1
35	Idaho	10.7	12	Kentucky	29.6
31	Illinois	13.5	13	Oklahoma	29.2
21	Indiana	20.3	14	South Carolina	25.8
19	Iowa	22.2	15	Arkansas	25.2
17	Kansas	23.9	16	North Carolina	24.3
12	Kentucky	29.6	17	Kansas	23.9
8	Louisiana	35.8	18	Delaware	23.3
47	Maine	(8.4)	19	Iowa	22.2
28	Maryland	16.6	20	Nebraska	21.3
23	Massachusetts	19.2	21	Colorado	20.3
33	Michigan	11.6	21	Indiana	20.3
31	Minnesota	13.5	23	Arizona	19.2
7	Mississippi	39.4	23	Massachusetts	19.2
27	Missouri	17.7	25	Virginia	19.1
2	Montana	53.0	26	Wisconsin	18.8
20	Nebraska	21.3	27	Missouri	17.7
5	Nevada	40.0	28	Maryland	16.6
50	New Hampshire	(18.2)	29	Utah	16.3
42	New Jersey	2.9	30	Texas	15.7
9	New Mexico	32.1	31	Illinois	13.5
46	New York	(5.1)	31	Minnesota	13.5
16	North Carolina	24.3	33	Michigan	11.6
11	North Dakota	30.1	34	Wyoming	10.8
40	Ohio	7.6	35	Idaho	10.7
13	Oklahoma	29.2	36	Pennsylvania	10.3
44	Oregon	(3.0)	37	California	10.2
36	Pennsylvania	10.3	38	Washington	9.1
41	Rhode Island	6.3	39	Florida	8.7
14	South Carolina	25.8	40	Ohio	7.6
1	South Dakota	53.8	41	Rhode Island	6.3
6	Tennessee	39.5	42	New Jersey	2.9
30	Texas	15.7	43	Georgia	(1.7)
29	Utah	16.3	44	Oregon	(3.0)
49	Vermont	(14.0)	45	Hawaii	(3.3)
25	Virginia	19.1	46	New York	(5.1)
38	Washington	9.1	47	Maine	(8.4)
4	West Virginia	42.1	48	Connecticut	(10.9)
26	Wisconsin	18.8	49	Vermont	(14.0)
34	Wyoming	10.8	50	New Hampshire	(18.2)

District of Columbia 36.4

Source: Morgan Quitno Corporation using data from U.S. Department of Justice, Federal Bureau of Investigation "Crime in the United States" (Uniform Crime Reports, 1989 and 1993 editions)
*Violent crimes are offenses of murder, rape, robbery and aggravated assault.

Murders in 1989

National Total = 21,500 Murders*

<table>
<tr><th colspan="4">ALPHA ORDER</th><th colspan="4">RANK ORDER</th></tr>
<tr><th>RANK</th><th>STATE</th><th>MURDERS</th><th>% of USA</th><th>RANK</th><th>STATE</th><th>MURDERS</th><th>% of USA</th></tr>
<tr><td>14</td><td>Alabama</td><td>421</td><td>1.96%</td><td>1</td><td>California</td><td>3,158</td><td>14.69%</td></tr>
<tr><td>40</td><td>Alaska</td><td>42</td><td>0.20%</td><td>2</td><td>New York</td><td>2,246</td><td>10.45%</td></tr>
<tr><td>23</td><td>Arizona</td><td>237</td><td>1.10%</td><td>3</td><td>Texas</td><td>2,029</td><td>9.44%</td></tr>
<tr><td>26</td><td>Arkansas</td><td>203</td><td>0.94%</td><td>4</td><td>Florida</td><td>1,405</td><td>6.53%</td></tr>
<tr><td>1</td><td>California</td><td>3,158</td><td>14.69%</td><td>5</td><td>Illinois</td><td>1,051</td><td>4.89%</td></tr>
<tr><td>29</td><td>Colorado</td><td>146</td><td>0.68%</td><td>6</td><td>Michigan</td><td>993</td><td>4.62%</td></tr>
<tr><td>27</td><td>Connecticut</td><td>190</td><td>0.88%</td><td>7</td><td>Georgia</td><td>820</td><td>3.81%</td></tr>
<tr><td>44</td><td>Delaware</td><td>34</td><td>0.16%</td><td>8</td><td>Pennsylvania</td><td>753</td><td>3.50%</td></tr>
<tr><td>4</td><td>Florida</td><td>1,405</td><td>6.53%</td><td>9</td><td>Louisiana</td><td>653</td><td>3.04%</td></tr>
<tr><td>7</td><td>Georgia</td><td>820</td><td>3.81%</td><td>10</td><td>Ohio</td><td>652</td><td>3.03%</td></tr>
<tr><td>37</td><td>Hawaii</td><td>53</td><td>0.25%</td><td>11</td><td>North Carolina</td><td>584</td><td>2.72%</td></tr>
<tr><td>45</td><td>Idaho</td><td>26</td><td>0.12%</td><td>12</td><td>Maryland</td><td>544</td><td>2.53%</td></tr>
<tr><td>5</td><td>Illinois</td><td>1,051</td><td>4.89%</td><td>13</td><td>Virginia</td><td>480</td><td>2.23%</td></tr>
<tr><td>18</td><td>Indiana</td><td>353</td><td>1.64%</td><td>14</td><td>Alabama</td><td>421</td><td>1.96%</td></tr>
<tr><td>36</td><td>Iowa</td><td>54</td><td>0.25%</td><td>15</td><td>Tennessee</td><td>417</td><td>1.94%</td></tr>
<tr><td>30</td><td>Kansas</td><td>138</td><td>0.64%</td><td>16</td><td>Missouri</td><td>409</td><td>1.90%</td></tr>
<tr><td>20</td><td>Kentucky</td><td>293</td><td>1.36%</td><td>17</td><td>New Jersey</td><td>394</td><td>1.83%</td></tr>
<tr><td>9</td><td>Louisiana</td><td>653</td><td>3.04%</td><td>18</td><td>Indiana</td><td>353</td><td>1.64%</td></tr>
<tr><td>42</td><td>Maine</td><td>39</td><td>0.18%</td><td>19</td><td>South Carolina</td><td>320</td><td>1.49%</td></tr>
<tr><td>12</td><td>Maryland</td><td>544</td><td>2.53%</td><td>20</td><td>Kentucky</td><td>293</td><td>1.36%</td></tr>
<tr><td>21</td><td>Massachusetts</td><td>254</td><td>1.18%</td><td>21</td><td>Massachusetts</td><td>254</td><td>1.18%</td></tr>
<tr><td>6</td><td>Michigan</td><td>993</td><td>4.62%</td><td>22</td><td>Mississippi</td><td>253</td><td>1.18%</td></tr>
<tr><td>34</td><td>Minnesota</td><td>111</td><td>0.52%</td><td>23</td><td>Arizona</td><td>237</td><td>1.10%</td></tr>
<tr><td>22</td><td>Mississippi</td><td>253</td><td>1.18%</td><td>24</td><td>Oklahoma</td><td>210</td><td>0.98%</td></tr>
<tr><td>16</td><td>Missouri</td><td>409</td><td>1.90%</td><td>25</td><td>Washington</td><td>209</td><td>0.97%</td></tr>
<tr><td>46</td><td>Montana</td><td>23</td><td>0.11%</td><td>26</td><td>Arkansas</td><td>203</td><td>0.94%</td></tr>
<tr><td>41</td><td>Nebraska</td><td>40</td><td>0.19%</td><td>27</td><td>Connecticut</td><td>190</td><td>0.88%</td></tr>
<tr><td>35</td><td>Nevada</td><td>91</td><td>0.42%</td><td>28</td><td>Wisconsin</td><td>176</td><td>0.82%</td></tr>
<tr><td>43</td><td>New Hampshire</td><td>36</td><td>0.17%</td><td>29</td><td>Colorado</td><td>146</td><td>0.68%</td></tr>
<tr><td>17</td><td>New Jersey</td><td>394</td><td>1.83%</td><td>30</td><td>Kansas</td><td>138</td><td>0.64%</td></tr>
<tr><td>32</td><td>New Mexico</td><td>132</td><td>0.61%</td><td>31</td><td>Oregon</td><td>134</td><td>0.62%</td></tr>
<tr><td>2</td><td>New York</td><td>2,246</td><td>10.45%</td><td>32</td><td>New Mexico</td><td>132</td><td>0.61%</td></tr>
<tr><td>11</td><td>North Carolina</td><td>584</td><td>2.72%</td><td>33</td><td>West Virginia</td><td>121</td><td>0.56%</td></tr>
<tr><td>50</td><td>North Dakota</td><td>4</td><td>0.02%</td><td>34</td><td>Minnesota</td><td>111</td><td>0.52%</td></tr>
<tr><td>10</td><td>Ohio</td><td>652</td><td>3.03%</td><td>35</td><td>Nevada</td><td>91</td><td>0.42%</td></tr>
<tr><td>24</td><td>Oklahoma</td><td>210</td><td>0.98%</td><td>36</td><td>Iowa</td><td>54</td><td>0.25%</td></tr>
<tr><td>31</td><td>Oregon</td><td>134</td><td>0.62%</td><td>37</td><td>Hawaii</td><td>53</td><td>0.25%</td></tr>
<tr><td>8</td><td>Pennsylvania</td><td>753</td><td>3.50%</td><td>38</td><td>Rhode Island</td><td>49</td><td>0.23%</td></tr>
<tr><td>38</td><td>Rhode Island</td><td>49</td><td>0.23%</td><td>39</td><td>Utah</td><td>45</td><td>0.21%</td></tr>
<tr><td>19</td><td>South Carolina</td><td>320</td><td>1.49%</td><td>40</td><td>Alaska</td><td>42</td><td>0.20%</td></tr>
<tr><td>49</td><td>South Dakota</td><td>9</td><td>0.04%</td><td>41</td><td>Nebraska</td><td>40</td><td>0.19%</td></tr>
<tr><td>15</td><td>Tennessee</td><td>417</td><td>1.94%</td><td>42</td><td>Maine</td><td>39</td><td>0.18%</td></tr>
<tr><td>3</td><td>Texas</td><td>2,029</td><td>9.44%</td><td>43</td><td>New Hampshire</td><td>36</td><td>0.17%</td></tr>
<tr><td>39</td><td>Utah</td><td>45</td><td>0.21%</td><td>44</td><td>Delaware</td><td>34</td><td>0.16%</td></tr>
<tr><td>48</td><td>Vermont</td><td>11</td><td>0.05%</td><td>45</td><td>Idaho</td><td>26</td><td>0.12%</td></tr>
<tr><td>13</td><td>Virginia</td><td>480</td><td>2.23%</td><td>46</td><td>Montana</td><td>23</td><td>0.11%</td></tr>
<tr><td>25</td><td>Washington</td><td>209</td><td>0.97%</td><td>47</td><td>Wyoming</td><td>21</td><td>0.10%</td></tr>
<tr><td>33</td><td>West Virginia</td><td>121</td><td>0.56%</td><td>48</td><td>Vermont</td><td>11</td><td>0.05%</td></tr>
<tr><td>28</td><td>Wisconsin</td><td>176</td><td>0.82%</td><td>49</td><td>South Dakota</td><td>9</td><td>0.04%</td></tr>
<tr><td>47</td><td>Wyoming</td><td>21</td><td>0.10%</td><td>50</td><td>North Dakota</td><td>4</td><td>0.02%</td></tr>
<tr><td></td><td></td><td></td><td></td><td></td><td>District of Columbia</td><td>434</td><td>2.02%</td></tr>
</table>

Source: U.S. Department of Justice, Federal Bureau of Investigation
   "Crime in the United States 1989" (Uniform Crime Reports, August 5, 1990)
*Includes nonnegligent manslaughter.

Percent Change in Number of Murders: 1989 to 1993

National Percent Change = 14.1% Increase*

ALPHA ORDER				RANK ORDER		
RANK	STATE	PERCENT CHANGE		RANK	STATE	PERCENT CHANGE
28	Alabama	15.0		1	North Dakota	175.0
17	Alaska	28.6		2	South Dakota	166.7
7	Arizona	43.0		3	Vermont	90.9
24	Arkansas	21.7		4	Nevada	58.2
14	California	29.7		5	Nebraska	57.5
8	Colorado	41.1		6	Missouri	44.3
32	Connecticut	8.4		7	Arizona	43.0
38	Delaware	2.9		8	Colorado	41.1
44	Florida	(12.9)		8	Mississippi	41.1
41	Georgia	(3.8)		10	Minnesota	39.6
46	Hawaii	(15.1)		11	North Carolina	34.4
21	Idaho	23.1		12	Louisiana	33.8
18	Illinois	26.7		13	Oklahoma	30.0
23	Indiana	21.8		14	California	29.7
22	Iowa	22.2		14	Washington	29.7
26	Kansas	16.7		16	Utah	28.9
45	Kentucky	(15.0)		17	Alaska	28.6
12	Louisiana	33.8		18	Illinois	26.7
50	Maine	(48.7)		19	Wisconsin	26.1
27	Maryland	16.2		20	Tennessee	24.9
43	Massachusetts	(8.3)		21	Idaho	23.1
42	Michigan	(6.0)		22	Iowa	22.2
10	Minnesota	39.6		23	Indiana	21.8
8	Mississippi	41.1		24	Arkansas	21.7
6	Missouri	44.3		25	South Carolina	17.8
31	Montana	8.7		26	Kansas	16.7
5	Nebraska	57.5		27	Maryland	16.2
4	Nevada	58.2		28	Alabama	15.0
49	New Hampshire	(36.1)		29	Virginia	12.3
34	New Jersey	6.1		30	Pennsylvania	9.3
40	New Mexico	(1.5)		31	Montana	8.7
33	New York	7.7		32	Connecticut	8.4
11	North Carolina	34.4		33	New York	7.7
1	North Dakota	175.0		34	New Jersey	6.1
39	Ohio	2.3		35	Texas	5.8
13	Oklahoma	30.0		36	Oregon	4.5
36	Oregon	4.5		37	West Virginia	4.1
30	Pennsylvania	9.3		38	Delaware	2.9
47	Rhode Island	(20.4)		39	Ohio	2.3
25	South Carolina	17.8		40	New Mexico	(1.5)
2	South Dakota	166.7		41	Georgia	(3.8)
20	Tennessee	24.9		42	Michigan	(6.0)
35	Texas	5.8		43	Massachusetts	(8.3)
16	Utah	28.9		44	Florida	(12.9)
3	Vermont	90.9		45	Kentucky	(15.0)
29	Virginia	12.3		46	Hawaii	(15.1)
14	Washington	29.7		47	Rhode Island	(20.4)
37	West Virginia	4.1		48	Wyoming	(23.8)
19	Wisconsin	26.1		49	New Hampshire	(36.1)
48	Wyoming	(23.8)		50	Maine	(48.7)
				District of Columbia		4.6

Source: Morgan Quitno Corporation using data from U.S. Department of Justice, Federal Bureau of Investigation
"Crime in the United States" (Uniform Crime Reports, 1989 and 1993 editions)
*Includes nonnegligent manslaughter.

Murder Rate in 1989

National Rate = 8.7 Murders per 100,000 Population*

ALPHA ORDER

RANK	STATE	RATE
9	Alabama	10.2
18	Alaska	8.0
22	Arizona	6.7
15	Arkansas	8.4
7	California	10.9
35	Colorado	4.4
28	Connecticut	5.9
30	Delaware	5.1
6	Florida	11.1
2	Georgia	12.7
33	Hawaii	4.8
43	Idaho	2.6
12	Illinois	9.0
25	Indiana	6.3
47	Iowa	1.9
29	Kansas	5.5
19	Kentucky	7.9
1	Louisiana	14.9
41	Maine	3.2
5	Maryland	11.6
38	Massachusetts	4.3
8	Michigan	10.7
45	Minnesota	2.5
10	Mississippi	9.7
19	Missouri	7.9
42	Montana	2.9
45	Nebraska	2.5
17	Nevada	8.2
40	New Hampshire	3.3
30	New Jersey	5.1
14	New Mexico	8.6
3	New York	12.5
13	North Carolina	8.9
50	North Dakota	0.6
27	Ohio	6.0
23	Oklahoma	6.5
33	Oregon	4.8
25	Pennsylvania	6.3
32	Rhode Island	4.9
11	South Carolina	9.1
49	South Dakota	1.3
15	Tennessee	8.4
4	Texas	11.9
43	Utah	2.6
47	Vermont	1.9
19	Virginia	7.9
35	Washington	4.4
23	West Virginia	6.5
39	Wisconsin	3.6
35	Wyoming	4.4

RANK ORDER

RANK	STATE	RATE
1	Louisiana	14.9
2	Georgia	12.7
3	New York	12.5
4	Texas	11.9
5	Maryland	11.6
6	Florida	11.1
7	California	10.9
8	Michigan	10.7
9	Alabama	10.2
10	Mississippi	9.7
11	South Carolina	9.1
12	Illinois	9.0
13	North Carolina	8.9
14	New Mexico	8.6
15	Arkansas	8.4
15	Tennessee	8.4
17	Nevada	8.2
18	Alaska	8.0
19	Kentucky	7.9
19	Missouri	7.9
19	Virginia	7.9
22	Arizona	6.7
23	Oklahoma	6.5
23	West Virginia	6.5
25	Indiana	6.3
25	Pennsylvania	6.3
27	Ohio	6.0
28	Connecticut	5.9
29	Kansas	5.5
30	Delaware	5.1
30	New Jersey	5.1
32	Rhode Island	4.9
33	Hawaii	4.8
33	Oregon	4.8
35	Colorado	4.4
35	Washington	4.4
35	Wyoming	4.4
38	Massachusetts	4.3
39	Wisconsin	3.6
40	New Hampshire	3.3
41	Maine	3.2
42	Montana	2.9
43	Idaho	2.6
43	Utah	2.6
45	Minnesota	2.5
45	Nebraska	2.5
47	Iowa	1.9
47	Vermont	1.9
49	South Dakota	1.3
50	North Dakota	0.6
	District of Columbia	71.9

Source: U.S. Department of Justice, Federal Bureau of Investigation
   "Crime in the United States 1989" (Uniform Crime Reports, August 5, 1990)
*Includes nonnegligent manslaughter.

Percent Change in Murder Rate: 1989 to 1993

National Percent Change = 9.2% Increase*

<table>
<tr><td colspan="3">ALPHA ORDER</td><td colspan="3">RANK ORDER</td></tr>
<tr><th>RANK</th><th>STATE</th><th>PERCENT CHANGE</th><th>RANK</th><th>STATE</th><th>PERCENT CHANGE</th></tr>
<tr><td>24</td><td>Alabama</td><td>13.7</td><td>1</td><td>North Dakota</td><td>183.3</td></tr>
<tr><td>26</td><td>Alaska</td><td>12.5</td><td>2</td><td>South Dakota</td><td>161.5</td></tr>
<tr><td>11</td><td>Arizona</td><td>28.4</td><td>3</td><td>Vermont</td><td>89.5</td></tr>
<tr><td>16</td><td>Arkansas</td><td>21.4</td><td>4</td><td>Nebraska</td><td>56.0</td></tr>
<tr><td>19</td><td>California</td><td>20.2</td><td>5</td><td>Missouri</td><td>43.0</td></tr>
<tr><td>9</td><td>Colorado</td><td>31.8</td><td>6</td><td>Mississippi</td><td>39.2</td></tr>
<tr><td>30</td><td>Connecticut</td><td>6.8</td><td>7</td><td>Louisiana</td><td>36.2</td></tr>
<tr><td>38</td><td>Delaware</td><td>(2.0)</td><td>8</td><td>Minnesota</td><td>36.0</td></tr>
<tr><td>45</td><td>Florida</td><td>(19.8)</td><td>9</td><td>Colorado</td><td>31.8</td></tr>
<tr><td>43</td><td>Georgia</td><td>(10.2)</td><td>10</td><td>Oklahoma</td><td>29.2</td></tr>
<tr><td>47</td><td>Hawaii</td><td>(20.8)</td><td>11</td><td>Arizona</td><td>28.4</td></tr>
<tr><td>27</td><td>Idaho</td><td>11.5</td><td>12</td><td>North Carolina</td><td>27.0</td></tr>
<tr><td>14</td><td>Illinois</td><td>26.7</td><td>13</td><td>Nevada</td><td>26.8</td></tr>
<tr><td>21</td><td>Indiana</td><td>19.0</td><td>14</td><td>Illinois</td><td>26.7</td></tr>
<tr><td>18</td><td>Iowa</td><td>21.1</td><td>15</td><td>Wisconsin</td><td>22.2</td></tr>
<tr><td>23</td><td>Kansas</td><td>16.4</td><td>16</td><td>Arkansas</td><td>21.4</td></tr>
<tr><td>44</td><td>Kentucky</td><td>(16.5)</td><td>16</td><td>Tennessee</td><td>21.4</td></tr>
<tr><td>7</td><td>Louisiana</td><td>36.2</td><td>18</td><td>Iowa</td><td>21.1</td></tr>
<tr><td>50</td><td>Maine</td><td>(50.0)</td><td>19</td><td>California</td><td>20.2</td></tr>
<tr><td>28</td><td>Maryland</td><td>9.5</td><td>20</td><td>Utah</td><td>19.2</td></tr>
<tr><td>42</td><td>Massachusetts</td><td>(9.3)</td><td>21</td><td>Indiana</td><td>19.0</td></tr>
<tr><td>41</td><td>Michigan</td><td>(8.4)</td><td>22</td><td>Washington</td><td>18.2</td></tr>
<tr><td>8</td><td>Minnesota</td><td>36.0</td><td>23</td><td>Kansas</td><td>16.4</td></tr>
<tr><td>6</td><td>Mississippi</td><td>39.2</td><td>24</td><td>Alabama</td><td>13.7</td></tr>
<tr><td>5</td><td>Missouri</td><td>43.0</td><td>25</td><td>South Carolina</td><td>13.2</td></tr>
<tr><td>35</td><td>Montana</td><td>3.4</td><td>26</td><td>Alaska</td><td>12.5</td></tr>
<tr><td>4</td><td>Nebraska</td><td>56.0</td><td>27</td><td>Idaho</td><td>11.5</td></tr>
<tr><td>13</td><td>Nevada</td><td>26.8</td><td>28</td><td>Maryland</td><td>9.5</td></tr>
<tr><td>49</td><td>New Hampshire</td><td>(39.4)</td><td>29</td><td>Pennsylvania</td><td>7.9</td></tr>
<tr><td>34</td><td>New Jersey</td><td>3.9</td><td>30</td><td>Connecticut</td><td>6.8</td></tr>
<tr><td>40</td><td>New Mexico</td><td>(7.0)</td><td>31</td><td>New York</td><td>6.4</td></tr>
<tr><td>31</td><td>New York</td><td>6.4</td><td>32</td><td>West Virginia</td><td>6.2</td></tr>
<tr><td>12</td><td>North Carolina</td><td>27.0</td><td>33</td><td>Virginia</td><td>5.1</td></tr>
<tr><td>1</td><td>North Dakota</td><td>183.3</td><td>34</td><td>New Jersey</td><td>3.9</td></tr>
<tr><td>36</td><td>Ohio</td><td>0.0</td><td>35</td><td>Montana</td><td>3.4</td></tr>
<tr><td>10</td><td>Oklahoma</td><td>29.2</td><td>36</td><td>Ohio</td><td>0.0</td></tr>
<tr><td>39</td><td>Oregon</td><td>(4.2)</td><td>36</td><td>Texas</td><td>0.0</td></tr>
<tr><td>29</td><td>Pennsylvania</td><td>7.9</td><td>38</td><td>Delaware</td><td>(2.0)</td></tr>
<tr><td>46</td><td>Rhode Island</td><td>(20.4)</td><td>39</td><td>Oregon</td><td>(4.2)</td></tr>
<tr><td>25</td><td>South Carolina</td><td>13.2</td><td>40</td><td>New Mexico</td><td>(7.0)</td></tr>
<tr><td>2</td><td>South Dakota</td><td>161.5</td><td>41</td><td>Michigan</td><td>(8.4)</td></tr>
<tr><td>16</td><td>Tennessee</td><td>21.4</td><td>42</td><td>Massachusetts</td><td>(9.3)</td></tr>
<tr><td>36</td><td>Texas</td><td>0.0</td><td>43</td><td>Georgia</td><td>(10.2)</td></tr>
<tr><td>20</td><td>Utah</td><td>19.2</td><td>44</td><td>Kentucky</td><td>(16.5)</td></tr>
<tr><td>3</td><td>Vermont</td><td>89.5</td><td>45</td><td>Florida</td><td>(19.8)</td></tr>
<tr><td>33</td><td>Virginia</td><td>5.1</td><td>46</td><td>Rhode Island</td><td>(20.4)</td></tr>
<tr><td>22</td><td>Washington</td><td>18.2</td><td>47</td><td>Hawaii</td><td>(20.8)</td></tr>
<tr><td>32</td><td>West Virginia</td><td>6.2</td><td>48</td><td>Wyoming</td><td>(22.7)</td></tr>
<tr><td>15</td><td>Wisconsin</td><td>22.2</td><td>49</td><td>New Hampshire</td><td>(39.4)</td></tr>
<tr><td>48</td><td>Wyoming</td><td>(22.7)</td><td>50</td><td>Maine</td><td>(50.0)</td></tr>
</table>

District of Columbia   9.2

Source: Morgan Quitno Corporation using data from U.S. Department of Justice, Federal Bureau of Investigation "Crime in the United States" (Uniform Crime Reports, 1989 and 1993 editions)
Includes nonnegligent manslaughter.

Rapes in 1989

National Total = 94,504 Rapes*

ALPHA ORDER					RANK ORDER			

RANK	STATE	RAPES	% of USA
24	Alabama	1,276	1.35%
42	Alaska	279	0.30%
23	Arizona	1,286	1.36%
29	Arkansas	924	0.98%
1	California	11,966	12.66%
26	Colorado	1,202	1.27%
32	Connecticut	892	0.94%
35	Delaware	569	0.60%
4	Florida	6,299	6.67%
8	Georgia	3,150	3.33%
36	Hawaii	496	0.52%
44	Idaho	236	0.25%
7	Illinois	4,161	4.40%
15	Indiana	1,804	1.91%
38	Iowa	459	0.49%
30	Kansas	917	0.97%
30	Kentucky	917	0.97%
17	Louisiana	1,675	1.77%
45	Maine	229	0.24%
16	Maryland	1,783	1.89%
14	Massachusetts	1,881	1.99%
3	Michigan	6,624	7.01%
21	Minnesota	1,363	1.44%
27	Mississippi	1,017	1.08%
20	Missouri	1,587	1.68%
47	Montana	145	0.15%
39	Nebraska	381	0.40%
34	Nevada	662	0.70%
41	New Hampshire	327	0.35%
11	New Jersey	2,449	2.59%
33	New Mexico	702	0.74%
5	New York	5,242	5.55%
13	North Carolina	1,964	2.08%
50	North Dakota	78	0.08%
6	Ohio	4,872	5.16%
25	Oklahoma	1,209	1.28%
22	Oregon	1,314	1.39%
9	Pennsylvania	2,963	3.14%
43	Rhode Island	266	0.28%
19	South Carolina	1,632	1.73%
45	South Dakota	229	0.24%
12	Tennessee	2,270	2.40%
2	Texas	7,951	8.41%
37	Utah	489	0.52%
49	Vermont	131	0.14%
18	Virginia	1,638	1.73%
10	Washington	2,938	3.11%
40	West Virginia	347	0.37%
28	Wisconsin	993	1.05%
48	Wyoming	134	0.14%

RANK	STATE	RAPES	% of USA
1	California	11,966	12.66%
2	Texas	7,951	8.41%
3	Michigan	6,624	7.01%
4	Florida	6,299	6.67%
5	New York	5,242	5.55%
6	Ohio	4,872	5.16%
7	Illinois	4,161	4.40%
8	Georgia	3,150	3.33%
9	Pennsylvania	2,963	3.14%
10	Washington	2,938	3.11%
11	New Jersey	2,449	2.59%
12	Tennessee	2,270	2.40%
13	North Carolina	1,964	2.08%
14	Massachusetts	1,881	1.99%
15	Indiana	1,804	1.91%
16	Maryland	1,783	1.89%
17	Louisiana	1,675	1.77%
18	Virginia	1,638	1.73%
19	South Carolina	1,632	1.73%
20	Missouri	1,587	1.68%
21	Minnesota	1,363	1.44%
22	Oregon	1,314	1.39%
23	Arizona	1,286	1.36%
24	Alabama	1,276	1.35%
25	Oklahoma	1,209	1.28%
26	Colorado	1,202	1.27%
27	Mississippi	1,017	1.08%
28	Wisconsin	993	1.05%
29	Arkansas	924	0.98%
30	Kansas	917	0.97%
30	Kentucky	917	0.97%
32	Connecticut	892	0.94%
33	New Mexico	702	0.74%
34	Nevada	662	0.70%
35	Delaware	569	0.60%
36	Hawaii	496	0.52%
37	Utah	489	0.52%
38	Iowa	459	0.49%
39	Nebraska	381	0.40%
40	West Virginia	347	0.37%
41	New Hampshire	327	0.35%
42	Alaska	279	0.30%
43	Rhode Island	266	0.28%
44	Idaho	236	0.25%
45	Maine	229	0.24%
45	South Dakota	229	0.24%
47	Montana	145	0.15%
48	Wyoming	134	0.14%
49	Vermont	131	0.14%
50	North Dakota	78	0.08%
	District of Columbia	186	0.20%

Source: U.S. Department of Justice, Federal Bureau of Investigation
"Crime in the United States 1989" (Uniform Crime Reports, August 5, 1990)
*Forcible rape is the carnal knowledge of a female forcibly and against her will. Assaults or attempts to commit rape by force or threat of force are included. However, statutory rape without force and other sex offenses are excluded.

Percent Change in Number of Rapes: 1989 to 1993

National Percent Change = 10.9% Increase*

ALPHA ORDER			RANK ORDER		
RANK	STATE	PERCENT CHANGE	RANK	STATE	PERCENT CHANGE
30	Alabama	15.3	1	North Dakota	91.0
2	Alaska	79.9	2	Alaska	79.9
29	Arizona	15.7	3	Vermont	74.8
34	Arkansas	11.3	4	Utah	69.5
43	California	(1.7)	5	Idaho	64.4
12	Colorado	35.9	6	Montana	61.4
48	Connecticut	(10.3)	7	New Hampshire	52.6
46	Delaware	(5.3)	8	Iowa	49.5
26	Florida	16.8	9	Maine	43.7
50	Georgia	(22.3)	10	Kentucky	41.9
49	Hawaii	(20.6)	11	South Dakota	38.9
5	Idaho	64.4	12	Colorado	35.9
44	Illinois	(2.8)	13	Oklahoma	31.7
18	Indiana	23.8	14	Nevada	27.8
8	Iowa	49.5	14	Wisconsin	27.8
35	Kansas	10.8	16	Virginia	27.2
10	Kentucky	41.9	17	Texas	24.8
37	Louisiana	8.5	18	Indiana	23.8
9	Maine	43.7	19	Maryland	22.5
19	Maryland	22.5	20	North Carolina	21.1
40	Massachusetts	6.6	21	Wyoming	20.1
42	Michigan	1.8	22	New Mexico	19.9
28	Minnesota	16.5	23	Missouri	19.3
36	Mississippi	10.6	24	Oregon	18.3
23	Missouri	19.3	25	Nebraska	17.3
6	Montana	61.4	26	Florida	16.8
25	Nebraska	17.3	27	South Carolina	16.7
14	Nevada	27.8	28	Minnesota	16.5
7	New Hampshire	52.6	29	Arizona	15.7
47	New Jersey	(9.6)	30	Alabama	15.3
22	New Mexico	19.9	31	Washington	15.2
45	New York	(4.5)	32	Tennessee	12.1
20	North Carolina	21.1	33	Ohio	11.7
1	North Dakota	91.0	34	Arkansas	11.3
33	Ohio	11.7	35	Kansas	10.8
13	Oklahoma	31.7	36	Mississippi	10.6
24	Oregon	18.3	37	Louisiana	8.5
38	Pennsylvania	7.8	38	Pennsylvania	7.8
39	Rhode Island	7.5	39	Rhode Island	7.5
27	South Carolina	16.7	40	Massachusetts	6.6
11	South Dakota	38.9	41	West Virginia	5.2
32	Tennessee	12.1	42	Michigan	1.8
17	Texas	24.8	43	California	(1.7)
4	Utah	69.5	44	Illinois	(2.8)
3	Vermont	74.8	45	New York	(4.5)
16	Virginia	27.2	46	Delaware	(5.3)
31	Washington	15.2	47	New Jersey	(9.6)
41	West Virginia	5.2	48	Connecticut	(10.3)
14	Wisconsin	27.8	49	Hawaii	(20.6)
21	Wyoming	20.1	50	Georgia	(22.3)
				District of Columbia	74.2

Source: Morgan Quitno Corporation using data from U.S. Department of Justice, Federal Bureau of Investigation
"Crime in the United States" (Uniform Crime Reports, 1989 and 1993 editions)
*Forcible rape is the carnal knowledge of a female forcibly and against her will. Assaults or attempts to commit rape by force or threat of force are included. However, statutory rape without force and other sex offenses are excluded.

Rape Rate in 1989

National Rate = 38.1 Rapes per 100,000 Population*

RANK	STATE	RATE
30	Alabama	31.0
5	Alaska	52.9
22	Arizona	36.2
17	Arkansas	38.4
15	California	41.2
22	Colorado	36.2
37	Connecticut	27.5
1	Delaware	84.5
6	Florida	49.7
7	Georgia	48.9
14	Hawaii	44.6
43	Idaho	23.3
24	Illinois	35.7
25	Indiana	32.3
49	Iowa	16.2
21	Kansas	36.5
40	Kentucky	24.6
18	Louisiana	38.2
46	Maine	18.7
19	Maryland	38.0
27	Massachusetts	31.8
2	Michigan	71.4
29	Minnesota	31.3
16	Mississippi	38.8
31	Missouri	30.8
48	Montana	18.0
42	Nebraska	23.6
4	Nevada	59.6
33	New Hampshire	29.5
28	New Jersey	31.7
12	New Mexico	45.9
34	New York	29.2
32	North Carolina	29.9
50	North Dakota	11.8
13	Ohio	44.7
20	Oklahoma	37.5
9	Oregon	46.6
40	Pennsylvania	24.6
39	Rhode Island	26.7
10	South Carolina	46.5
26	South Dakota	32.0
11	Tennessee	46.0
8	Texas	46.8
35	Utah	28.6
44	Vermont	23.1
38	Virginia	26.9
3	Washington	61.7
46	West Virginia	18.7
45	Wisconsin	20.4
36	Wyoming	28.2

RANK	STATE	RATE
1	Delaware	84.5
2	Michigan	71.4
3	Washington	61.7
4	Nevada	59.6
5	Alaska	52.9
6	Florida	49.7
7	Georgia	48.9
8	Texas	46.8
9	Oregon	46.6
10	South Carolina	46.5
11	Tennessee	46.0
12	New Mexico	45.9
13	Ohio	44.7
14	Hawaii	44.6
15	California	41.2
16	Mississippi	38.8
17	Arkansas	38.4
18	Louisiana	38.2
19	Maryland	38.0
20	Oklahoma	37.5
21	Kansas	36.5
22	Arizona	36.2
22	Colorado	36.2
24	Illinois	35.7
25	Indiana	32.3
26	South Dakota	32.0
27	Massachusetts	31.8
28	New Jersey	31.7
29	Minnesota	31.3
30	Alabama	31.0
31	Missouri	30.8
32	North Carolina	29.9
33	New Hampshire	29.5
34	New York	29.2
35	Utah	28.6
36	Wyoming	28.2
37	Connecticut	27.5
38	Virginia	26.9
39	Rhode Island	26.7
40	Kentucky	24.6
40	Pennsylvania	24.6
42	Nebraska	23.6
43	Idaho	23.3
44	Vermont	23.1
45	Wisconsin	20.4
46	Maine	18.7
46	West Virginia	18.7
48	Montana	18.0
49	Iowa	16.2
50	North Dakota	11.8

	District of Columbia	30.8

Source: U.S. Department of Justice, Federal Bureau of Investigation
   "Crime in the United States 1989" (Uniform Crime Reports, August 5, 1990)
*Forcible rape is the carnal knowledge of a female forcibly and against her will. Assaults or attempts to commit rape by force or threat of force are included. However, statutory rape without force and other sex offenses are excluded.

Percent Change in Rape Rate: 1989 to 1993

National Percent Change = 6.6% Increase*

<table>
<tr><td colspan="3"><u>ALPHA ORDER</u></td><td colspan="3"><u>RANK ORDER</u></td></tr>
<tr><td>RANK</td><td>STATE</td><td>PERCENT CHANGE</td><td>RANK</td><td>STATE</td><td>PERCENT CHANGE</td></tr>
<tr><td>24</td><td>Alabama</td><td>13.2</td><td>1</td><td>North Dakota</td><td>99.2</td></tr>
<tr><td>3</td><td>Alaska</td><td>58.4</td><td>2</td><td>Vermont</td><td>72.3</td></tr>
<tr><td>39</td><td>Arizona</td><td>4.4</td><td>3</td><td>Alaska</td><td>58.4</td></tr>
<tr><td>28</td><td>Arkansas</td><td>10.4</td><td>4</td><td>Utah</td><td>55.9</td></tr>
<tr><td>45</td><td>California</td><td>(8.5)</td><td>5</td><td>Montana</td><td>55.0</td></tr>
<tr><td>13</td><td>Colorado</td><td>26.5</td><td>6</td><td>Idaho</td><td>51.5</td></tr>
<tr><td>47</td><td>Connecticut</td><td>(11.3)</td><td>7</td><td>Iowa</td><td>50.6</td></tr>
<tr><td>46</td><td>Delaware</td><td>(8.9)</td><td>8</td><td>New Hampshire</td><td>50.5</td></tr>
<tr><td>34</td><td>Florida</td><td>8.2</td><td>9</td><td>Maine</td><td>42.2</td></tr>
<tr><td>50</td><td>Georgia</td><td>(27.6)</td><td>10</td><td>Kentucky</td><td>39.4</td></tr>
<tr><td>49</td><td>Hawaii</td><td>(24.7)</td><td>11</td><td>South Dakota</td><td>39.1</td></tr>
<tr><td>6</td><td>Idaho</td><td>51.5</td><td>12</td><td>Oklahoma</td><td>31.5</td></tr>
<tr><td>43</td><td>Illinois</td><td>(3.1)</td><td>13</td><td>Colorado</td><td>26.5</td></tr>
<tr><td>16</td><td>Indiana</td><td>21.1</td><td>14</td><td>Wisconsin</td><td>23.5</td></tr>
<tr><td>7</td><td>Iowa</td><td>50.6</td><td>15</td><td>Wyoming</td><td>21.6</td></tr>
<tr><td>30</td><td>Kansas</td><td>9.9</td><td>16</td><td>Indiana</td><td>21.1</td></tr>
<tr><td>10</td><td>Kentucky</td><td>39.4</td><td>17</td><td>Virginia</td><td>19.3</td></tr>
<tr><td>27</td><td>Louisiana</td><td>10.7</td><td>18</td><td>Nebraska</td><td>17.8</td></tr>
<tr><td>9</td><td>Maine</td><td>42.2</td><td>19</td><td>Missouri</td><td>17.5</td></tr>
<tr><td>21</td><td>Maryland</td><td>15.8</td><td>19</td><td>Texas</td><td>17.5</td></tr>
<tr><td>38</td><td>Massachusetts</td><td>5.0</td><td>21</td><td>Maryland</td><td>15.8</td></tr>
<tr><td>42</td><td>Michigan</td><td>(0.4)</td><td>22</td><td>North Carolina</td><td>14.7</td></tr>
<tr><td>25</td><td>Minnesota</td><td>12.5</td><td>23</td><td>New Mexico</td><td>13.5</td></tr>
<tr><td>31</td><td>Mississippi</td><td>9.8</td><td>24</td><td>Alabama</td><td>13.2</td></tr>
<tr><td>19</td><td>Missouri</td><td>17.5</td><td>25</td><td>Minnesota</td><td>12.5</td></tr>
<tr><td>5</td><td>Montana</td><td>55.0</td><td>25</td><td>South Carolina</td><td>12.5</td></tr>
<tr><td>18</td><td>Nebraska</td><td>17.8</td><td>27</td><td>Louisiana</td><td>10.7</td></tr>
<tr><td>41</td><td>Nevada</td><td>2.2</td><td>28</td><td>Arkansas</td><td>10.4</td></tr>
<tr><td>8</td><td>New Hampshire</td><td>50.5</td><td>29</td><td>Oregon</td><td>10.1</td></tr>
<tr><td>48</td><td>New Jersey</td><td>(11.4)</td><td>30</td><td>Kansas</td><td>9.9</td></tr>
<tr><td>23</td><td>New Mexico</td><td>13.5</td><td>31</td><td>Mississippi</td><td>9.8</td></tr>
<tr><td>44</td><td>New York</td><td>(5.8)</td><td>31</td><td>Ohio</td><td>9.8</td></tr>
<tr><td>22</td><td>North Carolina</td><td>14.7</td><td>33</td><td>Tennessee</td><td>8.5</td></tr>
<tr><td>1</td><td>North Dakota</td><td>99.2</td><td>34</td><td>Florida</td><td>8.2</td></tr>
<tr><td>31</td><td>Ohio</td><td>9.8</td><td>35</td><td>Pennsylvania</td><td>7.7</td></tr>
<tr><td>12</td><td>Oklahoma</td><td>31.5</td><td>36</td><td>West Virginia</td><td>7.5</td></tr>
<tr><td>29</td><td>Oregon</td><td>10.1</td><td>37</td><td>Rhode Island</td><td>7.1</td></tr>
<tr><td>35</td><td>Pennsylvania</td><td>7.7</td><td>38</td><td>Massachusetts</td><td>5.0</td></tr>
<tr><td>37</td><td>Rhode Island</td><td>7.1</td><td>39</td><td>Arizona</td><td>4.4</td></tr>
<tr><td>25</td><td>South Carolina</td><td>12.5</td><td>39</td><td>Washington</td><td>4.4</td></tr>
<tr><td>11</td><td>South Dakota</td><td>39.1</td><td>41</td><td>Nevada</td><td>2.2</td></tr>
<tr><td>33</td><td>Tennessee</td><td>8.5</td><td>42</td><td>Michigan</td><td>(0.4)</td></tr>
<tr><td>19</td><td>Texas</td><td>17.5</td><td>43</td><td>Illinois</td><td>(3.1)</td></tr>
<tr><td>4</td><td>Utah</td><td>55.9</td><td>44</td><td>New York</td><td>(5.8)</td></tr>
<tr><td>2</td><td>Vermont</td><td>72.3</td><td>45</td><td>California</td><td>(8.5)</td></tr>
<tr><td>17</td><td>Virginia</td><td>19.3</td><td>46</td><td>Delaware</td><td>(8.9)</td></tr>
<tr><td>39</td><td>Washington</td><td>4.4</td><td>47</td><td>Connecticut</td><td>(11.3)</td></tr>
<tr><td>36</td><td>West Virginia</td><td>7.5</td><td>48</td><td>New Jersey</td><td>(11.4)</td></tr>
<tr><td>14</td><td>Wisconsin</td><td>23.5</td><td>49</td><td>Hawaii</td><td>(24.7)</td></tr>
<tr><td>15</td><td>Wyoming</td><td>21.6</td><td>50</td><td>Georgia</td><td>(27.6)</td></tr>
<tr><td></td><td></td><td></td><td></td><td>District of Columbia</td><td>82.1</td></tr>
</table>

Source: Morgan Quitno Corporation using data from U.S. Department of Justice, Federal Bureau of Investigation
"Crime in the United States" (Uniform Crime Reports, 1989 and 1993 editions)
*Forcible rape is the carnal knowledge of a female forcibly and against her will. Assaults or attempts to commit rape by
force or threat of force are included. However, statutory rape without force and other sex offenses are excluded.

Robberies in 1989

National Total = 578,326 Robberies*

ALPHA ORDER					RANK ORDER			
RANK	STATE	ROBBERIES	% of USA		RANK	STATE	ROBBERIES	% of USA
21	Alabama	5,515	0.95%		1	New York	103,983	17.98%
42	Alaska	356	0.06%		2	California	96,431	16.67%
22	Arizona	4,944	0.85%		3	Florida	51,188	8.85%
31	Arkansas	2,660	0.46%		4	Illinois	39,138	6.77%
2	California	96,431	16.67%		5	Texas	37,913	6.56%
28	Colorado	2,984	0.52%		6	New Jersey	21,139	3.66%
17	Connecticut	6,956	1.20%		7	Michigan	20,616	3.56%
37	Delaware	934	0.16%		8	Ohio	18,635	3.22%
3	Florida	51,188	8.85%		9	Pennsylvania	18,025	3.12%
10	Georgia	17,450	3.02%		10	Georgia	17,450	3.02%
38	Hawaii	925	0.16%		11	Maryland	15,589	2.70%
45	Idaho	152	0.03%		12	Massachusetts	11,980	2.07%
4	Illinois	39,138	6.77%		13	Louisiana	10,397	1.80%
20	Indiana	5,671	0.98%		14	Missouri	10,060	1.74%
36	Iowa	1,108	0.19%		15	North Carolina	8,770	1.52%
32	Kansas	2,508	0.43%		16	Tennessee	7,926	1.37%
29	Kentucky	2,836	0.49%		17	Connecticut	6,956	1.20%
13	Louisiana	10,397	1.80%		18	Washington	6,672	1.15%
43	Maine	293	0.05%		19	Virginia	6,494	1.12%
11	Maryland	15,589	2.70%		20	Indiana	5,671	0.98%
12	Massachusetts	11,980	2.07%		21	Alabama	5,515	0.95%
7	Michigan	20,616	3.56%		22	Arizona	4,944	0.85%
25	Minnesota	4,128	0.71%		23	South Carolina	4,574	0.79%
33	Mississippi	2,053	0.35%		24	Oregon	4,282	0.74%
14	Missouri	10,060	1.74%		25	Minnesota	4,128	0.71%
46	Montana	137	0.02%		26	Oklahoma	4,070	0.70%
40	Nebraska	837	0.14%		27	Wisconsin	3,659	0.63%
30	Nevada	2,784	0.48%		28	Colorado	2,984	0.52%
44	New Hampshire	264	0.05%		29	Kentucky	2,836	0.49%
6	New Jersey	21,139	3.66%		30	Nevada	2,784	0.48%
34	New Mexico	1,607	0.28%		31	Arkansas	2,660	0.46%
1	New York	103,983	17.98%		32	Kansas	2,508	0.43%
15	North Carolina	8,770	1.52%		33	Mississippi	2,053	0.35%
50	North Dakota	61	0.01%		34	New Mexico	1,607	0.28%
8	Ohio	18,635	3.22%		35	Rhode Island	1,122	0.19%
26	Oklahoma	4,070	0.70%		36	Iowa	1,108	0.19%
24	Oregon	4,282	0.74%		37	Delaware	934	0.16%
9	Pennsylvania	18,025	3.12%		38	Hawaii	925	0.16%
35	Rhode Island	1,122	0.19%		39	Utah	898	0.16%
23	South Carolina	4,574	0.79%		40	Nebraska	837	0.14%
48	South Dakota	84	0.01%		41	West Virginia	793	0.14%
16	Tennessee	7,926	1.37%		42	Alaska	356	0.06%
5	Texas	37,913	6.56%		43	Maine	293	0.05%
39	Utah	898	0.16%		44	New Hampshire	264	0.05%
47	Vermont	102	0.02%		45	Idaho	152	0.03%
19	Virginia	6,494	1.12%		46	Montana	137	0.02%
18	Washington	6,672	1.15%		47	Vermont	102	0.02%
41	West Virginia	793	0.14%		48	South Dakota	84	0.01%
27	Wisconsin	3,659	0.63%		49	Wyoming	81	0.01%
49	Wyoming	81	0.01%		50	North Dakota	61	0.01%
						District of Columbia	6,542	1.13%

Source: U.S. Department of Justice, Federal Bureau of Investigation
   "Crime in the United States 1989" (Uniform Crime Reports, August 5, 1990)
*Robbery is the taking or attempting to take anything of value by force or threat of force.

Percent Change in Number of Robberies: 1989 to 1993

National Percent Change = 14.1% Increase*

<table>
<tr><td colspan="3"><u>ALPHA ORDER</u></td><td colspan="3"><u>RANK ORDER</u></td></tr>
<tr><td>RANK</td><td>STATE</td><td>PERCENT CHANGE</td><td>RANK</td><td>STATE</td><td>PERCENT CHANGE</td></tr>
<tr><td>24</td><td>Alabama</td><td>21.1</td><td>1</td><td>Alaska</td><td>105.9</td></tr>
<tr><td>1</td><td>Alaska</td><td>105.9</td><td>2</td><td>Montana</td><td>98.5</td></tr>
<tr><td>17</td><td>Arizona</td><td>29.7</td><td>3</td><td>Mississippi</td><td>79.4</td></tr>
<tr><td>32</td><td>Arkansas</td><td>13.8</td><td>4</td><td>Nevada</td><td>69.7</td></tr>
<tr><td>16</td><td>California</td><td>31.1</td><td>5</td><td>Wisconsin</td><td>56.2</td></tr>
<tr><td>11</td><td>Colorado</td><td>39.4</td><td>6</td><td>North Carolina</td><td>52.4</td></tr>
<tr><td>44</td><td>Connecticut</td><td>(7.3)</td><td>7</td><td>South Carolina</td><td>49.2</td></tr>
<tr><td>10</td><td>Delaware</td><td>39.9</td><td>8</td><td>Virginia</td><td>41.9</td></tr>
<tr><td>43</td><td>Florida</td><td>(4.4)</td><td>9</td><td>Tennessee</td><td>41.6</td></tr>
<tr><td>40</td><td>Georgia</td><td>(1.7)</td><td>10</td><td>Delaware</td><td>39.9</td></tr>
<tr><td>15</td><td>Hawaii</td><td>31.2</td><td>11</td><td>Colorado</td><td>39.4</td></tr>
<tr><td>22</td><td>Idaho</td><td>22.4</td><td>12</td><td>New Mexico</td><td>39.2</td></tr>
<tr><td>31</td><td>Illinois</td><td>13.9</td><td>13</td><td>Maryland</td><td>38.4</td></tr>
<tr><td>26</td><td>Indiana</td><td>20.7</td><td>14</td><td>Iowa</td><td>36.9</td></tr>
<tr><td>14</td><td>Iowa</td><td>36.9</td><td>15</td><td>Hawaii</td><td>31.2</td></tr>
<tr><td>20</td><td>Kansas</td><td>24.7</td><td>16</td><td>California</td><td>31.1</td></tr>
<tr><td>25</td><td>Kentucky</td><td>20.8</td><td>17</td><td>Arizona</td><td>29.7</td></tr>
<tr><td>28</td><td>Louisiana</td><td>17.2</td><td>18</td><td>South Dakota</td><td>27.4</td></tr>
<tr><td>46</td><td>Maine</td><td>(9.9)</td><td>19</td><td>Missouri</td><td>25.8</td></tr>
<tr><td>13</td><td>Maryland</td><td>38.4</td><td>20</td><td>Kansas</td><td>24.7</td></tr>
<tr><td>48</td><td>Massachusetts</td><td>(11.8)</td><td>21</td><td>Minnesota</td><td>23.4</td></tr>
<tr><td>34</td><td>Michigan</td><td>9.6</td><td>22</td><td>Idaho</td><td>22.4</td></tr>
<tr><td>21</td><td>Minnesota</td><td>23.4</td><td>23</td><td>Utah</td><td>21.4</td></tr>
<tr><td>3</td><td>Mississippi</td><td>79.4</td><td>24</td><td>Alabama</td><td>21.1</td></tr>
<tr><td>19</td><td>Missouri</td><td>25.8</td><td>25</td><td>Kentucky</td><td>20.8</td></tr>
<tr><td>2</td><td>Montana</td><td>98.5</td><td>26</td><td>Indiana</td><td>20.7</td></tr>
<tr><td>37</td><td>Nebraska</td><td>6.3</td><td>27</td><td>Pennsylvania</td><td>19.6</td></tr>
<tr><td>4</td><td>Nevada</td><td>69.7</td><td>28</td><td>Louisiana</td><td>17.2</td></tr>
<tr><td>29</td><td>New Hampshire</td><td>16.3</td><td>29</td><td>New Hampshire</td><td>16.3</td></tr>
<tr><td>33</td><td>New Jersey</td><td>10.3</td><td>30</td><td>Ohio</td><td>14.7</td></tr>
<tr><td>12</td><td>New Mexico</td><td>39.2</td><td>31</td><td>Illinois</td><td>13.9</td></tr>
<tr><td>41</td><td>New York</td><td>(1.8)</td><td>32</td><td>Arkansas</td><td>13.8</td></tr>
<tr><td>6</td><td>North Carolina</td><td>52.4</td><td>33</td><td>New Jersey</td><td>10.3</td></tr>
<tr><td>49</td><td>North Dakota</td><td>(13.1)</td><td>34</td><td>Michigan</td><td>9.6</td></tr>
<tr><td>30</td><td>Ohio</td><td>14.7</td><td>35</td><td>Washington</td><td>8.0</td></tr>
<tr><td>42</td><td>Oklahoma</td><td>(3.3)</td><td>36</td><td>Texas</td><td>6.7</td></tr>
<tr><td>45</td><td>Oregon</td><td>(8.2)</td><td>37</td><td>Nebraska</td><td>6.3</td></tr>
<tr><td>27</td><td>Pennsylvania</td><td>19.6</td><td>38</td><td>Wyoming</td><td>0.0</td></tr>
<tr><td>46</td><td>Rhode Island</td><td>(9.9)</td><td>39</td><td>West Virginia</td><td>(1.4)</td></tr>
<tr><td>7</td><td>South Carolina</td><td>49.2</td><td>40</td><td>Georgia</td><td>(1.7)</td></tr>
<tr><td>18</td><td>South Dakota</td><td>27.4</td><td>41</td><td>New York</td><td>(1.8)</td></tr>
<tr><td>9</td><td>Tennessee</td><td>41.6</td><td>42</td><td>Oklahoma</td><td>(3.3)</td></tr>
<tr><td>36</td><td>Texas</td><td>6.7</td><td>43</td><td>Florida</td><td>(4.4)</td></tr>
<tr><td>23</td><td>Utah</td><td>21.4</td><td>44</td><td>Connecticut</td><td>(7.3)</td></tr>
<tr><td>50</td><td>Vermont</td><td>(49.0)</td><td>45</td><td>Oregon</td><td>(8.2)</td></tr>
<tr><td>8</td><td>Virginia</td><td>41.9</td><td>46</td><td>Maine</td><td>(9.9)</td></tr>
<tr><td>35</td><td>Washington</td><td>8.0</td><td>46</td><td>Rhode Island</td><td>(9.9)</td></tr>
<tr><td>39</td><td>West Virginia</td><td>(1.4)</td><td>48</td><td>Massachusetts</td><td>(11.8)</td></tr>
<tr><td>5</td><td>Wisconsin</td><td>56.2</td><td>49</td><td>North Dakota</td><td>(13.1)</td></tr>
<tr><td>38</td><td>Wyoming</td><td>0.0</td><td>50</td><td>Vermont</td><td>(49.0)</td></tr>
</table>

District of Columbia   8.6

Source: Morgan Quitno Corporation using data from U.S. Department of Justice, Federal Bureau of Investigation
"Crime in the United States" (Uniform Crime Reports, 1989 and 1993 editions)
*Robbery is the taking or attempting to take anything of value by force or threat of force.

Robbery Rate in 1989

National Rate = 233.0 Robberies per 100,000 Population*

<table>
<tr><td colspan="3"><u>ALPHA ORDER</u></td><td colspan="3"><u>RANK ORDER</u></td></tr>
<tr><td>RANK</td><td>STATE</td><td>RATE</td><td>RANK</td><td>STATE</td><td>RATE</td></tr>
<tr><td>22</td><td>Alabama</td><td>133.9</td><td>1</td><td>New York</td><td>579.3</td></tr>
<tr><td>38</td><td>Alaska</td><td>67.6</td><td>2</td><td>Florida</td><td>404.0</td></tr>
<tr><td>20</td><td>Arizona</td><td>139.0</td><td>3</td><td>Illinois</td><td>335.7</td></tr>
<tr><td>27</td><td>Arkansas</td><td>110.6</td><td>4</td><td>Maryland</td><td>332.1</td></tr>
<tr><td>5</td><td>California</td><td>331.8</td><td>5</td><td>California</td><td>331.8</td></tr>
<tr><td>33</td><td>Colorado</td><td>90.0</td><td>6</td><td>New Jersey</td><td>273.3</td></tr>
<tr><td>12</td><td>Connecticut</td><td>214.8</td><td>7</td><td>Georgia</td><td>271.1</td></tr>
<tr><td>21</td><td>Delaware</td><td>138.8</td><td>8</td><td>Nevada</td><td>250.6</td></tr>
<tr><td>2</td><td>Florida</td><td>404.0</td><td>9</td><td>Louisiana</td><td>237.3</td></tr>
<tr><td>7</td><td>Georgia</td><td>271.1</td><td>10</td><td>Texas</td><td>223.1</td></tr>
<tr><td>34</td><td>Hawaii</td><td>83.2</td><td>11</td><td>Michigan</td><td>222.3</td></tr>
<tr><td>48</td><td>Idaho</td><td>15.0</td><td>12</td><td>Connecticut</td><td>214.8</td></tr>
<tr><td>3</td><td>Illinois</td><td>335.7</td><td>13</td><td>Massachusetts</td><td>202.6</td></tr>
<tr><td>30</td><td>Indiana</td><td>101.4</td><td>14</td><td>Missouri</td><td>195.0</td></tr>
<tr><td>42</td><td>Iowa</td><td>39.0</td><td>15</td><td>Ohio</td><td>170.9</td></tr>
<tr><td>31</td><td>Kansas</td><td>99.8</td><td>16</td><td>Tennessee</td><td>160.4</td></tr>
<tr><td>36</td><td>Kentucky</td><td>76.1</td><td>17</td><td>Oregon</td><td>151.8</td></tr>
<tr><td>9</td><td>Louisiana</td><td>237.3</td><td>18</td><td>Pennsylvania</td><td>149.7</td></tr>
<tr><td>43</td><td>Maine</td><td>24.0</td><td>19</td><td>Washington</td><td>140.1</td></tr>
<tr><td>4</td><td>Maryland</td><td>332.1</td><td>20</td><td>Arizona</td><td>139.0</td></tr>
<tr><td>13</td><td>Massachusetts</td><td>202.6</td><td>21</td><td>Delaware</td><td>138.8</td></tr>
<tr><td>11</td><td>Michigan</td><td>222.3</td><td>22</td><td>Alabama</td><td>133.9</td></tr>
<tr><td>32</td><td>Minnesota</td><td>94.8</td><td>23</td><td>North Carolina</td><td>133.5</td></tr>
<tr><td>35</td><td>Mississippi</td><td>78.3</td><td>24</td><td>South Carolina</td><td>130.2</td></tr>
<tr><td>14</td><td>Missouri</td><td>195.0</td><td>25</td><td>Oklahoma</td><td>126.2</td></tr>
<tr><td>47</td><td>Montana</td><td>17.0</td><td>26</td><td>Rhode Island</td><td>112.4</td></tr>
<tr><td>40</td><td>Nebraska</td><td>52.0</td><td>27</td><td>Arkansas</td><td>110.6</td></tr>
<tr><td>8</td><td>Nevada</td><td>250.6</td><td>28</td><td>Virginia</td><td>106.5</td></tr>
<tr><td>44</td><td>New Hampshire</td><td>23.8</td><td>29</td><td>New Mexico</td><td>105.2</td></tr>
<tr><td>6</td><td>New Jersey</td><td>273.3</td><td>30</td><td>Indiana</td><td>101.4</td></tr>
<tr><td>29</td><td>New Mexico</td><td>105.2</td><td>31</td><td>Kansas</td><td>99.8</td></tr>
<tr><td>1</td><td>New York</td><td>579.3</td><td>32</td><td>Minnesota</td><td>94.8</td></tr>
<tr><td>23</td><td>North Carolina</td><td>133.5</td><td>33</td><td>Colorado</td><td>90.0</td></tr>
<tr><td>50</td><td>North Dakota</td><td>9.2</td><td>34</td><td>Hawaii</td><td>83.2</td></tr>
<tr><td>15</td><td>Ohio</td><td>170.9</td><td>35</td><td>Mississippi</td><td>78.3</td></tr>
<tr><td>25</td><td>Oklahoma</td><td>126.2</td><td>36</td><td>Kentucky</td><td>76.1</td></tr>
<tr><td>17</td><td>Oregon</td><td>151.8</td><td>37</td><td>Wisconsin</td><td>75.2</td></tr>
<tr><td>18</td><td>Pennsylvania</td><td>149.7</td><td>38</td><td>Alaska</td><td>67.6</td></tr>
<tr><td>26</td><td>Rhode Island</td><td>112.4</td><td>39</td><td>Utah</td><td>52.6</td></tr>
<tr><td>24</td><td>South Carolina</td><td>130.2</td><td>40</td><td>Nebraska</td><td>52.0</td></tr>
<tr><td>49</td><td>South Dakota</td><td>11.7</td><td>41</td><td>West Virginia</td><td>42.7</td></tr>
<tr><td>16</td><td>Tennessee</td><td>160.4</td><td>42</td><td>Iowa</td><td>39.0</td></tr>
<tr><td>10</td><td>Texas</td><td>223.1</td><td>43</td><td>Maine</td><td>24.0</td></tr>
<tr><td>39</td><td>Utah</td><td>52.6</td><td>44</td><td>New Hampshire</td><td>23.8</td></tr>
<tr><td>45</td><td>Vermont</td><td>18.0</td><td>45</td><td>Vermont</td><td>18.0</td></tr>
<tr><td>28</td><td>Virginia</td><td>106.5</td><td>46</td><td>Wyoming</td><td>17.1</td></tr>
<tr><td>19</td><td>Washington</td><td>140.1</td><td>47</td><td>Montana</td><td>17.0</td></tr>
<tr><td>41</td><td>West Virginia</td><td>42.7</td><td>48</td><td>Idaho</td><td>15.0</td></tr>
<tr><td>37</td><td>Wisconsin</td><td>75.2</td><td>49</td><td>South Dakota</td><td>11.7</td></tr>
<tr><td>46</td><td>Wyoming</td><td>17.1</td><td>50</td><td>North Dakota</td><td>9.2</td></tr>
<tr><td></td><td></td><td></td><td></td><td>District of Columbia</td><td>1,083.1</td></tr>
</table>

Source: U.S. Department of Justice, Federal Bureau of Investigation
   "Crime in the United States 1989" (Uniform Crime Reports, August 5, 1990)
*Robbery is the taking or attempting to take anything of value by force or threat of force.

Percent Change in Robbery Rate: 1989 to 1993

National Percent Change = 9.8% Increase*

ALPHA ORDER			RANK ORDER		
RANK	STATE	PERCENT CHANGE	RANK	STATE	PERCENT CHANGE
22	Alabama	19.1	1	Montana	90.6
2	Alaska	81.1	2	Alaska	81.1
26	Arizona	17.2	3	Mississippi	77.9
29	Arkansas	12.9	4	Wisconsin	50.8
19	California	22.1	5	North Carolina	44.1
14	Colorado	29.7	6	South Carolina	43.9
42	Connecticut	(8.4)	7	Iowa	38.2
10	Delaware	34.5	8	Tennessee	37.2
47	Florida	(11.5)	9	Nevada	35.7
43	Georgia	(8.5)	10	Delaware	34.5
16	Hawaii	24.5	11	Virginia	33.3
31	Idaho	12.7	12	New Mexico	31.6
28	Illinois	13.6	13	Maryland	30.9
25	Indiana	18.1	14	Colorado	29.7
7	Iowa	38.2	15	South Dakota	28.2
18	Kansas	23.8	16	Hawaii	24.5
24	Kentucky	18.8	17	Missouri	24.0
21	Louisiana	19.5	18	Kansas	23.8
46	Maine	(11.2)	19	California	22.1
13	Maryland	30.9	20	Pennsylvania	19.6
48	Massachusetts	(13.3)	21	Louisiana	19.5
34	Michigan	7.3	22	Alabama	19.1
23	Minnesota	18.9	23	Minnesota	18.9
3	Mississippi	77.9	24	Kentucky	18.8
17	Missouri	24.0	25	Indiana	18.1
1	Montana	90.6	26	Arizona	17.2
35	Nebraska	6.5	27	New Hampshire	14.7
9	Nevada	35.7	28	Illinois	13.6
27	New Hampshire	14.7	29	Arkansas	12.9
33	New Jersey	8.3	30	Ohio	12.8
12	New Mexico	31.6	31	Idaho	12.7
40	New York	(3.1)	32	Utah	11.4
5	North Carolina	44.1	33	New Jersey	8.3
44	North Dakota	(9.8)	34	Michigan	7.3
30	Ohio	12.8	35	Nebraska	6.5
41	Oklahoma	(3.5)	36	West Virginia	0.7
49	Oregon	(14.6)	37	Texas	0.6
20	Pennsylvania	19.6	37	Wyoming	0.6
45	Rhode Island	(10.1)	39	Washington	(2.1)
6	South Carolina	43.9	40	New York	(3.1)
15	South Dakota	28.2	41	Oklahoma	(3.5)
8	Tennessee	37.2	42	Connecticut	(8.4)
37	Texas	0.6	43	Georgia	(8.5)
32	Utah	11.4	44	North Dakota	(9.8)
50	Vermont	(50.0)	45	Rhode Island	(10.1)
11	Virginia	33.3	46	Maine	(11.2)
39	Washington	(2.1)	47	Florida	(11.5)
36	West Virginia	0.7	48	Massachusetts	(13.3)
4	Wisconsin	50.8	49	Oregon	(14.6)
37	Wyoming	0.6	50	Vermont	(50.0)

District of Columbia		13.5

Source: Morgan Quitno Corporation using data from U.S. Department of Justice, Federal Bureau of Investigation "Crime in the United States" (Uniform Crime Reports, 1989 and 1993 editions)
Robbery is the taking or attempting to take anything of value by force or threat of force.

Aggravated Assaults in 1989

National Total = 951,707 Aggravated Assaults*

<table>
<tr><td colspan="4"><u>ALPHA ORDER</u></td><td colspan="4"><u>RANK ORDER</u></td></tr>
<tr><td>RANK</td><td>STATE</td><td>ASSAULTS</td><td>% of USA</td><td>RANK</td><td>STATE</td><td>ASSAULTS</td><td>% of USA</td></tr>
<tr><td>17</td><td>Alabama</td><td>17,117</td><td>1.80%</td><td>1</td><td>California</td><td>172,581</td><td>18.13%</td></tr>
<tr><td>41</td><td>Alaska</td><td>1,946</td><td>0.20%</td><td>2</td><td>New York</td><td>91,571</td><td>9.62%</td></tr>
<tr><td>20</td><td>Arizona</td><td>14,853</td><td>1.56%</td><td>3</td><td>Florida</td><td>81,683</td><td>8.58%</td></tr>
<tr><td>29</td><td>Arkansas</td><td>7,610</td><td>0.80%</td><td>4</td><td>Texas</td><td>63,996</td><td>6.72%</td></tr>
<tr><td>1</td><td>California</td><td>172,581</td><td>18.13%</td><td>5</td><td>Illinois</td><td>54,261</td><td>5.70%</td></tr>
<tr><td>22</td><td>Colorado</td><td>11,304</td><td>1.19%</td><td>6</td><td>Michigan</td><td>37,527</td><td>3.94%</td></tr>
<tr><td>27</td><td>Connecticut</td><td>8,538</td><td>0.90%</td><td>7</td><td>Ohio</td><td>26,950</td><td>2.83%</td></tr>
<tr><td>39</td><td>Delaware</td><td>2,208</td><td>0.23%</td><td>8</td><td>Georgia</td><td>25,937</td><td>2.73%</td></tr>
<tr><td>3</td><td>Florida</td><td>81,683</td><td>8.58%</td><td>9</td><td>Massachusetts</td><td>25,797</td><td>2.71%</td></tr>
<tr><td>8</td><td>Georgia</td><td>25,937</td><td>2.73%</td><td>10</td><td>North Carolina</td><td>24,584</td><td>2.58%</td></tr>
<tr><td>42</td><td>Hawaii</td><td>1,530</td><td>0.16%</td><td>11</td><td>Pennsylvania</td><td>23,845</td><td>2.51%</td></tr>
<tr><td>40</td><td>Idaho</td><td>2,168</td><td>0.23%</td><td>12</td><td>New Jersey</td><td>23,129</td><td>2.43%</td></tr>
<tr><td>5</td><td>Illinois</td><td>54,261</td><td>5.70%</td><td>13</td><td>Maryland</td><td>22,236</td><td>2.34%</td></tr>
<tr><td>19</td><td>Indiana</td><td>14,907</td><td>1.57%</td><td>14</td><td>South Carolina</td><td>22,050</td><td>2.32%</td></tr>
<tr><td>33</td><td>Iowa</td><td>5,942</td><td>0.62%</td><td>15</td><td>Louisiana</td><td>21,532</td><td>2.26%</td></tr>
<tr><td>31</td><td>Kansas</td><td>6,510</td><td>0.68%</td><td>16</td><td>Missouri</td><td>20,578</td><td>2.16%</td></tr>
<tr><td>25</td><td>Kentucky</td><td>9,256</td><td>0.97%</td><td>17</td><td>Alabama</td><td>17,117</td><td>1.80%</td></tr>
<tr><td>15</td><td>Louisiana</td><td>21,532</td><td>2.26%</td><td>18</td><td>Tennessee</td><td>16,505</td><td>1.73%</td></tr>
<tr><td>45</td><td>Maine</td><td>1,115</td><td>0.12%</td><td>19</td><td>Indiana</td><td>14,907</td><td>1.57%</td></tr>
<tr><td>13</td><td>Maryland</td><td>22,236</td><td>2.34%</td><td>20</td><td>Arizona</td><td>14,853</td><td>1.56%</td></tr>
<tr><td>9</td><td>Massachusetts</td><td>25,797</td><td>2.71%</td><td>21</td><td>Washington</td><td>12,641</td><td>1.33%</td></tr>
<tr><td>6</td><td>Michigan</td><td>37,527</td><td>3.94%</td><td>22</td><td>Colorado</td><td>11,304</td><td>1.19%</td></tr>
<tr><td>30</td><td>Minnesota</td><td>6,947</td><td>0.73%</td><td>23</td><td>Virginia</td><td>10,445</td><td>1.10%</td></tr>
<tr><td>34</td><td>Mississippi</td><td>4,833</td><td>0.51%</td><td>24</td><td>Oklahoma</td><td>10,358</td><td>1.09%</td></tr>
<tr><td>16</td><td>Missouri</td><td>20,578</td><td>2.16%</td><td>25</td><td>Kentucky</td><td>9,256</td><td>0.97%</td></tr>
<tr><td>48</td><td>Montana</td><td>630</td><td>0.07%</td><td>26</td><td>Oregon</td><td>8,895</td><td>0.93%</td></tr>
<tr><td>36</td><td>Nebraska</td><td>3,245</td><td>0.34%</td><td>27</td><td>Connecticut</td><td>8,538</td><td>0.90%</td></tr>
<tr><td>35</td><td>Nevada</td><td>3,410</td><td>0.36%</td><td>28</td><td>New Mexico</td><td>8,314</td><td>0.87%</td></tr>
<tr><td>44</td><td>New Hampshire</td><td>1,238</td><td>0.13%</td><td>29</td><td>Arkansas</td><td>7,610</td><td>0.80%</td></tr>
<tr><td>12</td><td>New Jersey</td><td>23,129</td><td>2.43%</td><td>30</td><td>Minnesota</td><td>6,947</td><td>0.73%</td></tr>
<tr><td>28</td><td>New Mexico</td><td>8,314</td><td>0.87%</td><td>31</td><td>Kansas</td><td>6,510</td><td>0.68%</td></tr>
<tr><td>2</td><td>New York</td><td>91,571</td><td>9.62%</td><td>32</td><td>Wisconsin</td><td>6,006</td><td>0.63%</td></tr>
<tr><td>10</td><td>North Carolina</td><td>24,584</td><td>2.58%</td><td>33</td><td>Iowa</td><td>5,942</td><td>0.62%</td></tr>
<tr><td>50</td><td>North Dakota</td><td>274</td><td>0.03%</td><td>34</td><td>Mississippi</td><td>4,833</td><td>0.51%</td></tr>
<tr><td>7</td><td>Ohio</td><td>26,950</td><td>2.83%</td><td>35</td><td>Nevada</td><td>3,410</td><td>0.36%</td></tr>
<tr><td>24</td><td>Oklahoma</td><td>10,358</td><td>1.09%</td><td>36</td><td>Nebraska</td><td>3,245</td><td>0.34%</td></tr>
<tr><td>26</td><td>Oregon</td><td>8,895</td><td>0.93%</td><td>37</td><td>Utah</td><td>2,985</td><td>0.31%</td></tr>
<tr><td>11</td><td>Pennsylvania</td><td>23,845</td><td>2.51%</td><td>38</td><td>Rhode Island</td><td>2,335</td><td>0.25%</td></tr>
<tr><td>38</td><td>Rhode Island</td><td>2,335</td><td>0.25%</td><td>39</td><td>Delaware</td><td>2,208</td><td>0.23%</td></tr>
<tr><td>14</td><td>South Carolina</td><td>22,050</td><td>2.32%</td><td>40</td><td>Idaho</td><td>2,168</td><td>0.23%</td></tr>
<tr><td>47</td><td>South Dakota</td><td>647</td><td>0.07%</td><td>41</td><td>Alaska</td><td>1,946</td><td>0.20%</td></tr>
<tr><td>18</td><td>Tennessee</td><td>16,505</td><td>1.73%</td><td>42</td><td>Hawaii</td><td>1,530</td><td>0.16%</td></tr>
<tr><td>4</td><td>Texas</td><td>63,996</td><td>6.72%</td><td>43</td><td>West Virginia</td><td>1,463</td><td>0.15%</td></tr>
<tr><td>37</td><td>Utah</td><td>2,985</td><td>0.31%</td><td>44</td><td>New Hampshire</td><td>1,238</td><td>0.13%</td></tr>
<tr><td>49</td><td>Vermont</td><td>509</td><td>0.05%</td><td>45</td><td>Maine</td><td>1,115</td><td>0.12%</td></tr>
<tr><td>23</td><td>Virginia</td><td>10,445</td><td>1.10%</td><td>46</td><td>Wyoming</td><td>991</td><td>0.10%</td></tr>
<tr><td>21</td><td>Washington</td><td>12,641</td><td>1.33%</td><td>47</td><td>South Dakota</td><td>647</td><td>0.07%</td></tr>
<tr><td>43</td><td>West Virginia</td><td>1,463</td><td>0.15%</td><td>48</td><td>Montana</td><td>630</td><td>0.07%</td></tr>
<tr><td>32</td><td>Wisconsin</td><td>6,006</td><td>0.63%</td><td>49</td><td>Vermont</td><td>509</td><td>0.05%</td></tr>
<tr><td>46</td><td>Wyoming</td><td>991</td><td>0.10%</td><td>50</td><td>North Dakota</td><td>274</td><td>0.03%</td></tr>
<tr><td></td><td></td><td></td><td></td><td></td><td>District of Columbia</td><td>5,775</td><td>0.61%</td></tr>
</table>

Source: U.S. Department of Justice, Federal Bureau of Investigation
    "Crime in the United States 1989" (Uniform Crime Reports, August 5, 1990)
*Aggravated assault is an attack for the purpose of inflicting severe bodily injury.

Percent Change in Number of Aggravated Assaults: 1989 to 1993

National Percent Change = 19.3% Increase*

ALPHA ORDER

RANK	STATE	PERCENT CHANGE
10	Alabama	40.5
3	Alaska	67.9
13	Arizona	34.0
15	Arkansas	32.4
38	California	12.5
22	Colorado	25.9
47	Connecticut	(12.2)
16	Delaware	32.2
17	Florida	31.6
35	Georgia	14.2
46	Hawaii	(8.0)
31	Idaho	14.9
32	Illinois	14.8
25	Indiana	23.6
29	Iowa	16.0
21	Kansas	26.9
12	Kentucky	35.6
7	Louisiana	42.7
48	Maine	(15.2)
36	Maryland	13.1
11	Massachusetts	38.0
27	Michigan	19.2
34	Minnesota	14.3
18	Mississippi	30.4
30	Missouri	15.8
5	Montana	52.1
23	Nebraska	24.8
1	Nevada	88.9
50	New Hampshire	(41.8)
44	New Jersey	1.3
8	New Mexico	42.1
45	New York	(6.3)
24	North Carolina	24.7
37	North Dakota	12.8
41	Ohio	5.5
9	Oklahoma	42.0
40	Oregon	8.3
42	Pennsylvania	3.6
32	Rhode Island	14.8
20	South Carolina	27.8
4	South Dakota	60.9
6	Tennessee	50.0
14	Texas	32.6
26	Utah	21.3
49	Vermont	(30.1)
28	Virginia	18.0
19	Washington	28.0
2	West Virginia	72.2
43	Wisconsin	1.8
39	Wyoming	9.7

RANK ORDER

RANK	STATE	PERCENT CHANGE
1	Nevada	88.9
2	West Virginia	72.2
3	Alaska	67.9
4	South Dakota	60.9
5	Montana	52.1
6	Tennessee	50.0
7	Louisiana	42.7
8	New Mexico	42.1
9	Oklahoma	42.0
10	Alabama	40.5
11	Massachusetts	38.0
12	Kentucky	35.6
13	Arizona	34.0
14	Texas	32.6
15	Arkansas	32.4
16	Delaware	32.2
17	Florida	31.6
18	Mississippi	30.4
19	Washington	28.0
20	South Carolina	27.8
21	Kansas	26.9
22	Colorado	25.9
23	Nebraska	24.8
24	North Carolina	24.7
25	Indiana	23.6
26	Utah	21.3
27	Michigan	19.2
28	Virginia	18.0
29	Iowa	16.0
30	Missouri	15.8
31	Idaho	14.9
32	Illinois	14.8
32	Rhode Island	14.8
34	Minnesota	14.3
35	Georgia	14.2
36	Maryland	13.1
37	North Dakota	12.8
38	California	12.5
39	Wyoming	9.7
40	Oregon	8.3
41	Ohio	5.5
42	Pennsylvania	3.6
43	Wisconsin	1.8
44	New Jersey	1.3
45	New York	(6.3)
46	Hawaii	(8.0)
47	Connecticut	(12.2)
48	Maine	(15.2)
49	Vermont	(30.1)
50	New Hampshire	(41.8)

District of Columbia 55.9

Source: Morgan Quitno Corporation using data from U.S. Department of Justice, Federal Bureau of Investigation
"Crime in the United States" (Uniform Crime Reports, 1989 and 1993 editions)
*Aggravated assault is an attack for the purpose of inflicting severe bodily injury.

Aggravated Assault Rate in 1989

National Rate = 383.4 Aggravated Assaults per 100,000 Population*

ALPHA ORDER

RANK	STATE	RATE
11	Alabama	415.7
17	Alaska	369.3
10	Arizona	417.7
22	Arkansas	316.3
3	California	593.8
18	Colorado	340.8
28	Connecticut	263.6
20	Delaware	328.1
1	Florida	644.6
13	Georgia	403.0
42	Hawaii	137.6
33	Idaho	213.8
8	Illinois	465.4
26	Indiana	266.5
34	Iowa	209.2
29	Kansas	259.1
30	Kentucky	248.3
6	Louisiana	491.4
45	Maine	91.2
7	Maryland	473.7
9	Massachusetts	436.3
12	Michigan	404.7
41	Minnesota	159.6
38	Mississippi	184.4
14	Missouri	398.9
49	Montana	78.2
36	Nebraska	201.4
24	Nevada	306.9
44	New Hampshire	111.8
25	New Jersey	299.0
4	New Mexico	544.1
5	New York	510.1
16	North Carolina	374.1
50	North Dakota	41.5
31	Ohio	247.1
21	Oklahoma	321.3
23	Oregon	315.4
37	Pennsylvania	198.0
32	Rhode Island	234.0
2	South Carolina	627.8
46	South Dakota	90.5
19	Tennessee	334.1
15	Texas	376.6
39	Utah	174.9
47	Vermont	89.8
40	Virginia	171.3
27	Washington	265.5
48	West Virginia	78.8
43	Wisconsin	123.4
35	Wyoming	208.6

RANK ORDER

RANK	STATE	RATE
1	Florida	644.6
2	South Carolina	627.8
3	California	593.8
4	New Mexico	544.1
5	New York	510.1
6	Louisiana	491.4
7	Maryland	473.7
8	Illinois	465.4
9	Massachusetts	436.3
10	Arizona	417.7
11	Alabama	415.7
12	Michigan	404.7
13	Georgia	403.0
14	Missouri	398.9
15	Texas	376.6
16	North Carolina	374.1
17	Alaska	369.3
18	Colorado	340.8
19	Tennessee	334.1
20	Delaware	328.1
21	Oklahoma	321.3
22	Arkansas	316.3
23	Oregon	315.4
24	Nevada	306.9
25	New Jersey	299.0
26	Indiana	266.5
27	Washington	265.5
28	Connecticut	263.6
29	Kansas	259.1
30	Kentucky	248.3
31	Ohio	247.1
32	Rhode Island	234.0
33	Idaho	213.8
34	Iowa	209.2
35	Wyoming	208.6
36	Nebraska	201.4
37	Pennsylvania	198.0
38	Mississippi	184.4
39	Utah	174.9
40	Virginia	171.3
41	Minnesota	159.6
42	Hawaii	137.6
43	Wisconsin	123.4
44	New Hampshire	111.8
45	Maine	91.2
46	South Dakota	90.5
47	Vermont	89.8
48	West Virginia	78.8
49	Montana	78.2
50	North Dakota	41.5
	District of Columbia	956.1

Source: U.S. Department of Justice, Federal Bureau of Investigation
"Crime in the United States 1989" (Uniform Crime Reports, August 5, 1990)
Aggravated assault is an attack for the purpose of inflicting severe bodily injury.

Percent Change in Rate of Aggravated Assaults: 1989 to 1993

National Percent Change = 14.8% Increase*

ALPHA ORDER

RANK ORDER

RANK	STATE	PERCENT CHANGE	RANK	STATE	PERCENT CHANGE
9	Alabama	38.2	1	West Virginia	75.8
4	Alaska	47.7	2	South Dakota	60.9
21	Arizona	21.1	3	Nevada	51.2
13	Arkansas	31.5	4	Alaska	47.7
39	California	4.7	5	Montana	46.0
25	Colorado	17.1	6	Louisiana	45.6
47	Connecticut	(13.2)	7	Tennessee	45.3
15	Delaware	27.1	8	Oklahoma	41.7
20	Florida	21.9	9	Alabama	38.2
37	Georgia	6.3	10	Massachusetts	35.7
46	Hawaii	(12.7)	11	New Mexico	34.4
38	Idaho	6.0	12	Kentucky	33.5
30	Illinois	14.4	13	Arkansas	31.5
21	Indiana	21.1	14	Mississippi	29.3
26	Iowa	17.0	15	Delaware	27.1
16	Kansas	25.9	16	Kansas	25.9
12	Kentucky	33.5	17	Nebraska	25.1
6	Louisiana	45.6	18	Texas	25.0
48	Maine	(16.3)	19	South Carolina	23.2
36	Maryland	6.9	20	Florida	21.9
10	Massachusetts	35.7	21	Arizona	21.1
27	Michigan	16.7	21	Indiana	21.1
35	Minnesota	10.2	23	North Carolina	18.0
14	Mississippi	29.3	24	North Dakota	17.3
31	Missouri	14.1	25	Colorado	17.1
5	Montana	46.0	26	Iowa	17.0
17	Nebraska	25.1	27	Michigan	16.7
3	Nevada	51.2	28	Washington	16.0
50	New Hampshire	(42.7)	29	Rhode Island	14.6
43	New Jersey	(0.5)	30	Illinois	14.4
11	New Mexico	34.4	31	Missouri	14.1
45	New York	(7.6)	32	Utah	11.3
23	North Carolina	18.0	33	Wyoming	10.9
24	North Dakota	17.3	34	Virginia	10.8
40	Ohio	3.7	35	Minnesota	10.2
8	Oklahoma	41.7	36	Maryland	6.9
42	Oregon	0.7	37	Georgia	6.3
41	Pennsylvania	3.6	38	Idaho	6.0
29	Rhode Island	14.6	39	California	4.7
19	South Carolina	23.2	40	Ohio	3.7
2	South Dakota	60.9	41	Pennsylvania	3.6
7	Tennessee	45.3	42	Oregon	0.7
18	Texas	25.0	43	New Jersey	(0.5)
32	Utah	11.3	44	Wisconsin	(1.6)
49	Vermont	(31.2)	45	New York	(7.6)
34	Virginia	10.8	46	Hawaii	(12.7)
28	Washington	16.0	47	Connecticut	(13.2)
1	West Virginia	75.8	48	Maine	(16.3)
44	Wisconsin	(1.6)	49	Vermont	(31.2)
33	Wyoming	10.9	50	New Hampshire	(42.7)

	District of Columbia	62.9

Source: Morgan Quitno Corporation using data from U.S. Department of Justice, Federal Bureau of Investigation
"Crime in the United States" (Uniform Crime Reports, 1989 and 1993 editions)
*Aggravated assault is an attack for the purpose of inflicting severe bodily injury.

Property Crimes in 1989

National Total = 12,605,412 Property Crimes*

<table>
<tr><td colspan="4">ALPHA ORDER</td><td colspan="4">RANK ORDER</td></tr>
<tr><td>RANK</td><td>STATE</td><td>CRIMES</td><td>% of USA</td><td>RANK</td><td>STATE</td><td>CRIMES</td><td>% of USA</td></tr>
<tr><td>25</td><td>Alabama</td><td>166,244</td><td>1.32%</td><td>1</td><td>California</td><td>1,681,516</td><td>13.34%</td></tr>
<tr><td>46</td><td>Alaska</td><td>22,567</td><td>0.18%</td><td>2</td><td>Texas</td><td>1,234,977</td><td>9.80%</td></tr>
<tr><td>13</td><td>Arizona</td><td>265,284</td><td>2.10%</td><td>3</td><td>Florida</td><td>975,042</td><td>7.74%</td></tr>
<tr><td>32</td><td>Arkansas</td><td>98,213</td><td>0.78%</td><td>4</td><td>New York</td><td>926,596</td><td>7.35%</td></tr>
<tr><td>1</td><td>California</td><td>1,681,516</td><td>13.34%</td><td>5</td><td>Illinois</td><td>558,803</td><td>4.43%</td></tr>
<tr><td>22</td><td>Colorado</td><td>184,692</td><td>1.47%</td><td>6</td><td>Michigan</td><td>487,682</td><td>3.87%</td></tr>
<tr><td>28</td><td>Connecticut</td><td>154,119</td><td>1.22%</td><td>7</td><td>Ohio</td><td>465,143</td><td>3.69%</td></tr>
<tr><td>45</td><td>Delaware</td><td>28,998</td><td>0.23%</td><td>8</td><td>Georgia</td><td>407,868</td><td>3.24%</td></tr>
<tr><td>3</td><td>Florida</td><td>975,042</td><td>7.74%</td><td>9</td><td>New Jersey</td><td>360,532</td><td>2.86%</td></tr>
<tr><td>8</td><td>Georgia</td><td>407,868</td><td>3.24%</td><td>10</td><td>Pennsylvania</td><td>359,008</td><td>2.85%</td></tr>
<tr><td>36</td><td>Hawaii</td><td>66,723</td><td>0.53%</td><td>11</td><td>North Carolina</td><td>309,323</td><td>2.45%</td></tr>
<tr><td>43</td><td>Idaho</td><td>37,278</td><td>0.30%</td><td>12</td><td>Washington</td><td>291,472</td><td>2.31%</td></tr>
<tr><td>5</td><td>Illinois</td><td>558,803</td><td>4.43%</td><td>13</td><td>Arizona</td><td>265,284</td><td>2.10%</td></tr>
<tr><td>18</td><td>Indiana</td><td>225,592</td><td>1.79%</td><td>14</td><td>Massachusetts</td><td>263,780</td><td>2.09%</td></tr>
<tr><td>31</td><td>Iowa</td><td>108,349</td><td>0.86%</td><td>15</td><td>Louisiana</td><td>239,235</td><td>1.90%</td></tr>
<tr><td>29</td><td>Kansas</td><td>115,146</td><td>0.91%</td><td>16</td><td>Virginia</td><td>237,757</td><td>1.89%</td></tr>
<tr><td>30</td><td>Kentucky</td><td>110,328</td><td>0.88%</td><td>17</td><td>Missouri</td><td>231,874</td><td>1.84%</td></tr>
<tr><td>15</td><td>Louisiana</td><td>239,235</td><td>1.90%</td><td>18</td><td>Indiana</td><td>225,592</td><td>1.79%</td></tr>
<tr><td>40</td><td>Maine</td><td>42,116</td><td>0.33%</td><td>19</td><td>Maryland</td><td>220,955</td><td>1.75%</td></tr>
<tr><td>19</td><td>Maryland</td><td>220,955</td><td>1.75%</td><td>20</td><td>Tennessee</td><td>195,854</td><td>1.55%</td></tr>
<tr><td>14</td><td>Massachusetts</td><td>263,780</td><td>2.09%</td><td>21</td><td>Wisconsin</td><td>191,869</td><td>1.52%</td></tr>
<tr><td>6</td><td>Michigan</td><td>487,682</td><td>3.87%</td><td>22</td><td>Colorado</td><td>184,692</td><td>1.47%</td></tr>
<tr><td>23</td><td>Minnesota</td><td>178,252</td><td>1.41%</td><td>23</td><td>Minnesota</td><td>178,252</td><td>1.41%</td></tr>
<tr><td>35</td><td>Mississippi</td><td>83,980</td><td>0.67%</td><td>24</td><td>South Carolina</td><td>168,772</td><td>1.34%</td></tr>
<tr><td>17</td><td>Missouri</td><td>231,874</td><td>1.84%</td><td>25</td><td>Alabama</td><td>166,244</td><td>1.32%</td></tr>
<tr><td>44</td><td>Montana</td><td>31,285</td><td>0.25%</td><td>26</td><td>Oklahoma</td><td>161,558</td><td>1.28%</td></tr>
<tr><td>38</td><td>Nebraska</td><td>61,413</td><td>0.49%</td><td>27</td><td>Oregon</td><td>159,119</td><td>1.26%</td></tr>
<tr><td>37</td><td>Nevada</td><td>62,732</td><td>0.50%</td><td>28</td><td>Connecticut</td><td>154,119</td><td>1.22%</td></tr>
<tr><td>42</td><td>New Hampshire</td><td>37,945</td><td>0.30%</td><td>29</td><td>Kansas</td><td>115,146</td><td>0.91%</td></tr>
<tr><td>9</td><td>New Jersey</td><td>360,532</td><td>2.86%</td><td>30</td><td>Kentucky</td><td>110,328</td><td>0.88%</td></tr>
<tr><td>34</td><td>New Mexico</td><td>89,693</td><td>0.71%</td><td>31</td><td>Iowa</td><td>108,349</td><td>0.86%</td></tr>
<tr><td>4</td><td>New York</td><td>926,596</td><td>7.35%</td><td>32</td><td>Arkansas</td><td>98,213</td><td>0.78%</td></tr>
<tr><td>11</td><td>North Carolina</td><td>309,323</td><td>2.45%</td><td>33</td><td>Utah</td><td>92,577</td><td>0.73%</td></tr>
<tr><td>50</td><td>North Dakota</td><td>16,485</td><td>0.13%</td><td>34</td><td>New Mexico</td><td>89,693</td><td>0.71%</td></tr>
<tr><td>7</td><td>Ohio</td><td>465,143</td><td>3.69%</td><td>35</td><td>Mississippi</td><td>83,980</td><td>0.67%</td></tr>
<tr><td>26</td><td>Oklahoma</td><td>161,558</td><td>1.28%</td><td>36</td><td>Hawaii</td><td>66,723</td><td>0.53%</td></tr>
<tr><td>27</td><td>Oregon</td><td>159,119</td><td>1.26%</td><td>37</td><td>Nevada</td><td>62,732</td><td>0.50%</td></tr>
<tr><td>10</td><td>Pennsylvania</td><td>359,008</td><td>2.85%</td><td>38</td><td>Nebraska</td><td>61,413</td><td>0.49%</td></tr>
<tr><td>39</td><td>Rhode Island</td><td>48,372</td><td>0.38%</td><td>39</td><td>Rhode Island</td><td>48,372</td><td>0.38%</td></tr>
<tr><td>24</td><td>South Carolina</td><td>168,772</td><td>1.34%</td><td>40</td><td>Maine</td><td>42,116</td><td>0.33%</td></tr>
<tr><td>48</td><td>South Dakota</td><td>18,230</td><td>0.14%</td><td>41</td><td>West Virginia</td><td>41,154</td><td>0.33%</td></tr>
<tr><td>20</td><td>Tennessee</td><td>195,854</td><td>1.55%</td><td>42</td><td>New Hampshire</td><td>37,945</td><td>0.30%</td></tr>
<tr><td>2</td><td>Texas</td><td>1,234,977</td><td>9.80%</td><td>43</td><td>Idaho</td><td>37,278</td><td>0.30%</td></tr>
<tr><td>33</td><td>Utah</td><td>92,577</td><td>0.73%</td><td>44</td><td>Montana</td><td>31,285</td><td>0.25%</td></tr>
<tr><td>47</td><td>Vermont</td><td>22,429</td><td>0.18%</td><td>45</td><td>Delaware</td><td>28,998</td><td>0.23%</td></tr>
<tr><td>16</td><td>Virginia</td><td>237,757</td><td>1.89%</td><td>46</td><td>Alaska</td><td>22,567</td><td>0.18%</td></tr>
<tr><td>12</td><td>Washington</td><td>291,472</td><td>2.31%</td><td>47</td><td>Vermont</td><td>22,429</td><td>0.18%</td></tr>
<tr><td>41</td><td>West Virginia</td><td>41,154</td><td>0.33%</td><td>48</td><td>South Dakota</td><td>18,230</td><td>0.14%</td></tr>
<tr><td>21</td><td>Wisconsin</td><td>191,869</td><td>1.52%</td><td>49</td><td>Wyoming</td><td>17,246</td><td>0.14%</td></tr>
<tr><td>49</td><td>Wyoming</td><td>17,246</td><td>0.14%</td><td>50</td><td>North Dakota</td><td>16,485</td><td>0.13%</td></tr>
<tr><td></td><td></td><td></td><td></td><td></td><td>District of Columbia</td><td>49,235</td><td>0.39%</td></tr>
</table>

Source: U.S. Department of Justice, Federal Bureau of Investigation
 "Crime in the United States 1989" (Uniform Crime Reports, August 5, 1990)
*Property crimes are offenses of burglary, larceny-theft and motor vehicle theft.

Percent Change in Number of Property Crimes: 1989 to 1993

National Percent Change = 3.1% Decrease*

<table>
<tr><td colspan="3"><u>ALPHA ORDER</u></td><td colspan="3"><u>RANK ORDER</u></td></tr>
<tr><td>RANK</td><td>STATE</td><td>PERCENT CHANGE</td><td>RANK</td><td>STATE</td><td>PERCENT CHANGE</td></tr>
<tr><td>16</td><td>Alabama</td><td>3.2</td><td>1</td><td>Alaska</td><td>27.6</td></tr>
<tr><td>1</td><td>Alaska</td><td>27.6</td><td>2</td><td>Mississippi</td><td>25.4</td></tr>
<tr><td>25</td><td>Arizona</td><td>(0.3)</td><td>3</td><td>Montana</td><td>23.7</td></tr>
<tr><td>14</td><td>Arkansas</td><td>4.1</td><td>4</td><td>Nevada</td><td>17.5</td></tr>
<tr><td>24</td><td>California</td><td>(0.2)</td><td>5</td><td>Tennessee</td><td>16.5</td></tr>
<tr><td>36</td><td>Colorado</td><td>(4.2)</td><td>6</td><td>Maryland</td><td>14.8</td></tr>
<tr><td>45</td><td>Connecticut</td><td>(10.8)</td><td>7</td><td>North Carolina</td><td>11.7</td></tr>
<tr><td>20</td><td>Delaware</td><td>1.1</td><td>8</td><td>South Dakota</td><td>7.8</td></tr>
<tr><td>23</td><td>Florida</td><td>0.2</td><td>9</td><td>Hawaii</td><td>5.7</td></tr>
<tr><td>41</td><td>Georgia</td><td>(7.2)</td><td>9</td><td>Wyoming</td><td>5.7</td></tr>
<tr><td>9</td><td>Hawaii</td><td>5.7</td><td>11</td><td>North Dakota</td><td>5.5</td></tr>
<tr><td>13</td><td>Idaho</td><td>5.1</td><td>12</td><td>South Carolina</td><td>5.3</td></tr>
<tr><td>33</td><td>Illinois</td><td>(2.5)</td><td>13</td><td>Idaho</td><td>5.1</td></tr>
<tr><td>21</td><td>Indiana</td><td>0.7</td><td>14</td><td>Arkansas</td><td>4.1</td></tr>
<tr><td>42</td><td>Iowa</td><td>(8.6)</td><td>15</td><td>Louisiana</td><td>3.9</td></tr>
<tr><td>30</td><td>Kansas</td><td>(1.6)</td><td>16</td><td>Alabama</td><td>3.2</td></tr>
<tr><td>34</td><td>Kentucky</td><td>(3.9)</td><td>17</td><td>Minnesota</td><td>2.9</td></tr>
<tr><td>15</td><td>Louisiana</td><td>3.9</td><td>18</td><td>West Virginia</td><td>2.8</td></tr>
<tr><td>46</td><td>Maine</td><td>(10.9)</td><td>19</td><td>Virginia</td><td>2.2</td></tr>
<tr><td>6</td><td>Maryland</td><td>14.8</td><td>20</td><td>Delaware</td><td>1.1</td></tr>
<tr><td>39</td><td>Massachusetts</td><td>(6.8)</td><td>21</td><td>Indiana</td><td>0.7</td></tr>
<tr><td>44</td><td>Michigan</td><td>(9.4)</td><td>22</td><td>Oregon</td><td>0.3</td></tr>
<tr><td>17</td><td>Minnesota</td><td>2.9</td><td>23</td><td>Florida</td><td>0.2</td></tr>
<tr><td>2</td><td>Mississippi</td><td>25.4</td><td>24</td><td>California</td><td>(0.2)</td></tr>
<tr><td>31</td><td>Missouri</td><td>(1.8)</td><td>25</td><td>Arizona</td><td>(0.3)</td></tr>
<tr><td>3</td><td>Montana</td><td>23.7</td><td>26</td><td>Wisconsin</td><td>(0.5)</td></tr>
<tr><td>29</td><td>Nebraska</td><td>(1.1)</td><td>27</td><td>Utah</td><td>(0.8)</td></tr>
<tr><td>4</td><td>Nevada</td><td>17.5</td><td>28</td><td>Vermont</td><td>(0.9)</td></tr>
<tr><td>50</td><td>New Hampshire</td><td>(18.0)</td><td>29</td><td>Nebraska</td><td>(1.1)</td></tr>
<tr><td>43</td><td>New Jersey</td><td>(8.8)</td><td>30</td><td>Kansas</td><td>(1.6)</td></tr>
<tr><td>34</td><td>New Mexico</td><td>(3.9)</td><td>31</td><td>Missouri</td><td>(1.8)</td></tr>
<tr><td>47</td><td>New York</td><td>(12.1)</td><td>32</td><td>Washington</td><td>(2.0)</td></tr>
<tr><td>7</td><td>North Carolina</td><td>11.7</td><td>33</td><td>Illinois</td><td>(2.5)</td></tr>
<tr><td>11</td><td>North Dakota</td><td>5.5</td><td>34</td><td>Kentucky</td><td>(3.9)</td></tr>
<tr><td>38</td><td>Ohio</td><td>(5.1)</td><td>34</td><td>New Mexico</td><td>(3.9)</td></tr>
<tr><td>39</td><td>Oklahoma</td><td>(6.8)</td><td>36</td><td>Colorado</td><td>(4.2)</td></tr>
<tr><td>22</td><td>Oregon</td><td>0.3</td><td>36</td><td>Pennsylvania</td><td>(4.2)</td></tr>
<tr><td>36</td><td>Pennsylvania</td><td>(4.2)</td><td>38</td><td>Ohio</td><td>(5.1)</td></tr>
<tr><td>48</td><td>Rhode Island</td><td>(15.3)</td><td>39</td><td>Massachusetts</td><td>(6.8)</td></tr>
<tr><td>12</td><td>South Carolina</td><td>5.3</td><td>39</td><td>Oklahoma</td><td>(6.8)</td></tr>
<tr><td>8</td><td>South Dakota</td><td>7.8</td><td>41</td><td>Georgia</td><td>(7.2)</td></tr>
<tr><td>5</td><td>Tennessee</td><td>16.5</td><td>42</td><td>Iowa</td><td>(8.6)</td></tr>
<tr><td>49</td><td>Texas</td><td>(17.1)</td><td>43</td><td>New Jersey</td><td>(8.8)</td></tr>
<tr><td>27</td><td>Utah</td><td>(0.8)</td><td>44</td><td>Michigan</td><td>(9.4)</td></tr>
<tr><td>28</td><td>Vermont</td><td>(0.9)</td><td>45</td><td>Connecticut</td><td>(10.8)</td></tr>
<tr><td>19</td><td>Virginia</td><td>2.2</td><td>46</td><td>Maine</td><td>(10.9)</td></tr>
<tr><td>32</td><td>Washington</td><td>(2.0)</td><td>47</td><td>New York</td><td>(12.1)</td></tr>
<tr><td>18</td><td>West Virginia</td><td>2.8</td><td>48</td><td>Rhode Island</td><td>(15.3)</td></tr>
<tr><td>26</td><td>Wisconsin</td><td>(0.5)</td><td>49</td><td>Texas</td><td>(17.1)</td></tr>
<tr><td>9</td><td>Wyoming</td><td>5.7</td><td>50</td><td>New Hampshire</td><td>(18.0)</td></tr>
<tr><td></td><td></td><td></td><td colspan="2">District of Columbia</td><td>3.8</td></tr>
</table>

Source: Morgan Quitno Corporation using data from U.S. Department of Justice, Federal Bureau of Investigation
"Crime in the United States" (Uniform Crime Reports, 1989 and 1993 editions)
*Property crimes are offenses of burglary, larceny-theft and motor vehicle theft.

Property Crime Rate in 1989

National Rate = 5,077.9 Property Crimes per 100,000 Population*

ALPHA ORDER				RANK ORDER		
RANK	**STATE**	**RATE**		**RANK**	**STATE**	**RATE**
32	Alabama	4,037.0		1	Florida	7,695.1
28	Alaska	4,282.2		2	Arizona	7,460.2
2	Arizona	7,460.2		3	Texas	7,268.4
31	Arkansas	4,082.0		4	Georgia	6,337.3
8	California	5,785.8		5	Washington	6,122.1
11	Colorado	5,568.0		6	Hawaii	6,000.3
20	Connecticut	4,758.2		7	New Mexico	5,870.0
27	Delaware	4,308.8		8	California	5,785.8
1	Florida	7,695.1		9	Nevada	5,646.4
4	Georgia	6,337.3		10	Oregon	5,642.5
6	Hawaii	6,000.3		11	Colorado	5,568.0
41	Idaho	3,676.3		12	Louisiana	5,459.5
19	Illinois	4,793.3		13	Utah	5,423.4
33	Indiana	4,033.5		14	Michigan	5,259.2
39	Iowa	3,815.1		15	New York	5,162.1
24	Kansas	4,582.0		16	Oklahoma	5,011.0
47	Kentucky	2,960.2		17	Rhode Island	4,846.9
12	Louisiana	5,459.5		18	South Carolina	4,805.6
43	Maine	3,446.5		19	Illinois	4,793.3
22	Maryland	4,707.2		20	Connecticut	4,758.2
26	Massachusetts	4,461.0		21	North Carolina	4,707.4
14	Michigan	5,259.2		22	Maryland	4,707.2
30	Minnesota	4,094.9		23	New Jersey	4,660.4
45	Mississippi	3,204.1		24	Kansas	4,582.0
25	Missouri	4,494.6		25	Missouri	4,494.6
38	Montana	3,881.5		26	Massachusetts	4,461.0
40	Nebraska	3,812.1		27	Delaware	4,308.8
9	Nevada	5,646.4		28	Alaska	4,282.2
44	New Hampshire	3,427.7		29	Ohio	4,264.6
23	New Jersey	4,660.4		30	Minnesota	4,094.9
7	New Mexico	5,870.0		31	Arkansas	4,082.0
15	New York	5,162.1		32	Alabama	4,037.0
21	North Carolina	4,707.4		33	Indiana	4,033.5
49	North Dakota	2,497.7		34	Tennessee	3,964.7
29	Ohio	4,264.6		35	Vermont	3,955.7
16	Oklahoma	5,011.0		36	Wisconsin	3,942.2
10	Oregon	5,642.5		37	Virginia	3,898.9
46	Pennsylvania	2,981.8		38	Montana	3,881.5
17	Rhode Island	4,846.9		39	Iowa	3,815.1
18	South Carolina	4,805.6		40	Nebraska	3,812.1
48	South Dakota	2,549.7		41	Idaho	3,676.3
34	Tennessee	3,964.7		42	Wyoming	3,630.7
3	Texas	7,268.4		43	Maine	3,446.5
13	Utah	5,423.4		44	New Hampshire	3,427.7
35	Vermont	3,955.7		45	Mississippi	3,204.1
37	Virginia	3,898.9		46	Pennsylvania	2,981.8
5	Washington	6,122.1		47	Kentucky	2,960.2
50	West Virginia	2,216.2		48	South Dakota	2,549.7
36	Wisconsin	3,942.2		49	North Dakota	2,497.7
42	Wyoming	3,630.7		50	West Virginia	2,216.2
					District of Columbia	8,151.5

Source: U.S. Department of Justice, Federal Bureau of Investigation
"Crime in the United States 1989" (Uniform Crime Reports, August 5, 1990)
*Property crimes are offenses of burglary, larceny-theft and motor vehicle theft.

Percent Change in Property Crime Rate: 1989 to 1993

National Percent Change = 6.7% Decrease*

ALPHA ORDER				RANK ORDER		
RANK	STATE	PERCENT CHANGE		RANK	STATE	PERCENT CHANGE
13	Alabama	1.5		1	Mississippi	24.4
4	Alaska	12.3		2	Montana	18.8
39	Arizona	(10.0)		3	Tennessee	12.8
12	Arkansas	3.3		4	Alaska	12.3
32	California	(7.0)		5	North Dakota	9.6
41	Colorado	(10.9)		6	Maryland	8.5
44	Connecticut	(11.9)		7	South Dakota	7.8
21	Delaware	(2.8)		8	Wyoming	6.8
34	Florida	(7.1)		9	Louisiana	6.0
47	Georgia	(13.7)		10	North Carolina	5.6
15	Hawaii	0.3		11	West Virginia	4.9
23	Idaho	(3.1)		12	Arkansas	3.3
21	Illinois	(2.8)		13	Alabama	1.5
18	Indiana	(1.4)		13	South Carolina	1.5
35	Iowa	(7.7)		15	Hawaii	0.3
19	Kansas	(2.3)		16	Minnesota	(0.9)
28	Kentucky	(5.5)		16	Nebraska	(0.9)
9	Louisiana	6.0		18	Indiana	(1.4)
45	Maine	(12.1)		19	Kansas	(2.3)
6	Maryland	8.5		20	Vermont	(2.5)
36	Massachusetts	(8.3)		21	Delaware	(2.8)
43	Michigan	(11.4)		21	Illinois	(2.8)
16	Minnesota	(0.9)		23	Idaho	(3.1)
1	Mississippi	24.4		24	Missouri	(3.2)
24	Missouri	(3.2)		25	Wisconsin	(3.9)
2	Montana	18.8		26	Virginia	(4.0)
16	Nebraska	(0.9)		27	Pennsylvania	(4.3)
29	Nevada	(6.0)		28	Kentucky	(5.5)
49	New Hampshire	(19.3)		29	Nevada	(6.0)
40	New Jersey	(10.4)		30	Ohio	(6.6)
38	New Mexico	(9.1)		31	Oregon	(6.7)
46	New York	(13.3)		32	California	(7.0)
10	North Carolina	5.6		32	Oklahoma	(7.0)
5	North Dakota	9.6		34	Florida	(7.1)
30	Ohio	(6.6)		35	Iowa	(7.7)
32	Oklahoma	(7.0)		36	Massachusetts	(8.3)
31	Oregon	(6.7)		37	Utah	(9.0)
27	Pennsylvania	(4.3)		38	New Mexico	(9.1)
48	Rhode Island	(15.5)		39	Arizona	(10.0)
13	South Carolina	1.5		40	New Jersey	(10.4)
7	South Dakota	7.8		41	Colorado	(10.9)
3	Tennessee	12.8		42	Washington	(11.2)
50	Texas	(21.9)		43	Michigan	(11.4)
37	Utah	(9.0)		44	Connecticut	(11.9)
20	Vermont	(2.5)		45	Maine	(12.1)
26	Virginia	(4.0)		46	New York	(13.3)
42	Washington	(11.2)		47	Georgia	(13.7)
11	West Virginia	4.9		48	Rhode Island	(15.5)
25	Wisconsin	(3.9)		49	New Hampshire	(19.3)
8	Wyoming	6.8		50	Texas	(21.9)

District of Columbia   8.4

Source: Morgan Quitno Corporation using data from U.S. Department of Justice, Federal Bureau of Investigation
"Crime in the United States" (Uniform Crime Reports, 1989 and 1993 editions)
*Property crimes are offenses of burglary, larceny-theft and motor vehicle theft.

Burglaries in 1989

National Total = 3,168,170 Burglaries*

ALPHA ORDER

RANK	STATE	BURGLARIES	% of USA
22	Alabama	47,224	1.49%
47	Alaska	4,358	0.14%
16	Arizona	59,284	1.87%
32	Arkansas	28,738	0.91%
1	California	410,468	12.96%
24	Colorado	41,475	1.31%
26	Connecticut	40,035	1.26%
44	Delaware	6,072	0.19%
3	Florida	289,254	9.13%
8	Georgia	110,215	3.48%
37	Hawaii	14,939	0.47%
42	Idaho	8,843	0.28%
5	Illinois	125,441	3.96%
18	Indiana	54,201	1.71%
34	Iowa	24,052	0.76%
31	Kansas	29,871	0.94%
29	Kentucky	30,526	0.96%
13	Louisiana	64,184	2.03%
41	Maine	9,810	0.31%
19	Maryland	52,735	1.66%
14	Massachusetts	63,004	1.99%
6	Michigan	113,579	3.59%
27	Minnesota	39,042	1.23%
30	Mississippi	30,018	0.95%
17	Missouri	58,594	1.85%
46	Montana	5,575	0.18%
39	Nebraska	12,010	0.38%
35	Nevada	15,607	0.49%
43	New Hampshire	8,157	0.26%
11	New Jersey	75,548	2.38%
33	New Mexico	26,146	0.83%
4	New York	211,130	6.66%
9	North Carolina	98,792	3.12%
50	North Dakota	2,369	0.07%
7	Ohio	111,057	3.51%
20	Oklahoma	50,411	1.59%
25	Oregon	40,197	1.27%
10	Pennsylvania	85,925	2.71%
38	Rhode Island	12,045	0.38%
21	South Carolina	48,914	1.54%
48	South Dakota	3,394	0.11%
15	Tennessee	59,621	1.88%
2	Texas	342,346	10.81%
36	Utah	15,311	0.48%
45	Vermont	5,835	0.18%
23	Virginia	46,156	1.46%
12	Washington	73,563	2.32%
40	West Virginia	11,635	0.37%
28	Wisconsin	35,683	1.13%
49	Wyoming	3,001	0.09%

RANK ORDER

RANK	STATE	BURGLARIES	% of USA
1	California	410,468	12.96%
2	Texas	342,346	10.81%
3	Florida	289,254	9.13%
4	New York	211,130	6.66%
5	Illinois	125,441	3.96%
6	Michigan	113,579	3.59%
7	Ohio	111,057	3.51%
8	Georgia	110,215	3.48%
9	North Carolina	98,792	3.12%
10	Pennsylvania	85,925	2.71%
11	New Jersey	75,548	2.38%
12	Washington	73,563	2.32%
13	Louisiana	64,184	2.03%
14	Massachusetts	63,004	1.99%
15	Tennessee	59,621	1.88%
16	Arizona	59,284	1.87%
17	Missouri	58,594	1.85%
18	Indiana	54,201	1.71%
19	Maryland	52,735	1.66%
20	Oklahoma	50,411	1.59%
21	South Carolina	48,914	1.54%
22	Alabama	47,224	1.49%
23	Virginia	46,156	1.46%
24	Colorado	41,475	1.31%
25	Oregon	40,197	1.27%
26	Connecticut	40,035	1.26%
27	Minnesota	39,042	1.23%
28	Wisconsin	35,683	1.13%
29	Kentucky	30,526	0.96%
30	Mississippi	30,018	0.95%
31	Kansas	29,871	0.94%
32	Arkansas	28,738	0.91%
33	New Mexico	26,146	0.83%
34	Iowa	24,052	0.76%
35	Nevada	15,607	0.49%
36	Utah	15,311	0.48%
37	Hawaii	14,939	0.47%
38	Rhode Island	12,045	0.38%
39	Nebraska	12,010	0.38%
40	West Virginia	11,635	0.37%
41	Maine	9,810	0.31%
42	Idaho	8,843	0.28%
43	New Hampshire	8,157	0.26%
44	Delaware	6,072	0.19%
45	Vermont	5,835	0.18%
46	Montana	5,575	0.18%
47	Alaska	4,358	0.14%
48	South Dakota	3,394	0.11%
49	Wyoming	3,001	0.09%
50	North Dakota	2,369	0.07%
	District of Columbia	11,780	0.37%

Source: U.S. Department of Justice, Federal Bureau of Investigation
   "Crime in the United States 1989" (Uniform Crime Reports, August 5, 1990)
*Burglary is the unlawful entry of a structure to commit a felony or theft. Attempts are included.

Percent Change in Number of Burglaries: 1989 to 1993

National Percent Change = 10.5% Decrease*

ALPHA ORDER				RANK ORDER		
RANK	STATE	PERCENT CHANGE		RANK	STATE	PERCENT CHANGE
17	Alabama	(3.5)		1	South Dakota	15.7
3	Alaska	12.3		2	Mississippi	13.2
16	Arizona	(2.7)		3	Alaska	12.3
25	Arkansas	(7.3)		4	Nevada	10.8
11	California	0.9		5	Montana	7.5
35	Colorado	(13.2)		6	Maryland	6.7
45	Connecticut	(19.9)		7	North Carolina	6.6
8	Delaware	2.8		8	Delaware	2.8
35	Florida	(13.2)		9	New Jersey	1.6
42	Georgia	(18.0)		10	Tennessee	1.1
31	Hawaii	(10.9)		11	California	0.9
41	Idaho	(16.9)		12	Wyoming	0.7
21	Illinois	(5.3)		13	North Dakota	0.0
30	Indiana	(10.2)		14	Minnesota	(2.3)
40	Iowa	(14.5)		15	South Carolina	(2.5)
19	Kansas	(4.1)		16	Arizona	(2.7)
26	Kentucky	(8.1)		17	Alabama	(3.5)
27	Louisiana	(8.4)		18	Utah	(3.9)
29	Maine	(9.2)		19	Kansas	(4.1)
6	Maryland	6.7		20	Massachusetts	(4.4)
20	Massachusetts	(4.4)		21	Illinois	(5.3)
42	Michigan	(18.0)		22	Virginia	(6.1)
14	Minnesota	(2.3)		23	West Virginia	(6.3)
2	Mississippi	13.2		24	Wisconsin	(6.4)
27	Missouri	(8.4)		25	Arkansas	(7.3)
5	Montana	7.5		26	Kentucky	(8.1)
32	Nebraska	(11.2)		27	Louisiana	(8.4)
4	Nevada	10.8		27	Missouri	(8.4)
49	New Hampshire	(29.0)		29	Maine	(9.2)
9	New Jersey	1.6		30	Indiana	(10.2)
33	New Mexico	(12.2)		31	Hawaii	(10.9)
39	New York	(13.9)		32	Nebraska	(11.2)
7	North Carolina	6.6		33	New Mexico	(12.2)
13	North Dakota	0.0		34	Ohio	(12.3)
34	Ohio	(12.3)		35	Colorado	(13.2)
46	Oklahoma	(20.8)		35	Florida	(13.2)
47	Oregon	(22.7)		37	Rhode Island	(13.6)
44	Pennsylvania	(18.4)		38	Vermont	(13.7)
37	Rhode Island	(13.6)		39	New York	(13.9)
15	South Carolina	(2.5)		40	Iowa	(14.5)
1	South Dakota	15.7		41	Idaho	(16.9)
10	Tennessee	1.1		42	Georgia	(18.0)
50	Texas	(31.7)		42	Michigan	(18.0)
18	Utah	(3.9)		44	Pennsylvania	(18.4)
38	Vermont	(13.7)		45	Connecticut	(19.9)
22	Virginia	(6.1)		46	Oklahoma	(20.8)
48	Washington	(23.8)		47	Oregon	(22.7)
23	West Virginia	(6.3)		48	Washington	(23.8)
24	Wisconsin	(6.4)		49	New Hampshire	(29.0)
12	Wyoming	0.7		50	Texas	(31.7)

District of Columbia   (2.1)

Source: Morgan Quitno Corporation using data from U.S. Department of Justice, Federal Bureau of Investigation "Crime in the United States" (Uniform Crime Reports, 1989 and 1993 editions)
*Burglary is the unlawful entry of a structure to commit a felony or theft. Attempts are included.

Burglary Rate in 1989

National Rate = 1,276.3 Burglaries per 100,000 Population*

ALPHA ORDER				RANK ORDER		

RANK	STATE	RATE		RANK	STATE	RATE
23	Alabama	1,146.8		1	Florida	2,282.8
38	Alaska	826.9		2	Texas	2,014.9
5	Arizona	1,667.2		3	Georgia	1,712.5
20	Arkansas	1,194.4		4	New Mexico	1,711.1
11	California	1,412.3		5	Arizona	1,667.2
15	Colorado	1,250.4		6	Oklahoma	1,563.6
16	Connecticut	1,236.0		7	Washington	1,545.1
33	Delaware	902.2		8	North Carolina	1,503.5
1	Florida	2,282.8		9	Louisiana	1,464.7
3	Georgia	1,712.5		10	Oregon	1,425.4
14	Hawaii	1,343.4		11	California	1,412.3
36	Idaho	872.1		12	Nevada	1,404.8
27	Illinois	1,076.0		13	South Carolina	1,392.8
32	Indiana	969.1		14	Hawaii	1,343.4
37	Iowa	846.9		15	Colorado	1,250.4
21	Kansas	1,188.7		16	Connecticut	1,236.0
39	Kentucky	819.1		17	Michigan	1,224.8
9	Louisiana	1,464.7		18	Rhode Island	1,206.9
40	Maine	802.8		18	Tennessee	1,206.9
26	Maryland	1,123.5		20	Arkansas	1,194.4
28	Massachusetts	1,065.5		21	Kansas	1,188.7
17	Michigan	1,224.8		22	New York	1,176.2
35	Minnesota	896.9		23	Alabama	1,146.8
24	Mississippi	1,145.3		24	Mississippi	1,145.3
25	Missouri	1,135.8		25	Missouri	1,135.8
46	Montana	691.7		26	Maryland	1,123.5
42	Nebraska	745.5		27	Illinois	1,076.0
12	Nevada	1,404.8		28	Massachusetts	1,065.5
43	New Hampshire	736.9		29	Vermont	1,029.1
31	New Jersey	976.6		30	Ohio	1,018.2
4	New Mexico	1,711.1		31	New Jersey	976.6
22	New York	1,176.2		32	Indiana	969.1
8	North Carolina	1,503.5		33	Delaware	902.2
50	North Dakota	358.9		34	Utah	897.0
30.	Ohio	1,018.2		35	Minnesota	896.9
6	Oklahoma	1,563.6		36	Idaho	872.1
10	Oregon	1,425.4		37	Iowa	846.9
45	Pennsylvania	713.7		38	Alaska	826.9
18	Rhode Island	1,206.9		39	Kentucky	819.1
13	South Carolina	1,392.8		40	Maine	802.8
49	South Dakota	474.7		41	Virginia	756.9
18	Tennessee	1,206.9		42	Nebraska	745.5
2	Texas	2,014.9		43	New Hampshire	736.9
34	Utah	897.0		44	Wisconsin	733.2
29	Vermont	1,029.1		45	Pennsylvania	713.7
41	Virginia	756.9		46	Montana	691.7
7	Washington	1,545.1		47	Wyoming	631.8
48	West Virginia	626.5		48	West Virginia	626.5
44	Wisconsin	733.2		49	South Dakota	474.7
47	Wyoming	631.8		50	North Dakota	358.9
					District of Columbia	1,950.3

Source: U.S. Department of Justice, Federal Bureau of Investigation
"Crime in the United States 1989" (Uniform Crime Reports, August 5, 1990)
*Burglary is the unlawful entry of a structure to commit a felony or theft. Attempts are included.

Percent Change in Burglary Rate: 1989 to 1993

National Percent Change = 13.9% Decrease*

ALPHA ORDER

RANK	STATE	PERCENT CHANGE
14	Alabama	(5.1)
10	Alaska	(1.2)
30	Arizona	(12.1)
21	Arkansas	(8.0)
17	California	(6.0)
40	Colorado	(19.2)
43	Connecticut	(20.9)
9	Delaware	(1.1)
41	Florida	(19.6)
46	Georgia	(23.7)
37	Hawaii	(15.5)
45	Idaho	(23.3)
15	Illinois	(5.6)
30	Indiana	(12.1)
32	Iowa	(13.7)
13	Kansas	(4.8)
22	Kentucky	(9.6)
20	Louisiana	(6.6)
25	Maine	(10.4)
6	Maryland	0.8
17	Massachusetts	(6.0)
42	Michigan	(19.8)
16	Minnesota	(5.8)
2	Mississippi	12.3
24	Missouri	(9.7)
4	Montana	3.3
26	Nebraska	(11.0)
27	Nevada	(11.4)
48	New Hampshire	(30.1)
8	New Jersey	(0.3)
38	New Mexico	(16.9)
36	New York	(15.1)
6	North Carolina	0.8
3	North Dakota	4.0
33	Ohio	(13.8)
44	Oklahoma	(21.0)
47	Oregon	(28.1)
39	Pennsylvania	(18.5)
33	Rhode Island	(13.8)
17	South Carolina	(6.0)
1	South Dakota	15.7
11	Tennessee	(2.0)
50	Texas	(35.6)
28	Utah	(11.8)
35	Vermont	(15.0)
28	Virginia	(11.8)
49	Washington	(30.9)
12	West Virginia	(4.4)
22	Wisconsin	(9.6)
5	Wyoming	1.8

RANK ORDER

RANK	STATE	PERCENT CHANGE
1	South Dakota	15.7
2	Mississippi	12.3
3	North Dakota	4.0
4	Montana	3.3
5	Wyoming	1.8
6	Maryland	0.8
6	North Carolina	0.8
8	New Jersey	(0.3)
9	Delaware	(1.1)
10	Alaska	(1.2)
11	Tennessee	(2.0)
12	West Virginia	(4.4)
13	Kansas	(4.8)
14	Alabama	(5.1)
15	Illinois	(5.6)
16	Minnesota	(5.8)
17	California	(6.0)
17	Massachusetts	(6.0)
17	South Carolina	(6.0)
20	Louisiana	(6.6)
21	Arkansas	(8.0)
22	Kentucky	(9.6)
22	Wisconsin	(9.6)
24	Missouri	(9.7)
25	Maine	(10.4)
26	Nebraska	(11.0)
27	Nevada	(11.4)
28	Utah	(11.8)
28	Virginia	(11.8)
30	Arizona	(12.1)
30	Indiana	(12.1)
32	Iowa	(13.7)
33	Ohio	(13.8)
33	Rhode Island	(13.8)
35	Vermont	(15.0)
36	New York	(15.1)
37	Hawaii	(15.5)
38	New Mexico	(16.9)
39	Pennsylvania	(18.5)
40	Colorado	(19.2)
41	Florida	(19.6)
42	Michigan	(19.8)
43	Connecticut	(20.9)
44	Oklahoma	(21.0)
45	Idaho	(23.3)
46	Georgia	(23.7)
47	Oregon	(28.1)
48	New Hampshire	(30.1)
49	Washington	(30.9)
50	Texas	(35.6)

District of Columbia   2.3

Source: Morgan Quitno Corporation using data from U.S. Department of Justice, Federal Bureau of Investigation
"Crime in the United States" (Uniform Crime Reports, 1989 and 1993 editions)
*Burglary is the unlawful entry of a structure to commit a felony or theft. Attempts are included.

Larceny and Theft in 1989

National Total = 7,872,442 Larcenies and Thefts*

ALPHA ORDER					RANK ORDER			

RANK	STATE	THEFTS	% of USA
25	Alabama	106,771	1.36%
46	Alaska	15,811	0.20%
13	Arizona	181,574	2.31%
33	Arkansas	63,084	0.80%
1	California	972,603	12.35%
21	Colorado	128,195	1.63%
28	Connecticut	91,483	1.16%
45	Delaware	20,294	0.26%
3	Florida	583,702	7.41%
8	Georgia	255,578	3.25%
36	Hawaii	47,374	0.60%
42	Idaho	26,825	0.34%
5	Illinois	362,556	4.61%
16	Indiana	149,514	1.90%
29	Iowa	79,801	1.01%
30	Kansas	77,802	0.99%
32	Kentucky	71,611	0.91%
15	Louisiana	152,209	1.93%
39	Maine	30,067	0.38%
20	Maryland	137,043	1.74%
17	Massachusetts	146,925	1.87%
6	Michigan	307,096	3.90%
22	Minnesota	122,673	1.56%
35	Mississippi	49,266	0.63%
18	Missouri	146,269	1.86%
44	Montana	23,892	0.30%
37	Nebraska	46,403	0.59%
38	Nevada	40,686	0.52%
41	New Hampshire	27,087	0.34%
10	New Jersey	213,878	2.72%
34	New Mexico	58,201	0.74%
4	New York	544,459	6.92%
12	North Carolina	191,783	2.44%
50	North Dakota	13,370	0.17%
7	Ohio	306,609	3.89%
27	Oklahoma	92,270	1.17%
26	Oregon	103,690	1.32%
9	Pennsylvania	216,566	2.75%
40	Rhode Island	27,104	0.34%
24	South Carolina	107,845	1.37%
48	South Dakota	14,057	0.18%
23	Tennessee	109,908	1.40%
2	Texas	741,660	9.42%
31	Utah	73,210	0.93%
47	Vermont	15,466	0.20%
14	Virginia	172,645	2.19%
11	Washington	196,122	2.49%
43	West Virginia	26,608	0.34%
19	Wisconsin	140,040	1.78%
49	Wyoming	13,593	0.17%

RANK	STATE	THEFTS	% of USA
1	California	972,603	12.35%
2	Texas	741,660	9.42%
3	Florida	583,702	7.41%
4	New York	544,459	6.92%
5	Illinois	362,556	4.61%
6	Michigan	307,096	3.90%
7	Ohio	306,609	3.89%
8	Georgia	255,578	3.25%
9	Pennsylvania	216,566	2.75%
10	New Jersey	213,878	2.72%
11	Washington	196,122	2.49%
12	North Carolina	191,783	2.44%
13	Arizona	181,574	2.31%
14	Virginia	172,645	2.19%
15	Louisiana	152,209	1.93%
16	Indiana	149,514	1.90%
17	Massachusetts	146,925	1.87%
18	Missouri	146,269	1.86%
19	Wisconsin	140,040	1.78%
20	Maryland	137,043	1.74%
21	Colorado	128,195	1.63%
22	Minnesota	122,673	1.56%
23	Tennessee	109,908	1.40%
24	South Carolina	107,845	1.37%
25	Alabama	106,771	1.36%
26	Oregon	103,690	1.32%
27	Oklahoma	92,270	1.17%
28	Connecticut	91,483	1.16%
29	Iowa	79,801	1.01%
30	Kansas	77,802	0.99%
31	Utah	73,210	0.93%
32	Kentucky	71,611	0.91%
33	Arkansas	63,084	0.80%
34	New Mexico	58,201	0.74%
35	Mississippi	49,266	0.63%
36	Hawaii	47,374	0.60%
37	Nebraska	46,403	0.59%
38	Nevada	40,686	0.52%
39	Maine	30,067	0.38%
40	Rhode Island	27,104	0.34%
41	New Hampshire	27,087	0.34%
42	Idaho	26,825	0.34%
43	West Virginia	26,608	0.34%
44	Montana	23,892	0.30%
45	Delaware	20,294	0.26%
46	Alaska	15,811	0.20%
47	Vermont	15,466	0.20%
48	South Dakota	14,057	0.18%
49	Wyoming	13,593	0.17%
50	North Dakota	13,370	0.17%
	District of Columbia	29,164	0.37%

Source: U.S. Department of Justice, Federal Bureau of Investigation
"Crime in the United States 1989" (Uniform Crime Reports, August 5, 1990)
*Larceny and theft is the unlawful taking of property without use of force, violence or fraud. Attempts are included. Motor vehicle thefts are excluded.

Percent Change in Number of Larcenies and Thefts: 1989 to 1993

National Percent Change = 0.7% Decrease*

ALPHA ORDER			RANK ORDER		
RANK	STATE	PERCENT CHANGE	RANK	STATE	PERCENT CHANGE
22	Alabama	4.8	1	Alaska	34.1
1	Alaska	34.1	2	Montana	28.2
40	Arizona	(4.9)	3	Mississippi	26.8
11	Arkansas	7.4	4	Tennessee	25.3
37	California	(2.8)	5	Maryland	19.3
36	Colorado	(2.7)	6	North Carolina	14.8
42	Connecticut	(6.1)	7	Nevada	13.4
26	Delaware	2.8	8	Idaho	11.1
23	Florida	3.4	9	Hawaii	9.6
38	Georgia	(3.4)	10	South Carolina	9.0
9	Hawaii	9.6	11	Arkansas	7.4
8	Idaho	11.1	12	Louisiana	7.3
29	Illinois	(0.5)	13	Oregon	6.9
25	Indiana	3.0	13	West Virginia	6.9
44	Iowa	(8.3)	15	Wyoming	6.5
33	Kansas	(1.6)	16	Vermont	6.2
35	Kentucky	(2.6)	17	South Dakota	6.1
12	Louisiana	7.3	18	Minnesota	5.8
46	Maine	(10.4)	19	North Dakota	5.3
5	Maryland	19.3	20	Virginia	4.9
43	Massachusetts	(7.1)	20	Washington	4.9
41	Michigan	(5.5)	22	Alabama	4.8
18	Minnesota	5.8	23	Florida	3.4
3	Mississippi	26.8	24	Oklahoma	3.1
30	Missouri	(0.6)	25	Indiana	3.0
2	Montana	28.2	26	Delaware	2.8
28	Nebraska	0.9	27	Pennsylvania	1.9
7	Nevada	13.4	28	Nebraska	0.9
50	New Hampshire	(14.5)	29	Illinois	(0.5)
45	New Jersey	(8.4)	30	Missouri	(0.6)
34	New Mexico	(2.5)	30	Wisconsin	(0.6)
49	New York	(11.6)	32	Utah	(0.8)
6	North Carolina	14.8	33	Kansas	(1.6)
19	North Dakota	5.3	34	New Mexico	(2.5)
39	Ohio	(3.5)	35	Kentucky	(2.6)
24	Oklahoma	3.1	36	Colorado	(2.7)
13	Oregon	6.9	37	California	(2.8)
27	Pennsylvania	1.9	38	Georgia	(3.4)
48	Rhode Island	(11.1)	39	Ohio	(3.5)
10	South Carolina	9.0	40	Arizona	(4.9)
17	South Dakota	6.1	41	Michigan	(5.5)
4	Tennessee	25.3	42	Connecticut	(6.1)
46	Texas	(10.4)	43	Massachusetts	(7.1)
32	Utah	(0.8)	44	Iowa	(8.3)
16	Vermont	6.2	45	New Jersey	(8.4)
20	Virginia	4.9	46	Maine	(10.4)
20	Washington	4.9	46	Texas	(10.4)
13	West Virginia	6.9	48	Rhode Island	(11.1)
30	Wisconsin	(0.6)	49	New York	(11.6)
15	Wyoming	6.5	50	New Hampshire	(14.5)

District of Columbia   8.0

Source: Morgan Quitno Corporation using data from U.S. Department of Justice, Federal Bureau of Investigation
"Crime in the United States" (Uniform Crime Reports, 1989 and 1993 editions)
*Larceny and theft is the unlawful taking of property without use of force, violence or fraud. Attempts are included. Motor vehicle thefts are excluded.

Larceny and Theft Rate in 1989

National Rate = 3,171.3 Larcenies and Thefts per 100,000 Population*

ALPHA ORDER

RANK ORDER

RANK	STATE	RATE		RANK	STATE	RATE
40	Alabama	2,592.8		1	Arizona	5,106.1
20	Alaska	3,000.2		2	Florida	4,606.6
1	Arizona	5,106.1		3	Texas	4,365.0
39	Arkansas	2,621.9		4	Utah	4,288.8
13	California	3,346.5		5	Hawaii	4,260.3
8	Colorado	3,864.8		6	Washington	4,119.3
30	Connecticut	2,824.4		7	Georgia	3,971.1
19	Delaware	3,015.5		8	Colorado	3,864.8
2	Florida	4,606.6		9	New Mexico	3,809.0
7	Georgia	3,971.1		10	Oregon	3,677.0
5	Hawaii	4,260.3		11	Nevada	3,662.1
38	Idaho	2,645.5		12	Louisiana	3,473.5
15	Illinois	3,109.9		13	California	3,346.5
37	Indiana	2,673.2		14	Michigan	3,311.7
33	Iowa	2,809.9		15	Illinois	3,109.9
16	Kansas	3,096.0		16	Kansas	3,096.0
47	Kentucky	1,921.4		17	South Carolina	3,070.8
12	Louisiana	3,473.5		18	New York	3,033.2
42	Maine	2,460.5		19	Delaware	3,015.5
22	Maryland	2,919.5		20	Alaska	3,000.2
41	Massachusetts	2,484.8		21	Montana	2,964.3
14	Michigan	3,311.7		22	Maryland	2,919.5
31	Minnesota	2,818.1		23	North Carolina	2,918.6
48	Mississippi	1,879.7		24	Nebraska	2,880.4
28	Missouri	2,835.2		25	Wisconsin	2,877.3
21	Montana	2,964.3		26	Oklahoma	2,862.0
24	Nebraska	2,880.4		27	Wyoming	2,861.7
11	Nevada	3,662.1		28	Missouri	2,835.2
43	New Hampshire	2,446.9		29	Virginia	2,831.2
34	New Jersey	2,764.7		30	Connecticut	2,824.4
9	New Mexico	3,809.0		31	Minnesota	2,818.1
18	New York	3,033.2		32	Ohio	2,811.1
23	North Carolina	2,918.6		33	Iowa	2,809.9
45	North Dakota	2,025.8		34	New Jersey	2,764.7
32	Ohio	2,811.1		35	Vermont	2,727.7
26	Oklahoma	2,862.0		36	Rhode Island	2,715.8
10	Oregon	3,677.0		37	Indiana	2,673.2
49	Pennsylvania	1,798.7		38	Idaho	2,645.5
36	Rhode Island	2,715.8		39	Arkansas	2,621.9
17	South Carolina	3,070.8		40	Alabama	2,592.8
46	South Dakota	1,966.0		41	Massachusetts	2,484.8
44	Tennessee	2,224.9		42	Maine	2,460.5
3	Texas	4,365.0		43	New Hampshire	2,446.9
4	Utah	4,288.8		44	Tennessee	2,224.9
35	Vermont	2,727.7		45	North Dakota	2,025.8
29	Virginia	2,831.2		46	South Dakota	1,966.0
6	Washington	4,119.3		47	Kentucky	1,921.4
50	West Virginia	1,432.8		48	Mississippi	1,879.7
25	Wisconsin	2,877.3		49	Pennsylvania	1,798.7
27	Wyoming	2,861.7		50	West Virginia	1,432.8
					District of Columbia	4,828.5

Source: U.S. Department of Justice, Federal Bureau of Investigation
"Crime in the United States 1989" (Uniform Crime Reports, August 5, 1990)
Larceny and theft is the unlawful taking of property without use of force, violence or fraud. Attempts are included. Motor vehicle thefts are excluded.

Percent Change in Rate of Larcenies and Thefts: 1989 to 1993

National Percent Change = 4.4% Decrease*

ALPHA ORDER			RANK ORDER		
RANK	STATE	PERCENT CHANGE	RANK	STATE	PERCENT CHANGE
16	Alabama	3.1	1	Mississippi	25.7
4	Alaska	18.0	2	Montana	23.2
48	Arizona	(14.1)	3	Tennessee	21.4
11	Arkansas	6.6	4	Alaska	18.0
41	California	(9.5)	5	Maryland	12.8
41	Colorado	(9.5)	6	Louisiana	9.5
34	Connecticut	(7.2)	7	North Dakota	9.4
25	Delaware	(1.2)	8	West Virginia	9.1
30	Florida	(4.2)	9	North Carolina	8.6
43	Georgia	(10.1)	10	Wyoming	7.6
15	Hawaii	4.0	11	Arkansas	6.6
18	Idaho	2.5	12	South Dakota	6.1
24	Illinois	(0.8)	13	South Carolina	5.1
22	Indiana	0.8	14	Vermont	4.5
35	Iowa	(7.5)	15	Hawaii	4.0
28	Kansas	(2.3)	16	Alabama	3.1
30	Kentucky	(4.2)	17	Oklahoma	2.9
6	Louisiana	9.5	18	Idaho	2.5
46	Maine	(11.6)	19	Minnesota	1.9
5	Maryland	12.8	20	Pennsylvania	1.8
38	Massachusetts	(8.6)	21	Nebraska	1.1
35	Michigan	(7.5)	22	Indiana	0.8
19	Minnesota	1.9	23	Oregon	(0.5)
1	Mississippi	25.7	24	Illinois	(0.8)
27	Missouri	(2.0)	25	Delaware	(1.2)
2	Montana	23.2	26	Virginia	(1.5)
21	Nebraska	1.1	27	Missouri	(2.0)
40	Nevada	(9.3)	28	Kansas	(2.3)
50	New Hampshire	(15.9)	29	Wisconsin	(4.0)
43	New Jersey	(10.1)	30	Florida	(4.2)
37	New Mexico	(7.8)	30	Kentucky	(4.2)
47	New York	(12.8)	32	Washington	(5.0)
9	North Carolina	8.6	33	Ohio	(5.1)
7	North Dakota	9.4	34	Connecticut	(7.2)
33	Ohio	(5.1)	35	Iowa	(7.5)
17	Oklahoma	2.9	35	Michigan	(7.5)
23	Oregon	(0.5)	37	New Mexico	(7.8)
20	Pennsylvania	1.8	38	Massachusetts	(8.6)
45	Rhode Island	(11.3)	39	Utah	(9.0)
13	South Carolina	5.1	40	Nevada	(9.3)
12	South Dakota	6.1	41	California	(9.5)
3	Tennessee	21.4	41	Colorado	(9.5)
49	Texas	(15.5)	43	Georgia	(10.1)
39	Utah	(9.0)	43	New Jersey	(10.1)
14	Vermont	4.5	45	Rhode Island	(11.3)
26	Virginia	(1.5)	46	Maine	(11.6)
32	Washington	(5.0)	47	New York	(12.8)
8	West Virginia	9.1	48	Arizona	(14.1)
29	Wisconsin	(4.0)	49	Texas	(15.5)
10	Wyoming	7.6	50	New Hampshire	(15.9)

District of Columbia 12.9

Source: Morgan Quitno Corporation using data from U.S. Department of Justice, Federal Bureau of Investigation
"Crime in the United States" (Uniform Crime Reports, 1989 and 1993 editions)
*Larceny and theft is the unlawful taking of property without use of force, violence or fraud. Attempts are included. Motor vehicle thefts are excluded.

Motor Vehicle Thefts in 1989

National Total = 1,564,800 Motor Vehicle Thefts*

<u>ALPHA ORDER</u>

RANK	STATE	THEFTS	% of USA
27	Alabama	12,249	0.78%
43	Alaska	2,398	0.15%
15	Arizona	24,426	1.56%
33	Arkansas	6,391	0.41%
1	California	298,445	19.07%
26	Colorado	15,022	0.96%
17	Connecticut	22,601	1.44%
42	Delaware	2,632	0.17%
4	Florida	102,086	6.52%
11	Georgia	42,075	2.69%
37	Hawaii	4,410	0.28%
46	Idaho	1,610	0.10%
6	Illinois	70,806	4.52%
18	Indiana	21,877	1.40%
36	Iowa	4,496	0.29%
31	Kansas	7,473	0.48%
30	Kentucky	8,191	0.52%
16	Louisiana	22,842	1.46%
44	Maine	2,239	0.14%
12	Maryland	31,177	1.99%
9	Massachusetts	53,851	3.44%
7	Michigan	67,007	4.28%
23	Minnesota	16,537	1.06%
35	Mississippi	4,696	0.30%
13	Missouri	27,011	1.73%
45	Montana	1,818	0.12%
39	Nebraska	3,000	0.19%
32	Nevada	6,439	0.41%
41	New Hampshire	2,701	0.17%
5	New Jersey	71,106	4.54%
34	New Mexico	5,346	0.34%
2	New York	171,007	10.93%
22	North Carolina	18,748	1.20%
49	North Dakota	746	0.05%
10	Ohio	47,477	3.03%
21	Oklahoma	18,877	1.21%
25	Oregon	15,232	0.97%
8	Pennsylvania	56,517	3.61%
29	Rhode Island	9,223	0.59%
28	South Carolina	12,013	0.77%
48	South Dakota	779	0.05%
14	Tennessee	26,325	1.68%
3	Texas	150,971	9.65%
38	Utah	4,056	0.26%
47	Vermont	1,128	0.07%
20	Virginia	18,956	1.21%
19	Washington	21,787	1.39%
40	West Virginia	2,911	0.19%
24	Wisconsin	16,146	1.03%
50	Wyoming	652	0.04%

<u>RANK ORDER</u>

RANK	STATE	THEFTS	% of USA
1	California	298,445	19.07%
2	New York	171,007	10.93%
3	Texas	150,971	9.65%
4	Florida	102,086	6.52%
5	New Jersey	71,106	4.54%
6	Illinois	70,806	4.52%
7	Michigan	67,007	4.28%
8	Pennsylvania	56,517	3.61%
9	Massachusetts	53,851	3.44%
10	Ohio	47,477	3.03%
11	Georgia	42,075	2.69%
12	Maryland	31,177	1.99%
13	Missouri	27,011	1.73%
14	Tennessee	26,325	1.68%
15	Arizona	24,426	1.56%
16	Louisiana	22,842	1.46%
17	Connecticut	22,601	1.44%
18	Indiana	21,877	1.40%
19	Washington	21,787	1.39%
20	Virginia	18,956	1.21%
21	Oklahoma	18,877	1.21%
22	North Carolina	18,748	1.20%
23	Minnesota	16,537	1.06%
24	Wisconsin	16,146	1.03%
25	Oregon	15,232	0.97%
26	Colorado	15,022	0.96%
27	Alabama	12,249	0.78%
28	South Carolina	12,013	0.77%
29	Rhode Island	9,223	0.59%
30	Kentucky	8,191	0.52%
31	Kansas	7,473	0.48%
32	Nevada	6,439	0.41%
33	Arkansas	6,391	0.41%
34	New Mexico	5,346	0.34%
35	Mississippi	4,696	0.30%
36	Iowa	4,496	0.29%
37	Hawaii	4,410	0.28%
38	Utah	4,056	0.26%
39	Nebraska	3,000	0.19%
40	West Virginia	2,911	0.19%
41	New Hampshire	2,701	0.17%
42	Delaware	2,632	0.17%
43	Alaska	2,398	0.15%
44	Maine	2,239	0.14%
45	Montana	1,818	0.12%
46	Idaho	1,610	0.10%
47	Vermont	1,128	0.07%
48	South Dakota	779	0.05%
49	North Dakota	746	0.05%
50	Wyoming	652	0.04%
	District of Columbia	8,291	0.53%

Source: U.S. Department of Justice, Federal Bureau of Investigation
"Crime in the United States 1989" (Uniform Crime Reports, August 5, 1990)
*Includes the theft or attempted theft of a self-propelled vehicle. Excludes motorboats, construction equipment, airplanes and farming equipment.

Percent Change in Number of Motor Vehicle Thefts: 1989 to 1993

National Percent Change = 0.2% Decrease*

ALPHA ORDER				RANK ORDER		
RANK	STATE	PERCENT CHANGE		RANK	STATE	PERCENT CHANGE
12	Alabama	15.5		1	Mississippi	88.6
17	Alaska	12.6		2	Nevada	59.3
3	Arizona	39.2		3	Arizona	39.2
7	Arkansas	22.3		4	North Dakota	26.5
25	California	7.0		5	Idaho	25.2
26	Colorado	6.9		6	New Mexico	22.5
42	Connecticut	(13.7)		7	Arkansas	22.3
43	Delaware	(16.1)		8	Florida	20.0
8	Florida	20.0		9	Hawaii	19.8
35	Georgia	(2.4)		10	Iowa	19.4
9	Hawaii	19.8		11	Oregon	15.6
5	Idaho	25.2		12	Alabama	15.5
38	Illinois	(7.7)		13	Louisiana	15.4
18	Indiana	11.8		14	Tennessee	14.5
10	Iowa	19.4		15	Wisconsin	13.8
22	Kansas	9.3		16	Montana	13.6
33	Kentucky	0.0		17	Alaska	12.6
13	Louisiana	15.4		18	Indiana	11.8
48	Maine	(25.6)		19	Wyoming	11.7
23	Maryland	8.8		20	Utah	11.1
39	Massachusetts	(8.9)		21	Washington	10.0
41	Michigan	(13.0)		22	Kansas	9.3
37	Minnesota	(6.4)		23	Maryland	8.8
1	Mississippi	88.6		24	Nebraska	8.0
28	Missouri	6.1		25	California	7.0
16	Montana	13.6		26	Colorado	6.9
24	Nebraska	8.0		26	North Carolina	6.9
2	Nevada	59.3		28	Missouri	6.1
46	New Hampshire	(19.2)		29	South Dakota	5.1
47	New Jersey	(20.9)		30	South Carolina	4.3
6	New Mexico	22.5		31	Ohio	1.7
40	New York	(11.1)		32	West Virginia	1.0
26	North Carolina	6.9		33	Kentucky	0.0
4	North Dakota	26.5		34	Virginia	(2.2)
31	Ohio	1.7		35	Georgia	(2.4)
45	Oklahoma	(17.7)		36	Pennsylvania	(6.2)
11	Oregon	15.6		37	Minnesota	(6.4)
36	Pennsylvania	(6.2)		38	Illinois	(7.7)
49	Rhode Island	(29.9)		39	Massachusetts	(8.9)
30	South Carolina	4.3		40	New York	(11.1)
29	South Dakota	5.1		41	Michigan	(13.0)
14	Tennessee	14.5		42	Connecticut	(13.7)
44	Texas	(17.3)		43	Delaware	(16.1)
20	Utah	11.1		44	Texas	(17.3)
50	Vermont	(32.3)		45	Oklahoma	(17.7)
34	Virginia	(2.2)		46	New Hampshire	(19.2)
21	Washington	10.0		47	New Jersey	(20.9)
32	West Virginia	1.0		48	Maine	(25.6)
15	Wisconsin	13.8		49	Rhode Island	(29.9)
19	Wyoming	11.7		50	Vermont	(32.3)

District of Columbia (2.8)

Source: Morgan Quitno Corporation using data from U.S. Department of Justice, Federal Bureau of Investigation
   "Crime in the United States" (Uniform Crime Reports, 1989 and 1993 editions)
*Includes the theft or attempted theft of a self-propelled vehicle. Excludes motorboats, construction equipment, airplanes and farming equipment.

Motor Vehicle Theft Rate in 1989

National Rate = 630.4 Motor Vehicle Thefts per 100,000 Population*

ALPHA ORDER				RANK ORDER		
RANK	**STATE**	**RATE**		**RANK**	**STATE**	**RATE**
33	Alabama	297.5		1	California	1,026.9
22	Alaska	455.0		2	New York	952.7
10	Arizona	686.9		3	Rhode Island	924.1
36	Arkansas	265.6		4	New Jersey	919.2
1	California	1,026.9		5	Massachusetts	910.7
23	Colorado	452.9		6	Texas	888.5
9	Connecticut	697.8		7	Florida	805.7
26	Delaware	391.1		8	Michigan	722.6
7	Florida	805.7		9	Connecticut	697.8
12	Georgia	653.7		10	Arizona	686.9
25	Hawaii	396.6		11	Maryland	664.2
45	Idaho	158.8		12	Georgia	653.7
13	Illinois	607.4		13	Illinois	607.4
26	Indiana	391.1		14	Oklahoma	585.5
46	Iowa	158.3		15	Nevada	579.6
34	Kansas	297.4		16	Oregon	540.1
40	Kentucky	219.8		17	Tennessee	532.9
19	Louisiana	521.3		18	Missouri	523.6
43	Maine	183.2		19	Louisiana	521.3
11	Maryland	664.2		20	Pennsylvania	469.4
5	Massachusetts	910.7		21	Washington	457.6
8	Michigan	722.6		22	Alaska	455.0
28	Minnesota	379.9		23	Colorado	452.9
44	Mississippi	179.2		24	Ohio	435.3
18	Missouri	523.6		25	Hawaii	396.6
39	Montana	225.6		26	Delaware	391.1
42	Nebraska	186.2		26	Indiana	391.1
15	Nevada	579.6		28	Minnesota	379.9
37	New Hampshire	244.0		29	New Mexico	349.9
4	New Jersey	919.2		30	South Carolina	342.1
29	New Mexico	349.9		31	Wisconsin	331.7
2	New York	952.7		32	Virginia	310.9
35	North Carolina	285.3		33	Alabama	297.5
49	North Dakota	113.0		34	Kansas	297.4
24	Ohio	435.3		35	North Carolina	285.3
14	Oklahoma	585.5		36	Arkansas	265.6
16	Oregon	540.1		37	New Hampshire	244.0
20	Pennsylvania	469.4		38	Utah	237.6
3	Rhode Island	924.1		39	Montana	225.6
30	South Carolina	342.1		40	Kentucky	219.8
50	South Dakota	109.0		41	Vermont	198.9
17	Tennessee	532.9		42	Nebraska	186.2
6	Texas	888.5		43	Maine	183.2
38	Utah	237.6		44	Mississippi	179.2
41	Vermont	198.9		45	Idaho	158.8
32	Virginia	310.9		46	Iowa	158.3
21	Washington	457.6		47	West Virginia	156.8
47	West Virginia	156.8		48	Wyoming	137.3
31	Wisconsin	331.7		49	North Dakota	113.0
48	Wyoming	137.3		50	South Dakota	109.0
					District of Columbia	1,372.7

Source: U.S. Department of Justice, Federal Bureau of Investigation
   "Crime in the United States 1989" (Uniform Crime Reports, August 5, 1990)
Includes the theft or attempted theft of a self-propelled vehicle. Excludes motorboats, construction equipment, airplanes and farming equipment.

Percent Change in Rate of Motor Vehicle Thefts: 1989 to 1993

National Percent Change = 4.0% Decrease*

<table>
<tr><td colspan="3">ALPHA ORDER</td><td colspan="3">RANK ORDER</td></tr>
<tr><td>RANK</td><td>STATE</td><td>PERCENT CHANGE</td><td>RANK</td><td>STATE</td><td>PERCENT CHANGE</td></tr>
<tr><td>11</td><td>Alabama</td><td>13.5</td><td>1</td><td>Mississippi</td><td>87.0</td></tr>
<tr><td>32</td><td>Alaska</td><td>(0.9)</td><td>2</td><td>North Dakota</td><td>31.6</td></tr>
<tr><td>4</td><td>Arizona</td><td>25.8</td><td>3</td><td>Nevada</td><td>27.4</td></tr>
<tr><td>5</td><td>Arkansas</td><td>21.4</td><td>4</td><td>Arizona</td><td>25.8</td></tr>
<tr><td>30</td><td>California</td><td>(0.4)</td><td>5</td><td>Arkansas</td><td>21.4</td></tr>
<tr><td>31</td><td>Colorado</td><td>(0.6)</td><td>6</td><td>Iowa</td><td>20.5</td></tr>
<tr><td>41</td><td>Connecticut</td><td>(14.7)</td><td>7</td><td>Louisiana</td><td>17.7</td></tr>
<tr><td>44</td><td>Delaware</td><td>(19.4)</td><td>8</td><td>New Mexico</td><td>15.8</td></tr>
<tr><td>13</td><td>Florida</td><td>11.2</td><td>9</td><td>Idaho</td><td>15.5</td></tr>
<tr><td>37</td><td>Georgia</td><td>(9.2)</td><td>10</td><td>Hawaii</td><td>13.7</td></tr>
<tr><td>10</td><td>Hawaii</td><td>13.7</td><td>11</td><td>Alabama</td><td>13.5</td></tr>
<tr><td>9</td><td>Idaho</td><td>15.5</td><td>12</td><td>Wyoming</td><td>12.8</td></tr>
<tr><td>35</td><td>Illinois</td><td>(8.0)</td><td>13</td><td>Florida</td><td>11.2</td></tr>
<tr><td>16</td><td>Indiana</td><td>9.5</td><td>14</td><td>Tennessee</td><td>10.9</td></tr>
<tr><td>6</td><td>Iowa</td><td>20.5</td><td>15</td><td>Wisconsin</td><td>9.9</td></tr>
<tr><td>18</td><td>Kansas</td><td>8.5</td><td>16</td><td>Indiana</td><td>9.5</td></tr>
<tr><td>33</td><td>Kentucky</td><td>(1.6)</td><td>17</td><td>Montana</td><td>9.1</td></tr>
<tr><td>7</td><td>Louisiana</td><td>17.7</td><td>18</td><td>Kansas</td><td>8.5</td></tr>
<tr><td>48</td><td>Maine</td><td>(26.6)</td><td>19</td><td>Nebraska</td><td>8.3</td></tr>
<tr><td>24</td><td>Maryland</td><td>2.9</td><td>20</td><td>Oregon</td><td>7.5</td></tr>
<tr><td>39</td><td>Massachusetts</td><td>(10.4)</td><td>21</td><td>South Dakota</td><td>5.0</td></tr>
<tr><td>42</td><td>Michigan</td><td>(14.9)</td><td>22</td><td>Missouri</td><td>4.6</td></tr>
<tr><td>38</td><td>Minnesota</td><td>(9.8)</td><td>23</td><td>West Virginia</td><td>3.0</td></tr>
<tr><td>1</td><td>Mississippi</td><td>87.0</td><td>24</td><td>Maryland</td><td>2.9</td></tr>
<tr><td>22</td><td>Missouri</td><td>4.6</td><td>25</td><td>Utah</td><td>1.9</td></tr>
<tr><td>17</td><td>Montana</td><td>9.1</td><td>26</td><td>North Carolina</td><td>1.1</td></tr>
<tr><td>19</td><td>Nebraska</td><td>8.3</td><td>27</td><td>South Carolina</td><td>0.6</td></tr>
<tr><td>3</td><td>Nevada</td><td>27.4</td><td>28</td><td>Ohio</td><td>0.0</td></tr>
<tr><td>45</td><td>New Hampshire</td><td>(20.5)</td><td>29</td><td>Washington</td><td>(0.3)</td></tr>
<tr><td>47</td><td>New Jersey</td><td>(22.3)</td><td>30</td><td>California</td><td>(0.4)</td></tr>
<tr><td>8</td><td>New Mexico</td><td>15.8</td><td>31</td><td>Colorado</td><td>(0.6)</td></tr>
<tr><td>40</td><td>New York</td><td>(12.4)</td><td>32</td><td>Alaska</td><td>(0.9)</td></tr>
<tr><td>26</td><td>North Carolina</td><td>1.1</td><td>33</td><td>Kentucky</td><td>(1.6)</td></tr>
<tr><td>2</td><td>North Dakota</td><td>31.6</td><td>34</td><td>Pennsylvania</td><td>(6.2)</td></tr>
<tr><td>28</td><td>Ohio</td><td>0.0</td><td>35</td><td>Illinois</td><td>(8.0)</td></tr>
<tr><td>43</td><td>Oklahoma</td><td>(17.9)</td><td>36</td><td>Virginia</td><td>(8.2)</td></tr>
<tr><td>20</td><td>Oregon</td><td>7.5</td><td>37</td><td>Georgia</td><td>(9.2)</td></tr>
<tr><td>34</td><td>Pennsylvania</td><td>(6.2)</td><td>38</td><td>Minnesota</td><td>(9.8)</td></tr>
<tr><td>49</td><td>Rhode Island</td><td>(30.1)</td><td>39</td><td>Massachusetts</td><td>(10.4)</td></tr>
<tr><td>27</td><td>South Carolina</td><td>0.6</td><td>40</td><td>New York</td><td>(12.4)</td></tr>
<tr><td>21</td><td>South Dakota</td><td>5.0</td><td>41</td><td>Connecticut</td><td>(14.7)</td></tr>
<tr><td>14</td><td>Tennessee</td><td>10.9</td><td>42</td><td>Michigan</td><td>(14.9)</td></tr>
<tr><td>46</td><td>Texas</td><td>(22.1)</td><td>43</td><td>Oklahoma</td><td>(17.9)</td></tr>
<tr><td>25</td><td>Utah</td><td>1.9</td><td>44</td><td>Delaware</td><td>(19.4)</td></tr>
<tr><td>50</td><td>Vermont</td><td>(33.3)</td><td>45</td><td>New Hampshire</td><td>(20.5)</td></tr>
<tr><td>36</td><td>Virginia</td><td>(8.2)</td><td>46</td><td>Texas</td><td>(22.1)</td></tr>
<tr><td>29</td><td>Washington</td><td>(0.3)</td><td>47</td><td>New Jersey</td><td>(22.3)</td></tr>
<tr><td>23</td><td>West Virginia</td><td>3.0</td><td>48</td><td>Maine</td><td>(26.6)</td></tr>
<tr><td>15</td><td>Wisconsin</td><td>9.9</td><td>49</td><td>Rhode Island</td><td>(30.1)</td></tr>
<tr><td>12</td><td>Wyoming</td><td>12.8</td><td>50</td><td>Vermont</td><td>(33.3)</td></tr>
<tr><td></td><td></td><td></td><td colspan="2">District of Columbia</td><td>1.6</td></tr>
</table>

Source: Morgan Quitno Corporation using data from U.S. Department of Justice, Federal Bureau of Investigation
"Crime in the United States" (Uniform Crime Reports, 1989 and 1993 editions)
*Includes the theft or attempted theft of a self-propelled vehicle. Excludes motorboats, construction equipment, airplanes and farming equipment.

VII. APPENDIX

Resident State Population in 1993

National Total = 257,908,000*

ALPHA ORDER					RANK ORDER			

RANK	STATE	POPULATION	% of USA		RANK	STATE	POPULATION	% of USA
22	Alabama	4,187,000	1.62%		1	California	31,211,000	12.10%
48	Alaska	599,000	0.23%		2	New York	18,197,000	7.06%
23	Arizona	3,936,000	1.53%		3	Texas	18,031,000	6.99%
33	Arkansas	2,424,000	0.94%		4	Florida	13,679,000	5.30%
1	California	31,211,000	12.10%		5	Pennsylvania	12,048,000	4.67%
26	Colorado	3,566,000	1.38%		6	Illinois	11,697,000	4.54%
27	Connecticut	3,277,000	1.27%		7	Ohio	11,091,000	4.30%
46	Delaware	700,000	0.27%		8	Michigan	9,478,000	3.67%
4	Florida	13,679,000	5.30%		9	New Jersey	7,879,000	3.05%
11	Georgia	6,917,000	2.68%		10	North Carolina	6,945,000	2.69%
40	Hawaii	1,172,000	0.45%		11	Georgia	6,917,000	2.68%
42	Idaho	1,099,000	0.43%		12	Virginia	6,491,000	2.52%
6	Illinois	11,697,000	4.54%		13	Massachusetts	6,012,000	2.33%
14	Indiana	5,713,000	2.22%		14	Indiana	5,713,000	2.22%
30	Iowa	2,814,000	1.09%		15	Washington	5,255,000	2.04%
32	Kansas	2,531,000	0.98%		16	Missouri	5,234,000	2.03%
24	Kentucky	3,789,000	1.47%		17	Tennessee	5,099,000	1.98%
21	Louisiana	4,295,000	1.67%		18	Wisconsin	5,038,000	1.95%
39	Maine	1,239,000	0.48%		19	Maryland	4,965,000	1.93%
19	Maryland	4,965,000	1.93%		20	Minnesota	4,517,000	1.75%
13	Massachusetts	6,012,000	2.33%		21	Louisiana	4,295,000	1.67%
8	Michigan	9,478,000	3.67%		22	Alabama	4,187,000	1.62%
20	Minnesota	4,517,000	1.75%		23	Arizona	3,936,000	1.53%
31	Mississippi	2,643,000	1.02%		24	Kentucky	3,789,000	1.47%
16	Missouri	5,234,000	2.03%		25	South Carolina	3,643,000	1.41%
44	Montana	839,000	0.33%		26	Colorado	3,566,000	1.38%
37	Nebraska	1,607,000	0.62%		27	Connecticut	3,277,000	1.27%
38	Nevada	1,389,000	0.54%		28	Oklahoma	3,231,000	1.25%
41	New Hampshire	1,125,000	0.44%		29	Oregon	3,032,000	1.18%
9	New Jersey	7,879,000	3.05%		30	Iowa	2,814,000	1.09%
36	New Mexico	1,616,000	0.63%		31	Mississippi	2,643,000	1.02%
2	New York	18,197,000	7.06%		32	Kansas	2,531,000	0.98%
10	North Carolina	6,945,000	2.69%		33	Arkansas	2,424,000	0.94%
47	North Dakota	635,000	0.25%		34	Utah	1,860,000	0.72%
7	Ohio	11,091,000	4.30%		35	West Virginia	1,820,000	0.71%
28	Oklahoma	3,231,000	1.25%		36	New Mexico	1,616,000	0.63%
29	Oregon	3,032,000	1.18%		37	Nebraska	1,607,000	0.62%
5	Pennsylvania	12,048,000	4.67%		38	Nevada	1,389,000	0.54%
43	Rhode Island	1,000,000	0.39%		39	Maine	1,239,000	0.48%
25	South Carolina	3,643,000	1.41%		40	Hawaii	1,172,000	0.45%
45	South Dakota	715,000	0.28%		41	New Hampshire	1,125,000	0.44%
17	Tennessee	5,099,000	1.98%		42	Idaho	1,099,000	0.43%
3	Texas	18,031,000	6.99%		43	Rhode Island	1,000,000	0.39%
34	Utah	1,860,000	0.72%		44	Montana	839,000	0.33%
49	Vermont	576,000	0.22%		45	South Dakota	715,000	0.28%
12	Virginia	6,491,000	2.52%		46	Delaware	700,000	0.27%
15	Washington	5,255,000	2.04%		47	North Dakota	635,000	0.25%
35	West Virginia	1,820,000	0.71%		48	Alaska	599,000	0.23%
18	Wisconsin	5,038,000	1.95%		49	Vermont	576,000	0.22%
50	Wyoming	470,000	0.18%		50	Wyoming	470,000	0.18%
						District of Columbia	578,000	0.22%

Source: U.S. Bureau of the Census
   Press Release CB93-219 (December 29, 1993)
*Resident population. Includes armed forces residing in each state.

Resident State Population in 1992

National Total = 255,082,000*

ALPHA ORDER

RANK	STATE	POPULATION	% of USA
22	Alabama	4,138,000	1.62%
48	Alaska	588,000	0.23%
23	Arizona	3,832,000	1.50%
33	Arkansas	2,394,000	0.94%
1	California	30,895,000	12.11%
26	Colorado	3,465,000	1.36%
27	Connecticut	3,279,000	1.29%
46	Delaware	691,000	0.27%
4	Florida	13,483,000	5.29%
11	Georgia	6,773,000	2.66%
40	Hawaii	1,156,000	0.45%
42	Idaho	1,066,000	0.42%
6	Illinois	11,613,000	4.55%
14	Indiana	5,658,000	2.22%
30	Iowa	2,803,000	1.10%
32	Kansas	2,515,000	0.99%
24	Kentucky	3,754,000	1.47%
21	Louisiana	4,279,000	1.68%
39	Maine	1,236,000	0.48%
19	Maryland	4,917,000	1.93%
13	Massachusetts	5,993,000	2.35%
8	Michigan	9,434,000	3.70%
20	Minnesota	4,468,000	1.75%
31	Mississippi	2,615,000	1.03%
15	Missouri	5,191,000	2.04%
44	Montana	822,000	0.32%
36	Nebraska	1,601,000	0.63%
38	Nevada	1,336,000	0.52%
41	New Hampshire	1,115,000	0.44%
9	New Jersey	7,820,000	3.07%
37	New Mexico	1,582,000	0.62%
2	New York	18,109,000	7.10%
10	North Carolina	6,836,000	2.68%
47	North Dakota	634,000	0.25%
7	Ohio	11,021,000	4.32%
28	Oklahoma	3,205,000	1.26%
29	Oregon	2,972,000	1.17%
5	Pennsylvania	11,995,000	4.70%
43	Rhode Island	1,001,000	0.39%
25	South Carolina	3,603,000	1.41%
45	South Dakota	708,000	0.28%
17	Tennessee	5,025,000	1.97%
3	Texas	17,683,000	6.93%
34	Utah	1,811,000	0.71%
49	Vermont	571,000	0.22%
12	Virginia	6,394,000	2.51%
16	Washington	5,143,000	2.02%
35	West Virginia	1,809,000	0.71%
18	Wisconsin	4,993,000	1.96%
50	Wyoming	465,000	0.18%

RANK ORDER

RANK	STATE	POPULATION	% of USA
1	California	30,895,000	12.11%
2	New York	18,109,000	7.10%
3	Texas	17,683,000	6.93%
4	Florida	13,483,000	5.29%
5	Pennsylvania	11,995,000	4.70%
6	Illinois	11,613,000	4.55%
7	Ohio	11,021,000	4.32%
8	Michigan	9,434,000	3.70%
9	New Jersey	7,820,000	3.07%
10	North Carolina	6,836,000	2.68%
11	Georgia	6,773,000	2.66%
12	Virginia	6,394,000	2.51%
13	Massachusetts	5,993,000	2.35%
14	Indiana	5,658,000	2.22%
15	Missouri	5,191,000	2.04%
16	Washington	5,143,000	2.02%
17	Tennessee	5,025,000	1.97%
18	Wisconsin	4,993,000	1.96%
19	Maryland	4,917,000	1.93%
20	Minnesota	4,468,000	1.75%
21	Louisiana	4,279,000	1.68%
22	Alabama	4,138,000	1.62%
23	Arizona	3,832,000	1.50%
24	Kentucky	3,754,000	1.47%
25	South Carolina	3,603,000	1.41%
26	Colorado	3,465,000	1.36%
27	Connecticut	3,279,000	1.29%
28	Oklahoma	3,205,000	1.26%
29	Oregon	2,972,000	1.17%
30	Iowa	2,803,000	1.10%
31	Mississippi	2,615,000	1.03%
32	Kansas	2,515,000	0.99%
33	Arkansas	2,394,000	0.94%
34	Utah	1,811,000	0.71%
35	West Virginia	1,809,000	0.71%
36	Nebraska	1,601,000	0.63%
37	New Mexico	1,582,000	0.62%
38	Nevada	1,336,000	0.52%
39	Maine	1,236,000	0.48%
40	Hawaii	1,156,000	0.45%
41	New Hampshire	1,115,000	0.44%
42	Idaho	1,066,000	0.42%
43	Rhode Island	1,001,000	0.39%
44	Montana	822,000	0.32%
45	South Dakota	708,000	0.28%
46	Delaware	691,000	0.27%
47	North Dakota	634,000	0.25%
48	Alaska	588,000	0.23%
49	Vermont	571,000	0.22%
50	Wyoming	465,000	0.18%
	District of Columbia	585,000	0.23%

Source: U.S. Bureau of the Census
Press Release CB93-219 (December 29, 1993)
*Resident population. Includes armed forces residing in each state.

Resident State Population in 1991

National Total = 252,137,000*

ALPHA ORDER

RANK	STATE	POPULATION	% of USA
22	Alabama	4,090,000	1.62%
48	Alaska	569,000	0.23%
23	Arizona	3,746,000	1.49%
33	Arkansas	2,371,000	0.94%
1	California	30,407,000	12.06%
26	Colorado	3,370,000	1.34%
27	Connecticut	3,290,000	1.30%
46	Delaware	681,000	0.27%
4	Florida	13,273,000	5.26%
11	Georgia	6,628,000	2.63%
40	Hawaii	1,135,000	0.45%
42	Idaho	1,038,000	0.41%
6	Illinois	11,525,000	4.57%
14	Indiana	5,607,000	2.22%
30	Iowa	2,790,000	1.11%
32	Kansas	2,491,000	0.99%
24	Kentucky	3,715,000	1.47%
21	Louisiana	4,244,000	1.68%
39	Maine	1,236,000	0.49%
19	Maryland	4,863,000	1.93%
13	Massachusetts	5,995,000	2.38%
8	Michigan	9,375,000	3.72%
20	Minnesota	4,426,000	1.76%
31	Mississippi	2,592,000	1.03%
15	Missouri	5,156,000	2.04%
44	Montana	807,000	0.32%
36	Nebraska	1,590,000	0.63%
38	Nevada	1,288,000	0.51%
41	New Hampshire	1,108,000	0.44%
9	New Jersey	7,773,000	3.08%
37	New Mexico	1,547,000	0.61%
2	New York	18,047,000	7.16%
10	North Carolina	6,749,000	2.68%
47	North Dakota	633,000	0.25%
7	Ohio	10,940,000	4.34%
28	Oklahoma	3,168,000	1.26%
29	Oregon	2,919,000	1.16%
5	Pennsylvania	11,949,000	4.74%
43	Rhode Island	1,004,000	0.40%
25	South Carolina	3,561,000	1.41%
45	South Dakota	702,000	0.28%
17	Tennessee	4,952,000	1.96%
3	Texas	17,352,000	6.88%
35	Utah	1,767,000	0.70%
49	Vermont	568,000	0.23%
12	Virginia	6,288,000	2.49%
16	Washington	5,016,000	1.99%
34	West Virginia	1,799,000	0.71%
18	Wisconsin	4,947,000	1.96%
50	Wyoming	458,000	0.18%

RANK ORDER

RANK	STATE	POPULATION	% of USA
1	California	30,407,000	12.06%
2	New York	18,047,000	7.16%
3	Texas	17,352,000	6.88%
4	Florida	13,273,000	5.26%
5	Pennsylvania	11,949,000	4.74%
6	Illinois	11,525,000	4.57%
7	Ohio	10,940,000	4.34%
8	Michigan	9,375,000	3.72%
9	New Jersey	7,773,000	3.08%
10	North Carolina	6,749,000	2.68%
11	Georgia	6,628,000	2.63%
12	Virginia	6,288,000	2.49%
13	Massachusetts	5,995,000	2.38%
14	Indiana	5,607,000	2.22%
15	Missouri	5,156,000	2.04%
16	Washington	5,016,000	1.99%
17	Tennessee	4,952,000	1.96%
18	Wisconsin	4,947,000	1.96%
19	Maryland	4,863,000	1.93%
20	Minnesota	4,426,000	1.76%
21	Louisiana	4,244,000	1.68%
22	Alabama	4,090,000	1.62%
23	Arizona	3,746,000	1.49%
24	Kentucky	3,715,000	1.47%
25	South Carolina	3,561,000	1.41%
26	Colorado	3,370,000	1.34%
27	Connecticut	3,290,000	1.30%
28	Oklahoma	3,168,000	1.26%
29	Oregon	2,919,000	1.16%
30	Iowa	2,790,000	1.11%
31	Mississippi	2,592,000	1.03%
32	Kansas	2,491,000	0.99%
33	Arkansas	2,371,000	0.94%
34	West Virginia	1,799,000	0.71%
35	Utah	1,767,000	0.70%
36	Nebraska	1,590,000	0.63%
37	New Mexico	1,547,000	0.61%
38	Nevada	1,288,000	0.51%
39	Maine	1,236,000	0.49%
40	Hawaii	1,135,000	0.45%
41	New Hampshire	1,108,000	0.44%
42	Idaho	1,038,000	0.41%
43	Rhode Island	1,004,000	0.40%
44	Montana	807,000	0.32%
45	South Dakota	702,000	0.28%
46	Delaware	681,000	0.27%
47	North Dakota	633,000	0.25%
48	Alaska	569,000	0.23%
49	Vermont	568,000	0.23%
50	Wyoming	458,000	0.18%
	District of Columbia	594,000	0.24%

Source: U.S. Bureau of the Census
  Press Release CB93-219 (December 29, 1993)
*Resident population. Includes armed forces residing in each state.

Urban Population in 1993

National Total = 203,306,162 Urban Population*

RANK	STATE	POPULATION	% of USA
22	Alabama	3,399,065	1.67%
45	Alaska	409,945	0.20%
20	Arizona	3,633,939	1.79%
32	Arkansas	1,609,504	0.79%
1	California	30,594,127	15.05%
23	Colorado	3,208,477	1.58%
24	Connecticut	3,086,065	1.52%
43	Delaware	611,628	0.30%
4	Florida	12,937,368	6.36%
10	Georgia	5,558,656	2.73%
40	Hawaii	914,776	0.45%
42	Idaho	715,640	0.35%
NA	Illinois**	NA	NA
15	Indiana	4,661,803	2.29%
30	Iowa	1,919,787	0.94%
29	Kansas	2,074,830	1.02%
28	Kentucky	2,408,748	1.18%
21	Louisiana	3,537,890	1.74%
41	Maine	892,999	0.44%
14	Maryland	4,698,976	2.31%
9	Massachusetts	5,999,742	2.95%
7	Michigan	8,446,953	4.15%
19	Minnesota	3,650,623	1.80%
33	Mississippi	1,494,206	0.73%
16	Missouri	4,057,993	2.00%
47	Montana	407,883	0.20%
36	Nebraska	1,193,493	0.59%
35	Nevada	1,219,162	0.60%
39	New Hampshire	984,474	0.48%
8	New Jersey	7,879,000	3.88%
34	New Mexico	1,322,854	0.65%
2	New York	17,339,782	8.53%
12	North Carolina	5,304,742	2.61%
46	North Dakota	408,755	0.20%
6	Ohio	9,776,241	4.81%
26	Oklahoma	2,605,326	1.28%
27	Oregon	2,543,497	1.25%
5	Pennsylvania	10,984,114	5.40%
38	Rhode Island	1,000,000	0.49%
25	South Carolina	2,857,398	1.41%
44	South Dakota	424,578	0.21%
18	Tennessee	3,990,059	1.96%
3	Texas	16,438,651	8.09%
31	Utah	1,658,629	0.82%
49	Vermont	312,729	0.15%
11	Virginia	5,442,934	2.68%
13	Washington	4,770,656	2.35%
37	West Virginia	1,038,723	0.51%
17	Wisconsin	4,052,489	1.99%
48	Wyoming	345,829	0.17%

RANK	STATE	POPULATION	% of USA
1	California	30,594,127	15.05%
2	New York	17,339,782	8.53%
3	Texas	16,438,651	8.09%
4	Florida	12,937,368	6.36%
5	Pennsylvania	10,984,114	5.40%
6	Ohio	9,776,241	4.81%
7	Michigan	8,446,953	4.15%
8	New Jersey	7,879,000	3.88%
9	Massachusetts	5,999,742	2.95%
10	Georgia	5,558,656	2.73%
11	Virginia	5,442,934	2.68%
12	North Carolina	5,304,742	2.61%
13	Washington	4,770,656	2.35%
14	Maryland	4,698,976	2.31%
15	Indiana	4,661,803	2.29%
16	Missouri	4,057,993	2.00%
17	Wisconsin	4,052,489	1.99%
18	Tennessee	3,990,059	1.96%
19	Minnesota	3,650,623	1.80%
20	Arizona	3,633,939	1.79%
21	Louisiana	3,537,890	1.74%
22	Alabama	3,399,065	1.67%
23	Colorado	3,208,477	1.58%
24	Connecticut	3,086,065	1.52%
25	South Carolina	2,857,398	1.41%
26	Oklahoma	2,605,326	1.28%
27	Oregon	2,543,497	1.25%
28	Kentucky	2,408,748	1.18%
29	Kansas	2,074,830	1.02%
30	Iowa	1,919,787	0.94%
31	Utah	1,658,629	0.82%
32	Arkansas	1,609,504	0.79%
33	Mississippi	1,494,206	0.73%
34	New Mexico	1,322,854	0.65%
35	Nevada	1,219,162	0.60%
36	Nebraska	1,193,493	0.59%
37	West Virginia	1,038,723	0.51%
38	Rhode Island	1,000,000	0.49%
39	New Hampshire	984,474	0.48%
40	Hawaii	914,776	0.45%
41	Maine	892,999	0.44%
42	Idaho	715,640	0.35%
43	Delaware	611,628	0.30%
44	South Dakota	424,578	0.21%
45	Alaska	409,945	0.20%
46	North Dakota	408,755	0.20%
47	Montana	407,883	0.20%
48	Wyoming	345,829	0.17%
49	Vermont	312,729	0.15%
NA	Illinois**	NA	NA
	District of Columbia	578,000	0.28%

Source: Morgan Quitno Corporation using data from U.S. Department of Justice, Federal Bureau of Investigation
"Crime in the United States 1993" (Uniform Crime Reports, December 4, 1994)
*Estimated totals for urban areas, defined by the F.B.I. as Metropolitan Statistical Areas and other cities outside such areas. National total is only for states reporting.
**Not available.

Rural Population in 1993

National Total = 28,905,838 Rural Population*

<u>ALPHA ORDER</u>

RANK	STATE	POPULATION	% of USA
18	Alabama	787,935	2.73%
42	Alaska	189,055	0.65%
33	Arizona	302,061	1.04%
17	Arkansas	814,496	2.82%
24	California	616,873	2.13%
31	Colorado	357,523	1.24%
41	Connecticut	190,935	0.66%
46	Delaware	88,372	0.31%
22	Florida	741,632	2.57%
4	Georgia	1,358,344	4.70%
38	Hawaii	257,224	0.89%
30	Idaho	383,360	1.33%
NA	Illinois**	NA	NA
10	Indiana	1,051,197	3.64%
14	Iowa	894,213	3.09%
27	Kansas	456,170	1.58%
3	Kentucky	1,380,252	4.77%
21	Louisiana	757,110	2.62%
32	Maine	346,001	1.20%
36	Maryland	266,024	0.92%
47	Massachusetts	12,258	0.04%
12	Michigan	1,031,047	3.57%
15	Minnesota	866,377	3.00%
7	Mississippi	1,148,794	3.97%
6	Missouri	1,176,007	4.07%
28	Montana	431,117	1.49%
29	Nebraska	413,507	1.43%
43	Nevada	169,838	0.59%
44	New Hampshire	140,526	0.49%
48	New Jersey	0	0.00%
34	New Mexico	293,146	1.01%
16	New York	857,218	2.97%
1	North Carolina	1,640,258	5.67%
39	North Dakota	226,245	0.78%
5	Ohio	1,314,759	4.55%
23	Oklahoma	625,674	2.16%
25	Oregon	488,503	1.69%
9	Pennsylvania	1,063,886	3.68%
48	Rhode Island	0	0.00%
19	South Carolina	785,602	2.72%
35	South Dakota	290,422	1.00%
8	Tennessee	1,108,941	3.84%
2	Texas	1,592,349	5.51%
40	Utah	201,371	0.70%
37	Vermont	263,271	0.91%
11	Virginia	1,048,066	3.63%
26	Washington	484,344	1.68%
20	West Virginia	781,277	2.70%
13	Wisconsin	985,511	3.41%
45	Wyoming	124,171	0.43%

<u>RANK ORDER</u>

RANK	STATE	POPULATION	% of USA
1	North Carolina	1,640,258	5.67%
2	Texas	1,592,349	5.51%
3	Kentucky	1,380,252	4.77%
4	Georgia	1,358,344	4.70%
5	Ohio	1,314,759	4.55%
6	Missouri	1,176,007	4.07%
7	Mississippi	1,148,794	3.97%
8	Tennessee	1,108,941	3.84%
9	Pennsylvania	1,063,886	3.68%
10	Indiana	1,051,197	3.64%
11	Virginia	1,048,066	3.63%
12	Michigan	1,031,047	3.57%
13	Wisconsin	985,511	3.41%
14	Iowa	894,213	3.09%
15	Minnesota	866,377	3.00%
16	New York	857,218	2.97%
17	Arkansas	814,496	2.82%
18	Alabama	787,935	2.73%
19	South Carolina	785,602	2.72%
20	West Virginia	781,277	2.70%
21	Louisiana	757,110	2.62%
22	Florida	741,632	2.57%
23	Oklahoma	625,674	2.16%
24	California	616,873	2.13%
25	Oregon	488,503	1.69%
26	Washington	484,344	1.68%
27	Kansas	456,170	1.58%
28	Montana	431,117	1.49%
29	Nebraska	413,507	1.43%
30	Idaho	383,360	1.33%
31	Colorado	357,523	1.24%
32	Maine	346,001	1.20%
33	Arizona	302,061	1.04%
34	New Mexico	293,146	1.01%
35	South Dakota	290,422	1.00%
36	Maryland	266,024	0.92%
37	Vermont	263,271	0.91%
38	Hawaii	257,224	0.89%
39	North Dakota	226,245	0.78%
40	Utah	201,371	0.70%
41	Connecticut	190,935	0.66%
42	Alaska	189,055	0.65%
43	Nevada	169,838	0.59%
44	New Hampshire	140,526	0.49%
45	Wyoming	124,171	0.43%
46	Delaware	88,372	0.31%
47	Massachusetts	12,258	0.04%
48	New Jersey	0	0.00%
48	Rhode Island	0	0.00%
NA	Illinois**	NA	NA
	District of Columbia	0	0.00%

Source: Morgan Quitno Corporation using data from U.S. Department of Justice, Federal Bureau of Investigation
   "Crime in the United States 1993" (Uniform Crime Reports, December 4, 1994)
*Estimated totals for rural areas, defined by the F.B.I. as other than Metropolitan Statistical Areas and other cities outside such areas. National total is only for states reporting.
**Not available.

Percent of Population Covered in the F.B.I.'s Uniform Crime Report in 1993

National Percent = 94.73% of Population Covered*

ALPHA ORDER			RANK ORDER		
RANK	STATE	PERCENT	RANK	STATE	PERCENT
9	Alabama	99.86	1	Alaska	100.00
1	Alaska	100.00	1	Hawaii	100.00
15	Arizona	99.77	1	Vermont	100.00
13	Arkansas	99.79	4	Texas	99.97
43	California	89.58	5	Louisiana	99.95
6	Colorado	99.92	6	Colorado	99.92
46	Connecticut	85.02	7	Idaho	99.91
25	Delaware	99.00	8	Montana	99.88
27	Florida	98.32	9	Alabama	99.86
36	Georgia	97.17	9	North Carolina	99.86
1	Hawaii	100.00	11	North Dakota	99.84
7	Idaho	99.91	12	Virginia	99.80
18	Illinois	99.54	13	Arkansas	99.79
37	Indiana	97.08	13	Wyoming	99.79
23	Iowa	99.11	15	Arizona	99.77
33	Kansas	97.43	16	Michigan	99.58
26	Kentucky	98.79	17	Utah	99.57
5	Louisiana	99.95	18	Illinois	99.54
24	Maine	99.03	19	Nebraska	99.50
32	Maryland	97.72	20	South Carolina	99.48
30	Massachusetts	97.97	21	Rhode Island	99.40
16	Michigan	99.58	22	Nevada	99.35
40	Minnesota	92.36	23	Iowa	99.11
49	Mississippi	81.12	24	Maine	99.03
31	Missouri	97.90	25	Delaware	99.00
8	Montana	99.88	26	Kentucky	98.79
19	Nebraska	99.50	27	Florida	98.32
22	Nevada	99.35	28	Oklahoma	98.30
48	New Hampshire	82.58	29	Washington	98.14
38	New Jersey	96.50	30	Massachusetts	97.97
39	New Mexico	95.05	31	Missouri	97.90
44	New York	88.69	32	Maryland	97.72
9	North Carolina	99.86	33	Kansas	97.43
11	North Dakota	99.84	34	Oregon	97.23
42	Ohio	91.34	35	Wisconsin	97.20
28	Oklahoma	98.30	36	Georgia	97.17
34	Oregon	97.23	37	Indiana	97.08
50	Pennsylvania	75.45	38	New Jersey	96.50
21	Rhode Island	99.40	39	New Mexico	95.05
20	South Carolina	99.48	40	Minnesota	92.36
45	South Dakota	86.71	41	Tennessee	92.27
41	Tennessee	92.27	42	Ohio	91.34
4	Texas	99.97	43	California	89.58
17	Utah	99.57	44	New York	88.69
1	Vermont	100.00	45	South Dakota	86.71
12	Virginia	99.80	46	Connecticut	85.02
29	Washington	98.14	47	West Virginia	83.19
47	West Virginia	83.19	48	New Hampshire	82.58
35	Wisconsin	97.20	49	Mississippi	81.12
13	Wyoming	99.79	50	Pennsylvania	75.45
				District of Columbia	100.00

Source: Morgan Quitno Corporation using data from U.S. Department of Justice, Federal Bureau of Investigation "Crime in the United States 1993" (Uniform Crime Reports, December 4, 1994)

*The Uniform Crime Reporting (UCR) Program is a nationwide, cooperative statistical effort of more than 16,000 city, county and state law enforcement agencies voluntarily reporting data on crimes brought to their attention. During 1993, law enforcement agencies active in the UCR Program represented more than 245 million U.S. inhabitants or almost 95 percent of the population.

VIII. SOURCES

Administrative Office of the U.S. Courts
Statistics Division
One Columbus Circle
Washington, DC   20544
202-273-2290

American Correctional Association
8025 Laurel Lakes Court
Laurel, MD   20707-5705
301-206-5051

Bureau of the Census
3 Silver Hill & Suitland Roads
Suitland, MD   20746
301-457-2794

Bureau of Justice Assistance Clearinghouse
Box 6000
Rockville, MD   20850
800-688-4252

Bureau of Justice Statistics Clearinghouse
Box 6000
Rockville, MD   20850
800-732-3277

Corrections Compendium
CEGA Publishing
P.O. Box 81826
Lincoln, NE   68501-1826
402-464-0602

Drugs and Crime Data Center & Clearinghouse
1600 Research Boulevard
Rockville, MD   20850
800-666-3332

Federal Bureau of Investigation
J. Edgar Hoover FBI Building
9th Street and Pennsylvania Avenue, NW
Washington, DC   20535
202-324-3000

Juvenile Justice Clearinghouse
Box 6000
Rockville, MD   20850
800-638-8736

National Archive of Criminal Justice Data
Inter-University Consortium for Political
  and Social Research
P.O. Box 1248
Ann Arbor, MI   48106
800-999-0960

National Association of State Alcohol and Drug Abuse Directors, Inc.
444 North Capitol Street, NW
Suite 642
Washington, DC   20001
202-783-6868

National Center for State Courts
300 Newport Avenue
Williamsburg, VA   23185
804-253-2000

National Institute of Justice
National Criminal Justice Reference Service (NCJRS)
Box 6000
Rockville, MD 20850
800-851-3420

Substance Abuse and Mental Health Services Administration
U.S. Department of Health
  and Human Services
5600 Fishers Lane
Rockville, MD   20857
301-443-4795

Victims of Crime Resource Center
Box 6000
Rockville, MD   20850
800-627-6872

IX. INDEX

IX. INDEX (continued)

IX. INDEX (continued)

IX. INDEX (continued)

Arrests

Corrections

Drugs and Alcohol

Finance

Law Enforcement

Offenses

CHAPTER INDEX

HOW TO USE THIS INDEX

Place left thumb on the outer edge of this page. To locate the desired entry, fold back the remaining page edges and align the index edge mark with the appropriate page edge mark.

Other books by Morgan Quitno Press:
- *City Crime Rankings*
- *State Rankings 1995*
- *Health Care State Rankings 1995*

Call toll free: 1-800-457-0742